Handbook of
BEREAVEMENT RESEARCH

Handbook of
BEREAVEMENT RESEARCH

CONSEQUENCES, COPING, AND CARE

Edited by
Margaret S. Stroebe, Robert O. Hansson,
Wolfgang Stroebe, and Henk Schut

AMERICAN PSYCHOLOGICAL ASSOCIATION
WASHINGTON, DC

Fifth Printing March 2007

Published by
American Psychological Association
750 First Street, NE
Washington, DC 20002

Copies may be ordered from
APA Order Department
P.O. Box 92984
Washington, DC 20090-2984

In the UK and Europe, copies may be ordered from
American Psychological Association
3 Henrietta Street
Covent Garden, London
WC2E 8LU England

Typeset in Goudy by EPS Group Inc., Easton, MD
Printer: United Book Press, Inc., Baltimore, MD
Cover Designer: Kathleen Sims Graphic Design, Washington, DC
Editor/Project Manager: Debbie K. Hardin, Charlottesville, VA

The opinions and statements published are the responsibility of the authors, and such opinions and statements do not necessarily represent the policies of the APA.

Library of Congress Cataloging-in-Publication Data
Handbook of bereavement research : consequences, coping & care / edited by
    Margaret S. Stroebe . . . [et al.].
       p. cm.
    Includes bibliograpical references and index.
    ISBN 1-55798-736-X (alk. paper)
    1. Grief.   2. Bereavement—Psychological aspects.   3. Death—Psychological
aspects. I. Stroebe, Margaret S.
BF575.G7H355 2001
155.9'37'072—dc21

00-0067633

British Library Cataloguing-in-Publication Data
A CIP record is available from the British Library.

Printed in the United States of America

For

Mary and Ken
(Margaret S. Stroebe and Wolfgang Stroebe)

Kathleen and Julie
(Robert O. Hansson)

Cobi and Niels
(Henk Schut)

CONTENTS

PREFACE

Since our first acquaintance in the early 1980s, collaboration between the first three editors of this volume has focused on synthesizing scientific knowledge about the phenomena and manifestations of bereavement. Our interest has been to provide a comprehensive review, emphasizing theoretical approaches and scientific methodology. We have tried throughout our joint work to identify developments and ongoing controversies and to encourage debate about them. In the third of our collaborative productions —this volume—we invited a fourth editor, Henk Schut, to join us. Together we designed a completely new volume, commissioning chapters by leading experts from countries throughout the world (including Australia, Canada, Germany, Israel, The Netherlands, the United Kingdom, and the United States). This volume, then, builds on, but leaves intact, the work that we have published together already, involving different teams of authors. The foundations laid by those authors remain fundamental, but the structure and content of the new volume has changed radically to reflect contemporary research developments.

There are always two narratives to tell about editing a volume such as this: namely, the scientific justification, which we elaborate in the next chapter, and the personal story of its creation. The latter is remarkable. In many respects, the authors of this volume became an academic community. There is no doubt that the editors, with the help of electronic mail, became more engrossed and involved in this virtual community and its joint venture than in their own real communities for many periods during the production of this volume. There has been generous sharing of academic ideas and openness to others' perspectives in a manner that has been unprecedented in our experience. There has also been sharing of more personal matters, some of which made the completion of chapters extremely difficult. An unexpectedly large number of our contributors have endured not only one but sometimes even two or three life crises during the writing of their chapters. We are extremely grateful for the commitment that everyone has shown despite personal demands and difficulties. It is good to be able to report that not all the critical life events were negative ones. One author became the proud father of twins and a temporary burden to his coauthor, who never complained; another was taken by surprise at the upheaval of getting married and unable to concentrate on completing her chapter during the week of the wedding (we did grant a short extension of deadline). Thus first and foremost we thank our authors for their dedication to this enterprise and for their marvelous contributions.

There are also many other people who deserve our thanks in bringing this volume to completion, including colleagues, friends, and family members. We are very grateful to Warren Jones and John Harvey, who provided insightful and constructive reviews of this whole volume. We received marvelous cooperation, also, from the APA editorial team, in particular Margaret Schlegel and Debbie Hardin.

Finally, in our efforts to produce a beautiful book, we searched long and hard for the perfect pictorial representation. Once seen, there was no doubt about this. The cover photo reflects an underlying theme of the volume—namely, cultural differences in patterns of grief and mourning. As many of the authors have noted, in the early twenty-first century there is growing awareness of the need to extend research interest beyond the predominantly Western cultural scene. The photograph was taken by our colleague Professor Louk Hagendoorn, who kindly gave permission for its appearance in this context and whom we wish to thank very much. The depicted shrines are located at Pashupatinath, which lies in the valley of Kathmandu. This small village on the banks of the sacred River Bagmati incorporates a large number of Hindu temples and shrines. The photograph shows the area rising from the river above cremation ghats. Such places of commemoration reflect a society's perspective on death, illustrating placement of the dead among the living, as addressed in this book.

CONTRIBUTORS

John Archer, University of Central Lancashire, Preston, Lancashire, United Kingdom

Deshratn Asthana, University of Miami School of Medicine, Miami, Florida

Teri T. Baldewicz, Duke University Medical Center, Durham, North Carolina

David E. Balk, Oklahoma State University, Stillwater

Nancy T. Blaney, University of Miami School of Medicine, Miami, Florida

George A. Bonanno, Columbia University, New York

Jack E. Burkhalter, Memorial Sloan-Kettering Cancer Center, New York

Joshua Cohen, University of Miami School of Medicine, Miami, Florida

Alicia Skinner Cook, Colorado State University, Fort Collins

Charles A. Corr, Southern Illinois University—Edwardsville

Denise T. D. de Ridder, Utrecht University, Utrecht, The Netherlands

Matthew Dobson, University of Queensland and Royal Brisbane Hospital, Herstone, Queensland, Australia

Stephen Fleming, York University, Toronto, Ontario, Canada

Susan Folkman, Center for AIDS Prevention Studies, Department of Medicine, University of California—San Francisco

Karl Goodkin, University of Miami School of Medicine, Miami, Florida

Martica Hall, Western Psychiatric Institute and Clinic, Pittsburgh, Pennsylvania

Robert O. Hansson, University of Tulsa, Tulsa, Oklahoma

Nancy S. Hogan, University of Miami, Miami, Florida

Michael Irwin, University of California School of Medicine—San Diego

Selby C. Jacobs, Yale University School of Medicine, New Haven, Connecticut

Dennis Klass, Webster University, St. Louis, Missouri

Mahendra Kumar, University of Miami School of Medicine, Miami, Florida

Barbara Leeds, University of Miami School of Medicine, Miami, Florida

Ruth Malkinson, School of Social Work, Tel Aviv University, Ramat-Aviv, Israel

Christine Minkov, University of Queensland and Royal Brisbane Hospital, Herstone, Queensland, Australia

Rudolf H. Moos, Department of Veterans Affairs Health Care System and Stanford University Medical Center, Palo Alto, California

Miriam S. Moss, The Edward and Esther Polisher Research Institute, Philadelphia Geriatric Center, Philadelphia, Pennsylvania

Sidney Z. Moss, The Edward and Esther Polisher Research Institute, Philadelphia Geriatric Center, Philadelphia, Pennsylvania

Janice Winchester Nadeau, Minnesota Human Development Consultants, Minneapolis

Robert A. Neimeyer, University of Memphis, Memphis, Tennessee

Susan Nolen-Hoeksema, University of Michigan, Ann Arbor

Kevin Ann Oltjenbruns, Colorado State University, Fort Collins, Colorado

Colin Murray Parkes, St. Christopher's Hospice, London

James W. Pennebaker, The University of Texas, Austin

Holly G. Prigerson, Yale University School of Medicine, New Haven, Connecticut

Beverley Raphael, University of Queensland and Royal Brisbane Hospital, Herstone, Queensland, Australia

David Rigg, University of Miami School of Medicine, Miami, Florida

Bernard Rimé, University of Louvain, Louvain-la-Neuve, Belgium

Paul Robinson, North York General Hospital, Toronto, Ontario, Canada

Paul C. Rosenblatt, University of Minnesota, St. Paul

Simon Shimshon Rubin, University of Haifa, Mount Carmel, Haifa, Israel

Jeanne A. Schaefer, Department of Veterans Affairs Health Care System and Stanford University Medical Center, Palo Alto, California

Henk Schut, Utrecht University, Utrecht, The Netherlands

Ester R. Shapiro, University of Massachusetts, Boston

Paul Shapshak, University of Miami School of Medicine, Miami, Florida

Phillip R. Shaver, University of California—Davis

Roxane Cohen Silver, University of California—Irvine

Margaret S. Stroebe, Utrecht University, Utrecht, The Netherlands

Wolfgang Stroebe, Utrecht University, Utrecht, The Netherlands

Caroline M. Tancredy, University of California—Davis

Maaike Terheggen, Utrecht University, Utrecht, The Netherlands

Mary D. Tyll, University of Miami School of Medicine, Miami, Florida

Jan van den Bout, Utrecht University, Utrecht, The Netherlands

Guus L. van Heck, Tilburg University, Tilburg, The Netherlands

Tony Walter, The University of Reading, Reading, United Kingdom

Robert S. Weiss, Gerontology Institute, University of Massachusetts, Boston

Camille B. Wortman, State University of New York—Stony Brook

Emmanuelle Zech, University of Louvain, Louvain-la-Neuve, Belgium

Wen Li Zheng, University of Miami School of Medicine, Miami, Florida

Handbook of
BEREAVEMENT
RESEARCH

1

INTRODUCTION: CONCEPTS AND ISSUES IN CONTEMPORARY RESEARCH ON BEREAVEMENT

MARGARET S. STROEBE, ROBERT O. HANSSON,
WOLFGANG STROEBE, AND HENK SCHUT

Although still a comparatively young field of research, the scientific study of bereavement has already passed through a number of identifiable generations, each being characterized by attention to a distinct set of important issues, theoretical advancements, and unique implications for society. Systematic shifts in the focus and character of bereavement research during the latter half of the twentieth century are reflected in the content of three volumes that we have edited. Each of these volumes was designed to provide an overview of contemporary scientific knowledge about bereavement, bringing together leading scholars in the field, integrating traditional and novel conceptions of grief, and seeking to structure the research field for the future. Two of them were published over the past couple of decades (Hansson, Stroebe, & Stroebe, 1988; Stroebe, Stroebe, & Hansson, 1993). The third, this volume, has been compiled in recognition of developments in the bereavement field since the first two publications. During the past decade alone, an increasing volume of sound scientific research has contributed to knowledge, and the scope of investigation has extended considerably. Even a casual examination shows evidence of ingenious research designs, novel theoretical integration, lively disputes, and unusual scientifically based intervention programming. It seems timely to produce an entirely *new* edited volume, covering a different scope and adopting a new structure, to represent these exciting developments.

Looking back briefly at the history of bereavement research, to place the current volume in perspective: The stage was set for the theoretical analysis of grief close to the turn of the twentieth century, with the publication of the classic paper by Freud (1917/1957) titled, "Mourning and Melancholia." However, it was not until the 1940s that the empirical study of grief and its consequences gained comparable momentum with Lindemann's (1944) renowned publication, "Symptomatology and Management of Acute Grief." With these cornerstones laid, what was to characterize more recent directions in scientific research? First, there had to be more systematic mapping of the manifestations and duration of grief, to gain understanding about the vulnerabilities of grieving individuals and indications for providing care in contemporary society. The focus was very much on the reactions of grieving individuals, on intrapersonal processes. Following this, there was a broadening of interest to examine interpersonal issues as well, including social risk factors, the effectiveness of intervention, and the consequences of bereavement on social networks. As before, empirical research was still to a large extent issue- rather than theory-generated, despite the psychoanalytic foundations laid early on and the subsequent theoretical developments emerging from—or in reaction to—this tradition.

Most recently—as reflected in this volume—bereavement researchers have come to recognize and investigate more complex phenomena of bereavement on various bio-, psycho-, and social levels, using more sophisticated methodologies and applying finer-grained theorizing. Basic to much of this research has been the search for *processes* underlying the manifestations of grief. We had to decide how to select, organize, and structure contemporary research in a manner that would best reflect the most topical themes, issues, and controversies. Our starting point was to follow our own guidelines for future research, drawn up in the final editorial chapter of the previous volume (Stroebe et al., 1993). Further ideas came from systematic review of the emerging literature and from conference presentations reporting new studies. This culminated in a structure designed around the three themes in our subtitle, "Consequences, Coping, and Care," because these seemed to best represent those areas in which most expansion and development has taken place in the 1990s. We elaborate on these later on.

Several principles characterize the approach of this handbook. As before, our approach is founded on the premise that bereavement needs to be understood from a sound base of theoretically oriented and empirically derived knowledge and not purely on subjective descriptive accounts. Our bias is toward methodologically stringent empirical research rather than clinical reports (although, as will be evident, the latter are of considerable value as an integral part of designing research and in illustrating the phenomena of bereavement). It must be recognized, though, that it takes time for such a database and orientation to reach maturity. This book can be viewed as the effort of the editors and authors alike to share contemporary ideas, discuss cutting-edge issues, and identify controversies, thereby trying to move the field forward in ways that will further not only scientific but also applied interests.

It is also important to realize that this is not a source book for practitioners wanting practical tips, but rather a research-oriented review of the current state of scientific knowledge in the field of bereavement. Although this latter approach may appear rigorously academic in a sensitive area, it must be said that underlying the work of all those included is concern about the impact of loss on bereaved individuals and groups. Although it is a normal event occurring in most people's lives, the understanding is that bereavement can cause much suffering, associated with severe consequences to health and well-being, and sometimes with effects as devastating as death of the bereaved person him- or herself. Ultimately, research on bereavement should not only lead to deeper scientific understanding, but this should be practically useful too.

Finally, it will become evident that although we advocate for narrowness in concentrating on just one life stressor, bereavement, this is matched by broadness in scientific approaches represented in the volume. The work of researchers from disciplines as different as gerontology, medicine, sociology, epidemiology, social psychology, and clinical psychology is discussed in the volume, and the authors themselves are drawn from as wide a variety of disciplines. Thus it is truly multidisciplinary, and this too is fundamental to our approach: Our understanding is that the study of bereavement will progress from a synthesis across disciplines. To quote the late Henri Tajfel, "All of us in our various disciplines . . . are dealing with a common knot of problems seen from different perspectives, and it would be futile to claim a monopoly of some kind of a 'basic truth' or conceptual priority for any one of these perspectives" (1981, p. 224).

FUNDAMENTAL CONCEPTS IN THE STUDY OF BEREAVEMENT

Over the years, reasonable agreement among researchers has been reached with respect to a number of basic concepts and manifestations associated with bereavement. It is useful to outline these as background to the subsequent chapters. First, we briefly describe the key definitions, and then we elaborate a little on the state of knowledge and current debate on the three themes of the book—consequences, coping, and care.

Definitions

Although it is difficult to draw categorical distinctions between the terms *bereavement*, *grief*, and *mourning*, or *normal* versus *pathological grief*, it is important at the outset to indicate how we use these terms.

Bereavement, Grief, and Mourning

The term *bereavement* is understood to refer to the objective situation of having lost someone significant. Across the life span, people have to face the death of parents, siblings, partners, friends, or even their own children. Although most people manage to come to terms with this over the course of time, it is associated with intense distress for most people. This usual reaction to bereavement is termed *grief*, defined as a primarily emotional (affective) reaction to the loss of a loved one through death. It incorporates diverse psychological (cognitive, social–behavioral) and physical (physiological–somatic) manifestations. Sometimes *mourning* is used interchangeably with *grief*, particularly among those following the psychoanalytic tradition. Our preference is to define mourning as the social expressions or acts expressive of grief that are shaped by the practices of a given society or cultural group. Clearly, there is sometimes a lack of distinction between grief and mourning—for example, it may be difficult to ascertain whether an overt act of crying may reflect an emotional, personal reaction or the following of a societal norm to weep on a certain occasion. Likewise, ritual crying may make a bereaved person feel his or her grief more keenly.

Normal and Pathological Grief

Distinctions between normal and pathological grief are difficult to make, partly because definitions of pathological (or complicated; traumatic) grief have been empirically rather than theoretically derived; also because complicated grief is not a single syndrome with clear diagnostic criteria (although, as evidenced in this volume, considerable effort is being made to derive diagnostic criteria by a number of different research teams); also because setting a cutoff point between what is normal and what is not is a dubious endeavor (e.g., differences in cultural manifestations need to be taken into account); and finally, because it is sometimes difficult to differentiate pathological grief from related disorders (depression, anxiety disorders, posttraumatic stress disorder).

At the risk of oversimplification, it is perhaps useful to define *pathological grief* as a deviation from the (cultural) norm (i.e., that could be expected to pertain, according to the extremity of the particular bereavement event) in the time course or intensity of specific or general symptoms of grief. Subtypes that have become well-known are chronic, absent, and delayed grief. The latter two categories are currently debated, whereas chronic grief seems more accepted. It remains to be seen how the symptomatology and manifestations of complicated grieving will be included in future diagnostic category systems, and how, should this happen, such inclusion could in turn affect conceptualization of pathological grief.

Given that grief is a normal reaction to the death of a loved one, it does not usually require the help of professional counselors or therapists: The majority of bereaved people can be said to have no pathological indications, and only in a minority of cases is there a need for referral.

Consequences

The first of our three major themes, "consequences," should be as important a focus today as it was in the pioneering days of bereavement research. There is a danger that it is no longer considered topical or newsworthy to study the psychological and physical effects of loss, because these have been the subject of so much investigation in the past. In fact, we still know too little about such things as male grief reactions or somatization of grief in non-Western cultures. It is also important to remember that the consequences may be different now from what they used to be, given the societal changes within which grieving takes place.

Reactions to Bereavement

Much is now known about typical manifestations of grief. Focus in the past has been on the *symptomatology* of grief—understandably, because researchers were concerned to establish what precisely the mental and physical health consequences of bereavement were, given the association of grief with suffering and indications that effects on health could be severe. Review of the literature shows consensus among investigators in descriptions of normal grief reactions (cf. Shuchter & Zisook, 1993; Stroebe, Stroebe, Schut, & van den Bout, 1998). The following dimensions can be identified: Affective manifestations include depression, despair and dejection, anxiety, guilt, anger and hostility, anhedonia, and loneliness. Behavioral manifestations include agitation, fatigue, crying, and social withdrawal. Cognitive manifestations include preoccupation with thoughts of the deceased, lowered self-esteem, self-reproach, helplessness and hopelessness, a sense of unreality, and problems with memory and concentration. Physiological and somatic manifestations include loss of appetite, sleep disturbances, energy loss and exhaustion, somatic complaints, physical complaints similar to those the deceased had endured, changes in drug intake, and susceptibility to illness and disease.

It has come to be recognized that the previous description may be culturally specific. There may be (sub)cultural differences in the relative frequency of symptoms across these different dimensions—for example, grieving males may cry less but show greater tendency to increase alcohol intake; there may be more somatization of grief in non-Western cultures. Some of the ongoing research on such differential patterns is included in this volume.

Also reflected in this volume is the concern among researchers recently to extend investigation beyond the symptomatology of grief to include examination of a broader range of consequences, including such aspects as changes in ongoing relationships with others (e.g., worsening or improving of marital relationships), the creation of a narrative or biography about the deceased, and positive effects, even "growth," that a loss may actually have on a bereaved individual. In fact, there is growing concern that limiting to, and labeling, grief reactions as *symptomatology* causes "medicalization"—that is, bereavement comes to be seen as an illness and medical problem.

Health Consequences of Bereavement

As noted previously, the first wave of empirical research investigated mental and physical health consequences, including mortality. Although it is still debatable which subgroups of bereaved individuals are most vulnerable, that the health of bereaved people in general is at risk (compared to their nonbereaved counterparts) has by now been well-established. There is no longer any doubt that the costs of bereavement in terms of health can be extreme. Bereaved individuals suffer elevated risks of depression, anxiety, and other psychiatric disorders, somatic complaints and infections, and a variety of other physical illnesses. They have higher consultation rates with doctors, use more medication, are hospitalized more often, and have more days of disability. The risk of mortality is associated with many different causes, including, particularly, suicide. Most recently, as evident in this volume, research has shown biological links between grief and these increased risks of morbidity and mortality.

Coping

In this volume we treat "coping," our second major theme, separately from "consequences." Indeed, it is important for theoretical and empirical research purposes to try to distinguish coping with bereavement from symptomatology, difficult though this may be at times. One reason for this is that we need to learn more about the *cognitive processes* underlying adaptation to loss: What is it about the ways that people go about their grieving that leads to better or poorer health outcome?

Processes, Strategies, and Styles

Coping refers to processes, strategies, or styles (depending on the researcher's focus) of managing (reducing, mastering, tolerating) the situation in which bereavement places the individual. By contrast, the symptoms described earlier can be seen instead as outcomes: If coping is effective, symptomatology should be reduced, and the outcome more positive for the individual. Well-acknowledged in the past was the importance of *grief work*, which is understood to refer to the cognitive process of confronting the reality of a loss through death, of going over events that occurred before and at the time of death, and of focusing on memories and working toward detachment from the deceased. As we shall see, much research has addressed the question of the adequacy of this construct in describing adaptive ways of coping with bereavement.

A few things need to be remembered in connection with coping. Clearly, mental and physical symptomatology levels are dependent on many factors other than the strategies of coping that a person has at his or her disposal (e.g., type of death; relationship to the deceased may make a difference)—the way one copes does not fully determine the outcome. Also, there is a thin line between the concepts of *coping* and *symptomatology*. Crying has been described previously as a symptom, and yet shedding tears has been shown to alleviate distress (bringing about physiological changes), thus perhaps, on occasion, assisting the coping process. Finally, variables can be examined both as process and product of grief. Thus the interest of one study may be to establish how creating a biography about the deceased leads to relocation (finding a place for the deceased in ongoing life), whereas in another, relocation may be studied as a variable that could potentially lead to reduction of symptomatology.

Despite these cautions, in our view, the basic distinction between symptoms and coping is useful, particularly to retain clarity in the design of research (e.g., in any particular study what are the process versus outcome variables?), and theoretical interpretation of study results.

Phases, Stages, or Tasks of Grief

Phasal conceptualizations of grief typically postulate a succession from an initial stage of shock, with numbness and denial, through yearning and protest, to despair, followed by gradual adjustment and acceptance of the loss (cf. Bowlby, 1980). Phases should be regarded as descriptive guidelines, not as set rules or prescriptions regarding where bereaved people ought to be at any particular duration of bereavement. There is much overlap, and passing back and forth through these phases. It is also important to note the general view these days that bereaved individuals do not "get over" their loss and back to normal but rather adapt and adjust to the changed situation. Thus labels such as "resolution" or "completion" of grief are deemed inappropriate.

In accordance with the effortful struggle to come to terms with loss that is typical of grief, task models have more recently been suggested, notably that of Worden (1991), the four tasks postulated being (a) accepting the reality of loss; (b) experiencing the pain of grief; (c) adjusting to an environment without the deceased; and (d) "relocating" the deceased emotionally and moving on with life.

It must be emphasized that not all grieving individuals show indications of going through all the phases or tasks or in the sequence suggested. Furthermore, such processes may be culturally specific.

Care

The final theme, "care," focuses on ways that bereavement research can inform health care professionals and members of informal networks surrounding bereaved persons. This includes knowledge about the nature of complications in the grieving process, the types of psychological and pharmacological interventions that are now available, and assessment of the effectiveness of such programs.

Types of Intervention for Bereaved Individuals

Grief is a normal reaction to the death of a loved one, one that most persons manage to come to terms with over the course of time. Although it is associated with a period of intense suffering for most people, it does not usually require the help of professional counselors or therapists. For a minority, however, mental or physical ill health is extreme and sometimes persistent. Bereavement is thus a concern for the planning of preventive care and it is of clinical relevance. Progress has been made in designing and implementing services for bereaved individuals. A range of support programs are available and appropriate to assist bereaved persons through their grief process.

It is useful in this context to distinguish between grief counseling and grief therapy (cf. Worden, 1991). *Grief counseling* refers to the facilitation through counseling of the process (tasks) of normal, uncomplicated grieving to alleviate suffering and help bereaved individuals to adjust well within a reasonable time. *Grief therapy*, on the other hand, refers to those specialized techniques of intervention that guide an abnormal or complicated grief reaction (e.g., chronic grief)—one that could be said to have "gone wrong" for some reason—toward a normal coping process. Although in practice the distinction between these two types of intervention is harder to make, it helps to classify the wide range of support programs for bereaved people that are by now available. These encompass counseling support schemes such as Widow-to-Widow, the mutual help program developed in the United States (see Silverman, 1986), or Cruse, the British organization for bereavement care (see Parkes, 1996), on the one hand, and a wide range of therapy programs, including various behavior and cognitive therapy techniques, on the other.

SCOPE AND CONTENT OF THIS VOLUME

The themes of consequences, coping, and care incorporate a number of research domains that are at the frontiers of research about bereavement. However, before delving into these topics, it is important to address major conceptual, methodological, and ethical issues in bereavement research.

Theory, Methodology, and Ethical Issues

Part I begins with three very different theoretical chapters. The first two of these are by the well-known pioneers and leading scholars in bereavement research, Parkes and Weiss. Together and individually, these two have made a large contribution in terms of both theoretical and empirical knowledge about bereavement and loss (e.g., Parkes, 1996; Parkes & Weiss, 1995; Weiss, 1975).

In chapter 2, Parkes provides a comprehensive historical perspective, tracing the origin and evolution of ideas in the field of bereavement and weaving together many of the theoretical and intervention principles that form the basis of contemporary knowledge. Parkes calls for integration of what we know about the nature and consequences of loss, the attachment process, and trauma and stress more generally (including psychological, physiological, and social components). As will be seen in the remaining chapters of the handbook, other authors share his concern about the still-fragmented view (and research base) on bereavement. Some encouraging attempts at integration are already being made, as will be discussed. Consistent with his own research in this area (e.g., Parkes, Laungani, & Young, 1997), he also stresses the need for cross-cultural comparisons in our analyses of the nature of grief and grieving. This is a major theme in a number of chapters in this book.

It is true that researchers' descriptions of grief have outstripped our ability to explain and understand it. We lack a general theory of grief that explains why it happens in response to only certain losses. Fundamental questions continue to puzzle: What is the role of security and attachment in the grieving process? How and why does grief abate? Is it functional?

How can we understand individual differences, and how can others help in the grieving process? Such basic questions are addressed in Weiss's innovative theoretical analysis in chapter 3. Starting with observations of bereavement phenomena that need explanation, Weiss proposes an extension of the attachment theory perspective, based on analysis of the type of lost relationship. He argues that grief is a response to loss of relationships of attachment (child; parent; pairbond partner), whereas the ending of other relationships, although important, are not bonds of attachment and give rise to distress but not to grief.

In recent years, bereavement research has been undertaken from a variety of theoretical perspectives. In addition to attachment theory and the early psychodynamic approaches, stress-coping theory has become an influential framework. The authors of chapter 4, Shaver and Tancredy, have strong backgrounds in attachment theory (e.g., Cassidy & Shaver, 1999) but argue the need for an even broader consideration—namely that emotion theory in general should be applied in interpretation of the phenomena of bereavement and grief. For example, they point out that features such as intrusive thoughts are not bereavement-specific but that all emotions have such "mind-narrowing" effects. Likewise, emotions generally are functional, and suggest the need to explore the adaptive functions of grief. They also criticize interpretations of Bowlby's (1980) ideas, contrasting their own attachment theorist's perspective with many in the bereavement research field. It is interesting to compare the views expressed in this chapter with those of Parkes (chapter 2), Klass and Walter (chapter 19), and M. Stroebe and Schut (chapter 17).

Grief is a complex emotional syndrome, associated with a myriad of reactions and diverse ways of coping. As such, it is difficult for scientists to "measure" phenomena associated with it. Methodological techniques have recently expanded to enable more sophisticated analysis of these phenomena. Can we capture the essence of the grieving process in "snapshot" measures using questionnaire methodology, or do we need "rolling film" information obtained in interview transcripts and using qualitative analysis? These issues are addressed by two researchers with deep interest in the conceptualization and adequacy of measurement—Neimeyer and Hogan (chapter 5). They provide a critical review of quantitative and qualitative methods and argue for methodological pluralism. As they note, there is no golden standard in the measurement of grieving, but there are a number of promising new approaches that suggest useful future directions.

The field of bereavement research has lagged behind the disciplines of medicine and clinical psychology in its consideration of ethical issues, and yet the researcher is confronted with unique and complex ethical challenges. The topic is of growing importance, given the expansion of bereavement research, and, most particularly, given the vulnerability of bereaved people and the demands that are put on them when they are asked to participate in research. In chapter 6, Cook draws on her own professional experience and theoretical knowledge to provide a comprehensive examination of ethical issues as applied to bereavement research, illustrating many of the ethical dilemmas that occur in research settings. She considers a variety of issues, including research participants' rights, dignity, and well-being; assessment of the risks versus benefits of bereavement research; and a novel suggestion for including potential participants in discussion of research ethics.

Consequences: The Bereaved Individual Across the Life Span

Parts II and III (consequences) cover contemporary empirical research focusing on new intrapersonal (Part II) and interpersonal (Part III) directions, although there is necessarily some overlap. Bereavement research has grown out of a long tradition focusing on intrapersonal processes and consequences. Research is still needed at this level, and the lifespan perspective of Part II identifies a theme where this is particularly necessary. Choice of this topic reflects our concern to extend understanding beyond the traditional concentration on spousal loss, or, more recently, separate treatment of the grieving experience at different phases of life. These chapters, taken together, provide an overview of the developmental process of grieving, showing how this perspective can add to our understanding of grieving. Thus the section applies life span developmental theory to the understanding of bereavement.

Chapter 7 by Schaefer and Moos represents an important extension to the study of bereavement. We have become used to thinking in medical model terms, whereby outcome of bereavement is a mental or physical health variable. Yet multifaceted as it is, the bereavement experience leads to many different types of consequences. Although it would be a mistake to look exclusively at positive outcomes (bereaved people who struggle to get through each day would surely confirm this), the enrichment of life through bereavement is one of the aspects that scientific study needs to uncover. These authors emphasize the potential for personal growth and transformations following a period of successful coping and adaptation (e.g., increased self-understanding, maturity, coping skills, ability to regulate affect), providing a theoretical framework to understand how personal, developmental, and environmental factors may foster this potential.

Following this chapter, specific bereavement phenomena at different periods of the lifespan are investigated, each by experts specializing in a particular developmental period. Chapter 8 by Oltjenbruns focuses on early experiences of loss among children. Oltjenbruns outlines developmental characteristics of childhood to give the necessary background for understanding the bereavement process. The implications of developing capacities on children's understandings of bereavement become evident, for example, as Oltjenbruns identifies a "regrief" phenomenon—children as they mature will revisit a significant loss that had occurred earlier in childhood, this time from a different, more mature point of view. Thus we need to consider developmental status (e.g., the availability of language to shape and express meaning; understanding the permanence of death; the available repertoire of coping mechanisms) as a moderator of bereavement experience.

Along similar lines, Balk and Corr (chapter 9) examine developmental phases that take place during adolescence and what this might mean for young people in these age groups who become bereaved. The focus is on death of siblings, parents, friends, and peers. The authors identify specific adolescence-related difficulties that may be encountered following loss, including those related to developmental processes themselves, to the forging of relationships marked by belonging, and developing a confident self-image. Conversely, Balk and Corr also discuss the potential for adolescents emerging from grief experiences to be more emotionally experienced and mature than their nonbereaved peers.

One of the hardest upsets of the expected life cycle is the experience of losing a child. Why and how does this type of loss so deeply affect the lives of bereaved parents? The authors of chapter 10, Rubin and Malkinson, have done much of their research in their home country, Israel, where so many families have experienced such bereavements. They examine the adaptation of bereaved parents to loss of a child, framing their analysis in terms of Rubin's two-track model, a perspective that is applicable to parental loss across the life cycle. Their dual analysis tracks the course of bereavement in terms of the bereaved person's own symptoms, reactions, and functioning on the one hand and his or her evolving experience of the relationship with the deceased, on the other. They also elaborate on risk and mitigating factors in parental reactions to their bereavement that have applied clinical implications.

Older persons are not only subject to declining personal health but they have to deal with the deaths of those close to them with increasing frequency. There is likelihood of multiple and sequential losses and bereavement overload. In chapter 11 Moss, Moss, and Hansson, all of whom have worked closely with elderly persons for many years, address how a number of age-related issues influence the ability and motivation of older adults to cope with and adapt to bereavement. Critical issues that these authors discuss include diminishing physiological function and adaptive reserves, social isolation, and increased dependency on support relationships that may become strained, less accessible, and mismatched to the older person's needs. Understanding the bereavement experience in elderly individuals requires a broad theoretical approach. To this end, the authors' orientation rests on a psychosocial model of bereavement rather than a medical model.

Consequences: The Bereaved Individual in Social Context

The second part of the consequences focus of this book places the bereaved individual within the social group in which grieving takes place. Grieving does not occur in isolation but in interaction with others. There is an interdependence of grieving within family and societal groups. What, then, are the implications for the individual of grieving among others? What effects does a bereavement have on the social group itself? Part III of the volume extends traditional approaches to document new ways to understand grief at this interindividual level.

However, although we have taken the social context as a major theme in the volume, we need to keep a balance in perspectives, and explore alternatives. Thus the first chapter in this section, by Archer (chapter 12), addresses the biological functions–universals of grief, and the potential of evolutionary theory for understanding grief and grieving. This provides a fascinating contrast with the remaining chapters in this section. A basic question posed by Archer is whether grief is adaptive, which he approaches by examining how general it is in the natural world and by exploring the biological background of the adaptive significance of grief. Contrasting also with attachment approaches, which emphasize differences in the strength of attachments, Archer examines whether a Darwinian framework can predict variations in grieving according to the nature of the relationship with the deceased: Can evolutionarily important variables—notably kinship and reproductive value (age)—predict individual variations in anything other than a very general way?

Although universals can be identified, cross-cultural differences in grieving have been documented for a great diversity of cultures. The cultural relativity of grieving is examined in chapter 13 by Rosenblatt, well-known for his theoretical analyses of grief in social and cultural context. He examines a wide range of bereavement phenomena across cultural groups, placing these within social constructionism, a perspective that denies the universality of bereavement reactions. Indeed, it is difficult, having read this chapter, to assume the generalizability of measures of any aspect of bereavement. Cultural differences are linked to a variety of phenomena, including understandings of what has been lost in death, death rituals, cultural constructions of the survivor's ongoing and future relationship with the deceased, and cultural constructions of what is deviant grieving.

Shifting attention from cultural construction to interpersonal construction, in chapter 14 Shapiro takes a broad integrative perspective, following a mainly psychodynamic viewpoint on family systems but also examining the relevance of other theoretical perspectives. She applies this interpersonal framework in both social and developmental contexts, to illuminate influences on our actual (and internally represented) relationships and their importance to the self and the self's capacity to adapt and adjust after a death. She shows how relational resources moderate the impact of diverse stressors associated with death, ideas that link nicely with other chapters in the volume concerned with adult attachment, meaning-making, and continuing bonds.

"Grief is a family affair," as Winchester-Nadeau notes in her introduction to chapter 15, and yet, in the past, there has been more concentration on the ways that individuals, rather than families, make meaning of their loss. She argues that making sense of a death is not just an individual task but also a collaborative process of social cognition. Reporting her innovative empirical research with families, Winchester-Nadeau shows how studying family grief is not only theoretically important but also helps us to direct effective intervention, which likewise can usefully shift from an intrapersonal to an interpersonal approach. Winchester-Nadeau's research is exemplary of the way that an in-depth, qualitative analysis adds to understanding of complex phenomena of grief.

Research on risk factors has had a fairly long tradition. Given this, it is surprising how few of the beliefs that we have about high-risk categories (unexpected death; loss of a child; social isolation; lack of religion, and so forth) have actually been adequately researched, or—if they have —how few of these actually turn out to be "bereavement risk factors." Finally in this section, in chapter 16 W. Stroebe and Schut reexamine research on risk factors, setting stringent methodological standards for empirical research, and, unusually for this topic, adopting a theoretical framework (cognitive stress theory). They explore the extent to which interpersonal as well as the more frequently researched intrapersonal factors serve, on the one hand, protective or ameliorative functions against detrimental consequences of loss, or, on the other hand, increase the chances that adjustment will be difficult.

Coping: Basic Concepts and Their Measurement

Coping has become a dominant theme of bereavement research during the past decade. Given the establishment of health effects of bereavement, particularly among high-risk persons, researchers became concerned to identify effective ways of coping and to explore cognitive mechanisms underlying adjustment to this stressor. Thus to begin with in Part IV, new conceptual approaches to coping with bereavement are examined before turning, in Part V, to empirical research programs that have probed the mechanisms.

What is adaptive coping with bereavement? This is the question posed by M. Stroebe and Schut in chapter 17. They review theoretical analyses that provide insight into this fundamental question, exploring first the general stress and trauma theories, then theories and models that have been applied in particular to bereavement, and finally the more specific models of coping with bereavement. The latter category includes both intra- and interpersonal models. The chapter closes with a description of the authors' own dual-process model of coping with bereavement, which is an attempt to integrate much that is offered in the previous perspectives, and, in addition, to include a dynamic process of *oscillation*, one that captures the active, effortful nature of coping with bereavement.

More than a decade ago, Wortman and Silver (1989) wrote a highly influential paper titled, "The Myths of Coping With Loss," that caused lay persons and bereavement professionals alike to rethink their beliefs about how people (should) go about their grieving. For example, does successful adjustment require confronting or working through feelings? Must the bereaved individual endure a period of intense distress, and is failure to do so indicative of a problem? Ten years on, we invited them to take up the challenge that some of the editors, among others, posed to them. We criticized their interpretation of much of the empirical research on which their arguments were based (M. Stroebe, van den Bout, & Schut, 1994). How could they answer these criticisms, and what new evidence could they bring to bear on their "myths"? In chapter 18 Wortman and Silver provide an eloquent rejoinder, revisiting the myths to reexamine their earlier conclusions.

One could add an old "myth" to those considered by Wortman and Silver, namely that "bonds to the deceased have to be broken." This was integral to Freud's position and characteristic perhaps of Bowlby's early research done somewhat later. Recently, systematic investigation has been made of the role and functions of continuing bonds with the deceased. The authors of chapter 19, Klass and Walter, have contributed to this endeavor in a number of intriguing ways, and they draw their research together to argue their case for the importance of retaining bonds. They conclude that sensing the presence of the deceased cannot be labeled pathological. Many people talk to the deceased and find it meaningful. The dead also play a role in the moral lives of the living. Furthermore, conversation with the dead has, they argue, replaced ritual as the normative way in which the bond is maintained.

Although models of bereavement in recent years have increasingly focused on coping, efforts to develop valid measures of coping with bereavement have not kept pace with theoretical development. We invited experts from the general coping research field, van Heck and de Ridder, to consider bereavement. In chapter 20 they grapple with the problem of how to measure coping with bereavement, given the shortcomings of established coping scales and the poor application of generic coping measures to the specific stressor(s) of bereavement. For example, these instruments do not systematically include all the domains of coping that are relevant to bereavement (e.g., proactive as well as reactive coping strategies–behaviors; planful versus habitual or automatic coping). It becomes evident that conceptual analysis of the demands of coping with the loss of a loved one are needed, and that further empirical work is needed to catalog coping efforts that work. Clearer distinction between coping and outcome variables is also needed: Frequently instruments confound these two (e.g., the inclusion of distress items).

Coping: Exploration of the Mechanisms

One of the most fascinating new directions that research on bereavement has taken recently has been the examination of cognitive mechanisms underlying effective coping. Part V of the volume provides detailed coverage of leading empirical research investigations designed to probe such processes.

First, in chapter 21 Hall and Irwin provide an unusual analysis at the physiological level to further understanding of biological "feedback" in the coping process. This approach upturns the typical way of looking at physiological phenomena as outcomes of bereavement, looking rather at these as part of the coping process. The authors put forward a conceptual model, providing a useful framework within which the diverse lines of research can be understood. The chapter also addresses the implications of methodology in studies thus far, to clarify restrictions (e.g., causal modeling) in what we can really say about the topic. Although they show that neuroendocrine, immune, and sleep profiles are altered in association with bereavement, there is as yet no evidence of direct neurobiological pathways or physiological "signaling" of risk for poor health consequences. The authors suggest how these could be further examined.

Physiological changes have been investigated in connection with processing on a more psychological level—namely, in the research of Bonanno (chapter 22) representing as it does a new wave of research interest in the field. He identified "dissociation" between psychological and physiological reactions during disclosure following bereavement. Bonanno presents a theoretical analysis of this phenomenon, distinguishing emotion from grief, focusing on emotional dissociation, and reviewing his own research that derives from this analysis. His data on emotional dissociation add another thread of argument with respect to the controversy about the value of grief work. He suggests a competing position, based on a social-functional view of emotion. He argues that his own research on both dissociation and facial expression of emotion contradicts the grief work notion, providing support instead for his social–functional view.

The theme of disclosure is central to the next contribution. On the one hand, research by Pennebaker and colleagues, covering several domains, indicates that disclosure of upsetting experiences, through writing or talking, is beneficial for physical health. On the other hand, an equally strong body of research by Rimé and colleagues on the impact of social sharing of emotion indicates that sharing does not alleviate the emotional impact of the event, although people maintain the subjective feeling that this actually does help. We invited Pennebaker, Zech, and Rimé (chapter 23) to join forces in a single chapter to try to disentangle the similarities and differences between these two lines of research, focusing on the application of their more general trauma research to the specific area of bereavement. The result is a fine-grained analysis of the general processes and their specific application to bereavement that should help focus future research.

Drawing the fine line between adaptive "grief work" and less-adaptive "rumination" is difficult, and yet this needs to be done if we are to make useful predictions about the relationship of these processes to outcome. A fine body of empirical research has been conducted by Nolen-Hoeksema and colleagues, concentrating specifically on rumination. This research ranges from laboratory investigations to studies of reactions to natural disasters, many of which were conducted longitudinally. Nolen-Hoeksema reviews her series of studies in chapter 24, expounding the implications for interventions with the bereaved individual and for theories of adaptation to loss. In particular, she examines the relationships between ruminative coping and the search for meaning in loss, "grief work," and the assimilation of loss into one's schemas or world views. Nolen-Hoeksema's work is particularly important in that it identifies pathways whereby rumination may lead to an intensification of grief.

A lesson offered by Folkman (chapter 25), one of the most experienced researchers in the field, is "Listen carefully to what your respondents are trying to tell you!" It was the gay caregivers in her longitudinal study of partners of men with AIDS who alerted her to the role that positive emotions play in coping with caregiving and (for many) bereavement. Despite the burden on them, these men were gaining strength by finding positive things in their arduous daily lives. This caused Folkman to build questions about positive affect and (re)appraisal carefully into her investigation and to look at their role in coping. Ultimately, this led to revision of cognitive-stress theory, a perspective that has become a major force in the study of critical life events (Lazarus & Folkman, 1984). In this chapter, focusing closely on its application to bereavement, Folkman describes the original theory, her recent adaptations of it, and the empirical research on which her revised ideas are based. Just as Nolen-Hoeksema identified pathways in ruminative coping, so did Folkman for the opposite effect of positive emotions.

Care: Intervening in the Coping Process

Part VI, taking up the theme of care more centrally than in the previous chapters, draws the link between theory and intervention because, as mentioned earlier, in this volume we focus more on conceptual under-pinnings and scientific understanding of intervention than on providing practical guidelines for professionals and lay people.

The section begins with a scholarly presentation of the state of knowl-edge about psychotherapeutic and pharmacological intervention for be-reaved people by Raphael, Minkov, and Dobson (chapter 26). Their mes-sage that "there can be no justification for routine intervention for bereaved persons . . . for grief is not a disease" comes across loud and clear. Anchoring their analysis in theory, the authors explore ways that attach-ment and psychodynamic theories can inform practice. They review the range of available interventions and their application. They address key questions, such as whether complicated forms of grieving need the support of drugs, or whether professional therapy is sufficient. They argue the need for psychopharmacological interventions to be administered in a condition-specific manner and for the "grief process" to be looked after whatever the diagnosis.

Diagnostic issues are integral to the care process. Exemplary of efforts in the clinical research community to develop a consensus of diagnostic criteria for pathological, or traumatic, or complicated grief is the extended research of Prigerson and Jacobs. Chapter 27, in which they present their research on this topic, gives insight too into the lengthy process of research and deliberation that goes into the derivation and testing of criteria. This process involves evaluation of research about the symptomatology of "trau-matic grief" (their preferred descriptor). Does this satisfy requirements for establishing a distinct clinical entity? Is this useful or harmful? What cri-teria are justified? Prigerson and Jacobs consider these key issues in the light of preliminary empirical testing and suggest ways to solve one of the most difficult problems—namely, how to distinguish normal from traumatic reactions.

Many of the chapters in this volume have emphasized the centrality of meaning-making in the process of coming to terms with a bereavement. Surely, then, if something has "gone wrong" in the grieving process, it should be possible to influence meaning-making and further the process of adaptation. Combining their skills as theoreticians and clinicians, this is exactly what Fleming and Robinson propose in chapter 28. Particularly valuable in this endeavor is cognitive–behavior therapy. The authors re-view the basic claims of this approach and its applicability to intervention with bereaved individuals, covering issues of attachment to the deceased, traumatic grief complications, and the impact of counterfactual thinking on the nature and dynamics of grief, showing how the bereaved individual's distress may be perpetuated in a cognitive–affective loop that can be ad-dressed usefully and, it is hoped, altered in intervention.

Just as investigation of physiological correlates is rarely considered within an analysis of the coping process itself, so are they unusual in intervention studies. A notable exception is the research of Goodkin and his colleagues, presented in chapter 29. Quite uniquely, they investigated physiological changes following bereavement support-group intervention for HIV+ and at-risk men and women. In this presentation of their work, Goodkin and colleagues examine physiological mechanisms through which bereavement may exacerbate declining function of the immune and neuroendocrine systems. They go on to investigate how social support and successful coping may minimize disruption to these physiological systems and progression of disease. Never before has the body of research on physiological mechanisms underlying bereavement phenomena suggested causal effects on health care use and that this relationship can be modified by psychosocial intervention.

Another myth about bereavement could be that "intervention helps the bereaved." This is an assumption that is voiced by many, including health care professionals working with bereaved individuals. But what evidence is there for this belief? Does help really *help*, and if so, for whom and at what duration of bereavement? Fortunately, an increasing body of empirical research has recently been gathering to put the myth to the test and to examine such questions. In chapter 30 Schut, M. Stroebe, van den Bout, and Terheggen critically examine the results of these empirical studies on the efficacy of grief counseling and grief therapy, arguing the need for refinements in methodology in future studies, and, in their conclusions, upturning some of the common assumptions and suggesting that we may need to reconsider strategies for providing care.

CONCLUSION

As noted at the outset, the purpose in compiling this volume was to bring together leading experts from different disciplines and with different approaches to provide a source of contemporary scientific knowledge in the field. It will become evident on reading these chapters that an enormous amount has been learned in recent years about the consequences of bereavement, about ways of coping with this life event, and about effective ways of caring for bereaved individuals. It can be said that bereavement is now an established scientific discipline. Nevertheless, as one must expect, there are limits to our current knowledge, and there are major remaining (even newly created) controversies, even between the covers of this volume. In chapter 31, the editors, M. Stroebe, Hansson, W. Stroebe, and Schut, take a new look at the current state of knowledge, attempting to consolidate themes and emerging issues from the volume. We identify what we see as the major controversies, the most significant lines for future investigation, and the main implications for policy making.

REFERENCES

Bowlby, J. (1980). *Attachment and loss. Vol. 3. Loss: Sadness and depression.* London: Hogarth.

Cassidy, J., & Shaver, P. R. (1999). *Handbook of attachment: Theory, research and clinical applications.* New York: Guilford Press.

Freud, S. (1957). Mourning and melancholia. In J. Strachey (Ed. and trans.), *Standard edition of the complete works of Sigmund Freud.* London: Hogarth Press. (Original work published 1917)

Hansson, R. O., Stroebe, M., & Stroebe, W. (1988). Bereavement and widowhood. *Journal of Social Issues, 44,* whole issue.

Lazarus, R., & Folkman, S. (1984). *Stress, appraisal, and coping.* New York: Springer.

Lindemann, E. (1944). Symptomatology and management of acute grief. *American Journal of Psychiatry, 101,* 141–148.

Parkes, C. M. (1996). *Bereavement: Studies of grief in adult life* (3rd ed.). London: Routledge.

Parkes, C. M., Laungani, P., & Young, B. (1997). *Death and bereavement across cultures.* London: Routledge.

Parkes, C. M., & Weiss, R. S. (1995). *Recovery from bereavement* (2nd ed.). Northvale, NJ: Jason Aronson.

Shuchter, S., & Zisook, S. (1993). The course of normal grief. In M. Stroebe, W. Stroebe, & R. O. Hansson (Eds.), *Handbook of bereavement: Theory, research and intervention* (pp. 23–43). New York: Cambridge University Press.

Silverman, P. (1986). *Widow to widow.* New York: Springer.

Stroebe, M., Stroebe, W., & Hansson, R. (Eds.). (1993). *Handbook of bereavement: Theory, research and intervention.* New York: Cambridge University Press.

Stroebe, M., Stroebe, W., Schut, H., & van den Bout, J. (1998). Bereavement. In H. Friedman, N. Adler, & R. D. Parke (Eds.), *Encyclopedia of mental health.* San Diego, CA: Academic Press.

Stroebe, M., van den Bout, J., & Schut, H. A. W. (1994). Myths and misconceptions about bereavement: The opening of a debate. *Omega: Journal of Death and Dying, 29,* 187–203.

Tajfel, H. (1981). *Human groups and social categories.* Cambridge: Cambridge University Press.

Weiss, R. S. (1975). *Marital separation.* New York: Basic Books.

Worden, J. W. (1991). *Grief counseling and grief therapy: A handbook for the mental health practitioner.* New York: Springer.

Wortman, C., & Silver, R. (1989). The myths of coping with loss. *Journal of Consulting and Clinical Psychology, 57,* 349–357.

I

THEORY, METHODOLOGY, AND ETHICAL ISSUES

2

A HISTORICAL OVERVIEW OF THE SCIENTIFIC STUDY OF BEREAVEMENT

COLIN MURRAY PARKES

It has been a privilege, in my lifetime, to witness the emergence of bereavement as a topic of scientific study, to have known many of the pioneers in this field, and to have played a part in blazing the trail. In this chapter I shall attempt to summarize what I see as the most significant developments and to draw some conclusions.

Research relevant to an understanding of bereavement comes from many sources. These sources can be subdivided into studies of losses and their consequences, studies of the attachments that precede these losses, and studies of other types of psychological trauma. Work in each of these three fields has usually taken little regard of the other two. Thus an entire literature has grown up around the psychopathology and phenomenology of loss, which pays little attention to the literature on attachment and child development or that on the psychology and physiology of stress; yet all of these fields of study must be integrated if we are to obtain a balanced view of bereavement.

To some extent this results from the fact that the people doing the research come from many different disciplines. Physicians, pediatricians, psychiatrists, psychoanalysts, psychologists, sociologists, anthropologists, ethologists, physiologists, and endocrinologists have all made important contributions to our knowledge of bereavement, and each has seen it from their own special point of view and described it in their own particular language. This inevitably has led to isolation and fragmentation when researchers confine their communication to a small group of people who share their frame of reference and to confusion and dissent when people from one field assume that others share a common language and viewpoint. We find psychologists blaming doctors for seeing grief as an illness, sociologists blaming psychologists for drawing universal conclusions from the study of one particular culture, psychiatrists blaming physicians for ignoring the psyche, and ethologists accusing all the rest of anthropocentrism. This said, however painful it may be, communication across these boundaries is always worth the effort, and books such as this one, which bring together researchers from a variety of disciplines and points of view, can do much to remove our blinkers and expand our view of the field.

EARLY VIEWS OF GRIEF

Interest in loss as a potential cause of physical and mental illness goes back a long way. Thus Robert Burton, in *The Anatomy of Melancholie* (1621), refers to grief or sorrow as "The epitome, symptome and chief cause" of melancholia or, as it would be termed today, clinical depression. In the same century we find "griefe" acceptable as a cause of death in Heberden's *Bills of Mortality of the City of London* for 1657. The idea that grief itself can take a pathological form was current by 1703 when Vogther, in *Altdorf*, published a thesis, "*De Morbis Moerentium*," in which he prescribed a variety of medications for pathological grief. The dangers of bereavement were also emphasised by Benjamin Rush, one of the signatories of the American Declaration of Independence, who advised bereaved people to avoid reminders of their loss and to take "liberal doses of opium" (1835). He too saw grief as a potential cause of death and described postmortem findings in people who had died of rupture of the auricles and ventricles of the heart following bereavement, literally dying from a "broken heart."

An attempt to explain the roots of grief was made by Charles Darwin in his little-known book, *The Expression of the Emotions in Man and Animals* (1872). He observed that many animal species cry aloud when separated from those to whom they are attached. Sorrowing human beings attempt to inhibit that cry, and Darwin speculated that the distinctive expression of grief was produced by the "grief muscles" that are less under the control of the will than other facial muscles.

FREUD AND WORLD WAR I

Freud's influential paper *Mourning and Melancholia*, first published when the western world was wracked with grief (1917/1953), was based on clinical observation. In this paper he described the similarities and differences between grief (or "mourning," as it is still termed by psychoanalysts) and melancholia. He recognized that bereavement is sometimes a cause of depression and suggested that this is most likely to arise if it follows the death of someone who has been ambivalently loved. He coined the term "grief work" on the supposition that grief is a job of psychological work that we neglect at our peril.

Interest in other types of psychological trauma arose at this time from the work of army medical officers who were treating "shell shock." Faced with the multiple traumas of trench warfare, losses of friends, severe physical privation, and the immediate danger of death, in a situation from which there was no honorable escape, many soldiers developed psychiatric symptoms that would today be diagnosed as hysteria (dissociative syndromes) or as posttraumatic stress disorder. These often responded to "abreaction," a form of treatment that involved injecting the patient with a sedative drug and prompting him or her to "re-live" the traumatic experiences that he or she had suffered. Following this treatment the patient's symptoms often improved and many of them were able to return to the war front. In both Freud's approach to the treatment of melancholia and the treatment of the war neuroses the emphasis was on finding ways of helping people to abandon defensive avoidance and face painful realities.

ERIC LINDEMANN AND WORLD WAR II

Despite the influence of Freud's paper on our thinking about depression it was not until another world war that Kardiner published his *Traumatic Neuroses of War* (1941) and two systematic descriptive studies of bereaved psychiatric patients were published by Lindemann (1944) and Anderson (1949). Kardiner challenged the then-current psychoanalytic view that current events were traumatic because they rearoused conflicts derived from infancy. He suggested that major traumatic events disorganize the ego and bring about both numbness and intrusive memories.

More directly focused on bereavement were Lindemann's study of 101 patients who sought help at a clinic that he set up following a fire in the Coconut Grove night club in Boston, Massachusetts (1944), and Anderson's study of 100 patients whom he treated for "morbid grief reactions" at a psychiatric unit in England (1949). Lindemann's masterly description of acute grief did much to create the current view of what is "normal," and he went on to describe various deviations from the norm, or *formes fruste*, as he called them, which he attributed to the repression or avoidance of grief. Finally he suggested a simple therapy by which people could be induced to express their grief and return to the "normal" pattern. He noted, but failed to recognize the significance of the phenomenon of "chronic grief," a severe and lasting reaction to bereavement that was the most common psychiatric problem found by Anderson. Anderson also pointed out that there is a wide range of other psychiatric disorders that can be triggered by bereavement, including anxiety states (in 59% of his patients) and manic depression (15%).

Lindemann's paper attracted much more attention than Anderson's and was very influential. It established views of "morbid grief" and its treatment that are still accepted today, but his failure to recognize that other psychiatric reactions to bereavement cannot be so easily explained or treated has caused later workers to question his conclusions and, indeed, to throw doubt on the whole concept of grief work (Wortman & Silver, 1989).

My own first studies of bereavement confirmed the claims that had been made that bereavement can cause psychiatric problems. I examined the case records of 3245 adult psychiatric patients admitted to two psychiatric units in London between 1949 and 1951. The incidence of death of a spouse during the six months before onset of the psychiatric illness was six times greater than would have been expected from the rates of bereavement obtainable from mortality figures among people of the same age. Further study of 94 bereaved patients from this sample confirmed the patterns of morbidity that had been described by Anderson (Parkes, 1965).

STUDIES OF STRESS

A related field in which progress was being made at this time was the broader field of the psychophysiology of stress. As early as 1929, Cannon had made the remarkable claim that psychological situations as varied as rage, hunger, fear, and pain produced a common bodily response. This was attributable to the stimulation of the sympathetic nervous system and the inhibition of the parasympathetic. Subsequent research revealed the important role played by nor-epinephrine (adrenaline) and the corticoid and pituitary hormones in response to the wide variety of situations that are lumped together under the rubric of "stress." By analogy with physical stress the circumstances that caused these traumas were termed "stressors" and the effect on the individual "strain."

Psychologists and physiologists used a wide range of techniques to study this field in both humans and other animals, leading to major advances in neuroendocrinology and psychophysiology. Their research explains many of the physical symptoms that arise following bereavements and other major stressors and helps us to distinguish between the physiological responses that, however unpleasant, are transient and do no lasting damage, and the occasional pathological responses that are evidence of stress-related illness and may do permanent damage or even cause death. Although these are undoubtedly important to the study of bereavement, and likely to become more so as our knowledge grows, it is only in recent years that findings are emerging that are specific to situations of loss rather than nonspecific reactions to a wider range of stressors (see, for instance, Jacobs's 1993 review of this field as it applies to bereavement).

There is no space in this chapter to review the numerous studies of stress management and crisis intervention. Much of this now seems simplistic, but it presented clinicians and counselors with the possibility that psychiatric and psychosomatic disorders could be prevented if prompt action was taken in the wake of traumatic life events, and it played an important part in the emergence of the community mental health programs that were brought into being in the United States by President John F. Kennedy's Community Mental Health Centers Act of 1964.

EMPIRICAL STUDIES OF UNCOMPLICATED OR "NORMAL" GRIEF

Despite Lindemann's delineation of "normal" grief, no systematic studies had examined samples of unselected bereaved people as opposed to people seeking psychiatric help. The first person to attempt this was Peter Marris, whose book *Widows and Their Families* described the results of interviews with 72 widows in East London (1958). As might be expected, he found a lower incidence of many of the "symptoms" that had been reported in bereaved people who sought psychiatric help and threw doubt on the "normality" of these samples. On the other hand, he was able to confirm that features such as hallucinations and a sense of the presence of the dead person near at hand were no less common in unselected widows than they had been in the psychiatric samples. Certainly these features could not be taken as symptoms of psychiatric illness.

Up to this time all studies had been cross-sectional, and little had been written about the changes that take place over time and the sequence of events. Working in close collaboration with John Bowlby, who, with James Robertson, was carrying out similar studies of children separated from their parents, I undertook a longitudinal study of unselected widows who were followed through the first year of bereavement. This revealed changes in the psychological features of grief that resembled the sequence of changes that had been reported by Robertson and Bowlby in separated children (1952). Although there was wide variation within the sample, it was possible to discern an overall pattern, and Bowlby and I published a descriptive classification of the phases of grief, which comprised (a) numbness, (b) yearning and searching, (c) disorganization and despair, and (d) reorganization (Bowlby & Parkes, 1970). This classification has given rise to a great deal of controversy and spawned a number of alternative classifications (which are reviewed by Marrone, 1997).

The sequence was never intended to be more than a rough guide, and it was recognized from the start that people would move back and forth through the sequence rather than following a fixed passage. Even so it was adopted with enthusiasm by some psychotherapists and counselors who saw in it a resemblance to Freud's stages of psychosexual development. According to this model psychoneuroses arise if people become stuck or "fixated" at one of the stages. The aim of therapy is to help the client to move forward by confronting the repressed ideas and memories that are perpetuating the fixation. Applying this model in a rigid way to bereaved people, some therapists attempted to force them to fit a pattern with which they felt very uncomfortable.

Figure 2-1 shows the level of overall distress reported week by week by each widow in my sample during the first three months of bereavement (Parkes, 1970). It illustrates the variety of affective responses that were found. It also indicates that those people who showed the least amount of distress during the first two weeks of bereavement were *more* disturbed three months later than those who expressed their grief to the full right from the start. Thus it provided some evidence to support the idea that grief can be delayed but not avoided.

THE PREDICTION OF BEREAVEMENT RISK

Given the variation that was apparent, the next step was clearly to study a larger sample to discover why some people coped well with bereavement and emerged stronger and wiser and others suffered lasting psychiatric and other problems. At the invitation of Gerald Caplan, who had pioneered crisis intervention in the United States, I took over the direction of the Harvard Bereavement Study, a short longitudinal study of widows and widowers in Boston, Massachusetts, who were interviewed at intervals through their first four years of bereavement. The findings of this study enabled us to identify before, or at the time of a bereavement, the "risk factors" that predicted later adjustment. It also enabled us to clarify some of the causal links that led up to problematic reactions (Parkes & Weiss, 1983).

THE DEVELOPMENT OF SERVICES FOR BEREAVED PEOPLE

These findings proved extremely valuable when, later, I returned to England to work at St. Christopher's Hospice in Sydenham, where Cicely

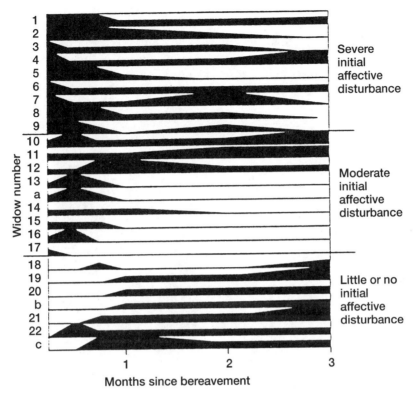

Figure 2-1. Severity of Emotional Disturbance in Twenty-Five Widows During the First Three Months of Bereavement (Parkes, 1970). Reprinted by permission of Routledge.
Note: Each widow is given a number except three widows who did not complete the follow-up and were excluded from the main study. They are indicated with the letters a, b, and c.

Saunders was pioneering the first of the modern hospices. In this setting I was able to set up the first hospice bereavement service using carefully selected and trained volunteers to act as counselors to "high-risk" bereaved people who had been identified by hospice staff using the criteria that we had identified in the Harvard study.

Another member of Caplan's team in Boston had been David Maddison, who carried out his own studies of bereavement risk in Boston and Sydney, Australia (Maddison & Viola, 1968; Maddison, Viola, & Walker, 1969; Maddison & Walker, 1967). His findings confirmed and extended my own, and we both went on to use the findings in clinical practice. Beverley Raphael was a member of Maddison's team. She and I set up two very similar evaluative studies using the Harvard risk assessment to identify bereaved people at risk and offering counseling to a random half of the high-risk groups (Parkes, 1979; Raphael, 1977). The main difference between the two studies was that in Raphael's case the counseling was given by a highly professional psychiatrist (herself) and, in my study at St. Christopher's Hospice, by trained volunteer counselors.

Followed up at c. 20 months after bereavement both studies showed statistically significant findings (see Figure 2-2). The high-risk bereaved

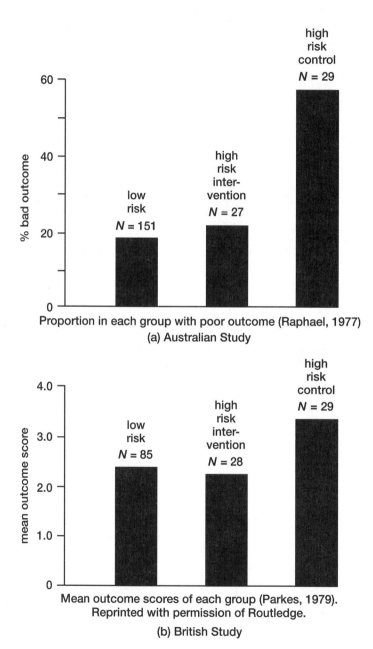

Figure 2-2. Bereavement Outcome in High- and Low-Risk Groups With and Without Intervention

without counseling had poorer outcome scores on a number of measures than the low-risk bereaved, confirming the predictive power of the risk assessment. The high-risk bereaved without counseling also had significantly poorer outcome than those who had received counseling. The effect of the counseling had been to reduce the risk of poor outcome in the high-risk group to about the same level as that of the low-risk group. In other, subsequent, random allocation studies of bereavement counseling, only the minority of bereaved people who are at special risk, as shown by high levels of emotional disturbance, have been shown to benefit from counseling (see, for instance, Murphy et al., 1998; Schut, Stroebe, van den Bout, & Keijser, 1996; Vachon, Lyall, Rogers, Freedman, & Freeman, 1980; see also chapter 30, this volume).

Subsequent developments in services for the bereaved in Australia, Britain, and the United States were influenced in different ways by these studies and by others that were also carried out at this time. In Australia, Raphael assisted in the inception of a National Association for Loss and Grief (NALAG), which provided training for psychiatrists, psychologists, and social workers. The emphasis was, and remains, the provision of competent professional services. From the start funeral directors played a part in NALAG, and in recent years they have partly taken over the provision of professional counseling services. New Zealand has followed the example of Australia and has its own New Zealand Association for Loss and Grief (NZALAG).

In Britain most hospices and palliative care services now offer bereavement counseling by trained volunteers, as does Cruse Bereavement Care, a large national organization with branches in most parts of the United Kingdom. In addition there are a number of local bereavement services that are loosely linked through the National Association of Bereavement Services. All of these organizations make use of volunteers who are carefully selected, trained, and supervised (usually by professionals). This model of counseling by these volunteers subsequently spread to the United States with the spread of the Hospice Movement to that country.

Another source of help for the bereaved that originated in Britain was the Compassionate Friends, a mutual help group for parents who have lost a child; this organization was started by a hospital chaplain, Simon Stevens, and subsequently spread to America.

A powerful advocate of mutual help for bereaved people is Phyllis Silverman. She too worked in Caplan's Laboratory of Community Psychiatry in the late 1960s, where she started a Widow-to-Widow Program (1969). Mutual help groups subsequently sprung up for bereaved people in many situations, including people bereaved by murder, suicide, and other trauma. It is not easy to evaluate such groups scientifically, but one attempt, by Vachon et al. (1980), did indicate that for those bereaved people who were most depressed (but not for others), a mutual help group with professional support could lead to marked improvement.

Mutual help groups remained the predominant source of help for bereaved people in the United States for many years. Recently, however, thanks partly to the influence of the Association for Death Education and Counselling and partly to the provision of professional counseling by funeral services, counseling by professional psychologists, and counselors has become widespread.

Ramsay's treatment of "morbid grief" by "forced (later "guided") mourning" accepted the prevalent idea that avoidance of grief was the principle cause of pathology, although he attempted to explain this using the language of learning theory rather than psychoanalysis (1979). When, subsequently, his approach was subjected to a well-conducted random-allocation study by Mawson, Marks, Ramm, and Stern (1981), the results indicated that, although the method succeeded with a minority of research participants, it was not uniformly successful.

Several other techniques have been proposed for use in the therapy of pathological grief. These include Volkan's use of linking objects (1972, 1981), the empty chair, and similar techniques derived from Gestalt therapy (Perls, Hefferline, & Goodman (1951) and Rando and van der Hart's use of therapeutic rituals (Rando, 1985; van der Hart 1988). Although each of these make sense in certain clinical situations, none of them has, to my knowledge, been subjected to any kind of scientific evaluation.

More recently Schut, de Keijser, van den Bout, & Stroebe (1996) have developed a combination of psychotherapy and art therapy for bereaved in-patients that has been subjected to systematic comparison with a traditional psychotherapeutic approach in a therapeutic community. The new combined therapy proved significantly more effective.

In the same year these authors published another important study that compared two types of therapy with a waiting list control group. Women were found to benefit from a form of therapy that helped them to rethink and restructure their lives and to find fresh meanings. Men, on the other had, were found to benefit more from a traditional type of therapy aimed at helping them to express the wide range of emotions that accompany grief (Schut, Stroebe, van den Bout, & de Keijser, 1996).

STUDIES OF OTHER CULTURES

Most of the early studies of the psychology of bereavement were conducted by psychiatrists on samples of White, Christian widows. This has resulted in a culturally biased view of "normal grief." Gorer's classic study of mourning customs in Britain (1965) suggested that the mores of southern England that pertained in the 1960s were highly deviant from most other countries, but he made no attempt to establish the "norm" for the world. Subsequently Rosenblatt, Walsh, and Jackson (1976) reviewed evidence from a stratified sample of 78 world cultures that had been studied by anthropologists. They demonstrated the wide range of variation that exists between cultures. More recently Wolfgang and Margaret Stroebe have gone to the extreme of questioning the universality of grief (Stroebe & Stroebe, 1987). In the concluding statement to their book Rosenblatt et al. wrote,

> Despite warnings that American customs and grief behavior may be peculiar to America, it seems that American practices and behaviors are a relatively safe base from which to generalize about the species. We have assumed in our research that people everywhere experience grief, that people everywhere experience the death of close kin as a loss and mourn for that loss. Judging by the richness of our findings, our assumptions have been correct. (1976, p. 124)

Rosenblatt may, subsequently, have had second thoughts on this issue, but I would maintain that there is something that all who suffer a major loss have in common and that the word "grief" does have a universal meaning that transcends culture.

Cross-cultural differences are, however, very great and need to be studied if we are to learn how to mitigate some of the suffering caused by grief. It may well be that certain types of reaction to bereavement are "normal" within certain subcultures and "abnormal" in others, but we should not assume that it follows that what is "normal" is necessarily right, healthy, or harmless. One has only to think of the once-widespread practice of suttee in India, in which a widow burns herself on the funeral pyre of her husband, to recognize this error. Likewise the attribution of deviance from the norm is no evidence that a custom is wrong, unhealthy, or harmful despite the tendency in every society to think it so.

There are some societies in which overt expression of grief is encouraged by traditions, rituals, and belief systems. There are others in which it is discouraged. Systematic cross-cultural studies are needed if we are to discover the reasons for and the advantages and disadvantages associated with each type of response. In the absence of these it does appear that it is societies that have recently experienced war or see themselves as "warriors" that are most likely to minimize mourning.

SEX DIFFERENCES

Some of the largest differences exist within cultures. Thus Rosenblatt et al. found that although there are some cultures in which men appear to mourn as much as women, wherever a sex difference occurs it is the women who show their grief more than the men. This is born out in numerous studies of western cultures and may also reflect the "macho," warrior identity of western men in the wake of two world wars.

Is there a price to be paid for these sex differences? Psychoanalytic theory would lead us to expect to find that the repression of emotion would lead to a higher incidence of mental illness among bereaved men than women. In fact most studies indicate the opposite. Women are much more likely to admit to psychiatric symptoms and to seek psychiatric help during the first year after bereavement than men. This does not necessarily mean that avoidance of grief is not sometimes harmful and it is not unreasonable to attribute some psychological and, indeed, some somatic disorders to the avoidance of grief. Thus men are much more likely to die of a cardiac condition during the first year after the death of their wives than women are after the death of their husbands. (This evidence is reviewed in Parkes, 1996.) Furthermore, as discussed previously, Schut, Stroebe et al. (1996; also chapter 30, this volume) have found that men benefit more than women from counseling that helps them to express their grief. By contrast women seem to have less difficulty in expressing grief and other emotions but may need help in rethinking and restructuring their lives and finding fresh meanings.

AGE DIFFERENCES

Most of the earlier studies of bereavement have focused on young and middle-aged persons. More recently Lund (1989) and his colleagues have carried out extensive research with elderly bereaved people. Age emerges as another determinant of the reaction to bereavement, with elderly people usually found to mourn less than younger people. To some extent this may result from the fact that bereavements in old age are seldom unexpected and untimely. Hence older people are better prepared for the losses that are an increasing occurrence in old age. This said, bereavements are a common cause of depression in old age, and many of those who seek help from bereavement counselors are elderly. It is often the secondary consequences of bereavement, social isolation and lack of care, that contribute to loneliness and depression and aggravate the somatic illnesses to which people in this age group are prone.

At the other extreme of age we have losses in childhood, whose short- and long-term consequences have proved so profound that they have become a major field of study in their own right. In fact, it was John Bowlby's review of the consequences for children of parental loss and homelessness for the World Health Organization, published in 1953 as *Child Care and the Growth of Love*, that revolutionized the field of child development research and led to the inception of attachment theory. In that report Bowlby concluded,

> The proper care of children deprived of a normal home life can now be seen to be not merely an act of common humanity, but essential to the mental health and social welfare of a community. For, when care is neglected, as happens in every country in the Western world today, they grow up to reproduce themselves. Deprived children . . . are the source of social infection as real and serious as are carriers of diphtheria or typhoid. And, just as preventive measures have reduced these diseases to negligible proportions, so can determined action greatly reduce the number of deprived children in our midst and the growth of adults liable to produce more of them. (p. 239)

THE DEVELOPMENT OF ATTACHMENT THEORY

Bowlby emphasized the damaging effects of "maternal deprivation" and, in a world in which men were expected to play little part in child-rearing, this conclusion may well have been justified. But his words met considerable opposition from the women's movement, who saw Bowlby's position as an attack on their own aspirations toward liberation from the drudgery of house work and child care. Subsequent research showed that the sex of a child's caregiver was of less importance than the quality of care, and Bowlby himself soon began to refer to the "mother *or mother figure*" as the essential requisite. Even this was seen as sexist by some fathers, who did not wish to be seen as "mother figures."

There is no space in this chapter to consider Bowlby's trenchant criticisms of aspects of Freudian and Kleinian psychoanalysis or to review the huge body of scientific evidence that he amassed in his three-volume work, *Attachment and Loss* (1969, 1973, 1980). Suffice it to say that no serious student of bereavement or of child development can afford to ignore this major work, whose influence continues today. In the words of Anthony Storr, "I think he really saved psychoanalysis from being totally discredited" (quoted in Karen, 1994, p. 431).

A major contributor to our understanding of attachments is one of Bowlby's former trainees, Mary Salter Ainsworth. She developed the first systematic way of studying parent–child attachments, the Strange Situation Test (Ainsworth, Blehar, Waters, & Wall (1978). This constitutes a standard laboratory situation in which young children and their mothers (or fathers) can be studied before, during, and after a brief period of separation. Despite the brevity of the separations (only a few minutes) Ainsworth was able to describe patterns of behavior that have proved highly predictive of the subsequent attachments made by these children throughout their childhood and into adult life. Although psychiatrists had long recognized the baneful influence of parents who reject their children and Bowlby had added maternal deprivation as a pathogen, it was Ainsworth who made the important distinction between secure and insecure attachments. A mother may love her child very much and still harm him or her if her behavior evokes insecurity. Ainsworth delineated four patterns of attachment (Ainsworth, et al., 1978); the fourth has since been reinvestigated by one of her former trainees, Mary Main (Main & Hesse, 1990). These are summarized in the section that follows.

Secure (Ainsworth's Category B)

Parents whose sensitivity and responsiveness to their infants' needs for security and a safe base from which to explore the world are adequate, have children who tolerate brief separations without great distress, and respond rapidly and warmly to their mother's comforting behavior when she returns.

Insecure

Anxious Ambivalent (Ainsworth's Category C)

Mothers who are overanxious and insensitive to their infants and discourage exploration have children who show great distress during periods of separation and who both cling to and angrily cry at their mother when she returns.

Avoidant (Ainsworth's Category A)

The children of mothers who cannot tolerate closeness and punish attachment behavior learn to inhibit clinging and crying. When their mother leaves the room they appear detached and uncaring. When she returns they often ignore or turn away from her. However uncaring they may appear they show evidence of physiological arousal in a rapid heart rate throughout the period of separation.

Disorganized/Disoriented (Ainsworths' Category D)

This group of children exhibits a wide variety of disorganized behaviors when separated. They often "freeze" and may show stereotyped behavior after mother returns. Main and Hesse (1990) showed that most of the mothers have suffered major losses or other trauma that remained unresolved at the time when the strange situation test was carried out.

Although most of the initial studies focused on mother–child dyads, subsequent studies of father–child dyads have shown that secure parenting from either parent can, to a degree, mitigate the effects of insecure parenting from the other. Follow-up studies of Ainsworth's dyads and similar studies in other parts of the world (described in Parkes, Stevenson-Hinde, & Marris, 1991) have shown that these patterns are remarkably stable and occur in many different cultures, although in different proportions determined by the patterns of childrearing within the culture. My own recent work suggests that they also influence the reaction when these attachments come to an end. Secure children remain secure in their relationships not only to their mother but to other subsequent people to whom they become attached in childhood and adult life.

These attachment patterns have been spelled out in some detail, because I believe them to play an important part in subsequent reactions to loss. I have developed a retrospective attachment questionnaire to study the attachment patterns of adults (Parkes, 1991). Among the bereaved people referred to me for psychiatric treatment most report clear evidence of negative parental influences, leading to vulnerability in childhood and predicting the type and intensity of the symptoms that they experience following bereavements in adult life. Many had been anxious/ambivalent children (category II 1), who lacked trust in themselves; their relationships in adult life are often conflicted, and my work suggests that they are prone to lasting grief when these relationships end. Others were avoidant children (category II 2), who lack trust in others; they tend to be compulsively independent, wary of closeness, and have aggressive, assertive relationships in later life. When the relationships end they do not cry and are unable to express grief. Disorganized children (category II 3) are deeply unhappy, and as adults they lack trust in themselves *and* others; they fit best Seligman's picture of "learned helplessness" (1975), which he identified as a common precursor of depression. They easily become depressed and inclined to alcoholism when faced with loss. Only a minority were securely attached, and they most often sought psychiatric help after an unusually traumatic type of bereavement (e.g., multiple or unexpected and untimely losses, homicides, suicides, and so forth).

TRAUMATIC TYPES OF BEREAVEMENT

Unexpected and untimely deaths, particularly when associated with violence and the witnessing of horrific events, have emerged from many studies as predictors of poor outcome following bereavement (Parkes, 1996). These traumatic types of bereavement include studies in war zones and disaster areas where sudden, unexpected deaths are often multiple and associated with witnessing horrific events. Horowitz, Wilner, and Alvarez (1979) described the way in which traumatized persons oscillate between intrusive recollection of the traumatic event and avoidance. Their Impact of Events Scale includes subscales of intrusion and avoidance. The intrusion scale measures the presence of intrusive memories and, for this reason, has been used as a measure of grief. However, it does not make a clear distinction between the preoccupation with happy memories of a lost person, which is a normal feature of the reaction to bereavement, and intrusive memories of a painful or life-threatening event, which is a diagnostic symptom of the condition that has since come to be called posttraumatic stress disorder (PTSD).

This term was adopted by the authors of the third edition of the *Diagnostic Statistical Manual* of the American Psychiatric Association in 1980 (*DSM-III*). It established PTSD as a distinct mental illness and, where attributable to human agency, grounds for compensation in law. Suddenly psychological trauma became a respectable topic of study, and a plethora of research followed. The condition received so much attention that it is sometimes, mistakenly, thought to be the most common consequence of psychological trauma. Work by Pynoos and others (1987) has established that, although PTSD can coexist with grief, it is a quite different phenomenon, with different causes and features. Although PTSD is relatively rare following bereavement, it does occur, and may then lead to avoidance of stimuli likely to evoke grief. This, in turn, is likely to interfere with the course of grieving. For a more extended review of the cognitive–behavioral models that have been put forward to explain PTSD, a paper by Lee and Turner is recommended (1997).

The term traumatic grief has also been used as an alternative to the unsatisfactory terms pathological or morbid grief by Prigerson et al. (1997; and chapter 26, this volume), who are currently attempting to refine the diagnostic criteria. It is unfortunate that this term is easily confused with the reactions to traumatic bereavement described earlier.

CONFRONTATION AND AVOIDANCE

Another important finding to come out of Horowitz's research is his classification of people as "avoiders" or "sensitizers" (1986). He suggested that sensitizers are more prone to obsessive preoccupation with memories but, again, did not make a clear distinction between painful and happy memories. These ideas have recently undergone further development in the hands of Stroebe and her colleagues (M. Stroebe & Schut 1999; and chapter 17, this volume) in their dual process model of bereavement. They highlight the way in which bereaved people oscillate between the pangs of grief (separation orientation), in which attention is focused on the lost person, and the less dramatic but equally important periods of apathy and direction of attention away from the loss and toward other life tasks (restoration orientation). Only in the infrequent event that one or both of these processes becomes inhibited can the grief be said to have become pathological.

LOSSES OTHER THAN THOSE BY DEATH

Losses by death are not, of course, the only or the most frequent losses to be encountered, and there is a growing literature on the effects of other types of loss. These studies are reviewed in a recent book edited by Parkes and Markus (1998). One of the first was Fried's comparison of bereavement and loss of a home in the face of compulsory relocation (1962). There followed a comparison by Fitzgerald of bereavement and loss of sight (1970). These studies and my own systematic comparison of reactions to bereavement and loss of a limb (Parkes, 1972, 1975) revealed the similarities and differences between these reactions and enabled me to recognize the significance of the psychosocial transitions that accompany bereavement and many other losses. Marris's important book, *Loss and Change* (1974), is based on his own observations as a sociologist of the impact of a variety of situations of loss, and this has been followed by a more recent study of uncertain situations in which it is unclear whether or not a loss is impending (Parkes, Stevenson-Hinde, & Marris, 1991).

PSYCHOSOCIAL TRANSITIONS

In all of these studies it is clear that it takes time for people to accept the implications of change, even change for the better. Our first inclination is to resist acknowledging that a major change will take place or has taken place. Only with time and support do we undertake the major task of relearning our assumptions about the world. The change in the structures of meaning that invest our lives are gradual and involve incorporating and reinterpreting the past rather than giving it up. Another more recent attempt to tackle the same problem is the recent book *Continuing Bonds* (Klass, Silverman, & Nickman, 1996).

CONCLUSION

Despite the differences in viewpoint and orientation that are apparent from this review, a consensus is gradually emerging that is backed by a great deal of research. There is now a growing acceptance that there is a common core to grief that is rooted in the attachments that we make to the people and objects around us. How that grief is expressed and how we go about the process of relearning that inevitably follows a loss is determined by social and other factors that are identifiable and, often, predictable.

Most people who experience a bereavement are part of a social network of caring people whose attachments to each other are supportive.

Indeed, families exist for the support of their members and, most of the time, they fulfil this function well. The failure of many of the evaluations that have been carried out to show differences between those who receive intervention and control groups suggests that current methods of counseling are only needed by and effective for a minority of high-risk bereaved people. In the western world most people come through bereavement without the need for counseling or other support, but there is a minority who will suffer serious consequences to their physical or mental health unless they are given appropriate help from professional or trained volunteer counselors.

To refine our approaches we need systematic comparisons between people from different cultures, people experiencing different types of loss, and people receiving different types of intervention and no intervention. Although families and friends will continue to meet the needs of most bereaved people, those who offer counseling and other professional and voluntary support should meet proper standards of selection, training, and supervision and should keep abreast of the research that continues to expand our knowledge. Journals such as *Omega*, *Death Studies*, and *Mortality* provide the academic and scientific forum, and *Bereavement Care*, *The Forum Newsletter* (from ADEC), *Grief Matters* (from NALAG), and the newsletter from the American Academy of Bereavement are written in nontechnical language. Both types of journals are needed and must take full and impartial account of developments in this exciting and growing field of knowledge.

REFERENCES

Ainsworth, M. D. S., Blehar, M. C., Waters, E., & Wall, S. (1978). *Patterns of attachment: A psychological study of the strange situation*. Hillsdale, NJ: Erlbaum.

American Psychiatric Association. (1980). *Diagnostic and statistical manual of mental disorders* (3rd ed.). Washington, DC: Author.

Anderson, C. (1949). Aspects of pathological grief and mourning. *International Journal of Psychoanalysis, 30*, 48–55.

Bowlby, J. (1953). *Child care and the growth of love*. London: Pelican.

Bowlby, J. (1969). *Attachment and loss. Vol. 1. Attachment*. London: Hogarth.

Bowlby, J. (1973). *Attachment and loss. Vol. 2. Separation, anxiety and anger*. London: Hogarth.

Bowlby, J. (1980). *Attachment and loss. Vol. 3. Loss: Sadness and depression*. London: Hogarth.

Bowlby, J., & Parkes, C. M. (1970). Separation and loss within the family. In E. J. Anthony (Ed.), *The child in his family* (pp. 197–216). New York: Wiley.

Burton, R. (1621). *The anatomy of melancholie*. Amsterdam: Theatrum Orbis Terrarum.

Cannon, W. B. (1929). *Bodily changes in pain, hunger, fear and rage* (2nd ed.). London: Appleton.

Darwin, C. (1872). *The expression of the emotions in man and animals*. London: Murray.

Fitzgerald, R. G. (1970). Reactions to blindness: An exploratory study in adults with recent loss of sight. *Archives of General Psychiatry, 22,* 370–379.

Freud, S. (1953). Mourning and melancholia. *The standard edition of the complete psychological works of Sigmund Freud* (Vol. 14) (James Strachey, ed., in collaboration with Anna Freud, assisted by Alix Strachey and Alan Tyson). London: Hogarth. (Original work published 1917)

Fried, M. (1962). Grieving for a lost home. In L. J. Duhl (Ed.), *The environment of the metropolis*. New York: Basic Books.

Gorer, G. (1965). *Death, grief and mourning in contemporary Britain*. London: Cresset.

Heberden. (1657). *Bill of mortality of the city of London*.

Horowitz, M. (1986). *Stress response syndromes*. Northvale, NJ: Aronson.

Horowitz, M., Wilner, N., & Alvarez, W. (1979). Impact of Event Scale: A measure of subjective stress. *Psychosomatic Medicine, 41,* 209–218.

Jacobs, S. (1993). *Pathologic grief: Maladaptation to loss*. Washington, DC: American Psychiatric Press.

Kardiner, A. (1941). *The traumatic neuroses of war*. New York: Hoeber.

Karen, R. (Ed.). (1994). *Becoming attached: Unfolding the mystery of the infant-mother bond and its impact on later life* (p. 131). New York: Warner.

Klass, D., Silverman, P. R., & Nickman, S. (Eds.). (1996). *Continuing bonds: New understandings of grief*. Washington, DC: Taylor & Francis.

Lee, D., & Turner, S. (1997). Cognitive-behavioural models of PTSD. In D. Black, M. Newman, J. Harris-Hendriks, & G. Mezey (Eds.), *Psychological trauma: A developmental approach* (pp. 60–80). London: Gaskell.

Lindemann, E. (1944). The symptomatology and management of acute grief. *American Journal of Psychiatry, 101,* 141–148.

Lund, D. A. (Ed.). (1989). *Older bereaved spouses: Research with practical applications*. New York: Taylor & Francis/Hemisphere.

Maddison, D. C., & Viola, A. (1968). The health of widows in the year following bereavement. *Journal of Psychosomatic Research, 12,* 297–306.

Maddison, D. C., Viola, A., & Walker, W. (1969). Further studies in conjugal bereavement. *Australian and New Zealand Journal of Psychiatry, 3,* 63–66.

Maddison, D. C., & Walker, W. L. (1967). Factors affecting the outcome of conjugal bereavement. *British Journal of Psychiatry, 113,* 1057–1067.

Main, M., & Hesse, E. (1990). Parents' unresolved traumatic experiences are related to infant disorganised attachment status: Is frightened and/or frightening parental behavior the linking mechanism? In M. Greenberg, D. Cicchetti, & M. Cummings (Eds.), *Attachment in the preschool years* (pp. 161–185). Chicago: University of Chicago Press.

Marris, P. (1958). *Widows and their families*. London: Routledge.

Marris, P. (1974). *Loss and change*. London: Routledge & Kegan Paul.

Marrone, R. (1997). *Death, mourning and caring*. Pacific Grove, CA: Brooks/Cole.

Mawson, D., Marks, I. M., Ramm, L., & Stern, L. S. (1981). Guided mourning for morbid grief: A controlled study. *British Journal of Psychiatry, 138,* 185–193.

Murphy, S. A., Johnson, C., Cain, K. C., Gupta, A. D., Dimond, M., & Lohan, J. (1998). Broad-spectrum treatment for parent bereaved by violent deaths of 12–18 year old children: A randomized controlled trial. *Death Studies, 22,* 209–235.

Parkes, C. M. (1965). Bereavement and mental illness. Part I. A clinical study of the grief of bereaved psychiatric patients. Part II. A classification of bereavement reactions. *British Journal Medical Psychology, 38,* 1–26.

Parkes, C. M. (1970). The first year of bereavement: A longitudinal study of the reaction of London widows to the death of their husbands. *Psychiatry, 33,* 442–467.

Parkes, C. M. (1972). Components of the reaction to loss of a limb, spouse or home. *Journal of Psychosomatic Research, 16,* 343–349.

Parkes, C. M. (1975). Psychosocial transition: Comparison between reactions to loss of a limb and loss of a spouse. *British Journal of Psychiatry, 127,* 204–210.

Parkes, C. M. (1979). Terminal care: Evaluation of in-patient service at St. Christopher's Hospice. Pt I. Views of surviving spouse on effects of service on the patient. Pt II. Self-assessment of effects of the service on surviving spouses. *Postgraduate Medical Journal, 55,* 517–527.

Parkes, C. M. (1991). Attachment, bonding and psychiatric problems after bereavement in adult life. In C. M. Parkes, J. Stevenson-Hinde, & P. Marris (Eds.), *Attachment across the life cycle* (pp. 268–292). London: Routledge.

Parkes, C. M. (1996). *Bereavement: Studies of grief in adult life* (3rd ed.). London: Routledge.

Parkes, C. M., & Markus, A. C. (1998). *Coping with loss*. London: BMJ Books.

Parkes, C. M., Stevenson-Hinde, J., & Marris, P. (Eds.). (1991). *Attachment across the life cycle*. London: Routledge.

Parkes, C. M., & Weiss, R. S. (1983). *Recovery from bereavement*. New York: Basic Books.

Perls, F., Hefferline, R., & Goodman, P. (1951). *Gestalt therapy: Excitement and growth in the human personality*. New York: Delta.

Prigerson, H. G., Bierhals, A. J., Kasl, S. V., Reynolds, C. F., III, Shear, M. K., Day, N., Berry, L. C., Newsom, J. T., & Jacobs, S. (1997). Traumatic grief as a risk factor for mental and physical morbidity. *American Journal of Psychiatry, 54,* 617–623.

Pynoos, R .S., Frederick, C., Nader, K., Arroyo, W., Steinberg, A., Eth, S., & Nunez, F. (1987). Life threat and post-traumatic reactions in school-age children. *Archives of General Psychiatry, 44*, 1057–1063.

Ramsay, R. W. (1979). Bereavement: A behavioural treatment for pathological grief. In P. O. Sjoden, S. Bayes, & W. S. Dorkens (Eds.), *Trends in behaviour therapy* (pp. 217–248). New York: Academic Press.

Rando, T. A. (1985). Creating therapeutic rituals in the psychotherapy of the bereaved. *Psychotherapy, 22*, 236–240.

Raphael, B. (1977). Preventive intervention with the recently bereaved. *Archives of General Psychiatry, 34*, 1450–1454.

Robertson, J., & Bowlby, J. (1952). Responses of young children to separation from their mothers. *Courier of the International Children's Centre, Paris*, II, 131–140.

Rosenblatt, P. C., Walsh, R. P., & Jackson, D. A. (1976). *Grief and mourning in cross-cultural perspective*. Washington, DC: HRAF Press.

Rush, B. (1835). *Medical inquiries and observations upon the diseases of the mind*. Philadelphia: Grigg & Elliott.

Schut, H., de Keijser, J., van den Bout, J., & Stroebe, M. S. (1996). Cross-modality grief therapy: Description and assessment of a new program. *Journal of Clinical Psychology, 52*, 357–365.

Schut, H. A. W., Stroebe, M., van den Bout, J., & de Keijser, J. (1997). Intervention for the bereaved: Gender differences in the efficacy of two counseling programs. *British Journal of Clinical Psychology, 36*, 63–72.

Seligman, M. E. P. (1975). *Helplessness*. San Francisco: Freeman.

Silverman, P. R. (1969). The Widow-to-Widow Program. *Mental Hygiene, 35*, 333.

Stroebe, M., & Schut, H. (1999). The dual process model of coping with bereavement: Rationale and description. *Death Studies, 23*, 197–224.

Stroebe, W., & Stroebe, M. S. (1987). *Bereavement and health: The psychological and physical consequences of partner loss*. Cambridge: Cambridge University Press.

Vachon, M. L. S., Lyall, W. A. L., Rogers, J., Freedman, B. A., & Freeman, S. J. (1980). A controlled study of self-help intervention for widows. *American Journal of Psychiatry, 137*, 1380–1384.

van der Hart, O. (Ed.). (1988). *Coping with loss: The therapeutic value of leave-taking rituals*. New York: Irvington.

Vogther, C. B. (1703). *Disputation de Morbis Moerentium Altdorfii*. British Library Shelf 7306.I, 9(2).

Volkan, V. (1972). The linking objects of pathological mourners. *Archives of General Psychiatry, 27*, 215–221.

Volkan, V. (1981). *Linking objects and linking phenomena: A study of the forms, symptoms, metapsychology and therapy of complicated mourning*. New York: International University Press.

Wortman, C. B., & Silver, R.C. (1989). The myths of coping with loss. *Journal of Consulting and Clinical Psychology, 57*, 349–357.

3

GRIEF, BONDS, AND RELATIONSHIPS

ROBERT S. WEISS

In this chapter I extend the theory of grief proposed by Bowlby and Parkes, in which grief is seen as a response to loss of a relationship of attachment. I begin by describing the emotional state of grief. I then consider what must be the characteristics of an attachment bond if we assume that it is that bond whose interruption gives rise to grief. I suggest how the bond may be different in children's relationships with parents, in the relationship of spouses, and in parents' relationships with children. Finally, I argue that there is a class of close relationships maintained by another sort of bond, which I call affiliative, in which loss may trigger distress but does not give rise to grief.

THE CHARACTERISTICS OF GRIEF

By the term *grief* I mean the severe and prolonged distress that is a response to the loss of an emotionally important figure. Among adults, grief is provoked especially by loss of a husband, wife, or child; among children, grief is provoked by loss of a parent, although the loss of other figures, especially siblings, can sometimes also provoke grief.

The expression of grief appears in two forms. The first, which Bowlby characterized as "protest," is marked by preoccupation with the loss, waves of pain, agitation, tension, and vigilant attentiveness to the possibility that the lost figure may reappear (Bowlby, 1980, pp. 87–91). The second, which Bowlby characterized as "despair," is in level of attentiveness to the environment and physiological arousal, virtually the opposite of the first syndrome. Instead of vigilance, it is marked by apparent withdrawal of attention from ongoing life. Instead of agitation it is marked by persistent low moods and pervasive sadness (Bowlby, 1980, pp. 93–96). This second form of grief has at times been referred to as reactive depression, but it differs from depression in that a particular event, the return of the lost figure (were that possible), would restore well-being. It also differs in that it is without the alienation from self that seems pathognomic to depression.

Bowlby and Parkes referred to the syndromes of protest and despair as phases of grieving, implying by the term "phases" that there is a temporal sequencing in which protest appears first and then gives way to despair. However, survey data suggest that at best the sequencing of symptom sets is imperfect, and that it may not occur at all (Wortman & Silver, 1989). A plausible hypothesis is that throughout bereavement the phenomena of protest—vigilance, agitation, and yearning—emerge from a background of chronic despair, but as time goes on intervals of protest ordinarily occur less frequently and despair lightens (Osterweis, Solomon, & Green, 1994, p. 148).

Parkes (1996) suggested that the motive force for the syndrome of protest was a compulsion to search for the lost figure, together with anxious yearning for the figure's return. The restless energy that is part of the syndrome is consistent with a compulsion to search and there is often a vigilant scanning of the environment for indications of the lost figure's presence. Furthermore, part of the protest syndrome is a level of tension high enough to defeat efforts at rest and sleep. This is consistent with the idea that there has been loss of a security-fostering figure.

The physiological and emotional state of protest, in which attention and energy are fully mobilized by the threat of loss, might be described as an emergency reaction. If we assume, with Bowlby and Parkes, that the bond whose interruption gives rise to grief is the attachment bond, then it appears that an important characteristic of this bond is that the threat of persisting inaccessibility of its object triggers emergency reactions.

The syndrome of despair appears to stem from acceptance that efforts to restore the lost relationship are hopeless—from acceptance of loss. A remarkable characteristic of this syndrome is its persistence. More often than not it is the predominant emotional state through much of the first year of bereavement and continues as a kind of background state for at least another two or three years thereafter (Parkes & Weiss, 1983). Even many years after loss there may be vulnerability to upsurges of distress on anniversaries of the death or at times that would have been significant for the lost figure—as at a child's graduation (Rosenblatt, 1996). Evidently the bond whose interruption gives rise to grief can persist indefinitely, despite absence of reinforcement by interaction with the person with whom the bond had been established.

Grief states, including protest and despair, appear in adults after loss of a spouse or a child, and in children, and sometimes also in adults, after loss of a parent. There are differences in the nature of the grief states that follow each kind of loss. The grief states following loss of a spouse and loss of a child differ in that loss of a spouse brings a sense of having been abandoned, but only rarely, if ever, is this associated with loss of a child. The grief state following loss of a child is likely to include guilt for having failed the child, whereas after loss of a spouse both the spouse and the self can be seen as having responsibility for the ending of the relationship.

After loss of a child there is need to continue to act protectively toward the child. Although there may be similar feelings after loss of a spouse, they appear less intense and less persisting. Indeed, grief following loss of a child seems regularly to resist the fading that is ordinarily seen with grief following other forms of loss (Lehman, Wortman, & Williams, 1987; see also Finkbeiner, 1996). Parents' continued commitment to protect the child, together with their feeling that attending to other matters would mean that they have forgotten and so abandoned their child, may account for this persistence of grieving.

That the well-being of the other is a central concern among bereaved spouses and bereaved parents is supported by observation of their efforts to assuage their grief. These efforts often propose that the lost figure is, somehow, all right (e.g., is no longer suffering, or has gone to heaven). Bereaved parents and spouses, and sometimes bereaved children as well, act to keep the memory of the lost figure alive through recognition of such special days as anniversaries of the date of the death. They may display their continued commitment to the lost figure through visits to the grave, perhaps with gifts of flowers. Among bereaved parents especially, the impulse underlying these acts appears to be continued concern for the well-being of the other rather than of the self.

Fixity of object seems to be an aspect of the attachment bond. Grief states, irrespective of the nature of the loss, are not ended by replacement of the lost person. Despair continues even when what might seem to be substitutive relationships are available. Entering a new marriage does not end grieving for a spouse who died, though support can be found in the new partnership; having another child does not end grieving for a child who died. It is not loss of a role occupant that gives rise to grief; it is loss of a particular person. (In relation to loss of a spouse, see Glick, Weiss, & Parkes, 1974; in relation to loss of a child, see Finkbeiner, 1996.)

In all forms of bereavement feelings of guilt, anger, fearfulness, or anxiety frequently are intermeshed with protest and despair. The intensity of these feelings varies among the bereaved individuals; indeed, each is reported by only a minority of bereaved spouses (Shuchter & Zisook, 1993). However, these further emotional responses suggest some of the meanings that may be given to loss.

The occurrence of feelings of guilt and of anger suggests that the loss is seen as someone's fault. In instances of guilt and anger, the bereaved person seems to believe that the relationship ought to have continued and that someone is to blame for its ending. Feelings of guilt suggest that the bereaved person blames the self. Feelings of anger suggest that the bereaved person directs blame instead toward the object of the anger: the departed spouse or a physician or other third party. The belief that the loss is someone's fault appears most strongly among those who have lost children, where there had been expectation that the children would survive the griever; it appears least strongly among those whose parent or spouse dies in old age.

Fearfulness and anxiety, which appear especially as aspects of the grief that follows loss of a spouse, suggest that the lost relationship was relied on for reassurance of security. The lost figure may have directly provided such reassurance or may instead have strengthened the griever's self-confidence. Parents who have lost children, although they seem less likely to feel newly fearful, may now see the world as dangerous, unjust, and uncontrollable, and may be less certain of their ability to protect another person.

Loss of a parent seems to affect children and adults differently. Children, on loss of a parent, experience intense and persisting grief (Normand, Silverman, & Nickman, 1996). Adults on loss of a parent appear to experience an upsurge of previously dormant attachment feelings that now express themselves in grief like that of immature children for parents. However, the grief state in adults who have lost parents seems ordinarily short-lived, with limited expression of protest and a brief time of despair. (Exceptional cases of deep and persisting grief on the death of a parent are reported by Horowitz, Wilner, Marmar, & Krupnick, 1980.)

With the foregoing observations in mind, we can summarize the characteristics of the attachment bond whose severance gives rise to grief. The bond is formed with a particular figure. Following loss of that figure, substitutive figures will not interrupt distress. The bond is associated, at least in pair-bond relationships and parent–child relationships, with an expectation of permanence, and persists despite absence of reinforcement through interaction. The bond is in all instances associated with feelings of security, but not necessarily with feelings of *personal* security; in parent–child relationships, it is the security of the child, not that of the parent, that matters to the parent. Even in pair-bond relationships it is often the security of the other that matters. In both parent–child relationships and pair-bond relationships, threat triggers emergency reactions, but in parent–

child relationships it is almost always endangerment of the other, not of the self, that triggers these reactions.

Bowlby's primary concern was the relationship of the child to his or her parents. In his discussion of the attachment bond in that relationship he emphasized both the specificity of the attachment figures—that other caring adults could not replace absent parents—and also the persistence of the bond. He also emphasized the importance of proximity to a parent as necessary to the child's security should there be threat. He held that the attachment bond expressed itself in three ways, each of them expressive of the linkage between a child's sense of security and the child's access to an attachment figure: Proximity to the attachment figure provided the child with a safe haven from threat; the accessibility of the attachment figure provided a secure base from which the child might more confidently confront challenge; and separation from the attachment figure triggered separation anxiety, a state of anxious distress in the child in which the child's energy and attention were directed to regaining proximity to the attachment figure (Bowlby, 1969, 206–208; 1973, 56; 1988, 12, 121–123).

The defining characteristics of the attachment bond that might be inferred from the phenomena of grief are in some respects different from those emphasized by Bowlby. In particular, they give less weight to proximity to the attachment figure as the essential provider of security under conditions of threat. Instead they emphasize the reliability with which the bond gives rise to emergency reactions aimed at forestalling the threat.

Furthermore, in Bowlby's view of the child's relationship with his or her parent, it was the child's own security that was critical, and the child would display reactions when his or her security was threatened. A description of the attachment bond based on the nature of grief would note that emergency reactions can also have as their aim ensuring the security of the other. In a pair-bond relationship it may be either the security of the self or of the other that is critical, and in a parent's relationship with a child, it is the security of the other that matters.

REPRESENTATIONS AND THEIR ORGANIZATION

I now turn to the issue of how the attachment bond, as described in this chapter, may be maintained even in the absence of the attachment figure. Evidence for the surmise that the bond remains in place despite the death of the attachment figure is that, years after the figure's death, feelings and thoughts about the figure can be triggered by photographs, letters, or items of clothing. The feelings can be distressing if the representations of the other are linked to awareness of loss. But they can also be consoling insofar as they trigger a sense of the other as still accessible. Some widows and widowers report that they find it reassuring to invoke a sense of the presence of their deceased spouse (Glick, Weiss, & Parkes, 1974).

Observations such as these suggest that the bereaved person carries, in long-term memory, representations of the attachment figure's name, image, and voice, together with the feeling state of being in that figure's presence. The bereaved person must also maintain holistic representations of the figure that integrate the representations obtained through different modalities. Indeed, the ability to form holistic representations that integrate the input of different modalities seems virtually hardwired into mental functioning: It has been shown that we form such representations from the very beginning of life (Meltzoff & Borton, 1979).

To account for the different expressions of attachment in different relationships, it seems necessary to suppose that long-term memory also lodges not only one representation of the self but more than one such representation, perhaps including the self as needful and the self as competent to care for another. The representation of the self elicited by a relationship with a parent would then be different from the representation of the self elicited by a pairbond partner or a child.

Given a set of different representations of the self, a single emotional system, the attachment system, might underlie relationships that respond differently to threat. In an adult child's relationship to his or her parent, the self could be understood as needful; in that same parent's relationship to his or her own child, the self could be understood as protective. In a corresponding fashion, the other figure could be understood as protective should it be the parent, as needful should it be the child. In the relationship of spouses, it seems likely that the self could be understood either as needful or as protective, depending on circumstances and the partners' characteristics.

It seems likely that people also carry in their minds a representation of the class of relationships to which a particular relationship belongs. This would seem to be required by the observation that behavior in particular relationships can be affected by beliefs about the class of relationship. Thus beliefs about how parents should behave toward their children can affect how a parent actually behaves toward his or her own children. Conversely, experience in a particular relationship might affect beliefs about the class of relationship to which it belongs.

Something like this sort of brain modeling of others, of the self, and of relationships seems necessary if we are to explain the differences in grief states associated with loss of particular relationships. It seems necessary if we are to explain, especially, the observation that children experience loss of parents as abandonment by a protective figure, that conjugal bereavement can be experienced either as abandonment or as personal failure, and that bereaved parents blame themselves for having failed to protect their child.

REPRESENTATIONS IN THE ABSENCE OF DIRECT EXPERIENCE

Although mental representations of attachment figures seem to persist indefinitely, they are influenced by information. Direct experience with an attachment figure might corroborate and extend established representations or might modify them: Someone initially felt to be untrustworthy may prove his worth or someone initially trusted may disappoint, with consequent change in the mental representation of that person. Representation of a person can also be affected by others' reports. Indeed, a person's reputation might be thought of as information about a person that affects representations of that person.

Representations are also accessible to internal influences. Presumptions regarding the characteristics of others can tug representations their way. There may be tendencies to reduce cognitive dissonance, so that there is idealization of those already seen positively and dismissal or reinterpretation of positive information about those viewed negatively.

When interaction with the other is no longer possible, as after the death of a spouse, representation of the other's characteristics will depend on records, memories, internal processes, and the communications of others. It can matter more, now, what one is told about the other person, and the reduction of cognitive dissonance in positive or negative directions will be uncontested by actual experience.

Here we have an explanation for the idealization of the other that often follows conjugal bereavement. The widow's or widower's yearnings for the return of the other make likely, in a dissonance-reduction fashion, a tendency to focus attention on the positive qualities of the lost figure. There may be comfort, as well, in understanding the relationship as having been entirely satisfactory. The pressures toward idealization would then be heightened as friends and family, in their consolation of the bereaved person, emphasize their respect for the lost figure (Lopata, 1996).

Similar processes could produce the blanket condemnation of the other that often is seen in marital separation and divorce. Each former partner might be led by fear and anger to establish a negative representation of the other. Past experience might then be reinterpreted so that it is consistent with their negative representations. Present experience can be minimized and, to the extent it is inescapable, can be made consistent with the negative representations.

BONDS AND RELATIONSHIPS

It may be useful to distinguish between bonds and relationships. A bond might be defined as the mental representations of self and other, together with the feelings associated with these representations. So a child's bond of attachment to a parent would be those mental and emotional phenomena that lead the child to feel comfort in the parent's presence. They would include the child's representations of self and parent, and the feelings—security, connection, deference, awe—that are linked to the representations. Actual interactions would express the representations and feelings in expectations and behaviors.

Relationships are formed of all the events occurring between people, whereas bonds are the emotional linkages that underlie those events. A child's bond to a parent would include the child's representations of self, parent, and relationship to parent, together with the feelings these representations trigger and are triggered by. The child's relationship to the parent would include not only the child's thoughts, feelings, and behaviors in relation to the parent, but all the experiences the child has with the parent. At one point the child might ask the parent's help with a task, at another point the child might be taken somewhere by the parent, at another point the child and parent might have a dispute over bedtimes; all these events are part of their relationship.

Although bonds help decide important properties of relationships—for example, the relationship's contribution to feelings of security and the reliability of the relationship—bonds cannot predict the feelings of each participant toward the other. Consider the relationship of marriage. Fundamental to the functioning of marital relationships, with few exceptions, is a bond of attachment. But even though marriages in consequence foster feelings of security and well-being, in some troubled marriages such feelings are darkened by anger and distrust. Indeed, discomfort with a marital partner sufficient to give rise to separation and divorce can coexist with feeling lost without access to the other (Kitson & Holmes, 1992; Weiss, 1975).

In a similar way, children's relationships with parents and parents' with children can be freighted with a range of feelings unconnected to the attachment bond. The attachment bond is reliably linked to feelings of security and will reliably trigger emergency reactions under conditions of threat, but otherwise does not dictate the feelings to be found in the relationships in which it is embedded.

Bonds are more stable than the relationships they underlie. It has been noted that mental representations of attachment figures are accessible to information about the figure and also to internally driven reconstructions. The same may be said regarding representations of the self; success and failure, acquisition and loss, all affect how the self is understood. Mental representations of self and other undoubtedly are also accessible to feeling states, including feelings of well-being and of self-sufficiency, and so are likely to vary from time to time. The quality of relationships, including the extent to which they express need and trust, would vary accordingly.

Grief is a predictable consequence of the loss of a relationship of attachment. But other consequences of the loss of a relationship of attachment depend on the constellation of bonds and feelings carried by that relationship. Consider the effect of marital loss on self-esteem. Where there had been dependence on the relationship for support of self-esteem, loss of the relationship will bring with it self-doubt. But where the relationship had diminished self-esteem, as might happen in a marital relationship in which the bereaved partner had regularly been disparaged as incompetent, grieving may after a time be accompanied by improved self-esteem.

A SECOND CLASS OF RELATIONSHIPS

Bowlby believed that once a child's security needs were met, the child could give attention and energy to other matters. He wrote,

> Exploring the environment, including play and varied activities with peers, is . . . antithetic to attachment behavior. When an individual (of any age) is feeling secure he is likely to explore away from his attachment figure. (Bowlby, 1988, p. 121)

Bowlby viewed "play and varied activities with peers" as antithetic to attachment behavior, because children engaged in these activities gave no attention to the attachment issues of safeguarding a secure base and maintaining proximity to safe haven. Instead, they might seek out challenge and apparently manageable threat. Yet attachment-indifferent relationships are maintained by underlying bonds, just as are attachment relationships.

The bonds underlying relationships that are not attachment relationships have strong similarities to one another, and so can be thought of as a class of relational bonds, distinct from the attachment bonds underlying pair-bond relationships and parent–child relationships. I will refer to them as affiliative bonds and the relationships they sustain as affiliations or affiliative relationships.

Observation suggests that loss of an affiliative relationship does not give rise to grief, though it may well give rise to distress of another sort. As an example, consider the bond underlying work relationships. Work relationships are often of great emotional importance, and loss of work relationships can produce severe distress. However, the characteristics of that distress differ from the characteristics of the distress that follows loss of relationships of attachment: It is less immediate; it is focused more on loss of a social connection than of a particular figure; and it is more easily interruptible by new work relationships. This does not mean that work relationships are emotionally unimportant; only that they function differently from relationships of attachment.

Work bonds, like bonds of attachment, appear to be maintained by representations of self, other, and the relationship. However, the emotions linked to work bonds appear to have more to do with acceptance of self and other as appropriate or desirable partners and allies than they do with maintaining security. Crucial to the satisfactoriness of relationships of attachment is the other's accessibility. In work relationships, in contrast, what is most important is respect for the other's competence and reliability as a partner and ally, together with the other's apparent respect for the self.

Work relationships are just one instance of a relationship based on an affiliative bond. In children, affiliative bonds are embedded in relationships with peers and siblings. In adults, affiliative bonds are embedded in relationships with work colleagues, with friends, and with kin. In general, affiliative bonds are experienced as alliances. The other person is felt to be someone with whom can join forces in efforts to achieve goals or respond to challenge. (For further discussion, see Weiss, 1998.)

The affiliations differ, one from another, in their aims and, in consequence, in such characteristics as the anticipated permanence of the relationship and the meaning of the relationship's interruption. Work relationships are concerned with contributions to a shared enterprise and their continuation is understood to depend on the continued validity of the enterprise. People who change jobs expect to change work relationships. Friendship has as its basis the mutual enhancement of quality of life. It is understood as implying loyalty and affection. It is also anticipated as potentially lasting lifelong, but it is often the case that changed circumstances change the salience of the relationship. The third affiliative relationship, the kinship tie, has as its basis a sense of permanent membership in a collectivity in which each member feels obligated to give help to any other member who needs it, insofar as this is possible. Like friendships, kinship ties imply loyalty and affection, but even without loyalty and affection, they are understood as lifelong. Still, estrangements occur, and even without estrangement kin who live at a distance from one another may communicate only occasionally.

Affiliative bonds give rise to feelings of connectedness and to a sense of augmented resources. In other respects, different bonds seem to foster different feelings. In work relationships there are usually feelings linked to assessment of the other's competence and reliability and to assessments of the extent to which one is respected by the other; in friendships there is usually liking for the other, feelings of comfort with the other, and respect for the other; in kin ties there may be feelings of gratitude or resentment, of closeness or misuse, but withal a sense of permanent connection because of shared membership in a collectivity.

Affiliations, like attachments, strengthen feelings of security. Affiliations, however, do so indirectly by making available resources, including the energies and understandings of others, with which to achieve aims or respond to threat. Work relationships make possible the achievement of goals and projects unreachable alone, including the goal of earning a living;

friendships facilitate the management of social life as well as help in dealing with challenges of every sort; kinship ties provide a kind of safety net, a resource that can be called on at any time and that would be available should all else fail. In all these instances, it is the availability of help, not the assurance of safe haven, that fosters feelings of security. Affiliations strengthen one's confidence in one's ability to deal with challenge or threat.

Another difference between attachments and affiliations is in the importance of exclusivity. Attachments tend to be exclusive. At least one participant in an attachment relationship relies on the attentive presence of the other to provide a secure base. The beneficiary of the secure base is made less secure to the extent that the guarantor of the secure base also provides a secure base for another, because the guarantor may then be unavailable when needed. Parents who have more than a single child serve as attachment figures to all their children, but can find it difficult to respond to more than one needy child at once. Here is a root of sibling rivalry. (At the same time, and partially offsetting the rivalry of siblings, is the potential for alliance in a sibling relationship. So siblings are often rivals within the home and allies outside it.)

Affiliative relationships, because they are concerned with the management of challenge, are likely to welcome additional relationships of the same kind. Indeed, affiliative relationships often are components of aggregates: friendships are components of friendship networks, work relationships of work groups, and kinship ties of families. Social life often involves participation not in isolated affiliative relationships but rather in aggregates of affiliative relationships: Thus the work day brings people into organizational settings, friendships give rise to informal gatherings and organized parties, and kinship ties are celebrated through family events, such as Christmas dinners, that would be unsatisfactory if only two people were present.

AFFILIATIONS AND LOSS

Ending of affiliative relationships ordinarily produces distress, but this is not necessarily the case. Work relationships can be interrupted or ended without persisting distress or, often, without distress at all. Should a better job offer itself, an entire set of work relationships can ordinarily be left behind with little remorse. Unemployment is intensely painful, but that is because of the sense of social exclusion and personal failure associated with absence of employment, not because of loss of former associates.

The fading of friendships can, in a similar fashion, be taken in stride. Should a close friendship end in discord because of perceived insult or injury, there can be a sense of loss, but it will not approach in intensity or duration the emotional upheaval that follows marital separation. There may be a persisting sense of misuse or uneasiness associated with a loss of trust in the relationship, but this is quite different from grief.

Kin relationships, including the relationships of adults with siblings and parents as well as with more distant kin, can experience estrangements triggered by anger over long-past events or by current disputes or as a result of objectionable behavior or simply because of geographical distance and competing demands. The estrangement of kin, like the parting of friends, may be accompanied by hurt and a sense of loss, but, as with friendships, there will not be the compulsion to reinstate the relationship that follows estrangements in relationships of attachment. Although the estrangement of kin can foster feelings of bitterness, it does not dominate thoughts and feelings as would estrangement in a relationship of attachment.

To be sure, the death of a sibling or of a parent can trigger an upsurge of attachment feelings that had long been dormant. There can, in consequence, be a sense of having been abandoned to one's own resources, bereft of a critically important guarantor of security. However, grief following loss of close kin tends to be brief, and in most instances soon gives way to a return by the griever to an emotional state oriented to ongoing life (Cleiren, 1993, pp. 90, 248).

Loss of an affiliative relationship usually is distressing, sometimes severely so, but the characteristics of the distress are different from those of grief. The death of even the closest of friends, though it is likely to give rise to great sorrow, will not produce the syndrome of protest, with its compulsive searching, nor the syndrome of hopeless despair. Despite the sorrow, there almost surely will be no waves of pain, as there are in grief, no pining for the lost figure, no vigilant alertness to the figure's possible return. There may well be dismay that the loss occurred, possibly anger that it could not be prevented, and a sense of a world from which someone emotionally important has disappeared. There may well be persisting feelings of loyalty and affection. But there will be no seemingly interminable stretches of despair such as follow loss of an attachment figure.

One reason for the limited distress associated with loss of particular affiliative relationships is the much greater degree of substitutability among affiliates. Under conditions of threat, attachment relationships mobilize attention and energy in relation to that one person who is the attachment figure. It is access to, or the safety of, one's parent, one's spouse, or one's child that is important; others, no matter how plausible they may be as substitute figures, are irrelevant. Ordinarily, in affiliative relationships more than a single other will do. Under conditions of threat, although that friend who has skills or resources particularly useful in relation to the threat will be the most valued, any friend can be helpful. In dealing with a work task any coworker with appropriate skills can serve as a partner. In seeking help with a problem in living—need for a temporary residence, need for help with child care—any member of the kin group can be turned to.

RELATIONSHIPS AND MULTIPLE BONDS

As was noted previously, relationships can have more than a single bond embedded in them. Affiliative bonds seem easily to coexist; work relationships often have embedded in them, though perhaps only weakly, friendship bonds, as when colleagues go to lunch together, and kinship bonds, as when colleagues form a committee to provide help and companionship for one of their number who is ill or has been injured. In a similar fashion, friends can become a working party, and kin can enjoy each other as companions. Attachment relationships, too, seem able to embody more than a single form of attachment bond, though in child–parent and parent–child relationships one form would clearly predominate.

Relationships organized around attachment bonds may also have affiliative bonds embedded within them. This is especially true of the relationship of marriage. Marriages ordinarily embody not only a bond of attachment but also a work bond, as each partner relies on the other to contribute to the management of their shared home and family. There is in addition, in most marriages, a friendship bond, in which each partner relies on the other to share in social life and the interpretation of social experience. Marital partners are also, of course, each the other's next-of-kin, obligated to provide help as needed.

The recognition that multiple bonds exist in marital relationships provides a way of understanding the kinds of damage produced by the ending of the relationship. After the death of a spouse the grief that would have been a consequence simply of loss of an attachment figure is complicated by disorganization and, among parents of dependent children, by task overload, because of loss of a partner, by loneliness because of loss of a steady companion, and by a sense of vulnerability because of loss of a figure who had been counted on for support.

CONCLUSION

I have proposed a theory of grief as a response to the loss of relationships of attachment. Aspects of this theory include

(a) The grief of children, should parents die or permanently leave; of pair-bond partners at the ending of their relationship; and of parents who have lost children, all draw on the same emotional system. This is the attachment system Bowlby identified in children. Differences in the nature of grief can be linked to differences in identification of the self as a protecting or protected figure.

(b) The affective tone of a relationship is not predictable from knowledge of the bonds that maintain the relationship. Attachment bonds may maintain relationships that sustain both positive and negative feelings about the self and the other. Grief on loss of relationships is likely to be colored by the nature of the lost relationships.

(c) We maintain representations of ourselves and others that decide the emotions triggered by our relationships with them. The persistence of representations and associated feelings after the death of attachment figures is responsible for a sense of continued relationship to those figures.

(d) Grief may be complicated when the lost relationship had embedded within it other bonds. Marriage is a relationship especially likely to have embedded within it multiple bonds.

(e) Relationships can be important without having embedded within them the bond of attachment. Ending of relationships that are emotionally important yet not based on attachment bonds gives rise to distress but not to grief.

Although this theory of grief is consistent with observations, at least two key elements have not, to my knowledge, been demonstrated empirically. There has not been demonstration that there are indeed the two distinct emotional systems I propose, one engaged by attachment relationships and the other by affiliative relationships. Some support for this proposal is provided by studies of loneliness that give evidence that there are two distinct types, one corresponding to an absence of attachment figures, the other to an absence of affiliative relationships. Conclusive demonstration might require something like the use of brain-imaging techniques to show that a different configuration of sites is triggered by different relationships.

Also, there has not been work that might bear on the model I present of internalized representations of others and representations of the self that shift with the nature of the relationship. It is hard to imagine an alternative to this model that would fit observations of the way people function in relationships of attachment, but the functioning of representations has not been directly observed.

Other elements of the theory I propose seem to me to have stronger empirical support. There is observational evidence that persisting grief states of despair, perhaps interrupted by protest, occur only following loss of attachment figures. There is observational evidence, though it is not conclusive, that vulnerability to grief on loss of an attachment figure persists indefinitely. The specificity of attachment figures seems to be well-established.

The theory of grief presented in this chapter suggests approaches to explanation for a number of potentially perplexing observations. These include the occurrence of grief after loss of some kinds of close relationships but not others, and both the similarities and the differences in the grief syndromes that follow loss of a child, a spouse, and a parent. The theory draws on a more inclusive theory of the nature and functioning of social relationships. Its use of this more inclusive theory suggests that we can better understand social relationships by study of grief.

REFERENCES

Bowlby, J. (1969). *Attachment and loss. Vol. 1: Attachment*. New York: Basic Books.

Bowlby, J. (1973). *Attachment and loss. Vol. 2: Separation, anxiety and anger*. New York: Basic Books.

Bowlby, J. (1980). *Attachment and loss. Vol. 3: Loss: Sadness and depression*. New York: Basic Books.

Bowlby, J. (1988). *A secure base: Parent-child attachment and healthy human development*. New York: Basic Books.

Cleiren, M. (1993). *Bereavement and adaptation: A comparative study of the aftermath of death*. Washington, DC: Hemisphere.

Finkbeiner, A. (1996). *After the death of a child: Living with loss through the years*. New York: Free Press.

Glick, I. O., Weiss, R. S., & Parkes, C. M., (1974). *The first year of bereavement*. New York: John Wiley & Sons.

Horowitz, M. J., Wilner, N., Marmar, C., and Krupnick, J., (1980). Pathological grief and the activation of latent self-images, *American Journal of Psychiatry, 137*, 1157–1162.

Kitson, G., & Holmes, W. (1992). *Portrait of divorce: Adjustment to marital breakdown*. New York: Guilford Press.

Lehman, D. R., Wortman, C. B., & Williams, A. F. (1987). Long-term effects of losing a spouse or child in a motor vehicle crash. *Journal of Personality and Social Psychology, 52*, 228–231.

Lopata, H. (1996). Widowhood and husband sanctification. In D. Klass, P. R. Silverman, & S. L. Nickman (Eds.), *Continuing bonds: New understandings of grief* (pp. 149–162). Philadelphia: Taylor & Harris.

Meltzoff, A. N., & Borton, W. (1979). Intermodal matching by human neonates. *Nature, 282*, 403–404.

Normand, C. L., Silverman, P. R., & Nickman, S. L., (1996). Bereaved children's changing relationships with the deceased. In D. Klass, P. R. Silverman, & S. L. Nickman (Eds.), *Continuing bonds: New understandings of grief* (pp. 87–111). Philadelphia: Taylor & Harris.

Osterweis, M., Solomon, F., & Green, M. (Eds.). (1994). *Bereavement: Reactions, consequences, and care*. Washington, DC: National Academy Press.

Parkes, C. M. (1996). *Bereavement: Studies of grief in adult life* (3rd ed.). London: Routledge.

Parkes, C. M., & Weiss, R. S. (1983). *Recovery from bereavement*. New York: Basic Books.

Rosenblatt, P. C. (1996). Grief that does not end. In D. Klass, P. R. Silverman, & S. L. Nickman (Eds.), *Continuing bonds: New understandings of grief* (pp. 45–58). Philadelphia: Taylor & Harris.

Shuchter, C. R., & Zisook S. (1993). The course of normal grief. In M. S. Stroebe, W. Stroebe, & R. O. Hansson (Eds.), *Handbook of bereavement: Theory, research, and intervention* (pp. 23–43). Cambridge: Cambridge University Press.

Weiss, R. S. (1975). *Marital separation*. New York: Basic Books.

Weiss, R. S. (1998). A Taxonomy of relationships. *Journal of Personal and Social Relationships, 15,* 671–684.

Wortman, C. B., & Silver, R. C. (1989). The myths of coping with loss. *Journal of Consulting and Clinical Psychology, 57,* 349–357.

4

EMOTION, ATTACHMENT, AND BEREAVEMENT: A CONCEPTUAL COMMENTARY

PHILLIP R. SHAVER AND CAROLINE M. TANCREDY

Bereavement and grief have been the subjects of historical, artistic, and philosophical works for as long as people have composed stories about the important events in their lives. Despite such prolonged and intense scrutiny, bereavement has yet to inspire a single, widely accepted explanatory framework (see summaries by Archer, 1999; M. S. Stroebe, Hansson, & Stroebe, 1993). Indeed, the medical and social scientific literature on bereavement spawns one conceptual perspective after another, none of which, despite adding to our understanding of bereavement, seems to result in a winning theoretical conception. Each of the major approaches to grief tends to become the foundation for clinical interventions and advice meant to benefit grieving individuals. To the extent that the approaches differ, the advice can be extremely disparate. Freud's (1917/1957) "Mourning and Melancholia" inspired efforts to aid clients' "grief work" (acknowledgment and expression of painful emotions) and apparently caused bereaved individuals to feel worried or out of place if they failed to cry and express anger at the deceased person. Today, partly as a reaction against the grief-work concept, Bonanno and Kaltman (1999) suggest that the bereaved might watch comedy films because researchers have discovered that successful mourning often includes smiling and laughter. Probably no psychodynamic therapist has ever suggested to bereaved clients that they watch comedy films.

The purpose of this chapter is to consider whether it is possible for bereavement researchers to adopt strategies that encourage the integration of discoveries rather than the proliferation of isolated findings and approaches and the frequent straw-man characterization of previous theories. With a complex topic such as bereavement, it seems probable that most serious observations are correct. The problem is not so much to counter those observations but to figure out how they can all be incorporated, eventually, into a single theoretical framework. Because our own orientation grows out of research experiences in two topic areas—human emotions and attachment processes—we are especially interested in the ways in which bereavement theories dovetail or diverge from contemporary emotion theory (represented, for example, by Frijda, 1986, 1988; Lazarus, 1991, 1999) and attachment theory (Bowlby, 1969, 1973, 1980; Cassidy & Shaver, 1999). But we hope our comments will contribute to a larger theoretical effort that incorporates the best insights of these two approaches as well as other approaches described in this volume. Our chapter is divided into two main sections, one dealing with emotion theory and the other with attachment theory.

BEREAVEMENT IN THE CONTEXT OF CONTEMPORARY EMOTION THEORY

Contemporary emotion theory provides a useful framework for integrating bereavement data because it encompasses several theoretical perspectives that have already been applied to the study of bereavement, such as evolutionary theory, cognitive–behavioral approaches to psychotherapy, cognitive–appraisal approaches to emotion, and the study of personality and individual differences in emotional reactions. In this initial section of the chapter we first examine how grief is conceptualized and measured in current research. Specifically, we suggest that constructs such as stress and depression have dominated bereavement research somewhat at the expense of a consideration of a wider range of emotional processes. Second, we invoke a general model of appraisal, emotion, and emotion regulation that may contribute to a broader conceptualization of responses to bereavement. Essentially, we argue that grieving involves a host of emotional reactions, each of which can be understood partly in terms of the general nature of emotion. Third, we discuss how some of the data gathered by bereavement researchers fit into this framework. Fourth, because we are interested in retaining what is valuable and correct about previous theories, we point to instances of misrepresentation or rejection of ideas related to the emotion model that deserve to be retained and incorporated into current theories.

The Conceptualization and Measurement of Grief Processes and Outcomes

In the previous *Handbook of Bereavement*, several authors (e.g., Sanders, 1993; W. Stroebe & Stroebe, 1993; Wortman, Silver, & Kessler, 1993) presented data indicating that not all bereaved individuals react in the same way (i.e., some standard, predictable way) to bereavement, and that some of them hardly grieve at all. This high variability in emotional reaction is likely to characterize all complex events that have an emotional impact on some people. As explained in this section, no emotion follows automatically and directly from a particular objective event (Frijda, 1986; Lazarus, 1991, 1999; Oatley & Jenkins, 1996). We cannot understand a person's emotional reactions to the loss of a close-relationship partner without knowing something about the relationship, the person's needs and wishes regarding the relationship, the person's general orientation to emotional expression in general, the social environment's reactions to such expressions, and the extent to which the lost person is an important part of the bereaved individual's mental representational world.

In recent years, psychodynamic approaches to grief have been challenged by stress-and-coping, or cognitive coping, approaches. Although this change in theoretical orientation has been beneficial, because it makes contact with recent emotion theories and provides natural links between bereavement and poor health, reducing all emotional reactions to "stress," as Selye (1936, 1956/1976) did in his influential general adaptation model, also causes researchers to lose track of potentially important differences between, say, anxiety, anger, sadness, and despair, not to mention pride, love, and joy. (Selye chose to overlook even distinctions between stressors as different as heat, physical pain, and bereavement, the effects of which Mason et al., 1976, later showed to be mediated by cognitive–affective appraisals.) The stress concept encourages the use of one or a few outcome variables—usually either physical health, distress, or depression (viewed as a form of mental ill-health). Even in very recent studies, such as the one reported by Nolen-Hoeksema and Larson (1999), measures of emotional reactions tend to get combined.

> Many researchers have used measures of depression to assess grief-related symptoms, with the assumption that the depressive syndrome closely mirrors the grief syndrome. . . . We also included measures of anxiety and posttraumatic stress symptoms. . . . In some of our analyses, we combined all these emotional symptom measures into one general distress measure, in line with arguments that we must look at a wide

range of emotional symptoms among the bereaved, rather than just at symptoms of depression. (p. 9)

In Selye's work and the literature that has grown out of it, prolonged activation of the sympathetic component of the autonomic nervous system is viewed as damaging various bodily systems, including the immune system. In more psychological work on bereavement, the major dependent variable is often depression, as noted earlier by Nolen-Hoeksema and Larson. Even when stress-and-coping researchers include positive as well as negative emotions in their framework (e.g., Bonanno & Kaltman, 1999; chapters 22 and 25, this volume), the collection of positive and negative emotions is viewed as influencing a single outcome variable such as health or depression.

If the primary goal is to understand a particular person's grief reactions, it may be misleading to reduce everything to "stress and coping." Being angry and being lonely, for example, seem sufficiently different to warrant distinctions more precise than "stress versus nonstress." According to Lazarus's most recent thinking:

> [The] idea of stress is much simpler than that of emotions. Either as a single dimension, or with only a few functional categories, stress tells us relatively little about the details of a previous struggle to adapt. Emotion, conversely, includes at least 15 different varieties, greatly increasing the richness of what can be said about a person's adaptational struggle. . . . If we know what it means to experience each emotion—that is, the dramatic plot for each—then knowing the emotion being experienced provides a ready understanding of how it was brought about. This provides the advantage of substantial clinical insight about the dynamics of that person's adaptational life. We should not allow this potential gain to be forgotten in our research on stress. . . . (1999, pp. 33–34)

A Model of the Emotion Process

Figure 4-1, adapted from Shaver, Schwartz, Kirson, and O'Connor (1987) and Fischer, Shaver, and Carnochan (1990), is a general model of the process that underlies emotions. The model is based both on theoretical considerations (e.g., Frijda, 1986; Lazarus, 1991) and on ordinary people's accounts of their emotional experiences (e.g., Shaver et al., 1987; Smith & Ellsworth, 1985, 1987). At the extreme left-hand side of the figure, we show that the activation of an emotion depends on a perceived change in the environment, especially an unexpected or surprising or personally important change. (Bereavement certainly qualifies.) These changes are automatically, and often unconsciously, appraised in relation to a person's (the perceiver's) needs, goals, wishes, and concerns. If the perceived

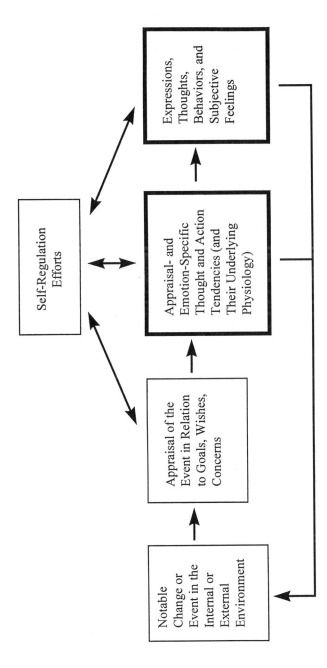

Figure 4-1. Flowchart Model of the Emotion Process

A particular pattern of event appraisals, made in relation to goals and concerns, triggers a particular emotion, viewed as a set of action tendencies with their supporting physiology (e.g., autonomic arousal). If not obstructed, suppressed, or altered by self-regulation efforts, the triggered emotion is expressed in behavior and in subjective experience. (The heavy lines indicate what we mean informally by the everyday term "emotion.") Self-regulation processes can alter appraisals, goals/concerns, action tendencies, physiological arousal, expressions, or acknowledged feelings. Emotions themselves, when registered as notable changes/events, can themselves become the objects of subsequent emotions (e.g., fear of becoming too angry). This appraisal of emotions is indicated by the return arrow along the bottom of the diagram.

Adapted from Shaver, Schwartz, Kirson, and O'Connor (1987) and Fischer, Shaver, and Carnochan (1990). Copyright 1987 by the American Psychological Association.

changes are favorable to goal attainment, the resulting emotions are likely to be positive. If the changes are unfavorable, the resulting emotions are likely to be negative. If the changes have both positive and negative implications for the person's wishes and needs, both positive and negative emotions will be evoked. The particular emotion or emotions that emerge depend on the specific pattern of concerns and appraisals that get activated. For most emotions it has been possible to describe the relevant appraisal patterns (e.g., Lazarus, 1991; Shaver et al., 1987; with respect to grief, see Field, Hart, & Horowitz, 1999). When the required appraisal pattern occurs, the emotion—which can be viewed as an organized, functional set of action tendencies (Frijda, 1986; Oatley & Jenkins, 1996)—follows automatically, with some of its parameters being determined by the specific meaning of the appraised situation. (For example, a person who is frightened by an oncoming train tries to jump *away* from it, but one who fears that he or she is about to miss an important train runs *toward* it.)

The physiological underpinnings of each emotion can be conceptualized as the bodily adjustments necessary to support the appraisal-evoked action tendencies. Although these underpinnings often include autonomic arousal, which is typically viewed as the physiological core of "stress," they cannot generally be reduced to autonomic arousal alone. When they are, such tendencies as yearning, searching, berating one's self or others, and resigning one's self to helplessness get ignored at the expense of failing to understand the nature of a bereaved person's experience.

Returning to the model in Figure 4–1, if there is no reason to postpone, dampen, redirect, or deny the emerging emotion, the emotion-generation process moves immediately from the action-tendency phase to the phase of observable and subjectively perceivable actions, expressions (verbal and nonverbal), and feelings. Often, however, there are other goals in play that make direct enactment and expression of the emotion undesirable. For example, Lepore, Silver, Wortman, and Wayment (1996) reported that high levels of intrusive thoughts about the death of one's infant predict later depression only for mothers who perceive their social environments as disapproving the expression of grief-related feelings.

The need to control emotional expressions and behavior causes emotional individuals to alter some combination of their appraisals, concerns, action tendencies, arousal level, facial expressions, and actions. For this reason, the "self-regulation" component of the model in Figure 4–1 is bidirectionally connected to the other components. The self-regulation component is roughly equivalent to what many investigators call "coping," but rather than view it as a separate process we include it as a normal part of emotion elicitation and regulation. (Such an integration is the major aim of Lazarus's 1999 book on emotions, stress, and coping. See also Bonanno & Kaltman, 1999.)

Because the "changes" and "events" referred to on the left-hand side of the model include changes in a person's internal environment, the process of emotion regulation is actually the same as the process of emotion generation. For example, if a person suddenly remembers his recently deceased spouse and begins to feel overcome by sadness while at work, the sudden change in emotional experience will itself become a central focus of concern, and the resulting action tendencies will include an effort to keep from expressing the sadness. (See Fischer et al., 1990, for additional discussion of this cycling quality of the emotional stream of consciousness.)

With Figure 4-1 in mind, it is easier to see why bereavement researchers (e.g., Shuchter & Zisook, 1993; Wortman et al., 1993) have repeatedly found that the emotions following bereavement differ widely from one individual to another and within individuals over time. If we wish to understand and help with a person's reactions to loss, we will presumably have to find out about his or her goals, concerns, appraisals, social environment, and self-regulatory efforts.

The Evolutionary Function of Emotions Pertaining to Bereavement

Most contemporary theorists view emotions as evolved patterns of experience and behavior that exist and persist because they are, or at least once were, functional (e.g., Bonanno & Kaltman, 1999; Ekman & Davidson, 1994; Oatley & Jenkins, 1996). Anger, for example, motivates people to seek justice following what they perceive to be an unfair or demeaning violation of personal rights or status (Lazarus, 1991; Shaver et al., 1987). Fear often motivates a person to escape or prepare to respond protectively to a threat. In the case of sadness and grief, it has not been as easy for researchers to agree on a likely function. There is some evidence and considerable intuitive support for the possibility that sadness—following, say, a failed project or the loss of an important relationship—contributes to the abandonment of unattainable goals (e.g., Archer, 1999; Klinger, 1975, 1977). If such goals were to be pursued intensely but unsuccessfully for a long period of time, energy and resources would be wasted. If this waste, in turn, reduced an individual's inclusive fitness, there would be an evolutionary advantage to other individuals who felt sad enough to withdraw, regroup, and invest efforts and energies elsewhere.

In the case of grief, which is best viewed as a complex of emotions rather than as a single emotion (chapter 22, this volume), some of the component emotions (e.g., anxiety and anger; yearning and pining) can be viewed as functional in the case of separation but not useful in the case of loss (Archer, 1999; Bowlby, 1980). Parts of the brain involved in separation–protest behavior evolved before mammals had the capacity to understand death and its permanence; thus for certain parts of the grief response there is no difference between extended separation and loss. The brain instigates search and protest action tendencies in both cases. The sadness component of grief may be different. It may result from an appraisal that the attachment figure, or target of caregiving (in the case of parents who lose a child), is permanently gone. It may be useful for bereaved individuals to think about their emotional reactions in these terms and for bereavement researchers to discover which parts of these emotional reactions are functional under modern circumstances and which are not.

Emotion, Cognition, and Grief Work

From Freud to the present, many researchers, clinicians, and bereaved individuals have been concerned about the intrusive nature of thoughts and feelings related to grief. Freud (1917/1957) wrote about the need to painfully detach libido from the mental representations of deceased partners; Horowitz (1986), Nolen-Hoeksema and Larson (1999), and Bonnano and Kaltman (1999) have written more recently about the troubling mental "intrusions" and "flashbacks" that afflict bereaved individuals. Looking at such experiences from the vantage point of a general model of the emotions makes the attention-commanding and mind-narrowing qualities of grief seem less exceptional. All emotions have an attention-commanding effect, and the more intense the emotion, the more powerful the effect. Shaver et al. (1987) empirically derived prototypes for each of five basic emotions—love, joy, anger, sadness, and fear—from research participants' accounts of actual and "typical" experiences. In each case, some of the prototypical reaction components involved cognitive narrowing: in the case of romantic love, for example, "being obsessed with the other, not being able to take one's eyes or thoughts off the other"; joy, "having a positive outlook, seeing only the bright side, having a high threshold for worry, and annoyance, feeling invulnerable"; anger, "narrowing of attention to exclude everything but the anger-provoking situation, thinking 'I'm right, everyone else is wrong'"; sadness, "having a negative outlook, seeing only the negative side of the situation, giving up, no longer trying to improve or control the situation"; and fear, "picturing a disastrous conclusion to events in progress."

Emotions are generally functional partly because they compel attention to the personally relevant events that cause them. Oatley and Jenkins (1996) explained how an emotion takes center stage and crowds out other mental (brain) processes. Memories and action tendencies related to the emotional situation currently at center stage become more accessible, and other kinds of memories and considerations become less accessible. Anything that calls attention to a person or situation that has caused us to experience strong emotions in the past—whether those emotions were positive or negative, and if negative, whether they included anger, fear, or sadness—will tend to reactivate those emotions and crowd out other kinds of mentation. (There is also a more general narrowing and focusing effect of physiological arousal.)

When viewed in the context of a general model of emotion, Freud's (1917/1957) often-criticized conception of the grief process continues to make sense. According to Freud, being emotionally bound to another person (which we might now call "being attached," as explained later) means investing libido in, or cathecting, one's mental representations of the person. In this theory, the close relationship partner—or more precisely, the partner as mentally represented—is called the "object" of an "instinct" (which is not as different as it may at first seem from Bowlby's conception of cognitive–affective "internal working models" of attachment figures). According to Freud, the cathexis connects, or binds, some of the mind's psychic (instinctual) energy to the object. If the relationship partner dies, Freud thought the bereaved person must, in effect, sort through mental representations of the lost partner and decathect each one to reclaim libido for subsequent relationships and commitments. This is the essence of his grief-work concept. Freud also spoke of hypercathexis, his name for the fact that encountering an emotionally painful memory or implicit assumption about a no-longer living partner is often painful, intrusive, and preoccupying, hence detrimental to other mental activities. To the extent that a bereaved individual is ambivalent about the lost partner, he or she may have trouble accomplishing decathexis (i.e., doing grief work), because ambivalence may contribute to continuing anger toward the partner, guilt feelings about being angry, and so on.

It is of course easy to criticize Freud's theory from a contemporary vantage point. We no longer believe in a literal libido or in the idea that mental energy invested in representations of one person is necessarily lost to other mental activities. We also no longer believe, as Freud may initially have done, that the goal of normal grieving is to disengage completely from memories of lost relationship partners (see the section on continuing bonds). Despite these criticisms, anyone who has lost a close relationship partner probably knows what Freud was referring to. In writer C. S. Lewis's famous account of grieving for his dead wife, he says,

> There are moments . . . when something inside me tries to assure me that I don't really mind so much, not so very much, after all. Love is not the whole of a man's life. I was happy before I ever met H. I've plenty of what are called "resources." People get over these things. Come, I shan't do so badly. One is ashamed to listen to this voice but it seems for a little to be making out a good case. *Then comes a sudden jab of red-hot memory and all this "commonsense" vanishes like an ant in the mouth of a furnace.* (1961, p. 7; emphasis ours)

This "jab of red-hot memory" is essentially what Freud meant by hypercathexis, and it is perfectly compatible with what we know about the general attention-grabbing and mind-narrowing effects of all strong emotions. Translated into contemporary cognitive and neuroscientific terms, Freud's and Lewis's observations are equivalent to saying that long-term memory is deeply mined throughout with affectively charged memories and representations of attachment figures (perhaps more so in the case of secure and preoccupied persons and less so in the case of avoidant persons, as explained later), including expectations about the attachment figures' future existence, assistance in times of need, and companionship. The normal processes of association and priming will occasionally activate one or more of these mental structures, surprising their "owner" with unexpected and unbeckoned emotions that are difficult to ignore. Grieving is partly a matter of bumping up against these thoughts and feelings over a period of months or years and acknowledging both their affective charge and their inadequacy as representations of current reality. They have to be reworked (entailing the creation of new or altered neural networks) or weakened by habituation.

Freud's observations, and perhaps even his decathexis metaphor, are still pertinent and need to be explained. It seems likely that recent and future advances in brain imaging will allow researchers to see which parts of the brain (e.g., the amygdala [LeDoux, 1995], the right frontal cortex [Davidson, 1995]) are involved when bereaved individuals free associate about lost loved ones and hit on memories that are emotionally glowing if not "red-hot." If so, it should also be possible to map differences between individuals that make reorganization of mental representations and associated emotions more difficult for some than for others. For present purposes, the issue is not the details of future brain-imaging studies but the idea that Freud's observations were probably not as mistaken as later critics have made them seem. The part of Freud's analysis that has been replaced or superseded in more recent work is his stock of neologisms and metaphors, not his focus on intrusive thoughts, their emotional quality, and the nature of mental reorganization following important losses (Fraley & Shaver, 1999; M. S. Stroebe & Schut, 1999). Freud's observations are still worth considering even if his metaphors seem misleading, just as "attachment," "affectional bonds," "stress" (based on a metaphorical reference to mental fatigue), and inherited "mental modules" may seem misleading 50 to 100 years from now.

Emotion in the Context of the Temporal Course of Grieving

When theorizing about grief, it may be useful to include both the possibility that there is a rough temporal course to mourning (Bowlby, 1980; Sanders, 1999) and the possibility that almost any emotion can occur at any point along the way (M. S. Stroebe & Schut, 1999; Wortman et al., 1993). Surely it is the case, on average, that bereaved individuals become less intensely emotional and less preoccupied with their loss over time. To the extent that a bereaved individual moves from an initial conviction that the lost individual is indispensable and therefore must be recovered to an acknowledgment that the person is—at least in the ordinary, everyday sense—gone, then there is likely to be a general progression from protest (anxiety, anger, searching), to intense sadness, to less intense and less frequent sadness.

Nevertheless, it is also possible for a bereaved individual to feel any emotion at any time, including (as Wortman et al., 1993, have documented; and Nolen-Hoeksema & Larson, 1999, Folkman [chapter 25, this volume], and M. S. Stroebe & Schut, 1999, have described), positive emotions (amid negative ones) in the early phases of grief and bursts of anger in the later phases. As indicated in Figure 4-1, mourning will involve a variety of different emotions, depending on which particular goals or concerns and which particular appraisals are salient at a given time. To the extent that the appraisal process sometimes focuses on the unfairness of the loss, the possibility that it need not have happened, or the insistent recognition that the lost person is still badly missed, then the emotions evoked by these appraisals may continue to be heterogeneous throughout the mourning period and beyond. As M. S. Stroebe and Schut (1999) explained in describing their dual process model of coping with bereavement, most bereaved individuals move back and forth between painful, and sometimes preoccupying, thoughts about the loss and more present-oriented or forward-looking thoughts related to adjustment, challenges, and the need to carry on with life. As a person's concerns and appraisals shift from aspects of the loss to aspects of the rest of life's demands and opportunities, a corresponding shift in emotions occurs naturally.

BEREAVEMENT IN THE CONTEXT OF CONTEMPORARY ATTACHMENT THEORY

Besides emotion theory, one of the most useful theoretical perspectives for thinking about bereavement is Bowlby and Ainsworth's attachment theory (e.g., Ainsworth, Blehar, Waters, & Wall, 1978; Bowlby, 1969, 1973, 1980; see also Cassidy & Shaver, 1999; chapter 3, this volume). One of Bowlby's most important books (Bowlby, 1980) is titled, *Loss: Sadness and Depression*, and another (Bowlby, 1979), *The Making and Breaking of Affectional Bonds*. His interest in attachment was originally sparked by noticing the effects of maternal loss on children's later psychopathology and delinquency, so in a sense the entire edifice of attachment theory was designed to explain the psychological impact of loss.

For our purposes, the theory can be summarized briefly: Human beings, like many of our primate and mammalian relatives, are born with several innate behavioral systems, including the "attachment behavioral system" and the "caregiving [parenting] system" (Bowlby, 1969). Human infants become emotionally attached to their primary caregivers, and once this happens they clearly prefer those caregivers, exhibit fear or wariness to strangers, and become distressed when separated from an attachment figure. In a complementary way, adults usually become emotionally invested in the children who are attached to them. Experiences with attachment figures are represented psychologically as "internal working models" (see Bretherton & Munholland, 1999, for a description and evaluation of this concept). Individual differences in these models are reflected in individual differences in reactions to separations from and reunions with attachment figures (Ainsworth et al., 1978; see Weinfield, Sroufe, Egeland, & Carlson, 1999, for a review). Similar individual differences in adults' attachment representations are predictive of differences in their parenting behavior toward infants and young children (e.g., George & Solomon, 1999; Hesse, 1999; Main, Kaplan, & Cassidy, 1985). They may also be related to pair-bond attachment and reactions to loss of a marital or romantic partner during adulthood (e.g., Fraley & Shaver, 1999; Shaver & Clark, 1994; chapter 2, this volume).

Researchers have identified four major patterns of attachment and corresponding patterns of adult caregiving. Ainsworth and her colleagues (1978) named three of the infant patterns "secure," "avoidant," and "anxious/ambivalent." Main and Solomon (1986, 1990) identified a fourth pattern and called it "disorganized/disoriented." In the literature on adult caregiving, the same four patterns are called "secure," "dismissing," "preoccupied," and "unresolved" (e.g., Hesse, 1999). In the literature on romantic pair-bonding, some combination of the child and caregiver type names are used (e.g., Shaver & Clark, 1994).

When studying bereavement, attachment theory is useful both as a way of thinking about what is "broken" or "lost" when a close-relationship partner dies and as a way of characterizing common individual differences in reactions to loss. In the remainder of this chapter we comment on the ways in which attachment theory has been used and misused in the bereavement literature and explain how the most recent version of the theory may prove useful in future studies of bereavement.

Attachment Theory and Various Kinds of Losses

Attachment theory leads us to expect that the loss of an attachment figure will be an important and troubling event, especially to the extent that a person is emotionally dependent on the lost attachment figure. It also leads us to expect that parents and caregivers will be upset about the death of the infants and children who are attached to them, although the precise nature of the grieving reaction may not be the same in the two cases. Of course, both kinds of losses are prominent in the large literature on bereavement.

One issue to which Bowlby, like many contemporary bereavement theorists, did not devote much attention is the possibility that genetic relatedness plays a role in attachment formation and grieving loss. In Archer's (1999) recent book, *The Nature of Grief*, which integrates aspects of attachment theory with the broader perspective of evolutionary psychology, this matter is given explicit attention. Archer considers the possibility that grieving is especially intense following the loss of someone who contributed to, or would eventually have contributed to, the bereaved individual's inclusive fitness. (See also chapter 12, this volume.) This may be one reason why grief is especially intense following the loss of a reproductively viable identical twin (Segal & Bouchard, 1993), with whom one shares 100 percent of one's genes; or an offspring who has reached reproductive age but not yet borne children; or a sibling of reproductive age; or a spouse whose contributions are still needed for reproduction, child care, and child support. Archer is also sensitive to the possibility that fitness-related grief is *mediated by attachment*. That is, people who are biologically important because of their implications for a griever's reproductive fitness are also likely to be the ones with whom the griever has strong emotional ties. It is not yet clear whether intense grief reactions are a result of broken affectional bonds, some more direct indicator of genetic similarity (e.g., physical appearance, known genetic relatedness), or both.

The distinction between attachment and nonattachment relationships, explained more fully by Weiss (chapter 3, this volume; see also Cassidy, 1999), raises broader issues concerning different kinds of relationships. In terms of the emotion model in Figure 4-1, it matters a great deal how a perceived loss (an important change, or event, in the environment) is related to a person's needs and wishes. If a child loses one of his or her parents, the intensity of the grief reaction may be determined by the extent to which the parent was perceived by the child to be the child's major source of protection and security (i.e., the child's primary attachment figure). In a prototypical attachment relationship, the child relies on the attachment figure (whom Bowlby characterized as a "stronger, wiser" other) for protection ("safe haven" and "secure base," in the theory's terms). This makes it easy to understand why, as Bowlby (1973, 1980) explained, the natural action tendencies and behavior following separation and loss include search, protest, calling, pleading, and berating.

The situation is somewhat different in the case of a parent whose child dies (chapter 3, this volume). In contemporary attachment theory (as explained by Cassidy, 1999, and George & Solomon, 1999) a parent is not said to be "attached" to his or her child (contrary to Archer and other bereavement theorists' broad use of the term attachment). Although both attachment and caregiving involve "affectional bonds," a parent who occupies the role of primary caregiver does not look to the child for protection, a safe haven, or a secure base. In the rare cases in which a parent *does* treat his or her child as an attachment figure (i.e., as a major source of protection and security), attachment theorists view it as a case of pathological "role reversal," which is likely to be psychologically damaging to the child. As Weiss (1993; chapter 3, this volume) explains, parental grief often includes intense wishes to protect and soothe the lost child, along with guilt and helplessness about not having successfully protected the child from pain and death. As with an attached individual's irrational search for a lost attachment figure ("irrational" because the figure is known to be unreachable), a parent may be moved to protect a no longer existent child and may feel guilty even though, realistically, the child's death was not the parent's fault.

In short, the various action tendencies experienced as part of a particular course of mourning are likely to depend on the nature of the relationship and the particular needs and beliefs underlying the bereaved individual's emotion-related appraisals. Without knowing something about those appraisals, we cannot understand why grief takes the form it does in a particular case.

Degree of Attachment

Unfortunately, given the potential importance to bereavement researchers of the distinctions between attachment and nonattachment, or affectionally bonded versus nonbonded relationships, attachment researchers have yet to provide the research community with measures of *degree* of attachment or bondedness, or even the presence versus absence of attachment or bonding. For various reasons, Ainsworth (1972) and other early investigators of infant attachment downplayed the issue of degree of attachment, preferring instead to assume that the most available, familiar caregiver (usually the mother in early studies of attachment) automatically becomes an attachment figure because the totally dependent child's attachment system requires that someone occupy that role. Researchers could therefore focus on what Ainsworth called "quality" of attachment (secure, avoidant, or anxious/ambivalent) rather than degree. Some writers (e.g., Weiss, 1982) have actually defined *attachment* in terms of the likelihood that a person would grieve intensely following the loss of a particular relationship, a strategy that does not help if we wish to understand grief in terms of prospectively measured attachment. Researchers who study adult romantic attachment have devised preliminary questionnaire measures to determine *who* a particular person's major attachment figures are (see Fraley & Davis, 1997; Hazan, Hutt, Sturgeon, & Bricker, 1991; Trinke & Bartholomew, 1997), and these may prove useful in future bereavement research. But they do not assess *degree* of attachment to a particular person.

The lack of measures of attachment points to an even more troubling fact: We do not really know, in depth, what "attachment" means. It is not the same as closeness, liking, or relationship satisfaction (popular constructs in the study of close relationships).[1] It is considered to be more primitive —more deeply rooted in evolutionarily older portions of the brain—than other social processes, which helps to explain why attachment can continue even when a parent or partner is abusive or neglectful and even after one divorces a troublesome spouse (Morgan & Shaver, 1999; Weiss, 1975). Polan and Hofer (1999) described how the loss of an attachment figure (in mice and rats) causes dysregulation of physiological systems, which suggests that attachment figures (mothers, in this case) provide not only a psychological safe haven and secure base but also considerable control over the attached infants' body temperature, sleep–wake cycles, and so on. We do not know yet whether human attachments also involve such physiological regulation as well as "felt security" (Sroufe & Waters, 1977). Thus if we wish to pursue Archer's (1999) interesting idea that degree of attachment explains intensity of grief following loss, we will have to go further than attachment researchers have gone so far in conceptualizing and measuring attachment.

Attachment Orientations and Reactions to Loss

Several studies have shown that people who react especially intensely to a particular loss—crying hysterically, being heavily preoccupied with the loss, ruminating about it, and experiencing it as catastrophic—are more likely than less distressed grievers to continue to be upset about the loss months and years later. This finding has been interpreted as meaning that "grief work," as outlined by Freud and endorsed by subsequent psychoanalysts, does not work (e.g., Wortman & Silver, 1989). Some researchers have even begun to question whether grieving, as conventionally understood, is necessary at all (for reviews, see Bonnano & Kaltman, 1999; chapter 22, this volume).

Research on attachment and loss (see Cassidy & Shaver, 1999, for an overview) can contribute to this discussion. First, people with different attachment patterns handle emotions differently. Those who have been

---

[1]Nolen-Hoeksema and Larson (1999, p. 45) provide two interesting examples:

> (a) Just as with spousal relationships, some relationships between adult children and parents are closer and more positive than others. Yet, in our study, there was no significant relationship between the bereaved adult children's level of distress and how close or conflictual their relationship with their deceased parent had been. Similarly, a larger study of bereaved adult children found no relationship between the closeness of the relationship with the deceased parent and the intensity of grief reactions (Umberson & Chen, 1994).
> (b) There was no relationship between how close and loving the siblings felt their relationship had been with the deceased and their levels of depression after the loss.

treated in ways that cause them to feel secure find it easier to access attachment-related emotional memories and to discuss them coherently (Hesse, 1999). Their primary attachment figures have generally encouraged them to acknowledge feelings and to understand their causes and implications.

Among individuals who do not have a secure orientation to attachment, three major patterns have been delineated, as we mentioned earlier: avoidant (or dismissing, in the case of adults), anxious/ambivalent (preoccupied), and disorganized/disoriented (unresolved). At the risk of oversimplifying, we can say that people with an avoidant or dismissing orientation suppress or avoid attachment-related emotions; those with an anxious or preoccupied orientation are highly emotional and expressive but unable to cope constructively with attachment-related feelings; and those with a disorganized or unresolved orientation have been traumatized in ways that damage their ability to think and talk coherently about attachment-related losses and abuse.

These different patterns are empirically based elaborations of distinctions made by Bowlby (1980) in his discussion of loss, especially the distinction between "chronic mourning" (related to anxious, dependent attachment) and "prolonged absence of conscious grieving" (related to avoidant, compulsively self-reliant attachment). (See Fraley & Shaver, 1999, for details and references.) Both Bowlby's original analysis of individual differences in grieving and the more recent attachment literature lead us to expect that prototypically secure individuals will react emotionally to the loss of an important relationship partner but will not feel overwhelmed by grief. They should also be able to assemble a coherent narrative about the loss and its aftermath and not suffer from intense self-blame or lowered self-esteem.

Dismissingly avoidant individuals are not likely to become emotional about such losses (Fraley, Davis, & Shaver, 1998). They may always, for example, have limited the extent to which they depended emotionally on their relationship partner. In contrast, preoccupied individuals, as the name implies, are probably among the people whom bereavement researchers have found to be very emotional and preoccupied following loss. If so, they were probably more emotional about and preoccupied with the relationship before the loss as well. It is therefore not surprising that they continue to be emotional and preoccupied months and years after the loss.

The Adult Attachment Interview (AAI) has high test–retest reliability and deals with an adult's memories, defenses, and discourse patterns related to childhood attachment experiences (George, Kaplan, & Main, 1996; Hesse, 1999). It could be used, either prospectively or (with caution) retrospectively, to examine the effects of attachment orientation on grief reaction. Even before such research is completed, simply keeping attachment patterns in mind may help researchers think about such controversial issues as "grief work" and "resolution." Avoidant individuals may grieve less without being "unresolved" in the attachment–theoretical sense. Preoccupied individuals may grieve more intensely, but without doing security-enhancing grief work, and later be "unresolved" in both the attachment sense and the sense commonly intended in the bereavement literature (M. S. Stroebe & Stroebe, 1991).

Unresolved/disorganized individuals are a special case. Discovery of this category among children (Main & Solomon, 1986, 1990) was based on the failure of certain infants and toddlers to fit any of Ainsworth's three patterns of infant attachment: secure, avoidant, and anxious/ambivalent. The disorganized infants seemed not to possess a coherent strategy for dealing with their attachment figure's behavior—behavior that Main and Hesse (1990, 1992) later described as "frightened or frightening." When a disorganized infant approached his or her attachment figure for protection, support, or soothing, the attachment figure seemed momentarily frightened, threatened, or distracted (perhaps even momentarily lost in a dissociative state). This caused the infant to engage in odd, disrupted behavior, meriting the label "disorganized/disoriented." Main and Hesse discovered, by studying the disorienting caregivers' AAI transcripts, that these transcripts were marked by indications of "unresolved grief," reflected in an inability to talk coherently (logically, fluently, understandably) about the loss. In other words, parents' unresolved grief, measured in a very specific, reliable way, predicted children's disorganized attachment.

The importance in this research of coherent discourse about emotions is reminiscent of Pennebaker's research on the health value of talking and writing about emotional and traumatic experiences (e.g., Pennebaker, Mayne, & Francis, 1997; see chapter 23, this volume). Archer (1999, pp. 123–124) commented as follows:

> Pennebaker's [research involves] precise linguistic analysis of writing about personal events. A reanalysis of six of his previous studies . . . found that people whose writings were characterized by an increase in the level of insight or words about causes over the writing period showed an improvement in health. The researchers concluded that it was the *change* in thinking patterns over time, not simply thinking about the loss, that predicted improved health. Indeed, they characterized thinking without cognitive restructuring as equivalent to rumination, which is associated with poor recovery.

Since the early work on disorganized attachment was published, attachment researchers working with more troubled samples have extended the notion of "unresolved grief" to include unresolved attachment-related *traumas* as well as losses, because a parent's inability to talk in an organized, coherent way about his or her own abuse also seems to presage having a disorganized/disoriented baby (see Lyons-Ruth & Jacobvitz, 1999, for a review).

Individual differences in attachment orientation, and the relation of these differences to ways of thinking and talking about attachment-related emotions, suggest both that particular patterns of grief must be viewed in the wider context of personality and attachment history and that resolution of grief is partly a matter of what Main and her colleagues (1985) have called "coherence of discourse" and "coherence of mind" (see Hesse, 1999, for a review). Resolution cannot be assessed simply in terms of depression or negative emotion. Nor should normal (presumably secure) grief work be confused with anxious/preoccupied hysteria and rumination.

Secure Attachment Orientation as a Model of "Healthy" Grief

If we wish to create a model of normal or healthy grieving, we might productively look at the typical behavior of secure individuals, in general and especially following loss. (In most samples, the majority of people are classified as secure.) Our prediction is that such people will, on average, experience and express emotions to a moderate degree (e.g., more than dismissing individuals but less than preoccupied ones; Mikulincer & Nachshon, 1991) and be able to provide a coherent account of their loss-related experiences (unlike unresolved/ disorganized individuals; see Hesse, 1999). They will successfully update their "internal working models" of the lost partner and their altered (but perhaps continuing) relationship with him or her. As explained in the next section of this chapter, which deals with the notion of "continuing bonds" (Klass, Silverman, & Nickman, 1996), updating need not involve detachment. It need only allow a person to assemble a workable and mostly present-oriented and forward-looking approach to life.

We would expect secure individuals to be more likely and able than insecure individuals to solicit and benefit from social support following loss (see Nolen-Hoeksema & Larson, 1999, and Mikulincer, Florian, & Weller, 1993, for relevant findings), to be more optimistic than insecure individuals (which Nolen-Hoeksema & Larson, 1999, reported to be associated with better adjustment following loss), and to be better able to move flexibly between the "loss oriented" and "restoration oriented" processes delineated in M. S. Stroebe and Schut's (1999) dual-process model of coping with bereavement. (The mental and behavioral flexibility of secure, and security-engendering, adults has been discussed recently by George & Solomon, 1999.) These predictions are all empirically testable.[2]

---

[2] Nolen-Hoeksema and Larson (1999; p. 76) have written,

> Traditional grief theories suggest that people who are more dependent on others for self-esteem will be more at risk for poor adjustment to loss ... more generally, some studies have found that people who are emotionally unstable, neurotic, insecure, or anxious tend to cope less adaptively and adjust more poorly to loss.

Attachment Theory and "Continuing Bonds"

Like Freud's theorizing about the decathexis of "lost object representations," Bowlby's (1980) analysis of grief in *Loss: Sadness and Depression* has been used as something of a strawman against which subsequent theoretical ideas could be contrasted. As an example we will consider *Continuing Bonds* (Klass et al., 1996), an extremely interesting and valuable book whose editors wish to replace the ideas of decathexis and detachment with the notion that grieving individuals often choose to construct continuing mental relationships with deceased attachment figures.[3] The editors and authors of this otherwise laudable volume seem to believe that they must set aside Bowlby (1980) to make room for their own observations and insights. Here are a few examples:

> In Bowlby's view . . . the attempt to restore proximity [to the deceased attachment figure] is inappropriate or nonfunctional. . . . Those who retain ties are considered maladjusted. This general impression that ties to the deceased need to be severed is referred to in this chapter as the *breaking bonds* hypothesis. (M. S. Stroebe, Gergen, Gergen, & Stroebe, 1996, p. 33)
>
> According to the attachment theory of bereavement resolution, ongoing attachment following a death is unhealthy, if not pathological. (Balk, 1996, p. 311)

As we showed earlier, in the section titled "Attachment Orientation and Reactions to Loss," contemporary attachment theorists conceptualize "unresolved grief," or unresolved losses and traumas, in terms of inability to think and talk coherently about loss and trauma, not in terms of failure to "detach." Even in Bowlby's day, attachment theory did not require that bereaved individuals sever all mental ties with their lost attachment figures. Moreover, in his book about loss Bowlby (1980) referred to the final phase of bereavement as "reorganization," not "detachment," a term he had used earlier (1969) to denote the third stage of young children's reaction to prolonged separation from parents. "Detachment" referred not to the final phase of grieving but rather to a defensive posture reflected in a relatively short-lived coolness toward temporarily absent parents when they returned home. Here is some of what Bowlby (1980) actually wrote about grief, its phases, and the role of "continuing bonds" (not his term, although he comes close to using it in the final quotation that follows) in the reorganization process:

> There is a tendency [with which Bowlby was explicitly disagreeing] to suppose that a normal healthy person can and should get over a bereavement not only fairly rapidly but also completely. (p. 8)
>
> I emphasize these [research] findings because I believe that clinicians

---

[3] This section is based on a more extensive critique by Fraley and Shaver (1999).

sometimes have unrealistic expectations of the speed and completeness with which someone can be expected to get over a major bereavement. (p. 101)

It seems likely that for many widows and widowers it is precisely because they are willing for their feelings of attachment to the dead spouse to persist that their sense of identity is preserved and they become able to reorganize their lives along lines they find meaningful. (p. 98)

During the months and years that follow he will probably be able to organize life afresh, fortified perhaps by *an abiding sense of the lost person's continuing and benevolent presence.* (p. 243, emphasis ours)

Our discomfort with continuing-bonds theorists' treatment of attachment theory is not just a matter of setting the scholarly record straight. Their enthusiasm for continuing bonds, and their strong presumption that all continuing bonds and unresolved elements of grief are beneficial, causes them to overlook signs of pathology (lack of resolution in the contemporary attachment–theoretical sense) in some of their interview transcripts. (See Fraley & Shaver, 1999, for details.)

In the previous *Handbook of Bereavement* (M. S. Stroebe et al., 1993, p. 463), the editors noted other examples of theory distortion:

> Much has been written on "stages" of grief. Most researchers [and Bowlby, we might add] would agree that these are to be taken only as general, flexible guidelines. However, Wortman, Silver, and Kessler argue that there are "stage theories" of grief, namely, those of Bowlby . . . and Horowitz . . . Yet Bowlby's theory is a theory of attachment, Horowitz's one of stress . . . References to phasal changes in both theories are . . . meant to be descriptive, not to be understood as set rules or prescriptions for where an individual ought to be in the "normal" grieving process. (p. 463)

Despite making such points, the Stroebes themselves classified Bowlby's attachment theory as a modernist "breaking bonds" theory (as opposed to the valorized postmodernist "continuing bonds" theory), and on another occasion characterized it as a "depression theory" rather than a "stress theory" (M. S. Stroebe et al., 1996; W. Stroebe & Stroebe, 1993). Neither of these latter designations seems to capture the essence of Bowlby's analysis, or its extensions in recent attachment research. Bowlby did not insist on the breaking of bonds, and he emphasized love, anger, and anxiety as well as sadness and depression (perhaps making him neither a stress theorist nor a depression theorist).

CONCLUSION

Bereavement theorists and researchers have made many important discoveries, as explained in the other chapters in this book. But there has been a tendency to move from one theoretical approach to another, often by attacking previous landmark theories in an unnecessarily harsh and distorting way. This is certainly understandable, and not at all unusual. Every creative person tends to heighten differences to earn a visible stall in the overly crowded marketplace of ideas (Bloom, 1983, 1997), and new approaches really do improve on aspects of earlier approaches. We contend, however, that the field of bereavement studies would be well-served by a more generous and inclusive policy of attempting to retain every valid insight that previous researchers and theorists have achieved. Presumably, all of these valid insights will eventually fit within a single overarching theoretical framework, as has happened many times in the physical and biological sciences. We see the beginnings of such an approach in the dual-process model, which includes both loss-oriented and restoration-oriented processes; the social–functional perspective outlined by Bonanno (chapter 22, this volume); and Archer's (chapter 12, this volume) evolutionary perspective. These theoretical frameworks can encompass both negative and positive emotions, and both decathexis/detachment and continuing bonds. In developing these frameworks further and, perhaps eventually, in attempting to integrate them, it will prove useful to keep both contemporary emotion theory and contemporary attachment theory in mind. An integration of these several perspectives will provide a solid foundation for future research and clinical interventions.

REFERENCES

Ainsworth, M. D. S. (1972). Attachment and dependency: A comparison. In J. L. Gewirtz (Ed.), *Attachment and dependency* (pp. 97–137). Washington, DC: V. H. Winston.

Ainsworth, M. D. S., Blehar, M. C., Waters, E., & Wall, S. (1978). *Patterns of attachment: A psychological study of the Strange Situation.* Hillsdale, NJ: Erlbaum.

Archer, J. (1999). *The nature of grief: The evolution and psychology of reactions to loss.* London and New York: Routledge.

Balk, D. E. (1996). Attachment and the reactions of bereaved college students: A longitudinal study. In D. Klass, P. R. Silverman, & S. L. Nickman (Eds.), *Continuing bonds: New understandings of grief* (pp. 311–328). Washington, DC: Taylor & Francis.

Bloom, H. (1983). *Agon: Towards a theory of revisionism.* Oxford: Oxford University Press.

Bloom, H. (1997). *The anxiety of influence: A theory of poetry* (2nd ed.). Oxford: Oxford University Press.

Bonanno, G. A., & Kaltman, S. (1999). The self-regulation of grief: Toward an integrative perspective on bereavement. *Psychological Bulletin, 125,* 760–776.

Bowlby, J. (1969). *Attachment and loss: Vol. 1. Attachment*. London: Hogarth.

Bowlby, J. (1973). *Attachment and loss: Vol. 2. Separation, anxiety and anger*. New York: Basic Books.

Bowlby, J. (1979). *The making and breaking of affectional bonds*. New York: Tavistock.

Bowlby, J. (1980). *Attachment and loss: Vol. 3. Loss: Sadness and depression*. New York: Basic Books.

oks. Bretherton, I., & Munholland, K. A. (1999). Internal working models in attachment relationships: A construct revisited. In J. Cassidy & P. R. Shaver (Eds.), *Handbook of attachment: Theory, research, and clinical applications* (pp. 89–111). New York: Guilford Press.

Cassidy, J. (1999). The nature of the child's ties. In J. Cassidy & P. R. Shaver (Eds.), *Handbook of attachment: Theory, research, and clinical applications* (pp. 3–20). New York: Guilford Press.

Cassidy, J., & Shaver, P. R. (Eds.). (1999). *Handbook of attachment: Theory, research, and clinical applications*. New York: Guilford Press.

Davidson, R. J. (1995). Cerebral asymmetry, emotion, and affective style. In R. J. Davidson & K. Hugdahl (Eds.), *Brain asymmetry* (pp. 361–387). Cambridge: MIT Press.

Ekman, P., & Davidson, R. J. (Eds.). (1994). *The nature of emotion: Fundamental questions*. New York: Oxford University Press.

Field, N. P., Hart, D., & Horowitz, M. J. (1999). Representations of self and other in conjugal bereavement. *Journal of Social and Personal Relationships, 16,* 407–414.

Fischer, K. W., Shaver, P. R., & Carnochan, P. (1990). How emotions develop and how they organize development. *Cognition and Emotion, 4,* 81–127.

Fraley, R. C., & Davis, K. E. (1997). Attachment formation and transfer in young adults' close friendships and romantic relationships. *Personal Relationships, 4,* 131–144.

Fraley, R. C., Davis, K. E., & Shaver, P. R. (1998). Dismissing avoidance and the defensive organization of emotion, cognition, and behavior. In J. A. Simpson & W. S. Rholes (Eds.), *Attachment theory and close relationships* (pp. 249–279). New York: Guilford Press.

Fraley, R. C., & Shaver, P. R. (1999). Loss and bereavement: Attachment theory and recent controversies concerning grief work and the nature of detachment. In J. Cassidy & P. R. Shaver (Eds.), *Handbook of attachment: Theory, research, and clinical applications* (pp. 735–759). New York: Guilford Press.

Freud, S. (1957). Mourning and melancholia. In J. Strachey (Ed. and Trans.), *The standard edition of the complete psychological works of Sigmund Freud* (Vol. 14, pp. 237–260). New York: Basic Books. (Original work published 1917)

Frijda, N. H. (1986). *The emotions*. Cambridge: Cambridge University Press.

Frijda, N. H. (1988). The laws of emotion. *American Psychologist, 43,* 349–358.

George, C., Kaplan, N., & Main, M. (1996). *Adult Attachment Interview* (3rd ed.). Unpublished manuscript, University of California, Berkeley.

George, C., & Solomon, J. (1999). Attachment and caregiving: The caregiving behavioral system. In J. Cassidy & P. R. Shaver (Eds.), *Handbook of attachment: Theory, research, and clinical applications* (pp. 649–670). New York: Guilford Press.

Hazan, C., Hutt, M. J., Sturgeon, J., & Bricker, T. (1991, April). *The process of relinquishing parents as attachment figures.* Paper presented at the biennial meetings of the Society for Research in Child Development, Seattle, WA.

Hesse, E. (1999). The Adult Attachment Interview: Historical and current perspectives. In J. Cassidy & P. R. Shaver (Eds.), *Handbook of attachment: Theory, research, and clinical applications* (pp. 395–433). New York: Guilford Press.

Horowitz, M. J. (1986). *Stress response syndromes.* Northvale, NJ: Aronson.

Klass, D., Silverman, P. R., & Nickman, S. L. (Eds.). (1996). *Continuing bonds: New understandings of grief.* Washington, DC: Taylor & Francis.

Klinger, E. (1975). Consequences of commitment to and disengagement from incentives. *Psychological Review, 82,* 1–25.

Klinger, E. (1977). *Meaning and void: Inner experience and the incentives in people's lives.* Minneapolis: University of Minnesota Press.

Lazarus, R. S. (1991). *Emotion and adaptation.* New York: Oxford University Press.

Lazarus, R. S. (1999). *Stress and emotion: A new synthesis.* New York: Springer.

LeDoux, J. E. (1995). Emotion: Clues from the brain. *Annual Review of Psychology, 46,* 209–235.

Lepore, S. J., Silver, R. C., Wortman, C. B., & Wayment, H. A. (1996). Social constraints, intrusive thoughts, and depressive symptoms among bereaved mothers. *Journal of Personality and Social Psychology, 70,* 271–282.

Lewis, C. S. (1961). *A grief observed.* London: Faber & Faber.

Lyons-Ruth, K., & Jacobvitz, D. (1999). Attachment disorganization: Unresolved loss, relational violence, and lapses in behavioral and attentional strategies. In J. Cassidy & P. R. Shaver (Eds.), *Handbook of attachment: Theory, research, and clinical applications* (pp. 520–554). New York: Guilford Press.

Main, M., & Hesse, E. (1990). Parents' unresolved traumatic experiences are related to infant disorganized attachment status: Is frightened and/or frightening parental behavior the linking mechanism? In M. T. Greenberg, D. Cicchetti, & E. M. Cummings (Eds.), *Attachment in the preschool years: Theory, research, and intervention* (pp. 161–182). Chicago: University of Chicago Press.

Main, M., & Hesse, E. (1992). Disorganized/disoriented infant behavior in the strange situation, lapses in the monitoring of reasoning and discourse during the parent's Adult Attachment Interview, and dissociative states. In M. Ammaniti & D. Stern (Eds.), *Attachment and psycho-analysis* (pp. 80–140). Rome: Guis, Laterza, & Figl.

Main, M., Kaplan, N., & Cassidy, J. (1985). Security in infancy, childhood, and adulthood: A move to the level of representation. In I. Bretherton & E.

Waters (Eds.), Growing points of attachment theory and research. *Monographs for the Society for Research in Child Development, 50,* 66–104.

Main, M., & Solomon, J. (1986). Discovery of a new, insecure-disorganized/disoriented attachment pattern. In T. B. Brazelton & M. W. Yogman (Eds.), *Affective development in infancy* (pp. 95–124). Norwood, NJ: Ablex.

Main, M., & Solomon, J. (1990). Procedures for identifying infants as disorganized/disoriented during the Ainsworth Strange Situation. In M. T. Greenberg, D. Cicchetti, & E. M. Cummings (Eds.), *Attachment in the preschool years* (pp. 121–160). Chicago: University of Chicago Press.

Mason, J. W., Maher, J. T., Hartley, L. H., Mougey, E., Perlow, M. J., & Jones, L. G. (1976). Selectivity of corticosteroid and catecholamine response to various natural stimuli. In G. Serban (Ed.), *Psychopathology of human adaptation* (pp. 147–171). New York: Plenum Press.

Mikulincer, M., Florian, V., & Weller, A. (1993). Attachment styles, coping strategies, and posttraumatic psychological distress: The impact of the Gulf War in Israel. *Journal of Personality and Social Psychology, 64,* 817–826.

Mikulincer, M., & Nachshon, O. (1991). Attachment styles and patterns of self-disclosure. *Journal of Personality and Social Psychology, 61,* 321–331.

Morgan, H., & Shaver, P. R. (1999). Attachment processes and commitment to romantic relationships. In J. M. Adams & W. H. Jones (Eds.), *Handbook of interpersonal commitment and relationship stability* (pp. 109–123). New York: Plenum Press.

Nolen-Hoeksema, S., & Larson, J. (1999). *Coping with loss.* Mahwah, NJ: Erlbaum.

Oatley, K., & Jenkins, J. M. (1996). *Understanding emotions.* Cambridge, MA: Blackwell.

Pennebaker, J. W., Mayne, T. J., & Francis, M. E. (1997). Linguistic predictors of adaptive bereavement. *Journal of Personality and Social Psychology, 72,* 863–871.

Polan, H. J., & Hofer, M. A. (1999). Psychobiological origins of infant attachment and separation responses. In J. Cassidy & P. R. Shaver (Eds.), *Handbook of attachment: Theory, research, and clinical applications* (pp. 162–180). New York: Guilford Press.

Sanders, C. M. (1993). Risk factors in bereavement outcome. In M. S. Stroebe, W. Stroebe, & R. O. Hansson (Eds.), *Handbook of bereavement: Theory, research, and intervention* (pp. 255–267). Cambridge: Cambridge University Press.

Sanders, C. M. (1999). *Grief: The mourning after: Dealing with adult bereavement* (2nd ed.). New York: Wiley.

Segal, N. L., & Bouchard, T. J. (1993). Grief intensity following the loss of a twin and other relatives: Test of kinship hypothesis. *Human Biology, 65,* 87–105.

Selye, H. (1936). A syndrome produced by diverse noxious agents. *Nature, 138,* 32.

Selye, H. (1976). *The stress of life.* New York: McGraw-Hill. (Original work published 1956)

Shaver, P. R., & Clark, C. L. (1994). The psychodynamics of adult romantic attachment. In J. M. Masling & R. F. Bornstein (Eds.), *Empirical perspectives on object relations theory* (pp. 105–156). Washington, DC: American Psychological Association.

Shaver, P. R., Schwartz, J., Kirson, D., & O'Connor, C. (1987). Emotion knowledge: Further exploration of a prototype approach. *Journal of Personality and Social Psychology, 52*, 1061–1086.

Shuchter, S. R., & Zisook, S. (1993). The course of normal grief. In M. S. Stroebe, W. Stroebe, & R. O. Hansson (Eds.), *Handbook of bereavement: Theory, research, and intervention* (pp. 23–43). Cambridge: Cambridge University Press.

Smith, C. A., & Ellsworth, P. C. (1985). Patterns of cognitive appraisal in emotion. *Journal of Personality and Social Psychology, 48*, 813–838.

Smith, C. A., & Ellsworth, P. C. (1987). Patterns of appraisal and emotion related to taking an exam. *Journal of Personality and Social Psychology, 52*, 475–488.

Sroufe, L. A., & Waters, E. (1977). Attachment as an organizational construct. *Child Development, 48*, 1184–1199.

Stroebe, M. S., Gergen, M., Gergen, K., & Stroebe, W. (1996). Broken hearts or broken bonds? In D. Klass, P. R. Silverman, & S. L. Nickman (Eds.), *Continuing bonds: New understandings of grief* (pp. 31–44). Washington, DC: Taylor & Francis.

Stroebe, M. S., Hansson, R. O., & Stroebe, W. (1993). Contemporary themes and controversies in bereavement research. In M. S. Stroebe, W. Stroebe, & R. O. Hansson (Eds.), *Handbook of bereavement: Theory, research, and intervention* (pp. 457–475). Cambridge: Cambridge University Press.

Stroebe, M. S., & Schut, H. (1999). The dual process model of coping with bereavement: Rational and description. *Death Studies, 23*, 197–224.

Stroebe, M. S., & Stroebe, W. (1991). Does "grief work" work? *Journal of Consulting and Clinical Psychology, 59*, 479–482.

Stroebe, W., & Stroebe, M. S. (1993). Determinants of adjustment to bereavement in younger widows and widowers. In M. S. Stroebe, W. Stroebe, & R. O. Hansson (Eds.), *Handbook of bereavement: Theory, research, and intervention* (pp. 208–226). Cambridge: Cambridge University Press.

Trinke, S. J., & Bartholomew, K. (1997). Hierarchies of attachment relationships in young adulthood. *Journal of Social and Personal Relationships, 14*, 603–625.

Weinfield, N. S., Sroufe, L. A., Egeland, B., & Carlson, E. A. (1999). The nature of individual differences in infant-caregiver attachment. In J. Cassidy & P. R. Shaver (Eds.), *Handbook of attachment: Theory, research, and clinical applications* (pp. 68–88). New York: Guilford Press.

Weiss, R. S. (1975). *Marital separation.* New York: Basic Books.

Weiss, R. S. (1982). Attachment in adults. In C. M. Parkes & J. Stevenson-Hinde (Eds.), *The place of attachment in human behavior* (pp. 171–184). New York: Basic Books.

Weiss, R. S. (1993). Loss and recovery. In M. S. Stroebe, W. Stroebe, & R. O.

Hansson (Eds.), *Handbook of bereavement: Theory, research, and intervention* (pp. 271–284). Cambridge: Cambridge University Press.

Wortman, C. B., & Silver, R. C. (1989). The myths of coping with loss. *Journal of Consulting and Clinical Psychology, 57,* 349–357.

Wortman, C. B., Silver, R. C., & Kessler, R. C. (1993). The meaning of loss and adjustment to bereavement. In M. S. Stroebe, W. Stroebe, & R. O. Hansson (Eds.), *Handbook of bereavement: Theory, research, and intervention* (pp. 349–366). Cambridge: Cambridge University Press.

5

QUANTITATIVE OR QUALITATIVE? MEASUREMENT ISSUES IN THE STUDY OF GRIEF

ROBERT A. NEIMEYER AND NANCY S. HOGAN

As the breadth and depth of this volume testifies, the scientific study of bereavement has burgeoned in recent decades, making it one of the most fertile domains of research in the field of thanatology, the study of death and dying. With more than 2000 published books and articles devoted to grief and mourning, one might assume that a great deal is now known about the human encounter with loss, providing a secure grounding for both grief theory and therapy. Unfortunately, however, this is not the case, owing in part to limitations in the most commonly used methods adopted to study bereavement-related phenomena. Our goal in this chapter is to survey and evaluate the most promising of these methods, remarking on the strengths and weaknesses of each, and formulating recommendations that, if followed by future investigators, could help ensure a higher "information yield" from scientific research on bereavement in the future.

SCOPE

As scientific research on grief and loss has grown, so too has the need to evaluate the methods with which it has been studied by investigators in psychology, medicine, and nursing, the major disciplines producing this literature. In part because of this disciplinary diversity, researchers have displayed a considerable range of methodological preferences in mapping the symptomatic, emotional, cognitive, behavioral, and social impact of bereavement. Thus although the majority of investigators in each of these fields continues to rely on generic measures of psychiatric symptomatology, psychologists have begun to use measures of coping processes, physicians have started to evaluate physiological sequelae of loss, and nurses have taken the lead in using qualitative methods for assessing the shared meanings of loss for survivors.[1] All three core disciplines have also made contributions to the development of the measurement strategy that will be the primary concern of this chapter—namely, self-report rating scales focusing specifically on personal reactions to bereavement.

The range of options that currently exists for the measurement of grief-related phenomena makes a comparison of their strengths and weaknesses essential. To date, however, such evaluations have been limited. Gabriel and Kirschling (1989) reviewed eight scales that had been used or described in the literature through the late 1980s; however, this review is now dated, and several of the scales they considered either have been revised or have been abandoned by subsequent investigators. The utility of their review is further compromised by the selective citation of only a single reliability score, a primary focus on the initial reports of scale authors, and inattention to important psychometric features of the various scales, such as their factorial validity. Many of these same shortcomings obtain in the case of the more recent review by Robinson and Pickett (1996), who uncritically summarized the validity claims of developers of four different measures of possible use in the study of adult sibling bereavement. Unfortunately, their evaluation is also constrained by the failure to consider several relevant psychometric features, such as test–retest stability estimates and factor structures for the scales they include. A more conceptually useful review was offered by Hansson, Carpenter, and Fairchild (1993), who discussed several important measurement issues (e.g., the need to assess processes as well as outcomes and to measure competencies as well as deficiencies in survivors). However, the authors provided only a cursory evaluation of a few of the most prominent grief scales, excluding most of those discussed in this chapter. Our goal in this review is to provide a reasonably comprehensive survey of the most widely used and most promising scales for the quantitative assessment of grief responses, including several recent instruments that were not considered by earlier reviewers. In addition, we will draw attention to the possible contributions of alternative qualitative methods that deserve greater consideration by grief re-

---

[1] Two of these areas—the measurement of coping and physiological changes in bereavement—are capably reviewed elsewhere in this book. The third, focusing on the distinctive contributions of qualitative methods in grief research, will be considered in this chapter.

searchers and conclude with some recommendations for the more progressive study of bereavement in the future.

PSYCHIATRIC SYMPTOM SCALES

Although we will focus on scales designed specifically for measuring various dimensions of grieving, it is worth emphasizing that most investigators of bereavement rely on generic measures of psychiatric symptomatology, as opposed to scales tailored to the assessment of grief per se. Thus studies frequently use "broad band" assessments of distress, such as the Brief Symptom Inventory (BSI; Gilbar & Dagan, 1995; Sable, 1991) and Symptom Checklist (SCL-90; Gillis, Moore, & Martinson, 1997), or scales focusing on prominent symptom clusters such as the Beck Depression Inventory (Stroebe, Stroebe, Abakoumkin, & Schut, 1996).[2] Although the use of such measures may be defensible on the basis of their typically respectable validity, reliability, and general relevance in assessing some common features of the aftermath of loss, they also have important and insufficiently recognized limitations. First, they are at best *nonspecific* measures, assessing only phenomena shared by bereaved individuals and psychiatric reference groups. As a result, they systematically preclude assessment of psychosocial responses that are unique to loss, such as attachment difficulties signaled by missing the deceased, striving to maintain a sense of connection to his or her memory, and so forth. Second, one can question whether grief, defined as a *normal* response to profound loss, is most appropriately assessed by measures designed to quantify degree of *psychopathology*. Granted, one may be interested in whether a bereaved individual experiences depression or anxiety secondary to the loss, just as a physician might be concerned about whether a patient might develop infection secondary to a compound fracture. But in each case, the presence or absence of secondary symptomatology sheds little light on the status of the original "injury." At a minimum, exclusive reliance on scales of psychiatric symptomatology precludes assessment of theoretically and practically important outcomes, such as processes of "meaning reconstruction" following loss (Neimeyer, 1998b; Neimeyer, 2001) or the "posttraumatic growth" evidenced by many be-

---

[2] This reliance on generic, as opposed to grief-specific measures is especially striking in what is otherwise the most methodologically rigorous subset of studies in the bereavement literature—namely, the two dozen randomized controlled trials of the efficacy of psychosocial interventions for grieving. Indeed, only a third of such studies measure grief outcomes per se, as opposed to more general outcomes associated with decreased "morbidity" on measures of depressive and anxious symptomatology. One ironic consequence of this methodological constriction is that such studies actually tell us less than they otherwise might about the efficacy of treatment in improving outcomes distinctive to bereavement, such as disruptions caused by the intrusion of images of the dead, yearning for the deceased, and so on. On the other hand, research using the best available grief measures rarely attains the level of design sophistication displayed by these outcome studies.

reaved individuals as a result of their encounter with personal tragedy (Tedeschi, Park, & Calhoun, 1998). Third, empirical research to be discussed later in the chapter has begun to demonstrate that symptoms of grieving form a separate cluster from those associated with depression (Byrne & Raphael, 1997; Prigerson et al., 1995a), raising important questions about their presumed equivalence by psychiatric researchers. Thus studies of bereaved populations that fail to measure what is distinctive to grieving should be considered at best incomplete. In view of the need to assess bereavement-specific responses, we will now turn to a review of the most prominent and promising measures of grief phenomena currently available.

GENERAL PURPOSE GRIEF SCALES

Literally dozens of measures of grieving have been proposed by various investigators, ranging from the informal construction of a few face-valid questions for use in a particular study to the design of elaborate multidimensional measures comprising more than 100 items. In this chapter we will consider seven scales with sufficient psychometric backing to warrant continued research, four of which represent general-purpose instruments for studying most bereaved populations and three of which are designed to shed light on unique groups of mourners. Our selection of these instruments was based on three considerations: (a) our belief that the current state of the art renders the use of idiosyncratic researcher-designed items obsolete, except perhaps where use of single screening items is defensible in epidemiological or survey research; (b) our decision to focus on those measures that have been used by multiple investigators, or in progressive and ongoing research programs, enabling a confident prediction that they will play an important role in the further development of this literature; and (c) our choice not to review a few measures that might yet be more thoroughly validated and widely adopted but which at present have had limited use (Jacobs et al., 1987; Murphy et al., 1998). For each measure reviewed, we will consider issues pertaining to its design, format, and scaling, and limitations and precautions, tabulating data on its internal consistency, test–retest reliability,[3] convergent and discriminant validity, construct validity, and factorial validity. Finally, we will also provide in tabular form an eval-

---

[3] Some readers might question our inclusion of test–retest reliability as a psychometric desideratum for a measure of grieving, arguing that grief is a dynamic process that fluctuates considerably over time. Although we are sympathetic to the view that grieving is a process rather than a trait, we believe that a useful measure should permit one to draw *some* inferences regarding the intensity and valence of this process over at least brief intervals. Equally important, the fact is that some of the most promising measures of grief responses have managed to demonstrate *both* meaningful stability over some months of bereavement, as well as clinical and scientific sensitivity. We revisit this larger conceptual point about the stability of measurement methods later in the chapter.

uation of the psychometric properties of each measure, as a guide to helping future investigators make methodological choices appropriate to the aims of their particular study.

Texas Revised Inventory of Grief (TRIG)

The Texas Revised Inventory of Grief (TRIG) (Faschingbauer, 1981) remains the most commonly used measure of bereavement symptomatology in the empirical literature. The TRIG was designed to assess grief "as a present emotion of longing, as an adjustment to a past life event with several stages, as a medical psychology outcome, and as a personal experience" (p. 1). As is true for most grief scales, items were rationally developed based on the literature on normative and atypical grief reactions, as well as the clinical experience of the scale's authors. A distinctive feature of the TRIG is its translation into Spanish, facilitating the sort of multicultural research that is unfortunately otherwise lacking in the area of bereavement (Grabowski & Frantz, 1993).

Item Format and Scaling

The TRIG includes two primary subscales focusing on past behavior (Part I; 8 items) and present feelings (Part II; 13 items). Both sets of items consist of simple declarative statements (e.g., I found it hard to sleep after the person died; I can't avoid thinking about the person who died), to which the research participant responds on a 5-point Likert scale ranging from "completely true" to "completely false." In addition, the inventory contains several additional (unscaled) items assessing the nature of the relationship (e.g., spouse, friend), perceived closeness to the deceased, length of time since the death, and other "related facts" (e.g., funeral attendance, anniversary reactions).

Because Part I by definition should be invariant over time if respondents accurately report their reactions at the time of the death, Part II is the primary measure used in studies of changing grief symptomatology over time. Psychometric properties of both subscales are reviewed in Table 5-1.

Limitations and Precautions

Some investigators have criticized the TRIG because a number of its items may actually permit little variation (e.g., At times I feel the need to cry for the person who has died), or because they overlap extensively with measures of depression, blurring the scale's distinctiveness (Burnett, Middleton, Raphael, & Martinek, 1997). Others have noted that it includes a number of benign items (e.g., Sometimes I very much miss the person who died) as well as redundancies (e.g., 3 of 13 questions in Part II focus on crying), while neglecting more threatening symptoms associated with guilt,

TABLE 5-1
Psychometric Properties of Best-Established General Purpose Measures of Grief

Criterion	Texas Revised; Inventory of Grief (TRIG Pt. I)	Texas Revised; Inventory of Grief (TRIG Pt. II)	Grief Experience Inventory (GEI)	Core Bereavement Items (CBI)	Inventory of Complicated Grief (ICG)
Internal consistency (Cronbach's alpha)	.77–.87 (Faschinbauer, 1981) .78–.89 (Longman, 1993)	.69–.89 (Faschinbauer, 1981) .90–.93 (Longman, 1993)	.34–.59 for validity scales; .52 to .84 for clinical scales (Sanders et al., 1985)	.91 (Burnett et al., 1997)	.94 (Prigerson et al., 1995b)
Test–retest reliability	Not reported	Not reported	.53–.61 for validity scales; .71–.87 for clinical scales over 9 weeks; much lower over 18 months (Sanders et al., 1985)	Not reported	.80 over 6 months of bereavement (Prigerson, 1995b)
Convergent and discriminant validity[a]	Not reported	.87 with ITG (Prigerson et al., 1995)	.3–.5 with MMPI scales (Sanders et al., 1985)	Not reported, though larger set of items from which CBI derived correlate with anxiety and depression, (Byrne & Raphael, 1997)	.87 with TRIG Part II, but ITG better discriminates good from poor outcome; .67 with depression (Prigerson et al., 1995b)

Construct validity	Not reported	Higher grief for intimate than nonintimate relationships (Faschinbauer, 1981; Gilbar & Dagan, 1995) No differences by relationship (Grabowski & Frantz, 1993)	Clinical scales discriminate between bereaved and nonbereaved groups, and are higher for bereaved parents than spouses (Sanders et al., 1985) Clinical scores higher for respondents indicating greater "trouble" with the death (Gamino et al., 1998)	Discriminates between bereaved parents > bereaved spouses > bereaved adult children; scores higher for unexpected than for expected deaths; scores diminish over time (Middleton et al., 1998)	ITG associated with lower quality of life (Prigerson et al., 1995b); predicts global functioning, mood, sleep quality, self-esteem 18 months after spousal loss (Prigerson et al., 1995a); scores 6 months after loss predict risk of cancer, high blood pressure, heart trouble, smoking, eating problems 1 to 2 years later (Prigerson et al., 1997)
Factorial validity	Exploratory factor analysis, with retention of items loading .40 (Faschinbauer, 1981)	Exploratory factor analysis, with retention of items loading .40 (Faschinbauer, 1981)	Items grouped rationally not empirically; factor analysis suggests three factors with dominant one measuring depression (Sanders et al., 1985)	Items grouped by "rational/empirical" strategy into subscales reflecting "images and thoughts," "acute separation," and "grief," but these scales highly intercorrelated (Burnett et al., 1997)	ITG refined through use of principal components analysis combined with TETRAD II to produce pure measure of complicated grief (Prigerson et al., 1995b).

[a]Convergent validity refers to correlations with established measures of grief symptoms; discriminant validity to freedom from social desirability confounds.

bitterness, performance disruption, and hallucinatory experiences (Prigerson et al., 1995b). More serious is the logical error made by the scale's developers in advocating that a comparison between Parts I and II "can provide information regarding a person's progress through the various stages of grief" (Faschingbauer, 1981, p. 10). Subsequent reviewers of the TRIG (e.g., Hansson, Carpenter, & Fairchild, 1993) have emphasized that such an inference is problematic because of the confounding effects of memory and present adjustment on the retrospective past behavior portion (not to mention the differing content and number of items on the two subscales). Nonetheless, inferences regarding temporal patterns in grieving based on the TRIG's two-part structure are far from uncommon in the published literature (Sable, 1991). Finally, a number of investigators (Pruchno, Moss, Burant, & Schinfeld, 1995) have tended to borrow a subset of TRIG items for use in their own research, disembedded from the context of the TRIG subscales as a whole. Because this compromises the validity of the instrument and precludes comparison of subscale results with those reported by other investigators, this practice is probably inadvisable.

Grief Experience Inventory (GEI)

The Grief Experience Inventory (GEI) evolved from "a set of items culled from the literature on bereavement [representing] actual statements made by individuals experiencing grief themselves or researchers' descriptions of grief as they observed it" (Sanders, Mauger, & Strong, 1985, p. 11). Initially presented in Q-sort form, the technique encountered serious methodological problems, leading the authors to reformat it as a self-report questionnaire. In its more widely used bereavement version, the inventory consists of 135 items, although a generic "loss" version consisting of 104 non–death-related items is also available.

Item Format and Scaling

Items are phrased as simple sentences (e.g., I feel restless; Looking at photographs of the deceased is too painful) to which the participant responds "true" or "false." Following the style of the MMPI, items are clustered into three validity scales (denial, atypical response, and social desirability) and nine rationally derived clinical scales (despair, anger/hostility, guilt, social isolation, loss of control, rumination, depersonalization, somatization, and death anxiety). Psychometric findings on the GEI are summarized in Table 5-1.

Limitations and Precautions

In addition to the difficulties with factor structure and internal consistency indicated in Table 5-1, the GEI has been criticized for its "true–

false" item formatting, which in effect reduces the possible variability in responses and hence the instrument's sensitivity to changes in grief intensity over time (Burnett et al., 1997; Lev & McCorkle, 1993). Furthermore, items such as, "I have dreamed of the deceased as being dead," if answered affirmatively and accurately, can never change over time (Burnett et al., 1997). Several items in the GEI have this past-tense formatting, such that they might better be conceived of as constant values rather than "variables" in the literal sense of the word. Critics have also pointed to the extensive redundancies among items, many of which involve trivial rewordings of the same idea (e.g., I tend to be more irritable with others; I find I am often irritated with others; I am often irritable). At a minimum, this suggests that many of the 135 items are superfluous, whereas other responses of probable high relevance to grief are altogether missing (e.g., items bearing on sadness over the loss, missing the lost person, or crying at reminders; Burnett et al., 1997). Finally, although the GEI's authors are clear in explaining that the denial scale was devised to detect "naïve defensiveness" as a response set rather than the psychological mechanism of denial featured in some theories of grief, some users seem to give the scale a more clinical interpretation (Gamino, Sewell, & Easterley, 1998).

Core Bereavement Items (CBI)

The brief Core Bereavement Items (CBI) scale represents a refinement of the Bereavement Phenomenology Questionnaire (BPQ), whose 76 items were drawn from the literature by Burnett, Middleton, Raphael, and Martinek (1997) to "provide a basis for the detailed description of the evolution of the overall bereavement response" (p. 52). The decision to distill a much smaller CBI from the parent measure reflected the authors' intent to construct a coherent scale of symptomatology endorsed with considerable frequency by diverse groups of bereaved persons (e.g., images and thoughts of the deceased, acute feelings of separation, and grief).[4]

Item Format and Scaling

The CBI contains 17 questions referring to commonly occurring symptoms (e.g., Do you experience images of events surrounding X's death? Do you find yourself missing X?), which the respondent is instructed to answer on a 4-point scale of frequency. Although the items originally were derived from three separate subscales of the BPQ, they are currently com-

---

[4]Although the CBI seems to have replaced the longer BPQ in most recently published research, it is worth noting that various forms of the BPQ continue to be cited occasionally, such as the 22-item format used by Byrne and Raphael (1997). We have chosen to focus on the CBI because it is the most psychometrically refined version and because its brevity is likely to make it appealing to other investigators.

bined into a single measure. Table 5–1 presents the psychometric information about the CBI available at this time.

Limitations and Precautions

As a recently devised instrument, further validational work on the CBI is needed, a point acknowledged by its authors (Burnett et al., 1997). Little is currently known about its relationship to broad-band scales of distress, its convergence with other measures of grieving, or its stability over even brief periods of time. In addition, its focus on "core" bereavement phenomena is both a strength (insofar as items will have high relevance for most grievers) and a limitation (insofar as it intentionally excludes less frequent symptoms of nonresolution, such as numbness, unreality, or anger, topics covered in the original BPQ). Thus the CBI is probably best suited to the study of "normal" grief responses, rather than the more complicated courses assessed by other instruments.

Inventory of Complicated Grief (ITG)

The Inventory of Complicated Grief (ITG) was constructed by Prigerson and her colleagues (1995b) to measure "symptoms of grief [that] form a unified component of emotional distress that is clearly distinguishable from the symptoms of depression and anxiety" (p. 66), reactions such as preoccupation with thoughts of the deceased, disbelief about the death, and nonacceptance of its reality. Moreover, by including more threatening symptomatology (e.g., jealousy of nonbereaved persons, identification symptoms), the ICG was designed to distinguish between "normal" grief and its more "pathological" forms. Subsequently, 11 of the 19 items (those associated uniquely with poor bereavement outcomes) have been incorporated into a modified scale by the same authors (titled the Inventory of Traumatic Grief), which may attract wider attention (see chapter 27, this volume).

Item Format and Scaling

The ICG consists of 19 statements (e.g., Ever since s/he died it is hard for me to trust people), which the respondent completes by checking the frequency of the experience on a 5-point scale ranging from "never" to "always." Unlike the TRIG and GEI, which assess past as well as present reactions, the ICG focuses on how the respondent feels at the moment, as a means of minimizing the potential confounds of memory on responses. Psychometric data on the ICG appear in Table 5-1.

Limitations and Precautions

Although promising, basic psychometric properties of the ICG deserve replication by independent investigators. In recent writings by Prigerson and her colleagues (1997, p. 618), the ICG is being reinterpreted as a measure of "traumatic grief," because in their view its content reflects "the two underlying dimensions of the syndrome (i.e., trauma and separation distress)." However, it is worth noting that the ICG was derived from research on apparently nontraumatically bereaved older spouses (most of whom died of cancer), rather than persons bereaved by violent, mutilating, sudden, or suicidal death. Thus the content and predictive validity of the instrument with more "objectively" traumatized samples remains to be established.

SPECIALIZED GRIEF SCALES

Although the instruments discussed previously have been designed to assess expressions of grieving that presumably are shared by a wide variety of bereaved populations, others have recently been developed that have special relevance to distinctive subgroups of the bereaved. Such subgroups have been identified based on the type of loss suffered (e.g., suicidal bereavement), the relationship to the deceased (e.g., adolescent siblings), or both (parents of a child who dies before or soon after birth). This level of specialization permits them to assess unique features of loss (e.g., survivor guilt, stigmatization) that fall outside the purview of most general scales. An overview of these instruments is provided in Table 5-2.

Perinatal Grief Scale (PGS)

The Perinatal Grief Scale (PGS) was devised by selecting items from the literature on grief in general and perinatal loss in particular. It was constructed to represent the reactions of women and their partners who had experienced spontaneous abortion, ectopic pregnancies, fetal death, and neonatal loss (Toedter, Lasker, & Alhadeff, 1988). The authors presumed that distinctive features of this loss, including having no object to mourn and the higher probability of maternal guilt, argued for assessment using a specially tailored scale rather than a generic grief inventory.

Item Format and Scaling

The original version of the PGS consisted of 104 items, reduced to 84 when those with low item-total correlations were discarded. Items take the form of simple statements (e.g., I find it hard to make decisions since the baby died), to which the participant responds on a 5-point Likert scale

TABLE 5-2
Psychometric Properties of Best-Established Specialized Grief Scales

Criterion	Perinatal Grief Scale (PGS)	Hogan Sibling Inventory of Bereavement (HSIB)	Grief Experience Questionnaire (GEQ)
Internal consistency (Cronbach's alpha)	Good alphas for 9 "theoretical" subscales (Stinson et al., 1992); but preferable to interpret empirically established subscales of abbreviated form: active grief .88–.93; difficulty coping .70–.97; despair .85–.91; total PGS .92–.96 (Toedter et al., in press)	.90–.95 for grief subscale; .88–.90 for personal growth (Blankenship, 1990; Hogan & Greenfield, 1991) .85–.93 for HSIB total completed by various family members (Hogan & Balk, 1990) .77 for grief and .62 for abbreviated version (Hogan & Balk, 1990)	.68–.89 for rationally derived subscales; .97 overall (Barrett & Scott, 1989) .79–.87 for empirical subscales (Bailley et al., 2000)
Test–retest reliability	.59 to .66 over one year for brief form (Potvin et al., 1989)	Not reported	Not reported

Convergent & discriminant validity	.73 with SCL-90 depression (Toedter et al., 1988); unspecified correlations with trauma (Hunfeld et al., 1993) & personal inadequacy (Hunfeld et al., 1997)	Not reported	Not reported
Construct validity	PGS associated with longer gestation, poorer ratings of mental and physical health (Hunfeld et al., 1993; Toedter et al., in press)	Higher HSIB scores associated with poorer adolescent self-concept (Hogan & Greenfield, 1991)	GEQ differentiates suicidally bereaved from those suffering accidental, unexpected natural, and expected natural losses (Barrett & Scott, 1989)
Factorial validity	Exploratory factor analysis established three subscales listed above for short and longer forms (Potvin et al., 1989; Toedter et al., 1988)	Exploratory factor analysis identified 24-item grief factor, 22-item personal growth factor (Hogan & DeSantis, 1996)	Principal components analysis identified 8 factors: abandonment/rejection, stigmatization, search for explanation, guilt, somatic reactions, personal responsibility, self-destructive orientation, & shame/embarrassment (Bailley et al., 2000)

ranging from "strongly agree" to "strongly disagree." Although statements were initially rationally drafted to conform to 21 dimensions of perinatal grief discussed in the literature (e.g., fear/vulnerability, replacement concerns), scaling ultimately was empirically based, resulting in three 11-item subscales assessing active grief, difficulty coping, and despair (Toedter et al., 1988). A shorter, 33-item version of the scale was introduced by Potvin, Lasker, & Toedter (1989) using a subset of the items refined by factor analysis. Data on the validity and reliability of the PGS appear in Table 5-2.

Limitations and Precautions

The distinctive content and economy of the abbreviated PGS, coupled with its apparent reliability and validity, suggest that it will find wider adoption than the original, lengthier form of the instrument. However, its ability to predict future psychological complications deserves greater attention, as well as its relevance to samples of greater ethnic diversity (Toedter, Lasker & Janssen, in press).

Hogan Sibling Inventory of Bereavement (HSIB)

The Hogan Sibling Inventory of Bereavement (HSIB) is distinctive not only in its focus of the loss of brothers and sisters during childhood or adolescence but also in its method of item development. Whereas the content of other grief scales was derived from items or themes in the literature, the HSIB was developed by analyzing conversations of bereaved children and adolescents during support group meetings to ensure that it reflected issues of genuine relevance to this population (Hogan & Greenfield, 1991). It therefore represents a rare example of a quantitative measure that is grounded in a qualitative methodology. Data on its psychometric features are presented in Table 5-2.[5]

Item Format and Scaling

The HSIB comprises 46 items, each of which begins with the stem, "Since my brother or sister died," and then concludes with a variety of personal reactions (e.g., I am uncomfortable when having fun; I have grown up faster than my friends). The respondent is asked to answer with a 1 to 5 rating representing how true the statement is for him or her now, from "almost always true" to "hardly ever true." A distinctive feature of the

---

[5] In addition to these published data, recent studies with Finnish and Norwegian adolescents generally support the internal consistency of the HSIB and the convergence of its grief subscale with a measure of traumatic intrusion symptoms (personal communication with S. Poijula and A. Dyregrov, respectively, 1999). Publication of these reports should add to the psychometric validation and refinement of the scale.

scale is its inclusion of two factors: a 24-item distress factor titled "grief," encompassing such areas as physical effects and desire for reunion with the sibling; and a 22-item adaptive-behavior factor titled "personal growth," assessing such outcomes as increased resiliency and ability to give and receive help (Hogan & DeSantis, 1996).

Limitations and Precautions

Because it was derived from the responses of bereaved children as well as adolescents, investigators might well find the HSIB attractive as a measure for preteen children. However, the instrument has been used to date only with adolescents (aged 13 to 18). Thus the appropriateness of the scale to younger children remains to be established, especially in view of the sophisticated content (e.g., referring to loss of control or changed priorities) of some items.

Grief Experience Questionnaire (GEQ)

The Grief Experience Questionnaire (GEQ) is distinctive in its focus on the presence or absence of certain factors believed to be unique to suicidal bereavement (Barrett & Scott, 1989). Although it also contains items assessing more generic grief reactions (e.g., shock, despair), the preponderance of the scale addresses topics that are more relevant to bereavement resulting from suicide (e.g., disgrace, feeling culpable for the death).

Item Format and Scaling

The GEQ is made up of 55 items, originally assigned on a rational basis to 11 subscales, 5 items per scale. Subscales addressed somatic reactions, general grief reactions, search for explanation, loss of social support, stigmatization, guilt, responsibility, shame, rejection, self-destructive behavior, and unique reactions, such as concealing the cause of the death (Barrett & Scott, 1989). Items begin with a common stem, with alternative endings that are rated on 1- to 5-point Likert scales, ranging from "never" to "almost always." An example is, "Since the death of [this person], how often did you: Feel like others may have blamed you for the death?" Reliability and validity information on the scale is summarized in Table 5-2.

Limitations and Precautions

In its more defensible factor-analyzed form (Bailley, Dunham, & Kral, 2000), the GEQ no longer has a distinctive subscale that assesses general grief reactions, making it potentially an inappropriate choice for the assessment of normative grieving. On the other hand, the instrument probably has wider applicability than to suicide bereavement per se, because items would seem to be equally pertinent to a range of potentially stigmatizing deaths, such as death from AIDS, drug overdose, and so on.

General Remarks

In summary, an evaluation of the psychometric properties of both general-purpose grief scales and more specialized instruments suggests that the measurement of grief has advanced substantially in recent years. No longer must (or should) researchers and clinicians rely exclusively on generic measures of psychological distress as proxies for the assessment of grief when investigating bereaved persons, because several of the present scales enable more specific measurement of relevant processes and outcomes. Moreover, as Table 5-3 indicates, the psychometric quality of this literature appears to have improved across time, with newer instruments generally evidencing greater validity and reliability than familiar (and more commonly used) alternatives. Although this suggests that the scientific study of grief is indeed progressive, it also implies that older instruments such as the TRIG or GEI may need to be substantially revised to justify their continued use.

What are the unique advantages of quantitative approaches to the assessment of grief, considered as a whole? Such scales have several legitimate uses, including (a) fine-grained measurement of grief responses in different groups of bereaved persons, (b) diagnosis of populations potentially "at risk" for complicated courses of grieving, and (c) tracking of attenuation or intensification of grief symptoms over time or in response to treatment. Moreover, their ability to assess grief intensity as a continuous

TABLE 5-3
Psychometric Properties of Leading Measures of Grief Symptomatology

Instruments	Internal Consistency	Test–Retest Reliability	Convergent & Discriminant Validity[a]	Construct Validity	Factorial Validity
General Scales					
TRIG[b]	+[c]	?	+	+	+
GEI	−−	−	+	+	−−
CBI	++	?	?	+	+
ICG	++	+	+	+	++
Special Scales					
PGS	++	−	+	+	+
HSIB	++	?	?	+	+
GEQ	+	?	?	+	+

[a] Convergent validity refers to correlations with established measures of grief symptomatology; discriminant validity refers to freedom from social desirability confounds.
[b] TRIG = Texas Revised Inventory of Grief; GEI = Grief Experience Inventory; CBI = Core Bereavement Items; ICG = Inventory of Complicated Grief; PGS = Perinatal Grief Scale; HSIB = Hogan Sibling Inventory of Bereavement; GEQ = Grief Experience Questionnaire.
[c] ++ = very favorable; + = favorable but preliminary; − = unfavorable; −− = very unfavorable; ? = little or no information available.

variable permits investigators to identify covariates of postbereavement functioning, such as closeness of attachment to the deceased, preexisting mental health risk factors in the bereaved person, and so on. On the other hand, we believe that standardized questionnaires also have intrinsic limitations that are best appreciated after considering alternative assessment methods. For this reason, we will offer some closing recommendations about the further refinement of the measurement of grieving after noting the relevance of an alternative paradigm for the assessment of loss experiences—namely, the domain of qualitative research.

QUALITATIVE STUDIES OF BEREAVEMENT

A very different methodological tradition from the quantitative assessment literature reviewed earlier is the domain of qualitative research, which encompasses a broad range of techniques for study design, data collection, analysis, and interpretation (Lincoln & Guba, 1985). As Thorson (1996) reminded us, empirical thanatology in many respects had its origins in such landmark qualitative research as Glaser and Strauss's (1969) classic field studies of "levels of awareness" in the social drama of dying and Kübler-Ross's (1969) intensive (if less systematic) interviews of hundreds of dying patients. Since these pioneering contributions, dozens of investigators in disciplines ranging from nursing to psychology have applied qualitative research strategies to the study of bereavement, in the process refining a number of techniques whose greater use could add depth to the assessment of the grieving process. Our purpose in this brief section is to highlight the most significant of these qualitative methods, concentrating on their essential features and providing references to some exemplary studies using each. First, however, it is important to underscore a few features of the epistemological orientation shared by such approaches, insofar as this tends to set them apart from traditional quantitative methods and suggests some of the distinctive contributions they might make to the study of grief and loss.

As a group, qualitative approaches express a constructivist philosophy (Neimeyer & Mahoney, 1995; Schwandt, 1994) that holds that human knowledge is socially and personally constructed, with no single view laying claim to universal validity or absolute truth. Seen from this vantage point, social realities are inherently multiplistic rather than singular, and the goal of research is less to generate incontestable "facts" than to discover and explore the unique and common perspectives of the individuals being studied (Neimeyer & Raskin, 2000). Such methods are especially valuable in generating theory where little good theory exists, in revealing how people make meaning of events, and in moving toward a deep understanding of a particular phenomenon rather than a nomothetic set of causal inferences presumed to generalize across different cultures and settings. For all of these reasons, qualitative methods can provide a useful counterbalance to the often atheoretical, objectivistic, superficial, and decontextualized study of grieving that typifies conventional studies of bereavement. We will concentrate on five promising methods that have been used in research on loss, including grounded theory, content analysis, focus groups, ethnography, and case study.

Grounded Theory

Since its introduction by sociologists Glaser and Strauss (1969), grounded theory has become the most widely used qualitative method in thanatology, with especially strong representation in nursing. The term *grounded theory* itself refers to the inductive method that is at the root of the approach, in which the "processes and products of research are shaped from the data rather than from preconceived logically deduced theoretical frameworks" (Charmaz, 1983, p. 110). The data can consist of any of several forms of "thick description" of the phenomena of interest, including carefully transcribed interviews, researcher field notes, diaries, and documents, which represent with as much fidelity as possible the experiences of the research participants. These materials are then painstakingly coded on a line-by-line basis or by "meaning units," often with the assistance of computerized systems that facilitate text and code management. Coding categories emerge from the data in response to the orienting question, "What do I see going on here?" The subjective hunches, preconceptions, and insights of the researcher are captured in memos that track along with the process of coding, often suggesting connections among the emerging codes, the existence of more abstract or "core" categories, and possible "negative cases" that contradict the overall pattern. An adequate grounded theory analysis should provide a comprehensive and clearly explicated account that is honest, plausible to the reader, confirmable by external "audit," and amenable to "member checks" by the original data contributors or others in a similar position. Lincoln and Guba (1985), Charmaz (1983), and Strauss and Corbin (1990) provide good introductions to this method.

The recent literature on parental grief following the death of a child includes several good examples of grounded theory studies. For instance, M. L. Braun and Berg (1994) analyzed the accounts of parental bereavement contributed by ten mothers and found that the "core variable" was their "prior meaning structure" that, if unable to accommodate the deaths of their children, resulted in considerable discontinuity and disorganization. These concepts were further clarified in terms of subcategories or properties, anchored in the words of the mothers themselves. For example, previous meaning structures included assumptions about the centrality of the child in the mother's sense of purpose, the nature of life, and the existence of order in the world, whereas disorientation implied such features as feeling out of touch, losing personal control, and losing a purpose in life. Other grounded theory studies include Hogan, Morse, and Tasón's (1996) development of an experiential theory of bereavement, Milo's (1997) revealing analysis of maternal responses to the deaths of children with developmental disabilities, Martin's (1998) book-length treatment of parental bereavement associated with SIDS, and Hagemeister and Rosenblatt's (1997) sensitive investigation of the changed sexual relationship between bereaved parents. The latter analysis is particularly interesting in suggesting the power of qualitative research to account for interactive phenomena (such as decline in the couple's sexual relations) in terms of the meanings given them by the participants (intercourse is how we made the child; now we are back together living life). Nadeau's (1997; see also chapter 15, this volume) thorough study of "family meaning making" in the wake of loss provides a further illustration of the potential of qualitative studies to reveal systemic as well as individual features of bereavement, such as the conversational attribution of meaning to coincidences surrounding a loved one's death.

Content Analysis

Originating within both sociology and psychology, content analysis is actually a hybrid method with qualitative and quantitative features. Unlike grounded theory analyses, in which researchers attempt to minimize their preconceptions regarding the phenomenon of interest, content analysts often approach a text with a formal categorical system in mind and then code material (e.g., interviews) in light of those categories. In most instances, the fundamental data consist of the frequencies of occurrence of each code, rendering the results amenable to quantitative summary or comparison with other measures. Gottschalk, Lolas, and Viney (1987) provide a good overview of content analytic methods.

In the area of grief research, this method is exemplified by the work of Richards and her associates (Richards, Acree, & Folkman, 1999; Richards & Folkman, 1997; see also chapter 25, this volume), who conducted a longitudinal study of the experience of 125 recently bereaved partners of men who died of AIDS. Coding open-ended interviews for spiritual content, they discovered that frequency of references to belief in a higher order early in bereavement correlated with higher levels of depression and anxiety but also with more adaptive ways of coping. Spirituality deepened for more than three quarters of the cohort across the next three to four years, and gradually transformed from a means of coping to a personal governing influence that provided value and direction in life. A more purely descriptive use of content analysis is illustrated by the research of Hogan and DeSantis (1992), who examined the frequency of various attachment themes in bereaved adolescents in response to the question, "If you could ask or tell your dead sibling something, what would it be?" In this case, reliable codes emerged from the data and conveyed common (e.g., reaffirmation of love) and uncommon categories (e.g., asking for advice and guidance) expressing their continued bond to their deceased brother or sister.

Focus Groups

Since the introduction of focus group interviewing by sociologists in the 1950s, it has been widely adopted by marketing researchers interested in people's perceptions of products, as well as by social activists attempting to understand the needs and problems confronted by various constituencies in the community. Participants typically form a relatively homogeneous group of 6 to 12 people, with a professional moderator setting the tone for the interaction, asking broad questions of relevance to the study, and facilitating or redirecting the sometimes challenging group dynamics that result (Patton, 1987). Focus groups can therefore be an efficient way to increase the number of participants in a qualitative study, yielding recorded conversations that can be subjected to closer analysis. They are not, however, without their drawbacks, as the constraints imposed by spending an hour or two with a group of perhaps eight or ten people obviously precludes a very personal or detailed exploration of the views or experiences of any one of them (Rubin & Rubin, 1995).

K. L. Braun and Nichols (1997) made innovative use of focus group methodology in their study of the ways in which different Asian-American cultures deal with death and loss. Convening five to eight informants in separate groups of Americans with Chinese, Japanese, Vietnamese, and Filipino ancestry, they interviewed them about traditional philosophies of life and death, burial, memorial and bereavement practices, and their views on a range of topics from suicide to euthanasia. Both commonalties and considerable differences emerged among the groups, as well as patterns of changing belief and ritualization with increasing acculturation to life in the United States. Focus group methods also informed Malacrida's (1998) research on parents' attempts to create meaning from miscarriage, stillbirth, and early infant death.

Ethnography

Originating in anthropology, enthography can be distinguished from other forms of qualitative research by its objectives more than its methods. Whereas most qualitative researchers strive to reveal the meanings and processes that characterize individuals (or perhaps families) who share some common experience, ethnographers ultimately pursue the goal of cultural interpretation. This does not necessarily mean that ethnographic work concentrates only on abstract social groupings—indeed, some of the finest examples of the genre focus on quite small groups of people—but instead, that the work involves a commitment to making sense of behavior in terms of a cultural patterning (Wolcott, 1990). Ethnographers rely heavily on interviews, observations, and "field notes" taken on site, which blend the *etic* categories of the investigator's own discipline with an *emic* account featuring informants' own words. Perhaps less formally "unitized" and coded than texts subjected to grounded theory or content analysis, these notes and observations can inform ethnographers' attempts to elucidate the implicit order in the scenes and settings where unique cultures "take place." Several fascinating "microethnographies" of this kind focusing on world views associated with bulimia, sexual abuse, and other distinctive "cultures" have been provided in a recent anthology by Ellis and Bochner (1996).

An impressive qualitative study of this kind was performed by Klass (1995, 1997, 1999), who conducted long-term ethnographic research on the Compassionate Friends, a support group for bereaved parents. The central concern of Klass's ethnography was the changing worldviews of the parents, which were supported by specialized forms of communication (e.g., commemorative newsletter articles) and practices (e.g., candlelight vigils) shared by other group members. Of particular interest was his subtle analysis of the interaction between group culture and the parents' inner world, tracing the evolution of their continuing bond with their children across the various phases of bereavement, from "newly bereaved," through "well along in their grief," to "resolved as much as it will be." Additional forms of ethnographic research on loss—including poignant "autoethnographies" of the author's own losses—have been described by Ellis (1998).

Case Study

Having its beginnings in the clinical sciences, the case study is a time-honored "N of 1" investigation of the unique features of a single individual or event. A common starting point for such a study is simple curiosity about a case that went particularly well or poorly, whose in-depth study might reveal the subtleties of the phenomenon in a way that suggests avenues for future exploration (Maione, 1997). Legitimate data for a case study might include video or audio tapes of therapeutic interactions, test results and archival documents, clinical case notes, or interviews. Whereas many forms of qualitative study strive for at least some degree of generalization to similar cases, the case study is typically more bounded, taking as its main objective a thorough description of a single individual.

Recent case studies in the area of bereavement include Balk and Vesta's (1998) analysis of four years of unique journal entries by a young woman, Rhonda, which took the form of an extended missive to her deceased father. The journal reveals her ongoing symbolic relationship with her father, her struggle to cope with the loss, and the life lessons that resulted, all of which were pervaded by the core theme of "finding herself." Narrative methods of case study are also central to the "meaning reconstruction" approach to loss being pursued by Neimeyer and his collaborators (Neimeyer, 1998b, 2001; Neimeyer, Keesee, & Fortner, 2000), who have devised various reflexive forms of writing and interviewing to prompt exploration of the significance of a loss for one's ongoing life. Finally, Hébert (1998) has made use of alternative case studies to suggest important differences in a family's accommodation to perinatal death in the West versus in the Muslim Middle East. Thus such studies can be used to illustrate a theory or exemplify a method, as well as to focus on the distinctive features of a particular person or family's way of mourning.

General Comments

In summary, numerous qualitative research methods exist that have demonstrated relevance to the study of bereavement, many of which expand considerably the characteristic focus of quantitative measures on an individual's grief symptomatology. Because of their special congruence with a constructivist orientation, such approaches are ideally suited to reveal the unique meanings that inform the reactions of individuals or cultural groups to death and loss, thereby both broadening and deepening the scholarly study of bereavement. However, such approaches are not without their limitations, as their descriptive intent constrains the extent to which they can provide causal explanations for grief phenomena, demonstrate the efficacy of particular interventions, or identify correlates of intensified grieving as assessed by other quantitative measures. For this reason, we will conclude with a few recommendations to other researchers and professionals interested in using qualitative and quantitative approaches in their own future work.

CONCLUSION

Although the human experience of bereavement has often been studied, it has not often been studied well. Indeed, a close inspection of the literature on the measurement of grief reveals a remarkable constriction in method, such that the majority of studies preemptively rely on experimenter-designed but essentially unvalidated questionnaires purporting to measure bereavement responses. By focusing in this review on better-established measures of responses to bereavement, we have tried to alert researchers to promising assessment techniques that could provide a more adequate grounding for future studies. In our concluding remarks we will share a few additional observations and recommendations on these measurement issues, leaving it to other authors in this volume to provide substantive recommendations appropriate to their respective areas.

First, there is little justification for future studies to assess bereavement as an exclusively psychopathological process. Adopting a narrow focus on psychiatric symptomatology as an operational definition of grieving is as indefensible as equating "intelligence" with one's ability to perform long division or defining "self-esteem" in terms of how one feels about one's golf game. At best, a focus on psychiatric "morbidity" should complement, not substitute, for a broader assessment of the impact of bereavement on one's health, social relationships, relationship to the deceased person, styles of coping, meaning reconstruction, and identity transformation, all of which in turn will reciprocally influence one's style of grieving.

Second, future researchers need to give more than fleeting attention to the reliability and validity of the scales they adopt or devise for the measurement of grief phenomena. Indeed, by any rigorous standards of psychometric adequacy, even the most promising of existing measures—like those reviewed in this chapter—are rarely impressive. The best of these measures can claim internal consistency, perhaps some occasional correlation with another measure of psychological distress, some ability to distinguish relevant samples of bereaved persons from comparison groups, and a tentative factor structure based on more than the intuition of its authors. But even these results are virtually never replicated, and given the few failed replication attempts that do exist (e.g., investigating the ability of a scale to measure change in grief symptomatology over time), the current evidence for the validity of these instruments should be considered provisional rather than definitive.

Third, and equally serious, major lacunae exist that are shared by the majority of existing quantitative instruments. For example, less than half of the instruments reviewed have demonstrated any test–retest reliability, a basic desideratum for any measure that purports to assess a reasonably stable state or process. Although grieving undoubtedly has its vicissitudes, if there is literally *no* predictability in the course of bereavement from one day, hour, or moment to the next, then the entire premise of measuring it might be called into question, as the resulting score would pertinence as soon as it is calculated. In view of this consideration, a more enlightened strategy might be to study the *meaningful variation* of an instrument's reliability over time or type of loss, and so on. For instance, an investigator might hypothesize that a scale would show greater stability over the second year of bereavement than the first, given the emotional turbulence that might characterize early grieving. Alternatively, a researcher might predict that traumatically bereaved individuals might show more fluctuation than survivors of expected loss, given the alternation of intrusive and avoidant symptoms in the former case. The point is simply that if a given measure has not shown a modicum of temporal stability, then its use in measuring presumed decreases in grieving over time or in assessing the efficacy of pharmacological or psychosocial treatments for bereaved persons is at best premature.

Another gap in the literature that invites attention is the astonishing tendency of investigators to proliferate new instruments without pausing to evaluate their relationship to existing measures. Indeed, with the exception of the rare study correlating another scale with the TRIG, *the seven leading measures reviewed in this chapter have never been compared with one another*. In addition to weakening their claim to convergent validity, this tendency to treat each scale as if it were the only available measure of grief symptomatology makes it difficult to assess their unique strengths and weaknesses and whether they are measuring the same or different constructs. For example, although it is plausible that the ICG provides a complementary measure of traumatic grief that supplements a more general scale of normative bereavement like the CBI, this judgment cannot be made with confidence in the absence of studies comparing them. Just as striking is the virtually complete inattention to social desirability confounds and other response sets, which may contribute unknown amounts of "error variance" to measures whose preferred responses are transparent to even the most naive research participant. Likewise, the fact that no existing measure of grief has been subjected to a confirmatory factor analysis (or even the replication of an exploratory factor analysis) means that prudent researchers should remain skeptical about the interpretation of subscales until such research is conducted.

It is worth emphasizing that the incompleteness of this research domain derives from factors other than the intrinsic difficulty of conducting scientific studies on topics concerning death and dying. A comparison with the other large empirical literature in thanatology, the study of death attitudes, reveals that instrumentation for the assessment of death anxiety, fear, threat, and acceptance more often satisfies criteria of psychometric adequacy like those tabulated in this review (Neimeyer, 1994, 1998a). Instead, it seems more likely that shortcomings in the available literature on the measurement of grief derive from the tendency to rush toward application, before conducting the serious work of instrument development required to place full confidence in the resulting research. This pattern of hasty use of a scale that should still be undergoing validation is compounded by the apparent "territoriality" of grief researchers, such that research on or with various instruments tends to be undertaken by small clusters of researchers who routinely ignore one another's work. To some extent, this pattern might be the result of the recency of most of these instruments, so that further psychometric studies of these scales by independent investigators might be conducted in the future. We believe that the majority of the measures reviewed warrant this further development, and hope that these remarks might point to some useful directions that such research could take.

A fourth point concerns the possible contributions of qualitative research to the study of bereavement. Essentially, we advocate a stance of *methodological pluralism*, respecting both numbers and narratives and the distinctive forms of understanding that each can promote. Even at this germinal stage in the application of qualitative paradigms to the study of loss, it is clear that they begin to paint a picture of bereavement that is far more complex and less tidy than that suggested by the artificially simplified and controlled canvasses of quantitative questionnaires. This is not to say, however, that the results of such studies are without meaningful patterning. To the contrary, they hint that there are multiple levels of order nested in the manifest "disorder" of grieving, ranging from regularities in the meanings attached to particular losses by those who suffer them, to communication practices that distinguish one culture of loss from another. Because they are less apt to be constrained by investigator preconceptions than are quantitative approaches relying on ready-made questionnaires, qualitative approaches such as grounded theory, content analysis, focus groups, ethnography, and case study are better positioned to introduce novelty, scope, and depth to the study of bereavement. Like the quantitative measures we have reviewed in this chapter, such methods also have their own limitations and must meet their own standards of adequacy, defined in terms of credibility, reproducibility, applicability, and the like (Strauss & Corbin, 1990). But if used creatively and critically, qualitative approaches can help suggest more trenchant theories of bereavement, which can then be tested and refined using more precise quantitative methods.

Finally, a further word about the use of "mixed methods" is in order. Because most grief researchers operate exclusively within either a quantitative or qualitative frame of reference (which may be reinforced by disciplinary allegiances to one method or the other), few exploit the possibilities for integration of both methods *in the same research program*. Yet this more eclectic approach may have significant advantages, even in the focused domain of instrument development. For example, as an alternative to the common tendency of test developers to intuitively construct scale items on the basis of their reading of the existing scientific literature, a sounder approach might be to defer to the "real" experts on loss—bereaved people—to define the relevant content of scale questions. This could take the form of conducting grounded-theory analyses of interviews with people mourning a death, organizing focus groups of bereaved persons, and so on, to identify the symptoms, themes, and practices that characterize their reaction to a loss. Questionnaire items could then be designed to capture these responses, contributing greater "content validity" to the resulting measure. A rare example of this method is provided by the ongoing development of the Hogan Grief Reactions Checklist (HGRC),[6] a 61-item self-report questionnaire whose items were empirically derived from newsletters of bereavement support groups, interviews, and focus groups conducted with bereaved individuals. Significantly, it was the mourners themselves who judged the relevance of candidate items to their experience, with care being taken to include those who had lost family members as a result of different kinds of deaths (suicide, homicide, accident, illness) and who had different forms of kinship to the deceased (parent, child, sibling, spouse). Once approved, final items were then subjected to additional psychometric refinement to meet conventional criteria of reliability, convergent, construct, and factorial validity. Although the HGRC awaits more widespread use by other investigators, it exemplifies the strategic blending of qualitative and quantitative approaches that could promote more progressive measurement in the area of bereavement.

Although there is as yet no gold standard in the measurement of grieving, there are nonetheless a number of promising new approaches to assessing grief within both the quantitative and qualitative research traditions. We hope that our attempt to highlight the problems and prospects in this field will suggest useful directions for future research and that through attention to these issues, scientific study might make a more profound contribution to our understanding of the experience of loss.

REFERENCES

Bailley, S. E., Dunham, K., & Kral, M. J. (in press). Factor structure of the Grief Experience Questionnaire (GEQ) and its sensitivity to suicide bereavement. *Death Studies, 24.*

Balk, D. E., & Vesta, L. C. (1998). Psychological development during four years of bereavement: A longitudinal case study. *Death Studies, 22,* 23–41.

Barrett, T. W., & Scott, T. B. (1989). Development of the Grief Experience Questionnaire. *Suicide and Life-Threatening Behavior, 19,* 201–215.

Blankenship, M. (1990). *Adolescent sibling bereavement: Family factors associated with adjustment to loss.* Unpublished master's thesis, Bowling Green State University, Bowling Green, Ohio.

Braun, K. L., & Nichols, R. (1997). Death and dying in four Asian American cultures. *Death Studies, 21,* 327–359.

Braun, M. L., & Berg, D. H. (1994). Meaning reconstruction in the experience of bereavement. *Death Studies, 18,* 105–129.

Burnett, P., Middleton, W., Raphael, B., & Martinek, N. (1997). Measuring core bereavement phenomena. *Psychological Medicine, 27,* 49–57.

---

[6] A preliminary study using this scale is reported by Hyrkas, Kunonen, and Paunonen (1997). A full report of the psychometric development of this new measure is now nearing completion and is available from the second author.

Byrne, G., & Raphael, B. (1997). The psychological symptoms of conjugal bereavement in elderly men over the first 13 months. *International Journal of Geriatric Psychiatry, 12,* 241–251.

Charmaz, K. (1983). The grounded theory method. In R. Emerson (Ed.), *Contemporary field research* (pp. 109–126). Boston: Little, Brown.

Ellis, C. (1998). Exploring loss through autoethnographic inquiry. In J. Harvey (Ed.), *Perspectives on loss: A sourcebook* (pp. 49–68). Philadelphia: Brunner/Mazel.

Ellis, C., & Bochner, A. P. (Eds.). (1996). *Composing ethnography.* Walnut Creek, CA: AltaMira.

Faschingbauer, T. R. (1981). *Texas Revised Inventory of Grief Manual.* Houston, TX: Honeycomb.

Gabriel, R. M., & Kirschling, J. M. (1989). Assessing grief among the bereaved elderly: A review of existing measures. *Bereavement Care, 29–54.*

Gamino, L. A., Sewell, K. W., & Easterling, L. W. (1998). Scott & White grief study: An empirical test of predictors of intensified mourning. *Death Studies, 22,* 333–355.

Gilbar, O., & Dagan, A. (1995). Coping with loss: Differences between widows and widowers of deceased cancer patients. *Omega, 31,* 207–220.

Gillis, C. L., Moore, I. M., & Martinson, I. M. (1997). Measuring parental grief after childhood cancer: Potential use of the SCL-90R. *Death Studies, 21,* 277–287.

Glaser, B. G., & Strauss, A. L. (Eds.). (1969). *Time for dying.* Chicago: Aldine.

Gottschalk, L., Lolas, F., & Viney, L. (Eds.). (1987). *Content analysis of verbal behavior.* Berlin: Springer Verlag.

Grabowski, J., & Frantz, T. T. (1993). Latinos and anglos: Cultural experiences of grief intensity. *Omega, 26,* 273–285.

Hagemeister, A. K., & Rosenblatt, P. C. (1997). Grief and the sexual relationship of couples who have experienced a child's death. *Death Studies, 21,* 231–251.

Hansson, R. O., Carpenter, B. N., & Fairchild, S. K. (1993). Measurement issues in bereavement. In M. S. Stroebe, W. Stroebe, & R. O. Hansson (Eds.), *Handbook of bereavement* (pp. 62–74). Cambridge: Cambridge University Press.

Hébert, M. P. (1998). Perinatal grief in its cultural context. *Death Studies, 22,* 61–78.

Hogan, N. S., & Balk, D. E. (1990). Adolescent reactions to sibling death: Perceptions of mothers, fathers, and teenagers. *Nursing Research, 39,* 103–106.

Hogan, N., & DeSantis, L. (1992). Adolescent sibling bereavement: An ongoing attachment. *Qualitative Health Research, 2,* 159–177.

Hogan, N. S., & DeSantis, L. (1996). Basic constructs of a theory of adolescent sibling bereavement. In D. Klass, P. R. Silverman, & S. L. Nickman (Eds.), *Continuing bonds* (pp. 235–255). Philadelphia: Taylor & Francis.

Hogan, N. S., & Greenfield, D. B. (1991). Adolescent sibling bereavement symptomatology in a large community sample. *Journal of Adolescent Research, 6,* 97–112.

Hogan, N., Morse, J. M., & Tasón, M. C. (1996). Toward an experiential theory of bereavement. *Omega, 27,* 43–65.

Hunfeld, J., Wladimiroff, J., & Passchier, J. (1997). Prediction and course of grief four years after perinatal loss due to congenital abnormalities: A follow-up study. *British Journal of Medical Psychology, 70,* 85–91.

Hunfeld, J., Wladimiroff, J., Passchier, J., Venema-van Uden, U., Frets, P., & Verhage, F. (1993). Reliability and validity of the Perinatal Grief Scale for women who experienced late pregnancy loss. *British Journal of Medical Psychiatry, 66,* 295–298.

Hyrkas, K., Kunonen, M., & Paunonen, M. (1997). Recovering from the death of a spouse. *Journal of Advanced Nursing, 25,* 775–779.

Jacobs, S., Kasl, S., Ostfeld, A., Berkman, L., Kosten, T., & Charpentier, P. (1987). The measurement of grief: Bereaved versus nonbereaved. *Hospice Journal, 2,* 21–36.

Klass, D. (1995). Spiritual aspects of the resolution of grief. In H. Wass & R. A. Neimeyer (Eds.), *Dying: Facing the facts* (pp. 243–268). Philadelphia: Taylor & Francis.

Klass, D. (1997). The deceased child in the psychic and social worlds of bereaved parents during the resolution of grief. *Death Studies, 21,* 147–175.

Klass, D. (1999). *The spiritual lives of bereaved parents.* Philadelphia: Brunner-Mazel.

Kübler-Ross, E. (1969). *On death and dying.* New York: Macmillan.

Lev, E., & McCorkle, R. (1993). A shortened version of an instrument measuring bereavement. *International Journal of Nursing Studies, 30,* 213–226.

Lincoln, Y. S., & Guba, E. G. (1985). *Naturalistic inquiry.* Newbury Park, CA: Sage.

Longman, A. J. (1993). Effectiveness of a hospice community bereavement program. *Omega, 27,* 165–175.

Maione, P. V. (1997). Choice points: Creating clinical qualitative research studies. *The Qualitative Report, 3,* 1–10.

Malacrida, C. (1998). *Mourning the dreams.* Edmonton, Alberta: Qual Institute Press.

Martin, K. (1998). *When a baby dies of SIDS.* Edmonton, Alberta: Qual Institute Press.

Middleton, W., Raphael, B., Burnett, P., & Martinek, N. (1998). A longitudinal study comparing bereavement phenomena in recently bereaved spouses, adult children, and parents. *Australian and New Zealand Journal of Psychiatry, 32,* 235–241.

Milo, E. M. (1997). Maternal responses to the life and death of a child with developmental disability. *Death Studies, 21,* 443–476.

Murphy, S. A., Johnson, C., Cain, K. C., Das Gupta, A., Dimond, M., & Lohan, J. (1998). Broad-spectrum group treatment for parents bereaved by the violent deaths of their 12- to 28 year-old children: A randomized controlled trial. *Death Studies, 22*, 209–235.

Nadeau, J. W. (1997). *Families making sense of death.* Newbury Park, CA: Sage.

Neimeyer, R. A. (Ed.). (1994). *Death anxiety handbook: Research, instrumentation, and application.* New York: Taylor & Francis.

Neimeyer, R. A. (1998a). Death anxiety research: The state of the art. *Omega, 36*, 97–120.

Neimeyer, R. A. (1998b). *Lessons of loss: A guide to coping.* New York: McGraw Hill.

Neimeyer, R. A. (Ed.). (2001). *Meaning reconstruction and the experience of loss.* Washington, DC: American Psychological Association.

Neimeyer, R. A., Keesee, N. J., & Fortner, B. V. (2000). Loss and meaning reconstruction: Propositions and procedures. In R. Malkinson, S. Rubin, & E. Wiztum (Eds.), *Traumatic and non-traumatic loss and bereavement* (pp. 197–230). Madison, CT: Psychosocial Press.

Neimeyer, R. A., & Mahoney, M. J. (1995). *Constructivism in psychotherapy.* Washington, DC: American Psychological Association.

Neimeyer, R. A., & Raskin, J. (Eds.). (2000). *Constructions of disorder.* Washington, DC: American Psychological Association.

Patton, M. Q. (1987). *How to use qualitative methods in evaluation.* Newbury Park, CA: Sage.

Potvin, L., Lasker, J., & Toedter, L. (1989). Measuring grief: A short version of the Perinatal Grief Scale. *Journal of Psychopathology and Behavioral Assessment, 11*, 29–45.

Prigerson, H. G., Beirhals, A. J., Kasl, S. V., Reynolds, C. F., Shear, M. K., Day, N., Berry, L. C., Newson, J. T., & Jacobs, S. (1997). Traumatic grief as a risk factor for mental and physical morbidity. *American Journal of Psychiatry, 154*, 616–623.

Prigerson, H. G., Frank, E., Kasl, S., Reynolds, C., Anderson, B., Zubenko, G. S., Houck, P. R., George, C. J., & Kupfer, D. J. (1995a). Complicated grief and bereavement related depression as distinct disorders: Preliminary empirical validation in elderly bereaved spouses. *American Journal of Psychiatry, 152*, 22–30.

Prigerson, H. G., Maciejewski, P., Newson, J., Reynolds, C. F., Bierhals, A. J., Miller, M., Fasiczka, A., Doman, J., Houck, P. R. (1995b). Inventory of Complicated Grief: A scale to measure maladaptive symptoms of loss. *Psychiatry Research, 59*, 65–79.

Pruchno, R. A., Moss, M. S., Burant, C. J., & Schinfeld, S. (1995). Death of an institutionalized parent: Predictors of bereavement. *Omega, 31*, 99–119.

Richards, A. T., Acree, M., & Folkman, S. (1999). Spiritual aspects of loss among partners of men with AIDS: Postbereavement follow-up. *Death Studies, 23*, 105–127.

Richards, T. A., & Folkman, S. (1997). Spiritual aspects of loss at the time of a partner's death from AIDS. *Death Studies, 21*, 515–540.

Robinson, L., & Pickett, M. (1996). Assessment of adult sibling grief: A review of measurement issues. *The Hospice Journal, 11*, 1–18.

Rubin, H. J., & Rubin, I. S. (1995). *Qualitative interviewing.* Thousand Oaks, CA: Sage.

Sable, P. (1991). Attachment, loss of spouse, and grief in elderly adults. *Omega, 23*, 129–142.

Sanders, C. M., Mauger, P. A., & Strong, P. N. (1985). *A Manual for the Grief Experience Inventory.* Blowing Rock, NC: Center for the Study of Separation and Loss.

Schwandt, T. A. (1994). Constructivist, interpretivist approaches to human inquiry. In N. K. Denzin & Y. Lincoln (Eds.), *Handbook of qualitative research* (pp. 118–134). Newbury Park, CA: Sage.

Stinson, K. M., Lasher, J. N., Lohman, J., & Toedter, L. J. (1992). Parents' grief following pregnancy loss: A comparison of mothers and fathers. *Family Relations, 41*, 218–223.

Strauss, A., & Corbin, J. (1990). *Basics of qualitative research.* Newbury Park, CA: Sage.

Stroebe, W., Stroebe, M., Abakoumkin, G., & Schut, H. (1996). The role of loneliness and social support in adjustment to loss: A test of attachment versus stress theory. *Journal of Personality and Social Psychology, 70*, 1241–1249.

Tedeschi, R., Park, C., & Calhoun, L. (Eds.). (1998). *Posttraumatic growth: Positive changes in the aftermath of crisis.* Mahwah, NJ: Erlbaum.

Thorson, J. A. (1996). Qualitative thanatology. *Mortality, 1*, 177–190.

Toedter, L. J., Lasker, J. N., & Alhadeff, J. M. (1988). The Perinatal Grief Scale: Development and initial validation. *American Journal of Orthopsychiatry, 58*, 435–449.

Toedter, L. J., Lasker, J. N., & Janssen, H. (in press). International comparison of studies using the Perinatal Grief Scale. *Death Studies, 24.*

Wolcott, H. F. (1990). Making a study "more ethnographic." In H. F. Wolcott (Ed.), *Writing up qualitative research* (pp. 79–111). London: Sage.

6

THE DYNAMICS OF ETHICAL DECISION MAKING IN BEREAVEMENT RESEARCH

ALICIA SKINNER COOK

Scientific studies on grief and loss have proliferated over the past several decades as research on bereavement is increasingly accepted as a "legitimate" area of inquiry. This research has been guided by a diverse and scholarly literature on professional ethics in psychology that has also grown over the years. This literature has assisted investigators in interpreting and applying the general guidelines provided in the American Psychological Association's code of ethics (Thompson & Fata, 1997).

Publications on ethical issues related to bereavement research in particular have been limited but are increasingly needed as researchers expand their investigations to broader populations and more sensitive areas of study. In 1995 a special issue of *Death Studies* was published in which several authors explored the unique ethical questions and dilemmas that bereavement researchers face (Balk & Cook, 1995). Included in this special issue was a list of ethical guidelines developed by Parkes (1995) specifically

The author wishes to thank Dr. Kevin A. Oltjenbruns for her valuable input during the preparation of this chapter.

for grief and loss research. These guidelines offer valuable guidance to both experienced and inexperienced researchers in conducting ethical research; however, they do not address the ethical complexities involved when con-ducting research with bereaved individuals and families.

An examination of ethical issues must begin with the basic moral principles that form the foundation of functioning at the highest ethical level as a professional: autonomy (freedom to choose), nonmaleficence (avoiding doing harm), beneficence (promoting good), justice (fairness), fidelity (establishing trust and honoring commitments), and veracity (truthfulness; Kitchener, 1984; Meara, Schmidt, & Day, 1996). Numerous professional associations and government organizations have used these principles to establish standards for ethical research behavior. As early as 1981 Davis observed that principles of ethical human experimentation had been formalized into at least 33 different guidelines and codes of ethics, and all of them incorporate in some way the following standards: (a) ethical methods should be used to recruit participants, with sensitivity to potential conflicts of interest; (b) participants must volunteer on the basis of having all the information necessary to make an informed decision and be allowed to withdraw from the research whenever they desire; (c) all unnecessary risks (including matters of confidentiality as well as psychological and social risks) should be eliminated; (d) the benefits of the research to the individ-ual participants or to society (but preferably to both) should outweigh any risks; and (e) only qualified researchers should conduct scientific research.

This chapter analyzes these key ethical issues as applied to bereave-ment research and discusses the dynamic process of ethical decision making (see Figure 6-1). Within this framework factors contributing to ethical dilemmas are addressed, considering the full range of research situations and audiences. The chapter concludes with an emphasis on the importance of using scientific means to help determine ethical criteria in research with bereaved populations.

RECRUITING PARTICIPANTS

Critical variables related to recruitment of participants in bereave-ment studies include methods used to identify and approach participants, timing of research solicitation in relation to the loss event, and consider-ation of circumstances related to the loss.

Recruitment Methods

Although unintentional, methods of recruitment in psychological studies may actually add to the stress of bereaved individuals, influence

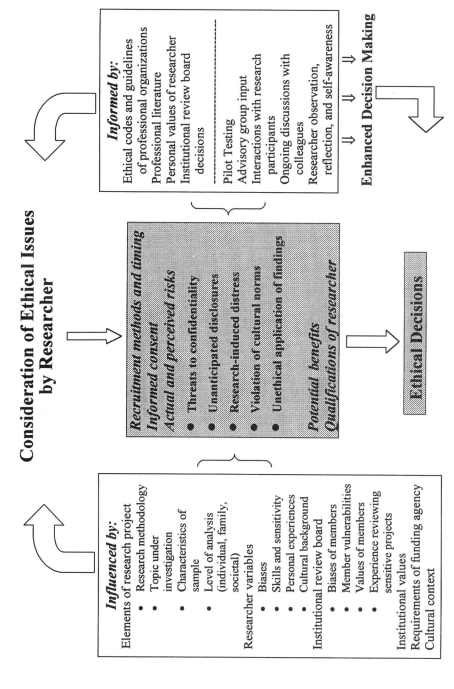

Figure 6-1. The Dynamics of Ethical Decision Making in Research

participation rates of certain subgroups, and result in socially desirable responses from participants. Many investigators studying bereavement seek the assistance of organizations or agencies (e.g., hospices, hospitals, oncology clinics, funeral homes) as avenues for accessing potential participants. Personnel from these groups have often provided services to either the bereaved or deceased family member and are therefore in a position to serve as a trusted source, attesting to the legitimacy of the investigators. At times, the study may be presented as a collaborative project; in other situations agency personnel simply serve as advance informants. Both approaches avoid the receipt of an unexpected (and sometimes unwelcome) solicitation letter or telephone call.

Endorsement of the project by health care personnel, however, may be perceived as subtle pressure to participate. Potential participants may fear that a decision not to participate may jeopardize their receipt of future services or that the quality of these services may be diminished, despite assurances to the contrary. They may also feel guilty for declining, especially if they value the services provided by the contact person or agency. Additional limitations of this method include having a biased sample. For example, families receiving hospice services tend to be White and middle-class (Strahan, 1994). Because of the nature of services offered by hospices, might participants also tend to be more open, more accepting of death, and more likely to seek social support than bereaved individuals who have not used hospice services? Systematic biases in sample selection can distort findings and interfere with our understanding of the grief experience.

To avoid conflict of interest issues and to obtain a more representative sample, some researchers prefer to seek participants from public documents (e.g., death certificates, obituary columns in local newspapers). This method may also be viewed as giving more freedom to the bereaved to decline to participate, because it will usually be a less "socially contaminated" request. However, this approach can be perceived as unfeeling and exploitative as a result of the impersonal nature of the request. In addition to being seen as an unwelcome intrusion or a source of potential harassment during an emotionally difficult time, research solicitations can be interpreted as threatening in other ways as well. For example, an unanticipated call to an elderly widow may result in feelings of vulnerability, even if she declines the request. She may speculate that other strangers may have also examined the obituary column and are also aware that she is now widowed and living alone, thus resulting in undue fear and concern. In a follow-up survey of widowed individuals who declined to participate in a bereavement study, M. Stroebe and Stroebe (1989) in fact found that more widows than widowers refused to be interviewed because they were suspicious or anxious about the interview.

Other characteristics of bereaved people can also affect responses to research recruitment. M. Stroebe and Stroebe (1989) found that depression interacted with gender in affecting rates of participation; lower participation rates were associated with higher levels of depression for men and lower levels of depression for women. Do gender and emotional state (or other characteristics) also interact with methods of recruitment, thus further adversely or positively affecting participation rates? For example, socially isolated males may be less likely to answer their telephones or read unsolicited mail, thus reducing their chances of responding in the affirmative to a research request. Follow-up studies on reasons for nonparticipation, examined differentially for different types of investigations (e.g., qualitative, experimental, intervention studies), are critical to facilitate better understanding of the bereavement data researchers actually collect and to assist in making ethical decisions that avoid distortions of the findings.

Type of recruitment can also affect honesty of responses, which raises ethical issues related to dilemmas the researcher may create for bereaved participants. For example, if names of bereaved individuals are obtained from religious leaders for a study on strengthening religious beliefs following a loss, participants may tend to give socially desirable responses, overemphasizing certain thoughts and actions and not revealing others. They may also experience a moral or spiritual crisis if faced with inconsistencies between what they truly feel and what they think individuals with strong religious faith *should* believe.

Timing of Recruitment

Research studies should be designed within the framework of research goals, but what does it mean to study the "bereaved" and what time frame is appropriate for identifying this population? It is generally acknowledged in the professional literature that grief endures months, even years, following a loss. For instance, Worden (1991) cited studies that suggest that fewer than half of widows have achieved emotional stability at the end of the first year following their loss, and for others three to four years appear to be required. Given this information, is additional justification needed to study bereaved individuals during the first few days or weeks following a loss, considering this would likely be a time of heightened vulnerability and stress? On the other hand, might the avoidance of this sensitive time interfere with our understanding of the unique needs of recently bereaved people as well as the identification of critical "early" variables that might assist or hinder the process of recovery? Through past research efforts, our understanding of grief and the needs of the bereaved have been greatly expanded. Might further expansion through scientific study be limited by being overly cautious in our ethical approach? An additional factor is accessibility. Neal, Carder, and Morgan (1996) demonstrated that recently bereaved husbands and wives are easier to locate and recruit versus those who have been widowed longer. Targeting recently bereaved individuals for a study may result in a more representative sample as well.

Other timing issues also have relevance for ethical consideration. Certain times of the year (e.g., holidays, birthday of the deceased, anniversary date of the death) can be particularly difficult for bereaved individuals and can elicit a strong emotional reaction, at times similar to the acute grief experienced initially following the loss (Cook & Oltjenbruns, 1998). Do bereavement researchers have an ethical responsibility to track dates that are likely to have special emotional significance to survivors? Should these dates be avoided when conducting research unless they are the focus of the study? If so, how might the results of studies be affected? Should research still be undertaken on or near these dates, openly acknowledging that it is a sensitive time?

Interface With Circumstances Related to Loss

Certain types of losses can raise additional ethical issues related to recruitment of participants. Consider the case of a researcher who is studying adaptation of families following death of a child by homicide. Research findings indicate that survivors of homicide victims often experience a pervasive fear for their own personal safety as well as a hypervigilance when relating to strangers (Cook & Oltjenbruns, 1998). Might an unexpected call from a researcher be perceived and responded to differently by bereaved parents in this situation versus parents who have lost a child as a result of terminal illness? Researchers must be prepared for myriad interpretations a request for research participation may elicit. In certain situations involving homicide (e.g., gang-related deaths), bereaved parents might think that their participation will be viewed as "cooperation with authorities" and thus they may fear retribution and have concern for the safety of themselves and their surviving children. In some disenfranchised communities (particularly in situations involving questionable deaths), bereaved parents may in fact suspect that the research project is a "cover" for an investigation into their own possible role in the death of their child. It is critical for a researcher in such instances to identify him- or herself, explain his or her affiliation, disclose where the information regarding the bereavement was obtained, and explain how the data collected will be used. These actions alone, however, may not be sufficient to alleviate concern.

This discussion on recruitment methods, timing, and consideration of loss circumstances implies that the bereavement researcher must have more information about potential participants than would typically be the case in other types of studies. Would the gathering of this information to make more informed ethical decisions be perceived as an infringement of privacy? In addressing one set of ethical concerns, is the researcher actually creating another ethical dilemma?

INFORMED CONSENT

Given that bereaved people are motivated (and at times desperate) to find meaning in their loss, might they also be too vulnerable to refuse requests for participation? If driven to participate in hope of finding answers to their questions (e.g., "Why me?" "Why him?" "Why now?") shortly following a loss, would these same individuals be as willing to participate during a later stage of bereavement? Given their emotional state, are they even capable of giving informed consent?

The Capacity of the Bereaved to Give Informed Consent

Two decades ago, Macklin (1978), a bioethicist, raised the question, "Is it likely that consent can be both voluntarily and rationally informed for bereaved individuals?" She concluded that it is "probably not, given our knowledge of human behavior in times of grief. Consent given under such trying circumstances may not meet the test of being freely and rationally given" (p. 22). Her statement seems to assume that the grief experience is similar for everyone and to question the capacity of all bereaved individuals to give their informed consent.

More recently, Wortman and Silver (1989), after conducting a systematic literature review, have challenged a number of prevalent assumptions commonly held about grief. They stated that "we are just beginning to realize the full range of what may be considered 'normal' grieving" (p. 355). Recognizing the variability of grief appears to be central to the question of the ethics of studying bereaved individuals. Variability will be determined not only by factors related to characteristics of the griever (i.e., personality) and the nature of the relationship with the deceased but also by the circumstances surrounding the loss. For example, a significant number of deaths in the United States are the result of violent acts. These deaths are typically sudden and often times random (thus unanticipated). Is the relevant question in these circumstances, "What is the capacity of a *traumatized* person to give informed consent?" Perhaps as our understanding of the full range of grief experiences grows, so will our understanding of the capacity of bereaved individuals to cope and make decisions (including decisions related to participation in a research project).

Is Consent Truly Informed and Freely Given?

When consent is obtained, the question can be asked, "Is it truly informed consent?" Are participants aware of the full range of emotions that may be evoked and the issues that may be discussed? Because of the unpredictable, unfolding nature of certain types of research methodologies (e.g., qualitative interviews), it may be difficult to warn individuals of all the specific issues that may arise and how they might react to them (LaRossa, Bennett, & Gelles, 1981). Cook and Bosley (1995) found that bereaved adults who participated in their study of funeral rituals reported the experience to be very positive, but many of them experienced intense emotions during the interview and found that emotional issues arose that they did not anticipate (despite being informed about the questions in advance).

Research on bereavement often involves entire family systems or subsystems within families (e.g., siblings, marital dyads) rather than just individuals. Rosenblatt (1995) has commented that additional dynamics and ethical complexities often come into play when conducting research with bereaved families. In his study of farm families following a loss, Rosenblatt found in some instances that family members who by themselves would not have agreed to participate "were drawn into the study because a spouse, parent, or offspring was interested in participating. They did not say no to the family member or to me, but they would not have said yes had they not been pressed by a family member" (p. 142). Extra precautions must be taken to ensure that individual family members are willing participants and that their participation is not coerced by others within the family system. Additional steps can include giving multiple opportunities for each participant to change his or her mind and offering the option of interviewing subsystems (i.e., husband and wife only, parent and child only) instead of the entire family. Some researchers have suggested using a provisional consent procedure that involves giving family members the opportunity to stop the researcher during the interview or at least to avoid a particularly difficult question (Ramos, 1989; Thorne, 1980).

Influence of Culture on Consent

Research ethics must be considered in context. The model for informed consent has been developed through the lens of Western researchers and without full acknowledgment of the cultural variations influencing how "consent" is perceived and communicated. Ethics do not occur in a social vacuum. Christakis (1992) suggested that because ethics are socially constructed they can vary somewhat according to the cultural setting in which they are formulated, as the following statement illustrates.

> The concept of voluntary consent, for instance, seems straightforward yet actually involves a number of cultural complexities. For example, persons from some cultural groups might be unfamiliar with the concept of declining to participate or to answer questions. Members of oppressed minority groups may not fully understand the issue of consent. Also, the Western notion of consent is based on the primacy of individual rights. In cultures in which concern for the group takes

precedence over that of the individual, the notion of consent may need to be expanded to group level concerns. (Cook, 1997, pp. 90–91)

In Slagter's (1996) study of ethics and cross-cultural research, one of the investigators surveyed suggested that it might be appropriate for informed consent requests to involve opportunities for discussion. Slagter recommended that instead of solely relying on paper and pencil consent forms, consideration should be given to also using interview methods to obtain consent.

ASSESSMENT OF ACTUAL AND PERCEIVED RISKS

A basic tenet in research ethics is to do no harm. To avoid causing harm unknowingly, a full assessment of potential risks associated with the study should be identified to the extent possible and disclosed to participants. Ethics review boards are specifically charged with the responsibility of reviewing proposals for elements of risk, and risk is always relative to the vulnerabilities of the research participants. Risks in bereavement research can include issues such as threats to confidentiality, unanticipated disclosures, research-induced distress, and violation of cultural norms. In some circumstances, unethical application of findings can potentially occur, particularly with exceptionally vulnerable and oppressed populations.

Threats to Confidentiality

The concept of confidentiality is typically viewed as respecting the privacy of information shared by an individual and protecting his or her identity. The basic concept of confidentiality should be applied to families as well, but unique confidentiality concerns may arise during the course of a family interview. For example, a husband may disclose private information about his wife or a child may reveal "family secrets" that are not the main focus of the study (and thus not covered in the signed consent form). Not only may information be shared that individual family members did not agree to, researchers may unknowingly ask family members to describe thoughts and feelings not previously shared within the context of the family. As a consequence, one family member may divulge this new information to others (e.g., a sibling may tell her best friend about her brother's disclosure during the research interview). These situations require special sensitivity as the rights and needs of all family members are considered.

Even when data are obtained through the use of mailed questionnaires, confidentiality may be unknowingly violated, albeit through indirect means. For example, in studies of effects of loss on couples, two questionnaires may be mailed to a family simultaneously. While completing the questionnaires in a spouse's presence, the husband or wife may inquire about the responses of the other. Depending on the previous communication between the couple, one or both bereaved adults may feel that participation in the study resulted in an invasion of privacy beyond what was originally anticipated. (It should be noted that these potentially problematic outcomes might occur even if the individuals decide not to participate in the study. Simply receiving the questionnaire in the mail may prompt unanticipated discussion.) Conversations prompted by the act of completing the research instrument may also affect the validity of the data; responses can be enhanced by insights gained or distorted in an effort to maintain privacy.

External threats to the protection of confidentiality can exist as well. For example, researchers studying anticipatory grief among young adults with AIDS should be aware that public health reporting laws can result in a forced breach of confidentiality in some cases (Melton & Gray, 1988).

Unanticipated Disclosures

It is also often times difficult to anticipate all the ethical issues that may arise during a research project. Rosenblatt (1995) related the experience of having bereaved persons tell him at the end of a qualitative research interview that they had revealed some aspects of their loss for the first time. Unanticipated disclosures can pose ethical dilemmas that the researcher had not expected before the interview.

Some disclosures can have legal ramifications, particularly if they involve the role of a surviving family member in the death. Consider a large-scale study of neonatal deaths in an urban community in which a participant confides that her husband, in a fit of anger, pushed her to the ground during the seventh month of her pregnancy, resulting in a premature birth. She then goes on to disclose other episodes of spousal abuse, asking the investigator not to tell anyone. What are the risks to the investigator if he or she does not comply with legal reporting requirements? How are these responsibilities balanced with previous assurances of confidentiality by the researcher and informed consent on the part of the participant?

Research-Induced Distress

How do researchers know if participation in their study has caused distress and what steps should be taken to provide appropriate assistance to anyone who experiences negative outcomes? It is unusual for participants in most scientific psychological studies to report harm resulting from the experience, and bereavement research is no exception. It is nonetheless common practice (and required in some instances) for researchers to provide resources to contact if research participants do have concerns. Some researchers provide this information routinely, and others give it on a perceived need basis. Is this practice sufficient? It could be argued that because the bereaved are more likely to be emotionally vulnerable than are research samples obtained from the general population, it is an ethical necessity to follow up with participants to inquire about their well-being. On the other hand, are participants likely to interpret this behavior by researchers as a kind and caring gesture or as an indication that they are "at risk" in some way? Might follow-up also be seen as going beyond the bounds of the original consent form and as an intrusion beyond what was originally agreed to?

The choice of research methodologies can also affect the ability to evaluate effects of the study on emotional states. For example, most quantitative studies do not provide an opportunity to assess directly the impact on participants by observing their reactions. Interview studies, in contrast, allow for direct responses to emotional expressions and the chance to intervene and terminate an interview if it is perceived as too stressful. On the other hand, are not individuals themselves more likely to terminate the research session when they are alone (and under no perceived social pressure) versus in the presence of a researcher? Ethical trade-offs appear to exist, no matter what approach is used.

In a recent article on future directions in bereavement research, Lund and Caserta (1998) stated that although a great deal is known about the bereavement process itself, we have much more to learn about the most effective ways to intervene. Research involving intervention, although certainly needed as these authors have suggested, raise additional ethical questions. Balk (1995) conducted a study of a social support intervention with 180 college students. A traditional control group design was used at the insistence of the funding agency; the bereaved students were assigned randomly to control or support groups and nonbereaved students formed a second control group. The pre–post design involved multiple assessments measuring depression, stress, and coping at five- to six-week intervals. Members of both control groups were not given any type of alternative treatment or placebo; they were only sent the research findings at the end of the project.

Of the students who dropped out of Balk's (1995) study after the first assessment, 80% were in the bereaved control group. Those who dropped out from this group tended to be males and older than the rest of the sample. Notably, they did not have depression or distress scores that differed significantly from the bereaved students remaining in the study; both showed mild mood disturbances and fairly high levels of distress. Balk concluded,

> It is possible that filling out the data instruments intensified distress
> for both the bereaved control and bereaved support group members.

In the first meeting of their support groups, bereaved students indicated that filling out the instruments made conscious many painful thoughts and feelings associated with the death they were grieving. One of the issues thus raised is to what extent completing the instruments worked as an intervention by eliciting thoughts, images, and feelings that had perhaps gone unrecognized by the students. (p. 135)

Although Balk's (1995) intervention study demonstrated effectiveness of support groups in mediating stress among bereaved college students, he was left with the following question: "Do scholars have an obligation to do more for participants (particularly in bereaved samples) than place them in a control group?" Balk acknowledged that, as a research issue, the refusal to use control groups could be seen as a breach of ethics itself because the investigator would be using procedures whose efficacy, quality, and testability are questionable. In the end, however, perhaps the most scientifically appropriate design resulted in less persuasive outcome data as a result of the high drop-out rate among the bereaved controls. Balk suggested consideration of cross-over, reversal, and multiple baseline designs with bereaved populations as alternative options to the control group design used in his study.

Violation of Cultural Norms

Certain risks may not be anticipated or perceived by the researcher because of cultural or ethnic differences. In Slagter's (1996) study of researchers engaged in cross-cultural research, one respondent said, "As a social scientist I must typically be concerned about psychological/psychic 'damage' to research participants. To the extent that stimuli and assessment can be experienced differently across cultures, my protections against such damage may be less than adequate if too specific to Western cultures" (p. 38). Another respondent said, "Most cross-cultural research in the field of psychology tends to use instruments conceptualized by Western researchers and standardized by sampling predominately middle-class whites. Some of them may violate cultural values or beliefs when directly used on people from other cultures" (p. 38). Some cultural groups, for example, consider it unlucky even to be asked about anything connected to death.

Unethical Application of Findings

Once a study is completed, publication of findings is a professional obligation; in fact, failure to disseminate research findings can be viewed as unethical. Information, which is widely available, can lead to a better understanding of the human response to loss and enhance the effectiveness of intervention efforts. However, Simpson (1993a, 1993b) has raised a number of ethical concerns in the larger sociopolitical global context, giving us a different way of looking at ways increased knowledge can be misused at times. For example, he suggested that knowledge of trauma and grief reactions can be perversely used by repressive regimes to perpetuate oppression. Furthermore, inhabitants of regions of the world suffering warfare and disaster may be used as experimental subjects, at times without their informed consent, for eager researchers who reside in safe countries and who may be naive with regard to the ramifications of their research outcomes.

POTENTIAL BENEFITS OF RESEARCH PARTICIPATION

Boss (1987) has asserted that although researchers must be concerned about the dangers of research, our sensitivity to the risks should not obscure an equal sensitivity to the benefits that research may bring to individuals and families as well. A full assessment of risks must be balanced with identification of benefits, and benefits are always relative to the ability of the participants or others to profit from the research experience and findings. Effective support and intervention for bereaved populations develop from a sound base of theoretically oriented and empirically derived knowledge (Stroebe, Stroebe, & Hansson, 1988), thus justifying the need for this type of research in general. In addition to the broader benefits for society and for improving our efforts to offer bereavement support, what particular benefits might research hold for the actual participants involved?

Self-Reports by Respondents

Curiously, the same response by participants may be seen as a risk by some and as a benefit by others. For example, bereavement researchers report that individuals often cry when interviewed about a deceased family member. In most Western societies, expressing sadness and shedding tears are associated with stress and negative events. Ethics review committees are at times concerned that asking questions about a loss will unduly upset individuals. Thus research that results in this type of behavior is often seen as having a negative impact. Contrary to this expectation, bereaved research participants often seem to welcome the opportunity to express their feelings and to discuss their losses.

Lehman, Ellard, and Wortman (1986) asked 94 bereaved individuals to identify both helpful and unhelpful attempts by others to support them in their grief. One of the responses perceived to be most helpful was the provision of opportunities to discuss their feelings. The least helpful responses were giving advice and encouraging recovery, perceived by many as ignoring the feelings of the bereaved and curtailing opportunities to share concerns. It is important to recognize that at least in American society (and many others), opportunities for bereaved persons to have their grief acknowledged are often limited. The larger society often expects people to resolve their grief quickly and to "get on with their lives," sending a message that their grief is not legitimate and that the depth of their loss is not fully recognized. Participating in a research study can, for some grievers, be an outlet for thoughts and feelings not previously shared with available support systems.

In their follow-up study of bereaved individuals who had participated in a study the previous month on funeral rituals, Cook and Bosley (1995) inquired about the perceived benefits, if any, of their research experience. The sample unanimously agreed that it was beneficial to have the opportunity to share their feelings, and all thought they had helped others by participating in the study. In particular, they perceived that their willingness to share their stories of sorrow as part of a research project would educate others and promote understanding of the impact of death on survivors. Although this study has limited generalizability, it does provide some evidence for positive benefits of participation under certain circumstances. A more recent study, using the same instrument with Bosnian refugee families in Norway, reported similar positive benefits of research participation (Dyregrov, Dyregrov, & Raundalen, 2000).

Experimental Studies

But are the participants the best ones to decide if their participation is in fact beneficial or harmful? Pennebaker (1989) concluded that we should not rely solely on self-reports of distress but instead focus more on objective physiological measures. Pennebaker and O'Heeron (1984) found that among individuals whose spouses had died unexpectedly by suicide or automobile accident, the more the survivors have talked with others about their spouse's death, the healthier they were and the less they ruminated about their spouse a year after the death. Similar findings were also obtained among Holocaust survivors when long-term health outcomes were studied (Pennebaker, Barger, & Tiebout, 1989). Not only does talking about a traumatic event appear to be beneficial when examined scientifically, but there appear to be health risks in not confiding.

In a series of studies on disclosure of traumatic events, Pennebaker and his colleagues (1989) asked participants to either talk or write about their most upsetting personal experiences and to discuss aspects of the experience that they have not previously discussed with others. The majority of individuals disclosed issues surrounding interpersonal conflict, intimacy, and loss from death or divorce. These investigators found that the mere venting of negative feelings exacerbates these feelings immediately after each study. For example, disclosure of loss issues may involve feelings of sadness, depression, guilt, or anger. However, these feelings do not seem to persist over time. Furthermore, the expression of both deep feelings and related thoughts can lead to insight and have long-term positive health consequences. In one Pennebaker and Beall (1986) experiment, those research participants who wrote about their thoughts *and* emotions evidenced improved health relative to participants who wrote only about their emotions or facts surrounding their traumatic experiences.

What is the process by which insight can result in positive physical and mental health benefits? According to Pennebaker (1989), when individuals confront traumatic experiences significant changes occur in the body. When talking or writing about traumatic events, compared to superficial topics, research participants show improved immune function as well as other positive physiological indicators as they repeatedly confront and thereby resolve the trauma. On a psychological level, confronting a trauma helps individuals to better understand and assimilate the event. In other words, "Individuals translate the event into language. Once coded linguistically, individuals can more readily understand, find meaning in, or attain closure of the experience" (p. 231), and a reconstruction of thoughts, emotions, beliefs, and self-perception takes place. A critical dimension to confronting personal experiences appears to be the assimilation of a variety of types of information.

In Pennebaker's studies, questions have typically been open-ended and participants are asked to write or talk about a traumatic experience. Bereavement studies, in contrast, typically have a specific content focus and thus may probe more deeply into particular variables of interest associated with the grief experience (e.g., feelings of anger, isolation). Do questions about a significant and emotional life event, particularly when not fully processed, influence how this particular event is framed psychologically? Might targeted questioning and probing act as an "unintended intervention" by suggesting an interpretation or meaning to a loss? For example, might questions related to "death as desertion" contribute to the cognitive structure from which the event may be viewed in the future?

RESEARCHER QUALIFICATIONS

Researcher qualifications are considered when members of institutional review boards assess research proposals involving human participants, but little discussion of this topic can be found in the professional literature. Although a particular research design may pose no ethical problems, the actual implementation of a study can be problematic and will depend on the skills and sensitivities of the researcher.

Definition of "Qualified"

Cook (1995) has raised the following questions in this regard: "What precisely is meant by the term *qualified*? Should the researcher have expertise in the subject matter that is the focus of the investigation? Experience with the research methodologies used? Clinical experience?" (p. 117). Studies that ask individuals about emotional, painful issues such as personal loss can require an expanded ethical assessment of the necessary qualifications for investigators.

When speaking of researcher qualifications, the discussion usually centers around the principal investigator(s), but what about the qualifications of those who are more directly involved in data collection efforts (e.g., distributing questionnaires, interviewing bereaved families)? These research assistants are in a position to exacerbate or alleviate potential stresses associated with the research project, but their training and preparation can be overlooked in a review of qualifications. Furthermore, there is little agreement about the additional skills these individuals may need to be considered "qualified." Do they need an understanding of grief and loss? Should they have clinical training? Turnbull, McLeod, Callahan, and Kessler (1988) have recommended that inexperienced interviewers be given extensive training to equip them to handle the intense affect that is evoked when discussing significant life events such as loss of a loved one. Such steps can enhance the quality of information obtained from the study, as well as increase the comfort level of both the interviewer and the interviewee.

At times community volunteers may be involved in data collection; should they have formal training regarding the ethical issues that may arise in the course of the study or is it the responsibility of the principal investigators to monitor this aspect of the project? Although the project director may have the ultimate responsibility for the ethical conduct of the study, do not all individuals involved in the project have responsibility for their own ethical (or unethical) actions and thus deserve to be prepared for potential ethical dilemmas they may encounter?

Biases

In socially and emotionally sensitive research, the definition of "qualified" can also include awareness of personal and professional biases. A growing body of research suggests that individuals systematically differ in the ways they formulate ethical appraisals of research, and the background characteristics of individuals who make these decisions account for some of these differences (Kimmel, 1991). The general nature of ethical principles in fact allows for interpretation as these principles are applied in varying contexts, with diverse populations, and in different circumstances.

Researchers thus can be assumed to have their own biases, which are shaped over time and which are never completely independent of the topic under investigation. For example, interviewer characteristics as well as the concerns interviewers have about the questions they ask can affect the validity of responses (Lee, 1993). Although a powerful influence on the research process, investigator bias has received little attention as it relates to ethics.

Morse (1994) recommended reflection on personal motives for conducting a particular study as a critical stage in the research process. Researchers need to separate their own needs, vulnerabilities, and expectations from the bereaved individuals and families they are studying. Unexamined emotional biases and unresolved personal issues of the investigator can convey unintentional messages to participants about the form and expression of their grief. If investigators use this forum as an unconscious way to resolve some of their own issues related to personal losses, there could be unintended consequences for those agreeing to be participants in the study. For example, if an investigator still has strong guilt over a child's death, then he or she may ask questions that focus excessively on guilt as a major component of bereavement. If this component is not expressed by participants, the researcher's own experience may influence interpretations of the findings (e.g., an interpretation of repressed feelings).

Stereotypes and cultural assumptions can also lead to misunderstandings and erroneous conclusions when the investigator and research participants come from different cultural backgrounds. Rooda (1993) found that nurses in clinical settings are likely to have more positive perceptions of patients from their own ethnic and cultural groups than of other patients. These types of tendencies can easily transfer to research settings and result in lack of attention to important ethical concerns when research involves participants from diverse cultural or ethnic groups. Also, members of dominant cultural groups tend to define normalcy in terms of their own experiences; thus ethnocentric perceptions and values can enter into research decisions and interpretation of findings. For example, cultural values and mores perceived as healthy in a dominant culture may be perceived as unhealthy and inappropriate in others (e.g., openly crying in the presence of others). The influence of culture on our perceptions cannot be overemphasized.

INSTITUTIONAL REVIEW BOARDS

Institutional review boards (IRBs) are charged with the responsibility of reviewing the ethics of individual research projects and giving (or denying) approval for investigations to be undertaken. Although having various titles in different countries, these boards or committees exist to ensure that researchers respect participants' rights and minimize risks; but are the actions of those who provide this oversight unbiased?

Bereavement research, in particular, has unique aspects that may influence the response of IRB members. Bereavement research cannot be separated from the contemporary context in which it occurs, including public and professional attitudes toward death, the openness with which it can be discussed, and the appropriateness of studying responses to loss of a loved one. Contemporary western society, for example, remains uncomfortable with the notion of death and those who are associated with it. These attitudes can spill over into professional decisions that can interfere with advancement in this field of study. Socially sensitive research projects often receive extra scrutiny; in fact one study found that such projects are twice as likely to be rejected as are other proposals (Ceci, Peters, & Plotkin, 1985). Does the caution used with socially and emotionally sensitive research affect the type and number of studies conducted on bereavement, particularly with certain populations (e.g., parents of murdered children)? Seiler and Murtha (1980) have suggested that seemingly arbitrary delays and rejections of research approval by IRBs can affect a researcher's choice of topics and limit the development of knowledge in particular areas.

Approval of grief studies in particular is complicated by the very nature of the phenomenon under investigation and the interplay of social and emotional responses to loss. For example, committee members who have experienced significant losses may project their own concerns and experiences onto the pool of potential research participants, thus subjecting the research proposal to extra scrutiny and perhaps delays in approval. Does this close examination of the ethical issues involved benefit the entire process, particularly because the concerned IRB member could legitimately be seen as representative of the group that will be studied and thus contribute valuable insights? Or should individuals with recent personal losses, which may interfere with their objectivity, remove themselves from the review process?

ADEQUACY OF EXISTING ETHICAL GUIDELINES

Researchers generally acknowledge that much of what we know about grief is obtained from research on dominant cultures. More attention has recently been paid to research that facilitates our understanding of the experience of grief among minority groups as well. At the same time, colleagues from many countries are increasingly collaborating in research projects that cross national boundaries and require cross-cultural communication regarding the ethics of research. Although professional peers in the international community often feel they speak the same language with regard to statistical techniques or other aspects of scientific inquiry, the same cannot necessarily be said for the nuances of ethical concerns.

Many national governments and professional associations have developed their own ethical codes and regulations for research involving human participants, but they often do not address issues that arise in cross-cultural situations. In a survey of researchers who had recently published articles in selected cross-cultural psychology journals, Slagter (1996) found that research guidelines were often perceived as inadequate by researchers engaged in cross-cultural research, and at times these guidelines actually contributed to ethical dilemmas (as with the case of informed consent discussed earlier). When guidelines do not address important ethical issues in cross-cultural research, researchers are on their own to address some very complex issues. This situation can be particularly problematic for researchers studying sensitive areas such as bereavement, because people tend to identify with their cultural backgrounds during a life crisis more than at any other time (Cook & Dworkin, 1992). Christakis (1992) summarized the issue as follows:

> An incomplete fit between the ethical expectations of researchers and subjects raises an important question: Is it possible to formulate ethical rules governing the conduct of investigators from one cultural background performing research on subjects from another? (p. 1080)

As the global academic community works more closely to integrate knowledge and understand differences, we must seek to learn more about the fundamental ethical principles and guidelines on which research by international colleagues is based as well as the ethics of those we seek to study. Valid cross-cultural research involves an attitude of openness and respect for divergent views, knowledge of the culture being studied, close collaboration with colleagues belonging to the cultural community in which the research is conducted, and modification or expansion of ethical procedures to fit with the social and ethical reality of the research participants (Welfel, 1998). Guidelines are needed that minimize ethnocentrism, avoiding approaches and interpretations rooted in the researchers' own cultural experiences that do not take into account the values and beliefs of those being studied.

INVOLVING RESEARCH PARTICIPANTS IN ETHICAL DECISION MAKING

Federal regulations and professional guidelines for evaluating research ethics are typically based on a cost–benefit model and provide minimum standards (Office for Protection From Research Risks, 1991); they do not substitute for the ethical sensitivities of the researcher. For investigators seeking to increase their ethical sensitivities and determine acceptable and appropriate actions within this context, give-and-take interaction with individuals from the targeted research sample can be very helpful. In fact, Brody, Gluck, and Aragon (1997) state that one of the most valuable perspectives on the issue of informed consent is that of the research participant. Although a largely ignored area of study, participant involvement is increasingly recognized as an important element of a full ethical analysis. Findings from research comparing ethical judgments of participants and researchers consistently demonstrate differences of opinion (Michaels & Oetting, 1979; Sullivan & Dieker, 1973). Although it may not be feasible (or ethical) to involve research participants in all aspects of research decision making, a useful substitute may be a group of similar individuals who are beyond the stage of acute bereavement or those who work with the bereaved on a daily basis. These groups could offer useful perspectives regarding the possible impact of researchers' actions on the bereaved individuals and families to be studied.

In qualitative studies, a researcher can learn the following from the bereaved through interviews: their understandings of the research, their perceived relationship with the researcher, and their reactions to the questions they are asked, as well as their own ethical dilemmas and the ways they prefer to resolve these dilemmas (Rosenblatt, 1995). Likewise in quantitative research in which less personal contact typically occurs during the course of the investigation, potential participants can also be viewed as partners in solving difficult ethical dilemmas. Quality bereavement research, like other types of research, typically begins with pilot testing. In these pilot projects, longer term bereaved groups can be asked how soon after their loss they would have felt comfortable having a researcher contact them, without undue distress. Input can also be gathered on preferred debriefing methods, the need and timing for follow-up to ensure no harm has been done, and the provision of information on helpful resources.

Melton, Levine, Koocher, Rosenthal, and Thompson (1988) have proposed using community consultation as a way of informing research that is socially sensitive or poses difficult ethical dilemmas. They suggest assembling groups of prospective participants for the purpose of discussing research plans, with the goal of conducting the research in a way that would be approved by the community being studied (the "bereaved community" in this instance). At these meetings prospective participants or similar groups could (a) provide support for each other's efforts to secure what they consider adequate explanations, (b) learn that their questions and concerns will be dealt with responsively and respectfully by researchers, and (c) offer suggestions and criticisms of the research effort. This approach may be particularly useful when studying individuals from minority groups.

CONCLUSION

As researchers continue to expand their knowledge of grief and loss, they will be faced with new ethical challenges. Scientific rigor must be matched with ethical rigor; ethics go hand in hand with scientific inquiry, and it is difficult to separate scientific issues from related ethical concerns. Bersoff (1994) has asserted that codes of ethics can build an ethical floor but they may not urge us to reach for the ceiling. Only by continuing to raise ethical concerns and adequately addressing them can advancement occur. These developments can be promoted by ongoing discussion of ethical considerations within the field of thanatology and refinement of ethical guidelines, particularly as research increasingly involves more complex dynamics (e.g., multiple family members, diverse ethnic and cultural communities, increase in study of traumatic deaths).

Researchers of sensitive topics such as bereavement must be more acutely aware of their ethical responsibilities than those who research more innocuous topics (Lee, 1993). Bereavement research will be enhanced when researchers and others involved in the research endeavor examine their own biases, acknowledge their limitations, and become more aware of the many ways they can potentially influence the research process. A full ethical analysis, however, includes involvement of those we seek to study. Ethical decision making is a dynamic and complex process with many players and a variety of perspectives.

A decade ago Kimmel (1991) concluded that

> if the relative importance of the many factors that influence judgments pertinent to ethical decision making can be enumerated, clarified, and weighed in subsequent research—on topics such as the influence of individual personality differences, the impact of early experience and socialization, moral ideology, the subject matter and content of evaluated research, and the impact of institutional values on review board members—researchers may then be able to deal effectively with their ethical dilemmas and obtain a fuller understanding of their differences through reasoned and informed discussion. (p. 788)

Much of what we "know" about the ethics of bereavement research still remains largely untested; systematic empirical analyses of current practices in the field and outcomes are largely absent. Issues of helpfulness and harmfulness must be established scientifically, with attention given to sample bias, nonrespondents, and limited generalizability in some cases. A clear understanding of risks and benefits associated with bereavement research should be increasingly guided by empirical research as psychologists and other professionals strive to enhance the process of ethical decision making.

REFERENCES

Balk, D. E. (1995). Bereavement research using control groups: Ethical obligations and questions. *Death Studies, 19*, 123–138.

Balk, D. E., & Cook, A. S. (1995). Special issue on ethics and bereavement research. *Death Studies, 19*, 103–197.

Bersoff, D. N. (1994). Explicit ambiguity: The 1992 ethics code as an oxymoron. *Professional Psychology: Research and Practice, 25*, 382–386.

Boss, P. (1987). The role of intuition in family research: Three issues of ethics. *Contemporary Family Therapy, 9*, 146–159.

Brody, J. L., Gluck, J. P., & Aragon, A. S. (1997). Participants' understanding of the process of psychological research: Informed consent. *Ethics & Behavior, 7*, 285–298.

Ceci, S. J., Peter, D., & Plotkin, J. (1985). Human subjects review, personal values, and the regulation of social science research. *American Psychologist, 40*, 994–1002.

Christakis, N. A. (1992). Ethics are local: Engaging cross-cultural variation in the ethics for clinical research. *Social Science Medicine, 35*, 1079–1091.

Cook, A. S. (1995). Ethical issues in bereavement research: An overview. *Death Studies, 19*, 103–122.

Cook, A. S. (1997). Investigator bias in bereavement research: Ethical and methodological implications. *Canadian Journal of Nursing Research, 29*, 87–93.

Cook, A. S., & Bosley, G. (1995). The experience of participating in bereavement research: Stressful or therapeutic? *Death Studies, 19*, 157–170.

Cook, A. S., & Dworkin, D. S. (1992). *Helping the bereaved: Therapeutic interventions for children, adolescents, and adults.* New York: Basic Books.

Cook, A. S., & Oltjenbruns, K. A. (1998). *Dying and grieving: Life span and family perspectives* (2nd ed.). Fort Worth, TX: Harcourt Brace.

Davis, S. (1981). Ethical considerations in gerontological nursing research. *Geriatric Nursing, 2*, 269–272.

Dyregrov, K., Dyregrov, A., & Raundalen, M. (2000). Refugee families' experience of research participation. *Journal of Traumatic Stress, 13*, 413–426.

Kimmel, A. L. (1991). Predictable biases in the ethical decision making of American psychologists. *American Psychologist, 46*, 786–788

Kitchener, K. S. (1984). Intuition, critical evaluation and ethical principles: The foundation for ethical decisions in counseling psychology. *The Counseling Psychologist, 12*, 43–55.

LaRossa, R., Bennett, L. A., & Gelles, R. J. (1981). Ethical dilemmas in qualitative research. *Journal of Marriage and Family Therapy, 43*, 303–313.

Lee, R. M. (1993). *Doing research on sensitive topics.* London: Sage.

Lehman, D. R., Ellard, J. H., & Wortman, C. B. (1986). Social support for the bereaved: Recipients' and providers' perspectives on what is helpful. *Journal of Consulting and Clinical Psychology, 54*, 438–446.

Lund, D. A., & Caserta, M. S. (1998). Future directions in adult bereavement research. *Omega, 36,* 287–303.

Macklin, R. (1978). Case studies in bioethics: Studying grief without consent–Commentary. *Hastings Center Report, 9*(4), 22.

Meara, N. M., Schmidt, L. D., & Day, J. D. (1996). Principles and virtues: A foundation for ethical decisions, policies and character. *The Counseling Psychologist, 24,* 4–77.

Melton, G. B., & Gray, J. N. (1988). Ethical dilemmas in AIDS research: Individual privacy and public health. *American Psychologist, 43,* 60–64.

Melton, G. B., Levine, R. J., Koocher, G. P., Rosenthal, R., & Thompson, W. C. (1988). Community consultation in socially sensitive research: Lessons from clinical trials of treatment for AIDS. *American Psychologist, 43,* 573–581.

Michaels, T. F., & Oetting, E. R. (1979). The informed consent dilemma: An empirical approach. *Journal of Social Psychology, 109,* 223–230.

Morse, J. M. (1994). Designing funded qualitative research. In N. K. Denzin & Y. S. Lincoln (Eds.), *Handbook of qualitative research* (pp. 220–235). Thousand Oaks, CA: Sage.

Neal, M. B., Carder, P. C., & Morgan, D. L. (1996). Use of public records to compare respondents and nonrespondents in a study of recent widows. *Research on Aging, 18,* 219–242.

Office for Protection From Research Risks. (1991). *Code of federal regulations, Title 45, Part 46—Protection of human subjects* (revised June 18, 1991). Washington, DC: U.S. Government Printing Office.

Parkes, C. M. (1995). Guidelines for conducting ethical bereavement research. *Death Studies, 19,* 171–181.

Pennebaker, J. W. (1989). Confession, inhibition, and disease. In L. Berkowitz (Ed.), *Advances in experimental social psychology* (Vol. 22). San Diego, CA: Academic Press.

Pennebaker, J. W., Barger, S. D., & Tiebout, J. (1989). Disclosure of traumas and health among Holocaust survivors. *Psychomatic Medicine, 51,* 577–589.

Pennebaker, J. W., & Beall, S. K. (1986). Confronting a traumatic event: Toward an understanding of inhibition and disease. *Journal of Abnormal Psychology, 95,* 274–281.

Pennebaker, J. W., & O'Heeron, R. C. (1984). Confiding in others and illness rate among spouses of suicide and accidental death victims. *Journal of Consulting and Clinical Psychology, 93,* 473–476.

Ramos, M. C. (1989). Some ethical implications of qualitative research. *Research in Nursing and Health, 12,* 57–63.

Rooda, L. A. (1993). Knowledge and attitudes of nurses toward culturally different patients: Implications for nursing education. *Journal of Nursing Education, 32,* 209–213.

Rosenblatt, P. C. (1995). Ethics of qualitative interviewing with grieving families. *Death Studies, 19,* 139–155.

Seiler, I. M., & Murtha, J. M. (1980). Federal regulation of social research using human subjects: A critical assessment. *American Sociologist, 15,* 146–157.

Simpson, M. A. (1993a). Bitter waters: The effects on children of the stresses of unrest and oppression. In J. Wilson & B. Raphael (Eds.), *International handbook of traumatic stress syndromes* (pp. 601–624). New York: Plenum Press.

Simpson, M. A. (1993b). Traumatic stress and the bruising of the soul: The effects of torture and coercive interrogation. In J. Wilson & B. Raphael (Eds.), *International handbook of traumatic stress syndromes* (pp. 667–684). New York: Plenum Press.

Slagter, T. (1996). *An exploration of ethical principles in human subjects research and their relevancy to cross-cultural contexts.* Master's thesis, Colorado State University, Fort Collins.

Strahan, G. W. (1994). *An overview of home health and hospice care patients: Preliminary data from the 1993 national home and hospice care survey.* U.S. Department of Health and Human Services, Advance Data, No. 257, 1–12.

Stroebe, M. S., & Stroebe, W. (1989). Who participates in bereavement research? A review and empirical study. *Omega, 20,* 1–29.

Stroebe, M. S., Stroebe, W., & Hansson, R. O. (1988). Bereavement research: An historical introduction. *Journal of Social Issues, 44,* 1–18.

Sullivan, D. S., & Dieker, T. E. (1973). Subject-experimenter perceptions of ethical issues in human research. *American Psychologist, 28,* 587–591.

Thompson, A., & Fata, M. (1997). Relating the psychological literature to the American Psychological Association ethical standards. *Ethics and Behavior, 7,* 79–88.

Thorne, B. (1980). "You still takin' notes": Fieldwork and problems of informed consent. *Social Problems, 27,* 284–297.

Turnbull, J. E., McLeod, J. D., Callahan, J. M., & Kessler, R. C. (1988). Who should ask? Ethical interviewing in psychiatric epidemiology studies. *American Journal of Orthopsychiatry, 58,* 228–239.

Welfel, E. R. (1998). *Ethics in counseling and psychotherapy: Standards, research, and emerging issues.* Pacific Grove, CA: Brooks/Cole.

Worden, J. W. (1991). *Grief counseling and grief therapy* (2nd ed.) New York: Springer.

Wortman, C., & Silver, R. (1989). The myths of coping with loss. *Journal of Consulting and Clinical Psychology, 57,* 349–357.

II

CONSEQUENCES:
THE BEREAVED INDIVIDUAL
ACROSS THE LIFE SPAN

7

BEREAVEMENT EXPERIENCES AND PERSONAL GROWTH

JEANNE A. SCHAEFER AND RUDOLF H. MOOS

Life crises and transitions forge our identities by initiating changes that challenge our basic values, placing new demands on us, and disrupting significant relationships and established roles. Although much of the research on adaptation to life crises emphasizes the painful emotions and psychological symptoms they generate, these events often are an impetus for personal growth (Tedeschi & Calhoun, 1995; Tedeschi, Park, & Calhoun, 1998b). A wide variety of crises—natural disasters, war and combat, physical illness, divorce, and bereavement—can be catalysts for personal transformation. It is quite common for people to emerge from these crises with enhanced social and personal resources and new coping skills (Schaefer & Moos, 1998).

Of all life's crises, the death of someone we love is one of the most emotionally wrenching. For many individuals and their families, adjustment to bereavement is a lengthy process that is a result, in part, of the

This work was supported by the Department of Veterans Affairs Office of Research and Development (Health Services Research and Development Service) and by NIAAA Grant AA06699. Shira Luft provided valuable assistance with the literature review for this chapter; she identified, retrieved, and organized a large number of articles.

145

disruptions in their roles and relationships with others. When a family member dies, a crisis ensues and the family must be recreated to cope with existing tasks and new demands (Shapiro, 1996). Loss of a family member also can interfere with developmental tasks, such as the transfer of primary attachments from the family of origin to a family of procreation, launching children, and supporting them in initiating new family systems (Jordan, Kraus, & Ware, 1993).

Despite the far-reaching, painful changes that occur following the loss of a loved one, bereavement, like other life crises, can foreshadow personal transformation. Personal growth in bereaved individuals often is reflected in increased independence, self-reliance, and self-efficacy; more wisdom, maturity, compassion, and understanding of others; and changes in life perspective and strengthened religious beliefs (Calhoun & Tedeschi, 1990; Kessler, 1987; Simon & Drantell, 1998).

Research on personal growth is a developing field. As yet, there is no consensus in the literature regarding the definition of personal growth, nor is there a clear distinction between personal growth and adjustment (for a discussion of issues related to the conceptualization of personal growth, see Park, 1998; Tedeschi, Park, & Calhoun, 1998a). In this chapter, we consider personal growth to have occurred when individuals' social resources or coping skills (proximal outcomes) or personal resources (ultimate outcomes) are enhanced after bereavement occurs.

We view personal growth as more than a readaptation in psychological functioning (less depression, anxiety, distress, decreased grief reactions) in the postbereavement period. Nevertheless, because the outcomes examined in the bereavement literature typically focus on adaptation, we comment on both personal growth and adaptation. Moreover, we believe that individuals who successfully adapt to bereavement may be more likely to experience personal growth.

BEREAVEMENT: SUCCESSFUL ADAPTATION AND PERSONAL GROWTH

Some of the processes through which bereaved individuals come to experience personal growth include grieving itself, introspection and the search for meaning, and redefining roles and relationships. In a study of adults who lost a child, parent, or sibling, Hogan, Morse, and Tason (1996) identified several processes that occur in bereavement: getting the news, responding to the news, facing realities, becoming engulfed in suffering, emerging from suffering, and getting on with life. Personal growth occurred across all phases of the bereavement process but manifested itself most after the bereaved person emerged from the acute pain of grief. Some bereaved individuals engaged in intense introspection, a process that fostered their ultimate personal growth.

In their search for meaning, some bereaved individuals came to see themselves as less judgmental and more compassionate and tolerant. Others reevaluated their priorities and concluded that work and money were not as important as family. Knowing that death could occur at anytime, bereaved individuals rededicated their life with more purpose and regard to their remaining loved ones. The desire to derive some good from the death and give meaning to their loved one's life led bereaved individuals to help others who were grieving and to be empathic toward them (Hogan et al., 1996).

Nerken (1993) asserted that growth occurs when bereaved individuals grieve actively, confront their loss, and attempt to understand it through self-reflection. Growth is reflected in increased empathy, self-awareness, and self-confidence. Hogan and DeSantis (1996) described a trajectory for personal growth in adolescents who lost a sibling to death. Before their sibling's death, the adolescents were focused on developing a sense of their personal identity and asking "Who am I?" After their sibling's death, the bereaved adolescents redefined their roles and interrelationships and asked, "Who am I now?" Their search for an answer led them to set new priorities, to shift focus from themselves to others, and to appreciate life's finiteness and the value of relationships.

Adults' Responses to Bereavement

Over the course of a lifetime, most people have multiple encounters with bereavement. We focus on adults' adaptation and personal growth following three types of bereavement experiences: death of a spouse, parent, and child.

Death of a Spouse

There is great variability in individuals' responses to loss of a spouse; some people experience intense distress following the loss of a spouse, whereas others do not (Wortman & Silver, 1990). In general, widowers have more negative bereavement outcomes than widows do (Cleiren, 1993). However, many older surviving spouses are quite resilient, even though bereavement is highly stressful. Although depression, confusion, and loneliness are typical, older bereaved spouses also are aware of the opportunity for personal growth that their loss presents. They show positive coping skills that contribute to feelings of confidence and pride in how they deal with the loss of their spouse (Lund, 1989).

Thomas, Digiulio, and Sheenan (1988) found that widows had high self-esteem and well-being that was comparable to nonbereaved persons. Overall, 24% of widows noted positive changes after widowhood, primarily viewing themselves as stronger and more independent, whereas 39% reported mixed effects and 30% reported negative outcomes. Likewise, Arbuckle and de Vries (1995) studied people's long-term adjustment to late-life loss and found that widowed respondents expressed greater self-efficacy than married nonbereaved adults. The authors speculated that self-efficacy was enhanced in the widowed group as a result of having survived the death of a spouse and having lived independently thereafter for a number of years. Increases in self-esteem and independence that widows experienced mirror similar changes reported by women following separation and divorce (Nelson, 1989, 1994; Wallerstein, 1986).

Death of a Parent

The death of one's parent is a normative life-span transition for many middle-aged people. Moss and Moss (1989) have asserted that a parent's death can provide a "developmental push" that prompts adult children to review their own life and identity, revise their goals, and grow closer to siblings as a result of sharing their grief.

Although people typically do not lose their parents during early adulthood, when such an unexpected, "off-time" loss occurs, positive outcomes may ensue. In a study of college students who lost a parent, Schwartzberg and Janoff-Bulman (1991) found that bereavement generated changes in the students' beliefs and world view: 45% reprioritized their goals, 35% gained a deeper understanding of life, 30% questioned their personal invulnerability, and 30% became more religious.

In another study, Edmonds and Hooker (1992) investigated positive changes in secular (life goals) and cosmic (belief in God) meaning among college students who had recently experienced the death of a close family member, mostly parents or grandparents who served as surrogate parents. More than 70% of the students experienced a positive change in their goals and 25% experienced a positive change in their belief in God. Students who experienced less grief-related distress were more likely to report a positive change in goals and had more purpose in life.

Death of a Child

Coping with the death of a child typically is a more difficult task than is coping with the loss of another family member (Cleiren, 1993), in part because parents and children share an intense emotional bond, and death shatters parents' hoped for immortality via their child. Nevertheless, some bereaved parents report positive changes, especially in their marital and family relationships. Miles and Crandall (1983) found that parents who lost a child experienced increased compassion and understanding of others who had endured a similar loss, appreciated life more, and recognized the importance of spending time with family and the value of loved ones.

In a study of accidental death, Shanfield and Swain (1984) focused on parents who had lost a young adult child in a traffic accident two years earlier. Some parents reported improvements in their marital and family life in the year after their child's death. More than a third of parents experienced increased marital satisfaction, more than half were closer to their spouse, and more than two thirds were closer to their other children. Bereaved families also were better able to resolve conflicts and talk to each other about emotional issues (for a somewhat different perspective, see Lehman, Lang, Wortman, & Sorenson, 1989).

In a follow-up of families whose child had died from cancer seven to nine years earlier, Martinson, McClowry, Davies, and Kulenkamp (1994) noted considerable variation in outcomes. Although their child's death contributed to divorce in a small number of couples, of couples in intact marriages many reported no change in their marital relationship, and about 40% viewed their marriage as improved. Parents also felt better prepared to handle subsequent health problems, made the family a priority over work and other activities, developed more appreciation of the daily activities of life, demonstrated more ability to empathize with others' problems, and reported a clearer understanding of God. Similarly, Shanfield, Benjamin, and Swain (1984) found that more than 60% of parents whose adult child died from cancer experienced some personal growth.

Successful Adaptation and Personal Growth in Children

Death of a parent or sibling has a profound impact on a child. Some children experience lingering symptoms of grief (Hogan & Greenfield, 1991; Simon & Drantell, 1998), disruptions in meeting normal developmental tasks, and behavioral and psychological problems, such as disturbances in sleep and eating habits, poor relationships with peers, declining school performance, preoccupation with thoughts of the dead sibling, and thoughts of suicide (Balk, 1990). Despite these temporary negative outcomes, coping with bereavement often eventually brings about positive changes, especially increased maturity (Balk, 1990; Davies, 1991; Martinson & Campos, 1991; Martinson, Davies, & McClowry, 1987; Simon & Drantell, 1998; Tyson-Rawson, 1996).

Balk (1983) found that adolescents who lost a sibling emerged from bereavement with increased maturity that derived, in part, from having coped successfully with their sibling's death and negotiating role changes, such as becoming the oldest child. Some adolescents also showed improved relationships with family and friends and learned the importance of valuing people while they are alive.

In a study of the long-term effects of sibling bereavement, Davies (1991) discovered that adults who had lost a sibling in childhood reported increased maturity that was reflected in greater insights into life and death. Their encounter with death made them face their own mortality, enhanced their understanding of the meaning of life, and enabled them to help others who experienced bereavement. Notably, the surviving siblings felt somewhat estranged from their peers and perceived as trivial some of their interests and activities. As a consequence, the sibling survivors withdrew and were rather detached from the normal experiences of growing up, such as peer friendships and social activities.

Martinson and Campos (1991) examined the long-term effects of bereavement on adolescents seven to nine years after their sibling died from cancer at home. Although almost 20% of the adolescents indicated that their sibling's death continued to have a negative impact on their life, most of them reported that the death enhanced their personal growth as well as that of their family. Adolescents matured because of experiences associated with the impending death, such as taking on adult responsibilities when their parents were at the hospital with their sibling, coping with the emotional pain of observing their sibling's suffering, and caring for and comforting their sibling.

Oltjenbruns (1991) discovered that more than 95% of late adolescents identified at least one positive outcome following the death of a family member or friend. The most commonly cited positive outcome was a deeper appreciation of life. Other outcomes included better communication skills and problem-solving skills, stronger bonds with other people, increased emotional strength, and greater empathy. Some adolescents also noted that they were less afraid of death, more independent, and clearer about their priorities.

CONCEPTUAL MODEL OF POSITIVE OUTCOMES
OF LIFE CRISES

We have developed a conceptual model (Figure 7-1) for understanding positive outcomes of life crises and transitions (Schaefer & Moos, 1992). In this chapter, we apply this model to bereavement experiences and use it to address the following questions: Are some individuals especially likely to emerge from bereavement with a new sense of self, increased maturity, and a greater appreciation for life? If so, are these individuals' preexisting personal and social resources and coping skills associated with positive outcomes? Do the circumstances of the death have an impact on whether bereaved individuals experience personal growth? What preexisting coping strategies help bereaved individuals experience positive personal transformations?

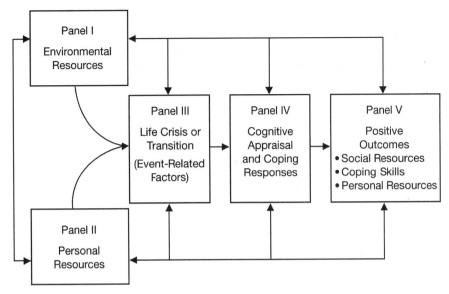

Figure 7-1. A conceptual model for understanding positive outcomes of life crises and transitions.

According to the model, individuals' existing environmental and personal resources influence the life crises and transitions they confront and shape their appraisal and coping responses to these events. In turn, these resources may contribute to positive outcomes following life crises and transitions. The bidirectional paths in the model present these processes as transactional and show that reciprocal feedback can occur at each stage.

The environmental system includes individuals' financial, home, and community living situation and their relationships with and social support from family, friends, and coworkers. The personal system comprises individuals' sociodemographic characteristics and personal resources such as self-confidence, resilience, and existing coping skills. The repertoire of coping skills that individuals possess before bereavement is a personal resource that they can draw on when a loved one dies. Event-related factors include such characteristics as the nature and timing of the crisis, the context within which it occurs, and its suddenness and controllability.

In this model, coping is regarded as a pivotal process through which personal and social resources foreshadow enhanced psychological functioning in the aftermath of a life crisis (Holahan & Moos, 1994). We view coping as both process and outcome, depending on when it occurs in relation to bereavement. Coping responses individuals use in the course of bereavement reflect the coping process. The new coping skills individuals develop as a result of their bereavement experiences are personal growth outcomes that can later serve as personal resources when future crises occur.

We categorize coping responses into approach and avoidance coping.

Approach coping includes the tendency to analyze the crisis in a logical way, reappraise it in a more positive light, and take actions to solve the problem, or seek support. Avoidance coping encompasses attempts to minimize the problem, seek alternative rewards, express emotions, or decide that nothing can be done to change the situation (Moos & Schaefer, 1993).

Individuals experience both proximal and ultimate outcomes following a crisis (Schaefer & Moos, 1992). The proximal outcomes encompass (a) enhanced social resources, including better relationships with family and friends and development of new confidants and support networks; and (b) expanded coping skills, such as the ability to regulate affect, seek help, and think through a problem logically. The ultimate outcomes are enhanced personal resources, such as increased self-understanding, empathy, maturity, and altruism.

We now use this model to guide a discussion of the determinants of personal growth that may occur in conjunction with bereavement. We concentrate on the impact that peoples' existing personal and environmental resources and the circumstances of the death have on their appraisal and coping strategies. We also examine how these factors influence peoples' adaptation to bereavement and potential personal growth. We close with a discussion of directions for future research on the connections between bereavement and personal growth.

CONTEXTUAL FACTORS AND PERSONAL GROWTH FOLLOWING BEREAVEMENT

In keeping with our conceptual model for understanding the positive outcomes of life crises (Figure 7-1), we postulate that successful adaptation and personal growth following bereavement results from the dynamic interplay of the environmental and personal resources individuals have available to them before and at the time of the death, the circumstances of the death, and how they appraise and cope with it.

Environmental Resources

Social networks often enable individuals to summon effective coping strategies and redefine a stressful event in a more positive light. We focus on two social resources that have been linked to better bereavement outcomes and personal growth: social support and positive family functioning.

Social Support

Social support may mitigate the negative effects of bereavement (Cleiren, 1993). For example, Dimond, Lund, and Caserta (1987) discovered that older adults who had larger and stronger social networks experienced more life satisfaction after their spouse's death. Likewise, Martinson and Campos (1991) found that bereaved adolescents who tended to rely on their family for support were able to view their sibling's death in a positive light and to experience personal growth as a result of it. In contrast, adolescents who did not view their family as a source of support reported a negative impact following their sibling's death.

Community services that foster family communication and support also facilitate personal growth in bereaved family members. Lauer, Mulhern, Bohne, and Camitta (1985) compared children whose siblings died at home after being treated in a home care program with children whose siblings died while hospitalized. The home care group received information about their dying sibling and support from their parents. Among these children, 85% reported greater family closeness and enhanced relationships with their parents. In contrast, fewer than 20% of the children with hospitalized siblings reported these positive outcomes.

Not only do individuals' social resources influence their bereavement outcomes, but bereavement can provide an impetus for people to strengthen old ties and find new sources of social support. Norris and Murrell (1990) compared older widows and widowers' adjustment to that of individuals who lost a parent or child and to a nonbereaved group. Widows and widowers were more likely to acquire new interests than were the comparison groups, even though initially they experienced more distress and depression. Widows and widowers also increased their social embeddedness over time, indicating that they were making efforts to cope with their loss and reduce their distress and depression.

Positive Family Functioning

Bereavement typically occurs within the context of a family, which can be a key resource that facilitates adaptation and personal growth among vulnerable individuals. Kissane, Bloch, and McKenzie (1997) found that the overall level of family coping predicted bereavement outcomes of the spouse and children in families in which a parent died of cancer. The spouse and children in families that were more cohesive and expressive, and resolved conflicts effectively, showed less depression and distress and better social adjustment. Likewise, among bereaved caregivers of men who died of AIDS, those who experienced fewer problems in their relationships with their own family and their partner's family showed fewer intrusive thoughts about the loss and a less depressed mood in the year after their partner's death (Nolen-Hoeksema, McBride, & Larson, 1997).

Other factors indicative of family functioning and stability also have been linked to family members' personal growth. Among bereaved parents, greater mutual interdependence, an unambivalent relationship with the dead child, and the child not having problems (such as with drugs or alcohol) at the time of death predicted parents' personal growth, as reflected in increased marital and family satisfaction (Shanfield & Swain, 1984).

Personal Resources

Maturity and previous experience with bereavement and religiosity have been linked to better adaptation to bereavement and personal growth. We examine these factors. For a discussion of the associations between other personal resources, such as personality factors and personal growth, see Tennen and Affleck (1998).

Maturity and Previous Bereavement

A person's age and developmental stage may influence the experience of personal growth following bereavement. Along this line, Zisook, Shuchter, Sledge, and Mulvihill (1993) found that older widows and widowers viewed themselves as being less depressed, less anxious, and better adjusted to widowhood than did younger persons. Younger widowers may have more difficulty adapting because they have responsibilities that older widowers do not have, such as being a single parent and handling financial burdens such as mortgages and car payments. Older widowers also may be more successful in coping because previous experience with loss taught them to accept the inevitability of death.

Experience with loss may enhance coping skills and constitute a personal resource that can contribute to better outcomes (Aldwin, Sutton, & Lachman, 1996). In this vein, Shanfield and Swain (1984) found that older parents who reported more previous losses viewed the death of their adult child in a traffic accident as less painful than younger parents did. They noted that the coping skills and maturity that older parents acquired from prior bereavement experiences seemed to protect them from psychiatric distress.

Religiosity

Religion is an integral part of many people's lives that influences their appraisal of a death and often helps them to find meaning in the loss. Smith, Range, and Ulmer (1992) found that individuals with a stronger belief in an afterlife recovered better from bereavement. Findings from a study of caregivers of men with AIDS also suggest that religious beliefs facilitate adaptive coping during bereavement. Folkman (1997) noted that spirituality and religiosity facilitated caregivers' positive reappraisals and problem-focused coping, which, in turn, were linked to positive psychological states after their partner's death.

Religious beliefs may influence personal growth indirectly as a result of their association with social and coping resources. For example, in a study of parents whose baby died from sudden infant death syndrome, McIntosh, Silver, and Wortman (1993) found that parents who participated more in religious activities had more social support and were better able to find meaning in the death, which, in turn, enhanced their well-being.

Park and Cohen (1993) also identified indirect pathways by which religious beliefs influence personal growth. They found that intrinsic religiousness (holding faith as a supreme value and as providing meaning and motivation in one's life) was associated with students' attributing the death of a close friend to a loving God and to their use of positive reinterpretation coping—that is, looking at the death in an adaptive way. In turn, students who relied more on positive reinterpretation coping reported more personal growth. Students with more extrinsic religiousness (viewing religion as providing safety, comfort, and social standing) also relied more on positive reinterpretation coping, which, again was associated with more personal growth.

Event-Related Factors

In crises induced by physical illness, disasters, and violent crime, adaptation in part depends on event-related factors such as the severity of the loss, the threat to life, proximity and amount of exposure to the event, and its scope (Carr et al., 1995; Fromm, Andrykowski, & Hunt, 1996; Lonigan, Shannon, Taylor, Finch, & Sallee, 1994; Nader, Pynoos, Fairbanks, & Frederick, 1990; Phifer & Norris, 1989; Rieker, Edbril, & Garnick 1985). Through their effect on the coping tasks individuals encounter, event-related factors influence the nature and extent of personal growth. For example, the death of a child presents bereaved parents with the task of finding meaning in a devastating loss. Parents who are unable to accomplish this task may experience a prolonged grief reaction and subsequently be less likely to experience personal growth.

Our knowledge of the specific aspects of a death that affect bereaved individuals' experience of personal growth is quite limited. We examine the relationship between such factors as the extent to which the death was expected, the cause of death (accidental, natural, suicide), and the relationship of the bereaved to the deceased (spouse, parent, sibling) and individuals' adaptation to bereavement.

Forewarning and Mode of Death

In general, people who have more warning of an impending death adapt better (Cleiren, 1993). In turn, those who adapt better may be more likely to experience personal growth. Smith et al. (1992) found that bereaved individuals who had at least two weeks forewarning of the death of a family member or friend who died of natural causes reported less emotional pain as a result of not being able to make sense of the death than did individuals who confronted an unanticipated natural death or a sudden death as a result of an accident, suicide, or homicide. Likewise, Borne and Raphael (1994) determined that elderly widowers who were able to anticipate their wife's death had less severe bereavement reactions six weeks after her death.

Forewarning of a death may facilitate adjustment to bereavement by providing a chance for the survivor to talk with the dying person and work out some grief before the death. O'Bryant (1991) discovered that widows who had forewarning of their husband's death and had the opportunity to discuss their relationship and financial future with him had more positive affect in bereavement. Similarly, Parkes and Weiss (1983) found that bereaved spouses experienced better postbereavement outcomes when their partner's terminal illness lasted longer, thereby providing them with time to discuss impending death with their partner.

Rando (1983) ascertained that the amount of time parents had to prepare for the death of their child influenced adjustment. Parents whose child died soon after being diagnosed with cancer and those whose child died long after the initial diagnosis adjusted more poorly than did parents whose child died between 6 and 17 months after diagnosis. Death soon after diagnosis left little time to prepare, whereas a lingering death with multiple remissions may have given parents false hope that their child might be cured.

Cause of death also is an important factor that may influence adaptation and growth. In this vein, it is especially difficult to come to terms with death that results from murder or is associated with stigma (AIDS or suicide; Jordan et al., 1993). According to Smith et al. (1992), individuals bereaved because of natural death were able to find more meaning in the death than were people who confronted deaths from accidents, suicide, or homicide. Park and Folkman (1997) noted that people who are able to reconcile their values with their appraisal of the meaning of a crisis are likely to have better psychological adjustment.

The Bereaved's Relationship to the Deceased

The kinship relationship between the bereaved person and the deceased is a better predictor of bereavement outcomes than is mode of death (Cleiren, 1993). Although we did not find any bereavement studies that showed a link between the kinship relationship and personal growth, there is evidence of an association between kinship and individuals' adaptation to bereavement.

The severity of the loss and the meaning an individual attributes to the death of a loved one is closely tied to the bereaved person's relationship with the deceased. Sanders (1980) compared the intensity of bereavement reactions to the loss of a spouse, child, or parent. Parents who lost a child experienced more intense grief reactions than adult children who lost a parent. In part, these findings reflect the developmental timing of the death, which is much more "out of order" in the case of a child's than a parent's death. Gamino, Sewell, and Easterling (1998) also noted that bereaved individuals experienced more intense grief reactions when the death involved a younger person.

Similarly, Cleiren, Diekstra, Kerkhof, and van der Wal (1994) found that, compared to other bereaved individuals, parents who lost a child experienced the most difficulty finding meaning in the death. Mothers showed the most severe loss reactions; they were more depressed than other bereaved groups and were the most pessimistic about being able to handle the loss. Other factors indicative of the relationship between the bereaved individual and the deceased, such as a conflicted, ambivalent, or dependent relationship, also contribute to more intense grief reactions (Gamino et al., 1998).

Cognitive Appraisal and Coping Responses

Appraisal and coping processes are closely linked to each other and to successful adaptation to life crises. Individuals who view new tasks and roles as a challenge may cope more actively with their losses and subsequently be more apt to be transformed by them. Moreover, cognitive coping strategies, such as positive reappraisal, can help individuals alter the meaning of a traumatic event and thereby minimize its threat (Park & Folkman, 1997). For example, Taylor (1983) found that searching for meaning helped cancer patients understand their plight, regain mastery over their life, and renew their self-esteem. The meaning that patients acquired from their illness experiences led to a new attitude toward life, increased self-knowledge, and reordered priorities.

As part of the UCSF Coping Project, Folkman and her colleagues (Folkman, 1997; Stein, Folkman, Trabasso, & Richards, 1997) examined coping among caregivers of men who died of AIDS. Men who searched for and were able to find positive meaning (positive reappraisal, spiritual beliefs, and practices) experienced less depression and more positive states of mind during caregiving and bereavement one year later, and focused more on getting on with their life after their partner's death. Caregivers who developed long-term goals for themselves and their partners during the caregiving period also reported more psychological well-being after bereavement.

In general, people who respond to crises with approach coping fare better than those who rely on avoidance (Moos & Schaefer, 1993). Consistent with this idea, Aldwin et al. (1996) found that individuals who relied more on instrumental coping and less on escapism to handle their problems were more likely to report positive long-term outcomes following a low point in their lives, such as bereavement.

Positive Outcomes

Despite the grief and loss that the death of a loved one brings, it is not uncommon for bereaved individuals to confront the experience in a way that leads to personal growth. The stress and coping framework we use is one of several models that may help to explain the positive trans-formations some individuals undergo in the aftermath of life crises (O'Leary, Alday, & Ickovics, 1998). Some models focus on the slow and incremental change that occurs during psychotherapy (Nerken, 1993), whereas others emphasize the sudden or unexpected changes that may re-sult from crises (Aldwin, 1994; Miller & C'de Baca, 1994; O'Leary & Ickovics, 1995; Tedeschi & Calhoun, 1995). These models can help plan research to specify the environmental and personal resources and coping factors that may stimulate positive outcomes following crises.

In our model of personal growth, the social and personal resources (panels I and II in Figure 7-1) that individuals possess before bereavement are seen as influencing their appraisal of loss and the coping strategies they use to manage their grief (panel IV). In turn, these resources and coping processes predict postbereavement outcomes (panel V). As shown in Table 7-1, we categorize the new resources individuals acquire following bereave-ment into proximal and ultimate outcomes. New postbereavement social resources (such as improved marital relationships, and increased closeness to family members and friends) and coping skills (enhanced ability to think through a problem logically or ask for help) are proximal outcomes. These typically precede and contribute to enhanced personal resources, such as increased self-esteem, maturity, and life satisfaction. In turn, as shown in the model, enhanced personal resources can contribute to the further de-velopment of individuals' social resources and coping skills.

FUTURE DIRECTIONS FOR BEREAVEMENT RESEARCH

More than 35 years ago, Caplan (1964) noted that life crises are "turning points" that can contribute to personal growth. However, empir-ical research in this area has focused primarily on how life crises, including bereavement, lead to distress, depression, and impaired functioning. Re-search on the potential connections between bereavement and personal growth necessitates a fundamental paradigm shift. Because this area of re-search still is in the early stage of development, we focus more on concep-

TABLE 7-1

Key Coping Process Indicators and Proximal and Ultimate Positive
Outcomes that May Be Associated With Bereavement

Coping Process Indicators	Proximal Outcomes	Ultimate Outcomes
Cognitive Coping Strategies ■ Search for meaning ■ Logical analysis ■ Positive reappraisal ■ Acceptance Behavioral Coping Strategies ■ Help seeking ■ Problem solving ■ Expressing feelings	Enhanced Social Resources ■ Better relationships with and increased closeness to family members and friends ■ New relationships with friends and confidants ■ Increases in social support networks New Coping Skills ■ Longer term enhanced cognitive and behavioral coping skills in the areas shown under coping process indicators	Enhanced Personal Resources ■ Increased self esteem and self-efficacy ■ Greater independence and maturity ■ More compassion, empathy, and tolerance ■ Greater appreciation of life, more life satisfaction and well-being ■ Changes in goals, values, and world view ■ Better communication skills increased ability to resolve conflicts ■ Increased altruism

tual issues than on the complex methodological problems that also must be addressed.

To systematically examine the relationship between bereavement and personal growth, we need to conceptualize the cognitive processes that contribute to personal growth and to develop reliable and valid procedures to measure interim and long-term personal growth outcomes. In this vein, Park, Cohen, and Murch (1996) formulated the Stress Related Growth Scale (SRGS), which includes items that tap positive changes in personal resources, including life philosophy, in social relationships, and in coping skills. Park and her colleagues found that college students who had more intrinsic religiosity, had more satisfying social support, experienced more recent positive life events (personal and social resources), used more positive reinterpretation and acceptance coping, and reported more personal growth as reflected in higher SRGS scores. Longitudinal studies that use measures such as the SRGS can enhance our understanding of the specific dimensions of personal growth that ensue in different populations of bereaved individuals across the life span.

In addition to using a guiding conceptual model and developing better measures of coping processes and personal growth outcomes, bereavement researchers should consider the pre- and postcrisis environment, take a life-course perspective, and examine bereavement within a family and community context.

The Pre- and Postcrisis Environment

It is important to consider the potential effects of the pre- and post-bereavement environment on an individual's adaptation to loss. Most likely, the personal growth associated with bereavement has its origins in factors that occur before a loved ones' death. For example, Stein and her colleagues (1997) found that caregivers who reported more positive appraisals during caregiving developed more long-term goals for themselves, and, in turn, reported more psychological well-being at bereavement and better recovery a year later. Prospective longitudinal studies are needed to examine the role that personal resources, appraisal, and coping before bereavement play in later adaptation to loss.

A postbereavement environment marked by secondary stressors may thwart successful adaptation and personal growth. According to Pearlin, Aneshensel, and LeBlanc (1997), "stress proliferation" is the tendency for a primary stressor (caring for a dying family member) to generate additional secondary stressors (such as social isolation or financial problems). The care of a terminally ill family member and subsequent bereavement frequently results in an increase in stressors in multiple life domains. To understand the conditions under which bereavement does or does not foster adaptation and growth, it is important to assess stressors in various life domains and the resources individuals have available to cope with them.

The Life Stressors and Social Resources Inventory (LISRES; Moos & Moos, 1994) is one measure that bereavement researchers can use to assess individuals' overall pattern of life stressors and social resources. For example, we used the LISRES (Moos, 1995) to describe the postbereavement environment of Dorothy M., a 38-year-old mother of two who lost her husband in a car accident. Immediately after her husband's death, Dorothy experienced a high level of stressors in multiple life domains, including financial difficulties, interpersonal problems with her children, and excessive demands from her mother and in her job. Fortunately, Dorothy had supportive coworkers and two close women friends. Ultimately, with the help of her social resources, Dorothy established a more supportive social environment, improved her relationship with her mother and on the job, and experienced increased self-confidence. This case study illustrates the importance of assessing stressors and resources in each domain of an individual's life.

A Life Course Perspective

Longitudinal studies are needed to understand how the process of adaptation to bereavement can transform people. It may take months or even years for some bereaved individuals to make sense of their loss, find meaning in it, and mature from the experience. Moreover, individuals' trajectory of personal change may be influenced by the point in their life at which the loss occurs and the developmental tasks that arise.

Research with a life course perspective can help to clarify the relationships between normal developmental transitions, bereavement, and personal growth. We need to address such issues as the role of previously acquired personal and social resources in individuals' adaptation to bereavement; and the ways bereavement task demands and life-stage personal and social resources and developmental tasks, such as those associated with adolescence or middle age, interact to promote or impede adaptation and personal growth.

Bereavement Within a Family and Community Context

People rarely grieve in isolation. Families and communities are the context within which bereavement and growth occur. For example, Malone (1981) wrote movingly of her family's experience of gathering together over the Christmas holiday to care for and help her terminally ill sister Bobby fulfill her last wish to die at home. In the process of helping Bobby negotiate her last crisis, the family learned much about life, love, and caring. Caregiving may foster a sense of cohesion among family members that can serve as a resource that, in turn, fosters personal growth at the individual and family level.

The broader social milieu also may facilitate coping with death. For example, Elizur and Kaffman (1982) determined that the environment of the Israeli kibbutz helped bereaved children to cope with the death of their fathers. Children in the kibbutz became attached to family and friends living there, slept in communal children's homes, and were not as dependent on their relatives. In contrast, bereaved nonkibbutz children interacted less with family members, had less day-to-day stability, and more behavioral and psychological problems.

The traditional society of the Amish provides another example of cultural coping with death and bereavement. Among the Amish, death is seen as an integral part of life, and religious beliefs make death less frightening and lead to acceptance of it. Most Amish die at home surrounded by family members. Once death occurs, the Amish community offers support to grieving family members for at least a year (Bryer, 1979). Multicultural research may help us gain a better understanding of how communities and cultures shape individuals' bereavement outcomes via their impact on bereaved individuals' values and the coping and social resources they have available.

We know little about the phenomenon of personal growth at the community level or about the reciprocal relationships between community-level coping and the growth that individual members of the community experience. Thus it would be valuable for researchers to identify the types and patterns of change communities undergo when they confront bereavement and to examine the interactions between community coping and resources and individual's bereavement outcomes.

CONCLUSION

Bereavement is a universal crisis that transforms many of us in positive ways. We need to examine individuals' bereavement outcomes in light of other ongoing changes in their life, family, and community. The challenge facing researchers is to gain a better understanding of how, when, and why personal growth occurs in bereaved individuals, families, and communities. The answer lies in developing and testing integrated models of personal growth that take into account the interrelationships between the nature and context of the bereavement, personal and social resources, and appraisal and coping processes. Research on bereavement and personal growth should be pursued in conjunction with research on other life crises. This approach will stimulate a cross-fertilization of ideas and enable us to obtain more generalizable information about how life crises may foreshadow growth.

REFERENCES

Aldwin, C. M. (1994). Transformational coping. In C. M. Aldwin (Ed.), *Stress, coping, and development: An integrative perspective.* New York: Guilford Press.

Aldwin, C. M., Sutton, K. J., & Lachman, M. (1996). The development of coping resources in adulthood. *Journal of Personality, 64,* 837–871.

Arbuckle, N. W., & de Vries, B. (1995). The long-term effects of later life spousal and parental bereavement on personal functioning. *Gerontologist, 35,* 637–647.

Balk, D. (1983). Effects of sibling death on teenagers. *Journal of School Health, 53,* 14–18.

Balk, D. E. (1990). The self-concepts of bereaved adolescents: Sibling death and its aftermath. *Journal of Adolescent Research, 5,* 112–132.

Borne, G. J. A., & Raphael, B. (1994). A longitudinal study of bereavement phenomena in recently widowed elderly men. *Psychological Medicine, 24,* 411–421.

Bryer, K. B. (1979). The Amish way of death: A study of family support systems. *American Psychologist, 34,* 255–261.

Calhoun, L. G., & Tedeschi, R. G. (1990). Positive aspects of critical life problems: Recollections of grief. *Omega, 20,* 265–272.

Caplan, G. (1964). *Principles of preventive psychiatry.* New York: Basic Books.

Carr, V. J., Lewin, T. J., Webster, R. A., Hazell, P. L., Kenardy, J. A., & Carter, G. L. (1995). Psychosocial sequelae of the 1989 Newcastle earthquake: I. Community disaster experiences and psychological morbidity 6 months post-disaster. *Psychological Medicine, 25*, 539–555.

Cleiren, M. (1993). *Bereavement and adaptation: A comparative study of the aftermath of death.* Washington, DC: Hemisphere.

Cleiren, M., Diekstra, R., Kerkhof, A., & van der Wal, J. (1994). Mode of death and kinship in bereavement: Focusing on "who" rather than "how." *Crisis, 15*, 22–36.

Davies, B. (1991). Long-term outcomes of adolescent sibling bereavement. *Journal of Adolescent Research, 6*, 83–96.

Dimond, M., Lund, D. A., & Caserta, M. S. (1987). The role of social support in the first two years of bereavement in an elderly sample. *The Gerontologist, 27*, 599–604.

Edmonds, S., & Hooker, K. (1992). Perceived changes in life meaning following bereavement. *Omega, 25*, 307–318.

Elizur, E., & Kaffman, M. (1982). Children's bereavement reactions following death of the father. *Journal of the American Academy of Pediatrics, 21*, 474–480.

Folkman, S. (1997). Positive psychological states and coping with severe stress. *Social Science and Medicine, 45*, 1207–1221.

Fromm, K., Andrykowski, M. A., & Hunt, J. (1996). Positive and negative psychosocial sequelae of bone marrow transplantation: Implications for quality of life assessment. *Journal of Behavioral Medicine, 19*, 221–240.

Gamino, L. A., Sewell, K. W., & Easterling, L. W. (1998). Scott & White Grief Study: An empirical test of predictors of intensified mourning. *Death Studies, 22*, 333–355.

Hogan, N. S., & DeSantis, L. (1996). Adolescent sibling bereavement: Toward a new theory. In C. A. Corr & D. E. Balk (Eds.), *Handbook of adolescent death and bereavement* (pp. 173–195). New York: Springer.

Hogan, N. S., & Greenfield, D. B. (1991). Adolescent sibling bereavement symptomatology in a large community sample. *Journal of Adolescent Research, 6*, 97–112.

Hogan, N., Morse, J. M., & Tason, M. C. (1996). Toward an experiential theory of bereavement. *Omega, 33*, 43–65.

Holahan, C. J., & Moos, R. H. (1994). Life stressors and mental health: Advances in conceptualizing stress resistance. In W. R. Avison & I. H. Gotlib (Eds.), *Stress and mental health: Contemporary issues and prospects for the future* (pp. 213–238). New York: Plenum Press.

Jordan, J. R., Kraus, D. R., & Ware, E. S. (1993). Observations on loss and family development. *Family Process, 32*, 425–440.

Kessler, B. G. (1987). Bereavement and personal growth. *Journal of Humanistic Psychology, 27*, 228–247.

Kissane, D. W., Bloch, S., & McKenzie, D. P. (1997). Family coping and bereavement outcome. *Palliative Medicine, 11,* 191–201.

Lauer, M. E., Mulhern, R. K., Bohne, J. B., & Camitta, B. M. (1985). Children's perceptions of their sibling's death at home or hospital: The precursors of differential adjustment. *Cancer Nursing, 8,* 21–27.

Lehman, D. R., Lang, E. L., Wortman, C. B., & Sorenson, S. B. (1989). Long-term effects of sudden bereavement: Marital and parent-child relationships and children's reactions. *Journal of Family Psychology, 2,* 344–367.

Lonigan, C. J., Shannon, M. P., Taylor, C. M., Finch, A. J., Jr., & Sallee, F. R. (1994). Children exposed to disaster: II. Risk factors for the development of post-traumatic symptomatology. *Journal of the American Academy of Child and Adolescent Psychiatry, 33,* 94–105.

Lund, D. A. (1989). Conclusions about bereavement in later life and implications for interventions for future research. In D. A. Lund (Ed.), *Older bereaved spouses: Research with practical applications* (pp. 217–231). New York: Hemisphere.

Malone, C. R. (1981). A special Christmas: An account of the last Christmas of Barbara Mackenzie Rogers Hepner. *Topics in Clinical Nursing, 3,* 39–43.

Martinson, I. M., & Campos, R. G. (1991). Adolescent bereavement: Long-term responses to a sibling's death from cancer. *Journal of Adolescent Research, 6,* 54–69.

Martinson, I. M., Davies, E. B., & McClowry, S. G. (1987). The long-term effects of sibling death on self-concept. *Journal of Pediatric Nursing, 2,* 227–235.

Martinson, I. M., McClowry, S. G., Davies, B., & Kulenkamp, E. J. (1994). Changes over time: A study of family bereavement following childhood cancer. *Journal of Palliative Care, 10,* 19–25.

McIntosh, D. N., Silver, R. C., & Wortman, C. B. (1993). Religion's role in adjustment to a negative life event: Coping with the loss of a child. *Journal of Personality and Social Psychology, 65,* 812–821.

Miles, M. S., & Crandall, E. K. B. (1983). The search for meaning and its potential for affecting growth in bereaved parents. *Health Values: Achieving High Level Wellness, 7,* 19–23.

Miller, W. R., & C'de Baca, J. (1994). Quantum change: Toward a psychology of transformation. In T. Heatherton & J. Weinberger (Eds.), *Can personality change?* (pp. 253–281). Washington, DC: American Psychological Association.

Moos, R. (1995). Development and application of new measures of life stressors, social resources and coping responses. *European Journal of Psychological Assessment, 11,* 1–13.

Moos, R., & Moos, B. (1994). *Life stressors and social resources inventory adult form manual.* Odessa, FL: Psychological Assessment Resources.

Moos, R. H., & Schaefer, J. A. (1993). Coping resources and processes: Current concepts and measures. In L. Goldberger & S. Breznits (Eds.), *Handbook of stress: Theoretical and clinical aspects* (2nd ed., pp. 234–257). New York: Free Press.

Moss, M. S., & Moss, S. Z. (1989). The death of a parent. In R. A. Kalish (Ed.), *Midlife loss: Coping strategies* (pp. 89–114). Newbury Park, CA: Sage.

Nader, K., Pynoos, R., Fairbanks, L., & Frederick, C. (1990). Children's PTSD reactions one year after a sniper attack at their school. *American Journal of Psychiatry, 147,* 1526–1530.

Nelson, G. (1989). Life strains, coping, and emotional well-being: A longitudinal study of recently separated and married women. *American Journal of Community Psychology, 17,* 459–483.

Nelson, G. (1994). Emotional well-being of separated and married women: Long-term follow-up study. *American Journal of Orthopsychiatry, 64,* 150–160.

Nerken, I. R. (1993). Grief and the reflective self: Toward a clearer model of loss resolution and growth. *Death Studies, 17,* 1–26.

Nolen-Hoeksema, S., McBride, A., & Larson, J. (1997). Rumination and psychological distress among bereaved partners. *Journal of Personality and Social Psychology, 72,* 855–862.

Norris, F. H., & Murrell, S. A. (1990). Social support, life events, and stress as modifiers of adjustment to bereavement in older adults. *Psychology and Aging, 5,* 429–436.

O'Bryant, S. L. (1991). Forewarning of a husband's death: Does it make a difference for older widows? *Omega, 22,* 227–239.

O'Leary, V. E., Alday, C. S., & Ickovics, J. R. (1998). Models of life change and posttraumatic growth. In R. G. Tedeschi, C. L. Park & L. G. Calhoun (Eds.), *Posttraumatic growth: Positive changes in the aftermath of crises* (pp. 127–151). Mahwah, NJ: Erlbaum.

O'Leary, V. E., & Ickovics, J. R. (1995). Resilience and thriving in response to challenge: An opportunity for a paradigm shift in women's health. *Women's Health: Research on Gender, Behavior, and Policy, 1,* 121–142.

Oltjenbruns, K. A. (1991). Positive outcomes of adolescents' experience with grief. *Journal of Adolescent Research, 6,* 43–55.

Park, C. L. (1998). Implications of posttraumatic growth for individuals. In R. G. Tedeschi, C. L. Park, & L. G. Calhoun (Eds.), *Posttraumatic growth: Positive changes in the aftermath of crises* (pp. 153–177). Mahwah, NJ: Erlbaum.

Park, C. L., & Cohen, L. H. (1993). Religious and nonreligious coping with the death of a friend. *Cognitive Therapy and Research, 17,* 561–577.

Park, C. L., Cohen, L. H., & Murch, R. L. (1996). Assessment and prediction of stress-related growth. *Journal of Personality, 64,* 71–105.

Park, C. L., & Folkman, S. (1997). Meaning in the context of stress and coping. *Review of General Psychology, 1,* 115–144.

Parkes, C. M., & Weiss, R. S. (1983). *Recovery from bereavement.* New York: Basic Books.

Pearlin, L. I., Aneshensel, C. S., & LeBlanc, A. J. (1997). The forms and mechanisms of stress proliferation: The case of AIDS caregivers. *Journal of Health and Social Behavior, 38,* 223–236.

Phifer, J. F., & Norris, F. H. (1989). Psychological symptoms in older adults following natural disaster: Nature, timing, duration, and course. *Journal of Gerontology: Social Sciences, 44,* S207–S217.

Rando, T. A. (1983). An investigation of grief and adaptation in parents whose children have died from cancer. *Journal of Pediatric Psychology, 8,* 3–20.

Rieker, P. P., Edbril, S. D., & Garnick, M. B. (1985). Curative testis cancer therapy: Psychological sequelae. *Journal of Clinical Oncology, 3,* 1117–1126.

Sanders, C. M. (1980). A comparison of adult bereavement in the death of a spouse, child, and parent. *Omega, 10,* 303–322.

Schaefer, J. A., & Moos, R. H. (1992). Life crises and personal growth. In B. N. Carpenter (Ed.), *Personal coping: Theory, research, and application* (pp. 149–170). Westport, CT: Praeger.

Schaefer, J. A., & Moos, R. H. (1998). The context for posttraumatic growth: Life crises, individual and social resources, and coping. In R. G. Tedeschi, C. L. Park, & L. G. Calhoun (Eds.), *Posttraumatic growth: Positive changes in the aftermath of crises* (pp. 99–125). Mahwah, NJ: Erlbaum.

Schwartzberg, S. S., & Janoff-Bulman, R. (1991). Grief and the search for meaning: Exploring the assumptive worlds of bereaved college students. *Journal of Social and Clinical Psychology, 10,* 270–288.

Shanfield, S. B., Benjamin, A. H., & Swain, B. J. (1984). Parents' reactions to the death of an adult child from cancer. *American Journal of Psychiatry, 141,* 1092–1094.

Shanfield, S. B., & Swain, B. J. (1984). Death of adult children in traffic accidents. *Journal of Nervous and Mental Disease, 172,* 533–538.

Shapiro, E. R. (1996). Family bereavement and cultural diversity: A social developmental perspective. *Family Process, 35,* 313–332.

Simon, L., & Drantell, J. J. (1998). *A music I no longer heard: The early death of a parent.* New York: Simon & Schuster.

Smith, P. C., Range, L. M., & Ulmer, A. (1992). Belief in afterlife as a buffer in suicidal and other bereavement. *Omega, 24,* 217–225.

Stein, N., Folkman, S., Trabasso, T., & Richards, T. A. (1997). Appraisal and goal processes as predictors of psychological well-being in bereaved caregivers. *Journal of Personality and Social Psychology, 72,* 872–884.

Taylor, S. E. (1983). Adjustment to threatening events: A theory of cognitive adaptation. *American Psychologist, 38,* 1161–1173.

Tedeschi, R. G., & Calhoun, L. G. (1995). *Trauma and transformation: Growing in the aftermath of suffering.* Thousand Oaks, CA: Sage.

Tedeschi, R. G., Park, C. L., & Calhoun, L. G. (1998a). Posttraumatic growth: Conceptual issues. In R. G. Tedeschi, C. L. Park, & L. G. Calhoun (Eds.), *Posttraumatic growth: Positive changes in the aftermath of crises* (pp. 1–22). Mahwah, NJ: Erlbaum.

Tedeschi, R. G., Park, C. L., & Calhoun, L. G. (Eds.). (1998b). *Posttraumatic growth: Positive changes in the aftermath of crisis*. Mahwah, NJ: Erlbaum.

Tennen, H., & Affleck, G. (1998). Personality and transformation in the face of adversity. In R. G. Tedeschi, C. L. Park, & L. G. Calhoun (Eds.), *Posttraumatic growth: Positive changes in the aftermath of crises* (pp. 65–98). Mahwah, NJ: Erlbaum.

Thomas, L. E., Digiulio, R. C., & Sheehan, N. W. (1988). Identity loss and psychological crisis in widowhood: A re-evaluation. *International Journal of Aging and Human Development, 26*, 225–239.

Tyson-Rawson, K. J. (1996). Adolescent responses to the death of a parent. In C. A. Corr & D. E. Balk (Eds.), *Handbook of adolescent death and bereavement* (pp. 155–172). New York: Springer.

Wallerstein, J. S. (1986). Women after divorce: Preliminary report from a 10-year follow-up. *American Journal of Orthopsychiatry, 56*, 65–67.

Wortman, C. B., & Silver, R. C. (1990). Successful mastery of bereavement and widowhood: A life-course perspective. In P. B. Baltes & M. M. Baltes (Eds.), *Successful aging* (pp. 225–264). Cambridge: Cambridge University Press.

Zisook, S., Shuchter, S. R., Sledge, P., & Mulvihill, M. (1993). Aging and bereavement. *Journal of Geriatric Psychiatry and Neurology, 6*, 137–143.

8

DEVELOPMENTAL CONTEXT OF CHILDHOOD: GRIEF AND REGRIEF PHENOMENA

KEVIN ANN OLTJENBRUNS

A child's understanding (or misunderstanding) of the concept of death, particular manifestations of grief, and availability of certain coping mechanisms are all related to developmental capacity. This chapter will highlight how a stage of development (including its reflection in the presence of certain capabilities, the need to master particular tasks, and the definition of primary psychosocial needs) provides a foundation for a child's response to loss. This perspective, in turn, serves as scaffolding for professionals to use as they build deeper insight into childhood bereavement processes.

As time passes and the bereaved child moves through later stages, the context for understanding an earlier loss and for coming to terms with its impact changes over time. Within this milieu of maturing developmental capacities and shifting developmental tasks, an individual who experi-

In addition to the editors, the author would like to thank the following individuals for their valuable assistance: Alicia Cook, Rosemary Holland, and Peggy Short.

ences a significant loss during childhood will often "regrieve" the loss at a later time from a different and more mature vantage point.

In this chapter, I will begin by focusing on the importance of understanding the developmental characteristics of childhood in conjunction with the bereavement process and the regrief phenomenon. I will then briefly outline previous research that has been done on childhood bereavement that has not specifically taken into account developmental variables, which I believe has led to sometimes inconclusive and contradictory findings. Finally, I make some recommendations for future research that better integrates what we have learned about child development and bereavement that may help move the field forward in terms of both research and intervention.

CHARACTERISTICS OF DEVELOPMENTAL SUBSTAGES

Three substages make up the childhood years. Although there is no universal agreement about the actual demarcation of these periods, for purposes of this chapter I have operationally defined them as follows: *early* (spanning from approximately 2 to 4 years of age), *middle* (from approximately 4 to 7), and *late* (from approximately 7 to 11). Because developmental capacities in various realms (e.g., cognitive, psychosocial, coping) unfold gradually, these time periods are somewhat blurred. Nonetheless, it is important to understand that a young child is significantly different than one in middle or late childhood.

Cognitive–Language Capacity

Very young children think qualitatively differently than do older children. Most do not understand the universality, permanence, and nonfunctionality aspects of death (i.e., cessation of all bodily function such as feeling, breathing, eating) until they enter what Piaget (1963) described as the concrete operational stage. A preschool child who believes that death is reversible logically asks such questions as, "When will mama be coming back?" Repeated comments to the contrary cannot be understood until the child has the cognitive ability to understand the permanence of death. Major characteristics of children's thinking, specifically in relation to the concept of death and time perspective, are summarized in Table 8-1, together with a summary of psychosocial crises, coping mechanisms, and developmental tasks.

Often, young children do not have the language capacity to describe their emotions or to ask for what they need. They are often unable to draw comfort from spoken statements in the same way an adult can; instead, children frequently communicate with others in behavioral or symbolic ways (Moody & Moody, 1991). For example, regression to an earlier level of functioning or acting out behaviors may be a way of communicating the need for attention. A sense of pain and isolation following the death of a parent may be expressed through play activities or artwork. These behavioral manifestations are external clues that provide insights into the young child's emotional state and serve as helpful assessment tools to understand the child's coping (Cook & Dworkin, 1992; Fleming & Balmer, 1991).

Psychosocial Crises

Particular issues become paramount over time as individuals face normative psychosocial crises. Although Erikson (1963) defined these crises in terms of polar differences, the level of resolution actually occurs somewhere along a continuum from positive to negative. Specific outcomes of a normative crisis may be altered by many factors, including the experience of a nonnormative crisis such as death of a loved one. For example, Erikson identified the middle childhood psychosocial crisis as that of initiative versus guilt. A sense of comfort and ease while exploring the physical and social world marks a positive resolution of this crisis and manifests a sense of initiative. On the other hand, a negative resolution is reflected in a sense of guilt and its accompanying restrictions. Guilt may occur even in situations in which it is unwarranted by real circumstances because a child cannot always differentiate between reality and fantasy. A child who loses a parent to death may wrongly believe that she or he was responsible for the illness or the death. Unless a sensitive and caring adult reassures the child that this is not the case, he or she will be all the more at risk for responding negatively to the normative crisis of initiative versus guilt.

Childhood Coping

An individual's coping mechanisms clearly affect how that person responds to stressful situations, including death of a loved one. The child's repertoire of coping strategies is much more limited than the adult's. This restriction of options is tied to such factors as the child's narrower life experiences, immature cognitive capacities, and shorter attention span.

Coping mechanisms frequently used by young children include regression, repression, denial, and displacement. During middle and late childhood, children become more capable of describing their feelings, verbalizing their needs, and seeking social support. As children mature, they experience a developmental shift in problem-focused coping, and older children begin to feel they have more control over their environment (Aldwin, 1994).

Lacking personal maturity, children often mirror the type of coping or communication styles modeled by adults who are close to them (Bowlby,

TABLE 8-1
Developmental Context for Childhood Bereavement

Child's Developmental Capacity and Challenges

Cognitive/Language

Understanding of concept of death

Understanding of concept of time

Sources: Gibbons, 1992; Koocher, 1974; Lonetto, 1980; Nagy, 1948; Piaget, 1963; Speece & Brent, 1984, 1992, 1996.

Early Childhood (2–4 years)
- Preoperational stage
- Egocentric
- Concrete, literal, euphemisms confusing
- Focus on the here and now
- Believe death is reversible, temporary
- Believe dead people act and perceive
- Do not understand death is universal

Middle Childhood (4–6 years)
- Magical thinking, diminishes over time
- Understand death is irreversible, final
- Understand dead people are nonfunctional
- Understand death is universal (age 5–)

Late Childhood (7–11 years)
- Concrete operational stage
- Understand death is final
- Have increased understanding of future
- More realistic understanding of causality of death

Psychosocial Crisis

Source: Erikson, 1963.

Early Childhood
- Autonomy vs. shame and doubt

Middle Childhood
- Initiative vs. guilt

Late Childhood
- Industry vs. inferiority

Coping (As Compared to Adults)

Sources: Aldwin, 1994; Sorenson, 1993.

- More limited repertoire of coping strategies
- (Often) little experience dealing with previous loss
- Regression tendencies (young children)
- Diminished comfort drawn from words—immature language capacity

Developmental Tasks

Sources: Cook & Oltjenbruns, 1998; Havighurst, 1956; Newman & Newman, 1999.

Early Childhood
- Increase mastery of motor skills
- Increase independence
- Enhance language capacity
- Develop imagination
- Increase self-control/regulation

Middle Childhood
- Explore physical and social environments
- Develop conscience
- Increase sense of gender identification
- Internalize parental values
- Recognize another's emotional state
- Learn cooperative behavior
- Lay foundation for self-esteem

Late Childhood
- Develop numerous skills valued by one's society (e.g., reading, math, science, sports, art)
- Do meaningful work
- Develop self-evaluation skills
- Develop self-confidence
- Develop interdependence

1980; Elizur & Kaffman, 1983) and may constrain their emotional reactions in response to parental influences (Shapiro, 1994). Many believe that young children simply cannot tolerate long periods of intense emotional pain and that, as a measure of self-protection, they will vacillate between experiencing their loss and engaging in other activities.

This shifting back and forth between grief on the one hand and engagement in normal activities on the other brings to mind a model developed by Stroebe and Schut (1999) to describe coping behavior of adults. These authors described a dual-process model of bereavement, explaining that adults oscillate between two different orientations. When focused on the "loss orientation," individuals deal with and process various aspects of the loss experience. While engaged in the "restoration orientation," however, they disengage from their grief in an attempt to adapt to the demanding changes triggered by the loss and to cope with the many activities of daily life. Although this conceptual model was originally presented in terms of adult loss, it seems to hold merit in the study of childhood bereavement as well.

Developmental Tasks

Developmental tasks are those major tasks, defined by one's culture, that are to be mastered at a specific life stage if one is to be successful in a particular society. These tasks relate to various developmental realms, including the physical, social, emotional, and psychological. Failure to master tasks at a particular stage leads to greater difficulty in dealing successfully with those of later life stages (Havighurst, 1956). Persons often continue to deal with some variation of an earlier developmental task or crisis through subsequent life stages; for example, most individuals continually struggle with issues of independence. Although striving for autonomy is a primary focus of early childhood, seeking a balance between independence and interdependence becomes an important challenge as one is faced with the ongoing tasks of developing peer relations, then close friendships, and then intimate relationships during successive life stages.

Although all children struggle to master normative developmental tasks, bereaved children are also challenged to master the tasks of mourning. The interface between the two will be discussed in the next section.

Developmental Capacity and Tasks of Mourning

Based primarily on their work with adults, numerous authors have defined "tasks of mourning" as activities that facilitate the resolution of a significant loss. Table 8-2 compares Worden's (1991) adult-based model to a paradigm developed by Baker, Sedney, and Gross (1992, 1996) that specifically highlights children's tasks. Worden's model was chosen because it

TABLE 8-2
Adult Tasks of Mourning Compared to Children's

Adult's Tasks of Mourning (Worden, 1991)	Child's Tasks of Mourning (Baker, Sedney, & Gross, 1992, 1996)	Developmental Context: Child's Life Stage as an Influence on Grief (Cook & Oltjenbruns, 1998)
Accept the reality of the loss	Understand that someone has died	Mature understanding is tied to the cognitive capacity to understand that death is permanent.
Experience the pain or emotional aspects of the loss	Face the psychological pain of the loss	Immaturity of child's coping mechanisms influences certain grief responses.
	Cope with periodic resurgence of pain	As developmental tasks shift and cognitive capacity matures, individuals often regrieve an earlier loss.
Adjust to an environment in which the deceased is missing	Invest in new relationships	Child's developmental needs help to define significance of the loss during a particular life stage.
	Develop a new sense of identity that includes experience of the loss	A significant loss during childhood is often regrieved—for example, during adolescence a young person struggles with the primary task of refining personal identity.
Emotionally relocate the deceased; move on with life	Reevaluate the relationship to the person who is lost	Over time, children use a variety of strategies to retain a connection with the deceased.
(Note: This relocation process still allows for a "connection" to the deceased.)	Maintain an internal relationship with person who has died	
	Return to age-appropriate developmental tasks	If the child is unable to master particular tasks at this time, future success in various developmental areas will be jeopardized.

is one of the most frequently cited in the professional literature base. The third column of the table provides commentary on how the developmental context during childhood affects the grief process.

Developmental Tasks and Disabling Grief

The best criteria to use to recognize or define a complicated grief response among adults have been debated by many (Demi & Miles, 1987; Middleton, Raphael, Martinek, & Misso, 1993; Rando, 1993). Webb

(1993) contended that the best term to describe a complicated grief re-action among children is that of "disabling grief." She defined the concept in terms of a developmental context and stressed that "we must determine the extent to which a child can carry out his/her usual activities and pro-ceed with his/her developmental tasks despite the grief. When the child's social, emotional, or physical development shows signs of interference, the grief process can justifiably be considered 'disabling'" (p. 21). One goal of bereavement intervention for children, then, must be to create a devel-opmentally appropriate and supportive environment that allows children to continue mastery of tasks crucial to each particular life stage (Wolfe & Senta, 1995).

OVERVIEW OF CHILDREN AND GRIEF

Literally hundreds of essays, case studies, and research articles have been published in the area of children and grief. Because it is not possible to thoroughly explore all of these works in a single chapter, the focus will be on three important domains: common manifestations of grief, children's attempts to keep a connection to the deceased, and methodological issues related to the study of childhood bereavement.

Until the 1970s (in the United States) a common philosophy was to treat grieving children from a rather exclusionary perspective. This was predicated on the belief that to protect them from the pain of the loss, children must be sheltered both from full knowledge about the death and others' reactions to the loss. Although this may have seemed logical in many ways, the outcome of such "protection" often resulted in a child's increased sense of isolation, a belief that others had minimized the signif-icance of the loss, a diminished trust in those around them, misconceptions about what really happened, and more (Attig, 1995; Stillion & Wass, 1979; Wass, 1991). The philosophy of how to treat bereaved children and how to integrate them into the broader network of grievers is tied to cultural beliefs, and one perspective should not be regarded as universal. Although the knowledge base regarding children's capacity to mourn and their need to be informed and included has expanded over recent years, many children remain the "forgotten mourners" as a result of individual circumstances and misguided interventions (Wolfelt, 1983).

Common Manifestations of Children's Grief

Grief is a multidimensional response to loss. Certain manifestations have been found to be more prevalent during early childhood; these in-clude regression, helplessness, magical thinking related to guilt over causing death, or wishful thinking that the deceased would return. In contrast, others (e.g., school problems, anger, hypochondriasis, identification with deceased) more often arise during late childhood (Elizur & Kaffman, 1982; Gudas, 1993; Van Eerdewegh, Bierie, Parrilla, & Clayton, 1982). Although bearing some similarity to an adult's bereavement reaction, children's grief differs in the constellation of responses, their intensity, and their duration (Deveau, 1997). Childhood bereavement should not be regarded "as a different version of adult mourning but rather as one unique to the child's capacities" (Sekaer & Katz, 1986, p. 292). Figure 8-1 includes a listing of manifestations of grief commonly exhibited by children as they reflect the somatic, intrapsychic, and behavioral realms.

Many reactions are more prevalent in the months immediately following the death than they are in the long term; others do not appear

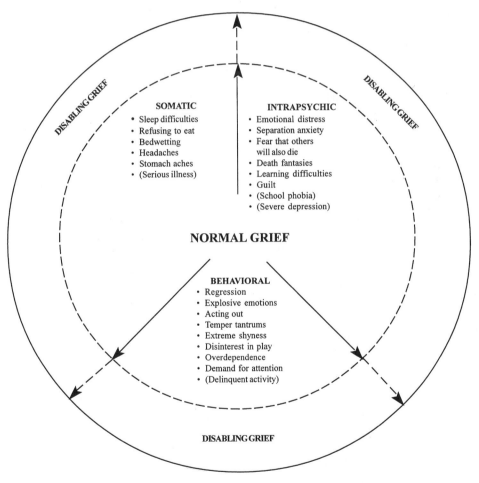

Figure 8-1. Common Manifestations of Grief Among Children
Note: Manifestations listed in parentheses are more commonly found among a clinical sample than a community-based sample.

until a couple of years later. Furthermore, there is a somewhat curvilinear relationship between the magnitude of certain feelings or behaviors and length of time since the death. Worden and Silverman (1996) explain.

> There were initial behavioral/emotional responses that distinguished bereaved children from non-bereaved. However, most of these differences attenuated by the end of the first year of bereavement. By two years, there were marked significant differences in how these bereaved children saw themselves in terms of school performance, general behavioral conduct, and overall self esteem, although the mean . . . scores on the three CBCL scales were not statistically significantly different between bereaved and controls, there was a significantly higher percentage of bereaved children in the seriously disturbed group than in the control group (p. 99).

Although most children experience some of these grief responses they will most likely not experience all of them. The intensity of responses, together with their duration, also varies. A particular child's bereavement experience is mediated by many variables. These are summarized in Table 8-3.

Re-Grief Phenomenon

As children mature and new capacities emerge, they begin to process the experience of death from a very different vantage point than was possible earlier. Various developmental theorists suggest "that one can review and reinterpret previous stages in the light of new insight and/or new experiences . . . themes of earlier stages may re-emerge at any point, bringing a new meaning or a new resolution to an earlier conflict" (Newman & Newman, 1999, p. 17). Loss of a parent relationship can be interpreted in many different ways depending, in part, on one's developmental stage. A young child may miss a parent as nurturer, primary caregiver, and provider. Alternatively, an adolescent may struggle with the loss of a parent in relation to self-identity; for example, the adolescent may wonder about the influence of the deceased parent on his or her life and may question how life would have been different had the parent survived. Later, as individuals refine their own spiritual beliefs, the parent's death might take on new meaning as it is put in a philosophical rather than a functional context. "Developmental transitions . . . may precipitate a resurgence of grief which provide opportunities for further accommodation of the loss in relation to the current life stage. . . . Issues of bereavement are superimposed on those of development" (Miller, 1995, p. 101).

Continuing Bonds With the Deceased

Earlier psychoanalytic perspective argued the necessity of decathecting one's energy from the lost object (Furman, 1974). In contrast, more

TABLE 8-3
Variables Influencing Child's Bereavement Outcome

	Variables Related to . . .			
Death	Deceased	Surviving Parent	Family	Surviving Child
■ Inability to anticipate ■ Type of death ■ Reaction of surviving parent ■ Lack of preparation for the funeral	■ Gender of deceased ■ Nature of predeath relationship	■ Level of dysfunction or vulnerability ■ Discrepancy of perception between parent and child ■ Consistency of discipline provided to child	■ Size ■ Cohesiveness ■ Coping style ■ Socioeconomic status ■ (In)ability to provide support	■ Age ■ Gender ■ Birth order ■ Understanding of concept of death ■ Earlier psychological difficulties

Sources: Krupnick, 1984; Worden, 1996.

recent work in the field of thanatology has led to the understanding that many children find it important to continue a connection with the person who has died as they deal with their grief and accommodate to the loss. Over time, children use various strategies in their efforts to retain a continuing bond. Attending to the importance of normal developmental shifts, Silverman, Nickman, and Worden (1992) noted,

> This inner representation or construction leads the child to remain in a relationship with the deceased, and this relationship changes as the child matures and as the intensity of the grief lessens. . . . The emphasis should be on negotiating and renegotiating the meaning of the loss over time, rather than on letting go. (p. 502)

Relationship Between Early Loss and Psychological Outcomes

A number of researchers have found the incidence of parental death during one's childhood to be significantly higher in certain populations of depressed patients as compared to the general population (Beck, Sethi, & Tuthill, 1963; Brown, 1961; Caplan & Douglas, 1969; Forrest, Fraser, & Priest, 1965; Greer, 1964; Mireault & Bond, 1992; Wolfenstein, 1966). Early parent death was found to be more prevalent in severely depressed patients (rather than in all depressed patients; Birtchnell, 1970a). As would be expected with a clinical sample, researchers found bereaved children to be at very high risk for manifesting some type of psychopathology.

From data such as these, many earlier researchers postulated that early parental death causes adult depression. More recent studies have contradicted these earlier findings. This difference in conclusion can be attributed to many factors, such as sampling biases, lack of appropriate control groups, lack of attention to mediating factors, and inconsistent definition of the dependent variable of depression (Harris, Brown, & Bifulco, 1986; Tennant, 1988; Tennant, Bebbington, & Hurry, 1980).

Evidence has mounted that parental death, in and of itself, does not necessarily increase risk of depression. When looking for risk factors, a multidimensional perspective must be taken, examining both individual and family variables (Saler & Skolnick, 1992). For example, there is evidence that the lack of adequate parental care following the death is a more powerful predictor of later adult impairment than the simple fact that a parent has died (Harris, Brown, & Bifulco, 1986).

Positive Outcomes of Childhood Bereavement

Given that so many early studies of childhood bereavement focused on potential for later dysfunction, many have assumed that loss brings only pain. Difficult and challenging as the grief experience is, most children seem to have the capacity to deal effectively with a significant loss. Some researchers have even discovered what may be regarded as positive outcomes derived from a childhood bereavement experience (Davies, 1991, 1999). For example, in one study of siblings bereaved during childhood, a number of participants (primarily, those with a higher self concept) reported that they were more mature as a result of having to deal with their sibling's illness and death, had better coping skills, and valued other people more than they had before the loss experience (Martinson, Davies, & McClowry, 1987). Furthermore, some survivors of childhood loss have noted enhanced creative abilities and psychosocial functioning in later years (Aldwin, 1994). More generally speaking, as one reviews studies of children and stress, it becomes evident that children are remarkably resilient (Garmezy & Rutter, 1983).

STUDY OF CHILDHOOD BEREAVEMENT

Although literally hundreds of studies have been published in regard to childhood bereavement, there is no clear understanding of how a child grieves. We must continue to strengthen research methodologies, be clear about what questions we want to answer, and examine findings in terms of the many variables that are known to have some effect on bereavement outcome.

Trends in the Study of Childhood Bereavement

A number of trends in childhood bereavement research activities are apparent as one moves from the 1950s to the current time frame. During the 1950s to the mid-1980s, a preponderance of the research was based on case studies or very small samples drawn from clinical settings. These efforts were typically retrospective in nature, and findings were often interpreted from a psychoanalytic perspective (Altschul, 1988; Birtchnell, 1970b; Cain, Fast, & Erickson, 1964; Furman, 1974; Kliman, 1968).

> By the 1980's . . . researchers began to move away from describing the pathology to identifying the developmental, environmental, and individual psychosocial attributes . . . that impact response to death. Research methodology moved from predominantly case studies and retrospective descriptive studies to exploratory/descriptive studies using objective measures. (Walker, 1993, p. 327)

As years have passed, researchers have come to understand that mourning is a normal process and not necessarily one resulting in psychopathology or developmental dysfunction.

General Critique of Research Methodologies

Childhood bereavement literature must be read with a critical eye based on an awareness of many factors that may ultimately confound the findings. Lack of attention to such detail over time has contributed to what is a somewhat contradictory, and often confusing, perspective of children's experience of grief and its related outcomes. Shortcomings in many research studies include such factors as sample selection, data-gathering techniques, mediating variables not taken into account in the experimental design, and weaknesses in interpretation of data. Many of these are noted in Table 8-4.

TABLE 8-4
General Critique of Methodology Used in Childhood
Bereavement Studies

Research Design

- Data are often gathered years after the death, leading to paucity of information about acute grief reactions of children. Sometimes intent is to determine long-term outcomes. Other times the design is retrospective in nature and depends on participants' memories of death event and of time thereafter. Participants' recall may be different from reality of actual events and reactions.
- Most studies are cross-sectional in design. Because grief process shifts over time, more longitudinal prospective studies are needed.
- Parent is usually an informant regarding child's grief; parents' own grief may affect perceptions of child's experience. In addition, parent is not likely to be aware of full range of child's reactions—particularly those that are not reflected outwardly.
- Bereaved children are rarely asked to give input about their own grief. This can lead to misleading conclusions. When included as informants, children often report presence of thoughts and emotions that their parents did not report; parents also sometimes report reactions that the child did not note as being present.
- There is almost no systematic building of research agendas; rarely does one study build on the findings of another.
- Extremely wide band of time (marking time since death) in many subject pools may lead to contamination of findings by numerous intervening historical variables.

Sample

- Samples are often small in size.
- Nonbereaved control group is rarely included.
- Participants from minority groups are rarely included.
- Sample frequently crosses developmental substages and often includes those grieving various types of deaths. Varied time frames since the death occurred are used. These differences are rarely included in either analysis or interpretation.
- When samples are drawn from clinical population or other nonrepresentative sample, findings are often generalized to larger population.

Table Continues

TABLE 8-4
(*Continued*)

Measurement Tools/Interview Strategies

- Data gathering techniques often reflect narrow focus of childhood bereavement rather than reflecting the many dimensions of childhood grief.
- Measures used often are not developed to examine "grief" per se—but rather such things as depression, general health, etc. Although related, these measure phenomena different from grief.
- No standardized instrument is consistently being used other than the Child Behavior Checklist (CBCL). CBCL was not developed to measure grief responses per se; it focuses on behaviors rather than emotions or thoughts. Although many common facets of grief are found in a given CBCL scale, separate manifestations are not indicated in the "Total Score" or "Internalizing Behaviors" or "Externalizing Behaviors." Rarely are scores of a particular item reported.
- Little detail, if any, is provided in regard to specific interview questions used.
- Few studies use measures intended to examine presence of positive outcomes of loss experience.

Analysis

- Even when variables are identified that are likely to have an effect on outcome (e.g., developmental stage of bereaved child; time since death; suddenness of death), they are rarely analyzed in relation to bereavement outcome.

Reporting

- Details of sample and research design rarely reported in detail needed to ensure replication of the study and to assist in interpretation of findings.
- Many studies report as "fact" a bereavement outcome that is not warranted as a part of the design or sample.

Interpretation

- Often, mediating factors (risk/protective) or confounding variables are not discussed in relation to findings.
- Although most studies involve children of various developmental stages, age span is rarely considered in interpretation of data.
- Most researchers do not know (or report) level of functioning or emotional state prior to death (e.g., that which is measured by CBCL or other experiences); therefore, reader does not know whether a given loss precipitated presence of particular emotions, behaviors, etc.

OVERVIEW OF SPECIFIC RESEARCH STUDIES EXAMINING CHILDHOOD BEREAVEMENT

Although it is recognized that the death of a grandparent (Hatter, 1996) or the death of a friend is a significant loss (Toray & Oltjenbruns, 1996), there has been almost no systematic study of these grief experiences. The death of a sibling or a parent has been the focus of almost all of the research related to childhood bereavement. Significant studies in these two arenas will be highlighted in upcoming sections. Although the nature of the relationship severed does have an impact, the grief of a child following the death of a sibling is similar in many respects to the grief experience following the death of a parent (Silverman, 2000).

Grief Following Death of a Sibling During Childhood

Table 8-5 provides a summary of salient points related to grief following death of a sibling. This set of studies is not meant to be exhaustive but rather illustrative. For a more thorough review, see Davies (1999), in which she summarizes research studies published between the years 1964 to 1995.

Grief Following Death of a Parent During Childhood: The Harvard Childhood Bereavement Study

Although there have been hundreds of studies over the years examining bereavement outcome following death of a parent during childhood, this section focuses on a particular hallmark study, the Harvard Childhood Bereavement Study, implemented by principle investigators Phyllis Silverman and William Worden, together with their colleagues. This longitudinal effort has a much stronger methodology than most other studies in the field; it served as the central focus of the chapter related to childhood bereavement in the 1993 *Handbook on Bereavement: Theory, Research and Intervention* (Stroebe, Stroebe, & Hansson, 1993). Table 8-6 summarizes the overall design of the child bereavement study.

To examine various facets of childhood bereavement, a number of researchers drew subsets of data from the larger pool collected for the overall childhood bereavement study. A few outcomes are reported in this chapter. For example, the process of reconstructing the deceased parent seems to help many children cope with the loss; both children and the surviving parent may be actively engaged in that effort.

Silverman et al. (1992) reported that a child's strategies for remaining connected to the deceased parent are consistent with his or her level of cognitive development and that those strategies change over time. They include,

- Attempting to "locate" the deceased (e.g., in heaven),
- Experiencing the deceased,
- Remembering various facets of the deceased and interactions with that parent, and
- Keeping a belonging of the deceased.

Surviving parents contribute to the reconstruction of the deceased by

- Talking about the deceased parent,
- Providing the child with opportunities to participate in memorializing activities,

- Giving mementos of the deceased to the child,
- Remaining alert to the child's feelings about the deceased,
- Helping the child find language to express feelings,
- Showing respect for the deceased, and
- Honoring the child's relationship to the parent who died. (Nickman, Silverman, & Normand, 1998; Silverman & Nickman, 1996)

Children's gender and age, together with the suddenness of the death and gender of the parent who died, affected various outcomes, including the children's affective experiences, their efforts to maintain connection to the deceased parent, involvement in social networks and support systems, and changes in family routines (Silverman & Worden, 1992). Drawing data from the four-month and one-year time frames, these two researchers found little indication overall of serious dysfunctional behavior among the children studied up to the one-year mark. However, by changing the time frame studied and including data gathered at the two-year mark, Worden and Silverman (1996) found higher levels of social withdrawal, anxiety, and social problems, as well as lower levels of self-esteem and self-efficacy, in the bereaved group compared to the control group. Twenty-one percent of the bereaved group showed serious problems two years following the death. Most differences between the two groups were not apparent until two years after the death. This is a crucial insight for researchers as well as support personnel. Methodological designs that collect data during the time frame immediately after death will not be sensitive to the possibility of delayed reactions. Those who provide support need to be aware of possible problems developing in the time frame extending beyond the first year of bereavement.

RECOMMENDATIONS FOR FUTURE STUDY

Much is yet to be done in the ongoing study of childhood bereavement. Certainly various methodological concerns noted earlier must be addressed if researchers are to continue building our knowledge base. Many important questions are yet to be answered.

Developmental Lens

As noted earlier, it is crucial to examine a child's bereavement experience within a developmental context. Even when there has been a fairly wide age span among those included in the sample, many researchers have interpreted their findings as if the broad-based group was homogeneous in nature. Although a few have created research designs with atten-

TABLE 8-5
Grief Following Death of a Sibling

Author/Year	Sample	Death Experience	Research Design	Mediating Factors	Bereavement Outcomes
	■ Size ■ Age ■ Gender ■ Ethnicity ■ Clinical or commu- nity ■ Control group	■ Who died ■ Type of death ■ Time since death	■ Question ■ Methods ■ Instruments used		
Birenbaum, 1989	■ 61 participants, 13 completed all 4 time frames ■ 4 to 17 years of age ■ Not reported ■ Not reported ■ Community sample ■ No control group	■ Sibling ■ Terminal phase of cancer ■ 2 weeks, 4 months, 12 months after ill child's death	■ Examine relationship between parents' communication and child's grief ■ Child Behavior Checklist— parent as information (inter- nal, external, and social com- petence) ■ Parent–Sibling Communica- tion Instrument—used before sick child's death		■ Before the death, the more open the communication, the more social competence found—not found other three times ■ After the death, the more open the communication, the fewer behavior problems noted
Birenbaum, Robinson, Phillips, Stewart, McCown, 1990	■ 61 participants total but only 31 at any of the four points of assessment; 13 completed all 4 time frames ■ 4–16 years ■ Predominantly Cau- casian ■ Community sample ■ No control group but used normative data on CBCL	■ Sibling ■ Cancer ■ Predeath ■ 2 weeks after, 4 months after, 1 year after	■ Investigate behavioral adjust- ment during terminal illness and 1 year following death ■ Child Behavior Checklist (ex- ternal, internal and social competence) from parent ■ Child Behavior Checklist (ex- ternal, internal, and adaptive functioning) from teacher		■ "Referable Scores"—signifi- cant behavior problems signif- icantly higher than that of normative group ■ Referable scores vary some- what over time frame of study; ranging from 16% at 4 months to 30% at both pre- death and 1 month after; 27% at one year ■ Social competence signifi- cantly lower than normative sample ■ Adaptive functioning similar to norm

Study	Sample	Death characteristics	Purpose/Methods	Variables	Findings
Davies, 1988a, 1988b	■ 34 participants ■ 14 were ages 6 to 11 years ■ 20 were ages 12–16 years ■ 21 females, 13 males ■ No control ■ Data compared to norm group	■ Sibling ■ Cancer ■ 2 to 36 months	■ Examine predeath relationship between siblings and bereavement responses (a) ■ Examine relationship of family environment to surviving sibling behavior (b) ■ Mothers completed Achenbach Child Behavior Checklist (a and b) ■ Closeness index derived from interview with family members (a)	■ Closeness (a) ■ Shared life space ■ Mutuality of relationship ■ Family Environment (b)	■ Trend for greater closeness to predict increased internalizing behavior scores (a) ■ Cohesion in the families was significantly related to lower behavior problem scores in the children (b)
Finke, Birenbaum, Chand, 1994	■ 38 participants; missing data on 3 ■ Ages not reported ■ 13 males, 22 females ■ No control group	■ Sibling ■ Before death ■ Also 2 weeks after death	■ Describe grief experience 2 weeks following sibling's death ■ Parent was informant ■ Questionnaire—Sibling Background Interview; Sibling Experience With Death Interview	■ Gender—no difference ■ Age—difference in shared activities ■ Family size on effect on grief experience	■ Most likely to hear about death from mother—were given a variety of reasons for the death ■ 7 children told nothing about the death ■ Most common reaction during this two week interval was crying
Mahon & Page, 1995	■ 18 participants ■ 4 to 23 years; mean of 11.4 years; standard deviation of 5.8 years ■ 10 females; 8 males ■ 9 families White; 2 African American ■ Community sample ■ No control group	■ Sibling ■ Varied causes ■ 3 months to 58 months; mean of 24 months; standard deviation of 17.6 months	■ Constant comparative technique ■ Two semistructured questionnaires for background—one for siblings; one for parents ■ Open-ended questionnaire; interview regarding experience	■ Availability of mother ■ Presence of friends ■ Having possessions of deceased sibling	Many common patterns: ■ Vivid memories of how they learned of death ■ Sadness coexisting with other feelings—often relief ■ Confusion ■ Anger ■ Need to be alone ■ Felt isolated ■ Felt they were being judged in regard to how they were grieving ■ Protective of parents ■ Sense of responsibility

Table Continues

TABLE 8-5 (Continued)

Author/year	Sample	Death Experience	Research Design	Mediating Factors	Bereavement Outcomes

McCown & Davies, 1995	■ 90 participants
	■ 48 females, 42 males
	■ 4–16 years, mean of 9.9 years; standard deviation of 4 years
		■ Sibling, ages 2 months to 20 years
		■ Varied causes, cancer most frequent
			■ Describe behaviors in children after sibling's death
			■ Child Behavior Checklist—reports by mothers
				■ Age—younger children showed more problems	■ Highest incidence of behavioral problems occurred in preschool (4–5) and school age children (6–11)
					■ Most frequent behavior was "demands a lot of attention"
					Most common behaviors in girls:
					■ Aggression Subscale:
					  ■ Argues
					  ■ Demands attention
					  ■ Jealous
					  ■ Stubborn, sullen, or irritable
					■ Depression Subscale
					■ Self-conscious or easily embarrassed
					Most common behaviors in boys:
					■ Aggression Subscale:
					  ■ Argues
					  ■ Demands attention
					  ■ Disobedience
					  ■ Showing off, clowning
					■ Hyperactive Subscale
					  ■ Cannot concentrate
					■ Reported that few somatic problems were found–only two found in 25%+
					  ■ Does not eat well
					  ■ Nightmares

■ Has been standardized by sex for ages 4 to 18 years
■ Behaviors are grouped into eight syndrome subscales
Total score is made up of
■ Internalizing behaviors, which measures such things as crying, sleep disturbances, fears, self-consciousness, nightmares, sadness, guilt, tiredness, somatic complaints
■ Externalizing behaviors, which measures hyperactivity, demands for attention, disobedience, impulsiveness, poor school performance, inability to concentrate.

TABLE 8-6
Methodological Notes: The Harvard Childhood Bereavement Study

Sample

Bereaved Sample
- 70 families experiencing the death of a parent
  - 62 of the deaths natural
  - 60% expected; 40% sudden
  - 70% Catholic, 23% Protestant; 6% Jewish; 1% other
- 125 children
  - 65 boys; 60 girls
  - 74% experience father loss; 26% mother loss
  - Nonclinical, community-based sample
  - Ages between 6 and 17 years
    - 62 were between ages 6–11 at Time 1 (four months following death)
    - 63 were between 12–16 years
    - Mean of 11.6 years

Nonbereaved Control Group
- Matched by age, gender, grade in school, family religion, and community

Design

- Data collected at three different points after death: 4 months, 1 year, 2 years
- Both child and surviving parent served as informants

Measurements

Child	Parent
■ Semistructured interview ■ Nowicki and Strickland Locus of Control Scale ■ Harter's Self-Perception ■ Smilansky's Understanding of Death	■ Semistructured interview ■ Family Adaptation and Cohesion Evaluation Scales ■ Family Crisis Oriented Personal Evaluation Scale ■ Family Inventory of Life Events ■ CES-Depression Scale ■ Child Behavior Checklist

Sources: Nickman et al., 1998; Silverman & Nickman, 1996; Silverman et al., 1992; Silverman & Worden, 1992; Worden & Silverman, 1996; Worden, 1996.

---

tion to developmental stages, it is important that thanatologists strengthen efforts in this regard. The following suggestions for future research simply illustrate the many questions yet to be studied from a developmental context:

- Do certain risk factors increase the likelihood of negative bereavement outcomes during particular substages of childhood?
- Do certain protective factors enhance the likelihood of positive bereavement outcomes during particular substages of childhood?
- Are certain types of support or intervention strategies more

effective during one substage of childhood compared to another?

- What coping strategies are more helpful to children dealing with a death during particular life stages? Can these be taught?
- Are there certain facets of unfolding cognitive capacity that serve as the underpinnings for anticipatory grief?
- Does the "dual process" model of bereavement posited by Stroebe and Schut (1999) have relevance for the substages of childhood?

Not only should there be an ongoing focus on developmentally based questions, there needs to be more attention given to the interpretation of findings within a developmental context for all studies. Even when researchers have in the past presented findings in terms of age or stage differences, they have most often simply reported similarities and differences between various age groups along a particular dimension of interest. With the exception of examining children's concept of death, there has been little attempt to actually interpret the findings in relation to developmental stage issues. This lack of discussion greatly diminishes our understanding of childhood bereavement processes. For example, Kaffman and Elizur (1979) and Elizur and Kaffman (1982, 1983) reported age-related differences in aggressive behaviors following the death of a father. Although they compared young children and school-age children, they did not interpret these findings in terms of differential cognitive and language capabilities, coping mechanisms, or other age-related variables.

Those who design studies in which the sample crosses substages must be attuned to the fact that bereaved children of various ages have different normative capacities (e.g., cognitive, language, socioemotional, coping) and struggle with mastering different developmental tasks. Age or stage of the sample should be examined as an independent variable, not simply recorded as a descriptor of the individuals who make up the sample. To date, the field does not have a coherent understanding of developmental trends or of the processes underlying change in regard to children's grief as they mature over time.

McCown and Pratt (1985) illustrated how increased insight can be derived when research findings are interpreted from a developmental perspective. These researchers studied children across various substages of childhood to better understand grief following the death of a sibling. Using the standardized Child Behavior Checklist, they found that children who were grieving the death of a sibling exhibited significantly more behavioral problems than did children in the standardized norm group. These problems included withdrawal, clinging to adults, nightmares, running away, excessive talking, arguing, and hyperactivity. Of the three age groups studied (ages 4 to 5, 6 to 11, and 12 to 16), the 6- to 11-year-olds showed the greatest level of disturbance. McCown and Pratt interpreted this finding by noting,

> Several explanations are possible. First, the 6- to 11-year olds fall within the psychosocial stage described by Erikson as Industry versus Inferiority. The loss of a sibling at this phase may lead to a sense of self-vulnerability and inferiority. A second potential explanation for problems may be related to the 6- to 11-year olds' death conceptualization. . . . School age children 6 to 11 make a transition from preoperational to concrete operational modes of thinking. They find death bewildering and seek a cause and explanation. For the child in this age group who is making the transition to concrete thought, the event and cause of sibling death may evoke confusion. The increased behavior problems may be a reflection of that confusion and concern. (1985, p. 333)

The fact that three substages were studied and reported separately instead of a longer, more inclusive age span provides insights not possible had the data been collapsed with no attention given to relevant developmental issues.

Cross-Cultural Lens

Although this particular chapter focuses primarily on the developmental context, it is important to note that there are also many questions to be answered in relation to childhood bereavement issues examined from a cross-cultural perspective. (Ideally, these two perspectives should be integrated, as they are in the real world.) The thanatology literature contains references to varying child mortality rates in countries across the world and also includes some information about children's involvement in funeral rituals. Little emphasis, however, has been put on the study of similarities and differences among children's grief in relation to various ethnic or cultural backgrounds. As we design studies to provide us with this insight, we must be sensitive to both within-group and between-group differences.

"A systemic developmental perspective on childhood bereavement emphasizes the interweaving of the child's stage of development, family relationships, and culture in determining his or her grief reaction and the impact of death and grief on his or her ongoing development" (Shapiro, 1994, p. 85). One's cultural background may actually define the significance of the loss event and prescribe what resources are available to the child. A research agenda in this arena should include attention to differential definitions of loss, similarities and differences among bereavement outcomes, factors that make children less vulnerable to negative outcomes and more likely to experience positive outcomes. Again, these should be examined in reference to a developmental context.

Other Recommendations

Effort should be made in the future to determine the difference between particular manifestations of grief and the underlying dynamic or function. For example, are regressive behaviors among young children simply manifestations of grief or are they, as many suggest, coping mechanisms intended to gain attention from adults in their social environment? In parallel fashion, are aggressive behaviors simply manifestations of anger or are they instrumental coping mechanisms intended to gain adult attention (McCown & Davies, 1995)?

Although more attention has been given to the regrief phenomenon in recent years, we know relatively little about the following:

- What factors have an effect on an individual's regrief experience and enhance likelihood of a positive outcome?
- The interface between the regrief phenomenon and the child's efforts to reconstruct the individual who died. (This inner representation changes over time, and is influenced by ongoing development and maturation, as noted by Silverman et al., 1992).

CONCLUSION

Because of many factors, the research related to childhood bereavement outcomes is inconclusive and often contradictory. These factors include use of measurements not intended to capture the multidimensional aspects of grief; use of such a variety of instruments or interview protocols that it is difficult to compare one study's findings to another; research designs that do not take into account individuals' physical, psychological, social, or behavioral states before the death event; little attention given —in either design or interpretation—to many potentially confounding variables such as developmental stage.

Clearly, the field would be better served if we were able to determine how to create a long-term, collaborative research agenda that would allow us to more effectively build on each other's efforts. To deepen our understanding of childhood bereavement outcomes, it could also be helpful to use the meta-analysis statistical technique. Done well, a meta-analysis "sets the bar" at the very outset for what studies are sufficiently sound to include in the analysis. Alternatively, much is to be gained by the type of integrative review and model development done by Davies (1999).

Although discussion of intervention is not a focus of this particular chapter, the research highlighted would suggest that support over an extended period of time be made available to children. Certain reactions do not become apparent until a couple of years after the death; yet many believe the need for support dissipates after the first anniversary of the death. An argument for ongoing support is also reflected in the interactive processes of regrieving the loss and reconstructing the deceased.

REFERENCES

Aldwin, C. M. (1994). *Stress, coping, and development: An integrative perspective.* New York: Guilford Press.

Altschul, S. (1988). *Childhood bereavement and its aftermath.* Madison, CT: International Universities Press.

Attig, T. (1995). Respecting bereaved children and adolescents. In D. W. Adams & E. J. Deveau (Eds.), *Helping children and adolescents cope with death and bereavement.* (pp. 43–60). Amityville, NY: Baywood.

Baker, J. E., Sedney, M. A., & Gross, E. (1992). Psychological tasks for bereaved children. *American Journal of Orthopsychiatry, 62,* 105–116.

Baker, J. E., Sedney, M. A., & Gross, E. (1996). How bereaved children cope with loss: An overview. In C. Corr & D. Corr (Eds.), *Handbook of childhood death and bereavement* (pp. 109–130). New York: Springer.

Beck, A. G., Sethi, B., & Tuthill, R. W. (1963). Childhood bereavement and adult depression. *Archives of General Psychiatry, 9,* 295–302.

Birenbaum, L. K. (1989). The relationship between parent-sibling communication and coping of siblings with death experience. *Journal of Pediatric Oncology Nursing, 6,* 86–91.

Birenbaum, L. K., Robinson, M. A., Phillips, D. S., Stewart, B. J., & McCown, D. E. (1990). The response of children to the dying and death of a sibling. *Omega, 20,* 213–218.

Birtchnell, J. (1970a). Recent parent death and mental illness. *British Journal of Psychiatry, 116,* 289–297.

Birtchnell, J. (1970b). Depression in relation to early and recent parent death. *British Journal of Psychiatry, 116,* 299–306.

Bowlby, J. (1980). *Attachment and loss. Vol. 3. Loss: sadness, and depression.* New York: Basic Books.

Brown, F. (1961). Depression and childhood bereavement. *Journal of Mental Science, 107,* 754–757.

Cain, A., Fast, I., & Erickson, M. (1964). Children's disturbed reactions to the death of a sibling. *American Journal of Orthopsychiatry, 34,* 741–745.

Caplan, M. G., & Douglas, V. (1969). Incidence of parental loss in children with depressed mood. *Journal of Child Psychology and Psychiatry, 10,* 225–232.

Cook, A. S., & Dworkin, D. (1992). *Helping the bereaved: Therapeutic interventions for children, adolescents, and adults.* New York: Basic Books.

Cook, A. S., & Oltjenbruns, K. A. (1998). *Dying and grieving: Lifespan and family perspectives.* Fort Worth, TX: Harcourt & Brace.

Davies, B. (1988a). Shared life space and sibling bereavement responses. *Cancer Nursing, 11,* 339–347.

Davies, B. (1988b). The family environment in bereaved families and its relationship to surviving sibling behavior. *Children's Health Care, 17,* 22–32.

Davies, B. (1991). Responses of children to the death of a sibling. In D. Papadatou & C. Papadatos (Eds.), *Children and death* (pp. 125–133). New York: Hemisphere.

Davies, B. (1999). *Shadows in the sun. The experiences of sibling bereavement in childhood.* Philadelphia: Brunner/Mazel.

Demi, A. S., & Miles, M. S. (1987). Parameters of normal grief: A Delphi study. *Death Studies, 11,* 397–412.

Deveau, E. J. (1997). The pattern of grief in children and adolescents. In J. D. Morgan (Ed.), *Readings in thanatology* (pp. 359–390). Amityville, NY: Baywood.

Elizur, E., & Kaffman, M. (1982). Children's bereavement reactions following death of the father: II. *Journal of the American Academy of Child Psychiatry, 21,* 474–480.

Elizur, E., & Kaffman, M. (1983). Factors influencing the severity of childhood bereavement reactions. *American Journal of Orthopsychiatry, 53,* 669–676.

Erikson, E. (1963). *Childhood and society.* (2nd ed.). New York: Norton.

Finke, L. M., Birenbaum, L. K., & Chand, N. (1994). Two weeks post-death report by parents of sibling's grieving experience. *Journal of Child and Adolescent Psychiatric Nursing, 7,* 17–25.

Fleming, S., & Balmer, L. (1991). Group intervention with bereaved children. In D. Papadatou & C. Papadatos (Eds.), *Children and death* (pp. 105–124). New York: Hemisphere.

Forrest, A. D., Fraser, R. H., & Priest, R. G. (1965). Environmental factors in depressive illness. *British Journal of Psychiatry, 111,* 243–253.

Furman, E. (1974). *A child's parent dies: Studies in childhood bereavement.* New Haven, CT: Yale University Press.

Garmezy, N., & Rutter, M. (1983). *Stress, coping, and development in children.* New York: McGraw-Hill.

Gibbons, M. B. (1992). A child dies, a child survives: The impact of sibling loss. *Journal of Pediatric Health Care, 6,* 65–72.

Greer, S. (1964). The relationship between parental loss and attempted suicide: A control study. *British Journal of Psychiatry, 110,* 698–705.

Gudas, L. J. (1993). Concepts of death and loss in childhood and adolescence: A developmental perspective. In C. F. Saylor (Ed.), *Children and disasters* (pp. 67–84). New York: Plenum Press.

Harris, T., Brown, G. W., & Bifulco, A. (1986). Loss of parent in childhood and adult psychiatric disorder: The role of lack of adequate parental care. *Psychological Medicine, 16,* 641–659.

Hatter, B. S. (1996). Children and death of a parent or grandparent. In C. Corr

& D. Corr (Eds.), *Handbook of childhood death and bereavement* (pp. 131–148). New York: Springer.

Havighurst, R. J. (1956). *Human development and education*. New York: McKay.

Kaffman, M., & Elizur, E. (1979). Children's bereavement reactions following the death of the father. *International Journal of Family Therapy, 1*, 203–229.

Kliman, G. W. (1968). *Psychological emergencies of childhood*. New York: Grune & Stratton.

Koocher, G. P. (1974). Talking with children about death. *American Journal of Orthopsychiatry, 44*, 404–411.

Krupnick, J. (1984). Bereavement during childhood and adolescence. In M. Osterweis, M. Solomon, & M. Green (Eds.), *Bereavement: Reactions, consequences, and care* (pp. 99–141). Washington, DC: National Academy Press.

Lonetto, R. (1980). *Children's conceptions of death*. New York: Springer.

Mahon, M., & Page, M. (1995). Childhood bereavement after the death of a sibling. *Holistic Nursing Practice, 9*, 15–26.

Martinson, I. M., Davies, E. B., & McClowry, S. G. (1987). The long-term effects of sibling death on self-concept. *Journal of Pediatric Nursing, 2*, 227–235.

McCown, D., & Davies, B. (1995). Patterns of grief in young children following the death of a sibling. *Death Studies, 19*, 41–53.

McCown, D., & Pratt, D. (1985). Impact of sibling death on children's behavior. *Death Studies, 9*, 323–335.

Middleton, W., Raphael, B., Martinek, N., & Misso, V. (1993). Pathological grief reactions. In M. S. Stroebe, W. Stroebe, & R. O. Hannson (Eds.), *Handbook of bereavement: Theory, research and intervention* (pp. 44–61). Cambridge: Cambridge University Press.

Miller, M. A. (1995). Re-grief as narrative: The impact of parental death of child and adolescent development. In D. W. Adams & E. J. Deveau (Eds.), *Helping children and adolescents cope with death and bereavement* (pp. 99–113). Amityville, NY: Baywood.

Mireault, G. C., & Bond, L. A. (1992). Parental death in childhood: Perceived vulnerability and adult depression and anxiety. *American Journal of Psychiatric Nursing, 62*, 517–524.

Moody, R. A., & Moody, C. P. (1991). A family perspective: Helping children acknowledge and express grief following the death of a parent. *Death Studies, 15*, 587–602.

Nagy, M. (1948). The child's theories concerning death. *Journal of Genetic Psychology, 73*, 3–27.

Newman, B. M., & Newman, P. R. (1999). *Development through life: A psychosocial approach*. New York: Brooks/Cole-Wadsworth.

Nickman, S. L., Silverman, P. R., & Normand, C. (1998). Children's construction of a deceased parent: The surviving parent's contribution. *American Journal of Orthopsychiatry, 68*, 126–134.

Piaget, J. (1963). *The origins of intelligence in children.* New York: International Universities Press.

Rando, T. (1993). *Treatment of complicated mourning.* Champaign, IL: Research Press.

Saler, L., & Skolnick, N. (1992). Childhood parental death and depression in adulthood: Roles of surviving parent and family environment. *American Journal of Orthopsychiatry, 62,* 504–516.

Sekaer, C., & Katz, S. (1986). On the concept of mourning in childhood. *The Psychiatric Study of the Child, 41,* 287–314.

Shapiro, E. R. (1994). *Grief as a family process: A developmental approach to clinical practice.* New York: Guilford Press.

Silverman, P. R. (2000). *Never too young to know: Death in children's lives.* New York: Oxford University Press.

Silverman, P. R., & Nickman, S. (1996). Children's construction of their dead parents. In D. Klass, P. R. Silverman, & S. L. Nickman (Eds.), *Continuing bonds* (pp. 73–86). Washington, DC: Taylor & Francis.

Silverman, P. R., Nickman, S., & Worden, J. W. (1992). Detachment revisited: The child's reconstruction of a dead parent. *American Journal of Orthopsychiatry, 62,* 494–503.

Silverman, P. R., & Worden, W. (1992). Children's reactions in the early months after the death of a parent. *American Journal of Orthopsychiatry, 62,* 93–104.

Sorenson, E. S. (1993). *Children's stress and coping: A family perspective.* New York: Guilford Press.

Speece, M. W., & Brent, S. B. (1984). Children's understanding of death: A review of three components of a death concept. *Child Development, 55,* 1671–1686.

Speece, M. W., & Brent, S. B. (1992). The acquisition of a mature understanding of three components of the concept of death. *Death Studies, 16,* 211–229.

Speece, M. W., & Brent, S. B. (1996). The development of children's understanding of death. In C. Corr & D. Corr (Eds.), *Handbook of childhood death and bereavement* (pp. 29–50). New York: Springer.

Stillion, J., & Wass, H. (1979). Children and death. In H. Wass (Ed.), *Dying: Facing the facts* (pp. 208–235). Washington, DC: Hemisphere.

Stroebe, M. S., & Schut, H. (1999). The dual process model of bereavement: Rationale and description. *Death Studies, 23,* 197–224.

Stroebe, M. S., Stroebe, W., & Hansson, R. O. (1993). *Handbook of Bereavement: Theory, research, and intervention.* Cambridge: Cambridge University Press.

Tennant, C. (1988). Parental loss in childhood: Its effect in adult life. *Archives of General Psychiatry, 45,* 1045–1050.

Tennant, C., Bebbington, P., & Hurry, J. (1980). Parental death in childhood and risk of adult depressive disorders: A review. *Psychological Medicine, 10,* 289–299.

Toray, T., & Oltjenbruns, K. A. (1996). Building friendships during childhood:

Significance of the death of a peer. In C. Corr & D. Corr (Eds.), *Handbook of childhood death and bereavement* (pp. 165–178). New York: Springer.

Van Eerdewegh, M. Bierie, M., Parrilla, R., & Clayton, P. (1982). The bereaved child. *British Journal of Psychiatry, 140,* 23–29.

Walker, C. L. (1993). Sibling bereavement and grief responses. *Journal of Pediatric Nursing, 8,* 325–334.

Wass, H. (1991). Helping children cope with death. In D. Papadatou & C. Papadatos (Eds.), *Children and death* (pp. 11–32). New York: Hemisphere.

Webb, N. (1993). *Helping bereaved children: A handbook for practitioners.* New York: Guilford Press.

Wolfe, B. S., & Senta, L. M. (1995). Interventions with bereaved children nine to thirteen years of age: From a medical center-based young person's grief support program. In D. W. Adams & E. J. Deveau (Eds.), *Helping children and adolescents cope with death and bereavement* (pp. 203–227). Amityville, NY: Baywood.

Wolfelt, A. (1983). *Helping children cope with grief.* Muncie, IN: Accelerated Development.

Wolfenstein, M. (1966). How is mourning possible? *Psychoanalytic Study of the Child, 21,* 93–123.

Worden, J. W., & Silverman, P. R. (1996). Parental death and the adjustment of school-age children. *Omega, 33,* 91–102.

Worden, W. (1991). *Grief counseling and grief therapy: A handbook for the mental health practitioner.* (2nd ed.). New York: Springer.

Worden, W. (1996). *Children and grief: When a parent dies.* New York: Guilford Press.

9

BEREAVEMENT DURING ADOLESCENCE: A REVIEW OF RESEARCH

DAVID E. BALK AND CHARLES A. CORR

The unique developmental challenges facing persons during the formative adolescent years distinguish bereavement during this period from other portions of the life cycle, even though, understandably, there are some similarities between bereaved adolescents and bereaved adults. Thus the study of bereavement during adolescence deserves the particular attention of researchers. The objective of this chapter is to examine adolescent bereavement, provide a synthesis of adolescent bereavement research, and identify issues for future research.

Although adolescent bereavement research has had a short history, a historical approach is a useful principal for organizing the chapter, because understanding its origins helps a reader see what has been accomplished in this field, understand the current limitations, and appreciate the advances made in some studies. A secondary organizing mechanism of the chapter is "development during adolescence." Adolescent bereavement cannot reliably be understood or investigated unless placed in the overall context of the developmental tasks and transitions facing adolescents.

The effects of bereavement are severe, and unresolved bereavement has been linked to agitated depression, chronic illness, enduring and intense clinical reactions such as guilt, and significant disturbances in self-esteem, job and school performance, and interpersonal relationships (Balk, 1983, 1990, 1996; Balk & Corr, 1996; Balk & Hogan, 1995; Balk et al., 1998; Balk & Vesta, 1998; DeVaul, Zisook, & Faschingbauer, 1979; Hogan, 1986; Hogan & DeSantis, 1996a, 1996b; Jacobs, 1999; Lindemann, 1944; Osterweis, Solomon, & Green, 1984; Parkes, 1998, Raphael, 1983; Silver & Wortman, 1980; Silverman & Worden, 1992; M. Stroebe, Stroebe, & Hansson, 1993; W. Stroebe & Stroebe, 1987; Tyson-Rawson, 1996; Worden, 1996). Unanticipated negative outcomes can include secondary losses and incremental grief (Cook & Oltjenbruns, 1998) as un-affected friends fear coming into contact with a grieving adolescent, frequently dismiss the intensity and duration of grief, find an adolescent's ongoing grief both disquieting and wearisome, and shun the griever (Balk & Vesta, 1998).

The chapter focuses on two central topics: (a) adolescent bereavement over different types of loss; and (b) issues at stake in the adolescent bereavement research domains. However, to enhance understanding of these major concerns, background information on the phases of adolescent development and on the nature and experience of adolescent encounters with death and bereavement needs first to be presented.

PHASES OF ADOLESCENT DEVELOPMENT

Adolescent development can be divided into three phases: early adolescence, middle adolescence, and later adolescence. Early adolescence is viewed to extend from approximately the ages of 10 to 14 and is marked by the onset of puberty. Middle adolescence extends from the ages of 15 to 17, and later adolescence extends from 18 to 22. Of course, these age ranges are likely conditioned by Western cultural biases in developed countries, particularly the United States. Coming of age in some cultures may have no such three-part phase.

Reaching the age of 22 does not propel one automatically out of later adolescence and into responsible adulthood. Some persons throughout their adult years remain ambivalent about accepting responsibility, forging a separate identity, and sustaining interpersonal intimacy. In short, "the end of adolescence is less easily identified than its beginning, although separation from home and financial independence are the typical markers that herald an individual's passage from later adolescence to young adulthood" (Balk, 1995a, p. 7). A model proposed by Fleming and Adolph (1986), to be discussed shortly, provides a link between phases of adolescent development and grief during the adolescent years.

ADOLESCENT ENCOUNTERS WITH DEATH
AND BEREAVEMENT

Adolescents are not innocent of encounters with death and bereavement. As early as 1979, Ewalt and Perkins concluded from a survey of 148 students in high school English classes that adolescents were more experienced with death and bereavement than had been realized. More recent data on adolescent violence in the United States indicate that Black adolescents in particular are likely to know someone who was murdered (Federal Bureau of Investigation, 1992).

Five surveys taken in the late 1980s and early 1990s with a representative sample of the undergraduate population at Kansas State University indicate that at any time at least 23% of students are in the first year of grief over a family member's death, and at least 27% are in the first year of grief over a friend's death. The percentages increase to around 47% in each category when the deaths occurred in the past two years (Balk, 1997). These findings have now been replicated in studies at Oklahoma State University (Balk, Wettemann, & Hair, 1998; Wettemann, 1999). A notable proportion of grief-stricken students may be found on many campuses (LaGrand, 1986; Rickgarn, 1987, 1996; Tyson-Rawson, 1993, 1996; Wrenn, 1999).

Studies such as these, assessing the prevalence of bereavement experience within college student populations, have provided initial information necessary to developing intervention programs and outcome studies. As will be shown, some investigators of college student bereavement have also investigated the effectiveness of interventions with grieving students.

The phases of adolescent development and the critical life tasks associated with each phase suggest a model for what is at stake developmentally for grieving adolescents. For example, Fleming and Adolph (1986) have proposed that bereavement requires adolescents to cope behaviorally, cognitively, and affectively with five core issues that vary according to the maturational phase of the adolescent. These five core issues are (a) trusting in the predictability of events, (b) gaining a sense of mastery and control, (c) forging relationships marked by belonging, (d) believing the world is fair and just, and (e) developing a confident self-image.

Coping with bereavement during adolescence thus involves an interplay with the tasks and conflicts of each maturational phase of adolescence. This suggests, then, that researchers need to study how, why, and when such dynamics occur as bereaved adolescents mature. A few studies (e.g., Fleming & Balmer, 1996; Worden, 1996) have examined adolescent bereavement within the context of adolescent development. However, most studies have not explicitly examined adolescent bereavement within the notion of developmental phases and critical life tasks.

ADOLESCENT BEREAVEMENT OVER DIFFERENT
TYPES OF LOSS

Most research into adolescent bereavement has focused on sibling death and parental death, with a growing interest emerging also in bereavement over the death of friends. Although not reviewed in this chapter, there have also been studies of adolescents' grieving the deaths of their own children (Bright, 1987; Shaefer, 1996; Wheeler, 1997) and the deaths of pets (Brown, 1993; Jarolmen, 1996).

Deaths of Siblings

Research on adolescent sibling bereavement has suffered from design flaws. It has often relied on cross-sectional designs gathering retrospective data. In addition, studies commonly lack control groups and include bereaved individuals for whom time since death varies widely. Adolescent sibling bereavement research still needs a rigorous, longitudinal, control group design.

Research attention was first drawn to sibling bereavement during adolescence in a study by Balk (1981), which focused on such variables as self-concept and family communication and coherence. A few years later, Hogan (1986) conducted a study on the process of adolescent sibling bereavement and adaptation. A contribution from Hogan's study was the development of a valid and reliable instrument, the Sibling Inventory of Bereavement (SIB; Hogan, 1990). Both Balk's and Hogan's early studies, however, were limited by reliance on retrospective methodology, lack of control groups, and samples influenced by parental participation in mutual support groups focused on bereavement. In addition, there was wide dispersion in time since the death. One or more of these limitations has characterized adolescent bereavement research into the 1990s.

Hogan and Balk (1990) assessed the perceptions of mothers, fathers, and adolescents about adolescent sibling bereavement. The adolescents completed the SIB in terms of their own reactions. The mother and the father completed the instrument as they thought their adolescent would answer. Of particular interest, mothers' and fathers' perceptions of their adolescent's grief and self-concept differed significantly. Fathers' responses were in agreement with their children's self-reports. However, mothers considered their adolescents' grief to be more enduring than was reflected in the reports of fathers or adolescents. Mothers also had more favorable views of their adolescents' self-concepts than what either the fathers or the adolescents themselves reported. Hogan and Balk noted that these findings raise serious questions about the common reliance in the literature on mothers' views about their bereaved children and indicated that fathers' reports about adolescent sibling bereavement should be given more credence.

Hogan and Greenfield (1991) found an inverse relationship between intensity of bereavement and self-concept scores, and inferred that adolescents with low self-concepts and enduring acute grief 18 months after the death were particularly vulnerable to long-term negative outcomes. Self-concept struggles are highly relevant to developing a confident self-image and to gaining a sense of mastery and control (Fleming & Adolph, 1986).

There appear also to be important age-related (within adolescence) issues in bereavement. For example, in a study of 40 adolescents grieving a sibling's death (Balmer, 1992), older adolescents reported greater experience of psychological distress, whereas younger bereaved adolescents reported more physiological distress.

Fleming and Balmer (1996) explored these issues further, with an eye to life tasks and phases of development, as proposed earlier in the Fleming and Adolph (1986) model. They suggested that younger adolescents, more self-conscious than older adolescents about appearing different than their peers, are less likely to talk with friends about their grief. Such reticence would leave younger adolescents vulnerable to psychosomatic symptoms such as headaches and stomach pains, and indicate problems associated with the core issues of forging relationships and achieving a sense of belonging.

Fleming and Balmer reasoned that developmental maturity, in both thinking and identity formation, enables older bereaved adolescents to discuss their grief with peers. However, experience with bereaved college students indicates less willingness on the part of nongrieving peers to engage in such discussions (see Balk, Tyson-Rawson, & Colletti-Wetzel, 1993).

Fleming and Balmer implied that maturity eliminates denial as an ongoing coping strategy for later adolescents; lack of denial produces more psychological distress than reported by younger adolescents. It is consistent, then, that older adolescents assessed by Balmer (1992) reported lower self-esteem and higher depressive symptoms. Some other researchers also have reported responses that differed according to the age of the bereaved adolescents. In contrast to the reactions of adolescents 13 to 16 years of age, adolescents 17 to 19 years of age were more angry about their sibling's death, particularly if the sibling had been younger than they (Balk, 1981, 1983). In one study of adolescent parental grief, however, younger adolescents (15 years of age and below) had lower grades on their report cards than did adolescents who were older than 15 when the parent died (Gray, 1987).

Deaths of Parents

The early studies of adolescent parental grief manifested the same limitations found in much of the research into adolescent sibling grief. A notable exception is the longitudinal work done in the early 1990s at Massachusetts General Hospital. Silverman, Worden, and Nickman (1992; Silverman & Worden, 1992; Worden, 1996; Worden & Silverman, 1993) studied the trajectory of grief experienced by children and adolescents during the first two years following the death of a parent. Their Child Bereavement Study provided multiple measures of change over time. In addition, nonbereaved youth participated in the study as controls, allowing comparisons to determine if changes over time were attributable to bereavement. Because sufficient numbers of children and adolescents were included in the study, the researchers were also able to compare bereaved adolescents with bereaved children to identify any differences associated with age.

Worden (1996) used Fleming and Adolph's (1986) model when discussing outcomes for the adolescents in the Child Bereavement Study. For example, one of the Fleming and Adolph tasks involves the predictability of events. Worden reported that bereaved adolescents were more anxious and fearful over time, compared to nonbereaved adolescents, and thought it reasonable that such reactions stemmed from "the lack of predictability in their lives caused by the death of a parent" (Worden, 1996, p. 90). Development of self-image is another normative task. The self-image of bereaved adolescents in the Child Bereavement Study manifested itself in differing ways: Although bereaved adolescents considered their conduct and academic performance inferior to that of their nonbereaved peers, they also considered themselves more mature than nonbereaved youth. Worden (1996, p. 90) suggested that "perhaps this was compensatory behavior on their part to make up for deficits in esteem."

Bereaved adolescents in the Child Bereavement Study displayed more difficulties getting along with others than did nonbereaved peers. Worden concluded that the bereaved adolescents were managing less effectively the core developmental issue of gaining a sense of belonging.

Tyson-Rawson (1993, 1996) engaged in a grounded-theory analysis of the responses of female college students whose fathers had died. More than half of her small sample indicated a continuing presence of their fathers in their lives. From a systems theory perspective, she examined adolescent grief over parental death within the contexts of both family and peer relations. She found that few peers were willing to talk with her research participants about the bereavement or even about their fathers. Bereaved college students find it dismaying that few nonbereaved peers are willing to talk to them about their experience. It is dismaying to them that few peers feel comfortable in the presence of someone who is bereaved. Wrenn

(1999), for instance, noted that one of the central issues for grieving college students is learning "how to respond to people who ignore their grief, or who tell them that they need to get on with life, that it's not good for them to continue to grieve" (p. 134). Tyson-Rawson also reported on the complex issues facing a family as it struggles to deal with the death of a parent, including (a) finding a language to talk about the person who died; (b) reallocating roles within the family structure; and (c) dealing with dissynchronous expressions of grief (for instance, a son and a daughter bereft over a father's death may manifest their feelings of loss differently than each other and differently than their mother).

From a different perspective, Balk and Vesta (1998) conducted a longitudinal case study of a college student whose father had died. This study used multiple measures gathered several times, used both quantitative and qualitative methods, and made comparisons to a larger sample of bereaved college students. Discrepancies between quantitative and qualitative observations, however, led the authors to question the validity of data. They leaned toward "trusting (the student's) nondirected, open-ended comments as more descriptive of her" (Balk & Vesta, 1998, p. 37). Thus various strengths of this case study—longitudinal design, multiple and repeated measures, and multiple methods—appeared to butt into issues separating quantitative and qualitative research. That is, rigorous quantitative measurement provides precision but may be unable to investigate beyond the surface of bereavement phenomena. Sophisticated qualitative methodology achieves gains in understanding human experiences but offers unsure powers of generalizing bereavement results to larger populations. We return to this issue when discussing quantitative and qualitative methodology.

Important advances have thus been made in understanding adolescent bereavement over parental death as researchers used longitudinal methodology and, in some cases, examined bereavement phenomena using qualitative methods. The Child Bereavement Study (Worden, 1996) set an example of a carefully designed quantitative study of the trajectory of bereavement over parental death. The Balk and Vesta (1998) study showed that quantitative measures possess limitations and accented the need for triangulation using both qualitative and quantitative procedures. Tyson-Rawson (1996) used grounded theory methods and family systems theory to explore the ramifications of a father's death in college students' lives.

Deaths of Peers and Friends

Grief over the deaths of peers and friends is an understudied area in adolescent bereavement research. This oversight is odd, given the increased importance that peers gain in the lives of adolescents and an increased mortality during adolescence because of accidental death, homicide, and suicide. Research on this topic has shared many of the limitations characteristic of the research literature on sibling bereavement during adolescence. However, descriptive findings have laid the beginnings for further work.

In a case study of the reactions of high school students 18 months after the death of a popular peer, McNeil, Silliman, and Swihart (1991) reported that the youth had camouflaged from adults and each other their ongoing anger, distress, and confusion about the death. The research process brought these feelings into the open and led the researchers to discuss obligations to bereaved adolescent research participants. For example, McNeil et al. (1991) noted that bereavement research has an emotional impact on the participants, and they wrote, "in the process of seeking answers to the puzzles of grief, researchers must also provide some dependable sources of immediate or eventual therapeutic support" (p. 140). They linked this obligation to the common requirements for human participants research and considered such an obligation "a mark of professional integrity" (p. 140).

O'Brien, Goodenow, and Espin (1991) studied adolescents' responses to the nonsuicide deaths of peers. The researchers noted that reactions to suicide had dominated literature on adolescent reactions to peer death. They interviewed ten college students who in high school had lost a friend to death. The students said the death had made a lasting change in their lives, unlike other deaths that they had experienced. They had found it difficult talking about the death of a friend, particularly when neither their parents nor their peers had been willing to do so. Before meeting the researchers, no one else seemed interested in the adolescents' grief experience or even knew how to talk with them about the death.

Oltjenbruns (1996) noted that grief following the death of a friend is disenfranchised and often tainted with survivor guilt. She pointed out that such grief can affect relationships with other friends and may eventually lead to estrangement of other friends and an increase in grief. Oltjenbruns termed these phenomena incremental grief and secondary loss. We might ask, therefore, are secondary losses obstacles to developing intimacy? Do crises over secondary losses lead to learning new ways of achieving the fundamental task of developing intimacy?

Oltjenbruns (1991) also examined positive outcomes following bereavement over a friend's death. Nearly all persons interviewed mentioned at least one positive outcome, such as gaining a deeper appreciation of life, strengthening problem-solving skills, improving communication skills, and acquiring emotional strength.

ISSUES AT STAKE IN THE ADOLESCENT BEREAVEMENT RESEARCH DOMAINS

The chapter concludes with a consideration of five issues: (a) the need for cultural pluralism, (b) the need for scientific openness, (c) methodological issues, (d) extension of research topics, and (e) ethical obligations.

The Need for Cultural Pluralism

Most research on adolescent bereavement has been done with middle-class, White populations in the United States. Some studies, however, have examined adolescents from other cultures.

Eisenbruch (1991) studied the reactions of Cambodian adolescent refugees, some of whom were placed in foster care in the United States and some in group care in Australia. The adolescents had been subjected to deeply shocking experiences in Cambodia, resulting in posttraumatic stress disorders. However, their displacement into a foreign culture produced what Eisenbruch termed "cultural bereavement." In many cases, cultural bereavement manifestations incorporated what outsiders would consider posttraumatic stress disorder. This cultural bereavement took many forms, and allowed some adolescents to understand their distress by providing a framework for interpreting their many losses.

Israeli researchers (Bachar, Caneti, Bonne, Denour, & Shalev, 1997) reported on the psychological well-being and psychiatric symptoms of bereaved and nonbereaved Israeli adolescents who ranged in age from 13 to 17. Twenty-three adolescents were grieving war-related deaths, 19 were grieving deaths resulting from vehicular accidents, and 829 were not bereaved. Instruments used included the Brief Symptom Inventory, the General Well-Being Scale, the Parental Bonding Instrument, and the Perceived Social Support—Family/Friend Measure (Derogatis & Spencer, 1982; Dupuy, 1975; Parker, Tulping, & Brown, 1979; Procidano & Heller, 1983). Adolescents grieving war-related deaths differed from their peers grieving deaths resulting from accidents: The former group had higher well-being scores and lower psychiatric symptom scores than the adolescents bereaved as a result of accidental deaths. The war-bereaved adolescents' well-being and psychiatric symptom scores indicated that they were healthier than the normal nonbereaved population. The issue of constructing meaning out of the death was seen to play a prominent part in coping with a battlefield death versus an accidental death.

Other examples of research sensitive to cultural diversity include Oltjenbruns's (1989, 1991) studies of grief reactions of Hispanic college students and Barrett's (1991, 1993) examinations of the reactions of African American youth to violence and death. In a study of homicidal violence, Barrett (1996) posed several theses to explain African American adolescent violence, including a subculture of violence, Black rage, economic deprivation, and the politics of the economics of crime.

The Need for Scientific Openness

The need for greater scientific openness is well-illustrated by considering the topics religion and spirituality, and researchers' appreciation of both quantitative and qualitative research.

Scholarly Inattention to Religion and Spirituality

Research into adolescent bereavement would benefit from studies on the role of spirituality and religion in the lives of grieving adolescents. We sense a degree of inattention to spirituality and religion on the part of some researchers. Perhaps there is a concern over being tainted with belief in superstition.

There have been some examinations of the role of religion for bereaved adolescents. For example, Balk (1983, 1990), Floerchinger (1991), Gray (1987), and LaGrand (1986) have noted that many bereaved adolescents report religion as helpful. Models for coping with life crises also see potential value for both religion and spirituality (Moos & Schaefer, 1986; Pargament, 1997). However, it is clear that religion and spirituality are distinct. It is possible to be spiritual without being religious, and perhaps possible to be religious without being spiritual. What may be required is more careful consideration of what it means to be religious and what it means to be spiritual (see Balk, 1999; Balk & Hogan, 1995).

Religion involves organized, systematic efforts to provide access to the sacred, although these efforts can at times become influenced with desire for control of, rather than openness to, what is holy. Spirituality connotes the human ability to seek meaning and connectedness, experience wonder and transcendence, and express awe.

We assert that all who grieve are engaged in a spiritual task—that is, in a profound quest for meaning. Bereaved adolescents and bereaved adults alike acknowledge that grief leads them to ask questions and to search for meaning; those are spiritual tasks. Researchers need to let the bereaved tell their stories, some of which have religious as well as spiritual themes.

Openness Toward Quantitative and Qualitative Research

The dichotomy between qualitative and quantitative research methodologies is evident in the bereavement research field. This dichotomy manifests itself in two ways. Rather than seeing in rigorous, systematic qualitative inquiry a rich means for understanding experiences filled with human volition, meaning, and wonder, some scholars dismiss qualitative approaches as merely anecdotal and unreliable. Similarly, rather than seeing in rigorous, quantitative inquiry a means to achieve precision, validity, and reliability in knowledge, some scholars dismiss quantitative approaches as vain efforts to use both numbers and very carefully designed procedures to explain phenomena.

Methodological Issues

Most studies in the field of bereavement research, certainly in adolescent bereavement research, are retrospective and cross-sectional. They usually lack control groups. Very little is known about the trajectory of adolescent grief because few studies have used longitudinal designs. The premier example of a longitudinal study of grief of children and adolescents following the death of a parent is the Child Bereavement Study mentioned earlier (Silverman et al., 1992; Silverman & Worden, 1992; Worden, 1996; Worden & Silverman, 1993). Because of the careful design of this study, the authors can describe changes at four months, one year, and two years following the death. Because of the presence of control group participants, changes over time for bereaved and nonbereaved youth can be compared.

Some of Balk's work with bereaved college students at Kansas State University was longitudinal. Published results include (a) analyses of Thematic Apperception Test (TAT) stories written by bereaved and nonbereaved college students (Balk et al., 1998); (b) an examination of bereaved college students' attachment to the person who died (Balk, 1996); and (c) a case study following a college student for four years after the death of her father (Balk & Vesta, 1998).

Because the favored research methods in bereavement research with adolescents have been cross-sectional and retrospective, scholars have produced singular snapshots of adolescent grief but have yet to produce a motion picture of how the snapshots fit together over time. Cross-sectional studies that gather data at one point in time, that ask persons to compare the present with what things used to be like, and that then make inferences about changes over time, do not yield such a picture.

Longitudinal studies could help us to answer such important questions as, "What is the trajectory of adolescent grief?"; "How does the trajectory of grief change as adolescents move from one phase of adolescence into another?"; "How does attachment influence the trajectory of grief for adolescents?"; "Does an ongoing attachment to the deceased emerge as time elapses from a death?"; "What models of development can best explain changes over time as bereaved early adolescents grow into adults?"; "Do interventions make any lasting changes for the better in the lives of bereaved participants?" These questions present an agenda for the next generation of adolescent bereavement research studies.

Extensions of Research Topics

Asking whether interventions make any lasting changes for the better in the lives of bereaved participants infers a need for intervention-outcome studies. Knowledge is needed about outcomes following bereavement, and that need links into the call for carefully designed longitudinal studies. Interventions designed to assist bereaved adolescents should be empirically tested. Researchers have an ethical obligation to do more than gather information: We are obligated to apply our scholarship to assist persons in need (Balk, 1995b, in press).

Outcome Studies

How do adolescents emerge from grief work? Some scholars are convinced that adolescents emerge from their bereavement more emotionally and interpersonally mature than unaffected persons their own age (Balk, 1981; Hogan, 1986; Oltjenbruns, 1991). One sign of the maturity forged in the crucible of grief is the typical grit and strength that bereaved adolescents develop to endure someone else's sorrow and pain. They do not literally or figuratively flee when someone else is in emotional distress.

However, the outcomes for some bereaved adolescents seem troubling. Findings from the Child Bereavement Study (Worden, 1996) indicated that bereaved adolescents lagged behind their nonbereaved peers on several important developmental tasks and core issues. Hogan and DeSantis (1992) reported that ongoing, intense grief reactions were associated with adolescents whose self-concepts were weak. It seems likely that bereavement itself did not cause these adolescents to have ongoing problems but rather they brought predisposing conditions of vulnerability to the crises they were facing.

Bereavement Interventions

There is some literature on interventions with bereaved adolescents. Seldom are the studies longitudinal, and seldom do they involve control groups. However, some cases such as postventions in a high school following a suicide defy the normal notion of establishing a control group. The term *postvention* "refers to all the activities and support that help with the traumatic aftereffects among survivors of profound loss experiences" (Hill & Foster, 1996, p. 250).

Interventions with bereaved adolescents have included support groups and self-help groups (Berson, 1988; Riordan & Beggs, 1987; Tedeschi, 1996), postvention efforts within school systems (Catone & Schatz, 1991; Hill & Foster, 1996; Komar, 1994), campus-wide efforts with college students (Rickgarn, 1996), and therapy (Valentine, 1996). Cates (1986) has reported on an approach with adolescents in residential treatment. Lang (1992) reviewed art therapy as an intervention with bereaved adolescents.

An apparently successful—but time-limited—alternative was provided in a mutual support group intervention offered at Kansas State University in college classrooms and off-campus buildings. This intervention involved bereaved students meeting twice a week over a four-week period for two or more hours in a meeting facilitated by a graduate student in marriage and family therapy. The meetings focused on a framework for coping with life crises and on the sharing of personal experiences. This intervention needs to be studied further to ensure that it is effective over more than the duration of the support sessions (Balk et al., 1993). Strengths of this intervention study were the use of both a bereaved control group and a nonbereaved control group; multiple measures repeated on several occasions; and the use of both quantitative and qualitative methodology. Calculations of statistical power demonstrated treatment effects in some variables. Drawbacks to this intervention study were a wide variation in time since the deaths and unexpected attrition by members of the bereaved control group (Balk & Howard, 1999).

Anschuetz (1990) developed and implemented a group counseling model with bereaved adolescents between the ages of 14 and 18. The deaths had occurred within the past twelve months. Five or six bereaved adolescents made up each group, and coleaders facilitated each group. Outcomes included increased personal insight and the use of a safe environment in which to express concerns over school, families, and friends. Anschuetz concluded that many stakeholders in the adolescents' lives remain unaware of the concerns of bereaved adolescents, and she suggested more efforts be exerted to teach counselors about bereavement. A strength of this study is the limits on time since the death. A drawback is the lack of a control group.

Intervention studies with bereaved adolescents need to include several characteristics to increase the prospects of meaningful results. In addition to using multiple measures, uniform periods of time since the deaths, a clear developmental framework, designs overcoming threats to statistical power, and the presence of control groups, intervention studies need to reduce attrition. These considerations involve both a design issue and an ethical issue: When intervention studies contain design flaws, they obstruct meaningful analysis and generalization. When they are flawed by threats that can be foreseen and checked—such as high attrition rates from a control group that jeopardize a study—issues of design competency and ethical obligations intermingle (Balk, 1995b).

Ethical Obligations

What are the ethical obligations scholars incur when they study bereaved individuals? (See chapter 6, this volume). Our test case is the study of bereaved students on college campuses.

University researchers contract ethical obligations when they conduct research with bereaved college students. These obligations fundamentally are of a practical nature and arise for several reasons. These reasons include

(a) what grief entails; (b) the incidence and prevalence of grief on college campuses; (c) the impact of grief on late adolescent developmental transitions; (d) the basic notion of scholarship; and (e) the idea that universities are communities of scholarship, care, and compassion. University researchers who study bereaved college students are obligated to extend their research from a scholarship of discovery to a scholarship of application (Boyer, 1990; Glassick, Huber, & Maeroff, 1997). In short, we contend that university researchers who study bereaved college students should apply their research findings and work within the university so that programmatic efforts are made to assist bereaved students.

CONCLUSION

Research into bereavement during adolescence needs a theoretical synthesis that will provide clear explanation, suggest the course interventions should take with grieving adolescents at risk for pathologic reactions, and prompt further studies. We do not have that theoretical synthesis now. Two beginnings have been supplied in the writings of Fleming and Adolph (1986) and Hogan and DeSantis (1996a, 1996b).

Components of what a theoretical synthesis requires are suggested by the structure of this chapter: an understanding of adolescence, appreciation for the developmental tasks and transitions facing adolescents, analysis of the impact and the trajectory of adolescent grief over the deaths of friends and family members, and openness to quantitative and qualitative methods.

First, the theory must incorporate knowledge about adolescent development, including the growing evidence for phases in a progression from early through middle to later adolescence. Specifically, this developmental approach will focus some attention on the developmental tasks and transitions that adolescence presents to youth and look at the influence of grief in meeting these tasks and moving through these transitions. Further, this approach will assume a life-span developmental focus, looking for ongoing changes attributable to coping with grief and looking to see if nonbereaved peers experience such changes.

Second, longitudinal studies are needed to chart the trajectory of adolescent grief. These studies can be quantitative or qualitative and can even provide a happy comingling of each approach if the researchers have the appropriate team assembled.

Third, openness to the use of multiple methods is needed, most particularly an openness to the value of quantitative and qualitative approaches. We need some very carefully designed qualitative studies, such as would be suggested by grounded theory (Glaser & Strauss, 1967; Strauss & Corbin, 1990, 1994) to determine just what the data suggest about a theory of adolescent bereavement. At the same time we need to proceed on the other front of testing hypotheses, an approach that assumes a certain theoretical perspective is in place already. This two-fold approach is, thus, paradoxical. Perhaps what is more accurate to say is that hypothesis testing will be provisional in nature until an established theory of adolescent development captures the minds and imaginations of researchers.

Fourth, the unique developmental tasks and transitions of adolescence intertwine with the demands and effects of grief. Adults in the midst of grief normally are not faced with completing such momentous developmental challenges as forging an autonomous identity, making career decisions, and entering into stable, intimate relationships (Balk, 1995a; Erikson, 1968). No claim is being made that grief is more intense for adolescents than for persons in other times of the life cycle; for one thing there have yet to be extended studies of the trajectory of adolescent grief and other studies comparing the trajectories of adult and adolescent grief. We contend that the consequences of bereavement are unique for adolescents, given the momentous developmental tasks that poorly managed grief can obstruct (perhaps that even well-managed grief can obstruct). Although there is optimism about the resiliency of youth (Bandura, 1964; Best, Hauser, & Allen, 1997; Jew & Green, 1998; Weiss, 1979) and some evidence that adolescents typically benefit from managing life crises (Balk, 1981; Hogan, 1986; Offer, 1969), it would be a mistake to assume that bereavement does not place adolescents in harm's way. A theory of adolescent grief will need to link developmental transitions and tasks to the experiences and outcomes of adolescent bereavement.

REFERENCES

Anschuetz, B. L. (1990). *The development and implementation of a group counselling intervention model with bereaved adolescents.* Unpublished doctoral dissertation, University of Toronto, Ontario.

Bachar, E., Caneti, L., Bonne, O., Denour, A., & Shalev, A. Y. (1997). Psychological well-being and ratings of psychiatric symptoms in bereaved Israeli adolescents: Differential effect of war- versus accident-related bereavement. *Journal of Nervous and Mental Disease, 185,* 402–406.

Balk, D. E. (1981). *Sibling death during adolescence: Self concept and bereavement reactions.* Unpublished doctoral dissertation, University of Illinois, Champaign-Urbana.

Balk, D. E. (1983). Adolescents' grief reactions and self-concept perceptions following sibling death: A study of 33 teenagers. *Journal of Youth and Adolescence, 12,* 137–161.

Balk, D. E. (1990). The self-concepts of bereaved adolescents: Sibling death and its aftermath. *Journal of Adolescent Research, 5,* 112–132.

Balk, D. E. (1995a). *Adolescent development: Early through late adolescence.* Pacific Grove, CA: Brooks/Cole.

Balk, D. E. (1995b). Bereavement research using control groups: Ethical obligations and questions. *Death Studies, 19*, 123–138.

Balk, D. E. (1996). Attachment and the reactions of bereaved college students: A longitudinal study. In D. Klass, P. R. Silverman, & S. L. Nickman (Eds.), *Continuing bonds: New understandings of grief* (pp. 311–328). Washington, DC: Taylor & Francis.

Balk, D. E. (1997). Death, bereavement, and college students: A descriptive analysis. *Mortality, 2*, 207–220.

Balk, D. E. (Ed.). (1999). Spirituality and bereavement. *Death Studies, 23*(6). [Special issue].

Balk, D. E. (in press). College student bereavement, scholarship, and the university: A call for university engagement. *Death Studies.*

Balk, D. E., & Corr, C. A. (1996). Adolescents, developmental tasks, and encounters with death and bereavement. In C. A. Corr & D. E. Balk (Eds.), *Handbook of adolescent death and bereavement* (pp. 3–24). New York: Springer.

Balk, D. E., & Hogan, N. S. (1995). Religion, spirituality, and bereaved adolescents. In D. Adams & E. Deveau (Eds.), *Beyond the innocence of childhood. Volume 3. Helping children and adolescents cope with death and bereavement* (pp. 61–88). Amityville, NY: Baywood.

Balk, D. E., & Howard, T. L. (1999). *Social support with bereaved college students: Power analysis of a preventive intervention research.* Manuscript submitted for review.

Balk, D. E., Lampe, S., Sharpe, B., Schwinn, S., Holen, K., Cook, L., & Dubois, R. (1998). TAT results in a longitudinal study of bereaved college students. *Death Studies, 22*, 3–21.

Balk, D. E., Tyson-Rawson, K., & Colletti-Wetzel, J. (1993). Social support as an intervention with bereaved college students. *Death Studies, 17*, 427–450.

Balk, D. E., & Vesta, L. (1998). Psychological development during four years of bereavement: A longitudinal case study. *Death Studies, 22*, 23–41.

Balk, D. E., Wettemann, B. A., & Hair, C. (1998). *Students and their life experiences.* Unpublished manuscript, Oklahoma State University, Stillwater.

Balmer, L. E. (1992). *Adolescent sibling bereavement: Mediating effects of family environment and personality.* Unpublished doctoral dissertation, York University, Toronto, Ontario.

Bandura, A. (1964). The stormy decade: Fact or fiction? *Psychology in the Schools, 1*, 224–231.

Barrett, R. K. (1991). Homicide and suicide: Who is at risk. *The American Black Male, 3*(2), 4–8; *3*(3), 4–6.

Barrett, R. K. (1993). Urban adolescent homicidal violence: An emerging public heath concern. *The Urban League Review, 16*, 67–75.

Barrett, R. K. (1996). Adolescents, homicidal violence, and death. In C. A. Corr

& D. E. Balk (Eds.), *Handbook of adolescent death and bereavement* (pp. 42–64). New York: Springer.

Berson, R. J. (1988). A bereavement group for college students. *American Journal of College Health, 37*, 101–108.

Best, K. M., Hauser, S. T., & Allen, J. P. (1997). Predicting young adult competencies: Adolescent era parent and individual differences. *Journal of Adolescent Research, 12*, 90–112.

Boyer, E. L. (1990). *Scholarship reconsidered: Priorities of the professoriate.* Princeton, NJ: Carnegie Foundation for the Advancement of Teaching.

Bright, P. D. (1987). Adolescent pregnancy and loss. *Maternal-Child Nursing Journal, 16*, 1–12.

Brown, B. H. (1993). *Adolescent bereavement and pet death: Linkages among bonding, bereavement, and gender.* Unpublished doctoral dissertation, University of Virginia, Charlottesville.

Cates, J. A. (1986). Grief therapy in residential treatment: A model for intervention. *Child Care Quarterly, 15*, 147–158.

Catone, W. V., & Schatz, M. T. (1991). The crisis moment: A school's response to the event of suicide. *School Psychology International, 12*, 17–23.

Derogatis, L. R., & Spencer, P. M. (1982). *The Brief Symptom Inventory: Administration, scoring, and procedures. Manual I.* Baltimore: Clinical Psychometrics Research.

DeVaul, R. A., Zisook, S., & Faschingbauer, T. R. (1979). Clinical aspects of grief and bereavement. *Primary Care, 6*, 391–402.

Dupuy, D. F. (1975). *Utility of the National Center for Health Statistics' General Well-Being Schedule in the assessment of self representations of subjective well-being.* Paper presented at the National Conference on the Evaluation of Drug, Alcohol, and Mental Health Programs.

Eisenbruch, M. (1991). From post-traumatic stress disorder to cultural bereavement: Diagnosis of Southeast Asian refugees. *Social Science and Medicine, 33*, 673–680.

Erikson, E. H. (1968). *Identity: Youth and crisis.* New York: Norton.

Ewalt, P. L., & Perkins, L. (1979). The real experience of death among adolescents: An empirical study. *Social Casework, 60*, 547–551.

Federal Bureau of Investigation. (1992). *Crime in the United States. 1991. Uniform crime reports.* Washington, DC: U.S. Department of Justice.

Fleming, S. J., & Adolph, R. (1986). Helping bereaved adolescents: Needs and responses. In C. A. Corr & J. N. McNeil (Eds.), *Adolescence and death* (pp. 97–118). New York: Springer.

Fleming, S. J., & Balmer, L. E. (1996). Bereavement in adolescence. In C. A. Corr & D. E. Balk (Eds.), *Handbook of adolescent death and bereavement* (pp. 139–154). New York: Springer.

Floerchinger, D. S. (1991). Bereavement in late adolescence: Interventions on college campuses. *Journal of Adolescent Research, 6*, 146–156.

Glaser, B., & Strauss, A. L. (1967). *The discovery of grounded theory: Strategies for qualitative research.* Chicago: Aldine.

Glassick, C. E., Huber, M. T., & Maeroff, G. I. (1997). *Scholarship assessed: Evaluation of the professoriate.* San Francisco: Jossey-Bass.

Gray, R. (1987). Adolescent response to the death of a parent. *Journal of Youth and Adolescence, 16,* 511–525.

Hill, D. C., & Foster, Y. M. (1996). Postvention with early and middle adolescents. In C. A. Corr & D. E. Balk (Eds.), *Handbook of adolescent death and bereavement* (pp. 250–272). New York: Springer.

Hogan, N. S. (1986). *An investigation of the adolescent sibling bereavement process and adaptation.* Unpublished doctoral dissertation, Loyola University, Chicago.

Hogan, N. S. (1990). Hogan Sibling Inventory of Bereavement. In J. Touliatos, B. Perlmutter, & M. Strauss (Eds.), *Handbook of family measurement techniques* (p. 524). Newbury Park, CA: Sage.

Hogan, N. S., & Balk, D. E. (1990). Adolescent reactions to sibling death: Perceptions of mothers, fathers, and teenagers. *Nursing Research, 39,* 103–106.

Hogan, N. S., & DeSantis, L. (1992). Adolescent sibling bereavement: An ongoing attachment. *Qualitative Health Research, 2,* 159–177.

Hogan, N. S., & DeSantis, L. (1996a). Adolescent sibling bereavement: Toward a new theory. In C. A. Corr & D. E. Balk (Eds.), *Handbook of adolescent death and bereavement* (pp. 173–195). New York: Springer.

Hogan, N. S., & DeSantis, L. (1996b). Basic constructs of a theory of adolescent sibling bereavement. In D. Klass, P. R. Silverman, & S. L. Nickman (Eds.), *Continuing bonds: New understandings of grief* (pp. 235–256). Washington, DC: Taylor & Francis.

Hogan, N. S., & Greenfield, D. B. (1991). Adolescent sibling bereavement: Symptomatology in a large community sample. *Journal of Adolescent Research, 6,* 97–112.

Jacobs, S. (1999). *Traumatic grief: Diagnosis, treatment, and prevention.* Philadelphia: Brunner/Mazel.

Jarolmen, J. J. (1996). *A comparison of the human grief reaction: Focusing on pet loss and bereavement.* Unpublished doctoral dissertation, Rutgers University.

Jew, C. L., & Green, K. E. (1998). Effects of risk factors on adolescents' resiliency and coping. *Psychological Reports, 82,* 675–678.

Komar, A. A. (1994). Adolescent school crises: Structure, issues and techniques for postventions. *International Journal of Adolescence & Youth, 5,* 35–46.

LaGrand, L. E. (1986). *Coping with separation and loss as a young adult: Theoretical and practical implications.* Springfield, IL: Charles C. Thomas.

Lang, L. A. (1992). *Expressions of grief: Art therapy used as an intervention in the treatment of bereaved adolescents.* Unpublished Master's thesis, Ursuline College, Pepper Pike, OH.

Lindemann, E. (1944). Symptomatology and management of acute grief. *American Journal of Psychiatry, 101,* 141–148.

McNeil, J. N., Silliman, B., & Swihart, J. J. (1991). Helping adolescents cope with the death of a peer. *Journal of Adolescent Research, 6*, 132–145.

Moos, R. H., & Shaefer, J. A. (1986). Life transitions and crises: A conceptual overview. In R. H. Moos (Ed.), *Coping with life crises: An integrated approach* (pp. 3–28). New York: Plenum Press.

O'Brien, J. M., Goodenow, C., & Espin, O. (1991). Adolescents' reactions to the death of a peer. *Adolescence, 26*, 431–440.

Offer, D. (1969). *The psychological world of the teenager.* New York: Basic Books.

Oltjenbruns, K. A. (1989). *Ethnicity and the grief response: Mexican-American and Anglo college students.* Unpublished doctoral dissertation, University of Colorado at Boulder.

Oltjenbruns, K. A. (1991). Positive outcomes of adolescents' experience with grief. *Journal of Adolescent Research, 6*, 43–53.

Oltjenbruns, K. A. (1996). Death of a friend during adolescence: Issues and impacts. In C. A. Corr & D. E. Balk (Eds.), *Handbook of adolescent death and bereavement* (pp. 196–215). New York: Springer.

Osterweis, M., Solomon, F., & Green, M. (Eds.). (1984). *Bereavement: Reactions, consequences, and care.* Washington, DC: National Academy Press.

Pargament, K. I. (1997). *The psychology of religion and coping: Theory, research, practice.* New York: Guilford Press.

Parker, G., Tulping, H., & Brown, L. B. (1979). A parental bonding instrument. *British Journal of Medical Psychology, 65*, 78–86.

Parkes, C. M. (1998). *Bereavement: Studies of grief in adult life* (3rd ed.). Madison, WI: International Universities Press.

Procidano, M. E., & Heller, K. (1983). Measures of perceived social support from friends and from family: Three validation studies. *American Journal of Community Psychology, 11*, 1–23.

Raphael, B. (1983). *The anatomy of bereavement.* New York: Basic Books.

Rickgarn, R. L. V. (1987). The death response team: Responding to the forgotten grievers. *Journal of Counseling and Development, 66*, 197–199.

Rickgarn, R. L. V. (1996). The need for postvention on college campuses: A rationale and case study findings. In C. A. Corr & D. E. Balk (Eds.), *Handbook of adolescent death and bereavement* (pp. 273–292). New York: Springer.

Riordan, R. J., & Beggs, M. S. (1987). Counselors and self-help groups. *Journal of Counseling and Development, 65*, 427–429.

Shaefer, S. J. M. (1996). *Adolescent mothers: Functioning after bereavement.* Unpublished doctoral dissertation, University of Maryland at Baltimore.

Silver, R. L., & Wortman, C. B. (1980). Coping with undesirable life events. In J. Garber & M. E. P. Seligman (Eds.), *Human helplessness: Theory and applications* (pp. 279–340). New York: Academic Press.

Silverman, P. R., Nickman, S., & Worden, J. W. (1992). Detachment revisited: The child's reconstruction of a dead parent. *American Journal of Orthopsychiatry, 62*, 494–503.

Silverman, P. R., & Worden, J. W. (1992). Children's reactions in the early months after the death of a parent. *American Journal of Orthopsychiatry, 62*, 93–104.

Strauss, A., & Corbin, J. (1990). *Basics of qualitative research: Grounded theory procedures and techniques.* Newbury Park, CA: Sage.

Strauss, A., & Corbin, J. (1994). Grounded theory methodology. In N. K. Denzin & Y. S. Lincoln (Eds.), *Handbook of qualitative research* (pp. 273–285). Thousand Oaks, CA: Sage.

Stroebe, M. S., Stroebe, W., & Hansson, R. O. (1993). *Handbook of bereavement: Theory, research, and intervention.* New York: Cambridge University Press.

Stroebe, W., & Stroebe, M. (1987). *Bereavement and health.* New York: Cambridge University Press.

Tedeschi, R. G. (1996). Support groups for bereaved adolescents. In C. A. Corr & D. E. Balk (Eds.), *Handbook of adolescent death and bereavement* (pp. 293–311). New York: Springer.

Tyson-Rawson, K. J. (1993). *College women and bereavement: Late adolescence and father death.* Unpublished doctoral dissertation, Kansas State University, Manhattan.

Tyson-Rawson, K. J. (1996). Adolescent responses to the death of a parent. In C. A. Corr & D. E. Balk (Eds.), *Handbook of adolescent death and bereavement* (pp. 155–172). New York: Springer.

Valentine, L. (1996). Professional interventions to assist adolescents who are coping with death and bereavement. In C. A. Corr & D. E. Balk (Eds.), *Handbook of adolescent death and bereavement* (pp. 312–328). New York: Springer.

Weiss, R. S. (1979). Growing up a little faster: The experience of growing up in a single-parent household. *Journal of Social Issues, 35*, 97–111.

Wettemann, B. A. (1999). *Bereavement and college students.* Unpublished manuscript, Oklahoma State University, Stillwater.

Wheeler, S. R. (1997). *The impact of early pregnancy loss on adolescent women age 13–19.* Unpublished doctoral dissertation, Indiana University, Bloomington.

Worden, J. W. (1996). *Children and grief: When a parent dies.* New York: Guilford Press.

Worden, J. W., & Silverman, P. R. (1993). Grief and depression in newly widowed parents with school-age children. *Omega, 11*, 355–361.

Wrenn, R. L. (1999). The grieving college student. In J. D. Davidson & K. J. Doka (Eds.), *Living with grief: At work, at school, at worship* (pp. 131–141). Levittown, PA: Brunner/Mazel.

10

PARENTAL RESPONSE TO CHILD LOSS ACROSS THE LIFE CYCLE: CLINICAL AND RESEARCH PERSPECTIVES

SIMON SHIMSHON RUBIN AND RUTH MALKINSON

> And the king was much moved, and went up to the chamber over the gate, and wept: and as he went, thus he said, O my son Absalom, my son, my son Absalom! would God I had died for thee, O Absalom, my son, my son! —2 Samuel 18:33

The impetus for living things to reproduce and create offspring who will survive them is so basic to life that it is one of the fundamental truths of our world, like gravity or the sun. Through it, continuity and a kind of immortality are achieved. The human impetus to reproduce and create offspring embraces both the biological and the symbolical. People both create life and give meaning to that life as part of existence and self-preservation (Neimeyer, Keese, & Fortner, 2000). When one's child dies, however, a significant portion of the parent's life energy can effectively die with that child. This can have negative results for the individual, the family, and the community (Rubin, 1993). The majority of parents, al-

The authors wish to thank Naamah Bar-On and Dafnah Haimovitz for their assistance in the preparation of this chapter.

219

though deeply and permanently affected by the loss, do find a path to a productive and loving resumption of life.

In this chapter, we focus primarily on the impact of child loss on parents and on why and how this type of loss so severely disrupts the life patterns of those affected. In the opening section, we consider the parent–child bond and its meaning for parents. From there, we present a conceptual framework for viewing response to loss in the Two-Track Model of Bereavement (Rubin, 1984a, 1992, 2000; Rubin, Malkinson, & Witztum, 2000). We then illustrate this approach with select research, which sets forth a perspective of parental loss across the life cycle. Risk and mitigating factors in parental response to loss give an applied clinical dimension to this devastating life event and the processes by which it is woven into the fabric of parental and familial life.

The life span development of the human individual is mediated by culture and meaning systems, gender and biology, and personality features that develop in the crucible of the family of origin in the first years of life. Development, however, is a life-long process. The close kinship ties of the marital and parent–child bonds will affect the individual life trajectory in myriad ways. Although these may be less pervasive and formative than the early development of the human infant and young child, they are perhaps no less important. These attachment bonds of the nuclear family are linked to the very core of human existence (Bowlby, 1969).

As the child becomes an adult, he or she rejoins with his or her own parents in a fuller unfolding of human potential and experience. When that adult becomes a parent, a dimension of human potential linked to the parents of origin is opened (Anthony & Benedek, 1970; Sandler & Sandler, 1978; Stern, 1995). The importance and the significance of the parental role and the parental bond to children will undergo many changes over time. They will not end with any developmental milestone of the child, however, and as paradoxical as it may seem, certainly not with the death of a child (Klass, Silverman, & Nickman, 1996; Schiff, 1977).

The loss of a child can refer to things so disparate as the loss of a fetus or the death of a grown daughter or son who are themselves mature grandparents (Moss & Moss, 1996). In their impact on siblings and other family members, these losses will trigger many responses and share common features. They will be difficult to grieve for and to integrate into each person's life history (Rubin et al., 2000). Typically, however, it is the loss of a child to a mother and father that will possess the meaning and power to shake the adult personality to its very roots (Rubin, 1993). Many parents find themselves searching for what they did to cause this tragedy to befall them. Scientific and religious interpretations may be thinly veiled attempts to find these reasons.

Familial bereavement is known to be a major life crisis, and the loss process that parents undergo is particularly extensive and profound (Malkinson & Bar-Tur, in press; Rando, 1993; Rosenblatt & Burns, 1986; Walsh & McGoldrick, 1991). Parents' mourning for a dead child, as well as their emergence from it, have been described as unusually difficult and prolonged (Gorer, 1965; Klass, 1988; Lehman, Lang, Wortman, & Sorenson, 1989; Rubin, 1990, 1993). In the next section, a number of factors that make child loss so painful to bear are considered.

THE PARENT–CHILD BOND

The parental attachment bond to children is a result of powerful biological, evolutionary, and psychological forces operating to ensure that children will come into the world and be cared for (Anthony & Benedek, 1970). To survive, the human individual must regard the self and those things considered important to the self as deserving of protection. When the survival of the other is felt to be vital for the survival of the self, the self may engage in altruistic behavior that readily serves its own purposes. Spousal bonds are one kind of relationship in which the value of self and other function together in an adaptive state for all (Lopata, 1981). Children are a variation, and many would argue, the primary reason for the utility of couple bonds. Parents' spend emotional, financial, and physical resources for the benefit of their children and yet experience this as a giving to the self.

The ability of parents to establish a unique and meaningful love relationship with each of their children is an important feature of human attachment. The number of children is not the major predictor of the amount of love and attention a child will get in the family. It is rather the parent's reservoir of emotional resources that is the better predictor of the emotional experience afforded children (Rubin, 1993). When a child dies, the complex interplay of elements that are shaken precipitate a crisis of emotion and experience that is devastating as well as pervasive for parents (Breznitz, 2000; Lehman, Wortman & Williams, 1987).

The parent–child tie is by nature a dynamic and shifting relationship primed to weather a wide range of variation and stress over a lifetime (Bornstein, 1995; Fivaz-Depersuing et. al., 1994). Love and aggression, immature and mature sexuality, cooperation and competition, hope and disappointment will characterize the parent–child attachment bond across the life cycle (Belsky, 1988). The study of object relations has devoted much attention to the conceptualization of relationships (Bowlby, 1969, 1973, 1980; Rubin, 1999; Sandler & Sandler, 1978). This field has focused on the schema we have of people and the manner in which these schema reflect how we think of them and the interactions with their inner psychological representations within ourselves.

The parental representations of their own children have been studied from before birth. It has been shown that the nature and quality of the cognitive–emotional schema that prospective parents construct of their future child is a measurable and important feature of the developing relationship (Oppenheim, Koren-Kane, & Sagi, 2000; Stern, 1995). The attitudes and relationship to the schema of the child will undergo change as parents and child mature (Levi, 1989). Neither proximity nor distance, neither life nor death, neither conscious awareness nor studied avoidance are the major determinants of the internal representation and the covert relationship to them. Simply put, significant others are represented in the mind's eye significantly and complexly. These representations are no less a mental fact after a person's death—and often become even more so after it (Blatt, 1994; Horowitz, Wilner, Marmar, & Krupnick, 1980; Rubin, 1984a, 1984b, 1998).

A TWO-TRACK MODEL OF BEREAVEMENT: FUNCTIONING AND RELATIONSHIP TO THE DECEASED ACROSS THE LIFE CYCLE

Significant interpersonal loss can be conceptualized as a process that will affect subsequent modes of functioning. Indeed, disruption in function serves as a powerful indicator of the response to loss in the initial weeks and months following a death (Rubin et al., 2000). Perhaps more significantly in the long run, however, are the constellation and ways in which the deceased are conceptualized and remembered. These may serve as a *lifelong* measure of the response to loss (Rubin, 1984a, 1985, 1998, 1999, 2000). This bifocal approach to the understanding, measure, and intervention with loss is reflected in the Two-Track Model of Bereavement.

In our combined classical and empirically oriented Western view of the world, dysfunction is often equated with negative response. However, the reparative aspects of "not carrying on" should not be overlooked (Engel, 1961). Earlier in the century, Freud wrote that the depressive response to loss was normal and undeserving of intervention (1917/1957). This approach reflected his society's tolerance of grief and dysfunction as normative following loss (Siggins, 1966). Research on this topic suggests that dysfunction and depressive affect following loss vary greatly and are in fact deserving of more careful specification before reasoned conclusions can be drawn (Bowlby, 1980; Dichterman, 1989; Prigerson et al., 1995; Rubin & Schechter, 1997; Tamir, 1987). With problems in overt functioning, much of what is observed is relatively evident as suffering following loss. Less overt psychological construction of the loss and the deceased, however, deserves at least equal attention (Beutler, Machado, & Neufeldt, 1994; Horowitz et al., 1997; Strupp, 1969). A cardinal feature of relationships is that their mental representations affect the interaction and thus are of significant import in the bereavement process (Bowlby, 1980; Sandler & Sandler, 1978; Volkan, 1981).

The Two-Track Model of Bereavement includes the following main features: First, the bereavement response occurs along two main axes, each of which is multidimensional. The first axis or track is how people function naturally and how this functioning is affected by the cataclysmic life experience that loss may entail. The second is how people are involved in maintaining and changing their relationships with the memories and mental representations of the deceased. The bereaved individual may not always appreciate the extent or be aware of the nature of this relationship and their investment in it or of its consequences. Nonetheless, this component is critical for what the human bereavement response involves throughout the life cycle.

Second, the implications of the Two-Track Model of Bereavement are relevant for theory, research, and clinical and counseling interventions. One can always examine how far the bereaved person's response on each of the tracks is consistent with expectations along particular dimensions of functioning and relationship. Given the variation and fluctuation that characterize the process of response to loss, discrepancies will be interpreted differently by different people.

Third, the clinical implications of the model derive directly from the focus on both the functional and relational aspects of the response to loss. Interventions may deal directly with one or both domains of the response to loss (Rubin, 1999b). There is clearly some mutual interaction between the tracks of function and relationship to the deceased. A tabular representation of the model in clinical use is contained in Exhibit 10-1.

In considering these features of the response to loss, we engage in an examination of the bereaved individual's life from a variety of vantage

EXHIBIT 10-1
The Two-Track Model of Bereavement: A Multidimensional View

Track I: Functioning	Track II: Relationship to the Deceased
■ Anxiety ■ Depressive affect and cognitions ■ Somatic concerns ■ Symptoms of a psychiatric nature ■ Familial relationships ■ General interpersonal relations ■ Self-esteem and self-worth ■ Meaning structure ■ Work ■ Investment in life tasks	■ Imagery and memory ■ Emotional distance ■ Positive affect vis-à-vis deceased ■ Negative affect vis-à-vis deceased ■ Preoccupation with loss and the lost ■ Idealization ■ Conflict ■ Features of loss process (shock, searching, disorganization, and reorganization) ■ Impact on self-perception ■ Memorialization and transformation of the loss and the deceased

Source: Rubin, 1999.

points. Track I, general functioning, reflects the individual's adaptive re-action to life across a number of domains. Embodied in the Track I formulation, the individual's functioning across affective, interpersonal, somatic, and classical psychiatric indicators are considered. These components are often cited in the literature as characterizing response to bereavement (Bowlby, 1980; Rubin et al., 2000; Stroebe & Stroebe, 1987). For example, anxious and depressive features are central to the clinical assessment of individual functioning and remain so in assessment following loss (Strupp, Horowitz, & Lambert, 1997). Family as well as other relationships can provide much information about the bereaved person. Evaluating the extent and quality of interpersonal interactions reflect the emotional strength of the bereaved individual and the emotional support these interactions may provide. The state of the bereaved person's meaning matrixes that includes religious and other world-views is important (Parkes, 1975; Parkes, Laungani, & Young, 1997). These can indicate whether the bereaved individual has been disconnected from fundamental belief networks that provide critical inner emotional support and organization. For example, a parent may feel that the loss of a child is a failure of God. If, however, that failing seriously distances him or her from the previous positively experienced relationship with a spouse, faith community, or God, the consequences can be debilitating. The person may be cast adrift from the matrix of much that was familiar and supportive. Finally, the investment in life tasks manifests the ability of the bereaved person to be absorbed by something other than his or her own grief and mourning (Wikan, 1988). As is true for the bereaved person's ability to manage interpersonal relationships and work, the ability to invest in life tasks in a balanced fashion is a benchmark for understanding the response to loss.

Track II, the relationship to the deceased, captures the salient features of the interpersonal relationship to the deceased. First, the extent of the imagery and memories that the bereaved individual can and does experience sets the stage for the understanding of the relationship to the deceased. A bereaved individual who constantly avoids or is constantly involved with the overt or covert stimuli of the deceased is not maintaining an adaptive balance in dealing with the reorganization of loss. Likewise, the positive and negative affects associated with memories of the deceased; the extent of preoccupation with the loss; and the indications of idealization of and conflict with the deceased, provide a picture of the bereaved person's cognitive and emotional view of the deceased. The bereaved person's response to loss can be filtered through the features, but not necessarily the sequence, of the now-classic stage theory of Bowlby and Parkes (Bowlby, 1980; Parkes, 1986). The bereaved individual's description of the loss and the deceased will convey elements of shock, disorganization, and reorganization. The preponderance of each of these features, and their complex interplay, reflect the mix of the dynamic ways in which the deceased and the loss are currently integrated by the bereaved person. Proceeding further, we consider the extent to which thinking about the deceased leads to a negative self-view (e.g., I feel guilty whenever I think of the deceased; Horowitz et. al., 1980; Horowitz et al., 1984). These help us understand the ways in which the bereaved person constructs the relationship with the deceased (Rubin, 1996; Sadeh, Rubin, & Berman, 1993). Finally the memorialization process can teach us about the way in which the bereaved individual has transformed the relationship with the deceased into something more. It is the way in which the loss of a person has been transformed into something beyond grief and mourning and shades into the life fabric that is of interest (Malkinson & Witztum, in press; Pollock, 1989; Rubin et al., in press). We turn now to research studies that follow this perspective on loss.

REPRESENTATIVE RESEARCH FINDINGS REGARDING FUNCTIONING AND RELATIONSHIP TO THE DECEASED CHILD ACROSS THE LIFE CYCLE

Two sets of studies that examined various types of child loss can further illustrate both the use of the model as well as characteristic features of child loss at different points in the life cycle.

Young Parents and Young Children

The Chicago SIDS (Sudden Infant Death Syndrome) study using the Two-Track Model involved mothers who had lost children recently (7 months before), not recently (an average of 4.5 years before), and mothers who had not suffered child loss (Rubin, 1981). It was hypothesized that recently bereaved mothers would manifest difficulties in functioning and that the nonrecently bereaved mothers would be quite similar to the no-child loss mothers on functioning (Track I). The results confirmed the hypotheses. Recently bereaved mothers had heightened anxiety, a more negative perception of the world, and lowered resilience. The nonrecently bereaved and nonbereaved mothers were not distinguishable from each other. In comparison with the recently bereaved mothers, they had less anxiety, a more positive view of the world, and were relatively resilient to the shocks of life (see Figure 10-1). The entire group of bereaved mothers were examined for other aspects of their response to loss. Persistent changes in the relationship to other children and to the meaning and priorities of life were characteristic features of their response to loss. This reorganization following loss tended to occur within the first year following death and to remain consistent years later and to be relatively refractory to change.

On the relational track, it was hypothesized that recently bereaved

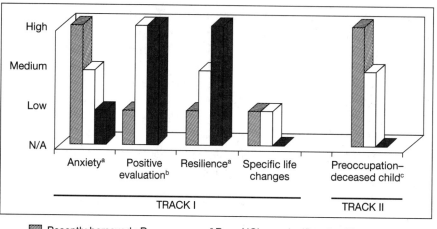

Legend:
Recently bereaved : R   [a] R vs. NCL are significantly different
Non-recently bereaved : NR   [b] R vs. NR + NCL are significantly different
No child loss : NCL   [c] R vs. NR are significantly different

Figure 10-1. Chicago SIDS Study
Source: Rubin, 1981.

mothers would differ from the nonrecently bereaved individuals in the intensity of the relationship to the deceased. Track II measures reflecting the nature of the continuing investment in the relationship to the deceased confirmed this hypothesis. Although consistent and powerful attachment to the lost child was characteristic of all the bereaved mothers, the recently bereaved mothers were more preoccupied with the deceased. Overall, however, a continuing involvement with the deceased emerged as a normative feature of this type of child loss. Without doubt, the particular characteristics of SIDS, with its unknown and confusing etiology, bring with it a shock to parents, children, and the extended support system (DeVries, Lana, & Flack, 1994; Powell, 1995; Rubin, 1981). The suddenness, the etiological ambiguity, and the Western societal expectation that parents will successfully raise their children to maturity are part of the background to this type of loss (Kirkely-Best & Kellner, 1982). Continuing advances in the prevention of SIDS further contribute to the persistent sense of guilt and responsibility that accompany this loss. These results are consistent with many other studies suggesting that loss of pregnancy and young children can be a devastating experience for parents (Peppers & Knapp, 1980). We shall return to this in the concluding section.

Middle-Aged Parents and Adult Children

As children (and parents) mature, the response to loss takes on a somewhat different characteristic. The sense of total responsibility for the welfare of the child gives way to a partnership with the child, who assumes responsibility as well. The greater self-definition of the child who has grown into a unique personality transforms this loss into a combination of a lost relationship that was and lost potential relationship that could have been. In a series of studies it was possible to examine the responses of bereaved parents of adult children—sons lost to war in Israel (Rubin, 1987, 1992). Once again, the Two-Track Model of Bereavement was used as the conceptual paradigm. The research evaluated parents who had lost sons 4 and 13 years previously, in the 1973 Yom Kippur War and in the 1982 Lebanon war (Rubin, 1992, 1993, 1996). Their questionnaires and interview data were compared with those of parents who had not lost children. As before, separating the bereaved person by length of time since loss helped examine bereavement as a process continuing for many years.

In these studies, it was hypothesized that 4-year bereaved, 13-year bereaved, and no child loss groups would differ from each other as a function of time elapsed since loss. On Track I assessing functioning, the bereaved persons reported significantly more anxiety than the nonbereaved parents. (See Figure 10-2.) On a range of other indexes of function comparing the three groups, parents bereaved 4 years earlier tended to have greater affective, somatic, social, and psychological distress than did the nonbereaved parents. Parents bereaved 13 years earlier evinced a mixed picture as a result of gender differences. The 13-year bereaved fathers tended to resemble their nonbereaved counterparts whereas the 13-year bereaved mothers tended to resemble their more recently bereaved counterparts.

On the relational track, it was hypothesized that a continuing in-

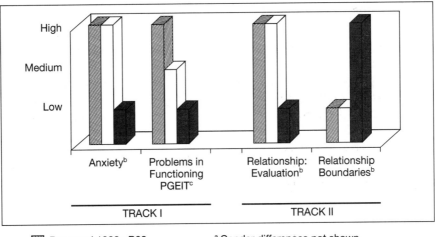

	Bereaved 1982 : B82	[a] Gender differences not shown
	Bereaved 1973 : B73	[b] B82 + B73 vs. NCL : significant difference
	No child loss : NCL	[c] B82 vs. NCL : significant difference

Figure 10-2. Israel War Bereaved Study[a]
Source: Rubin, 1992, 1993.

volvement with the deceased would characterize all the bereaved parents. Furthermore, it was predicted that the bereaved parents' relationship to the deceased would differ from the nonbereaved parents' relationship to living children. The results confirmed these hypotheses. On Track II (and similar to the case of SIDS loss), indications of a continuing involvement with the deceased were normative for parents of the deceased both 4 and 13 years after loss. On comparison between the relationship to living and deceased children, sharp distinctions were found. The bereaved parents evaluated their children more positively than did the parents of the living children. Particularly striking were indications that bereaved parents experienced their deceased children as being closer and more involved with them than nonbereaved parents experienced their living children (Blatt, 1994; Sadeh et al., 1993). The results pointed to a paradoxical feature of bereavement: The death of the son and the loss of the living contact with him often led to an increase in the strength of the relationship with the now internalized and remembered son. In many cases, the positive evaluation, investment, and involvement with the deceased remained disproportionately elevated for many years, and at considerable cost to the interpersonal relationships with other children (Rubin, 1993, 1996).

As part of the attempt to study the information provided by the participants in depth, the bereaved parents' semistructured interviews were analyzed and coded according to three sets of variables: (a) the relationship with the deceased, (b) the relationship to a living sibling of the deceased, and (c) the ability to invest interest in life tasks (Ariel-Henig, 1999). Among the results of interest were that indications of conflict with the deceased in the interview were associated with written measures of difficulties in the resolution of the relationship (Track II). Rumination on the deceased and distress when thinking about him or her are examples of these difficulties. Conflict with the deceased, however, was not related to functional difficulties such as anxiety, depression, somatic difficulties, and so forth. This buttresses the distinction between a complex of indicators associated with functioning and a complex of indicators associated with relationship to the deceased.

Similarly, where difficulties in the relationship with a living child (sibling of the deceased) were present, they were associated with difficulties in general functioning rather than with problems in the relationship to the deceased. The measures of resilience, assessing investment in life activities, were robust indicators of adaptation. The greater the investment in life tasks, the better both the functioning and the relationship to the deceased.

Although these results are specific to parents of adult children who were lost to war, additional studies suggest that such losses as a result of motor vehicle accidents were similar in impact (Shalev, 1999). The extensive clinical and research literature on the impact of losses of schoolage, adolescent, and adult children are consistent with the picture of a pervasive, overwhelming, and persistent response to loss (DeVries et al., 1994; Lehman et al., 1987; Murphy et. al., 1998; Rando, 1986, 1993; Videka-Sherman, 1982).

Aged Parents and Older Children

The life progression of adults confronts many parents with child loss at later stages of life. The loss of middle-aged and elderly children to older and aged parents forces this issue on many parents (DeVries et al., 1994; Moss & Moss, 1996). Yet aging parents who have lost children earlier in life continue to deal with the meaning of these losses and continue to be affected even as they age. In the 10-year follow-up study of Israeli war-bereaved parents (Rubin, 1992), one third out of the original group of bereaved parents completed written measures and were reinterviewed (Ben-Israel Reuveni, 1999). The results suggested that the mourning process continued for parents originally bereaved 4 years and then 14 years removed from the loss. A reduction in problems in functioning and a lesser degree of distress over the relationship to the deceased characterized them. By contrast, there were no indications of significant change in either functioning or relationship to the deceased for parents who had been bereaved 13 years and who were then bereaved for 23 years.

In another study, analysis of a series of interviews obtained in individual, couple, and group formats of war-bereaved parents who had lost children as long as 33 years previously shed additional light on this process (Malkinson & Bar-Tur, 1999, in press). In addition to the losses often associated with aging that parents described, many also described continued difficulties in coming to terms with the loss of their child. Poignantly, a number expressed their fear that the deceased sons would "die forever" when they themselves died. The actual death of the son awaits the second symbolic death—the loss of the child's inner representation, which would occur on the death of the parents themselves.

Older bereaved parents also tended to reevaluate their grief as experienced shortly after the death and years and decades later (Ben-Israel Reuveni, 1999; Malkinson & Bar-Tur, in press). A central theme dealt with the marital relationship and the relationship with the surviving children. In retrospect, a number bemoaned their intense emotional involvement with the deceased son rather than with the living children. They realized how difficult their grieving and response to loss had been for the other members of the family. Many felt that the continued emotional involvement with the lost son had persisted disproportionately and had affected their ability to fully engage with their families, which themselves were developing and changing (Lopata, 1981). Responsibility to the deceased child coexisted alongside that to the surviving children, even though the parents expressed greater guilt with regard to the living children. These bereaved parents seemed to live in two separate worlds—the real and an alternate reality. Often it is the deceased child who is perceived as the more accessible and the more real of the children. As one parent put it, "Our children have left home. We are at home with him [the deceased child], he is there with us" (Malkinson & Bar-Tur, 1999).

Overall, our results suggest that on both functional and relational aspects of response to loss, the passage of time blurs distinctions between the groups of bereaved parents and types of loss (Shalev, 1999). Although the impact of child loss is life-long, it seems to reach a state of relative steady influence over time, although the meaning of the loss continues to change throughout the life cycle (Neimeyer et al., 2000). The extent to which change proceeds differently along the functional and relational tracks of the Two-Track Model is an important question for further study. Research from both the SIDS and war-bereaved parents suggests that some changes occur relatively early and remain relatively impervious to change (e.g., change in relationship to other children, continuation of some depressive features; Dichterman, 1989; Rubin, 1982, 1993). Regarding the extent of involvement with the deceased, the results suggest that distress over this relationship may be on a slowly diminishing curve, but beyond some time point, the involvement itself does not significantly change. Measures of involvement with the relationship to the deceased support the notion of strong and powerful investment in the relationship. In many ways, many of the bereaved parents of adult children saw the relationship to the deceased son as either the closest or one of the closest relationships they had ever had (Ben-Israel Reuveni, 1999).

The loss of younger and older children has been studied under a variety of circumstances and with varying methodologies. The results are generally consistent with the reality of an ongoing relationship to the deceased and a transformation over time of the meaning of loss and of the relationship with the deceased (Klass 1988, 1996).

RISK FACTORS AND MITIGATING FACTORS IN PARENTAL RESPONSE TO LOSS

Child loss is a disruptive and life-shattering experience for families, yet features exist that can exacerbate or mitigate it (Smeding, 1996). The importance of support, self-help groups, and counseling and psychotherapy is well-known (Klass, 1988; Lieberman, 1993; Murphy et al., 1998; Raphael, 1983; Videka-Sherman & Lieberman, 1985; Worden, 1992). The meaning of support in bereavement has been shown to encompass both active support (problem solving and other types of instrumental assistance) and emotional support (willingness to listen; Lehman et al., 1987; Schechter, 1994; Stylianos & Vachon, 1993). The ability to listen to the bereaved individual and to respond with simple human presence is a very powerful ingredient in human relatedness (Havens, 1988).

For parents of young children, loss meets them at a point at which many are engaged in tasks of raising a family, juggling work and family obligations, and trying to establish themselves as adults (Gilbert & Smart, 1992; Levinson, 1978). The loss of a young child during pregnancy or shortly thereafter is the loss of hopes, dreams, and expectations invested in the hoped-for child. As mothers tend to bond with the fetus earlier and more deeply in the pregnancy stage than do fathers, the reaction to the loss is often colored by differing phases of intensity of attachment by the parents. The ability of the young couple to muster their mutual support system may be greatly stressed at this time. This can combine with other gender differences in response to adversity, which can be considerable (Schwab, 1996). The social support matrix of family, friends, and community may likewise not fully understand the impact of the loss, assuming that there is little grief for those who were never born or died shortly after birth. When they are aware of and supportive of the grief, however, their contribution is considerable (Giladi, 1993). Treating stillbirth as a recognized event, holding and seeing the child before burial, and naming the child and conducting a burial are all variations that can make the grief process real. Such features can bring the grieving parents closer to their own realization of loss (Kirkely-Best & Kellner, 1982). As such, their grief may be experienced, traversed, and assimilated in ways that enable better integration and outcome (Bowlby, 1980).

The loss of a young infant to illness, SIDS, or accident share characteristics with the losses just described. Many people find it hard intuitively to understand why the grief for a child who has not lived long enough to define him- or herself should be so prolonged or intense. The guilt that parents feel for the loss of a young infant, one who is totally dependent on them, is one of the most poignant features of these losses. In SIDS, for example, the lack of a clear disease process may leave parents unsure about the "scientific" and objective reason why their baby died. Many of the parents we studied believed that a formal scientific understanding of the disease process would allow them to put aside their doubts about their own contributions to their child's death. Data from parents who have lost children to such "scientifically" clear losses as cancer quickly remind us that parental guilt for young children may be exacerbated by an unclear disease process, but it is by no means dependent on it (Bowlby, 1980; Gaylin, 1968; Gourevitch, 1973; Miles & Demi, 1986).

As part of normal family planning, as part of the coping process, and as part of the meaning reassessment, younger parents deal with the question of whether or when to have another child. There can be little doubt that many consider the bringing of a new child into the family to be a part of the recovery process. On the other hand, the clinical literature has raised serious questions about bringing a new child into the world when the mourning process has not been adequately addressed (Rubin & Nassar, 1993). When having another child is presented as a means of avoiding grief, the possibility exists for confused boundaries between the deceased and the subsequent child. When the parents have traversed their grief, the likelihood of healthy and adaptive attachment process to the living child is increased (Cain & Cain, 1964; Powell, 1995). The need to maintain an ongoing attachment to the unique child who died, and to allow for the formation of a distinct attachment bond to the unique child who is to enter the family, are important benefits to experiencing the grief and loss process.

As the individual children who die are older (and as the parents age), there is greater recognition of the uniqueness of the loss, and often greater support for the family experiencing the loss. The twin extremes of sudden death or a more lingering expected death as a result of illness can overwhelm and erode the strengths and resilience of parents and exceed their ability to process loss. Yet coping with loss, traversing grief and acute mourning, and reorganizing one's relationship to the living and the dead are a series of tasks that have a sharp beginning, but literally no end as long as life is lived and experienced.

Parents' patterns of grief affect the surviving children who themselves go through a grief process in mourning the death of a brother or a sister (Balk, 1991; Silverman, 2000a, 2000b). Grief and mourning over the loss of a close and intimate sibling relationship that could have lasted for many years can reoccur throughout the life-cycle (Robinson & Mahon, 1997). For the surviving sibling adapting to loss often involves "a double loss"— that of the relationship with brother or sister and the loss of parents who are immersed in their grief and lack the energy to function as parents to the surviving children (Fanos, 1996; McKown & Davies, 1995; Rubin, 1986; Sanders, 1989; Stephenson, 1986). The loss is affected to some degree by the quality of the relationship before the loss, but in any event will leave the surviving sibling with a feeling of emptiness and yearning. The loss can be experienced as that of a close friend, a dependent little brother, or a valued older sister. In any event, feelings of guilt for surviving, for not having taken enough care of or with the sibling, and anger at the parental comparisons with the often idealized internal image in the parent's and the surviving sibling's mind can make these losses confusing (Frydman-Helfant, 1994). The younger the surviving sibling, the more confusing these responses (Rubin, 1999b).

CONCLUSION

Ultimately, there are no significant deaths that are not in and of themselves notable risk factors because of their ability to derail a life trajectory and to distort adequate functioning. Yet among bereaved individuals are many who find within themselves and their surroundings the requisite support and resources to reorganize their lives following the death of their loved child. There is no single correct path or proper time frame to transform the loss into a meaningful but balanced part of one's history and memory (Malkinson, Rubin, & Witztum, 1993, 2000).

Losses occurring under conditions of trauma, losses not recognized by the individual or society, losses in which interpersonal conflict is a major feature of the relationship, and losses that are not grieved for in ways suitable to the bereaved person impose burdens on him or her and interfere with grief and mourning (Bowlby, 1980, 1990; Doka, 1989; Exline, Dorrity, & Wortman, 1996; Janoff-Bulman, 1992; Rando, 1993; Van der Kolk, Mcfarlane, & Weisaeth, 1996). In similar fashion, but with opposite results, there are few aspects of the circumstances of loss, the individual, the support system, or the family that cannot become integrated into the mitigation or healing features in the response to loss. The losses of children will require a continuing life-long accommodation, at some level, to the shifting meanings of the loss and to the bonds and ongoing relationship to the memories and thoughts associated with the deceased (Silverman, Nickman, & Worden, 1992; S. Silverman, 1997; M. Stroebe, Gergen, Gergen, & Stroebe, 1992). Continuing to address the meanings associated with the loss, the ongoing reevaluation of what was lost, and awareness of how one has changed are significant features of the accommodation to loss. These responses can, over time, provide considerable solace for the bereaved individual.

> April 12, 1929
> My daughter who died would have been thirty-six years old today.
> . . .
> Although we know that after such a loss the acute state of mourning will subside, we also know we shall remain inconsolable and will never find a substitute. No matter what may fill the gap, even if it be filled completely, it nevertheless remains something else. And actually this is how it should be. It is the only way of perpetuating that love which we do not want to relinquish. (Freud's Letter to Binswanger, 1929a; E. Freud, 1961, p. 386)

REFERENCES

Anthony, E. J., & Benedek, T. (Eds.). (1970). *Parenthood: Its psychology and psychopathology.* Boston: Little Brown.

Ariel-Henig, L. (1999) *Listening to bereavement: Analyzing interviews with war bereaved parents.* Unpublished master's thesis, University of Haifa.

Balk, D. E. (1991). Death and adolescent bereavement: Current research and future directions. *Journal of Adolescent Research, 6,* 7–27.

Belsky, J. (1988). *Clinical implications of attachment*. Hillsdale, NJ: Erlbaum.

Ben-Israel Reuveni, O. (1999) *The effect of time on the adjustment of war bereaved parents: Functioning, relationship and marital adjustment*. Unpublished master's thesis, University of Haifa.

Beutler, L. E., Machado, P. P. P., & Neufeldt, S. (1994). Therapist variables. In S. L. Garfield & A. E. Bergin (Eds.), *Handbook of psychotherapy and behavior change* (4th ed., pp. 259–269). New York: Wiley.

Blatt, S. J. (1994). *Therapeutic change*. New York: Plenum Press.

Bornstein, M. C. (Ed.). (1995). *Handbook of parenting, Vols. 1–3*. Mahweh, NJ: Erlbaum.

Bowlby, J. (1969). *Attachment and loss: Vol. 1. Attachment*. London: Hogarth.

Bowlby, J. (1973). *Attachment and loss: Vol. 2. Separation*. London: Hogarth.

Bowlby, J. (1980). *Attachment and loss: Vol. 3. Loss: Sadness and depression*. London: Hogarth.

Bowlby, J. (1990). *Charles Darwin: A biography*. London: Hutchinson.

Breznitz, S. (2000). Preface. In R. Malkinson, S. Rubin, & E. Witztum (Eds.), *Traumatic and non-traumatic loss and bereavement: Clinical theory and practice*. Madison, CT: Psychosocial Press/International Universities Press.

Cain, A. C., & Cain, B. S. (1964). On replacing a child. *Journal of the American Academy of Child Psychiatry, 3*, 443–456.

DeVries, B., Lana, R. D., & Flack, V. D. (1994). Parental bereavement over the life course: A theoretical intersection and empirical review. *Omega, 29*, 47–69.

Dichterman, D. (1989). *Personality and interpersonal history and their relationship to long-term outcome to child loss in Israel*. Unpublished master's thesis, University of Haifa.

Doka, K. (1989). *Disenfranchised grief*. Lexington, MA: Lexington Books.

Engel, G. L. (1961). Is grief a disease? *Psychosomatic Medicine, 23*, 18–22.

Exline, J. J., Dorrity, K., & Wortman, C. (1996). Coping with bereavement: A research review for clinicians. *In Session: Psychotherapy in Practice, 2*, 3–20.

Fanos, J. H. (1996). *Sibling loss*. New Jersey: Erlbaum.

Fivaz-Depersuing, E., Stern, D. N., Burgin, D., Byng-Hall, J., Corboz-Warnery, A., Lamour, M., & Lebovici, S. (1994). The dynamics of interfaces. *Infant Mental Health Journal, 15*, 69–89.

Freud, E. L. (Ed.). (1961). *Letters of Sigmund Freud*. New York: Basic Books.

Freud, S. (1957). *Mourning and melancholia, Standard edition of the complete psychological works of Sigmund Freud*. London: Hogarth Press. (Original work published 1917)

Frydman-Helfant, S. (1994). *Sibling bereavement*. Unpublished master's thesis, University of Haifa.

Gaylin, W. (1968). (Ed.). *The meaning of despair*. New York: Jason Aronson.

Giladi, A. (1993). "The child was small . . . not so the grief for him: Al-Sakhawi's consolation treatise for bereaved parents. *Poetics Today, 14*, 367–386.

Gilbert, K. R., & Smart, L. S. (1992). *Coping with infant or fetal loss: The couple's healing process*. New York: Brunner/Mazel.

Gorer, G. (1965). *Death, grief and mourning in contemporary Britain*. London: Tavistock.

Gourevitch, M. (1973). A survey of family reactions to disease and death in a family member. In E. J. Anthony & C. Koupernik (Eds.), *The child in his family* (pp. 21–28). New York: Wiley.

Havens, L. L. (1988). *Making contact: Uses of language in psychotherapy*. Boston: Harvard University Press.

Horowitz, M. J., Siegel, B., Holen, A., Bonanno, G. A., Milbrath, C., & Stinson, C. S. (1997). Diagnostic criteria for complicated grief disorder. *American Journal of Psychiatry, 154*, 904–910.

Horowitz, M. J., Weiss, D., Kaltreider, N., Krupnick, J., Wilner, N., Marmar, C., & DeWitt, K. (1984). Reactions to the death of a parent: Results from patients and field subjects. *Journal of Nervous and Mental Disease, 172*, 383–392.

Horowitz, M. J., Wilner, N., Marmar, C., & Krupnick, J. (1980). Pathological grief and the activation of latent self-images. *American Journal of Psychiatry, 137*, 1157–1160.

Janoff-Bulman, R. (1992). *Shattered assumptions. Towards a new psychology of trauma*. New York: Free Press.

Kirkley-Best, E., & Kellner, K. R. (1982). The forgotten grief: A review of the psychology of stillbirth. *American Journal of Orthopsychiatry, 52*(3), 420–429.

Klass, D. (1988). *Parental grief: Solace and resolution*. New York: Springer.

Klass, D. (1996). The deceased child in the psychic and social worlds of bereaved parents during the resolution of grief. In D. Klass, P. R. Silverman, & S. Nickman (Eds.), *Continuing bonds* (pp. 199–215). Washington, DC: Taylor & Francis.

Klass, D., Silverman, P. R., & Nickman, S. (Eds.). (1996). *Continuing bonds*. Washington, DC: Taylor & Francis.

Lehman, D. R., Lang, E. L., Wortman, C. B., & Sorenson, S. B. (1989). Long-term effects of sudden bereavement: Marital and parent-child relationships and children's reactions. *Journal of Family Psychology, 2*, 344–367.

Lehman, D. R., Wortman, C. B., & Williams, A. F. (1987). Long-term effects of losing a spouse or child in a motor vehicle crash. *Journal of Personality and Social Psychology, 52*, 218–231.

Levi, P. (1989). *The mirror maker: Stories and essays*. New York: Schocken.

Levinson, D. (1978). *Seasons of a man's life*. New York: Knopf.

Lieberman, M. (1993). Bereavement self-help groups. In M. S. Stroebe, W. Stroebe, & R. O. Hansson (Eds.), *Handbook of bereavement* (pp. 411–426). Cambridge: Cambridge University Press.

Lopata, H. Z. (1981). Widowhood and husband sanctification. *Journal of Marriage and the Family, 43,* 439–450.

Malkinson, R., & Bar-Tur, L. (1999). The aging of grief in Israel: A perspective of bereaved parents. *Death Studies, 23,* 413–431.

Malkinson, R., & Bar-Tur, L. (in press). The aging of grief; Parental grief of Israeli soldiers. In J. H. Harvey & B. G. Pauwels (Eds.), *Post-traumatic stress: Theory, research and application.* Philadelphia: Brunner/Mazel.

Malkinson, R., Rubin, S. & Witztum, E. (Eds.). (1993). *Loss and bereavement in Jewish society in Israel.* Israel: Canah/Ministry of Defense.

Malkinson, R., Rubin, S. & Witztum, E. (Eds.). (2000). *Traumatic and non-traumatic loss and bereavement: Clinical theory and practice.* Madison, CT: Psychosocial Press/International Universities Press.

Malkinson, M., & Witztum, E. (2000). Commemoration and bereavement: Cultural aspects of collective myth and the creation of national identity. In R. Malkinson, S. Rubin, & E. Witztum (Eds.), *Traumatic and non-traumatic loss and bereavement: Clinical theory and practice* (pp. 295–320). Madison, CT: Psychosocial Press/International Universities Press.

McKown, D. E., & Davies, B. (1995). Patterns of grief in young children following the death of a sibling. *Death Studies, 19,* 41–53.

Miles, M. S., & Demi, A. S. (1986). Guilt in bereaved parents. In T. A. Rando (Ed.), *Parental loss of a child* (pp. 97–118). Champaign: Research Press.

Moss, M. S., & Moss, S. Z. (1996). Death and bereavement. In R. Blieszner & V. H. Bedford (Eds.), *Aging and the family: Theory and research.* Westport, CT: Praeger.

Murphy, S. A., Johnson, C., Cain, C. K., Gupta, A. D., Diamond, M., & Lohan, J. (1998). Broad-spectrum group treatment for parents bereaved by the violent deaths of their 12- to 28-year-old children: A randomized controlled trial. *Death Studies, 22,* 209–235.

Neimeyer, R., Keese, B. V., & Fortner, M. (2000). Loss and meaning reconstruction: Propositions and procedures. In R. Malkinson, S. Rubin, & E. Witztum (Eds.), *Traumatic and non-traumatic loss and bereavement: Clinical theory and practice* (pp. 197–230). Madison, CT: Psychosocial Press/International Universities Press.

Oppenheim, D., Koren-Kane, N., & Sagi, A. (2000). *Mothers' empathic understanding of their pre-schoolers' internal experience: Relations with early attachment.* Unpublished manuscript.

Parkes, C. M. (1975). What becomes of redundant world models? A contribution to the study of change. *British Journal of Medical Psychology, 48,* 131–137.

Parkes, C. M. (1986). *Bereavement: Studies of grief in adult life* (2nd ed.). Harmondsworth, UK: Penguin.

Parkes, C. M., Laungani, P., & Young, B. (Eds.). (1997). *Death and bereavement across cultures.* New York: Routledge.

Peppers, L. G., & Knapp, R. J. (1980). *Motherhood and mourning: Perinatal death.* New York: Praeger.

Pollock, G. (1989). *The mourning-liberation process*. New York: International Universities Press.

Powell, M. (1995). Sudden Infant Death Syndrome: The subsequent child. *British Journal of Social Work, 25*, 227–240.

Prigerson, H. G., Frank, E., Kasel, S. V., Reynolds, C. F., Anderson, B., Zubenko, G. S., Houck, P. R., George, C. J., & Kupfer, D. J. (1995). Complicated grief and bereavement-related depression as distinct disorders: Preliminary empirical validation in elderly bereaved spouses. *American Journal of Psychiatry, 152*, 22–30.

Rando, T. A. (Ed.). (1986). *Parental loss of a child*. Champaign: Research Press.

Rando, T. A. (1993). *Treatment of complicated mourning*. Champaign: Research Press.

Raphael, B. (1983). *The anatomy of bereavement*. New York: Basic Books.

Robinson, L., & Mahon, M. (1997). Sibling bereavement: A conceptual analysis and review. *Death Studies, 9–10*, 447–499.

Rosenblatt, P. G., & Burns, L. H. (1986). Long-term effects of perinatal loss. *Journal of Family Issues, 7*, 237–253.

Rubin, S. (1981). A two-track model of bereavement: Theory and application in research. *American Journal of Orthopsychiatry, 51*, 101–109.

Rubin, S. (1982). Persisting effects of loss: A model of mourning. In C. Spielberger & I. Sarason (Eds.), N. Milgram (guest editor), *Stress and Anxiety Vol. VIII* (pp. 275–282). Washington, DC: Hemisphere.

Rubin, S. (1984a). Mourning distinct from melancholia. *British Journal of Medical Psychology, 57*, 339–345.

Rubin, S. (1984b). Maternal attachment and child death: On adjustment, relationship and resolution. *Omega, 15*, 347–352.

Rubin, S. (1985). The resolution of bereavement: A clinical focus on the relationship to the deceased. *Psychotherapy: Theory, Research, Training and Practice, 22*, 231–235.

Rubin, S. (1986). Child death and the family: Parents and children confronting loss. *International Journal of Family Therapy, 7*, 377–388.

Rubin, S. (1987). *The long-term adaptation of parents bereaved by war*. Unpublished research report submitted to the Department of Rehabilitation, Ministry of Defense, State of Israel.

Rubin, S. (1990). Death of the future: An outcome study of bereaved parents in Israel. *Omega, 20*, 323–339.

Rubin, S. (1992). Adult child loss and the Two-track Model of Bereavement. *Omega, 24*, 183–202.

Rubin, S. (1993). The death of a child is forever: The life course impact of child loss. In M. S. Stroebe, W. Stroebe, & R. O. Hansson (Eds.), *Handbook of bereavement* (pp. 285–299). Cambridge: Cambridge University Press.

Rubin, S. (1996). The wounded family: Bereaved parents and the impact of adult child loss. In D. Klass, P. R. Silverman, & S. Nickman, *Continuing bonds:*

Understanding the resolution of grief (pp. 217–232). Washington, DC: Taylor & Francis.

Rubin, S. (1998). Reconsidering the transference paradigm in treatment with the bereaved. *American Journal of Psychotherapy, 52,* 215–228.

Rubin, S. (1999a). Psychodynamic psychotherapy with the bereaved: Listening for conflict, relationship and transference. *Omega, 39,* 83–98.

Rubin, S. (1999b). The Two-Track Model of Bereavement: Overview, retrospect and prospect. *Death Studies, 23*(8), 681–714.

Rubin, S. (2000). Psychodynamic perspectives on treatment with the bereaved: Modifications of the therapeutic/transference paradigm. In R. Malkinson, S. Rubin, & E. Witztum (Eds.), *Traumatic and non-traumatic loss and bereavement: Clinical theory and practice* (pp. 117–141). Madison, CT: Psychosocial Press/ International Universities Press.

Rubin, S., Malkinson, R., & Witztum, E. (1999). *The pervasive impact of war-related loss and bereavement in Israel. International Journal of Group Tensions, 28*(1/2), 137–153.

Rubin, S., Malkinson, R., & Witztum, E. (2000). An overview of the field of loss. In R. Malkinson, S. Rubin, & E. Witztum (Eds.), *Traumatic and non-traumatic loss and bereavement: Clinical theory and practice* (pp. 5–40). Madison, CT: Psychosocial/International Universities Press.

Rubin, S., Malkinson, R., & Witztum, E. (in press). The sacred and the secular: The changing face of death, loss and bereavement in Israel. In J. Morgan & P. Laungani (Eds.), *Cross-cultural issues in the care of the dying and the grieving.*

Rubin, S., & Nassar, H. Z. (1993). Psychotherapy and supervision with a bereaved Moslem family: An intervention that almost failed. *Psychiatry, 56,* 338–348.

Rubin, S., & Schechter, N. (1997). Exploring the social construction of bereavement: Perceptions of adjustment and recovery for bereaved men. *American Journal of Orthopsychiatry, 67,* 279–289.

Sadeh, A., Rubin, S., & Berman, E. (1993). Parental and relationship representations and experiences of depression in college students. *Journal of Personality Assessment, 60,* 192–204.

Sanders, C. M. (1989). *Grief: The mourning after.* New York: Wiley.

Sandler, J., & Sandler, A. M. (1978). On the development of object relationships and affects. *International Journal of Psychoanalysis, 59,* 285–296.

Schechter, N. (1994). *Perceived loss of spouse and children: Adaptation and the Two-Track Model of Bereavement.* Unpublished master's thesis, University of Haifa.

Schiff, H. (1977). *The bereaved parent.* New York: Crown.

Schwab, R. (1996). Gender differences in parental grief. *Death Studies, 20,* 103–113.

Shalev, R. (1999). *Comparison of war-bereaved and motor vehicle accident-bereaved parents.* Unpublished master's thesis, University of Haifa.

Siggins, L. D. (1966). Mourning: A critical survey of the literature. *International Journal of Psychoanalysis, 47,* 14–25.

Silverman, P. R. (2000a). *Never too young to know: Death in children's lives.* New York: Oxford University Press.

Silverman, P. R. (2000b). Children as part of a family drama: An integrated view of childhood bereavement. In R. Malkinson, S. Rubin, & E. Witztum (Eds.), *Traumatic and non-traumatic loss and bereavement: Clinical theory and practice* (pp. 67–90). Madison, CT: Psychosocial Press/International Universities Press.

Silverman, P. R., Nickman, S., & Worden, J. W. (1992). Detachment revisited: The child's reconstruction of a dead parent. *American Journal of Orthopsychiatry, 62*(4), 494–503.

Silverman, S. M. (1997). Justice Joseph Story and death in early 19th-century America, *Death Studies, 21,* 397–416.

Smeding, R. (1996). *Education or interpretation: Development of a teaching model for palliative and bereavement care.* Unpublished PhD thesis, Union Institute, Cincinnati, Ohio.

Stephenson, J. (1986). Grief of siblings. In T. A. Rando (Ed.), *Parental loss of a child* (pp. 321–338). Champaign, Il: Research Press.

Stern, D. (1995). *The mothering constellation.* New York: Basic Books.

Stroebe, M. S., Gergen, M. M., Gergen, K. J., & Stroebe, W. (1992). Broken hearts or broken bonds. *American Psychologist, 47,* 1205–1212.

Stroebe, M. S., Stroebe, W., & Hansson, R. O. (Eds.). (1993). *Handbook of bereavement.* Cambridge: Cambridge University Press.

Stroebe, W., & Stroebe, M. S. (1987). *Bereavement and health: The psychological and physical consequences of partner loss.* New York: Cambridge University Press.

Strupp, H. (1969). *Patients view their psychotherapy.* Baltimore: Johns Hopkins Press.

Strupp, H. H., Horowitz, L. M., & Lambert, M. J. (1997). *Measuring patient changes in mood, anxiety and personality disorders towards a core battery.* Washington, DC: American Psychological Association.

Stylianos, S. K., & Vachon, M. (1993). The role of social support in bereavement. In M. S. Stroebe, W. Stroebe, & R. O. Hansson (Eds.), *Handbook of bereavement* (pp. 397–410). Cambridge: Cambridge University Press.

Tamir, G. (1987). *Functioning and attachment in war bereaved Israeli parents.* Unpublished master's thesis, University of Haifa.

Van der Kolk, B. A., McFarlane, A. C., & Weisaeth, L. (Eds.). (1996). *Traumatic stress: The effects of overwhelming experience on mind, body, and society.* New York: Guilford Press.

Videka-Sherman, L. (1982). Coping with the death of a child: A study over time. *American Journal of Orthopsychiatry, 52,* 688–699.

Videka-Sherman, L., & Lieberman, M. (1985). The effects of self-help and the psychotherapy intervention on child loss: The limits of recovery. *American Journal of Orthopsychiatry, 55,* 70–82.

Volkan, V. D. (1981). *Linking objects and linking phenomena.* New York: International Universities Press.

Walsh, F., & McGoldrick, M. (Eds.). (1991). *Living beyond loss.* New York: W.W. Norton.

Wikan, U. (1988). Bereavement and loss in two Muslim communities: Egypt and Bali compared. *Social Science and Medicine, 27,* 451–460.

Worden, J. W. (1992). *Grief counseling and grief therapy: A handbook for the mental health practitioner* (2nd ed.). New York: Springer.

11

BEREAVEMENT AND OLD AGE

MIRIAM S. MOSS, SIDNEY Z. MOSS, AND ROBERT O. HANSSON

Most people who die in the United States are elderly, yet researchers in gerontology and thanatology historically have tended to ignore each other. Although there have been some concerted efforts to bridge the gap between the two fields, there is still a paucity of research and clinical material that examines the interface between dying, death, bereavement, and old age.

Our goal in this chapter will be to focus on old age as a relevant context in which to understand the bereavement experience. To that end, we have divided the chapter into three sections. In the first section, we discuss a number of broad, aging-related issues that have potential implications for bereavement. In the second section, we review more specifically what has been learned from studies of the bereavement reactions of older adults. In the third section we examine the bereavement experiences of close family members after the death of an old person. Throughout, our theoretical orientation rests on a broad psychosocial model of bereavement rather than a medical model.

BROADER AGING-RELATED ISSUES

We address four general issues in this section that influence the ability of older adults to cope with and adapt to important life stressors—among them, bereavement. These issues are also important to consider in understanding the impact of the death of an old person.

Age-Related Changes in Physiological Functioning

Normal aging processes mandate significant changes in physiological function and adaptive reserves for older persons. In addition to appearance, strength, and endurance, longitudinal studies document cumulative degeneration in the major human biological systems (e.g., endocrine, cardiovascular, skeletal, immune, the nervous systems: Hayflick, 1994). At some point for every older person such changes impact physical and cognitive functioning. They degrade the individual's capacity for self-repair, for example, after physical trauma, illness, or surgery (Rowe, 1985). They are also associated with increased incidence of chronic illness, increased vulnerability to disease, and diminished adaptive reserves (Rowe, 1985). Age-related changes in physiological and functional status thus provide an important context in which to view older persons and bereavement.

Interpersonal Contexts of Aging

Relationships serve most of the supportive functions for older persons that they do for younger persons, and generally increase in importance with increased age, frailty, and dependence on assistance in tasks of daily living (Hansson & Carpenter, 1994). Most older persons are not socially isolated. They live with family or within practical reach of family members. Generally they do have strong family supports.

There are, however, many constraints on the availability of family that could be expected to diminish family members' ability and motivation to provide support for an older bereaved person: (a) The death of a family member can affect the family as a functioning collective, undermining communication, solidarity, ability to make decisions, and confidence in the family's ability to cope (Hansson, Vanzetti, Fairchild, & Berry, 1999). (b) Both a declining birth rate and increased longevity have resulted in families that are more vertical in structure, having more generations to care for but fewer young people to help. (c) Disability of older persons has been deferred. This means that caregiving duties may be undertaken at an older age, when the caregiver is also older and more frail (Cantor, 1991). (d) Relationships in later life can become less accessible, strained, interpersonally problematic, and mismatched to an older person's needs. For example, the social networks of older people are often narrowed as a result of poor health, deaths, and relocation of family and friends. In spite of these constraints and the limitations of family resources, families usually do provide considerable support to their elders.

The seminal gerontological paradigm of "environmental docility" views older persons who are less competent in terms of either their physical health, psychological, or social status as having a narrower range of adaptability to any form of environmental stress (Lawton & Simon, 1968; Nahemow, 2000). This suggests that less competent older persons would be expected to be more immediately threatened by a deteriorating, less supportive social or family environment—in other words, a "poor fit" to current needs.

Regulation of Emotion in Later Life

Data from the Boston Normative Aging Study recently suggested important age-related differences in appraisal of life stressors, in the emotions thus experienced, and in patterns of coping (Aldwin, Sutton, Chiara, & Spiro, 1996). The study found that as men age they are less likely to report life problems. Compared to middle-aged men, they indicated feeling less "challenged" and less "annoyed" by recently experienced problems. Although they were more likely to be dealing with deaths of significant persons, they were no more likely to see bereavements in terms of threat or loss. Compared to middle-aged men, they reported less frequent use of instrumental coping strategies or of social support. They reported levels of confidence similar to middle-age men with respect to their ability to cope with any current or future problems.

It may be that older persons tend to narrow their involvements to avoid especially challenging events and to reduce their social networks by focusing on emotionally rewarding relationships (Carstensen, Gross, & Fung, 1997; Lang & Carstensen, 1994). They may also be more accepting of the realities of later life. Adaptive shifts in coping styles may reflect changing life problems in the later years (e.g., shifts from acute to chronic health conditions). Older persons may learn from experience how to prevent or to manage chronic or expected difficulties, reducing the need for reactive coping strategies (Aldwin et al., 1996).

Older persons do not typically report declines in emotional well-being. They score higher than younger persons on measures of emotional control and mood stability (Lawton, Kleban, Rajagopal, & Dean, 1992). At a time when many life stressors may seem inevitable, older persons are increasingly effective in using cognitive strategies in regulating their emotions (Carstensen et al., 1997; Lazarus & Folkman, 1984; Schulz & Heckhausen, 1998). These strategies may include lowering their goal-standards for coping with difficulty, comparing themselves only with other older persons who have similarly suffered, and reappraising negative events to find something positive in them. Barnes, Harvey, Carlson, and Haig (1996) found older bereaved persons more likely than younger persons to have engaged in extensive account-making about their loss (searching for a private meaning in the loss) and more likely to have confided these accounts to others.

Finally, Lawton et al. (1992) reported a greater sense of emotional moderation in older persons—in other words, reacting to fewer worries (and pleasures) and expressing fewer positive and negative feelings. They also found a reduction in physiological responsiveness when upset or emotionally excited. This dampening of emotional responsiveness would be expected to affect the intensity of grief reactions.

Ageism

Our socially and culturally rooted assumptions about older people also provide an important context for understanding their bereavement experience (Butler, 1969; Rubinstein, 1995; Thompson, 1995). An ageist perspective views older people as a homogeneous and less valued group, as frail, rigid, sexless, and isolated.

Elderly people, however, are a highly diverse population, spanning a wide age range (over 65 to past 100) and varying considerably in cognitive competence, emotional resilience, and personal history (all of which affect their responses to stressful life events such as the death of a loved one). Even among the very old (80+), there are important differences. About one fourth live in nursing homes, one fifth live in the community and are dependent on others for care in their activities of daily living, leaving more than half in advanced old age who live relatively independently.

Ageist perspectives tend to overlook or devalue the older person's past, their current feelings, competence, significance to others, and their multiple roles in the world. Unfortunately many older persons internalize this negative and stereotypic perspective; the result is a devaluing of self and age-peers.

OLDER PERSON AS BEREAVED

Old age is a time of multiple and sequential losses. It might be argued that successful adaptation to past losses leads to the development of a world view and a concept of self that would facilitate adaptation to later losses (Hansson, Remondet, & Galusha, 1993; Wortman & Silver, 1992). At the same time, one runs the risk of bereavement overload (Kastenbaum, 1969; Parkes & Weiss, 1983) and a cumulative negative effect (Norris & Murrell, 1990).

When ageist beliefs are internalized by bereaved older persons, they may devalue themselves and their feelings. They may be encouraged by family and friends to put aside their grief and may take on a facade of normal functioning, controlling both their thoughts and expression of feelings (Rubin, 1993). People may view older persons' normal responses to bereavement as problems of old age (e.g., fatigue, confusion, loneliness, and social withdrawal; Kalish, 1985). As we describe later, younger family members may be viewed as those primarily bereaved, with the older person considered a secondary griever (Littlewood, 1992). The focus on the younger nuclear family tends to place the bereaved elder on the periphery.

The relationship of the bereaved person to the deceased may also play a central role in the meaning and impact of the loss (Raphael, 1983). In the following sections, we highlight some findings and themes in older persons' bereavement for sibling, spouse, child, and grandchild.

Sibling Death

Perhaps the most frequent death of a close family member in later years is the death of a sibling. More than two fifths of elderly persons experience the death of a sibling after the age of 60 (S. Z. Moss & Moss, 1989) and nearly 10% of persons after the age of 65 have had a sibling die in the previous year (Hays, Gold, & Pieper, 1997).

Sibling bereavement in old age, however, has received little research or clinical attention. This may in part reflect the fact that few elderly siblings coreside, few provide primary caregiving, and few seek counseling around sibling ties or sibling bereavement (Bedford, 1994; S. Z. Moss & Moss, 1989). When a sibling dies, the spouse and adult children are generally expected to be most affected. Sibling death may not even be viewed by others as a significant loss for older persons (Cornoni-Huntley et al., 1990; Murrell & Himmelfarb, 1989). There are few social supports for older persons after their sibling dies, although surviving siblings can provide mutual comfort through reminiscence (Rosenblatt & Elde, 1990; Walter, 1996).

The functional and cognitive status of bereaved siblings appears not to differ from those who have lost spouses (Hays et al., 1997). Siblings of the deceased, however, have lower self-rated health than do spouses (Hays et al., 1997). Middle-aged surviving siblings have been found to have poorer health than nonbereaved individuals (Perkins & Harris, 1990). This may reflect the siblings' shared genetic inheritance with the deceased. The biogenetic tie between siblings can intensify the real and the perceived threat of the surviving sibling's death.

A qualitative study of 20 older persons (average age 77) about a sibling who had died since the elder was age 60 described both the impact on self (increased vulnerability and sense of personal resiliency) and impact on family alignments (symbolizing a sense of family incompleteness, as well as serving to maintain or strengthen existing ties with surviving kin). Siblings emphasized the continuity of their tie with the deceased (S. Z. Moss & Moss, 1989).

Widowhood

The death of a spouse in old age implies more than the loss of a beloved partner–attachment figure (Lopata, 1996). During a marriage of many years, there forms a system of roles, traditions, and interdependencies, which are in turn reflected in an identity shared by the couple. Many important roles (wife, companion, life-partner, "other-half"), which previously defined who I am and were the source of personal rewards, are also lost with a death. The bond persists, however, and the tie continues beyond the death (Moss & Moss, 1996a).

A wide variety of factors can influence adaptation among older widowed persons (Lopata, 1996). Women age 65 and older, for example, are three times more likely than men to be widowed and twice as likely to be living alone (U.S. Bureau of the Census, 1997). Moreover, in a modern, highly mobile society, families are often geographically distant, reducing their effectiveness as a support system, and limiting family awareness of the widowed persons' needs. It is thus important for widowed persons to effectively assert their needs. Yet many older widows (especially) who were raised in simpler times, in smaller and more tightly woven communities, were not encouraged to learn the skills that would assist them in accessing or developing new support relationships outside of the family (Lopata, 1996).

Another theme involves the difficulty encountered by newly widowed persons in maintaining previously enjoyed "couple-companionate" relationships. They are now a "fifth-wheel" and fit less well into the activities of their married friends. Age peers of widowed women are increasingly likely to be widows and their contacts tend to be primarily female. The formation of new romantic relationships is constrained by the attitudes of family members, by an unwillingness to give up a newly achieved independence, by a reluctance to nurse another aging partner in the last years, and for widows by the relative unavailability of male partners (O'Bryant & Hansson, 1995). No wonder loneliness is among the most frequently mentioned consequences of widowhood (Lopata, 1996; Lund, Caserta, & Dimond, 1993).

There is much diversity in the adjustment process among older widowed persons, with some experiencing long and difficult bereavements and some responding well to the adaptive challenges associated with their new circumstance (e.g., Lund et al., 1993). Most live alone (O'Bryant & Hansson, 1995), and many learn new skills and develop in positive ways (Fry, 1998; Lund et al., 1993).

Research suggests that the initial bereavement experience of older widows may be less intense than that of younger widows (e.g., Sanders, 1993; Stroebe & Stroebe, 1987), but that emotional and physical distress associated with grief decline more slowly among older persons (e.g., Sanders, 1981; Thompson, Gallagher-Thompson, Futterman, Gilewski, & Peterson, 1991). The death of a spouse of many years would be expected to result in greater disorganization of the roles, commitments, and patterns of a widow's life (Lopata, 1996). For older persons, conjugal bereavement may also trigger a complex of interactions unique to later life. That is, the death of a spouse is only one of many important life stressors that tend to cluster in old age. Among elderly persons, one's grief may interact with or exacerbate a variety of other, more systemic, age-related changes and events such as chronic illness or disability, loss of independence, or involuntary relocation (O'Bryant & Hansson, 1995). As with the first onset of an age-related disability, widowhood may also come to symbolize for the bereaved individual a "line between not being old and being old" (Kemp, 1985).

Researchers thus continue to find it relevant to include elderly widowed persons as research participants in studies on a wide variety of topics —for example, depressive symptoms associated with bereavement (Mendes de Leon, Kasl, & Jacobs, 1994), criteria for "complicated" grief (Prigerson et al., 1995; chapter 26, this volume), suicidal ideation among bereaved individuals (Szanto, Prigerson, Houck, Ehrenpreis, & Reynolds, 1997), the dynamics of ethnic identity (Luborsky & Rubinstein, 1997), and the impact of widowhood on health and nutritional habits (Rosenbloom & Whittington (1993).

Parental Bereavement

Parents are expected to die before their children (Rando, 1986). Too frequently, however, older persons suffer the loss of a child. One large sample found that of all elderly persons who had ever been parents, 10% had a child die when the parent was at least 60 years old (Moss, Lesher, & Moss, 1986). As many as one fourth of all women over age 65 who have a living son may expect their son to predecease them (Metropolitan Life Insurance Company, 1977).

Most research comparing the impact of family deaths on persons across the life course has found that the death of an adult child elicits more intense reactions such as despair, somatization, anger, and guilt than other deaths (Cleiren, 1993; Hays et al., 1997; Owen, Fulton, & Markusen, 1983; Sanders, 1989). Arbuckle and De Vries (1995), however, compared the bereavement experience of older parents and spouses and found few differences.

Although most adult children of elderly parents die as a result of illness, much of the reported research on the death of adult children focuses on deaths resulting from war, suicide, or accident (e.g., Levav, Friedlander, Kark, & Peritz, 1988; Rubin, 1992; Shanfield & Swain, 1984). These studies have found that parents of deceased adult children experience a loss of continuity, persistent intense sadness, survival guilt, yearning, and pre-occupation with the deceased.

It is not clear how age of the elderly parent is a factor in bereavement. In several studies of parent bereavement the child died before the onset of the parent's old age, yet they yielded important findings to be pursued in understanding the experience of the very old. For example, Rubin (1993) found the persistence of intense grief over 14 years. Fish (1986) found that older fathers (mean age 47) grieved more intensely than younger fathers (mean age 31). Arbuckle and De Vries (1995) studied the first wave of a national sample of persons age 57 and over. In comparing the impact of the death of a spouse and of an adult child, age of the bereaved person explained little unique variance to a wide range of outcome variables.

De Vries, Davis, Wortman, and Lehman (1997) included analysis of the first wave and the second wave (two and a half years later) in the previously mentioned longitudinal study. They reported that bereaved parents (mean age 77) were initially more depressed than a control group of nonbereaved parents, and their level of depression did not decline. Further, the health status of the bereaved parents declined at a more rapid rate than the nonbereaved.

Research that focuses on bereaved elderly parents is rare in spite of the fact that adult children play a major part in the social and emotional world of parents throughout their lifetime. There are differences in the meanings of the loss and the shape of bereavement over the life course to the end of life (De Vries, Dalla Lana, & Falck, 1994; Rando, 1986). The loss of normal reciprocity and mutual emotional support between parent and child would be intensified if the child had been an active or potential source of caregiving for the bereaved parent. Goodman, Black, and Rubinstein (1996) in their qualitative study of elderly men found that narcissism could be a powerful buffer against the pain in the death of their adult child.

There are cultural differences in the reaction to the death of a child; for Jewish women the loss remains more central to their lives than for non-Jewish women (Goodman, Rubinstein, Alexander, & Luborsky, 1991). Lesher and Bergey (1988) described a small group (18) of institutionalized elderly Jewish women who continued to mourn, often with clinical depression, an average of six years after the death of an adult child.

Finally, we suggest that when an adult child dies the bereaved old parent may play a peripheral role in regard to terminal care decisions, funeral plans, as well as mourning after the death. In spite of the fact that the loss can have profound meaning and impact, the surviving parent's grief is often seen as secondary to that of the spouse and offspring of their child.

Death of a Grandchild

The untimely death of a grandchild has rarely been examined as an experience of old age. An exception is Fry's (1997) study of bereaved Canadian grandparents (mean age 65) that found themes similar to those of a death of a child: intense emotional upset, survivor guilt, regrets about the relationship with the deceased child, and a need to restructure relationships with the surviving family. Grandparents, however, tend to control their grief and bereavement behavior, yielding to the priority of their adult child's grief. Also, they attempt to shield their child from the deep pain of the loss, and in so doing assert their own protective role as parent (Rando, 1986).

WHEN AN OLDER PERSON DIES

We have focused so far on the bereavement *of* the older person, not bereavement *for* the older person (M. S. Moss & Moss, 1989). Age of the deceased (though generally highly correlated with age of the bereaved individual) can be more significant in the outcome of bereavement than age of the bereaved person (Cleiren, 1993). This is reflected in the commonplace query after a person dies: "How old was he or she?" The answer helps to set the context of the loss and the parameters of bereavement.

Although one in eight persons are over 65, almost three quarters (73%) of all persons who die in the United States are at least 65 years old; of those, two thirds are between 65 and 85, and one third are over 85 (Rosenberg, Ventura, & Maurer, 1996). No longer is death in old age the rare privilege of the few as it was several centuries ago (Institute of Medicine, 1997). Women have greater longevity than men: 33% of women die at age 85 and older compared with 15% of men who die at that age (Brock & Foley, 1998).

In the United States, 53% of older persons die in hospitals and 17% in nursing homes (Brock & Foley, 1998). Based on the finding that 71% of all hospice recipients are age 65 and older (National Hospice Organization, 1995), we estimate that one in five older persons who die receive hospice services.

It is difficult to predict the timing or quality of end of life for elderly persons. The terminal decline in cancer tends to be relatively predictable, but less than one fourth of older persons die from cancer. Most die from other chronic diseases (e.g., heart disease, cerebral vascular disease, chronic lung disease, diabetes), in which the terminal trajectory often fluctuates between severe crises and improvements (Lynn, Wilkinson, Cohn, & Jones, 1998).

A few major retrospective studies of the end of life experience of older persons have been undertaken (Brock & Foley, 1998; Lawton, Moss, & Glicksman, 1990; Lentzner, Pamuk, Rhodenhiser, Rothenberg, & Powell-Griner, 1992). There is considerable range in the functioning and quality of life in the final year. For example, for a sample of elderly individuals (mean age 77) not residing in an institution, most (60%) were completely mentally clear over the year, many (41%) were never or seldom depressed. Although one half (51%) reported increased pain over the year, one quarter seldom or never felt pain or physical discomfort (Lawton et al., 1990).

Death of an Elderly Parent

This section examines themes that emerge when younger persons experience the death of a close elderly person, specifically the death of an elderly parent and its impact on an adult child. This in many ways is the prototype of the death of old people: It is anticipated and it is normative. Parents are expected to die before their children die.

Parent death may be seen as a psychosocial loss, outside the context of the medical model of bereavement, which focuses on illness, treatment, and recovery. Analyses of the impact of the death of an elderly parent have focused on six interrelated domains: anticipation, disenfranchisement, circumstances of the death, impact on the self, social construction of the loss, and maintenance of the tie with the deceased.

Anticipation

From early childhood on there are dual expectations about a parent's life course: On the one hand there is the anticipation that in the remote future the parent will predecease the child, and on the other hand there is a strong feeling that one's parent is invincible. There is often a progression of illness or frailty for an elderly parent that leads to anticipation of death (Fitzgerald, 1994). Family members may see decline in cognitive or physical functioning and experience "partial grief" for what is lost (Berezin, 1977; Kowalski, 1986). Part of the anticipation may involve "adaptation anxiety," which includes both worry about how the parent will handle dying and how the child will adjust to the dying and death (Moss & Moss, 1996b). In general, there is no consistent evidence that overall anticipation of the death of an older person lessens the intensity of later responses to bereavement (Lund, 1989).

Children may see each remission by their parent as a confirmation of the parent's strength. As long as the parent lives, the parent continues to be a buffer against the child's own death. This illusion of the parent's invincibility is a way in which the child holds on to the bond. Thus before the death there are strong, often simultaneous elements of holding on to the parent and letting go of the parent.

Disenfranchisement

Ageism is often translated into disenfranchised grief (Doka, 1989). It denigrates the dying and deceased older person, such that family members are given little social permission to express many dimensions of their loss. There is evidence that fewer funeral rituals mark the death of older persons (Kalish, 1985; Owen, Fulton, Markusen, 1983; Rosenblatt, Walsh, & Jackson, 1976). There is little support for adult children to engage in a long, intense process of bereavement for an elderly parent. Although most deaths across the life cycle may be seen as untimely because they occur too soon, lingering deaths of the very frail old parent who is in pain can be seen as too late (Marshall, 1996) and may evoke less intense grief.

Circumstances of the Death

The impact of the death of a parent can be influenced by the parent's living arrangement and quality of life at the end of life (Lynn et al., 1997). Research on children of recently deceased widowed parents examined four contexts of the last year of life: *coresident heavy caregiving* by the child, *nursing home*, relatively *independent* parents, and *geographically distant* parents (Moss, Moss, Rubinstein, & Resch, 1993; Moss, Resch, & Moss, 1997). Children who have been a heavy caregiver for a parent who has died tend to have greater emotional upset, more health problems, and stronger active and symbolic ties to the parent. Children of parents who had lived in a nursing home tend to express less emotional upset, greater control of expressions of grief, less sense of personal finitude, and less strong ties with the parent than those whose children provided heavy care at home. Acceptance of the death was greater for the caregivers and for children of parents in nursing homes than for children of independent parents. The impact of the death of distant mothers was not found to differ from any of the other three groups, suggesting that geographic distance does not dilute the quality of the parent–child tie (Moss, Moss, & Moles, 1985; Silverstein & Angelelli, 1998).

Pruchno, Moss, Burant, and Schinfeld (1995) examined in a prospective study the impact of the death of parents who had died in nursing homes. Almost half (46%) of the surviving children indicated that they had a harder time adjusting to the death than they had expected. Overall the greater the stress experienced by the adult child before the parent's death (e.g., the child's upset about the nursing home experience), the more difficult was the bereavement process (also see Aneshensel, Pearlin, Mullan, Zarit, & Whitlatch, 1995; Bass & Bowman, 1990). There tends to be no significant relationship between the parent's cognitive status and bereavement outcomes (Pruchno et al., 1995).

For family caregivers of elderly persons with dementia, bereavement is less stressful when the elder's personhood was perceived as having been lost before death (Aneshensel et al., 1995). Surviving children have indicated that the person they grieved for was the former vital and strong parent as well as the senile parent. There is evidence that basic themes in family caregivers' bereavement for persons with Alzheimer's disease are similar whether the elder died at home or in a nursing home (Aneshensel et al., 1995).

Impact on the Self

Parent death may be both expected and timely. Complicated or pathological grief tend to be rare for surviving adult children. There is contradictory research evidence on the impact of parental death on depression and sense of personal competence for the surviving child. With the loss of the parental buffer against the child's eventual death, sons and daughters often have a sense of increased personal finitude (Douglas, 1991; Kowalski, 1986; Scharlach, 1991; Scharlach & Fredriksen, 1993). The concept of acceptance of the death is ubiquitous but complex, and Bower (1997) has suggested that acceptance is reflective of the internal conflict between the social evaluation of a timely loss and the emotional pain evoked by the loss.

Social Construction

The expectations of other persons play a significant role in the social construction of feeling and the expression of emotions (Hochschild, 1979). In qualitative interviews, adult children frequently have spoken of controlling and managing their grief (Klapper, Moss, Moss, & Rubinstein, 1994). Some tried to avoid "selfish grief," feeling that it would be selfish to wish their parent were still alive because the parent would continue to suffer. Many spoke of family traditions, current family expectations, as well as "folk knowledge" (Bruner, 1990) as guides to their feelings, attitudes, and behaviors.

There tends to be a continuity of collective family identity that includes both living and dead members. Themes such as parental favoritism and rivalry may persist well after the death. The death of an elderly parent may have unique meanings for each surviving child based on their past relationship with the parent and their own losses over the life course. Nadeau (1998) emphasized that adult children often evaluate their own responses in comparison with their siblings.

The role of gender, of both the parent and the child, has been found to be significant in the reaction to parental death (Moss et al., 1997; Umberson & Chen, 1994). Bereaved sons tend to emphasize themes of control, action, cognition, and privacy (Moss, Rubinstein, & Moss, 1997), which are quite different from the traditional feminine style of bereavement responses emphasizing relationship loss, the value in social support, and expression and sharing of emotions (Martin & Doka, 1998).

Maintenance of the Tie While Letting Go

Although there is a strong sense of letting go in emotional upset, loss of a buffer against death, acceptance of the death, and a feeling of relief that caregiver's or parent's suffering may be ended, the child–parent bond persists after parental death and continues to give meaning to the loss (Horacek, 1991). Whether the child models herself after the parent or tries to break free of the parent's expectations (Pincus, 1974; Robbins, 1990) or whether memories and associations are comforting or painful (Umberson & Chen, 1994), these elements are part of the bereavement process. Holding on and letting go are inseparable. For example, although sadness represents a recognition of the reality of the loss, it also holds on to thoughts of the deceased and reflects the viability of the continuing tie. Alternately, although a sense of presence of the elder represents holding on, it is a constant reminder of the reality of the loss.

These domains in the adult child's bereavement may offer a template for understanding the ways other kin relate to the death of an elderly person, whether it be a grandparent, a parent-in-law, a sibling, or a parent of an elderly person.

CONCLUSION

Although younger persons may react more intensely to deaths of significant family members, and untimely deaths of young people may evoke particularly strong reactions among survivors, old age is the time of the life course when death occurs most frequently. Older people make up most of the deaths in the United States, and older people are more frequently bereaved than younger ones. We have emphasized the interplay between emotional and cognitive aspects of the bereavement experience of elderly individuals. Further we have suggested that bereavement is largely a normative process of adaptation to loss. Bereaved persons described earlier emphasize themes of continuity of self and shifts in self, continuity and change in family, and maintenance and weakening of the tie with the deceased. Understanding of processes of bereavement in old age—such as control of grief, reframing of the loss, and barriers to social support—may well yield considerable insights about bereavement involving younger persons.

Many areas are yet to be explored about bereaved older persons: the interface between their frailty, health values (Tsevat et al., 1998), attitudes toward their own deaths, and their reactions to the death of others; the ways that bereavement makes a difference in the network of personal relationships; the meaning and impact of multiple, sequential deaths; the differential coping styles of subgroups of elderly people—masculine and feminine, ethnic and religious, young old and old-old, relatively healthy and relatively frail, cognitively alert and Alzheimer patients. Further, we need to know more about how the death of an old person is experienced by caregivers in their own home, in the hospital, or in a nursing home; how the pattern of terminal decline affects bereavement; the range of contemporary rituals around the death of elderly persons; how the old person's death differentially affects multiple generations in the family. We welcome the increasing attention that is being paid to death and old age and suggest that the later years are a fertile and appropriate area for continuing exploration.

REFERENCES

Aldwin, C. M., Sutton, K. J., Chiara, G., & Spiro, A. (1996). Age differences in stress, coping, and appraisal: Findings from the Normative Aging Study. *Journal of Gerontology: Psychological Sciences, 51B*, 4, P179–188.

Aneshensel, C. S., Pearlin, L. I., Mullan, J. T., Zarit, S. H., & Whitlatch, C. J. (1995). *Profiles in caregiving: The unexpected career.* New York: Academic Press.

Arbuckle, N. W., & De Vries, B. (1995). The long term effects of late life spousal and parental bereavement on personal functioning. *The Gerontologist, 35,* 637–647.

Barnes, M. K., Harvey, J. H., Carlson, H., & Haig, J. (1996). The relativity of grief: Differential adaptation reactions of younger and older persons. *Journal of Personal and Interpersonal Loss, 1,* 375–392.

Bass, D. M., & Bowman, K. (1990). The transition from caregiving to bereavement: The relationship between care related strain and adjustment to death. *The Gerontologist, 30,* 35–42.

Bedford, V. H. (1994). Sibling relationships in middle and old age. In R. Blieszner & V. H. Bedford (Eds.), *Handbook of aging and the family* (pp. 201–222). Westport, CT: Greenwood Press.

Berezin, M. A. (1977). Partial grief for the aged and their families. In E. M. Pattison (Ed.), *The experience of dying* (pp. 279–286). Englewood Cliffs, NJ: Prentice Hall.

Bower, A. (1997). The adult child's acceptance of parent death. *Omega, 35,* 67–96.

Brock, D. B., & Foley, D. J. (1998). Demography and epidemiology of dying in the U.S. with emphasis on deaths of older persons. *The Hospice Journal, 13,* 49–60.

Bruner, J. (1990). *Acts of meaning.* Cambridge, MA: Harvard University Press.

Butler, R. N. (1969). Ageism: Another form of bigotry. *The Gerontologist, 9*, 243–246.

Cantor, M. H. (1991). Family and community: Changing roles in an aging society. *The Gerontologist, 31*, 337–346.

Carstensen, L. L., Gross, J. J., & Fung, H. H. (1997). The social context of emotional experience. *Annual Review of Gerontology and Geriatrics, 17*, 325–352.

Cleiren, M. P. H. D. (1993). *Bereavement and adaptation.* Washington, DC: Hemisphere Press.

Cornoni-Huntley, J., Blazer, D. G., Laferty, M. E., Everett, D. F., Brock, D. B., & Farmer, M. E. (Eds.). (1990). *Established populations for the epidemiologic studies of the elderly*, Vol. II: Resource data book, NIA Publication No. 90–945, National Institute on Aging, U.S. Department of Health and Human Services, Washington, DC.

De Vries, B., Dalla Lana, R., & Falck, V. (1994). Parental bereavement over the life course: A theoretical intersection and empirical review. *Omega, 29*, 47–69.

De Vries, B., Davis, C. G., Wortman, C. B., & Lehman, D. R. (1997). Long-term psychological and somatic consequences of later life parental bereavement. *Omega, 35*, 97–117.

Doka, K. J. (1989). Disenfranchised grief. In K. Doka (Ed.), *Disenfranchised grief: Recognizing hidden sorrow* (pp. 3–11). Lexington, MA: Lexington Books.

Douglas, J. D. (1990). Patterns of change following parent death in midlife adults. *Omega, 22*, 123–137.

Fish, W. C. (1986). Differences in grief intensity of bereaved parents. In T. A. Rando (Ed.), *Parental loss of a child* (pp. 415–430). Champaign, IL: Research Press.

Fitzgerald, M. (1994). Adults' anticipation of the loss of their parents. *Qualitative Health Research, 4*, 463–479.

Fry, P. S. (1997). Grandparents' reactions to the death of a grandchild: An exploratory factor analysis. *Omega, 35*, 119–140.

Fry, P. S. (1998). Spousal loss in late life: A 1-year follow-up of perceived changes in life meaning and psychosocial function following bereavement. *Journal of Personal and Interpersonal Loss, 3*, 369–391.

Goodman, M., Black, H. K., & Rubinstein, R. L. (1996). Paternal bereavement in older men. *Omega, 33*, 303–322.

Goodman, M., Rubinstein, R. L., Alexander, B. B., & Luborsky, M. (1991). Cultural differences among elderly women in coping with the death of an adult child. *Journal of Gerontology: Social Sciences, 46*, S321–329.

Hansson, R. O., & Carpenter, B. N. (1994). *Relationships in old age: Coping with the challenge of transition.* New York: Guilford Press.

Hansson, R. O., Remondet, J. H., & Galusha, M. (1993). Old age and widowhood: Issues of personal control and independence. In M. S. Stroebe, W. Stroebe, & R. O. Hansson (Eds.), *Handbook of bereavement* (pp. 367–380). Cambridge: Cambridge University Press.

Hansson, R. O., Vanzetti, N. A., Fairchild, S. K., & Berry, J. O. (1999). The impact of bereavement on families. In B. De Vries (Ed.), *End of life issues: Interdisciplinary and multidimensional perspectives* (pp. 99–117). New York: Springer.

Hayflick, L. (1994). *How and why we age*. New York: Ballantine Books.

Hays, J. C., Gold, D. T., & Pieper, C. F. (1997). Sibling bereavement in late life. *Omega, 35,* 25–42.

Hochschild, A. R. (1979). Emotion work, feeling, rules and social support. *American Journal of Sociology, 85,* 551–573.

Horacek, B. J. (1991). Toward a more viable model of grieving and consequences for older persons. *Death Studies, 15,* 459–472.

Institute of Medicine. (1997). *Approaching death: Improving care at the end of life.* M. J. Field & C. K. Cassel (Eds.). Washington, DC: National Academy Press.

Kalish, R. A. (1985). The social context of death and dying. In R. H. Binstock & E. Shanas (Eds.), *Handbook of aging and the social sciences* (2nd ed., pp. 149–170). New York: Van Nostrand Reinhold.

Kastenbaum, R. (1969). Death and bereavement in later life. In A. H. Kutscher (Ed.), *Death and bereavement* (pp. 27–54). Springfield, IL: Charles Thomas.

Kemp, B. (1985). Rehabilitation and the older adult. In J. E. Birren & K. W. Schaie (Eds.), *Handbook of the psychology of aging* (2nd ed., pp. 647–663). New York: Van Nostrand Reinhold.

Klapper, J., Moss, S., Moss, M., & Rubinstein, R. L. (1994). The social context of grief among adult daughters who have lost a parent. *Journal of Aging Studies, 8,* 29–43.

Kowalski, N. C. (1986). Anticipating the death of an elderly parent. In T. A. Rando (Ed.), *Loss and anticipatory grief* (pp. 187–199). Lexington, MA: Lexington Books.

Lang, F. R., & Carstensen, L. L. (1994). Close emotional relationships in late life: Further support for proactive aging in the social domain. *Psychology and Aging, 9,* 315–324.

Lawton, M. P., Kleban M. H., Rajagopal, D., & Dean, J. (1992). Dimensions of affective experience in three age groups. *Psychology and Aging, 7,* 171–184.

Lawton, M. P., Moss, M. S., & Glicksman, A. (1990). The quality of the last year of life of older person. *Milbank Quarterly, 68,* 1–28.

Lawton, M. P., & Simon, B. B. (1968). The ecology of social relationships in housing for the elderly. *The Gerontologist, 8,* 110–115.

Lazarus, R. S., & Folkman, S. (1984). *Stress, appraisal and coping.* New York: Springer.

Lentzner, H. R., Pamuk, E. R., Rodenhiser, E. P., Rothenberg, R., & Powell-Griner, E. (1992). The quality of life in the year before death. *American Journal of Public Health, 82,* 1093–1098.

Lesher, E. C., & Bergey, K. J. (1988). Bereaved elderly mothers: Changes in health, functional activities, family cohesion and psychological well-being. *International Journal of Aging and Human Development, 26,* 81–90.

Levav, I., Friedlander, Y., Kark, J., & Peritz, E. (1988). An epidemiological study of mortality among bereaved parents. *New England Journal of Medicine, 319,* 457–461.

Littlewood, J. (1992). *Aspects of grief: Bereavement in adult life.* New York: Routledge.

Lopata, H. Z. (1996). *Current widowhood: Myths and realities.* Thousand Oaks, CA: Sage.

Luborsky, M. R., & Rubinstein, R. L. (1997). The dynamics of ethnic identity and bereavement among older widowers. In J. Soklovsky (Ed.), *The cultural context of aging* (pp. 304–315). Westport, CT: Bergie & Garvey.

Lund, D. A. (1989). Conclusions about bereavement in later life and implications for interventions and future research. In D. A. Lund (Ed.), *Older bereaved spouses* (pp. 217–231). New York: Hemisphere.

Lund, D. A., Caserta, M. S., & Dimond, M. R. (1993). The course of spousal bereavement. In M. S. Stroebe, W. Stroebe, & R. O. Hansson (Eds.), *Handbook of bereavement: Theory, research, and intervention* (pp. 240–254). Cambridge: Cambridge University Press.

Lynn, J., Teno, J. M., Phillips, R. S., Wu, A. W., Desbiens, N., Harrold, J., Claessens, M. T., Wenger, N., Kreling, B., & Connors, A. F., Jr. (1997). Perceptions by family members of the dying experience of older and seriously ill patients. *Annals of Internal Medicine, 126,* 97–106.

Lynn, J., Wilkinson, A., Cohn, F., & Jones, S. B. (1998). Capitated risk-bearing managed care systems could improve end-of-life care. *Journal of American Geriatric Society, 46,* 322–330.

Marshall, V. W. (1996). Death, bereavement and the social psychology of aging and dying. In J. D. Morgan (Ed.), *Ethical issues in the care of the dying and bereaved aged* (pp. 57–73). Amityville, NY: Baywood.

Martin, T. L., & Doka, K. J. (1998). Revisiting masculine grief. In K. J. Doka & J. D. Davidson (Eds.), *Living with grief: Who we are, how we grieve* (pp. 133–142). Philadelphia: Brunner/Mazel.

Mendes de Leon, C. F., Kasl, S. V., & Jacobs, S. (1994). A prospective study of widowhood and changes in symptoms of depression in a community sample of the elderly. *Psychological Medicine, 24*(3), 613–624.

Metropolitan Life Insurance Company. (1977). Current patterns of dependency. *Statistical Bulletin, 58.*

Moss, M., Lesher, E. L., & Moss, S. Z. (1986). Impact of the death of an adult child on elderly parents: Some observations. *Omega, 17,* 209–218.

Moss, M. S., & Moss, S. Z. (1989). Death of the very old. In R. A. Kalish (Ed.), *Midlife loss* (pp. 121–145). Newbury Park, CA: Sage.

Moss, M. S., & Moss, S. Z. (1996a). Remarriage of widowed persons: A triadic relationship. In D. Klass, P. R. Silverman, & S. L. Nickman (Eds.), *Continuing bonds: New understandings of grief* (pp. 163–178). Washington, DC: Taylor & Francis.

Moss, M. S., & Moss, S. Z. (1996b). Anticipating the death of an elderly parent. In J. D. Morgan (Ed.), *Ethical issues in the care of the dying and bereaved aged* (pp. 111–130). Amityville, NY: Baywood.

Moss, M. S., Moss, S. Z., & Moles, E. L. (1985). The quality of relationships between elderly parents and their out-of-town children. *The Gerontologist, 25,* 134–140.

Moss, M. S., Moss, S. Z., Rubinstein, R., & Resch, N. (1993). The impact of elderly mother's death on middle-aged daughters. *International Journal of Aging and Human Development, 37,* 1–22.

Moss, M. S., Resch, N., & Moss, S. Z. (1997). The role of gender in middle-age children's responses to parent death. *Omega, 35,* 43–65.

Moss, S. Z., & Moss, M. S. (1989). The impact of the death of an elderly sibling. *American Behavioral Scientist, 33,* 94–106.

Moss, S. Z., Rubinstein, R. L., & Moss, M. S. (1997). Middle-aged son's reactions to father's death. *Omega, 34,* 259–277.

Murrell, S. A., & Himmelfarb, S. (1989). Effects of attachment bereavement and the pre-event conditions on subsequent depressive symptoms in older adults. *Psychology and Aging, 4,* 166–172.

Nadeau, J. W. (1998). *Families making sense of death.* Thousand Oaks, CA: Sage.

Nahemow, L. (2000). The ecological theory of aging. In R. L. Rubinstein, M. Moss, & M. Kleban (Eds.), *The many dimensions of aging* (pp. 22–40). New York: Springer.

National Hospice Organization. (1995). *Census Survey.* Arlington, VA: National Hospice Organization.

Norris, F. H., & Murrell, S. A. (1990). Social support, life events and stress as modifiers of adjustment to bereavement by older adults. *Psychology and Aging, 5,* 429–436.

O'Bryant, S. L., & Hansson, R. O. (1995). Widowhood. In R. Blieszner & V. H. Bedford (Eds.), *Handbook of aging and the family* (pp. 440–458). Westport, CT: Greenwood Press.

Owen, G., Fulton, R., Markusen, E. (1983). Death at a distance: A study of family survivors. *Omega, 13,* 191–225.

Parkes, C. M., & Weiss, R. S. (1983). *Recovery from bereavement.* New York: Basic Books.

Perkins, H. W., & Harris, L. B. (1990). Familial bereavement and health in adult life course perspective. *Journal of Marriage and the Family, 52,* 233–241.

Pincus, L. (1974). *Death in the family.* New York: Pantheon Books.

Prigerson, H. G., Frank, E., Kasl, S. V., Reynolds III, C. F., Anderson, B., Zubenko, G. S., Houck, P. R., George, C. J., & Kupfer, D. J. (1995). Complicated grief and bereavement-related depression as distinct disorders: Preliminary empirical validation in elderly bereaved spouses. *American Journal of Psychiatry, 152,* 22–30.

Pruchno, R. A., Moss, M. S., Burant, C. J., & Schinfeld, S. (1995). Death of an institutional parent: Predictors of bereavement. *Omega, 31,* 99–119.

Rando, T. (1986). Death of the adult child. In T. Rando (Ed.), *Parental loss of a child* (pp. 221–238). Champaign, IL: Research Press.

Raphael, B. (1983). *The anatomy of bereavement.* New York: Basic Books.

Robbins, M. A. (1990). *Midlife women and death of mother.* New York: Peter Lang.

Rosenberg, H. M., Ventura, S. J., & Maurer, J. D. (1996). Births and deaths United States 1995. *Monthly Vital Statistics Report, National Center for Health Statistics, 45,* Suppl. 2.

Rosenblatt, P., & Elde, C. (1990). Shared reminiscence about a deceased parent: Implications for grief education and grief counseling. *Family Relations, 39,* 206–210.

Rosenblatt, P. C., Walsh, P. R., & Jackson, D. A. (1976). *Grief and mourning in cross-cultural perspective.* New Haven, CT: HRAF Press.

Rosenbloom, C. A., & Whittington, F. J. (1993). The effects of bereavement on eating behaviors and nutrient intakes in elderly widowed persons. *Journal of Gerontology: Social Sciences, 4,* S223–S229.

Rowe, J. W. (1985). Health care of the elderly. *New England Journal of Medicine, 312, 13,* 827–835.

Rubin, S. S. (1992). Adult child loss and the two-track model of bereavement. *Omega, 24,* 183–202.

Rubin, S. S. (1993). The death of a child is forever: The life course impact of child loss. In M. S. Stroebe, W. Stroebe, & R. O. Hansson (Eds.), *Handbook of Bereavement: Theory, research and intervention* (pp. 285–299). Cambridge: Cambridge University Press.

Rubinstein, R. L. (1995). Narratives of elder parental death: A structural and cultural analysis. *Medical Anthropology Quarterly, 9,* 258–277.

Sanders, C. M. (1981). Comparison of younger and older spouses in bereavement outcome. *Omega, 11,* 217–232.

Sanders, C. M. (1989). *Grief: The mourning after: Dealing with adult bereavement.* New York: John Wiley.

Sanders, C. M. (1993). Risk factors in bereavement outcome. In M. S. Stroebe, W. Stroebe, & R. O. Hansson (Eds.), *Handbook of bereavement: Theory, research and intervention* (pp. 256–267). Cambridge: Cambridge University Press.

Scharlach, A. E. (1991). Factors associated with filial grief following the death of an elderly parent. *American Journal of Orthopsychiatry, 6,* 307–313.

Scharlach, A. E., & Fredriksen, K. I. (1993). Reactions to the death of a parent during midlife. *Omega, 27,* 307–317.

Schulz, R., & Heckhausen, J. (1998). Emotion and control: A life-span perspective. *Annual Review of Gerontology and Geriatrics, 17,* 185–205.

Shanfield, S., & Swain, B. (1984). Death of adult children in traffic accidents. *Journal of Nervous and Mental Disease, 172,* 533–538.

Silverstein, M., & Angelelli, J. J. (1998). Older parents' expectations of moving closer to their children. *Journal of Gerontology: Social Sciences, 53,* S153–S163.

Stroebe, W., & Stroebe, M. (1987). *Bereavement and health.* New York: Cambridge University Press.

Szanto, K., Prigerson, H., Houck, P., Ehrenpreis, L., & Reynolds III, C. F. (1997). Suicidal ideation in elderly bereaved: The role of complicated grief. *Suicide and Life-Threatening Behavior, 27,* 194–207.

Thompson, L. W., Gallagher-Thompson, D., Futterman, A., Gilewski, M. J., & Peterson, J. (1991). The effects of late-life spousal bereavement over a 30-month interval. *Psychology and Aging, 6,* 434–441.

Thompson, N. (1995). *Age and dignity: Working with older people.* Vermont: Ashgate & Aldershot.

Tsevat, J., Dawson, N. V., Wu, A. W., Lynn, J., Soukup, J. R., Cook, E. F., Vidaillet, H., & Phillips, R. S. (1998). Health values of hospitalized patients 80 years or older. *Journal of American Medical Association, 279,* 371–375.

Umberson, D., & Chen, M. D. (1994). Effects of a parent's death on adult child: Relationship salience and reaction to loss. *American Sociological Review, 59,* 152–168.

U.S. Bureau of the Census. (1997). *Statistical Abstract of the United States: 117th Edition.* Washington, DC.

Walter, T. (1996). A new model of grief: Bereavement and biography. *Mortality, 1,* 7–25.

Wortman, C., & Silver, R. C. (1992). Reconsidering assumptions about coping with loss: An overview of current research. In L. Montada, S. H. Filipp, & M. J. Lerner (Eds.), *Life crises and experiences of loss in adulthood* (pp. 341–365). Hillside, NJ: Erlbaum.

III

CONSEQUENCES:
THE BEREAVED INDIVIDUAL
IN SOCIAL CONTEXT

12

GRIEF FROM AN EVOLUTIONARY PERSPECTIVE

JOHN ARCHER

An evolutionary approach to grief raises two issues: first, whether grief itself is adaptive, and if not, how it arose through the process of natural selection; second, whether variations in grief following loss of different forms of relationship can be understood in terms of evolutionary principles. I first review evidence that grief is a universal human reaction and that a similar process occurs following both separation and loss of affectional bonds in social animals. I then consider the first of the two main questions —whether grief is adaptive. I argue that grief is associated with features that would be maladaptive in terms of natural selection. Its evolutionary origin can be understood in terms of a trade-off of these costs with other benefits—namely the existence of mechanisms for ensuring the stability of important social bonds.

In examining individual differences in grief from an evolutionary perspective, it is assumed that how we feel about someone when they have died depends on how we felt toward them when they were alive. This in turn depends on several sets of evolutionary principles concerning kinship,

I thank the editors and Nancy Segal for their helpful comments on this chapter.

age, and sex. These principles must necessarily operate through proximal mechanisms. Previous analyses have involved the strength of attachment as the mediating mechanism underlying broad differences in grief for different categories of relationships. An evolutionary approach can supplement our knowledge of how attachment develops by emphasizing responses to specific evolved cues in addition to general processes such as exposure learning.

We begin with the biological background to the adaptive significance of grief by examining how general it is in the natural world.

THE GENERALITY OF GRIEF IN THE NATURAL WORLD

Grief would seem to be a human universal. It is described in works of literature from ancient times to the present day and throughout the contemporary world in nonscientific and scientific accounts alike (Archer, 1999). Rosenblatt, Walsh, and Jackson (1976) used the Human Relations Area Files, which are records based on anthropological findings that are used as material for cross-cultural comparisons, to examine grief and found that the familiar reactions to a bereavement, such as distress, crying, anger, and aggression, were similar across those cultures for which there was evidence. Some reactions, such as crying and self-injury, were more common among women, whereas others, such as anger, were more common among men. W. Stroebe and Stroebe (1987) concluded from ethnographic evidence that crying was a consistent response to bereavement despite cultural practices that tend either to prolong or curtail the open expression of grief.

It is not surprising that grief is a human universal because a reaction similar to human grief occurs in social birds and mammals when they lose a significant other either through death or separation. Darwin (1872) described monkeys as "weeping" through grief, and since Darwin's observations scattered but unsystematic observations of animal grief have accumulated (Averill, 1968; Bowlby, 1961; Pollock, 1961). For example, jackdaws and geese frantically searched and called for a lost mate and also showed such signs of depression as a lack of interest in social contacts. A dog that has lost its owner appeared to search, and showed aggression and agitation. In general, social animals showed protest, increased activity, hostility, and depression when an attachment figure was lost. Later studies of young primates separated from their parents found comparable reactions (Field, 1996; Mineka & Suomi, 1978). Adult primates showed calling, distress, and depressive reactions when separated from a sexual partner or their peer groups. Butterfield (1970) found increased activity in the male and increased calling by the female when mated pairs of zebra finches were separated. In another pair-bonded species, the Mongolian gerbil, Hendrie and Starkey (1998) found reduced social contact with other animals following separation from the partner.

There is then, widespread evidence that reactions broadly similar to those of human grief occur among social birds and mammals when they are separated from a parent, offspring, or mate. There are, however, two aspects of animal grief that require further consideration: first for what types of relationship it occurs and second the extent to which it really is equivalent to the human form.

What is "a significant other" for a nonhuman animal? For humans, we are used to thinking of a loved-one, a close personal relationship. A clearer definition of such relationships can be derived from attachment theory combined with modern evolutionary thinking. Harlow and Harlow (1965) referred to all biologically important relationships as involving "affectional systems," emotional bonds between the individuals concerned. Parents and offspring and mates are the examples that most readily spring to mind, but the Harlows's list also included relationships between siblings and between young peer companions. In evolutionary terms, these relationships can be summed up as being important for overall (or "inclusive") fitness (Hamilton, 1964; Trivers, 1971). In general, they involve aiding relatives or those that are important for reproduction or parenting, or those who provide other forms of mutual benefit.

A second aspect of animal grief is whether it really is equivalent to the human form. Adult humans show distress reactions when separated from a loved one (Vormbrock, 1993), but these differ in important ways from the grief that occurs when the separation is understood to be permanent as a result of death (Archer, 1999). Although children may use the word "dead" at 3 to 4 years of age (e.g., Barrett, 1998), it is only at around 6 to 7 years of age that they come to regard death as irreversible (Koocher, 1973; Nagy, 1948; Speece & Brent, 1984; see also Archer, 1999). Before this age, they generally mix up departure and death. One important consequence of this is that an equivalent reaction is shown to separation and to death at these young ages. It is the *separation* that produces the reactions of sorrow among young children.

Even those animals closest to the human species in evolutionary terms are nowhere near to a 5-year-old child in terms of cognitive development (Archer, 1992). We should therefore expect a similar lack of distinction between reactions to separation and death among all nonhuman species. The available evidence indicates that this is so. Primates, such as baboons, gorillas, and chimpanzees, respond to the death of a loved one in a manner different from that of humans: Mothers will carry a dead infant around for some time, gradually leaving it for longer and longer periods until it is abandoned altogether (Altmann, 1980; Schaller, 1963; van Lawick-Goodall, 1968).

There is, therefore, a form of grief widespread in social birds and mammals, but it is equivalent to the grief of young children rather than to that of adult humans. The same reactions are found both to separation from, and the death of, a significant other. They involve active distress (often accompanied by calling and hostility) and passive–depressive behavior. The grief of adult humans is more complex, but it is built on the basic separation reaction. There are defensive reactions, which serve (in the short term, anyway) to avoid or mitigate the mental pain of grief; there are attributions of responsibility, which can lead to blaming others or to self-blame; there are intrusive thoughts; and there are changes to the person's self-concept (Archer, 1999).

WHY GRIEF IS MALADAPTIVE

Whether or not a feature is adaptive in evolutionary terms depends on its net contribution to fitness—that is, the perpetuation of genes from that individual in succeeding generations. If a gene contributes to producing an individual that is in better health, or can obtain more of life's essential resources, or can attract mates, or can produce viable offspring, or can feed and protect them so that they successfully reproduce, it will increase fitness. Such a gene will tend to spread in the population at the expense of alternatives at the same location on the chromosomes. Genes will also tend to spread as a result of help given to close kin, individuals sharing as a result of common descent a high proportion of genes that are generally uncommon in the population.

When tested against these criteria, grief does not aid fitness. Indeed, the reverse is the case: Its common features would lead to a lowering of fitness. In humans, grief is associated with poor health, leading to higher mortality rates, loss of appetite, loss of weight, depression, increased alcohol and drug consumption, and a loss of sexual interest and functioning.

The mortality of bereaved people is higher than in control samples (Lichtenstein, Gatz, & Berg, 1998; Stroebe & Stroebe, 1993), although the evidence for this is stronger for men than for women (e.g., Gallagher-Thompson, Futterman, Farberow, Thompson, & Peterson, 1993; Helsing & Szklo, 1981; Young, Benjamin, & Wallis, 1963) and in some studies only found for men (Smith & Zick, 1996). These deaths arise from a variety of causes, including heart disease, cancer, violence, suicide, and cirrhosis of the liver.

Clearly, there are a variety of mediating influences between a bereavement and subsequent death of the bereaved individual. Other evidence indicates increased somatic symptoms indicative of greater physiological stress among bereaved people compared with control samples (e.g., Gallagher-Thompson et al., 1993; Parkes & Brown, 1972; Windholz, Marmar, & Horowitz, 1985). The health consequences are worse when the grief is stronger (Prigerson et al., 1997). Specific indicators of physiological stress, such as secretion of corticosteroids from the adrenal cortex, are also increased following bereavement (Biondi & Picardi, 1996; Goodkin et al.,

1996), larger increases being associated with greater distress (Hofer, Wolff, Friedman, & Mason, 1972; Kim & Jacobs, 1993). There is widespread evidence for the suppression of reproductive function as a consequence of stress (Sapolsky, 1994). In the case of bereavement, Fenster et al. (1997) found a decline in sperm quality following the death of a close family member.

Studies of immune system functioning indicate changes in immunomodulation, notably lower natural killer cell activity, following bereavement (e.g., Goodkin et al., 1996; Kemeny et al., 1995; Schleifer, Keller, Carnerino, Thornton, & Stein, 1983), which are associated with depression in some studies (Herbert & Cohen, 1993; Irwin & Pike, 1993).

This evidence all points to poorer health following bereavement, which in the ancestral environment would adversely affect survival of the individual and therefore indirectly their chances of leaving viable offspring. Threats to individual survival will also adversely affect the survival chances of existing offspring. In nonindustrial societies, there are very pronounced practical disadvantages associated with the death of a father at a young age. For example, children of the Ache people of Paraguay are deliberately killed when their father dies in a club fight, such are their poor survival prospects (Hill & Kaplan, 1988). The death of a mother at an early age is likely to have even greater deleterious consequences (Hill & Hurtado, 1996; Voland, 1988).

There are also psychological consequences of bereavement that will adversely affect survival prospects. One of these, unfamiliar in Western cultures, is self-injury, which is widely reported in historical writings and accounts of preindustrial societies (Borgquist, 1906; Rosenblatt et al., 1976; W. Stroebe & Stroebe, 1987). Others, associated with anxiety and depression, are an inability to concentrate or to sleep and loss of appetite (e.g., Clayton, Desmarais, & Winokur, 1968; Hobson, 1964; Parkes, 1970; Shuchter & Zisook, 1993).

It is clear, therefore, that grief has detrimental effects. Some commentators (Crawford, Salter, & Jang, 1989; Izard, 1991; Tobach, 1970) have suggested that there might be indirect benefits—for example, that it evokes help or sympathy from others. There is, however, no evidence that the expressions of grief do generally evoke sympathy or that they occur more often when other people are present. In nonhuman primates, very obvious signs of grief are greeted with apparent indifference by social companions (Seyfarth & Cheney, 1992), and in humans sadness is strongest when the bereaved person is alone (Nesse, 1991).

HOW GRIEF AROSE THROUGH NATURAL SELECTION

If grief has such a negative impact on fitness, this raises the question of how it could have arisen through the process of natural selection. Why were individuals who grieved not replaced by those who greeted the death of a mate or offspring with emotional indifference? Such individuals would, it seems, be better able to carry on with essential maintenance activities and be more motivated and able to find a mate and raise offspring.

There are, however, two further considerations. Any individual characteristic such as grief has to be viewed as part of the individual's overall behavioral repertoire. It may be part of a wider set of reactions that, when taken together, are adaptive. In addition, every adaptive feature involves a trade-off between its benefits and its costs. Fighting has evolved throughout the animal kingdom, because it pays in terms of obtaining scarce resources and fending off danger (Archer, 1988a). Yet it involves costs in terms of the risk of injuries and the energy that needs to be expended.

Badcock (1990), Bowlby (1980), and Parkes (1972) have all suggested that grief is a cost incurred in pursuit of something that has an important adaptive consequence. The exact nature of the adaptive consequence varies in the three accounts, but it can be summed up as the persistence of important social bonds when the individual concerned is absent.

Bowlby (1980) argued that separation reactions have a clear adaptive function in that they aid reunion and maintain attachment to the other individual. Separation is a common occurrence among animals, and therefore separation reactions frequently come into play. Death of a significant other is much less common. Bowlby argued that the mechanisms controlling separation reactions are not sufficiently flexible to be suppressed in cases of death. In addition, animals cannot distinguish between death and separation (see earlier discussion). Bowlby's position is, therefore, that the maladaptive grief response is the necessary cost of the adaptive separation reaction.

Like Bowlby, Badcock (1990) also emphasized the common occurrence of individuals being separated and returning at a later time. However, he considered the evolution of grief within the context of evolving humans, when, as indicated earlier, it has a more widespread occurrence among social animals. Badcock's main point was the necessity of being able to resume a relationship when that individual returns. Grief enables this to occur by preventing the social network being rapidly rearranged to accommodate their absence. This applies most obviously to sexual partners, and it is in fact difficult to see how it would apply to parents who lose offspring. In the case of offspring who lose parents, it is even more difficult to understand how mechanisms that prevent finding substitutes would be appropriate. Nevertheless, Badcock's suggestion could be an important adjunct to Bowlby's emphasis on the role of separation reactions in promoting reunification. As well as doing so, they preserve the integrity of the relationship for those statistically more numerous occasions when the separation is temporary. As the pioneer of the study of grief, A. F. Shand, wrote, "The bond which joy alone forms with an object would in its absence be quickly dissolved, were there no sorrow to reinforce it" (Shand, 1914, p. 333).

Parkes (1972) emphasized the importance of stability in the mechanisms that underlie relationships. Any relationship is represented in the brain by a stable internal model associated with emotions and feelings toward that individual. The internal model does not change even when that individual ceases to be in the external world. It requires a gradual and painful process (grief) to achieve change in the internal model to conform to the new reality caused by a loss. Grief is therefore the cost of possessing brain mechanisms that represent significant aspects of the outside world as stable. They are not in fact stable, but it is generally advantageous to operate as if they were. Parkes's explanation emphasizes the need to experience important aspects of the outside world as unchanging, whereas Badcock located the need for stability in relationships.

Parkes's view is broadly similar to that of Klinger (1975), who was concerned with how individuals disengaged from a particular goal following any form of frustration and disappointment associated with it. To disengage, the individual first goes through a process of more persistent goal-directed activity, followed by a passive or avoidant action that aids switching from the current goal to another activity. Klinger emphasized the importance of disengagement mechanisms for preventing being locked on to inappropriate incentive-related cues. However, the reason that disengagement mechanisms are necessary in the first place is the stability of internal representations of goal-related activities despite disconfirmation by the external world. Klinger viewed grief as a more prolonged and complex disengagement process occurring when there are a series of related "goals" associated with a biologically important attachment.

These speculations can be integrated as follows. For social relations to endure despite separations, there must be mechanisms to cause social bonds to persist when the other is absent. These mechanisms are based on ones that ensure stable internal representations of important features of an animal's environment. In the case of relationships, they involve the presence of an enduring mental model of the other, which is continually checked with the input from the outside world. When there are signs of a discrepancy between this input and the mental model, an emotional reaction—distress—is generated. This also facilitates searching for the other individual. Grief is a by-product of these mechanisms, whose primary function is to maintain social relationships that are crucial for fitness.

EVOLUTIONARY PRINCIPLES UNDERLYING INDIVIDUAL DIFFERENCES IN GRIEVING

The assumption behind the following evolutionary analysis of individual differences in grief is that although grief is not adaptive, the intensity of grief will broadly follow the strength of the relationship with the dead person. This in turn will be influenced by evolutionary principles relating to kinship, the ages of the deceased and the bereaved, and the sex of the bereaved.

All forms of social relationship have originated and been perpetuated through natural selection because they provide a net contribution to passing on copies of an individual's genes to succeeding generations. The warm feelings we have for others are the consequences of mechanisms that aided our ancestors' survival. One feature of these feelings is that they generally operate in a discriminating way. People find young children attractive (e.g., Sternglanz, Gray, & Murakami, 1977) and their own children especially so (e.g., Daly & Wilson, 1988b); in addition, we are attracted to people of the opposite sex who show characteristics related to reproductive fitness (e.g., Singh, 1993, 1995).

The strength of feeling one individual has for another also arises from general processes, such as exposure learning, resulting from their mutual interactions over a period of time. This has been emphasized in attachment theory (Bowlby, 1969). In addition, evolutionarily important cues, such as those indicating kinship, or age, or health, are likely to facilitate or hinder the development of bonds between individuals. For example, analyses of child abuse indicate that parental feelings are facilitated in the case of natural offspring and more difficult in the case of step-children (Daly & Wilson, 1988a, 1988b).

In understanding the impact of kinship, age, and sex on grief, we can be guided in each case by principles derived from theoretical analyses of the evolution of social behavior. Hamilton's principle of inclusive fitness applies to kinship, Fisher's principle of reproductive value to age, and modern sexual selection theory to sex differences.

Animals form their primary relationships with close kin, who help and are in turn helped by them. The obvious example is parents caring for their offspring. Whereas offspring are the primary means of passing on parental genes, a sexually reproducing parent and its offspring only share, on average, .5 of the genes that are rare in the population as a whole (a figure that is known as *the coefficient of relatedness*). An individual who helped a dependent younger sibling to survive to maturity would also be helping a relative with the same coefficient of relatedness. It was this insight that led Hamilton (1964) to introduce the concept of *inclusive fitness*. This describes the overall contribution to perpetuating copies of an individual's genes when aiding relatives (other than offspring) is included. Hamilton's mathematical analysis indicated that the tendency to aid other individuals would follow the degree of kinship. Thus cousins (whose coefficient of relatedness is .125) would be aided to a lesser extent than siblings (.5), who in turn would be aided less than an identical twin (1.0).

If we assume that the strength of relationships with kin broadly fol-

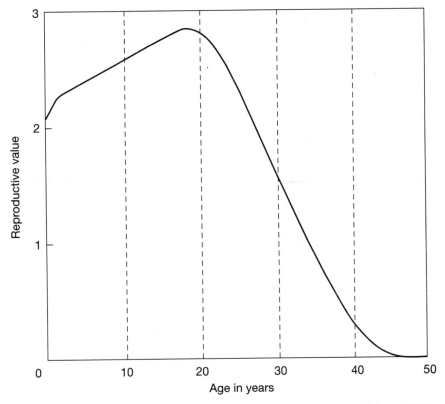

Figure 12-1. Reproductive value of Australian women in 1910 (Fisher, 1930).

lows their coefficient of relatedness, we have a clear starting point for an evolutionary analysis of grief following the loss of different relatives.[1] If other variables were constant, we would expect a greater intensity of grief for an identical twin than for another sibling, and a higher intensity for a full sibling than for a half-sibling, which in turn would be greater than for a cousin.

Of course, other variables are usually not constant, and in particular we have to consider the ages of the people concerned. The net contribution of another animal to passing on an individual's genes to succeeding generations depends on its *reproductive value*, a term introduced by Fisher (1930), originally to describe the expected contribution of a child to its parents' fitness. Figure 12-1 shows Fisher's graph of reproductive value against age for a human population in which infant and child mortality was high by modern western standards (Australian women in 1911). Except under modern conditions, where infant and child mortality are low, reproductive value increases from the beginning of life to an optimal value in

[1] We should note that this analysis does not cover relationships between nonrelatives, in particular spouses, which are—in evolutionary terms—built upon mutual benefit.

young adulthood, thus reflecting the lower survival chances at young ages. Thereafter it declines as more of the expected reproductive life is used up, to reach zero when reproduction ends.

Reproductive value can be used to describe the average utility of individuals of different ages for passing on copies of a relative's genes to future generations. From this, we can make predictions about how that relative should feel about them, which in turn will influence how intense grief will be when they have died. We would predict that as offspring get older, parents will value them more; but as the parents get older they will be valued less by their offspring. Daly and Wilson (1988a) used this reasoning to predict changes in homicide rates between parents and their offspring, homicide being viewed as an indication of the extent to which feelings become more antagonistic and less altruistic.

The change in reproductive value with age can be used to predict that parents' grief for the loss of a child will increase from early pregnancy to young adulthood, and that sons' and daughters' grief for a parent will decline with parental age.

Sexual selection is a particularly important principle for explaining a wide range of sex differences in social behavior (Archer, 1996a, 1996b; Buss, 1994; Daly & Wilson, 1988a). Several aspects of the modern version of sexual selection set out by Trivers (1972) are important when considering grief. Two are considered next.

The first is that females, and particularly female mammals, devote much more time and energy (*parental investment*) to the reproductive process than do males. Although in species with paternal care and protection, such as humans, this may be partly made up as the offspring grow older; during pregnancy and early neonatal life, the imbalance in parental investment is considerable. We should expect the feelings for the developing fetus and infant to reflect this and to be generally greater for women than for men. Grief following the loss of an offspring early in its life will reflect the strength of these feelings.

A second principle concerns paternity certainty. In animals with internal fertilization and parental care, it is always possible for the male to care for offspring that are not his. In evolutionary terms this is highly maladaptive: Various mechanisms for reducing the possibility—from killing existing offspring to guarding a mate—are found in animals, and there are human counterparts of these (Buss, 1994; Daly & Wilson, 1998a). Another consequence of paternity uncertainty is that the strength of relationships on the paternal side are likely to be on average weaker than those on the maternal side (where there is no uncertainty in genetic relatedness at the parental level).[2] This leads to the prediction that grief for a child's death

---

[2] There is of course the possibility of paternity certainty at the grandparental level, but this complication is omitted from the present discussion.

will be stronger among maternal than paternal grandparents and among maternal uncles and aunts than paternal ones.

THE IMPACT OF KINSHIP ON THE INTENSITY OF GRIEF

Identical or monozygotic (MZ) twins share all the same genes. From this consideration alone, we might expect MZ twins to form the closest of all human relationships (Segal, 1993). However, this expectation may depend on whether humans are sensitive to cues indicating genetic relatedness outside the normal range, which usually does not exceed a coefficient of relatedness of .6 (Wilson, 1995). In humans, MZ twins may have been insufficiently frequent or predictable in the ancestral environment for selection to have operated on them to produce an especially close relationship. There is, however, another way in which this might have come about, which is that cues for recognizing close kin, such as perceived similarity (Segal & Ream, 1998; Segal & Bouchard, 1993), operate to an even greater degree in MZ twins. Thus a close relationship among MZ twins would have arisen because they recognize each other as being more alike than dizygotic (DZ) twins, or other siblings, do. Studies of reunited MZ twins who were reared apart indicate that they form especially close relationships, suggesting that variables other than shared upbringing and similar treatment by others are indeed operating (Segal, 1993).

Three studies have compared the grief shown by MZ and DZ twins. In two independent samples involving more than 600 twins, MZs reported more intense grief than DZs (Segal & Ream, 1998; Segal, Welson, Bouchard, & Gitlin, 1995; Woodward, 1988). Segal and Bouchard (1993) also compared grief for a cotwin with that experienced when another relative had died using a single-item measure. Twins (both sorts combined, but 70% MZ) were grieved over more intensely than the person's mother, father, grandmother, grandfather, aunt, uncle, and surprisingly—spouse. Except for the latter difference, the other results have been confirmed with a larger sample (Segal, 1997): In this case, when the two types of twin were analyzed separately, MZs showed more intense grief for a cotwin than for a spouse, whereas the reverse was the case for DZs.

In contrast to these differences involving twins, Segal and Bouchard (1993) and Segal (1997) appeared to find no differences between the grief expressed for mothers or fathers, grandparents, aunts and uncles, using a single-item measure (based on inspection of fig. 1 in both papers). Littlefield and Rushton (1986) asked bereaved parents to estimate the perceived grief of other relatives, and used these estimates along with direct ratings of the parents' own grief, to test a number of evolutionarily derived hypotheses, but did not specifically test for differences between relatives.

It is possible to use data from both papers to undertake a simple assessment of estimated intensity of grief based on the coefficient of relatedness. Mean ratings for grief following death of relatives whose coefficient of relatedness is .5 can be compared with the mean ratings for those whose value is .25. If we ignore the additional complication of paternity uncertainty, parents fall into the first category and grandparents, aunts, and uncles into the second. Segal and Bouchard (1993) were assessing the grief experienced by twins for other relatives. The mean ratings for parents and other relatives (from their fig. 1), were 4.17 and 3.11, respectively. The difference in terms of effect size is a large one ($g = 1.00$).[3] Littlefield and Rushton (1986) were concerned with the grief of parents for their offspring, and they compared this with estimates of how other relatives felt following the same death. Because we are dealing with death of an offspring whose mean age was 14 years, from an evolutionary perspective we should expect much higher overall ratings (based on the reproductive value of the deceased). This is supported by mean parental ratings of 5.58 from both mothers and fathers (derived from tab. 1 in Littlefield & Rushton, 1986). The other relatives had a mean value of 4.02 (based on mother's ratings)[4] and 4.10 (based on the fathers' ratings). This produces the very large effect sizes of $g = 1.32$ (mothers' ratings) and the $g = 1.42$ (fathers' ratings) for the comparison of those related by .5 and those related by .25.

THE IMPACT OF AGE-RELATED CHANGES IN REPRODUCTIVE VALUE ON THE INTENSITY OF GRIEF

As shown in Figure 12-1, reproductive value increases from conception until early adulthood and thereafter declines, reaching zero at the end of reproductive life. Crawford et al. (1989) asked Canadian adults to rate the expected intensity of grief experienced by parents for each of two differently aged offspring who had died in a car crash. Each person made a series of these judgments, with the ages of the offspring varying from one day up to 50 years, with 10 age categories in all. The relative judgments for each age category were converted into standard scores,[5] and the scores for the 10 ages were compared with the reproductive values (see earlier discussion) for the Canadian population, which the authors calculated from census data. Both the judgments and the reproductive values were calculated sep-

---

[3] Calculations were undertaken using D-STAT (Johnson, 1989). Standard deviations were pooled. The sample sizes were based on the data points from Segal and Bouchard being largely independent, and those from Littlefield and Rushton being from the same sample. Although this is not quite correct in the first case, the effect sizes are so large that the main findings are likely to hold up despite this.
[4] Mothers' and fathers' ratings were calculated separately rather than relying on the composites used by Littlefield and Rushton, since these involved problems of inter-rater reliability and inflated sample sizes (Archer, 1988b).
[5] Z-scores.

arately for males and females. (See Figure 12-2 for the association for daughters.) Except at younger ages when the grief ratings are much lower than the reproductive values, the two show a reasonable correspondence. The pooled correlation coefficient for sons and daughters and men and women raters was $r = .64$. The reproductive values of the Canadian population are, like those of most modern Western nations, much higher from 0 to 18 years than is the case for populations with high infant and child mortality. With this in mind, Crawford et al. also calculated the association between the grief ratings for the 10 ages and the reproductive values of !Kung hunter–gatherers, which begins at the lower level associated with

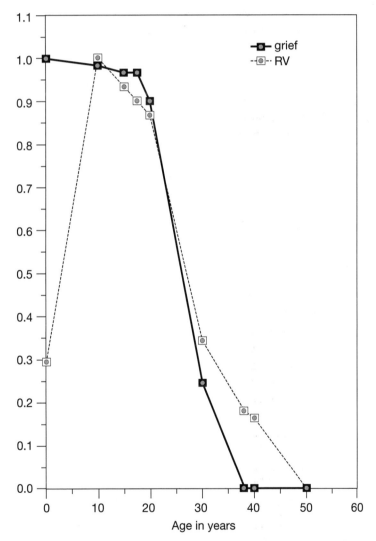

Figure 12-2. Graph showing estimated parental grief and reproductive value at different offspring ages for daughters (based on Crawford et al., 1989, fig. 2).

higher early mortality rates. They found the higher correlation of $r = .92$, suggesting that people's intuitive feelings may reflect ancestral rather than contemporary western demographic patterns.

This study was based on the empathy felt by others toward bereaved parents. Direct comparisons of the intensity of grief experienced for offspring at different ages are more difficult to make because there are few studies of parental grief that span a wide enough age range. Littlefield and Rushton (1986) did find a small correlation ($r = .11$) between grief intensity and the child's age, controlling for parent's age, but because "child" in this study ranged from 0 to 45 years of age, the correlation does not take account of the increase followed by a decrease in reproductive value with age (and indeed in the study by Crawford et al. correlations between grief and age were lower).

If we examine narrower age ranges, it is apparent that there is an association between the offspring's age and grief intensity at young ages. Several studies (Archer, 1999) show an association between gestational age and grief for perinatal deaths. For example, Toedter, Lasker, and Alhadeff (1988) found a partial correlation of .47, which indicates a considerable effect over this restricted age range. Overall, the findings for specific ages show a steady increase in grief intensity from early pregnancy loss through to young adulthood.

If we examine studies from the descending part of the reproductive value curve, there is evidence for a lowering of grief with increasing age of the deceased. Segal and Bouchard (1993) and Segal et al. (1995) found this among samples of adult twins. Grief for a parent who dies when an offspring is an adult is generally less intense than that for other forms of bereavement, such as loss of a spouse or a child (Bass, Noelker, Townsend, & Deimling, 1990; Leahy, 1993; Middleton, Raphael, Burnett, & Martinek, 1998; Owen, Fulton, & Markusen, 1983; Sanders, 1989).

THE IMPLICATIONS OF SEXUAL SELECTION FOR GRIEF

Two considerations from modern sexual selection were outlined earlier. The first was that female mammals show much higher parental investment early in life than males do. We should therefore expect grief to be greater among mothers than fathers, and that this applies particularly to early losses. This is generally found to be the case. However, because most studies do not include nonbereaved controls, it is seldom possible to tell whether this finding reflects preexisting sex differences in depression and other signs of distress or a greater impact of the loss among women. One exception is the study by Lang and Gottlieb (1993), who found that although women from a control sample showed higher scores than men on measures of distress that were not specific to grief, these differences were smaller than those between the bereaved men and women.

The second consideration is paternity certainty. An obvious prediction is that children would on average grieve more strongly for mothers than for fathers. This was found to be the case using data from Segal and Bouchard (1993, fig. 1): The effect size was $g = .50$ ($p = .06$).[6] Paternity certainty might also be a consideration in relation to the greater parental grief of mothers than fathers, but as we have seen there are other influences operating in this case.

Perhaps the most appropriate test of the impact of paternity uncertainty is a comparison of the grief of grandparents, and of aunts and uncles, from the two sides of the family. It was possible to make these calculations from data presented by Littlefield and Rushton (1986, tab. 1). As indicated previously, these are ratings of the estimated intensity of grief for the loss of a child, made by mothers and fathers independently. Rather than use the authors' composite ratings (see footnote 3), ratings from the two sources were kept separate. According to the fathers' ratings there were no differences between maternal and paternal grandmothers, maternal and paternal grandfathers, and maternal and paternal aunts and uncles ($g = .11$, 0, and 0, respectively). However, according to the mothers' ratings, the relative from the maternal side of the family grieved more intensely than the corresponding one from the paternal side in each case ($g = .30$, .43, and .56; all values exceed $p = .05$). These findings are particularly interesting because the mothers are much more likely than fathers to be aware of the reality of paternity uncertainty.

CONCLUSION

In the first part of this chapter, grief was placed into an evolutionary perspective by discussing evidence that human grief is similar to a set of responses to loss widely found in other social mammals. Grief itself does not aid survival and reproductive prospects (fitness), and indeed would appear to be maladaptive. Yet it can be understood as a consequence of the way in which affectional bonds are formed and maintained. It is the existence of these affectional bonds that are highly adaptive.

Three sets of evolutionary principles were applied to understanding differences in the intensity of grief. The first was reproductive value, and one study indicated that peoples' intuitive understanding of parental grief following the loss of an offspring at different ages followed reproductive value. Data on parental grief was generally insufficient to test this association for experienced grief, except for restricted age ranges, where the as-

[6] Using D-STAT (Johnson, 1989).

sociation was generally found. Some preliminary assessments of whether grief for kin followed the coefficient of relatedness indicated that it generally did. Predictions based on parental investment and paternity uncertainty were also supported by the available data.

Many of these evolutionary predictions lead to the same conclusions that would be derived from considering the way in which attachment developed, in particular that parent-to-offspring attachment would increase with age in the early years and that attachment would be strongest among close kin, who generally spend more time together. However, other predictions, such as different intensities of grief by maternal and paternal relatives, would not be expected from considering proximal mechanisms only. The challenge for future research from this perspective is to identify circumstances in which predictions based on attachment and on evolutionary principles are divergent. This could also lead to the enrichment of our understanding of attachment mechanisms, to include not only general processes such as exposure learning but also evolved cues associated with age, kinship, and paternity certainty.

REFERENCES

Altmann, J. (1980). *Baboon mothers and infants.* Cambridge, MA: Harvard University Press.

Archer, J. (1988a). *The behavioural biology of aggression.* Cambridge: Cambridge University Press.

Archer, J. (1988b). The sociobiology of bereavement: A reply to Littlefield and Rushton. *Journal of Personality and Social Psychology, 55,* 272–278.

Archer, J. (1992). *Ethology and human development.* Hemel-Hempstead, UK: Harvester-Wheatsheaf.

Archer, J. (1996a). Evolutionary social psychology. In M. Hewstone, W. Stroebe, & G. Stephenson (Eds.), *Introduction to social psychology: A European perspective* (pp. 24–45). Oxford: Blackwell.

Archer, J. (1996b). Sex differences in social behavior: Are the social role and evolutionary explanations compatible? *American Psychologist, 51,* 909–917.

Archer, J. (1999). *The nature of grief: The evolution and psychology of reactions to loss.* London: Routledge.

Averill, J. R. (1968). Grief: Its nature and significance. *Psychological Bulletin, 70,* 721–748.

Badcock, C. (1990). *Oedipus in evolution: A new theory of sex.* Oxford: Blackwell.

Barrett, H. C. (1998, July 8–12). *Children's early understanding of death: An evolutionary approach.* Paper presented at Human Behavior and Evolution Society 10th Annual Meeting, University of California, Davis.

Bass, D. M., Noelker, L. S., Townsend, A. L., & Deimling, G. T. (1990). Losing an aged relative: Perceptual differences between spouses and adult children. *Omega, 21*, 21–40.

Biondi, M., & Picardi, A. (1996). Clinical and biological aspects of bereavement and loss-induced depression: A reappraisal. *Psychotherapy and Psychosomatics, 65*, 229–245.

Borgquist, A. (1906). Crying. *American Journal of Psychology, 17*, 149–205.

Bowlby, J. (1961). Processes of mourning. *International Journal of Psychoanalysis, 42*, 317–340.

Bowlby, J. (1969). *Attachment and loss. Vol. 1. Attachment.* London: Hogarth Press and Institute of Psychoanalysis.

Bowlby, J. (1980). *Attachment and loss. Vol. 3. Loss: Sadness and depression.* London: Hogarth Press and Institute of Psychoanalysis.

Buss, D. M. (1994). *The evolution of desire: Strategies of human mating.* New York: Basic Books

Butterfield, P. A. (1970). The pair bond in the zebra finch. In J. H. Crook (Ed.), *Social behaviour in birds and mammals* (pp. 249–278). London: Academic Press.

Clayton, P., Desmarais, L., & Winokur, G. (1968). A study of normal bereavement. *American Journal of Psychiatry, 125*, 168–178.

Crawford, C. B., Salter, B. E., & Jang, K. L. (1989). Human grief: Is its intensity related to the reproductive value of the deceased? *Ethology and Sociobiology, 10*, 297–307.

Daly, M., & Wilson, M. (1988a). *Homicide.* New York: Aldine de Gruyter.

Daly, M., & Wilson, M. (1988b). Evolutionary social psychology and family homicide. *Science, 242*, 519–524.

Darwin, C. (1872). *The expression of the emotions in man and animals.* London: Murray.

Fenster, L., Katz, D. F., Wyrobek, A. J., Pieper, C., Rempel, D. M., Oman, D., & Swan, S. H. (1997). Effects of psychosocial stress on human semen quality. *Journal of Andrology, 18*, 194–202.

Field, T. (1996). Attachment and separation in young children. *Annual Review of Psychology, 47*, 541–561.

Fisher, R. A. (1930). *The Genetical Theory of Natural Selection.* Oxford, UK: Clarendon Press.

Gallagher-Thompson, D., Futterman, A., Farberow, N., Thompson, L. W., & Peterson, J. (1993). The impact of spousal bereavement on older widows and widowers. In M. S. Stroebe, W. Stroebe, & R. O. Hansson (Eds.), *Handbook of bereavement: Theory, research and intervention* (pp. 227–239). New York: Cambridge University Press.

Goodkin, K., Feaster, D. J., Tuttle, R., Blaney, N. T., Kumar, M., Baum, M. K., Shapshak, P., & Fletcher, M. A. (1996). Bereavement is associated with time-dependent decrements in cellular immune function in asymptomatic human immunodeficiency virus type 1-seropositive homosexual men. *Clinical and Diagnostic Laboratory Immunology, 3*, 109–118.

Hamilton, W. D. (1964) The genetical evolution of social behavior, I and II. *Journal of Theoretical Biology*, 7, 1–52.

Harlow, H. F., & Harlow, M. K. (1965). The affectional systems. In A. M. Schrier, H. F. Harlow, & F. Stollnitz (Eds.), *Behavior of nonhuman primates*, Vol. 2 (pp. 287–334). New York: Academic Press.

Helsing, K. J., & Szklo, M. (1981). Mortality after bereavement. *American Journal of Epidemiology*, 114, 41–52.

Hendrie, C. A., & Starkey, N. J. (1998). Pair-bond disruption in Mongolian gerbils: Effects on subsequent social behavior. *Physiology and Behavior*, 63, 895–901.

Herbert, T. B., & Cohen, S. (1993). Depression and immunity: A meta-analytic review. *Psychological Bulletin*, 113, 472–486.

Hill, K., & Hurtado, A. M. (1996). *Ache life history: The ecology and demography of a foraging people*. New York: Aldine de Gruyter.

Hill, K., & Kaplan, H. (1988). Tradeoffs in male and female reproductive strategies among the Ache: Part 2. In L. Betzig, M. Borgerhoff Mulder, & P. Turke (Eds.), *Human reproductive behaviour: A Darwinian perspective* (pp. 291–305). Cambridge, UK, and New York: Cambridge University Press.

Hobson, C. J. (1964). Widows of Blackton. *New Society*, 4(104), 13–16.

Hofer, M. A., Wolff, C. T., Friedman, S. B., & Mason, J. (1972). A psychoendocrine study of bereavement: Part 1. 17-hydroxycorticosteroid excretion rates of parents following death of their children from leukemia. *Psychosomatic Medicine*, 34, 481–491.

Irwin, M., & Pike, J. (1993). Bereavement, depressive symptoms and immune function. In M. S. Stroebe, W. Stroebe, & R.O. Hansson (Eds.), *Handbook of bereavement: Theory, research and intervention* (pp. 175–195). New York: Cambridge University Press.

Izard, C. E. (1991). *The psychology of emotions*. New York: Plenum Press.

Johnson, B. T. (1989). *Software for the meta-analytic review of research literatures*. Hillsdale, NJ: Erlbaum.

Kemeny, M. E., Weiner, H., Duran, R., Taylor, S. E., Visscher, B., & Fahey, J. L. (1995). Immune system changes after the death of a partner in HIV-positive gay men. *Psychosomatic Medicine*, 57, 547–554.

Kim, K., & Jacobs, S. (1993). Neuroendocrine changes following bereavement. In M. S. Stroebe, W. Stroebe, & R. O. Hansson (Eds.), *Handbook of bereavement: Theory, research and intervention* (pp. 143–159). New York: Cambridge University Press.

Klinger, E. (1975). Consequences of commitment to and disengagement from incentives. *Psychological Review*, 82, 1–25.

Koocher, G. P. (1973). Childhood, death and cognitive development. *Developmental Psychology*, 9, 369–375.

Lang, A., & Gottlieb, L. N. (1993). Parental grief reactions and marital intimacy following infant death. *Death Studies*, 17, 233–255.

Leahy, J. M. (1993). A comparison of depression in women bereaved of a spouse, child, or a parent. *Omega, 26,* 207–217.

Lichtenstein, P., Gatz, M., & Berg, S. (1998). A twin study of mortality after spousal bereavement. *Psychological Medicine, 28,* 635–643.

Littlefield, C. H., & Rushton, J. P. (1986). When a child dies: The sociobiology of bereavement. *Journal of Personality and Social Psychology, 51,* 797–802.

Middleton, W., Raphael, B., Burnett, P., & Martinek, N. (1998). A longitudinal study comparing bereavement phenomena in recently bereaved spouses, adult children and parents. *Australian and New Zealand Journal of Psychiatry, 32,* 235–241.

Mineka, S., & Suomi, S. J. (1978). Social separation in monkeys. *Psychological Bulletin, 85,* 1376–1400.

Nagy, M. (1948). The child's theories concerning death. *The Journal of Genetic Psychology, 73,* 3–27.

Nesse, R. M. (1991). What good is feeling bad? The evolutionary benefits of psychic pain. *The Sciences* (November/December), 30–37.

Owen, G., Fulton, R., & Markusen, E. (1983). Death at a distance: A study of family survivors. *Omega, 13,* 191–225.

Parkes, C. M. (1970). The first year of bereavement: A longitudinal study of the reaction of London widows to the death of their husbands. *Psychiatry, 33,* 444–467.

Parkes, C. M. (1972). *Bereavement: studies of grief in adult life.* London: Tavistock.

Parkes, C. M., & Brown, R. J. (1972). Health after bereavement: A controlled study of young Boston widows and widowers. *Psychosomatic Medicine, 34,* 499–461.

Pollock, G. H. (1961). Mourning and adaptation. *International Journal of Psychoanalysis, 42,* 341–361.

Prigerson, H. G., Bierhals, A. J., Kasl, S. V., Reynolds, C. F., III, Shear, M. K., Day, N., Beery, L. C., Newsom, J. T., & Jacobs, S. (1997). Traumatic grief as a risk factor for mental and physical morbidity. *American Journal of Psychiatry, 154,* 616–623.

Rosenblatt, P. C., Walsh, R., & Jackson, D. A. (1976). *Grief and mourning in cross-cultural perspective.* New Haven, CT: Human Relations Area File Press.

Sanders, C. M. (1989). *Grief: The mourning after: Dealing with adult bereavement.* New York: Wiley.

Sapolsky, R. M. (1994). *Why zebras don't get ulcers: A guide to stress, stress-related diseases, and coping.* New York: W. H. Freeman.

Schaller, C. B. (1963). *The mountain gorilla.* Chicago: University of Chicago Press.

Schleifer, S. J., Keller, S. E., Camerino, M., Thornton, J. C., & Stein, M. (1983). Suppression of lymphocyte stimulation following bereavement. *Journal of the American Medical Association, 250,* 374–377.

Segal, N. L. (1993). Twin, sibling and adoption methods: Tests of evolutionary hypotheses. *American Psychologist, 48,* 943–956.

Segal, N. L. (1997). Twin research perspective on human development. In N. L. Segal, G. E. Weisfeld, & C. C. Weisfeld (Eds.), *Uniting psychology and biology: Integrative perspectives on human development* (pp. 145–173). Washington, DC: American Psychological Association.

Segal, N. L., & Bouchard, T. J. (1993). Grief intensity following the loss of a twin and other relatives: Test of kinship hypotheses. *Human Biology, 65,* 87–105.

Segal, N. L., & Ream, S. L. (1998). Decreases in grief intensity for deceased twin and non-twin relatives: An evolutionary perspective. *Personality and Individual Differences, 25,* 317–325.

Segal, N. L., Welson, S. M., Bouchard, T. J., & Gitlin, D. G. (1995). Comparative grief experiences of bereaved twins and other bereaved relatives. *Personality and Individual Differences, 18,* 525–534.

Seyfarth, R., & Cheney, D. (1992). Inside the mind of a monkey. *New Scientist, 133,* 25–29.

Shand, A. F. (1914). *The foundations of character.* London: Macmillan.

Shuchter, S. R., & Zisook, S. (1993). The course of normal grief. In M. S. Stroebe, W. Stroebe, & R. O. Hansson (Eds.), *Handbook of bereavement: Theory, research and intervention* (pp. 23–43). New York: Cambridge University Press.

Singh, D. (1993). Adaptive significance of female physical attractiveness: Role of waist-to-hip ratio. *Journal of Personality and Social Psychology, 65,* 293–307.

Singh, D. (1995). Female judgements of male attractiveness and desirability for relationships: Role of waist-to-hip ratio and financial status. *Journal of Personality and Social Psychology, 69,* 1089–1101.

Smith, K. R., & Zick, C. D. (1996). Risk of mortality following widowhood: Age and sex differences by mode of death. *Social Biology, 43,* 59–71.

Speece, M. W., & Brent, S. B. (1984). Children's understanding of death: A review of three components of a death concept. *Child Development, 55,* 1671–1686.

Sternglanz, S. H., Gray, J. L., & Murakami, M. (1977). Adult preferences for infantile facial features: An ethological approach. *Animal Behaviour, 25,* 108–115.

Stroebe, M. S., & Stroebe, W. (1993). The mortality of bereavement: A review. In M. S. Stroebe, W. Stroebe, & R. O. Hansson (Eds.), *Handbook of bereavement: Theory, research and intervention* (pp. 175–195). New York: Cambridge University Press.

Stroebe, W., & Stroebe, M. S. (1987). *Bereavement and health.* Cambridge: Cambridge University Press.

Tobach, E. (1970). Notes on the comparative psychology of grief. In B. Schoenberg, A. C. Carr, D. Peretz, & A. H. Kutscher (Eds.), *Loss and grief: Psychological management in medical practice* (pp. 347–354). New York: Columbia University Press.

Toedter, L. J., Lasker, J. N., & Alhadeff, J. M. (1988). The Perinatal Grief Scale: Development and initial validation. *American Journal of Orthopsychiatry, 58,* 435–449.

Trivers, R. L. (1971). The evolution of reciprocal altruism. *Quarterly Review of Biology, 46*, 35–57.

Trivers, R. L. (1972). Parental investment and sexual selection. In B. B. Campbell (Ed.), *Sexual selection and the descent of man* (pp. 136–179). Chicago: Aldine.

van Lawick-Goodall, J. (1968). The behaviour of free-living chimpanzees in the Gombe Stream Reserve. *Animal Behaviour Monographs, 1*, 161–311.

Voland, E. (1988). Differential infant and child mortality in evolutionary perspective: Data from late 17th to 19th century Ostfriesland (Germany). In L. Betzig, M. Borgerhoff Mulder, & P. Turke (Eds.), *Human reproductive behaviour: A Darwinian perspective* (pp. 253–261). Cambridge: Cambridge University Press.

Vormbrock, J. (1993). Attachment theory as applied to wartime and job-related marital separation. *Psychological Bulletin, 114*, 122–144.

Wilson, D. S. (1995, March 8). Commentary on identical twins. *Human Behavior and Evolution Society Electronic List.*

Windholz, M. J., Marmar, C. R., & Horowitz, M. J. (1985). A review of the research on conjugal bereavement: Impact on health and efficacy of intervention. *Comprehensive Psychiatry, 26*, 433–447.

Woodward, J. (1988). The bereaved twin. *Acta Geneticae Medicae et Gemellologia, 37*, 173–180.

Young, M., Benjamin, B., & Wallis, C. (1963). The mortality of widows. *The Lancet, 7305*, 454–456.

13

A SOCIAL CONSTRUCTIONIST PERSPECTIVE ON CULTURAL DIFFERENCES IN GRIEF

PAUL C. ROSENBLATT

> In Kaliai ... people ... almost always attribute death to ... a spirit or (more frequently) a hostile human being. ... The Kaliai believe that a human agent may cause death by an act of violence; by shame or slandering other persons, thereby causing them to commit suicide (they call this "killing with talk") or—most commonly ... —by the practice of malevolent magic; by sorcery. As one of our consultants declared, "If we had no sorcerers, we'd have no death." (Counts & Counts, 1991, p. 193)

A social constructionist perspective on cultural differences in grieving raises challenging questions about grief, culture, and social construction. This chapter offers a constructionist view on grief theories that assume fundamental commonality across humans in grieving and on cross-cultural research that could be taken as support for the idea that such fundamental commonality exists. While the chapter offers support for the notion that there is commonality among grieving humans, it also questions how great and significant that commonality is. Human grieving seems to be quite malleable. Exploring that malleability in cross-cultural perspective, it is clear that cultural differences in reactions to loss are linked to many factors. Those factors include cultural understandings of what has been lost with a death, death rituals, cultural constructions of a survivor's ongoing and future relationship with the deceased, and the cultural construction of culturally deviant grieving. With so much variability across cultures in how grief is understood, the conceptions other cultures offer of grieving may be valuable supplements or alternatives to contemporary psychological conceptions of grieving. To see and understand beyond contemporary psychological conceptions, we need to learn, understand, and become fluent in the language and realities of people in societies very different from those of most of us who have been writing about grief.

A SOCIAL CONSTRUCTIONIST PERSPECTIVE

A social constructionist perspective on grieving denies the essentiality and universality of thoughts, feelings, and words said in or about bereavement. From a social constructionist perspective, whatever anyone, including scholars of bereavement, might call "bereavement" is a social construction. It is inextricably entangled in culture-based social construction processes, social interactions among those writing about grief, the ways their spoken and written language shape and limit what can be said about grief, and their own socially constructed experiences of loss and grief.

From a social constructionist perspective, everything that we may say, as social scientists writing about grief, is shaped by our current sociocultural environment. Because that environment is ever-changing, we are always in a position of revising what we think and say. But it is difficult to say, and possibly even fruitless to try to say, how much what we experience as developments in our thinking about grief are achievements of scientific progress and how much they are achievements of remaining in the flow of an ever-changing sociocultural environment. From a constructionist perspective, the basic terms used in this chapter—*death, grief, feeling, culture, society, ethnographic evidence, deviance, religion,* and *gender*—are socially constructed. Treating them as static, clearly knowable concepts obscures the fluidity and diversity of meanings and usages of each term and how much our constructing the terms as we do depend on ignoring information that could challenge our constructions (cf. Rosenblatt, 1994; Rosenblatt & Wright, 1984). In fact, each term I use in this chapter could be accompanied by a long footnote pointing out the assumptions, simplifications, ethnocentrism, and selectivity of perception that allow me to use the term as though it has a solid and more or less universally agreed on meaning. But writing from a social constructionist perspective is like all other theory and research work in psychology and the social sciences: a conceptual building operation that requires positing a temporarily solid base to illuminate a topic of interest.

From a constructionist perspective, each bereaved person is as much a player as anyone else in constructing whatever is going on. Each person is active in a network of interacting individuals, families, groups, institutions, and ways of thinking. A comprehensive constructionist analysis would illuminate this network of mutual interactions in all their systemic complexity and subtlety.

In an essay on grief and culture, it may help to illustrate how an awareness of the ways constructed realities, even those constructed by social scientists, may be too simple is to explore the concept of "a culture." "A culture" is a reified abstraction, a category that serves as a container for lots of other abstractions that are based on inevitably selective observations made by certain people at certain times. Even if we grant some sort of reality to a culture, say the culture of the Navajo Indians, a culture is not monolithic and invariant. It is inhomogeneous and complex, filled with contradictions and ambiguities, and ever in process.

Social construction is, in part, a process of distilling, sorting out, and perhaps temporarily coming to terms with complexity, contradictions, ambiguity, and processes in the sociocultural environment. So any simple characterization of a culture's pattern of grieving or of death ritual is misleading. It almost certainly is too simple to rely on in trying to understand or help a person or family from that culture (Rosenblatt, 1993, 1997). Even in what seems from a distance to be a homogeneous and unchanging culture, there may be a great deal of diversity and change. For example, Barker (1985), writing about the Maisin of Papua New Guinea, said that each of the 10 deaths that occurred while he was doing his fieldwork was treated differently by the Maisin. Further, a characterization of a culture as though it is distinct, concrete, and free-standing obscures the dynamic interactions among what we may conceive of as separate cultures. Those interactions guarantee that new complexities, contradictions, interpretations, belief systems, translations, and other ingredients for social construction are always being imported or created.

One kind of support for social constructionist perspectives on bereavement is evidence of historical, cultural, ethnic, and other differences in grieving. Such evidence shows that much about human grieving is not constant. Grieving varies markedly across places, times, and groups in how, when, or even whether emotions that might be taken as grief are expressed, how much bereaved individuals seem to be preoccupied by the death, and how much the death alters daily routines and interactions. Grieving varies markedly across cultures in how a death is understood, the possibility for future reunion with the dead, the meaning of various forms of emotion following the death, the things to say to self and others following a death, and the things believed about death. When there is obvious emotional expression of grief, there are variations across historical periods and groups in terms of which family members and associates of the deceased express strong grief feelings. There are also enormous variations across historical periods and groups in how grief is expressed; tears and what Euro-Americans would label sorrow do not constitute a universal emotional language of loss.

In the next section of this chapter, I argue that there are what seem to be near-constants if not universals in grieving (cf. Counts & Counts, 1991; Klass, 1999). However, I think that there is no solid epistemological ground to stand on in making such a claim. Much of what is written about grieving comes from the perceptions, writing, and editing of educated Americans and Europeans. When my collaborators and I wrote *Grief and Mourning in Cross-Cultural Perspective* (Rosenblatt, Walsh, & Jackson, 1976), we relied on sources by Europeans and Americans and sources from other languages and cultures that were selected, translated, and edited by Europeans and Americans. Almost everything we read was written in English. At that time, before social constructionist thinking was well-developed, there seemed to be no great risk to looking at grief everywhere from the standpoint of one language and what is arguably a single culture. I believed that there were real realities that objective observers with sufficient time, opportunity, and local language skill could report. Now I believe an observer's culture and language in knowing and an observer's culture and language of writing strictly limit what an observer can know and communicate. And I now believe that a reader's own cultural and language limitations affect what the observer can grasp of what is written about another culture and language. So now I have very serious reservations about our finding that certain things are common in grief across cultures. What seems to be an objective reality of common experience and expression may only be an artifact of the limitations of culture and language in our sources and ourselves. So I offer the following section of the chapter with a strong warning to the reader to be skeptical.

DEATHS SEEM TO BE DIFFICULT FOR PEOPLE EVERYWHERE

Our study of 78 of the world's cultures (Rosenblatt et al., 1976) documented that deaths seemed to be difficult for many people in every culture. The difficulty was expressed through tears, anger, personal disorganization, lamentation, depressed affect, or difficulty engaging in some or all of what before the death would be normal activities.

The one culture in our study about which there was doubt concerning the commonality of strong grief feelings following a death was the Balinese. But more recent research by Wikan (1990) has demonstrated conclusively that deaths are in fact difficult for the Balinese. Wikan showed how grieving Balinese do not stop feeling sad, distressed, and disorganized even though they successfully put on a smooth, unruffled, even happy exterior. They are strongly supported, even coerced in their efforts to appear as though not bereaved by concerned acquaintances, friends, and relatives— people who work at cheering them and offering ways to define the loss as insubstantial. Underlying these processes are Balinese concerns about the vulnerability of the bereaved to illness and to malevolent acts of others. The concerns arise from beliefs and values regarding something that might be glossed in English as sorcery, regarding illness and health, and regarding social order in Balinese life.

Perhaps it seems obvious why deaths would be difficult for people everywhere, but from the constructionist perspective of this chapter, it should not be obvious. What another person means to one, what the other person does for one and with one, the place of the other in one's life, the meaning of the other's death, and whether death is understood to cut off relationship with the deceased are all socially constructed. Even "death" itself has different meanings from culture to culture. Hence it would seem implausible, from a constructionist perspective, that deaths would be difficult for many people in so many cultures. This finding, if it can be trusted, could be taken as a threat to social constructionist thinking and as an argument that human nature puts limits on constructed variability.

CHALLENGE TO THE CLAIM OF GRIEF UNIVERSALITY

In any culture in which the aftermath of death is described in some detail, it is always clear that there are substantial variations in grieving among people who, based on their relationship with the deceased, seem as though they would grieve in the same way. For example, based on my own research in the United States (Rosenblatt, 2000), I have seen how one parent who loved his child dearly remains depressed and cries recurrently for decades, whereas another parent who loved his child dearly never cries and seems, in a matter of weeks, to be free of depression and sorrow. What is universal when there are such wide individual variations?

Wide variations among cultures in how and how much people typically grieve also pose a challenge to the claim of grief universality. In the Rosenblatt et al. (1976) study, there were cultures in which anger and aggression were a central part of grief and cultures in which they were seemingly never expressed in grief, cultures in which self-mutilation was a part of grief and cultures in which it was not. There were cultures in which grief for a close family member would often go on for years and cultures in which grief, at least on the surface, typically disappeared quickly. The Balinese were anomalous in the study because the ethnographic literature said that they rarely or never cried in bereavement, and yet there were other cultures in which tears were common in bereavement. Those kinds of findings make clear that any theory of grieving that claims that grief is basically the same across all humankind must account for a lot of variability and must be careful not to overstate what is common to all grieving humans.

DIVERSITY OF CULTURAL CONSTRUCTIONS IN BEREAVEMENT

Caught between the notion that grief following a major loss is basically human and the notion that grief varies enormously across individuals and cultures, a next step might be to explore the ways we can make sense of differences across cultures in the construction of bereavement. What is linked to those construction differences? As the linkages are explored, we move away from a shouting contest between those who think grief is basically the same across all humans and those who say that little that follows loss is common across cultures. Instead, we move to theory, research questions, and practice ideas about how to make sense of grief in various contexts.

One place to look in trying to make sense of diversity in reactions to a loss is to look at cultural differences in what is understood to have been lost with a death. In comparing cultures, there is a sense that what is perceived as lost with a death is enormously variable from culture to culture. For example, Leavitt (1995) wrote about a Bumbita Arapesh (Papua New Guinea) young man enumerating what he had lost because his father had died. (The contrast that I draw is with what I presume one would hear from many young men in North America and Europe.) Included in the Bumbita man's enumeration of what he had lost were mentorship at becoming an effective man, help obtaining a wife, the strength that a young man in that culture is said to sap from his father, and the opportunity to show his father that he can work. These losses are not what would be shared with many young men in Europe and North America. I believe, moreover, that these losses would seem even more exotic if they had not been glossed with English language terms—if, for example, we had a fully nuanced Arapesh sense of what "mentorship" is in father–son relationships.

Another way to look at cultural differences in bereavement is to look at the construction of the relationship of survivors with the person who has died. There is considerable evidence that many people in the United States continue a relationship in various forms with loved ones who have died (Rosenblatt, 2000). The continuation of relationship of survivors with people who have died seems to be a fact of life for some survivors in many cultures (see Rosenblatt et al., 1976, discussions of "ghosts"). But even if such continuation can be found commonly, the forms and meanings of such continuation may be strongly affected by the cultural context. Consider grief among the Toraja of Indonesia as described by Hollan (1995) and Wellenkamp (1991). The Toraja value emotional equanimity, so bereaved individuals are encouraged not to be preoccupied with the dead or to dwell on memories of them. But Toraja dead still are in relationship to the living and may communicate with them via dreams, often dreams that foretell future prosperity. Such dreams are culturally expected and are encouraged. People grow up knowing of such dreaming and how to interpret it, so after a death of someone close to them, they may eagerly await such dreams. For Europeans and Americans who have continuing connections with the deceased, the usual forms of such connection might be a sense of presence, internal conversation, connections through prayer, or dreams that may be taken as a meaningful message but not with the expectation that the dreaming will tell of future prosperity.

There are enormous differences from society to society (and within societies) in how grief is shaped, the meaning of the shaping, and the consequences of resisting shaping processes. For example, grief often occurs in a sociopolitical or economic environment that demands public words, emotional expressions, and actions that are different from private social constructions. In the past in North America and Britain, that meant that many people felt constrained to display their "mourning" publicly, through clothing, actions, and demeanor that expressed a public grief that not infrequently was more intense, prolonged, or unambivalent than the private socially constructed reality (Lerner, 1975). The discomfort, inconvenience, and expense of those requirements were factors in the ending of the wearing of mourning (Lerner, 1975). In Britain another factor may have been a shift in the public construction of grieving about soldiers killed in World War I. Lerner (1975) argued that then the public construction was that the soldiers died as heroes, so there was an expectation that bereaved individuals would celebrate their death. Public grieving for their death was thought of as unpatriotic, something that would discount the heroism of the dead (and undermine the resolve of the British to carry on the war). However, Cannadine (1981, p. 218) argued that the decline of wearing mourning at that time resulted from a collective realization that with so many war dead, wearing mourning was "recognized as being inadequate, superfluous and irrelevant."

Nowadays, billions of people live in countries that demand a decorum that accepts or even honors a grimly oppressive political regime. In such a situation, many people must hide feelings and actions that violate the regime's idea of loyal subject. Failure to conceal feelings and actions the regime might consider inappropriate would risk loss of job, property, freedom, or even life for one's self and one's family and friends. For example, there are many stories from the "dirty war" in Argentina and "La Violencia" in Guatemala, where people whose relatives or friends had been "disappeared" by the agents of the military dictatorship had to act in public as though they did not grieve the disappearance (Hollander, 1997; Zur, 1998, p. 211). This is not to say that it is only the modern totalitarian state that coerces social constructions of grief that deny feelings. For example, in Central America, there is a history of coerced denial of grief in some local cultures—for example, Mayan widows coerced to act as though their conjugal relationship had never existed (Zur, 1998, pp. 58–59).

In these situations, it seems clear that people can achieve multiple, even contradictory social constructions of a death and their grief, with one (or perhaps more than one) construction in public and another (or perhaps more than one) in private. It also seems clear that some bereaved people experience that as difficult and strongly prefer greater consistency in social construction across all situations. This is not to say that everyone prefers to grieve freely and in an invariant constructive environment. Some grieving people in the United States say that they prefer to move between situations in which they can and do grieve strongly and situations in which the expectation is that they will distance their grieving (Rosenblatt, 2000).

The coercion of grieving along certain routes and not others does not necessarily go uncontested. The complexities and contradictions of cultural forces guarantee that all the force shaping grief is not unidirectional. For example, sometimes the local cultural construction of reality demands a public challenge of an oppressive regime, even if there are risks in that. Consider the public testimonies of people who lost family members to the death squads, military massacres, and calculated starvation strategies of the elites in El Salvador and Guatemala. Those testimonies, which have fueled worldwide pressure on the elites to end their wars with their own people, come out of cultural situations that give such testimonies meaning (Westerman, 1994). People deliver their testimony in hopes of ending the pattern of violence, so that some good might come from the deaths and other losses they have experienced, and out of liberation theology ideas of active community participation (Westerman, 1994). The testimony may also arise from religious beliefs requiring that the story of a death be collectively developed and told (cf. Zur, 1998, pp. 170–172). So even as people who have experienced a loss resist certain aspects of the sociocultural environment, they are responsive to others. Contesting certain forces in the environment does not mean that people are grieving in a sociocultural vacuum.

SOCIAL CONSTRUCTION AND THE MALLEABILITY OF GRIEF

People who are newly bereaved are surrounded by others whose own grieving offers models of bereavement decorum and who may even try to influence them about what to feel and do. There will be rituals that define the bereaved person and the bereaved person's feelings and actions. Included in those rituals may be eulogies, laments, prayers to and for the dead, funeral statements that define the bereaved individual, storytelling about the deceased and about grieving, the transmission of information about the deceased, and much else that shapes or creates the grieving. Also included in the rituals are many nonverbal defining symbols—for example, of the movement of the deceased to a more distant place or of the transformation of the deceased's relationship with the living. Further, in many cultures death rituals go on for months or even years following a death, which gives many opportunities for communal social construction processes to operate.

The construction of grief actually begins long before most people are bereaved. Grief is constructed throughout the life span, in the full context of life in culture and society. Those of us who study grief typically "punctuate" that context by beginning our examination of a survivor's grieving at the time the survivor first knows of a death or first anticipates that a death will happen soon. But everyone we study has had a lifetime of social construction about emotion, emotional control, the meaning of death, the etiquette of grieving, and much else that is relevant to what we call "bereavement."

With a lifetime of experience pushing for one way of grieving versus another, and with all the richness of interactions and rituals that go on following a death, it should not be surprising that cultures vary widely in how death is dealt with. Consider a small bit of what may seem strange to many in North America and Europe about the Kwanga of Papua New Guinea, as described by Brison (1992, 1995). Kwanga believe that most deaths are caused by sorcery. People talk about the deceased and most of those grieving for the deceased as passive victims of sorcery. They speculate about who is at fault for the sorcery. Anger at the perpetrator is an appropriate feeling and revenge is appropriate but also risky, because one should be careful not to provoke a powerful man who may have the resources to engage a sorcerer. The social construction process involves a great deal of community discussion (including two full days following the death) that constitutes a kind of sorcery inquest (dominated by men) and also can involve a great deal of lamenting and weeping (especially by women). Also, women's keening may erupt recurrently, even long after the burial. The sorcery inquest and the keening may identify actions of immediate family members that provoked the fatal sorcery, so anger may be directed at immediate family members as well as known sorcerers and powerful people who may have hired a sorcerer. Also included in the keening and sorcery inquests are narratives about emotions, emotional control, and reunion with the deceased. So with the Kwanga we see a social construction process arriving at a place that may seem quite unusual to most North Americans and Europeans.

I do not want to overstate how exotic and diverse the social contexts of bereaved people are in cross-cultural perspective. Even in the most exotic of cultural settings, there are likely to be cultural elements that seem familiar to somebody whose perspective is grief in North America or Europe. For example, one aspect of social construction among the Kwanga (Brison, 1992, 1995) that may reflect what goes on in many societies is the withholding of information from bereaved individuals. Among the Kwanga, this withholding is intended to control the rage of the bereaved, so a sorcery inquest is not only a matter of defining the sources of the death but also of not revealing things that could lead to violence.

Information control in dealing with bereavement can be seen in other societies as well. For example, Good and Good (1988) described an instance in which an Iranian man was not told of his mother's death until he was with family and friends. The information was withheld because people feared that it would not be safe for him to learn about it while alone. I take it that the information control also meant that when he did learn about his mother's death, family and friends knew that he was in a social construction environment that could shape his understandings and feelings.

SOCIAL CONSTRUCTION THROUGH DEATH RITUALS

Every death is unique, and cultures, families, and lives are complex, with many competing shoulds, values, needs, and demands. So it stands to reason that some sort of process must go on to work out what to make of a death, how to deal with it, and what to make of how it is dealt with. One obvious place to look for such processes is death rituals, obvious because such rituals are generally present, public, and well-attended, at least for adult deaths (Rosenblatt et al., 1976).

Death rituals in many societies are more elaborate and spread over much more time than would be typical for death in most cultures of North America and Europe (Rosenblatt et al., 1976). The rituals accomplish a great many things, including disposal of the remains of the deceased and defining the death (perhaps framing it in terms of religious texts, past deaths, and societal values). The public attendance means that many people participate in the construction process and witness the participation of others. Death rituals typically resolve what to do with the property, rights, and obligations of the deceased, identify who is most bereaved, define appropriate feelings, and decide who will provide what sort of support to those who are most bereaved. They also define the relationship of living with the dead and of living with the living now that the death has occurred; who has the right to grieve in what way; who will pay for what; and who will do what with the body. Death rituals involve words. They involve symbolic actions, perhaps self-mutilation, voluntary isolation, recurrent handling of the bodily remains of the deceased over months or years, not bathing for a period of time, animal sacrifices, and destruction of the property of the deceased. Death rituals also often involve symbolic materials, prayers, music, physical actions, effort, expenditure, transformations of appearance for the most bereaved, shared expressions of all sorts, and symbolic transformations in relationships, location, status.

In a sense (and reflecting Barker, 1985, talking about the Maisin of New Guinea), looking at the social interactions associated with death rituals, what follows a death may be as much discussion, interpretation, and social transaction as it is ritual. Even if the outcome of the social interaction is what is typical in that society following a death, that in itself is an achievement of social construction. And it is not only the death and grieving that are dealt with through social construction processes following a death. Death rituals and the interactions associated with them speak to all of a society's values, structures, and perspectives. They are not only about death but also about gender relations, the place of work in people's lives, political power, social status, social order, the meaning of things, etiquette, proper ways to eat and to dress, health, and innumerable other things.

Grieving can be understood in some sense as a public performance that does not necessarily fit private thoughts and feelings. However, the social construction that goes on through death rituals should not be understood as imposing realities, meanings, and actions that are totally divorced from what a person privately experiences (Kapferer, 1979). The rituals and the person exist in a shared environment of cultural values, cultural beliefs, people, and so on. So even if there are ways in which ritual and social interactions can be understood to coerce and shape grief, Kapferer (1979) argued that the cultural construction of what is going on includes a sense for participants that there is a connection between what is coerced and what is assumed by the bereaved individual and those around him or her to be going on in some private, personal reality. An important reason that the connection is likely to be assumed is that sense needs to be made of the public, ritual requirements (Kapferer, 1979).

Death ritual is important in many cultures and is not divorced from other aspects of a culture, but it would be remiss to overlook the ways that much else that is built into culture is entangled in grief construction. Among the many other sociocultural pieces that may operate within a culture to define grief and death are folktales, prayer, song, poetry, somatization of emotional pain, private conversation, consultation with spiritualists, participation in support groups, religious beliefs, and beliefs about what "proper" women and men are like.

CULTURAL CONSTRUCTIONS OF DEVIANT GRIEVING

As part of the dynamic process of socially constructing grief, deviant grieving is typically resisted by family, community, and the larger society. For example, Maschio (1992) wrote about a widow who fought to continue her grieving for her husband when those who had the role of ending her public display of grieving tried to quiet her. She wanted to continue not eating pork and wearing soot marks on her face and a loin cloth of her dead husband around her neck. Her resistance to ending her public display of grieving provoked anger in others. She was scolded. Her public grieving reminded others of how hard it was for them to keep their own grief to themselves and also of the shame they would feel were they to grieve publicly after the time they were expected to stop. At the same time people constructed her public grieving, her public grieving was part of the social construction environment for people dealing with their own losses.

Social reactions to deviant grieving seem not to be simply a matter of people wanting one pattern rather than another. There generally are risks involved in the deviance, risks to the bereaved individual, to the family of the individual, or to the whole community. For example, deviant grieving may be understood to risk ill health, insanity, misfortune caused by the gods, or the deceased returning to take the life of someone in the community. Deviant grieving may cut one off from family and family support. It may risk misfortune for the whole community.

The concept of "deviance" seems to presume a clear set of standards for evaluating grieving. Yet in many societies there are multiple standards —for example, in Tana Toraja on the island of Sulawesi in Indonesia, Christian beliefs coexist and are in dialogic relationship with what could be called indigenous beliefs (Adams, 1993). Such a pattern of contradiction between earlier ways of grieving and more recent ones that arrived with missionaries or other outsiders is common around the world. Among the consequences of the multiplicity of standards is that there are many people in the world who know that whatever they do in their grieving will be judged deviant by the standards of some of the people in their immediate social environment. Consider the Maisin people, living with the conflict between more recently adopted Christian standards for grieving and standards that antedate the Christian standards (Barker, 1985). By older standards, burial within the village, mourning for years, and engaging in a final funeral ceremony years after the death are proper and have been observed by some people even after conversion to Christianity (Barker, 1985). By the mission standards, those may all be inappropriate. One might look at the older pattern and say that it is in some sense more basically human— for example, it fits evidence that normal grief can be long-term, even lifelong (Klass, Silverman, & Nickman, 1996). However, the traditional pattern, according to Barker, was not only about grief but about competition among widows, the relationships among kin groups, beliefs about regeneration following a loss, and other matters that seem not to be the kind of dynamics underlying continuing grief as described in Klass, Silverman, and Nickman (1996). So in cultural groups such as the Maisin, reactions to "deviant grief" may have much to do with the cultural construction of kin relationships, Christianity, and much else that is not grief.

From another perspective, what seems to be deviant grieving may be understood as a challenge to the power of certain people in the community to define aspects of reality or to control the person who grieves. In that sense, grieving can be understood as one of the many arenas in social life in which power moves are carried out and power relationships are constructed. Whatever else some aspect of grieving may represent and express, it can also be a move in relations of power. For example, a person may use mechanisms within the grieving process that effectively block others from altering some of what the person communicates in grief (Briggs, 1993).

From another perspective, deviance and opposition to it occur in a cultural dialectic in which deviance and nondeviance both make sense culturally. That is, even deviance typically has culturally defined meaning.

"Deviance" can also be a matter of not yet knowing what one should know about grieving. Herzfeld (1993), for example, reporting research on the island of Crete in Greece, described a 15-year-old lamenting her father's death. Community members responded to her lamenting with words that supported her but also told her to lament properly given that her father had been quite old. Herzfeld shows that people are not automatically shaped by the social construction environment in which they grieve. The 15-year-old did not change her laments to fit the social demands directed at her.

CONCLUSION

Although by some evidence deaths could be said to be difficult for people everywhere, this chapter questions the base of that evidence and suggests that much that is connected to grieving varies greatly from culture to culture. A lot will vary from individual to individual within a culture. The variability fits a social constructionist perspective in showing that grieving is malleable, that there is not a simple biological or developmental process that controls and shapes how people grieve a death, how long they grieve, or what meanings they give to the death. This is not to deny that there is something basically human in grieving but to urge caution in claiming too much or in relying for evidence on a single set of cultural lenses. I will enjoy, value, and use the chapters in this book that seem to say that there is a core of species-wide grief processes, but I also wonder if that core is very substantial after we modify our theories to take into account cultural and individual differences. Whether the core is substantial or not is, I suppose, a matter of socially constructed judgment, but I think theories of bereavement can be magnificently insightful and extremely useful even if they do not apply to all humans.

Consistent with a constructionist perspective, it is clear that in many cultures important social construction work is carried out or consolidated through death rituals, and in many cultures those rituals extend months or years beyond a death, which affords considerable opportunity for the rituals to shape grieving. In addition, there is information from some societies about social reactions to grieving that is judged by some in the society to be deviant. From that information it is clear that deviant grieving can bring into play efforts by others to influence how the deviant grieves—another sign that grieving is embedded in sociocultural processes that construct everything connected to the death.

The quest for grief universals and universal processes is predicated on an essentialist reality. That reality helps us to learn more about human grieving, but it also guarantees that we miss a lot. To learn what we may be missing, it would be very useful to understand grieving from the perspectives of many different languages and cultures, to understand things in people's own terms. That means learning new languages and social realities and observing social processes through the filters of different cultures and languages. I hope that one of the great achievements of psychology and the social sciences will be to learn how to abandon our carefully developed scholarly vocabulary and theoretical achievements to be fully open to the vocabulary and understandings of people in societies very different from our own. Such work can move us to perspectives and understandings that are beyond what we can talk about now, things that cannot even be translated into the current languages of scholarship. We would then be better able to understand people within a culture and we also would be able to use what they have taught us as conceptual tools for looking at people in other cultures. For future handbooks of bereavement theory and research, we would have a new lexicon of terms dealing with grief that would be drawn from exotic languages and cultures. For example, from the Kwanga as described by Brison (1992, 1995), we could talk about *nogat bun* ("without bones"—the numbness felt by a newly bereaved person). From the Ifaluk, a Pacific atoll society as described by Lutz (1985), we could talk about *lalomweiu*, a loneliness/sadness and neglect of other relationships that involves excessive thinking/feeling about someone lost to one through separation or death. We could also talk about the Ifaluk concept of *fago* (Lutz, 1985), a blend of sadness, love, and compassion following a loss. If we let such a lexicon challenge our own psychological and social science terms and theories in looking at grief, we might come to see grief among any people we study, teach, and live with in new ways. We could come to see our own ideas about grief as only one of many useful but limited ways of thinking about grief.

REFERENCES

Adams, K. M. (1993). The discourse of souls in Tana Toraja (Indonesia): Indigenous notions and Christian conceptions. *Ethnology, 32*, 55–68.

Barker, J. (1985). Missionaries and mourning: Continuity and change in the death ceremonies of a Melanesian people. *Studies in Third World Cultures, 25*, 263–294.

Briggs, C. L. (1993). Personal sentiments and polyphonic voices in Warao women's ritual wailing: Music and poetics in a critical and collective discourse. *American Anthropologist, 95*, 929–957.

Brison, K. J. (1992). *Just talk: Gossip, meetings, and power in a Papua New Guinea village*. Berkeley: University of California Press.

Brison, K. J. (1995). You will never forget: Narrative, bereavement, and worldview among Kwanga women. *Ethos, 23*, 474–488.

Cannadine, D. (1981). War and death, grief and mourning in modern Britain. In J. Whaley (Ed.), *Mirrors of mortality: Studies in the social history of death* (pp. 187–242). New York: St. Martin's Press.

Counts, D. A., & Counts, D. R. (1991). Loss and anger: Death and the expression of grief in Kaliai. In D. R. Counts & D. A. Counts (Eds.), *Coping with the final tragedy: Cultural variation in dying and grieving* (pp. 191–212). Amityville, NY: Baywood.

Good, M. D., & Good, B. J. (1988) Ritual, the state, and the transformation of emotional discourse in Iranian society. *Culture Medicine and Psychiatry, 12*, 43–63.

Herzfeld, M. (1993). In defiance of destiny: The management of time and gender at a Cretan funeral. *American Ethnologist, 20*, 241–255.

Hollan, D. (1995). To the afterworld and back: Mourning and dreams of the dead among the Toraja. *Ethos, 23*, 424–436.

Hollander, N. C. (1997). *Love in a time of hate: Liberation psychology in Latin America*. New Brunswick, NJ: Rutgers University Press.

Kapferer, B. (1979). Emotion and feeling in Sinhalese healing rites. *Social Analysis, 1*, 153–176.

Klass, D. (1999). *Developing a cross-cultural model of grief: The state of the field*. Omega, 39, 153–178.

Klass, D., Silverman, P. R, & Nickman, S. L. (Eds.). (1996). *Continuing bonds: New understandings of grief*. Washington, DC: Taylor & Francis.

Leavitt, S. C. (1995). Seeking gifts from the dead: Long-term mourning in a Bumbita Arapesh cargo narrative. *Ethos, 23*, 453–473.

Lerner, J. C. (1975). Changes in attitudes toward death: The widow in Great

Britain in the early twentieth century. In B. Schoenberg, I. Gerber, A. Wiener, A. H. Kutscher, D. Peretz, & A. C. Carr (Eds.), *Bereavement: Its psychosocial aspects* (pp. 91–118). New York: Columbia University Press.

Lutz, C. (1985). Depression and the translation of emotional worlds. In A. Kleinman & B. Good (Eds.), *Culture and depression: Studies in the anthropology and cross-cultural psychiatry of affect and disorder* (pp. 63–100). Berkeley: University of California Press.

Maschio, T. (1992). To remember the faces of the dead: Mourning and the full sadness of memory in southwestern New Britain. *Ethos, 20,* 387–420.

Rosenblatt, P. C. (1993). Cross-cultural variation in the experience, expression, and understanding of grief. In D. P. Irish, K. F. Lundy, & V. J. Nelson (Eds.), *Ethnic variations in dying, death, and grief: Diversity in universality* (pp. 13–19). Washington, DC: Taylor & Francis.

Rosenblatt, P. C. (1994). *Metaphors of family systems theory: Toward new constructions.* New York: Guilford.

Rosenblatt, P. C. (1997). Grief in small scale societies. In C. M. Parkes, P. Laungani, & B. Young (Eds.), *Death and bereavement across cultures* (pp. 27–51). London: Routledge.

Rosenblatt, P. C. (2000). *Parent grief: Narratives of loss and relationship.* Philadelphia: Brunner/Mazel.

Rosenblatt, P. C., Walsh, R. P., & Jackson, D. A. (1976). *Grief and mourning in cross-cultural perspective.* New Haven, CT: Human Relations Area Files Press.

Rosenblatt, P. C., & Wright, S. E. (1984). Shadow realities in close relationships. *American Journal of Family Therapy, 12*(2), 45–54.

Wellenkamp, J. C. (1991) Fallen leaves: Death and grieving in Toraja. In D. R. Counts & D. A. Counts (Eds.), *Coping with the final tragedy: Cultural variation in dying and grieving* (pp. 113–134). Amityville, NY: Baywood.

Westerman, W. (1994). Central American refugee testimonies and performed life histories in the sanctuary movement. In R. Benmayor & A. Skotnes (Eds.), *International Yearbook of Oral History and Life Stories, Vol. III. Migration and Identity* (pp. 167–181). New York: Oxford University Press.

Wikan, U. (1990). *Managing turbulent hearts: A Balinese formula for living.* Chicago: University of Chicago Press.

Zur, J. N. (1998). *Violent memories: Mayan war widows in Guatemala.* Boulder, CO: Westview.

14

GRIEF IN INTERPERSONAL PERSPECTIVE: THEORIES AND THEIR IMPLICATIONS

ESTER R. SHAPIRO

Grief as a human experience powerfully exposes the interpersonal construction of what only appears to be an isolated, individual self. From birth to death, our shared adaptations to both ordinary and extraordinary family life cycle transitions are structured through mutually responsive re-actions. Infant research offers compelling evidence that we are born neu-rodevelopmentally immature and interpersonally well-designed to evoke precisely the social interactions we need to complete ourselves (Schore, 1994; Zeanah, 1999). Through complex choreography of interpersonal in-teractions, first with family and then with a widening circle of partners, we engage in the life-long transactions that coconstruct a negotiated, pro-visional, collaborative self. A loved one's death shakes the foundation of this interpersonally created and maintained self, disrupting relational sys-tems of affect regulation, attachment, identity, and social role. Bereaved individuals must rebuild relational resources to meet intensified emotional needs and undertake social transitions, just when both actual and symbolic relational worlds have been profoundly diminished.

This chapter applies an interpersonal framework to illuminate grief's profound disruptions, highlighting the relational resources families use to moderate multiple stressors associated with death and its circumstances and to support ongoing development (Shapiro, 1994, 1996b, 1996c, 1997). I first briefly review early psychodynamic theory on grief and then explore more fully recent relational theories and research to illuminate grief's profound disruptions. I will then build on this interpersonal model of bereavement by reviewing family systems theory and the cross-cultural literature on bereavement. Finally, I will review the burgeoning social systems–developmental literature. Integrating these approaches using a social developmental model, recommendations are made for the most promising direction in research and practice from an interpersonal perspective.

DEFINING THE INTERPERSONAL DOMAIN: THE NEED FOR A COMPREHENSIVE CONCEPTUAL APPROACH

An interpersonal approach can help bridge the realistic worlds of death and its circumstances, and the subjective, symbolized worlds of internal emotional regulation and meaning, clarifying current paradoxes of grief and growth. Since Freud's time, clinically based theories have asserted that bereaved individuals experience increased risk of psychopathology. The grief literature lacks agreement in conceptualizing and operationalizing pathological versus successful bereavement. Current controversies include tension between models proposing detachment from the deceased as promoting recovery (Frankiel, 1994) and those emphasizing restructured attachment and continuing bonds (Klass, Silverman, & Nickman, 1996); and researchers focusing on functional outcomes as compared to psychological distress (Calter, Case, Saldinger, & Lohnes, 1999). The available, methodologically sound prospective and longitudinal research suggests that even the most agonizing grief experiences result in a broad range of functional outcomes, determined by multiple, interdependent factors. When studied systematically using appropriate control groups or normed measures, adaptive outcomes seem more often positive than previously assumed for children (Silverman, 2000), adults (McCrae & Costa, 1993) and families (Kissane et al., 1996a, 1996b). However, for a substantial subset of bereaved adults, sequelae such as increased depression and decreased life satisfaction may persist for years (Wortman, Silver, & Kessler, 1993). A focus on family relationships links adaptation to death and its circumstances with responses to ongoing demands of family life and shared growth.

Although strong interpersonal trends have emerged in the grief literature, their usefulness is limited by fragmentation and lack of systematic conceptualization. The interpersonal dimension of grief broadly defined overlaps with chapters reviewing social, cultural, and family systems perspectives. This chapter focuses on interpersonal action and its symbolization as critical dimensions of psychological organization disrupted by grief. Bereavement is defined as a here and now, interpersonally negotiated life-long process in a sociocultural context rather than as individual, decontextualized, and finite. Interpersonal grief processes are examined both as external communicative behavior and as negotiated, intersubjective representations of action templates, maintained and reorganized through current actions with others. This approach offers an interpersonal framework for understanding the dual process of grief (M. Stroebe & Schut, 1999): first, grief as disruption of interpersonal strategies for affect regulation, self-definition, and social role functioning, which must be restored; and second, grief as intensification of loss-related emotions and cognitions that must be managed in the absence of habitual strategies for stability. This chapter explores interpersonal strategies for stable coping with discontinuities precipitated by death that families mobilize to protect ongoing development. The limited empirical research addressing interpersonal factors in bereavement is reviewed. The chapter concludes by outlining an individualized intervention approach enhancing use of relational resources to moderate multiple stressors accompanying death and its aftermath.

THEORETICAL SOURCES IN THE GRIEF LITERATURE: FROM INTRAPSYCHIC TO INTERPERSONAL PSYCHIC STRUCTURE

Psychoanalysis looms large as a source of both enduringly useful and destructive grief beliefs. Contemporary psychoanalytic writers agree that the intense disruption accompanying a loved one's death is a result both of intensified affects and of reorganization of psychic structure. However, newer definitions of psyche emphasize real actions in relationships as organizing our capacities for creating emotional stability and establishing a sense of self. Psychoanalytically informed object relations and attachment theories have been applied to bereavement as useful antidotes to the Freudian approach. However, these important contributions remain limited by the assumption that early experiences determine psychic structure. This section will review relational psychoanalytic theories of bereavement, emphasizing contemporary interpersonal perspectives that help conceptualize grief as disrupting life-long, transactional constructions of psychological structure.

So why begin with Freud? Freud's "Mourning and Melancholia" (1917/1957) accurately described the phenomenology of grief as a confrontation with the many pathways by which our mind's most casual associations lead, agonizingly and inexorably, to the lost loved one. Freud argued that grief's intensity and duration resulted from the reorganization of psychic structure precipitated by a loved one's death. Recognition that grief disrupts characteristic controls of intense emotions, requiring reorganization of essential constituents of self, offers valuable contributions to current models. However, Freud's definition of identification as failure of the normal detachment from the love object required for recovery pathologized nearly all grief reactions. Freud's bereavement theory remains influential because an individualized model promising that emotional catharsis will be followed by detachment and a full recovery powerfully appeal to modern, Western cultural beliefs in the encapsulated, isolated self controlling fate (Cushman, 1994; Stroebe et al., 1992). It is ironic to note that Freud's enduring attachments to his deceased daughter and grandson eloquently testify to the need for alternative models (Shapiro, 1996a).

Object relations theory offers a crucial step toward an interpersonal model, viewing the individual's inner life as built from internalized representations of real relationships with early caretaking figures. Relationship templates established early in childhood become the operating principles by which the maturing self and new relationships are understood and invested with emotional meaning. Object relations theory suggests that a loved one's death requires reorganization of the internal object world. The Tavistock Center under John Bowlby's direction stimulated extensive work applying object relations and attachment theories to loss (Bretherton, 1991; Cassidy & Shaver, 1999). Bowlby's attachment theory (1969, 1973, 1980) has been widely used to study both childhood and adult grief. Bowlby incorporated an ethological perspective on survival benefits of attachment bonds. Initially proposing an early imprinting maintained for life (P. Bateson, 1991), Bowlby and others later argued that early maternal separation leads to attachment disturbances through enduring disruptions in caretaker–infant relationships (Lyons-Ruth & Block, 1996; Rutter, 1991; Tremblay & Allen, 1998). Ainsworth's operationalization of attachment in the strange situation (Ainsworth, Blehar, Waters, & Wall, 1978) helped empirically test hypotheses linking attachment security to a broad range of developmental contexts and outcomes (Bretherton & Waters, 1985; Cassidy & Shaver, 1999).

Bowlby also integrated information-processing theory with psychodynamic concepts of defense to describe how attachment experiences become internal working models of relationships designed to maintain psychological stability throughout development. When experiencing overwhelming emotions and attachment disruptions, individuals dissociate to reestablish emotional stability. Dissociation blocks full access to painful emotions and related associations, creating constricted areas of inner experience and relational adaptations unavailable for new learning (Bowlby, 1980). More recent work on internal working models uses script theories of event representation to explore the organizational complexity characterizing real relationship representations. Information derived from experiences is organized to produce representational schemas preserving spatiotemporal and causal relations, simulating real-world event structures

(Bretherton & Munholland, 1999; Bretherton, Ridgeway, & Cassidy, 1990).

Bowlby and colleagues suggest that adulthood attachment bonds are derived from the same emotional system underlying child attachment (Main, 1991; Main, Kaplan, & Cassidy, 1985; Weiss, 1993). Adult socio-emotional functioning relies on maintaining secure images of attachment figures. A close family death disrupts attachment security and elicits an adult version of the infant's response to attachment threat or loss (Parkes, Stevenson-Hinde, & Marris, 1991; Weiss, 1993). Recent research has empirically tested the value of adult attachment models of grief in predicting outcomes of conjugal bereavement. W. Stroebe, M. Stroebe, Abakoumkin, and Schut (1996) tested an attachment model in conjugal loss, and found it to better predict the mediating effect of social support than did a stress and coping model. They found that emotional loneliness, unique to a primary attachment bond such as marriage, could not be assuaged by social support the way social loneliness could. Van Doorn, Kasl, Beery, Jacobs, and Prigerson (1998) studied marital quality and attachment style among caregivers of terminally ill spouses and their impact on traumatic grief and depressive symptoms before and then 3, 6, and 13 months postloss. They found that security-increasing marriages and insecure attachment styles each put spouses at risk for elevated traumatic grief symptoms but not for depression.

The mechanisms through which attachment security is reestablished or internal working models are repaired after a loved one's death have not yet been articulated theoretically or tested empirically. However, adult attachment research on intergenerational transmission of attachment security begins to suggest variables involved in both disruption and repair of attachment bonds after loss. Main and colleagues have been exploring pathways by which parental transmission affects childhood attachment status in the next generation, empirically testing an adult attachment inventory (Hesse, 1999; Main & Goldwyn, 1984) that analyzes parental organization of their own childhood narratives as predictors of their children's attachment status. Their findings suggest that coherent, complex parental narratives with perspective on even negative experiences are significantly associated with secure attachment in their children. Recent work identifies parent–infant interactions involved in transmission, suggesting that disorganizing or frightening interactions with roots in unresolved parental loss and emotional dissociation lead to disrupted infant attachment (Lyons-Ruth & Block, 1996; Lyons-Ruth & Jacobvitz, 1999; Schuengel, Bakermans-Kranenburg, & Van Ijzendoorn, 1999). Schuengel et al. (1999) argued that these interpersonal disruptions characterize unresolved loss as distinct from successful suppression of grief, which does not interfere with parental internal working models and subsequent parent–child transactions.

The need for more complex models of attachment development and disruption are suggested by research on adult outcomes for parentally bereaved children. Recent studies suggest that although bereaved children are likely to experience anguish and report emotional distress, they do not show any more psychological disturbance than their same-age peers (Calter et al., 1999; Clark, Pynoos, & Gobel, 1994; Silverman, 2000). Caretaking disruptions rather than loss itself seem to be associated with negative outcomes (Harris & Bifulco, 1991; Hurd, 1999; Lyons-Ruth & Block, 1996), creating vulnerabilities that increase susceptibility to adult life stressors. This research suggests that the impact of childhood grief cannot be understood outside of the material and symbolic relational resources available to support ongoing development. Adult attachment findings on intergenerational transmission further suggest that the capacity to create more complex, coherent relationship representations may protect from the deleterious effects of childhood losses and subsequent vulnerabilities in coping with adult life stress.

Another important contribution in conceptualizing and testing a psychodynamic interpersonal approach to bereavement is found in Horowitz's work on role relationship models (Horowitz, 1986, 1989; Horowitz, Bonanno, & Holen, 1993; Horowitz, Wilner, Marmar, & Krupnick, 1980). Horowitz views bereavement as a stress response syndrome, in which schemas of self, constructed through relational interactions, are challenged by death and its circumstances. Because schemas are strategies for establishing cognitive and emotional control, stressful life events destabilize habitual, characterological control strategies. In research studying narratives generated by bereaved participants, Horowitz and colleagues (1993) used the role relationship schemas approach to assess both death's meanings and associated self-construals, suggesting that grief reactivates latent self-images previously located in the partner through projective identification.

Recent research builds on the theoretical work of Horowitz and colleagues to study transformations of relational representations to the deceased spouse and the relationship of these construals to bereavement outcomes. Field, Nichols, Holen, & Horowitz (1999) studied continuing attachment and adjustment in 70 mid-life conjugally bereaved participants, using a monologue role play with the deceased spouse conducted at 6, 14, and 25 months postloss. They found that attachment through fond memories was related to less distress, whereas use of the deceased's possessions for comfort predicted less decrease in grief-specific symptoms over time. Bonnano, Notarius, Gunzerath, Keltner, & Horowitz (1998; chapter 22, this volume) developed a measure of ambivalence based on an algorithmic combination of separate positive and negative evaluations of the spouse, comparing conjugally bereaved participants with a nonbereaved comparison group. They found that bereaved participants recollected their relationships as better adjusted but were more ambivalent. Yet once initial outcome was controlled, ambivalence about spouses, although associated with increased distress and poorer perceived health, did not predict long-term grief outcome. These findings suggest that relationship representations shift to regulate overwhelming emotions and that early self-regulating strategies can themselves create difficulties in longer term adaptation.

Empirical research on therapeutic interactions help illuminate how early relational representations can be restructured through current interpersonal processes. Horowitz et al. (1993) tested a brief psychodynamic psychotherapy intervention for bereaved individuals, based on the role relationship model. His work and that of other psychodynamic psychotherapy researchers (Miller, Luborsky, Barber, & Docherty, 1993) suggests that therapeutic relationships offer opportunities to meaningfully reactivate relational templates and effectively restructure internalized relationship schemas. These researchers find that schemas can be restructured explicitly, through standard psychodynamic interventions such as stated interpretations of current relationship patterns, their historical sources, and their projection onto the therapist. However, their research suggests that schemas can also be restructured implicitly, through strategic design of the therapeutic relationship to contradict habitual dysfunctional patterns no longer useful to current adaptation.

In addition to work on adult attachment and on role relationship schemas, object relations theory has also been extended to study interpersonal collaborations through which spouses repeat historical relationship internalizations (Dicks, 1967). Pincus (1974), whose approach to bereavement developed at the Tavistock Center integrates object relations and systems theory, argued that conjugal grief requires reintegration of aspects of self previously located in the spouse through mechanisms of projection, identification, and projective identification. Death disrupts the deceased spouse's role in an interactionally constructed "shared personality." Bereaved survivors must reintegrate projected aspects of self into new, more complex identity and behavioral repertoires. Pincus used clinical examples to describe grieving adults who adopted one personality style during marriage but after their spouse's death revealed hidden capacities in emotional and interpersonal functioning. Pincus's case studies offer a valuable conceptualization of couples' mutual regulation transactions disrupted by death, but does not address gendered psychosocial roles in accounting for death's disruption of the collaborative self.

EXPANDING THEORETICAL SOURCES FOR AN INTERPERSONAL MODEL OF GRIEF

So far, this review suggests that interpersonal factors offer an important link between grief experience and bereavement outcomes in the quality of the actual relationships available to the bereaved individual after a loved one's death and in the characteristics of evolving relational representations of self and deceased. Further, the work of Horowitz and colleagues suggests that the psychological structures regulating intense emotions and meaning making, derived from internalized relationship representations, are amenable to intervention through interpersonally oriented psychotherapy. Interpersonal psychodynamic approaches to bereavement can be usefully expanded to further clarify interpersonal factors in grief process and outcome by applying models emphasizing the organization and reorganization of psychic structure through here-and-now interpersonal interactions. Recent work in interpersonal psychoanalysis, in self-psychology, and in infant research on internalization of relational transactions can usefully contribute to an understanding of interpersonal factors in bereavement.

Harry Stack Sullivan and the interpersonal school of psychoanalysis view personality as made up of the relatively enduring patterns of recurrent interpersonal situations that characterize a human life (Sullivan, 1953). Current work has shifted from use of "interpersonal" to "relational," clarifying the distinction between Sullivan's here and now behavioral emphasis and interpersonal approaches emphasizing symbolic representation of relational experiences (Mitchell, 1988; Skolnick & Warshaw, 1991). Integrating theories of intersubjectivity with psychoanalytic developmental models (Winnicott, 1965), Benjamin (1998), Pizer (1997), and others suggest that relational processes of mutual recognition help establish capacities to view self and others empathically and multidimensionally as experiencing subjects rather than projective objects. These capacities are interpersonally constructed through negotiated transactions balancing self-assertion and maintained connection in caretaker–infant relationships. According to these theorists, a loved one's death disrupts interpersonally fine-tuned mutual regulation processes and corresponding symbolizations of relationships.

Self-psychologists (Kohut, 1977) describe self-regulation and intersubjectivity as relational, and view the psyche as organized through internalization of attuned, empathic transactions creating regulatory "self-objects." Grief requires transformation of internalized self-objects (Hagman, 1995), and traumatic experiences are mediated by empathic relational processes (Stolorow & Atwood, 1992). Stolorow (1999) applies a self-psychological approach to his own experience of conjugal bereavement. He suggests that grief shatters absolute assumptions about the world's safety and continuity, creating an experience of isolation or singularity, preventing the bereaved from experiencing the empathic attunement offered by others.

Another useful interpersonal approach with implications for understanding bereavement emerges from Wachtel's (1993) integration of psychodynamic with behavioral and family systems perspectives, which he calls "cyclical psychodynamics." Wachtel highlights repetitive cycles of interpersonal interaction, which create cycles of reciprocal causation between intrapsychic processes and current relationships in daily living. Psychological states are elements in a vicious circle in which current transactions, selected for their resonance with the past, reconfirm past expectations. Although these patterns may originate in earlier events, knowing their origins can no more change current symptomatology than can addiction be cured by knowing its etiology. Change requires correction of current interpersonal habits and the intense emotions that were controlled or defended against by these actions. Wachtel's interpersonal approach is consistent with that of Horowitz and colleagues but further implies that a loved one's death may precipitously disrupt a previously coherent, habitual relationship between here-and-now interpersonal transactions and life-long defensive strategies for emotional control.

Relational psychoanalysts have turned to infant research as illuminating microtransactions in infant–caretaker dyads, which form the internalized relational structures regulating affect, cognition, and behavior and which are disrupted by a loved one's death. Infant researchers have generated models of therapeutic intervention addressing both relational action and its representation (Beebe & Lachmann, 1998; Lachmann & Beebe, 1997). Contemporary research suggests that infants are highly organized toward basic developmental tasks of self-regulation through systematic engagement of their social world (Beebe & Lachman, 1998; Lyons-Ruth & Zeanah, 1999; Schore, 1994). Research studying socioemotional regulation through caretaker–infant interaction documents young infants' sophisticated participation in shared action sequences regulating affective responses (Beebe, Lachmann, & Jaffe, 1997; Tronick, 1989, 1998). Stern (1985) suggested that the mood, quality, and rhythm of parent–infant interaction evolves into stable representations of interactions that have been generalized (RIGS), establishing the foundation for later self-regulation. Social critics argue that Stern's decontextualized views of mother–infant relationships obscure the role of idealized maternal images in constructing gender bias (Benjamin, 1988) and consumer cultures of narcissism (Cushman, 1994). Infant researchers critique Stern's emphasis on harmonious attunement in the mother–infant relationship, suggesting that restoration of synchrony after expectable disruptions is a more useful focus (Beebe & Lachmann, 1998; Tronick, 1989). Approaches that apply infant research models to explore the transactions necessary for restoration of synchrony after disruption offer a potentially useful approach in the restoration of stable interactions and their internal representations after a loved one's death.

IMPLICATIONS FOR AN INTERPERSONAL MODEL OF BEREAVEMENT

Contemporary interpersonal psychodynamic approaches suggest several useful concepts for understanding bereavement. First, psychic structure is redefined as organized through patterns of relationship and their representation throughout life. A transactional self is built from complex, multidimensional interpersonal expectancies in infancy, which continue to be reorganized through life-long processes of relational adaptation. Second, habitual patterns of interaction help stabilize schemas of emotional control or socioemotional regulation. Third, stressful life events contribute to the complexity and flexibility with which relationship schemas are organized so as to respond to ongoing developmental challenges. Fourth, interventions that use relationships strategically as sources of both emotional regulation and meaning making can help establish more complex perspectives on previously overwhelming experiences as well as more multidimensional and functionally adaptive relationship representations.

From this perspective, a family death disrupts highly interrelated interpersonal strategies for self-definition and emotional control, and shatters continuity of self-construal, which relies on coherence between early relationship experiences and adult relationships. Individual grief reactions for children and adults can be redefined as intersubjectively negotiated and symbolized, mutually regulating, self-organizing interactions designed to restabilize templates for self-with-others disrupted by the death. However, these interpersonal developmental models remain fundamentally dyadic. Further, they do not address factual circumstances of the death, demands of the psychosocial transition, and stressors or resources in a broader sociocultural context, which influence the need to deploy defensive coping strategies for stability (Shapiro, 1994).

FAMILY SYSTEMS THEORY AND FAMILY THERAPY

Family systems theory adds triadic and systemic concepts to the interpersonal dimensions of bereavement. A systemic focus helps formulate how interactions after a family member's death are reorganized to solve new problems of social role disruption, and affect regulation and meaning making. Further, a family systems approach to bereavement is compatible with individual approaches emphasizing relationships (Moos, 1995; Shapiro, 1994). Family systems theory views families as governed by the same rules that organize other complex biological systems (G. Bateson, 1972, 1979; Piercy & Sprenkle, 1998). The family is seen as an organized whole with interdependent constituent members, with patterns of relationships themselves making up the family structure. Further, systems are circular rather than linear in causality: Actions by any member affect all others and change their functioning. The same triggering event can lead to different outcomes through the interplay of responses and patterns of relationships. Family systems theory has been critiqued for viewing families outside their sociocultural context, although new work includes critical cultural perspectives that socially contextualize family functioning (Luepnitz, 1988; McGoldrick, 1998).

Processes of adaptation and self-regulation in family systems include both stabilizing mechanisms for maintaining continuity, or homeostasis, and transformational mechanisms for adapting to change, or morphogenesis (Shapiro, 1994). Earlier work with extremely disturbed families highlighted homeostatic mechanisms designed to maintain family stability and to rigidly control change. More recent writings emphasize balance of change and continuity as families adapt to change while maintaining a sense of cohesiveness and stability (Falicov, 1998; Walsh, 1982). Family systems theorists have also identified the balance of connection and self-assertion characterizing healthy family relationships. Earlier work described a continuum of differentiation of self from family, with extreme overinvolvement and emotional reactivity or "enmeshment" at one end and extreme isolation or "disengagement" at the other. In highly enmeshed families, individual self-assertion presents a potential threat to family stability and is strictly controlled. Recent work emphasizes the balance of self-assertion and connection achieved through negotiated inclusion of differences, permitting actual rather than fictitious family cohesiveness. Family power imbalances can distort the inclusive negotiation of perceptions and emotions, as can children's protective sensitivity to parental stress (Shapiro, 1994).

Family systems theorists have historically focused on patterns of communication as they organize emotional responsiveness and reflect shared patterns of adaptation. Any individual's symptom expresses a shared process conveying the family's rules for establishing stable organization. Family interactions provide a constant flow of nonverbal and verbal information that communicates acceptable ideas and controls emotions potentially disruptive of family cohesiveness and stability. Individual symptoms are viewed as functional in family organization, maintaining family homeostasis while representing or "meta-communicating" problematic, censored aspects of family experience. Most schools of family therapy, including current narrative models, work on family communication to help create more inclusive organizing structures with more flexible adaptation to changing circumstances (Piercy & Sprenkle, 1998).

The family systems bereavement literature has been primarily generated by intergenerational therapists focusing on patterns of emotional relatedness established in families of origin and imposed on current relationships (Shapiro, 1994; Walsh & McGoldrick, 1991). The more stress families experience during the intergenerational life cycle, the more likely that past images or patterns of relationship will be inflexibly preserved at the expense of realistic engagement in current relationships. Intergenerational patterns designed to manage overwhelming grief become a central focus. Paul and Grosser's (1965) classic work on operational mourning suggested that disturbances throughout the family life cycle might result from failures of mourning in the previous generation. Bowen (1976) and Herz (1989) applied Bowen's work on differentiation of self from family of origin, proposing that the anxiety and stress accompanying a death increase a family's fusion, mutual emotional reactivity, and reliance on overly rigid structures for emotional stability. Following a family death, relationships shift to closed communication systems, to protect against anxiety generated by open discussion and establish new equilibrium. Although a family member's death is always a severe disruption, the family's previous adaptation, level of differentiation, and communication style are crucial elements of a family's grief reaction, as are the deceased's functional and emotional roles. Simply helping families express feelings during a crisis does not necessarily increase levels of emotional integration and successful adaptation. A family death and associated disruptions can cause an "emotional shock wave," which may trigger additional, disruptive life events and even more rigid strategies for stabilization.

Walsh and McGoldrick (1991) discussed family grief reactions from a systemic framework that includes intergenerational and family life cycle perspectives. They describe two major adaptive tasks in response to a family death: first, shared acknowledgment of the death's reality and experience of loss; second, reorganization of the family system to enable reinvestment in other relationships and life pursuits (McGoldrick and Walsh, 1991). They stress the importance of open communication of feelings while recognizing that family members may be out of phase with each other's grief. Other writers have used specific concepts in structural family therapy to analyze family bereavement, including disruptions of the structures that maintain family homeostatic balance (Bowlby-West, 1983; Jordan, Kraus, & Ware, 1993).

Gregory Bateson (1972, 1979, 1992) has been highly influential in the family therapy field, historically for bridging anthropology and communication theory, most recently inspiring work on shared meaning making or family epistemology (Friedman, 1993; White & Epston, 1990). Beginning with work on family narratives, more recent writings emphasize the role of cultural beliefs and injustice as contexts for negotiation of shared meanings. Focusing on bereavement as a systemic process, Walker (1991) described work with families who have a member dying of AIDS. Her teams' work explored AIDS' cultural meanings and impact on diverse families' mutual adaptations and shared, negotiated meaning making. Because AIDS is often associated with lifestyles some societies consider both deliberately chosen and morally reprehensible, families experience social pressure to expel the dying family member or define his or her death as punishment for transgressions. Walker and her team helped families create a new narrative that moved from shame to pride and allowed loving inclusion of the dying individual.

The published literature on family bereavement is primarily clinical, focusing on shifts in family expressiveness, communication, cohesion, and conflict resolution after the death (Kissane & Bloch, 1994). Research studying family bereavement variables has focused on family conflict, cohesion, and communication after a family death. Silverman and Weiner (1995) examined parent–child communication in bereaved Israeli families in which one parent had died, and found that some families closed off communication for purposes of mutual protection from painful feelings. Nelson and Frantz (1996) compared family relationships after a death by suicide and by other causes, finding that expressiveness and cohesion were associated with better outcomes for both types of death.

Kissane and colleagues on the Melbourne Family Grief Study (Kissane et al., 1996a, 1996b; Kissane, Bloch, & McKenzie, 1997) assessed participants from 115 families at 6 weeks, 6 months, and 13 months after the death of a parent on measures of grief intensity, psychological status, social adjustment, and family coping. Individual responses on the Family Environment Scale and the Family Adaptability and Cohesion Evaluation Scales (Faces III) were clustered to identify a predominant style for each family and analyzed to generate five family types. The two well-functioning types, supportive and conflict-resolving, showed better grief resolution and functional adaptation when compared to sullen, hostile, or intermediate family types. Well-functioning families were most cohesive, reported using more family coping strategies such as shared expressiveness and mutual support, and tolerated differences well. Intermediate families, identified as "ordinary" in earlier research, showed intermediate levels of cohesion but lowest levels of both achievement orientation and control. Family characteristics were consistent over the period of evaluation and follow-up, except for sullen families who by 13 months had shifted into either hostile or intermediate groups. The family typology clusters accounted for 15.7% of the variance in depression and 27.9% of variance in social functioning (Kissane et al., 1996b). Family coping was the best predictor of bereavement outcome, accounting for up to 38% of the variance in grief, 64% in distress, 53% in depression, and 46% in social adjustment. Kissane et al. (1996a, 1996b, 1997) concluded that although most grieving families can use their own resources for successful coping, high-risk families can be helped by appropriate interventions targeting family interaction and shared coping.

INTERPERSONAL DOMAIN IN SOCIOCULTURAL CONTEXT

An understanding of interpersonal dimensions in grief requires a sociocultural context. The grief literature has used the concept of psychosocial transitions (Parkes, 1993; Silverman, 2000) to address social role transformations and related sense of identity disrupted by death. Harvey (1996, 1997) used a social psychological, interpersonal narrative approach to account making following loss. He argues that storytelling includes components of socially guided meaning making and of sharing or confiding. Symbolic interactionism has also been used to analyze grief's disruption of the ongoing social actions and related meanings from which we derive a sense of self (Rosenblatt, 1993). Recent work in symbolic interactionism has focused on the role of interpersonal transactions and their symbolization in affect control (MacKinnon, 1994). Some meaning-making processes address elements of the loss itself, including its causality, whereas others reflect the meaning of death in one's life. Nolen-Hoeksema and colleagues (Davis, Nolen-Hoeksema, & Larson, 1998) reported that a focus on understanding the death and its circumstances was associated with improved short-term adjustment, but finding benefit from the death was associated with longer term adjustment. Wortman, Silver, and Kessler's (1993) longitudinal research on parental coping with an adult child's death has recently focused on attributions of personal responsibility as problematic self-stabilizing strategies temporarily reducing stress but creating negative longer term outcomes (Lepore, Silver, Wortman, & Wayment, 1996). Research on attributions and meaning making can usefully incorporate a sociocultural perspective. Cultures differ radically in their construal of the material as compared to spiritual relationship between life and death, or of the causal role played by individual agency, impersonal fate, and community actions as explanations for death and its meaning (Fadiman, 1997).

The cross-cultural literature on grief helps us further contextualize the interpersonal transactions configuring bereavement. Each culture defines grief and reconstruction consistent with beliefs regarding life, death, and the afterlife, emphasizing certain aspects of the broad range of human responses while de-emphasizing others, striving to preserve its own social continuity (Metcalf & Huntington, 1991; Rosaldo, 1989). Bereavement rituals create avenues for public articulation of deeply felt emotions such as sorrow and anger, and provide community comfort for those emotions. At the same time, these rituals restore the social order disrupted by the death. Social norms prescribe solutions for management of the feelings associated with grief, recreating life structures, and reestablishing a meaningful sense of identity in connection with surviving family members and the wider community. Romanoff and Terenzio (1998) have suggested that successful grief rituals need to simultaneously address intrapsychic self-transformation, social status transition, and continuation of connection with the deceased affirmed in a communal context. They further argued that useful cultural rituals address evolution of grief over time, not just immediately after the death (see also Klass, Silverman, & Nickman, 1996).

Cultural anthropologists use the concept of "liminality" to describe the bereaved person's transitional experience during this period of psychic and social transformation (Metcalf & Huntington, 1991; Turner, 1967). Although bereavement rituals offer meaningful support to grieving families, their social and individual functions are not necessarily in harmony. Rituals designed to reassure the wider community of its continuity may clash with individual or family needs. In North American culture, which emphasizes the isolated individual, scientific rather than spiritual explanations, and "letting go and moving on" after death, social sanctions pressure the bereaved individual to rapidly "recover." Other cultures affirm collectivity of the self in life (Tedlock & Manheim, 1995) and spiritual and psychological continuity between the dead and the living, potentially constraining the bereaved's individual choice in rebuilding their lives.

Recent research affirms the importance of meaning-making processes in grief outcomes (chapter 15, this volume) and suggests how cultural differences in social responses help achieve a sense of meaning (Rosaldo, 1989; chapter 19, this volume). Communities and cultures often prescribe ways of thinking about accountability and meaning for a particular death, leaving families to struggle with the consequences of these social constructions. A family's access to social support will also be determined by cultural attitudes toward their experience of death and expression of grief. Lepore et al. (1996) found that social constraints on discussion of infant death interfered with maternal processing of the experience. Rosenblatt (1993) described the bereaved individual's interpersonal attunement to communication of a death's social meanings and accompanying self-censorship. Shared expression and reflection within families and communities, and with others who have undergone similar experiences, can help the bereaved go beyond narrow social mandates to more inclusive, complex, multidimensional perspectives.

SOCIAL–SYSTEMS DEVELOPMENTAL MODELS AND THEIR IMPLICATIONS

The past several decades have seen the burgeoning of a social–systems developmental literature exploring human development under conditions of adversity, including a family member's death. This approach is useful in building an interpersonal model of bereavement, as it helps organize the complex, interdependent factors contributed by individual, dyadic, familial, and cultural domains to a continuum of adaptive or symptomatic outcomes. Sources in this literature include the ecology of human development (Belsky, 1993; Bronfenbrenner, 1979; Bronfenbrenner, Moen, & Garbarino, 1984); developmental psychopathology that studies resilience under circumstances of adversity (Cicchetti & Cohen, 1995a, 1995b; Cicchetti & Garmezy, 1993; Coie et al., 1993; McLoyd, 1990; Rolf, Masten, Cicchetti, Nuechterlein, & Weintraub, 1990; Werner, 1993); and systems developmental models (Sameroff, 1995), which approach development in terms of mutually regulating transactions. These models view human development as progressing through mutually adaptive transactions in interdependent "nested structures" of family and extended family, peer, institutional, community, and cultural relationships and contexts. Developmental outcomes are determined by the child and family's distinctive use of resources to manage the risks posed by potential stressors. Supportive resources and sources of stress are found across interdependent individual, family, community (neighborhood, school), and cultural domains, and change configuration and impact over the course of development.

These approaches have generated a substantial body of empirical research identifying risk and protective factors that contribute to a continuum of resilient or disrupted development in both normal and at-risk populations of children and adults (Cicchetti & Cohen, 1995a, 1995b). This literature offers strong links between theory, research, and application in designing prevention programs maximizing resources and minimizing stresses in at-risk populations (Coie et al., 1993). Developmental transitions are seen as powerful opportunities for altering the balance of stresses and supports to improve outcomes. Cicchetti (1989) used organizational and dialectical theories of development to propose that during developmental transitions, when new cognitive, social, and emotional capacities emerge, new competencies are especially responsive to more favorable developmental circumstances. Interventions can be designed that leverage normally occurring developmental shifts to enhance new use of existing resources and successful development of new competencies (Shapiro, 1994, 1996a).

This approach has recently been applied to the existing literature on adolescent bereavement (Clark et al., 1994), suggesting that grief poses both immediate, direct disruption, and a cascade of secondary related disruptions combining to create configurations of risk and protective factors contributing to later outcomes. A risk and protective factors approach to predicting positive or negative outcomes after exposure to adversity has been used more frequently in research on exposure to traumatic stress or community violence (Garbarino, Dubrow, Kostelny, & Pardo, 1992; Pynoos, Steinberg, & Wraith, 1995; Richters & Martinez, 1993) and poverty (Halpern, 1999; McLoyd, 1990). Pynoos et al. (1995) have suggested that childhood traumatic grief especially burdens ongoing development, because traumatized children experiencing posttraumatic stress disorder must reconstruct an image of the deceased loved one interfered with by the death's violence. Richters and Martinez (1993) found that outcomes for children exposed to community violence were worse when their mothers experienced intense anxiety themselves. Richters and Martinez (1993) and Garbarino et al. (1992) suggested that meaning making emphasizing vengeance can provide immediate relief from intense feelings of rage and helplessness but are associated with poorer longer term outcomes.

CONCLUSION

This chapter has focused on theories that have ranged from the dyadic to the cross-cultural as a way of organizing the focus on interpersonal aspects of grief. This interpersonal model proposes that both child and adult grief reactions are collaboratively constructed through interpersonal, familial, and social interactions and their shared symbolization. A family death interrupts negotiated, provisional conversations between self, family, social community, and culture evolving over the life course. These conversations are designed to use available individual, familial, and social resources to solve both existing problems of shared development and new problems of social role functioning, affect regulation, attachment, identity, and meaning making created by the timing and circumstances of the death. The greater the domains of family life disrupted by a death, the greater the demands made on existing sources of continuity and stability to restore the interrupted work of family development. In the absence of instrumental resources such as economic security or social support, individuals and families are forced to rely on interpersonally negotiated emotional controls as strategies for stability of last resort.

A social developmental model recognizes grief symptomatology as a substantially culturally determined process. Yet an interpersonal approach, like all the grief literature, must differentiate normal and pathological grief reactions. Development and psychopathology defines symptoms as self-regulating strategies that interfere with a next step in development (Sameroff & Emde, 1989). The balance of stressors and resources creates a continuum of optimal, normative, or pathological grief reactions and determines a family's tolerance for ongoing family change. Interpersonal control strategies in response to overwhelming grief, such as interactions suppressing differences in shared experience or restricting destabilizing change, interfere with the individual and family capacity for open communication, cohesion, and mutual support, narrowing the capacity for flexible coping with future developmental challenges (Shapiro, 1994, 1996c).

In testing a social developmental model of family bereavement empirically, we need to begin with the call for overall improvement of bereavement research addressed throughout this volume. Especially important are systematic use of empirically tested outcome variables, comparison of bereavement samples with normative samples, clarity about sample characteristics such as type of death, clarification of mediating variables associated with the circumstances of the death such as accompanying disruptions, and distinctions between short-term and long-term grief outcomes. Further, this approach requires research methods capable of studying interpersonal relationship variables, such as communication or cohesion, and private representations of relationships, such as adult attachment models. Although age is more frequently used as a marker for development in bereavement research, additional family demographic variables such as stage of the family life cycle and family structure (number of children, adults in household) need to be considered. Because of the complexity and uniqueness of the configurations of factors affecting developmental outcomes, we need models that permit the study of variability in the organization of these pathways. The social sciences are only recently developing theoretical and methodological tools permitting systematic study of multiple variables interacting over time in complex developmental transitions. Guidelines for such research can be found in the literatures on development and psychopathology and on risk and resilience described earlier. Prospective, longitudinal research assessing sources of risk and protective factors in multiple domains can illuminate the complex pathways through which a family death affects shared development throughout the life cycle.

Implications for Interventions

The limited research literature on grief interventions presents conceptual and methodological problems (Kato & Mann, 1999) and offers contradictory guidelines. As a field, we have learned caution from historical prescriptions later proved unfounded (Wortman & Silver, 1989). It is important to recognize the limits of our knowledge about risks or protective factors associated with optimal long-term outcomes, and to respect any family's struggles, within their own cultures and communities, to make sense of death and its implications over time. The field's truism that detachment was required for healthy grief has given way to a more finely tuned recognition that enduring connections to the deceased that emphasize living images (Silverman, 2000) and fond memories (Field, Nichols, Holen, & Horowitz, 1999) are associated with positive outcomes. The Freudian concept of "working through" grief has yielded to a recognition that individuals and families process grief in a complex balance with other ongoing life tasks (Shapiro, 1994; Stroebe & Schut, 1999; chapter 22, this volume). Although appropriately trained professionals can offer useful help, community-based volunteers who offer support and access to resources, or bereaved survivors, can often be even more helpful to bereaved individuals (Klass, 1996; Silverman, 2000).

The review in this chapter suggests a few key elements that can help both individuals and families achieve more favorable interpersonal reorganization after a family death (Shapiro, 1994, 1995, 1996b). First, bereaved people need instrumental social support, which is practical help with the work of daily family survival such as child care, housework, or finances, to manage daily life disruptions. Without practical help, families become too burdened with real life problems to afford the luxury of exploring the enormous shifts in images of self, relationships, and meaning precipitated by the death. Second, a grieving family's next priority is reestablishing mechanisms for stable, shared emotional regulation. Open expression of feelings, valued highly in both psychodynamic and stage models of grief, can become destabilizing to a family's interpersonally negotiated rules for shared emotional stability. For example, many families find that their grief is triggered by the grief of a family member, and create implicit rules for permissible communication of thoughts and feelings. Grieving children are especially concerned about emotionally protecting their parents to minimize the emotional and practical disruption of caretaking safety in their daily lives. The greater the stressors and discontinuities, and the fewer the social supports, the more likely families will be to rely on interpersonal control strategies that limit their adaptive flexibility. For some families, the dead cannot be spoken about at all, for fear that a fragile family member might not be able to tolerate the emotions triggered by a reminder. Such families inhibit their growing children, whose maturing cognitive capacities generate new questions about the death and its meaning, from exploring the experience of the death and their images of the deceased family member in ways that enhance ongoing development (Shapiro, 1994; Silverman, 2000). Supports that increase stability, continuity, and cohesion can be introduced at every level of the family system, and can range from mundane management of practical household tasks, to strategies for improving family communication, to spiritual connections with religious communities and ancestral beliefs. These supports help the family as a unit, through interpersonal communications and their symbolization, to integrate experience and adapt to changes with fewer attempts to control thoughts and feelings in ways that impede shared development.

Interventions featuring systematic, individualized assessment and collaborative planning to diminish stressors and identify existing and new resources increase the likelihood of more favorable integration of experiences and successful adaptation to the changing circumstances. Such a multisystemic model of treatment has been empirically tested in work with delinquent adolescents, demonstrating that a complex conceptual model can be systematically applied to design highly individualized interventions improving outcomes (Henggeler et al., 1996, 1998). Therapeutic relationships can offer supportive interpersonal resources permitting safer exploration, perspective-taking, and integration of emotionally overwhelming concerns for both individuals and families. Kissane et al. (1996, 1997) suggested that assessment of high-risk families can help identify those most needing therapy. The research findings overall suggest that useful family interventions can help explore and expand family communication, cohesion, and shared narratives of the loss and its implications. Therapeutic group interventions can be especially useful to bereaved children (Lohnes & Coltody, 1994), especially when paired with interventions that enhance the parent's responsiveness (Baker, 1997). An interpersonal approach in social and developmental context offers guidelines for assessing collaboratively, with families and their communities, the best use of relational resources for ameliorating the anguish of a family death and supporting the most favorable configuration of circumstances for life and growth after grief.

REFERENCES

Ainsworth, M., Blehar, M., Waters, E., & Wall, S. (1978). *Patterns of attachment: A psychological study of the strange situation.* Hillsdale, NJ: Erlbaum.

Baker, J. (1997). Minimizing the impact of parental grief on children: Parent and family interactions. In C. Figley & B. Bride (Eds.), *Death and trauma: The traumatology of grieving* (pp. 139–157). Washington, DC: Taylor & Francis.

Bateson, G. (1972). *Steps to an ecology of mind.* New York: Ballantine.

Bateson, G. (1979). *Mind and nature: A necessary unity.* New York: Bantam.

Bateson, G. (1992). *Sacred unity: Further steps to an ecology of mind.* New York: Harper Collins.

Bateson, P. (1991). *The development and integration of behaviour: Essays in honour of Robert Hinde.* Cambridge, England: Cambridge University Press.

Beebe, B., & Lachmann, F. (1998). Co-constructing inner and relational processes: Self-and mutual regulation in infant research and adult treatment. *Psychoanalytic Psychology, 15,* 480–516.

Beebe, B., Lachmann, F., & Jaffe, J. (1997). Mother-infant interaction structures and presymbolic self- and object representations. *Psychoanalytic Dialogues, 7,* 133–182.

Belsky, J. (1993). Etiology of child maltreatment: A developmental-ecological analysis. *Psychological Bulletin, 114,* 413–434.

Benjamin, J. (1988). *The bonds of love: Psychoanalysis, feminism and the problem of domination.* New York: Pantheon.

Benjamin, J. (1998). *Shadow of the other: Intersubjectivity and gender in psychoanalysis.* New York: Routledge.

Bonnano, G., Notarius, C., Gunzerath, L., Keltner, D., & Horowitz, M. (1998). Interpersonal ambivalence, perceived relationship adjustment, and conjugal loss. *Journal of Consulting and Clinical Psychology, 66,* 1012–1022.

Bowen, M. (1976). Family reaction to death. In P. Guerin (Ed.), *Family therapy* (pp. 335–348). New York: Gardner.

Bowlby, J. (1969). *Attachment and loss. Vol. 1. Attachment.* New York: Basic Books.

Bowlby, J. (1973). *Attachment and loss. Vol. 2. Separation.* New York: Basic Books.

Bowlby, J. (1980). *Attachment and loss. Vol. 3: Loss.* New York: Basic Books.

Bowlby-West, L. (1983). The impact of death on the family system. *Journal of Family Therapy, 5,* 279–294.

Bretherton, I. (1991). The roots and growing points of attachment theory. In C. Parkes, J. Stevenson-Hinde, & P. Marris (Eds.), *Attachment across the life cycle* (pp. 9–32). New York: Routledge.

Bretherton, I., & Munholland, K. (1999). Internal working models in attachment relationships: A construct revisited. In J. Cassidy & P. Shaver (Eds.), *Handbook of attachment theory and research* (pp. 89–113). New York: Guilford Press.

Bretherton, I., Ridgeway, D., & Cassidy, J. (1990). Assessing internal working models of the attachment relationship: An Attachment Story Completion Task for 3-year olds. In M. Greenberg, D. Cicchetti, & E. Cummings (Eds.), *Attachment during the preschool years* (pp. 273–308). Chicago: University of Chicago Press.

Bretherton, I., & Waters, E. (1985). Growing points in attachment theory and research. *Monographs of the Society for Research in Child Development, 50*(1–2, Serial # 209).

Bronfenbrenner, U. (1979). *Ecology of human development.* Cambridge, MA: Harvard University Press.

Bronfenbrenner, U., Moen, P., & Garbarino, J. (1984). Families and communities. In H. Parke (Ed.), *Review of Child Development Research* (pp. 251–278). Chicago: University of Chicago Press.

Byng-Hall, J. (1995). Creating a secure family base: Some implications of attachment theory for family therapy. *Family Process, 34,* 45–58.

Calter, N., Case, A., Saldinger, A., & Lohnes, K. (1999, June). *Child bereavement outcomes.* Paper presented at the Childhood Grief Support Services conference, Ann Arbor, MI.

Cassidy, J., & Shaver, P. (1999). *Handbook of attachment theory and research.* New York: Guilford Press.

Cicchetti, D. (1989). How research on child maltreatment has informed the study of child development: Perspectives from developmental psychopathology. In D. Cicchetti & V. Carson (Eds.), *Child maltreatment: Theory and research on the causes and consequences of child abuse and neglect* (pp. 377–431). Cambridge: Cambridge University Press.

Cicchetti, D., & Carlson, V. (1989). *Child maltreatment: Theory and research on the causes and consequences of child abuse and neglect.* Cambridge: Cambridge University Press.

Cicchetti, D., & Cohen, D. (1995a). *Development and psychopathology, Volume I: Theory and methods.* New York: John Wiley & Sons.

Cicchetti, D., & Cohen, D. (1995b). *Development and psychopathology, Volume II: Risk, disorder and adaptation.* New York: John Wiley & Sons.

Cicchetti, D., & Garmezy, N. (Eds.). (1993). *Milestones in the Development of Resilience.* Special Issue, *Development and Psychopathology, 5,* 497–775.

Clark, D., Pynoos, R., & Gobel, A. (1994). Mechanisms and processes of adolescent bereavement. In R. Haggard, N. Garmezy, M. Rutter, & L. Sheerod (Eds.), *Stress, risk and resilience in children and adolescents: Processes, mechanisms and interventions* (pp. 100–146). Cambridge: Cambridge University Press.

Coie, J., Watt, N., West, S., Hawking, J., Asarnow, J., Markman, H., Ramey, S., Shure, M., & Long, B. (1993). The science of prevention: A conceptual framework and some directions for a national research program. *American Psychologist, 48,* 1013–1022.

Cushman, P. (1994). *Constructing the self, constructing America: A cultural history of psychotherapy.* Boston: Addison Wesley.

Davis, C., Nolen-Hoeksema, S., & Larson, J. (1998). Making sense of loss and benefitting from the experience: Two construals of meaning. *Journal of Personality and Social Psychology, 75,* 561–574.

Dicks, H. (1967). *Marital tensions.* New York: Basic Books.

Fadiman, A. (1997). *The spirit catches you and you fall down: A Hmong child, her American doctors, and the collision of two cultures.* New York: Farrar, Strauss & Giroux.

Falicov, C. (1998). *Latino families in therapy.* New York: Guilford Press.

Field, N., Nichols, C., Holen, A., & Horowitz, M. (1999). The relation of continuing attachment to adjustment in conjugal bereavement. *Journal of Consulting and Clinical Psychology, 67,* 212–218.

Frankiel, R. (1994). *Essential papers on object loss.* New York: New York University Press.

Freud, S. (1957). Mourning and melancholia. In J. Strachey (Ed. & Trans.), *The standard edition of the complete psychological works of Sigmund Freud* (Vol. 14, pp. 239–260). New York: Norton. (Original work published 1917)

Friedman, S. (Ed.). (1993). *The new language of change.* New York: Guilford Press.

Garbarino, J., Dubrow, N., Kostelny, K., & Pardo, C. (1992). *Children in danger: Coping with the consequences of community violence.* San Francisco: Jossey Bass.

Hagman, G. (1995). Death of a selfobject: Toward a self psychology of the mourning process. In A. Goldberg (Ed.), *Progress in self psychology, Vol. 11* (pp. 189–205). Hillsdale, NJ: Analytic Press.

Halpern, R. (1999). Poverty and infant development. In C. Zeanah (Ed.), *Handbook of infant mental health* (2nd ed., pp. 73–86). New York: Guilford Press.

Harris, T., & Bifulco, A. (1991). Loss of parent in childhood, attachment style, and depression in adulthood. In C. Parkes, J. Stevenson-Hinde, & P. Marris (Eds.), *Attachment across the life cycle* (pp. 234–267). New York: Routledge.

Harvey, J. (1996). *Embracing their memory: Loss and the social psychology of storytelling.* New York: Allyn & Bacon.

Harvey, J. (1997). (Ed.). *Perspectives on loss: A sourcebook.* Philadelphia: Brunner/Mazel.

Henggeler, S., Schoenwald, S., Bardwin, C., Rowland, M., & Cuningham, P. (1998). *Multi-systemic treatment of antisocial behavior in children and adolescents.* New York: Guilford Press.

Henggeler, S., Schoenwald, S., & Pickrel, S. (1995). Multisystemic therapy: Bridging the gap between university- and community-based treatment. *Journal of Consulting and Clinical Psychology, 63,* 709–717.

Herz, F. (1989). The impact of death and serious illness on the family life cycle.

In B. Carter & M. McGoldrick (Eds.), *The changing family life cycle: A framework for family therapy* (2nd ed., pp. 457–482). Boston: Allyn & Bacon.

Hesse, E. (1999). The Adult Attachment Interview: Historical and current perspectives. In J. Cassidy & P. Shaver (Eds.), *Handbook of attachment theory and research* (pp. 735–759). New York: Guilford Press.

Horowitz, M. (1986). *Stress response syndromes.* New York: Aronson.

Horowitz, M. (1989). A model of mourning: Change in schemas of self and other. *Journal of the American Psychoanalytic Association, 38,* 297–324.

Horowitz, M., Bonanno, G., & Holen, A. (1993). Pathological grief: Diagnosis and explanations. *Psychosomatic Medicine, 55,* 260–273.

Horowitz, M., Wilner, N., Marmar, C., & Krupnick, J. (1980). Pathological grief and the activation of latent self-images. *American Journal of Psychiatry, 137,* 1157–1162.

Hurd, R. (1999). Adults view their childhood bereavement experiences. *Death Studies, 23,* 17–41.

Jordan, J. R., Kraus, D. R., & Ware, E. S. (1993). Observations on loss and family development. *Family Process, 32,* 425–440.

Kato, P., & Mann, T. (1999). A synthesis of psychological interventions for the bereaved. *Clinical Psychology Review, 19,* 275–296.

Kissane, D., & Bloch, S. (1994). Family grief. *British Journal of Psychiatry, 164,* 728–740.

Kissane, D., Bloch, S., Dowe, D., Snyder, R., Onghena, P., McKenzie, D., & Wallace, C. (1996a). The Melbourne family grief study, I: Perceptions of family functioning in bereavement. *American Journal of Psychiatry, 153*(5), 650–658.

Kissane, D., Bloch, S., & McKenzie, D. (1997). Family coping and bereavement outcome. *Palliative Medicine, 11,* 191–201.

Kissane, D., Bloch, S., Onghena, P., McKenzie, D., Snyder, R., & Dowe, D. (1996). The Melbourne family grief study, II: Psychosocial morbidity and grief in bereaved families. *American Journal of Psychiatry, 153,* 659–666.

Klass, D. (1996). The deceased child in the psychic and social worlds of bereaved parents during the resolution of grief. In D. Klass, P. Silverman, & S. Nickman (Eds.), *Continuing bonds: New understandings of grief* (pp. 199–216). Washington, DC: Taylor and Francis.

Klass, D., Silverman, P., & Nickman, S. (1996). *Continuing bonds: New understandings of grief.* Washington, DC: Taylor & Francis.

Kohut, H. (1977). *The restoration of the self.* New York: International Universities Press.

Lachmann, F., & Beebe, B. (1997). Trauma, interpretation, and self-state transformations. *Psychoanalysis and Contemporary Thought, 20,* 269–291.

Lepore, S., Silver, R., Wortman, C., & Wayment, H. (1996). Social constraints, intrusive thoughts, and depressive symptoms among bereaved mothers. *Journal of Personality and Social Psychology, 70,* 271–282.

Lohnes, K., & Coltody, N. (1994). Preventive intervention groups for parentally bereaved children. *American Journal of Orthopsychiatry, 64,* 594–603.

Luepnitz, D. (1988). *The family interpreted.* New York: Basic Books.

Lyons-Ruth, K., & Block, D. (1996). The disturbed caregiving system: Relations among childhood trauma, maternal caregiving, and infant affect and attachment. *Infant Mental Health Journal, 17,* 257–275.

Lyons-Ruth, K., & Jacobvitz, D. (1999). Attachment disorganization: Unresolved loss, relational violence, and lapses in behavioral and attentional strategies. In J. Cassidy & P. Shaver (Eds.), *Handbook of attachment theory and research* (pp. 520–554). New York: Guilford Press.

Lyons-Ruth, K., & Zeanah, C. (1999). The family context of infant mental health: I. Affective development in the primary caregiving relationship. In C. Zeanah (Ed.), *Handbook of infant mental health* (pp. 14–37). New York: Guilford Press.

MacKinnon, N. (1994). *Symbolic interactionism as affect control.* Albany: State University of New York Press.

Main, M. (1991). Metacognitive knowledge, metacognitive monitoring, and singular (coherent) vs. multiple (incoherent) model of attachment: Findings and directions for future research. In C. Parkes & P. Marris (Eds.), *Attachment across the life cycle* (pp. 127–159). London: Routledge.

Main, M., & Goldwyn, R. (1984). Predicting rejection of her infant from mother's representation of her own experiences: Implications for the abused-abusing intergenerational cycle. *Child Abuse and Neglect, 8,* 203–217.

Main, M. Kaplan, N., & Cassidy, J. (1985). Security in infancy, childhood and adulthood: A move to the level of representation. In I. Bretherton & E. Waters (Eds.), *Growing points of attachment theory and research. Monographs of the Society for Research in Child Development, 50,* 66–104.

McCrae, R., & Costa, P. (1993). Psychological resilience among widowed men and women: A 10 year follow-up. In M. Stroebe, W. Stroebe, & R. Hansson (Eds.), *Handbook of bereavement: Theory, research and intervention* (pp. 196–207). New York: Cambridge University Press.

McGoldrick, M. (1998). *Re-visioning family therapy: Race, culture and gender in clinical practice.* New York: Guilford Press.

McGoldrick, M., & Walsh, F. (1991). A time to mourn: Death and the family life cycle. In R. Walsh & M. McGoldrick (Eds.), *Living beyond loss* (pp. 30–49). New York: W. W. Norton.

McLoyd, V. (1990). The impact of economic hardship on black families and children: Psychological distress, parenting, and socioemotional development. *Child Development, 61,* 311–346.

Metcalf, P., & Huntington, R. (1991). *Celebrations of death: The anthropology of mortuary ritual.* New York: Cambridge University Press.

Miller, N., Luborsky, L., Barber, J., & Docherty, J. (1993). *Psychodynamic treatment research: A handbook for clinical practice.* New York: Basic Books.

Mitchell, S. (1988). *Relational concepts in psychoanalysis.* Cambridge, MA: Harvard University Press.

Moos, N. (1995). An integrative model of grief. *Death Studies, 19,* 337–364.

Nelson, B., & Frantz, T. (1996). Family interactions of suicide survivors and survivors of non-suicidal death. *Omega: Journal of Death and Dying, 33,* 131–146.

Parkes, C. (1993). Bereavement as a psychosocial transition: Processes of adaptation to change. In M. Stroebe, W. Stroebe, & R. Hansson (Eds.), *Handbook of bereavement: Theory, research and intervention* (pp. 91–101). New York: Cambridge University Press.

Parkes, C., Stevenson-Hinde, J., & Marris, P. (Eds.). (1991). *Attachment across the life cycle.* London: Routledge.

Paul, N., & Grosser, G. (1965). Operational mourning and its role in conjoint family therapy. *Community Mental Health Journal, 1,* 339–345.

Piercy, F., & Sprenkle, D. (1998). *Family therapy sourcebook* (2nd ed.). New York: Guilford Press.

Pincus, L. (1974). *Death and the family: The importance of mourning.* New York: Pantheon.

Pizer, St. (1997). *Building bridges: The negotiation of paradox in psychoanalysis.* Mawah, NJ: Analytic Press.

Pynoos, R., Steinberg, A., & Wraith, R. (1995). A developmental model of childhood traumatic stress. In D. Cicchetti & D. Cohen (Eds.), *Development and psychopathology, Volume II: Risk, disorder and adaptation* (pp. 96–161). New York: John Wiley.

Richters, J., & Martinez, P. (1993). Violent communities, family choices, and children's chances: An algorithm for improving the odds. *Development and Psychopathology, 5,* 609–628.

Rolf, J., Masten, A., Cicchetti, D., Nuechterlein, K., & Weintraub, S. (1990). *Risk and protective factors in the development of psychopathology.* Cambridge: Cambridge University Press.

Romanoff, B., & Terenzio, M. (1998). Rituals and the grieving process. *Death Studies, 22,* 697–711.

Rosaldo, R. (1989). Grief and a headhunter's rage. In R. Rosaldo (Ed.), *Culture and truth: The remaking of social analysis* (pp. 1–21). Boston: Beacon Press.

Rosenblatt, P. (1993). Grief: The social context of private feelings. In M. Stroebe, W. Stroebe, & R. Hansson (Eds.), *Handbook of bereavement: Theory, research and intervention* (pp. 102–111). Cambridge: Cambridge University Press.

Rutter, M. (1991). Maternal deprivation revisited. In P. Bateson (Ed.), *The development and integration of behaviour: Essays in honour of Robert Hinde* (pp. 331–374). Cambridge: Cambridge University Press.

Sameroff, A. (1995). General systems theory and developmental psychopathology. In D. Cicchetti & D. Cohen (Eds.), *Development and psychopathology, Volume I: Theory and methods* (pp. 659–695). New York: John Wiley & Sons.

Sameroff, A., & Emde, R. (1989). *Relationship disturbances in early childhood.* New York: Basic Books.

Schore, A. (1994). *Affect regulation and the origin of the self: The neurobiology of emotional development*. Mahwah, NJ: Erlbaum.

Schuengel, C., Bakermans-Kranenburg, M., & Van Ijzendoorn, M. (1999). Frightening maternal behavior linking unresolved loss and disorganized infant attachment. *Journal of Consulting and Clinical Psychology, 67* 54–63.

Shapiro, E. (1994). *Grief as a family process: A developmental approach to clinical practice*. New York: Guilford Press.

Shapiro, E. (1995). Grief and trauma in family developmental and cultural context. *Clinical Quarterly, 5*, 1–6.

Shapiro, E. (1996a). Family development in cultural context: Implications for prevention and early intervention with Latino families. *New England Journal of Public Policy, 11*, 113–128.

Shapiro, E. (1996b). Grief in Freud's life: A relational developmental model of bereavement. *Psychoanalytic Psychology, 13*, 547–566.

Shapiro, E. R. (1996c). Family bereavement and cultural diversity: a social developmental perspective. *Family Process, 35*, 313–332.

Shapiro, E. (1997). The healing power of culture stories: What writers can teach psychotherapists. *Cultural Diversity and Mental Health, 4*, 91–101.

Silverman, P. (2000). *Never too young to know: Death in children's lives*. New York: Oxford University Press.

Silverman, P., & Weiner, A. (1995). Parent-child communication in bereaved Israeli families. *Omega: Journal of Death and Dying, 31*, 275–293.

Skolnick, N., & Warshaw, S. (1991). *Relational perspectives in psychoanalysis*. Hillsdale, NJ: Analytic Press.

Stern, D. (1985). *The interpersonal world of the infant*. New York: Basic Books.

Stolorow, R. (1999). The phenomenology of trauma and the absolutisms of everyday life: A personal journey. *Psychoanalytic Psychology, 16*, 464–468.

Stolorow, R., & Atwood, G. (1992). *Contexts of being: The intersubjective foundations of psychological life*. Hillsdale, NJ: Analytic Press.

Stroebe, M., Gergen, M., Gergen, K., & Stroebe, W. (1992). Broken hearts or broken bonds: Love and death in historical perspective. *American Psychologist, 47*, 1205–1212.

Stroebe, M., & Schut, H. (1999). The dual process model of coping with bereavement: rationale and description. *Death Studies, 23*, 197–224.

Stroebe, W., Stroebe, M., Abakoumkin, G., & Schut, H. (1996). The role of loneliness and social support in adjustment to loss: A test of attachment versus stress theory. *Journal of Personality and Social Psychology, 70*, 1241–1249.

Sullivan, H. (1953). *The interpersonal theory of psychiatry*. New York: Norton.

Tedlock, D., & Mannheim, B. (Eds.). (1995). *The dialogic emergence of culture*. Urbana: University of Illinois Press.

Tremblay, G., & Allen, I. (1998). Children's adjustment to parental death. *Clinical Psychology: Science and Practice, 5*, 424–438.

Tronick, E. (1989). Infant development and mother/infant interaction. *American Psychologist, 44,* 112–119.

Tronick, E. (1998). Dyadically expanded states of consciousness and the process of therapeutic change. *Infant Mental Health Journal, 19,* 290–299.

Turner, V. (1967). *The forest of symbols.* Ithaca, NY: Cornell University Press.

Van Doorn, C., Kasl, S., Beery, L., Jacobs, S., & Prigerson, H. (1998). The influence of marital quality and attachment styles on traumatic grief and depressive symptoms. *Journal of Nervous and Mental Disease, 186*(9), 566–573.

Wachtel, P. (1993). *Therapeutic communication: Principles and effective practice.* New York: Guilford Press.

Walker, G. (1991). *In the midst of winter: Systemic therapy with families, couples and individuals with AIDS infection.* New York: Norton.

Walsh, F. (1982). *Normal family processes.* New York: Guilford Press.

Walsh, R., & McGoldrick, M. (Eds.). (1991). *Living beyond loss.* New York: W. W. Norton.

Weiss, R. (1993). Loss and recovery. In M. Stroebe, W. Stroebe, & R. Hansson (Eds.), *Handbook of bereavement: Theory, research and intervention* (pp. 271–284). Cambridge: Cambridge University Press.

Werner, E. (1993). Risk, resilience and recovery: Perspectives from the Kauai longitudinal study. *Development and Psychopathology, 5,* 503–516.

White, M., & Epston, D. (1990). *Narrative means to therapeutic ends.* New York: W. W. Norton.

Winnicott, D. (1965). The *maturational process and the facilitating environment.* New York: International Universities Press.

Wortman, C., & Silver, R. (1989). The myths of coping with loss. *Journal of Consulting and Clinical Psychology, 57,* 349–357.

Wortman, C., Silver, R., & Kessler, R. (1993). The meaning of loss and adjustment to bereavement. In M. Stroebe, W. Stroebe, & R. Hansson (Eds.), *Handbook of bereavement: Theory, research and intervention* (pp. 349–366). Cambridge: Cambridge University Press.

Zeanah, C. (Ed.). (1999). *Handbook of infant mental health* (2nd ed.). New York: Guilford Press.

15

MEANING MAKING IN FAMILY BEREAVEMENT: A FAMILY SYSTEMS APPROACH

JANICE WINCHESTER NADEAU

Few events affect families more than the death of a family member. When someone in a family dies, the shock wave is felt throughout the family. Most studies have focused on individuals, however. Studying family grief yields important data that can help build useful theory and direct effective intervention. Although there are undoubtedly many ways that family grief could be explored, this chapter focuses on how family members coconstruct the meaning of a death. This process of coconstruction is referred to as *family meaning making*. The way in which a family construes the loss of a family member greatly influences how they will grieve. A family that construes the death of a family member as a long-awaited relief from pain is likely to grieve differently from the family who construes a death as something they should have prevented.

When grieving families are seen through the lens of family meaning making, much of what is important about family grief comes into view. Family patterns are vividly revealed. Multigenerational effects can be identified. The interweaving of family structure, family process, and family meaning making can be seen. Ways in which certain meanings affect the course of family grief become apparent, and an array of family interventions suggest themselves.

In this chapter the findings from a study of 10 grieving families (Nadeau, 1998) are used to illustrate family meaning making. An attempt is made to show how thinking of families from a meaning-making perspective reveals grief's broader face and shifts our focus from the intrapersonal to the interpersonal.

A QUALITATIVE STUDY OF FAMILY MEANING MAKING

I noticed over 20 years of working with grieving families in intensive care units, in emergency rooms, and in counseling offices that most families, on receiving news of a family member's death, started trying to make sense of what had happened by talking with other family members. Their process was highly interactive and sometimes sounded litany-like. Comments such as "they lived a long life," "this is how she would have wanted to die," "why didn't we get a second opinion," or "it must have been his time," were made, agreed with, questioned, and repeated. Sometimes family members spliced their phrases together, arriving at some joint conclusion. Their conclusions, which I now would call, "family meanings," tended to set a mood or tone for the family's mourning. I questioned how one would capture this process in a formal study and not lose the spontaneity. What theories would inform such a study and what methods would be useful?

As family qualitative research came more into its own, methods emerged that showed promise for studying families in grief. I interviewed 10 nonclinical, multigenerational families using research methods influenced by grounded theory (Glaser & Strauss, 1967; Strauss & Corbin, 1990). It was possible to ask questions of families as groups by conducting intensive interviews with multiple family members in their homes. The use of open-ended questions directed to the family as a whole enabled most families to "forget themselves" long enough to engage in what looked like a natural family process. Interviews were transcribed verbatim and content analyzed. Findings revealed that families used certain methods or strategies to make meaning. The meanings that they made were identified and classified into a typology. Forty-eight family members were interviewed. Some were interviewed twice, once alone and once with other family members.

Theories Pertinent to Understanding Family Meaning Making

The theories that were the most useful in studying family meaning making were *symbolic interaction theory* and *family systems theory*. Symbolic interaction theory grew out of the philosophical writings of James (1890), Cooley (1902, 1909), Dewey (1922), Thomas (1923), and Mead (1932, 1934, 1936, 1938) in the Chicago School of Sociology. These theorists postulated that reality is socially constructed, and that people construct meaning through the use of everyday conversation. With this theory we could expect to see family members attempting to make sense of their experience by talking to each other about the death that had occurred.

Thomas (1923), most well-known for his descriptions of self-fulfilling prophecy, asserted that when people define situations as real, they are real in their consequences. We could anticipate, then, that the family, who construes the death of a family member as a relief from pain rather than as something that should have been prevented, would experience different consequences.

Berger and Luckmann (1966), building on the theories of the early interactionists, spoke directly to the loss of significant others through death. These theorists contend that death constitutes a crisis situation that requires intense measures of reality maintenance. They emphasized that, although reality is socially defined, the definitions are always embodied in concrete individuals and groups of individuals. Families create and maintain their own realities or "family worlds," as Hess and Handel (1959) first called them. Within this conceptual framework, family conversation is seen as the apparatus by which reality is constructed and maintained.

There are three concepts from family systems theory that are useful in thinking about family meaning-making patterns: roles, rules, and boundaries. *Roles* are the expectations attached to a given position in the family, including family positions such as mother and father (Stryker, 1972). Other roles, less attached to position, include peacemaker, scapegoat, and family star. When a family member dies, the roles once held by the lost member are lost. The family casts about for new actors.

Rules are prescriptions for familial responses to a wide range of possible inputs (Broderick & Smith, 1979). Rules can be thought of as unspoken understandings within the family that govern all family interactions, including how the family is to grieve. Families with a wide range of rules are more flexible and are better able to adapt to new conditions. When someone in the family dies, current rules may be inadequate and new rules may be needed.

Boundaries delineate the elements belonging to the system in question and those belonging to its environment (Broderick & Smith, 1979). There are family boundaries separating a given family from its environment, boundaries separating generations within the family, and boundaries separating subgroups of family members. The concept of boundaries becomes of greatest importance when considering how meanings get constructed within certain boundaries and, in turn, how meanings help to maintain boundaries. The meaning of the loss may be different for the one who is left alone in a former two-person coalition or alliance than it is for those family members whose alliances and coalitions remain intact.

Conceptually, it is useful to think of family grief as a complex interaction of family meaning-making processes, family structure, and family dynamics. Family meaning making can be studied in terms of the processes used to make meaning and the meanings themselves. Family structure may be studied in terms of boundaries, and family dynamics in terms of roles and rules.

Methods Pertinent to the Study of Family Meaning Making

This study drew heavily on grounded theory methods developed by Glaser and Strauss (1967) and Strauss and Corbin (1990). Family meaning making, as it was conceptualized in this study, had not been previously described. Qualitative methods that would assume little but allow for theories to be inductively developed from the data were needed.

Family research presents certain unique problems, such as how to capture families doing what they naturally do, and how to find language with which to describe family-level phenomena. In this study, Milan circular questioning was used to get family members to lose themselves in conversations. Milan circular questioning comes from a model of family therapy developed by Selvini, Boscolo, Cecchin, and Prata (Boscolo, Cecchin, Hoffman, & Penn, 1987) in Milan, Italy. A critical part of circular questioning in family therapy is to ask family members in the presence of other members how they think someone in the family would respond to a particular question. An adaptation of this method, developed by Wright (n.d.), asks family members to speak for absent members. In this study, Wright's adaptation was used and expanded to include asking the family how the member who had died might answer. This technique was immensely effective in stimulating spontaneous family dialogue, revealing family patterns, and increasing the amount of systemic data.

Another challenge in family research is to collect data that represents the family perspective. In this study the challenge was met in part by collecting data from multiple family members from more than one generation and by interviewing some family members both alone and with other family members. This made comparisons among interviews possible and revealed many more family patterns. (For specifics, see Nadeau, 1998.)

Families were interviewed primarily in their homes using intensive, unstructured interviews as described by Lofland and Lofland (1984). First genograms were drawn to identify the family players. This was a relatively nonthreatening way to join with the family, to capture family structure, and to identify potential respondents. Families were asked open-ended questions about 25 areas related to the death. Interviews were audiotaped, transcribed verbatim, and content analyzed by traditional, noncomputerized methods. There were 33 interviews, totaling 70 hours and yielding 3000 pages of hard copy. Open coding was used to code data related to meaning making. Codes were grouped into categories using a word processing program. Categories were then related to one another by using axial coding (Strauss & Corbin, 1990). The findings that emerged included strategies that families use to make meaning, the meaning statements themselves, and family patterns associated with the meaning-making process.

Issues of Validity, Reliability, and Generalizability

In this qualitative study, issues of reliability, validity, and generalizability were addressed differently than they would be in a quantitative study. Rosenblatt and Fischer (1993) argued that the nature of qualitative knowledge and truth can be very different from the nature of nonqualitative knowledge and truth and, therefore, require different methods of establishing reliability and validity. In qualitative research, the term "verification of the data" is sometimes used to distinguish its methods from those associated with quantitative research.

According to Miles and Huberman (1984), verification of data in qualitative studies goes on continuously as data are collected. When a finding begins to emerge, the investigator checks it out with other informants. Validity checks occur when data are examined for their plausibility and confirmability. Validity can be established, according to Rosenblatt and Fischer (1993), by the internal patterning and coherence of a complex set of interviews without rigorous quantification. Validity analysis involves careful examination of the consistency of data. Data that deviate are explored as a check on the validity of the coding and analysis or as sources of additional theorizing.

For example, one of the findings in this study was that families make sense of a death by comparing it to other deaths inside and outside of the family. Validity analysis included checking each use of comparison to see that it was associated with meaning statements. This was done for each of the family meaning-making strategies identified in the study.

Validity was enhanced in three other ways. One was the generation of the interview guidelines by talking to grieving family members in a pilot study. Fruitful lines of questioning became the 25 questions asked of families in the main study. The questions were circulated to several colleagues in the family field and changes were made as necessary.

A second check on validity was returning repeatedly to the study data during the analysis. Sections of the transcripts rich in meaning-making activity were examined three times: once to identify family themes, once to code the meaning statements, and once to code the meaning-making processes. As the study was being conducted, interview data were shared with four colleagues as a check on the validity of the coding scheme. Before the results were reported, the coding scheme was used by Strauss and Corbin (1990) in a grounded theory workshop for the National Council on Family Relations and was judged to be appropriately coded and methodologically sound.

A third check on validity is the presentation of ample amounts of verbatim data in research reports. This practice allows consumers to judge for themselves whether the conclusions drawn seem valid.

Multiple attempts to ensure reliability of the data were used. Those having to do with the questions themselves included asking relevant and clear questions and asking several questions about the same thing. Those having to do with interview technique included conducting lengthy interviews (one and a half to three and half hours each), interviewing multiple family members, interviewing some members twice, and calculating the level of agreement between interviews.

Perhaps the most important method was the technique of verifying meanings as they were stated. This technique drew heavily on the psychotherapy training and experience of the interviewer and involved listening for meaning statements and repeating them back to respondents throughout the interview. This technique allowed speakers to correct the researcher and to elaborate.

Generalization, as it is generally thought of, is problematic in qualitative studies because qualitative findings are highly personal in nature, long interviews yield highly particularized data, and we do not know how "typical" our respondents are. The focus is on generalizability to theory as opposed to generalizations to populations (Moon, Dillon, & Sprenkle, 1990). Strauss and Corbin (1990) contended that it is instances of the concepts being studied that need to be sampled, not the individuals themselves. As grounded theory is tested by its application to broader samples and new populations, inconsistencies are noted, current theory is modified or discarded. The process is one of constant comparison of new data to evolving theory.

In qualitative studies generalizability is less of a goal than it is in quantitative studies. The goals of qualitative research, according to Rosenblatt and Fischer (1993), are to show that some phenomenon exists, to reveal the complexity of the data, and to provide illustrations.

LIMITATIONS OF THE STUDY

The study had four major limitations. One limitation was that the study was essentially designed and carried out by a single investigator. In spite of ongoing consultation with other qualitative researchers, critical decisions about such things as when to use interview probes, how to select, interpret, and summarize data, were made essentially by one person. Researcher bias can be assumed to have occurred.

A second limitation was the homogeneity of the population studied, including the types of deaths. Families were all White, middle-class Midwesterners in families who were open enough to allow an interviewer into their worlds. Only one death was accidental and none were by suicide. There were no deaths of children and there were no AIDS or SIDS deaths. One can imagine that the meanings attached to such deaths would be significantly different, as might be the processes by which families construe such deaths.

A third limitation was that not all the members of each family were interviewed. Aside from the problematic issue of what constitutes "family" was the question of how family members who declined to be interviewed would have differed from the family members who participated. An attempt was made to address this limitation by using the Milan method of circular questioning. Members who were present were asked to "mind read" absent members and to rank them in terms of agreement with the meanings articulated by those present. This technique was very useful in revealing family patterns but it was no substitute for the real presence of missing members.

A fourth limitation of the study was that it represented only the first phase of a grounded theory study. Ideally, one would return to the population studied to test the theories that had evolved, to look for inconsistencies and changes over time. This process would continue until there were no new data, a state called "category saturation" (Strauss & Corbin, 1990). A good example in this study would be to return to families with the meanings identified in previous interviews to ascertain levels of agreement and persistence of previously stated meanings over time.

LOCATING FAMILIES

Ten families were found through funeral homes and clergy in a two county area in Midwestern United States. All were White, mostly of Northern European descent. There were 26 females and 22 males. With the exception of a 5-year-old and two younger teenagers who joined interviews for short periods of time, the ages of respondents ranged from 18 to 74. The ages of the members who had died ranged from 39 to 91. The time that had elapsed since the death of a family member was from $4\frac{1}{2}$ months to 22 months. Nine died of natural causes and one died accidentally.

FINDINGS: AN OVERVIEW

Findings emerged as three main categories: the strategies by which families made sense of the death, a typology of the meanings themselves, and related patterns of family meaning making. The strategies included storytelling, using dreams, making comparisons, characterizing the deceased, "coincidancing," and using "family speak." These are illustrated in the following section.

Meanings were defined as cognitive representations of reality held in the minds of individual family members but constructed interactively with others in the family. Meaning statements numbered in the hundreds. Some were made in direct response to questions asked about how the family had made sense of their loss but more were found embedded in the stories families told. Some meanings came in the form of beliefs. Others sounded more like interpretations of the facts of the death, such as whether the death was preventable. Meaning statements were grouped on the basis of their similarity. The ten groupings or types were (a) statements about what the death was not, (b) statements about how there was no sense to be made, (c) statements about how the death was unfair or unjust, (d) philosophical statements, (e) religious statements, (f) statements about the afterlife, (g) statements about the nature of the death, (h) statements about the attitude of the deceased toward death, (i) statements about how the death changed the family, and (j) statements about lessons learned and truths realized. Selected meanings are presented in the following section.

Also found were a number of related family features that affected how families made sense of their experiences. These features included such things as sharing patterns in families, the systems levels at which meaning making took place, and factors that either stimulated or inhibited family meaning making. For instance, in regard to sharing, most family members said that they could share most anything with other family members, but in subsequent interviews they failed to do so. Useful data were collected about what would affect talking about the death within the family. Examples were found of meaning making at all levels of the family system, from the individual level to full family groups. Factors that either stimulated or inhibited meaning making were discovered and are also illustrated in the next section.

TWO FAMILIES IN CONTRAST

The two families described in this section were chosen because they differed substantially in most of the family characteristics relevant to family meaning making. Furthermore, there were members in each of these families who were interviewed more than once, making the data more comparable.

The Munson Family

Claude Munson, age 72, died on the couch as his wife, Evelyn, prepared their dinner in the adjoining room. (See Figure 15-1.) Struck by the sudden quietness, Evelyn rushed in to check his pulse. Finding none, she called for help. "Help came too late," she said, "he was gone."

Twelve months later, Claude and Evelyn's sons, Darren and Sam, were interviewed along with their wives. The Munsons were typical in that many of their meanings were beliefs about the afterlife. The four were asked where they thought Claude went after his death. Sam, the youngest son, shared that his father's spirit had "hung around" the hospital awhile but it had departed for heaven at about the time the hearse got stuck going up cemetery hill.

Darren, the older son, said that his father was simply in the cemetery. Claude's spirit, according to Darren, persisted only in that it was with loved ones as they remembered him. Deb, Sam's wife, was astounded that Darren did not espouse what she believed to be typical Catholic beliefs. There ensued a lively family discussion stimulated by Deb's questions to Darren and his wife, Marie.

Marie confessed that she struggled with what to believe. She was emphatic about how no one who had behaved badly on earth could go automatically to heaven. It was clear from other parts of the interview that she saw Claude as having behaved poorly on earth.

The Munson family was one of several who could not agree on something as seemingly factual as the cause of death, much less what meanings Claude's death held. Some said it was alcohol that killed Claude; others denied the alcoholism and pointed to kidney disease. His wife referred back to wounds he had sustained in World War II. The meanings family members attached to Claude's death depended greatly on what "facts" they recognized as valid. Those family groupings who thought his death was from alcoholism blamed Claude for not abstaining. Their grief was laced with anger and blaming. Those who thought his death was from other causes felt less angry and more accepting.

The Munson family had few family rituals and infrequent contact. Darren and Sam, who lived in the same town, had seen each other only once in the year following their father's death, and that was in passing each other on the golf course. One of their most problematic meanings was a question of whether Evelyn had purposely neglected to call 911 when her husband's heart stopped. Some believed that she had not called, and others believed she *had* called but that the paramedics were delayed at a house fire. Those who believed that Evelyn chose not to call the 911

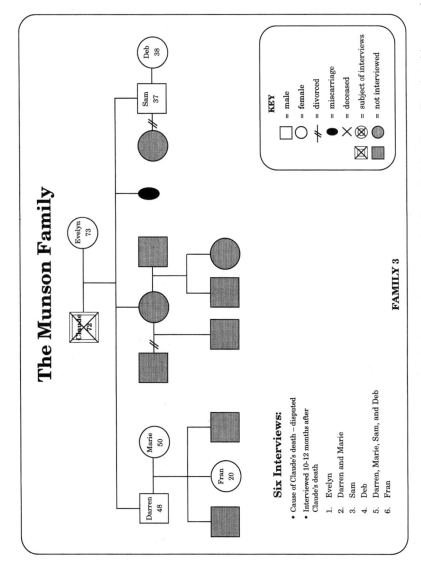

The Munson Family

Six Interviews:

- Cause of Claude's death – disputed
- Interviewed 10-12 months after Claude's death

1. Evelyn
2. Darren and Marie
3. Sam
4. Deb
5. Darren, Marie, Sam, and Deb
6. Fran

KEY

☐ = male
◯ = female
⚭ = divorced
● = miscarriage
✕ = deceased
⊗ = subject of interviews
▨ = not interviewed

FAMILY 3

Figure 15-1. The Munson Family. From Nadeau (1998). Copyright © 1998 by Sage Publications. Reprinted by permission of Sage Publications, Inc.

emergency number construed Claude's death as preventable. Their grief was laced with far more anger and resentment than those who believed Evelyn had called.

In this interview it was possible to catch a glimpse of how families tend to forget themselves when open-ended questions are asked of them as a group. This family launched into what seemed to be their natural, albeit cautious, dialogue. Their meanings converged and diverged as did most families', this family being one with the most divergence.

Even when families seemed to forget themselves in the interview there was still a difference in what they would share, depending on who was present. In an earlier interview with Marie and Darren alone, Marie openly expressed her contempt for Claude. When Sam and Deb were present she was not willing to be as frank but her anger was palpable in the room.

One goal of the study was to understand differences in how the same family members answered the same questions in different interviews. Families were asked about sharing patterns: Did they share their thoughts with other family members, and what determined their willingness to share? Members said that they could share if their meanings were not too different from others, if sharing something did not cause discomfort, hurt someone else, or upset the family balance. Others said they would share if they had something to say and if they thought someone would listen. Many family members said they could share anything with their family, but when certain family members were present they failed to do so.

Certain family meaning-making strategies were apparent in the Munson family data. The term *strategy* was used in the analysis to designate the methods families used to make sense of losing a family member. Deb used the strategy of *questioning* to find out what others in the family believed and, perhaps, to keep from being asked questions herself. Questioning was a strategy used by the majority of families in the study.

Deb also exemplified what was called *the in-law effect*. The term *meaning-making stimulator* was used to designate factors that stimulated the processes of family meaning construction. When there was an in-law present at the interviews, meaning-making activity was more vigorous. In-laws stimulate meaning making, perhaps because they are not susceptible to the same family rules. Also, in-laws may be ignorant of family history and family taboos, so they may rush in where members would not. Other meaning-making stimulators found in the study included abundant family rituals, frequent contact among family members, sudden deaths, and deaths of relatively young family members.

The Munson family was limited by a number of factors called *meaning-making inhibitors*. These factors restricted the interactions necessary to make sense of the deaths and were found in all 10 families. In the Munson family, one meaning-making inhibitor was the existence of cut-offs. A *cut-off* is an extended cessation of contact between members or groups of family members. Darren and Sam were no longer in contact with their sister, Jackie, whom they said continued to drink with Claude in spite of his advanced disease. In the previous generation, Evelyn had been cut-off from most of her siblings.

Other meaning-making inhibitors were family rules. The Munson family had rules against open sharing. Jackie had canceled her interview at the last minute, saying she did not want to "stir things up." Other inhibitors apparent in this family were the lack of family contact and the paucity of family rituals. It was a sad moment when at the end of the interview Darren shared his wish that they could have had this talk before his father died. He would have liked to know how his father viewed his own death.

Finally, the Munson family interview illustrates how family grief can be explored in terms of the interaction of family structure, family dynamics, and family meaning making. The in-law effect and cut-offs were structural features of the Munson family that stimulated or inhibited the family meaning-making process. The sharing patterns that emerged, governed by family rules, can be seen as helping to determine what meanings were constructed and with whom. As family members make meaning together they may make meaning in preexisting subsystems as the Munsons did or set new boundaries around subsystems by constructing new meanings.

The Primo Family

Ronnie Primo, age 39, was killed in an airplane crash. He was flying with two of his high school friends, one of whom was the pilot. (See Figure 15–2.) It was the first time the pilot had taken passengers. Ronnie had diapered their new baby, kissed his wife and their 3-year-old daughter, and left the house. Two hours later, the sheriff came to tell Rena that Ronnie and his friends were dead.

Twenty-two months after Ronnie's death 11 members of the Primo family were interviewed. The Primos stand in stark contrast to the Munsons in terms of their cohesiveness, family rules, frequency of contact, and richness of family rituals. After Rena lost her husband, her parents moved in with her to help with the children. Most other family members lived next door or a few houses away.

Storytelling was the most common meaning-making strategy. It was used by all the families in the study. The richest data in the study came from four Primo family members, who were interviewed as a family group and then each one separately. They were asked whether they had been able to make sense of Ronnie's death. They did what most families in the study did: They said there was no sense to be made, then they went on at length about what his death might mean.

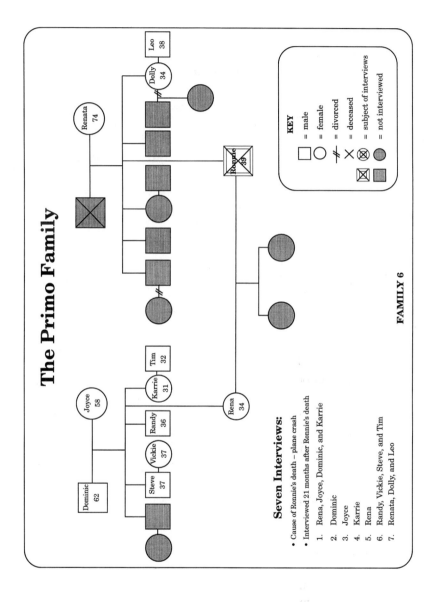

The Primo Family

KEY

□ = male	○ = female	⧣ = divorced
☒	⊠ = subject of interviews	✕ = deceased
⊗ ● = not interviewed		

FAMILY 6

Seven Interviews:

- Cause of Ronnie's death – plane crash
- Interviewed 21 months after Ronnie's death

1. Rena, Joyce, Dominic, and Karrie
2. Dominic
3. Joyce
4. Karrie
5. Rena
6. Randy, Vickie, Steve, and Tim
7. Renata, Dolly, and Leo

Figure 15-2. The Primo Family. From Nadeau (1998). Copyright © 1998 by Sage Publications. Reprinted by permission of Sage Publications, Inc.

Rena, the young widow, said that there was no sense to be made of Ronnie's dying. "What was done was done," she said, "Ronnie should not have flown with such an inexperienced pilot." The fact that Ronnie chose to take the risk made her "mad." The meaning that Ronnie could have prevented his own death but failed to do so resulted in feelings of subdued anger, not only for Rena but for everyone in the family.

One of the features of meaning making found in connection with the "no sense to be made" category of meanings was how sudden deaths and deaths of younger people like Ronnie tended to be viewed as more senseless than the deaths of older members. This was particularly true if the older member had been ill for a long time and was perceived to be ready to die. There was considerably more meaning-making activity around the younger, more sudden deaths. *Comparing* the current death with other deaths inside and outside the family was a common meaning-making strategy. Rena and her mother, Joyce, compared the deaths of Rena's niece from brain cancer and Ronnie's accidental death with expected deaths of older people.

The Primo family was particularly skilled in using *cooperative interrupting* (Tannen, 1990) to weave their meanings together. Cooperative interrupting consists of breaking into someone's sentence, in support of the speaker's meaning. Tannen contrasts this to *uncooperative interrupting* in which the interrupter breaks in and changes the subject. Cooperative interrupting seemed to move the meaning-making process along in some family way. This pattern was far more prevalent in the Primo family than it was in the less cohesive Munson family.

Elements of everyday conversation such as cooperative interrupting and questioning were referred to as *family speak*. Some form of family speak was present in all of the group interviews. Family speak also manifested itself as referencing other members' meanings, agreeing, disagreeing, finishing others' sentences, elaborating, and echoing others' meanings. Meanings constructed by family speak could not be assigned to a particular family member but seemed to be products of family conversation.

One of the questions in the interview guidelines was how the meanings that family had given the death affected the way they grieved. Rena said that her belief that Ronnie could have prevented his own death made her "mad." Ronnie's sister in-law, Karrie, said that thinking of Ronnie's death as meaningless made her grief "harder" and left her without hope. Her feelings of hopelessness, she said, stemmed from the suddenness by which Ronnie had "disappeared from the family" and the fact that Ronnie and Rena's girls were growing up fatherless.

Rena and Joyce compared their reaction to Ronnie's death with their reaction to the death of Karrie's mother-in-law, Jackie, who had died more recently. Rena made the point that accidental deaths were the most senseless and shocking of all deaths. As she started to elaborate, her mother finished her sentence by saying that a person does not have time to prepare. Then Rena's sister, Karrie, interrupted with the notion that in a slower death like Jackie's there is time to make some memories by doing and saying important things. In some ways, Karrie said, this made Jackie's death easier. With multiple phases spliced together, the Primo family came to the conclusion that all deaths are senseless unless the person who dies is old and has been suffering.

Among the other meaning-making strategies used by the Primos were *characterization and "coincidancing."* Members characterized Ronnie as being a high risk-taker, very vain, and never wanting to grow old. Characterizing Ronnie in this way allowed them to construct the meaning that if he had to die, he would have liked dying young and having a front-page news story. The family recited these meanings over and over as part of their *litany of loss* and, seemingly, drew some comfort from doing so.

"Coincidancing" was the term coined for how families used unexplainable, co-occurring events to make sense of the loss of their family member. Karrie and Joyce reported that at the exact time of the plane crash they each experienced physical symptoms that they construed as premonitions. Each family in the study was able to identify some coincidental event or events that occurred near the time of the death to which they attached meaning. Coincidental events were seen as a sort of "family ink blot" on which family meanings could be projected.

IMPLICATIONS FOR THEORY, RESEARCH, AND PRACTICE

Proponents of qualitative research would argue that studies such as this one have the potential for bridging theory, research, and practice. Theorists may find substantive data that support current theory or suggest new theories. Researchers may be challenged to use more systemic methods. Practitioners may recognize family behavioral patterns and see the relevance of such research for their practice.

Building Theory

Theory built from a family systems perspective would broaden and deepen our understanding of grief in some significant ways. It would expand grief theory to include the context of family grief not as an "add on" to individual grief theory but as an integration of the individual and the extra-individual. Studying the family system from a meaning-making perspective provides substantive data with which to build substantive theory.

A family systems perspective has the potential for providing a non-pathologizing conceptualization of grief. It counters models of grief that assume pathology and promote inappropriate intervention based on the reification of medical diagnoses. It supports the contention that grief is a natural process, not a disease to be cured.

Building family grief theory could be accomplished by integrating family meaning making, family structure, and family process. The relatedness of systems concepts to family grief can be explored and family variables can be identified and studied. For instance, the Primo family's meaning-making processes revealed that they were a highly cohesive, open family. Their family boundary was permeable enough to allow outsiders like the researcher and their pastor into their family world. The generational boundary around Dominic and Joyce, Ronnie's in-laws, was apparent when Joyce tried to talk Dominic out of believing that he could have used his influence to persuade Ronnie not to fly. Dominic made meaning with his daughter, Rena, when they examined the autopsy report together. The meaning they made was that Ronnie had died from the crash, not from the fire that followed. The subsystem boundary around Rena and Dominic was strengthened by their shared meaning.

There are suggestions in the data about how certain meanings have different consequences in terms of the course of grief. The family meaning-making framework provides a test for Thomas's theory (1923) that when people define situations as real, they are real in their consequences. Karrie Primo identified how believing that there was no sense to be made of Ronnie's death made her grief "harder" and how having warning in the case of her mother-in-law's death made it easier in some ways. Rena's grief lessened by letting go of her fear that her husband had burned to death.

Contributing to Research

There is value in expanding the unit of analysis to the family. Systemic data lead to new insights and point the way to a broad array of systemic interventions. This study demonstrates that there is value in using qualitative methods to capture the particulars of the family grief. The most fruitful family data resulted from interviewing family members together, using a style of interviewing that facilitated the emergence of their natural processes. Family patterns were best revealed when the family interviews were followed by individual interviews so that comparisons could be made.

Using the technique of Milan circular questioning was shown to be immensely useful in expanding systemic data and could be used to collect data about any part of family life. Asking how missing and deceased members would answer a given question increases the amount of systemic data and raises aspects of grief that would not be as likely to emerge otherwise.

Interviewing multiple family members from multiple generations revealed multiple realities and multigenerational effects. These important dimensions of grief are less likely to emerge even in qualitative studies if interviews are limited to individuals.

Implications for Intervention

Thinking of families from a meaning-making perspective helps us to listen differently and to ask more sensitive questions. It provides a way of talking about family grief as the interaction of family structure and family processes. It helps maintain a systemic focus, to see the family as a unit rather than as a collection of individuals.

In therapy, the family meaning-making framework can provide a model for assessment. When intervention is deemed appropriate, the meaning-making framework may provide direction and open up an array of family interventions that otherwise might not be considered.

Families may benefit from family grief therapy if the way they have construed a death is problematic or there is a preponderance of factors that inhibit family meaning making. The Primo's original belief that Ronnie had burned to death in the plane crash was extremely painful to them, but they were able to gather additional data from the medical examiner and to share that data within the family. Their new meaning was that Ronnie had died from the sudden descent, not from burning to death.

By contrast, the Munsons were distressed by their belief that their mother had purposefully failed to call 911 when their father's heart had stopped. The inhibitory effects of their family communication rules kept them from learning that their mother *had* called 911 but that the medics were at a house fire.

Interventions, when they are called for, may be targeted at reducing the factors that inhibit family meaning making and enhancing factors that stimulate family meaning making. Help may consist of developing new family rules that call for open communication, reconnecting family members who have been cut-off, increasing the frequency of family gatherings and family rituals, and helping families to process the difficult particulars of how their family member died. From a family therapy perspective, a therapeutic goal might be to help family members feel safe enough to share their meanings within the family.

Intervention may consist of encouraging strategies that families tend to use naturally. For instance, storytelling could be fostered by gathering multiple members, representing more than one generation, and taking advantage of the "in-law" effect by including as many in-laws as possible.

The Milan method of circular questioning (Boscolo et al., 1987) can be used to elicit family dialogue, to engage shy members, and to raise family patterns of interaction. This method may be particularly useful with families who tend to be more closed and defensive because it is a nonconfrontive approach. Progress in therapy can be checked by noticing changes in meanings over time.

One intervention that is not limited to family therapy settings is the fostering of family rituals (Imber-Black, 1992). Rituals are rich in meaning.

They support differences among members and provide for both continuity and change. Rituals allow families to dip into their pain and then to back away from it. They allow families to hang on to old meanings that serve them well, let go of meanings that no longer serve, and create new meanings.

CONCLUSION

Looking at family grief from a meaning-making perspective provides a systems view with substance. Meanings are important determinants of how families will survive the loss of a loved one, therefore understanding how families coconstruct meaning is worthwhile. The meaning-making framework takes us beyond the intrapsychic dimension of grief and opens up a new vista of possibilities. The potential it has for demedicalizing and depathologizing grief is significant.

In the future we need to study family meaning making in families who have lost members to all kinds of deaths, including AIDS, SIDS, and deaths of children. We need to study families over time to see how meaning systems change. We need to know the long-term consequences of both positive and negative meanings. We need to ask whether the same family processes prevail in the wake of nondeath losses. Our knowledge base would be built by identifying the characteristics of families who are successful meaning makers, perhaps by comparing them to families who are less successful. There is much more to be learned about family meaning making and grief.

REFERENCES

Berger, P. L., & Luckmann, T. (1966). *The social construction of reality*. New York: Doubleday.

Boscolo, L., Cecchin, G., Hoffman, L., & Penn, P. (1987). *Milan systemic family therapy*. New York: Basic Books.

Broderick, C., & Smith, J. (1979). General systems approach to the family. In W. Burr, R. Hill, F. I. Nye, & I. L. Reiss (Eds.), *Contemporary theories about the family* (Vol. II, pp. 112–128). New York: Free Press.

Cooley, C. H. (1902). *Human nature and the social order*. New York: Scribner's.

Cooley, C. H. (1909). *Social organization*. New York: Scribner's.

Dewey, J. (1922). *Human nature and conduct*. New York: Scribner's.

Glaser, B. G., & Strauss, A. L. (1967). *The discovery of grounded theory: Strategies for qualitative research*. Hawthorne, NY: Aldine.

Hess, R. D., & Handel, G. (1959). *Family worlds: A psychological approach to family life*. Chicago: Chicago University Press.

Imber-Black, E. (1992). *Rituals for our times*. New York: Harper Collins.

James, W. (1890). *Principles of psychology, vol. 2*. New York: Holt.

Lofland, J., & Lofland, L. H. (1984). *Analyzing social settings*. Belmont, CA: Wadsworth.

Mead, G. H. (1932). *The philosophy of the present*. Chicago: Open Court.

Mead, G. H. (1934). *Mind, self and society*. Chicago: University of Chicago Press.

Mead, G. H. (1936). *Movements of thought in the nineteenth century*. Chicago: University of Chicago Press.

Mead, G. H. (1938). *The philosophy of the act*. Chicago: University of Chicago Press.

Miles, G. B., & Huberman, M. A. (1984). *Qualitative data analysis*. Beverly Hills, CA: Sage.

Moon, S. M., Dillon, D. R., & Sprenkle, D. H. (1990). Family therapy and qualitative research. *Journal of Marital and Family Therapy, 16*, 357–373.

Nadeau, J. W. (1998). *Families making sense of death*. Thousand Oaks, CA: Sage.

Rosenblatt, P. C., & Fischer, L. R. (1993). Qualitative family research. In P. B. Boss, W. J. Doherty, R. LaRossa, W. R. Schumm, & S. K. Steinmetz (Eds.), *Source book of family theories and methods: A contextual approach*. New York: Plenum Press.

Strauss, A., & Corbin, J. (1990). *Basics of qualitative research*. Newbury Park, CA: Sage.

Stryker, S. (1972). Symbolic interaction theory: A review and some suggestions for comparative family research. *Journal of Comparative Family Studies, 3*, 17–32.

Tannen, D. (1990). *You just don't understand*. New York: William Morrow.

Thomas, W. I. (1923). *The unadjusted girl*. Boston: Little, Brown.

Wright, S. (n.d.). *Adapting Milan style systemic therapy from family therapy to family research*. Unpublished manuscript.

16

RISK FACTORS IN BEREAVEMENT OUTCOME: A METHODOLOGICAL AND EMPIRICAL REVIEW

WOLFGANG STROEBE AND HENK SCHUT

The study of risk factors in bereavement outcome is important for practical as well as theoretical reasons. Early identification of individuals at risk can help to solve the dilemma that bereavement poses to the helping professions. Bereavement is frequent and most people suffer terribly, at least in the short term. However, the majority of bereaved people manage to adjust to the loss without professional help. They would not be helped, and indeed might even be harmed, by receiving clinical therapy (chapter 29, this volume). Yet a minority of bereaved people are at risk of suffering lasting health consequences. Because they might be helped by psychological or medical therapy, early identification of this risk group is important.

The study of risk factors also plays an important role in developing and testing theoretical explanations of the health impact of bereavement. Because theories of bereavement identify situational or personal characteristics likely to be associated with poor bereavement outcome, the study of

The authors are indebted to Robert Weiss for many insightful and stimulating comments on earlier drafts of this manuscript.

these risk factors can be used as a method of testing such theoretical predictions. However, before we review the research on risk factors, a number of conceptual and methodological issues need to be clarified.

CONCEPTUAL AND METHODOLOGICAL ISSUES

There is still a great deal of confusion in the bereavement literature about the nature of risk factors and about the methodological features of the designs that are appropriate for assessing their impact. In this first part of the chapter we distinguish different types of risk factors and discuss the types of designs that should be used in studying their effects.

Conceptual Issues

A risk factor is an aspect of personal behavior or lifestyle, an environmental exposure or an inborn or inherited characteristic, which, on the basis of epidemiological evidence, is known to be associated with health-related conditions considered important to prevent (Last, 1995, p. 148). Thus the (relative) risk of disease of those in whom the risk factor is present is higher than that of those in whom the risk factor is absent. Risk factors in bereavement outcome increase the risk of disease by *moderating* either the health impact of the loss experience (impact factors) or the speed of the recovery (recovery factors).

These risk factors can be either bereavement-specific or general. *Bereavement-specific risk factors* are aspects of the bereavement situation that influence bereavement impact or recovery. For example, the circumstances surrounding a loss are a bereavement-specific risk factor. More severe health consequences occur following, for instance, a sudden rather than an expected loss (Sanders, 1983). *General risk factors* are personality or social context variables that affect the health of bereaved and nonbereaved individuals. They can be divided into factors that do not moderate the effects of bereavement and factors that have *bereavement-specific effects*. For example, socioeconomic status is positively associated with health (Adler et al., 1994), but does not appear to moderate bereavement effects (W. Stroebe & Stroebe, 1987). There is no evidence that high socioeconomic status helps the bereaved individual to cope with his or her loss. In contrast, lack of social support has not only been found to be associated with health impairment in the general population (e.g., Berkman & Syme, 1979), it has also been suspected of intensifying the impact of bereavement on health and of slowing down the recovery process (Sanders, 1993).

Methodological Issues

Both longitudinal and cross-sectional designs have been used in the study of risk factors in bereavement outcome. Longitudinal studies use designs in which a cohort of people is followed to allow repeated measurement of variables with the same individuals over time. In contrast, cross-sectional studies use a design by which variables are assessed in different groups at the same point in time. In this section we will discuss potential problems that might arise with each of these types of designs in bereavement research.

Longitudinal Designs

Valid *longitudinal* designs involve at least two levels of the risk factor, and at least two points of measurement, assessing health either before and after the loss experience or at two (or more) time points following the loss. In both cases, the impact of the risk factor would be reflected by a risk factor by time interaction. For example, one would expect partner loss to result in more health deterioration or slower recovery in low-social support as compared to high-social support groups. The *general* health effect of lack of social support would be controlled for in this design, because, as long as the level of support remains stable, the general health effect would be the same at all points of measurement (i.e., even before bereavement).

It is important to note, however, that if health assessments are only available for the time following bereavement, a number of complications can arise that might easily result in a misinterpretation of findings. First, the absence of an interaction between risk factor and time of measurement indicates only that the general risk factor did not affect the recovery process. It does not rule out the possibility that the risk factor moderated the impact of the loss experience. If one wants also to draw inferences about the effect of the risk factor as a moderator of bereavement impact, matched nonbereaved control groups should be added to the design.

More problematic is the fact that if only two points of measurement have been taken after bereavement, a risk factor by time interaction might reflect the effect of the risk factor on bereavement impact, rather than on recovery. If a risk factor intensifies the impact of bereavement, the health of the high-risk group will be worse at bereavement than that of the low-risk group. If the risk factor does not impair the recovery process, it is likely that the health of both groups will sooner or later return to baseline (i.e., the level of a nonbereaved comparison group). If they recover at precisely the same rate, the low-risk group, having suffered much less health impairment, will reach this baseline sooner than the high-risk group. However, if improvements in health and well-being are only assessed at two points that are widely separated in time (e.g., 4 months and 18 months after the loss), both groups are likely to have returned to baseline before the second measurement has been taken. The comparison of the health improvement between the two points in time will therefore indicate a greater health improvement for the high-risk than for the low-risk group. To validly assess the speed of recovery of both groups, one would need at least two points of measurement taken before either of the two groups has adjusted to the loss (i.e., returned to baseline). This would require the taking of several measurements, spaced more closely during the first year of bereavement. If this strategy is chosen, then individual growth modeling should be used for data analysis rather than the more familiar MANOVAs (Willet & Sayer, 1994; Willet, Singer, & Martin, 1998).

Cross-Sectional Designs

These designs will differ depending on whether general or bereavement-specific risk factors are being assessed. For *general risk factors*, one needs a factorial design in which the presence or absence of bereavement is crossed with two (or more) levels of the risk factor. By comparing the health impact on the nonbereaved control group with that on the group of bereaved individuals, we will be able to separate the general from the bereavement-specific effects. For example, to assess whether lack of social support intensifies the impact of bereavement one would assess the level of depressive symptomatology of married and recently bereaved individuals who either have low or high levels of social support. The general effect of social support would be reflected by a social support main effect on depression. The bereavement-specific effects of social support would be reflected by a social support by bereavement interaction, with the difference in depression between the high- and the low-social support groups being greater for the bereaved than the nonbereaved individuals. Without a nonbereaved control group, it would be impossible to distinguish whether the difference in depression likely to be observed between well-supported and not well-supported bereaved individuals reflected a general or a bereavement-specific effect of social support. One obvious disadvantage of the use of nonbereaved controls is that it precludes comparisons involving grief-specific measures.

Cross-sectional designs could also be used to assess the bereavement-specific effects of a general risk factor in recovery from bereavement. However, it is not only easier but also preferable on methodological grounds to use longitudinal designs for this purpose. The preponderance of cross-sectional designs in the study of moderators of the impact of bereavement is a result of the fact that it is difficult to obtain prebereavement measures of health status or of psychological risk factors.

For *bereavement-specific risk factors*, which are by definition exclusive to bereaved samples, nonbereaved controls are not necessary. However, even though bereavement-specific risk factors cannot have a health effect on the general population, they may be correlated with other variables that do have such an effect. For example, the relative frequency of accidental deaths is higher among younger age groups. Because the age of marital partners is correlated, one would expect bereaved individuals who experienced sudden losses to be younger than bereaved individuals who lost their partners following a chronic illness. Thus if one assessed the relative impact of expected versus sudden losses by comparing the physical health of two groups of bereaved individuals, one would have to either match them by age or control age statistically to avoid confounding the impact of age with that of the mode of death.

Implications

Why is it important to distinguish general from bereavement-specific effects of risk factors when both are seen as causes to health deterioration? The answer to this question is easier for issues of theory testing. To test the prediction from stress theory that social support is a coping resource that helps bereaved individuals to recover from the loss, it is important to know whether better health of bereaved individuals who enjoy high levels of support is a general difference or a result of the impact of social support on the process of coping (for a discussion of this point, see Cohen & Wills, 1985). This knowledge is also useful for the design of interventions aimed at helping these bereaved individuals. The answer is less easy for use of risk factors in the *prediction* of the health effects of bereavement. If one wants to know which bereaved individuals are likely to suffer from depression or some physical ailments, then the risk is higher the greater the number of risk factors, regardless of whether the effects of these risk factors are general or bereavement-specific. However, if one wants to identify those who are likely to suffer the greatest health *deterioration* following bereavement, then one has to separate the bereavement-specific effects from the general effects of a risk factor, because only the bereavement-specific effects increase the magnitude of the health deterioration.

EMPIRICAL FINDINGS

This section will present the evidence for the impact of risk factors on bereavement outcome. We will categorize them into factors that are associated with the bereavement situation (e.g., mode of death), with the person (e.g., personality, religiosity, age, gender) and with the interpersonal context (e.g., social support, kinship relationship). Our discussion of risk factors will be limited in three ways. We will focus mainly on one type of bereavement—partner loss—because most research has been conducted on this type of bereavement. For the same reasons, we will focus on health consequences and distress as outcomes of bereavement. Other outcomes, such as the potential impact on stimulating personal growth or on altering interpersonal relationships will not be discussed (for a discussion of these outcomes, see chapter 7, this volume). Finally, we restrict our review to those risk factors that have been studied most extensively.

Situational Risk Factors: Mode of Death

Most people would agree that the circumstances of the death of a partner are likely to affect the course of bereavement. Thus the situation of a person whose spouse dies in a car accident on his or her way to work differs in ways that are likely to affect the course of bereavement from that of an individual who loses his or her partner after an illness lasting for several years. The assumption that the abruptness of the change and the period of time that the individual has to adjust to the loss should affect health outcomes is consistent with both stress and attachment theory. Stress theories would argue that adjustments to change that take place over a lengthy period of time (i.e., death after a long illness) should be less stressful than adjustments to a sudden change of the same magnitude. According to attachment theory, the sudden loss of an attachment figure might destroy the surviving individual's feeling of safety and security. For the person who has experienced loss without forewarning, there is no situation that feels safe—loss can come again out of the blue. The result might be persisting vigilance (R. Weiss, personal communication, 1999).

The empirical evidence on the impact of sudden loss is inconsistent. Some studies found lack of forewarning to have a negative effect on health outcome (Ball, 1977; Lundin, 1984; Parkes, 1975; Sanders, 1983; W. Stroebe, Stroebe, & Domittner, 1987, 1988), but others did not (e.g., Bornstein, Clayton, Halikas, Maurice, & Robins, 1973; Breckenridge, Gallagher, Thompson, & Peterson, 1986; Maddison & Walker, 1967). One reason for these discrepancies could be individual differences in reactions to sudden loss. For example, in the Tübingen Study of Bereavement, in which the health of a sample of recently bereaved individuals was repeatedly assessed over a period of two years following their loss, the main effect of expectedness was marginally significant and limited to the first point of measurement (W. Stroebe et al., 1988). However, when the bereaved individuals were further divided into groups according to whether they held internal or external control beliefs, this personality variable was found to moderate the impact of expectedness. Unexpected losses resulted in higher levels of depression and somatic complaints only among those who believed that they had little control over their lives (W. Stroebe et al., 1988). A similar pattern was found for individuals who had high self-esteem (W. Stroebe et al., 1987). The expectedness of loss resulted in differential effects on well-being only for individuals with low rather than high self-esteem.

This moderator role of internal control beliefs and self-esteem is consistent with an interpretation in terms of attachment theory. Sudden losses might be less threatening to individuals with high self-esteem and high internal control beliefs because they feel that even though the threat cannot be anticipated, it could be dealt with, should it arise. Age might be another variable that moderates the impact of unexpected loss. Research participants in the studies of Bornstein and colleagues (1973) and Breckenridge and colleagues (1986) were elderly. As Parkes (1975) has argued, for this age group even sudden death could hardly be totally unexpected and would also not be as untimely as sudden deaths that occurred in a younger age group.

Suicide deaths might also be expected to result in greater problems of adjustment than deaths from other causes. However, there is little empirical evidence to support this contention. In fact, the few studies that compared the psychological consequences of bereavements because of suicide with that of other forms of losses have typically failed to find any marked differences in bereavement outcome (Barret & Scott, 1987, reported in Cleiren, 1991; Farberow, Gallagher-Thompson, Gilewski, & Thompson, 1992; Shepherd & Barraclough, 1974; Sherkat & Reed, 1992).

Personal Risk Factors

The following section will discuss risk factors that are associated with the bereaved person. Our discussion of personal risk factors will cover both factors related to individual differences (e.g., differences in personality or religiosity) and factors related to sociodemographic or group differences (e.g., gender, age).

Personality Traits

It would seem plausible that individuals with well-adjusted personalities who feel in control of their lives should be better able to withstand the impact of stressful life events such as bereavement than persons who are poorly adjusted and believe that they have little control. Consistent with this assumption, Vachon and her colleagues (1982) reported that their "enduring high distress group," whose level of distress had remained high two years after their loss, had lower scores on ego strength and higher scores on guilt proneness and anxiety on Cattell's 16 Personality Factor Questionnaire than the widowed individuals characterized as "enduring low distress group." However, because these personality traits are likely to be related to measures of distress in nonbereaved populations as well, these findings may merely reflect the general correlation between these personality measures and distress.

In the Tübingen Study of Bereavement, the interaction between marital status and either self-esteem or internal locus of control was not significant. Thus there was no indication that individuals with high self-esteem or internal locus of control were better able to cope with the loss of their partners than individuals with low self-esteem or low internal control beliefs (W. Stroebe et al., 1987, 1988). However, as we reported earlier, high self-esteem and high internal control beliefs were found to buffer bereaved people against the impact of a particularly stressful type of loss —losses that happen suddenly and without any forewarning.

With attachment theory emerging as one of the major theoretical accounts of processes of coping with bereavement (e.g., Bowlby, 1971; Weiss, 1975; chapters 3 and 4, this volume), it is surprising that little research has been conducted on attachment styles as predictors of differential adjustment to bereavement. Attachment theory suggests that whether an individual reacts to loss with normal grief responses or develops one of the variants of pathological grief (e.g., chronic grief or delayed grief) depends on certain childhood experiences, in particular the pattern of parental attachment (e.g., Bowlby, 1981). Those who have been treated in ways that cause them to feel secure find it easier to access attachment-related emotional memories and discuss them coherently (chapter 4, this volume). These individuals are likely to resolve their grief and adjust to their loss. In contrast, individuals who do not have a secure orientation to attachment are likely to encounter problems in coping with their loss experiences. For example, individuals with an anxious–ambivalent attachment style are highly emotional but unable to cope constructively with attachment-related feelings. These individuals have been found to show patterns of chronic grieving, characterized by an extension of the period of grieving that can be indefinite in extreme cases (Parkes & Weiss, 1983). One could speculate further that this extension of their grieving process could be a result of a heightened tendency to engage in ruminative coping. Ruminative coping is defined as "passively and repetitively focusing on one's symptoms of distress and the circumstances surrounding those symptoms" (Nolen-Hoeksema, McBride, & Larson, 1997, p. 855). It has been shown to be associated with extended periods of depressed mood following a loss experience but has not yet been linked to differences in attachment style.

Individuals with an avoidant style of insecure attachment are assumed to suppress or avoid attachment-related emotions (chapter 4, this volume). It would therefore be plausible to relate this attachment style to "delayed grief," a pathological style of grieving in which normal grief reactions occur only after an extensive delay, during which the expression of grief is inhibited. However, few cases of delayed grief have been reported in the literature. Furthermore, a study by Bonanno and Field (in press) found no evidence that avoidance, defined as minimal facial expression of negative emotions or verbal expression of negative content, or dissociation of negative emotion, assessed six months after the loss, was related to delayed symptom elevation more than four years later.

Religiosity

Another individual difference variable that one would expect to moderate coping with bereavement is religious beliefs. It is plausible that being religious helps individuals adjust to the loss of a loved one. Religion could influence bereavement outcome through two mechanisms. First, religion may provide a belief system or perspective that enables individuals to deal differently and perhaps better with crises in general and death in particular. Second, religious participation may be associated with integration into a social network or community (McIntosh, Silver, & Wortman, 1993; Stroebe & Stroebe, 1987). Yet findings on the role of religious beliefs in coping with loss have been rather mixed. Some investigators claim positive associations (e.g., Bohannon, 1991; Clayton, Halikas, & Robins, 1973; Glick, Weiss, & Parkes, 1974; Gray, 1987; Heyman & Gianturco, 1973; Levy, Martinowski, & Derby, 1994; Nolen-Hoeksema & Larson, 1999; Sherkat & Reed, 1992), others report either no difference (e.g., Burks, Lund, Gregg & Bluhm, 1988; Lund, Caserta & Dimond, 1986; Schut, 1992; W. Stroebe et al., 1987) or even greater maladjustment among the more religious bereaved individuals (e.g., Amir & Sharon, 1982; Rosik, 1989).

Most of these studies lack appropriate control groups, which renders their findings inconclusive. For example, religiosity was confounded with ethnicity in the study of Amir and Sharon (1982) conducted in Israel. The religious individuals were mainly Middle Eastern, whereas the nonreligious were Western. Because the Western widows were more educated than the Eastern widows and because education was found to be highly correlated with adjustment in an earlier study of bereavement in Israel (Purisman & Maoz, 1977), differences in education offer a plausible alternative interpretation for the negative association reported by Amir and Sharon (1982). The study of Rosik (1989) found extrinsic but not intrinsic religiosity (Allport & Ross, 1967) associated with more grief and depression. Because Rosik (1989) did not use a nonbereaved control group, and because extrinsic religiosity (i.e., religiosity that sees religion as a means to ends, such as provision of security, solace, sociability, and status) is associated with poor mental health in the general population (Batson, Schoenrade, & Ventis, 1993), this finding may merely reflect the effect of a general risk factor.

Many of the studies that report a positive effect of religious beliefs on coping are similarly problematic. Two of these studies used the evaluations of bereaved respondents' reports on how helpful they found religion as a dependent measure (Glick et al., 1974; Heyman & Gianturco, 1973). Such reports are inconclusive, because the fact that individuals find a coping mechanism helpful does not necessarily indicate that this mechanism *actually* does facilitate adjustment. However, even the results of the studies that used measures of health as an outcome variable are difficult to interpret because of the absence of nonbereaved control groups. Because some forms of religious orientation (namely, intrinsic religious orientation; Allport & Ross, 1967) are positively associated with mental health in the general population (Batson et al., 1993), positive correlations of religiosity and health in bereaved individuals may merely reflect an association that exists in the general population.

Yet two studies that attempted to avoid these problems by using longitudinal designs concluded that being religious facilitated adjustment to loss. Thus in a longitudinal study conducted by Levy et al. (1994), religiosity discriminated between groups of bereaved individuals who had different trajectories in their depressive symptomatology over time (stable high, stable low, ascending, descending). However, because stable scores may reflect a main effect of religiosity, it is unclear whether this study really demonstrated a supportive role of religion in coping with loss. More clear-cut conclusions can be drawn from the results of a study by Nolen-Hoeksema and Larson (1999). Participants in this study who attended religious services at least occasionally had lower levels at depression at 13 and 18 but not at 6 months after the bereavement than those who did not.

Furthermore, there is also empirical support for the mechanisms assumed to mediate the relationship between religiosity and health. Thus Nolen-Hoeksema and Larson (1999) found a positive association between church attendance and levels of social support. Sherkat and Reed (1992), who observed an inverse relationship between frequent church attendance (but not personal prayer) and depression, reported that this association became insignificant once social support was being controlled for. Finally, McIntosh and colleagues (1993) found in a study of mothers who had lost a child to sudden infant death syndrome that social support mediated the association between church attendance and well-being. This study also provided evidence for the second mechanisms linking religion and health outcome—the role of religious beliefs. Importance of religion was positively related to cognitive processing and finding meaning in death. Furthermore, through these coping processes, religious beliefs were indirectly related to greater well-being and less distress among parents 18 months after their infants' death. Taken together, these studies offer some support for the assumption that religious beliefs can be helpful in coping with the loss of a loved one.

Gender

Gender is a general as well as a bereavement-specific risk factor. There is a consistent pattern of gender differences with respect to health-related variables. Males have higher mortality rates than females, females have higher depression rates than males (Verbrugge, 1989; Verbrugge & Wingard, 1987). The bereavement-specific effects are also quite consistent, at least with regard to the impact of the loss of a partner (M. Stroebe & Stroebe, 1983): When compared to same-sex, nonbereaved individuals, losing a partner results in greater increases in the mortality and depression rates of widowers.

The gender pattern is most consistent for the mortality of bereaved individuals. As M. Stroebe and Stroebe (1983) concluded in a review of the early literature, mortality rates for widowers (compared to married men) are relatively higher than those for widows (compared to married women). This trend has been replicated in more recent studies. For example, Goldman, Korenman, and Weinstein (1995), who performed extensive baseline controls, still found widowers to have higher odds of dying (about 25%) as compared to married men. They concluded that the same may be true for widows, but the coefficients for women were smaller and the estimated effects were insignificant. Similarly, Rogers (1995) found that being conjugally bereaved was more detrimental for men than for women. The data of large prospective cohort studies conducted in The Netherlands (Joung, 1996) and Finland (Martikainen & Valkonen, 1996) show the same pattern, even after controlling for many of the potentially confounding factors. (For a recent review, see M. Stroebe, Stroebe, & Schut, in press.)

In view of the fact that the bereavement-specific and the general gender differences work in opposite directions for depression, it is hardly surprising that findings are less consistent than for mortality. Many of the early studies of the depression in bereavement, which compared depression rates of widows and widowers directly without using nonbereaved control groups, concluded that bereavement resulted in higher levels of depression among widows than widowers (e.g., Carey, 1977; Jacobs, Kasl, Ostfeld, Berkman, & Charpentier, 1986) or that there were no substantial differences. Given that women have higher depression rates than men in the general population, the outcome of *direct* comparisons of depression rates of widows and widowers should depend on the relative magnitude of the two opposing gender differences (i.e., general versus bereavement-specific). Because the gender differences in bereavement outcome are likely to weaken over time, the pattern of gender differences inferred from direct comparisons of widows and widowers is likely to vary with the time interval between bereavement and health measurement. Whereas the bereavement-specific gender effect is likely to be dominant in the immediate period after bereavement, the general gender effect is likely to become dominant at longer time intervals.

Studies that used the appropriate nonbereaved, same-sex comparisons generally found widowers to show relatively greater elevations in depressive symptomatology than widows (e.g., Cramer, 1993; Radloff, 1975; Umberson, Wortman, & Kessler, 1992). A cross-sectional study of elderly bereaved and married men and women in The Netherlands, which replicated this pattern for the first two years following bereavement, suggested that the relative difference in depression levels dissipated over time (Nieboer, Lindenberg, & Ormel, 1998). However, such findings may merely reflect the fact that differences in impact are attenuated over time, because most individuals adjust to their loss in the long run.

Although there is now a reasonably sound body of evidence to support the conclusion that men suffer more severe health consequences from partner loss than women, the reasons for this gender difference are still not well-understood. In an earlier review, M. Stroebe and Stroebe (1983) suggested that gender differences in the social support received by widows and widowers were responsible for the differential bereavement outcome. This interpretation was based on two assumptions—namely that widows received more social support than widowers and that this difference was responsible for the differential impact of the loss experience. Although the evidence as to the existence of such gender differences in social support following bereavement is quite persuasive, a study that assessed whether these differences mediated the gender difference in health outcome did not support the hypothesis (W. Stroebe, Stroebe, & Abakoumkin, 1999). Thus although widows receive more social support than widowers, this difference does not appear to be responsible for their greater well-being.

A second interpretation in terms of gender differences in coping styles assumes that there are gender differences in coping with bereavement and that the strategies used by women are more effective than those used by men. There is ample support for the first assumption, indicating that women prefer emotion-focused and men problem-focused coping styles (e.g., Billings & Moos, 1981; Folkman & Lazarus, 1980). However, the evidence is inconclusive with regard to the superiority of the emotion-focused coping in adjustment to grief. In our view, the limited evidence available on this issue supports the assumption that *both* coping styles are essential in coping with the loss of a loved one (M. Stroebe & Schut, 1999).

Attention and avoidance of both the direct emotional impact of the loss itself and of its secondary consequences is necessary for successful coping (see chapter 17, this volume). Confrontation of a loss (i.e., including grief work) is essential for a healthy recovery, and this comes easily to women. However, if it is also relentless, no progress toward recovery is made: It is necessary to attend to other things as well. This, however, is demanded of women who have the caring role, who have to attend to the household and to other tasks. It is our contention that, by totally immersing themselves in their work, men, who are generally more avoidant in their coping style, can more easily and completely block their emotions and not attend to the tasks defined in grief work. Thus we would argue that the gender differences in bereavement outcome are a result of the fact that external constraints prevent men but not women from exclusively engaging in their preferred style of coping (M. Stroebe et al., in press).

Age

Age and health are inversely related. It would therefore have been plausible that bereavement resulted in more health impairment among the old than the young. However, the opposite appears to be the case. It is the younger age groups who suffer more severe health consequences as a result of bereavement. This pattern emerges most clearly from mortality statistics, where widowed-to-married ratios are more excessive in younger than older age groups both in cross-sectional (e.g., Kraus & Lilienfeld, 1959) and longitudinal studies (e.g., Helsing & Szklo, 1981). The same pattern has been reported for grief symptoms (e.g., Ball, 1977) and other psychological and physical symptoms (e.g., Maddison & Walker, 1967) in studies of widows.

Sanders (1981) suggested that this age difference may be particularly marked for the initial impact of bereavement, but may disappear over time because of the greater speed of recovery of the younger widows. It would seem plausible that the young suffer more initially, because the loss is likely to have been sudden and unexpected, but that they are better able to cope in the long term because of their greater access to resources. However, this pattern could also be a result of an artifact. If one assumes that most bereaved individuals adjust over time and that therefore their health approaches the prebereavement baseline, then one would expect that initial differences in impact would dissipate in the course of the recovery process.

Little is known about the reasons for the greater health impact of bereavement in younger age groups. The most plausible interpretation is in terms of age differences in the expectedness of loss. Because accidents are the leading cause of death in the age group of 25 to 44 years, deaths in this age group are much more likely to be sudden and unexpected than among the older groups for whom diseases of the heart and cancers are the major killers. Thus the age difference might reflect the greater impact of losses that are unexpected rather than the outcome of a long period of illness.

The findings of a study that suggested a curvilinear relationship, with the impact of bereavement being strongest for middle-aged individuals, would appear to be inconsistent with this interpretation (Perkins & Harris, 1990). However, because this study of individuals who suffered a familial bereavement (loss of a sibling, spouse, child, or parent) did not control for type of bereavement, the weaker health effects among the young group (20 to 39) could have been a result of the fact that the proportion of deaths of parents were particularly high among the youngest group. The loss of a parent in adolescence is associated with less health deterioration than the loss of a sibling or spouse (Leahy, 1992; Nolen-Hoeksema & Larson, 1999). To clarify these inconsistencies, studies are needed that assess the role of expectedness of loss in mediating the impact of age of bereaved individuals on bereavement outcome.

Interpersonal Risk Factors

In this section we will discuss risk factors that are associated with the interpersonal context surrounding the loss. We will focus on two major factors—namely social support and kinship relationship. In discussing the impact of the kinship relationship that existed between the bereaved individual and the person who died, we will also broaden our discussion of bereavement, which has so far mainly focused on the loss of a partner.

Lack of Social Support

It is generally accepted that lack of social support is a bereavement-specific as well as a general risk factor. More precisely, social support from family and friends is assumed to have both a positive effect on health in general and to protect individuals against the health impact of bereavement (e.g., Sanders, 1993; Stroebe & Stroebe, 1987). As we have argued in an earlier publication, this assumption follows from stress theory, which attributes the impact of bereavement on well-being to stressful deficits caused by the loss (W. Stroebe, Stroebe, Abakoumkin, & Schut, 1996). Stress theory assumes that these deficits can be compensated through social support from family and friends (Lazarus & Folkman, 1984). In contrast, attachment theory denies that supportive friends can compensate the loss of an attachment figure and predicts main effects of marital status and social support that would reflect the general effect of social support (e.g., Bowlby, 1971, 1979; Weiss, 1975; chapter 4, this volume). Attachment theory further predicts that social support and partner loss affect health and well-being by separate pathways. The loss of a partner and thus of an important attachment figure results in emotional loneliness—the feeling of utter aloneness, even when one is with others. Emotional loneliness can only be remedied by the integration of another emotional attachment or the reintegration (after separation) of the one who has been lost. However, social support should reduce social loneliness that results from the absence of an engaging social network. In line with attachment theory, we observed a main effect of bereavement (but not social support) on emotional loneliness, a main effect of social support (but not bereavement) on social loneliness, and main effects of both social support and bereavement on measures of depression (W. Stroebe et al., 1996). We could further demonstrate that the impact of bereavement on depressive symptomatology was indeed mediated by emotional loneliness, whereas the impact of social support on depression was mediated by social loneliness.

In view of the strong support for attachment theory provided in our study, it is puzzling that four of the seven studies that used appropriate designs (i.e., included bereavement and levels of social support as factors) reported bereavement by social support interactions (Feld & George, 1994; Krause, 1986; Norris & Murrell, 1990; Schwarzer, 1992). This pattern reflects buffering effects of social support in bereavement and is thus consistent with stress rather than attachment theory. Of the studies that observed no buffering effects (Greene & Feld, 1989; Murphy, 1988; W. Stroebe et al. 1996), we were the only ones who found evidence for a main effect. The other studies found no effect (Murphy, 1988), or even a negative effect of social support (Greene & Feld, 1989).

How can we explain these inconsistencies? The major difference between our study and the studies in which social support buffered the impact of the loss experience on health and well-being is in the age of the widowed individuals studied. Whereas the mean age of the widows and widowers in our study was 53 years, the mean ages of the samples of the other studies ranged from 66 years to 73 years. But why should social support be more effective in alleviating the negative impact of bereavement for older than younger age groups? A potential explanation can be derived from the dual-process model of bereavement (M. Stroebe & Schut, 1999). According to this model, the loss of a partner results in two sources of stress: those directly associated with the loss of the loved person and those that come about as secondary consequences of loss, such as changes in life that occur because the deceased is no longer present. If one assumes that this second stress component increases with age, it would be plausible that, with advancing age, social support should become increasingly important for coping with bereavement. Obviously, further research is needed to test this hypothesis.

Kinship

A second interpersonal factor that moderates the impact of bereavement on health and well-being is the kinship relationship between the deceased and the bereaved individual. Comparative studies of the kinship relationship have consistently shown that the loss of an adult child results in more intense, or more persistent, grief and depression than the loss of a spouse, parent, or sibling (Cleiren, 1991; Leahy, 1992; Nolen-Hoeksema & Larson, 1999; Sanders, 1979). Thus in a study of women who had recently lost a husband, parent, or child, Leahy (1992) found the loss of an adult child to be associated with the highest and loss of a parent with the lowest depression scores. Similarly, in a comparison of men and women who had lost a spouse, a child, or a parent, Sanders (1979) concluded that those who experienced the death of a child revealed more intense grief reactions than did those bereaved individuals who had experienced the death of either a spouse or parent. Finally, studies by Cleiren (1991) and Nolen-Hoeksema and Larson (1999) also found the loss of a child to result in higher levels of depression than either the loss of a sibling, spouse, or parent. Because depression in all of these studies has been assessed some time after the loss experience, it is unclear whether these differences reflect differences in impact or in the rate of recovery. Furthermore, none of these studies appears to have controlled for age of the bereaved individual, even though the widowed tend to be older than the other kinship groups. However, the differences in depression measures are too substantial to be attributed to these age differences.

That the loss of a child, and particularly an adult child, result in more intense or more persistent grieving than the loss of a partner is theoretically interesting, because it appears to be inconsistent with stress theory. Both the loss of a spouse and of a child imply the loss of an attachment relationship. However, the death of a marital partner is characterized by a number of additional losses, namely the loss of a working relationship with the spouses sharing responsibility for home maintenance, child rearing, and the management of everyday lives. In addition, many marital relationships also provide companionship. The loss of these additional resources should make loss of a marital partner more stressful than the loss of a child.

According to the interpretation of attachment theory suggested by Weiss in this book (chapter 3, this volume; also personal communication, 1999) the nature of grief depends on the bonds that were severed, and these bonds are different in different relationships. Marital relationships involve the bond of attachment, with each spouse serving at times as the provider of a secure base to the other spouse and at other times as the beneficiary of the other spouse's provision of a safe haven. But marital relationships also embody the bond of partnership and of a working relationship in running the household and bringing up children.

The parent–child and the child–parent relationship is mainly characterized by attachment. Although Bowlby (1971) in his early writing distinguished between the care-giving system of the parents and the security-seeking system of the offspring, he seems to have abandoned this distinction in his later writing (Archer, 1999). From a developmental perspective, the distinction between the two systems may have been important, because there is reason to believe that when children grow up and leave home, the attachment relationship between children and parents recedes, whereas this may be less the case for the care-giving system of the parents. That children separate emotionally from their parents is important for growing up, and typically other attachment figures (e.g., spouses) take over the role of the provider of secure base. This type of substitution is less likely to take place in the attachment of parents to their children. When children grow up and leave home, the parents' care-giving system simply becomes dysfunctional, but the child as an object of attachment is not being replaced by other attachment figures. Thus the death of a child may mobilize the care-giving system in full force. Some parents may remain mobilized by the need to do something, anything, partly because unceasing mobilization proves to them that they are doing everything possible (Weiss, personal communication, 1999).

Evolutionary psychology would add to this account the concepts of inclusive fitness, parental investment, and reproductive value (for reviews, see Archer, 1999; also chapter 12, this volume). Because natural selection operates at the level of the genes, we care for our relatives to the extent to which they share our genes (inclusive fitness) and are likely to pass them on to future generations (i.e., reproductive value). Because each biological parent shares 50 percent of his or her genes with a child, and because the same is true for siblings, inclusive fitness would not account for the differences in grief across the kinship relations discussed earlier. However, the usefulness of any individual with whom one shares genes, in passing on these genes (i.e., reproductive value) is dependent on their age. Because parents are older than their children, their reproductive value is lower than that of their children. This could account for some of the difference in grief intensity observed between the loss of a child and the loss of a parent in adolescence. A second factor contributing to this difference is the fact that parents have invested a great deal in their children and "lose" this investment when a child dies. Because we invest much less in our siblings than in our children, grief over siblings should always be less than over children. It should further decrease with increasing age, having reached a maximum in adolescence, when the reproductive value of siblings is highest.

CONCLUSION

Theories of bereavement describe the mechanisms by which bereavement affects the health of bereaved individuals. The impact of risk factors on bereavement outcome has therefore to be mediated by the mechanisms postulated by a given theory. Our discussion indicated that stress theory does well in explaining the pattern of findings of studies of risk factors. The two major exceptions were the role of kinship relations and of social support as moderators of the grief relationship. That the loss of a child results in more intense grief and more severe depressive symptomatology is difficult to explain in terms of stress theory. It is in this instance that attachment theory offers a more convincing explanation. The case of social support is interesting because it suggests that the interpretation in terms of attachment theory may be most appropriate for younger age groups, whereas stress theory may be more applicable for elderly bereaved people. The distinction between different types of bonds suggested by Weiss (chapter 2, this volume; personal communication, 1999) offers a potential solution to these inconsistencies. Whereas variations in the impact of the loss of attachment relationships can best be predicted by attachment theory, the effects of the loss of these other bonds is better accounted for by stress theory.

We would like to conclude this chapter with a few methodological and conceptual comments. Methodologically, there is still a great deal to criticize, and little to praise, in research on risk factors in bereavement outcome. The major weakness is the absence of appropriate control groups or statistical controls. Although there has been some improvement in recent times, there are still too many studies that do not include nonbereaved control groups or, in the case of bereavement-specific risk factors, control for general risk factors associated with the variation in the bereavement-specific risk factor.

A second weakness is that most studies use designs that merely relate variations in risk factors to variations in health outcomes. Whereas such designs allow us to test predictions about the association between risk factors and bereavement outcome, they do not allow us to assess the assumed mediators and their role in mediating the relationship between risk factors and health outcome. To test hypotheses about assumed mediating variables, the variables have to be assessed, and mediating has to be tested for (for a discussion, see Baron & Kenny, 1986). The studies of McIntosh and colleagues (1993) and W. Stroebe and colleagues (1996, 1999) demonstrate the power of these types of analyses.

A third methodological weakness is that, because risk factors are seen as "causes" or "independent variables" in these analyses, it is typically assumed that they do not change during the period of observation. This assumption may often be unwarranted. For example, bereaved individuals often increase their smoking or alcohol consumption to cope with their grief (W. Stroebe, 2000). Similarly, in cases in which the deceased spouse was the main wage earner of the family, marital bereavement can result in a sudden drop in socioeconomic status (Sanders, 1993). Finally, heavy reliance on social support from others might reduce the availability of social support during the course of recovery (Stroebe & Stroebe, 1996). Because these changes in the levels of risk factors would in turn affect the health of the bereaved person during the recovery process, it is important to assess risk factors repeatedly during the course of a study.

Finally, a conceptual shortcoming of research on risk factors is the disregard of the social context both in defining risk factors and outcome variables. It is no coincidence that most of the risk factors that have been studied have been associated with aspects of the bereavement situation or the bereaved individual. Only two interpersonal risk factors—that is risk factors that are determined by a particular relationship that exists between the bereaved individual and others—have been studied: social support and kinship relations. Other potential interpersonal risk factors may be the concordance that exists in coping styles of parents grieving over the loss of a child or in the way family members construct the meaning of a loss. Furthermore, the relational context might not only be important as a determinant of risk but also as a mediating process or outcome variable. The loss of a child has an impact on the marital relationship, which in turn may moderate the grief reaction. Similarly, the loss of a spouse is likely to change the relationship individuals have with their friendship circle, and this in turn could affect the coping process. Conceptual integration of such social context variables would enrich research on risk factors in bereavement outcome.

REFERENCES

Adler, N. E., Boyce, T., Chesney, M. A., Cohen, S., Folkman, S., Kahn, R. L., & Syme, S. L. (1994). Socioeconomic status and health: The challenge of the gradient. *American Psychologist, 49*, 15–24.

Allport, G. W., & Ross, J. M., (1967). Personal religious orientation and prejudice. *Journal of Personality and Social Psychology, 5*, 432–443.

Amir, Y., & Sharon, I. (1982). Factors in the adjustment of war widows in Israel. In C. D. Spielberger, I. G. Sarason, & N. A. Milgram (Eds.), *Stress and anxiety* (Vol. 8). Washington, DC: Hemisphere.

Archer, J. (1999). *The nature of grief.* London: Routledge.

Ball, J. F. (1977). Widow's grief: The impact of age and mode of death. *Omega, 7*, 307–333.

Baron, R. M., & Kenny, D. A. (1986). The moderator–mediator variable distinction in social psychological research: Conceptual, strategic and statistical considerations. *Journal of Personality and Social Psychology, 51*, 1173–1182.

Barret, T. W., & Scott, T. B. (1987). *Suicide vs. other bereavement recovery patterns.* Paper presented at the joint meeting of the American Association of Suicidology and the International Association for Suicide Prevention, San Francisco.

Batson, C. D., Schoenrade, P., & Ventis, W. L. (1993). *Religion and the individual.* New York: Oxford University Press.

Berkman, L. F., & Syme, S. L. (1979). Social networks, host resistance, and mortality: A nine-year follow-up of Alameda County residents. *American Journal of Epidemiology, 109*, 186–204.

Billings, A. G., & Moos, R. H. (1981). The role of coping responses and social resources in attenuating the stress of life events. *Journal of Behavioral Medicine, 4*, 139–157.

Bohannon, J. R. (1991). Religiosity related to grief levels of bereaved mothers and fathers. *Omega, 23,* 153–159.

Bonanno, G. A., & Field, N. P. (in press). Examining the delayed grief hypothesis across five years of bereavement. *American Behavioral Scientist.*

Bornstein, P., Clayton, P. J., Halikas, J. A., Maurice, W. L., & Robins, E. (1973). The depression of widowhood after 13 months. *British Journal of Psychiatry, 122,* 561–566.

Bowlby, J. (1971). *Attachment and loss* (Vol. 1). *Attachment.* Harmondsworth, UK: Pelican Books.

Bowlby, J. (1979). *The making and breaking of affectional bonds.* London: Tavistock.

Bowlby, J. (1981). *Attachment and loss. Vol. 3. Loss: Sadness and depression.* Harmondworth, UK: Penguin Books.

Breckenridge, J., Gallagher, D., Thompson, L., Peteson, J. (1986). Characteristic depressive symptoms of bereaved elders. *Journal of Gerontology, 41,* 163–168.

Burks, V. K., Lund, D. A., Gregg, C. H., & Bluhm, H. P. (1988). Bereavement and remarriage for older adults. *Death Studies, 12,* 51–60.

Carey, R. G. (1977). The widowed: A year later. *Journal of Counseling Psychology, 24,* 125–131.

Clayton, P., Halikas, J. A., & Robins, E. (1973). Anticipatory grief and widowhood. *British Journal of Psychiatry, 122,* 47–51.

Cleiren, M. P. H. D. (1991). *Adaptation after bereavement.* Leiden, The Netherlands: DSWO Press.

Cohen, S., & Wills, T. A. (1985). Stress, social support, and the buffering hypothesis. *Psychological Bulletin, 98,* 310–357.

Cramer, D. (1993). Living alone, marital status, gender and health. *Journal of Applied and Community Social Psychology, 3,* 1–15.

Farberow, N. L., Gallagher-Thompson, D., Gilewski, M., & Thompson, L. (1992). Changes in grief and mental health of bereaved spouses of older suicides. *Journal of Gerontology, 47,* 357–366.

Feld, S., & George, L. K. (1994). Moderating effects of prior social resources on the hospitalizations of elders who become widowed. *Journal of Aging and Health, 6,* 275–295.

Folkman, S., & Lazarus, R. (1980). An analysis of coping in a middle-aged community sample. *Journal of Health and Social Behavior, 2,* 219–239.

Glick, I., Weiss, R. S., & Parkes, C. M. (1974). *The first year of bereavement.* New York: Wiley.

Goldman, N., Korenman, S., & Weinstein, R. (1995). Marital status and health among the elderly. *Social Science and Medicine, 40,* 1717–1730.

Gray, R. E. (1987). Adolescent response to the death of a parent. *Journal of Youth and Adolescence, 16,* 511–525.

Greene, R., & Feld, S. (1989). Social support coverage and the well-being of elderly widows and married women. *Journal of Family Issues, 10,* 33–51.

Helsing, K. J., & Szklo, M. (1981). Mortality after bereavement. *American Journal of Epidemiology, 114,* 41–52.

Heyman, D. K., & Gianturco, D. T. (1973). Long-term adaptation by the elderly to bereavement. *Journal of Gerontology, 28,* 359–362.

Jacobs, S., Kasl, S. V., Ostfeld, A. M., Berkman, L., & Charpentier, P. (1986). The measurement of grief: Age and sex variation. *British Journal of Medical Psychology, 59,* 305–310.

Joung, I. (1996). *Marital status and health: Descriptive and explanatory studies.* Unpublished Dissertation, Erasmus University, Rotterdam.

Kraus, A. S., & Lilienfeld, A. M. (1959). Some epidemiological aspects of the high mortality rate in the young widowed group. *Journal of Chronic Diseases, 10,* 207–217.

Krause, N. (1986). Social support, stress, and well-being among older adults. *Journal of Gerontology, 41,* 512–519.

Last, J. M. (Ed.). (1995). *A dictionary of epidemiology* (3rd ed.). New York: Oxford University Press.

Lazarus, R. S., & Folkman, S. (1984). *Stress, appraisal, and coping.* New York: Springer.

Leahy, J. M. (1992). A comparison of depression in women bereaved of a spouse, child, or a parent. *Omega, 26,* 207–218.

Levy, L. H., Martinowski, K. S., & Derby, J. F. (1994). Differences in patterns of adaptation in conjugal bereavement: Their sources and potential significance. *Omega, 29,* 71–87.

Lund, D., Caserta, M., & Dimond, M. (1986). Gender differences through two years of bereavement among the elderly. *The Gerontologist, 26,* 314–320.

Lundin, T. (1984). Morbidity following sudden and unexpected bereavement. *British Journal of Psychiatry, 144,* 84–88.

Maddison, D. C., & Walker, W. L. (1967). Factors affecting the outcome of conjugal bereavement. *British Journal of Psychiatry, 113,* 1057–1067.

Martikainen, P., & Valkonen, T. (1996). Mortality after death of a spouse in relation to duration of bereavement in Finland. *Journal of Epidemiology and Community Health, 50,* 264–268.

McIntosh, D. N., Silver, R., & Wortman, C. B. (1993). Religion's role in adjustment to a negative life event: Coping with the loss of a child. *Journal of Personality and Social Psychology, 65,* 812–821.

Murphy, S. A. (1988). Mental distress and recovery in a high-risk bereavement sample three years after untimely death. *Nursing Research, 37,* 30–35.

Nieboer, A. P., Lindenberg, S. M., & Ormel, J. (1998). Conjugal bereavement and well-being of elderly men and women: A preliminary study. *Omega, 38,* 113–142.

Nolen-Hoeksema, S., & Larson, J. (1999). *Coping with loss.* Mahwah, NJ: Erlbaum.

Nolen-Hoeksema, S., McBride, A., & Larson, A. (1997). Rumination and psychological distress among bereaved partners. *Journal of Personality and Social Psychology, 72*, 855–862.

Norris, F. H., & Murrell, S. A. (1990). Social support, life events, and stress as modifiers of adjustment to bereavement in older adults. *Psychology and Aging, 5*, 429–436.

Parkes, C. M. (1975). Unexpected and untimely bereavement: A statistical study of young Boston widows and widowers. In B. Schoenenberg, J. Gerber, A. Wiender, D. Kutscher, D. Peretz, & A. Cam (Eds.), *Bereavement: Its psychological aspects* (pp. 119–138). New York: Columbia University Press.

Parkes, C. M., & Weiss, R. S. (1983). *Recovery from bereavement*. New York: Basic Books.

Perkins, H. W., & Harris, L. B., (1990). Familial bereavement and health in adult life course perspective. *Journal of Marriage and the Family, 52*, 233–241.

Purisman, R., & Maoz, B. (1977). Adjustment and war bereavement—some considerations. *Journal of Medical Psychology, 50*, 1–9.

Radloff, L. (1975). Sex differences in depression. The effects of occupation and marital status. *Sex Roles, 1*, 249–265.

Rogers, R. G. (1995). Marriage, sex, and mortality. *Journal of Marriage and the Family, 57*, 515–526.

Rosik, C. H. (1989). The impact of religious orientation in conjugal bereavement among older adults. *International Journal of Aging and Human Development, 28*, 251–260.

Sanders, C. M. (1979). A comparison of adult bereavement in the death of a spouse, child, and parent. *Omega, 10*, 303–322.

Sanders, C. (1981). Comparison of younger and older spouses in bereavement outcome. *Omega, 11*, 217–231.

Sanders, C. M. (1983). Effects of sudden versus chronic illness death on bereavement outcome. *Omega, 13*, 227–241.

Sanders, C. M. (1993). Risk factors in bereavement outcome. In M. S. Stroebe, W. Stroebe, & R. O. Hansson (Eds.), *Handbook of bereavement* (pp. 255–270). New York: Cambridge University Press.

Schut, H. A. W. (1992). *Omgaan met de dood van de partner* (Coping with the loss of a partner). Unpublished PhD dissertation, Utrecht, The Netherlands.

Schwarzer, C. (1992). Bereavement, received social support, and anxiety in the elderly: A longitudinal analysis. *Anxiety Research, 4*, 287–296.

Shepherd, D., & Barraclough, B. M. (1974). The aftermath of suicide. *British Medical Journal, 2*, 600–603.

Sherkat, D. W., & Reed, M. D. (1992). The effects of religion and social support on self-esteem and depression among the suddenly bereaved. *Social Indicators Research, 26*, 259–275.

Stroebe, M. S., & Schut, H. W. (1999). The dual process model of coping with bereavement: Rationale and description. *Death Studies, 23*, 197–224.

Stroebe, M. S., & Stroebe, W. (1983). Who suffers more? Sex differences in health risks of the widowed. *Psychological Bulletin, 93,* 297–301.

Stroebe, M. S., Stroebe, W., & Schut, H. (in press). Gender differences in adjustment to bereavement: An empirical and theoretical review. *General Psychology Review.*

Stroebe, W. (2000). *Social psychology and health* (2nd ed.). Buckingham: Open University Press.

Stroebe, W., & Stroebe, M. S. (1987). *Bereavement and health.* New York: Cambridge University Press.

Stroebe, W., & Stroebe, M. (1996). The social psychology of social support. In E. T. Higgins & A. W. Kruglanski (Eds.), *Social psychology: Handbook of basic principles* (pp. 597–621). New York: Guilford Press.

Stroebe, W., Stroebe, M., & Abakoumkin, G. (1999). Does differential social support cause sex differences in bereavement outcome? *Journal of Applied Social and Community Psychology, 9,* 1–12.

Stroebe, W., Stroebe, M., Abakoumkin, G., & Schut, H. (1996). The role of loneliness and social support in adjustment to loss: A test of attachment versus stress theory. *Journal of Personality and Social Psychology, 70,* 1241–1249.

Stroebe, W., Stroebe, M., & Domittner, G. (1987). *Kummerbewältigung und Kummereffekt: Psychische und physische Reaktionen von Verwitweten* (Coping with grief: Psychological and physical reactions of bereaved). Technical Report, Tübingen.

Stroebe, W., Stroebe, M., & Domittner, G. (1988). Individual and situational differences in recovery from bereavement: A risk group identified. *Journal of Social Issues, 44,* 143–158.

Umberson, D., Wortman, C. B., & Kessler, R. C. (1992). Widowhood and depression: Explaining long-term gender differences in vulnerability. *Journal of Health and Social Behavior, 33,* 10–24.

Vachon, M. L. S., Rogers, J., Lyall, W. A. L., Rogers, J., Lancee, W. J., Sheldon, A. R., Freeman, S. J. (1982). Predictors and correlates of adaptation to conjugal bereavement. *American Journal of Psychiatry, 137,* 1380–1384.

Verbrugge, L. M. (1989). The twain meet: Empirical explanations of sex differences in health and mortality. *Journal of Health and Social Behavior, 30,* 282–304.

Verbrugge, L. M., & Wingard, D. L. (1987). Gender differential in health and mortality. *Women and Health, 12,* 103–145.

Weiss, R. (1975). *Loneliness: The experience of emotional and social isolation.* Cambridge: MIT Press.

Willet, J. B., & Sayer, A. G. (1994). Using covariance structure analysis to detect correlates and predictors of individual change over time. *Psychological Bulletin, 116,* 363–380.

Willet, J. B., Singer, J. D., & Martin, N. C. (1998). The design and analysis of longitudinal studies of development and psychopathology in context: Statistical models and methodological recommendations. *Development and Psychopathology, 10,* 395–426.

IV

COPING:
BASIC CONCEPTS AND
THEIR MEASUREMENT

17

MODELS OF COPING WITH BEREAVEMENT: A REVIEW

MARGARET S. STROEBE AND HENK SCHUT

For most of the twentieth century, it was generally believed that to get over the loss of a loved one it was necessary to do one's "grief work." Yet people grieve in different ways, some more effectively than others. This has raised important questions about potential links between processes (ways of coping) and outcomes (e.g., health consequences). In recent decades, researchers have also begun to question the adequacy of the "grief work hypothesis" (cf. Rosenblatt, 1983; Rosenblatt, Walsh, & Jackson, 1976; Stroebe, 1992; Wortman & Silver, 1989).

This chapter seeks to determine the nature of adaptive coping with bereavement and provides a review of the scientific research on the issue. It is first necessary to establish what is meant by "adaptive coping" in terms of the processes that lead to abatement of grief and in terms of types of outcomes or ultimate adaptation. Current theories of grief (and of related phenomena) can then be evaluated with respect to their ability to explain the impact and significance of different ways of coping with bereavement.

At the start of the twenty-first-century, a number of quite different theoretical approaches have been proposed to explain such processes. These can be classified into three categories: (a) general stress and trauma theories; (b) general theories of grief; and (c) models of coping specific to bereavement (see Table 17-1). We follow this structure in the rest of the chapter, finally presenting our own dual-process model of coping with bereavement (M. Stroebe & Schut, 1999; in press), which integrates elements from a number of the other perspectives.

THE CONCEPT OF (ADAPTIVE) COPING

Coping is generally understood to encompass "the person's cognitive and behavioral efforts to manage (reduce, minimize, master, or tolerate) the internal and external demands of the person–environment transaction that is appraised as taxing or exceeding the resources of the person" (Folkman, Lazarus, Gruen, & De Longis, 1986, p. 572). Bereaved people use certain ways of coping to manage the stressful situation that follows the loss of the significant person and the negative emotional reaction of grief. This implies that certain coping strategies would lead to reduction in negative consequences of grief. Whether or not these strategies are successful, however, is not part of the definition of coping (cf. W. Stroebe, 2000). For purposes of the present discussion, then, we define "adaptive strategies" as those that actually lead to a reduction in the negative psychosocial and physical health consequences of bereavement or to a lowering of grief.

The theoretical perspectives to be reviewed postulate different effective strategies (if they discuss adaptive coping at all). In addition to the broader notion of "grief work" postulated by psychoanalysts (e.g., Freud, 1917/1957) and attachment theorists (e.g., Bowlby, 1980), more specific processes such as "disclosure" (e.g., Pennebaker, 1995) have been examined. Similarly, the specification of "negative effects" has broadened. Some investigators have concentrated on the intensity and duration of grief or depression (e.g., Shuchter & Zisook, 1993), others on categories of pathologic grief or psychiatric conditions (e.g., Jacobs, 1993), and still others on physical health consequences, including mortality (see W. Stroebe & Stroebe, 1987).

At the outset, we need to point out that assessment of adaptive coping strategies or styles is difficult (see W. Stroebe, 2000, for a review). For example, different strategies may be more effective at different durations or for coping with different aspects of bereavement; a strategy may be useful short-term but harmful long-term; it may positively affect physical health but increase distress. Methodologically, too, many of the empirical studies have shortcomings. For example, assessments are not frequently made longitudinally (coping strategy at the first measurement point predicting outcome at the second), and sometimes have even been conducted retrospectively. Finally, definitions of coping strategies or styles often include outcome as well as process variables. For example, some of the scales

TABLE 17-1
Coping With Bereavement: Principles of Adaptation in Theories and Models

I. General Life Event Theories (stress; trauma)
- Cognitive stress theory: Emotion- problem-focused coping; confrontation–avoidance
- Stress response syndromes: Cognitive regulation (intrusion/avoidance)
- Emotional disclosure and sharing: Communication with others about the loss
- Assumptive world views: Revision of assumptions/meanings

II. General Grief-Related Theories
- Psychoanalytic theory: Grief work
- Attachment theory: Grief work
- Psychosocial transition model: Revision of assumptions; working through
- Two-track model: Two-track processing ($\rightarrow$ transformation of attachment and recovery)

III. Specific Coping With Bereavement Models (intra-; interpersonal)
- Task model: Four tasks (working through)
- Cognitive process models:
  - (a) Rumination/distraction
  - (b) Positive psychological states
  - (c) Confrontation–avoidance
- Incremental grief model: Symmetry and congruence within bereaved (family) groups
- "New model" of grief: Biography (re)construction in (family) groups
- Meaning reconstruction: Six principles to shape adaptation (inter)personally

IV. Integrative Models
- Four-component model: Appraisal/evaluation processing and changed representations as part of emotion regulation (dissociation of negative; enhancement of positive)
- Dual-process model: Confrontation–avoidance of loss- vs. restoration-oriented stressors; positive–negative meaning (re)construction; oscillation (cognitive control)

used to assess emotion-focused coping contain items that confound coping strategy with coping outcome (e.g., including questions about distress or low self-esteem among those on controlling emotions).

It becomes evident that criteria for "adaptive coping," both with respect to strategies and the negative effects, will be hard to formulate. With these cautions in mind, we can proceed to examine the theoretical perspectives for information about the differential effectiveness of coping strategies with respect to physical and psychological well-being following bereavement.

STRESS AND TRAUMA THEORIES

Stress theories and trauma theories provide explanations for how persons respond to stressful life events in general (e.g., victimization; war; traffic accidents; and bereavement), and include, for the most part, consideration of patterns of reactions and detrimental consequences (outcomes) associated with such events. These two approaches have resulted in independent lines of research, each of which has been influential, although their impact on bereavement has been realized only within the past decade.

Cognitive Stress Theory

Cognitive stress theory (cf. Lazarus & Folkman, 1984) incorporates principles of coping that are useful for the analysis of grieving. Consistent with the general theory, bereavement would be seen as a stressor, a life event that poses demands on the individual, which could tax or exceed the resources available, thereby endangering health and well-being. Appraisal by the individual determines the extent to which bereavement is considered challenging or stressful. A range of different coping strategies has been empirically derived. These could potentially be associated with adaptation to bereavement, but so far, only limited evidence is available.

The cognitive-stress theory is useful in the bereavement context for a number of other reasons. It provides a framework for the fine-grained definition of characteristics of the stressor (bereavement), coping process and related strategies (e.g., confrontation–avoidance), and outcomes (e.g., mental or physical health detriments), from which cause–effect relationships can be derived (cf. chapter 25, this volume). Bereavement is a global stressor. Making the picture more complicated, it involves a number of simultaneous, ongoing specific stressors (e.g., to do with the loss of an attachment figure; financial, and skills loss). Although the model acknowledges the possibility that different specific stressors coexist, it does not describe a process of concurrent appraisal and coping with the different stressors, as happens when coming to terms with a bereavement. Rather, the model details appraisal and coping with one stressor at a time (cf. Folkman et al., 1991, fig. 1).

Predictions about strategies of effective coping with bereavement within this framework remain unclear. This is not surprising given the number and variety of empirically derived strategies, the different stressors described previously, and duration-related changes in bereavement reactions. Nevertheless, two general types of coping strategies—namely, problem- versus emotion-focused coping, and confrontation versus avoidance, are especially relevant. These have been postulated as instrumental in dealing with stressful situations in general (cf. de Ridder, 1997).

Problem-focused coping is directed at managing and changing the problem causing the distress, whereas emotion-focused is directed at managing the resulting emotion (Billings & Moos, 1981; Lazarus & Folkman, 1984). The former is more appropriate in situations that are changeable, the latter in unchangeable situations. Some aspects of bereavement may be better dealt with in an emotion-focused manner, because they are unchangeable (the deceased cannot be brought back), others in a problem-focused way, because they can be altered (e.g., earning money to repair the finances). Folkman (chapter 25, this volume) acknowledges that coping processes used will be mixed and change over time. However, it is not clear how this applies in the complex situation confronting bereaved people. Similarly, it is hard to differentiate between adaptive and maladaptive emotion-focused coping with bereavement on the basis either of the definition or of the tools (coping scales) used to measure this dimension. In the case of bereavement, emotion-focused coping cuts across categories such as working through versus avoidance, including rumination, suppression, and denial.

Successful outcome appears to require both problem- and emotion-focused coping strategies. The theory does not postulate either problem- or emotion-focused coping. And predictions are not straightforward even if one argues for different focuses for different aspects. For example, emotion-focused strategies are not necessarily best used for dealing with unchangeable aspects. When coping with the loss of a loved one, it might be argued that grief needs to be suppressed, because lack of control over it presents difficulties for the self and others. On the other hand, it would seem intuitively reasonable, also, that it helps to "give sorrow words." To make matters even more complex, emotion-focused coping is defined as both control of emotions and the expression of them.

The other dimension noted previously, "confrontation-avoidance," is similarly difficult to apply, given the multiple stressors associated with bereavement. For example, a bereaved individual might avoid certain emotional responses (e.g., avoid crying over the personal loss), but confront other aspects of the experience (e.g., guilt at some action toward the deceased before death). Because bereavement involves multiple stressors, some changeable and some not, one cannot simply confront or avoid as a coping strategy. Different stressors will be confronted or avoided at different times. It is difficult to see how this relates to outcome.

Although this analysis leaves us with problems in deriving predictions from cognitive-stress theory about adaptive coping with bereavement, the basic framework can be used to develop a much finer-grained analysis than is provided in "grief work theories." It is important to note that it pinpoints the mediating role of cognitive appraisal in adjustment to loss. These issues are considered in greater detail by Folkman (chapter 25, this volume), and in our discussion later in the chapter on bereavement-specific models.

Trauma Theory

Trauma theory has produced three independent bodies of research: Horowitz's (1986) analysis in terms of "stress response syndromes," the work of Pennebaker (1995) on disclosure in trauma management, and Janoff-Bulman's (1992) "assumptive world views." These approaches are specific to traumatic life experiences and attempt to explain patterns of response occurring as a consequence of deeply disturbing, even horrendous events. Clearly, bereavement can sometimes be a traumatic experience (see M. Stroebe, Schut, & Stroebe, 1998, for consideration of overlap versus distinction in the two fields).

Stress Response Syndromes

A landmark in the scientific study of trauma is Horowitz's (1983, 1986) analysis of "stress response syndromes." This work describes the normal manifestations of human reactions following traumatic events, which may sometimes increase in intensity and frequency to an extent that can be diagnosed as posttraumatic stress disorder (Kleber & Brom, 1992). Of particular importance, Horowitz (1983, 1986) identified the antithetical reactions of intrusion–avoidance as distinctive features of traumatic reactions. Intrusion is the compulsive reexperiencing of feelings and ideas surrounding the event, including sleep and dream disturbance and hypervigilance. Avoidance signifies a denial process, including reactions such as amnesia, inability to visualize memories, and evidence of disavowal. The description of a person's intrusion–avoidance pattern (too much–too little) helps to define the extremity of a person's reaction to a traumatic event.

There is a subtle but fundamental difference between Horowitz's (1986) concern with intrusion–avoidance processes and our interest in effective coping. Horowitz's purpose was to determine how much impact the event had, intrusion–avoidance thus being a "symptomatic" process useful for classification of pathology. By contrast, our research question involves whether intrusion–avoidance coping strategies lead to adjustment to the event. Intrusion–avoidance reactions may then parallel the confrontation–avoidance dimension discussed in the previous section. In fact, in Horowitz's terms, intrusion–avoidance is not presented as a dynamic coping process but as an indicator of disturbance in reactions (although, to make matters complicated, below a specified clinically relevant level, intrusion–avoidance represents a normal coping process). Furthermore, intrusion–avoidance processes are typically measured only in relation to the traumatic event itself, and as we have already seen many other (secondary) aspects of the loss need to be taken into consideration in bereavement. Of concern also, the theoretical model does not (maybe even need to) distinguish between intrusion–avoidance of painful versus happy memories (cf. chapter 2, this volume). It is perhaps also true that intrusion–avoidance reactions to trauma (including traumatic bereavement) incorporate comparatively more involuntary processing (lack of personal control) than (nontraumatic) bereavement.

Again, it seems that although reactions to traumas in general and bereavements in particular share certain features, to understand the latter we need a more differentiated analysis of the nature of the stressor and the cognitions involved in intrusion–avoidance. It is noteworthy that both of the theoretical perspectives described so far include a confrontation–avoidance dimension in reactions to stressful life events. This dimension is far less apparent in the general bereavement models.

Emotional Disclosure and Social Sharing

There is by now overwhelming evidence that traumatic experiences cause mental and physical health problems (for a review, see Pennebaker, 1995). Some empirical evidence has also shown that engaging in written or verbal disclosure about traumatic events, and the personal upset of these experiences, helps adjustment and lowers mental and physical health risk (e.g., Pennebaker, 1989, 1993). This theme has been central to the fine-grained analyses by Pennebaker and colleagues in the United States and also by Rimé and colleagues in Belgium. This impressive body of research is reviewed by Pennebaker, Zech, and Rimé (chapter 23, this volume).

Relating this work to the current interest, we need to ask whether adaptive coping necessitates—or at least significantly involves—talking or writing about feelings associated with the loss. As Pennebaker et al. (chapter 23, this volume) acknowledge, there is no simple answer to this question. It is not just a case of expressing emotions to do with grief or sharing feelings with others to "get over" a trauma. Their work, in fact, represents an attempt to unravel the social and cognitive dynamics associated with the health benefits of disclosure. Of particular interest, the research distinguishes between the effects of naturally occurring disclosure and disclosure interventions on adjustment. It also distinguishes emotional recovery from the traumatic event from the negative mental and physical health consequences of the event. The research of Rimé and colleagues (e.g., Finkenauer & Rimé, 1998; Rimé, Finkenauer, Luminet, Zech, & Philippot, 1998) showed that, contrary to lay beliefs, social sharing does not lead to emotional recovery, although it does serve other cognitive, psychological, and social functions (which, though important, are not our current interest). By contrast, Pennebaker and colleagues (e.g., Pennebaker, 1993; Pennebaker & Beall, 1986; Pennebaker & Francis, 1986) found the expected effects in their intervention studies, with respect to mental and, particularly, physical health. It is important to note that they were able to design studies that would distinguish between disclosure that simply reflects grief (the more grief-stricken are more likely to talk about their emotions) and disclosure that actually affects grief (talking or writing improved mental or physical health). Although short-term increases in depression rates, for example, were to be found, long-term, the benefits of disclosure became apparent.

At first, Pennebaker's search for an explanation (i.e., what is it about disclosure that reduces symptomatology) concentrated less on the beneficial effects of the disclosure process per se and more on an inhibitory model (see Pennebaker, 1989; chapter 23, this volume), suggesting that the act of holding back one's thoughts and feelings involved biological work that was stressful. Recently, more cognitive and social factors have been included in the explanatory framework. Pennebaker has suggested that disclosure helps the individual to organize the experience; to clarify psychological state to others; and to translate emotional experiences into the medium of language. Pennebaker's conclusions are important (1997; chapter 23, this volume): For a disclosure intervention to be effective, the person must actively work through an upsetting experience. Those who benefited most were the ones who showed cognitive change across the course of the intervention. Those who did not but remained highly (expressively) emotional did not experience the health benefits.

Combined, these results suggest that social sharing does not further emotional recovery but that disclosure intervention is indeed effective in improving the health status of bereaved people who have suffered a traumatic bereavement or who are unable to talk naturally about their loss or come to terms with it (chapter 23, this volume). Given the high rates of natural social sharing of negative emotions (following Rimé and collaborators' findings), one would expect a lot of disclosure of grief to take place —most persons would be expected to share naturally and not to need intervention for this. Perhaps disclosure interventions are most appropriate for those for whom expression is inhibited and grief thereby complicated.

Defining these conditions and circumstances, and identifying the processes involved in cognitive change, are likely to be topics for future research.

Assumptive World Views

The work of Janoff-Bulman and colleagues (e.g., Janoff-Bulman, 1992; Janoff-Bulman & Berg, 1998) has emphasized the crucial role of meaning in the process of recovery from traumatic life events. These investigators have argued that the fundamental assumptions people hold about themselves, the world, and the relation between these two, which normally go unquestioned and unchallenged, are shattered by traumatic events such as the death of a loved one. Three assumptions were postulated to reside at the core of our inner worlds—namely, that we are worthy, that the world is benevolent, and that what happens to us "makes sense" (e.g., Janoff-Bulman, 1992). When death of a loved one (particularly if it has been traumatic) shatters these basic assumptions the survivor struggles to integrate the experience of the event into these broader meaning structures.

How are people supposed to cope effectively with the resulting situation, when "the terror of their own fragility is overwhelming" (Janoff-Bulman & Berg, 1998, p. 39)? Coping is said to involve rebuilding the inner world, to reestablish meaning, to adjust old assumptions or, at least partly, to accept new ones (that may be less positive–illusionary). Over time, most survivors reestablish an assumptive world that is not completely threatening. Presumably, effective coping from this perspective would be to search for meaning and to integrate the event into broader positively meaningful structures (rather than focusing on the malevolence of the world, etc.). By implication, this would involve a confrontational strategy. It is difficult, however, to distinguish between bereaved persons who do this effectively and those who do not. Meaning is an elusive concept in general. Defining "finding meaning" following bereavement has been problematic, and findings have been equivocal (e.g., when operationalized in terms of "spiritual beliefs" or "death occurring in the fullness of time"). In fact, the theory, like those described previously, focuses more on describing and understanding trauma reactions than on adaptive versus maladaptive coping. Nevertheless, the meaning variables identified by Janoff-Bulman (1992) can be integrated usefully into a bereavement-specific coping framework, as we will illustrate later in the chapter.

GENERAL THEORIES OF GRIEF

Psychoanalytic (Freud, 1917/1957) and attachment (Bowlby, 1980) perspectives are highly influential general theories of grief (for more detailed accounts, see W. Stroebe & Stroebe, 1987). It is important to emphasize the distinction made earlier between these more general theories of grief, which are designed to explain the manifestations and processes of grief, and models specific to coping with bereavement, which try to distinguish and elucidate adaptive versus maladaptive ways of grieving. The general theories should be able to explain the broad range of phenomena that make up grief, including not only mental and physical health reactions and elevated mortality risk but also the somewhat less expected phenomena that are sometimes associated with bereavement (e.g., anger, searching for the deceased, positive meaning-making, creativity). As part of their explanatory framework for this broad range of consequences of bereavement, these theories may—explicitly or implicitly—include an analysis of coping strategies or mechanisms, because these may add explanatory power. This is where the general theories become interesting in the present context: We can examine their potential to provide insights into how bereaved persons grieve. Given our narrow focus, analyses of other grief phenomena such as the symptomatology of grief (e.g., Shuchter & Zisook, 1993), or predictors of outcome (e.g., Sanders, 1989) will be referred to only briefly. Though relevant, these topics are peripheral to our current focus on effective ways of coping.

Psychoanalytic Theory

The concept of "grief work" defined in our introduction has been fundamental to the psychoanalytic perspective on adaptive coping. Its origins are typically traced to the seminal paper by Freud (1917/1957). Freud proposed that when a loved one dies, the bereaved person is faced with the struggle to sever ties and detach energy invested in the deceased person. The psychological function of grief, therefore, is to free the individual of his or her bond to the deceased, achieving a gradual detachment by means of reviewing the past and dwelling on memories of the deceased. Thus successful adaptation will involve working through loss; grief cannot otherwise be overcome. Freud talked of "the work which mourning performs" (1917/1957, p. 253) and described the "reality testing" of those who have lost a loved one, through which they gradually come to realize that the person no longer exists.

The grief work concept retains its theoretical and practical significance, even today (cf. Bowlby, 1980; Parkes, 1996; Raphael, Middleton, Martinek, & Misso, 1993). However, it has also received much critical examination (cf. Bonanno, 1998; M. Stroebe, 1992; M. Stroebe & Schut, 1999; Wortman & Silver, 1987, 1989; see also chapter 22, this volume). The concept was also incorporated into Bowlby's (1980) attachment framework, which we consider next. We will therefore summarize the main points of criticism after describing this latter perspective.

Attachment Theory

According to Bowlby (1980), working through grief is important for the purpose of rearranging representations of the lost person and, relatedly, of the self (for detailed accounts, see Archer, 1999; chapter 4, this volume). This working through takes place through a sequence of overlapping, flexibly occurring phases. This well-known "phase" or "stage" model incorporates four phases: shock, yearning and protest, despair, and recovery. Although working through these phases is viewed to enable detachment (labeled reorganization in his later work), or the breaking of affectional bonds (Bowlby, 1979), it is also considered to further the continuation of the bond. This implies a relocation of the deceased so that adjustment can gradually be made to the physical absence of this person in ongoing life (see Fraley & Shaver, 1999; chapter 4, this volume).

Psychoanalytic and attachment theory differ with respect to the function that grief work was said to serve. In psychoanalytic theory, grief work brings about a severance of the "attachment to the non-existent object" (Freud, 1917/1957, p. 166). In attachment theory, it reflects a characteristic response of many species following the disruption of a strong affectional bond—namely, to try to recover proximity. In the case of separation through death, proximity cannot be reestablished, resulting in protest and despair. The biological function of grieving—to end separation—is then dysfunctional. It is beyond the scope of this chapter to debate the psychological versus biological explanations of these impactful theories.

It is more important to consider the evidence that links grief work to adaptation. In a review of theoretical and empirical research on grief work, M. Stroebe (1992) summarized a number of shortcomings associated with the grief-work hypothesis (i.e., the notion that one has to confront the experience of bereavement to come to terms with loss and avoid detrimental health consequences). For example, the definition of grief work lacks clarity because it does not differentiate between negatively associated rumination and more positively associated aspects of working through. Also, there has been a diversity in operationalizations, including outcome variables among the coping strategy variables (e.g., including despair, yearning, and pining). Empirical support has been equivocal (cf. Bonanno, 1998; Bonanno & Kaltman, 1999; M. Stroebe & Stroebe, 1991; Wortman & Silver, 1987, 1989; chapters 18 and 22, this volume), with a number of studies failing to show that those who work through grief adjust better than those who do not. Finally, there seems to be a lack of applicability in certain cultures, where there is apparent adaptation without confrontation or "working through" of grief (for a review, see W. Stroebe & Stroebe, 1987).

In our view, despite these critical points, the grief work concept remains a powerful analytic tool for understanding the way people adapt to bereavement. It captures at least part of the essence of coming to terms with loss, at least in our own culture. It must also be noted that although the major theorists did consider grief work to be fundamental to adaptive grieving, their writing reflects an awareness of greater complexity (cf. M. Stroebe, 1997; M. Stroebe & Schut, 1999). Further specification of the concept could be productive, however.

Bereavement as a Psychosocial Transition

Although comparable in some respects to Janoff-Bulman's (1992) analysis of traumas as disruptions of assumptive world views, Parkes's psychosocial transition model provides specific description of what actually changes in bereavement:

> When somebody dies a whole set of assumptions about the world that relied upon the other person for their validity are suddenly invalidated. Habits of thought which have been built up over many years must be reviewed and modified, a person's view of the world must change . . . it inevitably takes time and effort. (Parkes, 1996, p. 90)

Following this model, a gradual changing of assumptions is needed, deeply bound up, as these are, with one's "internal model" of the world (and the self within it). Continued resistance to change will inhibit adaptation, although at first it may be functional, because change needs to be interpreted in terms of old assumptions, in the absence, still, of revised ones. Parkes (1996), like the major theorists before him (himself an attachment theorist), accepted that grief work was an essential part of adaptive grieving. He specified component, interdependent parts of the process: First, there is preoccupation with thoughts of the lost person. Second, there is painful repetitious recollection of the loss experience, or "worry work," to accept the irrevocability of loss. Third, there is an attempt to make sense of loss, to fit it into one's set of assumptions about the world (one's "assumptive world") or to modify those assumptions if need be.

The Two-Track Model

Rubin's (1981; Rubin & Schechter, 1997) two-track model of bereavement addressed the bereavement process and its outcome. It does not focus on the coping process per se, but it has relevance for the analysis of adaptational coping. Examining the phenomena of child loss specifically, Rubin postulated two tracks. Track I was an outcome track, describing the biopsychosocial reactions to bereavement. Track II focused on the attachment to the deceased, describing ways that this becomes transformed and a new still-ongoing relationship to the deceased established. These two dimensions comprise a dual-axis paradigm in that the intense preoccupation with the deceased "sets in motion" the bereavement response (Rubin, 1993). Although compatible with and similar in some ways to cognitive-stress theory, described previously, Rubin's model does not provide an analysis of cognitive structures or processes, as does Folkman (e.g., Folkman et al., 1991). On the other hand, it suggests a dynamic mechanism associated with the attachment bond, which is an important addition to previous formulations, as is the identification and clear distinction of the two tracks.

MODELS OF COPING WITH BEREAVEMENT: FROM INTRA- TO INTERPERSONAL PERSPECTIVES

Finally, we come to the bereavement-specific coping models. There have been a number of new approaches in recent years, following (perhaps even suggesting) exciting new trends in scientific research in general. Although the models have been designed specifically for bereavement, it will become evident that, just as the general theories have applications to the specific stressor of bereavement, so do these bereavement-specific models have potential application to other stressors (e.g., loss of livelihood, terminal illness). That is, the postulated adaptive ways of coping with bereavement may (sometimes) be appropriate for helping us understand coping with other stressors.

Two recent research developments have been especially important to understanding adaptive coping: (a) the specification of cognitive tasks and processes in the coping process and (b) the extension of analysis beyond the intrapersonal to interpersonal perspectives. These perspectives are well-represented in this volume. This section is therefore confined to describing how each would answer our specific coping–adaptation question.

Intrapersonal Coping Models

Among intrapersonal models of coping, a clear distinction can be drawn between task and process models. The former involve a more precise definition of the stressors that need working through, the latter involve more precise definition (than offered in the "grief work" notion) of mechanisms underlying (mal)adaptive coping. Detailed description is important for the development of the dual-process model.

The Task Model

Rather than conceptualizing the grieving process in terms of "phases" or "stages" as described previously under attachment theory, Worden (1982/1991) described "tasks" that the bereaved person has to perform to adjust to bereavement. Such a model represents coping as a more dynamic process because the griever is presented as actively working through grief (rather than more passively experiencing it), which represents the reality that most grievers report. The grief process is viewed to encompass four tasks, namely accepting the reality of loss; experiencing the pain of grief; adjusting to an environment without the deceased; and "relocating" the deceased emotionally.

It is clear that not all grievers undertake these tasks, and not in a set order. In general, however, completion of the work associated with each task should facilitate adaptation. This formulation incorporates an implicit "time" dimension: Different coping tasks are appropriate at different durations of bereavement, which is a useful consideration in making predictions about adaptive coping. Nevertheless, in our view, additional tasks need to be performed, such as working toward acceptance of the changed world, not just the reality of loss. One needs to take time out from grieving, as well as experiencing pain. The subjective environment itself (not just adjustment to the environment) needs to be reconstructed. Finally, we need to specify that bereaved people work toward developing new roles, identities, and relationships, not just relocating the deceased and "moving on."

Cognitive Process Models

In earlier research it was not easy to define precisely what was meant by "grief work." More recently a number of investigators have provided theoretical analyses of components in this process of coping with loss. The dimensions that have received most research attention—also major components in general coping research (see de Ridder, 1997)—are positive and negative appraisal processes and confrontation versus avoidance strategies.

Rumination. People whose style it is to confront and talk about negative aspects of their loss over time do not do as well as those who refrain (more) from this type of disclosure. A few investigators have gone a step further, controlling for the amount of distress at the outset of evaluation and showing the impact of disclosure of negative emotions on later recovery. Nolen-Hoeksema (e.g., Nolen-Hoeksema & Larson, 1999; Nolen-Hoeksema, Parker, & Larson, 1994; chapter 24, this volume) showed that a ruminative style of coping—that is, focusing on distressing aspects and meanings in a repetitive and passive manner—was associated with higher depression levels months later. This was independent of depression level early on. Those with a distractive style became less depressed over time. Support came from studies by Bonanno (chapter 22, this volume). Capps and Bonanno (2000) showed that disclosure of negatively valanced emotions predicted increased distress and somatic complaints.

Nolen-Hoeksema (Nolen-Hoeksema & Jackson, 1996; chapter 24, this volume) suggested pathways whereby ruminative coping may lead to a lengthening and worsening of the impact of loss: first, through enhancing the effects of depressed mood on thinking; second, through interfering with everyday instrumental behavior (reducing motivation to act that would normally increase the sense of control and lift mood); third, through interfering with effective problem-solving (because they think negatively about themselves and their lives); and fourth, through reducing necessary social support (perhaps because persistent ruminations violate social norms of coping). One might infer, then, that adaptation would be associated with more active, problem-solving, distractive, outgoing styles of coping.

Positive psychological states. Along similar lines, it has recently been shown that disclosing or confronting positive aspects associated with loss leads to recovery. Just as rumination was shown to play a mediating role in hampering adjustment, so has the role of positive affect been shown to further adjustment. It has even been shown that the occurrence of smiling and laughter during the grieving process is positively related to later adjustment (Keltner & Bonanno, 1997). Being able to find positive meaning in bereavement-related stressful events brings about or enhances positive affect and reduces distress. Positive emotional states—even laughter—emerge as part of the effective coping process (cf. Folkman & Moskowitz, 2000). Again, the same stringent methodological requirements, with baseline controls, have been included in the research that backs up these interpretations (Bonanno & Kaltman, 1999; chapters 22 and 25, this volume).

In the same way that pathways were included to explain why rumination led to poor adjustment, so have they been postulated for positive affect following a bereavement, by Folkman (1997; chapter 25, this volume) in her revised cognitive-stress model. First, meaning-based processes (e.g., positive reappraisals) lead to positive psychological states. Second, negative psychological states may motivate people to search for and create positive psychological states to gain relief (coping as a response to distress). Third, positive psychological states lead back to appraisal and coping, so that coping efforts are sustained.

Recent research has led us to conclude that the occurrence of positive emotions per se may not be sufficient to affect outcomes: Positive affect alone may not be efficacious in adaptive coping (cf. Pennebaker, Mayne, & Francis, 1997). Rather, it is positive meaning construction and reconstruction that makes up adaptive coping. This suggestion derives from analysis of differential results of studies of positive affect versus those where positive reappraisal seems to have been possible (cf. Schut, Stroebe, & Stroebe, 1999).

Confrontation–avoidance processes. It is apparent that grief work or disclosure would involve confrontation rather than avoidance—the benefits of which have been discussed previously. Denial or avoidance of grief has been considered maladaptive, notably in psychoanalytic formulations. Recently, however, investigators have provided evidence that avoidant strategies may be more functional than had previously been assumed. For example, Bonanno, Keltner, Holen, and Horowitz (1995; chapter 22, this volume) found a dissociation between physiologically measured arousal and indices of psychological upset among bereaved men who were placed in an "empty chair" situation, meaning that they were to imagine the presence of the deceased person in this chair, as someone to communicate with. High physiological arousal but low psychological confrontation were associated with good outcome (measured at a later time point). Thus although too complete a denial has frequently been associated with pathological forms of grieving (e.g., Jacobs, 1993), this study suggests that some degree of avoidance may be healthy. Evidence in support of this has begun to accumulate from other sources, including the benefits of keeping secrets (Kelly & McKillop, 1996) and, in certain circumstances, suppressing extremely traumatic experiences (Kaminer & Lavie, 1993). These studies all point to the possibility that at times it is potentially adaptive to "keep grief within" and regulate grieving. "Involuntary" nondisclosure may, however, have negative consequences: Lepore, Silver, Wortman, and Wayment (1996) found that bereaved mothers who perceived their social environments as constraining against disclosure and who had high initial levels of intrusive thoughts about their loss were more depressed in the long term. We would suggest that personal control over the regulation (confrontation–avoidance) of grieving may be critical. This needs further examination.

Taken together, how are the adaptive effects of confrontation versus avoidance to be understood? Bereaved individuals need to confront pain and work through loss, which is an effortful process. Yet they also need to fight against the reality of loss (cf. Janoff-Bulman, 1992). On the other hand, denial is also effortful. What empirical studies so far seem to indicate is that too much confrontation or too much avoidance is detrimental to adaptation. Both processes may be linked with detrimental health effects if undertaken relentlessly, causing exhaustion. Scientific analysis needs to explore and represent the tendency, even necessity, to confront combined with the tendency to avoid, deny, or suppress aspects of grieving as part of the adaptive coping process.

Interpersonal Coping Perspectives

There has been increasing interest in the interpersonal aspects of loss in the past several years, such that examination of more interactive coping processes is possible. It is important not simply to add a social dimension but to use this approach to try to provide an integrated scientific analysis (cf. M. Stroebe, Stroebe, & Schut, 1999).

Model of Incremental Grief

Basic to Cook and Oltjenbrun's (1998) model of incremental grief is the understanding that one loss can often trigger another loss. As a result, there is a magnification of grief, occurring with each added loss. These investigators describe the "dissyncrony of grief" among bereaved persons (particularly families), as different persons grieving together over the loss of a loved one exhibit discrepant coping styles. Asymmetry and incongruence in grieving is said to lead to secondary loss, meaning a change between the grievers in their relationship. The latter is an additional source of stress for the survivors. The argument, then, is that loss of a child (primary loss) would trigger change in the relationship with one's partner (secondary loss), and precipitate yet another loss, possibly divorce (tertiary loss). Thus "incremental loss" denotes "the additive factor of grief due to multiple related losses" (Cook & Oltjenbruns, 1998, p. 160). In this manner, Cook and Oltjenbruns (1998; chapter 8, this volume) place individual coping reactions within the context of the social environment in which they take place.

It seems fair to assume that poor adaptation to grief would be predicted in cases in which incremental grieving takes place. More specifically, one would predict that the outcome would be poor in cases of asymmetry and incongruence (this could potentially include individual health deficits as well as divorce). In contrast, couples coping "congruently" would probably be expected to adjust more easily—perhaps there is such a thing as "decremental" grieving? These analyses, then, introduce an important new dimension in understanding processes of adaptive coping and complement the more intrapersonal, cognitive-level perspectives described so far. Still needed, however, are operationalizations of "(in)congruence" and investigations of relationships to health detriments–benefits.

Social Construction Models

As described previously, Janoff-Bulman (e.g., Janoff-Bulman & Berg, 1998) argued the need to examine assumptive world views and the process of meaning (re)construction with respect to reactions to traumas in general. Likewise, one of the most significant new developments in the study of bereavement has been a recognition of grieving as a process of meaning reconstruction. This research has roots in symbolic interactionism and in family systems theory (see Rosenblatt, 1993; chapter 13, this volume). Similar to the approach of Cook and Oltjenbruns (1998), this type of research has focused on social process. Meaning is negotiated between (grieving) family members, and the process of coming to terms with bereavement is an ongoing effort. Assumptions about the relationship to the deceased are actively explored and adjusted, rather than static, entrenched phenomena. Bereaved people develop "narratives" about the nature of the deceased's life and death, and these "social constructions" themselves can affect the outcome of grief.

Some investigators have been more interested in how groups of bereaved people make meaning, for example among family members, during their bereavement (e.g., Nadeau, 1998; chapter 15, this volume) or in understanding grief "as an interpersonally constructed family developmental process in sociocultural context" (chapter 14, this volume; see also Shapiro, 1994) or in endeavoring to understand grief as a social construction per se (chapter 13, this volume) rather than exploring the ways that social constructions relate to outcome specifically. Though of related interest, these particular investigations are not, then, directly relevant to the question of adaptive coping.

Walter's new model of grief. Although not strictly a "coping model," Walter's (1996) new model of grief describes the "process" (as well as "purpose") of grief in such a way that we can draw hypotheses about adaptive coping. Walter (1996) proposes that the purpose of grief is to grasp the reality of the death. This is accomplished through "the construction of a durable biography that enables the living to integrate the memory of the dead into their ongoing lives" (p. 7). This is achieved principally through talking to others who knew the deceased. According to Walter, even if talking does not help adjustment in terms of recovery from distress, it does help in the process of biography construction, the dimension along which adjustment should, he says, be measured. Walter argued that grieving is done when a durable biography has been constructed that enables the living to integrate the memory of the dead into their ongoing lives. The emphasis is on talking rather than feeling and on a nonmedical outcome of grieving—namely, the relocation of the deceased: Adaptive coping would necessitate talking to people. Only if this is done can a durable biography be derived, and the deceased can move on and stop grieving, having found an ongoing place for the deceased. This novel perspective supplements the more traditional ones that have dominated the research field (see M. Stroebe, 1997, and Walter, 1997, for discourse on this model).

The meaning reconstruction model. Also in contrast to the emphasis in previous approaches on stages, tasks, or symptoms, Neimeyer's recent work (1998; Neimeyer, Keesee, & Fortner, 1998) has emphasized the extent to which one's adaptation to loss is shaped by personal, familial, and cultural factors. He suggested that meaning reconstruction is the central process of grieving (along similar lines, then, to Walter). He proposed six principles or "propositions" that would help in the construction of a more adequate theory of coping with bereavement, compatible with this perspective. Similar to Janoff-Bulman (1992), the first proposition concerned the (in)validation of beliefs, or experience for which there are no existing constructions; the second involved the personal nature of grief (our sense of who we are); the third, "grieving is something we do, not something that is done to us" (p. 101); the fourth requires reconstructing the personal world of meaning; the fifth focused on the functions (not just symptomatology) of grief feelings as signals of meaning-making efforts; and finally, the sixth places the griever in social context: We (re)construct our identities in negotiation with others.

How could these principles operate to bring about adaptation? The process of adaptation would entail confronting and exploring these concerns of loss. It involves an ongoing process of confrontation of the meaning of the deceased person for the bereaved individual and articulation of the personal construction of the relationship. Coping effectively with grief entails meaning reconstruction, or rebuilding of previously held beliefs, and negotiation and renegotiation over time. Lack of adaptation will occur if the bereaved person cannot explore and articulate his or her ongoing construction of the relationship with the deceased. It is interesting in this context to consider the cognitive–behavioral therapy approach, which is well-suited to assist bereaved persons who have trouble doing this (chapter 28, this volume).

Integrative Models of Coping With Bereavement

In our view (cf. Stroebe & Schut, 1998) a bereavement-specific rather than general model of adaptive coping is needed, although useful guidelines in the development of such a model can be derived from the more general theories. Our reasoning is that the manifestations of bereavement are complex and largely idiosyncratic to this particular stressor. We have reviewed very different types of investigation, and a diversity of mechanisms at different levels of analysis (e.g., intra- versus interpersonal) that provide insights into the processes of adaptive coping with bereavement. Is it possible to draw these threads together and to develop a model that incorporates the various components identified so far? Attempts at integration have been made by Bonanno and Kaltman (1999) and M. Stroebe & Schut (1999; in press).

The Four Component Model

Bonanno and Kaltman (1999) considered bereavement in terms of four components. The first of these is the *context of the loss*, which refers to risk factors such as type of death, age, gender, social support, and cultural setting. The second factor is the *continuum of subjective meanings associated with loss*, ranging from appraisals and evaluations of everyday matters and problems as well as existential concerns about the meaning of life and death. The third is the *changing representations of the lost relationship over time*, which plays an important role in the grieving process: "There appears to be an optimal or manageable level of grief that allows for the reorganization of the bereaved survivor's representational world into a supportive and ongoing bond with the deceased" (p. 770). The fourth factor—and the most important for current concerns—is that *the role of coping and emotion-regulation processes* highlights the range of coping strategies that may "potentially mollify or exacerbate the stress of loss" (p. 770). This component draws on the cognitive stress perspective described previously and on emotion theory. It is important to note that according to the latter perspective, "emotion is not a unitary phenomenon but, rather, manifests in multiple channels, including experiential, expressive, and physiological responses" (Bonanno & Kaltman, 1999, p. 771). They further argued that emotion regulation research can be used to show ways to draw these perspectives together, by showing how regulation of emotion may at times involve deliberate or strategic processing, at others, more spontaneous or automatic regulatory processing and thereby not available to conscious awareness—or easily captured by self-report instruments.

Bonanno and Kaltman (1999) identified an important aspect of emotion regulation in bereavement that would enhance adjustment—namely, the regulation or even dissociation of negative emotions and the enhancement of positive emotions: "These processes foster adjustment to loss because they help maintain relatively high levels of functioning, and thus contribute to retrospective reappraisals that the pain of loss can be coped with and that life can go on after the death of a loved one" (p. 771).

A unique aspect of Bonanno and Kaltman's (1999) model is the focus on emotion theory and on the identification of spontaneous or automatic processes. There is also some empirical support for this approach (e.g., Bonanno & Keltner, 1997; Bonanno et al., 1995). Adaptive ways of grieving may be better understood, then, if such processes are included in the analysis. Furthermore, this perspective adds weight to the argument that positive emotions foster adjustment. It also supports Folkman's (1997; chapter 25, this volume) analysis of positive appraisal pathways and her contention that negative emotion exacerbates grief. Similarly, it is consistent with Nolen-Hoeksema's analysis of ruminative pathways (Nolen-Hoeksema & Jackson, 1996; chapter 24, this volume).

The Dual Process Model of Coping With Bereavement

The different theories and models discussed previously complement and overlap one another with regard to our basic question: What is adaptive coping? Indeed, we have been influenced by many of these lines of argument in the formulation of our own dual process model of coping with bereavement (DPM; M. Stroebe & Schut, 1999; in press). As such, the DPM represents an attempt to integrate existing ideas rather than an altogether new model. Next we define the main parameters of the DPM, referring back to the detail provided in the models described so far.

Examination of previous formulations showed the need for precise definition of stressors associated with bereavement. The DPM defines two broad types of stressor. In grieving, people have to deal with a number of diverse stressors, which can be classified into those that are loss- versus restoration-oriented. "Loss-orientation" refers to the bereaved person's concentration on and processing of some aspect of the loss experience itself. The focus of attachment theory on the nature of the lost relationship would be consistent with this, as would the integration of grief work in this orientation. *Restoration-orientation* refers to the focus on secondary stressors that are also consequences of bereavement. Cognitive stress theory is applicable in assuming that a range of substressors may occur. Both orientations are sources of stress, are burdensome, and are associated with distress and anxiety. Both are, then, involved in the coping process and are attended to in varying degrees (according to individual and cultural variations). As a consequence, one can speak of "tasks" of grieving but, as noted previously, these are more extensive than described already.

It is important to represent confrontation versus avoidance of these two types of stressor as dynamic and fluctuating and also as changing over time. The DPM specifies a dynamic coping process (the regulatory process of "oscillation") that distinguishes it from these models. It is proposed that a bereaved person will alternate between loss- versus restoration-oriented coping. At times the bereaved will confront aspects of loss, at other times avoid them, and the same applies to the tasks of restoration. Sometimes, too, there will be "time out," when grieving is left alone. What emerges is a more complex regulatory process of confrontation and avoidance than that described earlier in the models of confrontation (disclosure) versus avoidance (denial). The DPM postulates that oscillation between the two types of stressors is necessary for adaptive coping. These two structural components are depicted in Figure 17-1.

Some of the models described showed the need to represent cognitive processes: meanings, assumptions, and types of expression associated with good versus poor adaptation. Drawing on the cognitive process models of positive versus negative (re)appraisal described, the DPM provides an analysis of cognitions related to the confrontation–avoidance process. Following these models, and the confrontation-avoidance analysis presented earlier, there are good reasons to argue the need for oscillation between positive and negative affect–(re)appraisal as an integral part of the coping process. Persistent negative affect enhances grief, yet working through grief, which includes rumination, has been identified as important in coming to terms with a bereavement. On the other hand, positive reappraisals sustain the coping effort. Yet if positive psychological states are maintained relentlessly, grieving is neglected. How can these aspects be integrated? Folk-

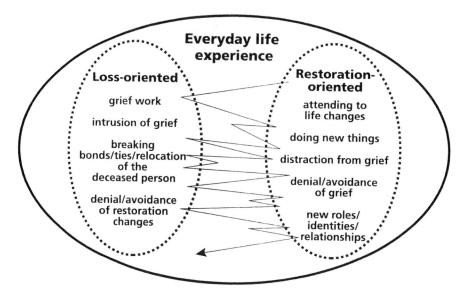

Figure 17-1. A Dual Process Model of Coping With Bereavement. Copyright Stroebe and Schut, 2001.

man's (1997; Folkman & Moskowitz, 2000; chapter 25, this volume) integration of positive meaning states in the revision of stress-coping theory can be incorporated into the DPM. Following the work of Nolen-Hoeksema (Nolen-Hoeksema & Jackson, 1996; chapter 24, this volume), also needed is integration of negative appraisals. This can be done by introducing pathways, again partially following these previous investigators, as shown in Figure 17-2.

Following this model, adaptive coping would require oscillation between positive and negative (re)appraisal (note our previous argument suggesting that positive emotions alone are not enough) in relationship not only to loss- but also restoration-orientation. This cognitive analysis provides a framework within which to address the types of assumptive worlds, meaning systems or life narratives of bereaved people, that many theorists have identified as critical to adaptive coping. Important for future research will be the analysis of regulatory control processes. For example, when and how does oscillation take place? To what extent is it (in)voluntary and how does this affect adaptive coping? Although these are questions for further examination, the introduction of the regulatory process of oscillation in the DPM amends previous grief work conceptions to include facilitative functions of periodic withdrawal from grieving, as emphasized by Rosenblatt (1983).

The DPM is also integrative in the sense that it is broadly applicable. For example, it lends itself to the analysis of between- and within-cultural group differences in ways of coping with grief; pathological grief manifes-

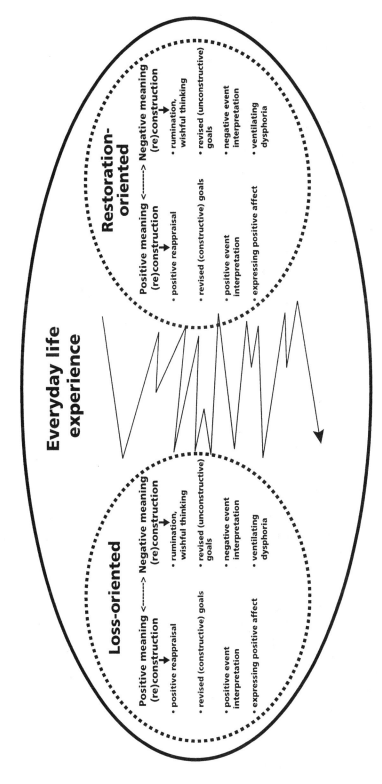

Figure 17-2. A Dual Process Model of Coping With Loss: Pathways. Copyright Stroebe and Schut, 2001.

tations; and duration of bereavement changes in adaptive coping (see M. Stroebe & Schut, 1999). Furthermore, although the analysis so far has been essentially intrapersonal, an interpersonal framework can be superimposed (cf. M. Stroebe et al., 1999). To take just one example: Individuals (and groups) differ in the extent to which they are loss- or restoration-oriented. Women tend to be more loss-oriented in their grieving than men (cf. Dijkstra, van den Bout, Stroebe, Schut, & Stroebe, 1999). The "profile" of coping with grief as represented in Figures 17-1 and 17-2 would be different for men and women. Because bereaved people typically grieve in families or other small groups, it would be predicted that lack of congruence in ways of grieving could lead to conflicts and poorer adaptation of the grievers. Parallels with Cook and Oltjenbruns's (1998) incremental grief model are evident. Furthermore, although the DPM was originally developed as a framework for understanding partner loss, it has application to other types of bereavement (e.g., parents grieving the loss of their child), and maybe even to stressors other than bereavement. It is also evident that the range of outcomes that can be examined within the DPM framework is not limited to health-related ones but that variables as different as the creation of a biography about the deceased, following the social constructionist focus described previously, or marital conflict (cf. Dijkstra & Stroebe, 1998) can be introduced for examination.

CONCLUSION

A scientific model of coping with bereavement is necessary for a number of reasons. It provides a basis for testing the validity of assumptions that people have about the coping process: Should we, following the poets, "give sorrow words," or should we "keep grief within"? Without a systematic analysis, how are we to know which assumption is valid, or whether people's beliefs about what is best for them, actually is (cf. chapter 18, this volume)? Further, we need theories to guide the planning of research. The task of scientists is to search for regularities, so that predictions can be made, for example, about the likelihood of poor adjustment. Theories of coping can also provide guidelines for the process of collecting valid data. Questionnaires for measuring coping used to be developed on the basis of clinical experience or intuition. Currently, theoretical models are deemed important for the development of assessment instruments: "Rational, theory-driven strategies are to be recommended over inductive, empirical approaches which run the risk of coincidental solutions" (chapter 20, this volume). Finally, there is applied as well as scientific motivation behind the model-building on adaptive coping. In understanding how people come to terms with loss, we learn much about the nature of grief itself, but we also need answers to questions about effective coping to help those who suffer extremely.

REFERENCES

Archer, J. (1999). *The nature of grief: The evolution and psychology of reactions to loss*. London: Routledge.

Billings, A. G., & Moos, R. H. (1981). The role of coping responses and social resources in attenuating the stress of life events. *Journal of Behavioral Medicine, 4*, 139–157.

Bonanno, G. (1998). The concept of "working through" loss: A critical evaluation of the cultural, historical, and empirical evidence. In A. Maercker, M. Schuetzwohl, & Z. Solomon (Eds.), *Posttraumatic stress disorder: Vulnerability and resilience in the life-span* (pp. 221–247). Göttingen, Germany: Hogrefe & Huber.

Bonanno, G. A. & Eddins, C. (2000). *Talking about the loss of a spouse: Different dimensions of verbal disclosure predict different outcomes*. Unpublished manuscript.

Bonanno, G., & Kaltman, S. (1999). Toward an integrative perspective on bereavement. *Psychological Bulletin, 125*, 760–776.

Bonanno, G. A., & Keltner, D. (1997). Facial expressions of emotion and the course of conjugal bereavement. *Journal of Abnormal Psychology, 106*, 126–137.

Bonanno, G. A., Keltner, D., Holen, A., & Horowitz, M. J. (1995). When avoiding unpleasant emotions may not be such a bad thing: Verbal-autonomic response dissociation and midlife conjugal bereavement. *Journal of Personality and Social Psychology, 69*, 975–989.

Bowlby, J. (1979). *The making and breaking of affectional bonds*. London: Tavistock.

Bowlby, J. (1980). *Attachment and loss. Vol. 3. Loss: Sadness and depression*. London: Hogarth.

Capps, L., & Bonanno, G. A. (2000). Narrating bereavement: Thematic and grammatical predictors of adjustment to loss. *Discourse Processes, 30*, 1–25.

Cook, A., & Oltjenbruns, K. (1998). *Dying and grieving: Lifespan and family perspectives*. Ft. Worth, TX: Harcourt Brace.

Dijkstra, I., & Stroebe, M. (1998). The impact of a child's death on parents: A myth (not yet) disproved? *Journal of Family Studies, 4*, 159–185.

Dijkstra, I., van den Bout, J., Stroebe, W., Schut, H., & Stroebe, M. (1999). Coping with the death of a child. A longitudinal study of discordance in couples. *Gedrag & Gezondheid, 27*, 103–108.

Finkenauer, C., & Rimé, B. (1998). Socially shared emotional experiences vs. emotional experiences kept secret: Differential characteristics and consequences. *Journal of Social and Clinical Psychology, 17*, 295–318.

Folkman, S. (1997). Positive psychological states and coping with severe stress. *Social Science and Medicine, 45*, 1207–1221.

Folkman, S., Chesney, M., McKusick, L., Ironson, G., Johnson, D., & Coates, T. (1991). Translating coping theory into an intervention. In J. Eckenrode (Ed.), *The social context of coping* (pp. 239–260). New York: Plenum Press.

Folkman, S., Lazarus, R. S., Gruen, R. J., & De Longis, A. (1986). Appraisal, coping, health status and psychological symptoms. *Journal of Personality and Social Psychology, 50*, 571–579.

Folkman, S, & Moskowitz, J. (2000). *Positive affect and the other side of coping. American Psychologist, 55*, 647–654.

Fraley, R. C., & Shaver, P. (1999). Loss and bereavement: Attachment theory and recent controversies concerning "grief work" and the nature of detachment. In J. Cassidy & P. R. Shaver (Eds.), *Handbook of attachment: Theory, research, and clinical applications* (pp. 735–759). New York: Guilford Press.

Freud, S. (1957). Mourning and melancholia. In J. Strachey (Ed. & Trans.), *Standard edition of the complete psychological works of Sigmund Freud.* London: Hogarth. (Original work published 1917)

Horowitz, M. (1983). Psychological response to serious life events. In S. Breznitz (Ed.), *The denial of stress.* New York: International Universities Press.

Horowitz, M. (1986). *Stress response syndromes.* Northvale, NJ: Aronson.

Jacobs, S. (1993). *Pathologic grief: Maladaptation to loss.* Washington, DC: American Psychiatric Press.

Janoff-Bulman, R. (1992). *Shattered assumptions: Towards a new psychology of trauma.* New York: Free Press.

Janoff-Bulman, R., & Berg, M. (1998). Disillusionment and the creation of value: From traumatic losses to existential gains. In J. H. Harvey (Ed.), *Perspectives on loss: A sourcebook* (pp. 35–47). Philadelphia: Taylor & Francis.

Kaminer, H., & Lavie, P. (1993). Sleep and dreams in well-adjusted and less adjusted Holocaust survivors. In M. Stroebe, W. Stroebe, & R. O. Hansson (Eds.), *Handbook of Bereavement: Theory, research and intervention* (pp. 331–345). New York: Cambridge University Press.

Kelly, A. E., & McKillop, K. J. (1996). Consequences of revealing personal secrets. *Psychological Bulletin, 120*, 450–465.

Keltner, D., & Bonanno, G. (1997). A study of laughter and dissociation: Distinct correlates of laughter and smiling during bereavement. *Journal of Personality and Social Psychology, 73*, 687–702.

Kleber, R., & Brom, D. (1992). *Coping with trauma: Theory, prevention, and treatment.* Amsterdam: Swets & Zeitlinger.

Lazarus, R., & Folkman, S. (1984). *Stress, appraisal and coping.* New York: Springer.

Lepore, S. J., Silver, R., Wortman, C., & Wayment, H. A. (1996). Social constraints, intrusive thoughts, and depressive symptoms among bereaved mothers. *Journal of Personality and Social Psychology, 70*, 271–282.

Nadeau, J. (1998). *Families making sense of death.* Thousand Oaks, CA: Sage.

Neimeyer, R. (1998). *The lessons of loss: A guide to coping.* Raleigh, NC: McGraw-Hill.

Neimeyer, R., Keesee, N., & Fortner, B. (1998). Loss and meaning reconstruction: Propositions and procedures. In S. Rubin, R. Malkinson, & E. Witztum (Eds.), *Traumatic and non-traumatic bereavement* (pp. 5–40). Madison, CT: International Universities Press.

Nolen-Hoeksema, S., & Jackson, B. (1996). *Ruminative coping and the gender differences in depression.* Paper presented at the American Psychological Association Meeting, Toronto, August 10.

Nolen-Hoeksema, S., & Larson, J. (1999). *Coping with loss.* Mahwah, NJ: Erlbaum.

Nolen-Hoeksema, S., Parker, L. E., & Larson, J. (1994). Ruminative coping with depressed mood following loss. *Journal of Personality and Social Psychology, 67,* 92–104.

Parkes, C. M. (1996). *Bereavement: Studies of grief in adult life* (3rd ed.). New York: International Universities Press.

Pennebaker, J. (1989). Confession, inhibition and disease. In L. Berkowitz (Ed.), *Advances in experimental social psychology* (Vol. 22, pp. 211–244). San Diego, CA: Academic Press.

Pennebaker, J. (1993). Putting stress into words: Health, linguistic, and therapeutic implications. *Behavior Research and Therapy, 31,* 539–548.

Pennebaker, J. (1995). *Emotion, disclosure, and health.* Washington, DC: American Psychological Association.

Pennebaker, J. (1997). Writing about emotional experiences as a therapeutic process. *Psychological Science, 8,* 162–166.

Pennebaker, J., & Beall, S. (1986). Confronting a traumatic event: Toward an understanding of inhibition and disease. *Journal of Abnormal Psychology, 95,* 274–281.

Pennebaker, J., & Francis, M. (1986). Cognitive, emotional, and language processes in disclosure. *Cognition and Emotion, 10,* 601–626.

Pennebaker, J., Mayne, T. J., & Francis, M. E. (1997). Linguistic predictors of adaptive bereavement. *Journal of Personality and Social Psychology, 72,* 863–871.

Raphael, B., Middleton, W., Martinek, N., & Misso, V. (1993). Counseling and therapy of the bereaved. In M. Stroebe, W. Stroebe, & R. O. Hansson (Eds.), *Handbook of bereavement: Theory, research and intervention* (pp. 427–453). New York: Cambridge University Press.

de Ridder, D. (1997). What is wrong with coping assessment? A review of conceptual and methodological issues. *Psychology and Health, 12,* 417–431.

Rimé, B., Finkenauer, C., Luminet, O., Zech, E., & Philippot, P. (1998). Social sharing of emotion: New evidence and new questions. In W. Stroebe & M. Hewstone (Eds.), *European Review of Social Psychology* (Vol. 9, pp. 145–189). Chichester, UK: Wiley.

Rosenblatt, P. (1983). *Bitter, bitter tears: Nineteenth century diarists and twentieth century grief theories.* Minneapolis: University of Minnesota Press.

Rosenblatt, P. (1993). Grief: The social context of private feelings. In M. Stroebe, W. Stroebe, & R. O. Hansson (Eds.), *Handbook of bereavement: Theory, research and intervention* (pp. 102–111). New York: Cambridge University Press.

Rosenblatt, P., Walsh, R., & Jackson, D. (1976). *Grief and mourning in cross-cultural perspective.* New Haven, CT: Human Relations Area Files.

Rubin, S. (1981). A two-track model of bereavement: Theory and application in research. *American Journal of Orthopsychiatry, 51,* 101–109.

Rubin, S. (1993). The death of a child is forever: The life course impact of child loss. In M. Stroebe, W. Stroebe, & R. O. Hansson (Eds.), *Handbook of bereavement: Theory, research and intervention* (pp. 285–299). New York: Cambridge University Press.

Rubin, S., & Schechter, N. (1997). Exploring the social construction of bereavement: Perceptions of adjustment and recovery for bereaved men. *American Journal of Orthopsychiatry, 67,* 279–289.

Sanders, C. (1989). *Grief: The mourning after.* New York: Wiley.

Schut, H., Stroebe, M., & Stroebe, W. (1999, August 20–24). *Positive and negative emotions in bereavement: Theoretical and empirical analysis.* Paper presented at the American Psychological Association Annual Conference, Boston.

Shapiro, E. (1994). *Grief as a family process: A developmental approach to clinical practice.* New York: Guilford Press.

Shuchter, S., & Zisook, S. (1993). The course of normal grief. In M. Stroebe, W. Stroebe, & R. O. Hansson (Eds.), *Handbook of bereavement: Theory, research and intervention* (pp. 23–43). New York: Cambridge University Press.

Stroebe, M. (1992). Coping with bereavement: A review of the grief work hypothesis. *Omega: Journal of Death and Dying, 26,* 19–42.

Stroebe, M. (1997). From mourning and melancholia to bereavement and biography: An assessment of Walter's New Model of Grief. *Mortality, 2,* 155–162.

Stroebe, M., & Schut, H. (1998, May 25–27). *(Why) do we need a stressor-specific model of coping with bereavement?* Second Dutch Conference on Psychology and Health, Rolduc, The Netherlands.

Stroebe, M., & Schut, H. (1999). The Dual Process Model of Coping with Bereavement: Rationale and description. *Death Studies, 23,* 197–224.

Stroebe, M., & Schut, H. (in press). Meaning making in the Dual Process Model. In R. Neimeyer (Ed.), *Meaning reconstruction and the experience of loss.* Washington, DC: American Psychological Association.

Stroebe, M., Schut, H., & Stroebe, W. (1998). Trauma and grief: A comparative analysis. In J. Harvey (Ed.), *Perspectives on loss: A sourcebook.* Washington, DC: Taylor & Francis.

Stroebe, M., & Stroebe, W. (1991). Does "grief work" work? *Journal of Consulting and Clinical Psychology, 59,* 479–482.

Stroebe, M., Stroebe, W., & Schut, H. (1999, August 20–24). *The social context of grief and grieving: A theoretical and empirical analysis.* Paper presented at the American Psychological Association Annual Conference, Boston.

Stroebe, W. (2000). *Social Psychology and Health.* Milton Keynes, UK: Open University Press.

Stroebe, W., & Stroebe, M. (1987). *Bereavement and health.* New York: Cambridge University Press.

Walter, T. (1996). A new model of grief: Bereavement and biography. *Mortality, 1,* 7–25.

Walter, T. (1997). Letting go and keeping hold: A reply to Stroebe. *Mortality, 2,* 263–266.

Wortman, C. B., & Silver, R. C. (1987). Coping with irrevocable loss. In G. R. Vandenbos & B. K. Bryant (Eds.), *Cataclysms, crises and catastrophes: Psychology in action* (pp. 189–235). Washington, DC: American Psychological Association.

Wortman, C. B., & Silver, R. C. (1989). The myths of coping with loss. *Journal of Consulting and Clinical Psychology, 57,* 349–357.

Worden, W. (1982/1991) *Grief counseling and grief therapy: A handbook for the mental health practitioner.* New York: Springer.

18

THE MYTHS OF COPING WITH LOSS REVISITED

CAMILLE B. WORTMAN AND ROXANE COHEN SILVER

In a well-publicized legal case in Arizona, John Henry Knapp was convicted of the murder of his two young daughters, who died in a fire that destroyed their one-bedroom trailer. The principal evidence offered against Knapp was that immediately after the fire, he was outwardly calm and talkative and showed no overt display of distress. He was ultimately sentenced to death and remained in prison for 13 years. At that point, new evidence emerged about the origin of the fire that exonerated Knapp, and he was released (Brill, 1983).

As this example illustrates, societal beliefs about the grieving process can exert a powerful influence on how bereaved individuals are treated. For the past two decades, we have attempted to address the following question: Are there certain beliefs or assumptions about how people should react to the loss of a loved one that are prevalent in Western culture? To determine whether such assumptions exist, we reviewed a number of theoretical models of reactions to loss, such as Freud's (1917/1957) grief work perspective and Bowlby's (1980) early attachment model of grief (see also Bonanno & Kaltman, 1999). We also examined books and articles written by and for clinicians and other health care providers that describe how bereaved individuals typically respond following a loss and what reactions are considered to be "normal." Finally, we reviewed books and articles written by and for bereaved individuals themselves (Silver & Wortman, 1980; Wortman & Silver, 1987, 1989).

Drawing from this material, we have maintained that in the United States today, there are strong and powerful assumptions about how people should react to the loss of a loved one. In previous papers, we have identified and discussed several different assumptions that are prevalent in Western culture (Silver & Wortman, 1980; Wortman & Silver, 1987, 1989, 1992; Wortman, Silver, & Kessler, 1993). First is that following a loss, individuals will go through a period of intense distress. Positive emotions are implicitly assumed to be absent during this period. Second it is assumed that failure to experience such distress is indicative of a problem. Third it is believed that successful adjustment to the loss requires that individuals confront and "work through" their feelings. Fourth, continued attachment to the person who died has generally been viewed as pathological, and the necessity of breaking down the attachment to the loved one is often considered to be a key component of the mourning process. Fifth, it is assumed that within a year or two, people will recover from the loss and return to earlier levels of functioning.

We maintain that it is extremely important to articulate assumptions about the grieving process that may be implicit in Western culture, and to subject these assumptions to careful scientific scrutiny. If it is generally assumed that the coping process should unfold in a particular way, bereaved individuals who do not conform to these expectations may receive harsh treatment, as was the case for Knapp. If counseling for bereaved individuals is based on erroneous assumptions, it may ultimately prove unhelpful. Friends and family members may have difficulty offering appropriate forms of support to a bereaved person if they are misinformed about the grieving process. Finally, those who have encountered a loss may be confused and distressed by their own responses if they have misconceptions about how they are supposed to react.

In our earlier papers (Silver & Wortman, 1980; Wortman & Silver, 1987, 1989) we carried out a systematic evaluation of the aforementioned assumptions, focusing on the best scientific evidence available at the time of our reviews. Because beliefs concerning the grieving process are firmly entrenched in our culture, we anticipated that they would be supported by the empirical data. Although the data were not always consistent, and although some of the assumptions had not been heavily researched, our review provided virtually no support for any of the assumptions we examined. For this reason, we came to label them "myths of coping with loss."

Some of our colleagues praised us for challenging the validity of prevailing assumptions and calling attention to the absence of empirical support for them (e.g., Bonanno & Kaltman, 1999; Fraley & Shaver, 1999). In contrast, others were more critical of our efforts. Some questioned our operational definitions of certain constructs (e.g., Fraley & Shaver, 1999) or our interpretations of specific studies (e.g., M. Stroebe, van den Bout, & Schut, 1994). Others maintained that we overstated the degree to which researchers and clinicians believe the myths we identified (e.g., Parkes, 1998; M. Stroebe et al., 1994). Such scrutiny of our position is not surprising when one considers that in many cases, treatment practices are based on the validity of these assumptions. For example, many current treatments are specifically designed to help individuals "work through" their loss or break down their attachment to the deceased (see, e.g., Worden, 1991). If assumptions about the importance of these processes are shown to lack support, some of the most widely used treatment approaches in the field could be questioned.

Now that nearly a decade has passed and new research has been completed, we felt it would be worthwhile to revisit the so-called myths of coping that we identified earlier. In this chapter, we draw from a series of recent, methodologically rigorous studies to reevaluate assumptions about the grieving process that we identified earlier. We then explore the implications of our review for subsequent research on, and interventions for, bereaved individuals.

NEW RESEARCH EVIDENCE PERTAINING TO THE "MYTHS OF COPING"

In the past decade, many new studies relevant to the myths of coping have been conducted (see Bonanno & Kaltman, 1999, for a review). Some new cross-sectional studies have examined the reactions of bereaved individuals from a few months to several decades after the loss (e.g., Wortman, Kessler, Bolger, House, & Carnelley, 1999). Others have begun assessing bereaved individuals within the first few months after the death and have continued assessments at various points thereafter (see, e.g., Bonanno, Keltner, Holen, & Horowitz, 1995; Murphy, 1997). Still others have focused on individuals whose spouse or partner is ill, and assessed relevant variables before, and at various intervals after, the death (e.g., Folkman, Chesney, Collette, Boccellari, & Cooke, 1996; Nolen-Hoeksema, McBride, & Larson, 1997). Finally, some followed large community samples across time and studied those who became bereaved between measurement periods (see, e.g., Carnelley, Wortman, & Kessler, 1999; Harlow, Goldberg, & Comstock, 1991; Mendes de Leon, Kasl, & Jacobs, 1994).

As was the case years ago, most bereavement studies focus on the loss of a spouse. However, there have been some new and important studies on reactions to the loss of a child (e.g., Murphy, 1997) or parent (Silverman,

Nickman, & Worden, 1992), as well as studies that have compared reactions to various types of familial loss (e.g., Cleiren, 1993; Cleiren, Diekstra, Kerkhof, & van der Wal, 1994). In most investigations, the group being studied is heterogeneous with respect to cause of death. However, some have focused on specific kinds of losses, such as parents whose children experienced a sudden, violent death (Murphy, 1997) or gay male caregivers whose partner died of AIDS (Folkman et al., 1996). A few studies have compared two or more groups of respondents who died under different circumstances (e.g., natural causes, accident, or suicide; see Cleiren, 1993; Cleiren et al., 1994).

Because of the number of excellent studies that have appeared in the past decade, we are now able to put the myths of coping to a rigorous test. These new studies include a wider variety of bereaved samples and research designs, and a greater number of operational definitions of key constructs. Thus we are now able to consider whether these myths hold true across various kinds of bereavement and deaths that occur under various conditions.

The Expectation of Intense Distress

As we discussed in earlier papers (Wortman & Silver, 1987, 1989), when a major loss is experienced, it is assumed that the normal way to react is with intense distress or with depression. As we previously noted, many of the most prevalent theories in the area of loss, such as classic psychoanalytic models (e.g., Freud, 1917/1957) and Bowlby's (1980) attachment model, are based on the assumption that at some point, individuals will confront the reality of their loss and experience a period of depression. Of course, no theorists took the extreme position that all individuals who experienced a loss would go through a full major depression. However, it was generally believed that most people experienced "intense emotional distress ... with features similar in nature and intensity to those of clinical depression" (Osterweis, Solomon, & Green, 1984, p. 18). This view is still very much in evidence today. For example, Sanders (1999) has maintained that once the bereaved individual has come to grips with the loss, he or she will go through a phase of grief that "can be one of the most frightening periods in the grief process because it seems so like clinical depression" (p. 78).

The studies reviewed in our original papers indicated that, depending on the sample and the assessment procedure used, from about 20 to 35% of people who lost a spouse experienced depression in the first few months after the death (cf. Wortman & Silver, 1989). Very similar results have emerged from subsequent studies of conjugal loss. For example, in a prospective study of individuals over the age of 65 who became widowed following a large baseline survey, 37.5% reported high depressive symptomatology during the first year of bereavement (Mendes de Leon et al., 1994; see Bonanno et al., 1995; and Bruce, Kim, Leaf, & Jacobs, 1990, for similar findings).

Two recent studies have found somewhat higher rates of depression following the loss of a loved one. In their study of caregivers of gay men who died of AIDS, Folkman et al. (1996) reported that 1 month after the loss, 75 to 80% of the respondents were evidencing clinically significant levels of depression. Similarly, in her study on the sudden, traumatic death of a child, Murphy (1997) reported that four months postdeath, more than 80% of the mothers and more than 60% of the fathers rated themselves as highly distressed. Murphy's scores are comparable to those obtained in our study of reactions to the loss of an infant to SIDS, where approximately 70% were classified as depressed at the initial assessment three weeks after the death (Wortman & Silver, 1987). It is interesting to note that both Folkman and Murphy emphasized that, despite the severity of the stressor their respondents were facing and the short period of time that had passed, a "significant minority" of respondents reported low levels of depressive mood or did not rate themselves as highly distressed.

When we have presented these data, colleagues have sometimes pointed out that those respondents who do not exhibit pathological or major depression may still be evidencing significant but less intense levels of depression. The aforementioned studies do not really speak to this issue, because they do not include measures of mild or subsyndromal depression. However, a prospective study of conjugally bereaved individuals over age 45 conducted by Bruce et al. (1990) did include a measure of dysphoria as well as depression. Dysphoria was defined as two weeks or more of feeling "sad, blue, depressed or when you lost all interest and pleasure in things you usually cared about or enjoyed." About 60% of the respondents had experienced dysphoria, but a significant minority (almost 40%) did not go through even a two-week period of sadness following their loss. Even more striking results have been reported by Zisook, Paulus, Shuchter, and Judd (1997) in their study of elderly widows and widowers. Research participants' ratings on symptom inventories were used to classify them into DSM-IV categories of major depression, minor depression, subsyndromal depression (endorsing any two symptoms from the DSM-IV symptom list), and no depression (endorsing one or no items reflecting depression). Two months after bereavement, 20% were classified as showing major depression, 20% were classified as exhibiting minor depression, 11% were classified as evidencing subsyndromal depression, and 49% were classified as evidencing no depression. These studies provide compelling evidence that following the loss of a spouse, a substantial minority of respondents show few signs of sadness. Comparable findings have been reported by Cleiren

(1993) in his study of how adults react to the loss of a spouse, child, sibling, or parent.

In our original articles, we noted that many people not only exhibited less distress than anticipated but actually experience positive emotions far more frequently than might have been expected. At three weeks following the loss of a baby to SIDS, parents reported experiencing positive emotions such as happiness as frequently as they experienced negative feelings (Wortman & Silver, 1987). Similar findings have been obtained in more recent studies. When caregivers of men who died of AIDS were asked to talk about their experiences and then emotions were coded from the dialogue, about 80% evidenced positive emotions and only 61% of respondents showed negative emotions (Stein, Folkman, Trabasso, & Christopher-Richards, 1997; see also Folkman, 1997). Comparable findings were obtained by Bonanno and Keltner (1997), who coded facial expressions of conjugally bereaved respondents while they were describing their relationship with the deceased. Videotapes of interviews were coded for the presence of genuine or "Duchenne" laughs or smiles, which involve movements in the muscles around the eyes. Not only was positive emotion exhibited by the majority of participants, but its presence was correlated with reduced grief 14 and 25 months postloss (see also chapter 22, this volume). These studies suggest that it is indeed normal to experience positive emotions following a major loss.

Viewing the Failure to Experience Distress as Problematic

Historically, the absence of grief following bereavement has been viewed as an indication that the grieving process was abnormal or "pathologic" (e.g., Deutsch, 1937; Marris, 1958; Osterweis et al., 1984). As M. Stroebe, Hansson, and Stroebe (1993) have indicated, however, there are many possible reasons why an individual may not exhibit intense distress following loss that would not necessarily be considered pathological (e.g., early adjustment following an expected loss, perhaps coupled with relief following an end to suffering). Nonetheless, available evidence suggests that most practicing clinicians continue to maintain either explicitly or implicitly that there is something wrong with individuals who do not exhibit grief or depression. In a survey of researchers and clinicians in the field of loss (Middleton, Moylan, Raphael, Burnett, & Martinek, 1993), respondents were asked to indicate whether certain variants of the grieving process occur, and if so, to describe their features. A majority (65%) agreed that "absent grief" exists, that it typically occurs as a result of intrapsychic causes such as denial or inhibition, and that it is generally maladaptive in the long run. This is because it is assumed that if grief is not expressed, a "delayed grief reaction" will surface at some point in the future or health problems will subsequently emerge (Worden, 1991).

In our earlier papers, we reviewed a number of studies that indicated that a delayed grief reaction is very rare. New studies support this conclusion. For example, in a study that followed the conjugally bereaved for five years, Bonanno and his associates reported that virtually no participants showed a delayed grief reaction (Bonanno et al., 1995; Bonanno & Field, in press; Bonanno, Znoj, Siddique, & Horowitz, 1999). A small number of respondents did report increased somatic complaints at later points in time, although these complaints were not related to frequency of visits to medical professionals (see also Middleton, Burnett, Raphael, & Martinek, 1996). Nonetheless, in the previously described survey by Middleton et al. (1993), a substantial majority (76.6%) of researchers and clinicians indicated that delayed grief does occur.

"Absent grief" has also been viewed as evidence for a character weakness in the survivor. For example, Horowitz (1990) has suggested that among those who show little overt grief are "narcissistic personalities" who "may be too developmentally immature to have an adult type of relationship and so cannot exhibit an adult type of mourning at its loss" (p. 301). Although such a view is often espoused in the clinical literature, it has not, to our knowledge, been put to an empirical test.

A prospective longitudinal study by Wheaton (1990) has helped to clarify one important reason why some bereaved individuals may not exhibit intense distress following loss. In a provocative analysis, Wheaton (1990) argued that for some people, the death of a loved one may represent the end of a chronically stressful situation, such as a bad marriage or heavy caregiving responsibilities. In fact, he demonstrated that when the marriage is viewed as a chronic stressor, mental health actually increases following the death of a spouse.

In sum, research continues to support our original conclusion that the failure to experience grief appears not to portend subsequent difficulties.

The Importance of "Working Through" The Loss

It is widely assumed in Western culture that to adapt successfully to a major loss, a person must "work through" what has happened. M. Stroebe (1992) has defined working through as "a cognitive process of confronting a loss, of going over the events before and at the time of the death, of focusing on memories and working towards detachment from the deceased" (p. 20). Although there is some debate about exactly what it means to "work through" a loss, most grief theorists agree that it requires an active, ongoing effort to come to terms with the death (Rando, 1993; M. Stroebe, 1992). Attempts to deny its implications, or avoid feelings or thoughts about it, are ultimately regarded as unproductive. Grief work has also been described as having an "obsessional" quality, in which the bereaved person repeatedly reviews thoughts about the loved one and his or her death

(Sanders, 1999). This process is seen as being invariably painful, but it is believed that the pain must be confronted and experienced (see, e.g., Rando, 1993; Worden, 1991).

In our original papers, we were unable to locate any studies designed specifically to test the value of "working through" the loss. However, we reported some data from our own research on SIDS loss that we felt was relevant to this concept. We identified items thought to reflect parents' active attempts to make sense of and process the death, including searching for an answer for why the baby had died, thinking of ways the death could have been avoided, and being preoccupied with thoughts about the loss. The more parents engaged in these activities at three weeks after their loss, the more distressed they were 18 months later. In her review of the literature on "working through," M. Stroebe (1992) was critical of our interpretation, suggesting that what we had termed "working through" probably was, at least in part, an indication of rumination. Stroebe acknowledged, however, that shortly after a loss, it may be difficult to tell when a bereaved person's review of thoughts and feelings about a loved one represents rumination and when it represents "working through" (cf. Nolen-Hoeksema et al., 1997).

During the past decade, a number of new studies have appeared in the literature regarding the value of working through a loss. These studies have assessed one or more constructs that seem relevant to the process of working through, including thinking about one's relationship with the loved one (Nolen-Hoeksema et al., 1997); expressing high distress on self-report measures of emotion (Cleiren, 1993); verbally expressing negative feelings or showing negative facial expressions (Bonanno & Keltner, 1997); confronting thoughts and reminders of the loss versus avoiding reminders and using distraction (M. Stroebe & Stroebe, 1991); disclosing or expressing one's thoughts and feelings to others (Lepore, Silver, Wortman, & Wayment, 1996); and expressing one's feelings through writing about the loss (Pennebaker, Mayne, & Francis, 1997).

When "working through" is defined in these ways, there is little indication that bereaved individuals who show evidence of "working through" their loss ultimately cope better than those who do not. In a study of gay men who lost a partner to AIDS, Nolen-Hoeksema et al. (1997) found that those who thought about their life without the partner, and how they had changed as a result of the loss, showed positive morale shortly after the death, but showed more persistent depression over the 12 months following the loss. Evidencing high self-reported distress shortly after the loss has consistently been shown to be a powerful predictor of poor grief resolution (see, e.g., Cleiren, 1993; or see M. Stroebe, 1992, for a review). Bonanno and Keltner (1997) found that those who expressed negative feelings or manifested negative facial expressions in an interview showed higher interviewer-rated grief 14 months postloss, even when initial levels of grief were controlled. In a study designed specifically to compare those who used avoidant versus more confrontative coping styles in dealing with conjugal loss, Bonanno et al. (1995; in press) asked bereaved individuals to speak about their lost loved one and then complete scales indicating what they were experiencing. Physiological data assessing their cardiovascular reactivity were simultaneously collected. Those who evidenced emotional avoidance (i.e., little emotion relative to their physiological scores) showed low levels of interviewer-rated grief throughout the two-year study. There was no relationship between initial emotional avoidance and the delayed emergence of grief symptoms. Although respondents with an avoidant style did show higher levels of somatic complaints at six months postloss, these symptoms did not persist beyond the six-month assessment and were unrelated to medical visits.

Results in all of the aforementioned studies run directly counter to what the "working through" hypothesis would predict. There are a few studies that provide support for the value of "working through" a loss under some conditions or on some measures but not others. M. Stroebe and Stroebe (1991) found that 18 months following the loss of a spouse, there were no differences between widows who confronted their loss (i.e., did not avoid reminders and disclosed their feelings to others) and those who did not. In fact, widowers who confronted their grief showed lower depression scores over time. One study focusing on disclosure of feelings found that talking about the loss of an infant to SIDS resulted in lower subsequent rates of depression if people in the social environment were supportive of emotional disclosures but higher rates of depression if they reacted negatively to emotional disclosures (Lepore et al., 1996). Finally, writing about a trauma resulted in fewer health visits than writing about a trivial event (Pennebaker, 1997; Pennebaker et al., 1997). Those who demonstrated this effect showed an increase in the use of causal and insight words, suggesting successful "working through." However, writing about trauma had no effect on self-reported psychological distress. Finally, there are two studies suggesting that certain kinds of emotional avoidance may be detrimental in coping with the loss of a loved one. Nolen-Hoeksema and Larson (1999) and Rubin (1996) have reported that avoiding loss through increased reliance on alcohol or substance abuse is associated with prolonged distress.

All of the previously reviewed studies focused on bereaved respondents recruited from the general population. What about individuals who participate in grief counseling or grief therapy? It is widely accepted that such treatments can facilitate the process of "working through" a loss, and indeed some treatments are specifically designed to confront feelings about the deceased gradually (Mawson, Marks, Ramm, & Stern, 1981; Volkan, 1981). Although a review of the grief treatment literature is beyond the scope of this chapter, a recent meta-analysis of studies on grief therapy raises serious questions about the efficacy of bereavement interventions. Fortner and Neimeyer (cited in Neimeyer, 2000) located all scientifically adequate outcome evaluations of grief therapy published between 1975, when the first such studies appeared, and 1998. Of these 23 studies, grief therapy was provided by professional therapists in 19 of them and by non-professionals in the remainder. The analysis revealed a significant but small effect size (.15). This means that the average participant in grief therapy was better off than only 55% of bereaved persons who received no treatment for anxiety or depression. It is interesting to note that these investigators found that 38% of those who received grief counseling showed deterioration as a result of their treatment. According to Neimeyer (2000), this rate is many times higher than the 5% rate typically shown in psychotherapy for various problems. Treatment outcome was found to be completely unrelated to the length of treatment, to the level of training of the therapist, and to the type of treatment approach (individual, family, or group). Better outcomes were achieved by clients for whom more time had passed since the loss. The results revealed that when normal grievers were offered counseling, this resulted in no positive effect and a 50% probability of deterioration. In studies dealing with grief following a sudden, traumatic death or chronic grief, a reliable positive effect was found ($d = .38$), and the potential for deterioration was substantially lower (17%) than for normal grievers.

Why are these treatment effects so modest, even for traumatic or chronic grief reactions? According to Neimeyer (2000), grief therapy studies typically offer treatments that are not based on well-delineated conceptual models and are often not described in any detail. When it is described, "it tends to be based on suspiciously simplistic models, such as stage theories of grieving that have been largely repudiated by contemporary theorists and researchers" (Neimeyer, 2000, p. 8). As Foa and Meadows (1997) have indicated, there have been major advances in what is regarded as a methodologically sound treatment study over the past decade. As a result, methods that were acceptable, or even common in earlier studies, are no longer considered scientifically rigorous today. Parameters of a methodologically rigorous study include such features as reliable and valid measures, clearly defined treatment programs that are manualized and replicable, and random assignment of research participants to various treatment and control conditions (see Foa & Meadows, 1997, for a more complete list of parameters that a treatment study must include to meet the "gold standard" of treatment outcome studies today).

Although we have not encountered many such studies in the field of bereavement, there are outstanding research programs on treatment for rape victims that can be interpreted as showing that "working through" the implications of a traumatic event can be beneficial (Foa & Rothbaum, 1997; Resick & Schnicke, 1992). These authors have each developed brief but remarkably effective treatments for rape victims based on having them repeatedly reexperience the event within the context of individual therapy. They then perform in vivo exposure "homework" in which they confront avoided places and things. Frank, Prigerson, Shear, and Reynolds (1997) have recently adapted Foa and Rothbaum's approach to people suffering from intense or prolonged grief, and preliminary results appear highly encouraging.

In summary, this review indicates that there are several different ways of working through versus avoiding the thoughts and feelings associated with a loss. As Archer (1999) has noted, at this point we have little empirical data regarding how these approaches to grieving are related to one another, and little evidence that the "confrontative" strategies are associated with better outcomes than the "avoidant" ones. In fact, confrontative strategies such as thinking about one's relationship with the loved one or how the death occurred often portend subsequent difficulties. Avoidant coping strategies may predict or facilitate subsequent adjustment as long as they do not take maladaptive forms such as enhanced use of alcohol or drugs. When one moves from bereavement studies on the general population to treatment studies, the evidence in favor of working through does not improve. Although most treatments are designed to facilitate working through, a recent review suggests that as a whole, such treatments are rarely effective, but conceptual and methodological problems make many bereavement studies difficult to interpret. Two conceptually grounded and methodologically rigorous treatment programs on rape suggest that therapy can indeed help people work through a trauma. We believe these programs hold great promise for application to bereaved individuals.

The Necessity of Breaking Down Attachments

An important element in working through loss involves dealing with one's attachment to the lost loved one. Historically, Freud (1917/1957) and other psychoanalytic writers emphasized the importance of breaking down the affective bonds to the deceased. According to this view, grief work is completed only when the bereaved person withdraws energy from the deceased person and has freed him- or herself from attachment to an unavailable individual. This view continued to be influential for many years, with its advocates maintaining that if attachments are not broken down, the bereaved person will be unable to invest energy in new relationships and pursuits (see, e.g., Rando, 1984; Raphael, 1983).

These views about the importance of breaking down attachments were not shared by Bowlby (1980). As Fraley and Shaver (1999) pointed out in an insightful analysis, Bowlby maintained in his later writings that continuing attachments to the deceased, such as sensing his or her presence or talking with him or her, can provide an important sense of continuity and facilitate adaptation to the loss (see also chapter 4, this volume). A similar view has been advocated recently by Klass, Silverman, and Nickman (1996). Although they were trained to expect grief resolution to be accompanied by breaking down attachments to the lost loved one, these investigators reported that this is not what they observed in their research or their clinical interviews with bereaved individuals. Instead, their work suggested that it is common for bereaved individuals to remain connected to the deceased and that these connections "provided solace, comfort, and support, and eased the transition from the past to the future" (p. xvii).[1]

When our earlier papers were written, the prevailing view among clinicians was that breaking down attachments was indeed essential for mourning (see, e.g., Rando, 1984; Raphael, 1983; Worden, 1982). Therefore, we were surprised to find several well-controlled studies suggesting that continued and persistent attachments to the deceased were very common (see, e.g., Parkes & Weiss, 1983; Rees, 1971). Parkes and Weiss (1983) speculated that forms of attachment such as sensing the presence of the deceased facilitated recovery. At that time, however, there was little empirical data linking attachment to the deceased to subsequent adjustment.

Recent studies continue to provide evidence that continued attachments to the deceased are quite common. For example, Zisook and Shuchter (1993) reported that 13 months after a spouse's death, 63% of respondents agreed that they feel their spouse is with them at times, 47% felt that he or she is watching out for them, and 34% talked with their spouse regularly. Similarly, in their study of how children cope with the loss of a parent, Silverman and Nickman (1996) reported that four months after the death, it was common for children to maintain an active and apparently beneficial tie to the deceased. The clear majority of children (74%) located their parents in heaven, and most viewed the parent as watching out for them. It was also common for children to reach out to the deceased to maintain a connection, with almost 60% talking with him or her and 43% indicating that they received an answer. Types of connections identified in other new studies include incorporation of virtues of the deceased into one's own character (Normand, Silverman, & Nickman, 1996), using the deceased as a role model, turning to the deceased for guidance regarding a particular problem, and reflecting on the death to clarify one's current values (Marwit & Klass, 1996).

These types of continued connections with the deceased can be viewed as comforting to bereaved individuals. Nonetheless, as Fraley and Shaver (1999) have emphasized, many of these same studies have reported

---

[1]Klass et al. (1996) contrasted their view that continued attachment can be beneficial with Freud and Bowlby's views that such attachments are indicative of pathology. Fraley and Shaver (1999) maintained, however, that Klass et al. have failed to recognize Bowlby's opinion regarding the value of attachments, as reflected in his later writings, and that it is actually almost identical to the view they espouse.

that among a significant minority of survivors, ongoing connections with the deceased were not always comforting. For example, 57% of the children in the study by Silverman and Nickman (1996) indicated that they were "scared" by the idea that their parents could watch them from heaven. In fact, some children regarded their deceased parent as a ghost "whose presence was frightening, unpredictable, and out of their control" (Normand et al., 1996, p. 88; see also Tyson-Rawson, 1996).

The literature is clear in suggesting that it is indeed common for individuals to maintain an attachment to the deceased, that this link can be perceived as comforting or frightening, and that there are many different forms that this attachment may take. What is less clear, however, is whether there is a relationship between specific attachment behaviors and subsequent resolution of grief. In the only study we could locate on this issue, interviewers rated the extent to which bereaved respondents manifested four different kinds of attachment six months following loss, and subsequently asked them to engage in a monologue role play with their deceased spouse (Field, Nichols, Holen, & Horowitz, 1999). This exercise has been found to be a powerful vehicle for confronting bereaved individuals with the reality of their loss. Results indicated that bereaved individuals who sought comfort through memories of their loved ones experienced less distress in the monologue. However, those who tended to hang on to possessions, or sought comfort through contact with the deceased's belongings, showed greater distress during it. The investigators also examined the relationship between attachment behaviors and grief symptomology and resolution over time. They found that those bereaved individuals who hung on to the deceased's possessions, or attempted to gain comfort through contact with the possessions, evidenced higher grief-specific symptoms over a two-year period, and less of a decrease in grief symptoms over time. These findings suggest that whether continuing attachment with the deceased is adaptive or maladaptive may depend on the form that this attachment takes. Many forms of attachment identified in earlier studies, such as adopting virtues of the deceased, were not examined in this study, and thus no information is available about their adaptive value.

The Expectation of Recovery

Once they have completed the process of "working through" the loss, it is generally believed that bereaved individuals will achieve a state of recovery where they can encounter reminders without pain and they can return to normal levels of functioning. Those who fail to recover after an "appropriate" amount of time are often viewed as displaying "chronic grief" (see, e.g., Jacobs, 1993), which is widely regarded as an indication of "pathological mourning" (Middleton et al., 1993). Although Lindemann (1944) originally maintained that, with appropriate psychiatric intervention, it was usually possible to resolve a grief reaction in four to six weeks, many have suggested that this view was overly optimistic (see, e.g., Rando, 1993). In fact, Worden (1991) wrote that he would be suspicious "of any full resolution that takes under a year, and for many, two years is not too long" (p. 18). However, there are many textbooks as well as articles in the popular press that suggest that after approximately one year, individuals who lose a spouse should be "back to normal" (see Wortman et al., 1999, for a more detailed discussion).

Moreover, within a relatively brief period of time, individuals are expected to be able to remember the deceased and confront reminders of the loss without intense emotional pain (Parkes & Weiss, 1983; Rando, 1993). Many people continue to view recovery as the endpoint of the bereavement process and still evaluate bereaved people by judging whether they are taking "too long" to reach this endpoint. However, it appears that views of the recovery process are beginning to change (Silverman & Klass, 1996). Rando (1993) has pointed out that terms like "resolution" and "recovery" are not applicable to most losses because they imply a type of once-and-for-all closure that typically does not occur. Similarly, Miller and Omarzu (1998) emphasized that many are gradually acknowledging that bereaved individuals may never return to their preloss state. In fact, they maintain that this may not even be an optimal goal. They suggest that rather than expecting a return to the status quo, bereavement researchers should remain open to the notion that people may continue to negotiate and process their loss for many years.

In individual studies, the question of whether a bereaved person has "recovered" from the loss has been approached in several different ways. In cross-sectional studies, investigators have attempted to determine whether those who have been bereaved for many years show fewer symptoms of grief or distress than those bereaved more recently (see, e.g., Barrett & Schneweis, 1980). In longitudinal studies beginning before the loved one has died, recovery has been defined as a return to the baseline level of depression (e.g., Harlow et al., 1991); those who become depressed following the first interview and remain depressed over time are viewed as exhibiting "chronic grief" and as not recovering. In studies that have included a control group of married individuals who do not become bereaved, recovery has been defined as the length of time it takes bereaved individuals to reach the depression score of married individuals (e.g., Bruce et al., 1990). In each of these kinds of studies, recovery has also been conceptualized by examining whether or when bereaved respondents score below a cut-off designed to reflect a particular symptom or diagnosis—usually depression, which is considered the cardinal symptom of grief.

Although cross-sectional studies are generally viewed as less valuable in studying the grieving process than longitudinal ones (Wortman, Sheedy, Gluhoski, & Kessler, 1992), they are uniquely valuable in examining the issue of long-term recovery. There are virtually no longitudinal studies that have followed individuals more than a few years after the loss, but cross-sectional studies can provide information about how respondents are doing several years or decades later. For example, Lehman, Wortman, and Williams (1987) study on the long-term impact of losing a spouse or child in a motor vehicle accident four to seven years after loss found that the majority of respondents had painful memories about their loved one in the previous month. In one cross-sectional investigation, Barrett and Schneweis (1980) interviewed a large representative sample of elderly people who had lost their spouses; respondents were divided at the median (8.5 years) by length of bereavement. Results revealed no significant differences on the vast majority of measures included in the study, such as happiness and loneliness.

Long-term cross-sectional data on recovery are also available from Rubin's (1996) study of two groups of bereaved parents in Israel: one who lost their sons 4 years earlier in the Lebanon war and another who lost their sons 13 years earlier in the Yom Kippur war. In both cases, bereaved parents were compared with control parents who had not lost their sons on a wide range of measures, and there were demonstrable differences between the bereaved and nonbereaved parents. Moreover, these effects were apparent for at least a decade. For example, the bereaved parents were more anxious than the nonbereaved parents, and the passage of time did not affect this outcome. Time also failed to differentiate between the two bereaved groups on other important measures, including preoccupation with the loss and somatic symptoms.

Wortman et al. (1999) conducted a study involving a nationally representative sample of approximately 800 conjugally bereaved individuals who lost their spouses anywhere from 1 to 60 years before data collection. The study included several dependent measures designed to clarify the recovery process, such as the frequency of memories and conversations about the deceased and whether these were perceived as painful. Results of this study indicate that the process of adjustment continues for many years. Individuals initially reported that they experienced painful feelings when they thought or talked about their spouses, but the frequency of such painful feelings appeared to decline over time. Nonetheless, it took respondents nearly 40 years to reach a point at which they experienced such negative feelings "rarely." For most respondents, such negative thoughts never seem to fade completely. Similarly slow declines were found for so-called anniversary reactions—experiencing particular occasions when the sadness and loneliness that they experienced right after the death returned to them.

Moreover the difference in depression scores between widowed and married respondents remained significant as long as 15 years after the loss, and it took the widowed respondents more than 30 years to reach the level of depression of married respondents. The difference in life satisfaction between married and control respondents was significant as long as 7.5 years following the loss, and it took respondents more than 15 years to reach the level of life satisfaction of married respondents.

The results obtained in these cross-sectional studies are supported in an elegant cotwin longitudinal study of response to widowhood conducted by Lichtenstein, Gatz, Pedersen, Berg, and McClearn (1996). More than 2000 Swedish twins participated in a survey every three years for 12 years. Those who lost a spouse between any two intervals were classified as bereaved. Rates of depression were high in both the short-term bereaved (less than 5 years; 51%) and the long-term bereaved individuals (on average 13 years for men and 17 for women; 37%). They were also quite high in the to-be-bereaved condition (married at one interview but bereaved by a subsequent interview; 41%). All were significantly higher than those of the married respondents. When these analyses were repeated comparing bereaved respondents with their cotwin control, it was found that those bereaved fewer than five years reported more depressive symptoms, more loneliness, and less life satisfaction than their twin. Among the long-term bereaved respondents, women were significantly more lonely, less satisfied, and tended to be more depressed than their cotwin control. Long-term bereaved men were also found to be significantly more lonely than their cotwin control, although there were no significant differences in life satisfaction or depression.

An interesting finding to emerge from this study was that when married respondents were compared with to-be-widowed respondents, the latter group was found to have an elevated depression score. This finding has important implications for interpreting other longitudinal studies on bereavement. Some studies have claimed that the effects of widowhood were resolved in a year because by that time, the depression scores had returned to baseline (see, e.g., Harlow et al., 1991). The Lichtenstein et al. (1996) study demonstrates, however, that many bereaved individuals become depressed before the death, either because of anticipatory grief, caregiver burden, or other unknown reasons. These results suggest that those planning future studies should obtain a baseline interview at least a couple of years before the widowhood experience.

Taken together, these data suggest that although some symptoms lessen over time, many bereaved individuals continue to experience distressing symptoms, painful memories, and impaired quality of life for several years following their loss.

CONCLUSION

In our earlier papers, we maintained that some of the most widely held and influential assumptions about the process of coping with the loss of a loved one were not supported, and were often contradicted, by the available data. In this paper, we have reviewed numerous studies that provide strong support for our original conclusions. We have presented clear evidence that a large minority of respondents fail to experience even mild depression following the loss of a spouse, child, parent, or sibling. Respondents in such studies fail to show delayed grief, or health problems as long as 25 months following the loss, although we cannot rule out the possibility that such problems will eventually emerge. In direct contradiction to the idea that it is necessary to pass through a period of depression, the expression of negative emotion in the first few months following a loss has repeatedly been shown to portend subsequent difficulties. Expression of positive emotions, in contrast, has been associated with less severe and long-lasting symptoms. These findings have emerged whether emotions are assessed through self-report, coded from narratives, or coded from facial expressions. Similarly, many studies have tested the "working through" hypothesis, defining the construct in various ways, and none has found clear support for the hypothesis that people who actively confront their thoughts and feelings about the loss show better long-term adjustment than those who use avoidant strategies. Grief treatments, which are generally expected to help people resolve their grief, have been found to be surprisingly ineffective and sometimes counterproductive. Numerous studies show that continuing attachment to the deceased is normal, although whether attachment is beneficial may depend on the form that it takes. There is also clear evidence to suggest that a substantial percentage of people experience distressing symptoms for many years following an important loss.

Given the striking absence of empirical support for the aforementioned ideas, it is important to ask whether they are still influential in the bereavement field today. As we noted earlier, some of these assumptions are in a state of transition, such as the view that it is important to break down ties to the deceased, which has recently been challenged by researchers and clinicians (Klass et al., 1996). These challenges have led to exciting and important new studies examining whether particular kinds of attachments are beneficial. The same is true for the assumptions about recovery. As researchers and clinicians are beginning to think about the recovery process in new ways, they note that people may not return to their preloss state. The coping task may not be to return to previous levels of functioning but to negotiate a meaningful life without the deceased. It is also likely that bereaved individuals experience important and enduring changes as a result of their loss. These changes may be negative, such as a permanent shift in the ability to regulate anxiety (Rubin, 1996), as well as positive, such as enhanced feelings of competence and self-esteem (Wortman et al., 1999; and see Updegraff & Taylor, in press, for a more detailed discussion of positive and negative changes following stressful life events).

We would maintain that assumptions about the importance of going through a period of distress, and of working through the loss, however, are still extremely influential. In what is arguably the most widely used book on grief counseling, Worden (1991) stated that "there are certain tasks of mourning that must be accomplished for equilibrium to be reestablished and for the process of mourning to be completed" (p. 10). One of these tasks is to acknowledge and work through the pain of the loss. Worden argued that "it is impossible to lose someone you have been deeply attached to without experiencing some level of pain" (p. 13). He also warns that if this task is not adequately completed, "therapy may be needed later on" (p. 14). The views of Worden and others have given rise to a veritable industry of professional grief counselors. The major tenet on which their work is based is that "you have to feel it in order to heal it" (Labi, 1999, p. 70).

The notion of working through grief is also the most important feature of a treatment called Critical Incident Stress Debriefing. Originally developed by Jeffrey Mitchell, then a paramedic, to help soldiers in World War II deal with the traumas of war, this procedure is widely used today throughout the world following disasters and traumatic incidents. In Littleton, Colorado, for example, counselors spent 1500 hours talking to students in the first week after the April 20, 1999, shooting in which 15 died (Labi, 1999). As Theodore Fineberg, a New York-based psychologist who flew to Littleton as part of a team sent by the National Association of School Psychologists, explained, "Debriefing is a therapeutic opportunity to get people to open up, to ask questions and unburden the psychic pain they are carrying around" (Labi, 1999, p. 69). Nonetheless, the empirical evidence in support of Critical Incident Debriefing Therapy is sorely lacking: In a recent meta-analysis of six controlled studies examining the impact of this procedure, two produced positive results, two produced negative findings, and two showed no differences (Rose & Bisson, 1998).

Overall, our review suggests a number of intriguing implications for continued research and clinical work. It would be useful to clarify *why* some people show little distress shortly after their loss (and also fail to show delayed grief reaction). There are many possible ways of understanding such a reaction. It could signal relief if the relationship had been stressful or if the bereaved person was involved in caregiving responsibilities before death. It could reflect a lack of attachment to the loved one, as many clinicians have claimed. It could also be indicative of an avoidant coping style, or stoicism, that is working effectively. Alternatively, it could indicate that the bereaved person was able to incorporate the loss into his or her existing view of the world—for example, viewing the loss as God's will and believing that the deceased is in a better place, or believing that bad things happen and there is nothing one can do about them (Wortman & Silver, 1992; and see Janoff-Bulman, 1992, for a fuller discussion of the role of world views in response to loss). Given the many reasons why people may fail to show distress following a major loss, our review raises serious questions regarding the widespread belief among clinicians that such individuals need to "work through" the loss. In fact, the previously discussed meta-analysis by Neimeyer (2000) suggests that among individuals who are not highly distressed, a grief-focused intervention can lead to a worse outcome than no intervention at all.

What about those individuals who show intense or prolonged distress following the death of a loved one? Is such a reaction indicative of the loss of a great love, perhaps coupled with strong dependence on the spouse who has died? Or is such a reaction merely a reflection of previous psychopathology on the part of the surviving spouse? It is hoped that prospective studies assessing bereaved individuals before the death and following them for a period of time afterward will help to unravel this mystery.

The studies reviewed provide no evidence to suggest that people who attempt to confront and process the loss do better than those who do not. But this does not mean that focusing on the death or expressing negative feelings necessarily causes a worse outcome than blocking or avoiding such thoughts and feelings. It is important to identify the factors that may lead some people to express negative feelings after a death. First, people may be more likely to express negative feelings if they experience more negative feelings. People may suffer more following a loss for many reasons, including the closeness of the attachment to the deceased (Cleiren, 1993), the manner of death, and the extent to which the death shatters previously held beliefs about themselves or their world (Janoff-Bulman, 1992). Certain deaths may not only cause more suffering but may raise more existential questions. Hence, certain types of loss, such as the death of a child because of a drunk driver, may be more difficult to work through than the death of a beloved but elderly spouse.

Given a loss that is difficult to work through, how should people be encouraged to deal with their grief? We suspect that many people who have experienced a particularly traumatic loss may not know how to process grief on their own and an unsupportive, constraining social network may even make matters worse (see Lepore et al., 1996). If they think about the loss and its implications, what determines whether they will move forward or whether they will become "stuck" in their grief (Holman & Silver, 1998), continuing a process of painful rumination with little progress? As M. Stroebe (1992) has suggested, individual coping styles may be important, with some people developing "approaching" or "avoidant" styles that work well for them. The ability to tolerate affect may also be important (cf. McCann & Pearlman, 1990). Those who become flooded with painful affect when they think about the loss may not be able to stay with their feelings long enough to gain insight. Individuals with more well-developed coping capacities and resources for self-soothing may be more able to process the event in manageable chunks, moving back and forth between approach and avoidant strategies to regroup. Unfortunately, no studies on working through have included such constructs as coping styles, self-capacities, or the impact of the loss on world views.

In our judgment, working through is an area in dire need of further investigation. More basic research is needed to examine the role played by such components of working through as thinking about the loss, talking, crying, writing, and distraction. We also need more information about the conditions under which particular types of working through are likely to facilitate coming to terms with the loss. It is hoped that such research will provide a solid basis on which to develop effective interventions for bereaved individuals. Given the large number of bereaved individuals who suffer significant distress following the loss, we believe it is remarkable that no standardized treatments for grief have been developed, tested, and found to be effective. This should be an important societal goal, because many experts in the area have emphasized that helping a client work through a loss requires consummate training, and that those who push too hard and too fast may do more harm than good (Pearlman & Saakvitne, 1995; Rando, 1993). Fortunately, as we described earlier, bereavement researchers have begun to adapt treatments from the trauma literature, based on an exposure model to bereaved individuals (Frank et al., 1997). Of course, development of effective treatments will not resolve the problem, because only a small percentage of those who experience major mental health problems following bereavement seek professional help (Jacobs, 1993). As health care providers, it behooves us to develop and evaluate specific tools that bereaved people can use on their own to assist in "working through" the loss. Participating in guided writing programs, keeping diaries, completing workbooks, and interacting with other bereaved persons on the Internet are but a few examples.

In closing, we believe that it is important to identify beliefs about coping with loss that are widely held in the culture and to subject them to careful empirical scrutiny. There is evidence that the research community is revising its views on these issues (e.g., M. Stroebe et al., 1994). However, we believe that these myths are still prevalent among clinicians and among the general public. It is our hope that this review will encourage further research on how to facilitate resolution of grief among those who seek counseling following their loss and also among those who are suffering but not receiving professional help. We also hope that the profound variability that exists in Western culture in response to loss will ultimately come to be acknowledged, so that bereaved individuals will be met consistently with compassion by those whom they encounter.

REFERENCES

Archer, J. (1999). *The nature of grief: The evolution and psychology of reactions to loss*. London: Routledge.

Barrett, C. J., & Schneweis, K. M. (1980). An empirical search for stages of widowhood. *Omega, 11,* 97–104.

Bonanno, G. A., & Field, N. P. (in press). Examining the delayed grief hypothesis across five years of bereavement. *American Behavioral Scientist.*

Bonanno, G. A., & Kaltman, S. (1999). Toward an integrative perspective on bereavement. *Psychological Bulletin, 125,* 760–786.

Bonanno, G. A., & Keltner, D. (1997). Facial expressions of emotion and the course of bereavement. *Journal of Abnormal Psychology, 106,* 126–137.

Bonanno, G. A., Keltner, D., Holen, A., & Horowitz, M. J. (1995). When avoiding unpleasant emotion might not be such a bad thing: Verbal-autonomic response dissociation and midlife conjugal bereavement. *Journal of Personality and Social Psychology, 46,* 975–989.

Bonanno, G. A., Znoj, H. J., Siddique, H., & Horowitz, M. J. (1999). Verbal-autonomic response dissociation and adaptation to midlife conjugal loss: A follow-up at 25 months. *Cognitive Therapy and Research, 23,* 605–624.

Bowlby, J. (1980). *Loss: Sadness and depression. Vol. 3. Loss: Sadness and depression.* New York: Basic Books.

Brill, S. (1983, December). An innocent man on death row. *The American Lawyer, 1,* 84–91.

Bruce, M. L., Kim, K., Leaf, P. J., & Jacobs, S. (1990). Depressive episodes and dysphoria resulting from conjugal bereavement in a prospective community sample. *American Journal of Psychiatry, 147,* 608–611.

Carnelley, K. B., Wortman, C. B., & Kessler, R. C. (1999). Impact of widowhood on depression: Findings from a prospective national survey. *Psychological Medicine, 29,* 1111–1123.

Cleiren, M. P. H. D. (1993). *Bereavement and adaptation: A comparative study of the aftermath of death.* Philadelphia: Hemisphere.

Cleiren, M. P. H. D., Diekstra, R. F. W., Kerkhof, A., & van der Wal, J. (1994). Mode of death and kinship in bereavement: Focusing on "who" rather than "how." *Crisis, 15,* 22–36.

Deutsch, H. (1937). Absence of grief. *Psychoanalytic Quarterly, 6,* 12–22.

Field, N. P., Nichols, C., Holen, A., & Horowitz, M. J. (1999). The relation of continuing attachment to adjustment in conjugal bereavement. *Journal of Consulting and Clinical Psychology, 67,* 212–218.

Foa, E. B., & Meadows, E. W. (1997). Psychosocial treatments for post traumatic stress disorder: A critical review. *Annual Review of Psychology, 48,* 449–480.

Foa, E. B., & Rothbaum, B. O. (1997). *Treating the trauma of rape.* New York: Guilford Press.

Folkman, S. (1997). Positive psychological states and coping with severe stress. *Social Science & Medicine, 45,* 1207–1221.

Folkman, S., Chesney, M., Collette, L., Boccellari, A., & Cooke, M. (1996). Post-bereavement depressive mood and its prebereavement predictors in HIV+ and HIV− gay men. *Journal of Personality and Social Psychology, 70,* 336–348.

Fraley, R. C., & Shaver, P. R. (1999). Loss and bereavement: Bowlby's theory and recent controversies concerning "grief work" and the nature of detachment. In J. Cassidy & P. R. Shaver (Eds.), *Handbook of attachment theory and research: Theory, research, and clinical applications* (pp. 735–759). New York: Guilford Press.

Frank, E., Prigerson, H. G., Shear, M. K., & Reynolds, C. F., III. (1997). Phenomenology and treatment of bereavement-related distress in the elderly. *International Clinical Psychopharmacology, 12*, S25–S29.

Freud, S. (1957). Mourning and melancholia. In J. Strachey (Ed.), *The standard edition of the complete psychological works of Sigmund Freud, Vol. 14*, (pp. 152–170). London: Hogarth Press. (Original work published 1917)

Harlow, S. D., Goldberg, E. L., & Comstock, G. W. (1991). A longitudinal study of the prevalence of depressive symptomatology in elderly widowed and married women. *Archives of General Psychiatry, 48*, 1065–1068.

Holman, E. A., & Silver, R. C. (1998). Getting "stuck" in the past: Temporal orientation and coping with trauma. *Journal of Personality and Social Psychology, 74*, 1146–1163.

Horowitz, M. J. (1990). A model of mourning: Change in schemas of self and other. *Journal of the American Psychoanalytic Association, 38*, 297–324.

Jacobs, S. (1993). *Pathologic grief: Maladaptation to loss.* Washington, DC: American Psychiatric Press.

Janoff-Bulman, R. (1992). *Shattered assumptions: Towards a new psychology of trauma.* New York: Free Press.

Klass, D., Silverman, P. R., & Nickman, S. L. (1996). *Continuing bonds: New understandings of grief.* Washington, DC: Taylor & Francis.

Labi, N. (1999, May 17). The grief brigade. *Time, 153*, 69–70.

Lehman, D. R., Wortman, C. B., & Williams, A. F. (1987). Long-term effects of losing a spouse or child in a motor vehicle crash. *Journal of Personality and Social Psychology, 52*, 218–231.

Lepore, S. J., Silver, R. C., Wortman, C. B., & Wayment, H. A. (1996). Social constraints, intrusive thoughts, and depressive symptoms among bereaved mothers. *Journal of Personality and Social Psychology, 70*, 271–282.

Lichtenstein, P., Gatz, M., Pedersen, N. L., Berg, S., & McClearn, G. E. (1996). A co-twin control study of response to widowhood. *Journal of Gerontology. Series B, Psychological Sciences & Social Sciences, 51*, 279–289.

Lindemann, E. (1944). Symptomatology and management of acute grief. *American Journal of Psychiatry, 101*, 1141–1148.

Marris, P. (1958). *Widows and their families.* London: Routledge & Kegan Paul.

Marwit, S. J., & Klass, D. (1996). Grief and the role of the inner representation of the deceased. In D. Klass, P. R. Silverman, & S. L. Nickman (Eds.), *Continuing bonds: New understandings of grief.* Washington, DC: Taylor & Francis.

Mawson, D., Marks, I. M., Ramm, L., & Stern, R. S. (1981). Guided mourning for morbid grief: A controlled study. *British Journal of Psychiatry, 138*, 185–193.

McCann, I. L., & Pearlman, L. A. (1990). *Psychological trauma in the adult survivor: Theory, therapy, and transformation.* New York: Brunner/Mazel.

Mendes de Leon, C. F., Kasl, S., V., & Jacobs, S. (1994). A prospective study of widowhood and changes in symptoms of depression in a community sample of the elderly. *Psychological Medicine, 24,* 613–624.

Middleton, W., Burnett, P., Raphael, B., & Martinek, N. (1996). The bereavement response: A cluster analysis. *British Journal of Psychiatry, 169,* 167–171.

Middleton W., Moylan, A., Raphael, B., Burnett, P., & Martinek, N. (1993). An international perspective on bereavement related concepts. *Australian and New Zealand Journal of Psychiatry, 27,* 457–463.

Miller, E. D., & Omarzu, J. (1998). New directions in loss research. In J. Harvey (Ed.), *Perspectives on loss: A sourcebook* (pp. 3–20). Washington, DC: Taylor & Francis.

Murphy, S. A. (1997). A bereavement intervention for parents following the sudden, violent deaths of their 12–28-year-old children: Description and applications to clinical practice. *Canadian Journal of Nursing Research, 29,* 51–72.

Neimeyer, R. A. (2000). Searching for the meaning of meaning: Grief therapy and the process of reconstruction. *Death Studies, 24,* 541–558.

Nolen-Hoeksema, S., & Larson, J. (1999). *Coping with loss.* Mahwah, NJ: Erlbaum.

Nolen-Hoeksema, S., McBride, A., & Larson, J. (1997). Rumination and psychological distress among bereaved partners. *Journal of Personality and Social Psychology, 72,* 855–862.

Normand, C. L., Silverman, P. R., & Nickman, S. L. (1996). Bereaved children's changing relationships with the deceased. In D. Klass, P. R. Silverman, & S. L. Nickman (Eds.), *Continuing bonds: New understandings of grief.* Washington, DC: Taylor & Francis.

Osterweis, M., Solomon, F., & Green, F. (1984). *Bereavement: Reactions, consequences, and care.* Washington, DC: National Academy Press.

Parkes, C. M. (1998). *Bereavement: Studies of grief in adult life* (3rd ed.). Madison, CT: International Universities Press.

Parkes, C. M., & Weiss, R. S. (1983). *Recovery from bereavement.* New York: Basic Books.

Pearlman, L. A., & Saakvitne, K. (1995). *Trauma and the therapist.* New York: Norton.

Pennebaker, J. W. (1997). Writing about emotional experiences as a therapeutic process. *Psychological Science, 8,* 162–166.

Pennebaker, J. W., Mayne, T. J., & Francis, M. E. (1997). Linguistic predictors of adaptive bereavement. *Journal of Personality and Social Psychology, 72,* 863–871.

Rando, T. A. (1984). *Grief, dying and death: Clinical interventions for caregivers.* Champaign, IL: Research Press.

Rando, T. A. (1993). *Treatment of complicated mourning*. Champaign, IL: Research Press.

Raphael, B. (1983). *The anatomy of bereavement*. New York: Basic Books.

Rees, W. D. (1971). The hallucinations of widowhood. *British Medical Journal, 4*, 37–41.

Resick, P. A., & Schnicke, M. K. (1992). Cognitive processing therapy for sexual assault victims. *Journal of Consulting and Clinical Psychology, 60,* 748–756.

Rose, S., & Bisson, J. (1998). Brief early psychological interventions following trauma: A systematic review of the literature. *Journal of Traumatic Stress, 11,* 697–710.

Rubin, S. S. (1996). The wounded family: Bereaved parents and the impact of adult child loss. In D. Klass, P. R. Silverman, & S. L. Nickman (Eds.), *Continuing bonds: New understandings of grief*. Washington, DC: Taylor & Francis.

Sanders, C. M. (1999). *Grief: The mourning after* (2nd ed.). New York: John Wiley & Sons.

Silver, R. L., & Wortman, C. B. (1980). Coping with undesirable life events. In J. Garber & M. E. P. Seligman (Eds.), *Human helplessness: Theory and applications* (pp. 279–340). New York: Academic Press.

Silverman, P. R., & Klass, D. (1996). Introduction: What's the problem? In D. Klass, P. R. Silverman, & S. L. Nickman (Eds.), *Continuing bonds: New understandings of grief* (pp. 3–27). Washington, DC: Taylor & Francis.

Silverman, P. R., & Nickman, S. L. (1996). Children's construction of their dead parents. In D. Klass, P. R. Silverman, & S. L. Nickman (Eds.), *Continuing bonds: New understandings of grief*. Washington, DC: Taylor & Francis.

Silverman, P. R., Nickman, S. L., & Worden, J. W. (1992). Detachment revisited: The child's reconstruction of a dead parent. *American Journal of Orthopsychiatry, 62,* 494–503.

Stein, N. L., Folkman, S., Trabasso, T., & Christopher-Richards, A. (1997). Appraisal and goal processes as predictors of well-being in bereaved care-givers. *Journal of Personality and Social Psychology, 72,* 863–871.

Stroebe, M. S. (1992). Coping with bereavement: A review of the grief work hypothesis. *Omega, 26,* 19–42.

Stroebe, M. S., & Stroebe, W. (1991). Does "grief work" work? *Journal of Consulting and Clinical Psychology, 59,* 479–482.

Stroebe, M. S., Hansson, R. O., & Stroebe, W. (1993). Contemporary themes and controversies in bereavement research. In M. S. Stroebe, W. Stroebe, & R. O. Hansson (Eds.), *Handbook of bereavement: Theory, research, and intervention* (pp. 457–476). Cambridge: Cambridge University Press.

Stroebe, M. S., van den Bout, J., & Schut, H. A. (1994). Myths and misconceptions about bereavement: The opening of a debate. *Omega, 29,* 187–203.

Tyson-Rawson, K. (1996). Relationship and heritage: Manifestations of ongoing attachment following father death. In D. Klass, P. R. Silverman, & S. L. Nickman (Eds.), *Continuing bonds: New understandings of grief* (pp. 125–145). Washington, DC: Taylor & Francis.

Updegraff, J. A., & Taylor, S. E. (in press). From vulnerability to growth: Positive and negative effects of stressful life events. In J. H. Harvey & E. D. Miller (Eds.), *Handbook of loss and trauma*. New York: Bruner/Mazel.

Volkan, V. (1981). *Linking objects and linking phenomena: A study of forms, symptoms, metapsychology and therapy of complicated mourning period*. New York: International Universities Press.

Wheaton, B. (1990). Life transitions, role histories, and mental health. *American Sociological Review, 55*, 209–223.

Worden, J. W. (1982). *Grief counseling and grief therapy: A handbook for the mental health practitioner* (1st ed.). New York: Springer.

Worden, J. W. (1991). *Grief counseling and grief therapy: A handbook for the mental health practitioner* (2nd ed.). New York: Springer.

Wortman, C. B., Kessler, R. C., Bolger, N., House, J., & Carnelley, K. (1999). *The time course of adjustment to widowhood: Evidence from a national probability sample*. Manuscript submitted for publication.

Wortman, C. B., Sheedy, C., Gluhoski, V., & Kessler, R. (1992). Stress, coping, and health: Conceptual issues and directions for future research. In H. S. Friedman (Ed.), *Hostility, coping, and health* (pp. 227–256). Washington, DC: American Psychological Association.

Wortman, C. B., & Silver, R. C. (1987). Coping with irrevocable loss. In G. R. Van den Bos & B. K. Bryant (Eds.), *Cataclysms, crises, and catastrophes: Psychology in action* (*Master Lecture Series*; pp. 189–235). Washington, DC: American Psychological Association.

Wortman, C. B., & Silver, R. C. (1989). The myths of coping with loss. *Journal of Consulting and Clinical Psychology, 57*, 349–357.

Wortman, C. B., & Silver, R. C. (1992). Reconsidering assumptions about coping with loss: An overview of current research. In S. H. Filipp, L. Montada, & M. Lerner (Eds.), *Life crises and experiences of loss in adulthood* (pp. 341–365). Hillsdale, NJ: Erlbaum.

Wortman, C. B., Silver, R. C., & Kessler, R. C. (1993). The meaning of loss and adjustment to bereavement. In M. S. Stroebe, W. Stroebe, & R. O. Hansson (Eds.), *Bereavement: A sourcebook of research and interventions* (pp. 349–366). London: Cambridge University Press.

Zisook, S., Paulus, M., Shuchter, S. R., & Judd, L. L. (1997). The many faces of depression following spousal bereavement. *Journal of Affective Disorders, 45*, 85–94.

Zisook, S., & Shuchter, S. R. (1993). Major depression associated with widowhood. *American Journal of Geriatric Psychiatry, 1*, 316–326.

19

PROCESSES OF GRIEVING: HOW BONDS ARE CONTINUED

DENNIS KLASS AND TONY WALTER

"Life is short but love is long."
Epitaph for 11-year-old boy, Mells churchyard, Somerset, 1960

As the television cameras zoom in on the mother of a Japanese Olympic gold medal winner, she holds up a small framed photograph of her husband, the champion's father, who has been dead for more than a decade. In the Japanese tradition, it is important to acknowledge that the father's spirit guides and participates in the successes of the family, including the seemingly individualistic accomplishment of athletic victory. In the Indian house of an extended Hindu family, every morning a fresh garland of flowers is placed around the photograph of the father of the present patriarch of the family. A Tibetan monk begins every meditation session with a series of exercises that call forth the presence of his deceased teacher.

Over our history as a species, humans' continued interaction with people after they have died is a far more common pattern than is severing the bonds with the dead, as Westerners have been advised to do through most of the twentieth century. As Geary (1994, pp. 1–2) noted about contemporary western society, "The dead are banished. . . . never before have humans been able to kill so many people so efficiently or to forget them so completely." Indeed, a professional concern with bereavement—how survivors live on after the death—arose in the modern West at precisely the time that public concern with the afterlife—how the dead themselves live on—waned (Ariès, 1981; Walter, 1996a). It is perhaps not surprising that academic models of bereavement have focused on the bereaved individual rather than on the relations between bereaved people and those they have lost. That bereaved people maintain a bond with their dead has been recognized by twentieth-century bereavement theorists (Silverman & Klass, 1996), but until recently the phenomenon was generally seen as hypercathexis, an intensification of the bond as a prelude to breaking it (Fenichel, 1945; Raphael, 1983), as an introjection in the psyche that is by definition pathological (Dietrich & Shabad, 1989; Schafer, 1968; Volkan, 1981; Volkan & Showalter, 1968) or as an indication of searching behavior that will prove unsuccessful and so eventually be extinguished (Parkes, 1972; Sanders, 1989). Bowlby (1980) wrote at some length about both the existence and healthiness of continuing bonds, but this aspect of his work seems to have been relatively uninfluential or even ignored; indeed, Fraley and Shaver (1999) and Shaver (chapter 4, this volume) claim Klass, Stroebe, and others misrepresent Bowlby on this point.

More recently, there has been more prominence given to studies that highlight the ongoing importance for bereaved people of relationships with the dead. Several studies from the late 1980s and early 1990s documenting this—for example, M. Stroebe, Gergen, Gergen, and Stroebe (1992), were brought together by Klass, Silverman, and Nickman (1996) in their volume *Continuing Bonds: New Understandings of Grief*, while simultaneously in England Walter (1996b) published "A New Model of Grief: Bereavement and Biography." Both publications argued that bereaved people often maintain a bond with the dead person, a bond that can continue for decades and that is not associated with measures of poor adjustment. Klass et al. said little, however, about the mechanisms by which bonds are maintained; Walter argued that bonds are maintained through conversation, without stating what other mechanisms might be available to people in the modern West. In this chapter, we will redress these lacunae in our 1996 publications and sketch some ways bonds are continued in contemporary society.

RELIGION, POLITICAL POWER, AND THE DEAD

First we will examine the wider context. We will look at how the bond in other societies is intertwined with membership in the tribe or nation and with the legitimization of religious power. In every society rituals for those who have died in war are part of the bond between citizens and their country (e.g., Winter, 1995). Among the Tallensi of Ghana, not everyone can become an ancestor—only those who in life held authority, which they continue to wield after death; appeal to their authority in turn legitimates that exercised by the living (Fortes, 1965; Hamilton, 1998). The connection between political power and interaction with the dead is often complex. There are any number of cultures and historical periods that demonstrate this connection, but we have chosen to look at critical eras of Japanese history, and then at Western European history.

In Japan, as in other Confucian societies, ancestor rituals that continue for 35 or 50 years after a person dies are an expression of filial piety and loyalty, virtues that are necessary for an orderly society. At critical points in Japanese history, ancestor rituals have been put to the service of national identity. There has been a connection between ancestor rituals and nationalism at least since the Nara era (eighth century), when the reverence for imperial ancestors was linked with reverence for individual family ancestors. In the Tokugawa period (1603–1868), as a way of eradicating Western influence, everyone was required to register as a parishioner of a Buddhist temple where the main emotional and ritual connection was the ancestor rites. During the Meiji Restoration (1868) when the emperor was returned to power, an attempt was made to establish Shinto as the national religion. That was not successful, but a link was made between Shinto emperor worship and ancestor rituals. The idea was that the state is the household writ large and the household is the state in microcosm and they are made one through the medium of ancestor rituals (Smith, 1974). The connection between ancestor rituals and emperor veneration was severed after 1945 but remains as a latent conservative political symbol.

We can see a similar dynamic in the West over the medieval period as Rome extended its influence into central Europe. In Germanic sagas before Roman hegemony, "The dead regularly return to inflict punishment, share meals, exact revenge, give advice, teach, offer advice or . . . to repent" (Geary, 1994, p. 83). The idea of purgatory was undeveloped, so relationships between the living and the dead were not yet fixed. Early in the period, the dead could be directly involved with the living, but with time the Church became the intermediary between the living and the dead. Prayers for the dead were offered in church, and if the dead were to speak they were likely to do so through a priest or monk. Saints could be prayed to rather than for, but the Church controlled access to the relics of the saints (Geary, 1994). As Roman Christianity spread north, the relics of saints associated with Rome were brought in to replace local saints. Even today, visitors to Cologne Cathedral can view bone fragments from several saints associated with papal power.

Western theology has been ambivalent about whether the presence of God is more important than the presence of those we have loved. There has been a continual tension between heaven as a human place from which there is rather easy intercourse between the dead and those who remain behind and heaven as a place for God alone, where the triviality of human relationships is replaced by communion with Him (McDannell & Lang, 1988). St. Augustine, for example, had no use for human relationships except as they were grounded in God, so no communication with the dead could be useful. The resolution of grief in Augustine, as it would be for every Western theology that reasserted the transcendence of God, is bonding with God, not with the deceased.

The historical evidence suggests that the balance between a God-centered and a human-centered heaven depends on larger historical dynamics. When the institutions of political and religious power are secure from rivals within the land and safe from their enemies without, interactions with the dead can be incorporated into the society in ways that support the standing order. But when family or friendship bonds with the dead diminish the power needed to legitimize the standing order, then interaction between the living and the dead is suppressed in favor of interaction with God, who more directly supports the political and religious authorities. This is clearly seen in the prohibition on contacting any spirits other than God just before Israel went into exile (McDannell & Lang, 1988).

By the mid- to late medieval period, the doctrine of purgatory had placed the dead firmly under the Church's authority, so the barrier between the living and the dead could be lifted. The dead had easy access to the world of the living because their final destination was not settled. Even those who were damned to hell could return to warn the living of the importance of confession, extreme unction, and absolution at the point of death. The dead might ask that sacraments or donations to the Church be made on their behalf, or that the living intercede, especially with the Virgin Mary, on their behalf. Thus death was not the end of the process of achieving heaven. The living could help the dead by their prayers, masses, and intercessions, and the dead could help the living with advice on proper belief and behavior and with practical matters such as the location of lost money (Finucane, 1996).

The rejection of human bonds that continued after death was carried to its logical extreme by early Protestants (Duffy, 1992). The antipapal nationalism behind the Protestant revolt meant that the Catholic control of the dead needed to be broken. The existence of purgatory was denied. Only heaven or hell were allowed as after-death possibilities. Indulgences (the trigger of the Reformation) were meaningless, as were prayers, masses, alms for the dead, and appeals to the saints. God alone had power and He ruled in individual souls and in the legitimate governments He had established on earth. All medieval manifestations of communion between living and the dead were swept away. "For most sixteenth-century Protestants apparitions could only be demonic, angelic or illusory" (Finucane, 1996, p. 92).

Later, as the Protestant hegemony became secure, the transcendent God of Calvin and Luther could be replaced by the more personal God of the Methodists and Baptists. The family became the microcosm of the larger society as it was in the Japanese imperial system. The modern heaven emerged, characterized by immediate separation of the soul from the body, so after death the body only needs "disposal," whereas the soul relates to human love and family bonds (Ariès, 1981; McDannell & Lang, 1988). In the face of early industrialism, spiritual authority passed from the father to the mother and the home became a "haven in a heartless world" (Lasch, 1977). The domestic God was reinforced by early nineteenth-century consolation literature that featured detailed descriptions of heaven and comforting messages from the residents there (Douglas, 1977). Later in the century, spiritualism affirmed the bonds between the living and the dead (Brandon, 1983; Kerr & Crow, 1983; Rosenblatt, 1983).

CONTINUING BONDS IN THE MODERN WEST

What can we say about bonds between the living and the dead in a nontraditional and largely secular contemporary society that values individual autonomy, youth, and progress and that resists the notion of being guided by older, let alone deceased, generations? Psychological and sociological research on the issue has hardly begun. There are many variables that need to be considered—for example, family styles, subcultural patterns, religious belief, personality constructs, attachment patterns, and ego developmental levels. Further, as has happened elsewhere in the study of death, when scholars begin discussing the matter, lay people will use the professional discussion to structure the way they experience their world and express their grief. For now it seems that four points can be made. (a) A significant enough portion of the population sense the presence of the dead that it cannot be labeled pathological or even hallucinatory. (b) Many people talk with the dead and find the conversations meaningful. (c) The dead often play a role in the moral lives of the living. (d) For a variety of reasons, conversation has replaced ritual as the normative way in which the bond with the dead is maintained. The rest of this chapter will explicate these four points.

Sensing the Presence of the Dead

The dead may appear unbidden to the living, who, in the contemporary West, have no cultural framework by which to integrate them into their lives. This was first brought to the attention of bereavement researchers by the Welsh physician, Dewi Rees (1971). Rees found that about half of widows and widowers had a sense of the presence of their dead spouse; this typically happened while awake and at home and was unrelated to gender, nationality, social class, or social isolation. Three quarters had never mentioned their experience to anyone else. Subsequent work has replicated his findings in a number of settings (Bennett, 1987; Glick, Weiss, & Parkes, 1974; Greeley, 1975; Haraldsson, 1988; Kalish & Reynolds, 1974; Olson, Suddeth, Paterson, & Egelhoff, 1985; Rogo, 1986; Rosenblatt, 1983; Shuchter & Zisook, 1993). Rees (1997) has helpfully reviewed this literature. The majority of these encounters are experienced as comforting, and though they tend to decline over time, there are plenty of examples of the dead appearing to comfort well-adjusted individuals decades later. We have yet to understand how sensing the dead functions in normal populations, its relative importance in contributing to the continuing bond, and how interactions with the dead interface with other experiences deemed hallucinatory (Bentall, 1990). Some initial findings have been presented by Datson and Marwit (1997) and Simon-Buller, Christopherson, and Jones (1988).

Parkes (1986) explained sensing the presence of the dead as "searching" behavior. Rees (1997) has been skeptical of this explanation because (a) the sense of presence is not usually initiated by the living, (b) does not match other search behavior in which people know exactly what they are looking for, and (c) is by no means uncommon years after the loss, long after the bereaved person has ceased searching.

Though Rees himself paid proper respect to this phenomenon, it is significant that in his original work he referred to "hallucinations" and that the advisers for his PhD were psychiatrists. The word "hallucination" is of recent Euro-American origin and no self-respecting anthropologist or student of comparative religion would use it to refer to experiences reported by non-Western peoples while fully awake and not under the influence of drugs. It is a sign of a more developed phenomenological approach that Rees (1997) has now dropped the term "hallucination" and refers instead to "continuing relationships with the dead." It is of course possible that sensing the presence of the dead is a hallucination or wishful thinking, but it is unscientific to assume this a priori, which is why we prefer a phenomenological approach.

Talking With the Dead

In life, intimate relationships are developed and sustained through physical contact (Berger & Kellner, 1964; Duck, 1994) and through everyday conversation. If the relationship is to continue after death, we might expect to find not only a sense of physical presence but also an ongoing conversation with, and about, them. This is reflected in a poem by Henry Scott Holland that contains the following lines:

> Call me by my old familiar name,
> speak to me in the easy way you always used. . . .
> Let my name be ever the household word it always was.

That families often ask that this poem to be read at funerals in the United Kingdom suggests that its sentiments resonate with a considerable number of bereaved Britons.

Little research has been done into the extent to which people talk to the dead. In Shuchter and Zisook's study of San Diego widows and widowers (1993), more than a third said they talked regularly with the deceased, a proportion declining only very slightly in the 13 months since the death. Silverman and Nickman (1996) found the cemetery to be a common place for adult children to talk to their dead parents. A BBC television documentary in which one author (Walter) participated filmed one man whose son had died at the age of 19 and who regularly popped into cemetery on his way to work "to have a chat with the lad." Other anecdotal examples abound of graveside conversations with the dead (e.g., Brabant, 1996). Cemetery behavior, however, has only recently been systematically documented—by Doris Francis and her colleagues in their valuable ethnography in London. (This is one of very few participant observation studies of the social world of bereaved people, a gap in bereavement research on the modern West. Such ethnographies abound in traditional societies.) Francis, Kellaher, and Lee found that men were particularly likely to come to the cemetery to have a chat (1997, pp. 18–19):

> Middle age is a time when parents die. For many men, the cemetery offers a unique link with their dads. Occasionally on a quiet day, we will come upon a young man, almost invisible, as he kneels down planting or arranging flowers in front of his father's grave.
>
> Men come to the cemetery when things are not going well: a divorce or a broken relationship, a difficult time at work, a realisation that the father is gone and there was never enough time to talk and to get his needed guidance for life.
>
> There appear to be definite rules guiding these conversations between father and son. The man must be alone and there should be no-one tending graves close by. Under such conditions, often while cleaning the stone or planting flowers, there is an openness in their "conversations" which they never experienced when the parent was alive. . . .
>
> For some men, the grave is the place to openly confront parents for abuse or lack of love and warmth needed when they were growing up. . . . For others, it is the place to reclaim and continue a too-short relationship.

Those who have lost a spouse may regularly talk with the departed, telling him or her about family events such as the birth of a new grandchild or recalling memories of things done together (Francis et al., 1997). Some of these graveside encounters seek moral guidance from the dead, others help the bereaved person work out issues of self and family identity, others simply continue the conversation that was the bread and butter of the marital relationship when the partner was alive or create the conversation that sadly never existed between father and son. What other situations apart from cemeteries are important sites for these conversations has yet to be systematically researched. Women are more likely to sense the presence of the dead within the family home (Bennett, 1987; Rees, 1997) and they are more likely to talk to them here as well.

The Dead as Moral Guides

The dead no longer control the conduct of the living, as they do in some societies that venerate the ancestors, but they do continue to give moral guidance. When Marwit and Klass (1995) investigated the existence and function of inner representations of the dead and the resolution of grief among students enrolled in university psychology classes in the American Midwest, they got high interrater reliability in identifying four functions, three of which can be characterized as providing moral guidance and the fourth which may be linked to moral behavior in a broader way. The three categories that are directly about moral guidance follow:

1. Role model, defined as global identification with the deceased. Example: "I remember him as the ideal dad; someone I would like to imitate as a parent."
2. Situation-specific guidance, defined as the living calling on the deceased for guidance in specific problematic situations. Example: "I always think about her when I'm trying to make a decision on some big event in my life. I think, what would she do? She is always in my thoughts and I try to build my life the way I think she would have liked for me to be."
3. Values clarification, defined as adopting (or in some cases rejecting) a moral position identified with that of the deceased. Example: "Thinking about him (a mentally handicapped brother) makes me more appreciative that I am alive. It has made me and my family more caring towards all underprivileged people."

The fourth category is remembrance formation (Tahka, 1984), identifying the deceased as a valued part of the survivor's biography. This often provides solace (Klass, 1993). Solace seems to be related to moral functioning in a deep way: Psychoanalyst Horton (1981) noted that the sociopathic criminals whom he tried to treat seemed to have no sense of solace in their lives.

In bereaved parent self-help groups, the parents' inner representations of their dead children provide behavioral norms that put the parents in touch with their better self. For example, as a way of helping participants get acquainted at the beginning of a training session for new group facilitators, one of the authors (Klass) asked each person to answer the question: "Where is your child in your decision to take on leadership of the meeting?" One person described her daughter as a person who was always helping others. She was the one whom her friends called for help. The mother remembered once waking up in the morning and finding her daughter with the telephone cradled on her shoulder, having fallen asleep listening to a friend who was in trouble. In being a group leader, the mother was continuing the kind of person that her daughter was, especially when talking on the phone to newly bereaved parents. A woman who was daunted by the challenging task of beginning a new meeting said she sometimes feels her son looking over her shoulder saying, "Come on mom, you can do it." Her son was a cheerleader in her inner world as she became a helper of other bereaved parents.

Talking About the Dead

The previous section mentioned that the dead may become a valued part of the survivor's biography. Rosenblatt and Elde (1990) and Walter (1996b, 1999a) have hypothesized that one significant way in which this can happen is through talking to others who knew the dead person. This may be particularly important in certain relationships in which chunks of the dead person's life are unknown to the mourner, as when a parent loses an adolescent or adult child. Koppelman (1994) details how one father engaged in lengthy conversations with his deceased 19-year-old son's peers to fill out his understanding of the son. Because of the fragmentation of modern life, particularly the split between home and work, it is typical of many bereavements that significant parts of the deceased's life are unknown to the mourner, leaving the deceased's identity incomplete. That death typically occurs in a hospital can mean that the events of the death itself are poorly known by even close mourners, who may need to talk with doctors, nurses, and ambulance staff about how the person died. Mourning can therefore include the attempt to complete the dead person's identity, to write "the last chapter" of their biography. This is done chiefly with others who knew him or her, along with discovering writings and other artefacts left behind by the deceased that flesh out the picture.

Telling the deceased's story may be particularly important in contemporary secular societies. Giddens (1991) and other sociologists have suggested that formal rituals decline with increasing individualism. The sacred reality of ritual may not mesh with the personal constructions of the varied individuals who participate in them today. The trauma of grief is eased now through the new individualized ritual of grief counseling and grief support groups. Indeed, even within formal funeral ritual, we find a trend toward reducing the religious rite of passage in favor of telling the story of the deceased (Walter, 1990). In Giddens's phrase, ritual has been replaced by discourse (see also Seale, 1998). We would argue that for most people the conversations that ease people through painful life changes are not with professional therapists but with friends and family. Therapists may be needed when these more ordinary conversations break down. We are not saying that traditional mourning rituals cannot involve informal conversation about the dead—the Jewish Shiva and its Hindu equivalent clearly do—but that the typically rather weak formal mourning rituals of modernity *require* conversation as a functional substitute.

This concept of survivors telling the deceased's story clearly has connections with narrative (McAdams, 1993; Sarbin, 1986) and constructivist (Neimeyer & Mahoney, 1995) therapies, and with the interest in narrative and storying to be found in gerontology (Haight, 1988), in the social psychology of illness (Frank, 1995; Kleinman, 1988) and in a number of other areas, yet strangely this fashionable idea has made little impact on studies of bereavement (rare exceptions being Neimeyer & Mahoney, 1995, and Walter, 1996b, 1999a). We have much still to learn about the relative importance of the narrating of the story of the deceased, either individually or communally, in relation to other grief processes (Stroebe, 1997). We do not know how conversationally constructing the deceased's biography is associated with solace or distress or indeed how solace and distress intermix. We do not know how external conversations with others function in comparison to internal conversations (Balk, 1996) or conversations with the dead. And we do not know whether it matters that the story told about the deceased be recognized as true by others. We suspect that there will be some circumstances in which different survivors need to construct a joint story, some circumstances in which this may not be possible and they will just have to live with different stories that they cannot share, and others in which it really matters little that each survivor may have a very different story.

Whether people do include the dead in the everyday conversations clearly depends in part on cultural norms. In the Jewish shiva, for example, mourners are expected to discuss the deceased; but the North American Apache are not allowed to speak the name of the dead, and the Hopi express no desire to recall the memory of their deceased (Mandelbaum, 1959). If the dead may be mentioned or addressed, there may be rules about how they may be included in conversation; in Britain, for example, one is supposed never to speak ill of the dead and many people are unwilling to mention the dead if they think it will upset others, whereas in Japan the living talk but the dead seldom respond.

Even if culture allows the dead to be talked about, social and geographical structure may hinder it. The dead cannot be included in everyday conversation if those who knew the dead do not live, work, or socialize together, as is becoming increasingly common in modern Westernized societies. In this case, the bond with the dead can be continued only internally within bereaved individuals: The dead cannot be part of the social life of ongoing residential or work groups. The relevant variables affecting social structure are longevity, geographical mobility, community size and stability, and the separation of home and work. We may broadly identify three types of social structure; these may be compared with Walter's (1994) traditional, modern and postmodern types of death.

Traditional Mourning

In cohesive and stable small-scale communities, those encountered daily by the mourner typically also knew the deceased. Though some individuals are closer than others to the deceased, nevertheless the whole community has lost a member, and the whole community mourns (e.g., Clark, 1982). This kind of mourning is still found in rural Ireland and may also be found in urban subcultures involving cohesive ethnic or religious minorities. In such a social context, it is not hard (if cultural norms allow) for the deceased's name to live on for at least a generation or two in everyday conversation.

Modern Bereavement

In larger scale, urban societies, the bereaved person is individuated out from the mass, and is surrounded by people who never knew the deceased and do not share the pain of the death. Everyday conversation becomes problematic. The roots of this lie in the following:

- Social fragmentation. The scale of modern urban living often leads to fragmented social relationships, so that the family I live with, the shopkeepers I buy from, the colleagues I work with, the copassengers I travel with on bus or train, the people I play sports with, are totally separate groups (Berger, Berger, & Kellner, 1974). So when a close family member dies, my colleagues at work are unlikely to have met her; likewise if a colleague drops dead at work, my family members are unlikely to have known her. Colleagues or family can say "I'm sorry" but they are not themselves sorry, because they never knew the deceased.

- Geographical mobility. Not living with, or very near, close kin is related to urbanism and to class (Fischer, 1977), but the key factor is geographical mobility (Wenger, 1995). The geographically mobile are those least likely to have daily face-to-face interactions with others who knew the deceased well or even at all.
- Longevity. The twentieth century was the first century in Western history in which the typical death is not that of a child. Most children reach adulthood, and many adults reach old age. So the typical death in old age happens after the children have moved out, leaving a widow or widower on his or her own and leaving adult children geographically separated both from the surviving parent and from each other.

We are describing trends that should not be exaggerated, because a fair amount of residential propinquity still exists. In England substantial proportions of elderly people live near adult children (Qureshi & Walker, 1989; Warnes, Howe, & Took, 1985; Wenger, 1995), and in the United States the extended family can still be important, the telephone and the automobile shrinking geographical distance (Litwak, 1965). Rosenblatt and Elde (1990) found that all of their adult Midwestern respondents had reminisced with siblings about their deceased parent. Most bereaved people are elderly, and though the elderly widow is likely to live on her own she is likely to have regular—if not daily—contact with kin, either face-to-face or on the telephone. Nevertheless, the trend is toward it becoming increasingly difficult for bereaved people together to construct the deceased as an honored ancestor, except in highly private and individualized ways. Group ancestors are less and less found in the modern West.

Occasionally in complex urban societies, a death may shake an entire community, in which case there is typically a reversion to communal mourning. The death of a schoolchild may shake the entire school; the death in peacetime of a soldier may affect the entire unit. As modern communication creates the global village, a new kind of communal—even global—mourning is possible when a prominent personality dies. This modern phenomenon was noted as the United States mourned the loss of President Kennedy (Greenberg & Parker, 1964), and was recently reenacted for Diana, Princess of Wales (Walter, 1999b).

Postmodern Communities of Bereaved Individuals

Because of social structure, culture, or other compounding factors, bereaved people may not be able to talk about the dead to those with whom they daily interact. In this context, recent decades have witnessed the rise of self-help groups in which bereaved people create a community not with those who knew the deceased but with strangers who have suffered the same category of loss. In his participant observation study of a chapter of a self-help group of bereaved parents, Klass (1988, 1996) found that the group encourages members to talk about their interactions with their dead children and to create rituals that evoke their presence, to such an extent that members begin to feel they know each others' children. In the group, the dead children continue to have the existence that is denied them in the rest of society. After a while, the affirmation of the continuing bond that the group has provided may be sufficient for the parent to leave the group, with the bond safely internalized within the parent. Klass has suggested that this process is not peripheral but is the key to the group's healing power.

It is not known how much social validation people need once the deceased is safely internalized. Nor is it known how the communal creation of a place for the dead functions in other self-help groups, support groups, or bereavement counseling. Textbooks on bereavement counseling focus much more on the feelings of the client rather than on the biography of the deceased (Walter, 1999a). Klass (1988) found that talking about and to the deceased was a useful technique in his counseling practice (also see Rynearson, 1987), and a number of counselors have informed Walter that they too encourage talking about the dead. A number of grief therapists also use the empty chair technique in which the client addresses feelings or thoughts to the deceased, or they use the presence of the dead to help clients "finish unfinished business." But whether counseling practice overall reflects the textbooks' silence about interacting with the dead is not known, because there has been no systematic research into what actually happens in one-to-one bereavement counseling. It is possible that those trained as generic counselors, especially according to the tenets of person-centered counseling, may be more open to accepting a client's expressed desire to talk about the dead than are those who have been trained specifically as bereavement counselors or trained in models that emphasize detachment from the deceased.

Insofar as counselors respond positively when a client wants to talk about the deceased, the counselor may need to shift focus. If a client is exploring feelings, these may be similar to those experienced by other bereaved people. But if the client is talking about the deceased, then he or she is telling the story of a unique person. Many bereaved people feel the one they have lost is extraordinary, and they want that extraordinariness confirmed (Shapiro, 1994). At this point, the counselor may need to display interest in the deceased as much as empathy with the bereaved person. The counselor might be on the lookout for the same kinds of dysfunctions in the bond with the deceased as can be seen in bonds with the living (Klass, 1988).

CONCLUSION

In this chapter, we have sketched what seem to us to be how bonds are maintained with the dead, even in the individualistic and secular culture that characterizes much of the modern West. This is not to deny that some people may prefer to forget the dead, temporarily (Rosenblatt, 1983, pp. 39–40) or permanently (Winter, 1997). Recognition that bonds often are maintained is widespread in popular culture, even if not within bereavement theory. *Badger's Parting Gifts* (Varley, 1984), a popular bereavement book for children, describes the deceased Badger's friends telling each other his story, gaining valued lessons from him, speaking directly to him, and even sensing his presence. The story depicts a community of animals for whom Badger is a valued ancestor, each animal having been influenced by him in a different way and yet able to share memories and create a joint ancestor.

The dead may have been banished from twentieth-century Western culture and from the scientific literature on bereavement, but they continue to inhabit the lives of many private individuals. Still, bonds to the dead are not independent of the social changes associated with modernity and with postmodernity: Both the living and the dead are now free agents. The dead freely help the living, without invitation. Except to keep their memory alive and honor them by the way we live, the living no longer have ways to help the dead. We see little today of the obligations and threats that characterized the relationship between the living and the dead in other times and places. The dead with whom we commune are freely chosen, just as are our communities, careers, and marriage partners. We construct our communities, and within them we construct our meanings and our own pantheon of ancestors.

REFERENCES

Ariès, P. (1981). *The hour of our death.* London: Penguin.

Balk, D. E. (1996). Attachment and the reactions of bereaved college students: A longitudinal study. In D. Klass, P. R. Silverman, & S. L. Nickman, (Eds.), *Continuing bonds: New understandings of grief* (pp. 311–328). Washington, DC: Taylor & Francis.

Bennett, G. (1987). *Traditions of belief: Women, folklore and the supernatural today.* London: Penguin.

Bentall, R. P. (1990). The illusion of reality: A review and integration of psychological research on hallucinations. *Psychological Bulletin, 107,* 82–95.

Berger, P., Berger, B., & Kellner, H. (1974). *The homeless mind: Modernization and consciousness.* London: Penguin.

Berger, P., & Kellner, H. (1964). Marriage and the construction of reality. *Diogenes, 46*, 1–25.

Bowlby, J. (1980). *Attachment and loss. Vol. 3. Loss: Sadness and depression.* New York: Basic Books.

Brabant, S. (1996). *Mending the torn fabric: For those who grieve and those who want to help them.* Amityville, NY: Baywood.

Brandon, R. (1983). *The spiritualists.* London: Weidenfeld & Nicolson.

Clark, D. (1982). *Between pulpit and pew: Folk religion in a North Yorkshire fishing village.* Cambridge: Cambridge University Press.

Datson, S., & Marwit, S. J. (1997). Personality constructs and perceived presence of deceased loved ones. *Death Studies, 21*, 31–46.

Dietrich, D. R., & Shabad, P. C. (1989). *The problem of loss and mourning: Psychoanalytic perspectives.* Madison, CT: International Universities Press.

Douglas, A. (1977). *The feminization of American culture.* New York: Alfred Knopf.

Duck, S. (1994). *Meaningful relationships: Talking, sense, and relating.* Newbury Park, CA: Sage.

Duffy, E. (1992). *The stripping of the altars: Traditional religion in England 1400–1580.* New Haven, CT: Yale University Press.

Fenichel, O. (1945). *The psychoanalytic theory of neurosis.* New York: Norton.

Finucane, R. C. (1996). *Ghosts: Appearances of the dead and cultural transformation.* Amherst, NY: Prometheus Books.

Fischer, C. (1977). Network analysis and urban studies. In C. Fischer, R. M. Jackson, C. A. Steuve, K. Gerson, L. M. Jones, & M. Baldassare (Eds.), *Networks and places: Social relations in the urban setting* (pp. 19–37). New York: Free Press.

Fortes, M. (1965). Reflections on ancestor worship in Africa. In M. Fortes & G. Dieterlen (Eds.), *African systems of thought* (pp. 122–124). London: Oxford University Press for International African Institute.

Fraley, R. C., & Shaver, P. R. (1999). Loss and bereavement: Attachment theory and recent controversies concerning "grief work" and the nature of detachment. In J. Cassidy & P. R. Shaver (Eds.), *Handbook of attachment: Theory, research, and clinical applications* (pp. 735–759). New York: Guilford.

Francis, D., Kellaher, L., & Lee, C. (1997). Talking to people in cemeteries. *Journal of the Institute of Burial and Cremation Administration, 65*, 14–25.

Frank, A. W. (1995). *The wounded storyteller: Body, illness, and ethics.* Chicago: Chicago University Press.

Geary, P. J. (1994). *Living with the dead in the middle ages.* Ithaca, NY: Cornell University Press.

Giddens, A. (1991). *Modernity and self-identity.* Oxford: Polity.

Glick, I. O., Weiss, R. S., & Parkes, C. M. (1974). *The first year of bereavement.* New York: Wiley.

Greeley, A. (1975). *The sociology of the paranormal: A reconnaissance.* Beverley Hills, CA: Sage.

Greenberg, B. S., & Parker, E. B. (Eds.). (1964). *The Kennedy assassination and the American public: Social communication in crisis.* Stanford, CA: Stanford University Press.

Haight, B. (1988). The therapeutic role of a structured life review process in homebound elderly subjects. *Journal of Gerontology, 43,* 40–44.

Hamilton, M. (1998). *Sociology and the world's religions.* Basingstoke, UK: Macmillan.

Haraldsson, E. (1988). Survey of claimed encounters with the dead. *Omega, 19,* 103–113.

Horton, P. C. (1981). *Solace, the missing dimension in psychiatry.* Chicago: University of Chicago Press.

Kalish, R. A., & Reynolds, D. K. (1974). Widows view death: A brief research note. *Omega, 5,* 187–192.

Kerr, H., & Crow. C. (Eds.). (1983). *The Occult in America: New historical perspectives.* Chicago: University of Illinois Press.

Klass, D. (1988). *Parental grief: Resolution and solace.* New York: Springer.

Klass, D. (1993). Solace and immortality: Bereaved parents' continuing bond with their children. *Death Studies, 17,* 343–368.

Klass, D. (1996). The deceased child in the psychic and social worlds of bereaved parents during the resolution of grief. In D. Klass, P. R. Silverman, & S. L. Nickman (Eds.), *Continuing bonds: New understandings of grief* (pp. 199–215). Washington, DC: Taylor & Francis.

Klass, D., Silverman, P. R., & Nickman, S. L. (Eds.). (1996). *Continuing bonds: New understandings of grief.* Washington, DC: Taylor & Francis.

Kleinman, A. (1988). *The illness narratives.* New York: Basic Books.

Koppelman, K. L. (1994) *The fall of a sparrow: Of death and dreams and healing.* Amityville, NY: Baywood.

Lasch, C. (1977). *Haven in a heartless world.* New York: Basic Books.

Litwak, E. (1965). Extended kin relations in an industrial democratic society. In E. Shanas & G. Streib (Eds.), *Social structure and the family: Generational relations* (pp. 290–323). Englewood Cliffs, NJ: Prentice Hall.

Mandelbaum, D. (1959). Social uses of funeral rites. In H. Feifel (Ed.), *The meaning of death.* New York: McGraw Hill.

Marwit, S. J., & Klass, D. (1995). Grief and the role of the inner representation of the deceased. *Omega, 30,* 283–298.

McAdams, D. (1993). *The stories we live by: Personal myths and the making of the self.* New York: William Morrow.

McDannell, C., & Lang, B. (1988). *Heaven, a history.* New Haven, CT: Yale University Press.

Neimeyer, R. A., & Mahoney, M. J. (Eds.). (1995). *Constructivism in psychotherapy.* Washington, DC: American Psychological Association.

Olson, P. R., Suddeth, J. A., Peterson, P. A., & Egelhoff, C. (1985). Hallucinations of widowhood. *Journal of the American Geriatric Society, 33,* 543–547.

Parkes, C. M. (1972). *Bereavement: Studies of grief in adult life*. London: Penguin.

Parkes, C. M. (1986). *Bereavement: Studies of grief in adult life* (2nd ed.). London: Tavistock.

Qureshi, H., & Walker, A. (1989). *The caring relationship: Elderly people and their families*. Basingstoke, UK: Macmillan.

Raphael, B. (1983). *The anatomy of bereavement*. New York: Basic Books.

Rees, D. (1971). The hallucinations of widowhood. *British Medical Journal, 4,* 37–41.

Rees, D. (1997). *Death and bereavement: The psychological, religious and cultural interfaces*. London: Whurr.

Rogo, D. S. (1986). *Life after death*. Wellingborough, UK: Aquarian Press.

Rosenblatt, P. (1983). *Bitter, bitter tears: Nineteenth-century diarists and twentieth century grief theories*. Minneapolis: University of Minnesota Press.

Rosenblatt, P., & Elde, C. (1990). Shared reminiscence about a deceased parent: Implications for grief education and grief counselling. *Family Relations, 39,* 206–210.

Rynearson, E. K. (1987). Psychotherapy of pathologic grief: Revisions and limitations. *Psychiatric Clinics of North America, 10,* 487–499.

Sanders, C. M. (1989). *Grief: The mourning after*. New York: Wiley.

Sarbin, T. R. (Ed.). (1986). *Narrative psychology: The storied nature of human conduct*. New York: Praeger.

Schafer, R. (1968). *Aspects of internalization*. New York: International Universities Press.

Seale, C. (1998). *Constructing death: A sociology of dying and bereavement*. Cambridge: Cambridge University Press.

Shapiro, E. R. (1994). *Grief as a family process: A developmental approach to clinical practice*. New York: Guilford Press.

Shuchter, S. R., & Zisook, S. (1993). The course of normal grief. In M. S. Stroebe, W. Stroebe, & R. O. Hansson (Eds.), *Handbook of Bereavement* (pp. 23–43). New York: Cambridge University Press.

Silverman, P. R., & Klass, D. (1996). Introduction: What's the problem? In D. Klass, P. R. Silverman, & S. Nickman (Eds.), *Continuing bonds: New understandings of grief* (pp. 3–27). Washington, DC: Taylor & Francis.

Silverman, P. R., & Nickman, S. L. (1996). Children's construction of their dead parents. In D. Klass, P. R. Silverman, & S. Nickman (Eds.), *Continuing bonds: New understandings of grief* (pp. 73–86). Washington, DC: Taylor & Francis.

Simon-Buller, S., Christopherson, V., & Jones, P. (1988). Correlates of sensing the presence of a deceased spouse. *Omega, 19,* 21–30.

Smith, R. J. (1974). *Ancestor worship in contemporary Japan*. Stanford, CA: Stanford University Press.

Stroebe, M. (1997). From mourning and melancholia to bereavement and biography: an assessment of Walter's new model of grief. *Mortality, 2,* 255–262.

Stroebe, M., Gergen, M. M., Gergen, K. J., & Stroebe, W. (1992). Broken hearts or broken bonds: Love and death in historical perspective. *American Psychologist, 47*, 1205–1212.

Tahka, V. (1984). Dealing with object loss. *Scandinavian Psychoanalytic Review, 7*, 13–33.

Varley, S. (1984). *Badger's parting gifts*. London: Random Century.

Volkan, V. (1981). *Linking objects and linking phenomena: A study of the forms, symptoms, metapsychology, and therapy of complicated mourning*. New York: International Universities Press.

Volkan, V., & Showalter, C. (1968). Known object loss, disturbance in reality testing, and "re-grief" work as a method of brief psychotherapy. *Psychiatric Quarterly, 42*, 358–374.

Walter, T. (1990). *Funerals—And how to improve them*. London: Hodder.

Walter, T. (1994). *The revival of death*. London & New York: Routledge.

Walter, T. (1996a). *The eclipse of eternity: A sociology of the afterlife*. Basingstoke, UK: Macmillan/New York: St. Martins Press.

Walter, T. (1996b). A new model of grief: Bereavement and biography. *Mortality, 1*, 7–25.

Walter, T. (1999a). *On bereavement: The culture of grief*. Buckingham: Open University Press.

Walter, T. (Ed.). (1999b). *The mourning for Princess Diana*. Oxford: Berg.

Warnes, A. M., Howes, D. R., & Took, L. (1985). Residential locations and intergenerational visiting in retirement. *Quarterly Journal of Social Affairs, 1*, 231–247.

Wenger, C. (1995). A comparison of urban with rural support networks: Liverpool and North Wales. *Ageing & Society, 15*, 59–81.

Winter, J. (1995). *Sites of memory, sites of mourning: The Great War in European cultural history*. Cambridge: Cambridge University Press.

Winter, J. (1997, April). *Remembering total war*. Paper presented to the Third International Conference on the Social Context of Death, Dying and Disposal, Cardiff, California.

20

ASSESSMENT OF COPING WITH LOSS: DIMENSIONS AND MEASUREMENT

GUUS L. VAN HECK AND DENISE T. D. DE RIDDER

Evidence suggests that coping strategies mediate between the confrontation with stressful situations and the consequences for health and well-being (Aldwin & Revenson, 1987). Still, it has proven rather difficult to determine which health outcomes may indicate beneficial effects of coping, as many indicators of health have proven insensitive for coping efforts because they are either theoretically irrelevant or too distal (Folkman, 1992). In spite of the somewhat disappointing results regarding its effectiveness, coping can be conceived of as a key concept in the study of human adaptation. Over the past two decades, numerous articles on coping have been published covering different types of stressors, including bereavement and grief (e.g., Brison & Leavitt, 1995; Herth, 1990; Shuchter & Zisook, 1993; M. S. Stroebe, 1992). However, despite the apparent popularity of the coping concept, little attention has been paid to assessment issues (De Ridder, 1997; Parker & Endler, 1992). This has resulted in many coping measures of poor validity and reliability (Cohen, 1991; Coyne & Gottlieb, 1996; De Ridder, 1997; Parker & Endler, 1992; Stone, Greenberg, Kennedy-Moore, & Newman, 1991; Stone & Kennedy-Moore, 1992; Stone, Kennedy-Moore, Greenberg, Newman, & Neale, 1992).

This chapter aims at a critical discussion of established psychometric assessment techniques for measuring ways of coping with loss and bereavement. Central issues to be addressed concern (a) the conceptual clarity of coping with loss and bereavement compared to coping with other kinds of stressful situations, (b) the reliability and validity of the current generation of psychometric instruments for measuring coping with loss and bereavement, and (c) the methodological limitations of present-day assessment of coping with stressors associated with loss and suggestions for future directions in the development of new assessment methods.

CONCEPTUAL ISSUES IN COPING WITH LOSS

In the past decades, the study of coping has been highly influenced by the authoritative cognitive–mediational theory of stress and coping proposed by Lazarus and his coworkers (e.g., Lazarus, 1966; Lazarus & Folkman, 1984). This approach implies that coping efforts are initiated by appraising a particular event as threatening, or involving loss, harm, or challenge. In addition to an evaluation of the personal significance of events, the approach also dictates that the subsequent attempts to deal with these conditions are dynamic, because they may change over time, and transactional, because they take into account the specific demands of the stressful encounter. Applied to the stressful conditions of loss and bereavement, the cognitive perspective suggests that to provide an adequate description of coping, one way or another, one should pay attention to the demands associated with loss and the changes in the coping process during specific stages of bereavement. However, as is the case in many other fields of coping with specific upsetting conditions such as, for example, health problems or work stress, a conceptual analysis of the ways the demands associated with loss and bereavement events may shape the coping process is absent. Hence a number of classic problems relating to conceptualizing coping with particular stressful conditions bear relevance for the study of coping with loss. They all relate to the issue of whether individuals are "allowed" to perform their habitual coping preferences in response to the typical demands of the loss situation or whether these coping responses are affected by the typical characteristics of the loss event.

Styles or Strategies?

Viewed from this perspective, an issue that is of utmost importance for the understanding of coping with loss and bereavement is the difference between situational coping strategies and dispositional coping styles. The former approach takes into account the impact of specific stressful situations on coping behaviors, and the latter term refers to habitual ways of dealing with stress in general, irrespective of the particular type of stressful adaptational tasks that individuals encounter in their lives. Although it is well-established that people possess stable and consistent coping preferences that are associated with personality traits (Van Heck & Vingerhoets, 1989), it is also true that to some extent people are able to vary their responses to stressful situations in accordance with the demands these situations place on psychological adaptation. Depending on what kind of questions are posed, one can either use an intraindividual approach, in which coping responses of the same person or group of persons are studied across different types of situations attempting to examine the process of coping. Or one may prefer an interindividual approach in which the focus is on individual differences in basic coping strategies that are used by individuals across different types of stressful situations.

Of course, within the context of bereavement studies, virtually all investigations have used a situation-specific assessment of coping, emphasizing the stressful event of the death of a loved one, asking respondents to indicate how they have been reacting following the loss experience. This is done using short descriptive narratives of the particular stressful episode elicited from the respondents or using a short indication of the relevant stressor provided by the investigators. This research strategy makes it possible to use off-the-shelf self-report checklists and questionnaires that were not originally designed for coping with loss—mostly while keeping all items of the complete scale, and sometimes tailored to fit the narrower focus on bereavement by eliminating inapplicable responses or adding a few new items. However, this has never been done in a systematic way. For example, there are no lists available that indicate which items of a particular well-known coping instrument should be selected for coping with bereavement and which modules of loss-specific items should be added to optimize these scales for bereavement research. Moreover, this tradition of using a situational format of scales that were originally designed for assessing dispositional coping styles has prevented the development of a tradition of constructing scales that are specific for dealing with a particular type of stressor, such as loss or bereavement. As such, there is no systematic information available that describes precisely the particular demands loss situations impose on individuals' coping strategies and to what extent these demands differ from other kinds of stressful conditions.

The Domain of Coping With Loss and the Representative Design

Another conceptual issue that is of relevance for assessing coping with loss and bereavement concerns the failure of present day coping instruments to encompass the full range of adaptive thought and behavior. For instance, Coyne and Gottlieb (1996) have pointed at the erroneous exclusion of anticipatory coping. In a similar way, Aspinwall and Taylor (1997) have criticized the restriction of coping to reactive efforts excluding proactive coping efforts in which people try to foresee potential stressors and build resources to increase their competence in dealing with these stressors once they have fully developed. In instances of loss situations (e.g., anticipated death of one's spouse caused by chronic disease), the introduction of a time perspective may improve our understanding of the full range of thoughts and cognitions helpful in dealing with loss. It has also been suggested that a more liberal approach to coping, including habitual and automatic behaviors, may provide a better understanding of the variety of strategic and tactical maneuvers people use when they face adverse conditions. With respect to the latter omission Coyne and Gottlieb (1996) argued that it makes no sense to stop labeling particular ways of dealing with problems as coping methods once they have become dependable and part of a routine strategy. However, such a criticism appears to be at odds with a feature of coping that is considered essential— namely that, by definition, it refers to attempts that go beyond routinized behaviors. Others (e.g., Parkes, 1996) have stated that excluding semiconscious and subconscious operations is too restrictive and therefore a serious omission. Furthermore, the absence of items reflecting "coping through emotional approach" or confusing emotional expression with active or passive emotional rumination (Stanton, Danoff-Burg, Cameron, & Ellis, 1994) and the contamination of emotion regulation with emotional distress (e.g., De Ridder, 1997) are considered annoying shortcomings that seriously affect the study of coping with loss. In general, the lack of representative design (Brunswik, 1956) has restricted the identification of strategies related to adaptive functioning and can lead to a distorted picture of individual coping efforts and the effectiveness of coping (see, e.g., Coyne & Gottlieb, 1996).

Decisions regarding the conceptualization of coping have been inaccurate, incomplete, sometimes overly restrictive, sometimes not restrictive enough. Examples of the latter are the use of scales originally designed for assessing subjective experiences of life events and difficulties as coping scales. The reactions that are assessed by these instruments reflect more the impact of stressful events than the individual's attempts to influence and moderate the effects of stress. For that reason, we do not consider instruments such as the Impact of Events Scale (Horowitz, Wilner, & Alvarez, 1979) or the Hopelessness Scale (Beck, Weissman, Lester, & Trexler, 1974) as proper coping scales. They adequately measure qualities of the experience of stress, but fail to assess coping with stress.

So, given the fact that current conceptualizations of coping leave much to be desired, one should expect that the scales that are most prominent in studies of coping with bereavement are to a certain extent open to question. This can be illustrated by closely examining two questions. A first major question is whether our current knowledge of the adaptive efforts of people having to deal with bereavement is adequately represented in the descriptions of the coping domain that underlie the coping assessment instruments that are most frequently used in coping research. A second question concerns the applicability of the responses incorporated in these instruments. Are they suitable for describing the coping efforts of people trying to come to terms with the death of a loved person?

Bereavement-Specific Coping

Are current listings of the numerous thoughts, feelings, and actions that have been reported by bereaved people mostly overlapping with theoretical frameworks describing the domains and facets of coping, stressor unspecified? The answer must be clear: No. Generic coping instruments, such as the Ways of Coping Questionnaire (WCQ; Folkman & Lazarus, 1988), the Coping Orientation to Problems Experienced (COPE ; Carver, Scheier, & Weintraub, 1989), or the Coping Inventory for Stressful Situations (CISS; Endler & Parker, 1990) are rather poor descriptors of the variety of coping efforts of bereaved individuals. An illustration of this point can be given by contrasting aspects of grief such as attempts to recover the dead person by actively seeking places associated with the dead person, conscious searching and calling for the deceased, developing a sense of presence of the dead person, and building a new image of the dead person. Crying and restless and aimless hyperactivity have also been described in the literature on coping with bereavement (e.g., Littlewood, 1992). This listing of coping efforts of bereaved individuals is far from exhaustive. Many more important strategies have been reported, such as identification phenomena—that is, the adoption of traits, mannerisms, or symptoms of the lost person (Parkes, 1996) or hallucinations or illusions of the presence of the lost person (Rees, 1971). Although it may sound strange that such irrational thoughts and behaviors as crying and hallucinating are conceived of as coping strategies, one ought to keep in mind that these behaviors may be helpful in regulating emotion or in reducing the threat of loss, the very objectives of coping efforts. Nevertheless, these coping strategies are missing in scales such as the WCQ, the COPE, or the CISS, to mention some of the more important instruments. The latter instruments are generic coping scales that could be applied to many different contexts. For this wide applicability, however, a high price has to be paid. Working with a generic instrument implies that the richness and domain specificity of coping has been sacrificed

(Coyne & Gottlieb, 1996). This richness of specific coping methods is fully present in coping with the loss of a person. This does not exclude, of course, that some of the phenomena that have emerged in studies of the reaction to bereavement are also found in a rather similar form following other types of loss—for instance, loss of a limb, loss of a home, or divorce. However, even if this is true, then still "there is no reason to believe that all types and degrees of loss give rise to identical reactions" (Parkes, 1996, p. 208).

When drawing conclusions from this state of affairs, it should be kept in mind that even within the category of generic instruments there are substantial differences regarding the level of abstraction of the concepts reflected in the scales. A large group of measures focuses on broad dimensions reflecting approach versus avoidance, elaborating on the classic fight versus flight distinction, such as denial–intrusion (Horowitz, 1979), cognitive avoidance–vigilance (Krohne, 1993), or rejection–attention (Mullen & Suls, 1982). Another authoritative distinction was proposed by Folkman and Lazarus (1980), distinguishing between problem-focused coping directed at changing the situation that is causing the discomfort and emotion-focused coping, directed at regulating distressing emotions. This view on the two major functions of coping is beyond doubt the most widely used way of categorizing coping responses, although the distinction between emotion-focused and problem-focused coping was originally intended to classify coping *aims* instead of coping *efforts*. Others have proposed combinations of these basic coping factors. For example, Endler and Parker (1990) have distinguished three dimensions: task-oriented, emotion-oriented, and avoidance-oriented coping. Hierarchical factor analyses of scales such as the WCQ have demonstrated convincingly that primary factors such as confrontive coping, distancing, self-controling, seeking social support, and so forth can be grouped on secondary or tertiary levels in terms of emotion orientation and problem orientation or avoidance versus approach (e.g., Tobin, Holroyd, Reynolds, & Wigal, 1989). Such broad basic dimensions, however, "do not adequately explain or predict intraindividual variations in the way given sources of stress are dealt with in specific contexts," according to Lazarus (1993, p. 241), who continues by stating that "unidimensional typologies are, perhaps, too restricted in what they say about complex adaptational struggles to have much utility in explaining and predicting what people do when confronted with the many forms of harm, threat, and challenge to which all persons are exposed" (Lazarus, 1993, p. 241). In spite of this criticism, identifying the "superstrategies" of avoidance versus approach coping or emotion-focused versus problem-focused coping has been welcomed as a useful distinction to understand concrete coping acts and coping strategies at a more abstract level (Krohne, 1993).

Appropriateness of Coping Items

Another issue concerns the question of whether or not items in the currently most popular coping instruments are appropriate for assessing coping with bereavement (Ben-Porath, Waller, & Butcher, 1991). Stone, Greenberg, Kennedy-Moore, and Newman (1991) have pointed out the degree of applicability of coping items to different kinds of problems and have found that many coping items stemming from well-known scales were not applicable to certain kinds of stressful events. The study by Stone and coworkers was not directed at bereavement or grief, for example. Rather, their study suggests that this particular problem could also play a role in research on coping with the loss of a loved person. An inspection of coping items shows that items differ considerably with respect to the applicability in the bereavement situation. To illustrate, let us take a look at the WCQ. In our opinion, items such as "tried to get the person responsible to change his or her mind," "realized I brought the problem on myself," or "I made a promise to myself that things would be different next time" have a very limited applicability with respect to coping with the death of a partner, child, friend, or relative. Other scales such as the COPE and the CISS seem to be better in this regard, although, as stated earlier, they may not encompass the full range of possible reactions to a loss event.

ASSESSMENT OF COPING WITH LOSS: EXISTING MEASURES

Although the earlier work on coping was characterized by ad hoc procedures such as in-depth clinical interviews, more recent coping studies show the use of standardized measures. We next will describe the questionnaires that are most widely used in bereavement research. First, we will discuss a number of general self-report scales aimed at assessing situational coping strategies. Second, we will describe scales specifically developed for bereavement coping.

General Self-Report Scales

Many general coping scales exist, such as the Miller Behavioral Style Scale (Miller, 1987), the Mainz Coping Inventory (Krohne, 1993), the Billings and Moos Coping Measure (Billings & Moos, 1981), the Ways of Coping Questionnaire (WCQ; Folkman & Lazarus, 1988), the Coping Strategy Indicator (CSI; Amirkhan, 1990, 1994), the Life Events and Coping Inventory for Children (Dise-Lewis, 1988), the Adolescent Coping Orientation for Problem Experiences Inventory (A-COPE; Patterson & McCubbin, 1987), the Life Situations Inventory (Feifel & Strack, 1989), the Coping Inventory for Stressful Situations (CISS; Endler & Parker, 1990), the COPE (Carver et al., 1989), the Constructive Thinking Inventory (Epstein & Meier, 1989), and the Stress and Coping Process Questionnaire (Perrez & Reicherts, 1992), to list only the best-known scales in the field. These scales differ in the number of coping dimensions that they aim to assess (from two in the Miller Behavioral Style Scale to as much as 13 in the COPE), whether they allow for a situation-specific assessment (e.g., provided in the WCQ and the COPE), the stability of the dimensional structure and other psychometric qualities such as internal consistencies and associations between the subscales (e.g., weak in the WCQ and strong in the CISS), and their focus on either an approach–avoidance distinction or a problem-focused versus an emotion-focused distinction. Detailed reviews of these scales are provided by Schwarzer and Schwarzer (1996) and by De Ridder (1997). Some of these scales may be considered less relevant for use in loss and bereavement research because they focus on anxiety-provoking situations (the Miller Behavioral Style Scale and the Mainz Coping Inventory), allow for the assessment of dispositional coping styles only (CISS, Constructive Thinking Inventory), have poor psychometric qualities (e.g., CSI), or identify only two or three "superstrategies" (CISS, the Mainz Coping Inventory, the Billings and Moos Coping Measure, the Life Situations Inventory). Therefore, we will limit our discussion of general coping scales to those that seem most relevant for use in assessing loss and bereavement coping and as such provide an illustration of the problems associated with applying general measures in the specific situational context of loss and bereavement.

The Ways of Coping Questionnaire (WCQ; Folkman & Lazarus, 1988) or an earlier version, the Ways of Coping Checklist (WCC; Folkman & Lazarus, 1980) is a measure belonging to the process approach of coping, although large numbers of researchers have used the scale in a disposition-centered way. In its original version, respondents are asked to provide a short description of the most stressful event they encountered during the previous months and subsequently answer 68 items reflecting eight scales: confrontive coping, distancing, self-controling, seeking social support, accepting responsibility, escape–avoidance, planful problem-solving, and positive reappraisal. Although the WCQ is considered the standard in the field, one of its major problems concerns the instability of factors from sample to sample and from stressor to stressor, which is a problem that affects most situational coping measures. As the authors encourage researchers to adapt the WCQ for their own research purposes, the WCQ offers possibilities to adjust the items to the topic under study; however, this comes at the cost of diminished possibilities to compare the results with the outcomes of other studies. Another problem is that the eight original scales do not appear to be of the same theoretical level. Also, it remains undetermined to what extent the eight factors are embedded in the initial dimensions of problem-focused and emotion-focused coping.

The 53-item COPE scale developed by Carver et al. (1989) is a multidimensional coping inventory to assess 13 facets of coping. Five facets, each measured by four items, cover the domain of problem-oriented coping: active coping, planning, suppression of competing activities, restraint coping, and seeking of instrumental social support. Another five facets reflect emotion-oriented coping: seeking of emotional social support, positive reinterpretation, acceptance, denial, and turning to religion. Finally, three facets measure focusing on and venting of emotions, behavioral disengagement, and mental disengagement. A positive feature of the COPE concerns the theoretically derived scales elaborating on the dimensions of problem-focused and emotion-focused coping. Another positive feature is the availability of both a dispositional and a situational version of the scales, which allows for an analysis of the impact of situational features on the reported coping attempts in comparison with the impact of personal dispositions such as coping styles, optimism, or self-efficacy.

The Stress and Coping Process Questionnaire (Perrez & Reicherts, 1992) is a measure aimed at identifying two classes of coping, self-directed strategies (e.g., search for information, suppression of information, reevaluation, palliation, and self-blame) and environment-directed strategies (e.g., instrumental action, avoidance, and hesitation), a distinction that bears strong resemblance to emotion-focused coping and problem-focused coping. Although the instrument has not been used much, its unique properties lie in the distinction between coping intentions and coping acts, which allows for a detailed account of the coping process. The instrument also provides hypothetical event scenarios of two classes of stressful events, ambiguous–threatening and loss–failure. As such it is not suitable for ready use in bereavement research, although it may definitely suggest a research strategy to disentangle the various aspects of the loss situation.

Bereavement-Specific Coping Scales

There is a remarkable scarcity of scales that are specifically developed for bereavement coping. This does not mean that there are no inventories that focus on grief reactions. As a matter of fact, there are quite a number of such instruments, as can be learned from recent summaries of questionnaire measures of grief (Archer, 1999; chapter 5, this volume).

Sometimes grief reactions are more or less distinguished from coping. A good example is a study by Caserta, Lund, and Dimond (1985) in which typical grief reactions, such as emotional shock, negative affect, and helplessness, are contrasted with coping subscales, emphasizing confronting the loss, learning new tasks, and other forms of positive coping. Another example can be found in the longitudinal work of Shuchter and coworkers (see, e.g., Shuchter & Zisook, 1993) in which a multidimensional widowhood questionnaire was used with separate dimensions reflecting (a) emotional and cognitive responses such as apathy, disorganization, expressions of emotional pain, anger, guilt, anxiety and feelings of loneliness; and (b) coping with emotional pain. Items with high loadings on the latter dimension measured coping efforts such as acceptance and disbelief, emotional control, rationalization, faith, avoidance, active distraction, involvement with others, expression and exposure, and use of alcohol, cigarettes, medication, and so forth.

Most of the time, however, the existing scales cover a variety of reactions reflecting, either (a) coping with items assessing recovery from, or resolution of, grief—for example, the Acceptance of Loss Scale (ALS; Osuji, 1985), focusing on acceptance, or the Grief Resolution Index (Remondet & Hansson, 1987), emphasizing acceptance, closure and reintegration; (b) manifestations of the altered patterns of perception, thought, emotion and actions that characterize grief—for example, the Grant Foundation Bereavement Inventory (see Balk & Vesta, 1998), which assesses aspects of the grief process with an emphasis on attachment, reunion fantasies, disbelief, identification phenomena, and feelings of disloyalty; or (c) a combination of "symptoms," on the one hand, and ways in which people seek to manage their grief, on the other hand—for example, the Grief Experience Inventory (GEI; Sanders, Mauger, & Strong, 1985, 1991). The latter scale contains 135 true–false items and measures nine facets of grief —for ·example, despair, anger–hostility, guilt, social isolation, loss of control, rumination, depersonalization, somatization, and death anxiety. The scale is frequently used, often in combination with a semistructured (e.g., Milo, 1997) or a structured interview (e.g., Rando, 1983). The internal consistency for the separate scales range from moderate to fairly good. However, as the instrument assesses a mixture of coping efforts and psychological and somatic symptoms, it is not a pure coping inventory. Somewhat in between the second and the third category one can place the Texas Revised Inventory of Grief (TRIG; Faschingsbauer, Zisook, & DeVaul, 1987). This questionnaire contains two subscales of 8 and 13 items, assessing (a) feelings and actions at the time of the death, and (b) present feelings. The focus of the scale is on the impact of the loss on emotions and activities. Only a couple of items reflect coping efforts. In spite of this confounding of grief work with symptomatology (see M. S. Stroebe, 1992, for a discussion of the confounding of the process of adjustment to bereavement with symptomatology), internal consistency is moderate to good (>.75 most of the time). In the context of a review of the most prominent grief scales for assessing personal reactions to bereavement, Neimeyer and Hogan (chapter 5, this volume) have covered the GEI and the TRIG in more detail. Their discussion of these scales presents details that underline our reservation to consider these scales as coping instruments.

Drawing up the Balance

To date, only a few of the existing general coping scales appear suitable for assessing coping in loss and bereavement research. Because most of the existing scales are aimed either at identifying coping *dispositions* and as such are not suitable for providing a balanced picture of dealing with the specific situation of loss or they are aimed at assessing only a few coping strategies or dispositions at the cost of providing a valid account of the coping process, only few scales remain. We have discussed the WCQ, the COPE, and the Perrez and Reicherts instrument as possible candidates for the assessment of coping with loss. However, although these instruments are able to detect a variety of coping responses and even may distinguish coping intention from actual efforts (as in the Perrez and Reicherts instrument), it must be emphasized that none of these instruments was specifically designed for assessing coping with loss and as such may need some revision before they may be used in loss studies. Moreover, these instruments suffer from the conceptual flaws discussed in the first section of this chapter. In contrast, the measures developed specifically for assessing coping with loss may provide a more valid analysis of what is at stake during the process of coping with loss. Most of these instruments, however, suffer from another serious limitation, because they relate only distantly to the essence of what coping is about, and mixing coping efforts with other concepts such as symptoms.

Considering this, one is tempted to endorse Coyne's and Gottlieb's (1996) extremely negative evaluation of conventional checklists of coping: "Despite the accumulation of hundreds of studies, there is little sense of progress being made in our understanding of the role of coping in adaptation to stress. What consistencies are claimed are global, overly simplistic, and virtually self-evident" (p. 960). In their view, existing measures "render an incomplete and distorted portrait of coping" (p. 959). They base their harsh judgment on the observation that the existing instruments are grounded in too narrow a conception of coping, on the insight that the typical coping studies are not faithful to a transactional model of stress and coping, on the establishment that statistical controls cannot eliminate the effects of key person and situation variables on coping, and on the finding that no consistent interpretation can be assigned to coping scale scores. Other authors who have critically evaluated coping assessment have also pointed to these shortcomings and have added other limitations, such as the absence of items reflecting coping through emotional approach, the neglect of gender differences, and the inappropriateness of exploratory factor analysis for the construction of coping measures (Coyne & Gottlieb, 1996; De Ridder, 1997; Parker & Endler, 1992; Stone et al., 1991; Stone & Kennedy-Moore, 1992; Stone et al., 1992). To balance these negative evaluations, in the next section we will specify a number of critical issues that must be addressed in future development of methods suitable for as-sessing coping with loss and bereavement.

ASSESSING COPING WITH LOSS: DETERMINING THE KEY ISSUES

Elaborating on the conceptual issues that were presented in the first section of this chapter, we propose that instruments for assessing coping with loss should meet the criterion of accounting for situational specificity to provide a valid account of the coping process. In addition, a rational, theory-driven strategy should be preferred over inductive, empirical ap-proaches that bear the risk of coincidental solutions. A rational strategy is based on a selection of items that are considered to be related to the construct of interest. In contrast, a large item pool can be collected and empirically reduced to a number of scales using linear statistical models, such as the principal axes factor analysis model or the principal compo-nents model. Most of the coping scales that are currently available were constructed using the latter approach. A major reason for this may be that few researchers have attempted to define the relevant aspects of coping with loss, departing from existing theories on adaptation to loss. In the subsequent section, we discuss a number of issues that we consider relevant for the assessment of loss-specific coping.

The Impact of Situational Demands

Before one is able to list the items that may be relevant for con-structing a coping with loss scale, it appears wise to break down the loss event in a number of features that are considered stressful by those who suffer loss. The concept of "adaptive tasks," referring to aspects of the situation that are perceived as requiring coping efforts, may be useful in identifying the adaptive demands that are associated with loss, as has been done, for example, in the field of chronic diseases to identify the various aspects of the major life event of being chronically ill and list numerous "minor events" (De Ridder, Schreurs, & Bensing, 1998; Moos & Schaefer, 1984). Such an approach may start with the inductive categorization of issues involved in dealing with loss, such as grief, defining new goals or "life tasks," reestablishing social relationships, and preserving emotional balance, combined with a rational ordering of what is known about these issues. Such an approach may not only be useful to identify different coping strategies for different aspects of loss in the next stage of scale development, but is also more in accordance with the transactional coping theory im-plying that event characteristics may affect the coping options. A loss event, for example, bears some sense of immediacy, objectivity (the disappearance of a loved person), and may have consequences for the entire life span (Mikulincer & Florian, 1996), all features that impose constraints on coping efforts.

Collecting a Relevant Item Pool

As was indicated in the first section of this chapter, another important issue in developing measures for coping with loss concerns the establishment of a representative design covering all possible coping efforts that are relevant for dealing with loss. Starting from what is known about the behavioral and cognitive efforts bereaved people use in dealing with several aspects of the loss event, and paying respect to gender and age issues, such a loss-specific item pool may prove a more valid and valuable point of departure for constructing scales than deriving items from general coping scales. It should also be recommended that in constructing scales from these items, a rational strategy is followed, starting from a higher order categorization covering at least two (problem-focused versus emotion-focused or approach versus avoidance), but preferably three superstrategies (problem-focused, avoidance of emotions, confrontation of emotions). Such an approach allows for a bereavement-specific account of the coping process without jeopardizing the analysis of loss coping with strategies for dealing with other stressful situations at the higher level of superstrategies. Special respect should be paid to a scale construction strategy that allows for the simultaneous use of different coping attempts. The general problem of the inappropriateness of factor analysis allowing for the use of a particular response at the cost of using another one (e.g., Stone et al., 1991) seems all the more relevant to coping with loss, because it may be assumed that during crises people will not limit their coping efforts to one particular strategy but will try different approaches simultaneously. The use of multidimensional scaling techniques may therefore prove an important contribution to the construction of valid scales for assessing coping with loss.

The Role of Appraisal

Elaborating on the recent interest of personal meaning of stressors as a means to understanding individual variations in coping responses (Lazarus, 1993), it should be recommended that an adequate coping measure should pay respect to the issue of event appraisal (or, for that matter, appraisal of aspects of events) either in terms of the four categories suggested by Lazarus (i.e., loss, harm, threat, or challenge) or in an even more detailed way, referring to emotions generated by the loss event (e.g., anxiety, guilt, grief). Although few researchers have attempted to operationalize stress appraisal (cf. Peacock & Wong, 1990), to provide a better understanding of possible coping scenarios it may be useful to distinguish between the type and intensity of emotions aroused by experiencing a loss situation and assess their impact on the use of particular coping efforts.

Emotion-Focused Coping

One of the systematically undervalued aspects of coping relates to the issue of emotion-focused coping, which has been portrayed in the literature as a less effective way of coping that should only be used when more superior attempts to control the situation by problem-focused or approach efforts fail. This evaluation comes from research literature that has repeatedly demonstrated that emotion-focused coping is positively associated with emotional distress. However, as Coyne and Gottlieb (1996) have warned, these findings could simply reflect a confounding of measures of emotion-focused coping with emotional distress. In the past years, it has been demonstrated that treating emotion-focused coping in this way underestimates its value, especially in situations that lie beyond direct control as is, for example, the case in loss situations. However, to appreciate the effects of emotion-focused coping an effort should be made to disentangle symptoms of emotional distress, expressing emotions, passive rumination, and active grief work, which together obscure the role of emotion-focused coping in dealing with loss situations (Stanton et al., 1994). This aspect is of particular relevance given that the concept of grief work is so prominent in bereavement research. Moreover, recent research points out that emotional expression is not always beneficial and that in particular cases keeping one's emotion to one's self should be preferred (cf. chapter 22, this volume). Therefore, future research should be aimed at identifying under which conditions which aspect of emotion-focused coping may be helpful and whether our stereotypical ideas about the negative role of inhibition of emotions and the positive role of emotional disclosure are still valid in the context of bereavement. In general, it is recommended that positive aspects of emotions associated with loss events should be considered (cf. chapter 25, this volume).

The Role of Significant Others

Although the role of social support in the coping process has been the subject of much debate in the general coping literature (Schreurs & De Ridder, 1997), this issue bears specific relevance for assessing coping with loss. Loss events may be considered as social events because most of the time several people are confronted with loss simultaneously—for example, spouse and children or, more distantly, other family members and close friends. This does not only draw attention to the concept of social support seeking as an important coping strategy. In fact, it suggests an entire new area of coping research that moves far beyond the traditional assessment of individual coping strategies. It requires a concept such as "family coping" to study how members of a family together cope with loss and especially how they deal with the alternating positions of support seeker and support provider. More attention to support seeking as a strategy in coping with loss is also relevant. Especially in elderly people, women are more likely to be confronted with the loss of their partners. Therefore, social support seeking is a strategy that is more frequently found in women (De Ridder, 2000). In this respect, it may also be wise to account for a more differentiated assessment of the global concept of support seeking, as has been suggested by Carver et al. (1989) in the COPE measure and by Hobfoll, Dunahoo, Ben-Porath, and Monnier (1994) in the Strategic Approach to Coping measure. In both measures it is acknowledged that social support seeking may either be emotion-focused (as in seeking comfort) or problem-focused (as in seeking advice) and may even be a sign of avoidance coping (as in visiting a friend to escape from the confrontation with one's grief and despair).

Gender-Specific Coping

As stated previously, elder women are more likely to be confronted with loss events because epidemiological research has demonstrated that men's life expectancy is significantly lower than women's. This fact, combined with observations from the general coping literature that gender differences in coping exist (for a review, see De Ridder, 2000) makes the issue of gender-specific coping with loss especially relevant (cf. M. S. Stroebe, 1992). However, few coping researchers have attempted to analyze the gender-specific use of particular coping strategies or even the comparability of the dimensional structure of coping scales among men and women. Exceptions are the study by Endler and Parker (1990), who found a similar scale structure for men and women in the dispositional CISS, and the study by Hobfoll and colleagues (1994), which demonstrated that women engage more in prosocial coping strategies and men more frequently are inclined to take it out on other persons. Also, though it has been the subject of debate, indications exist that women more frequently engage in emotion-focused coping than men, especially emotional expression (cf. Nolen-Hoeksema & Larson, 1999), even when they are confronted with similar stressful situations (e.g., Vingerhoets & Van Heck, 1990; for a review, see De Ridder, 2000).

Time-Related Changes in Coping Activity

As in general coping research, research on coping with loss is rarely concerned with issues that address the question of how coping processes may develop over an extended time period (for an exception, see Nolen-Hoeksema & Larson, 1999). Instead, researchers limit their efforts to cross-sectional or, less frequent, repeated measures of coping. Because it is known from theories of adaptation to loss that coping may take some time and may change during this period (Parkes, 1996), assessment of coping should pay more attention to this issue. To that purpose, several methodologies are available, such as the daily measure approach developed by Stone and colleagues (1992). Also, measuring coping with an experience sampling design has been reported (Peeters et al., 1999). Of course, the application of such methodologies requires complex data-sampling and data-analysis methods but may result in more fine-grained analyses of the way the coping process develops over time. As such this may help to identify a relevant time point for collecting data on coping in future research. Related to this issue is an equally neglected aspect. Until now, coping scales fail to deal adequately with the fact that people make use of parallel efforts. Most of the traditional scales focus on identifying particular coping efforts at the expense of the use of other coping mechanisms. In doing so, they fail to acknowledge that certain coping efforts do not exclude others. Finally, the time aspect also refers to the question of what coping measures are actually measuring. It is assumed, but not tested, that research participants are able to provide a reliable picture of what they have done to handle the stressful situation, although it has been reported that these answers may reflect at least four possibilities relating to a different interpretation of the time framework they should apply: the number of efforts, the time spent on applying the coping effort, the effort that was made to apply a particular strategy, and the successfulness of the effort (Stone et al., 1991). From this state of affairs, it may be recommended that more attention be paid to the instruction provided in self-report coping measures and that, whenever possible, multiple assessments should be made, as is, for instance, done in the Perrez and Reicherts scale (Stress and Coping Process Questionnaire; Perrez & Reicherts, 1992), differentiating between intentions and actual attempts.

The Applicability of Measurement Models

According to Gottlieb and Gignac (1996), there are serious limitations to the conventional practice of relying exclusively on linear correlations with distress to evaluate the effectiveness of coping efforts. A first problem concerns the confounding of the inherent stressfulness of some situations with the effectiveness of the particular coping strategies they elicit. In our opinion, however, another, even more serious problem refers to possible misleading results as a result of the fact that nonlinear relationships between coping measures and outcome measures are ignored. For instance, if people make only a very limited use of avoiding being with ople in general, then they run the risk that there is not enough time to think through the key issues without distraction. In contrast, extremely high scores on avoidance could reflect total withdrawal from interpersonal relationships with a resulting loss of needed social support. This example demonstrates a nonlinear relationship between coping efforts and health-related outcomes. Therefore, in future research analyses of the effectiveness of coping should be guided by theoretical considerations that lead to the use of appropriate measurement models. Researchers examining the effects of coping should be cognizant of the possible nonlinear relations in their data. In this respect, we would like to point to a related issue. In our view, the construction of coping scales could profit considerably from the use of nonlinear factor analysis and nonlinear item-response models, especially in the case of dichotomously scored coping items. Waller, Tellegen, McDonald, and Lykken (1996) have contrasted these relatively new measurement models with the more traditional approaches. They conclude that the nonlinear models should be more than mere curiosities to future workers in the field of personality.

CONCLUSION

In this chapter we have provided a critical analysis of the assessment of coping with loss. We have paid special attention to the conceptual flaws in the coping concept because these may be a major cause of the striking shortcomings of currently available coping scales. Of course, this state of affairs is not specific to the assessment of coping with loss but affects most coping research, especially when aimed to describe and analyze coping processes in specific stressful conditions. Drawing attention to the present limitations of assessing coping with loss, however, does not imply that attempts to analyze coping with loss should be left for more general assessment of coping. On the contrary, we feel that the current state of affairs is a challenge for future efforts to generate the next generation of coping with loss instruments, which will be able to draw a more valid picture of what is at stake during the experience of loss and how people attempt to deal with these experiences.

REFERENCES

Aldwin, C. A., & Revenson, T. A. (1987). Does coping help? A reexamination of the relationship between coping and mental health. *Journal of Personality and Social Psychology, 53,* 337–348.

Amirkhan, J. H. (1990). A factor analytically derived measure of coping: The

Coping Strategy Indicator. *Journal of Personality and Social Psychology, 59,* 1066–1075.

Amirkhan, J. H. (1994). Criterion validity of a coping measure. *Journal of Personality Assessment, 62,* 242–261.

Archer, J. (1999). *The nature of grief: The evolution and psychology of reactions to loss.* London: Routledge.

Aspinwall, L. G., & Taylor, S. E. (1997). A stitch in time: Self-regulation and proactive coping. *Psychological Bulletin, 121,* 417–436.

Balk, D. E., & Vesta, L. C. (1998). Psychological development during four years of bereavement: A longitudinal case study. *Death Studies, 22,* 23–41.

Beck, A. T., Weissman, A., Lester, D., & Trexler, L. (1974). The measurement of pessimism: The Hopelessness Scale. *Journal of Consulting and Clinical Psychology, 42,* 861–865.

Ben-Porath, Y. S., Waller, N. G., & Butcher, J. N. (1991). Assessment of coping: An empirical illustration of the problem of inapplicable items. *Journal of Personality Assessment, 57,* 162–176.

Billings, A. G., & Moos, R. H. (1981). The role of coping responses and social resources in attenuating the impact of stressful live events. *Journal of Behavioural Medicine, 4,* 139–157.

Brison, K. J., & Leavitt, S. C. (1995). Coping with bereavement: Long-term perspectives on grief and mourning. *Ethos, 23,* 395–400.

Brunswick, E. (1956). *Perception and the representative design of psychological experiments.* Berkeley: University of California Press.

Carver, C. S., Scheier, M. F., & Weintraub, J. K. (1989). Assessing coping strategies: A theoretically based approach. *Journal of Personality and Social Psychology, 56,* 267–283.

Caserta, M. S., Lund, D. A., & Dimond, M. F. (1985). Assessing interviewer effects in a longitudinal study of bereaved elderly adults. *Journal of Gerontology, 40,* 637–640.

Cohen, F. (1991). Measurement of coping. In A. Monat & R. S. Lazarus (Eds.), *Stress and coping: An anthology* (pp. 228–244). New York: Columbia University Press.

Coyne, J. C., & Gottlieb, B. H. (1996). The mismeasure of coping by checklist. *Journal of Personality, 64,* 959–991.

De Ridder, D. (1997). What is wrong with coping assessment? A review of conceptual and methodological issues. *Psychology and Health, 12,* 417–431.

De Ridder, D. (2000). Gender, stress, and coping: Do women handle stressful situations differently from men? In L. Sherr & J. St. Lawrence (Eds.), *Women, health, and the mind* (pp. 115–135). New York: Wiley.

De Ridder, D., Schreurs, K., & Bensing, J. (1998). Adaptive tasks, coping, and quality of life of chronically ill patients. The cases of Parkinson's disease and the Chronic Fatigue Syndrome. *Journal of Health Psychology, 3,* 87–101.

Dise-Lewis, J. E. (1988). The Life Events and Coping Inventory: An assessment of stress in children. *Psychosomatic Medicine, 50,* 484–499.

Endler, N. S., & Parker, J. D. A. (1990). *Coping Inventory for Stressful Situations (CISS): Manual.* Toronto: Multi-health Systems.

Epstein, S., & Meier, P. (1989). Constructive thinking: A broad coping variable with specific components. *Journal of Personality and Social Psychology, 57,* 332–350.

Faschingsbauer, T. R., Zisook, S., & DeVaul, R. (1987). The Texas Revised Inventory of Grief. In S. Zisook (Ed.), *Biopsychosocial aspects of bereavement* (pp. 111–124). Washington, DC: American Psychiatric Press.

Feifel, H., & Strack, S. (1989). Coping with conflict situations: Middle-aged and elderly men. *Psychology and Aging, 4,* 26–33.

Folkman, S. (1992). Making the case for coping. In B. N. Carpenter (Ed.), *Personal coping: Theory, research, and application* (pp. 31–46). Westport, CT: Praeger.

Folkman, S., & Lazarus, R. S. (1980). An analysis of coping in a middle-aged community sample. *Journal of Health and Social Behaviour, 21,* 219–239.

Folkman, S., & Lazarus, R. S. (1988). *Ways of Coping Questionnaire.* Palo Alto, CA: Mind Garden.

Gottlieb, B. H., & Gignac, M. A. (1996). Content and domain specificity of coping among family caregivers of persons with dementia. *Journal of Aging Studies, 10,* 137–155.

Herth, K. (1990). Relationship of hope, coping styles, concurrent losses, and setting to grief resolution in the elderly widow(er). *Research in Nursing and Health, 13,* 109–117.

Hobfoll, S. E., Dunahoo, C. L., Ben-Porath, Y., & Monnier, J. (1994). Gender and coping: The dual-axis model of coping. *American Journal of Community Psychology, 22,* 49–82.

Horowitz, M. J. (1979). Psychological response to serious life events. In V. Hamilton & D. M. Warburton (Eds.), *Human stress and cognition: An information processing approach* (pp. 237–265). Chichester: Wiley.

Horowitz, M. J., Wilner, N., & Alvarez, W. (1979). Impact of Events Scale: A measure of subjective stress. *Psychosomatic Medicine, 41,* 209–218.

Krohne, H. W. (1993). Vigilance and cognitive avoidance as concepts in coping research. In H. W. Krohne (Ed.), *Attention and avoidance: Strategies in coping with aversiveness* (pp. 19–50). Seattle, WA: Hogrefe & Huber.

Lazarus, R. S. (1966). *Psychological stress and the coping process.* New York: McGraw-Hill.

Lazarus, R. S. (1993). Coping theory and research: Past, present, and future. *Psychosomatic Medicine, 55,* 234–247.

Lazarus, R. S., & Folkman, S. (1984). *Stress, appraisal and coping.* New York: Springer.

Littlewood, J. (1992). *Aspects of grief. Bereavement in adult life.* London: Tavistock/Routledge.

Mikulincer, M., & Florian, V. (1996). Coping and adaptation to trauma and loss. In M. Zeidner & N. S. Endler (Eds.), *Handbook of Coping: Theory, Research, and Applications* (pp. 554–572). New York: Wiley.

Miller, S. M. (1987). Monitoring and blunting: Validation of a questionnaire to assess styles of information seeking under threat. *Journal of Personality and Social Psychology, 52*, 345–353.

Milo, E. M. (1997). Maternal responses to the life and death of a child with a developmental disability: A study of hope. *Death Studies, 21*, 443–476.

Moos, R. H., & Schaefer, J. A. (1984). Coping resources and processes: Current concepts and measures. In L. Goldberger & S. Breznitz (Eds.), *Handbook of stress: Theoretical and clinical aspects* (pp. 234–257). New York: Free Press.

Mullen, B., & Suls, J. (1982). The effectiveness of attention and rejection as coping styles. *Journal of Psychosomatic Research, 26*, 43–49.

Nolen-Hoeksema, S., & Larson, J. (1999). *Coping with loss*. Mahwah, NJ: Erlbaum.

Osuji, O. N. (1985). Personality factors in acceptance of loss among physically disabled. *Psychological Record, 35*, 23–28.

Parker, J. D. A., & Endler, N. S. (1992). Coping with coping assessment: A critical review. *European Journal of Personality, 6*, 321–344.

Parkes, C. M. (1996). *Bereavement. Studies of grief in adult life* (3rd ed.). London: Routledge.

Patterson, J. M., & McCubbin, H. I. (1987). Adolescent coping style and behaviour. *Journal of Adolescence, 10*, 163–186.

Peacock, E. J., & Wong, P. T. (1990). The Stress Appraisal Measure (SAM): A multidimensional approach to cognitive appraisal. *Stress Medicine, 6*, 227–236.

Perrez, M., & Reicherts, M. (1992). *Stress, coping, and health*. Seattle, WA: Hogrefe & Huber.

Peeters, M. L., Sorbi, M. J., Kruise, D. A., Kerssens, J. J., Verhaak, P. F. M., & Bensing, J. M. (1999). Electronic diary assessment of pain, disability, and psychological adaptation in patients differing in duration of pain. *Pain, 84*, 181–192.

Rando, T. A. (1983). An investigation of grief and adaptation in parents whose children have died from cancer. *Journal of Pediatric Psychology, 8*, 3–20.

Rees, W. D. (1971). The hallucinations of widowhood. *British Medical Journal, 4*, 37–41.

Remondet, J. H., & Hansson, R. O. (1987). Assessing a widow's grief: A short index. *Journal of Gerontological Nursing, 13*, 30–34.

Sanders, C. M., Mauger, P. A., & Strong, P. A. (1985). *A manual for the Grief Experience Inventory*. Palo Alto, CA: Consulting Psychologists Press.

Sanders, C. M., Mauger, P. A., & Strong, P. A. (1991). *A manual for the Grief Experience Inventory*. Charlotte, NC: Center for the Study of Separation and Loss.

Schreurs, K., & De Ridder, D. (1997). Integration of coping and social support perspectives: Implications for the study of adaptation to chronic diseases. *Clinical Psychology Review, 17,* 89–112.

Schwarzer, R., & Schwarzer, C. (1996). A critical survey of coping instruments. In M. Zeidner & N. S. Endler (Eds.), *Handbook of Coping: Theory, Research, and Applications* (pp. 107–132). New York: Wiley.

Shuchter, S. R., & Zisook, S. (1993). The course of normal grief. In M. S. Stroebe, W. Stroebe, & R. O. Hansson (Eds.), *Handbook of bereavement: Theory, research, and intervention* (pp. 23–43). New York: Cambridge University Press.

Stanton, A. L., Danoff-Burg, S., Cameron, C. L., & Ellis, A. P. (1994). Coping through emotional approach: Problems of conceptualization and confounding. *Journal of Personality and Social Psychology, 66,* 350–362.

Stone, A. A., Greenberg, M. A., Kennedy-Moore, E., & Newman, M. G. (1991). Self-report, situation-specific coping questionnaires: What are they measuring? *Journal of Personality and Social Psychology, 61,* 648–658.

Stone, A. A., & Kennedy-Moore, E. (1992). Assessing situational coping: Conceptual and methodological considerations. In H. S. Friedman (Ed.), *Hostility, coping and health* (pp. 203–214). Washington, DC: American Psychological Association.

Stone, A. A., Kennedy-Moore, E., Greenberg, M. A., Newman, M. G., & Neale, J. M. (1992). Conceptual and methodological issues in current coping assessments. In B. N. Carpenter (Ed.), *Personal coping. Theory, research and applications* (pp. 15–29). Westport, CT: Praeger.

Stroebe, M. S. (1992). Coping with bereavement: A review of the grief work hypothesis. *Omega: Journal of Death and Dying, 26,* 19–42.

Tobin, D. L., Holroyd, K. A., Reynolds, R. V., & Wigal, J. K. (1989). The hierarchical factor structure of the Coping Strategies Inventory. *Cognitive Therapy and Research, 13,* 343–361.

Van Heck, G. L., & Vingerhoets, A. J. J. M. (1989). Copingstijlen en persoonlijkheidskenmerken [Coping styles and personality characteristics]. *Nederlands Tijdschrift voor de Psychologie, 44,* 73–87.

Vingerhoets, A. J. J. M., & Van Heck, G. L. (1990). Gender, coping and psychosomatic symptoms. *Psychological Medicine, 20,* 125–135.

Waller, N. G., Tellegen, A., McDonald, R. P., & Lykken, D. T. (1996). Exploring nonlinear models in personality assessment: Development and preliminary validation of a negative emotionality scale. *Journal of Personality, 64,* 545–576.

V

COPING: EXPLORATION OF THE MECHANISMS

21

PHYSIOLOGICAL INDICES OF FUNCTIONING IN BEREAVEMENT

MARTICA HALL AND MICHAEL IRWIN

Psychological stress and depressive symptoms are thought to affect a variety of health outcomes and result in increased rates of cardiovascular and noncardiovascular diseases (Bruce, Seeman, Merrill, & Blazer, 1994; McEwen & Stellar, 1993; Musselman, Evans, & Nemeroff, 1998). As guided by the conceptual model shown in Figure 21-1, the experience of bereavement affects psychological adaptation. It is important to note that responses to bereavement are variable, and individual differences in background characteristics (e.g., age, gender, socioeconomic status), social support, coping, and self-concept (e.g., self-efficacy) can impinge on the perception of loss and on psychological and physical outcomes both directly and indirectly. In other words, the cascading relationships between environmental and personal factors are thought to lead to affective distress and depressive disorders in bereaved individuals.

The impact of bereavement on an individual is not trivial or limited to effects on emotional well-being or social functioning. The occurrence of depression, even subthreshold depressive symptoms that are common in bereavement, produces impairments in measures of physical functioning, pain, and general health, along with decrements in emotional health

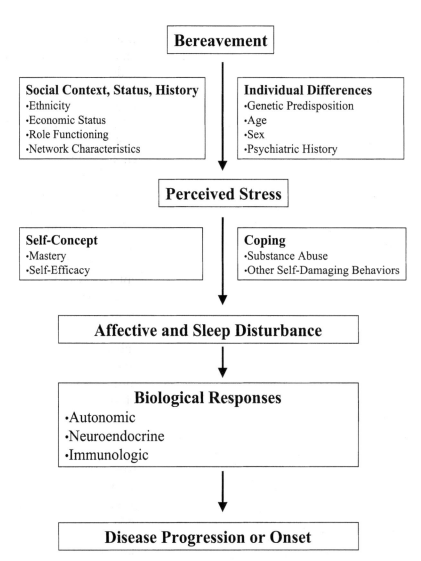

Figure 21-1. Conceptual model of the process whereby bereavement translates into adverse health outcomes. The impact of bereavement on perceived stress is modulated by social context, status, history, and individual differences, and the impact of perceived stress on affective and sleep disturbances is modulated by self-concept and coping.

(Broadhead, Blazer, George, and Tse, 1990; Bruce et al., 1994; VonKorff, Ormel, Katon, & Lin, 1992; Wells et al., 1989). Bruce et al. (1994) have further found that the onset of depressive symptoms can initiate a spiraling decline in physical and psychological health in older adults.

The notion that bereavement and associated depressive symptoms can increase one's risk for developing disease or influence the severity or rate of progression of disease is controversial. However, a number of previous cross-sectional and longitudinal studies involving measures of autonomic, neuroendocrine, and immune functions indicate multisystem physiological changes that occur during bereavement. In turn, dynamic fluctuations of physiologic systems in response to stressors such as bereavement lead to an accumulated wear and tear on the body (Seeman, Singer, Rowe, Horwitz, & McEwen, 1997), declines in cognitive and physical functioning in older adults (Seeman et al., 1997), and increased risk of cardiovascular, infectious, and inflammatory disorders (Hirsch, Hofer, Holland, & Solomon, 1984; Musselman et al., 1998; Sternberg, Chrousos, Wilder, & Gold, 1992). Despite the appeal of this hypothesis, the number of possible health outcomes and of processes that govern health outcomes pose a daunting task to the researcher interested in pathways to morbidity and mortality in bereaved individuals. An alternative hypothesis is that these physiological changes in association with bereavement provide an index of current functioning, and in some cases may predict subsequent psychological, physiological, and general functioning. In other words, physiological measures act as a signal of danger and are not, necessarily, a mechanism for adverse health outcomes.

In this chapter, we review the literature on physiological measures in studies of bereavement with an emphasis on evaluating these measures as signals, or indices, of current and future functioning. We have included a separate section for three domains of physiological measures studied in association with bereavement. Each domain of physiological measures (neuroendocrine functioning, immune system competence, sleep) may be viewed as a proxy measure of physiological dysregulation, because each is disturbed in association with acute and chronic stress and affective illness. First, we review the literature on neuroendocrine functioning in bereavement, which includes measures of the following hormones: cortisol, epinephrine, norepinephrine, and adrenocorticotrophic hormone (ACTH). Second, we review immunocompetence studies, which evaluate the number or function of various immune system components studied in bereavement, such as T-cells and natural killer (NK) cells. Third, we review bereavement-related changes in laboratory-assessed sleep, as well as subjective sleep quality.

In understanding this literature, it is important to recognize that the research design and analytic strategy used in these studies has critical implications for evaluating relationships among bereavement-related changes in physiology and functioning. The majority of the research on bereavement-related changes in physiology has evaluated relationships among physiological measures and current functioning, or changes in physiology across time. Far fewer studies have used design and analytic strategies that allow us to determine what impact bereavement-related changes in physiology may have on subsequent functioning. Thus little is known about whether bereavement-related changes in physiology are a correlate of, or a mechanism for, functioning. To account for and understand the processes that govern individual differences in response to bereavement, a number of these studies have also included measures of psychological issues common to bereavement including depression, anxiety, generalized distress, and coping styles. Again, the design of most of these studies only allows us to understand how the psychological constructs and physiological measures are related to one another; few studies allow us to evaluate which precedes the other. As a whole, these studies do provide a platform from which we can begin to understand, from an integrated perspective that includes measures of physiology and individual differences in psychological responses, how individuals cope with and adjust to bereavement.

NEUROENDOCRINE CORRELATES OF BEREAVEMENT

For the most part, neuroendocrine studies of bereavement have evaluated levels of the stress hormones cortisol, epinephrine, and norepinephrine. In these studies, higher levels of cortisol and the catecholamines (epinephrine and norepinephrine) are proxy measures for dysregulation of physiologic systems with implications, ultimately, for disease outcomes. A number of researchers have also used challenge studies, including the dexamethasone suppression test (DST) and the corticotrophin releasing hormone (CRH) test, to evaluate dysregulation of neuroendocrine function in bereavement. Among challenge studies, functioning is a measure of cortisol and adrenocorticotrophic hormone (ACTH) release, which should be suppressed following dexamethasone challenge (cortisol only) and heightened following CRH challenge (both cortisol and ACTH).

Cortisol and Catecholamines in Bereavement

The first evidence that cortisol is altered in association with bereavement was reported in a seminal series of studies published more than 20 years ago (Hofer, Wolff, Friedman, & Mason, 1972a, 1972b; Wolff, Friedman, Hofer, & Mason, 1964a; Wolff, Hofer, & Mason, 1964b). These researchers measured adrenocortical activity and coping efficacy in a sample of parents with fatally ill children, both before and following the loss of their child from cancer. Cortisol was measured indirectly via urinary excretion rates of the cortisol metabolite, 17-hydroxy corticosteroid (17-OHCS). Preloss 17-OHCS levels were negatively correlated with coping efficacy, as defined by clinical interviews (Wolff et al., 1964a). Wolff and colleagues reported that 17-OHCS values were highest among parents who were not effectively defending themselves against their impending loss. At six months and two years postloss, 17-OHCS levels remained elevated but were not strongly correlated with coping efficacy (Hofer et al., 1972a, 1972b). However, Hofer and colleagues did report qualitative differences in coping and grief among parents in the highest and lowest 17-OHCS quartiles at both postloss visits (Hofer et al., 1972b). Parents with heightened adrenocortical activity were described as more openly grieving, reporting more intrusive thoughts about their loss, and experiencing intense feelings of loss, whereas parents in the lowest 17-OHCS quartile were described as more guarded, avoiding reminders of their loss, and more reintegrated within their communities.

In a second series of papers on the neuroendocrine correlates of bereavement, Jacobs and colleagues characterized relationships among neuroendocrine activity, psychological distress, and health in a sample of men and women experiencing or anticipating spousal bereavement (Jacobs et al., 1985, 1986, 1987; Jacobs, Bruce, & Kim, 1997). The study sample included 67 men and women who had either recently lost a spouse (n = 43) or whose spouse had recently been hospitalized for a life-threatening illness (n = 24). Data were collected one and two months after the loss or hospitalization and at two subsequent times, 13 and 25 months later. At two months postloss or hospitalization, neuroendocrine function, as measured by urinary cortisol, epinephrine, and norepinephrine levels, was similar among the bereaved and nonbereaved groups (Jacobs et al., 1985, 1986). Although normal controls were not included in these studies, Jacobs and colleagues (Jacobs et al., 1986) reported that epinephrine and norepinephrine levels were significantly elevated in comparison to control data reported in the literature, a similar comparison was not made for cortisol levels. It is important to note that both groups of research participants were experiencing similar levels of stress; measures of unpleasant affect and coping were not significantly different among bereaved participants and those participants who were threatened with the loss of their spouse. Despite somewhat elevated levels of distress and neuroendocrine activation, these measures were not strongly correlated with one another. Among the bereaved participants only, elevated depression scores were more strongly correlated with heightened norepinephrine than epinephrine, and poorer coping was significantly correlated with heightened cortisol reactivity during the data collection process.

In comparison to the cross-sectional data, the follow-up data in this sample reveal stronger longitudinal relationships among neuroendocrine function, distress, and health. For example, bereavement-related stress at isolated times was not significantly associated with cortisol values, whereas changes in stress across a two-month period were a significant predictor of cortisol values (Jacobs et al., 1987). Regardless of bereavement status, participants whose separation anxiety increased across the two months immediately postloss or hospitalization had the highest urinary cortisol values, compared to participants who experienced diminishing or stable levels of grief during this time (Jacobs et al., 1987). These findings led Jacobs and colleagues to suggest that chronic stress may be an important determinant of neuroendocrine activity and, possibly, dysregulation in the hypothalamic-pituitary-adrenocortical (HPA) axis during bereavement. Neuroendocrine function at two months postloss or hospitalization was, in turn, a significant predictor of longer term reports of psychological and physical health. Elevated levels of epinephrine were predictive of greater hopelessness at 13 and 25 months postloss and hospitalization, whereas elevated cortisol levels were predictive of poorer self-reported health at 13 months, and lower levels of hopelessness at 25 months postloss and hospitalization. Thus chronic stress and neuroendocrine activation in the wake of bereavement appear to signal a modest risk for reports of poorer health and functioning.

Neuroendocrine Challenge Studies in Bereavement

Most of the challenge studies in bereavement have used the dexamethasone suppression test (DST) to evaluate the extent to which bereavement is associated with nonsuppression of cortisol. Nonsuppression was reported in three of four studies, with nonsuppression rates ranging from 10% to 39% of the sample (Das & Berrios, 1984; Kosten, Jacobs, & Mason, 1984; Shuchter, Zisook, Kirkorowicz, & Risch, 1986; Weller, Weller, Fristad, & Bowes, 1990). Two factors that appear to modulate nonsuppression are age of the sample and time since loss. Nonsuppression rates were higher in younger samples (Shuchter et al., 1986; Weller et al., 1990) and in studies conducted between two weeks and one month postloss (Das & Berrios, 1984; Shuchter et al., 1986; Weller et al., 1990). When Das and Berrios reexamined DST response in their sample of middle- to older-age participants at three months postloss, suppression rates were all within normal limits. Thus older participants studied between three and six months postloss showed normal responses to the DST (Das & Berrios, 1984; Kosten et al., 1984). The largest nonsuppression rate was seen in a study of children (mean age = 13 years) who had recently suffered the loss of one parent (Weller et al., 1990).

Each of the DST challenge studies examined the extent to which psychological responses to bereavement were associated with cortisol nonsuppression. Symptoms of depression were significantly correlated with postdexamethasone cortisol levels in two studies. Greater symptomatology on the Hamilton Rating Scale for Depression (HRSD; Hamilton, 1960) was associated with higher post-DST cortisol levels in elder individuals who were grieving the loss of their spouse (Kosten et al., 1984), and greater number of depressive symptoms was associated with higher post-DST cortisol levels in children who had recently lost a parent (Weller et al., 1990). In a study of spousal bereavement, baseline cortisol levels and anxiety were significantly higher in middle-age nonsuppressors, as compared to cortisol suppressors (Shuchter et al., 1986). It is interesting to note that Shuchter and colleagues reported that symptoms of anxiety were more strongly related to cortisol nonsuppression than were symptoms of depression. The only study that evaluated symptoms of grief in conjunction with response to the DST found no relationship between symptoms of grief and cortisol suppression (Das & Berrios, 1984). As was the case with nonsuppression rates, the strongest relationships among the psychological sequelae of bereavement and cortisol response was seen in the younger samples studied in closer proximity to their loss (Shuchter et al., 1986; Weller et al., 1990).

A close relationship between symptomatology and bereavement-related neuroendocrine dysregulation has also been reported in response to the corticotropin-releasing hormone (CRH) stimulation test (Roy, Gallucci, Avgerinos, Linnoila, & Gold, 1988). Roy and colleagues compared baseline cortisol levels and response to the CRH test in a sample of middle-age men and women who were recently bereaved (mean time since loss = 10 months), as compared to a sample of medication-free patients with major depression (mean age = 42 years), and a younger sample of healthy control participants (mean age = 29 years). The bereaved group was broken down into two subgroups, based on the presence of bereavement complicated by the presence of major depression. Other factors that significantly distinguished the depressed from the nondepressed bereaved subgroups included a stronger past history of depression, a greater proportion of women, and a longer time since loss. Grief scores did not distinguish the depressed from the nondepressed bereaved subgroups. Cortisol levels at baseline and in response to CRH stimulation were higher in the subgroup with bereavement-related depression than in bereaved participants without depression, depressed patients, and normal controls. Although baseline ACTH levels did not differ across groups, ACTH response to CRH stimulation was blunted among the subgroup with bereavement-related depression and the depressed patients, as compared to bereaved participants without depression and normal controls. It is notable that cortisol values at baseline and in response to CRH administration were higher among participants with bereavement-related depression than among nonbereaved patients with depression. This study suggests that the diathesis for depression, in association with chronic bereavement-related stress, may promote dysregulation of the HPA axis.

IMMUNE SYSTEM CORRELATES OF BEREAVEMENT

Research on the effects of bereavement on the immune system has used cross-sectional designs or repeated measures studies that extend, in general, to one year postloss. For the most part, these studies have used *ex vivo* techniques to evaluate both number and function of specific immune system components such as CD4 (t-helper), CD8 (t-suppressor), and natural killer cells. These studies have documented immune system differences among bereaved and nonbereaved comparison samples, as well as examining possible mediators of the bereavement-immunity relationship such as depression, social support, and elevated physiological arousal. Study samples have varied in terms of their age range and relationship of participant to the deceased, although the majority of studies have focused on older adults who have experienced the loss of a parent or spouse. Despite the wide variation in study design and sample characteristics, there is consistent evidence of persistent decrements in functional measures of immunocompetence among bereaved men and women, although the mechanisms of action remain poorly understood.

A pair of landmark studies established that bereavement is associated with impairments in immunologic functioning (Bartrop, Luckhurst, Lazarus, Kiloh, & Penny, 1977; Schleifer, Keller, Camerino, Thornton, & Stein, 1983). Bartrop and colleagues (1977) were the first to report an association between spousal loss and decreased lymphocyte responses to mitogenic challenges. Several important points emerged from the Schleifer and colleagues paper, which detailed immune responses during anticipatory bereavement and following loss. This study demonstrated that immune system changes were a consequence of bereavement and that decrements in lymphocyte function were apparent as early as one month after the loss. Second, the immune system did not habituate to the stress of anticipatory bereavement. In comparison to prebereavement levels, cell function dropped immediately following bereavement. Finally, decreases in immunocompetence were related to cellular function, not decreases in cell numbers. In an additional early study, Linn, Linn, and Jensen (1984) suggested that psychological reactions to bereavement were important determinants of immune system functioning in the wake of a significant loss. This idea has been echoed in a host of later studies that have demonstrated relationships among psychological factors such as social readjustment, social support, and symptoms of stress and depression to immunocompetence in bereaved participants (e.g., Esterling, Kiecolt-Glaser, & Glaser, 1996; Hall et al., 1998; Irwin, Daniels, Bloom, & Weiner, 1986; Irwin, Daniels, Bloom, Smith, & Weiner, 1987a; Irwin, Daniels, Smith, Bloom, & Weiner, 1987b; Zisook et al., 1994).

Studies of cell numbers have reported persistent shifts in the subset of T-cell populations, defined by subtle decreases in the number of T-suppressor cell population and an accompanying increase in the T-helper to T-suppressor cell ratio (Irwin et al., 1987a; Spratt & Denney, 1991). These shifts were seen in women who had lost, or were anticipating the loss of, their spouse, as well as parents who had suffered the sudden death of a child. In a more recent study, bereavement-related stress was associated with decreases in numbers of circulating natural killer cells in elderly men and women with bereavement-related depression (Hall et al., 1998). Bereavement-related changes in other cell populations such as B cells and monocytes have not been reported, and results of blastogenesis assays have also not revealed strong effects of bereavement on lymphocyte proliferation to mitogens (Bartrop et al., 1977; Spratt & Denney, 1991). These findings are consistent with a much larger literature that has demonstrated significant links between stress, depression, and immune system function (Herbert & Cohen 1993a, 1993b).

Natural killer cell function is the immune system component that has been most closely linked to bereavement. Irwin and colleagues have reported significant decreases in natural killer cell activity in women who were anticipating or had recently lost their spouse, as compared to an age-matched sample of nonbereaved women (Irwin et al., 1987a, 1987b; Irwin, Daniels, Risch, Bloom, & Weiner, 1988). Bereavement-related changes in natural killer cells have also been shown to persist across time. For example, significant decreases in natural killer cell function were reported in former caregivers of Alzheimer's disease patients who had lost their loved one on average two years earlier (Esterling, Kiecolt-Glaser, Bodnar, & Glaser, 1994). Esterling and colleagues went on to demonstrate that persistent bereavement- and caregiver-related reductions in IL-2 stimulated natural killer cell function were related to specific changes in the ability of natural killer cells to respond to a challenge, versus changes in supporting cell populations such as T- and B-lymphocytes, as well as granulocytes and macrophages (Esterling et al., 1996). Although one study did not find a group effect of bereavement on natural killer cell activity in a sample of widows at 2, 7, and 13 months postloss, these researchers reported significant decreases in natural killer cell activity among widows with major depression compared with widows without bereavement-related depression (Zisook et al., 1994). These results parallel an earlier report of anticipatory grief and bereavement in which changes in symptoms of depression were significantly correlated with changes in natural killer cell function (Irwin et al., 1987b).

As noted previously, several studies have examined psychological or physiological correlates of the bereavement-immunity relationship. Based on a much larger literature on stress, depression, and immune function (Herbert & Cohen, 1993a, 1993b), these researchers have reasoned that factors such as depressed mood, poor sleep, or elevated cortisol levels are pathways to immune system dysregulation in bereavement. Indeed, bereavement is not necessarily associated with decrements in enumerative and functional measures of the immune system (Spratt & Denney, 1991; Zisook et al., 1994). Data collected to date indicate that bereavement-related immune system changes are more strongly correlated with symptoms of depression and stress than with cortisol levels, although decreases in cortisol levels across time have been associated with increases in natural killer cell function (Irwin et al., 1987b). In addition, this research has demonstrated that immune system decrements and elevated symptoms of depression and stress coexist across time; these relationships have been shown to persist in men and women alike for as long as three years postloss (Esterling et al., 1996; Hall et al., 1998). Overall, these studies are consistent with demonstrated immunologic changes in association with depression and stress (Herbert & Cohen, 1993a, 1993b). Although these studies have demonstrated consistent relationships among bereavement-related changes in immunocompetence and psychological sequelae of bereavement, correlational study designs preclude evaluation of causal models among these variables. For example, although it might be argued that bereavement-related symptoms of stress and depression cause immune system decrements, it might also be argued that these factors are proxy measures for some other causal factor such as diet or other health behaviors. Conversely, it might also be argued that immune system changes cause symptoms of depression and stress. These issues cannot be resolved until experimental study designs are used to tease apart the unique contribution and temporal sequence of relationships among the psychological, physiological, and immunological consequences of bereavement.

The clinical significance of bereavement-related changes in immune function also awaits resolution. Among healthy populations, acute fluctuations in immune function related to bereavement have been within normal clinical values and are not likely to alter susceptibility to disease or illness processes. In contrast, the clinical significance of bereavement-related changes in immunity are more apparent in populations suffering from disorders of the immune system such as HIV infection and AIDS, as discussed previously. Before dismissing the significance of the bereavement–immunity relationship in healthy individuals, it is important to note that research to date has not evaluated the health effects of chronic, mild immunosuppression or its potential interaction with challenges to the immune system such as viral or bacterial pathogens. Certainly, bereavement is a risk factor for all-cause morbidity and mortality (Martikainen & Valkonen, 1998; Prigerson et al., 1997; Woof & Carter, 1997).

Two groups of researchers have evaluated the effects of bereavement on immune system measures among HIV seropositive men. Many of the immune system measures evaluated in these studies (e.g., T-helper cell numbers, serum neopterin levels, proliferative response to T-cells to mitogens) are associated with disease progression in HIV seropositive individuals and mortality associated with AIDS. In the first series of studies, Kemeny and colleagues demonstrated that the timing and significance of loss were important correlates of the bereavement–immunity relationship in HIV infected individuals. For example, bereavement was not a predictor of immune measures in a sample of HIV seropositive men who had lost a close friend to AIDS within the past year (Kemeny et al., 1994). Conversely, changes with implications for disease progression were seen in a sample of HIV seropositive men who had lost their partner to AIDS within the previous year (Kemeny et al., 1995). In the second study, the bereaved seropositive group had elevated serum neopterin levels and decreased T-lymphocyte proliferative response to the PHA mitogen, compared with three other groups: seropositive nonbereaved participants, seronegative bereaved participants, and seronegative nonbereaved participants. In a third study, Kemeny and colleagues reported that bereavement status was longitudinally associated with the decline in T-helper cell number across a three- to four-year period (Kemeny & Dean, 1995). Compared with nonbereaved HIV seropositive men, T-helper cells declined precipitously in the second year of follow-up and remained at significantly lower levels across the study period in bereaved HIV seropositive men. These effects remained significant after controlling for intervening drug therapies and initial cell counts, which did not differ at the one-year time point.

Goodkin and colleagues (1996) reported a significant change in the immune system profile of bereaved HIV seropositive men over a shorter time period, after controlling for psychosocial (e.g. stress and coping) variables and health-related behaviors. Regression analyses revealed that bereavement status was a significant correlate of natural killer cell cytotoxicity at 6 and 12 months postbereavement. A significant relationship between bereavement status and T-cell response to the PHA mitogen did not emerge until 12 months postbereavement. This study also revealed that the use of action-focused coping (e.g., planning, seeking instrumental support) was a significant correlate of immune function and thus might provide an opportunity for intervention. In a second study, Goodkin and colleagues (1998) demonstrated that participation in a support group was associated with an increase in T-helper cell counts and decreased number of physician visits in a sample of bereaved HIV seropositive men. Cortisol levels, which also decreased in the intervention group, and group attendance emerged as significant predictors of response to the support group intervention. This study provides the first evidence that bereavement has a causal effect on health care use as well as clinically significant immune system measures and that these relationships may be modified by psychosocial interventions.

SLEEP AS A CORRELATE OF BEREAVEMENT

Research on laboratory-assessed sleep in bereavement grew from descriptive studies that reported an increased incidence of sleep complaints and insomnia following bereavement (e.g., Clayton, 1974; Parkes &

Brown, 1972). Reports of bereavement-related sleep disruptions have been shown to be persistent and, in some cases, demonstrate a dose-response relationship with number of losses. For example, in a study of loss of a partner or close friend to AIDS, Martin (1988) reported that greater number of bereavement episodes were associated with increased incidence of sleep problems, after controlling for other variables that might affect sleep. The relationship between bereavement and sleep is especially intriguing to clinicians and researchers as bereavement-related sleep disruptions may signal vulnerability, or be a direct neurobiological pathway, to heightened psychiatric and medical morbidity and mortality in the wake of a significant loss (Reynolds et al., 1992). For example, the strong link between sleep and the immune system suggests that disrupted sleep following bereavement may affect health directly by suppressing the immune system (Irwin et al., 1996).

Laboratory studies of sleep during bereavement have all used a standard, three-night study series. In these studies, participants sleep in a private bedroom and adhere to their usual sleep–wake schedules. Although polysomnographic data are collected every night, sleep study measures represent averages from the second and third night of studies. The first night of data are not evaluated, as the novelty of the laboratory environment has been shown to disrupt sleep (Agnew, Webb, & Williams, 1966). Sleep measures evaluated in these studies include measures of sleep continuity, sleep architecture, and the temporal organization of sleep. Sleep continuity refers to one's ability to fall asleep and stay asleep and includes measures such as sleep latency (minutes to fall asleep after lights out), amount of wakefulness after sleep onset (WASO), and sleep efficiency (percentage of the night spent in sleep). Sleep architecture refers to the structure of sleep and generally refers to measures of the percentage of the night spent in each stage of sleep during nonrapid eye movement sleep (NREM, stages 1–4) and rapid eye movement sleep (REM). Measures of the temporal organization of sleep focus on departures from normative sleep, such as a reduced latency to REM sleep and a reduced delta sleep ratio (stronger generation of delta waves during the second, as opposed to the first, NREM period). These measures are of interest to clinicians and researchers because they are related to sleep disruptions in association with possible adverse outcomes of bereavement such as chronic stress responding and major depressive disorder (Buysse et al, 1998; Hall, Dahl, Dew, & Reynolds, 1995).

The first laboratory study of sleep in bereavement (Reynolds et al., 1992) compared EEG sleep measures in four groups of elderly men and women (mean age = 61 years): patients with bereavement-related major depressive disorder ($n = 15$), bereaved nondepressed participants ($n = 16$), nonbereaved patients with major depressive disorder ($n = 15$), and a group of age- and gender-matched healthy control participants ($n = 15$). Multivariate analyses revealed significant group differences in sleep continuity, sleep architecture, and measures of REM sleep. Sleep disruptions were most significant in depressed participants, irrespective of bereavement status. Major depression in both bereaved and nonbereaved patients was associated with poorer subjective sleep quality, alterations in the distribution of delta sleep across the night, a greater percentage of the night spent in REM sleep, and shorter latencies to REM sleep. In addition, sleep efficiency was significantly reduced in patients with bereavement-related depression (72%) compared with participants without major depression, whether they were bereaved (83%) or not (85%). Depressed patients who were not bereaved also had lower sleep efficiency scores (74%), although not significantly so. Secondary correlational analyses in the bereaved sample revealed that increased symptoms of depression were directly associated with poorer sleep efficiency and a heightened delta sleep ratio, after controlling for time since loss and symptoms of grief. These results suggest that sleep disruptions in the wake of bereavement are a function of level of distress; the sleep of bereaved elders without major depression did not differ from that of nonbereaved elders.

Subsequent studies have corroborated the observation that laboratory-assessed measures of sleep are not necessarily disrupted in the wake of bereavement. Pasternak and colleagues (1992) found no significant differences in EEG-assessed sleep in a sample of bereaved elders with subsyndromal depression compared with age- and gender-matched nonbereaved controls. Despite the absence of EEG-assessed sleep differences, subjective sleep quality ratings were significantly lower in the bereaved subsyndromal patients than in the comparison sample. A longitudinal study of laboratory sleep in nondepressed bereaved participants reported an increase in REM density that persisted through two years postloss (Reynolds et al., 1993). REM density is a measure of phasic activation of eye movements during REM sleep, and higher values have been associated with depression and poor affect balance (Nofzinger et al., 1994). In this study, no other significant differences were found between bereaved and nonbereaved participants.

These studies are consistent with the hypothesis that psychological resilience in the wake of bereavement is mirrored in relatively healthy sleep profiles (Reynolds et al., 1993). Before concluding that bereavement-related sleep disruptions are only seen in men and women with depression, it is important to emphasize that inclusion criteria for nondepressed participants in each of these studies excluded any bereaved individuals who had a positive history of affective illness. Evidence that some sleep disruptions persist during remission from bereavement-related depression (Pasternak et al., 1994) suggests that sleep disruptions may be seen in this vulnerable population, despite the absence of depression. In a study of elder individuals with bereavement-related depression, sleep profiles fluctuated as a function of remission from depression and treatment with nortriptyline.

Pasternak and colleagues observed sustained improvements in sleep quality and sleep efficiency, although treatment-related improvements in sleep architecture and the temporal organization of delta sleep returned to pretreatment levels after withdrawal from study medication. It thus appears that sleep profiles in the wake of bereavement may be affected by symptoms of depression, as well as other unidentified correlates of bereavement.

More recently, bereavement-related sleep disruptions have been linked to symptoms of stress and adverse health consequences. In a study of 40 bereaved elder individuals (mean age was 65 years and 75% of the sample was female), bereavement-related intrusive thoughts and avoidance behaviors were associated with longer sleep latencies and changes in the temporal organization of delta sleep (Hall et al., 1997). Stress-related difficulties in falling asleep and generating delta sleep during the first sleep cycle were seen after controlling for age, time since loss, and symptoms of depression. Symptoms of depression were associated with a shorter REM latency and a reduction in sleep efficiency after controlling for age and time since loss. These findings suggest that symptoms of stress and depression may have different effects on sleep following bereavement, although the cross-sectional design of the study does not allow the use of causal inferences.

The potential effects of bereavement-related sleep disruptions on morbidity and mortality were evaluated in a second, smaller study with this cohort (Hall et al., 1998). Blood samples were drawn on the second or third morning of sleep studies to evaluate the relationship between stress, sleep disruptions, and immune function in 29 bereaved elder individuals (mean age of the sample was 67 years, 68% were female). The conceptual model evaluated by this study hypothesized that stress would lead to sleep disruptions that in turn would lead to immunosuppression, as defined by reduced number and function of natural killer cells. Symptoms of stress, as measured by frequency of bereavement-related intrusive thoughts and avoidance behaviors, were significantly associated with sleep onset difficulties including longer sleep latencies and greater time spent awake during the first sleep cycle. Greater time spent awake during the first sleep cycle, in turn, was significantly associated with lower number of circulating natural killer cells, and accounted for 12% of the variance in this measure of immunocompetence. Study effects were observed after controlling for the effects of age and severity of depression; it should also be noted that severity of depression was not a significant correlate of sleep onset disruptions or immunocompetence. This study provided the first direct evidence that laboratory-assessed sleep disruptions, as defined by wakefulness during the sleep cycle, are a significant path between the stress of bereavement and natural killer cell number. Again, the cross-sectional nature of this study merely suggests, but does not prove, a causal relationship between stress, sleep, and immunocompetence, which may be one mechanism for increased morbidity and mortality following loss.

CONCLUSION

We have critically reviewed the literature on physiological indices of functioning in bereavement including neuroendocrine function, immune system competence, and sleep. These studies demonstrate that physiological functioning is indeed altered following loss, although many factors appear to dictate the timing, extent, and vulnerability to bereavement-related changes in functioning. At the most basic level, one can conclude that changes indicative of acute heightened arousal (e.g., increased circulating levels of catecholamines and cortisol, alterations in immunocompetence, subjective sleep complaints) are commonly seen during anticipatory bereavement and during the first few months following loss. More enduring alterations in neuroendocrine and immune parameters, as well as subjective and laboratory-assessed sleep disruptions, have also been observed in the years following loss. Who is at risk? Among the mediators that have been evaluated, younger age, symptoms of stress, and depression have emerged as the strongest risk factors for altered physiological functioning in bereavement, whereas physiological resiliency following loss is associated with the use of effective coping strategies, social support networks, and a healthy sleep profile.

Despite the wealth of evidence that neuroendocrine, immune, and sleep profiles are altered in association with loss, much additional work is needed to determine whether the imbalance in these various behavioral and physiological systems leads to an increased incidence of morbidity and mortality. In the first instance, a much greater understanding of the dynamic variability in levels of physiological regulation is required. For example, psychobiological reactivity to acute laboratory challenge might be used to uncover physiological abnormalities that are not always captured at rest or at a single point in time. Cohen and Manuck (1995) have suggested that individual differences in response to acute challenges provide a stable disposition that is replicable over time with implications for successful characterization of vulnerability risk in the stress–disease relationship. Second, the relevance of these psychobiological abnormalities to the onset and progression of physical disease remains a critical question. Evaluation of changes in disease-specific biological measures is needed to provide insights into the mechanisms underlying the association between bereavement, depression, and physical illness. Finally, we recommend the use of longer term intervention studies and the use of specific measures of morbidity and mortality, which would allow evaluation of causal relationships among measures of physiological functioning, morbidity, and mortality in association with loss. Possible intervention strategies for research might focus on teaching coping skills, extending social support networks, stabilizing sleep–wake routines, and preventing bereavement-related depression. Potential clinical benefits of bereavement interventions include overall improvements in physiological and psychological functioning, reductions in health care use, as well as the potential for reduced incidence of morbidity and mortality in medically at risk older adult populations.

REFERENCES

Agnew, H. W., Jr, Webb, W. B., & Williams, R. L. (1966). The first night effect: An EEG study of sleep. *Psychophysiology, 2*, 263–266.

Bartrop, R. W., Luckhurst, E., Lazarus, L., Kiloh, L. G., & Penny, R. (1977). Depressed lymphocyte function after bereavement. *Lancet, 1*(8016), 834–836.

Broadhead, W. E., Blazer, D. G., George, L. K., & Tse, C. K. (1990). Depression, disability days, and days lost from work in a prospective epidemiologic survey. *Journal of the American Medical Association, 264*, 2524–2528.

Bruce, M. L., Seeman, T. E., Merrill, S. S., & Blazer, D. G. (1994). The impact of depressive symptomatology on physical disability: MacArthur studies of successful aging. *American Journal of Public Health, 84*, 1796–1799.

Buysse, D. J., Hall, M., Tu, X. M., Land, S., Houck, P. R., Cherry, C. R., Kupfer, D. J., & Frank, E. (1998). Latent structure of EEG sleep variables in depressed and control subjects: Descriptions and clinical correlates. *Psychiatry Research, 79*, 105–122.

Clayton, P. J. (1974). Mortality and morbidity in the first year of widowhood. *Archives of General Psychiatry, 30*, 747–750.

Cohen, S., & Manuck, S. B. (1995). Stress, reactivity, and disease. *Psychosomatic Medicine, 57*, 423–426.

Das, M., & Berrios, G. E. (1984). Dexamethasone suppression test in acute grief reaction. *Acta Psychiatrica Scandinavica, 70*, 278–281.

Esterling, B. A., Kiecolt-Glaser, J. K., Bodnar, J. C., & Glaser, R. (1994). Chronic stress, social support, and persistent alterations in the natural killer cell response to cytokines in older adults. *Health Psychology, 13*, 291–298.

Esterling, B. A., Kiecolt-Glaser, J. K., & Glaser, R. (1996). Psychosocial modulation of cytokine-induced natural killer cell activity in older adults. *Psychosomatic Medicine, 58*, 264–272.

Goodkin, K., Feaster, D. J., Asthana, D., Blaney, N. T., Kumar, M., Baldewicz, T., Tuttle, R. S., Maher, K. J., Baum, M. K., Shapshak, P., & Fletcher, M. A. (1998). A bereavement support group intervention is longitudinally associated with salutary effects on the CD4 cell count and number of physician visits. *Clinical and Diagnostic Laboratory Immunology, 5*, 382–391.

Goodkin, K., Feaster, D. J., Tuttle, R. S., Blaney, N. T., Kumar, M., Baum, M. K., Shapshak, P., & Fletcher, M. A. (1996). Bereavement is associated with time-dependent decrements in cellular immune function in asymptomatic human immunodeficiency virus type 1-seropositive homosexual men. *Clinical and Diagnostic Laboratory Immunology, 3*, 109–118.

Hall, M., Baum, A., Buysse, D. J., Prigerson, H. G., Kupfer, D. J., & Reynolds,

C. F. (1998). Sleep as a mediator of the stress-immune relationship. *Psychosomatic Medicine, 60,* 48–51.

Hall, M., Buysse, D. J., Dew, M. A., Prigerson, H. G., Kupfer, D. J., & Reynolds, C. F. (1997). Intrusive thoughts and avoidance behaviors are associated with sleep disturbances in bereavement-related depression. *Depression and Anxiety, 6,* 106–112.

Hall, M., Dahl, R. E., Dew, M. A., & Reynolds, C. F. (1995). Sleep patterns following major life events. *Directions in Psychiatry, 15,* 1–8.

Hamilton, M. (1960). A rating scale for depression. *Journal of Neurology, Neurosurgery and Psychiatry, 23,* 56–62.

Herbert, T. B., & Cohen, S. (1993a). Depression and immunity: A meta-analytic review. *Psychological Bulletin, 113,* 472–486.

Herbert, T. B., & Cohen, S. (1993b). Stress and immunity in humans: A meta-analytic review. *Psychosomatic Medicine, 55,* 364–379.

Hirsch, J., Hofer, M., Holland, J., & Solomon, F. (1984). Toward a biology of grieving. In M. Osterweis, F. Solomon, & M. Green (Eds.), *Bereavement Reactions, Consequences and Care* (pp. 145–175). Washington, DC: National Academy Press.

Hofer, M. A., Wolff, C. T., Friedman, S. B., & Mason, J. W. (1972a). A psychoendocrine study of bereavement. Part I. 17-hydroxycorticosteroid excretion rates of parents following death of their children from leukemia. *Psychosomatic Medicine, 34,* 481–491.

Hofer, M. A., Wolff, C. T., Friedman, S. B., & Mason, J. W. (1972b). A psychoendocrine study of bereavement. Part II. Observations on the process of mourning in relation to adrenocortical function. *Psychosomatic Medicine, 34,* 492–504.

Irwin, M., Daniels, M., Bloom, E. T., Smith, T. L., & Weiner, H. (1987a). Life events, depressive symptoms, and immune function. *American Journal of Psychiatry, 144,* 437–441.

Irwin, M., Daniels, M., Bloom, E. T., & Weiner, H. (1986). Life events, depression, and natural killer cell activity. *Psychopharmacology Bulletin, 22,* 1093–1096.

Irwin, M., Daniels, M., Risch, S. C., Bloom, E. T., & Weiner, H. (1988). Plasma cortisol and natural killer cell activity during bereavement. *Biological Psychiatry, 24,* 173–178.

Irwin, M., Daniels, M., Smith, T. L., Bloom, E. T., & Weiner, H. (1987b). Impaired natural killer cell activity during bereavement. *Brain, Behavior, and Immunity, 1,* 98–104.

Irwin, M., McClintick, J., Costlow, C., Fortner, M., White, J., & Gillin, J. C. (1996). Partial night sleep deprivation reduces natural killer and cellular immune responses in humans. *FASEB Journal, 10,* 643–653.

Jacobs, S., Bruce, M., & Kim, K. (1997). Adrenal function predicts demoralization after losses. *Psychosomatics, 38,* 529–534.

Jacobs, S., Mason, J., Kosten, T., Kasl, S., Ostfeld, A., Atkins, S., Gardner, C., &

Schreiber, S. (1985). Acute bereavement, threatened loss, ego defenses and adrenocortical function. *Psychotherapy and Psychosomatics, 44,* 151–159.

Jacobs, S. C., Mason, J., Kosten, T. R., Kasl, S. V., Ostfeld, A. M., & Wahby, V. (1987). Urinary free cortisol and separation anxiety early in the course of bereavement and threatened loss. *Biological Psychiatry, 22,* 148–152.

Jacobs, S. C., Mason, J. W., Kosten, T. R., Wahby, V., Kasl, S. V., & Ostfeld, A. M. (1986). Bereavement and catecholamines. *Journal of Psychosomatic Research, 30,* 489–496.

Kemeny, M. E., & Dean, L. (1995). Effects of AIDS-related bereavement on HIV progression among New York City gay men. *AIDS Education and Prevention, 7,* 36–47.

Kemeny, M. E., Weiner, H., Duran, R., Taylor, S. E., Visscher, B., & Fahey, J. L. (1995). Immune system changes after the death of a partner in HIV-positive gay men. *Psychosomatic Medicine, 57,* 547–554.

Kemeny, M. E., Weiner, H., Taylor, S. E., Schneider, S., Visscher, B., & Fahey, J. L. (1994). Repeated bereavement, depressed mood, and immune parameters in HIV seropositive and seronegative gay men. *Health Psychology, 13,* 14–24.

Kosten, T. R., Jacobs, S., & Mason, J. W. (1984). The dexamethasone suppression test during bereavement. *Journal of Nervous and Mental Disease, 172,* 359–360.

Linn, M. W., Linn, B. S., & Jensen, J. (1984). Stressful events, dysphoric mood, and immune responsiveness. *Psychological Reports, 54,* 219–222.

Martikainen, P., & Valkonen, T. (1998). Do education and income buffer the effects of death of spouse on mortality? *Epidemiology, 9,* 530–534.

Martin, J. L. (1988). Psychological consequences of AIDS-related bereavement among gay men. *Journal of Consulting and Clinical Psychology, 56,* 856–862.

McEwen, B. S., & Stellar, E. (1993). Stress and the individual. *Archives of Internal Medicine, 153,* 2093–2101.

Musselman, D. L., Evans, D. L., & Nemeroff, C. B. (1998). The relationship of depression to cardiovascular disease: Epidemiology, biology, and treatment. *Archives of General Psychiatry, 55,* 580–592.

Nofzinger, E. A., Schwartz, R. M., Reynolds, C. F., Thase, M. E., Jennings, J. R., Frank, E., Fasiczka, A. L., Garamoni, G. L., & Kupfer, D. J. (1994). Affect intensity and phasic REM sleep in depressed men before and after treatment with cognitive-behavioral therapy. *Journal of Consulting and Clinical Psychology, 62*(1), 83–91.

Parkes, C. M., & Brown, R. J. (1972). Health after bereavement—A controlled study of young Boston widows and widowers. *Psychosomatic Medicine, 34,* 449–461.

Pasternak, R. E., Reynolds, C. F., Hoch, C. C., Buysse, D. J., Schlernitzauer, M., Machen, M., & Kupfer, D. J. (1992). Sleep in spousally bereaved elders with subsyndromal depressive symptoms. *Psychiatry Research, 43,* 43–53.

Pasternak, R. E., Reynolds, C. F., Houck, P. R., Schlernitzauer, M., Buysse, D. J., Hoch, C. C., & Kupfer, D. J. (1994). Sleep in bereavement-related depression during and after pharmacotherapy with nortriptyline. *Journal of Geriatric Psychiatry and Neurology, 7,* 69–73.

Prigerson, H. G., Bierhals, A. J., Kasl, S. V., Reynolds, C. F., Shear, M. K., Day, N., Beery, L. C., Newsom, J. T., & Jacobs, S. (1997). Traumatic grief as a risk factor for mental and physical morbidity. *American Journal of Psychiatry, 154,* 616–623.

Reynolds, C. F., Hoch, C. C., Buysse, D. J., Houck, P. R., Schlernitzauer, M., Frank, E., Mazumdar, S., & Kupfer, D. J. (1992). Electroencephalographic sleep in spousal bereavement and bereavement-related depression of late life. *Biological Psychiatry, 31,* 69–82.

Reynolds, C. F., Hoch, C. C., Buysse, D. J., Houck, P. R., Schlernitzauer, M., Pasternak, R. E., Frank, E., Mazumdar, S., & Kupfer, D. J. (1993). Sleep after spousal bereavement: A study of recovery from stress. *Biological Psychiatry, 34,* 791–797.

Roy, A., Gallucci, W., Avgerinos, P., Linnoila, M., & Gold, P. (1988). The CRH stimulation test in bereaved subjects with and without accompanying depression. *Psychiatry Research, 25,* 145–156.

Schleifer, S. J., Keller, S. E., Camerino, M., Thornton, J. C., & Stein, M. (1983). Suppression of lymphocyte stimulation following bereavement. *Journal of the American Medical Association, 250,* 374–377.

Seeman, T. E., Singer, B. H., Rowe, J. W., Horwitz, R. I., & McEwen, B. S. (1997). Price of adaptation—Allostatic load and its health consequences—MacArthur studies of successful aging. *Archives of Internal Medicine, 157,* 2259–2268.

Shuchter, S. R., Zisook, S., Kirkorowicz, C., & Risch, C. (1986). The dexamethasone suppression test in acute grief. *American Journal of Psychiatry, 143,* 879–881.

Spratt, M. L., & Denney, D. R. (1991). Immune variables, depression, and plasma cortisol over time in suddenly bereaved parents. *Journal of Neuropsychiatry, 3,* 299–306.

Sternberg, E. M., Chrousos, G. P., Wilder, R. L., & Gold, P. W. (1992). The stress response and the regulation of inflammatory disease. *Annals of Internal Medicine, 117,* 854–866.

VonKorff, M., Ormel, J., Katon, W., & Lin, E. H. B. (1992). Disability and depression among high utilizers of health care. *Archives of General Psychiatry, 49,* 91–100.

Weller, E. B., Weller, R. A., Fristad, M. A., & Bowes, J. M. (1990). Dexamethasone suppression test and depressive symptoms in bereaved children: A preliminary report. *Journal of Neuropsychiatry & Clinical Neurosciences, 2,* 418–421.

Wells, K. B., Stewart, A., Hays, R. D., Burnam, M. A., Rogers, W., Daniels, M., Berry, S., Greenfield, S., & Ware, J. (1989). The functioning and well-being of depressed patients. Results from the Medical Outcomes Study. *Journal of the American Medical Association, 262,* 914–919.

Wolff, C. T., Friedman, S. B., Hofer, M. A., & Mason, J. W. (1964a). Relationship between psychological defenses and mean urinary 17-hydroxycorticosteroid excretion rates. I. A predictive study of parents of fatally ill children. *Psychosomatic Medicine, 26,* 576–591.

Wolff, C. T., Hofer, M. A., & Mason, J. W. (1964b). Relationship between psychological defenses and mean urinary 17-hydroxycorticosteroid excretion rates. II. Methodologic and theoretical considerations. *Psychosomatic Medicine, 26,* 592–609.

Woof, W. R., & Carter, Y. H. (1997). The grieving adult and the general practitioner: a literature review in two parts (Part 1). *British Journal of General Practice, 47,* 443–448.

Zisook, S., Shuchter, S. R., Irwin, M., Darko, D. F., Sledge, P., & Resovsky, K. (1994). Bereavement, depression, and immune function. *Psychiatry Research, 52,* 1–10.

22

GRIEF AND EMOTION: A SOCIAL–FUNCTIONAL PERSPECTIVE

GEORGE A. BONANNO

There is little doubt that for most people the death of a loved one is an intensely painful experience. However, there are considerable individual differences in duration and severity of grief (Bonanno & Kaltman, 1999; Wortman & Silver, 1989). Traditionally, bereavement theorists have assumed that recovery from loss is predicated on the concerted review and expression of the negative emotions brought about by grieving. This process, considered part of the "work" of mourning, is thought to foster acceptance of the finality of the loss and aid in the necessary severing of attachment to the lost relationship. More recently, consideration of the social and functional aspects of emotion during bereavement has suggested an alternative view that recovery is most likely to occur when negative grief-related emotions are regulated or minimized and when positive emotions are instigated or enhanced (Bonanno & Keltner, 1997). In this chapter, I will first consider the distinction between the constructs of grief and emotion. I will next outline the traditional grief work view of emotion during bereavement and the competing position based on a social–functional view of emotion. Finally, I will review recent empirical evidence pertaining to both the dissociation and facial expression of emotion during conjugal loss that contradicts the grief work predictions but provides clear support for the social–functional view of emotion during bereavement.

DISTINGUISHING EMOTION FROM GRIEF

An important concern in assessing the role of emotion in the grieving process is the conceptual distinction between the constructs of emotion and grief outcome. Grief and emotion each involve complex behavioral responses whose respective operational definitions have not been without controversy (for reviews of some of the key definitional issues regarding emotion, see Ekman, 1992, 1994; Izard, 1994; Oatley & Jenkins, 1996; Russell, 1994; and regarding grief, see Bonanno, 1998a; Bonanno & Kaltman, 1999; Hansson, Carpenter, & Fairchild, 1993). Grief is typically a highly emotionally distressing experience, and at a superficial level appears to share features with specific emotions, most notably sadness (Lazarus, 1991). Perhaps for this reason, some investigators have preferred to blur the distinction between the concepts and have described grief as a form of emotion (Averill & Nunley, 1993; Stearns & Knapp, 1996). However, a careful analysis of the available literature reveals that grief is most appropriately conceptualized as a complex molar experience that generates various molecular components, including a range of specific emotions. In this section, I review four of the more prominent distinctions between emotion and grief.

First, emotion and grief encompass dramatically different temporal intervals. Emotions are by definition ephemeral phenomena, generally lasting between a few seconds and several hours (Ekman, 1984; Izard, 1977). In contrast, grief is an enduring state that for most bereaved individuals persists between several months and several years (Parkes & Brown, 1972; Zisook, Devaul, & Click, 1982). In some cases, grief has been found to endure seven to eight years after the loss (Lehman, Wortman, & Williams, 1987; Lundin, 1984).

Second, myriad different emotions typically occur within the course of a single period of grief. Although the death of a loved one is most commonly associated with sadness, grieving is far from a one-dimensional emotional phenomenon. Rather, grief has been associated with a wide range of negative emotions, such as sadness, anger, contempt, hostility, fear, and guilt (Abraham, 1924; Belitsky & Jacobs, 1986; Bonanno & Keltner, 1997; Bonanno, Mihalecz, & LeJeune, 1999; Bowlby, 1980; Cerney & Buskirk, 1991; Kavanagh, 1990; Lazare, 1989; Osterweis, Solomon, & Green, 1984; Raphael, 1983), as well as genuinely positive emotional experiences related to amusement, happiness, and pride (Bonanno & Keltner, 1997; Bonanno et al., 1999; Keltner & Bonanno, 1997; Shuchter & Zisook,

1993). I will return to the range of emotional responses associated with grieving at a later point in this chapter.

Third, emotion and grief are associated with different types of underlying meaning structures. Emotions are typically linked to relatively simple and proximal appraisals of danger or benefit, coping potential, or their interaction with motivational states as they pertain to the immediate situation (Frijda, 1993; Lazarus, 1991; Roseman, Antoniou, & Jose, 1996). In many cases, emotional responses occur without the benefit of even these simple cognitive appraisals. For instance, there is now compelling evidence that the chemical and physical responses associated with basic emotions, such as fear, can be triggered solely on the basis of rapid, automated, subcortical processing of crude perceptual information (LeDoux, 1989, 1996). In contrast to the relatively simple appraisals underlying emotion (Scherer, 1993), grief is associated with a profound evaluation of encompassing and irrevocable loss—the sense that "a piece of me is missing" (Shuchter & Zisook, 1993)—that envelops the grieving person's identity and cognitive understanding of the world (Schwartzberg & Janoff-Bulman, 1991) and the future (Horowitz et al., 1997; Lehman et al., 1987; Shuchter & Zisook, 1993). The longer term appraisals associated with grieving typically encompass the bereaved person's evaluation and understanding of the entire course of bereavement as well as major portions of the bereaved person's life (Bonanno, 1997; Bonanno & Kaltman, 1999).

Fourth, emotion and grief evoke different types of coping responses. Emotion is intimately related to short-term coping responses aimed at either changing or maintaining the immediate psychological or physical state. Indeed, emotion and coping are so intimately related that Folkman and Lazarus (1988, 1990) have described coping as a mediator of emotion. Grieving, on the other hand, typically evokes longer term coping efforts aimed at ameliorating the enduring emotional upsets as well as myriad concrete disruptions wrought by the loss, such as changes in social roles, economic situation, or familiar configuration (Bonanno & Keltner, 1997; Izard, 1977; Lazarus, 1991; Shuchter & Zisook, 1993; W. Stroebe & Stroebe, 1987).

EMOTION FROM A TRADITIONAL GRIEF WORK PERSPECTIVE

Given the evidence for the independence of emotion and grief, I next move to a consideration of how these two constructs may be related to each other during bereavement and how emotional processing during the early stages of grieving might relate to long-term bereavement outcome. To this end, I will consider two perspectives on the role of emotion in bereavement, one derived from a traditional "grief work" perspective and the other based on predictions from a social–functional perspective on the general role played by emotions in maintaining social relations and adjustment to important life events.

The dominant perspective on bereavement over most of the past half-century has assumed that successful recovery from the death of a loved one requires a period of working through the thoughts, memories, and emotions associated with the lost relationship, with the ultimate goal of relinquishing the attachment bond to the deceased in preparation for new intimate relationships. The association of bereavement with "work" can be traced to the phrase the "work of mourning," coined by Freud (1917/1957, p. 166). Although Freud (1917/1957) couched his speculations about the grieving process as tentative, the metaphor of the "work of mourning" was nonetheless rapidly adopted by subsequent bereavement theorists (Deutsch, 1937; Lindemann, 1944) and has, until relatively recently, dominated the bereavement literature (Belitsky & Jacobs, 1986; Bowlby, 1980; Cerney & Buskirk, 1991; Horowitz, 1986; Lazare, 1989; Marris, 1958; Osterweis et al., 1984; Parkes & Weiss, 1983; Rando, 1984; Raphael, 1983; Sanders, 1993; Worden, 1991).

In Freud's view, mourning was a process by which bereaved individuals gradually reviewed "each single one of the memories and hopes which bound the libido to the object" until "detachment of the libido from it (is) accomplished" (1917/1957, p. 154). In cases of "pathological" grieving, Freud further speculated, the bereaved survivor is unable to engage in the normal work of mourning and instead retains an unconscious identification with the lost object. When this happens, negative feelings about the deceased or the loss are redirected inwardly in the form of depressive self-reproaches or guilt. More recently, bereavement theorists have concluded that the "verbal and emotional expression of inner experience is a highly adaptive means of coping with the painful aspects of grief" (Shuchter & Zisook, 1993, p. 33) and that bereaved individuals "have a need to express their responses to a loss or death" (Corr, Nabe, & Corr, 1994).

Although the grief work perspective has been widely endorsed in the bereavement literature (W. Stroebe & Stroebe, 1987), it has yet to generate convincing empirical support. In one of the first studies to directly examine grief work, M. Stroebe and Stroebe (1991) measured five different types of behaviors associated with confrontative grief work or its avoidance (e.g., confrontation versus suppression) based on self-report and interview data obtained in the initial months after the loss. They then compared these measures to self-reported depression over the course of the first two years of bereavement. None of the five grief work measures predicted depression for widows. However, two of the measures indicating the avoidance of grief work, distraction and suppression, predicted increased depression among widowers. At best, these results provided weak support for the grief work hypothesis and then only among bereaved men, prompting M. Stroebe and Stroebe (1991) to conclude that "the view 'Everyone needs to do grief work' is an oversimplification" (p. 481). A more recent set of studies, based on the analysis of narratives obtained from bereaved gay men, also failed to clearly support the assumed necessity of grief work. In these studies, bereaved men with the fewest psychological and physical difficulties at the one-year point in bereavement had initially shown *less* evidence of self-analysis in their narratives (Nolen-Hoeksema, McBride, & Larson, 1997) and had described *fewer* negative themes and *more* positive themes, beliefs, and appraisals (Stein, Folkman, Trabasso, & Christopher-Richards, 1997).

But what about the processing of emotion during bereavement? From a traditional perspective, the failure to engage in grief work is assumed to result from a defensive inhibition of the "natural release of affects related to the loss" (Raphael, Middleton, Martinek, & Misso, 1993), so that the guiding treatment goal for clinical interventions with bereaved individuals is often centered around the "expression of grieving affects" (Raphael, 1983, p. 368). Clinical theorists have recommended that bereaved individuals "express their yearning for the lost person and the angry protest at the desertion his death seems to represent" (Raphael, 1983, pp. 368–369), and "verbalize and ultimately make peace with their hostility" (Lazare, 1989, p. 393). In this context, the grief work perspective leads to the rather straightforward prediction that experiencing and expressing negative emotions in the early months after a loss will lead to reduced grief over the long-term course of bereavement. In particular, grief work theorists have emphasized the importance of experiencing and expressing negative emotions aimed directly at the deceased, such as anger and hostility (Belitsky & Jacobs, 1986; Bowlby, 1980; Cerney & Buskirk, 1991; Lazare, 1989; Raphael, 1983). By the same token, avoiding or minimizing the experience or expression of negative grief-related emotions should predict a more intense and protracted bereavement outcome.

Although relatively little attention has been paid by grief work theorists regarding factors that may moderate emotional expression during bereavement, it stands to reason that the consequences of experiencing and expressing grief-related emotion will vary depending on the quality of the relationship with the deceased. In other words, bereaved individuals whose relationship with the deceased was particularly conflicted would likely have a greater need to work through the painful feelings associated with that relationship and, consequently, should benefit most from experiencing and expressing negative emotions in the early months of bereavement.

What about positive emotions? Somewhat surprisingly, grief work theorists have been relatively silent on the possible role of positive emotions during bereavement. Indeed, it is difficult even to find reference to positive emotions in the bereavement literature. Extrapolation of a grief work prediction regarding the role of positive emotions in the grieving process is therefore somewhat tenuous. However, it is arguable that most grief work theorists would likely view positive emotions during bereavement as a form of denial that short-circuits or impedes the proper work of mourning. For instance, Sanders (1979) described a "denial group" of bereaved individuals, based on their responses to self-report scales, as "determined optimists" (p. 238). Denial has likewise been associated with exaggerated positive or "idealized" representations of the deceased (Raphael, 1983). Finally, Bowlby (1980) described a form of "disordered mourning" in which there is a prolonged absence of grieving despite "tell-tale signs that the bereaved person has in fact been affected and that his mental equilibrium is disturbed" (p. 153). Among the "tell-tale signs" indexed were the positive emotions of pride and cheerfulness, as well as optimism and the appearance of being "in good spirits" (p. 156).

THE SOCIAL AND FUNCTIONAL ASPECTS OF EMOTION DURING BEREAVEMENT

To provide an alternative perspective on the role of emotion during bereavement, Dacher Keltner and I recently compared predictions from the grief work perspective with those derived from a consideration of the social and functional aspects of emotion (Bonanno & Keltner, 1997). In general, a social–functional perspective on emotions emphasizes their evolutionary significance as mediators of the individual's adaptation to the social environment and to significant events. Emotions are thought to play an important role in regulating both intrapersonal functioning (e.g., activating situation-specific behavioral patterns, such as the anger or flight responses, or coordinating experiential, behavioral, and physiological response systems) and interpersonal or social functioning (e.g., communicating emotional states to others or evoking responses in others that help maintain social order; Barrett & Campos, 1987; Bonanno & Keltner, 1997; Darwin, 1872; Ekman, 1992; Keltner & Buswell, 1996; Levenson, 1994).

The application of a social–functional approach to emotion in the context of bereavement suggests essentially the opposite prediction to that of the grief work perspective—that the experience and expression of intense negative emotion associated with the loss will impede functioning and predict a more severe grief course (Bonanno & Keltner, 1997). In support of this prediction, there are abundant data available from a variety of situational contexts linking prolonged negative emotions with increased stress and health problems (Watson, 1988; Watson & Clark, 1984; Watson & Pennebaker, 1989), depression (Nolen-Hoeksema, 1987), disrupted social and personal relationships (Keltner, 1995; Keltner, Moffitt, & Stouthamer-Loeber, 1995; Lemerise & Dodge, 1993; Levenson & Gottman, 1983), and pessimism and hopelessness (Keltner, Ellsworth, & Edwards, 1993). In addition, the capacity to minimize negative emotions during bereavement should make it easier for a grieved person to continue to function in areas of personal importance, such as performing in the workplace or caring for others (Shuchter & Zisook, 1993; W. Stroebe & Stroebe, 1987). Finally, the minimization of negative emotions should facilitate adaptation to the many concrete difficulties occasioned by the loss of a loved one, such as adaptation to changes in economic or family configurations, by freeing up greater resources for problem-focused coping.

The social–functional perspective on emotion also offered important predictions regarding positive emotions during bereavement. In contrast to the grief work perspective's general lack of attention to positive emotions, a consideration of the social and functional aspects of emotion suggested that (a) the expression of positive emotions associated with a loss will predict improved functioning over time, and (b) that positive emotions, in particular laughter, will be associated with improved social relations and will evoke positive responses in others (Keltner & Bonanno, 1997).

EMPIRICAL EVIDENCE

There has been a paucity of empirical data on the role of emotion in bereavement. However, my colleagues and I recently examined the prevalence and predictive utility of the experience and expression of emotion, as well as the dissociation of emotion, in the context of a longitudinal study of midlife conjugal bereavement. These data provided clear support for the predictions of the social–functional view of emotion during bereavement and contradicted the traditional grief work perspective.

Emotional Dissociation

In the first of these studies, we reported data relevant to the experience of emotion, and to the avoidance or dissociation of emotion during the initial months after the death of a spouse (Bonanno, Keltner, Holen, & Horowitz, 1995; Bonanno, Znoj, Siddique, & Horowitz, in press). Before reviewing these findings, I will elaborate briefly on the distinction between normative or everyday emotional dissociation and pathological dissociations of awareness. Dissociative phenomena are generally thought to occur along a continuum ranging from normative, transient shifts in awareness to more severe or pathological dissociations of consciousness and identity (Bernstein & Putnam, 1986; Hilgard, 1986; James, 1890). At the normative end of the continuum are relatively transient dissociative shifts in awareness, such as those occurring during daydreaming or transient distraction (Singer, 1966). Normative dissociative shifts are frequently measured as discrepancies between different psychological processes, such as direct versus indirect measures of perception (Merikle & Reingold, 1992) or explicit versus implicit forms of memory (Schacter, 1987). At a slightly more extreme level are the dissociative lapses in memory that normally result from the hierarchical nature of personality organization (James, 1890) and state-dependent or context-dependent memory retrieval (Eich, 1980; Eich & Metcalfe, 1989). Moderate forms of dissociation are manifest as the transient loss or letting go of the self as a result of intense absorption in films or other media (Bonanno & Singer, 1993) or during the mild shifts in attention and consciousness that occur during hypnosis (Hilgard, 1986). Finally, at the extreme end of the continuum are clinically relevant experiences of derealization, depersonalization, and the pathological alterations in memory and identity that typically accompany posttraumatic stress disorder and dissociative identity disorder (Steinberg, 1994; van der Kolk, van der Hart, & Marmar, 1996).

Emotional dissociation, as conceptualized in our research (Bonanno et al., 1995; Bonanno et al., in press) and elsewhere (e.g., Newton & Contrada, 1992), is assumed to fall somewhere near the normative end of the continuum of dissociative phenomena. This assumption stems from the widely accepted view that emotions are not unitary phenomena but, rather, manifest in multiple response channels, including experiential, expressive, and physiological responses. These different types of emotional responses occur partially independently from one another, and may often be dissociated such that emotion may be present at one response channel and absent, or even contradicted, at another response channel (Buck, 1988; Ekman, 1992; Izard, 1977, 1992; Lang, 1979; Lang, Kozak, Miller, Levin, & McLean, 1980; Levenson, 1994; Leventhal, 1984, 1991; Schwartz, Fair, Greenberg, Freedman, & Klerman, 1974; Schwartz, Fair, Salt, Mandel, & Klerman, 1976). For example, a subjective emotional response may be experienced in the absence of overt behavioral expression (Schwartz et al., 1974). Similarly, observable emotional responses or physiological changes may be "dissociated" or not fully experienced at the level of subjective awareness (Lang, Levin, Miller, & Kozak, 1983; Izard, 1977; Leventhal, 1991; Schwartz, 1982).

When relatively little negative emotion is reported during potentially stressful situations despite evidence of threat reactivity at other emotion response channels, it is generally assumed that some form of emotion-focused coping process, such as emotional dissociation, is operative (Bonanno & Singer, 1990; Krohne, 1992; Lazarus, 1966; Newton & Contrada, 1992). One of the most robust measures of this type of normative, emotional dissociation is the discrepancy between self-reported negative emotion and autonomic responsivity, or *verbal–autonomic response dissociation*. Evidence for the construct validity of the verbal–autonomic dissociation score has come from studies showing that it is consistently observed among individuals categorized as repressors (Asendorpf & Scherer, 1983; Newton & Contrada, 1992; Weinberger & M. Davidson, 1994; Weinberger, Schwartz, & J. Davidson, 1979). In addition, verbal–autonomic response dissociation has been found to correlate meaningfully with clinical ratings of the avoidance of emotional awareness and with the occurrence of genuine laughter, but was unrelated to nongenuine or social laughter (Bonanno et al., 1995; Keltner & Bonanno, 1997). Finally, a recent study provided direct support for the distinction between verbal–autonomic dissociation as a potentially adaptive emotional regulatory mechanism and pathological dissociation as a clinically relevant split in consciousness and identity. In this study, both sexually abused adolescents and nonabused controls who showed verbal–autonomic dissociation as they described their most stressful experiences scored significantly *lower* on questionnaire measures of pathological dissociation (Bonanno, Noll, Putnam, Trickett, & Lomakina, 1999).

To examine the role of verbal–autonomic response dissociation during bereavement, Bonanno et al. (1995) asked recently conjugally bereaved participants to talk freely about their relationship to the deceased and about their feelings about the loss of that relationship at the six-month point in bereavement. Changes in autonomic arousal were monitored during the interview, and at the end of the interview participants were asked to report how much negative and positive emotion they had experienced. These data were then standardized and used to compute verbal–autonomic response dissociation scores. From a grief work perspective, verbal–autonomic response dissociation while discussing the loss would indicate the avoidance of emotional processing and, thus, should predict a more protracted grief course. In contrast, from a social–functional point of view, verbal–autonomic dissociation in this same situation would suggest the capacity to minimize or regulate emotions to allow or enhance social relations and normative functioning and thus should predict a less severe grief course.

In contrast to the grief work assumption but consistent with the social–functional view, verbal–autonomic response dissociation was evidenced most clearly by participants who showed relatively little grief, as measured by a structured clinical interview across 25 months of bereavement (Bonanno et al., 1995; Bonanno et al., in press). The degree that participants engaged in verbal–autonomic response dissociation was also inversely correlated with the interviewer ratings of grief at later assessments, and these correlations remained significant when initial levels of grief were statistically controlled. It is interesting to note that the use of verbal–autonomic dissociation while talking about the lost relationship was not without a cost. Bereaved individuals who showed verbal autonomic response dissociation at six months also reported concurrent elevations in somatic complaints (Bonanno et al., 1995). However, at the 14- and 25-month follow-up assessments, these participants no longer had high levels of somatic complaints. In addition, verbal–autonomic dissociation was unrelated to the frequency of visits to medical professionals (Bonanno et al., in press) and was not influenced by the remembered quality of adjustment in the conjugal relationship. When considered together, these findings suggest that the dissociation of emotional distress is a relatively effective means of coping with the pain of losing a spouse. Although the dissociation of distress was not without some initial cost, manifest as temporary increases in health difficulties, this cost appeared to be relatively minor and to dissipate relatively early in the course of bereavement.

An additional consideration we examined in this study was the question of delayed grief. From a grief work perspective, emotional dissociation may result in a short-lived reduction in overt symptoms but, owing to the necessity of the working-through process, it is assumed that unresolved grief will eventually manifest in the form of delayed symptoms (Bowlby, 1980; Deutsch, 1937; Horowitz, 1986; Osterweis et al., 1984; Parkes & Weiss, 1983; Rando, 1984; Raphael, 1983). To examine this assumption, we operationally defined delayed grief as an increase in grief symptoms to a level at or above the six-month sample median (Bonanno et al., 1995). At the 25-month point in bereavement, not a single participant in this study evidenced a delayed increase in grief symptoms (Bonanno et al., in press). We also used a similar operational definition of delayed somatic symptoms. In this case, six participants (20%) did report greater numbers of somatic complaints at later points in the study. However, these increases were unrelated to the verbal–autonomic dissociation score, fell within a standard deviation observed for this measure in the same sample and in a similar married sample (Bonanno, 1997), and were unrelated to the frequency of visits to medical professionals (Bonanno et al., 1995; Bonanno et al., in press). Based on the confluence of these results, it would appear that the increases in somatic complaints had little to do with grief work and are more appropriately explained as random method variance.

Facial Expressions of Emotion

Another facet of emotional processing during bereavement is its overt expression in the face. The coding of facial muscle displays offers several distinct methodological advantages for the study of emotion and bereavement. First, although humans possess a rich array of expressive behaviors (e.g., tone of voice, posture), facial expressions are a primary means by which emotion is communicated (Bowlby, 1980; Darwin, 1872; Ekman, 1992). Second, there are well-validated methods available that make it possible to reliably code facial expressions for a number of basic emotions (Ekman & Friesen, 1976). Third, because the coding is done from videotapes, it was possible to measure emotional expression without relying on participant self-report or even on participant knowledge that expressive behaviors were of interest to the researchers.

Keltner and I recently examined facial expressions of emotion from videotapes of the same bereavement interviews from which the verbal–autonomic data were obtained (Bonanno & Keltner, 1997). The results of these analyses were consistent with the verbal–autonomic findings, and again supported the predictions of the social–functional view of emotion: The more participants expressed negative emotion as they talked about their loss, the more likely they were to be still showing intense grief at later assessments. In addition, facial expressions of positive emotions associated with the loss were quite common, and predicted improved functioning over the longer term course of bereavement.

Minimizing Negative Emotion

The facial expression data collected at the six-month point in bereavement corroborated Shuchter and Zisook's (1993) conclusion that grieving evokes a wide range of negative emotions. Facial expressions of sadness and anger were the most common at six months, with both observed in 63% of the sample, followed by facial expressions of disgust (35%), contempt (32%), and fear (16%). Further, consistent with the social–functional view, six-month facial expressions of anger, contempt, disgust, and fear, as well as a composite score representing the general tendency to express negative emotion, were each positively correlated with increased interviewer ratings of grief at 14-months postloss. It is interesting to note that facial expressions of anger, the emotion most consistently believed by grief work theorists to require expression during bereavement (Belitsky & Jacobs, 1986; Cerney & Buskirk, 1991), were the most strongly associated with increased grief at 14 months, and were still correlated with increased grief at the 25-month point in bereavement.

Consistent with the social–functional perspective, these findings suggest that minimizing the expression of negative emotion in the early months of bereavement fosters recovery. An important consideration, however, was that by themselves these findings could not determine whether expressing negative emotions actually influenced later grief per se or whether more grieved individuals simply tended to express more negative emotion. In other words, it was possible that facial expressions of negative emotion were a by-product of grief, rather than a factor that influenced the subsequent course of grief. To address this concern, we reanalyzed the facial data but this time statistically controlled for both the initial level of grief and for the initial self-reported experience of emotion. In effect, we evened out the sample for initial differences in grief severity and negative emotion and thus isolated the degree that expressing negative emotion was related to later grief course. This was a relatively conservative procedure because the sample size for this study was small ($N = 38$), thus reducing statistical power, and initial grief symptoms generally account for quite a bit of the variance at later assessments.

Nonetheless, with initial grief and self-reported emotion controlled, facial expressions of negative emotion were still consistently correlated with increased grief at 14 months postloss. A similar but slightly less robust pattern of associations was also observed between facial expression of negative emotion and lower scores on a measure of perceived health at 14 and 25 months postloss. Finally, these effects were still found to be significant when the quality of adjustment in the lost conjugal relationship, as measured by the Dyadic Adjustment Scale (Spanier, 1976), was statistically controlled (Bonanno, 1995). Thus regardless of how much grief participants showed at the beginning of the study, regardless of how much emotion participants reported experiencing when they described their lost relationship, and regardless of the quality of adjustment in the lost relationship, minimizing the expression of negative emotion was consistently linked to reduced grief over time.

Accentuating Genuine Positive Emotion

Examining the facial expression data for positive emotions provided compelling evidence that grieving is not solely a negative or distressing experience. The use of facial coding to examine positive emotional expression offered the further methodological advantage that genuine positive emotion could be distinguished from social or polite facial displays. The genuine or "Duchenne" smile—named after Duchenne de Bologne (1862), who first identified it—is distinguished by the involvement of the orbicularis occuli muscles around the eyes. In contrast, superficial or polite smiles do not involve the orbicularis muscles. Duchenne laughs may also be distinguished from polite laughs. In this case, Duchenne laughs are open-mouth smiles that involve the orbicularis occuli muscles and frequent vocalizations (typically a "he he" sound that evolves into a "ha ha" sound). Only Duchenne laughs and smiles have been linked to genuine positive emotion and to positive interpersonal consequences (Duchenne de Bologne, 1862; Frank, Ekman, & Friesen, 1993). As expected, we also found that only Duchenne expressions were correlated with the experience of positive emotion during bereavement (Keltner & Bonanno, 1997). Further, in contrast to the traditional assumption that positive emotion is inconsequential during bereavement, Duchenne laughter and smiling were exhibited at least once by the majority of the participants (58% and 63%, respectively) as they described their lost relationship.

Finally, both Duchenne laughter and smiling were significantly correlated with reduced grief at 14 and 25 months postloss. Further, when initial grief and self-reported emotion were controlled, as described previously, Duchenne laughter and smiling still predicted reduced grief at 25 months. The links between Duchenne laughs and smiles and 25-month outcome suggests a somewhat different relationship to long-term grief than was evidence for facial expressions of negative emotions, which predicted increased grief primarily at the 14-month point in bereavement. However, such a result is not inconsistent with the social–function perspective, which assumes that positive and negative emotions serve different intrapersonal and interpersonal functions (Diener & Emmons, 1984; Watson & Clark, 1984) and thus would likely interact with long-term adaptive functioning in different ways.

Laughter During Bereavement

The coding of facial expressions during bereavement offered a rare opportunity to examine several additional social–functional assumptions specific to Duchenne laughter. The social–functional view of emotion suggests that genuine laughter serves an important interpersonal function by enhancing social relations and also plays a role in self-regulation by fostering dissociation from distress (Keltner & Bonanno, 1997).

The Interpersonal Benefits of Laughter

Laughter has been found to occur almost exclusively in social contexts (Provine & Fischer, 1989) and appears to serve a number of positive social functions, such as inducing positive emotion in others through contagion (Hatfield, Cacioppo, & Rapson, 1992; Provine, 1992), fostering group cohesiveness (Vinton, 1989), and enhancing solutions to interpersonal conflict (Keltner & Monarch, 1996). Laughter has also been associated with the personality trait of agreeableness (Keltner et al., 1998). The correlates of laughter during bereavement were consistent with this presumed social function. In addition to its association with reduced grief over time (Bonanno & Keltner, 1997), Duchenne laughter while talking about the loss of a spouse was associated with reports of better overall adjustment in the lost conjugal relationship, in particular with greater consensus in mutual decision making, and with reduced ambivalence in current important relationships (Keltner & Bonanno, 1997).

We also explored the impact the bereaved participants' laughter might have on other people. To do so, we showed soundless videotapes of the bereaved participants to untrained observers, informed the observers that the individuals in the videotapes were talking about the recent loss of a spouse, and then asked the observers to rate their honest responses to each participant. The amount that a bereaved individual showed Duchenne laughter when describing their loss was correlated with the observers' perceptions of adjustment and inversely correlated with observers' perceptions of suffering. More important, bereaved individuals who showed Duchenne laughter also evoked more amusement and overall positive emotion and less frustration in the observers. In contrast, non-Duchenne, or polite, laughter was unrelated to observers responses (Keltner & Bonanno, 1997). Thus even while talking about a painful topic such as the recent death of a spouse, genuine laughter has a contagious function that induces positive emotions in others.

Laughter as a Dissociation From Distress

In addition to its interpersonal functions, laughter appears to play a role in the dissociation of, or distancing from, distress. In general, positive emotions have been thought of as "undoers" of negative emotions (Fredrickson & Levenson, 1998; Levenson, 1988). Laughter has been associated with improved psychological functioning (Martin & Lefcourt, 1983; Nezu, Nezu, & Blisett, 1988) and reduced distress (Keltner & Monarch, 1996; Krokoff, 1991) during potentially stressful situations. Cognitive analyses of humor have suggested that laughter arises during distressing events when a novel perspective is adopted or when insight is gained into incongruities or violated expectations, resulting in a reduction in tension and a corresponding shift to a positive state (Martin & Lefcourt, 1983; Ruch, 1993). Consistent with this general argument, we found that the occurrence of Duchenne laughter while bereaved individuals described the lost conjugal relationship was significantly associated with the reduced experience of anger and distress, whereas non-Duchenne or polite laughter was not. Further, Duchenne laughter correlated with verbal–autonomic response dissociation, whereas non-Duchenne or polite laughter was linked to the heightened experience of distress (Keltner & Bonanno, 1997). Finally, an "on-line" contingency analysis of facial expressions and verbalized emotion themes showed that Duchenne laughter was most likely to occur when bereaved participants described anger at the deceased (Bonanno & Keltner, 1999), thus further suggesting the role of genuine laughter in the shift from negative to positive states.

CONCLUSION

Although the findings reviewed in this chapter were garnered using relatively sophisticated measurements of facial and physiological variables, they are not without their methodological limitations. First and foremost is the fact that these findings come from the same research participants in the same longitudinal bereavement project. Further, in absence of additional data, it might be argued that the salutary benefit of minimizing negative emotions and enhancing positive emotions is limited to the specific type of loss—for example, conjugal, or to the specific age group, who were midlife adults—considered in this particular study.

As such, these findings underscore the need for continued empirical investigation of the role of emotion in the grieving process and point to a number of promising avenues for future bereavement research. For instance, it should be of great interest to learn whether the expression of grief-related emotions varies, or promote different outcomes, across divergent cultural contexts. Discrete emotions theorists generally agree that human emotions serve similar functions and tend to be expressed and understood in a similar manner in all cultures (Ekman, 1992; Ekman, Friesen, & Ellsworth, 1972; Izard, 1977, 1994). However, the "display rules" of a particular culture will guide when, in what particular contexts, and to what extent each emotion may be expressed, suppressed, or masked (Ekman, 1972, 1993). How different cultures construe the mourning process will undoubtedly interact with emotion. For instance, most cultures view anger as a potentially volatile, even dangerous, emotion that must be controlled, regulated, or avoided during bereavement. However, despite this general propensity, there are also observable variations across cultures in the specific rules that govern when or to what extent, if at all, it is socially acceptable to express grief-related anger (Mandelbaum, 1959; Rosenblatt, 1993). Thus it is an empirical question as to whether the findings we described in this chapter —the inverse association between facial expressions of anger and long-term grief outcome (Bonanno & Keltner, 1997)—will generalize to other cultures outside the United States.

Another area ripe for further study is the role of laughter during bereavement. Again, it will be of interest to examine whether laughter exerts the same salutary function during bereavement when other cultural contexts are examined. However, there is still quite a bit to be learned about laughter's more general role in the grieving process. For example, Keltner and Bonanno's (1997) findings suggested both that laughter serves as a means of regulating or distancing the experience of negative emotions and that laughter fosters interpersonal relatedness. Each of these processes, or perhaps their combination, may account for the salutary influence of laughter on long-term functioning during bereavement. Keltner and Bonanno's (1997) findings could not address this point. Further empirical study is needed to expand our understanding of the functions of laughter and the factors that might mediate its salutary impact on bereavement.

Given these considerations, the empirical evidence reviewed in this chapter nonetheless provides preliminary support for the social–functional view of emotion during bereavement and underscores its considerable promise as a framework from which to further investigate the role of emotion in the grieving process. One of the outstanding limitations of the traditional grief work approach to bereavement has been its lack of theoretical specificity—the components of grief work have not been well-defined and have proved difficult to operationalize for application to an empirical context (Bonanno, 1998b; W. Stroebe & Stroebe, 1993). By contrast, the social–functional perspective on emotion during bereavement offers workable operational definitions and a clear, empirically derived set of predictions from which to guide subsequent empirical investigation. The social-functional perspective also offers the advantage of linking the phenomenon of grieving with the broader body of theoretical and empirical literatures on emotion and evolutionary theory. As such, the social-functional approach makes possible new insights into the ways that both positive and negative emotion may manifest during bereavement, interact with the experience of grief, and inform its ultimate severity and course. It is hoped that this chapter will inspire further empirical exploration in this important and as yet underresearched area.

REFERENCES

Abraham, K. (1924). A short study of the development of the libido; viewed in the light of mental disorders. In K. Abraham (Ed.), *Selected papers on psychoanalysis* (pp. 418–501). London: Hogarth Press.

Asendorpf, J. B., & Scherer, K. R. (1983). The discrepant repressor: Differentiation between low anxiety, high anxiety, and repression of anxiety by autonomic-facial-verbal patterns of behavior. *Journal of Personality and Social Psychology, 45*, 1334–1346.

Averill, J. R., & Nunley, E. P. (1993). Grief as an emotion and as a disease: A social-constructionist perspective. In M. S. Stroebe, W. Stroebe, & R. O. Hansson (Eds.), *Handbook of bereavement: Theory, research, and intervention* (pp. 367–380). Cambridge: Cambridge University Press.

Barrett, K. C., & Campos, J. J. (1987). Perspectives on emotional development II: A functionalist approach to emotions. In J. D. Osofsky (Ed.), *Handbook of Infant Development* (2nd ed., pp. 555–578). New York: Wiley-Interscience.

Belitsky, R., & Jacobs, S. (1986). Bereavement, attachment theory, and mental disorders. *Psychiatric Annals, 16*, 276–280.

Bernstein, E. M., & Putnam, F. W. (1986). Development, reliability, and validity of a dissociation scale. *Journal of Nervous and Mental Disease, 174*, 727–735.

Bonanno, G. A. (1995, June). Grief and the varieties of emotional response. In D. Keltner (Chair), *Universality, Variation, and Functions of Emotional Expression*. Symposium conducted at the American Psychological Society Convention, New York.

Bonanno, G. A. (1997, July). *Examining the "grief work" approach to bereavement*. Presented at the 5th International Conference on Grief and Bereavement, Washington, DC.

Bonanno, G. A. (1998a). Factors associated with the effective accommodation to loss. In C. Figley (Ed.), *The traumatology of grieving* (pp. 37–51). Washington, DC: Taylor & Francis.

Bonanno, G. A. (1998b). Emotional dissociation, self-deception, and adaptation to loss. In C. Figley (Ed.), *The traumatology of grieving* (pp. 89–105). Washington, DC: Taylor & Francis.

Bonanno, G. A., & Kaltman, S. A. (1999). Toward an integrative perspective on bereavement. *Psychological Bulletin, 125*, 760–776.

Bonanno, G. A., & Keltner, D. (1997). Facial expressions of emotion and the course of bereavement. *Journal of Abnormal Psychology, 106*, 126–137.

Bonanno, G. A., & Keltner, D. (1999). *The organization of discrete emotions: A contingency analysis of facial expressions, "on-line" verbal themes, and written self-report.* Manuscript submitted for publication.

Bonanno, G. A., Keltner, D., Holen, A., & Horowitz, M. J. (1995). When avoiding unpleasant emotion might not be such a bad thing: Verbal-autonomic response dissociation and midlife conjugal bereavement. *Journal of Personality and Social Psychology, 46*, 975–989.

Bonanno, G. A., Mihalecz, M. C., & LeJeune, J. T. (1999). *The core emotion themes of conjugal loss. Motivation and Emotion, 23*, 175–201.

Bonanno, G. A., Noll, J., Putnam, F., Trickett, P., & Lomakina, N. (1999). *Emotional dissociation and clinically relevant dissociative experiences: A study of the long-term consequences of childhood sexual abuse.* Manuscript submitted for publication.

Bonanno, G. A., & Singer, J. L. (1990). Repressive personality style: Theoretical and methodological implications for health and pathology. In J. L. Singer (Ed.), *Repression and dissociation* (pp. 435–470). Chicago: University of Chicago Press.

Bonanno, G. A., & Singer, J. L. (1993). Controlling the stream of thought through perceptual and reflective processing. In D. Wegner & J. Pennebaker (Eds.), *Handbook of mental control* (pp. 149–170). New York: Prentice-Hall.

Bonanno, G. A., Znoj, H. J., Siddique, H., & Horowitz, M. J. (in press). Verbal-autonomic response dissociation and adaptation to midlife conjugal loss: A follow-up at 25 months. *Cognitive Therapy and Research.*

Bowlby, J. (1980). *Attachment and loss. Vol. 3. Loss: Sadness and depression.* New York: Basic Books.

Buck, R. (1988). *Human motivation and emotion* (2nd ed.). New York: Wiley & Sons.

Cerney, M. W., & Buskirk, J. R. (1991). Anger: The hidden part of grief. *Bulletin of the Menninger Clinic, 55*, 228–237.

Corr, C. A., Nabe, C. M., & Corr, D. M. (1994). *Death and dying, life and living.* Pacific Grove, CA: Brooks/Cole.

Darwin, C. (1872). *The expression of emotion in man and animals.* London: Murray.

Deutsch, H. (1937). Absence of grief. *Psychoanalytic Quarterly, 6*, 12–22.

Diener, E., & Emmons, R. A. (1984). The independence of positive and negative affect. *Journal of Personality and Social Psychology, 47*, 1105–1117.

Duchenne de Bologne, G. B. (1862). *The mechanism of human facial expression* (R. A. Cuthbertson, Trans.). New York: Cambridge University Press.

Ekman, P. (1972). Universals and cultural differences in facial expressions of emotion. In J. Cole (Ed.), *Nebraska symposium on motivation* (pp. 207–283). Lincoln: University of Nebraska Press.

Ekman, P. (1984). Expression and the nature of emotion. In K. Scherer & P. Ekman (Eds.), *Approaches to emotion* (pp. 319–344). Hillsdale, NJ: Erlbaum.

Ekman, P. (1992). Are there basic emotions? *Psychological Review, 99,* 550–553.

Ekman, P. (1993). Facial expression and emotion. *American Psychologist, 48,* 384–392.

Ekman, P. (1994). Strong evidence for universals in facial expressions: A reply to Russell's mistaken critique. *Psychological Bulletin, 115,* 268–287.

Ekman, P., & Friesen, W. V. (1976). Measuring facial movement. *Journal of Environmental Psychology and Nonverbal Behavior, 1,* 56–75.

Ekman, P., Friesen, W. V., & Ellsworth, P. C. (1972). *Emotion in the human face: Guidelines for research and an integration of findings.* New York: Pergamon Press.

Eich, E. (1980). The cue-dependent nature of state-dependent memory. *Memory and Cognition, 8,* 157–173.

Eich, E., & Metcalfe, J. (1989). Mood-dependent memory for internal versus external events. *Journal of Experimental Psychology: Learning, Memory, and Cognition, 15,* 443–455.

Fredrickson, B. L., & Levenson, R. W. (1998). Positive emotions speed recovery from cardiovascular sequelae of negative emotions. *Cognition and Emotion, 12,* 191–220.

Folkman, S., & Lazarus, R. S. (1988). Coping as a mediator of emotion. *Journal of Personality and Social Psychology, 54,* 466–475.

Folkman, S., & Lazarus, R. S. (1990). Coping and emotion. In N. L. Stein, B. Leventhal, & T. Trabasso (Eds.), *Psychological and biological approaches to emotion* (pp. 313–332). Hillsdale, NJ: Erlbaum.

Frank, M., Ekman, P., & Friesen, W. V. (1993). Behavioral markers and recognizability of the smile of enjoyment. *Journal of Personality and Social Psychology, 64,* 83–93.

Freud, S. (1957). Mourning and melancholia. In J. Strachey (Ed.), *The standard edition of the complete psychological works of Sigmund Freud, Vol. 14* (pp. 152–170). London: Hogarth Press. (Original work published 1917)

Frijda, N. H. (1993). The place of appraisal in emotion. *Cognition and Emotion, 7,* 357–387.

Hansson, R. O., Carpenter, B. N., & Fairchild, S. K. (1993). Measurement issues in bereavement. In M. S. Stroebe, W. Stroebe, & R. O. Hansson (Eds.), *Handbook of bereavement: Theory, research, and intervention* (pp. 255–270). Cambridge: Cambridge University Press.

Hatfield, E., Cacioppo, J. T., & Rapson, R. (1992). Primitive emotional contagion. In M. S. Clark (Ed.), *Review of personality and social psychology, vol. 14* (pp. 151–177). Newbury Park, CA: Sage.

Hilgard, E. R. (1986). *Divided consciousness: Multiple controls in human thought and action* (3rd ed.). New York: Wiley & Sons.

Horowitz, M. J. (1986). *Stress response syndromes*. Northvale, NJ: Aronson.

Horowitz, M. J., Siegel, B., Holen, A., Bonanno, G. A., Milbrath, C., & Stinson, C. H. (1997). Diagnostic criteria for complicated grief disorder. *American Journal of Psychiatry, 154*, 904–910.

Izard, C. E. (1977). *Human emotions*. New York: Plenum Press.

Izard, C. E. (1992). Basic emotions, relations among emotions, and emotion-cognition relations. *Psychological Review, 99*, 561–564.

Izard, C. E. (1994). Innate and universal facial expressions: Evidence from developmental and cross-cultural research. *Psychological Bulletin, 115*, 288–299.

James, W. (1890). *The principles of psychology, Vol. 1*. New York: Dover.

Kavanagh, D. G. (1990). Towards a cognitive–behavioral intervention for adult grief reactions. *British Journal of Psychiatry, 157*, 373–383.

Keltner, D. (1995). The signs of appeasement: Evidence for the distinct displays of embarrassment, amusement, and shame. *Journal of Personality and Social Psychology, 68*, 441–454.

Keltner, D., & Bonanno, G. A. (1997). A study of laughter and dissociation: Distinct correlates of laughter and smiling during bereavement. *Journal of Personality and Social Psychology, 73*, 687–702

Keltner, D., Bonanno, G. A., Caspi, A., Kreuger, B., & Strouthamer-Loeber, M. (1998). *Personality and facial expressions of emotion*. Unpublished manuscript.

Keltner, D., & Buswell, B. N. (1996). Evidence for the distinctiveness of embarrassment, shame, and guilt: A study of recalled antecedents and facial expressions of emotion. *Cognition and Emotion, 10*, 155–171.

Keltner, D., Ellsworth, P. C., & Edwards, K. (1993). Beyond simple pessimism: Effects of sadness and anger on social perception. *Journal of Personality and Social Psychology, 64*, 740–752.

Keltner, D., Moffitt, T., & Stouthamer-Loeber, M. (1995). Facial expressions of emotion and psychopathology in adolescent boys. *Journal of Abnormal Psychology, 104*, 644–652.

Keltner, D., & Monarch, N. M. (1996). *Emotion, personality, and relationship satisfaction in romantic couples*. Unpublished manuscript.

Krohne, H. W. (1992). Vigilance and cognitive avoidance as concepts in coping research. In H. W. Krohne (Ed.), *Attention and avoidance strategies in coping with aversiveness* (pp. 19–50). Göttingen, Germany: Hograth & Huber.

Krokoff, L. J. (1991). Job distress is no laughing matter in marriage, or is it? *Journal of Social and Personal Relationships, 8*, 5–25.

Lang, P. J. (1979). Language, image, and emotion. In P. Pliner, K. R. Blankstein, & J. M. Spigel (Eds.), *Perception of emotion in self and others* (Vol. 5). New York: Plenum Press.

Lang, P. J., Kozak, M. J., Miller, G. A., Levin, D. N., & McLean, A. (1980).

Emotional imagery: Conceptual structure and pattern of somato-visceral response. *Psychophysiology, 17,* 179–192.

Lang, P. J., Levin, D. N., Miller, G. A., & Kozak, M. J. (1983). Fear behavior, fear imagery, and the psychophysiology of emotion: The problem of affective response integration. *Journal of Abnormal Psychology, 92,* 276–306.

Lazare, A. (1989). Bereavement and unresolved grief. In A. Lazare (Ed.), *Outpatient psychiatry: Diagnosis and treatment* (2nd ed., pp. 381–397). Baltimore: Williams & Wilkins.

Lazarus, R. S. (1966). *Psychological stress and the coping process.* New York: Oxford University Press.

Lazarus, R. S. (1991). *Emotion and adaptation.* New York: Oxford University Press.

LeDoux, J. (1989). Cognitive–emotional interactions in the brain. *Cognition and Emotion, 3,* 267–289.

LeDoux, J. (1996). *The emotional brain.* New York: Simon & Schuster.

Lehman, D. R., Wortman, C. B., & Williams, A. F. (1987). Long-term effects of losing a spouse or child in a motor vehicle crash. *Journal of Personality and Social Psychology, 52,* 218–231.

Lemerise, E. A., & Dodge, K. A. (1993). The development of anger and hostile interactions. In M. Lewis & J. M. Haviland (Eds.), *Handbook of emotions* (pp. 537–546). New York: Guilford Press.

Levenson, R. W. (1988). Emotion and the autonomic nervous system: A prospectus for research on autonomic specificity. In H. L. Wagner (Ed.), *Social psychophysiology and emotion: Theory and clinical applications* (pp. 17–42). London: Wiley & Sons.

Levenson, R. W. (1994). Human emotion: A functional view. In P. Ekman & R. J. Davidson (Eds.), *The nature of emotion: Fundamental questions* (pp. 123–126). Oxford: Oxford University Press.

Levenson, R. W., & Gottman, J. M. (1983). Marital interaction: Physiological linkage and affective exchange. *Journal of Personality and Social Psychology, 45,* 587–597.

Leventhal, H. (1984). A perceptual-motor theory of emotion. In L. Berkowitz (Ed.), *Advances in experimental social psychology* (Vol. 17, pp. 117–182). New York: Academic Press.

Leventhal, H. (1991). Emotion: Prospects for conceptual and empirical development. In R. G. Lister & H. J. Weingartner (Eds.), *Perspectives on cognitive neuroscience* (pp. 325–348). Oxford: Oxford University Press.

Lindemann, E. (1944). Symptomatology and management of acute grief. *American Journal of Psychiatry, 101,* 1141–1148.

Lundin, T. (1984). Long-term outcome of bereavement. *British Journal of Psychiatry, 145,* 434–428.

Mandelbaum, D. G. (1959). Social uses of funeral rites. In H. Feifel (Ed.), *The meaning of death* (pp. 189–217). New York: McGraw-Hill.

Marris, P. (1958). *Widows and their families.* London: Routledge & Kegan Paul.

Martin, R. A., & Lefcourt, H. M. (1983). The sense of humor as a moderator of the relation between stressors and moods. *Journal of Personality and Social Psychology, 45*, 1313–1324.

Merikle, P. M., & Reingold, E. M. (1992). Measuring unconscious perceptual processes. In R. F. Bornstein & T. S. Pittman (Eds.), *Perception without awareness* (pp. 55–80). New York: Guilford Press.

Newton, T. L., & Contrada, R. J. (1992). Repressive coping and verbal-autonomic response dissociation: The influence of social context. *Journal of Personality and Social Psychology, 62*, 159–167.

Nezu, A. M., Nezu, C. M., & Blisett, S. E. (1988). Sense of humor as a moderator of the relation between stressful events and psychological distress: A prospective analysis. *Journal of Personality and Social Psychology, 54*, 520–525.

Nolen-Hoeksema, S. (1987). Sex differences in unipolar depression: Evidence and theory. *Psychological Bulletin, 101*, 259–282.

Nolen-Hoeksema, S., McBride, A., & Larson, J. (1997). Rumination and psychological distress among bereaved partners. *Journal of Personality and Social Psychology, 72*, 855–862.

Oatley, K., & Jenkins, J. M. (1996). *Understanding emotions.* Cambridge, MA: Blackwell.

Osterweis, M., Solomon, F., & Green, F. (Eds.). (1984). *Bereavement: Reactions, consequences, and care.* Washington, DC: National Academy Press.

Parkes, C. M., & Brown, R. J. (1972). Health after bereavement: A controlled study of young Boston widows and widowers. *Psychosomatic Medicine, 34*, 449–461.

Parkes, C. M., & Weiss, R. S. (1983). *Recovery from bereavement.* New York: Basic Books.

Provine, R. R. (1992). Contagious laughter: Laughter is a sufficient stimulus for laughs and smiles. *Bulletin of the Psychonomic Society, 30*, 1–4.

Provine, R. R., & Fischer, K. R. (1989). Laughing, smiling, and talking: Relation to sleeping and social context in humans. *Ethology, 83*, 295–305.

Rando, T. A. (1984). *Grief, dying and death: Clinical interventions for caregivers.* Champaign, IL: Research Press.

Raphael, B. (1983). *The anatomy of bereavement.* New York: Basic Books.

Raphael, B., Middleton, W., Martinek, N., & Misso, V. (1993). Counseling and therapy of the bereaved. In M. S. Stroebe, W. Stroebe, & R. O. Hansson (Eds.), *Handbook of bereavement: Theory, research, and intervention* (pp. 427–456.) Cambridge: Cambridge University Press.

Roseman, I. J., Antoniou, A. A., & Jose, P. E. (1996). Appraisal determinants of emotion: Constructing a more accurate and comprehensive theory. *Cognition and Emotion, 10*, 241–277.

Rosenblatt, P. C. (1993). Grief: The social context of private feelings. In M. S. Stroebe, W. Stroebe, & R. O. Hansson (Eds.), *Handbook of bereavement: Theory, research, and intervention* (pp. 102–111). Cambridge: Cambridge University Press.

Ruch, W. (1993). Exhilaration and humor. In M. Lewis & J. M. Haviland (Eds.), *The handbook of emotion* (pp. 605–616). New York: Guilford Press.

Russell, J. A. (1994). Is there universal recognition of emotion from facial expression? A review of cross-cultural studies. *Psychological Bulletin, 115,* 102–141.

Sanders, C. M. (1979). The use of the MMPI in assessing bereavement outcome. In C. S. Newmark (Ed.), *MMPI: Clinical and research trends* (pp. 223–247). New York: Praeger.

Sanders, C. M. (1993). Risk factors in bereavement outcome. In M. S. Stroebe, W. Stroebe, & R. O. Hansson (Eds.), *Handbook of bereavement: Theory, research, and intervention* (pp. 255–270). Cambridge: Cambridge University Press.

Schacter, D. L. (1987). Implicit memory: History and current status. *Journal of Experimental Psychology: Learning, Memory, and Cognition, 13,* 501–518.

Scherer, K. R. (1993). Studying the emotion-antecedent appraisal process: An expert system approach. *Cognition and Emotion, 7,* 325–355.

Schwartz, G. E. (1982). Physiological patterning and emotion: Implications for the self-regulation of emotion. In K. R. Blankstein & J. Polivy (Eds.), *Self-control and self-modification of emotional behavior* (pp. 13–27). New York: Plenum Press.

Schwartz, G. E., Fair, P. L., Greenberg, P. S., Freedman, M., & Klerman, J. L. (1974). Facial electromyography in the assessment of emotion. *Psychophysiology, 11,* 237.

Schwartz, G. E., Fair, P. L., Salt, P., Mandel, M. R., & Klerman, J. L. (1976). Facial muscle patterning to affective imagery in depressed and nondepressed subjects. *Science, 192,* 489–491.

Schwartzberg, S. S., & Janoff-Bulman, R. (1991). Grief and the search for meaning: Exploring the assumptive worlds of bereaved college students. *Journal of Social and Clinical Psychology, 10,* 270–288.

Shuchter, S. R., & Zisook, S. (1993). The course of normal grief. In M. S. Stroebe, W. Stroebe, & R. O. Hansson (Eds.), *Handbook of bereavement: Theory, research, and intervention* (pp. 23–43). Cambridge: Cambridge University Press.

Singer, J. L. (1966). *The inner world of daydreaming.* New York: Random House.

Spanier, G. B. (1976). Measuring dyadic adjustment: New scales for assessing the quality of marriage and similar dyads. *Journal of Marriage and the Family, 38,* 15–28.

Stearns, P. N., & Knapp, M. (1996). Historical perspectives on grief. In R. Harr & W. G. Parrott (Eds.), *The emotions: Social, cultural, and biological dimensions* (pp. 132–150). Thousand Oaks, CA: Sage.

Stein, N. L., Folkman, S., Trabasso, T., & Christopher-Richards, A. (1997). Appraisal and goal processes as predictors of well-being in bereaved care-givers. *Journal of Personality and Social Psychology, 72,* 863–871.

Steinberg, M. (1994). Systematizing dissociation: Symptomatology and diagnostic assessment. In S. Spiegel (Ed.), *Dissociation: Culture, mind, and body*. Washington, DC: American Psychiatric Press.

Stroebe, M. S., & Stroebe, W. (1991). Does "grief work" work? *Journal of Consulting and Clinical Psychology, 59,* 479–482.

Stroebe, W., & Stroebe, M. S. (1987). *Bereavement and health*. Cambridge: Cambridge University Press.

Stroebe, W., & Stroebe, M. S. (1993). Determinants of adjustment to bereavement in younger widows and widowers. In M. S. Stroebe, W. Stroebe, & R. O. Hansson (Eds.), *Handbook of bereavement: Theory, research, and intervention* (pp. 208–226). Cambridge: Cambridge University Press.

van der Kolk, B., van der Hart, O., & Marmar, C. R. (1996). Dissociation and information processing in posttraumatic stress disorder. In B. van der Kolk, A. C. McFarlane, & L. Weisaeth (Eds.), *Traumatic stress: The overwhelming experience of mind, body, and society* (pp. 303–327). New York: Guilford Press.

Vinton, K. L. (1989). Humor in the work place: Is it more than telling jokes? *Small Group Behavior, 20,* 151–166.

Watson, D. (1988). Intraindividual and interindividual analyses of positive and negative affect: Their relation to health complaints, perceived stress, and daily activities. *Journal of Personality and Social Psychology, 54,* 1020–1030.

Watson, D., & Clark, L. A. (1984). Negative affectivity: The disposition to experience aversive emotional states. *Psychological Bulletin, 96,* 465–490.

Watson, D., & Pennebaker, J. W. (1989). Health complaints, stress, and distress: Exploring the central role of negative affectivity. *Psychological Review, 96,* 234–254.

Weinberger, D. A., & Davidson, M. N. (1994). Styles of inhibiting emotional expression: Distinguishing repressive coping from impression management. *Journal of Personality, 62,* 587–613.

Weinberger, D. A., Schwartz, G. E., & Davidson, J. R. (1979). Low-anxious and repressive coping styles: Psychometric patterns of behavioral and physiological responses to stress. *Journal of Abnormal Psychology, 88,* 369–380.

Worden, J. W. (1991). *Grief counseling and grief therapy: A handbook for the mental health practitioner*. New York: Springer.

Wortman, C. B., & Silver, R. C. (1989). The myths of coping with loss. *Journal of Consulting and Clinical Psychology, 57,* 349–357.

Zisook, S., Devaul, R. A., & Click, M. A. (1982). Measuring symptoms of grief and bereavement. *American Journal of Psychiatry, 139,* 1590–1593.

23

DISCLOSING AND SHARING EMOTION: PSYCHOLOGICAL, SOCIAL, AND HEALTH CONSEQUENCES

JAMES W. PENNEBAKER, EMMANUELLE ZECH, AND BERNARD RIMÉ

For the past several years, the first and the last authors have been engaged in overlapping projects that have attempted to understand some of the social and cognitive dynamics of emotional upheavals. Together with a large number of students and colleagues, we have attempted to learn how people naturally talk about—and sometimes avoid talking about—emotional events. Whereas Rimé's laboratory has focused more on how individuals socially share their emotions with others following an emotional event, Pennebaker and his colleagues have developed an intervention strategy wherein individuals are encouraged to disclose emotional upheavals.

On the surface, one would think that we had found that it is always good to talk about your problems and, if pressed to do so, talking or writing about these problems would help you even more. If this were true,

Preparation of this chapter was made possible by a grant from the National Institutes of Health (MH-52391) and by grants 8.4506.98 and 2.4546.97 of the Belgian National Fund for Scientific Research.

the implications for bereavement would be clear-cut: Express your emotions and talk about your feelings and you will be able to get on with life quickly.

If only life (and research) were this simple. As we have discovered, the picture is far more complex. Sometimes talking about our feelings or putting them into words by way of writing predicts better adjustment. But other times, social sharing may reflect very poor adjustment. In this chapter, we will attempt to sort out some of the complexities of social sharing and disclosure. We first begin by reviewing the findings on social sharing of emotion in the first part of the chapter (Rimé, Finkenauer, Luminet, Zech, & Philippot, 1998; Rimé, Philippot, Boca, & Mesquita, 1992). The second part of the chapter will then focus on disclosure interventions that have been effective in improving health (Pennebaker, 1997a, 1997b). We conclude the chapter with specific issues surrounding social sharing and disclosure and bereavement. At the outset, it should be stressed that the two research areas to be described differ from one another in two important respects. First, Rimé and colleagues mainly focused on the verbalization of *emotional events* and the effects it may have on the *emotional recovery from such events*. Emotional recovery is defined as the evolution over time of the arousal still elicited when a given emotional memory is reaccessed. Pennebaker and colleagues investigated more broadly the effects of the disclosure of *personal events* (which, by definition, are emotional) *on physical and psychological health*. Thus the two research areas differ in three subtle ways: (a) the independent variable—the verbalization of emotion versus an event that is generally emotional; (b) the type of dependent variable—emotional recovery versus physical health; (c) the mode of expression—oral verbalization of emotions that occurs between intimates versus written expression of emotional events.

THE SOCIAL SHARING OF EMOTIONAL EXPERIENCES

Most traumas, including the death of someone close, are potentially shattering experiences. These events can disrupt the survivors' social, emotional, and cognitive worlds. Although there has been frequent mention in the literature that traumatic situations cause people to talk about their experiences (e.g., Lehman, Wortman, & Williams, 1987; Schoenberg, Carr, Peretz, Kutscher, & Cherico, 1975), most evidence has been anecdotal. Based on some of our earlier investigations, we originally hypothesized that the urge to talk about the experience was a characteristic consequence not only of trauma but of every emotional experience (Rimé, 1987). This hypothesis led us to investigate "the social sharing of emotion," or, more specifically, the reevocation of an emotional experience in a socially shared language with some addressee, the latter being present at least at the symbolic level.

Basic Findings on the Social Sharing of Emotion

The first step in our research was simply to determine when individuals talked about emotional experiences with others. Using a recall procedure (e.g. Rimé, Mesquita, Philippot, & Boca, 1991), respondents were instructed to recall a recent personal emotional episode corresponding to a specified basic emotion (e.g., joy, anger, fear). They then answered questions about their sharing of this episode: Did they talk about it with others? With whom? How long after the emotion? How often? And so on. Further studies used research procedures intended to control for potential memory bias inherent to the recall procedure (e.g., selection, reconstruction). In follow-up procedures, people were contacted immediately after an emotional situation and were subsequently recontacted on several occasions. In diary procedures, participants reported daily about the most important emotional episode of the day. Finally, experimental studies using emotion-inducing movies of different levels of intensity assessed the subsequent social sharing among exposed participants.

Across studies, we found that emotional experiences were shared in about 90% of the cases (for a review, see Rimé et al., 1992). The modal pattern was for the social sharing of an emotion to be initiated early after the episode. It occurred during the same day as the episode in about 60% of the cases. This rate of social sharing was virtually identical for all emotions—both positive and negative—with the exception of shame and guilt, which were delayed somewhat longer. In general, the social sharing process occurred multiple times and involved several recipients. Recipients were typically intimates that included parents or close family members, best friends, or spouse or companion. People not belonging to this circle were rarely mentioned. Recipients varied as a function of age and gender. Among children and adolescents, parents were by far the most frequent targets of social sharing for both males and females. Among young adults (18–33 years), the role of family decreased markedly, especially among males. For both genders, spouses or companions as well as best friends emerged as the most common targets. Among adults (40–60 years), females showed a heterogeneous sharing network, and males often reported the spouse–companion as exclusive sharing recipient.

The data indicated that the degree of social sharing surrounding a given episode was a function of the disruptiveness of the event. That is, the more disruptive an event, the more frequently it was shared. Laboratory studies revealed that participants exposed to a highly emotional movie talked more about their emotional experience than participants exposed to a low or moderate emotional film. These findings suggested that emotional intensity needs to exceed a certain threshold to elicit social sharing (Luminet, Bouts, Delie, Manstead, & Rimé, 1999).

Other studies have investigated social sharing in different age and cultural groups, as well as personality variables related to social sharing. One study comparing a group of younger adults (25 to 40 years), older adults (60 to 75 years), and an elderly sample (76 to 94 years) showed that the rate of social sharing increased with age (Rimé, Finkenauer, & Sevrin, 1995). Several studies have investigated social sharing across cultures and have found remarkably similar social sharing rates around the world, including people in eastern Asian countries (Rimé, Yogo, & Pennebaker, 1996), large samples of Japanese students (Yogo & Onoe, 1998), and Indian adolescents (Singh-Manoux, 1998). The data from these various studies all confirmed that social sharing of emotion is a cross-cultural phenomenon. Yet there exist several cultural differences in sharing modalities.

Finally, we have conducted studies to test whether personality traits accounted for extent of social sharing of emotion (Luminet, Zech, Rimé, & Wagner, in press). Results indicated that general personality dimensions such as the "Big Five" have no predictive value for the social sharing of emotion. However, alexithymia, a very specific personality dimension concerned with difficulties in the identification and verbalization of emotional experiences (G. J. Taylor, Bagby, & Parker, 1997), has been found to be consistently negatively correlated with social sharing, at least for negative events.

Social Sharing of Emotion and Emotional Recovery

Clearly, people generally share their emotional experiences with others. When the memory of an emotional episode is accessed, the components of the corresponding emotional reaction (i.e., physiological, sensory, experiential) are also activated (e.g., Bower, 1981; Lang, 1983; Leventhal, 1984). That this is elicited during a social sharing situation was confirmed in one of our laboratory studies wherein participants had first to describe a past emotional experience and then report what they experienced when sharing (Rimé, Noël, & Philippot, 1991). Nearly all of the participants reported experiencing mental images of the emotional event as well as accompanying feelings and bodily sensations. Although the vivid sensory feelings and images were comparable for all types of emotions, the reactions produced different social sharing behaviors. Not surprisingly, reporting an experience of joy was rated as more pleasant than reporting an emotion of sadness, of fear, or of anger. However, more surprising was that reporting fear, sadness, or anger was rated by only a minority of the study participants as painful or extremely painful. Notwithstanding the reactivation of vivid images, feelings, and bodily sensations of a negative emotional experience, the sharing did not appear as aversive as one would have expected. This was further confirmed by participants' answers to the question of whether they would be willing to undertake the sharing of another emotional memory of the same type as the first one. Indeed, 94% of the participants gave a positive answer. These data confirmed the paradoxical character of social sharing situations. On the one hand, social sharing reactivates the various components of the emotion, which in the case of negative emotion should be experienced as aversive. On the other hand, sharing an emotion, whether positive or negative, is a natural behavior that people do willingly.

If people are so eager to engage in a social process in which they will experience negative affect, then they should be driven to do so by some powerful incentive. What could be the rewards they find? Common sense offers a ready-made answer to this question. Indeed, common sense assumes that verbalizing an emotional memory can transform it, and that after verbalization this memory would lose a significant part of its emotional load. One of our studies recently documented this. We found that 89% of respondents in a large sample of laypersons ($N = 1024$) endorsed the view that talking about an emotional experience is relieving. Virtually no one refuted this view (Zech, 2000). If this layperson belief was valid, if data could confirm that verbalizing brings "emotional recovery" or "emotional relief," then the paradox would clear up. People would tolerate reexperiencing because of the final profit. We thus examined this question in several studies (for a review, see Rimé et al., 1998).

Shared Versus Secret Emotional Events

Of all emotions, people are least likely to share feelings of shame or guilt (Finkenauer & Rimé, 1998a). Comparing secret and shared emotions offered an opportunity to test the common sense view (Finkenauer & Rimé, 1998b). Participants were asked if they could recall an important emotional life event that they kept secret. Among 373 respondents, 43% answered positively and 57% negatively. Consistent with Pennebaker (e.g., 1989), participants who had the memory of a nonshared emotion reported a higher number of illnesses than those who did not have such a memory. Further, we found that those who had not shared at least one emotion scored lower on various markers of life satisfaction, including ratings about their love life, physical appearance, financial situation, public self, and current life situation. However, in two different studies, when shared and secret emotional episodes were compared for the intensity of the emotion, these episodes still elicited when they were reactivated, no significant difference was observed (Finkenauer & Rimé, 1998a). Thus the nonexpression of an important emotional memory was found associated with poorer health and with lower psychological well-being. Paradoxically, however, as compared to shared emotions, emotional memories that were not shared were found no more no less emotionally arousing when reaccessed at the time of the investigation. In conclusion, the layperson's view was not supported by these data.

Social Sharing and Emotional Recovery

We further explored this question in a number of studies in which we observed participants following a given emotional event. The research design generally involved assessing (a) the initial intensity of the emotion elicited by the episode, (b) the extent of sharing that developed after, and (c) the intensity of the emotion elicited when the memory of the episode was activated later. We tested the hypothesis of a positive correlation between the amount of social sharing after the emotional event and the degree of emotional recovery—or the difference between (a) and (c). To our surprise, these studies never supported the prediction that sharing an emotion would reduce the emotional load. Our data were perfectly consistent in this regard. In sum, together with our studies on shared and secret emotional memories, our correlational findings overwhelmingly suggested that verbalizing an emotional experience does not contribute to emotional recovery as such.

It may be critical to consider *how* people socially share. That is, how do they talk when telling others about their emotions and emotional experiences? Pennebaker and Beall (1986), for example, observed that writing about factual aspects of an emotional episode did not affect health variables, whereas writing about emotional aspects did. Experiments involving various types of sharing were thus conducted to assess how far such a distinction also has consequences when emotional recovery is the assessed variable (Zech, 1999, 2000).

In three studies, we had students interview relatives about a negative emotional event of their recent past. In a fourth one, participants extensively shared with an experimenter the most upsetting event of their life. In each of these four studies, different sharing conditions were created by instructing participants to emphasize either the factual aspects of the episode or the feelings. Control conditions involved talking about a nonemotional topic. The emotional impact that the shared event still had when reaccessed was assessed through several indices (e.g., emotional intensity of the memory, intensity of bodily sensations when thinking about the event, intensity of action tendencies when thinking about the event, challenged basic beliefs) before the sharing interview, immediately after, and again a couple of days after. In one of the studies, additional assessments were conducted two months later. Contrary to what was expected, in each of these studies no effect of sharing type was found on these indices of emotional impact. But despite these negative findings, when compared to participants in either factual sharing condition or control conditions, participants in the felt-emotions condition *consistently* rated the sharing as being more beneficial to them in general (e.g., it was useful), as having relieved their emotions more (e.g., made them feel good), as having helped them more cognitively (e.g., it helped in putting order in themselves), and as being more beneficial interpersonally (e.g., they experienced comforting behaviors from the part of the recipient). Thus no changes were found in the impact of the emotional memory, suggesting that sharing emotional experiences failed to alleviate the load of the emotional memory. Nevertheless, in a paradoxical manner, participants who shared their emotions reported that the experience was ultimately beneficial compared to the controls.

Recovered or Unrecovered Events

Faced repeatedly with these unexpected negative findings regarding effects of sharing on emotional recovery, we finally wondered whether the notion of emotional recovery on which our studies relied made sense at all. Rimé, Hayward, and Pennebaker (1996) addressed this question. Students were asked to recall one emotional experience they "had recovered from" and one they "had not recovered from." For each, they rated initial and residual emotional impact, as well as initial and residual sharing. The data showed that the two types of episodes had initially elicited a comparable emotional impact. Consistent with our previous studies, they also failed to differ for initial sharing. Both were shared in a very large extent in the days and weeks after they occurred. However, confirming that the notion of "recovery" makes sense, the two types of episodes differed very markedly in their residual emotional impact and thus yielded marked differences in the recovery index. This index was indeed much lower for nonrecovered emotional memories than for recovered emotional memories. Moreover episodes not recovered elicited much more residual sharing than recovered ones. We could thus conclude that the notion of emotional recovery really makes sense. Emotional memories that people selected as "unrecovered" evidenced a stronger impact on subjective feelings and on social behavior than was the case for emotional memories that people selected as "recovered."

In eight different studies we conducted, participants rated the emotional intensity felt when remembering a recent emotional event ("residual emotional intensity") and the extent to which they (a) still felt the need to talk about it and (b) still talked about it ("residual social sharing"). The delay between the target emotional event and follow-up assessments varied from a week (Rimé, Zech, Finkenauer, Luminet, & Dozier, 1996) to several months (e.g., Luminet, Zech, et al., in press), or even several years (e.g., Rimé, Finkenauer, & Sangsue, 1994). Correlations were computed between residual emotional intensity and residual sharing for each data set. Across all studies, we found that the higher the residual emotional intensity, the higher the residual social sharing (for a review, see Rimé et al., 1998). This confirmed that nonrecovered emotional memories do surface more in sharing behaviors than recovered ones. How can we interpret this relation? On the one hand, talking about an emotional memory can reactivate event-related emotional feelings. On the other hand, residual event-related feelings elicit residual sharing. Does this mean that people who have failed to recover from an emotion keep talking about it without limits? Examining the size of the correlations revealed that in six of our eight studies, residual emotional intensity was linked more closely to the need for sharing than to actual residual sharing. In short, when people fail to recover from an emotional episode, they feel the need to talk about it and they actually do so to some extent. Certain social constraints (Pennebaker, 1993) are likely to moderate the relation between residual emotionality and actual residual sharing. However, such constraints will at the very least leave intact people's *needs* to share. In other words, as long as an emotional memory elicits actual emotional feelings, the person can be expected to feel the need to talk about it.

Summary

People who experience an emotion feel compelled to talk about it and to share it, preferably with their intimates. They do it quite willingly, despite the fact that the sharing process reactivates the negative aspects of the emotional experience. A very widespread belief exists according to which sharing an emotion should bring emotional relief. Yet both correlative and experimental studies that were conducted to test the validity of this belief consistently failed to support this world view. It does not seem that talking about an emotional memory has a significant impact on the emotional load associated with this memory. Nevertheless, people who share their emotions generally express the feeling that the process is beneficial. Whereas sharing was not found to have an impact on recovery, data were supportive of the opposite relation. Lack of recovery was markedly associated with the perpetuation of sharing, and even more markedly with the perpetuation of the need to share.

The abundance of the null findings finally led us to accept that despite stereotypes, socially sharing an emotion does not bring emotional relief as such. The data collected so far strongly suggest that socially sharing an emotion cannot change the emotional memory. After all, it does make sense with regard to adaptation. An emotional memory carries important information with respect to future situations. If we had the potential to alter the emotion-arousing capacities of such memories by merely talking about them, such equipment would deprive us of vital fruits of our experience (Rimé, 1999).

Social Sharing Within the Context of Bereavement

When someone within a social network dies, members of the network are naturally drawn together. During the grieving period—especially within the first few days or weeks—the survivors socially share their emotions and memories with each other. Many of the discussion topics surround the individual who died, of course, but funerals and grieving rituals often include the social sharing of other personal and family histories. Although our work to date has not found compelling evidence that social sharing leads to emotional recovery, our data suggested that it may serve several other important cognitive, psychological, and social functions. In this section, we briefly summarize the most important effects. Empirical research about them is only at an exploratory stage. Yet we found it useful to briefly review some of these emerging functions of the social sharing of emotion.

Constructing and Consolidating Memory

The roles we have within our social networks are not often discussed or clearly defined. One of the ironies of having someone important in our family, friendship network, or even culture die is that we openly discuss the person, our feelings about him or her, and become conscious of that person's influence on us. Although we had not originally been interested in the nature of bereavement per se, our research group became fascinated by the strong and immediate emotional response following the death of King Baudouin of Belgium (Finkenauer et al., 1998). The king had unexpectedly died after a reign of 42 years. In the immediate aftermath, rehearsal processes involving both social sharing and information-seeking behavior (i.e., following the media) took place in the country. In our surveys of a large sample of Belgium citizens, we found that the news of the king's death had been socially shared at a remarkably high rate. The sharing content focused more on the event—the news of the king's death—than on one's personal circumstances when first learning about the news. Rehearsal thereby contributed to the creation of a collective memory in the Belgian society. Yet by socially rehearsing the collective memory, people's memory for personal circumstances was indirectly strengthened, ending up in flashbulb memories.

Flashbulb memories are particularly detailed, long-lasting memories of the personal context in which people first heard about important, shocking news (Brown & Kulik, 1977). Social sharing thus appears as a particularly efficient means to ensure that emotional events are not forgotten. By talking about the emotional event, people gradually construct a social narrative and a collective memory. At the same time, they consolidate their own memory for personal circumstances in which the event took place. Although the king's death was undoubtedly far less personal than a family member's might have been, the same basic processes seemed at work. What was observed generally fits with classic views. Indeed, authors such as James (1890) or Mead (1934) stressed that people construct reality through social relationships and particularly through the use of everyday conversation. As far as bereavement is concerned, the death of a loved one generally introduces chaos in people's personal universe, which may end up in denial and in alteration of the sense of reality. When bereaved individuals socially share the loss of a loved one, they give both the death itself and its consequences *more reality*.

Processing and Completing the Emotional Memory

The death of a loved one very often challenges our beliefs of a coherent, predictable, and controllable world (Janoff-Bulman, 1992; Marris, 1958; Parkes, 1972). The overwhelming emotions that result from such challenges often drive individuals into a state of cognitive business (e.g., Martin & Tesser, 1989). They slip into a cycle of ruminative thinking, trying unsuccessfully to figure it all out. Based on our earlier work, we hypothesized that social sharing would help to undermine this cognitive business cycle. This led us to predict that emotional memories that were not shared would be associated with higher cognitive needs than emotional memories that were shared.

The comparison of shared and secret memories (Finkenauer & Rimé, 1998a) indeed revealed that secret memories elicited globally more cognitive effort than shared ones. Secret memories were associated with (a) greater search for meaning, (b) greater efforts at understanding what had happened, and (c) greater attempts at "putting order in what happened." Similar items were later included in several studies in which the memory of an emotional experience was investigated some time after the occurrence of the event. In each of these studies, participants also rated whether they still needed to talk about this memory. In the studies, a positive correlation was found between need for completion and need for sharing. Altogether, these data suggest that sharing contributes to the processing of the emotional information and to the completion of the cognitive needs that were elicited by the emotional event.

This function of social sharing is also much more relevant in the context of bereavement. Experiencing the death of a loved one (Cornwell, Nurcombe, & Stevens, 1977) often shatters people's basic beliefs that they live in an orderly, understandable, and meaningful world (e.g., Glick, Weiss, & Parkes, 1974). As a result, individuals frequently *search for some meaning* or try to make sense out of their negative experiences (Bulman & Wortman, 1977; Silver & Wortman, 1980; S. E. Taylor, 1983). Finding meaning in the loss of a loved one is thought to be one way of dealing with and adjusting to the event (McIntosh, Silver, & Wortman, 1993).

Through the use of social sharing, people can give both the death itself and its consequences *more sense and meaning* (see chapter 15, this volume).

Enhancing Interpersonal Relationships and Social Integration

Almost by definition, social sharing is associated with more salient emotional bonds among participants of the interaction. In a recent project, for example, we observed that when intense emotions are shared, listeners reduced their use of verbal mediators in their responses (Christophe & Rimé, 1997). As a substitute, they manifested nonverbal comforting behaviors, like hugging, kissing, or touching. This suggests that the sharing of an intense emotional experience can decrease the physical distance between two persons. The decrease of interpersonal distance can have lasting consequences for the relationship between the sharer and the listener. In this sense, sharing emotions may contribute to the development and maintenance of close relationships. This observation is consistent with findings from research on self-disclosure and liking. In a meta-analytic review, Collins and Miller (1994) indeed found that people who engage in intimate disclosures tend to be liked more than people who disclose less. Complementing this finding, they also found that disclosure causes people to like their listeners.

The potential contribution of the social sharing of emotion to the development and maintenance of close relationships may be of particular importance in the context of bereavement for several reasons. As mentioned before, emotions are very generally socially shared with intimates such as close family members, spouse or companion, and close friends. Losing one of them also means losing a partner for socially sharing one's emotions. This may be particularly problematic in the case of widowers, as shown in our studies: Male adults often reported their spouse–companion to be their exclusive sharing recipient. When this occurs, widowers are left with no sharing partner. Bereavement theories emphasize the importance of attachment and social bonds in both the impact of the loss of the loved one (e.g., the greater the attachment to the lost person, the higher the impact) and the way people will deal with this loss of their loved one (e.g., Bowlby, 1980; chapters 3, 14, and 17, this volume). Social sharing of emotion may contribute to the development of new relationships after the loss of a sharing partner. It may also help to maintain close and satisfying relationships with those who remain in the social network, thus providing the bereaved person with social support from family and friends.

DISCLOSURE AND HEALTH

The social sharing findings point to an inherent puzzle that has intrigued researchers, poets, and philosophers for generations: Talking about your problems is good for you, but at the same time, if you are talking about your problems, something is the matter with you. Stiles (1987) simplified this conundrum by comparing talking or disclosure with the fever you get when you are sick. The fever, he pointed out, serves as an indicator that a person is sick. At the same time, however, the fever reflects an active healing process by the body that generally helps to heal the person. Carrying the analogy even further, if the fever continues too long—beyond a few days—the fever is probably not effectively healing the problem and is merely signaling the insidiousness of the underlying disease.

The importance of the social sharing literature is that it is some of the first to look at the "fever" of social sharing of emotions in the real world under naturalistic conditions. About the same time that some of the first social sharing research was being conducted in Europe, a separate group in the United States was beginning to explore what happened when people were unable or unwilling to socially share emotional upheavals. Much of this research, which was based on an inhibitory model, suggested that the act of inhibiting or holding back one's thoughts, feelings, or behaviors involved biological work that was in and of itself stressful. If individuals were forced to actively inhibit over long periods of time, it was argued, they were more likely to suffer from a variety of psychosomatic diseases (for a discussion of this model, see Pennebaker, 1989, 1997b).

Evidence for this inhibition model and stress-related disease has come from a variety of sources. For example, Kagan, Reznick, and Snidman (1988) reported that inhibited children as young as two to four years old have higher resting cortisol and autonomic nervous system levels and are more prone to colds, ear infections, and allergies than less inhibited or shy children. Recent work by Cole, Kemeny, Taylor, and Visscher (1996) indicates that gay men who conceal their homosexual status are more likely to suffer from major illnesses such as cancer if they are HIV-negative and to die more quickly from AIDS if they are HIV-positive than men who are more open about their homosexuality. In our own research, we have consistently found that not talking about traumatic experiences is correlated with a variety of health problems among college students and adult samples (Pennebaker & Susman, 1988). Other studies indicate that the more bereaved individuals are able to talk about their spouses' death, the healthier they are in the year following the death (Pennebaker & O'Heeron, 1984).

Although our initial approach to traumatic experience and health focused on the idea of inhibition, this view has gradually evolved to incorporate more cognitive and social factors. Not talking about a significant emotional experience or trauma with others can certainly invoke inhibitory processes: the active restraining of the urge to share one's story. But at the same time not sharing one's story may produce a number of interesting cognitive side effects. Talking with others about an important event may help the person to organize the experience and come to terms with it. By the same token, talking with others may also clarify one's psychological state to others. The person's social network, then, can make accommodations based on what the traumatized or bereaved person is feeling and saying. Without talking, the traumatized individual will be less likely to come to terms with the event and will be more socially isolated to the degree that he or she is able to connect closely with others. Most recently, we have been examining the health and cognitive effects of translating emotional experiences into language. Although our original work focused more on self-reports of talking, beginning more than a decade ago we began to explore the nature of writing as a form of coping.

We developed a paradigm whereby people were induced to socially share or, in our words, to disclose their thoughts and feelings about emotional topics (Pennebaker & Beall, 1986). Returning to the fever analogy, we wanted to induce a fever (i.e., disclosure) in our participants to see if it really had a healing effect.

The Disclosure Paradigm: Parameters of Writing and Talking

Since the mid-1980s, several laboratories have been exploring the value of writing or talking about emotional experiences. Confronting deeply personal issues has been found to promote physical health, subjective well-being, and selected adaptive behaviors. In this section, the general findings and limitations of the disclosure paradigm are discussed. Whereas a few studies have asked individuals to disclose personal experiences through talking, most involve writing.

The standard laboratory writing technique has involved randomly assigning participants to one of two or more groups. All writing groups are asked to write about assigned topics for 3 to 5 consecutive days, 15 to 30 minutes each day. Writing is generally done in the laboratory with no feedback given. Those assigned to the control conditions are typically asked to write about superficial topics, such as how they use their time. The standard instructions for those assigned to the experimental group are a variation on the following:

> For the next (three) days, I would like for you to write about your very deepest thoughts and feeling about an extremely important emotional issue that has affected you and your life. In your writing, I'd like you to really let go and explore your very deepest emotions and thoughts. You might tie your topic to your relationships with others, including parents, lovers, friends, or relatives, to your past, your present, or your future, or to who you have been, who you would like to be, or who you are now. You may write about the same general issues or experiences on all days of writing or on different topics each day. All of your writing will be completely confidential. Don't worry about spelling, sentence structure, or grammar. The only rule is that once you begin writing, continue to do so until your time is up.

The writing paradigm is exceptionally powerful. Participants—from children to elderly people, from honor students to maximum security prisoners—disclose a remarkable range and depth of traumatic experiences. Lost loves, deaths, sexual and physical abuse incidents, and tragic failures are common themes in all of our studies. If nothing else, the paradigm demonstrates that when individuals are given the opportunity to disclose deeply personal aspects of their lives, they readily do so. Even though a large number of participants report crying or being deeply upset by the experience, the overwhelming majority report that the writing experience was valuable and meaningful in their lives.

Effects of Disclosure on Outcome Measures

Researchers have relied on a variety of physical and mental health measures to evaluate the effect of writing. As discussed in several recent reviews (e.g., Pennebaker, 1997a; Smyth, 1998), writing or talking about emotional experiences relative to writing about superficial control topics has been found to be associated with significant drops in physician visits from before to after writing among relatively healthy samples. Writing or talking about emotional topics has also been found to influence some immune function indices in beneficial ways, including t-helper cell growth (using a blastogenesis procedure with the mitogen PHA), antibody response to Epstein-Barr virus, and antibody response to hepatitis B vaccinations.

Self-reports also suggest that writing about upsetting experiences, although painful in the days of writing, produce long-term improvements in mood and indicators of well-being compared to controls. Although a number of studies have failed to find consistent mood or self-reported distress effects, a recent meta-analysis by Smyth (1998) on written disclosure studies indicates that, in general, writing about emotional topics is associated with significant improvements in psychological well-being. The degree to which writing can affect long-term measures of negative moods needs additional investigation.

Behavioral changes have also been found. Students who write about emotional topics evidence improvements in grades in the months following the study. Senior professionals who have been laid off from their jobs get new jobs more quickly after writing (Spera, Buhrfeind, & Pennebaker, 1994). Consistent with the direct health measures, university staff members who write about emotional topics are subsequently absent from their work at lower rates than controls.

It is interesting to note that relatively few reliable changes emerge using self-reports of health-related behaviors. That is, after writing, experimental participants do not exercise more or smoke less. The one exception is that the study with laid-off professionals found that writing reduced self-reported alcohol intake.

The studies that we have conducted represent only a portion of projects that have demonstrated the health benefits of disclosure. Esterling, Antoni, Kumar, and Schneiderman (1990) found that students who wrote essays conveying a great deal of emotion evidenced more efficient immune function than those whose essays failed to reveal emotion. Consistent effects have also been found across several studies that have examined the physiological effects of various psychotherapies. Although not a specific test of disclosure, Spiegel, Bloom, Kraemer, and Gottheil (1989) found that women suffering from advanced breast cancer who were randomly assigned to nonspecific group therapy lived, on average, 1.5 years longer than those in an information-only control group. Mumford, Schlesinger, and Glass (1983) summarized a large number of studies examining the links between psychotherapy and medical use. Overall, when psychotherapy was introduced as part of health maintenance organizations within companies, overall medical use and corresponding costs dropped significantly.

Procedural Differences That Affect the Disclosure Effects

Writing about emotional experiences influences measures of physical and mental health. In recent years, several investigators have attempted to define the boundary conditions of the disclosure effect. Some of the most important findings are as follows.

Writing versus talking about traumas. Few studies have directly compared the effects of writing alone versus talking either into a tape recorder or to a therapist. Talking to a therapist was found to induce less negative moods in the short term than writing alone but comparable long-term effects (Donnelly & Murray, 1991; Murray, Lamnin, & Carver, 1989). Another study found comparable effects of talking as compared to writing on Epstein-Barr virus antibody levels (Esterling, Antoni, Fletcher, Margulies, & Schneiderman, 1994). Murray and Segal (1994) also found similar effects of writing and talking. Although future studies are needed to test their comparable biological, mood, cognitive, and social effects, talking and writing about emotional experiences are both superior to writing about superficial topics.

It should be emphasized that talking into a tape recorder or even to a therapist within the context of a disclosure study is quite different from the ways people normally socially share or talk with a friend about a trauma. In the context of a disclosure study, the person is not seeking or receiving emotional support, and is not receiving concrete feedback from the listener. In that way, disclosure studies are not related to true interactions in that there is no two-way interaction possible. Consequently, comparisons between naturalistic talking about an emotional event and talking into a tape recorder are simply not possible.

Topic of disclosure. Whereas two studies have found that health effects only occur among individuals who write about particularly traumatic experiences (Greenberg & Stone, 1992; Lutgendorf, Antoni, Kumar, & Schneiderman, 1994), most studies have found that disclosure is more broadly beneficial. Choice of topic, however, may selectively influence the outcome. For beginning college students, for example, writing about emotional issues about coming to college influences grades more than writing about traumatic experiences (Pennebaker, 1997a). It is also of interest that a recent large-scale study by W. Stroebe, Stroebe, Schut, Zech, and van den Bout (1997) on bereaved adults failed to find benefits of writing, suggesting that some types of upheavals may benefit from writing more than others. More about writing and bereavement will be discussed in the following section.

Length or days of writing. Different experiments have variously asked participants to write for 1 to 5 days, ranging from consecutive days to sessions separated by a week, ranging from 15 to 30 minutes for each writing session. In Smyth's meta-analysis, he found that the more days over which the experiment lapses, the stronger the effects. This effect suggests that writing once each week over a month may be more effective than writing four times within a single week. Self-reports of the value of writing do not distinguish shorter writing from longer writing sessions.

Individual differences. Very few consistent personality or individual difference measures have distinguished who does versus does not benefit from writing. Most commonly examined variables unrelated to outcomes include anxiety (or negative affectivity), and inhibition or constraint. The one study that preselected participants on hostility found that those high in hostility benefited more from writing than those low in hostility (Christensen & Smith, 1994). In a recent study by Paez, Velasco, and Gonzalez (1999), individuals high in the trait of alexithymia benefited more from writing than those low in the trait. Alexithymia is characterized by the inability to label and understand one's own emotional state. Finally, in the Smyth (1998) meta-analysis, males were found to benefit more than females.

The interesting pattern that is emerging from this work is that people who naturally do not talk about their emotional state to a great degree (men, alexithymics, and those high in hostility) benefit more from writing about traumatic experiences than more open individuals. Extending this logic, people should benefit more from writing about stigmatizing traumatic experiences than experiences that are more socially acceptable. Consequently, among bereaved individuals, writing might be more effective in dealing with a stigmatized death (e.g., suicide, AIDS, murder) than if the death was expected and "acceptable" (e.g., cancer, heart disease).

Educational, linguistic, or cultural effects. Within the United States, the disclosure paradigm has benefited senior professionals with advanced degrees at rates comparable to maximum security prisoners with 6th-grade education (Richards, Beal, Seagal, & Pennebaker, 2000; Spera, Buhrfeind,

& Pennebaker, 1994). Among college students, we have not found differences as a function of the students' ethnicity or native language. The disclosure paradigm has produced consistently positive results among Spanish-speaking residents of Mexico City, multiple samples of adults and students in The Netherlands, and even English-speaking New Zealand medical students.

Summary. When individuals write or talk about personally upsetting experiences, significant health improvements have been found. The effects include both subjective and objective markers of health and well-being. The writing disclosure phenomenon appears to generalize across settings and several Western cultures. Future studies should confirm that the health and well-being effects are equivalent when talking or writing.

Implications for Bereavement: Determining If Writing or Talking About a Death Can Accelerate Coping

The growing body of research on disclosure strongly suggests that putting upsetting experiences into words is associated with improved physical and mental health. By extension, writing or talking about the death of someone close should accelerate coping. To the degree that loss of a loved one is a form of trauma, then, we would predict that writing about it would be associated with improved physical and mental health. It is interesting to note that the data on disclosure and coping among bereaved individuals is clearly mixed. Some studies indicate that disclosure is beneficial, whereas others find no effects of disclosure. In this section, we briefly review some of the relevant studies and conclude with a discussion of when written disclosure interventions might be most effective.

Determining When Writing or Talking Interventions Help in Bereavement

In one of our first correlational studies on disclosure, we found that individuals who had recently experienced the sudden and unexpected death of a spouse as a result of a car accident or suicide reported being in better health if they had talked about their spouse's death than if they had not (Pennebaker & O'Heeron, 1984). This study was a bit unorthodox in that health was measured by asking people to report their health in the year before the death of their spouse and also in the year following the death. The disclosure measures were only related to the change in reported health. In fact, had we only looked at the postdeath health measures, we would have found that disclosure was mildly associated with worse health. For a discussion of the problem of relying on one-time measures of self-reports and personality measures of anxiety or neuroticism, see Watson and Pennebaker (1989).

More persuasive are actual intervention studies. As discussed in the previous section, the writing intervention studies require people to write about traumatic experiences for several days. Across the multiple studies from our lab, approximately 20% of participants write about the death of a close friend or family member. Internal analyses of these studies find that those who write about death benefit to the same degree as people who write about other topics. On the surface, then, people demonstrate mental and physical health benefits from writing about death-related topics.

A more direct test is one recently reported by Segal, Bogaards, and Chatman (in press) with 30 elderly adults (mean age = 67.0) whose spouses had died on average 16 months before the study. Participants, who responded to newspaper advertisements, were randomly assigned to talk into a tape recorder on four occasions about the death of their spouse. Half of the participants underwent the disclosure intervention within two weeks of completing the initial batch of questionnaires. The control–delay treatment group participated in the disclosure sessions approximately six weeks after the initial questionnaires. Overall, the authors found that disclosure resulted in lower ratings of hopelessness, depression, and unwanted intrusive thoughts.

Failure to Find Benefits From Disclosure

Two research projects stand out in suggesting that writing or talking interventions may not be beneficial—at least with everyone. The first is an intriguing correlational project by Bonanno and his colleagues (e.g., Bonanno, Keltner, Holen, & Horowitz, 1995; Bonanno, Notarius, Gunzerath, Keltner, & Horowitz, 1998; chapter 22, this volume). In the study, approximately 44 adults who had faced the death of a spouse in the previous six months were asked to come into the laboratory and, while hooked up to multiple physiological sensors, talk about their spouse for approximately 6 to 10 minutes. In the studies, the authors found that the more emotional that participants were during the interview (and, by extension, the more they disclosed), the more poorly they were coping with their spouse's death eight months later. As suggested by our fever analogy, this study raises the distinction between disclosure as reflecting grief versus disclosure as *affecting* grief.

A broad intervention study has been reported by Wolfgang Stroebe and his colleagues (W. Stroebe et al., 1997; W. Stroebe, Stroebe, & Zech, 1996; Zech, 1999). In their study, 119 individuals, ranging in age from 23 to 76, were contacted on average seven months after the death of their spouse. They were randomly assigned to one of five conditions. In three conditions, participants had to write their reactions to the loss of their partner for half an hour on seven consecutive days. Respondents were asked to either write about their feelings about the loss, the facts and problems surrounding the loss, or both. Two control groups were not asked to write about the death of their spouse. The written essays were then mailed to the experimenters. Dependent measures were not only self-report measures of emotional impact and mental health given before and 15 days after the intervention, but also information about health problems and doctors visits based on reports from their general practitioners for a one-year period before and after the intervention (on 80 bereaved individuals). At follow-up, the experimental and control participants did not differ in terms of their long-term physical health or on any of the measures of emotional impact and mental health.

Untangling the Web: When Interventions May Be Most Helpful

As is apparent from the previously discussed studies, the effects of disclosure on bereavement present a confusing picture. However, closer analysis suggests the following resolutions:

1. Bereavement and loss are not unidimensional constructs. As M. Stroebe, Schut, and Stroebe (1998) noted, trauma and bereavement overlap but are not the same. If one's spouse dies suddenly and unexpectedly, the psychological, social, and cognitive effects can be different than if the spouse dies after a long illness. A sudden death is, by definition, more likely to be defined as traumatic. We would predict that people would benefit more from disclosure following a traumatic loss than from a predicted one. There are two reasons for this: (a) disclosure is particularly beneficial in helping people to come to terms with chaotic, unexplained events; and (b) people find it easier to talk with their friends about more predictable losses than more traumatic ones. Consequently, spouses who have had to face the gradual demise of their loved one will more likely have talked with many others about death, dying, and loss. Among these people, a disclosure intervention should have relatively minor impact.

2. Some people may benefit more from disclosure interventions than others. Recall that Smyth (1998) reported that males are more likely to demonstrate health improvements after writing than females. Similarly, Schut, Stroebe, de Keijser, and van den Bout (1997) discovered that the ways men versus women are *counseled* differentially predicts positive bereavement responses. Specifically, in this study highly distressed bereaved persons entered a counseling program. The interventions were done by trained experienced social workers (seven times over a period of 10 weeks). When men were asked to focus on the acceptance of emotions and emotional discharge (client-centered type of counseling), they were less

distressed (General Health Questionnaire scores; Goldberg & Hillier, 1979) than when asked to focus on problems that hinder the grief process (behavior therapy type). Women showed the opposite pattern.

3. Who signs up to participate in an intervention is relevant. One of the most difficult aspects of studying bereavement is in collecting truly random samples. The Stroebe group has been doing this by directly contacting individuals four to eight months after the death of their spouse. Other researchers, such as Segal et al. (in press) advertised for participants in the local newspaper. We suspect that those who seek out researchers (as in the Segal et al., in press) and those who are directly contacted represent very different groups. Because most people cope quite well with the death of a spouse—especially if it is not a traumatic death (cf., Wortman & Silver, 1989), disclosure interventions may only be effective with those coping poorly. A randomly selected sample, then, will be less likely to show the benefits of disclosure because most of the participants will be in relatively good shape. A sample that self-selects to participate in a study on spousal bereavement may, in fact, be made up of the very people who have not had the opportunity to work through their emotions.

4. It is important to distinguish between disclosure as an intervention versus a reflection of grief. It is a truism within the psychopathology world that the best predictor of future depression is a previous episode of depression. Similarly, if we have a group of bereaved spouses six months after the death, the best predictor of their grief responses two years later will be their current grief responses. Asking participants about their thoughts and feelings during a brief interview is a reflection of their grief rather than an intervention about their grief. From this perspective, the work of Bonanno and his colleagues makes perfect sense. Indeed, we find similar effects with gay men who are dealing with the death of their lovers from AIDS (Pennebaker, Mayne, & Francis, 1997).

For a disclosure session to be an intervention, the person must actively work through an upsetting experience. In our writing paradigm, for example, people write about emotional topics multiple times over several days. Indeed, when we analyze the language of their writing samples, the people who benefit most are the ones who show clear cognitive change from the first writing session to the last. Those who are highly emotional across all four days of writing but who do not show cognitive change do not experience any health benefits (cf., Pennebaker, 1997a).

5. Considering the type of dependent variable is essential. Whether emotional recovery, perceived benefits, or health measures are considered is fundamental. Whereas social sharing of emotion failed to predict beneficial effects on emotional recovery, data suggested that it opens to a number of other important beneficial emotional, cognitive, and social effects. Writing about emotional upheavals was also found beneficial for a variety of physical health and adaptive behaviors but not generally on subjective well-being or negative moods. The research so far has mainly focused on the intrapersonal effects of social sharing or disclosure of emotion—that is, the effects on emotional recovery, well-being, and physical health. However, in natural settings, the verbalization of emotion often implies interpersonal processes. These important social functions of the sharing of emotion are still largely open to investigation.

CONCLUSION

Any emotionally upsetting experience has the potential to aggravate mental and physical health problems. People who experience an emotion feel compelled to talk about it and to share it with others despite the fact that it reactivates the negative aspects of the emotional experience. Although people believe that talking about their emotions will help them, the degree to which people talk about these experiences may not help them to recover from the emotion. It is thus debatable whether sharing bereavement-related feelings would bring emotional relief. However, bereaved individuals may well feel that sharing their emotions with intimates is meaningful and beneficial for various reasons. In particular, the development and maintenance of close relationships that may be involved when one shares one's emotions may be a fundamental function of social sharing of emotion. Future research should examine this more closely.

On the other hand, there is now an impressive body of research to support the idea that having people write about emotional upheavals can improve physical and psychological health. Those who are most likely to benefit may be those who are not able to naturally talk to others about their emotional experiences.

During bereavement, people usually work through grief naturally and do not need intervention strategies to help them to cope with their grief. However, when bereaved individuals continue to show extreme grief reactions several months or years after the death, intervention may be needed. Clinicians and counselors could use natural social sharing in group or family sessions and the writing technique as a clinical tool for people who are having the greatest difficulty in coping with loss. These techniques may be useful for different reasons. First, when people *do not recover* because they were *inhibited by social constraints*, this might help to give a place where it is allowed to express one's emotions without the direct evaluation of another person. Because the writing intervention does not need a real recipient to be present, such a tool may be particularly useful in the case of social constraints. Second, in cases in which bereaved individuals continue to show extreme distress, these tools may be used as an interesting manner to induce the structuring of the thoughts and feelings and meaning making. Although investigations are needed regarding whether and how beneficial changes would occur among bereaved individuals, we are optimistic about using these low-cost effective techniques as a clinical tool for bereaved people.

In the past decade, some theoreticians and researchers have not supported the notion that expressing the negative emotions associated with grief is effective for its successful resolution (Bonanno et al., 1995; Bonanno & Keltner, 1997; M. Stroebe & Stroebe, 1991). Depending on the theoretical view of bereavement, other tasks may be equally essential for resolving grief. For example, Nadeau (chapter 15, this volume) argued that in cases when factors inhibit family meaning making, interventions may be directed to reducing these and enhancing factors that stimulate it. In this regard, the expression of the meanings associated with the changes in roles attached to a given person, with the rules of the family system, and with boundaries to the social environment may be more beneficial than the expression of only feelings. Because social sharing and writing paradigm instructions are flexible enough, future studies could apply specific instructions related to a specific model of bereavement.

REFERENCES

Bonanno, G. A., & Keltner, D. (1997). Facial expressions of emotion and the course of conjugal bereavement. *Journal of Abnormal Psychology, 106,* 126–137.

Bonanno, G. A., Keltner, D., Holen, A., & Horowitz, M. J. (1995). When avoiding unpleasant emotions might not be such a bad thing: Verbal-autonomic response dissociation and midlife conjugal bereavement. *Journal of Personality and Social Psychology, 69,* 975–989.

Bonanno, G. A., Notarius, C. I., Gunzerath, L., Keltner, D., & Horowitz, M. J. (1998). Interpersonal ambivalence, perceived relationship adjustment, and conjugal loss. *Journal of Consulting and Clinical Psychology, 66,* 1012–1022.

Bower, G. H. (1981). Mood and memory. *American Psychologist, 36,* 129–148.

Bowlby, J. (1980). *Attachment and loss. Vol. 3. Loss: Sadness and depression.* New York: Basic Books.

Brown, R., & Kulik, J. (1977). Flashbulb memories. *Cognition, 5,* 73–99.

Bulman, R., & Wortman, C. B. (1977). Attributions of blame and coping in the "Real World": Severe accident victims react to their lot. *Journal of Personality and Social Psychology, 35,* 351–363.

Christensen, A. J., & Smith, T. W. (1994). Cynical hostility and cardiovascular reactivity during self-disclosure. *Psychosomatic Medicine, 55,* 193–202.

Christophe, V., & Rimé, B. (1997). Exposure to the social sharing of emotion: Emotional impact, listener responses and secondary social sharing. *European Journal of Social Psychology, 27,* 37–54.

Cole, S. W., Kemeny, M. E., Taylor, S. E., & Visscher, B. R. (1996). Elevated physical health risk among gay men who conceal their homosexual identity. *Health Psychology, 15,* 243–251.

Collins, N. L., & Miller, L. C. (1994). Self-disclosure and liking: A meta-analytic review. *Psychological Bulletin, 116,* 457–475.

Cornwell, J., Nurcombe, B., & Stevens, L. (1977). Family response to loss of a child by Sudden Infant Death Syndrome. *The Medical Journal of Australia, 1,* 656–658.

Donnelly, D. A., & Murray, E. J. (1991). Cognitive and emotional changes in written essays and therapy interviews. *Journal of Social and Clinical Psychology, 10,* 334–350.

Esterling, B. A., Antoni, M. H., Fletcher, M. A., Margulies, S., & Schneiderman, N. (1994). Emotional disclosure through writing or speaking modulates latent Epstein-Barr virus antibody titers. *Journal of Consulting and Clinical Psychology, 62,* 130–140.

Esterling, B. A., Antoni, M. H., Kumar, M., & Schneiderman, N. (1990). Emotional repression, stress disclosure responses, and Epstein-Barr vital capsid antigen titers. *Psychosomatic Medicine, 52,* 397–410.

Finkenauer, C., Luminet, O., Gisle, L., van der Linden, M., El-Ahmadi, A., & Philippot, P. (1998). Flashbulb memories and the underlying mechanisms of their formation: Towards an Emotional-Integrative Model. *Memory and Cognition, 26,* 516–531.

Finkenauer, C., & Rimé, B. (1998a). Socially shared emotional experiences vs. emotional experiences kept secret: Differential characteristics and consequences. *Journal of Social and Clinical Psychology, 17,* 295–318.

Finkenauer, C., & Rimé, B. (1998b). Keeping emotional memories secret: Health and subjective well-being when emotions are not shared. *Journal of Health Psychology, 3,* 47–58.

Glick, I. O., Weiss, R. S., & Parkes, C. M. (1974). *The first year of bereavement.* New York: Wiley.

Goldberg, D. P., & Hillier, V. F. (1979). A scale version of the General Health Questionnaire. *Psychological Medicine, 9,* 139–145.

Greenberg, M. A., & Stone, A. A. (1992). Emotional disclosure about traumas and its relation to health: Effects of previous disclosure and trauma severity. *Journal of Personality and Social Psychology, 63*, 75–84.

James, W. (1890). *The principles of psychology.* New York: Holt.

Janoff-Bulman, R. (1992). *Shattered assumptions: Towards a new psychology of trauma.* New York: Free Press.

Kagan, J., Reznick, J. S., & Snidman, N. (1988). Biological bases of childhood shyness. *Science, 240*, 167–171.

Lang, P. J. (1983). Cognition in emotion: Concept and action. In C. Izard, J. Kagan, & R. Zajonc (Eds.), *Emotion, cognition, and behavior* (pp. 192–226). New York: Cambridge University Press.

Lehman, D. R., Wortman, B. C., & Williams, A. F. (1987). Long-term effects of losing a spouse or child in a motor vehicle crash. *Journal of Personality and Social Psychology, 52*, 218–231.

Leventhal, H. (1984). A perceptual-motor theory of emotion. In L. Berkowitz (Ed.), *Advances in experimental social psychology* (Vol. 17, pp. 117–182). Orlando, FL: Academic Press.

Luminet, O., Bouts, P., Delie, F., Manstead, A. S. R., & Rimé, B. (1999). *Social sharing of emotion: Experimental evidence.* Manuscript submitted for publication.

Luminet, O., Zech, E., Rimé, B., & Wagner, H. (in press). Predicting cognitive and social consequences of emotional episodes: The contribution of emotional intensity, the Five Factor Model and alexithymia. *Journal of Research in Personality.*

Lutgendorf, S. K., Antoni, M. H., Kumar, M., & Schneiderman, N. (1994). Changes in cognitive coping strategies predict EBV-antibody titre change following a stressor disclosure induction. *Journal of Psychosomatic Research, 38*, 63–78.

Marris, P. (1958). *Widows and their families.* London: Routledge & Kegan Paul.

Martin, L. L., & Tesser, A. (1989). Toward a motivational and structural theory of ruminative thought. In J. A. Bargh, & J. S. Uleman (Eds.), *Unintended thoughts* (pp. 306–325). New York: Guilford Press.

McIntosh, D. N., Silver, R. C., & Wortman, C. B. (1993). Religion's role in adjustment to a negative life event: Coping with the loss of a child. *Journal of Personality and Social Psychology, 65*, 812–821.

Mead, G. H. (1934). *Mind, self and society.* Chicago: University of Chicago Press.

Mumford, E., Schlesinger, H. J., & Glass, G. V. (1983). Reducing medical costs through mental health treatment: Research problems and recommendations. In A. Broskowski, E. Marks, & S. H. Budman (Eds.), *Linking health and mental health* (pp. 257–273). Beverly Hills, CA: Sage.

Murray, E. J., Lamnin, A. D., & Carver, C. S. (1989). Emotional expression in written essays and psychotherapy. *Journal of Social and Clinical Psychology, 8*, 414–429.

Murray, E. J., & Segal, D. L. (1994). Emotional processing in vocal and written expression of feelings about traumatic experiences. *Journal of Traumatic Stress, 7*, 391–405.

Paez, D., Velasco, C., & Gonzalez, J. L. (1999). Expressive writing and the role of alexithymia as a dispositional deficit in self-disclosure and psychological health. *Journal of Personality and Social Psychology, 77,* 630–641.

Parkes, C. M. (1972). *Bereavement: Studies of grief in adult life.* London: Tavistock.

Pennebaker, J. W. (1989). Confession, inhibition, and disease. In L. Berkowitz (Ed.), *Advances in experimental social psychology* (Vol. 22, pp. 211–244). New York: Academic Press.

Pennebaker, J. W. (1993). Mechanisms of social constraint. In D. M. Wegner & J. W. Pennebaker (Eds.), *Handbook of mental control* (pp. 200–219). Englewood Cliffs, NJ: Prentice Hall.

Pennebaker, J. W. (1997a). Writing about emotional experiences as a therapeutic process. *Psychological Science, 8,* 162–166.

Pennebaker, J. W. (1997b). *Opening up: The healing power of expressing emotions* (Rev. ed.). New York: Guilford Press.

Pennebaker, J. W., & Beall, S. K. (1986). Confronting a traumatic event: Toward an understanding of inhibition and disease. *Journal of Abnormal Psychology, 95,* 274–281.

Pennebaker, J. W., Mayne, T. J., & Francis, M. E. (1997). Linguistic predictors of adaptive bereavement. *Journal of Personality and Social Psychology, 72,* 863–871.

Pennebaker, J. W., & O'Heeron, R. C. (1984). Confiding in others and illness rates among spouses of suicide and accidental death. *Journal of Abnormal Psychology, 93,* 473–476.

Pennebaker, J. W., & Susman, J. R. (1988). Disclosure of traumas and psychosomatic processes. *Social Science and Medicine, 26,* 327–332.

Richards, J. M., Beal, W. E., Seagal, J. D., & Pennebaker, J. W. (2000). The effects of disclosure of traumatic events on illness behavior among psychiatric prison inmates. *Journal of Abnormal Psychology, 109,* 156–160.

Rimé, B. (1987). *Le partage social des émotions* [Social sharing of emotions]. Paper presented at the Symposium on Social Psychology and the Emotions, Maison des Sciences de l'Homme, Paris.

Rimé, B. (1999). Expressing emotion, physical health, and emotional relief: A cognitive-social perspective. *Advances in Mind-Body Medicine, 15,* 175–179.

Rimé, B., Finkenauer, C., Luminet, O., Zech, E., & Philippot, P. (1998). Social sharing of emotion: New evidence and new questions. In W. Stroebe & M. Hewstone (Eds.), *European review of social psychology* (Vol. 9, pp. 145–189). Chichester, UK: John Wiley & Sons.

Rimé, B., Finkenauer, C., & Sangsue, J. (1994). *How do you feel now? A retrospective investigation on the adjustment to positive and negative emotional events.* Unpublished manuscript, University of Louvain, Louvain-la-Neuve, Belgium.

Rimé, B., Finkenauer, C., & Sevrin, F. (1995). *Les émotions dans la vie quotidienne des personnes âgées: Impact, gestion, mémorisation, et réevocation* [Emotions in everyday life of the elderly: Impact, coping, memory, and reactivation]. Unpublished manuscript, University of Louvain, Louvain-la-Neuve, Belgium.

Rimé, B., Hayward, M. S., & Pennebaker, J. W. (1996). Characteristics of recovered vs. unrecovered emotional experiences. Unpublished raw data.

Rimé, B., Mesquita, B., Philippot, P., & Boca, S. (1991). Beyond the emotional event: Six studies on the social sharing of emotion. *Cognition and Emotion, 5,* 435–465.

Rimé, B., Noël, M. P., & Philippot, P. (1991). Episode émotionnel, réminiscences mentales et réminiscences sociales [Emotional episodes, mental remembrances and social remembrances]. *Cahiers Internationaux de Psychologie Sociale, 11,* 93–104.

Rimé, B., Philippot, P., Boca, S., & Mesquita, B. (1992). Long-lasting cognitive and social consequences of emotion: Social sharing and rumination. In W. Stroebe & M. Hewstone (Eds.), *European review of social psychology* (Vol. 3, pp. 225–258). Chichester, UK: John Wiley & Sons.

Rimé, B., Yogo, M., & Pennebaker, J. W. (1996). Social sharing of emotion across cultures. Unpublished raw data.

Rimé, B., Zech, E., Finkenauer, C., Luminet, O., & Dozier, S. (1996, July). *Different modalities of sharing emotions and their impact on emotional recovery.* Poster presented at the 11th General Meeting of the European Association for Experimental Social Psychology, Gmunden, Austria.

Schoenberg, B., Carr, A. C., Peretz, D., Kutscher, A. H., & Cherico, D. J. (1975). Advice of the bereaved for the bereaved. In B. Schoenberg, I. Gerber, A. Wiener, A. H. Kutscher, D. Perets, D., & A. C. Carr (Eds.), *Bereavement. Its psychosocial aspects* (pp. 362–367). New York: Columbia University Press.

Schut, H. A. W., Stroebe, M. S., de Keijser, J., & van den Bout, J. (1997). Intervention for the bereaved: Gender differences in the efficacy of two counselling programmes. *British Journal of Clinical Psychology, 36,* 63–72.

Segal, D. L., Bogaards, J. A., & Chatman, C. (in press). Emotional expression improves adjustment to spousal loss in the elderly. *Journal of Mental Health and Aging.*

Silver, R. E., & Wortman, C. B. (1980). Coping with undesirable life-events. In J. Garber & M. E. P. Seligman (Eds.), *Human helplessness: Theory and applications* (pp. 279–340). New York: Academic Press.

Singh-Manoux, A. (1998). *Les variations culturelles dans le partage social des émotions* [Cultural variations in social sharing of emotions]. Unpublished doctoral dissertation, Université de Paris X-Nanterre, France.

Smyth, J. M. (1998). Written emotional expression: Effect sizes, outcome types, and moderating variables. *Journal of Consulting and Clinical Psychology, 66,* 174–184.

Spera, S. P., Buhrfeind, E. D., & Pennebaker, J. W. (1994). Expressive writing and coping with job loss. *Academy of Management Journal, 37,* 722–733.

Spiegel, D., Bloom, J. R., Kraemer, H. C., & Gottheil, E. (1989). Effects of psychosocial treatment of patients with metastatic breast cancer. *Lancet, ii,* 888–891.

Stiles, W. B. (1987). "I have to talk to somebody." A fever model of disclosure.

In V. J. Derlega & J. H. Berg (Eds.), *Self-disclosure. Theory, research, and therapy* (pp. 275–282). New York: Plenum Press.

Stroebe, M. S., Schut, H., & Stroebe, W. (1998). Trauma and grief: A comparative analysis. In J. H. Harvey (Ed.), *Perspectives on loss: A sourcebook* (pp. 81–96). Philadelphia: Brunner/Mazel.

Stroebe, M. S., & Stroebe, W. (1991). Does "Grief work" work? *Journal of Consulting and Clinical Psychology, 59*, 1–4.

Stroebe, W., Stroebe, M., Schut, H., Zech, E., & van den Bout, J. (1997, June). *Must we give sorrow words?* Paper presented at the Third International Conference on Grief and Bereavement in Contemporary Society, Washington, DC.

Stroebe, W., Stroebe, M., & Zech, E. (1996, July). *The role of social sharing in adjustment to loss.* Paper presented at the 11th General Meeting of the European Association of Experimental and Social Psychology, Gmunden, Austria.

Taylor, S. E. (1983). Adjustment to threatening events. A theory of cognitive adaptation. *American Psychologist, 38*, 1161–1173.

Taylor, G. J., Bagby, R. M., & Parker, J. D. A. (1997). *Disorders of affect regulation. Alexithymia in medical and psychiatric illnesses.* Cambridge: Cambridge University Press.

Watson, D., & Pennebaker, J. W. (1989). Health complaints, stress, and distress: Exploring the central role of negative affectivity. *Psychological Review, 2*, 234–254.

Wortman, C. B., & Silver, R. C. (1989). The myths of coping with loss. *Journal of Consulting and Clinical Psychology, 57*, 349–357.

Yogo, M., & Onoe, K. (1998, August). *The social sharing of emotion among Japanese students.* Poster session presented at ISRE '98, Biannual Conference of the International Society for Research on Emotion, Wuerzburg, Germany.

Zech, E. (1999). Is it really helpful to verbalise one's emotions? *Gedrag en Gezondheid, 27*, 42–47.

Zech, E. (2000). *The impact of the communication of emotional experiences.* Doctoral dissertation, University of Louvain, Louvain-la-Neuve, Belgium.

24

RUMINATIVE COPING AND ADJUSTMENT TO BEREAVEMENT

SUSAN NOLEN-HOEKSEMA

The loss of a loved one often creates a host of negative emotions—sadness, anxiety, anger, guilt—with which people must cope. Much has been written about the ill effects of coping with these negative emotions by denying or suppressing them (Bowlby, 1980; Freud, 1917/1957; Lindemann, 1944). The research described in this chapter focuses on the opposite form of coping, ruminative coping. People engaged in ruminative coping persistently and repetitively focus on their negative emotions without taking action to relieve these emotions. In the context of bereavement, this involves chronically and passively focusing on grief-related emotions and symptoms.

In this chapter, I first define rumination and then describe studies showing that ruminative coping worsens and lengthens negative emotions as well as increasing the probability a depressed mood will become a depressive disorder. Second I describe studies that have investigated the mechanisms by which rumination enhances negative mood. Third I explore the question of why some people engage in ruminative coping and others do not. Fourth I address the implications of these studies for interventions with bereaved individuals.

Some of the studies I will discuss in this chapter have been conducted with nonbereaved populations, but I will highlight a large, longitudinal study of bereaved people that also demonstrates the deleterious effects of ruminative coping (Nolen-Hoeksema & Larson, 1999). This study focused on 455 people who lost a close loved one, usually to cancer. These adults were recruited through hospices and were interviewed before their loss, then reinterviewed 1, 6, 13, and 18 months after their loss. About one third of the participants were the spouses of the person who died, 40% were the adult children of the deceased, 14% were the parents of the deceased, 9% were the adult siblings of the deceased, and the remaining participants had other relationships to the deceased. Seventy-five percent of the participants were women, and 81% were White. About half had been the primary caregiver to their loved ones before the death.

DEFINITION OF RUMINATION

Rumination is defined as engaging in thoughts and behaviors that maintain one's focus on one's negative emotions and on the possible causes and consequences of those emotions (Nolen-Hoeksema, 1991). People engaging in ruminative coping think persistently and repetitively about how badly they feel ("I'm so sad," "I'm so unmotivated.") and about the circumstances surrounding their feelings ("Will I ever get over this?"). In many of our studies, we have used the Ruminative Responses Scale of the Response Styles Questionnaire to assess people's tendencies to ruminate when distressed (Nolen-Hoeksema & Larson, 1999; Nolen-Hoeksema & Morrow, 1991; Nolen-Hoeksema, Parker, & Larson, 1994). Respondents are asked to indicate how often they engage in each of 22 ruminative thoughts or behaviors when they feel sad, blue, or depressed. These 22 items describe responses to depressed mood that are self-focused (e.g., "I think, 'Why do I react this way?'"), symptom-focused (e.g., "I think about how hard it is to concentrate"), and focused on the possible consequences and causes of their mood (e.g., "I think, 'I won't be able to do my job if I don't snap out of this'"). The internal consistency of this scale is high (e.g., Cronbach's alpha = .89 in our bereavement study; Nolen-Hoeksema & Davis, 1999) and the scale has acceptable convergent and predictive validity (Butler & Nolen-Hoeksema, 1994; Nolen-Hoeksema & Morrow, 1991). For example, participants' responses to this scale correlated significantly (r = .62) with their use of ruminative responses to depressed mood in a 30-day diary study (Nolen-Hoeksema, Morrow, & Fredrickson, 1993). In addition, in a controlled laboratory study participants who scored above the median on the scale were significantly more likely than participants who scored below the median to choose to engage in an emotion-focused task rather than a task unrelated to emotion while they were in a depressed mood (Butler & Nolen-Hoeksema, 1994).

Rumination appears to be a stable individual difference variable—some people are consistently ruminators and others are not (Nolen-Hoeksema et al., 1993). For example, in our bereavement study the intraclass correlation for the Ruminative Responses Scale across five interviews spanning 18 months after the loss was .75 ($p < .0001$). In addition, people who engaged in more ruminative coping shortly after their loss showed little decrease in their tendency to ruminate over the 18 months we followed them (Nolen-Hoeksema & Davis, 1999).

People who score high on ruminative coping (whom I will hereafter refer to as *ruminators*) often say that they focus on their emotions to try to understand them and solve their problems. Correlational studies show, however, that ruminative coping and problem-solving coping are negatively correlated with each other (Nolen-Hoeksema & Larson, 1999; Nolen-Hoeksema & Morrow, 1991). Thus although ruminators may *think* their ruminations will help them solve their problems, they do not actively engage in effective problem-solving behaviors, such as making plans of action. As I will discuss later in this chapter, when ruminators do try to solve difficult personal problems, they appear to generate solutions that are less effective than those they may be capable of generating.

Bereaved ruminators may be searching for meaning and understanding of their loss, but often they are not finding meaning. In our longitudinal study of bereavement, we asked participants in all the postloss interviews whether they had been able to "make sense" of their loss. Throughout the study, including at the interview 18 months postloss, ruminators were less likely than nonruminators to say they were able to make sense of their loss (Nolen-Hoeksema & Larson, 1999).

Is ruminative coping simply a component of a more general personality orientation such as neuroticism (cf. Costa & McCrae, 1985; Eysenck & Eysenck, 1985)? We have found that ruminative coping is moderately correlated with neuroticism. Yet, in longitudinal analyses, ruminative coping was a significant predictor of changes in depression over a three-week period, after controlling for participants' levels of neuroticism. In contrast, neuroticism was not a significant predictor of changes in depression after controlling for ruminative coping (Nolen-Hoeksema, 1993). These results suggest that ruminative coping is related to neuroticism, but is a better predictor of changes in depression over time than neuroticism. Ruminative coping may be one mechanism by which global traits such as neuroticism are related to depression.

THE EFFECTS OF RUMINATION ON NEGATIVE MOOD

In a number of longitudinal studies, we have found that ruminators experience more prolonged periods of distress than nonruminators, even after statistically controlling for baseline levels of distress (Nolen-Hoeksema, McBride, & Larson, 1997; Nolen-Hoeksema & Morrow, 1991; Nolen-Hoeksema et al., 1993; Nolen-Hoeksema et al., 1994; see also Wood, Saltzberg, Neale, Stone, & Rachmiel, 1990). In our bereavement study, participants who had a more ruminative style of coping with their bereavement-related negative emotions were more depressed at each of the preloss and postloss interviews. Ruminators were also more likely than non-ruminators to have depressive symptoms severe enough to meet the criteria for major depressive disorder (ignoring the exclusion criterion for recent bereavement). The effects of ruminative coping on depressive symptoms and depressive disorders were significant even in longitudinal analyses in which we statistically controlled for previous levels of depression (Nolen-Hoeksema, 2000; Nolen-Hoeksema & Davis, 1999; Nolen-Hoeksema & Larson, 1999; see also Bonanno, Keltner, Holen, & Horowitz, 1995; Lund et al., 1985; Vachon et al., 1982). Other analyses suggest that rumination may prolong anxiety symptoms and angry moods, as well as depression (Nolen-Hoeksema & Larson, 1999; Rusting & Nolen-Hoeksema, 1998).

DETERMINING HOW RUMINATION PROLONGS DISTRESS

Rumination may prolong distress through a variety of cognitive and social mechanisms (Nolen-Hoeksema, 1991; see also Kuhl, 1981; Lewinsohn, Hoberman, Teri, & Hautzinger, 1985; Musson & Alloy, 1988). First, rumination may enhance the effects of distressed mood on thinking (Bower, 1981), drawing people's attention to the negative thoughts and memories made salient and accessible by negative mood. Second, rumination may interfere with good problem-solving, largely because people are thinking so negatively about themselves and their lives. Third, rumination may impair instrumental behaviors—that is, when people are ruminating, they are not engaging in the everyday activities that can increase their sense of control and lift their mood. Fourth, people who express their ruminative thoughts over and over with family members and friends may experience criticism and rejection from these family members and friends.

To investigate how rumination prolongs distress, we have conducted laboratory studies in which we have induced dysphoric participants and control groups of nondysphoric participants to ruminate by asking them to spend several minutes focusing on their current feeling states and how their lives are going. Participants are not told explicitly to focus on negative feeling states or aspects of their lives. Thus this rumination induction is not expected to have any effect on the moods of nondysphoric participants. But because dysphoric participants' feeling states and evaluations of their lives do tend to be negative, we expect that drawing their attention to them will increase their dysphoric mood. These lab studies also include a distraction condition, in which separate groups of dysphoric and nondysphoric participants spend several minutes focusing away from their feeling states and life circumstances and onto neutral images such as a plane flying overhead or the layout of the local mall. Again, because the content of the distraction induction is emotionally neutral, we expect it to have no effects on the moods of the nondysphoric participants. But because this distraction induction may temporarily cut off ruminations that the dysphoric people were naturally engaging in, we expect it to have temporary positive effects on their moods. These expectations have been confirmed in a large number of studies (Lyubomirsky, Caldwell, & Nolen-Hoeksema, 1998; Lyubomirsky & Nolen-Hoeksema, 1993; Lyubomirsky & Nolen-Hoeksema, 1995; Morrow & Nolen-Hoeksema, 1990; Nolen-Hoeksema, 1991; see also Fennell & Teasdale, 1984; Gibbons et al., 1985).

To investigate the effects of dysphoric rumination on cognition and motivation, we have presented the participants in each of the four groups described previously with tasks to measure their thoughts after they have ruminated or distracted. For example, in a series of studies we asked participants to generate memories from their past, then examined the qualities of those memories (Lyubomirsky et al., 1998). Dysphoric participants induced to ruminate generated more negative memories from their past and felt that negative events were more frequent in their lives than did dysphoric participants induced to distract or nondysphoric participants. These results obtained whether the autobiographical memories were prompted or recalled freely or whether the hedonic tone of these memories was determined by objective judges or the participants themselves. Rumination alone, in the absence of dysphoria, was not associated with remembering negative life events. In addition, rumination did not lead to changes in the moods of nondysphoric participants. These results suggest that rumination has adverse consequences only in the context of a dypshoric mood and bolster the argument that rumination affects cognition by enhancing the effects of negative mood on the accessibility of negative memories (Nolen-Hoeksema, 1991; for similar results see Carver, Blaney, & Scheier, 1979; Gibbons et al., 1985).

Similarly, when asked to make predictions about their own futures, dysphoric people induced to ruminate make more negative predictions (e.g., happy events such as a good marriage are more unlikely to happen to them) than dysphoric people induced to distract or nondysphoric people (Lyubomirsky & Nolen-Hoeksema, 1995; see also Carver et al., 1979; Pyszczynski, Holt, & Greenberg, 1987). In turn, hopelessness for a better future may contribute to more depressed mood in dysphoric ruminators and sap their motivation to improve their lives (cf. Abramson, Metalsky, & Alloy, 1989).

In other studies, participants have been asked to interpret hypothetical negative events, or simply to talk about the current events in their lives. Dysphoric people induced to ruminate made more self-defeating interpretations of hypothetical events than either dysphoric people induced to distract from their ruminations or nondysphoric people who ruminated or distracted (Lyubomirsky & Nolen-Hoeksema, 1995). When we have asked people to talk about ongoing events in their lives, we have found that dysphoric people induced to ruminate also talk more about problems in their lives, blame themselves more for their problems, feel less in control of their lives, and are less self-confident compared to dysphoric people who are distracted or the nondysphoric groups (Lyubomirsky, Tucker, Caldwell, & Berg, 1998). Thus whether they are interpreting hypothetical events or real events in their lives, dysphoric people who ruminate are more negative and self-derogatory than dysphoric people who did not ruminate or non-dysphoric people.

As noted, ruminators often say that they are ruminating to try to understand their problems and decide what to do about them. When we have had participants in our lab studies generate solutions to common interpersonal problems, however, we have found that dysphoric people induced to ruminate generate poorer solutions than dysphoric people distracted from their ruminations or nondysphoric people (Lyubomirsky & Nolen-Hoeksema, 1995). Thus even though distressed people often ruminate in an attempt to problem-solve, they may come to more depressogenic conclusions about their lives and make poorer decisions than if they did not ruminate.

Among bereaved people, ruminators may remember more negative memories with the deceased, such as all the times they fought with the deceased or ways in which they were not helpful to the deceased. Ruminators may interpret ongoing events in their lives more negatively, for example, believing that they cannot cope with living alone. Ruminators may be hopeless about the future, expecting that they will never find another person to share their lives with. Ruminators may make poor decisions, for example, around the settlement of the deceased's estate. These negative thoughts and expectations, and the consequences of poor decisions, then will feed the ruminators' distress.

We also have evidence that rumination interferes with instrumental behavior. In one of our laboratory studies, we asked dysphoric and non-dysphoric participants who had ruminated or distracted to rate a series of everyday activities (e.g., going for coffee with a friend, seeing a favorite movie) for how much each activity would lift their mood and how likely they would be to engage in that activity if they had the chance. The dysphoric participants who had been ruminating rated the activities just as useful in lifting their mood as the other groups of participants. But the dysphoric ruminators said they were significantly less likely to engage in these activities than the other groups said they were (Lyubomirsky & Nolen-Hoeksema, 1993). Thus although the dysphoric ruminators could acknowledge that engaging in these activities might lift their mood, they were not motivated to engage in the activities. This may be because the thoughts the participants were focused on—how tired and unmotivated they felt, how badly their lives were going—were so compelling that it was difficult for the participants to imagine putting aside these thoughts and engaging in pleasant, distracting activities.

Some bereaved people may be reluctant to give up their ruminations, their sadness, their guilt, their grief, because it represents for them their last and final tie to the deceased. They fear that if they no longer think, cry, or mourn, they will "lose" the deceased. There comes a time when most people realize that this is not so, that they can "forget" temporarily, or forget certain aspects or details of the deceased, and they do not lose their connection to the deceased. Also, they realize that letting go is not a betrayal of the deceased. Thus people who cling to their ruminations may be, in a way, clinging to the deceased loved one in the only way that is left to them.

Finally, rumination may impair social relationships. In our bereavement study, ruminators reached out for support from others around their loss more than nonruminators did (Nolen-Hoeksema & Davis, 1999). Ruminators may seek out others for support following a loss because they are more actively and persistently thinking about their loss, its meanings, and their own reactions to the loss than nonruminators and want to share these thoughts with others. But ruminators reported less satisfaction with the support they received than did nonruminators. This was true even after we statistically controlled for differences in levels of distress between ruminators and nonruminators, thus ruminators were not less satisfied with their social networks simply because they were more distressed (see also Lepore, Silver, Wortman, & Wayment, 1996).

People may be less supportive of bereaved ruminators than nonruminators because ruminators go over and over their loss and persistently discuss their feelings and grief-related symptoms without making much progress toward "resolving" their loss. Although family members and friends may want to be supportive of the ruminator, it is difficult emotionally and physiologically to listen to others recount a trauma and their feelings about the trauma (Schortt & Pennebaker, 1992). Thus they may withdraw from the ruminator, become annoyed with him or her, dismiss the ruminator's concerns, or criticize the ruminator for continuing to ruminate (see also Lehman, Ellard, & Wortman, 1986). As one of the participants in our study observed,

> Don't spend the whole time feeling sorry for yourself with other people, because people get very tired (of it). Even if they know you're hurting inside, they'll stay with you. But if you're going to be crying and just talking about yourself all the time and your problems, you isolate yourself very quickly.

In summary, rumination may prolong distress by making negative memories of the past, negative interpretations of the present, and negative predictions about the future more accessible and salient, by interfering with good problem solving, by impeding instrumental behavior, and by driving away social support. Each of these consequences of rumination can then feed depression and other negative emotions and symptoms following a loss.

DETERMINING WHY SOME PEOPLE RUMINATE AND OTHERS DO NOT

If rumination makes people feel badly, why do they do it? There may be self-perpetuating properties of dysphoric rumination that make it difficult for people to "pull out" of rumination once it starts. One self-perpetuating property of dysphoric rumination may be the lack of motivation dysphoric ruminators have to engage in activities that might lift their mood. In addition, we found that dysphoric people induced to ruminate actually believe they are gaining insight into themselves and their problems when they are ruminating, even though they are generating relatively poor solutions to their problems (Lyubomirsky & Nolen-Hoeksema, 1993). Ruminators often say that they feel they have stopped deluding themselves and are now seeing things for how bad they really are. Such thoughts are extremely compelling and would be difficult to put aside for the sake of lifting one's mood.

A number of personality characteristics may contribute to the tendency to ruminate. We have already noted that people who are neurotic are more prone to ruminate. In addition, people who feel less mastery over their lives or are less dispositionally optimistic are more likely to be ruminators (Nolen-Hoeksema & Larson, 1999). Ruminative coping remains a significant predictor of the duration of depressive symptoms after statistically controlling for these personality characteristics, suggesting it is a proximal and potent contributor to depressive symptoms.

Certain contextual factors may also contribute to rumination. People who are faced with multiple negative events or chronic situations that are difficult to control, or who have a history of uncontrollability in their lives, may be more likely to lapse into rumination. These negative events and chronic strains may convince some people that there is little they can do to control their lives. Yet we suspect that most people under such strains hold out some hope that there is something they can do to improve their situation and thus do not become fully hopeless and helpless (cf. Garber, Miller, & Abramson, 1980; Wortman & Brehm, 1975). Instead, they search for some understanding of why their lives are not going as they wish, why they feel frustrated and distressed so much of the time. This searching may be manifested as rumination.

In our bereavement study, people who were beset by multiple negative events around the time of their loss were more likely to be ruminating than those who did not experience other negative events in addition to their loss (Nolen-Hoeksema et al., 1994). Some of these events were related to the loss, such as financial strain. But many of these events were unrelated to the loss and just happened to have occurred around the time of the loss. These were significant negative events, such as a major traffic accident, one's child getting in trouble with the law, or being diagnosed with a serious illness one's self. Some of the people in our study who had such experiences said they thought they could have coped well with their loss, but the cumulation of negative events overwhelmed their coping resources, causing them to turn inward and become passive.

People in the bereavement study who did not have adequate social support also were more likely to be ruminating (Nolen-Hoeksema et al., 1994). Thus it seems that lack of social support can contribute to rumination, just as rumination may drive away social support. Two social support variables that were particularly strongly related to rumination were social isolation and social friction. People who were socially isolated had few or no others with whom they could talk after their loss. This isolation gave people ample opportunity to ruminate, and no objective feedback from others on the content of their ruminations.

Social friction represents more than just the absence of positive emotional support. Critical or hostile responses from others may give ruminators more troubles to ruminate about, and raise more questions in their minds about their own behaviors or emotional reactions. For example, a ruminator who lost a sister might wonder if she should have taken more time off to be with her sister while she was alive or if she will suffer the same early death as her sister. If this same ruminating woman is also told by other family members that she was not around enough when her sister was ill and that they do not understand her reactions to her sister's death, this will encourage the woman's existing ruminations and give her new concerns about which to ruminate. Comments by participants in our bereavement study illustrate how lack of social support could give a ruminator more to ruminate about. One woman who lost her mother said,

> My husband probably doesn't feel very comfortable talking about her death with me. Neither do my friends. They can't handle if I start talking about it and get upset. My friends couldn't possibly understand how it affected me.
>
> I think the stress that it puts on a marital relationship (is great). My husband has never experienced the death of a parent, or the illness of a parent, so he's not really good with compassion. He doesn't have the

foggiest idea. He says, "Well, it's been six months. You should be over this now." I felt invalidated by him along the way quite a bit.

Some of the participants in our bereavement study lost a loved one to complications from AIDS. These participants were more likely to be ruminating following their loss than people who lost a loved one to cancer or other non-AIDS illnesses. The loss of a loved one to a stigmatized illness such as AIDS may foster ruminations because other people are not as willing to talk about the illness and loss, and thus the bereaved person experiences more social isolation or friction. Indeed, the people who lost a loved one to AIDS reported more social isolation and friction than people who lost a loved one to a non-AIDS illness. Other circumstances surrounding many AIDS-related deaths may also make adjustment for survivors especially difficult. First, the people dying from AIDS-related causes are typically young adults, thus their deaths shatter those basic assumptions about a natural order to life and death. Second, death from AIDS-related causes is usually long, painful, and horrible, requiring family members to provide care giving for extended periods (Folkman, Chesney, Cooke, Boccellari, & Collette, 1994). The opportunistic infections and diseases that occur during advanced HIV infection create chronic and severe diarrhea, wasting, severe musculoskeletal pain, blindness, and dementia. Third, homosexual transmission accounts for more than 50% of AIDS cases in the United States (Centers for Disease Control and Prevention, 1995). If the surviving family members have not accepted their loved one's homosexuality or perhaps did not know about it before the AIDS diagnosis was made, they have another major adjustment in addition to their loss to contend with. Some comments by people who lost a loved one to AIDS suggest that all these factors can contribute to rumination:

> He died so young of such a terrible disease. He's gone and I'm here. It's not the natural order of things. It doesn't make sense at all. I've had so many losses in the past couple of years that I feel why J. because he was always so interested in health. Sometimes I think that he got his disease because of his life style. He liked to live in the fast lane. I wish something in my life would go well. I kind of think everything I touch is spoiled. I wish I could have talked more to my son, and when he told me he had AIDS I kind of accepted it, but we had a couple bad scenes about it.
>
> There's not enough information on AIDS because of the rejection/ stigma/shame of it. You can't say "AIDS" in many places, or you'll risk a lot.

SUMMARY OF FINDINGS

Ruminative coping involves passively and repetitively focusing on one's symptoms of distress and the possible causes and consequences of these symptoms. Ruminative coping appears to be a stable individual difference variable. People who ruminate when distressed have longer periods of depression, anxiety, and anger than people who do not ruminate. Rumination amplifies and maintains distress through several mechanisms. First, it enhances the effects of distressed mood on thinking, making negative thoughts and memories more salient and accessible by negative mood. Second, rumination interferes with good problem solving, perhaps because people are thinking so negatively about themselves and their lives. Third, rumination impairs instrumental behaviors by reducing people's motivation to engage in the everyday activities that can increase their sense of control and lift their mood. Fourth, ruminators do not receive the social support they want and need, perhaps because their persistent ruminations violate social norms for coping.

Many factors appear to contribute to rumination. First, there may be self-perpetuating characteristics of rumination that make it difficult to break ruminative cycles. When ruminating, people seem to lose their motivation to engage in behaviors they know would make them feel better. They also report feeling they are gaining insight into their problems, even though their ruminations are impairing their problem solving.

Second, personality characteristics such as neuroticism and dispositional pessimism seem to contribute to rumination. Third, people who are beset by multiple negative life events, or have a history of uncontrollable events in their past, seem more prone to ruminate. Fourth, people who have little social support are more likely to ruminate. Fifth, bereaved people who experience "nonnormative" losses, such as the loss of a child or the loss of someone to a stigmatized illness, may be more prone to ruminate.

IMPLICATIONS FOR INTERVENTIONS
WITH BEREAVED RUMINATORS

So what is a ruminator to do—suppress? One might conclude that the distraction induction we use in our laboratory studies is a suppression manipulation and that the success of the distraction induction in reducing dysphoric mood and improving thinking and problem solving in dysphoric people suggests that suppression is good for bereaved ruminators. I would argue that our distraction induction has very different effects from simply telling a person to stop thinking about dysphoria and grief. The distraction induction gives participants a set of neutral images to focus on, without an explicit demand to stop thinking about their moods. Thus it provides a pleasant alternative to negative thoughts, without inducing anxiety over whether one is going to be successful at not thinking about one's distress. In contrast, simply telling one's self to stop thinking (or being told by others to do so) without having positive distracters sets one up for the many failure experiences documented so nicely by Wegner and colleagues (Wegner, 1989; Wegner & Gold, 1995; Wegner, Schneider, Knutson, & McMahon, 1991). Research by Wenzlaff and colleagues (Wenzlaff, Wegner, & Roper, 1988) shows the differential effects of providing dysphoric people with positive distracters from their mood versus simply giving them instructions to suppress negative thoughts—positive distracters work whereas suppression does not.

Our research clearly suggests that dysphoric people can get temporary relief from their mood, and more important, can go on to think more constructively and problem solve more effectively if they use positive distracters to get their minds off their ruminations for a while. Similarly, cognitive–behavioral therapies for depressed people include behavioral activation elements—getting people to get out of the house and do something active and constructive—that serve as distracters from their ruminative thoughts, among other purposes (Beck, Rush, Shaw, & Emery, 1979). These interventions are highly effective for depressed people, and one predictor of the effectiveness of cognitive–behavioral therapy is the extent to which patients are willing to learn more active strategies for coping with their periods of depression (Burns & Nolen-Hoeksema, 1991). Several studies have shown that cognitive–behavioral interventions can be helpful for bereaved people as well (chapter 28, this volume).

As noted earlier, bereaved ruminators may be unwilling to give up their ruminations because they believe these ruminations maintain their ties to the deceased. Therapists may need to confront this belief, directly but gently, perhaps with cognitive–behavioral techniques. In addition, therapists may help bereaved ruminators to find other means of creating lasting ties to the deceased, such as creating a memorial fund or dedicating a piece of property or some other contribution to the deceased. These activities may also help the ruminator create some meaning in the loss, which will reduce ruminations. Or the bereaved ruminator may be willing to contract with the therapist to confine his or her ruminations to certain times of the day or week, much as worriers will sometimes contract with therapists to confine their worries to a designated worry hour. Strategies such as these can help bereaved ruminators agree to put some constraints on their ruminations without feeling they have abandoned or betrayed the memory of their deceased loved one.

Another way therapists may help ruminators reduce their ruminations is by helping them solve some of the concrete problems they face as a result of their loss, or in addition to their loss. As noted earlier, in our bereavement study people who were beset by multiple stressors around the same time as their loss became more ruminative over time. Therapists can help bereaved people find and make use of resources within the community for solving problems such as loss of finances, the need for full-time child care, and the need for vocational training. Therapists can also help ruminators engage in active problem solving during sessions and can contract with them to take specific problem-solving actions between sessions. Solving problems may give bereaved ruminators less to ruminate about and more opportunity to feel some control over their lives.

Each of these interventions can be conceived as helping ruminators engage in what Stroebe and Schut (1999) have called *dual process coping*. They suggest that long-term adjustment to loss requires that people express their grief some of the time but suppress it at other times to deal with the necessary activities of daily life. People who cannot express their grief may suffer maladjustment. But people who cannot suppress their grief, especially as the time since the loss increases, may also suffer maladjustment. One person in our study nicely described dual process coping:

> I know I have a great capacity to tolerate pain and all these different things—I'm a survivor—it happened that way. Sometimes I question myself as to whether I'm being very unemotional about things, and then I realize I understand what it is that's happened, and I don't try to make it more than it is. When I wake up in the morning, I still have children to feed and things to do. The old life-goes-on saying is true, so there's the reality of it all. You can't just get caught in one thing and dwell on it. I've tried to run away from things, but that's not going to work either. You have to face it sometime.

Helping bereaved ruminators to work more effectively with their social support network would appear to be another important focus of interventions. Although ruminators in our bereavement study were less satisfied with the support they were receiving from others, it was clear that supportive relationships with others did help ruminators, even more than social support helped nonruminators (Nolen-Hoeksema & Davis, 1999). Ruminators who were well-integrated into a social network, received emotional support from the people in that network, and felt comfortable discussing their loss with people in their network were less distressed throughout the 18 months following their loss than ruminators who were isolated, were deficient of emotional support and did not feel comfortable discussing their loss.

Social support may be especially helpful to ruminators for several reasons. First, supportive others are likely to help ruminators engage in dual process coping, rather than remaining mired in ruminations. For example, supportive others may help a ruminating widow engage in active problem solving in dealing with financial problems she faces following a loss, rather than only ruminating about those problems. Similarly, ruminators may also need supportive others to encourage and accompany them as they begin to resume everyday activities following a loss because they are less likely than nonruminators to engage in everyday instrumental activities that can lift distress somewhat and provide a sense of control or accomplishment, such as doing a hobby or maintaining an exercise program.

Supportive others may also help ruminators "work through" questions about the meaning of their loss, rather than only ruminating about these questions (Greenberg, 1995). For example, family members and friends may help a ruminating parent accept the loss of his child and understand it in the context of his existing world views. They may do this by talking with the ruminating parent about his religious or philosophical beliefs and how these beliefs help him to understand his loss. Or simply telling the story of his loss over and over to emotionally supportive others may help the ruminating parent to habituate to the story and shape the story to fit his belief system (Janoff-Bulman, 1992; Rachman, 1980).

For ruminators who do not have a social support network that helps them engage in dual process coping and deal more effectively with their ruminations, support groups might be helpful. Many of the people in our study who were in support groups expressed that listening to, and being listened to, by others who have had similar experiences to their own helped them to move beyond passive self-focus and rumination. For example, one woman who cared for her dying mother for many months said,

> I did a fair amount of feeling sorry for myself because I couldn't get out. It wasn't until I joined a support group and talked out some of these things that really I felt better about it. It was really great. In the group, I saw women who dealt with very difficult mothers; mine was sweet and gentle. So I said, "Gee, I don't have it bad." That was the surprising, beneficial part of it for me—listening to them.

Ruminators who lose a loved one to a stigmatized and isolating illness such as AIDS may benefit greatly from support groups. A woman who lost her 31-year-old son to AIDS said,

> The whole time he was sick, very few people called to say "How is he?" I'm sure if he had cancer, I would have been getting phone calls right and left. It was very hard. That's why this support group is so helpful. It's really for gay and lesbian people, but it's broken up into different groups, like significant others—we went to that one, the bereavement group, the HIV-positive group. They have facilitators in each group. It's great. Now we're into the bereavement group. There are other parents in that group as well as wives, significant others. Everyone is just able to talk about their feelings. It's the only place I can really talk and feel at ease. I know they'll understand. They're not judgmental. They've gone through it. So it really is a big help. It's just a wonderful group.

CONCLUSION

Suppression of grief-related distress may be maladaptive (cf. Folkman, Chesney, Collette, Boccellari, & Cooke, 1996; Stroebe & Schut, 1999).

There is increasing evidence, however, that rumination over grief-related distress is also maladaptive, prolonging that distress and making it more difficult for people to solve the problems they face following their loss. Suppression and rumination may represent the maladaptive extremes of what Stroebe and Schut (1999) have called restoration orientation and loss orientation following grief.

Helping bereaved people find an adaptive middle ground between suppression and rumination will not always be easy. Suppressors and ruminators may need different types of interventions (chapter 30, this volume). Similarly, there may be individual differences among ruminators in their responsiveness to certain interventions. Cognitive–behavioral strategies that help people engage in more active problem solving and reintegration into daily activities may be helpful for some ruminators. Other ruminators may resist such interventions and benefit more from traditional supportive therapy, if that therapy helps them move past simple ruminations and into understanding and acceptance of their loss. Simply educating a bereaved ruminator about the negative effects of rumination on thinking, problem solving, and mood, and on the self-perpetuating properties of rumination, may help ruminators to gain some distance from the ruminations and begin to move past them.

REFERENCES

Abramson, L. Y., Metalsky, G. I., & Alloy, L. B. (1989). Hopelessness depression: A theory-based subtype of depression. *Psychological Review, 96,* 358–372.

Beck, A. T., Rush, A. J., Shaw, B. F., & Emery, G. (1979). *Cognitive therapy of depression.* New York: Guilford Press.

Bonanno, G. A., Keltner, D., Holen, A., & Horowitz, M. J. (1995). When avoiding unpleasant emotions might not be such a bad thing: Verbal-autonomic response dissociation and midlife conjugal bereavement. *Journal of Personality and Social Psychology, 69,* 975–989.

Bower, G. H. (1981). Mood and memory. *American Psychologist, 36,* 129–148.

Bowlby, J. (1980). *Attachment and loss. Vol. 3. Loss: sadness and depression.* New York: Basic Books.

Burns, D. D., & Nolen-Hoeksema, S. (1991). Coping styles, homework compliance, and the effectiveness of cognitive-behavioral therapy. *Journal of Consulting and Clinical Psychology, 59,* 305–311.

Butler, L. D., & Nolen-Hoeksema, S. (1994). Gender differences in responses to a depressed mood in a college sample. *Sex Roles, 30,* 331–346.

Carver, C. S., Blaney, P. H., & Scheier, M. F. (1979). Focus of attention, chronic expectancy, and responses to a feared stimulus. *Journal of Personality and Social Psychology, 37,* 1186–1195.

Centers for Disease Control and Prevention. (1995). *HIV/AIDS surveillance report.* Atlanta: U.S. Department of Health and Human Services.

Costa, P. T., & McCrae, R. R. (1985). Hypochondriasis, neuroticism, and aging: When are somatic complaints unfounded? *American Psychologist, 40*, 19–28.

Eysenck, H. J., & Eysenck, M. W. (1985). *Personality and individual differences.* New York: Plenum Press.

Fennell, M. J., & Teasdale, J. D. (1984). Effects of distraction on thinking and affect in depressed patients. *British Journal of Clinical Psychology, 23*, 65–66.

Folkman, S., Chesney, M., Collette, L., Boccellari, A., & Cooke, M. (1996). Post-bereavement depressive mood and its prebereavement predictors in HIV+ and HIV− gay men. *Journal of Personality and Social Psychology, 70*, 336–348.

Folkman, S., Chesney, M. A., Cooke, M., Boccellari, A., & Collette, L. (1994). Caregiver burden in HIV-positive and HIV-negative partners of men with AIDS. *Journal of Consulting and Clinical Psychology, 62*, 746–756.

Freud, S. (1957). Mourning and melancholia. In J. Strachey (Ed.), *Standard edition of the complete work of Sigmund Freud.* London: Hogarth Press. (Original work published 1917)

Garber, J., Miller, S. M., & Abramson, L. Y. (1980). On the distinction between anxiety states and depression: Perceived control certainty, and probability of goal attainment. In J. Garber & M. E. P. Seligman (Eds.), *Human helplessness: Theory and applications* (pp. 131–172). New York: Academic Press.

Gibbons, F. X., Smith, T. W., Ingram, R. E., Pearce, K., Brehm, S. S., & Schroeder, D. (1985). Self-awareness and self-confrontation: Effects of self-focused attention on members of a clinical population. *Journal of Personality and Social Psychology, 48*, 662–675.

Greenberg, M. A. (1995). Cognitive processing of traumas: The role of intrusive thoughts and reappraisals. *Journal of Applied Social Psychology, 25*, 1262–1296.

Janoff-Bulman, R. (1992). *Shattered assumptions: Towards a new psychology of trauma.* New York: Free Press.

Kuhl, J. (1981). Motivational and functional helplessness: The moderating effect of state versus action orientation. *Journal of Personality and Social Psychology, 40*, 155–170.

Lehman, D. R., Ellard, J. H., & Wortman, C. B. (1986). Social support for the bereaved: Recipients' and providers' perspectives on what is helpful. *Journal of Consulting and Clinical Psychology, 54*, 438–446.

Lepore, S. J., Silver, R. C., Wortman, C. B., & Wayment, H. A. (1996). Social constraints, intrusive thoughts, and depressive symptoms among bereaved mothers. *Journal of Personality and Social Psychology, 70*, 271–282.

Lewinsohn, P. M., Hoberman, H., Teri, L., & Hautzinger, M. (1985). An integrative theory of depression. In S. Reiss & R. Bootzin (Eds.), *Theoretical issues in behavior therapy* (pp. 331–359). New York: Academic Press.

Lindemann, E. (1944). Symptomatology and management of acute grief. *American Journal of Psychiatry, 101*, 141–148.

Lund, D. A., Dimond, M. F., Caserta, M. S., Johnson, R. J., Poulton, J. L., & Connelly, J. R. (1985). Identifying elderly with coping difficulties after two years of bereavement. *Omega: Journal of Death and Dying, 16*, 213–224.

Lyubomirsky, S., Caldwell, N. D., & Nolen-Hoeksema, S. (1998). Effects of ruminative and distracting responses to depressed mood on retrieval of autobiographical memories. *Journal of Personality and Social Psychology, 75,* 166–177.

Lyubomirsky, S., & Nolen-Hoeksema, S. (1993). Self-perpetuating properties of dysphoric rumination. *Journal of Personality and Social Psychology, 65,* 339–349.

Lyubomirsky, S., & Nolen-Hoeksema, S. (1995). Effects of self-focused rumination on negative thinking and interpersonal problem solving. *Journal of Personality and Social Psychology, 69,* 176–190.

Lyubomirsky, S., Tucker, K. L., Caldwell, N. D., & Berg, K. (1999). Why ruminators are poor problem solvers: Clues from the phenomenology of dysphoric rumination. *Journal of Personality and Social Psychology, 77,* 1041–1060.

Morrow, J., & Nolen-Hoeksema, S. (1990). Effects of responses to depression on the remediation of depressive affect. *Journal of Personality and Social Psychology, 58,* 519–527.

Musson, R. F., & Alloy, L. B. (1988). Depression and self-directed attention. In L. B. Alloy (Ed.), *Cognitive processes in depression* (pp. 193–220). New York: Guilford Press.

Nolen-Hoeksema, S. (1991). Responses to depression and their effects on the duration of depressive episodes. *Journal of Abnormal Psychology, 100,* 569–582.

Nolen-Hoeksema, S. (1993). Sex differences in the control of depression. In D. Wegner (Ed.), *Handbook of mental control* (pp. 306–324). Englewood Cliffs, NJ: Prentice-Hall.

Nolen-Hoeksema, S. (2000). The role of rumination in depressive disorders and mixed anxiety/depressive symptoms. *Journal of Abnormal Psychology, 109,* 504–511.

Nolen-Hoeksema, S., & Davis, C. G. (1999). "Thanks for sharing that": Ruminators and their social support networks. *Journal of Personality and Social Psychology, 77,* 801–814.

Nolen-Hoeksema, S., & Larson, J. (1999). *Coping with loss.* Mahwah, NJ: Erlbaum.

Nolen-Hoeksema, S., McBride, A., & Larson, J. (1997). Rumination and psychological distress among bereaved partners. *Journal of Personality and Social Psychology, 72,* 855–862.

Nolen-Hoeksema, S., & Morrow, J. (1991). A prospective study of depression and posttraumatic stress symptoms after a natural disaster: The 1989 Loma Prieta earthquake. *Journal of Personality and Social Psychology, 61,* 115–121.

Nolen-Hoeksema, S., Morrow, J., & Fredrickson, B. L. (1993). Response styles and the duration of episodes of depressed mood. *Journal of Abnormal Psychology, 102,* 20–28.

Nolen-Hoeksema, S., Parker, L. E., & Larson, J. (1994). Ruminative coping with depressed mood following loss. *Journal of Personality and Social Psychology, 67,* 92–104.

Pyszczynski, T., Holt, K., & Greenberg, J. (1987). Depression, self-focused attention, and expectancies for positive and negative future events for self and others. *Journal of Personality and Social Psychology, 52*, 994–1001.

Rachman, S. (1980). Emotional processing. *Behavior Research and Therapy, 18*, 51–60.

Rusting, C. L., & Nolen-Hoeksema, S. (1998). Regulating responses to anger: Effects of rumination and distraction on angry mood. *Journal of Personality and Social Psychology, 74*, 790–803.

Schortt, J. W., & Pennebaker, J. W. (1992). Talking versus hearing about Holocaust experiences. *Basic and Applied Social Psychology, 13*, 165–179.

Stroebe, M., & Schut, H. (1999). The dual process model of coping with bereavement: Rationale and description. *Death Studies, 23*, 197–224.

Vachon, M. L. S., Rogers, J., Lyall, W. A. L., Lancee, W. J., Sheldon, A. R., & Freeman, S. J. J. (1982). Predictors and correlates of adaptation to conjugal bereavement. *American Journal of Psychiatry, 139*, 998–1002.

Wegner, D. M. (1989). *White bears and other unwanted thoughts: Suppression, obsession, and the psychology of mental control.* New York: Penguin Books.

Wegner, D. M., & Gold, B. (1995). Fanning old flames: Emotional and cognitive effects of suppressing thoughts of a past relationship. *Journal of Personality and Social Psychology, 68*, 782–792.

Wegner, D. M., Schneider, D. J., Knutson, B., & McMahon, S. R. (1991). Polluting the stream of consciousness: The effect of thought suppression on the mind's environment. *Cognitive Therapy and Research, 15*, 141–152.

Wenzlaff, R. M., Wegner, D. M., & Roper, D. W. (1988). Depression and mental control: The resurgence of unwanted negative thoughts. *Journal of Personality and Social Psychology, 55*, 882–892.

Wood, J. V., Saltzberg, J. A., Neale, J. M., Stone, A., & Rachmiel, T. B. (1990). Self-focused attention, coping responses, and distressed mood in everyday life. *Journal of Personality and Social Psychology, 58*, 1027–1036.

Wortman, C. B., & Brehm, J. W. (1975). Responses to uncontrollable outcomes: An integration of reactance theory and the learned helplessness model. In L. Berkowitz (Ed.), *Advances in experimental social psychology* (pp. 278–336). New York: Academic Press.

25

REVISED COPING THEORY AND THE PROCESS OF BEREAVEMENT

SUSAN FOLKMAN

No one would question the assumption that adjustment to and re-covery from the loss of a spouse, parent, child, or close friend is a compli-cated process that is influenced by the timing and nature of the death, aspects of the bereaved individual's personality, the bereaved individual's history, the individual's psychosocial and material resources, competing de-mands on those resources, and serendipity. Few also would question the assumption that the way the individual copes with loss is likely to affect the quality of adjustment and recovery. The widespread conviction that coping can make a difference in loss-related adjustment and recovery is reflected in the burgeoning popular literature. It is also reflected in the rich literature for counselors and clinicians on therapeutic approaches for be-reaved individuals.

Perhaps not surprisingly, research about how people actually cope with their loss and its effects on adjustment and recovery lags behind the popular and clinical literatures. Relatively few research groups have con-

The writing of this chapter was supported by grants 49985, 52517, and 58069 from the National Institute of Mental Health. I thank Judy Moskowitz for her thoughtful comments on a previous version of the chapter.

ducted systematic, longitudinal studies of what people actually think and do to come to terms with their loss and move ahead in their lives. The research of Wortman, Silver, and their colleagues (e.g., Wortman & Silver, 1987, 1989; Wortman, Silver, & Kessler, 1993), Janoff-Bulman (e.g., Janoff-Bulman, 1989), and Jacobs and his colleagues (e.g., Jacobs, Kasl, Schaefer, & Ostfeld, 1994) represent some of the few systematic longitudinal studies that focus specifically on the ways people cope with loss.

One reason for the relative paucity of research on coping with bereavement may be the absence of theoretical models of coping that apply specifically to bereavement. A number of theories identify phases of grief the individual needs to pass through or adaptive tasks that the bereaved individual needs to address (e.g., Bowlby, 1980; Glick, Weiss, & Parkes, 1974; Kübler-Ross, 1969), but for the most part, these theories do not posit the thoughts and behaviors that people use to cope with bereavement-related demands. In this regard, Stroebe and Schut's (1999) dual process model of coping with loss stands out as one of the very few theoretical models of bereavement that actually refers specifically to coping.

My goal in this chapter is to consider how stress and coping theory (Lazarus & Folkman, 1984), which was developed to examine how people appraise and cope with a wide variety of stressful encounters ranging from minor daily hassles to major life events, can be applied to the more specific case of understanding how people appraise and cope with bereavement. The first part of the chapter includes a brief description of stress and coping theory, its application in a longitudinal study of caregiving and bereavement, and some unexpected findings that motivated a revision of the model. The second part of the chapter examines three conceptual and methodological issues that need to be addressed to adapt the revised coping model to the study of bereavement.

It is important to note that coping may have a relatively small influence on adjustment and recovery compared to factors such as the timing and nature of the death, history, and personality. Nonetheless, as the extensive popular and clinical literatures indicate, coping is important because it is one of the few factors influencing bereavement outcomes amenable to brief interventions.

STRESS AND COPING THEORY

Coping is such a commonly used word that we might assume it has a common underlying meaning. But it does not. To some, coping refers to successfully overcoming whatever the stress of the day is. Within this definition, coping is equivalent to mastery. To others, coping refers to the quality of the coping process independent of its effects on an outcome.

The most well-known variant of this definition comes from the ego-psychology literature and the concept of ego processes that regulate anxiety. Within this framework, mature ego processes that involve a minimum of distortion (Menninger, 1963; Vaillant, 1977) are usually referred to as coping. The less mature ego processes are referred to as defense.

Lazarus and Folkman (1984), in contrast, define coping as the changing thoughts and acts that an individual uses to manage the external or internal demands of stressful situations. This definition does not imply that coping is equivalent to mastery, nor does it depend on an evaluation of the quality of the coping process. It is a descriptive, process-oriented approach, the evaluation of which depends on constraints and demands that are inherent in the context and the kinds of outcomes that are examined.

Lazarus and Folkman's (1984) definition has guided much of the coping research in recent years (Zeidner & Endler, 1996). This body of research tends to support several basic propositions about coping: (a) coping is contextual and influenced by appraised characteristics of the person–environment relationship; (b) coping is a process that changes as a situation unfolds; and (c) coping is multidimensional, including problem- and emotion-focused functions, approach–avoidance functions, and interpersonal and intrapersonal functions.

A representation of the Lazarus and Folkman (1984) model is shown in Figure 25-1. The theoretical model suggests an orderly and clearly articulated process. Actual coping processes are not nearly as orderly or as well articulated as the theoretical model suggests. Nevertheless, the model is a useful tool for imposing order and suggesting cause–effect relationships that can be examined through empirical research.

The coping process begins with a person and his or her beliefs, values, goals, and resources for coping, and an event or a condition that signals a change or a threatened change in the status of a valued goal. The person appraises the personal significance of the event or condition (primary appraisal) and his or her options for coping (secondary appraisal). Together, primary appraisal and secondary appraisal affect the particular emotion the person will experience (Lazarus, 1991b) and its intensity. The appraisal process also influences what the person does to cope with the distress and with the underlying problem. The mixture of coping processes the person uses is likely to change as an encounter unfolds because of shifts in the person–environment relationship. The shifts may be a result of adventitious changes in the environment, the effects of coping efforts directed at changing the environment, or coping efforts directed at altering the meaning of the event. Any shift in the person–environment relationship leads to a reappraisal of the situation, which in turn influences subsequent coping efforts.

This basic model has been useful in organizing research and testing relationships between coping and its antecedents and outcomes. However,

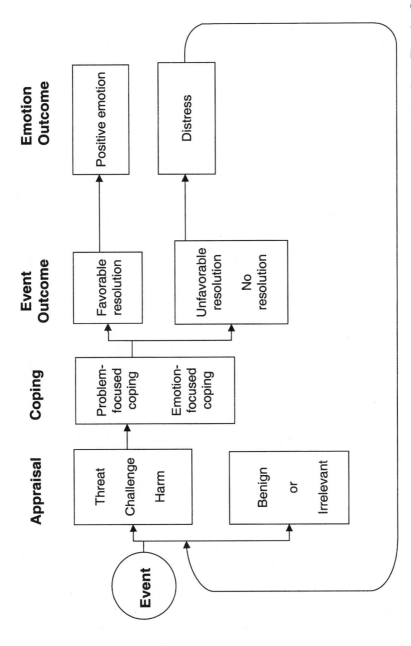

Figure 25-1. Original Stress and Coping Model. From Folkman (1997). Copyright 1997, with permission from Elsevier Science.

findings from a recently completed longitudinal study of coping in the caregiving partners of men with AIDS highlighted the need for an important modification to the model. Further, the study highlighted important questions that need to be addressed to adapt the model, including its revised form, to the study of bereavement.

A Challenge to the Model: Some Unexpected Findings

Between 1990 and 1997 my colleagues and I conducted a study of coping in the context of AIDS-related caregiving and bereavement. Participants in the study were 253 gay men who were the primary informal caregivers of partners with AIDS. We began with the premise that these caregivers had to be experiencing profound psychological stress. They were providing care to partners who mattered a great deal to them; the caregiving was likely to go on for many months, even years; and the disease was virulent, unpredictable, mostly uncontrollable, and ultimately it would claim the partner's life. The study was conducted during the years before the new treatments that may significantly prolong the lives of people with AIDS were available. Inevitably, this was also thus a study of bereavement. Nearly two thirds of the 253 caregivers who enrolled in the study became bereaved during their first two years of participation in the research, and 86% (n = 128) of those still in the study at the conclusion of the fifth year of participation were bereaved. If we could learn how these men managed to get through the process of caregiving, the time of their partner's death, and the subsequent period of bereavement, I believed we would learn some fundamental truths about the coping process.

As a study of bereavement, this study was unlike most others in several of its aspects. First, all of the deaths were expected and to a great extent planned for. Decisions about where the ill partner would die and how he would be memorialized were often made jointly by the caregiver and his partner, affairs were usually in order, and the formal health care providers usually respected wishes of the caregivers and their partners regarding treatment decisions. Most of the ill partners wanted to die at home, and most did (Cooke et al., 1998).

Second, prebereavement data were collected from all participants in bimonthly interviews. On average, participants were interviewed approximately seven times before their partners' deaths.

Third, interviews were conducted with all the newly bereaved caregivers soon after their partner's death, usually within two weeks of the partner's death, often within just a few days. A second interview was conducted two weeks later. These interviews were open-ended interviews and transcribed verbatim.

Fourth, the study included only men, and these men were middle-aged. The average age was about 39 when they entered the study. These men became bereaved off-time—in other words, at a time of life when most people are establishing relationships and building futures together. Many participants commented on this off-time quality, saying that burying a partner at this time of their lives was unnatural.

Finally, family caregivers of loved ones with terminal illnesses, such as cancer or Alzheimer's disease, usually do not have the same disease as the care recipient. In the case of AIDS-related bereavement, many of the bereaved are themselves infected with HIV. A number of HIV+ caregivers in our study, for example, wondered who would take care of them when their own disease progressed (Folkman, Chesney, & Christopher-Richards, 1994a).

We interviewed participants bimonthly for two years and semi-annually for three subsequent years. Interviews included assessments of domains called for by the model, including daily stress, coping resources (optimism, social support, religious beliefs), coping, and mental and physical health outcomes. The methods for the study are described in detail elsewhere (Folkman, 1997; Folkman, Chesney, Collette, Boccellari, & Cooke, 1996; Folkman, Chesney, Cooke, Boccellari, & Collette, 1994b; Moskowitz, Folkman, Collette, & Vittinghoff, 1996; Park & Folkman, 1997).

The study design allowed us to observe changes in mood during caregiving, at the time of the partners' deaths, and during the subsequent period of postbereavement. The findings regarding mood were rich. Not surprisingly, we found high levels of psychological distress. Throughout caregiving, participants' levels of depressive symptomatology, assessed with the Centers for Epidemiological Studies—Depression Measure (Radloff, 1977) were typically more than one standard deviation above the norm in the general community, rising to two standard deviations above the norm at the time of the ill partner's death (Folkman et al., 1996). At seven months following the partner's death, mean scores for depressive symptoms were still one standard deviation above the general community norm (Folkman et al., 1996), and the scores were virtually unchanged three years later (Moskowitz, Acree, & Folkman, 1998). This pattern is consistent with that reported in studies of the conjugally bereaved (e.g., Mullan, 1992; Norris & Murrell, 1990; Thompson, Gallagher, Cover, Gilewski, & Peterson, 1989; Zisook & Shuchter, 1986).

In contrast to the findings regarding negative mood, the findings regarding positive mood were startlingly different than what we had expected. With the exception of the weeks immediately surrounding the death of the partner, caregivers reported levels of positive psychological states that were high throughout caregiving and bereavement (Folkman, 1997). Our study included two measures of positive psychological states, the Positive States of Mind Scale (Horowitz, Adler, & Kegeles, 1988) and a modified version of the Bradburn (1969) positive affect scale. Except during the period surrounding the death of the partner, caregivers' reports of positive states of mind were comparable to those reported by Horowitz et al. (1988) in their community sample, and the frequency of positive affect reported on the Bradburn scale was comparable to the frequency of negative affect. We did not measure intensity or duration of affect, but that the frequencies of positive and negative affect were comparable (with the exception of the period surrounding death) was quite unexpected.

These findings raised several intriguing questions. First, what kinds of coping processes enable people to sustain positive affect during caregiving and bereavement? Second, does positive affect have adaptational significance in and of itself? A series of analyses from both quantitative and qualitative data helped us address these questions, and the findings led to a revision of the coping model.

Coping and Positive Affect

Although this volume focuses on bereavement, I include findings about caregiving as well as bereavement for two important reasons. First, many bereavements are preceded by a period of caregiving. Bereavement is not something that happens suddenly under these circumstances. It begins during caregiving, especially in diseases such as AIDS. Loss is not limited to the moment when the loved one dies. It begins much earlier. As one participant put it, "I'm losing him in bits and pieces. It's not like he's hit by a car and then gone. I lose him a little at a time, it's excruciating." The ways people maintain well-being while experiencing losses associated with caregiving may provide insight into the ways people cope with the ultimate loss, the death of the loved one.

We examined the relationship between coping and positive and negative affect using scales from the Ways of Coping (Moskowitz et al., 1996) and the modified Bradburn (1969) affect scales. This particular analysis included data at three months and one month before the death of the partner and three months and five months after the death of the partner. The findings indicated that two types of coping, active problem-focused coping and positive reappraisal, were especially important in maintaining positive affect.

Active problem-focused coping describes efforts to achieve specific, proximal goals. During caregiving, this type of coping was often directed at tasks such as changing bed linens, getting the ill partner to the clinic, or working out a problem with the insurance company. Active problem-focused coping was used more during caregiving than bereavement, and during caregiving, it was used most heavily during the month just before the partner died. It was inconsistently associated with lessened negative mood, but it was consistently associated with increased positive mood, controlling for the previous month's affect and for the other coping measures (Moskowitz et al., 1996).

We believe the reason active problem-focused coping has such a consistent relationship with positive affect is that its use gives the individual a sense of control in an illness context that usually makes people feel completely helpless. Further, when active problem-focused coping leads to a successful outcome, it also allows the individual to feel mastery, at least for the moment. This interpretation is consistent with Thompson's (Thompson, Nanni, & Levine, 1994) concept of central control versus consequential control. For the participants in this study, central control refers to control over the disease itself, and consequential control refers to the kinds of tasks that need attending to that follow from the illness. The disease was essentially not controllable, but the consequent caregiving tasks were.

Qualitative analyses also support this interpretation. Even during the hours surrounding the partner's death, which to the outsider might seem to be a period during which the caregiver is at his or her most helpless, caregivers reported many specific goals that they successfully achieved, such as giving the dying partner "permission to go," calling family members to the bedside, writing obituaries, and making arrangements for memorial services. Most caregivers, in fact, reported twice as many successes as they did failures with respect to achieving these goals, and usually the successes were accompanied by moments of positive affect (Stein, Folkman, Trabasso, & Richards, 1997).

The second type of coping associated with positive affect was positive reappraisal, which refers to cognitive strategies for reframing a situation to see it in a positive light (Moskowitz et al., 1996). Positive reappraisal was significantly and independently associated with increases in positive affect (Moskowitz et al., 1996).

We also assessed positive reappraisal as part of the final interview that was conducted at the conclusion of the participants' fifth year. We used a qualitative approach in which we asked bereaved participants to describe what they had learned from this whole period of their life, what they had gained, and how they felt different. These questions obviously pulled for positive as opposed to negative appraisals of the participants' experience. Nevertheless, the findings were interesting. The narratives were coded for the content and valence of statements about meaning. Of the 106 bereaved caregivers who completed this particular interview, 103 reported only positive meanings and 53 reported both positive and negative meanings or only negative meanings. The most frequently described meanings were similar to the kinds of positive meanings reported in other studies of bereavement and traumas (for review see Nolen-Hoeksema & Larson, 1999) and included positive appraisals of enhanced self-worth, strength, wisdom, and perspective. Nineteen people also said they no longer feared death.

Of greater interest than the content of the positive meanings was the fact that after taking into account psychosocial resources (social support, optimism), coping (assessed with the Ways of Coping) and health, meaning, which was scored simply as all positive meanings versus mixed meanings or only negative meanings, accounted for significant variance in positive affect, but not depressive symptoms, at the time of the final interview (Folkman, 1998).

Religious and spiritual beliefs and experiences through which people find existential meaning also were related to positive affect, but the relationship was complex. The qualitative data showed they supported positive affect, but the quantitative data showed they were also related to distress. These beliefs and experiences were described by participants in narratives given during interviews two and four weeks following their partners' deaths. An analysis of the narratives of 125 participants showed that 54% made explicit and spontaneous references to spiritual phenomena (Richards & Folkman, 1997). These phenomena included beliefs in spiritualism, a higher power, and oneness; a belief in the persistence of the relationship with the deceased; public and private rituals; and spiritual social support.

The complex relationship between spiritual beliefs and emotion was also observed in a study of religious participation and importance in parents who lost an infant to sudden infant death syndrome (SIDS; McIntosh, Silver, & Wortman, 1993). McIntosh et al. examined religious participation and importance in parents who lost an infant to SIDS. They were interested in understanding the role of religious participation and importance in relation to the cognitive processes associated with adjustment to bereavement. McIntosh et al. found that religious importance was related to working through the loss, which in turn was related to increased distress three weeks after the loss but decreased distress 18 months later. Religious importance could therefore be seen as causing distress, which was necessary for the longer term adjustment to the loss. Others have noted that spiritual and religious beliefs are often activated at the time of bereavement (Bowlby, 1980; Parkes, 1993; Parkes & Brown, 1972; Parkes & Weiss, 1983; Shuchter & Zisook, 1993). If nothing else, these studies illustrate that religious and spiritual aspects of coping with loss are multifaceted and multifunctioned (Pargament, 1997).

The Functions of Positive Affect During Caregiving and Bereavement

The pattern of cooccurrence of positive and negative affect suggested that positive affect may have adaptational significance in the coping process (Folkman & Moskowitz, 2000). The coping processes that generate positive affect and the positive affect itself appear to help sustain renewed problem- and emotion-focused coping efforts in dealing with the chronic stressful condition. Positive reappraisal processes, for example, can help the individual redefine and focus on positive meaning, which can help motivate the individual to reengage in efforts to cope with the ongoing stressor, and positive affect can energize goal-directed problem-focused behavior (Emmons & Kaiser, 1996). The mastery and control that are reinforced by accomplishing seemingly simple tasks can, in the midst of a stressful condition that is not within the person's control—as in the case of caregivers who could still administer good care to partners dying of a disease that could not be stopped—help strengthen resolve to keep providing that care.

Findings from our study also suggested that positive emotions may provide an important psychological time-out when distress becomes particularly intense. When we began our study, interviews focused on stressful events related to caregiving and other negative aspects of the caregiving situation. It was not long before we heard from our participants that they also wanted to tell us about positive events in their lives. Further, they wanted to end their interviews on a positive note.

We dealt with both issues by adding questions to the bimonthly interview concerning the positive meanings of caregiving and by concluding the interview with a question that asked participants to describe a positive meaningful event, something that helped them get through the day (Folkman, Moskowitz, Ozer, & Park, 1997). Reports of these positive events were not a rare occurrence. In fact, participants were able to report a positive meaningful event that helped them get through the day at nearly every occasion—specifically, in 99.5% of the 1794 interviews that asked about them (Folkman, 1997).

A content analysis of a sample of these events indicated that they were for the most part ordinary events of daily life such as getting positive feedback at work, the ill partner's expression of appreciation for something the caregiver did, seeing a beautiful sunset, or enjoying a good movie. These events not only provided respite, but they may also have helped restore psychosocial resources, including perceived social support, self-esteem, and hope (Folkman et al., 1997). This phenomenon is consistent with findings from studies of other intensely stressful contexts (e.g., Cohen & Hoberman, 1983; Hobfoll & Lilly, 1993; Wells, Hobfoll, & Lavin, 1999). The negative psychological states associated with significant and enduring stress may actually motivate people—consciously or unconsciously—to search for and create positive psychological states to gain relief, if only momentary, from the distress. The ability of caregivers to generate these positive events may help explain why the incidence of diagnosed clinical depression during any six-month period was no greater than in the general population.

That positive affect and emotion may have adaptational significance in the coping process is consistent with the social–functional interpretation of emotional expression (Barrett & Campos, 1987; Bowlby, 1980; Keltner, 1996; Lazarus, 1991a; chapter 22, this volume). According to this interpretation, emotion mediates the individual's adaptation to the social environment and to stressful life events by informing others of one's current state and evoking responses in others that directly influence well-being, relationship satisfaction, and adjustment.

Bonanno and Keltner (1997) tested this hypothesis by studying the facial expression of positive and negative emotion in conjugally bereaved adults six months after their loss, and their relation to grief-specific symptoms at 14 and 25 months after bereavement. The expressions were observed while participants discussed their relationship with the deceased spouse. Bonanno and Keltner (1997; see also chapter 22, this volume) found that the frequency of participants' facial expressions of positive emotion was comparable to their expression of negative emotion. This pattern parallels the one we observed in bereaved gay men at approximately the same point postbereavement (Folkman, 1997). Further, facial expressions of negative emotion at 6 months predicted increased grief at 25 months, and facial expressions of positive emotions predicted reduced grief at 25 months. Bonanno and Keltner suggested that the minimization of negative emotion may allow for more active problem-focused coping and facilitate supportive responses from others. They also suggest that the expression of positive emotion may signal a willingness or an ability to maintain contact with the social environment.

REVISED COPING THEORY

Our findings regarding positive affect and the coping processes that support it led to the revision of the coping model that is shown in Figure 25-2. The revision highlights the importance of positive affect in the coping process. The original model does not exclude positive affect, but its role is relatively incidental. In the original model, positive affect can be elicited during challenge appraisals in the form, for example, of excitement or eagerness, and in the outcome appraisal process when the outcome of the stressful encounter is favorable. The revised model, in contrast, gives positive affect multiple and important roles. Positive affect is included as an outcome of unresolved chronic stress that is prompted by the need to experience positive well-being in the midst of distress, it is maintained by a class of meaning-based coping processes that is distinct from those that regulate distress, and it functions to sustain coping over the long term.

APPLICATION OF REVISED COPING
THEORY TO BEREAVEMENT

One of the major reasons to conduct a longitudinal study of bereavement is to identify predictors of outcomes. This information is needed by both the lay person and clinician so that they can capitalize on factors

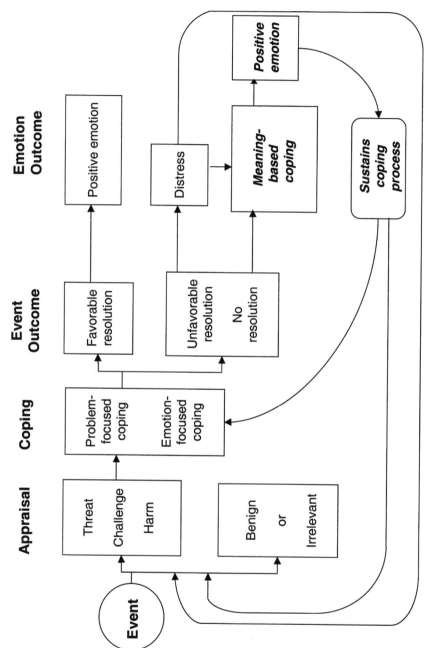

Figure 25-2. Revised Coping Model.

that facilitate adjustment and recovery and intervene with factors that impede adjustment and recovery. Identifying predictive factors is operationalized in many studies in a relatively simple way, through the group membership of study participants. Thus some studies investigate whether being young or old, male or female, or a spouse, parent, or child makes a difference in the response to bereavement (for review see Sanders, 1993). Other studies introduce additional moderating variables such as the quality of the relationship, childhood parental loss, prebereavement health, and personality disposition (cf. Sanders, 1993). Dispositional styles of coping, such as Miller's (Miller, Brody, & Summerton, 1988) monitoring–blunting style would also be included in this category. These variables are all technically appropriate as predictors because they existed as stable aspects of the person or the environment before bereavement.

Unlike age, personality disposition, or prebereavement parental loss, coping processes are not stable aspects of the person or the environment. Only to the extent that a particular type of coping represents a stable response to diverse stressors over time is that type of coping likely to function as a moderator. Positive reappraisal and cognitive escape–avoidance, for example, tend to be relatively stable types of coping (Carver, Scheier, & Weintraub, 1989; Folkman, Lazarus, Gruen, & DeLongis, 1986) that come closer to fitting the definition of coping style. Most types of coping, however, especially problem-focused coping and coping that involves the use of social support, are influenced by the immediate demands of the context.

Despite the fact that coping variables that are contextual do not behave like traditional predictor variables, their inclusion in research can provide important insight into the processes through which people adjust to and recover from bereavement. Lessons that we learned while conducting our longitudinal study of bereavement lead me to believe the predictive power of coping in studies of bereavement can be increased substantially if we address three important issues specific to bereavement: the nature of the focal stressful encounter, supplemental measurement approaches, and the nature of the outcome.

The Focal Stressful Encounter

We studied coping during bereavement in much the same way that we studied coping during caregiving. During caregiving, we asked participants to describe the most stressful event of the previous week related to their partner's death, and after the partner's death we asked for the most stressful event related to that event. Following the description of the stressful event, we asked participants to tell us how they coped with it. This method worked beautifully in the context of caregiving, in which the stressful demands of providing care for a person with a complicated and rapidly changing disease course are immediate, proximal, and usually clearly delimited. The stressful demands associated with loss, in contrast, are often existential and not easily defined by or reflected in the most stressful encounter of the previous week. During the early months of bereavement, the approach continued to work well because there were many stressful events related to settling the affairs of the deceased. Once this phase diminished in its prominence, the contextual approach did not work very well. Participants were often more involved in existential issues, and not in specific bereavement-related stressful encounters.

In retrospect, I believe we would have learned more if we had embedded our approach within one of the existing theories of bereavement. This would have led to reports of adaptationally significant stressful experiences rather than just the most stressful encounter of the week. Many kinds of adaptive tasks are defined in various theories of bereavement (for reviews see Nolen-Hoeksema & Larson, 1999; Stroebe & Schut, 1999). These tasks can include severing the relationship with the deceased, as described in psychoanalytic theory (e.g., Freud, 1917/1957), attachment theory (e.g., Bowlby, 1980; Parkes & Weiss, 1983), and the Two-Track Model (Rubin, 1981). Weiss (1988) for example, defines three specific adaptive tasks involved in this severing process: cognitive acceptance, emotional acceptance, and identity change.

Other theoretical approaches define adaptive tasks in terms of dealing with assumptions that are shattered by the loss, making sense of it, and, for some, ultimately finding meaning and purpose in it (e.g., Janoff-Bulman, 1989; Neimeyer, 1998). Still other approaches focus on adaptive tasks associated with a range of psychosocial transitions that are set into motion by loss ranging from changes in seemingly trivial everyday routines, to major life changes such as finding new housing or a job, to redefining one's self (Nolen-Hoeksema & Larson, 1999). Stroebe and Schut (1999, in press) combined many of these elements in their dual process model, which includes two orientations: loss-orientation, which refers to the processing of the loss experience itself, and restoration–orientation, which refers to secondary sources of stress, such as psychosocial transitions, and how they are coped with.

It is up to the researcher to decide which model is most appropriate for a particular study. Regardless of the model, the goal would be to elicit accounts of stress that are related to the adaptational tasks specified by the model. The adaptational tasks can be classified according to the theoretical model, and individual differences in coping with them should help account for bereavement-related outcomes, especially those that are affect-based.

Supplemental Measurement Approaches

The shift from specific stressful encounters to adaptationally significant stressful experiences has consequences for measurement. Coping within specific stressful encounters is often assessed with questionnaires that list coping strategies, such as the Ways of Coping (Folkman & Lazarus, 1988; Folkman, Lazarus, Dunkel-Schetter, DeLongis, & Gruen, 1986); the COPE (Carver et al., 1989); and the Coping Inventory for Stressful Situations (Endler & Parker, 1990a, 1990b). This kind of questionnaire is popular because of the relative ease of administration and analysis (for review see Schwarzer & Schwarzer, 1996). Although this approach has many methodological problems (Coyne & Racioppo, 2000; Stone, Greenberg, Kennedy-Moore, & Newman, 1991), it has been helpful in providing researchers with a common vocabulary of coping and some basic information on the nature of coping—that it is influenced by contextual factors, that it is multidimensional and dynamic, and that it is strongly related to affectively based outcomes, especially negative affect.

Coping strategy questionnaires, however, were not designed to assess coping with more general, existential kinds of stress that have to do with the adaptational tasks described by bereavement theorists. We found the richest material on coping with the broader, more existential kinds of stress in narrative accounts provided by participants. Qualitative analysis of bereavement narratives, for example, provided the important insight into the use of spirituality in coping with loss that was described earlier in this chapter. This use of spirituality was specific to adaptive tasks having to do with what Stroebe and Schut (1999) have called loss orientation.

The bereavement narratives also revealed thoughts and actions that caregivers who were by their partner's bedside at the time of death used to ease the pain at those specific moments. Although each account of a death was unique because of differences in the details of how the ill partner died and because of the unique qualities of each caregiver who told his story, several ways of coping were common in many of the narratives. The caregiver assured his partner of his love, told his partner that it was all right to die, allowed himself to feel relief when death finally came and the partner's suffering was ended, and took comfort in the deceased partner's peaceful appearance. Notice that these coping processes all supported positive affect at the moment of the partner's death. These kinds of thoughts and actions are clearly not captured on typical coping checklists. They emerged from the men's narratives, their stories of what happened.

Finally, adaptive tasks having to do with what Stroebe and Schut (1999) referred to as restoration–orientation are unlikely to be captured by the typical probe asking about a stressful event. Restoration–orientation coping is likely to involve proactive thoughts and actions that have to do with future-oriented planning and goals. The work of Aspinwall and Taylor (1997), who distinguish proactive coping from coping with extant stressor events, is to a certain degree consistent with the notion of restoration-orientated coping. The proactive coping described by Aspinwall and Taylor focuses on how people avoid and offset potential stressors. They stated that proactive coping requires different skills than does coping with extant stressors. Restoration-oriented coping is probably more complex than the type of proactive coping Aspinwall and Taylor envision, because the person engaged in restoration-oriented coping is doing so as a consequence of the extant stressor of loss and its sequelae. Thus, restoration-oriented coping involves dealing productively with extant stressors as well as the proactive coping described by Aspinwall and Taylor. The coping processes associated with restoration—orientation have yet to be described and catalogued. An important first step is to ask people to tell stories about this aspect of recovery from loss.

The Issue of Outcomes

In many ways, the design of our study of caregiving and bereavement seemed quite close to the standard recommended by many bereavement researchers (see Stroebe, Stroebe, & Hansson, 1993). The study was longitudinal, commencing before bereavement. We had comparison groups of HIV+ and HIV− nonbereaved caregivers, and we had an HIV+ comparison group of participants who were in relationships with healthy partners. The comparison group design allowed us to specify effects as a result of caregiving, bereavement, and HIV. We repeatedly assessed variables relevant to the theoretical model, including stress, coping, mood, and physical health (Folkman, 1997; Folkman et al., 1996).

The abundance of data created many options concerning the characterization of bereavement outcomes and ways to "predict" or "explain" these outcomes. Each characterization was scientifically legitimate, and each had different implications for interpreting our findings.

There are two major dimensions to the characterization of the psychological response to bereavement: content and form. The content has to do with the type of psychological response people have to bereavement, and it is the dimension that is usually emphasized in studies of response to bereavement. Often previous research on the course of grief, such as that described by Shuchter and Zisook (1993), guides the selection of variables that are to be examined. Studies that focus on the content of psychological response usually chart such outcomes over time (for a review see Byrne & Raphael, 1997). These studies often include a comparison with matched nonbereaved individuals so that the effects associated with bereavement can be more clearly observed. An example is a study by Byrne and Raphael (1997), who investigated the psychological symptoms experienced by recently widowed older men. They had a comparison group of elderly married men. The goal of these authors was to characterize bereavement in terms of depression, anxiety, and loneliness. They found that bereavement was manifest more in anxiety symptoms than in symptoms of loneliness or depression.

Much less attention is given to the form of the outcome. By form, I mean whether the outcome refers to a point or points in time or instead to the pattern of the outcome over time. Most studies just focus on the status of an outcome at one or more points in time. The determination of how the person is doing can be based on an a priori standard derived from some notion about what constitutes appropriate or normal levels of the outcome for a given time following bereavement, by comparing the bereaved individual with nonbereaved individuals, or by comparing the bereaved individual with others who became bereaved at about the same time. This is the simplest approach to characterizing bereavement response, but it is also the least informative.

Another way of looking at the response is according to the amount of change that has occurred during a given interval. People vary in the amount of distress they experience during the weeks immediately following bereavement. Two individuals may have the same scores at Time 2, but very different scores at Time 1. This raises an interesting question concerning the quality of recovery. Is the person who began with a higher score at Time 1, who therefore shows a greater decline in distress, doing better or worse than the person whose decline is less because he began with a lower level at Time 1? The answer may depend on the theoretical model. Those who hold that healthy recovery requires an intense distress reaction might say that the individual who began with the high level of distress had a healthier recovery than the person who began and ended with a relatively low level of distress. Others who argue that a high level of distress is not a necessary condition of recovery would say that the person with the smaller amount of change was doing better. In either case, both the intercept (the Time 1 score) and the degree of change (the Time 2 score, controlling for Time 1) contain important information.

A third approach, which depends on having at least three measurement points, is to look at the shape of slope of decline. Is there a steady linear decline in scores, or is the pattern irregular? In our study, in which we assessed depressed mood bimonthly for two years and semi-annually for three additional years, the modal pattern postbereavement was not the idealized steady, linear decline at the individual level (Moskowitz, Acree, & Folkman, 2000). We saw people whose drop in scores in depressed mood occurred relatively early in their bereavement process, others for whom the drop occurred relatively late, and still others who had erratic patterns with increases and decreases occurring throughout the measurement period. The rapid decline and the delayed decline can be captured statistically quite simply with a mean score for depressed mood over occasions. This score will give the overall sense of how depressed the person was over time. But a mean score does not capture the erratic quality of the third pattern.

What is needed is an approach that captures distinctions among trajectory patterns. This can be accomplished by classifying individual trajectories into categories that describe common variations in bereavement response. Although this approach still does not address the evaluation issues regarding which categories describe healthier or unhealthier bereavement response patterns, it does provide a way for representing what may be clinically meaningful variations in recovery patterns that can be used to enrich the evaluation process.

CONCLUSION

Bereavement confronts people with some of the most stressful adaptational challenges that humans experience. The challenge of understanding what bereaved individuals actually do to cope day in and day out as they try to meet these challenges provides an extraordinarily compelling agenda for coping research. Many of the coping challenges are profound and meaningful, and others are mundane and ordinary. All are a part of dealing with loss and getting on with one's life.

In this chapter I have described a theory of coping that, if properly adapted to the special characteristics of bereavement, should help define questions and interpret findings, thereby lending coherence to the emerging body of knowledge on coping and bereavement. A key element of this model is the inclusion of positive indicators of adjustment and recovery and processes that support the positive indicators. The model needs to be tailored for use in the context of bereavement by giving special attention to the definition of the focal stressful encounter, broadening assessment procedures to include narrative as well as quantitative approaches, and giving thought to the form as well as the content of the outcome variables. Research based on the adapted model should increase our understanding of bereaved individuals' appraisals of what it is that requires coping during bereavement, the various ways people cope with these appraised tasks over time, and how all of this helps explain adjustment to and recovery from loss. Ideally, results will serve the dual purposes of enriching theory and contributing to more effective clinical practice with bereaved individuals.

REFERENCES

Aspinwall, L. G., & Taylor, S. E. (1997). A stitch in time: Self-regulation and proactive coping. *Psychological Bulletin, 21*, 417–436.

Barrett, K. C., & Campos, J. J. (1987). Perspectives on emotional development II: A functionalist approach to emotions. In J. D. Osofsky (Ed.), *Handbook of infant development* (2nd ed., pp. 555–578). New York: Wiley.

Bonanno, G. A., & Keltner, D. (1997). Facial expressions of emotion and the course of conjugal bereavement. *Journal of Abnormal Psychology, 106,* 126–137.

Bowlby, J. (1980). *Attachment and loss. Vol. 3. Loss: Sadness and depression.* New York: Basic Books.

Bradburn, N. M. (1969). *The structure of psychological well-being.* Chicago: Aldine.

Byrne, G. J. A., & Raphael, B. (1997). The psychological symptoms of conjugal bereavement in elderly men over the first 13 months. *International Journal of Geriatric Psychiatry, 12,* 241–251.

Carver, C. S., Scheier, M. F., & Weintraub, J. K. (1989). Assessing coping strategies: A theoretically based approach. *Journal of Personality and Social Psychology, 56,* 267–283.

Cohen, S., & Hoberman, H. M. (1983). Positive events and social supports as buffers of life change stress. *Journal of Applied Social Psychology, 13,* 99–125.

Cooke, M., Gourlay, L., Collette, L., Boccellari, A., Chesney, M. A., & Folkman, S. (1998). Informal caregivers and the intention to hasten AIDS-related death. *Archives of Internal Medicine, 158,* 69–75.

Coyne, J. C., & Racioppo, M. W. (2000). Never the twain shall meet? *American Psychologist, 55,* 655–664.

Emmons, R. A., & Kaiser, H. A. (1996). Goal orientation and emotional well-being: Linking goals and affect through the self. In L. L. Martin & A. Tesser (Eds.), *Striving and Feeling* (pp. 79–98). Mahwah, NJ: Erlbaum.

Endler, N. S., & Parker, J. D. A. (1990a). *Coping Inventory for Stressful Situations.* Toronto: Multi Health Systems.

Endler, N. S., & Parker, J. D. A. (1990b). The multidimensional assessment of coping: A critical evaluation. *Journal of Personality and Social Psychology, 58,* 844–854.

Folkman, S. (1997). Positive psychological states and coping with severe stress. *Social Science and Medicine, 45,* 1207–1221.

Folkman, S. (1998, May). *New perspectives on coping.* Paper presented at the Second Dutch Conference on Psychology and Health, Kerkrade, The Netherlands.

Folkman, S., Chesney, M. A., & Christopher-Richards, A. (1994a). Stress and coping in partners of men with AIDS. *Psychiatric Clinics of North America, 17,* 35–55.

Folkman, S., Chesney, M. A., Collette, L., Boccellari, A., & Cooke, M. (1996). Post-bereavement depressive mood and its pre-bereavement predictors in HIV+ and HIV− gay men. *Journal of Personality and Social Psychology, 70,* 336–348.

Folkman, S., Chesney, M. A., Cooke, M., Boccellari, A., & Collette, L. (1994b). Caregiver burden in HIV+ and HIV− partners of men with AIDS. *Journal of Consulting and Clinical Psychology, 62,* 746–756.

Folkman, S., & Lazarus, R. S. (1988). *Ways of Coping Questionnaire.* Palo Alto, CA: Consulting Psychologists Press.

Folkman, S., Lazarus, R. S., Dunkel-Schetter, C., DeLongis, A., & Gruen, R.

(1986). The dynamics of a stressful encounter: cognitive appraisal, coping and encounter outcomes. *Journal of Personality and Social Psychology, 50,* 992–1003.

Folkman, S., Lazarus, R. S., Gruen, R., & DeLongis, A. (1986). Appraisal, coping, health status, and psychological symptoms. *Journal of Personality and Social Psychology, 50,* 571–579.

Folkman, S., & Moskowitz, J. T. (2000). Positive affect and the other side of coping. *American Psychologist, 55,* 647–654.

Folkman, S., Moskowitz, J. T., Ozer, E. M., & Park, C. L. (1997). Positive meaningful events and coping in the context of HIV/AIDS. In B. H. Gottlieb (Ed.), *Coping with chronic stress* (pp. 293–314). New York: Plenum Press.

Freud, S. (1957). Mourning and melancholia. In J. Strachey (Ed.), *Standard edition of the complete work of Sigmund Freud.* London: Hogarth Press. (Original work published 1917)

Glick, I. O., Weiss, R. S., & Parkes, C. M. (1974). *The first year of bereavement.* New York: Wiley.

Hobfoll, S. E., & Lilly, R. S. (1993). Resource conservation as a strategy for community psychology. *Journal of Community Psychology, 21,* 128–148.

Horowitz, M., Adler, N., & Kegeles, S. (1988). A scale for measuring the occurrence of positive states of mind: A preliminary report. *Psychosomatic Medicine, 50,* 477–483.

Jacobs, S., Kasl, S., Schaefer, C., & Ostfeld, A. (1994). Conscious and unconscious coping with loss. *Psychosomatic Medicine, 56,* 557–563.

Janoff-Bulman, R. (1989). Assumptive worlds and the stress of traumatic events: Applications of the schema construct. *Social Cognition, 7,* 113–136.

Keltner, D. (1996). Facial expressions of emotion and personality. In C. Malatesta-Magai & S. H. McFadden (Eds.), *Handbook of emotion, aging, and the lifecourse* (pp. 385–402). New York: Academic Press.

Kübler-Ross, E. (1969). *On death and dying.* New York: Macmillan.

Lazarus, R. S. (1991a). Cognition and motivation in emotion. *American Psychologist, 46,* 352–367.

Lazarus, R. S. (1991b). *Emotion and adaptation.* New York: Oxford University Press.

Lazarus, R. S., & Folkman, S. (1984). *Stress, appraisal, and coping.* New York: Springer.

McIntosh, D. N., Silver, R., & Wortman, C. B. (1993). Religion's role in adjustment to a negative life event: Coping with the loss of a child. *Journal of Personality and Social Psychology, 65,* 812–821.

Menninger, K. (1963). *The vital balance: The life process in mental health and illness.* New York: Viking.

Miller, S. M., Brody, D. S., & Summerton, J. (1988). Styles of coping with threat: Implications for health. *Journal of Personality and Social Psychology, 54,* 142–148.

Moskowitz, J., Acree, M., & Folkman, S. (1998, August). *Depression and AIDS-*

related bereavement: A 3-year follow-up. New perspectives on depression in AIDS-related caregiving and bereavement. Paper presented at the Annual Meeting of the American Psychological Association, San Francisco.

Moskowitz, J., Acree, M., & Folkman, S. (2000). *Capturing the bereavement response*. Manuscript in preparation.

Moskowitz, J. T., Folkman, S., Collette, L., & Vittinghoff, E. (1996). Coping and mood during AIDS-related caregiving and bereavement. *Annals of Behavioral Medicine, 18,* 49–57.

Mullan, J. T. (1992). The bereaved caregiver: A prospective study of changes in well-being. *The Gerontologist, 32,* 673–683.

Neimeyer, R. A. (1998). *Lessons of loss: A guide to coping.* Raleigh, NC: McGraw-Hill.

Nolen-Hoeksema, S., & Larson, J. (1999). *Coping with loss.* Mahwah, NJ: Erlbaum.

Norris, F. H., & Murrell, S. A. (1990). Social support, life events, and stress and modifiers of adjustment to bereavement by older adults. *Psychology and Aging, 5,* 429–436.

Pargament, K. I. (1997). *The psychology of religion and coping.* New York: Guilford Press.

Park, C. L., & Folkman, S. (1997). Stability and change in the psychosocial resources in caregivers of men with terminal-stage AIDS. *Journal of Personality, 65,* 421–447.

Parkes, C. M. (1993). Bereavement as a psychosocial transition: Processes of adaptation to change. In M. Stroebe, W. Stroebe, & R. O. Hansson (Eds.), *Handbook of Bereavement: Theory, research and intervention* (pp. 91–101). New York: Cambridge University Press.

Parkes, C. M., & Brown, R. (1972). Health after bereavement: A controlled study of young Boston widows and widowers. *Psychosomatic Medicine, 34,* 449–461.

Parkes, C. M., & Weiss, R. S. (1983). *Recovery from bereavement.* New York: Basic Books.

Radloff, L. S. (1977). The CES-D Scale: A self-report depression scale for research in the general population. *Applied Psychological Measurement, 1,* 385–401.

Richards, A., & Folkman, S. (1997). Spiritual aspects of bereavement among partners of men who died from AIDS. *Death Studies, 21,* 527–552.

Rubin, S. (1981). A two-track model of bereavement: Theory and application in research. *American Journal of Orthopsychiatry, 51,* 101–109.

Sanders, C. M. (1993). Risk factors in bereavement outcomes. In M. Stroebe, W. Stroebe, & R. O. Hansson (Eds.), *Handbook of Bereavement* (pp. 255–267). New York: Cambridge University Press.

Schwarzer, R., & Schwarzer, C. (1996). A critical survey of coping instruments. In M. Zeidner & N. S. Endler (Eds.), *Handbook of coping* (pp. 107–132). New York: John Wiley.

Shuchter, S. R., & Zisook, S. (1993). The course of normal grief. In M. S. Stroebe,

W. Stroebe, & R. O. Hansson (Eds.), *Handbook of Bereavement* (pp. 23–43). New York: Cambridge University Press.

Stein, N., Folkman, S., Trabasso, T., & Richards, T. A. (1997). Appraisal and goal processes as predictors of well-being in bereaved caregivers. *Journal of Personality and Social Psychology, 72,* 872–884.

Stone, A. A., Greenberg, M. A., Kennedy-Moore, E., & Newman, M. G. (1991). Self-report, situation-specific coping questionnaires: What are they measuring? *Journal of Personality and Social Psychology, 61,* 648–658.

Stroebe, M., & Schut, H. (1999). The dual process model of coping with bereavement: Rationale and description. *Death Studies, 23,* 197–224.

Stroebe, M., & Schut, H. (in press). Meaning making in the dual process model of coping with bereavement. In R. A. Neimeyer (Ed.), *Meaning reconstruction and the experience of loss.* Washington, DC: American Psychological Association.

Stroebe, M. S., Stroebe, W., & Hansson, R. O. (Eds.). (1993). *Handbook of bereavement.* New York: Cambridge University Press.

Thompson, L. W., Gallagher, D., Cover, H., Gilewski, M., & Peterson, J. (1989). Effects of bereavement on symptoms of psychopathology in older men and women. In D. A. Lund (Ed.), *Older bereaved spouses: Research with practical applications* (pp. 17–24). New York: Taylor & Francis/Hemisphere.

Thompson, S. C., Nanni, C., & Levine, A. (1994). Primary versus secondary and disease versus consequence-related control in HIV-positive men. *Journal of Personality and Social Psychology, 67,* 540–547.

Vaillant, G. E. (1977). *Adaptation to life.* Boston: Little, Brown.

Weiss, R. S. (1988). Loss and recovery. *Journal of Social Issues, 44,* 37–52.

Wells, J. D., Hobfoll, S. E., & Lavin, J. (1999). When it rains it pours; The greater impact of resource loss compared to gain on psychological distress. *Personality and Social Psychology Bulletin, 25,* 1172–1182.

Wortman, C., & Silver, R. (1987). Coping with irrevocable loss. In G. R. Van den Bos & B. K. Bryant (Eds.), *Cataclysms, crises, and catastrophies: psychology in action* (Vol. 6, pp. 189–235). Washington, DC: American Psychological Association.

Wortman, C., & Silver, R. (1989). The myths of coping with loss. *Journal of Consulting and Clinical Psychology, 57,* 349–357.

Wortman, C. B., Silver, R. C., & Kessler, R. C. (1993). The meaning of loss and adjustment to bereavement. In M. S. Stroebe, W. Stroebe, & R. O. Hansson (Eds.), *Handbook of bereavement* (pp. 349–366). New York: Cambridge University Press.

Zeidner, M., & Endler, N. S. (1996). *Handbook of Coping: Theory, Research, Applications.* New York: John Wiley & Sons.

Zisook, S., & Shuchter, S. R. (1986). The last four years of widowhood. *Psychiatric Annals, 15,* 288–294.

VI

CARE: INTERVENING IN THE COPING PROCESS

26

PSYCHOTHERAPEUTIC AND PHARMACOLOGICAL INTERVENTION FOR BEREAVED PERSONS

BEVERLEY RAPHAEL, CHRISTINE MINKOV, AND MATTHEW DOBSON

The questions that arise about intervention for bereaved people are multiple. The very first of these must be whether "intervention" is needed at all. Research and study of bereavement phenomenology, including reactions following many different kinds of deaths, has made it quite clear that for the majority of people, grief, although psychologically painful and distressing, is a normal process reflecting both the strengths and value of human attachments and the capacity to adapt to loss and adversity. The vast majority of people not only grieve "normally" but adapt to the loss and its consequences. Indeed, as Vaillant (1988) has pointed out, many of the internalizations that occur in relation to the loss of a loved one contribute positively to who we are as people. The learning associated with grieving and coming to terms with loss may also contribute positively to the ways in which we deal with other adversity and with change in our lives. Thus it must be stated at the outset that there can be *no justification for routine intervention* for bereaved persons in terms of therapeutic modalities—either psychotherapeutic or pharmacological—because grief is not a disease.

At the outset, however, response to those grieving is a basic human reaction of compassion, empathy with another's loss, the wish to comfort. This outreach, this acknowledgment, of the universality of grief is *not* a psychological or medical intervention. Yet it is automatically the first contact with bereaved individuals and part of all that may be done to comfort and assist those who have lost a loved one. Formal interventions for bereaved persons may be conceptualized and implemented from many sources. Any consideration of possible interventions also needs to take into account both the spectrum of interventions and the scientific evidence that validates their potential effectiveness. It must be clear what it is hoped that interventions will achieve: their aims and goals; the rationale for identifying these; and the basis for believing that the techniques and actions proposed will achieve better outcomes. The requirement "first to do no harm" should be paramount.

In this time of accountability it is critical that interventions for bereaved persons address these issues. There is also the need to consider the ethics of providing some therapeutic modality at such a time, which is often considered both a private and personal time, both spiritual and secular. It is a time of cultural rite and social presentation, of gradually facing reality, of challenge to belief and of finality. Thus it is a time when providing any intervention must be for specific purposes to which those receiving these can provide a knowledgeable consent and which are understood and provided in appropriate social, cultural and personal contexts.

With regard to the spectrum of interventions it is useful to consider Mrazek and Haggerty's (1994) conceptualization of the preventive, treatment, and maintenance interventions that may be needed and judgment concerning these in terms of the evidence of potential effectiveness, where this exists. For instance, significant interventions have been provided for bereaved persons who have been determined on the basis of scientific studies to be at high risk of pathological outcomes, and such interventions could be classified as preventive.

In this model preventive interventions may be *universal*—for the whole population; *selective*—for groups established to be at higher risk, for instance those bereaved by unexpected untimely deaths or those lacking social support; and *indicated*—those for bereaved individuals already demonstrating very high and continuing levels of bereavement-related symptomatology. There have been interventions of demonstrated effectiveness for those at high risk—for instance, selective interventions for populations with perceived lack of social support and high-risk circumstances of death (Raphael, 1977). Indicated interventions for those with high levels of grief-related distress (Vachon, Lyall, & Rogers, 1980) have also shown positive results. The concept of universal preventive intervention is more difficult and may apply to education of the community or indicate the need for changed social practice to support bereaved individuals. Although these may be hypothesized to lessen risk, there have not been systematic studies to test the effectiveness of such measures.

Identifying and treating bereavement pathologies is the next part of the spectrum, with intervention in this case, as elsewhere, emphasizing the earliest possible recognition of these pathologies and their effective treatment. Such interventions have been demonstrated to be effective, but they are inevitably more prolonged and complex (Marmar, Horowitz, Weiss, Wilner, & Kaltreider, 1988).

Not only are there significant difficulties in achieving effective interventions and improved outcomes in some bereavement pathologies (e.g., chronic grief), but there may be reason to consider maintenance interventions that aim to improve quality of life and assist the bereaved person to "live well" with their problem, lessening their tertiary morbidity and disability.

A number of factors are known to be relevant to intervention for bereaved persons. Age and psychosocial development at the time of bereavement are very relevant for the implications of loss—for instance the death of a parent for a child. Such variables require specific consideration when intervention is provided. Family context is also relevant and will be discussed in terms of new research that highlights patterns of family functioning and their relation to bereavement outcome. Grief may also be different for older people in terms of their nearness to the end of life— the purposes met by "going on" without the loved one. Language, culture, and social context will provide a background for intervention. Survival issues may also be critical, limiting opportunities for grief or its resolution at a particular time.

The theoretical frameworks in which bereavement processes are conceptualized will also influence the frameworks in which intervention is provided. Attachment theory and the work of John Bowlby (1969, 1973, 1980) has been the most influential (Middleton, Moylan, Raphael, Burnett, & Martinek, 1993), but other models may be relevant—for instance, bereavement as a change in assumptive worlds, and interventions that fit with such models may be more appropriate.

Although psychological understandings have increased there is not as yet a good basis for biological interventions. Pharmacological approaches should, for the most part, only be provided where there is an established disorder for which they are indicated. Thus a number of matters require consideration for a comprehensive overview of interventions that may be need to be provided. First, what systematic, replicable, and valid assessments indicate that intervention is needed; what guidelines should systematically influence what is done; by what measures are outcomes and effectiveness, evaluated? Any such "measure" and "systematization" must be balanced by humanity and sensitivity to the personal needs of the individual. Second, who will provide such interventions—what qualifications should they have; what personal qualities and abilities; where and how are such professionals to be identified and how are those that need them to be offered their services? Thus the delivery and effectiveness, the accessibility and acceptability of bereavement interventions must be clarified. The extension from bereavement research to appropriate practice, the monitoring of the quality and fidelity of interventions provided, is complex and requires organizational commitment; proof of relevance; and infrastructure to support such programs.

All these matters are more challenging because bereavement interventions have evolved from the wish to do good, to make better, to respond to distress. They have arisen from grassroots movements, experienced and charismatic counselors, and the identification of unmet need. They bring enthusiasm and belief and may strongly resent the new ethos of science and requirements for accountability. However, interventions are not to be lightly recommended, nor should they be lightly undertaken. They are of great potential value for those who need them, and, like all interventions, may be damaging for those who do not.

This chapter describes the basis for bereavement interventions in terms of populations and individuals for whom they may be appropriately applied, across the spectrum from prevention to treatment and maintenance. The relevance of such approaches from infancy to old age, and how they may be incorporated into care provision, will also be described.

SPECTRUM OF INTERVENTIONS

The concept of a spectrum of interventions from prevention to treatment and maintenance care has been applied in physical health, but best developed for mental health in terms of the model of Mrazek and Haggerty (1994). This model describes preventive interventions—for instance, universal approaches that may be applied for whole populations. Selective interventions are focused on populations at higher risk. Indicated interventions are for individuals at very high risk, perhaps in the prodromal period of onset of disorder, in which the person demonstrates at least some symptoms or distress indicating the likely onset of disorder. Case identification is the recognition of the disorder and its earliest effective management. Standard treatment of established conditions frequently applies to implementing evidence-based guidelines; and maintenance treatments apply to rehabilitation, support, compliance, and living as well as possible with whatever chronic disorder is residual (see Figure 26-1). Applying this model in terms of bereavement relies on a knowledge base of risk and protective factors and of the disorders that may arise, as well as their patterns and outcomes. Because grief itself is not a disorder.

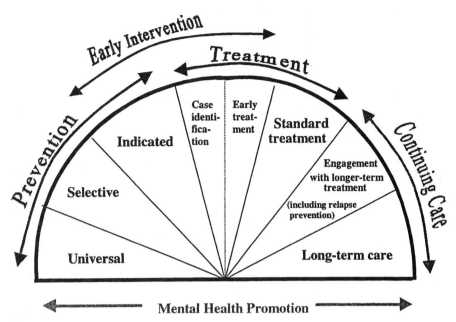

Figure 26-1. The Spectrum of Interventions for Mental Health Problems and Mental Disorders. Source: Adapted with permission from Mrazek & Haggerty (1994).

PREVENTIVE INTERVENTIONS FOR BEREAVED INDIVIDUALS

The concept of prevention in relation to bereaved people is based on knowledge that morbidity may arise for some bereaved people in terms of the development of bereavement pathologies such as chronic grief (Raphael & Minkov, 1999) or similar modalities (e.g., "traumatic" or complicated grief). Some bereaved people are also at higher risk of developing depressive and anxiety disorders in the postbereavement period. There may be other effects on health as well, including health behaviors, health care utilization, vulnerability to infection, and premature mortality. Although the majority of adults do not experience such outcomes, there is an increasing body of evidence that points to the risk factors associated with the individual, his or her social environment, and the loss that may indicate heightened likelihood of such problems. Preventive approaches then focus on reducing such risk factors and increasing protective factors to lessen the likelihood of adverse outcomes.

Preventive interventions for whole populations could include education about, and support for, "normal" bereavement. This should theoretically facilitate such processes in those affected by loss in the general population. More specifically, whole populations may become vulnerable when there has been massive loss—for instance, with genocide, war, disasters of larger scale. In these cases losses may be complex and may entail multiple loss of loved ones, family, community leaders, home, community, work, way of life, and so forth. However, there is no research establishing which programs of bereavement intervention are effective in such contexts.

PREVENTIVE INTERVENTIONS FOR INDIVIDUALS AT HIGHER RISK

Such interventions are targeted to individuals, who through screening or assessment or because of what is known of their experience, can be identified as more vulnerable to detrimental effects to their health and well-being.

Some will be at risk because of personal factors such as the nature of their relationship with the person who has died—for instance highly ambivalent or dependent relationships (Parkes & Weiss, 1983; Raphael, 1977). There may be personal characteristics of the individual that contribute to the ways in which he or she deals with adverse life experiences —for instance, vulnerability to responsiveness such as "neuroticism" or tendency to anxiety or depression through preexisting psychiatric vulnerability (Andrews, 1996). Past adverse life experiences that have not been mastered, such as the death of a parent in childhood, may increase vulnerability associated with subsequent loss (Brown, Harris, & Copeland, 1977).

Circumstances surrounding sudden, unexpected, and untimely losses have been shown to be associated with higher risk of adverse outcome (Parkes & Weiss, 1983; Raphael, 1977). A further factor of relevance in this context is particularly traumatic circumstances of death—for instance, gruesome, shocking, violent, mutilating deaths such as there are from homicide (Rynearson, 1996). In these instances the bereavement may become complicated by the development of posttraumatic stress disorder.

Other adverse life experiences in the time around and after the loss may also add to the vulnerability of individuals in terms of their capacity to deal with multiple concurrent severe stressors. The capacity of the social network to provide the support the bereaved person perceives as necessary, especially that which allows the expression of grief and resolution of the loss, has been shown to be a factor indicating greater vulnerability. Social network members, especially family, may themselves be affected by the loss and hence have difficulty in responding to the bereaved person's needs. Or there may be powerful social prescriptions that interfere with the capacity to respond to the bereaved person's needs—for example, about the privacy of grief or the proscription to not "speak ill" of the dead.

All these risk factors may be used to identify populations at higher risk of developing bereavement-related pathology or other morbidity. Selective interventions may be provided, such as crisis intervention or leader-guided or self-help groups that make use of psychotherapeutic principles. These interventions are provided to at-risk individuals or families to prevent grief-related pathologies.

Bereaved Widows

Interventions shown to be effective include *crisis intervention* for bereaved widows (selected on the basis of specific high-risk criteria; see Raphael, 1977). This modality uses six to eight sessions of focused counseling in the early weeks and months following the loss. It encourages the expression of separation distress, angry protest, and subsequent mourning for the dead person with review of the lost relationship in its positive and negative aspects and expression of relevant affects such as sadness. Other components include a specific review of the circumstances of the death and working through of the reactions to these. Opportunities to enhance supportive response from the social network are also incorporated. Information, recognition of the loss, acknowledgment of the deceased through the taking of a history of the lost relationship—these all contribute to facilitating a resolution process, specifically to diminish risk so that a more normal level of reaction and outcome is achieved. Psychodynamic principles inform this brief intervention process through, for example, recognition of transference and countertransference, which may be intense in this acute phase of lowered psychological defenses in the crisis period following the loss. Specific matters include the bereaved person's wish to replace the lost person and his or her anger toward the counselor because the counselor is there and the deceased is not (Raphael, 1983, 1997). The psychotherapeutic principles that inform this intervention are also relevant in bereavement-specific interventions for those who may have progressed to morbidity, but in this case are targeted at reducing risk and facilitating normal reactive processes (see also Parkes, 1980, 1986). It is noteworthy that much of the work in terms of prevention has focused on widows, although postbereavement risk, for instance in terms of mortality, may be greater for widowers.

Bereaved Parents

There have also been studies and intervention programs for parents following the death of a child, where the bereaved individual shows high levels of risk, especially where the death has occurred in traumatic circumstances. Grief after pregnancy loss has also been studied (e.g., Janssen, Cuisinier, de Graauw, & Hoogduin, 1997) showing that gestational age, preloss neurotic personality or psychiatric symptoms, and family composition (the absence of living children) were the strongest predictors of morbidity. Although not directly linked to these findings, a randomized controlled trial of selective perinatal bereavement counseling studied the effect of intervention for couples who experienced loss associated with fetal abnormality (Lilford, Stratton, Godsil, & Prasad, 1994). They found no difference between intervention and control groups, suggesting that it was inappropriate to provide counseling for all groups. They also suggested that it was likely that those who did attend and benefited from counseling were probably inherently better able to adjust to bereavement. All of this suggests that counseling should only be provided for those who need it—those who are at high risk or already demonstrating pathology.

Maternal grief after sudden infant death syndrome (SIDS) has been studied by a number of researchers. Ostfeld, Ryan, Hiatt, and Hegyi (1993) found that single mothers were more likely to be at risk for pathological grief but less likely to attend support groups and move on. Mothers whose infants had been discovered by another caregiver were more likely to reach out for the types of crisis intervention services and support offered to SIDS parents. Although it is difficult to draw conclusions from this study about modalities likely to be helpful, it highlights the variability of need and the fact that those who need intervention most may be least likely to avail themselves of preventive bereavement counseling in such circumstances.

Vance et al. (1991) also studied parental grief following stillbirth, neonatal death, and SIDS. Although they found mothers showed more anxiety and depression, fathers showed significant and virtually equal levels of morbidity when heavy drinking was taken into account. Using their findings and indicators of risk, a preventive intervention program for parents and siblings showed beneficial outcomes for those at higher risk. This provided a resource, information, and personal support program for family members and facilitated opportunities to express grief and sadness and to explore meaning and to move on (Murray, 1995, 1998). The value of this program is that it builds on the findings of a risk study and shows that these can be applied to broader populations of individuals, demonstrating particular benefits for those at higher risk. Its capacity for general and widespread use, its high level of acceptability, and its established effectiveness in such community-based settings make it extremely valuable.

Preventive intervention has also been carried out following the sudden and violent deaths of children, clearly very high risk bereavement situations. Murphy (1996) tested preventive intervention for 156 bereaved parents whose 12- to 28-year-old children had died by accident, homicide, or suicide in a multisite longitudinal cohort design, pre- and posttest. This involved both problem-focused and emotion-focused support. Both these dimensions were considered to be relevant, and selected intervention strategies included dealing with the parents' assumptions about the world, the experience of victimization, issues related to the family life cycle, and social support (see Schneiderman, Winders, Tallett, & Feldman, 1994; and chapter 30, this volume, for a more detailed review).

A review to determine whether child and parent bereaved programs are actually effective following the death of a child highlights both the variability of findings and the need for further research in this difficult but important field (Schneiderman et al., 1994).

Bereaved Children

Of great interest is the effect on children of losing a parent through death and whether or not preventive programs can lessen adverse impacts for them. Studies of parental bereavement intervention programs suggest that there may be significant benefits, although many are limited in both conceptual and methodological terms. Lohnes and Kalter (1994) described a model of time-limited intervention groups for such children and determined that there are common emergent themes that need to be taken into account. For instance, children continue to struggle with the stress well beyond the loss, and there is a need to maintain an internal representation of the dead parent that is an important component of the bereavement process. Such understandings are critical, because the child must take in the experience and respond in "doses" and time periods that can be modulated to his or her development, resiliency, and environment. Other work has emphasized the importance of a sense of ongoing family security after a parent dies and the continuity of a family environment of attachment and care. It is often only with this type of security assured that the child can deal with his or her loss, often much later on.

A family oriented prevention program for children in such circumstances has been described by Sandler, West, Baca, Pillow, and Gersten (1992) in the format of a family bereavement program. This program was specifically designed to improve variables in the family environment that were identified mediators of the effects of parental death on family mental health. This was a randomized controlled trial. The researchers found that the interventions led to parents experiencing increased warmth in their relationships with their children, increased satisfaction with their social support, and maintenance of family discussion of grief-related matters. On parent ratings there were decreases in conduct problems, depression, and overall problems in their older children. Significant correlations were also found between family environment variables and child mental health problems. These findings support the importance of a nurturing environment and parental effectiveness, as well as openness to grief issues, all theoretically relevant to prevention benefits for children following the death of a parent (e.g. West, Sandler, Pillow, Baca, & Gersten, 1991). Studies of young children (e.g., 2 to 8 years old) following the death of a parent confirm both the child's capacity to demonstrate sadness and grief as well as behavioral disturbances such as externalizing behaviors (mostly in boys) and internalizing behaviors (mostly in girls; Kranzler, Shaffer, Wasserman, & Davies, 1990; Raphael, Field, & Kvelde, 1980). The correlation between disturbance of the surviving parent and children was noted by both these groups, as was the impact of further adversity. In particular, it was often difficult for parents overwhelmed with their own grief, and often practical difficulties, to recognize and respond to their child's need. In addition, capacity to express grieving emotion correlated with symptom improvement (Kranzler et al., 1990). These findings further support the importance of a family-oriented approach for children in these circumstances and the common variables that heighten risk. However, it is still difficult to implement a program based on such findings (e.g., Christ, Siegel, Mesagno, & Langosch, 1991).

Kissane and his group have also developed a family-oriented preventive intervention model of bereavement. They have carried out a series of studies that have highlighted the value of a systems approach for identifying patterns of family vulnerability and as a basis for both preventive and treatment interventions (Kissane, 1998; Kissane & Bloch, 1994). Identifying dysfunctional families who are at risk and providing grief therapy for them as a preventive intervention aims to promote healthy family functioning during palliative care and bereavement. Family grief intervention has been successfully applied by psychoeducational bereavement support groups for families attending an outpatient cancer center (Goldstein, Alter, & Axelrod, 1996).

Other researchers have reported positive findings with intervention programs for children following parent death—for instance, Black and Urbanowitz's (1987) preventive group work with children following the death of a parent. Support groups for school-age children have also been described by Zambelli and DeRosa (1992), who suggest these can provide valuable social support for families and may also contribute new social meaning. Programs such as the Seasons for Growth, a structured group and support program for children in school settings, have also been evaluated positively (http://www.goodgrief.aust.com).

An important factor to consider in weighing these results is the finding of Gersten, Beals, and Kallgren (1991) that an epidemiological approach is the most sound basis for identifying bereaved children at risk and in need of intervention. Families recruited in such a fashion could be appropriately tested for the effectiveness of targeted interventions in reducing risk. However, many studies report on families referred to intervention by themselves or others, and these differ from such groups in ways that may produce significant evaluation bias—in other words, they are not representative so that the generalizing of any outcomes to the broader populations of bereaved children and families may not be possible.

BEREAVED ELDERLY INDIVIDUALS

The relevance of grief for older populations and the particular issues for preventive intervention with this group have been described by a number of researchers. For instance, a focus on enhancing a sense of control through self-help group intervention was found to be associated with decreased psychological distress (McKibbin, Guarnaccia, Hayslip, & Murdock, 1997). Another study of self-help groups also showed that the use of personal skills in the context of elderly bereaved individuals can reduce reports of depression and prolonged grief (Casserta & Lund, 1993). Because bereavement may be an important factor in precipitating depression in older people, programs focused on bereaved people who are at risk for pathological grief and bereavement in high-risk situations such as nursing homes (Murphy, Hanrahan, & Luchins, 1997) can be important in preventing depression. This is also relevant for caregivers of older people—for instance partners of those with Alzheimer's disease, where care givers experience significant grief. Bearing in mind the effectiveness of bereavement-related interventions in elderly individuals (e.g., Gerber, Wiener, & Battin, 1975) it is clearly worthwhile to incorporate bereavement programs into high-risk settings (Jorm, 1995). Building on interpersonal resources is important in self-help group effectiveness (Caserta & Lund, 1993). Suicide is also a higher risk for older bereaved people, especially older males, and this adds to the importance of focusing on bereaved populations in which suicidal ideation and death wishes are often prevalent (Byrne & Raphael, 1999).

Despite this growth of research in preventive intervention for bereaved adults, there is clearly a need for more sophisticated methodologies than have been available previously—for instance with conjugal bereavement (Windholtz, Marmar, & Horowitz, 1985) and following the death of a child or parent (Schneiderman et al., 1994). There is also the need to better link intervention studies to population-based epidemiology of bereavement and risk, so that studies of intervention may be more generalizable. This approach can contribute to improved outcomes not only for individuals but also for the population as a whole.

For adults at high risk there has also been a growing body of research dealing with interventions for specific risk situations—for instance, deaths from homicide (Rynearson, 1996); suicide (Dunne, 1992; Valente & Saunders, 1993); intensive care unit deaths (Tunnicliffe & Briggs, 1997); and HIV/AIDS (Sikkema, Kalichman, Kelly, & Koob, 1995; Worden, 1991).

There is a specific need for more systematic and epidemiologically based prevention trials so that effects of preventive intervention may be generalizable and a more appropriate basis for program implementation established.

EARLY INTERVENTION FOR BEREAVEMENT PATHOLOGY

Between prevention and treatment are a group of interventions, usually psychotherapeutically derived, that focus on individuals showing either very high levels of bereavement-related distress in the early postbereavement period or other signs of incipient pathology (bereavement pathology). Bereavement pathologies have recently been better clarified. However, although there is consensus about the presence of patterns of pathological grief (Middleton et al., 1993), there is not good agreement about their nature. Chronic grief is a widely recognized entity and recently established in population-based studies of bereavement to occur in approximately 9% of the population of adults experiencing a loss. This is a pattern of high and continuing levels of bereavement-specific distress (e.g., Raphael & Minkov, 1999). Other recently described pathologies include traumatic grief (not grief and PTSD but high levels of separation distress; Prigerson et al., 1999; chapter 27, this volume) and complicated grief disorder (Horowitz et al., 1997). These both show high levels of bereavement-specific distress, and like chronic grief, they can be clearly differentiated from major depression and anxiety disorders arising in association with bereavement.

These interventions that target early high levels of bereavement-specific distress that do not appear to be attenuating may either be considered *indicated preventive interventions* aimed at preventing the onset of these bereavement specific pathologies or indeed *early intervention* for incipient or prodromal pathology. The studies most directly relevant to such complications are those of Vachon et al. (1980) in which widows considered to be at high risk because of early high distress levels were provided with intervention by other widows trained to facilitate their resolution and recovery. The researchers found this intervention to be effective, compared to a high-risk control group. However, they concluded that these interventions, when viewed in the longer term, foreshortened the resolution period for those at higher risk, facilitating the lessening of grief at a rate more like those at lower risk. These findings suggest that in this instance the grief associated with the initial high distress had the propensity to be prolonged but perhaps not chronically so. Frank, Prigerson, Shear, and Reynolds (1997) have commented on the treatment of bereavement-related distress in elderly individuals. However, this deals with more prolonged distress at a later period following the loss and is more related to the treatment of chronic or traumatic grief. The emphasis in their model is on reliving the moment of the death and exposure to avoided circumstances or reminders of the loss, as well as saying "goodbye" to the deceased. There is as yet no data on outcomes, but this is much more in the realm of a treatment intervention. As described earlier, this is not unlike the guided mourning for situations of avoidant grief (Sireling, Cohen, & Marks, 1988).

PSYCHOTHERAPEUTIC AND OTHER TREATMENTS FOR BEREAVED INDIVIDUALS

The basis for treating bereaved people merges with that of prevention in that where there is specific bereavement-related pathology such as a pattern of abnormal grief, there will be attempts to facilitate normal grieving. The various modalities that have been used to achieve this will be discussed later in the chapter. In addition, there are the complications of bereavement that may require treatment, specifically the development of posttraumatic stress disorder, the development of bereavement-related depression or anxiety disorders, or the precipitation of other illness, for instance an episode of bipolar disorder.

Studies of treatment either involve outreach to affected populations or the treatment of those who present to clinics. A set of general principles still applies with respect to the bereavement—for instance, alongside the treatment of any established psychiatric disorder it is still likely to be of benefit to work with the process of grieving and to work toward resolution of the loss. Specific medications for bereavement-related disorders should be determined on the basis of the disorder and its appropriate treatment. Careful differential diagnosis of bereavement-related distress and other disorders is critical. Other problems best dealt with psychotherapeutically, such as concurrent or additional life stresses, social support, and social change, should also be assessed and incorporated in a comprehensive management plan.

TREATMENTS FOR BEREAVEMENT PATHOLOGIES

A number of groups have provided evidence about the effectiveness of a range of psychotherapeutic modalities. For instance, Schut, Stroebe, de Keijser, and van den Bout (1997) described an intervention program for widows (n = 23) and widowers (n = 23) who were suffering elevated distress 11 months after their loss. They were assigned to problem-focused or emotion-focused coping counseling. These researchers showed that men who were seen as more problem-focused benefited more from the emotion-focused counseling and that women benefited more from the problem-focused counseling. These interventions were effective in lessening distress, and the modality offered appeared to deal with those aspects of each group that might be considered to need more development.

Frank et al. (1997), as noted previously, provided intervention for a pattern of prolonged bereavement-related distress in elderly individuals as part of their studies of traumatic grief, thereby focusing on bereavement-related pathology and its treatment. However, the effectiveness of this program is yet to be established. Other work that focuses on prolonged or abnormal grief is that of Kleber and Brom (1992) in which a 12- to 15-session psychotherapeutic program showed benefits compared to wait-list controls, although avoidant behaviors were more resistant to intervention. This study dealt with facilitating normal grieving and the working through of the loss through psychodynamically oriented intervention, compared to other patterns of psychological intervention (hypnotherapy and behavioral). All were effective to a degree, with the psychotherapeutic interventions being most helpful for the avoidant phenomena.

Avoidant patterns of grief have been the specific focus of what has been termed guided mourning. This is a behaviorally based program carried out by nurse therapists who progressively encourage exposure to avoided situations such as visits to the grave (Sireling et al., 1988). Other modalities for grief pathologies include those identified by Lindemann (1944), the regrief work of Volkan (1972), and therapeutic leave-taking rituals of Van der Hart and Goosens (1987). The Horowitz group has provided the most detailed review of psychotherapy in a study of the effectiveness of this modality for abnormal grief and examined the relationship of process to outcomes (Horowitz, Marmar, Weiss, DeWitt, & Rosenbaum, 1984).

In each of these and other relevant cases and clinical descriptions, the psychotherapeutic aim is that of facilitating a "normal" grieving or bereavement process, whether through psychodynamic or behavioral intervention, or indeed other principles. This involves key elements of dealing with the circumstances of the death; reviewing the lost relationship; expressing the various affects of grief; mourning the deceased, both psychologically and in ritual; coming to some terms with the new realities that result from the loss, including any altered role or status; dealing with concurrent life stressors; and achieving the necessary tasks of a practical nature through this period. Most researchers (and clinicians) also acknowledge that this may be a time when earlier losses are reexperienced and new resolutions may be achieved. These interventions are brief, targeted, and do not usually engage the broader complex issues of the bereaved person's life unless specifically relevant to the loss, because to do so may be a defense against dealing with the loss. Such problems should be the aim of different, or later, therapeutic interventions. Always bereaved people must be understood, assessed, and managed in ways that recognize their social, cultural, and personal contexts, a potentially complex but vital framework.

POSTTRAUMATIC STRESS DISORDER AND BEREAVEMENT

Initially bereavement was seen as a traumatic stressor that could lead to stress response syndromes, but later, particularly with the development of the diagnostic criteria for PTSD in *DSM-IV*, it became increasingly clear that normal bereavement could not really be seen as a stressor meeting *DSM-IV*, criterion A (American Psychiatric Association, 1994). Raphael and Maddison (1976) observed a group of bereaved people who appeared to suffer from traumatic stress or traumatic neurosis effects that complicated their bereavement reaction after shocking and horrific circumstances of death. These researchers observed, as did Lindy, Green, Grace, & Tichener (1983) when providing psychotherapy to the survivors of a disaster, that it was often not possible to facilitate grief or provide bereavement counseling until the traumatic stress aspects had first been dealt with (Lindy et al., 1983). Nevertheless, work such as that of Kleber and Brom did not specifically separate these two sets of phenomena, and regarded them as one type of complication (Kleber & Brom, 1992).

There has been a growing interest in what has been called traumatic grief, but the term as currently used does not always clarify both the traumatic stress or PTSD phenomenology and the bereavement phenomenology and processes. Raphael and Martinek (1997) have described these in some depth from observational and clinical bases and highlight the differing patterns of arousal, affects (e.g., anxiety for fear–threat versus separation anxiety), and the differing preoccupations and intrusions. Nevertheless, the two sets of phenomena become complexly intermingled when particularly "traumatic" circumstances of the death lead to a matrix of symptoms in traumatic bereavements.

Rynearson (1996) has described this complex picture in those bereaved by homicide, and Black has described it for children whose fathers have killed their mothers (Black, Harris, & Kaplan, 1992). In both such circumstances the overlay of PTSD-type symptoms or syndromes complicates the bereavement and capacity to grieve.

Recently, Schut and colleagues have carried out systematic studies of PTSD and bereavement. They found this disorder to be frequent among bereaved individuals and often correlated with the perceived inadequacy of the goodbye said to the deceased. They concluded that creating opportunities for "saying farewell" to the deceased, for instance in grief therapy, may be important components that can facilitate recovery (Schut et al., 1997).

The dearth of good studies on effective treatment for PTSD, with the usual modalities being cognitive–behavioral therapy and pharmocological treatments, means that these should be considered early in the treatment program in relevant cases. Such interventions may be applied preventively for those showing high distress or dissociation in the acute period following the traumatization and loss (e.g.. Bryant, Harvey, Dang, & Sackville, 1998) to deal with the PTSD phenomena. Solomon (1999) has highlighted the value of this type of intervention in the early period after bereavement, at least more than two weeks after the traumatic episode versus "debriefing"-type models in the immediate postincident period. The bereaved individuals then gradually move on, with appropriate "dosing" of affect, to deal with the loss. Medications if required are usually antidepressants, although minor tranquilizers may be helpful in the acute phase. A melding of biopsychosocial assessments, with interventions dealing first with the trauma and then gradually with the loss, is most likely to achieve better outcomes, although there is a need for controlled trials to establish a scientific basis for these programs and their effectiveness.

However, difficulties arise here because these may be secondary "rewards" of victim status for chronic grievers. The identity and role of the "victim" may unconsciously become too valued and meaningful to be relinquished. Specific psychotherapeutic interventions may be needed to deal with this, as they may be for those who become obsessed by the search for justice. This latter frequently represents the unconscious (or conscious) wish to bring back the deceased, to have the world the way it once was. This search for justice through legal or other means may take many years or may not ever be achieved to the bereaved person's satisfaction. These processes may delay and prolong grief and lock the person into the trauma, preventing recovery (Raphael & Martinek, 1997).

In cases in which trauma has been massive—for instance the loss of a whole family in horrific ways—the bereaved person is likely to struggle for psychological and physical survival and only move to deal with both the trauma and the grief (Singh & Raphael, 1981) at a much later time. The double effects of trauma and loss contribute a major additional psychological burden to be dealt with, and this may occur over a considerable period, at a pace that is set by the bereaved individual. With the increases in violent deaths this is a growing and complex issue requiring sophisticated and highly skilled intervention and indeed much further research and study. On a more comprehensive basis, the issues of loss, trauma, identity, justice, and making meaning of what has happened have been drawn together in a conceptualization that is relevant to deal with mass trauma, conflict, and violence (Silove, 2000). This is relevant in that it recognizes both the adaptations that most people make to their grief and trauma, even in such overwhelming and horrific circumstances, and guides the type of interventions that may be needed.

DEPRESSION AND RELATED DISORDERS AND BEREAVEMENT

There has long been a conceptual difficulty in separating the phenomenology of bereavement reactions from those of depression. Indeed some researchers initially described the process of bereavement as a "reactive depression" (e.g., Parkes, 1972), and early studies used depression scales to measure the reaction to loss (Clayton, 1990).

Recent work has clearly differentiated both normal bereavement from depression and shown that abnormal bereavements such as chronic grief, complicated grief, or even "traumatic grief" can be clearly differentiated from major depression and from anxiety disorders and other psychiatric disorders, although there may for some be an increased risk of also developing major depression or anxiety syndromes in these circumstances (Horowitz et al., 1997; Prigerson et al., 1996; Raphael & Minkov, 1999).

Separating the clinical phenomenology of grief and depression is important to the assessment process. Freud's description of mourning and melancholia (1917/1957) provides the earliest attempt to do so. Table 26-1 shows some broad differences in phenomena.

Systematic research on bereavement and depression has mostly focused on the older years, but a number of recent reviews are helpful (e.g., Clayton, 1997). Taking a life span approach shows that children, particularly girls in the younger years (e.g., 2–8), may develop a pattern of internalizing behaviors, and even a level of depression in response to bereavement (Raphael, Field, & Kvelde, 1980; Weller, Weller, Fristad, & Bowes, 1990). However, the vulnerability of boys to depression as a consequence of parent death, and also parental depression (in the surviving parent), was shown by Van Erdewegh's studies of adolescents (Van Erdewegh, Clayton, & Van Eerdewegh, 1985). Nevertheless, these data are poorly developed and the influence of other variables, such as parental depression, family instability, and socioeconomic change need to be better identified.

TABLE 26-1
Phenomena of Bereavement and Depression

	Bereavement	Depression
Cognitive	Focus on lost person	Focus on negative interpretation of self, world
Affects	Yearning Separation anxiety Anger (externalizing) Sadness	Agitation Anxiety Anger (internalizing) Depressive feelings
Arousal	Present/seeks lost person Variable sleep disturbance	Reunion "sought" Withdrawal Sleep disturbance and sleep variation

Vulnerability to depression may not appear in childhood but in adult life, as Brown has demonstrated (Brown et al., 1977). Studies of adults (e.g., Middleton, Burnett, Raphael, & Martinek, 1996; Middleton, Raphael, Burnett, & Martinek, 1998) have shown that depressive and anxiety symptoms are common in bereaved people, but generally level off during the first year postloss, as does bereavement-related distress. Zisook, Shuchter, Sledge, Paulus, and Judd (1994) have described the spectrum of depressive phenomena after spousal bereavement with studies over a 25-month period following the loss compared to community controls. They found that both subsyndromal depression and major depression were prevalent through the first two years of widowhood. Other studies by Zisook's group (Zisook & Shuchter, 1993) have also shown the frequency and persistence of depression, especially if present in the early phase after the loss.

More extensive studies of depression in bereaved people have focused on later life. For instance, Rozenweig, Prigerson, Miller, & Reynolds (1997) describe major depression, anxiety, and substance abuse, as well as "complicated" grief as significant psychiatric complications of bereavement in elderly individuals. Reynolds (1992, 1997) also examined major depression in later life and its treatment in populations such as institutionalized elderly persons and those with neurological disability who are bereaved. He emphasized the importance of both psychotherapeutic and psychopharmacological aspects in treatment.

It is with these older populations that psychopharmocology in relation to postbereavement depressive disorders is most actively addressed. Workers in this field report that a combination of antidepressants and psychotherapy provides the best opportunity for improved outcomes. Miller, Wolfson, Frank, Cornes, and Silberman (1997) described their management of 180 older research participants with unipolar major depression who were trialed with nortriptylene and interpersonal psychotherapy by an experienced clinician. Eighty-one percent of these older people showed a full response acutely, and although they had not been identified in terms of the relationship of bereavement to depression, grief problems were central in almost a quarter of these. An open trial of antidepressant treatment for bereavement-induced late-life depression is also reported (Pasternak et al., 1991). This found that nortriptylene treatment was associated with significant symptomatic improvement in all areas of bereavement-related depression, but not with respect to the intensity of grief. This study highlighted the need for further research and emphasized again that treatment of any disorder postbereavement should be for that condition. However, work to facilitate normal grieving and resolution is still necessary where this is problematic. Furthermore, antecedent factors, such as depression before the bereavement and similar vulnerabilities, may well contribute. These separate psychiatric issues need also to be dealt with independently for their implications for treatment of depression in bereaved individuals at any stage of the life cycle. Psychotherapeutic interventions will inevitably be part of this and should be tailored both to developmental stage and to the modalities that are most likely to be effective for the particular pattern of illness. Cognitive–behavioral therapy and interpersonal psychotherapy are predominant modalities. Antidepressants should be used as appropriate to the syndrome of depression, and if very severe and nonresponsive, electroconvulsive therapy may also be required. Although reports to date focus on nortriptylene, new antidepressants may be relevant, but further trials for their value for such bereavement-related depressions are very necessary. Antidepressants are *not* treatment for bereavement without depression. Similar approaches may be necessary in relation to bipolar disorder, which may be precipitated by bereavement. Where there are high levels of preexisting psychiatric vulnerability or ongoing treatment of such disorders, a careful monitoring of medication in the postbereavement period as well as psychotherapy and a focus on grief resolution will all be critical to outcome.

Anxiety symptoms (separate from PTSD) are also found in bereaved individuals, and some may be at greater risk of anxiety disorders than depression. For instance, Byrne and Raphael (1994) found a closer relationship between bereavement phenomena and anxiety symptoms, whereas Middleton et al. (1998) pointed to a fairly consistent relationship with each. Anxiety disorders such as generalized anxiety disorder and phobic conditions have been described. It is important to understand the difference between anxiety symptoms of a general kind and the separation anxiety or distress that is part of normal grief but may be heightened in its more chronic or pathological forms.

Bearing in mind these clinical and phenomenological distinctions, as with depression, appropriate treatment for preexisting or precipitated disorders is relevant for the diagnosed condition, including antidepressants, anxiolytics and psychotherapy, or behavioral interventions, as well as grief counseling to facilitate the resolution of the loss.

SPECIAL ISSUES IN PSYCHOTHERAPY WITH BEREAVED PEOPLE

Psychotherapy with bereaved people, regardless of modality adopted, requires a dynamic understanding of bereavement and its effects. Such effects include lowered defensiveness in the acute period following loss; very intense affective response; painfulness of separation distress, yearning, and longing; pervasive angry protest; and the focus and sadness and exclusion of the psychological mourning processes. The bereaved individual may find it difficult to engage with the therapist; or may focus anger on the therapist because the therapist is alive to console the bereaved individual and the loved one is not; or may attach to the therapist as a replacement for the loved one; or struggle for survival psychologically and physically and resent those like the therapist who are able to get on with their lives. Although these issues are less obvious with chronically bereaved individuals than with acutely bereaved individuals, they are still relevant. As in all psychotherapy, particularly for those acutely distressed, there needs to be a mix of humanity and compassion; of professionalism and patience; of sensitive timing of progress. Overidentification with the bereaved individual and his or her suffering, immersion in this grief, a reluctance to accept that the aims of therapy may be to facilitate but not complete these grieving processes, are all issues of countertransference. For the therapist there is also the issue of the reawakening of personal losses, the fears of loss and death, and contagion from the bereaved individual. Trauma-related issues complicate this further. These and other parameters must be carefully monitored in this psychotherapy, as in all others.

RESEARCH FINDINGS AND IMPLICATIONS FOR PRACTICE

As noted in several parts of this review, intervention research requires much further development. In addition, many of the findings that are available are not necessarily epidemiologically based (Gersten et al., 1991) or generalizable because of the difficulties of recruitment (e.g., Schneiderman et al., 1994; Schlernitzauer et al., 1998). There is a powerful social movement of bereavement counseling, but this movement does not necessarily link closely with scientific evidence. There are thus critical tasks in extending the knowledge base about bereavement phenomenology and its assessment, psychotherapy in bereavement, and counseling and other interventions for both the prevention and treatment of bereavement-related pathologies and other disorders. There is the additional need to ensure that the knowledge available and developed is disseminated and incorporated in good practice in appropriate settings, from primary care (Woof, 1997), to self-help, to specialty mental health programs, to community education.

CONCLUSION

Psychotherapy and its conceptual basis is an essential component of the understanding and management of response to loss. Knowledge from attachment and psychodynamic theories can inform practice, both in terms of the interplay of social, cultural, psychological, and biological processes. Interventions for bereaved individuals may range from population-based approaches that incorporate these insights; to prevention counseling and programs for those at high risk of bereavement-related pathology; to the specific psychotherapeutic interventions for bereavement-specific morbidity; to the therapies relevant for bereavement-precipitated psychiatric morbidity. These principles also inform the interventions necessary to normalize the grief process that runs throughout this spectrum. Psychopharmacological interventions are relevant where indicated, for particular disorders that are either precipitated by bereavement or occur in bereaved populations. Such interventions should be specific to the conditions and based on best available evidence of what is effective. But here too, the grief process must be "looked after" in the management of those who are bereaved, whatever their diagnosis. This must also apply if they are physically ill, just as when they are psychiatrically unwell. Building these principles into research and practice, incorporating outcome measurement, evaluation, and monitoring, will all assist in the provision of best practice in bereavement-related prevention and care. Alongside this is the recognition and valuing of the multiplicity of human adaptations in those who do not require a therapeutic or preventive approach.

REFERENCES

American Psychiatric Association. (1994). *Diagnostic and statistical manual of mental disorders* (4th ed.). Washington, DC: Author.

Andrews, G. (1996). Comorbidity and the general neurotic syndrome. *British Journal of Psychiatry, 168*(Suppl. 30), 76–84.

Black, D., Harris, H. J., & Kaplan, T. (1992). Father kills mother: Post-traumatic stress disorder in the children. *Psychotherapy-Psychosomatics, 57*, 152–157.

Black, D., & Urbanowicz, M. A. (1987). Family intervention with bereaved children. *Journal of Child Psychology and Psychiatry, 28*, 467–476.

Bowlby, J. (1969). *Attachment. Vol 1. Attachment and loss.* London: Hogarth Press.

Bowlby, J. (1973). *Attachment and loss. Vol 2. Separation: Anxiety and anger.* London: Hogarth Press.

Bowlby, J. (1980). *Loss: Sadness and depression. Vol 3. Attachment and loss.* London: Hogarth Press.

Brown, G., Harris, T., & Copeland, J. (1977). Depression and loss. *British Journal of Psychiatry, 30*, 1–18.

Bryant, R. A., Harvey, A. G., Dang, S. T., & Sackville, T. (1998). Treatment of acute stress disorder: A comparison of cognitive-behavioural therapy and supportive counselling. *Journal of Consulting and Clinical Psychology, 66*, 862–866.

Byrne, G. J., & Raphael, B. (1999). Depressive symptoms and depressive episodes in recently widowed older men. *International Journal of Geriatric Psychiatry, 12*, 241–251.

Caserta, M. S., & Lund, D. A. (1993). Intrapersonal resources and the effectiveness of self-help groups for bereaved older adults. *Gerontologist, 33,* 619–629.

Christ, G. H., Siegel, K., Mesagno, F. P., & Langosch, D. (1991). A preventive intervention program for bereaved children: Problems of implementation. *American Journal of Orthopsychiatry, 61,* 168–178.

Clayton, P. J. (1990). Bereavement and depression. *Journal of Clinical Psychiatry, 51,* 34–40.

Clayton, P. J. (1997). The spectrum of depressive disorders following spousal bereavement—Discussion. *Journal of Affective Disorders, 45,* 1–2, 94–95.

Dunne, E. J. (1992). Psychoeducational intervention strategies for survivors of suicide. *Crisis, 13*(1), 35–40.

Frank, E., Prigerson, H. G., Shear, M. K., & Reynolds, C. F. (1997). Phenomenology and treatment of bereavement-related distress in the elderly. *International Clinical Psychopharmacology, 12*(Suppl. 7), S25–29.

Freud, S. (1957). Mourning and melancholia. In *Collected papers, Vol. IV.* London. Hogarth Press. (Original work published 1917)

Gerber, I., Wiener, A., & Battin, D. (1975). Brief therapy to the aged bereaved. In B. Schoenberg & I. Gerber (Eds.), *Bereavement: Its psychosocial aspects.* New York: Columbia University Press.

Gersten, J. C., Beals, J., & Kallgren, C. A. (1991). Epidemiology and preventive interventions: Parental death in childhood as a case example. *American Journal of Community Psychology, 19,* 481–500.

Goldstein, J., Alter, C. L., & Axelrod, R. (1996). A psychoeducational bereavement support group for families provided in an outpatient cancer centre. *Journal of Cancer Education, 11,* 233–237.

Horowitz, M. J., Marmar, C., Weiss, D. S., DeWitt, K. N., & Rosenbaum, R. (1984). Brief psychotherapy of bereavement reactions. The relationship of process to outcome. *Archives of General Psychiatry, 41,* 438–448.

Horowitz, M. J., Siegel, B., Holen, A., Bonanno, G., Milbrath, C., & Stinson, C. H. (1997). Diagnostic criteria for complicated grief disorder. *American Journal of Psychiatry, 154,* 904–910.

Janssen, H. J., Cuisinier, M. C., de Graauw, K. P., & Hoogduin, K. A. (1997). A prospective study of risk factors predicting grief intensity following pregnancy loss. *Archives of General Psychiatry, 54,* 56–61.

Jorm, A. F. (1995). The epidemiology of depressive states in the elderly: Implications for recognition, intervention and prevention. *Social Psychiatry and Psychiatric Epidemiology, 30,* 53–59.

Kissane, D. (1998). A controlled trial of family intervention to promote healthy family functioning in at-risk palliative care families. *Australian and New Zealand Journal of Psychiatry, 32*(Suppl. 8), A16.

Kissane, D. W., & Bloch, S. (1994). Family Grief. *British Journal of Psychiatry, 164,* 728–740.

Kleber, R. J., & Brom, D. (1992). *Coping with trauma: Theory, prevention and treatment.* Amsterdam: Swets & Zeitlinger.

Kranzler, E. M., Shaffer, D., Wasserman, G., & Davies, M. (1990). Early childhood bereavement. *Journal of American Academy of Child and Adolescent Psychiatry, 29*, 513–520.

Lilford, R. J., Stratton, P. Godsil, S., & Prasad, A. (1994). A randomised trial of routine versus selective counselling in perinatal bereavement from congenital disease. *British Journal of Obstetrics and Gynaecology, 101*, 291–296.

Lindemann, E. (1944). Symptomatology and management of acute grief. *American Journal of Psychiatry, 101*, 141–148.

Lindy, J. D., Green, B. L., Grace, M., & Tichener, J. (1983). Psychotherapy with survivors of the Beverly Hills Supper Club fire. *American Journal of Psychotherapy, 37*, 593–610.

Lohnes, K. L., & Kalter, N. (1994). Preventive intervention groups for parentally bereaved children. *American Journal of Orthopsychiatry, 64*, 594–603.

Marmar, C. R., Horowitz, M. J., Weiss, D. S., Wilner, N. R., & Kaltreider, N. B. (1988). A controlled trial of brief psychotherapy and mutual-help group treatment of conjugal bereavement. *American Journal of Psychiatry, 145*, 203–209.

McKibbin, C. L., Guarnaccia, C. A., Hayslip, B., & Murdock, M. E. (1997). Locus of control perceptions among conjugally bereaved older adults, a pilot study. *International Journal of Aging and Human Development, 44*, 37–45.

Middleton, W., Burnett, P., Raphael, B., & Martinek, N. (1996). The bereavement response: A cluster analysis. *British Journal of Psychiatry, 169*, 167–171.

Middleton, W., Moylan, A., Raphael, B., Burnett, P., & Martinek, N. (1993). An international perspective on bereavement related concepts. *Australian & New Zealand Journal of Psychiatry, 27*, 457–463.

Middleton, W., Raphael, B., Burnett, P., & Martinek, N. (1998). A longitudinal study comparing bereavement phenomena in recently bereaved spouses, adult children and parents. *Australian & New Zealand Journal of Psychiatry, 32*, 235–241.

Miller, M. D., Wolfson, L., Frank, E., Cornes, C., & Silberman, R. (1997). Using interpersonal psychotherapy (IPT) in a combined psychotherapy/medication research protocol with depressed elders. A descriptive report with case vignettes. *Journal of Psychotherapy Practise and Research, 7*, 47–55.

Mrazek, P. J., & Haggerty, R. J. (Eds.). (1994). *Reducing risks for mental disorders: Frontiers for preventive intervention research.* Washington, DC: National Academy Press.

Murphy, S. A. (1996). Parent bereavement stress and preventive intervention following the violent deaths of adolescent or young adult children. *Death Studies, 20*, 441–452.

Murphy, K., Hanrahan, P., & Luchins, D. (1997). A survey of grief and bereavement in nursing homes: The importance of hospice grief and bereavement for the end-stage Alzheimer's disease patient and family. *Journal of American Geriatric Society, 45*, 1104–1107.

Murray, J. (1995). *An ache in their hearts.* Resource package, Department of Child Health, University of Queensland.

Murray, J. (1998). Caring families affected by infant death: Evaluating an intervention. In J. Murray (Ed.), *Grief Matters* (p. 4). Melbourne, Australia: Centre for Grief Education.

Ostfeld, B. M., Ryan. T., Hiatt, M., & Hegyi, T. (1993). Maternal grief after sudden infant death syndrome. *Journal of Developmental and Behavioural Paediatrics, 14,* 156–162.

Parkes C. M. (1972). *Bereavement: Studies of grief in adult life.* New York: International Universities Press.

Parkes, C. M. (1980). Bereavement counselling: Does it work? *British Medical Journal, 281,* 3–10.

Parkes, C. M. (1986). *Bereavement: Studies of grief in adult life.* Harmondsworth, UK: Penguin Books.

Parkes, C. M., & Weiss, R. S. (1983). *Recovery from bereavement.* New York: Basic Books.

Pasternak, R. E., Reynolds, C. F., Schlernitzauer, M., Hoch, C. C., Buysse, D. J., Houck, P. R., & Perel, J. M. (1991). Acute open-trial nortriptyline therapy of bereavement-related depression in later life. *Journal of Clinical Psychiatry, 52,* 307–310.

Prigerson, H. G., Shear, M. K., Jacobs, S. C., Reynolds, C. F. III, Maciejewski, J. R., Davidson, J. R. T., Rosenheck, R., Pilkonis, P. A., Wortman, C. B., Williams, J. B. W., Widiger, T. A., Frank, E., Kupfer, D. J., & Zisook, S. (1999). Consensus criteria for traumatic grief: A preliminary empirical test. *British Journal of Psychiatry, 174,* 67–73.

Prigerson, H. G., Shear, M. K., Newsom, J. T., Frank, E., Reynolds, C. F., Maciejewski, P. K., Houck, P. R., Bierhals, A. J., & Kupfer, D. J. (1996). Anxiety among widowed elders: Is it distinct from depression and grief? *Anxiety, 2,* 1–12.

Raphael, B. (1977). Preventive intervention with the recently bereaved. *Archives of General Psychiatry, 34,* 1450–1454.

Raphael, B. (1983). *Anatomy of bereavement.* New York: Basic Books.

Raphael, B. (1997). The interaction of trauma and grief. In D. Black, M. Newman, J. Harris-Hendricks, & G. Mezey (Eds.), *Psychological trauma: A developmental approach* (pp. 31–43). London: Gaskell/Royal College of Psychiatrists.

Raphael, B., Field, J., & Kvelde, H. (1980). Childhood bereavement: A prospective study as a possible prelude to future preventive intervention. In E. J. Anthony & C. Chiland (Eds.), *Preventive psychiatry in an age of transition.* New York: Wiley.

Raphael, B., & Maddison, D. C. (1976). The care of bereaved adults. In O. W. Hill (Ed.), *Modern trends in psychosomatic medicine.* London: Butterworth.

Raphael, B., & Martinek, N. (1997). Assessing traumatic bereavements and PTSD. In J. P. Wilson & T. M. Keane (Eds.), *Assessing psychological trauma and PTSD* (pp. 373–395). New York: Guilford Press.

Raphael, B., & Martinek, N. (1998). Bereavements and trauma. In R. Jenkins &

T. Ustun (Eds.), *Preventing mental illness mental health promotion in primary care* (pp. 353–378). New York: Wiley.

Raphael, B., & Minkov, C. (1999). Abnormal grief. *Current Opinion in Psychiatry, 12*, 99–102.

Reynolds, C. F. (1992). Treatment of depression in special populations. *Journal of Clinical Psychiatry, 53*(Suppl.), 45–53.

Reynolds, C. F. (1997). Treatment of major depression in later life: A life cycle perspective. *Psychiatry Quarterly, 68*, 221–246.

Rozenweig, A., Prigerson, H., Miller, M. D., & Reynolds, C. F. (1997). Bereavement and late life depression: Grief and its complications in the elderly. *Annual Review of Medicine, 48*, 421–428.

Rynearson, E. K. (1996). Psychotherapy of bereavement after homicide: Be offensive. *Psychotherapy in Practice, 2*, 47–57.

Sandler, I. N., West, S. G., Baca, L., Pillow, D. R., & Gersten, J. C. (1992). Linking empirically-based theory and evaluation: The Family Bereavement Program. *American Journal of Community Psychology, 20*, 491–523.

Schlernitzauer, M., Bierhals, A. J., Geary, M. D., Prigerson, H. G., Stack, J. A., Miller, M. D., Pasternak, R. E., & Reynolds, C. F. (1998). Recruitment methods for intervention research in bereavement-related depression; Five years' experience. *American Journal of Geriatric Psychiatry, 6*, 67–74.

Schneiderman, G., Winders, P., Tallett, S., & Feldman, W. (1994). Do child and/or parent bereavement programs work? *Canadian Journal of Psychiatry, 39*, 215–217.

Schut, H. A., Stroebe, M. S., de Keijser, J., & van den Bout, J. (1997). Intervention for the bereaved: Gender differences in the efficacy of two counselling programmes. *British Journal of Clinical Psychology, 36*, 63–72.

Sikkema, K. J., Kalichman, S. C., Kelly, J. A., & Koob, J. J. (1995). Group intervention to improve coping with AIDS-related bereavement: Model development and an illustrative clinical example. *AIDS Care, 7*, 463–475.

Silove, D. (2000). A conceptual framework for mass trauma: Implications for adaptation, intervention and debriefing. In B. Raphael & J. Wilson (Eds.), *Stress debriefing: Theory, practice and evidence* (pp. 337–350). London: Cambridge University Press.

Singh, B., & Raphael, B. (1981). Post-disaster morbidity of the bereaved: A possible role for preventive psychiatry? *The Journal of Nervous and Mental Disease, 169*, 203–212.

Sireling, L., Cohen, D., & Marks, I. (1988). Guided mourning for morbid grief: A controlled replication. *Behavior Therapy, 19*, 121–132.

Solomon, Z. (1999). Interventions for acute trauma response. *Current Opinion in Psychiatry, 12*, 175–180.

Tunnicliffe, R., & Briggs, D. (1997). Introducing a bereavement support programme in ICU. *Nursing Standard, 11*, 38–40.

Vachon, M. L., Lyall, W. A., & Rogers, J. (1980). A controlled study of self-help interventions for widows. *American Journal of Psychiatry, 137*, 1380–1384.

Vaillant, G. E. (1988). Attachment, loss and rediscovery. *Hillside Journal of Clinical Psychiatry, 10,* 148–164.

Valente, S. M., & Saunders, J. M. (1993). Adolescent grief after suicide. *Crisis, 14*(1), 16–22.

Van der Hart, O., & Goosens, F. A. (1987). Leave taking rituals in mourning and therapy. *Israeli Journal of Psychiatry and Related Sciences, 24,* 87–98.

Van Erdewegh, M. M., Clayton, P. J., & Van Erdewegh, P. (1985). The bereaved child: Variables influencing early psychopathology. *British Journal of Psychiatry, 147,* 188–194.

Vance, J. C., Boyle, F. M., Najman, J. M., & Thearle, M. J. (1995). Gender differences in parental psychological distress following perinatal death or sudden infant death syndrome. *British Journal of Psychiatry, 167,* 806–811.

Vance, J. C., Foster, W. J., Najman, J. M., Embleton, G., Thearle, M. J., & Hodgen, F. M. (1991). Early parental responses to sudden infant death, stillbirth or neo-natal death. *Medical Journal of Australia, 155,* 292–297.

Volkan, V. (1972). A study of patient's "re-grief work." *Psychiatric Quarterly, 45,* 225–273.

Weller, E. B., Weller, R. A., Fristad, M. A., & Bowes, J. M. (1990). Dexamethasone suppression test and depressive symptoms in bereaved children: A preliminary report. *Journal of Neuropsychiatry and Clinical Neuroscience, 2,* 418–421.

West, S. G., Sandler, I., Pillow, D. R., Baca, L., & Gersten, J. C. (1991). The use of structural equation modelling in generative research: Toward the design of a preventive intervention for bereaved children. *American Journal of Clinical Psychology, 19,* 459–480.

Windholtz, M. J., Marmar, C. R., & Horowitz, M. J. (1985). A review of research on conjugal bereavement: Impact on health and efficacy of intervention. *Comprenesive Psychiatry, 26,* 433–447.

Woof, W. R. (1997). The future of bereavement care in British general practice. *European Journal of Cancer Care, 6,* 133–136.

Worden, J. W. (1991). Grieving a loss from AIDS. *Hospital Journal, 7,* 143–150.

Zambelli, G. C., & DeRosa, A. P. (1992). Bereavement support groups for school age children: Theory, intervention and case example. *American Journal of Orthopsychiatry, 62,* 484–493.

Zisook, S., & Shuchter, S. R. (1993). Uncomplicated bereavement. *Journal of Clinical Psychiatry, 54,* 365–372.

Zisook, S., Shuchter, S. R., Sledge, P. A., Paulus, M., & Judd, L. L. (1994). The spectrum of depressive phenomena after spousal bereavement. *Journal of Clinical Psychiatry, 55*(Suppl.), 29–36.

27

TRAUMATIC GRIEF AS A DISTINCT DISORDER: A RATIONALE, CONSENSUS CRITERIA, AND A PRELIMINARY EMPIRICAL TEST

HOLLY G. PRIGERSON AND SELBY C. JACOBS

This chapter will begin with an evaluation of recent research that has accumulated about traumatic grief (TG) symptomatology. More specifically, the available evidence will be reviewed to determine whether it satisfies requirements for the establishment of TG as a distinct clinical entity. Following this review, we will discuss some advantages and disadvantages of developing standardized criteria for TG. Given our belief that the advantages outweigh the disadvantages, we will then describe the logic behind the consensus criteria for TG proposed by a panel of experts. Results of a preliminary test of the proposed criteria set for TG will be reported, directions for their further refinement will be discussed, and assessment tools for TG presented. We will conclude by proposing ways to distinguish

Supported in part by NIMH grant MH-01100 and Claude D. Pepper Older Americans Independence Center grant P60-AG-10498-07. Portions of this chapter appear in H. G. Prigerson, M. K. Shear, S. C. Jacobs, C. F. Reynolds, P. K. Maciejewski, P. A. Pilkonis, C. Wortman, J. B. W. Williams, T. A. Widiger, R. A. Rosenheck, J. Davidson, E. Frank, D. J. Kupfer, & S. Zisook (1999). Consensus criteria for traumatic grief. A preliminary empirical between normal and TG reactions and by suggesting directions for future research.

BACKGROUND

The results of studies of several independent samples of bereaved individuals suggest that symptoms of pathological grief, or what we call "traumatic grief" (TG), form a unified syndrome (Burnett, Middleton, Raphael, & Martinek, 1997; Kim & Jacobs, 1991; Horowitz et al., 1997; Marwit, 1991, 1996; Prigerson, Bierhals, et al., 1996; Prigerson, Frank, et al., 1995; Prigerson, Maciejewski, et al., 1995) with symptoms that are distinct from those of bereavement-related depression and anxiety (Chen et al., 1999; Prigerson, Bierhals, et al., 1996; Prigerson, Frank, et al., 1995; Prigerson, Maciejewski, et al., 1995; Prigerson, Shear, et al., 1996). Research described in the section that follows will be evaluated to determine the extent to which TG symptomatology meets the *DSM-IV* definition of a mental disorder—that is, that it constitutes "a clinically significant behavioral or psychological syndrome or pattern that occurs in an individual and that is associated with present distress (e.g., painful symptom) or disability (i.e., impairment in one or more areas of functioning) or with a significant increased risk of suffering death, pain, disability, or an important loss of freedom" (American Psychiatric Association, 1994, xxi). The taxonomic principles outlined by Robins and Guze (1970) will be applied to an examination of recent studies of TG. The Robins and Guze (1970) principles include (a) the provision of a clinical description of the disorder, (b) laboratory studies that define the disorder, (c) the delimitation of the proposed disorder from other disorders, (d) follow-up studies of the disorder, and (e) family studies of the disorder. To the extent that the *DSM-IV* and Robins and Guze's (1970) requirements for a distinct psychiatric illness are

test. *British Journal of Psychiatry*, *174*, 67–73. Reproduced by permission of the Royal College of Psychiatrists.

The consensus panel comprised the following members: Holly G. Prigerson, PhD, conference organizer, Yale University, New Haven, CT; Charles F. Reynolds III, MD, conference coorganizer; David J. Kupfer, MD, conference coorganizer, University of Pittsburgh, Pittsburgh, PA; M. Katherine Shear, MD, conference coorganizer, University of Pittsburgh, Pittsburgh, PA; Selby C. Jacobs, MD, MPH, Yale University, New Haven, CT; Laurel C. Beery, BS, University of Pittsburgh, Pittsburgh, PA; Jonathan Davidson, MD, Duke University, Raleigh, NC; Ellen Frank, PhD, University of Pittsburgh, Pittsburgh, PA; Paul K. Maciejewski, PhD, Yale University, New Haven, CT; Paul A. Pilkonis, PhD, University of Pittsburgh, Pittsburgh, PA; Thomas Widiger, PhD, University of Kentucky, Janet B. W. Williams, DSW, New York State Psychiatric Institute, New York; Robert Weiss, PhD, University of Massachusetts, Boston, MA; Camille Wortman, PhD, Stony Brook, NY; Sidney Zisook, MD, University of California, San Diego, La Jolla, CA. We wish to thank Simona Noaghiul, MD, MPH, for her psychoanalytic insights.

The conference was supported by the Mental Health Clinical Research Center (Dr. Kupfer, director), the Late-Life Mood Disorders Center (Dr. Charles F. Reynolds III, director), and the Women's Initiatives in Service Effectiveness Center (Dr. M. Katherine Shear, director).

met, TG would appear to be a distinct disorder worthy of diagnosis and treatment.

TAXONOMIC PRINCIPLES FOR VALIDATING DIAGNOSTIC ENTITIES

Below we apply the Robins and Guze (1970) principles to the evidence currently available regarding TG.

Clinical Description

We have found the symptoms of TG to load on a unidimensional factor that is separate from depression in three independent samples of mid- to late-life widows and widowers (Prigerson, Bierhals, et al., 1996; Prigerson, Frank, et al., 1995; Prigerson, Maciejewski, et al., 1995). The internal consistencies found for scales assessing symptoms of TG have been high (Cronbach's alpha = .93 or above) among (a) elderly caregivers of terminally ill spouses (van Doorn, Kasl, Beery, Jacobs, & Prigerson, 1998), (b) young adults who lost a close friend to suicide (Prigerson et al., 1999), (c) both bereaved men and women studied separately (Chen et al., 1999), and (d) Belgian parents who have lost a child as a result of a traffic accident (Spooren, Henderick, & Jannes, in press). Cronbach's alpha of 0.95 was obtained for the current version of our traumatic grief scale, the Inventory of Traumatic Grief (see Appendix A), among a representative sample of 76 elderly widowed residents of Bridgeport, Connecticut, an average of 3.5 months after the loss.

Although the empirical evidence strongly supports the unity among the proposed TG symptoms, these symptoms could be conceptualized as falling into two categories: (a) symptoms of *separation distress*, such as preoccupation with thoughts of the deceased to the point of functional impairment, upsetting memories of the deceased, longing and searching for the deceased, loneliness following the loss; and (b) symptoms of *traumatic distress*, such as feeling disbelief about the death, mistrust, anger, and detachment from others as a result of the death, feeling shocked by the death, and the experience of somatic symptoms of the deceased. The presence of these dual elements of distress influenced our understanding and naming of this disorder.

Although we formerly referred to the disorder as "complicated grief," we prefer traumatic grief for several reasons. First is that we were dissatisfied with the word "complicated" because we considered it vague—it could refer to any of several symptoms of distress. We avoided the terms "pathologic," "neurotic," "distorted," "morbid," and "abnormal" grief because these adjectives seemed somewhat derogatory and value-laden; "unresolved" seemed unsatisfactory because it refers only to the chronicity of the symptoms. Second is that, similar to Horowitz et al. (1997), we consider the reaction to be a stress response syndrome and note that, as such, many of its symptoms resemble those of posttraumatic stress disorder (PTSD; e.g., disbelief, anger, shock, avoidance, numbness, a sense of futility about the future, a fragmented sense of security, trust, control). The trauma to which we refer, however, represents a specific type of trauma—what appears to be a "separation trauma." Accordingly, in several studies we find that the symptoms of traumatic distress load on a single factor with symptoms of separation distress (Prigerson, Bierhals, et al., 1996; Prigerson, Frank, et al., 1995; Prigerson, Maciejewski, et al., 1995). For these reasons we considered the term traumatic grief to capture accurately the phenomenology of the disorder because it refers to the two core components of the syndrome—symptoms of both "traumatic distress" and "separation distress" (grief).

These symptoms of mourning have been observed by authors as diverse as Freud (1917), Lindemann (1944), Bowlby (1973, 1980), Parkes (1987), Raphael and Martinek (1997), and Horowitz et al. (1997). For example, the Horowitz et al. (1997) criteria contain the following symptoms: intrusive thoughts, avoidant behaviors, yearnings, feeling alone and empty, and loss of interest in personal activities. Parkes (1987), Raphael and Martinek (1997), Middleton, Burnett, Raphael, and Martinek (1996), and others also have noted these symptoms. The similarity in the symptoms independently proposed by these diverse psychiatric researchers and experienced clinicians (e.g., yearning, searching, disbelief, loneliness, emptiness, numbness, anger, apathy) suggest a general agreement about the type of symptoms that a disorder of grief would comprise. Thus the symptoms described by diverse bereavement experts provide a clinical profile displaying many common features. The next steps would be to test the performance of a set of agreed on symptoms.

In addition to the symptoms that the disorder comprises, precipitating factors also help to clarify the clinical picture of TG. Results of a recent study demonstrated that a supportive, close, and security-increasing relationship to the deceased predicted severity of TG symptomatology but did not predict severity of depressive symptomatology (van Doorn et al., 1998). Consistent with these results, case studies of four participants with clinically significant levels of TG each revealed a symbiotic, or enmeshed, relationship to the deceased spouse (Prigerson, Shear, Bierhals, et al., 1997; Prigerson, Shear, Frank, et al., 1997).

Laboratory Studies

Several laboratory findings suggest the distinctiveness of the TG syndrome. In a study of late-life bereaved patients, McDermott, Prigerson, and

Reynolds (1997) found that symptoms of TG did not entail the electro-encephalographic (EEG) sleep physiology seen in depression. In addition, unlike symptoms of bereavement-related depression, the symptoms of TG have been shown to be relatively unresponsive to treatment with tricyclic antidepressants (Jacobs, Nelson, & Zisook, 1987; Pasternak et al., 1991; Reynolds et al., 1999), either alone or in combination with Interpersonal Psychotherapy (IPT; Reynolds et al., 1999). Shuchter, Zisook, Kirkorowicz, & Risch (1986) have reported rates of suppression following administration of the Dexamethasone Suppression Test (DST) among bereaved individuals to be associated with severity of phobic and interpersonal anxiety, but not with severity of depressive symptoms. Similarly, Jacobs (1987) observed urinary free cortisol and plasma growth hormone to be associated with severity of separation distress symptoms but not with symptoms of depression in a sample of mid- to late-life widows and widowers. Taken together, the results of these diverse tests suggest that the underlying physiology of TG may be dissimilar to that of depression. Physiological similarities to PTSD remains a question to be answered by future research.

Delimitation From Other Disorders

Much of the resistance to including TG as a distinct diagnostic entity may be rooted in the perception that a disorder of bereavement could be subsumed by established psychiatric disorders—specifically, major depressive disorder (MDD), adjustment disorder (AD), and posttraumatic stress disorder (PTSD). We will next describe why these disorders would not be appropriate for a diagnosis of TG.

Major Depressive Disorder

Several observations distinguish TG from MDD. TG symptoms have been shown to form a distinct symptom cluster apart from symptoms of depression (Chen et al., 1999; Prigerson, Maciejewski, et al., 1995; Prigerson, Shear, et al., 1996), to predict a wide variety of mental and physical health disorders adjusting for and separate from the outcomes associated with depression (Chen et. al., 1999; Prigerson, Bierhals, et al., 1997; Prigerson et al., 1999), to have a distinctive clinical course (Pasternak et al. 1991; Prigerson, Bierhals, et al., 1997; Prigerson, Maciejewski, et al., 1995; Prigerson, Shear, et al., 1996) and response to the DST (Shuchter et al., 1986). They also have distinct neuroendocrine responses (Jacobs, 1987) and responses to pharmacological treatment compared to those found for bereavement-related depression (Jacobs, 1987; Pasternak et al., 1991; Reynolds et al., 1999). They have distinct EEG sleep profiles from MDD (McDermott et al., 1997), and distinct risk factors from depression (Beery et al., 1997; Prigerson, Shear, et al., 1997; van Doorn et al., 1998). In a community sample of widows and widowers we have found that approximately 46% of participants who have syndromal level TG did *not* meet criteria for a diagnosis of MDD (Prigerson, Frank, et al., 1995). These findings indicate that many individuals who would meet criteria for TG would be missed by a diagnosis of MDD.

Adjustment Disorder

Although some clinicians might believe that TG could be subsumed by adjustment disorder (AD), there are several reasons why a diagnosis of AD would not be appropriate for individuals suffering from TG. First, AD does not include the specific clinical features of TG described previously (i.e., the clinical description is imprecise). Second, there is the stipulation that AD "must resolve within 6 months of the termination of the stressor" (American Psychiatric Association, 1994, p. 623), and this would overlook findings that TG symptomatology may last for years and sometimes decades following the loss (Horowitz et al., 1997; Prigerson, Maciejewski, et al., 1995; Prigerson, Shear, et al., 1997; Spooren et al., in press). Third, Criterion D for AD explicitly states that the symptoms cannot be a consequence of bereavement.

Posttraumatic Stress Disorder

Several aspects of TG indicate that, although appearing to be a stress response syndrome, it is not isomorphic with PTSD, as defined in the *DSM-IV*. The most important distinction is that the trauma in TG appears to be a result of separation, which causes separation distress, rather than a result of exposure to a particularly horrific or gruesome experience. Accordingly, PTSD criteria do not include the core symptoms of separation distress such as yearning or searching for the deceased or loneliness resulting from the loss of the loved one. The unbidden, intrusive thoughts about and longings for the deceased are related to a wish to be reunited with him or her, and in the case of TG, it is the absence of the person that is the source of the distress rather than fears that the horrifying event will be reexperienced (Raphael & Martinek, 1997). Reexperiencing the presence of the deceased, in fact, tends to be a source of comfort (Jacobs, 1993; Raphael & Martinek, 1997; Rees, 1971).

Unlike the criteria for complicated grief proposed by Horowitz et al. (1997), which specify avoidant behaviors as one of their two core criteria, as a study by Spooren et al. (in press) and our own preliminary testing of the proposed criteria will demonstrate, the PTSD symptom of avoidance does not adequately distinguish between "cases" and "noncases" of TG. Even in the report by Horowitz et al. (1997), the avoidance item at the recommended 14 months postloss assessment had a sensitivity of only 0.26. Consistent with previous poor performance of the avoidance items, preliminary Item Response Theory (IRT) analyses we have conducted on a community sample of 76 widowed persons in Connecticut revealed the avoidance item to yield the least amount of information for distinguishing between "cases" and "noncases" of TG. Thus the evidence appears to be mounting that avoidance is not an efficient marker for TG. Further research will need to confirm this hypothesis. To the extent it is validated, there will be a need to understand reasons why avoidance manifests itself in unique ways (e.g., denial, unconscious avoidance through dissociation).

Rather than avoidance, the more salient behavior is one of searching for reminders of the deceased. In TG, the hypervigilance relates to scanning the environment for cues of the deceased (Raphael & Martinek, 1997). Although both the criteria for PTSD and the Horowitz et al. (1997) criteria for complicated grief include sleep disturbances as a symptom of the disorder, in a recent EEG sleep study we found no evidence of hyperaroused sleep among participants with syndromal level TG (McDermott et al., 1997). In these ways, the "reexperiencing," "avoidance," and "hyperarousal" criteria for PTSD seem to resemble TG symptomatology, but they appear to have a different focus or significance among those suffering from a "separation trauma" (e.g., reexperiencing refers to thoughts of the person rather than the event; avoidant thoughts and behaviors appear to be less central than the numbness and dissociative features of the disorder; hyperarousal relates to searching for the missing loved one rather than being rooted in the threat posed by a dangerous event).

Additional evidence suggests a lack of diagnostic overlap between individuals with TG and those with PTSD. In a sample of 76 young adult friends who had been exposed to a close friend's suicide, we found that three of the seven (43%) who developed PTSD did not meet our criteria for "caseness" of TG. Of the 16 who met our criteria, 12 (75%) did *not* meet SCID criteria for PTSD (phi = .27; Prigerson et al., 1999). Thus although there is substantial overlap between symptoms of TG and those of PTSD, these two disorders do not appear to be isomorphic, and TG may prove to be a unique type of stress response syndrome.

Follow-Up Studies

Several studies indicate that individuals with syndromal-level TG represent a group with a poor prognosis. First, we find that for a significant minority of individuals, the severity of their TG will persist for years if not decades (Prigerson, Bierhals, et al., 1997; Prigerson, Maciejewski, et al., 1995; Prigerson, Shear, et al., 1997; 1997c; Spooren et al., in press). Second, studies of symptoms of TG assessed at six months postloss have been shown to predict mental and physical health problems (e.g., low self-esteem, poor subjective sleep, cardiac events, cancer), adverse health behaviors (increased alcohol consumption), and an interviewer's 25 months postloss assessment of the severity of their grief, after adjusting for baseline levels of depression, anxiety, age, gender, and previous pathology (Chen et al., 1999; Prigerson, Bierhals, et al., 1997; Prigerson, Frank, et al., 1995). Spooren et al. (in press) have found TG symptomatology to be significantly associated with somatic symptoms and enduring social dysfunction among Belgian parents surviving the death of their child from an automobile accident. The effects of TG on suicidality are particularly striking. Suicidal behaviors are a growing health concern among adolescent and elderly individuals (U.S. DHHS, 1990). We have found TG to be a risk factor for suicidality in both groups (Prigerson, Bierhals, et al., 1997, Prigerson et al., 1999; Szanto, Prigerson, Houck, & Reynolds, 1997).

Family Studies

To date, family studies have not been conducted that could support or refute a tendency for increased prevalence of TG in close relatives.

Taken together, the empirical studies described previously appear to satisfy most of the *DSM-IV* and Robins and Guze (1970) requirements for establishing TG as a distinct clinical entity. To the extent that available evidence is sufficient to justify the claim that TG represents a distinct disorder, it would appear that explicit and agreed on (i.e., standardized) criteria for this disorder are needed.

We are not the first to note the need for uniform diagnostic criteria for pathological grief. For decades, bereavement clinicians and researchers have expressed frustration over the lack of standardized diagnostic criteria for pathological grief (e.g., Corney & Horton, 1974; Jackson, 1957; Jacobs, 1993; Marwit, 1991, 1996; Parkes, 1987). From a clinical perspective, uniform criteria would enable the accurate detection, treatment, and reimbursement for treatment of individuals with this disorder. From a research perspective, studies of the prevalence, risk factors, outcomes, neurobiology, prevention and treatment of TG have been hampered by the absence of standardized criteria.

Nevertheless, there may be some unintended negative consequences of establishing TG as a new nosologic entity. As Averill and Nunley (1993), Eisenbruch (1990), Rosenblatt (1993), and W. Stroebe and Stroebe (1994) noted, societal norms and cultural beliefs shape reactions to loss. Thus establishing uniform criteria for TG may overlook important cultural, as well as individual, differences in reactions to loss. In addition, a variety of subtypes of grief may exist, making a single "duration" or "onset" time from the loss criterion an oversimplification of the "pathological grief" reaction—one that ignores differences between delayed and chronic grief, for example. The application of standardized criteria for a disorder of grief might promote an homogenized view of the ways in which maladaptive grief responses will present themselves and, thereby, reduce an appreciation for individual and cultural variations in reactions to loss.

As Say's law would predict, supply of a diagnosis for TG might create its own demand. Establishing a diagnosis for maladaptive grief might result in the "pathologizing," "medicalizing," or "stigmatizing" of normal reactions to loss. Developing TG as a disorder might encourage an insensitivity to the normal feelings of sadness and loss that accompany the death of a loved one by increasing the likelihood that a bereaved person will be diagnosed as having a "disorder." Averill and Nunley (1993) have suggested that professional systems of care for those with TG may undermine existing family and natural social supports. In light of these potential hazards associated with including TG in the diagnostic nomenclature, M. Stroebe et al. (2000) recommended that efforts to establish TG as a distinct diagnostic entity proceed, at the very least, in a self-conscious way, and emerge only after careful consideration has been given to the negative ramifications that might result.

Despite the potential adverse consequences of establishing standardized criteria for TG (consequences that could be said to result from standardized criteria for most, if not all, psychiatric disorders), we firmly believe this should not prevent efforts to identify and help those who might be at greatest risk for substantial, chronic physical and mental morbidity as a result of being traumatized by a significant loss. In light of the health consequences associated with marked and persistent levels of the TG symptoms, we consider the costs of misdiagnosis to be offset by the benefits of identifying and, ultimately, intervening on behalf of those who suffer the most from their grief. That is, the harm done by not diagnosing those at risk (false negatives) is, in our view, a greater concern than the misdiagnosis of those who are grieving normally (false positives). The development of highly sensitive, specific, and efficient criteria would minimize the likelihood of mislabeling individuals with TG and assist in the accurate detection of those truly suffering from this syndrome. The status quo has been to accept grief as a normal, natural response to loss, and the result has been the relative neglect among mental health professionals of the pain and suffering imposed by grief. The development and testing of efficacious treatments for those suffering from bereavement distress has lagged behind the treatment of other disorders, and lack of standardized criteria may largely be to blame.

In light of these considerations, and our conviction that there exists a definite subgroup of bereaved individuals who could benefit from professional intervention, we, together with our colleagues in Pittsburgh (see the note at the beginning of the chapter for a list of organizers and participants), convened a panel of leading experts in reactions to loss and trauma and in the formulation of diagnostic criteria for psychiatric disorders, to develop agreed on diagnostic criteria for TG. Although the level of sophistication and expertise of the panel members was impressive, we acknowledge that constraints in time, space, money, and availability limited the variety of perspectives represented among the panel members. We next will describe the development of the proposed criteria set by the expert panel. As we test and refine these criteria both in the United States and abroad, we will have an opportunity to modify the criteria, incorporating the views of other bereavement experts who were not able to be present at the workshop.

METHOD

Below is a description of the procedure through which consensus criteria for TG were formulated.

Development of Consensus Criteria

After a review of the available evidence that has emerged about TG, the panel agreed that elevated levels of grief symptomatology pose significant risks for mental and physical morbidity and adverse health behaviors. At the same time, the panel acknowledged that a wide range of "symptoms" that occur after a loss could be considered within normal limits. The question, then, was how best to define the boundary between normal and pathological. After considerable discussion, the panel agreed that certain marked symptoms of grief, persisting for more than two months, should be the critical factor for distinguishing between normal and pathological grief.

The rationale for the two-month duration criterion was as follows: Data from two separate samples demonstrated that a six-month assessment was superior to two- or three-months postloss assessments of TG for the prediction of adverse mental and physical health outcomes (Prigerson, Bierhals, et al., 1997; Prigerson, Frank, et al., 1995; Prigerson, Shear, et al., 1996). These results suggested that a six-month assessment of TG had good predictive validity. In addition, some members of the panel (including the authors of this chapter) were concerned that heightened symptoms of TG *before* six months might encroach on the range of a normal bereavement response. However, some panel members felt that it would be inhumane to insist that bereaved individuals suffer for half a year and preferred to follow the *DSM-IV* rule for major depressive disorder, which stipulates two months postloss as the point after which a diagnosis could be made. These individuals believed that benefits derived from early intervention would more than offset the costs of treating a subset of those individuals whose symptoms might resolve naturally. By focusing on a *duration* of at least two months rather than on the amount of time that had elapsed since the loss, confusion over the diagnosis of delayed reactions would be minimized (a diagnosis could be any time after the loss as long as the symptomatic distress endured at least two months), and those with extreme levels of distress early on could be diagnosed (and, presumably, treated) without delay. For these reasons the panel decided to propose at least two months duration for the chosen symptoms (Criterion C), but recognized that empirical work would ultimately determine when after the death, and how long, the symptoms should endure for a diagnosis of TG.

The panel then addressed the question of how to define the triggering event for TG. We discussed how a wide variety of losses might trigger a TG reaction and wondered whether losses other than a death should be included. Ultimately, we decided to limit the type of loss to a death and to define the criteria for loss as any death of a significant other (see Table 27-1, Criterion A1). We reasoned that once criteria for TG in response to the death of a significant other have been formulated and tested, it would be possible to test the criteria on those grieving over other losses (e.g., terminal illness, divorce).

The next task involved specifying the symptomatic criteria for TG. The panel decided that there were two basic symptom clusters that define TG—symptoms of separation distress and symptoms of traumatic distress (see Table 27-1).

Separation Distress

The group agreed that symptoms of separation distress were at the core of this grief-related disorder. In addition to having experienced the death of a significant other (Criterion A1), Criterion A2 requires that the response involves intrusive, distressing preoccupation with the deceased person (e.g., yearning, longing, or searching). Although loneliness was not explicitly mentioned among the proposed criteria, we have found loneliness to be closely associated with impairments in social functioning and physical health (e.g., Prigerson, Maciejewski, et al., 1995). For these reasons we added a loneliness item and considered it to fit best as a manifestation of separation distress.

Traumatic Distress

The panel decided to incorporate the symptoms of being traumatized by loss into a single cluster (Criterion B). These symptoms were intended to represent bereavement-specific manifestations of being traumatized by the death. The proposed traumatic distress symptoms included efforts to avoid reminders of the deceased; feelings of purposelessness and futility about the future; a sense of numbness or detachment resulting from the loss; feeling shocked, stunned, or dazed by the loss; having difficulty acknowledging the death; feeling that life was empty and unfulfilling without the deceased; having a fragmented sense of trust, security, and control; and

TABLE 27-1
Consensus Criteria Proposed for Traumatic Grief

	Best Threshold[a]	Sensitivity	Specificity
Criterion A			
1. Person has experienced the death of a significant other	N/A	N/A	N/A
2. Response involves distressing, *intrusive preoccupation*[b] with the deceased person (e.g., *yearning, longing,* or *searching* for the deceased)	2	0.69	0.77
	2	0.71	0.80
	3	0.63	0.66
Criterion B—In response to the death, the following symptoms are marked and persistent:			
1. Frequent efforts to avoid reminders of the deceased (e.g., thoughts, feelings, activities, people, places)	3	0.75	0.49
2. Purposelessness or feelings of futility about the future	2	0.86	0.55
3. Subjective sense of numbness, detachment, or absence of emotional responsiveness	3	0.95	0.31
4. Feeling stunned, dazed, or shocked	N/A	N/A	N/A
5. Difficulty acknowledging the death (e.g., disbelief)	3	0.73	0.69
6. Feeling that life is empty or meaningless	3	0.73	0.80
7. Difficulty imagining a fulfilling life without the deceased	3	0.58	0.65
8. Feeling that part of one's self has died	2	0.49	0.92
9. Shattered world view (e.g., lost sense of security, trust, control)	3	0.90	0.31
10. Assumes *symptoms* or harmful behaviors of, or related to, the deceased person	3	0.78	0.49
11. Excessive irritability, bitterness, or anger related to the death	3	0.90	0.49
Criterion C			
Duration of disturbance (symptoms listed) is at least two months	N/A	N/A	N/A
Criterion D			
The disturbance causes clinically significant impairment in social, occupational, or other important areas of functioning[c]	N/A	N/A	N/A

Note: N = 306 widowed research participants at seven months postloss.
[a] "Best Threshold" refers to level that provided the optimal balance of sensitivity and specificity. Coding was as follows: 0 = completely false; 1 = mostly false; 2 = true and false; 3 = mostly true; 4 = completely true. "N/A" indicates no available data for this item.
[b] Sensitivity and specificity refer to the italicized term.
[c] No data were available in the present analyses, but several studies show that these symptoms predict functional impairment.
From H. G. Prigerson, M. K. Shear, S. C. Jacobs, C. F. Reynolds III, P. K. Maciejewski, J. R. T. Davidson, R. A. Rosenheck, P. A. Pilkonis, C. B. Wortman, J. B. W. Williams, T. A. Widiger, E. Frank, D. J. Kupfer, & S. Zisook. (1999). Consensus Criteria for Traumatic Grief: A Preliminary Empirical Test. *British Journal of Psychiatry, 174,* 67–73. Reproduced by permission of the Royal College of Psychiatrists.

experiencing anger over the death. The facsimile illness symptom (i.e., experiencing symptoms or pain similar to that experienced by the deceased before to his or her death) was considered another aspect of being traumatized by the loss. This specific Criterion B item includes both symptoms of facsimile illness and the assumption of harmful behaviors of, or related to, the deceased. A new symptom based on feeling that a part of oneself had died was added to the traumatic distress cluster to capture the identification with the deceased, as well as the sense of dismemberment precipitated by the loss. Taken together, the items of Criterion B were intended to reflect the specific ways in which individuals with TG have been traumatized, or devastated, by their loss.

Preliminary Test of the Consensus Criteria for TG

Below is a description of the methods used to test the proposed consensus criteria for TG.

Sample

Analyses were conducted on data collected from Drs. Sidney Zisook and Stephen Shuchter's San Diego widowhood study. This project recruited all newly bereaved widows and widowers in San Diego County who could be identified by death certificates filed at the San Diego County Department of Health Services. Although a complete description of the study group is available elsewhere (Zisook, Schucter, & Lyons, 1987), we provide a brief description of the recruitment and composition of the study group. Widows and widowers (N = 2466) were mailed a description of the study two to three weeks after the death and were invited to volunteer to participate by returning a postcard indicating their willingness for a home interview. Of the 2466 postcards, 1028 (42%) were returned. Of the 1028 individuals who responded, 435 (42%) said they were or might be interested. All of these individuals were telephoned, and 350 (80%) agreed to participate. Seven weeks after the death of their spouses, these individuals were interviewed in their own homes. No demographic data were available for the nonparticipants, making it difficult to compare respondents with nonrespondents.

Of the 350 widows and widowers who entered the study, 308 (88%) completed the seven-month follow-up questionnaires. There were no differences in demographic factors, percentage of respondents meeting *DSM-III-R* (1987) criteria for MDD, or in mean levels of the TG symptoms at the baseline assessment between those who did or did not complete follow-up questionnaires. The reasons provided for not completing the questionnaire were feeling too busy [N = 5 (6%)], and finding questions about the loss too painful [N = 3 (5%)].

Research participants had a mean age of 61 years (SD = 10.4), 70% were female, and 95% were Caucasian. The mean number of years of schooling was 14.2 (SD = 2.6). Participants had been married an average of 32 years (SD = 14.2). Of the 308 participants, 43 (14%) had experienced a previous depressive episode, and 72 of 308 (23%) met *DSM-III-R* (1987) criteria for MDD at seven months.

Nearly all of the symptoms of the consensus criteria for TG could be found in the Widowhood Questionnaire (Zisook et al., 1987), which included questions assessing grief-specific feeling states, coping strategies, attachment behaviors, maintenance of old relationships, and self-concepts.

Analyses

A series of receiver operating characteristic (ROC) analyses were conducted to determine the operating characteristics for each item of the proposed criteria found in the Widowhood Questionnaire. Although the wording of the items in the Widowhood Questionnaire did not match exactly that of the proposed criteria, items that captured the basic nature of each criterion could be identified for all but the "stunned, dazed and shocked" item. Respondents were asked to determine the extent to which each statement was true for them (0 = completely false to 4 = completely true) at the time the questionnaire was completed (seven months postloss).

Items were examined to evaluate their ability to correctly identify individuals who did and did not meet criteria for "caseness" of TG. The criterion for a "true case" was a score in the upper quintile of the distribution of the summed score of all the proposed criteria, minus the missing "stunned" item. Determining "caseness" in the absence of a diagnostic "gold standard" represented a major challenge. As Kraemer (1992) has noted, a "gold standard" is one that is "considered one of the best diagnostic procedures known to date of this disorder" (p. 7). In contrast with Horowitz et al. (1997), who use a median-split, we chose the top 20% of the distribution of TG scores because this threshold has repeatedly been shown to be the best threshold for distinguishing individuals at risk for functional impairments (e.g., Prigerson, Frank, et al., 1995; Prigerson, Maciejewski, et al., 1995; Prigerson, Shear, et al., 1997). The upper 20% criterion is, in our estimation, one of the best empirically validated bases for determining "caseness." Furthermore, Horowitz et al. (1997) found clinician's global ratings of the presence or absence of "pathological grief" to have comparable sensitivity and specificity to a median-split using a grief symptom inventory, which suggests findings derived from use of a cutoff score may be comparable to those that use a clinician's evaluation.

A high priority was put on correctly identifying those who met criteria for TG (i.e., sensitivity). However, there was also concern for specificity because of the interest in distinguishing between normal and pathological grief reactions. These considerations guided the selection of the "best thresholds" presented in Tables 27-1 and 27-2. The "best threshold" was the level at which sensitivity was optimized with some consideration given to levels of specificity. So, for example, a sensitivity of 0.93 with specificity of 0.80 would be considered a better threshold than a sensitivity of 1.00 with a specificity of 0.17.

RESULTS

Using the upper 20% criterion for "caseness," each of the proposed separation distress items—preoccupation with thoughts of the deceased, yearning, and searching—had sensitivities and specificities in the range of 0.63 to 0.80 (Table 27-1). We then determined the optimal symptom number and threshold for a diagnosis of TG based on the separation distress criteria (Criteria A2) evaluated as a whole. Results indicated that if a respondent endorsed three of these four separation distress symptoms as being at least "sometimes true," then the sensitivity would be 0.83 and the specificity would be 0.80. Although the yearning item had the highest sensitivity among the proposed criteria, when the loneliness item was included, loneliness had the highest sensitivity (0.93). Yearning also had the highest specificity (0.80) for analyses with and without inclusion of the loneliness item.

For the Criterion B traumatic distress items, a sense of numbness, feelings of mistrust, and irritability had sensitivities of 0.90 or higher, but among the lowest specificities. Overall, the sensitivities for this cluster were above 0.73 for all but the "difficulty imagining a fulfilling life without the deceased" and the "feeling that a part of oneself has died" items. There were several indications that the former item was weak. Aside from low sensitivity, it had low specificity, and additional analyses revealed its item-total correlation to be 0.11. Furthermore, the internal consistency obtained for the entire set of items improved with the deletion of this item. For these reasons, we deleted the item. Similarly, we found that the PTSD symptom of avoidance not only had low specificity but its item-total correlation was extremely low ($r = 0.01$), and Cronbach's alpha improved with the deletion of this item in the second round of analyses. Consequently, we deleted the avoidance item. Although the "feeling that a part of oneself had died" item had the lowest sensitivity, it had the highest specificity, so this item was retained.

Refinement of Consensus Criteria

We then reran the analyses omitting the two poorly performing Criterion B items and found that the internal consistency of the entire criteria set improved (from Cronbach's alpha = 0.77 to 0.81). Among this more parsimonious set of items, we found that if a respondent endorsed four of the remaining eight Criterion B items as being "mostly true," the sensitivity would be 0.89 and the specificity would be 0.81. The reanalyses of the Criterion A2 items using the revised threshold score for caseness (i.e., upper 20% of the reduced set of items) revealed an improvement such that endorsing at least three of the four items as at least "sometimes true" yielded an improved sensitivity of 0.93 and specificity of 0.81 for the Criterion A2 items.

We then evaluated the diagnostic probabilities that would result from the combination of Criteria A2 and B. The results indicated that endorsing three of the four Criterion A items and four of the eight Criterion B items would yield a sensitivity of 0.93 and specificity of 0.93. Thus using both criteria conjointly, which is what would occur in clinical practice, would provide the highest rates of sensitivity and specificity. The refined criteria set based on these analyses can be found in Table 27-2.

Assessment Tools for Traumatic Grief

Stemming from the work on diagnostic criteria described earlier, we developed two assessment tools for TG. The first is a structured clinical interview called the Traumatic Grief Evaluation of Response to Loss (TRGR2L; available from the authors). This instrument has the rater evaluate the frequency and intensity of each of the proposed symptoms and provides instructions for determining whether or not the respondent would meet diagnostic criteria for TG. In our feasibility study of 76 widows, we found the kappa between the rater's global assessment of the respondent's grief and the diagnostic algorithm specified in the TRGR2L to be 0.71. The second assessment tool we developed is the Inventory of Traumatic Grief (ITG; Appendix A), which provides a self-report symptom severity score. The ITG also includes instructions to assist raters in determining whether or not the responses would meet the thresholds required for a diagnosis of TG. The ITG has been shown to be internally consistent (Cronbach's alpha = 0.95), and we have obtained perfect concordance between diagnoses for TG obtained using the ITG and those obtained using the TRGR2L in our feasibility study group. TG symptomatology and diagnoses using the ITG and TRGR2L have been shown to be significantly associated with quality of life domains assessed using the Medical Outcomes Survey SF-36 (unpublished data), suggesting criterion-related validity. Although these tools will be subject to further field testing, they have proven reliable and valid instruments for assessing TG and could be used in their present form for clinical or research purposes.

TABLE 27-2
Refined Criteria for Traumatic Grief

	Best Threshold[a]	Sensitivity	Specificity
Criterion A			
1. Person has experienced the death of a significant other	2	0.93	0.81
2. Response involves 3 of the 4 symptoms below experienced at least sometimes:			
2a. intrusive thoughts about the deceased			
2b. yearning for deceased			
2c. searching for the deceased			
2d. loneliness as result of the death			
Criterion B—In response to the death, 4 of the 8 following symptoms experienced as mostly true:	3	0.89	0.82
1. Purposelessness or feelings of futility about the future			
2. Subjective sense of numbness, detachment, or absence of emotional responsiveness			
3. Difficulty acknowledging the death (e.g., disbelief)			
4. Feeling that life is empty or meaningless			
5. Feeling that part of oneself has died			
6. Shattered world view (e.g., lost sense of security, *trust*, control)			
7. Assumes symptoms or harmful behaviors of, or related to, the deceased person			
8. Excessive irritability, bitterness, or anger related to the death			
Criterion C			
Duration of disturbance (symptoms listed) is at least two months	N/A	N/A	N/A
Criterion D			
The disturbance causes clinically significant impairment in social, occupational, or other important areas of functioning	N/A	N/A	N/A
Overall		0.93	0.93

Note: N = 306 widowed research participants at seven months postloss.

[a] Refers to the threshold level with the optimal balance of sensitivity and specificity. Coding: 0 = completely false; 1 = mostly false; 2 = true and false; 3 = mostly true; 4 = completely true.

From H. G. Prigerson, M. K. Shear, S. C. Jacobs, C. F. Reynolds III, P. K. Maciejewski, J. R. T. Davidson, R. A. Rosenheck, P. A. Pilkonis, C. B. Wortman, J. B. W. Williams, T. A. Widiger, E. Frank, D. J. Kupfer, & S. Zisook. (1999). Consensus Criteria for Traumatic Grief. A Preliminary Empirical Test. *British Journal of Psychiatry, 174*, 67–73. Reproduced by permission of the Royal College of Psychiatrists.

DISCUSSION

A review of empirical studies of TG was intended to highlight the extent to which TG would meet the *DSM-IV* definition for a mental disorder and would satisfy most of the requirements for validating a disorder established by Robins and Guze (1970). Although more data are needed, particularly in the area of biological and family studies, the available evidence suggests the validity of TG as a separate diagnostic entity. Consequently, explicit and agreed on criteria for this syndrome appear to be needed.

It was our belief that progress in establishing universally accepted criteria for TG could best be made if a group of experts gathered to (a) discuss the critical diagnostic issues and (b) achieve consensus on a preliminary criteria set. A consensus panel of leading experts convened for the purpose of developing a preliminary criteria set for TG. This chapter presents an agreed on criteria set for TG, provides a preliminary empirical test of the proposed criteria for TG, and suggests a refinement of the criteria based on the empirical results. Future research on a larger, representative sample of widowed persons for whom all the proposed items and responses are available will provide a more definitive testing of the consensus criteria.

Before a discussion of the results, we need to acknowledge the limitations of the data used in the preliminary test of the criteria. First, the study group used to test the criteria was not entirely random or unbiased. Only about 34% of the widowed participants who responded to the initial mailing ultimately enrolled in the study. The absence of information about nonparticipants prevents us from determining how refusers may have differed from participants. However, we know that participants were mostly White, middle-class, well-educated females, and their responses to widowhood may differ from those of other groups. If the reasons for refusal to participate were similar to those provided for dropping out of the study at follow-up, we might expect participants to be less distressed by the loss than the refusers. The low mean levels found for the proposed symptoms of TG suggests this may have been the case. To the extent that this is true, our results may reflect a conservative bias in the reporting of grief-related symptomatology. Although this suggests that scores corresponding to the upper 20% of the distribution might be higher in a more distressed sample, our preliminary analyses of 76 Connecticut widows and widowers an average of 3.5 months postloss found that 20% of this fairly representative community sample met criteria for TG using the algorithm validated in this chapter, suggesting the validity of the 20% prevalence rate. Still, given that this assessment was temporally closer to the loss, we would expect the prevalence to decline by a seven-month assessment. It remains an empirical question if, in a representative sample of widowed elders, 20% of them will meet diagnostic criteria for TG at seven months postloss. In light of the sample limitations inherent in the available data, we refrain from making definitive conclusions and await results from our longitudinal study of 260 representative community widows and widowers on whom we are collecting data on the proposed criteria for TG at 2, 6 and 15 months postloss—a sample on which we will be able to test for gender, cultural, racial, and socioeconomic differences in reactions to loss.

It is also important to acknowledge that the items from the Widowhood Questionnaire, although capturing the essence of most of the symptoms proposed for the disorder, did not contain the exact wording of the proposed criteria. For example, the best available item for "feelings of futility about the future" was an inverse coding of "feeling hopeful about the future"; the best item for feeling that life was "empty" was an inverse coding of feeling that life was "full." The poor performance of the "imagining a fulfilling life without the deceased" may have resulted from using "I will be able to love someone else" (reverse coded) as the best approximation of this item. Consequently, we would not recommend deleting this item until it has been tested explicitly. It is noteworthy that the capacity to love another did not appear to be a good predictor of "caseness" of TG. The Widowhood Questionnaire also did not contain an item to assess feeling stunned, dazed or shocked by the loss (Table 27-1, Criterion B5). Another limitation was that the questionnaire items were scored on a continuum that asked the participant whether the statement was 0 = completely false to 4 = completely true, rather than scoring items as present/absent. Lastly, the criterion for "caseness" of TG indicated the extent to which respondents were above or below the upper quintile of the distribution of the summary score for all the criteria instead of a diagnosis determined by a "gold standard."

Despite these limitations, because these analyses used what we considered to be the best available data to test our consensually agreed on criteria for TG, they represent an important step forward toward strengthening the empirical base for studies in this area.

Performance of the Consensus Criteria for TG

With respect to the Criterion A2 items, we found that as a group, and including a loneliness item, they had satisfactory operating characteristics. Although the rates for the individual items may not seem very high, they are quite similar to the scores reported by Horowitz et al. (1997) for similar items (e.g., at his 14 month postloss assessment, unbidden memories had sensitivity of 0.60 and specificity of 0.76; strong yearning had sensitivity of 0.66 and specificity of 0.97). The high rate of sensitivity achieved by endorsing three of four symptoms as true at least sometimes indicates that this initial criterion would perform well as a means of identifying individuals who have the disorder.

With respect to the Criterion B items, we found that omitting the "not fulfilled without the deceased" and the "avoidance" items enhanced parsimony and improved both the internal consistency and diagnostic accuracy of this "traumatic distress" set. Removing the "avoidance" item was consistent with the results of a study by Spooren et al. (in press), which found extremely low rates of avoidance among bereaved parents. It is also consistent with our preliminary IRT analyses and the view held by Raphael and Martinek (1997), who observed that in contrast with individuals with PTSD who intentionally avert reminders of the trauma, bereaved individuals wish to avoid reminders of the *absence* of the person. Consequently, rather than avoidance, bereaved individuals often seek out cues that remind them of the lost person. The removal of the avoidance item would mark a clear departure from the criteria for complicated grief proposed by Horowitz et al. (1997), which posit avoidance as one of the two criteria required for a diagnosis and highlights the distinction between TG and PTSD for which avoidance is one of the cornerstones of its diagnosis.

Preliminary analyses suggest that avoidance is a not a highly specific marker for the TG syndrome. According to Kaminer and Lavie (1993), avoidance may be a potentially *adaptive* way of coping with loss—what Parkes (1987) referred to as a way bereaved individuals may pace themselves or mitigate the pain associated with the loss. Avoidance may be a conscious process designed to keep out aversive thoughts, whereas disbelief over the death, feeling stunned, shocked, and dazed by the death may represent an active process of banishing from consciousness ideas that are unacceptable to it (through repression or dissociation). Given that the results presented are preliminary, we refrain from recommending the deletion of the avoidance item from the criteria set. In fact, we withhold recommendations regarding the deletion of any of the proposed items until their weak performance has been confirmed after extensive field testing.

The criteria we propose also differ from Horowitz et al. (1997) in that they specify that the diagnosis should not be made before 14 months postloss. The panel agreed, and preliminary analyses found in earlier reports (e.g., Prigerson, Bierhals, et al., 1997; Prigerson, Frank, et al., 1995), as well as the results of this study, suggest that individuals with marked and persistent symptoms of TG can be identified much earlier. Nevertheless, in the absence of analyses that test Criterion C's "at least 2 months duration" stipulation using the proposed criteria, we are unable to draw conclusions about the validity of our duration criterion. By contrast, recent studies (Chen et al., 1999; Prigerson, Bierhals, et al., 1997; Prigerson, Frank, et al., 1995; Prigerson, Maciejewski, et al., 1995; Spooren et al., in press) have demonstrated that symptoms of TG do predict "clinically significant impairment in social, occupational, or other important areas of functioning" (Criterion D).

Taken together, the results of the preliminary test suggest that the criteria proposed by the expert panel, on the whole, appear to have satisfactory operating characteristics and should perform well in determining which bereaved individuals may be suffering from TG.

Distinguishing TG From Normal Grief

To a large extent, normal grief reactions can be characterized by the absence of the specified levels of the proposed criteria. For example, individuals who are able to acknowledge the death (who do not feel disbelief); who do not feel extremely lonely or empty after the loss; who are able to feel emotionally connected to others; who feel that life still holds meaning and purpose; whose sense of self, personal efficacy, and trust in others has not been shaken by the loss; and who are not extremely angered over the loss, would appear to be adapting to life in the absence of the deceased. These survivors would be expected to feel sad about the loss and miss the deceased, particularly in the first few months following the loss, but would experience a gradual return over the first few years after the loss of the capacity for reinvestment in new interests, activities, and relationships. They would also experience an attenuation of their distress (i.e., not have marked and persistent levels of TG symptoms) and generally appear capable of adjusting to their new circumstances without undue difficulty.

CONCLUSION

Extensive field testing of the proposed criteria on representative samples of bereaved individuals will be required before standardized criteria can be proposed. Future studies will need to determine the optimal timing–duration criterion and to test for possible subtypes of TG. The syndrome we outline appears similar to that of "chronic grief" described by researchers such as Middleton et al. (1996), but future studies may find support for subtypes such as "delayed" or "inhibited" grief. Studies will need to determine if the symptomatic presentation differs based on the survivor's age, kinship, and connection to the deceased (e.g., parent, degree of closeness), and according to the traumatic circumstances of the death (e.g., suicide, homicide, accidents). Future work could also examine the extent to which this syndrome emerges after other types of losses (e.g., divorce). Following the lead of researchers such as Eisenbruch (1990), studies of TG begun in other countries (e.g., Pakistan, Norway, Egypt, Chile, Belgium) will inform us of the role of culture in reactions to bereavement. The proposal and preliminary testing of consensus criteria provide an initial step toward the international standardization of diagnostic criteria for TG.

REFERENCES

American Psychiatric Association. (1994). *Diagnostic and statistical manual of mental disorders* (4th ed.). Washington, DC: Author.

Averill, J. R., & Nunley, E. P. (1993). Grief as an emotion and as a disease: A social-constructionist perspective. In M. S. Stroebe, W. Stroebe, & R. O. Hansson (Eds.), *Handbook of bereavement: Theory, research and intervention* (pp. 23–43). New York: Cambridge University Press.

Beery, L. C., Prigerson, H. G., Bierhals, A. J., Santucci, L., Newsom, J. T., Maciejewski, P. K., Rapp, S., Fasiczka, A., & Reynolds, C. F. III. (1997). Traumatic grief, depression and caregiving in elderly spouses of the terminally ill. *Omega, 35,* 261–279.

Bowlby, J. (1973). *Attachment and loss. Vol 2: Separation, anxiety and anger.* London: Hogarth Press.

Bowlby, J. (1980). *Attachment and loss. Vol 3: Loss, sadness, and depression.* New York: Basic Books.

Burnett, P., Middleton, W., Raphael, B., & Martinek, N. (1997). Measuring core bereavement phenomena. *Psychological Medicine, 27,* 49–57.

Chen, J. C., Bierhals, A. J., Prigerson, H. G., Kasl, S. V., Mazure, C. M., Reynolds, C. F., Shear, M. K., Day, N., & Jacobs, S. C. (1999). Gender differences in health outcomes resulting from bereavement-related emotional distress. *Psychological Medicine, 29,* 367–380.

Corney, R., & Horton, F. (1974). Pathological grief following spontaneous abortion. *American Journal of Psychiatry, 121,* 825–827.

Eisenbruch, M. (1990). The cultural bereavement interview: A new clinical research approach for refugees. *Psychiatric Clinics of North America, 13,* 715–735.

Freud, S. (1917). Mourning and melancholia. *Internationale Zeitschrift für arzliche Psychoanalyse, 4,* 288–301.

Horowitz, M. J., Siegel, B., Holen, A., Bonnano, G. A., Milbrath, C., & Stinson, C. H. (1997). Criteria for complicated grief disorder. *American Journal of Psychiatry, 154,* 905–910.

Jackson, E. (1957). *Understanding grief: Its roots, dynamics, and treatment.* New York: Arbindon Press.

Jacobs, S. C. (1987). Psychoendocrine aspects of bereavement. In S. Zisook (Ed.), *Biopsychosocial aspects of bereavement* (pp. 139–155). Washington, DC: American Psychiatric Association Press.

Jacobs, S. C. (1993). *Pathological grief.* Washington, DC: American Psychiatric Association Press.

Jacobs, S. C., Nelson, J. C., & Zisook, S. (1987). Treating depressions of bereavement with antidepressants: a pilot study. *Psychiatric Clinics of North America, 10,* 501–510.

Kaminer H., & Lavie, P. (1993). Sleep and dreams in Holocaust survivors. In

M. S. Stroebe, W. Stroebe, & R. O. Hansson (Eds.), *Handbook of bereavement: Theory, research, and intervention* (pp. 331–343). New York: Cambridge University Press.

Kim, K., & Jacobs, S. C. (1991). Pathologic grief and its relationship to other psychiatric disorders. *Journal of Affective Disorders, 21,* 257–263.

Kraemer, H. C. (1992). *Evaluating medical tests: Objective and quantitative guidelines.* Newbury Park, CA: Sage.

Lindemann, E. (1944). Symptomatology and management of acute grief. *American Journal of Psychiatry, 101,* 141–148.

Marwit, S. J. (1991). DSM III-R, Grief reactions, and a call for revision. *Professional Psychology: Research and Practice, 22,* 75–79.

Marwit S. J. (1996). Reliability of diagnosing complicated grief: a preliminary investigation. *Journal of Consulting and Clinical Psychology, 64,* 538–563.

McDermott, O., Prigerson, H. G., & Reynolds, C. F. III. (1997). EEG sleep in complicated grief and bereavement-related depression: A preliminary report. *Biological Psychiatry, 41,* 710–716.

Middleton, W., Burnett, P., Raphael, B., & Martinek, N. (1996). The bereavement response: A cluster analysis. *British Journal of Psychiatry, 169,* 167–171.

Parkes, C. M. (1987). *Bereavement: Studies of grief in adult life* (2nd ed.). Madison, CT: International Universities Press.

Pasternak, R. E., Reynolds, C. F., Schlernitzauer, M., Hoch, C. C., Buysse, D. J., Houck, P. R., & Perel, J. M. (1991). Acute open-trial nortriptyline therapy of bereavement-related depression in late life. *Journal of Clinical Psychiatry, 52,* 307–310.

Prigerson, H. G., Bierhals, A. J., Kasl, S. V., Reynolds, C. F. III, Shear, M. K., Day, N., Berry, L. C., Newsom, J. T., & Jacobs, S. (1997). Traumatic grief as a risk factor for mental and physical morbidity. *American Journal of Psychiatry, 54,* 617–623.

Prigerson, H. G., Bierhals, A. J., Kasl, S. V., Reynolds, F. III, Shear, M. K., Newsom, J. T., & Jacobs, S. (1996). Complicated grief as a distinct disorder from bereavement-related depression and anxiety: A replication study. *American Journal of Psychiatry, 153,* 84–86.

Prigerson, H. G., Frank, E., Kasl, S. V., Reynolds, C. F. III, Anderson, B., Zubenko, G. S., Houck, P. R., George, C. J., & Kupfer, D. J. (1995). Complicated grief and bereavement-related depression as distinct disorders: Preliminary empirical validation in elderly bereaved spouses. *American Journal of Psychiatry, 152,* 22–30.

Prigerson, H. G., Kupfer, D. J., Beery, L. C., Bridge, J., Rosenheck, R. A., Maciejewski, P. K., Iyengar, S., & Brent, D. A. (1999). Traumatic grief as a risk factor for suicidal ideation among young adult men and women. *American Journal of Psychiatry, 156,* 1994–1995.

Prigerson, H. G., Maciejewski, P. K., Newsom, J., Reynolds, C. F. III, Frank, E., Bierhals, E. J., Miller, M., Fasiczka, A., Doman, J., & Houck, P. R. (1995).

The Inventory of Complicated Grief: A scale to measure maladaptive symptoms of loss. *Psychiatry Research, 59*, 65–79.

Prigerson, H. G., Shear, M. K., Bierhals, A. J., Wolfson, L., Erenpreis, L., & Reynolds, C. F. III. (1997). Case histories of complicated grief. *Omega, 35*, 9–24.

Prigerson, H. G., Shear, M. K., Frank, E., Silberman, R., & Reynolds, C. F. III. (1997). Traumatic grief: A case of loss-induced trauma. *American Journal of Psychiatry, 154*, 1003–1009.

Prigerson, H. G., Shear, M. K., Newsom, J., Frank, E., Reynolds, C. F. III, Houck, P. R., Bierhals, A., Kupfer, D. J., & Maciejewski, P. K. (1996). Anxiety among widowed elders: Is it distinct from depression and grief? *Anxiety, 2*, 1–12.

Raphael, B., & Martinek, N. (1997). Assessing traumatic bereavement and PTSD. In J. P. Wilson & T. M. Keane (Eds.), *Assessing psychological trauma and PTSD* (pp. 373–395). New York: Guilford Press.

Rees, W. D. (1971). The hallucinations of widowhood. *British Medical Journal, 4*, 37–41.

Reynolds, C. F., Miller, M. D., Pasternak, R. E., Frank, E., Perel, J. M., Cornes, C., Houck, P. R., Mazumdar, S., Dew, M. A., & Kupfer, D. J. (1999). Treatment of bereavement-related major depressive episodes in later life: A controlled study of acute and continuation treatment with nortriptyline and Interpersonal Psychotherapy. *American Journal of Psychiatry, 156*, 202–208.

Robins, L., & Guze, S. B. (1970). Establishment of diagnostic validity in psychiatric illness: Its application to schizophrenia. *American Journal of Psychiatry, 126*, 983–987.

Rosenblatt, P. C. (1993). Grief: The social context of private feelings. In M. S. Stroebe, W. Stroebe, & R. O. Hansson (Eds.), *Handbook of bereavement: Theory, research and intervention* (pp. 102–111). New York: Cambridge University Press.

Shuchter, S. R., Zisook, S., Kirkorowicz, C., & Risch, C. (1986). The dexamethazone test in acute grief. *American Journal of Psychiatry, 143*, 879–881.

Spooren, D. J., Henderick, H., & Jannes, C. (in press). A retrospective study of parents bereaved from a child in a traffic accident: Service satisfaction, available support, and psychiatric sequelae. *Omega*.

Stroebe, M., van Son, M., Stroebe, W., Kleber, R., Schut, H., & van den Bout, J. (2000). On the classification and diagnosis of pathological grief. *Clinical Psychology Review, 20*, 57–75.

Stroebe, W., & Stroebe, M. (1994). Is grief universal? Cultural variations in the emotional reaction to loss. In R. Fulton & R. Bendiksen (Eds.), *Death and identity* (pp. 177–209). Philadelphia: Charles Press.

Szanto, K., Prigerson, H. G., Houck, P. R., & Reynolds, C. F. (1997). Suicidal ideation in elderly bereaved: The role of complicated grief. *Suicide and Life-Threatening Behavior, 27*, 10–15.

U.S. Department of Health and Human Services. (1990). Healthy People 2000:

National health promotion and disease prevention objectives. (DHHS Pub. No. (PHS) 91-50212). Washington, DC: U.S. Government Printing Office.

van Doorn, C., Kasl, S. V., Beery, L. C., Jacobs, S. C., & Prigerson, H. G. (1998). Qualities of marriage associated with traumatic grief and depressive symptomatology. *Journal of Nervous and Mental Disease, 186,* 566–573.

Zisook, S., Shuchter, S. R., & Lyons, L. E. (1987). Predictors of psychological reactions during the early course of bereavement. *Psychiatric Clinics of North America, 19,* 355–367.

APPENDIX A
INVENTORY OF TRAUMATIC GRIEF (ITG)

Holly Prigerson, Stanislav Kasl, and Selby Jacobs

Please mark the box next to the answer that best describes how you have been feeling over the past *month*. The blanks refer to the deceased person over whom you are grieving.

Almost never = less than once a month
Rarely   = once a month or more, less than once a week
Sometimes   = once a week or more, less than once a day
Often   = once every day
Always   = several times every day

1. The death of _____ feels overwhelming or devastating.

Almost never	☐₁
Rarely	☐₂
Sometimes	☐₃
Often	☐₄
Always	☐₅

2. I think about _____ so much that it can be hard for me to do the things I normal do.

Almost never	☐₁
Rarely	☐₂
Sometimes	☐₃
Often	☐₄
Always	☐₅

3. Memories of _____ upset me.

Almost never	☐₁
Rarely	☐₂
Sometimes	☐₃
Often	☐₄
Always	☐₅

4. I feel that I have trouble accepting the death.

Almost never $\square_1$

Rarely $\square_2$

Sometimes $\square_3$

Often $\square_4$

Always $\square_5$

5. I feel myself longing and yearning for _____.

Almost never $\square_1$

Rarely $\square_2$

Sometimes $\square_3$

Often $\square_4$

Always $\square_5$

6. I feel drawn to places and things associated with _____.

Almost never $\square_1$

Rarely $\square_2$

Sometimes $\square_3$

Often $\square_4$

Always $\square_5$

7. I can't help feeling angry about _____'s death.

Almost never $\square_1$

Rarely $\square_2$

Sometimes $\square_3$

Often $\square_4$

Always $\square_5$

8. I feel disbelief over _____'s death.

Almost never $\square_1$

Rarely $\square_2$

Sometimes $\square_3$

Often $\square_4$

Always $\square_5$

9. I feel stunned, dazed, or shocked over _____'s death.

Almost never	☐₁
Rarely	☐₂
Sometimes	☐₃
Often	☐₄
Always	☐₅

10. Ever since _____ died it is hard for me to trust people.

No difficulty trusting others	☐₁
A slight sense of difficulty	☐₂
Some sense	☐₃
A marked sense	☐₄
An overwhelming sense	☐₅

11. Ever since _____ died I feel like I have lost the ability to care about other people or I feel distant from people I care about.

No difficulty feeling close or connected to others	☐₁
A slight sense of detachment	☐₂
Some sense	☐₃
A marked sense	☐₄
An overwhelming sense	☐₅

12. I have pain in the same area of my body, some of the same symptoms, or have assumed some of the behaviors or characteristics of _____.

Almost never	☐₁
Rarely	☐₂
Sometimes	☐₃
Often	☐₄
Always	☐₅

13. I go out of my way to avoid reminders that _____ is gone.

Almost never	☐₁
Rarely	☐₂
Sometimes	☐₃
Often	☐₄
Always	☐₅

14. I feel that life is empty or meaningless without _____.

No sense of emptiness or meaninglessness	☐₁
A slight sense of emptiness or meaninglessness	☐₂
Some sense	☐₃
A marked sense	☐₄
An overwhelming sense	☐₅

15. I hear the voice of _____ speak to me.

Almost never	☐₁
Rarely	☐₂
Sometimes	☐₃
Often	☐₄
Always	☐₅

16. I see _____ stand before me.

Almost never	☐₁
Rarely	☐₂
Sometimes	☐₃
Often	☐₄
Always	☐₅

17. I feel like I have become numb since the death of _____.

No sense of numbness	☐₁
A slight sense of numbness	☐₂
Some sense	☐₃
A marked sense	☐₄
An overwhelming sense	☐₅

18. I feel that it is unfair that I should live when _____ died.

No sense of guilt over surviving the deceased ☐₁

A slight sense of guilt ☐₂

Some sense ☐₃

A marked sense ☐₄

An overwhelming sense ☐₅

19. I am bitter over _____'s death.

No sense of bitterness ☐₁

A slight sense of bitterness ☐₂

Some sense ☐₃

A marked sense ☐₄

An overwhelming sense ☐₅

20. I feel envious of others who have not lost someone close.

Almost never ☐₁

Rarely ☐₂

Sometimes ☐₃

Often ☐₄

Always ☐₅

21. I feel like the future holds no meaning or purpose without _____.

No sense that the future holds no purpose ☐₁

A slight sense that the future holds no purpose ☐₂

Some sense ☐₃

A marked sense ☐₄

An overwhelming sense ☐₅

22. I feel lonely every since _____ died.

Almost never ☐₁

Rarely ☐₂

Sometimes ☐₃

Often ☐₄

Always ☐₅

23. I feel unable to imagine life being fulfilling without _____.

$$\text{Almost never} \quad \square_1$$
$$\text{Rarely} \quad \square_2$$
$$\text{Sometimes} \quad \square_3$$
$$\text{Often} \quad \square_4$$
$$\text{Always} \quad \square_5$$

24. I feel that a part of myself died along with the deceased.

$$\text{Almost never} \quad \square_1$$
$$\text{Rarely} \quad \square_2$$
$$\text{Sometimes} \quad \square_3$$
$$\text{Often} \quad \square_4$$
$$\text{Always} \quad \square_5$$

25. I feel that the death has changed my view of the world.

$$\text{No sense of a changed world view} \quad \square_1$$
$$\text{A slight sense of a changed world view} \quad \square_2$$
$$\text{Some sense} \quad \square_3$$
$$\text{A marked sense} \quad \square_4$$
$$\text{An overwhelming sense} \quad \square_5$$

26. I have lost my sense of security or safety since the death of _____.

$$\text{No change in feelings of security} \quad \square_1$$
$$\text{A slight sense of insecurity} \quad \square_2$$
$$\text{Some sense} \quad \square_3$$
$$\text{A marked sense} \quad \square_4$$
$$\text{An overwhelming sense} \quad \square_5$$

27. I have lost my sense of control since the death of _____.

$$\text{No change in feelings of being in control} \quad \square_1$$
$$\text{A slight sense of being out of control} \quad \square_2$$
$$\text{Some sense of being out of control} \quad \square_3$$
$$\text{A marked sense} \quad \square_4$$
$$\text{An overwhelming sense} \quad \square_5$$

28. I believe that my grief has resulted in significant impairment in my social, occupational or other areas of functioning.

No functional impairment ☐₁
Mild functional impairment ☐₂
Moderate ☐₃
Severe ☐₄
Extreme ☐₅

29. I have felt on edge, jumpy, or easily startled since the death.

No change in feelings of being on edge ☐₁
A slight sense of feeling on edge ☐₂
Some sense ☐₃
A marked sense ☐₄
An overwhelming sense ☐₅

30. Since the death, my sleep has been . . .

Basically okay ☐₁
Slightly disturbed ☐₂
Moderately disturbed ☐₃
Very disturbed ☐₄
Extremely disturbed ☐₅

31. How many months after your loss did these feelings begin?

_____ months

32. How many months have you been experiencing these feelings?

_____ months   (0 = never)

33. Have there been times when you did not have pangs of grief and then these feelings began to bother you again?

Yes ☐₁
No ☐₂

34. Can you describe how your feelings of grief have changed over time?

For Office Purposes Only

35. If interviewer-administered, does rater consider this respondent to have syndromal level Traumatic Grief?

Yes ☐₁

No ☐₂

36. Does respondent meet the following criteria for Traumatic Grief?

Criterion A1

- The death of a significant other is a prerequisite for completion of the ITG.

Criterion A2

Separation Distress: at least 3 of the 5 following symptoms must be greater than or equal to 4 ("often," "very," or "marked").

- Q2, Q3, Q5, Q6, Q22

Criterion B

Traumatic Distress: at least 6 of the 12 following symptoms must be greater than or equal to 4.

- Q4, Q7, Q8, Q9, Q11, Q13, Q14, Q17, Q19, Q21, Q23, Q26

Criterion C

- Q32 is greater than 2 months.

Criterion D

- Q28 is greater than or equal to 4 ("severe").

Yes ☐₁

No ☐₂

28

GRIEF AND COGNITIVE–BEHAVIORAL THERAPY: THE RECONSTRUCTION OF MEANING

STEPHEN FLEMING AND PAUL ROBINSON

Neimeyer (1998) has argued for the application of a "new wave" of grief theory, involving the need for increased attention to the cognitive processes entailed in mourning. Indeed, within the evolving, general conceptualizations of grief, there is growing understanding of the adjustment to bereavement as one of meaning reconstruction or the rebuilding of previously held assumptions (e.g., Janoff-Bulman & Berg, 1998). In their consideration of postmodern understandings of grief, Silverman and Klass (1996) further noted that the meaning of the loss is negotiated and re-negotiated over time. This represents a significant paradigm shift from the psychoanalytic emphasis on object loss, decathexis, and disengagement to the bereaved revisiting the experience and maintaining a constant, yet ever-changing, connection to the deceased. In effect, moving from a "going on" to an "ongoing" perspective of the loss. In our view, therefore, a therapeutic approach such as cognitive–behavioral therapy (CBT) seems most fitting as therapists assist bereaved individuals in exploring and articulating their ongoing construction of the relationship with the deceased.

This chapter begins with a brief overview of the origins and assumptions of CBT and the application of this approach to loss situations. Although the various techniques and strategies of CBT will be mentioned throughout our discussion, the details of such methods are not outlined and may be found in other resources. Instead, we will focus on several areas of interest that we feel are of central use in working effectively with bereaved clients. Following a discussion of the application of CBT to the more general issue of trauma and the specific issue of traumatic loss, we will highlight the cognitive tasks of meaning making and the phenomenon of counterfactual thinking. This latter notion is well-researched in social psychology but to our knowledge has not been integrated into the study and practice of cognitive therapy. Nevertheless, this a most relevant and useful body of research-based knowledge, of direct, immediate value in the therapeutic interaction with many bereaved individuals.

COGNITIVE–BEHAVIORAL THERAPY

Although various forms of cognitive–behavioral therapy (CBT) are practiced, each emphasizing or articulating different aspects of similar, general principles and methods, A. Beck (1963, 1964) and Ellis (1962) usually are acknowledged as the most productive and influential pioneers of CBT. Other major theorists contributing to the early development of these ideas include Kelly (1955), Lazarus (1976), Mahoney (1974), and Meichenbaum (1977; see Rachman, 1997, for a detailed discussion of the evolution of CBT). A. Beck noted that phenomenological approaches to psychology, structural theory, depth psychology, and cognitive psychology each contributed to the theoretical foundations of cognitive therapy. He also acknowledged the influence of Freudian theory, particularly the hierarchical structuring of cognition into primary and secondary processes and the view that pathogenic ideas undergird clinical symptomatology (A. Beck & Rush, 1995; A. Beck & Weishaar, 1989). George Kelly's (1955) formulation of personal constructs was another major influence on A. Beck's work, as was contemporary behaviorism (e.g., Bandura, 1977).

By 1988, Mahoney observed that a "cognitive revolution" was underway and that the cognitive theories and therapies were a major force in contemporary approaches to psychological services. At the same time, however, he also noted that there were clear signs of conceptual and practical differentiation among those who considered themselves "cognitivists." In particular, Mahoney (1988) contrasted traditional, "rationalist" cognitive therapy approaches (e.g., Ellis, 1962) with developmental or "constructivist" perspectives (e.g., Guidano & Liotti, 1983). Such a distinction reflected the growing influence of postmodernism, a reaction to the modernist belief in an objectively knowable world, a singular truth, quantitative scientific method, and numerous other points of comparison (see Neimeyer, 1995).

Mahoney's (1988) work, and earlier work by others such as Guidano and Liotti (1983), seemed to herald the onset of substantial debate and growth within the cognitive therapy community. Indeed, as most recently noted by Neimeyer (1998), it is not clear that constructivist psychotherapy (e.g., Neimeyer & Mahoney, 1995) should be considered within the sphere of cognitive therapy at this point. Nevertheless, constructivist notions inherent in the cognitive approach have continued to be articulated and integrated by many cognitive–behavioral theorists and therapists (e.g., Alford & Beck, 1997), such that the central importance of phenomenology and personal meaning in the therapeutic encounter continues to be emphasized. Indeed, as recently outlined by Clark and Steer (1996), the core tenet of the cognitive model is that people are actively involved in constructing their own realities.

Assumptions and Principles of CBT

Clark and Steer (1996) recently concluded that four intrinsic assumptions can be identified that guide cognitive theory and treatment. First, as already mentioned, it is assumed that individuals actively construct their reality, such that highly personal, idiosyncratic meanings are attached to events. Second, it is assumed that cognition mediates affect and behavior. Often the cognitive model is misunderstood as based on a "billiard ball" theory, in which cognition simply causes affective and behavioral difficulties. Instead, cognitive theorists posit that cognition, emotion, and behavior are reciprocally determining and interactive constructs. Third, cognition is knowable and accessible. This is not to say that all cognition is conscious or controlled but, rather, people can be guided to gain access to their faulty information processing. Fourth, cognitive change is central to human change processes. In other words, any affective or behavioral change can only occur coincident with change in the mediating cognitive products, processes, and structures. Of course, there are many ways this might be achieved, and by no means is CBT the only method by which cognitive shifts occur.

A final important aspect of the general cognitive model and associated assumptions relates to the notion of levels of cognitive functioning. Often a tripartite conceptualization is outlined (A. Beck, Rush, Shaw, & Emery 1979; Hollon & Kriss, 1984; Howes & Parrott, 1991), comprising (a) cognitive content or automatic thoughts, (b) cognitive processes or information-processing styles, and (c) cognitive structures or schemas. In a given, specific situation, automatic thoughts tend to occur rapidly and without intention. In contrast, cognitive processing styles and schemas are cross-situational tendencies, either "error" tendencies in the processing of information (e.g., selective abstraction, overgeneralization) or activated overarching schemas that are more absolute and core in nature. For example, an automatic thought about receiving a poor grade on an exam may be, "I knew I didn't do very well on this test," whereas an activated schema may take the form of a more general and absolute notion, such as "I am a failure." The therapist will want to be particularly alert for the presence of these more wide-ranging, often self-related schemas. It should be noted that A. Beck (1996; Alford & Beck, 1997) more recently outlined a global expansion of simple schema theory, a development that provides the scaffolding for a wholly integrated theory of personality and psychopathology.

A typical CBT session involves direct, collaborative discussion between client and therapist, in which the focus of the meeting is agreed on by both parties. The therapist assumes no a priori knowledge of the individual's meaning system and looks to the client for the provision of this. Although there may be some consideration of past experiences, there is an emphasis on the present, with an anticipation of the near future in which the client may observe–experiment with a "next step" toward reaching a previously agreed on goal. Thus much work is done between sessions by clients, with attention paid in the next session to the results of this activity.

The Socratic method and the therapist stance of "guided discovery" are fundamental to the standard CBT approach. According to Padesky (1996), Socratic questioning involves asking the client questions that the client has the knowledge to answer, drawing the client's attention to information that may be outside the client's current focus, and generally moving from the concrete to the more abstract, such that the client can apply the new information to either reevaluate a previous conclusion or construct a new idea. Clearly, this general approach allows for an emergence of the client's phenomenology and shows a respect for this. Moreover, this process of guided discovery enables clients to realize something they did not expect.

The treatment is not something "done" to the client but a process in which the client discovers and learns to use skills and strategies that can continue to be applied long after the contact with the therapist has ended. For those less familiar with CBT, fundamental approaches and techniques are well-outlined in material offered by J. Beck (1995); Freeman, Simon, Beutler, and Arkowitz (1989); Padesky and Greenberger (1995); and Persons (1989). Salkovskis (1996), Clark and Fairburn (1997), and Alford and Beck (1997) provide more advanced discussions of the contemporary practice of CBT, as well as current theoretical advances and future directions. Therapies that are primarily constructivist in nature lead to quite different therapeutic stances and techniques, as exemplified in the compendium edited by Neimeyer and Mahoney (1995).

The Application of CBT to Bereavement

Since its original development and application in the treatment of depression (A. Beck et al., 1979), CBT now has been applied and found effective in a wide range of psychological problems (see Barlow & Hoffman, 1997; Clark & Steer, 1996; Roth & Fonagy, 1996; and Wright & Beck, 1994, for more extensive reviews of the applications and efficacy of CBT). In addition to a proven effectiveness in the treatment of depression (e.g., Dobson, 1989), CBT is now a well-established therapeutic approach to various anxiety disorders, substance abuse, eating disorders, chronic pain, couples/marital problems, personality disorders, among numerous other applications (J. Beck, 1995).

The application of CBT to the realm of adjustment to loss and grief has been limited in comparison to the myriad pursuits noted previously. We refer the reader to our previous work in which much of the most relevant psychotherapy outcome research is summarized (Fleming & Robinson, 1991). In brief, the most common *behavioral* interventions used in the treatment of problematic grief responses have included flooding (Ramsey, 1977) and graduated exposure to grief-eliciting stimuli (Gauthier & Pye, 1979; Hodgkinson, 1982; Lieberman, 1978; Mawson, Marks, Ramm, & Stern, 1981; Melges & DeMaso, 1980; Turco, 1981). Only a handful of authors have outlined specific *cognitive* therapeutic approaches to grief (e.g., Abrahms, 1981; Woodfield & Viney, 1984). Powers and Wampold (1994) assessed the impact of numerous *cognitive–behavioral* strategies on postmorbid adjustment and concluded that the learning of health-protective behaviors (e.g., proper rest, nutrition, and so forth), the attribution of personal meaning to the loss, differentiating "letting go" from forgetting the deceased, and the ability to modulate the experience of the distressing components of grief were significantly related to adjustment in a sample of widows.

Aside from the Powers and Wampold (1994) research, a recent search to update the list of pertinent empirical research revealed few directly relevant citations. The reasons for this lack of formal reporting on the use of CBT in bereavement situations likely is a function of several factors, including the nature of grief as well as the nature of CBT and its traditional uses and emphases (see the observations of Moorey, 1996, described later). Moreover, it may be that quantitative, modernistic methodologies are not well-suited to the study of grief, at least as we are beginning to conceptualize it, such that emerging qualitative psychotherapy research methods simply lead to quite different interests and enquiries (Silverman & Klass, 1996). Regardless, quantitative outcome data assessing the efficacy of CBT with bereaved people are lacking.

Moorey (1996) recently addressed the issue of the use of CBT in realistically stressful, objectively negative situations. He argues that adverse life events pose two problems for standard cognitive therapy: First, how does CBT deal with realistic negative thoughts? Second, how does CBT apply to situations that are not static in nature but are processes of adjustment? Indeed, CBT most often has been applied in the treatment of static pathological states, conditions including cognitive distortion of reality in a manner associated with abnormal affective and behavioral symptomatology. Grief, on the other hand, is a natural, nonpathological condition of human existence, involving a continual, changing process of adjustment. In referring to those who are facing the death of a loved one or who have developed a serious illness like cancer, Moorey (1996) noted, "The negative thoughts verbalized by these patients may reflect an accurate appraisal of their surroundings. Even if these thoughts are distorted, it could be argued that they are often part of a natural sequence of reactions to stress, part of a natural process of grieving" (p. 451).

Thus it initially may appear that CBT is not an appropriate approach to the consideration of adjustment to loss. However, consistent with the conclusions of Moorey (1996), it is our experience that there are various ways in which the cognitive model, conceptualization, and techniques remain well-suited to bereavement situations. Whether an individual is seen as chronically grieving or somehow "stuck" in the process of adjustment, or is actively avoiding any degree of healthy confrontation–consideration of the related affective experience or processing of grief, or is experiencing guilt as a result of counterfactual thinking, there may be some degree of cognitive "distortion" contributing to these adjustment patterns. In these cases, the cognitive approach and exploration of one's personal view certainly seems appropriate. Of course, if one's grief process obviously is complicated by an affective, anxiety, or other disorder, CBT will be directly useful in attempting to assist the individual in managing these additional challenges. In passing, although consideration of masculine–feminine differences in responding to loss is beyond the scope of this chapter, Martin and Doka (1996) intimate that CBT, with its emphasis on thought processes and cognitive mastery, may be more suited to the male griever (or anyone with this particular personality style).

As Moorey pointed out, even in the case of seemingly "rational" responses to adverse life situations, there still may be aspects of a person's perspective that are somehow distorted and self-defeating. Thus it is an important therapeutic task to search beyond the surface level, apparently appropriate and entirely understandable perspectives, and identify other levels of idiosyncratic meaning that may be contributing to adjustment problems. Consistent with the cognitive model, the necessary intervention goes beyond the level of cognitive content to an exploration of the more central, self-related cognitive structures (Fleming & Robinson, 1991). For example, Horowitz (1997) argued that schematic change is a central process in mourning. Constructivist theory also posits that the attempt to reconstruct a world of meaning is the central process in the experience of grieving, a process that requires "transforming our identities so as to redefine our symbolic connection to the deceased while maintaining our relationship with the living" (Neimeyer, 1998, p. 98). For Parkes (1993), bereavement is a period of "psychosocial transition" during which one's habitual expectations and assumptions of the world are often invalidated and, as a consequence, revised. Janoff-Bulman (1992; Janoff-Bulman & Berg, 1998), based on her extensive work on "shattered assumptions" following trauma or loss, has concluded that the inner world of survivors must be "rebuilt" if they are to incorporate the traumatic experience and reinvest in living. Thus there appears to be much consensus with regard to the notion that these profound cognitive shifts must occur if adjustment is to be adaptive.

COGNITIVE–BEHAVIORAL THERAPY AND GRIEF

Although there is limited, direct application of CBT in the treatment of bereaved individuals, the remainder of this chapter will focus on how select CBT principles may be adapted to grief-related situations. Given the similarities between the acute phases of grief and posttraumatic stress disorder (PTSD) and the documented effectiveness of CBT with PTSD, the first section will explore how CBT treatment strategies might be implemented with those concomitantly experiencing grief and trauma. Next, the usefulness of CBT in facilitating meaning reconstruction and the rebuilding of one's assumptive world in the face of loss will be considered. Finally, this section will conclude with a discussion of a relatively new concept, counterfactual thinking, detailing how such thought processes operate, their potential to complicate the grief process, and how CBT principles can reduce or eliminate their destructive impact.

Posttraumatic Stress Disorder and Grief

Rando (1997) noted that uncomplicated grief reactions, particularly in the acute phase, bear a striking resemblance to PTSD in their salient symptoms, the oscillating pattern of intrusion—numbing–avoidance—and their treatment requirements. Simpson (1997) reported conspicuous similarities in the symptom picture of grief and PTSD after systematically comparing the *DSM-IV* criteria for PTSD with descriptions of grief proffered by prominent theorists (e.g., Parkes, 1972; Rando, 1984; Raphael, 1983; W. Stroebe & Stroebe, 1987; Worden, 1983). More specifically, "normal" grief and trauma share such responses as re-experiencing, avoidance–numbing, and increased arousal. Additional common reactions include guilt, shame, lasting changes in value systems and beliefs, and a search for meaning or purpose. Stroebe, Schut, and Stroebe (1998) also recognized the similarities and differences between traumatic stress reactions and adjusting to the death of a loved one. Finally, Fleming and Belanger (in press) have illustrated the parallels in commonly accepted strategies of intervention for PTSD and complicated grief responses.

Traumatic death increases the likelihood of grief complications as the survivor grapples with the impact of the trauma, the emotional, physical, behavioral, and cognitive vicissitudes inherent in the loss experience, and the interaction of the two. The prominent features of PTSD (arousal, numbness–avoidance, and re-experiencing) have the potential to complicate, impede, or exacerbate the grieving process (Nader, 1997). For example, trauma arousal may aggravate symptoms common to both phenomena, producing more severe sleep disturbances, concentration problems, disturbances in impulse control, prominent revenge fantasies, and unsettling rage (Stuckless, 1996).

When grieving a traumatic death, it is not uncommon for unbidden traumatic images to flood consciousness as one attempts to reminisce and fondly remember the deceased. Harrowing re-experiencing, then, has the potential to dislodge loss-related thoughts of the deceased or lead to a preoccupation with issues surrounding the trauma—for example, the pain of dying, the deceased's last conscious moments, what "caused" the death, and self-blame.

There are a variety of behavioral and cognitive–behavioral intervention strategies that have been used to reduce emotional flooding, increase sense of control, and positively affect hope in traumatized individuals. *Behavioral* approaches comprise an ensemble of therapeutic techniques, including systematic desensitization, flooding, and exposure (imaginal and *in vivo*). There are numerous and diverse theoretical models subsumed under the rubric of *cognitive–behavioral* therapy. One intervention strategy focuses on identifying and replacing faulty cognitions (A. T. Beck, 1976; J. Beck, 1995) or irrational belief systems (Ellis, 1994). Another approach, of which Meichenbaum's (1994) constructive narrative perspective is an example, emphasizes the "stories" or "accounts" developed by individuals in the face of loss and change as they struggle to find meaning and purpose in their lives. For Meichenbaum (1994) the challenge is to "transform and reframe (their) 'problem-saturated' trauma stories from one of shame and humiliation, guilt and fear, into 'solution-focused' stories of dignity and survival" (p. 105). Finally, the schema-based model (Janoff-Bulman, 1992; McCann & Pearlman, 1990) emphasizes how trauma disrupts and fragments the sense of self and shatters one's assumptive world.

Where there is a significant trauma overlay, then, it is suggested that trauma work be the primary focus of early intervention and, subsequently, the client's ability and willingness to deal with grief and the intrusive–

avoidant reactions to the traumatic event and traumatic death determines the rhythm of therapy (Rando, 1993, 1996). It is important to recognize that this distortion–irrational belief–constructivist–schema distinction is somewhat artificial and, in practice, cognitive–behavioral therapy can be characterized as a amalgam of these approaches; it is seldom, if ever, delivered in a "pure" form.

Meaning Making

Whether an individual is confronted with bereavement or some other traumatic life event, there may be a profound corresponding assault on the adaptive assumptions that give structure and meaning to life (Janoff-Bulman, 1992; Taylor, 1983; Thompson & Janigian, 1988). This is not always the case because experiences that somehow "fit" our constructions (e.g., the expected, appropriate death of an elderly person following a life well-lived) may provide validation of our assumptions and will not challenge our existing beliefs (Neimeyer, 1998). Thus in Piagetian terms, there may be either assimilation of the experience into existing cognitive structures or accommodation of our assumptions to allow for the irrefutable reality of the new, discrepant experience.

Thompson and Janigian (1988) also have observed that the disparity between beliefs and negative events can be resolved or lessened by changing one's cognitive representation (i.e., accommodation) or by changing one's perceptions such that the event seems less negative. In the latter instance, no change in the cognitive representation is necessary. These authors describe a "life scheme" framework for understanding how survivors search for and find meaning by using either or both of the processes of assimilation and accommodation. In many cases, a severely negative event challenges this life scheme or narrative that has provided order and purpose to one's life, with a resulting requirement that this scheme be modified if one is to reestablish order and purpose.

According to Janoff-Bulman (1992) there are three basic or fundamental assumptions threatened by grief and trauma—namely, the world is a benevolent place, the world is meaningful (i.e., it "makes sense"), and the self is worthy. Indeed, Janoff-Bulman and Berg (1998) stated that these comfortable assumptions are soon discovered to be "illusions" by those confronted with significant trauma or loss. Although these assumptions generally serve us well, they also are, at times, overgeneralized or overapplied. Thus it is not their positive valence but their overextension that accounts for their illusory nature. Extreme negative experiences cause an abrupt, terrifying disillusionment, with which survivors must then contend. The ideal outcome is a rebuilding process by which the survivor once again perceives the world and self in positive terms but, at the same time, incorporates the trauma–loss within the new assumptive world.

As Janoff-Bulman and Berg (1998) indicated, individuals who have experienced a significant trauma or loss generally cannot wholly embrace their old assumptions but, at the same time, they are not entirely accepting of the new ones, which often entail a perception of the world as malevolent and meaningless. Thus it is necessary that both views be incorporated into a perspective that fosters the reestablishment of a meaningful life. It is our experience that this is an important method by which individuals move from being victims of terrible misfortune to survivors.

Thompson (1998) further discussed how one modifies one's schemas or the cognitive representations of one's life. Specifically, she noted that this may be done through reordering one's priorities, changing to goals that can be reached despite the adversity, or adapting one's self-image in a positive way that incorporates the loss (e.g., a "coper" or "survivor"). She also suggested that adaptive assumptions are restored through reinterpretation of the event using a positive focus, changing perspective, or making social comparisons to others who are worse off. Reestablishing a sense of control is achieved in a couple of ways, including a simple acceptance of the situation as well as heightening awareness of areas in which one's attempts to exercise control have been successful. This latter strategy may be enacted by asking clients to monitor their decision making and control throughout the day. Presumably, perceptions of control are stronger if individuals are aware of their experience of exercising control (Langer, Blank, & Chanowitz, 1978). Counterfactual thinking, and its role in the reconstruction of one's world view and the re-establishment of control, is presented in the next section.

When a bereaved individual entertains extreme, absolutistic views (e.g., "the world is malevolent"), CBT suggests ways of fostering the development of more graduated, balanced beliefs. Much of this work has evolved as cognitive therapists have turned their attention to the treatment of personality disorders in which it is hypothesized that a central difficulty is the relatively continuous activation of negative core beliefs (A. Beck & Freeman, 1990; Young, 1990). A guided consideration of the evidence for and against a certain, affect-laden belief (e.g., Padesky & Greenberger, 1995), or the use of so-called schema-change methods (e.g., Padesky, 1994; Young, 1990) are two approaches that could be applied to the types of shattered assumptions outlined by Janoff-Bulman (1992). In the former approach, the therapist patiently explores with the client the evidence both for and against such an interpretation, then encourages consideration of an alternative or balanced construal that simultaneously acknowledges and contains these conflicting elements. This would be done repeatedly around specific incidents involving the activation of the extreme perspectives, allowing the survivor time and experience to elaborate and consolidate this modified outlook.

According to Padesky (1994), schemas or core beliefs tend to be extreme and absolute construals of self, others, or the world. They often are found when there is a corresponding high level of affect related to a particular event. Thus "the world is malevolent" would be understood as typical of this type of absolute belief. Once such a belief is identified, articulated in the client's words, and targeted for change, an appropriate CBT schema change process—such as the use of the "continuum" method—would be used. Because core beliefs or schemas are absolutes—and often polar opposites (e.g., benevolent vs. malevolent)—the continuum is used to chart the territory between these poles. Ideally, whether the client is considering a view of the world or a view of self ("I am unlovable" vs. "I am lovable"), the therapist gently uses the questioning of evidence to shift the client's evaluation to a midpoint on the continuum, thereby countering absolutistic thinking. Padesky (1994) has developed various strategies to maximize the use of continua. This technique promotes the establishment of a less absolute belief that allows for incorporation of the reality of the loss or trauma into the client's assumptive world.

As previously mentioned during the discussion of CBT and trauma, if one considers a person's life scheme to be a story with one's self as the protagonist (Thompson & Janigian, 1988), narrative psychotherapeutic approaches would appear to have much to offer in the treatment of bereaved individuals. These constructivist-based therapies are not outlined because of space limitations, but the general approach is exemplified by Gilligan and Price (1993), Meichenbaum (1994), and White and Epston (1990).

Counterfactual Thinking

As is clear from the preceding discussion of meaning-making, the cognitive aspects of adjustment to loss or trauma are varied and substantial in nature. Of late, considerable attention has been directed to an aspect of cognitive functioning—namely counterfactual thinking—that is pertinent to the experience of bereaved people. It is interesting to note that although this phenomenon has received much attention in social psychology, it has yet to be directly discussed in the context of cognitive therapy. Nevertheless, it seems a most useful body of knowledge as one is confronted with the bereaved client who is attempting to make sense of his or her world.

Counterfactual thinking is the generation of imagined alternatives to actual events. In this mental simulation of alternative outcomes, one attempts to undo, alter, or mutate some factual antecedent and contemplate its outcome. The essence of this process is captured by such reflections as "if only ... then. ..." For example, after a biopsy reveals a diagnosis of malignant melanoma, one might reflect, "If only I had not been exposed to the sun so much then I would not have this frightening, life-threatening condition." Or consider the contemplation of a bereaved father following the death of his son in a motor vehicle accident: "If only I had not permitted my son to drive the car that night, then he would still be alive today."

Broadly speaking, counterfactuals may be classified according to their direction—either upward or downward. Upward counterfactuals refer to postulating alternative circumstances that are an improvement on reality —for example, "If only I had been more cautious and taken another route home, then I would not have been mugged." Downward counterfactuals, in contrast, involve replaying an event with a more deleterious outcome; they often take the form of "it could have been worse" reflections. It is thought that these forms of counterfactual thinking have differing emotional consequences; more specifically, upward counterfactuals lead to negative affective repercussions and downward counterfactuals may improve one's affective response to misfortune (Kasimatis & Wells, 1995).

Both the directionality and the concomitant repercussions of counterfactual thinking have roots in social comparison theory (Festinger, 1954). Referring to our tendency to evaluate ourselves in comparison with others, Alcock, Carment, and Sadava (1998) noted that downward social comparison "with someone less able, less attractive or less powerful than ourselves" (p. 71) can enhance self-esteem. In contrast, upward social comparison may be either (a) ego-deflating if the comparison is to someone much better than ourselves or (b) ego-enhancing if this exercise illustrates fewer differences than expected.

Negative emotional experiences most commonly trigger counterfactual thinking. In contrast to positive outcomes, when confronted with an unexpected or unwanted outcome, one is more apt to adopt an "if only" mentality and automatically indulge in counterfactual generation (Gleicher et al., 1990; Landman, 1987). In one study of respondents who had experienced the death of a child or spouse in a motor vehicle accident, 48% reported they were still entertaining "if only . . . " scenarios 4 to 7 years after the accident (Davis, Lehman, Wortman, Silver, & Thompson, 1995). Further analyses revealed that 55% focused on altering their own behavior while the remainder generated counterfactuals directed at changing the deceased's behavior. It is interesting to note that although legally responsible for the motor vehicle accidents none of the respondents entertained counterfactuals aimed at undoing the perpetrator's behavior.

Davis et al. (1995) postulated this latter, curious finding of undoing their own (or the deceased's) behavior, but not the causal agent's, to be a function of the perceived mutability or changeability of the antecedent events and circumstances. In this study, because the actions and behaviors of the perpetrator were immutable, the content of the counterfactual process implicated a more mutable but perhaps less causally significant agent —namely, the actions of the bereaved individual or the deceased. Furthermore, interviews with mothers who had lost an infant to sudden infant death syndrome (Davis et al., 1995) and with quadriplegic and paraplegic respondents (Davis, Lehman, Silver, Wortman, & Ellard, 1996) consistently showed that, in the absence of any reasonable causal connection, participants tended to blame themselves for not preventing the mishap (as opposed to causal self-blame).

The acknowledgment that counterfactual thinking is triggered by unpleasant events, and that this process generates and amplifies negative emotions, does not preclude the possibility that there are some significant benefits accruing to the individual. Roese and Olson (1995) suggested that people are compelled to imagine alternative realities to brace themselves for the future (preparative function) or to enhance their current emotional state (an affective function).

The affective regulatory function is primarily served by the generation of downward counterfactuals involving statements such as "it could have been worse . . ." or "at least . . . didn't happen." The imagining of alternative outcomes that are evaluatively worse than reality can bring some measure of relief and self-soothing—for example, an individual depressed and demoralized about the loss of a leg in an industrial accident might reflect that "it could have been worse, I might have died" (McMullen, Markman, & Gavanski, 1995; Roese, 1997). In contrast, the preparatory function is best served by the production of upward counterfactuals. When one compares the actual outcome of misfortune with an imagined, more palatable alternative (upward comparison), the resulting negative affect will be amplified or intensified, especially if counterfactuals can be easily simulated (Boninger, Gleicher, & Strathman, 1994; Gleicher et al., 1990). Although such aversive or harmful exacerbation of negative affect tends to eventuate, this may well constitute a "bad news, good news" story, because an upward counterfactual "may be upsetting because it makes salient the deprived present state, yet it may also be uplifting if it gives hope for future betterment" (Roese, 1994, p. 806). In other words, the negative affect generated by the imagination of preferred alternative outcomes may be muted somewhat by the illumination of future courses of action designed to reduce the probability of similar misfortune occurring (McMullen et al., 1995; Roese, 1997).

In addition to the preparatory and affect-regulation functions of counterfactual thinking, Sherman and McConnell (1995) have proposed a third, related adaptive function—the induction of feelings of controllability. Such self-relevant counterfactuals as, "If only I had not allowed my son to take the car, he would still be alive today," lead to perceptions of personal causation and control and, frequently, to the ascription of self-blame and guilt, even when there is no objective causal connection. As a consequence, in the attribution of self-blame one reclaims a sense of control in the midst of chaos and intolerable randomness; the event sequence and the undesirable outcome are then rendered more understandable, predictable, and tolerable.

Notwithstanding the benefits derived from counterfactual thinking, Sherman and McConnell (1995) recognize that counterfactuals are basically schemas or scripts through which experience is organized and, as such, are subject to biases and errors in judgment that may have disastrous consequences for the individual. They propose that such processes as hindsight bias, faulty causal inferences, and succumbing to the "counterfactual fallacy" (Miller & Turnbull, 1990) introduce the potential for deleterious outcomes to the cognitive–emotional process of generating counterfactuals. In other words, there is a "darker side" to our seemingly compelling penchant for altering reality, and it is here, in considering the dysfunctional potential of counterfactual thinking, that CBT has much to offer. To appreciate the nature and dynamics of counterfactual thinking and implications for intervention, a brief case history will precede a more thorough treatment of hindsight bias, faulty causal inferences, and counterfactual fallacy.

> Sally and Ruth (not their real names) were driving in the country with their three children. Sally's daughter (age 3), her son (age 9), and Ruth's 3-year-old son were all belted into the rear seat of Sally's minivan. As they entered an intersection with the right of way, their vehicle was hit broadside by another minivan whose driver had failed to heed a stop sign. As a result of the collision, the rear seat was ejected from the van; both 3-year-olds were killed, and Sally, Ruth, and Sally's son sustained only minor injuries.

> Not unexpectedly, during the course of her psychotherapy with one of the authors (SF), Sally generated many self-implicating counterfactual possibilities related to this horrific accident. For example, the mental simulation of downward counterfactuals ("it could have been worse, my son might also have died") brought much-needed, but momentary, respite from the soul-crushing pain of the trauma and the death of her daughter. Although Sally clearly recognized that the perpetrator *caused* the motor vehicle accident (he was subsequently charged and convicted), she did not attempt to remove him from the scene or mutate his behavior in any way. Consistent with the literature, the content of Sally's upward counterfactuals was biased toward her behavior and how she could have *prevented* the accident. For example, "If only I had not stopped for gas, we would not have arrived at the intersection at that precise time."

> Another prominent counterfactual related to Sally's behavior at the accident scene. Immediately following impact, she struggled to reach the children (still strapped into the seat) and, gently, freed her unconscious daughter, lowered her to the roadway, and

attempted to revive her. In therapy, Sally reflected, "If only I had not moved my daughter, she might still be alive." Again, when actions–behaviors associated with the principal cause are perceived as immutable or unchangeable, other less causally significant but more mutable antecedents become the focus of undoing. In this instance, Sally was blaming herself and experiencing considerable guilt. As a consequence of her struggle to determine the cause of her daughter's death, Sally experienced self-blame and, ultimately, avoided the terror of randomness and arrived at a sense of perceived controllability and predictability.

Hindsight Bias

Hindsight bias, a term originating in social psychology (Fischhoff, 1975; Hawkins & Hastie, 1990), involves "the tendency for individuals with outcome knowledge (hindsight) to claim that they would have estimated a probability of occurrence for the reported outcome that is higher than they would have estimated in foresight (without the outcome information)" (1990, p. 311). In Sally's case, an example of hindsight bias is the statement, "I knew all along that something bad was going to happen that day." Outcome knowledge, then, led her to recall signs and signals that went unnoticed or were dismissed (or perhaps never existed)—signs and signals that should have alerted her to imminent danger. Sally erroneously claimed preoutcome knowledge of the inevitability of an event's occurrence (foresight) on the basis of outcome knowledge (hindsight). It is important to note that errors generated by hindsight-biased thinking jeopardize adaptive learning because, with the outcome perceived as inevitable and predetermined, there is nothing to learn. In addition, such faulty reasoning also contributes to causal inference errors and exacerbates self-blame. Davis et al. (1996) have illustrated that in the generation of counterfactual alternatives, individuals are likely to inflate or distort the importance of their roles and, as a consequence, experience extensive self-blame. In the previous case history, Sally may condemn herself for not responding preventively in the face of such an avoidable and foreseeable trauma.

Although not using the term "counterfactual thinking," Kubany (1998) recognized the potentially damaging consequences of outcome feedback on retrospective judgments and proposed a three-step, cognitive–behavioral intervention strategy. First, the concept of hindsight bias is explained and the therapist provides appropriate examples. Second, the therapist determines the extent to which the client falsely believes he or she "knew" what was going to happen before it was possible to have access to such information. Third, to assist clients in arriving at a more objective, accurate appraisal of their role and reduce self-blame, the therapist helps the client to appreciate the influence of hindsight-biased thinking and the "impossibility" of postoutcome data influencing preoutcome appraisals. Kubany (1998) also recommended the use of self-monitoring homework assignments—for example, monitoring and then changing "should" or "could have" statements as they betray a hindsight bias.

Causal Inferences

In addition to creating considerable guilt and self-blame, Sherman and McConnell (1995) cautioned that incorrect causal analyses threaten benefits such as an augmented sense of personal control, improved adjustment, and future preparedness. Kubany (1998) postulated a number of "thinking errors" that are likely to lead to faulty causal inferences and self-blame. First is not recognizing the countless, diverse influences outside of themselves that may have caused the focal event distorts the causal attribution process. Second is confusing thinking one "could have *prevented*" a tragedy with *causing* that same outcome. Third is failing to differentiate "responsibility as accountability" and "responsibility as power to cause or control outcomes" (e.g., parents are held accountable for the behavior of their children, however, if a child misbehaves in the schoolyard, the parent did not cause the inappropriate behavior to occur).

Kubany (1998) has formulated intervention strategies to deal specifically with the aforementioned faulty or sloppy cognitive processing of causal inferences. The initial phase is to distinguish causality and blame by focusing on issues of foreseeability, "knowingly" causing harm (what he terms "wrongdoing"), and hindsight bias. The remaining phases of addressing this particular aspect of treatment focus on a more objective analysis of perceived responsibility through listing people and factors external to the individual who might have causally contributed to the unfortunate outcome, estimating the percentage of outcome responsibility for each of these people–factors, and then revisiting the client's initial appraisal of their causal contribution.

Niedenthal, Tangney, and Gavanski (1994) explored the relationship between differing styles or patterns of counterfactual thinking and qualitatively differing affective experiences—namely, shame and guilt. The authors distinguished these two dysphoric emotions in noting that when one feels ashamed, "they feel they are a 'bad person' and that the self has been humiliated or disgraced," (p. 586) whereas feelings of guilt are associated with "a specific behavior or transgression" (p. 587) that does not extend to self-condemnation. Results revealed that feelings of shame stemmed from undoing distressing outcomes by mutating characteristics of one's *self* whereas guilt tended to follow counterfactual inferences mutating one's *behavior*. This distinction is strikingly similar to Janoff-Bulman's (1992) differentiation of characterological self-blame and behavioral self-blame, respectively. With its focus on persistent, distorted, and negative perceptions of self, experience, and the future, characterological self-blame may well lead to clinical depression. In contrast, behavioral self-blame is likely to result in a more benign affective disturbance without cognitive bias (Fleming & Robinson, 1991; Robinson & Fleming, 1989). In Sally's case, blaming herself for choosing the particular family van led to the eventual purchase of another, "safer" vehicle, thus increasing her sense of control.

Counterfactual Fallacy

Originally introduced by Miller and Turnbull (1990), the counterfactual fallacy "refers to the confusion of *what might have been* the case and what *ought to have been* the case" (p. 2). In other words, if counterfactual musings lead to the belief that an undesirable outcome *could* have been prevented or avoided, one may come to believe they *should* have prevented it, however unforeseeable. Sherman and McConnell (1995) posited that this fallacy "can affect both judgments of others and self-relevant judgments" and that "many of the negative affective responses directed toward the self . . . can be understood as consequences of the counterfactual fallacy" (p. 218). This assertion, however, has not been supported in limited field research (Davis & Lehman, 1995). Even if further research implicates the counterfactual fallacy in faulty causal inferences, Kubany's (1998) intervention strategies emphasizing psychoeducation, instruction, and self-monitoring homework assignments are admirably suited to illustrate the dysfunctional nature of this style of thinking and discourage its practice.

In our case illustration, although acknowledging that she did not *cause* her daughter's death, Sally was convinced that there must have been something she could have done to *prevent* it. Painfully reliving the event led Sally to *blame* herself for this tragedy as she had moved her unconscious daughter from the van's bench to the roadway. A psychoeducational focus explaining the cause–blame distinction and introducing conclusions from counterfactual research (e.g., the tendency to self-blame even when one's actions are not causally implicated) were effectively implemented. Simple homework assignments can also have a profound and positive therapeutic impact on perceived causality. In Sally's case, she was encouraged to thoroughly examine the autopsy report and, after formulating her questions and concerns, discuss issues of causality and self-blame with her physician. She was assured that the extent of her daughter's injuries indicated a sudden death, and neither moving the child nor attempting to resuscitate her would have contributed to the child's demise.

Given the therapeutic gains emanating from the exploration of self-blame, it is suggested that the aware clinician (a) be sensitive to the distinction between characterological self-blame and behavioral self-blame; (b) focus cognitive strategies and interventions on the destructive potential of attributing blame to enduring personality characteristics; (c) support shifting guilt to more adaptive, less destructive behavioral self-blame; and (d) resist the temptation to prematurely short circuit this potentially valuable exploration (e.g., by introducing the counterfactual fallacy).

CONCLUSION

Although we have seldom, if ever, used CBT in its pure form to guide intervention with bereaved individuals, we nonetheless feel that CBT, and its fundamental cognitive constructs and propositions that guide therapy implementation, offers many valuable therapeutic tools. Where there has been a traumatic death, the implementation of recognized CBT approaches to reduce traumatic arousal and facilitate trauma mastery is a necessary first step in competently treating survivors. Where grief shatters central, organizing beliefs regarding self and the world, CBT, with its focus on meaning reconstruction, offers invaluable insights into how core beliefs and schemas can be modified in the revision of one's assumptive world and the accommodation of the loss experience.

Finally, the generation of imagined alternatives to actual events, or counterfactual thinking, presents a challenge to grief therapists. Commonly triggered by unpleasant events, counterfactual thinking offers the potential benefits of providing relief from suffering, preparation for the future, and enhancing the illusion of control. One arrives at such benefits through navigating the treacherous psychological waters of self-blame and guilt—and CBT offers the knowledgeable practitioner many helpful suggestions about how this transition might be managed effectively.

REFERENCES

Abrahms, J. (1981). Depression versus normal grief following the death of a significant other. In G. Emery, S. Hollon, & R. Bedrosian (Eds.), *New directions in cognitive therapy* (pp. 255–270). New York: Guilford Press.

Alcock, J. E., Carment, D. W., & Sadava, S. W. (1998). *A textbook of social psychology*. Scarborough, Ontario, Canada: Prentice-Hall.

Alford, B., & Beck, A. T. (1997). *The integrative power of cognitive therapy*. New York: Guilford Press.

Bandura, A. (1977). Self-efficacy: Toward a unifying theory of behavioral change. *Psychological Review, 84*, 191–215.

Barlow, D., & Hoffman, S. (1997). Efficacy and dissemination of psychological treatments. In D. Clark & C. Fairburn (Eds.), *Science and practice of cognitive behaviour therapy* (pp. 95–117). Oxford: Oxford University Press.

Beck, A. T. (1963). Thinking and depression, I: Idiosyncratic content and cognitive distortions. *Archives of General Psychiatry, 9*, 324–333.

Beck, A. T. (1964). Thinking and depression, II: Theory and therapy. *Archives of General Psychiatry, 10*, 561–571.

Beck, A. T. (1976). *Cognitive therapy and emotional disorders.* New York: International Universities Press.

Beck, A. T. (1996). Beyond belief: A theory of modes, personality, and psychopathology. In P. Salkovskis (Ed.), *Frontiers of cognitive therapy* (pp. 1–25). New York: Guilford Press.

Beck, A. T., & Freeman, A. (1990). *Cognitive therapy of personality disorders.* New York: Guilford Press.

Beck, A. T., & Rush, A. J. (1995). Cognitive therapy. In H. Kaplan & B. Sadock (Eds.), *Comprehensive textbook of psychiatry/VI* (Vol. 2, 6th ed.; pp. 1847–1857). Philadelphia: Williams & Wilkins.

Beck, A. T., Rush, A. J., Shaw, B., & Emery, G. (1979). *Cognitive therapy of depression.* New York: Guilford Press.

Beck, A. T., & Weishaar, M. (1989). Cognitive therapy. In A. Freeman, K. Simon, L. Beutler, & H. Arkowitz (Eds.), *Comprehensive handbook of cognitive therapy* (pp. 21–36). New York: Plenum Press.

Beck, J. (1995). *Cognitive therapy: Basics and beyond.* New York: Guilford Press.

Boninger, D. S., Gleicher, F., & Strathman, A. (1994). Counterfactual thinking: From what might have been to what may be. *Journal of Personality and Social Psychology, 67*, 297–307.

Clark, D., & Fairburn, C. (Eds.). (1997). *Science and practice of cognitive behaviour therapy.* Oxford, England: Oxford University Press.

Clark, D., & Steer, R. (1996). Empirical status of the cognitive model of anxiety and depression. In P. Salkovskis (Ed.), *Frontiers of cognitive therapy* (pp. 75–96). New York: Guilford Press.

Davis, C. G., Lehman, D. R., Silver, R. C., Wortman, C. B., & Ellard, J. H. (1996). Self-blame following a traumatic event: The role of perceived avoidability. *Personality and Social Psychology Bulletin, 22*, 557–567.

Davis, C. G., Lehman, D. R., Wortman, C. B., Silver, R. C., & Thompson, S. C. (1995). The undoing of traumatic life events. *Personality and Social Psychology Bulletin, 21*, 109–124.

Dobson, K. (1989). A meta-analysis of the efficacy of cognitive therapy for depression. *Journal of Consulting and Clinical Psychology, 57*, 414–419.

Ellis, A. (1962). *Reason and emotion in psychotherapy.* Secaucus, NJ: Lyle Stuart.

Ellis, A. (1994). Post-traumatic stress disorder (PTSD): A rational emotive behavioral theory. *Journal of Rational-Emotive and Cognitive-Behavior Therapy, 12*, 3–25.

Festinger, L. (1954). A theory of social comparison processes. *Human Relations, 7*, 117–140.

Fischhoff, B. (1975). Hindsight does not equal foresight: The effect of outcome knowledge on judgment under uncertainty. *Journal of Experimental Psychology: Human Perception and Performance, 1*, 288–299.

Fleming, S. J., & Belanger, S. K. (in press). Trauma, grief, and surviving childhood sexual abuse. In R. Neimeyer (Ed.), *Meaning reconstruction and the experience of loss*. Washington, DC: American Psychological Association.

Fleming, S. J., & Robinson, P. J., (1991). The application of cognitive therapy to the bereaved. In T. M. Vallis, J. L. Howes, & P. C. Miller (Eds.), *The challenge of cognitive therapy: Applications to nontraditional populations* (pp. 135–158). New York: Plenum Press.

Freeman, A., Simon, K., Beutler, L., & Arkowitz, H. (Eds.). (1989). *Comprehensive handbook of cognitive therapy*. New York: Plenum Press.

Gauthier, J., & Pye, C. (1979). Graduated self-exposure in the management of grief. *Behavioral Analysis & Modification, 3*, 202–208.

Gilligan, S., & Price, R. (Eds.). (1993). *Therapeutic conversations*. New York: Norton.

Gleicher, F., Kost, K. A., Baker, S. M., Strathman, A. J., Richman, S. A., & Sherman, S. J. (1990). The role of counterfactual thinking in judgments of affect. *Personality and Social Psychology Bulletin, 16*, 284–295.

Guidano, V., & Liotti, G. (1983). *Cognitive processes and emotional disorders: A structural approach to psychotherapy*. New York: Guilford Press.

Hawkins, S. A., & Hastie, R. (1990). Hindsight: Biased judgments of past events after the outcomes are known. *Psychological Bulletin, 107*, 311–327.

Hodgkinson, P. (1982). Abnormal grief: The problem of therapy. *British Journal of Medical Psychology, 55*, 29–34.

Hollon, S., & Kriss, M. (1984). Cognitive factors in clinical research and practice. *Clinical Psychology Review, 4*, 35–76.

Horowitz, M. (1997). *Stress response syndromes*. Northvale, NJ: Jason Aronson.

Howes, J., & Parrott, C. (1991). Conceptualization and flexibility in cognitive therapy. In T. M. Vallis, J. Howes, & P. Miller (Eds.), *The challenge of cognitive therapy: Applications to nontraditional populations* (pp. 25–42). New York: Plenum Press.

Janoff-Bulman, R. (1992). *Shattered Assumptions: Towards a new psychology of trauma*. New York: Free Press.

Janoff-Bulman, R., & Berg, M. (1998). Disillusionment and the creation of value: From traumatic losses to existential gains. In J. H. Harvey (Ed.), *Perspectives on loss: A sourcebook* (pp. 35–47). Philadelphia: Taylor & Francis.

Kasimatis, M., & Wells, G. L. (1995). Individual differences in counterfactual thinking. In N. J. Roese & J. M. Olson (Eds.), *What might have been: The social psychology of counterfactual thinking* (pp. 81–101). Mahwah, NJ: Erlbaum.

Kelly, G. (1955). *The psychology of personal constructs*. New York: Norton.

Kubany, E. S. (1998). Cognitive therapy for trauma-related guilt. In V. M. Follette, J. I. Ruzek, & F. R. Abueg (Eds.), *Cognitive-behavioural therapies for trauma* (pp. 124–161). New York: Guilford Press.

Landman, J. (1987). Regret and elation following action and inaction. *Personality and Social Psychology Bulletin, 13*, 524–536.

Langer, E. J., Blank, A., & Chanowitz, B. (1978). The mindlessness of ostensibly thoughtful action. *Journal of Personality and Social Psychology, 35,* 635–642.

Lazarus, A. (1976). *Multimodal behavior therapy.* New York: Springer.

Lieberman, S. (1978). Nineteen cases of morbid grief. *British Journal of Psychiatry, 132,* 159–163.

Mahoney, M. (1974). *Cognition and behavior modification.* New York: Ballinger.

Mahoney, M. (1988). The cognitive sciences and psychotherapy: Patterns in a developing relationship. In K. Dobson (Ed.), *Handbook of cognitive-behavioral therapies* (pp. 357–386). New York: Guilford Press.

Martin, T., & Doka, K. J. (1996). Masculine grief. In K. J. Doka (Ed.), *Living with grief after sudden loss* (pp. 161–171). Bristol, PA: Taylor & Francis.

Mawson, D., Marks, I., Ramm, L., & Stern, R. (1981). Guided mourning for morbid grief: A controlled study. *British Journal of Psychiatry, 138,* 185–193.

McCann, I. L., & Pearlman, L. A. (1990). *Psychological trauma and the adult survivor: Theory, therapy, and transformation.* New York: Bruner/Mazel.

McMullen, M. N., Markman, K. D., & Gavanski, I. (1995). Living in neither the best nor the worst of all possible worlds: Antecedents and consequences of upward and downward counterfactual thinking. In N. J. Roese & J. M. Olson (Eds.), *What might have been: The social psychology of counterfactual thinking* (pp. 133–167). Mahwah, NJ: Erlbaum.

Meichenbaum, D. (1977). *Cognitive-behavior modification: An integrative approach.* New York: Plenum Press.

Meichenbaum, D. (1994). *A clinical handbook/practical therapist manual for assessing and treating adults with post-traumatic stress disorder (PTSD).* Waterloo, Ontario, Canada: Institute Press.

Melges, F., & DeMaso, D. (1980). Grief-resolution therapy: Reliving, revising, and revisiting. *American Journal of Psychotherapy, 34,* 51–61.

Miller, D. T., & Turnbull, W. (1990). The counterfactual fallacy: Confusing what might have been with what ought to have been. *Social Justice Research, 4,* 1–19.

Moorey, S. (1996). When bad things happen to rational people: Cognitive therapy in adverse life circumstances. In P. Salkovskis (Ed.), *Frontiers of cognitive therapy* (pp. 450–469). New York: Guilford Press.

Nader, K. O. (1997). Childhood traumatic loss: The interaction of trauma and grief. In C. R. Figley, B. E. Bride, & N. Mazza (Eds.), *Death and trauma: The traumatology of grieving* (pp. 17–41). Washington, DC: Taylor & Francis.

Neimeyer, R. (1995). Constructivist psychotherapies: Features, foundations, and future directions. In R. Neimeyer & M. Mahoney (Eds.), *Constructivism in Psychotherapy* (pp. 11–38). Washington, DC: American Psychological Association.

Neimeyer, R. (1998). *Lessons of loss: A guide to coping.* New York: McGraw-Hill.

Neimeyer, R., & Mahoney, M. (Eds.). (1995). *Constructivism in psychotherapy.* Washington, DC: American Psychological Association.

Niedenthal, P. M., Tangney, J. P., & Gavanski, I. (1994). "If only I weren't" versus "If only I hadn't": Distinguishing shame and guilt in counterfactual thinking. *Journal of Personality and Social Psychology, 67,* 585–595.

Padesky, C. (1994). Schema change processes in cognitive therapy. *Clinical Psychology and Psychotherapy, 1,* 267–278.

Padesky, C. (1996, May 13–14). *When there's not enough time: Innovations in cognitive therapy.* Cognitive therapy workshop presented in Toronto, Ontario, Canada.

Padesky, C., & Greenberger, D. (1995). *Clinician's guide to mind over mood.* New York: Guilford Press.

Parkes, C. M. (1972). *Bereavement: Studies of grief in adult life.* London: Tavistock.

Parkes, C. M. (1993). Bereavement as a psychosocial transition: Processes of adaptation to change. In M. S. Stroebe, W. Stroebe, & R. O. Hansson (Eds.), *Handbook of bereavement* (pp. 91–101). Cambridge: Cambridge University Press.

Persons, J. (1989). *Cognitive therapy in practice: A case formulation approach.* New York: Norton.

Powers, L. E., & Wampold, B. E. (1994). Cognitive-behavioral factors in adjustment to adult bereavement. *Death Studies, 18,* 1–24.

Rachman, S. (1997). The evolution of cognitive behaviour therapy. In D. Clark & C. Fairburn (Eds.), *Science and practice of cognitive behaviour therapy* (pp. 3–26). Oxford: Oxford University Press.

Ramsey, R. (1977). Behavioral approaches to bereavement. *Behavior Research and Therapy, 15,* 131–135.

Rando, T. A. (1984). *Grief, dying, and death: Clinical interventions for caregivers.* Champaign, IL: Research Press.

Rando, T. A. (1993). *Treatment of complicated mourning.* Champaign, IL: Research Press.

Rando, T. A. (1996). On treating those bereaved by sudden, unanticipated death. *In Session: Psychotherapy in Practice, 2/4,* 59–71.

Rando, T. A. (1997). Foreword. In C. R. Figley, B. E. Bride, & N. Mazza (Eds.), *Death and trauma: The traumatology of grieving* (pp. xv–xix). Washington, DC: Taylor & Francis.

Raphael, B. (1983). *The anatomy of bereavement.* New York: Basic Books.

Robinson, P. J., & Fleming, S. J. (1989). Differentiating grief and depression. *The Hospice Journal, 5,* 77–88.

Roese, N. J. (1994). The functional basis of counterfactual thinking. *Journal of Personality and Social Psychology, 66,* 805–818.

Roese, N. J. (1997). Counterfactual thinking. *Psychological Bulletin, 121,* 133–148.

Roese, N. J., & Olson, J. M. (1995). Counterfactual thinking: A critical overview. In N. J. Roese & J. M. Olson (Eds.), *What might have been: The social psychology of counterfactual thinking* (pp. 1–55). Mahwah, NJ: Erlbaum.

Roth, A., & Fonagy, P. (1996). *What works for whom? A critical review of psychotherapy research*. New York: Guilford Press.

Salkovskis, P. (Ed.). (1996). *Frontiers of cognitive therapy*. New York: Guilford Press.

Sherman, S. J., & McConnell, A. R. (1995). Dysfunctional implications of counterfactual thinking: When alternatives to reality fail us. In N. J. Roese & J. M. Olson (Eds.), *What might have been: The social psychology of counterfactual thinking* (pp. 199–231). Mahwah, NJ: Erlbaum.

Silverman, P., & Klass, D. (1996). Introduction: What's the problem? In D. Klass, P. Silverman, & S. Nickman (Eds.), *Continuing bonds: New understandings of grief* (pp. 3–27). Washington, DC: Taylor & Francis.

Simpson, M. A. (1997). Traumatic bereavements and death-related PTSD. In C. R. Figley, B. E. Bride, & N. Mazza (Eds.), *Death and trauma: The traumatology of grieving* (pp. 3–16). Washington, DC: Taylor & Francis.

Stroebe, W., & Stroebe, M. (1987). *Bereavement and health*. New York: Cambridge University Press.

Stroebe, M., Schut, H., & Stroebe, W. (1998). Trauma and grief: A comparative analysis. In J. H. Harvey (Ed.), *Perspectives on loss: A sourcebook* (pp. 81–96). Philadelphia: Taylor & Francis.

Stuckless, N. (1996). *The influence of anger, perceived injustice, revenge, and time on the quality of life of survivor-victims*. Unpublished doctoral dissertation, York University, Toronto, Ontario.

Taylor, S. (1983). Adjustment to threatening events: A theory of cognitive adaptation. *American Psychologist, 38*, 1161–1173.

Thompson, S. (1998). Blockades to finding meaning and control. In J. H. Harvey (Ed.), *Perspectives on loss: A sourcebook* (pp. 21–34). Philadelphia: Taylor & Francis.

Thompson, S., & Janigian, A. (1988). Life schemes: A framework for understanding the search for meaning. *Journal of Social and Clinical Psychology, 7*, 260–280.

Turco, R. (1981). Regrief treatment facilitated by hypnosis. *American Journal of Hypnosis, 24*, 62–64.

White, M., & Epston, D. (1990). *Narrative means to therapeutic ends*. New York: Norton.

Woodfield, R., & Viney, L. (1984). A personal construct approach to the conjugally bereaved woman. *Omega: Journal of Death and Dying, 15*, 1–13.

Worden, J. W. (1983). *Grief counseling and grief therapy*. New York: Springer.

Wright, J., & Beck, A. T. (1994). Cognitive therapy. In R. Hales, S. Yudofsky, & J. Talbot (Eds.), *The American psychiatric press textbook of psychiatry* (2nd ed.; pp. 1083–1114). Washington, DC: American Psychiatric Press.

Young, J. (1990). *Cognitive therapy for personality disorders: A schema-focussed approach*. Sarasota, FL: Professional Resource Exchange.

29

PHYSIOLOGICAL EFFECTS OF BEREAVEMENT AND BEREAVEMENT SUPPORT GROUP INTERVENTIONS

KARL GOODKIN, TERI T. BALDEWICZ, NANCY T. BLANEY,
DESHRATN ASTHANA, MAHENDRA KUMAR, PAUL SHAPSHAK,
BARBARA LEEDS, JACK E. BURKHALTER, DAVID RIGG,
MARY D. TYLL, JOSHUA COHEN, AND WEN LI ZHENG

This chapter discusses the physiological impact of bereavement in healthy individuals as well as in disease processes, such as HIV-1 infection and cancer. Physiological effects are subdivided into effects on neuroendocrines, the immune system, and clinical health. We present a stressor-support-coping (SSC) model predicting the occurrence of these effects. The model comprises three predictors: stressful life event burden, social support availability, and coping disposition. Finally, we present how these effects interdigitate with those of psychotherapeutic interventions aimed at grief and overall distress reduction after bereavement. The potential neuroendocrine, immune, and clinical health effects of bereavement also

We wish to acknowledge grant numbers R01 MH48628, 48628S, and 53802 from the NIMH to Dr. Goodkin. We also wish to acknowledge the individuals who took part in the research described in this chapter at such a difficult time in their lives.

671

are reviewed, focusing on how interventions might buffer or reverse these effects.

Several definitions are in order. *Bereavement* refers to the occurrence of loss of a loved one. *Grief* refers to a specific pattern of mood and behavior associated with such a loss. Grief includes depressed mood, yearning, loneliness, searching for the deceased, the sense of the deceased being present, and the sense of being in ongoing communication with that person. *Psychological distress* applies to a general dysphoric state resulting from one or more specific mood states and must be differentiated from the occurrence of a stressful life event, such as bereavement. *Stressors* cause *distress*, and specifically, the stressor of bereavement causes grief.

NEUROENDOCRINE SYSTEMS, THE IMMUNE SYSTEM, AND PHYSICAL HEALTH: A BACKGROUND FOR BEREAVEMENT RESEARCH

Complex neuroendocrine relationships mediate the link between bereavement and its immunological and physical health consequences. A series of systems interact, highlighted by the limbic-hypothalamic-pituitary-adrenal (LHPA) axis, the sympathetic adrenomedullary system, endorphins, and hormones derived from lymphocytes themselves. The LHPA axis is led by the hippocampus, a region of the brain that exerts an inhibitory effect on the secretion of corticotropin releasing hormone (CRH). The hypothalamus releases CRH, which stimulates corticotrophs—cells in the pituitary secreting adrenocorticotrophic hormone (ACTH). ACTH induces the adrenal cortex to secrete cortisol, which acts on the hypothalamus and the hippocampus in a negative feedback loop (by binding to glucocorticoid receptors) to decrease CRH release.

A second major neuroendocrine system is the sympathetic adrenomedullary system, located in the medulla (center) of the adrenal gland. The medulla secretes catecholamines—norepinephrine (NE) and epinephrine (E)—with NE additionally found in neurons secreting neuropeptide Y (NPY). Metabolites of these hormones also are of interest. A central nervous system metabolite of NE, 3-methoxy-4-hydroxyphenylglycol (MHPG), indicates NE activity in the brain. Peripheral metabolites include vanillylmandelic acid (VMA) and normetanephrines from NE and metanephrines from E. The sum of these metabolites yields a measure of catecholamine turnover in the whole body.

Note that the sympathetic system interacts with the LHPA axis. Hypothalamic secretion of CRH is under ongoing inhibitory control by central NE. Decrements in central NE activity, as in major depressive disorder, are associated with reduced inhibition of the LHPA axis, which increases CRH. Over time, this change in CRH release in the brain is associated with resistance to the inhibitory effect of cortisol—or exogenous gluco-corticoids, such as dexamethasone, a medication used to manipulate the LHPA axis in the dexamethasone suppression test (DST). Lack of the expected suppression of cortisol release in response to dexamethasone, described as "dexamethasone nonsuppression," has been observed in bereavement and in major depressive disorder. Dexamethasone nonsuppression reflects resistance to the negative feedback effect of glucocorticoids in the brain, and is related to binding of glucocorticoids to their receptors. Affinity for binding to receptors is expressed as the inverse of the "dissociation constant," K_d—the rate of spontaneous dissociation of glucocorticoids from their two types of receptors, types I and II. Glucocorticoid binding to type II receptors is more likely to show significant variation and reflect effects of psychosocial stressors like bereavement.

Endogenous opioids—analgesic substances—make up another neuroendocrine system mediating immune function changes. One endogenous opioid, β endorphin, has been associated with bidirectional changes. The pentapeptide hormones, leuenkephalin and metenkephalin, also have immunological effects (Wybran et al., 1987), although these may depend on their concentration and may be specific to the immune measure analyzed (Williamson, Knight, Lightman, & Hobbs, 1987). Hence relationships of the endogenous opioids may be difficult to evaluate for clinical significance.

In addition to these systems, lymphocytes secrete neuroendocrine hormones themselves. Their capacity to secrete ACTH has been referred to as the "lymphoid-adrenal" axis (Smith, Harbour-McMenamin, & Blalock, 1985). However, lymphocytes also can secrete CRH and other neuroendocrine hormones. This aspect of neuroendocrine activity has been least well evaluated in stressor research.

Each of these neuroendocrine systems interacts in an ongoing milieu, just as the psychosocial factors of stressor burden, social support, and coping style interact to create the background against which psychological distress is evaluated. The neuroendocrine systems just described are still incomplete representations of those relevant to stressor responses. The literature tends to highlight neuroendocrine hormones most commonly related to deleterious immune effects, resulting from activation of both the LHPA axis and the sympathetic adrenomedullary system, though the latter also is associated with immunological enhancement acutely. Immunological up-regulation (i.e., salutary effects) is less well studied than down-regulation (i.e., deleterious effects). Prolactin is known to increase immune measures, as do growth hormone and dehydroepiandrosterone (DHEA), an endogenous cortisol antagonist. The balance of up-regulatory and down-regulatory neuroendocrines should be accounted for in determining their immune effects.

The immune system has two arms—cellular and humoral. In the cellular system, lymphoid cells carry out immune responses; in the humoral system this is the task of antibodies. The cellular system contains two main subsets of immune cells—T lymphocytes (e.g., cytotoxic T lymphocytes), which require antigen priming to become active, and natural killer (NK) cells, which require no priming. The humoral immune system consists of B lymphocytes, which differentiate into plasma cells secreting antibodies on antigenic stimulation.

Immunological function is assessed in three major ways: phenotypic or enumerative measures (i.e., cell counts), cell function measures, and measures of immune secretory products. Enumerative measures include counts of CD4 cells—the target of HIV-1. CD4 cells include both "naive" cells not previously exposed to antigen and "memory" cells. The CD8 cell count includes both cytotoxic (immune effectors) and suppressor (down-regulatory) cells. NK cell number is measured by different cell surface protein markers (CD56 and/or CD16 positive; CD3 negative) than those for the CD4 and CD8 cells, both subsets of T (CD3 positive) lymphocytes.

An immune function measure frequently used in stressor research is artificial stimulation of lymphocyte growth *in vitro* using plant lectins such as phytohemagglutinin (PHA) for T cells and pokeweed for B cells. Different doses of these cell growth stimulants (or "mitogens") are used to more completely examine their effects. Outcomes are shown as net counts per minute (cpm, reflecting the net amount of additional radioactivity, beyond background level, incorporated into the DNA of newly synthesized cells), or as a stimulation index (SI, a ratio of the total radioactivity and the background level of radioactivity). Natural killer cell function is described as NK cell cytotoxicity (NKCC), expressed as percentage of target cells killed (typically the NK cell-sensitive K562 erythroleukemic cell line). Analogous to doses for mitogen, NKCC may be tested at different effector-to-target ratios. NKCC may also be expressed as kinetic lytic units in four hours, which is a measure of NK cell turnover.

Finally, soluble cellular products secreted by immune cells include cytokines, growth factors, and chemokines. We focus only on the cytokines, which include proinflammatory cytokines secreted by activated macrophages, such as tumor necrosis factor-alpha (α), interleukin (IL)-1, and IL-6. They also include cytokine subsets secreted by "T helper" cells (CD4 cells). One subset—Th1—is associated with increased cellular immune function and protection against HIV-1 disease progression. These cytokines include interferon-gamma (γ), IL-2, and IL-12. In contrast, Th2 cytokines are secreted by a different subset of CD4 cells and stimulate the humoral immune system. These cytokines include IL-4, IL-5, IL-6 (also pro-inflammatory), IL-10, and IL-13. The balance of Th1 to Th2 cytokines appears to predict HIV-1 clinical disease progression (Meyaard, Otto, Keet, Van Lier, & Miedema, 1994). Cortisol level has been associated with both a decrease in the Th1:Th2 cytokine balance and an increased likelihood of clinical disease progression (Clerici et al., 1994).

Neuroendocrine Effects of Bereavement

Because most studies of bereavement and immune function have not tested for neuroendocrine mediation of effects, documentation is limited for the presumed neuroendocrine mediation of immune effects related to psychosocial stressors. Exceptions include studies of Bartrop, Luckhurst, Lazarus, Kiloh, and Penny (1977) on proliferative response to mitogen, and Irwin, Daniels, Smith, Bloom, and Weiner (1987) on NKCC. Bartrop et al. (1977) showed no association of cortisol, prolactin, growth hormone, or thyroid hormone levels with postbereavement decrements in lymphocyte proliferative response, though a negative association between this measure and cortisol level has been described since the 1930s (Claman, 1972). Goodkin, Feaster, Tuttle, et al. (1996), however, found that controlling for other relevant neuroendocrine effects (E and NE) on lymphocyte proliferation to PHA revealed a significant negative association between plasma cortisol level and this immune measure.

Outside of psychoneuroimmunological studies, the LHPA axis is known to be altered in bereavement. Ten to 15% of bereaved individuals show DST nonsuppression one month postloss, the percentage increasing by six months postloss, especially among the clinically depressed (i.e., complicated bereavement; Das & Berrios, 1984; Kosten, Jacobs & Mason, 1984; Roy, Gallucci, Avgerinos, Linnoila, & Gold, 1988; Shuchter, Zisook, Kirkorowicz, & Risch, 1986). In complicated bereavement, ACTH (also known as corticotropin) response to CRH also is blunted, suggesting hypothalamic dysregulation and hypersecretion of CRH (Roy et al., 1988). One bereavement study showed that higher mean 24-hour urinary E output predicted greater helplessness and hopelessness over two years follow-up, and higher mean 24-hour urinary free cortisol output predicted lower helplessness and hopelessness, controlling for age, gender, and baseline symptom level (Jacobs, Bruce, & Kim, 1997). This study suggests a dysjunction between the adaptiveness of sympathetic adrenomedullary and LHPA axis activation postbereavement.

In a natural history study of HIV-1 infected homosexual men, plasma cortisol levels were higher among the bereaved than the nonbereaved individuals—as were plasma catecholamines (summed E and NE; Goodkin, Feaster, Tuttle, et al., 1996). As mentioned previously, a multiple regression analysis of NE, E, and cortisol showed a significant negative association of cortisol with concurrent lymphocyte proliferative response to PHA ($\log_{10}$ SI; $\beta = -2.08$, $p = .04$). The time course of these LHPA abnormalities postbereavement parallels that of decreased lymphocyte proliferative response postbereavement (Schleifer, Keller, Camerino, Thornton, & Stein, 1983), suggesting LHPA axis mediation of this immunological function. This finding may be relevant to HIV-1 clinical disease progression (Corley, 1996), among other diseases mediated by a Th1 to Th2 cytokine balance (Lucey,

Clerici, & Shearer, 1996). Clerici et al. (1994) hypothesized that increments in the ratio of cortisol to its endogenous antagonist (DHEA and its inactive, sulfated metabolite) suppress Th1 cytokine production (e.g., IL-2, interferon-γ [IFN-γ], and IL-12), favor Th2 cytokine production (e.g., IL-4, IL-5, IL-6, IL-10, and IL-13), induce apoptosis (i.e., "programmed cell death"), and directly increase HIV-1 transcription. Research on cortisol level should also control for level of cortisol binding globulin, as it is the free level of plasma cortisol that is biologically active. Work in bereavement in HIV-1 infection suggests that the expected increments in plasma cortisol are indeed found postbereavement, though in late-stage disease glucocorticoid resistance is common (Norbiato, Bevilacqua, Vago, Taddei, & Clerici, 1997).

Irwin, Daniels, Risch, Bloom, and Weiner (1988) found NKCC was negatively associated with serum cortisol level. It is interesting to note that NKCC decrements among study participants anticipating loss of a loved one did not show this relationship, though NKCC was decreased, suggesting that other neuroendocrine mechanisms (e.g., sympathetic adrenomedullary) may also warrant investigation. This dissociation has been supported by Goodkin, Feaster, Tuttle, et al. (1996), who reported a differential time course of immunological decrements postbereavement. NKCC decrements preceded decrements in lymphocyte proliferation to PHA, suggesting that adrenomedullary system activation may occur with anticipatory loss and may be associated with NKCC decrements preloss and early postloss, and LHPA axis stimulation and increased cortisol levels may be associated with longer term NKCC decrements postloss and the onset of decrements in lymphocyte proliferation to PHA, with a delay, following loss. This is consistent with viewing the sympathetic adrenomedullary system as the "acute alarm" or "fight–flight" system, and the LHPA axis as associated with longer term responses that lead to learned helplessness and decreased responsivity. The finding also suggests that anticipatory bereavement may differ fundamentally from response to actual loss, as suggested by others (Sweeting & Gilhooly, 1990).

Given that stressors have been associated with immune decrements in adrenalectomized mice (Keller et al., 1988; Keller, Weiss, Schleifer, Miller, & Stein, 1983) and that the expected relationships with cortisol are inconsistent in HIV-1 infected individuals (Kertzner et al., 1993), the sympathetic adrenomedullary system must be considered another potential source of immune deficits. Threat of bereavement has been associated with increased urinary catecholamine output (Jacobs et al., 1986), which is related to decreased lymphocyte proliferative response (Bourne et al., 1974; Crary et al., 1983; Livnat, Felten, Carlson, Bellinger, & Felten, 1985) and NK cell counts and cytotoxicity (Hodgson, Yirmiya, Chiappelli, & Taylor, 1999), as well as increased antibody titers to a latent virus—herpes simplex virus (McKinnon, Weisse, Reynolds, Bowles, & Baum, 1989). Although catecholamine increments have been associated with increased NKCC related to demargination of NK cells from the pool of cells adhering to the vascular walls (Schedlowski et al., 1993), chronic effects of catecholamine release differ. Irwin et al. (1991) found that plasma level of NPY was associated with NKCC decrements. As noted, the sympathetic adrenomedullary system and the LHPA axis interact with one another—with lowered central NE levels in depression decreasing basal inhibition of CRH release, although other neurotransmitters (e.g., arginine-vasopressin) also are involved (Holsboer, 1988). Hence both LHPA (CRH, ACTH, and cortisol) and sympathetic adrenomedullary (24-hour urinary whole body NE and E output; levels of NPY) changes may explain immune function decrements in bereavement.

The third potential source for bereavement-related immune function changes is the aforementioned endogenous opioid system. Animal and human studies show NKCC changes associated with β endorphin-like immunoreactivity (Kavelaars, Ballieux, & Heijnen, 1988, 1990; Shavit et al., 1985). Changes in peptide length related to different fragments of proopiomelanocorticotropin (POMC) affect NKCC differently, as do differing concentrations (Williamson et al., 1987). Hence the contribution of this system to immunomodulation in bereavement is complex to discern, as is true elsewhere.

The fourth, more recently described mechanism mediating between neuroendocrine and immune changes is stressor-induced immune changes in hormones released by the lymphocytes themselves. These changes have been shown to modulate immune function (Blalock, Harbour-McMenamin, & Smith, 1985; Smith et al., 1985). This has not been investigated in bereavement.

Across these four systems, the pattern of neuroendocrine-induced immunomodulatory effects differs for acute and chronic stressors. With acute stressors, LHPA activation causes hypercortisolemia, which ends a negative feedback loop to the brain—predominantly hypothalamus, also hippocampus (Holsboer, 1988). With chronic stressors (like bereavement), hypercortisolemia is associated with hippocampal neuronal damage (Sapolsky & Pulsinelli, 1985), loss of inhibitory cortisol feedback, and perpetually increased serum cortisol levels. This helps explain the longevity of postbereavement immune deficits. HIV-1 infection may potentiate this effect, because the hippocampus is rich in CD4 receptors—an HIV-1 binding site (Pert, Smith, Ruff, & Hill, 1988). The combined effects may be loss of inhibitory cortisol feedback through the hippocampus and disposition toward LHPA hyperactivity (Goodkin et al., 2000). Regarding HIV-1+ and HIV-1− serostatus, neuroendocrine and immunological effects of stressors differ (Goodkin, Feaster, et al., 1998; Kumar, Kumar, Morgan, Szapocznik, & Eisdorfer, 1993; Kumar, Morgan, Szapocznik, & Eisdorfer, 1991). Supporting the association of hypercortisolemia with hippocampal neuronal cell loss, Sheline, Wang, Gado, Csernansky, and Vannier (1996) reported decreased hippocampal volume in major depressive disorder, which occurs in complicated bereavement. Nemeroff et al. (1992) reported increased adrenal gland volume with major depressive disorder, confirming downstream effects of hippocampal and hypothalamic dysregulation. However, there is no conclusive evidence yet that hippocampal neuronal loss (and related LHPA axis inhibition downstream) occurs following bereavement (or other traumatic stressors), and the likelihood of this in posttraumatic stress disorder has been challenged (Yehuda, 1997).

Up-regulation of lymphocyte proliferation, as mentioned earlier, is related to prolactin and growth hormone levels. Hence the ratio of hormones up- and down-regulating this immune measure may be more important than studying any one neuroendocrine measure in isolation postbereavement. As a consequence, several neuroendocrine systems should be studied concurrently to understand (a) how postbereavement immune decrements are mediated, (b) how each mechanism contributes to changes longitudinally, and (c) how to intervene to prevent such immune decrements. The need to consider "neuroendocrine milieu" when analyzing effects of a specific hormone on an immune outcome parallels the need to consider "psychosocial context" when analyzing effects of a specific psychosocial variable (e.g., life stressor burden, social support availability, or coping style) on a mood outcome.

Bereavement and the Immune System

Bereavement is the extreme of a continuum of interpersonal separation showing immune decrements. Divorce, separation, marital discord, and even brief separation of mother and infant show immune decrements (Coe, Rosenberg, Fischer, & Levine, 1987; Kiecolt-Glaser, Fisher, et al., 1987; Kiecolt-Glaser & Glaser, 1988; Laudenslager, Captitanio, & Reite, 1985). Bartrop et al. (1977) were the first to demonstrate prospectively bereavement-related decreases in T cell lymphocyte proliferation. Responses to two T cell mitogens—PHA and concanavalin A—were significantly lower six weeks postbereavement than at weeks one to three, suggesting a cumulative, time-dependent stressor effect. Another prospective study replicating Bartrop et al. extended results to decreases in responses to a T cell-dependent B cell mitogen (pokeweed), and documented that return to immunological baseline required 4 to 14 months (Schleifer et al., 1983). The latter parallels the period of increased morbidity and mortality from a variety of illnesses postbereavement (Parkes, Benjamin, & Fitzgerald, 1969; Rees & Lutkins, 1967; Young, Benjamin, & Wallis, 1963). Subsequent research (Linn, Linn, & Jensen, 1984) controlled for depressed mood and found decrements in lymphocyte proliferative responses to PHA and to mixed lymphocyte cultures only in depressed individuals. Although three studies showed bereavement to be associated with decreased lymphocyte proliferative response, this *in vitro* measure may not have clinical significance. Further, physical health endpoints were not studied. Several other immune measures showed no bereavement association, and depressed mood level and depressive disorder history were not always controlled.

NKCC in bereavement has been examined by Irwin et al. (1987, 1988). Both cross-sectional and longitudinal studies of women anticipating or experiencing bereavement (within one to six months) have shown significantly lower NKCC in bereaved women than in nonbereaved controls. As in the study of Linn et al. (1984), these changes were associated with depressed mood. Of note, major depressive disorder has been associated with decreased NK cell counts in men but not in women (Evans et al., 1992), highlighting the issue of differentiating the circulating number of NK cells from their functional capacity. Although estrogens have generally been shown to decrease cell-mediated immunity, estrogen analogues may actually be more likely than endogenous 17β-estradiol to suppress NKCC (Uksila, 1985). This suggests a need to control for exogenous supplementation (oral contraceptives, estrogen replacement) in psychoneuroimmunological studies of women, especially the long-acting (three to six months duration) intramuscular contraceptive, medroxyprogesterone, which has been associated with decreased CD4 cell count. Changes in endogenous estrogens over the phases of the mensis also affect psychoneuroimmune relationships in women and must be controlled (Kiecolt-Glaser & Glaser, 1988). Other important control variables include current and historical alcohol and psychoactive substance use/abuse/dependence, exercise frequency, sleep efficiency, caffeine intake, cigarette smoking (current and total pack year history), history of sexual activity, nutritional status (global nutritional status as well as specific micronutrients, e.g., Ω_3 fatty acids, pyridoxine, cobalamin, folate, carotenoids, zinc, and selenium), and prescribed medication usage.

In HIV-1 infection, several studies have shown bereavement-related immune decrements, although effects are inconsistent. One study showed no immune differences between bereaved (solely loss of close friends) and nonbereaved homosexual men, regardless of HIV-1 serostatus (Kemeny et al., 1994). Among the nonbereaved HIV-1 seropositive men, higher depressed mood was associated with lower CD4 cell percentages, higher percentages of activated CD8 cells, and lower lymphocyte proliferative responses to PHA. These results were not seen among nonbereaved HIV-1 seronegative individuals or bereaved individuals, regardless of HIV-1 serostatus (Kemeny et al., 1994). However, even outside of bereavement in HIV-1 infection, the association of CD4 cell count with depressed mood has been inconsistent (Burack et al., 1993; Lyketsos et al., 1993). In contrast to the Kemeny et al. findings for loss of a close friend, a subsequent report on loss of an intimate partner (in the same cohort) found that bereavement was associated with increased serum neopterin level and decreased lymphocyte proliferative responses to PHA, and that these effects were not mediated by depressed mood (Kemeny et al., 1995). We also have reported that, independent of depressed mood level, the loss of an intimate partner or a close friend—controlling for relationship type—was associated with decreased functional immune responses (NKCC and lymphocyte proliferative response to PHA; Goodkin, Feaster, Tuttle, et al., 1996). Bereavement also has been associated with more rapid CD4 cell loss over a three- to four-year follow-up, beginning at two years postbereavement (Kemeny & Dean, 1995). However, in this study depressed mood, particularly self-reproach, predicted CD4 cell count decline, and grief reactions generally did not. Outside of HIV-1 infection, Spurrell and Creed (1993) reported that mildly elevated depressed mood in those anticipating bereavement was associated with increased lymphocyte proliferative response to PHA, and the opposite was true for patients with major depressive disorder. They suggested a potential "inverted U-shape curve" of depressed mood with this immune measure. Hence inconsistent bereavement effects observed in HIV-1 infection may, at least partly, be a result of nonlinear relationships of depressed mood with the immune outcome under study, as well as to inconsistent controls for this effect across studies.

Factors accounting for inconsistent bereavement effects related to depression include failure to control for type of loss, to differentiate grief from depressed mood, to use a clinical psychiatric interview for syndromal depression and other complicated bereavement reactions, and to use a clinical rating of depressed mood to complement self-reports. Also relevant is lack of a theoretically driven research model—such as the SSC model—to examine bereavement effects within their psychosocial context. This context comprises background life stressor burden, social support availability, and active versus passive dispositional and situational coping style. More consistent control is needed for other influences on immune measures as well, including alcohol and psychoactive substance use, nutritional status, exercise frequency, prescribed medications affecting immune function, cigarette smoking, caffeine intake, and sexual activity (Goodkin et al., 1994; Kiecolt-Glaser & Glaser, 1988).

Effects of Bereavement on Clinical Health

Bereavement has been extensively studied regarding its clinical health impact, with bereavement-related mortality particularly well studied, as loss of a loved one is more common in elderly individuals, who already have an increased mortality risk. Morbidity has been the focus in studies of those losing loved ones to lethal diseases (e.g., cancer, HIV-1 infection), because they are typically healthier. A number of studies have shown that bereavement is associated with physical health decrements (Clayton, 1974, 1979; Kaprio, Kosenvuo, & Rita, 1987; Lundin, 1984; Parkes & Brown, 1972). Increased morbidity and mortality from varied illnesses has been described in 40% of bereaved persons over the first six months, with a tenfold increase over the first year postloss (Parkes et al., 1969; Rees & Lutkins, 1967; Young et al., 1963), though this has not been found invariably. Although the bereavement–mortality association sometimes is found only for men (Helsing & Szklo, 1981), a well-controlled study of 12,522 spouse pairs in a prepaid heath care plan showed increased postbereavement mortality for both women and men, adjusting for age, education, and other mortality predictors (Schaefer, Quesenberry, & Wi, 1995). The highest relative risk (RR) was 7 to 12 months postbereavement (RR = 1.9 for women; 2.1 for men with few health problems). The RR decreased afterward but remained greater than 1.0 more than two years postbereavement. Controlling for previous medical history and effects of a shared environment did not fully account for bereavement effects.

In HIV-1 infection, no controlled research has been reported on the impact of bereavement on disease progression. As with studies of immune effects of bereavement in HIV-1 infection, studies of physical health outcomes associated with psychosocial context have been inconsistent. Although one study did not find stressful life events predicting progression to symptomatic HIV-1 infection (Kessler et al., 1991), Evans et al. (1997) found that severe stressful life events did predict clinical disease progression in a group of homosexual men followed up to 3.5 years. Following the same cohort up to 5.5 years, Leserman et al. (1999) reported that more rapid progression to AIDS was associated with greater life stressor burden, lower social support, and higher levels of depressive symptoms. Another study controlling for variables that could affect clinical progression (e.g., antiretroviral medications, substance use, nutritional status) found that increased life stressor count and decreased use of active coping predicted increased physical symptom burden six months later (Feaster et al., 2000). Moreover, the association of active coping style with decreased HIV-1 disease progression has been confirmed in a Dutch cohort (Mulder, Antoni, Duivenvooden, Kauffmann, & Goodkin, 1995). Similarly, and related to bereavement, another study reported that low availability of attachment was associated with more rapid CD4 cell count decline over five years (Theorell et al., 1995). In contrast, several studies of psychosocial factors and immune measures related to clinical progression of HIV-1 infection have found no association (Perry, Fishman, Jacobsberg, & Frances, 1992; Rabkin et al., 1991; Sahs et al., 1994). Differential use of control variables may account for discrepancies observed across both the immune and clinical health outcomes (Goodkin et al., 1994).

Longitudinal studies are needed of the impact of bereavement on several measures of clinical HIV-1 disease progression—Centers for Disease Control and Prevention clinical disease stage, time to AIDS, and time to death. Outside of HIV-1 infection, much bereavement-related morbidity and mortality is a result of cardiovascular disease. Indeed, recent hypotheses suggest that myocardial infarction may involve the behavioral-neuroendocrine-immune interactions more typically expected with mortality from cancer and infectious disease processes. In myocardial infarction, the connection may relate to cytomegalovirus and Chlamydia pneumoniae infection (Goodkin & Appels, 1997). Combining the potential for mortality as a result of myocardial infarction with mortality as a result of cancer and infectious diseases in the general population, a large proportion of increased morbidity and mortality not attributable to accidents, alcohol and substance use intoxication, and suicide following bereavement may be related to immunological decrements. In addition, the highly active anti-retroviral therapies (HAART) increase serum cholesterol and triglyceride levels, predisposing to myocardial infarction. Hence cardiovascular deaths may become more frequent in HIV-1 infection.

Health status is one step removed from immune function, which is itself one step removed from the multiple psychosocial changes occurring with bereavement. Our work suggests that psychosocial context is estimated to account for 10 to 15% of variance in HIV-1 disease progression, as much as 25 to 30% in immune measures, and more than 50% in psychological distress. Hence variance accounted for by SSC model predictors reduces sequentially across the domains of psychological distress, neuroendocrine-mediated immunological decrements, and clinical disease progression—a reduction related to additional control variables necessary to account for variance in these domains. Indeed, it is striking that the single life stressor of bereavement significantly accounts for more sick days and hospital admissions for a year postbereavement than those occurring in nonbereaved individuals (Parkes & Brown, 1972). Moreover, less severe stressors, such as the anticipatory losses of Alzheimer's caretakers (Kiecolt-Glaser et al., 1987; Kiecolt-Glaser, Dura, Speicher, Trask, & Glaser, 1991) also have been associated with clinical health changes. Hence the clinical health effects of bereavement may well be extended to life stressors more generally.

A PREDICTIVE "STRESSOR-SUPPORT-COPING" THEORETICAL MODEL FOR THE PHYSIOLOGICAL EFFECTS OF BEREAVEMENT

Much can be learned about psychosocial determinants of distress in AIDS-related bereavement by examining them in other diseases, such as women at risk for cervical intraepithelial neoplasia (CIN) and invasive cervical cancer. This is a sexually transmitted disease related to infection by human papillomavirus high-risk types (predominantly types 16, 18 and 33). These women manifest immunosuppression (Goodkin, Antoni, Helder, & Sevin, 1993; Goodkin, Antoni, Sevin, & Fox, 1993a, 1993b), and are also at risk for HIV-1 infection, if not coinfected.

The three principal variables characterizing psychosocial context in our studies are life stressor (S) burden, social support (S) availability, and coping (C) style; hence the SSC model (Baldewicz et al., 1998; Blaney et al., 1991, 1997; Feaster et al., 2000; Goodkin, 1989, 1990; Goodkin et al., 1993a, 1993b; Goodkin, Blaney, et al., 1999; Goodkin, Feaster, et al., 1998; Goodkin, Fletcher, & Cohen, 1995). The SSC model predicts that life stressors (particularly unpredictable, uncontrollable, and chronic) are associated with greater psychological distress. Social support (especially if available, satisfactory, and sufficient) may both directly and indirectly reduce such distress. The indirect effect is through buffering negative impacts of life stressors (Cohen & Wills, 1985). Passive, maladaptive coping styles —such as denial, or mental or behavioral disengagement (e.g., alcohol or substance use to manage a stressor)—are likely to increase psychological distress. In contrast, active coping styles (e.g., taking action to reduce stressor impact, creating a coping plan) are likely to decrease distress. The stressor, support, and coping variables of the SSC model are predictive of psychological distress (Baldewicz et al., 1998; Blaney et al., 1991, 1997; Feaster et al., 2000), immunological measures (Goodkin, Blaney, et al., 1992; Goodkin, Feaster, Tuttle, et al., 1996; Goodkin, Feaster, et al., 1998; Goodkin, Fuchs, Feaster, Leeka, & Rishel, 1992), and physical health outcome measures (Feaster et al., 2000; Goodkin, Feaster, et al., 1998).

Regarding cross-cultural effects, findings are similar in Dutch samples with HIV-1 infection (Mulder et al., 1995) and CIN (Visser et al., 2000). In addition, factor analysis of the COPE (Carver, Scheier, & Weintraub, 1989) has shown that the SSC model coping profile—composite scores for active coping, and disengagement and denial; subscale scores for focus on and venting of emotions, and turning to religion—held in a Dutch sample, although the religion emphasis was reduced (Goodkin, Blaney, et al., 1995). Subtle model differences by ethnic minority status have also emerged in our cervical cancer studies, with African Americans showing larger effects for life stressor burden than for coping strategies, and European Americans showing the reverse.

Effects of these variables on distress level have been confirmed in three other careful studies. In one, a longitudinal path analysis predicted depressed mood, controlling for distress and HIV-1-related symptoms at baseline (Folkman, Chesney, Pollack, & Coates, 1993). In this study, previous depressed mood, physical symptoms of HIV-1 infection, stressful life event burden, appraised controllability of these events, and coping strategy accounted for 60% of the variance in depressed mood one year later among HIV-1+ and HIV-1– homosexual men ($N = 425$). Stressors appraised as controllable were associated with involvement (active) coping and diminished depressed mood, and stressors associated with detachment (passive coping) were associated with increased depressed mood. A second study used a theoretical model—simultaneously assessing direct and buffering effects of distress predictors—and demonstrated that active coping decreased distress (Pakenham, Dadds, & Terry, 1994). A third study documented that greater "positive coping" (e.g., positive outlook) was associated with lower levels of depressive symptoms in a large sample ($N = 736$) (Fleishman & Fogel, 1994). Though passive, dispositional coping styles may be deleterious, selected situation-specific passive coping strategies (like turning to religion) associated with uncontrollable stressors (like bereavement) may be adaptive and actually reduce distress (Blaney et al., 1997).

A majority of HIV-1 infected women have shown significant psychological distress (Franke, Jager, Thomann, & Beyer, 1992). Although one study has shown no effect of depressed mood level on HIV-1 disease progression in women (Vedhara et al., 1999), these findings remain to be corroborated. A chronic, negative impact on psychological adjustment has already been well-demonstrated for conjugal bereavement in the general population (Jacobs, 1993; Zisook & Shuchter, 1991). Regarding theoretical SSC model predictions for women suffering the loss of a loved one, women might be expected to resolve their grief and overall distress more readily postbereavement as a result of broader and more flexible social support networks than those of men, who may be at greater risk for maladjustment. Men may more easily avoid grief work by working away from home and by a social environment less encouraging of emotional expression (W. Stroebe & Stroebe, 1993). Hence this may be an important gender difference in indications for bereavement intervention at the psychological level.

Regarding the clinical impact of bereavement, most depressions following bereavement are transient and require no professional attention (Breckenridge, Gallagher, Thompson, & Peterson, 1986; Wortman & Silver, 1989). However, psychological distress is quite common (Norris & Murrell, 1987). Depressions that persist through the first year are considered clinically significant (Jacobs, 1993) and severe psychiatric sequelae, including severe depression and psychosis, occur in 15% of bereaved individuals (Jacobs, 1993; Rynearson, 1990). In HIV-1 infection, bereavement may particularly predispose to severe psychiatric sequelae, because of confrontation with one's pending mortality. The potency of bereavement in HIV-1 infection is highlighted by (a) the chronicity of impact of losses typically experienced, and (b) the multiplicity of these losses and their cumulative impact on distress over time (Martin, 1988).

Earlier AIDS-related losses have not been found to exacerbate the psychological effects of a recent single loss (Martin & Dean, 1993; Neugebauer et al., 1992). Nevertheless, it has been suggested that multiple loss may be a traumatic stressor in HIV-1 infected individuals (Klein, 1994). Distress associated with traumatic stressors may manifest qualitatively differently from the general dysphoria noted with nontraumatic stressors. Women with HIV-1 infection have been noted to have an increased likelihood of both physical and emotional abuse. Such traumatic stressor exposure may increase the likelihood of trauma-specific distress during bereavement. Bereavement itself tends to manifest with both trauma-specific and general dysphoric aspects. This distinction parallels the difference between bereavement complicated by a major depressive disorder and bereavement complicated by a reaction more consistent with posttraumatic stress disorder (PTSD). The latter is associated with emotional numbing, avoidance of contact with others, hypervigilance, and an activated state, as opposed to a a lethargic, depressed state. Hence different psychological distress measures should be used to tease apart these types of distress.

Not surprisingly, PTSD-related immunological effects have been shown to differ from those associated with major depressive disorders, representing an increase rather than decrease in immune function (Dekaris et al., 1994; Laudenslager et al., 1998). If this type of reaction is more pronounced in multiple loss rather than after a single loss, it may be that the potential psychological and clinical health import of "multiple loss syndrome" has been largely overlooked to date. This divergence may gain more recognition as HIV-1 infected individuals more commonly experience multiple losses with longer survival time as a result of HAART.

BEREAVEMENT SUPPORT GROUP INTERVENTION EFFECTS

Psychological Effects

Our support group intervention aimed not only to accomplish grief work but also to modify the three underlying SSC model predictors of psychological distress and grief level–life stressors, social support and coping style (Goodkin, Blaney, et al., 1996). Social support is greatly decreased following bereavement and has been shown to be related to decrements in physical health among elderly individuals (Rodin, 1986). A high level of social support has been described as the single most consistent predictor of better psychological adjustment postbereavement (Gass, 1987; Windholtz, Marmar, & Horowitz, 1985). Those who perceive social support to be less adequate while caregiving in anticipation of loss show more intense grief symptoms postbereavement (Lennon, Martin, & Dean, 1990). Coping style has also been associated with adjustment to loss. In HIV-1 infection, homosexual male caregivers using distancing and self-blame showed more depressed mood seven months postloss, and those who reinterpreted the event as meaningful showed less depressed mood (Folkman, Chesney, Collette, Boccelari, & Cooke, 1996). Moreover, loss-associated life stressors—

for example, health bills, funeral arrangements, family conflicts, and moving—may compound the effects of loss. Although it has long been viewed that passive coping efforts, such as emotional venting, were most adaptive following a loss, more recently active coping strategies have been a focus of attention (Goodkin, Blaney, et al., 1996; Goodkin, Burkhalter, Blaney, Leeds, & Feaster, 1997; Jacobs, Kasl, Schaefer, & Ostfeld, 1994). It may be that the role of active coping strategies is more specifically associated with controllable life stressors attending a loss, rather than with the more commonly perceived-to-be uncontrollable event of the loss itself.

Bereavement support groups have been shown to reduce distress (Kay & Portillo, 1989; Marmar, Horowitz, Weiss, Wilner, & Kaltreider, 1988), including groups of HIV-1 infected individuals (Goodkin, Blaney, et al., 1999; Goodkin, Burkhalter, et al., 1997; McCallum, Dykes, Painter, & Gold, 1989; Sikkema, Kalichman, Kelly, & Koob, 1995). A landmark study of a support group intervention for terminal breast cancer patients, controlling for disease stage, showed that women receiving the group intervention increased survival time by approximately a factor of two. Further, the effect was correlated with the number of sessions attended (Spiegel, Bloom, Kraemer, & Gottheil, 1989; Spiegel, Bloom, & Yalom, 1981). Another study of terminal cancer patients showed enhanced immune function with mental imagery and relaxation training (Gruber, Hall, Hersh, & Dubois, 1988). The work of Fawzy et al. (Fawzy, Cousins, et al., 1990; Fawzy, Kemeny, et al., 1990; Fawzy et al., 1993) demonstrated that a brief group intervention focused on active coping in malignant melanoma patients was associated not only with reduced psychological distress but also with increased immunological function and longer survival time, though the path between these outcomes was not entirely supported.

Our research group studied 166 males (97 HIV-1 seropositive; 69 HIV-1 seronegative), randomly assigned to bereavement support groups of homogeneous HIV-1 serostatus or to a community comparison "standard of care" control condition (Goodkin, Blaney, et al., 1999). Participants were assessed at entry and at 10 weeks with psychosocial questionnaires, a semistructured interview for psychopathology, a medical history and physical examination, urine collection, and phlebotomy. For a composite score of psychological distress and grief as well as the distress component of this composite, scores were significantly lower postintervention by analyses against baseline scores, with and without control variables for other factors affecting distress level. For grief level, a significant relative reduction in grief for intervention versus control participants was found only in the analysis including control variables. Control participants showed no significant decrements in overall distress, though a significant decrement in grief level was observed. The trial demonstrated that a brief group intervention can significantly reduce overall distress and accelerate grief reduction in a sample of bereaved individuals unselected for psychopathology or for a high risk of maladjustment following loss.

Ethnicity-specific issues have been shown to have SSC model associations in natural history studies, as well as in the psychological effects of our bereavement support group intervention, over six time points and two years of follow-up. Although the support group intervention effects held for the entire sample, controlling for ethnicity, the distress reduction effects observed were not as great for Hispanic and African Americans as they were for European Americans. This may relate to a difference in the SSC model variable reflecting use of religion as a form of coping—used most frequently by African Americans, followed by Hispanic Americans, then European Americans. This suggests that one ethnicity-specific modification of our bereavement support group intervention might involve additional incorporation of a focus on religion and spirituality more explicitly across intervention topics.

Given the recent rapid growth of HIV-1 infection among women in the United States, it is important to determine whether a support group intervention that promotes grief resolution also improves the psychological, immune, and physical health of women experiencing AIDS-related losses. This is a particular concern as HIV-1 infected women, particularly minorities, have received inadequate research attention (e.g., risk behavior prediction; Stein, Newcomb, & Bentler, 1994), as well as on the bereavement issues discussed in this chapter (Goodkin, Blaney, et al., 1996). We have reported a pilot study of a bereavement support group intervention in women (Goodkin, Baldewicz, et al., 1998; Goodkin, Fletcher, et al., 1995), the majority African Americans and HIV-1 seropositive, with a minority of Hispanics and no European Americans. The intervention was adapted to be sensitive to HIV/AIDS issues of minorities, especially the increased heterogeneity of the type of losses (e.g., loss of a child). The avoidance coping strategy of psychoactive substance use was also a focus, because a large portion of the sample had current or previous alcohol and/or psychoactive substance use disorders. Other adaptations addressed the higher likelihood of traumatic stressors, below average socioeconomic status and educational level, as well as the lower participant comfort with the "culture" of a psychotherapy group. Our sample had a heavy loss burden—a total of 350 deaths were experienced by these women—$X = 19.44$/person, comparable to our sample of homosexual men. Grief level—the first tier of the intervention—was significantly reduced by the group. In addition, SSC model predictors of positive life event impact and social support weighted by satisfaction were increased by the intervention, as was active coping by suppression of competing activities and using instrumental social support. The clinical implications for AIDS-related bereavement in women are that both grief level and known predictors of maladjustment following a loss may be ameliorated by a brief, cost-effective group intervention.

Neuroendocrine Effects

Neuroendocrine effects of bereavement interventions studied to date have largely been limited to the LHPA axis and to the sympathetic adrenomedullary system. Future bereavement support group intervention research should extend to other neuroendocrine measures, particularly those likely to be associated with up-regulation of immune function.

LHPA Axis

Regarding our bereavement support group intervention in HIV-1+ and HIV-1− homosexual men, a three-time-point (baseline, 10 weeks, and at 6 months) repeated measures analysis of variance (RANOVA) showed a significant group effect in the time path of plasma cortisol change. The intervention group decreased, and the control group increased in plasma cortisol level. Among HIV-1+ individuals, intervention partcipants decreased mean plasma cortisol level 1.2 μg/dl by T3, whereas control participants increased 3.6 μg/dl by T3, a relative mean difference in change from baseline of 4.8 μg/dl. For HIV-1− individuals, intervention participants decreased mean plasma cortisol level 1.9 μg/dl by T3, whereas control participants increased 2.0 μg/dl by T3, a relative mean difference in change from baseline of 3.9 μg/dl. In an ANOVA including T1 and T3 alone, the intervention effect was statistically significant, whether or not baseline plasma cortisol level was controlled (Goodkin, Feaster, et al., 1998; see Figure 29-1). Recent studies suggest that the lower affinity glucocorticoid type II receptors are more involved in cortisol regulation in stressful situations, because their K_d is higher (on the order of 5nm) than type I receptors (K_d = 0.5nm), which are more likely to be saturated. If confirmed in bereavement, this may justify studying glucocorticoid receptor activation. We found extremely high mean levels of plasma CRH for both HIV-1− and HIV-1+ bereaved individuals (M_{CRH} = 359 pg/ml, sd = 304 for HIV-1+ individuals; M_{CRH} = 368 pg/ml, sd = 275, for HIV-1− individuals) compared to normal values (M = 1–15 pg/ml; Goodkin, Baldewicz, et al., 1999). Because plasma CRH does not reflect central level, this suggests production of immunoreactive CRH in the periphery, implying an unstudied immune–brain communication mechanism that may be important for future bereavement research.

Sympathetic Adrenomedullary System

Catecholamine measures also have shown significant effects in our bereavement support group intervention with HIV-1+ and HIV-1− homosexual men. In HIV-1+ individuals, a reduction postintervention was observed in MHPG obtained from the 24-hour urine. MHPG is known to

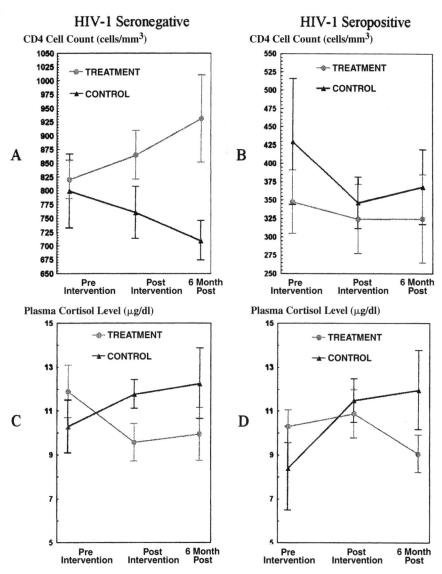

Figure 29-1. Impact of a Bereavement Support Group Intervention on CD4 Cell Count, Plasma Cortisol Level, and Health Care Visit Use in HIV-1 Seropositive and Seronegative Homosexual Men.

be elevated following bereavement, as well as in major depressive disorder (in a subset of cases), and posttraumatic stress disorder—two potential complicated bereavement reactions (Goodkin, Blaney, et al., 1996). In HIV-1− individuals, MHPG decrements were also found postintervention, as were decrements in NE and E. These findings are buttressed by our results for neuroendocrine-immune associations with bereavement itself— a trend for plasma norepinephrine to be higher among bereaved (p =

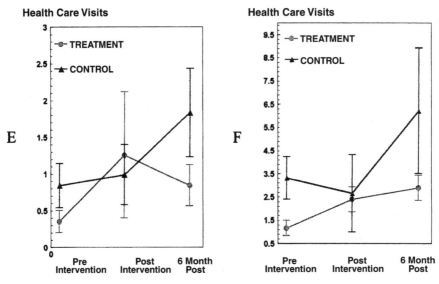

Figure 29-1. Continued

.09) than nonbereaved individuals (Goodkin, Feaster, et al., 1996). Summed plasma norepinephrine and epinephrine levels also were significantly higher among bereaved individuals (p = .02). VMA demonstrated an intervention-buffering effect against an increase observed in HIV-1+ control participants.

Immune Effects

Although immune effects of psychotherapy interventions have been reported, there has been little focus on bereavement support group interventions. Our intervention showed beneficial effects over six months follow-up for CD4 cell count, of central importance in HIV-1 infection (Goodkin, Feaster, et al., 1998; see Figure 29-1). Among HIV-1+ individuals, controls showed a noteworthy decrement compared to intervention participants. For HIV-1− individuals, intervention participants increased and controls decreased—a relative change between groups of greater than 200 cells/mm^3 (Goodkin, Feaster, et al., 1998).

Total lymphocyte count—which combined with CD4 cell count has been used to characterize level of immunological progression—increased pre- to postintervention (a trend) through six-months follow-up (a statistically significant change). The more reliable measure—total lymphocyte percentage—showed a significant increment 1.5 years following intervention by an ANOVA on simple change controlling for baseline values. However, results of other analyses were more robust for count than for the percentage measure.

Although CD56 (NK) cell count did not increase significantly pre-to postintervention, the more reliable measure, CD56 percentage, did increase significantly through six-months follow-up (by repeated measures ANOVA) as well as by ANOVA on simple change at 6 months, 18 months, and 24 months. Differences between intervention and control participants were more prominent for HIV-1+ than for HIV-1− individuals.

Regarding functional immune measures, lymphocyte proliferative response to PHA increased significantly following intervention—measured either as net cpm or as stimulation index (SI), from baseline to 6, 12, 18 and 24 months (at PHA doses of 20 μg/ml and at 10 μg/ml). Effects were more prominent for HIV-1+ than for HIV-1− individuals. At 10 μg/ml, net cpm did not show an effect at six months, whereas SI did. Both showed significant intervention effects at 12, 18, and 24 months. For NKCC, there was a change (in kinetic lytic units over 4 hours, KLU 4h, a measure of cell turnover after killing) from preintervention through six-months follow-up (RANOVA, $p = .052$), suggesting a possible buffer against a decrease compared to control participants.

In summary, these findings support the conclusion that our current, single-loss support group intervention is associated with significant improvement in psychological status as well as both neuroendocrine and immunological measures. Regarding the latter, this was observed for CD4 cell count (and the associated total lymphocyte count) and lymphocyte proliferative response to PHA, as well as some effects on NK cell percentage and on NKCC.

Virological Effects

The clinical relevance of these findings is substantiated by the virological effects of our intervention. To our knowledge, ours is the first report of a behavioral intervention affecting plasma load of HIV-1. In a subset of 36 HIV-1+ homosexual men, plasma viral load was measured using the Amplicor assay (Roche, Nutley, NJ). There was a significant intervention effect on plasma HIV-1 RNA copy number ($p = .01$), controlling for baseline antiretroviral medication use, prophylaxis against HIV-1 associated conditions, CD4 cell count, viral load, and CDC clinical disease stage (Goodkin, Baldewicz, Asthana, et al., in press). We did not use CDC immunological stage (based on three tiers of the CD4 cell count) because the continuous measure of CD4 cell count is the more sensitive control. Relative mean change between conditions ($0.78 \log_{10}$) was greater than the minimum suppression required to define a clinical benefit ($0.5 \log_{10}$) in antiretroviral medication trials, suggesting a clinically relevant virological effect from our bereavement support group intervention. Our previously reported effects for CD4 cell count and health care visit utilization may be mediated by an intervention-induced buffer against increased plasma viral load. This finding is of special import in that plasma viral load has been adopted as a principal outcome measure by the AIDS Clinical Trial Group (ACTG) as a result of cumulative data supporting its clinical prognostic value.

Physical Health Effects

Physical health effects of bereavement support group interventions have received little attention. In our randomized clinical trial, health care visit frequency significantly decreased postintervention and at six months (Goodkin, Feaster, et al., 1998; see Figure 29-1) and one-year follow-up. This suggests that the intervention not only had significant psychological, neuroendocrine, immunological, and virological benefits but also that these may have been transduced into clinical health benefits as well—at least up to one year, the period of greatest physical health decline following loss.

Regarding daily life activities, psychological dysfunction decreased immediately postintervention—an effect that persisted at 1.5 years. Overall dysfunction (psychological and physical) also was reduced at one year. Given that daily life dysfunction as well as number of health care visits showed salutary intervention effects in HIV-1 individuals as well, these findings may also extend to those in the general population suffering a loss.

To evaluate distress and dysfunction after a subsequent loss following the intervention, we analyzed responses in daily life activities for 118 subsequent losses. Thirty-one were sustained by HIV-1 seropositive intervention participants, 36 by HIV-1 seropositive controls, 42 by HIV-1 seronegative intervention participants, and nine by HIV-1 seronegative controls. Compared to controls, intervention participants showed significant reductions in overall distress and grief following a subsequent loss, controlling for serostatus, subsequent loss impact, psychotropic medication usage, psychosocial service use, order of the subsequent loss, and baseline grief and distress levels. Of the 118 subsequent losses, 50 were at least a second subsequent loss. Hence there were 68 participants with at least one subsequent loss. For those with more than one loss, we focused on the loss associated with the highest grief level; analyzing for a bereavement support group intervention effect, we replicated our results for index loss-induced grief level. Intervention participants showed significantly less grief. Subsequent loss affected functional status significantly less in intervention participants on both overall dysfunction and on psychosocial dysfunction, specifically, controlling as described previously (adding antiretroviral medication usage for total dysfunction). This suggests an inoculation effect of our bereavement support group intervention against the effects of subsequent loss that is sustained for up to two years.

CONCLUSION

Future studies in HIV-1 infection are necessary to determine whether a bereavement support group intervention decreases clinical disease progression. In addition to progression to clinically defined AIDS, changes in clinical disease stage within the CDC staging system (Centers for Disease Control, 1992) could also be examined. However, changes in CDC immunological staging would likely not prove of additional value, because the grid of clinical and immunological stage is not yet well-defined regarding its progression characteristics. Finally, an effect on mortality could also be studied. No evidence has yet accumulated regarding such effects for bereavement support groups in HIV-1 infection. However, studies (Evans et al., 1995; Leserman et al., 1997) suggest that severe stressors—presumably, a significant number of which were losses—are associated with both decreased cytotoxic T lymphocyte counts (effector cells targeting HIV-1 infected cells) and increased clinical disease progression. Outside of HIV-1 infection, bereavement support group interventions for losses unrelated to HIV/AIDS warrant examination. A related issue, still to be determined, is whether such interventions might have effects on specific causes of mortality (e.g., tumors significantly mediated by immunological surveillance; Garssen & Goodkin, 1999) and infections other than HIV-1, as well as mortality as a result of coronary artery disease (associated with *Chlamydia pneumoniae* and cytomegalovirus infections; Goodkin & Appels, 1997). Thus the physiological effects of a bereavement support group intervention may hold equally well for physically healthy individuals in the general population as for those suffering from HIV-1 infection, cancer, and other diseases.

REFERENCES

Baldewicz, T., Goodkin, K., Feaster, D., Blaney, N., Kumar, M., Kumar, A., Shor-Posner, G., & Baum, M. (1998). Plasma pyridoxine deficiency is related to increased psychological distress in recently bereaved homosexual men. *Psychosomatic Medicine, 60,* 297–308.

Bartrop, R. W., Luckhurst, L., Lazarus, L., Kiloh, L. G., & Penny, R. (1977). Depressed lymphocyte function after bereavement. *Lancet, 1,* 834–836.

Blalock J. E., Harbour-McMenamin D., & Smith E. M. (1985). Peptide hormones shared by the neuroendocrine and immunologic systems. *Journal of Immunology, 135*(2, Suppl.), 858s–861s.

Blaney, N. T., Goodkin, K., Feaster, D., Morgan, R., Millon, C., Szapocznik. J., & Eisdorfer, C. (1997). A psychosocial model of distress over time in early HIV-1 infection: The role of life stressors, social support and coping. *Psychology & Health, 12*(6), 633–653.

Blaney, N. T., Goodkin, K., Morgan, R. O., Feaster, D., Millon, C., Szapocznik, J., & Eisdorfer, C. (1991). A stress-moderator model of distress in early HIV infection: Concurrent analysis of life events, hardiness, and social support. *Journal of Psychosomatic Research, 35,* 297–305.

Bourne, H. R., Lichtenstein, L. M., Melmon, K. L., Henney, C. S., Weinstein, Y., & Shearer, G. M. (1974). Modulation of inflammation and immunity by cyclic AMP. *Science*, *184*, 19–28.

Breckenridge, J. A., Gallagher, D., Thompson, L. W., & Peterson, J. (1986). Characteristic depressive symptoms of bereaved elders. *Journal of Gerontology*, *41*, 163–168.

Burack, J. H., Barrett, D. C., Stall, R. D., Chesney, M. A., Ekstrand, M. L., & Coates, T. J. (1993). Depressive symptoms and CD4 lymphocyte decline among HIV-infected men. *Journal of the American Medical Association*, *270*, 2568–2573.

Carver, C. S., Scheier, M. F., & Weintraub, J. K. (1989). Assessing coping strategies: A theoretically based approach. *Journal of Personality and Social Psychology*, *56*, 267–283.

Centers For Disease Control. (1992). 1993 revised classification system for HIV infection and expanded surveillance case definition for AIDS among adolescents and adults. *Morbidity and Mortality Weekly Reports*, *41*, 1–19.

Claman, H. N. (1972). Corticosteroids and lymphoid cells. *New England Journal of Medicine*, *287*, 388–397.

Clayton, P. J. (1974). Mortality and morbidity in the first year of widowhood. *Archives of General Psychiatry*, *30*, 747–750.

Clayton, P. J. (1979). The sequelae and nonsequelae of conjugal bereavement. *American Journal of Psychiatry*, *136*, 1530–1534.

Clerici, M., Bevilacqua, M., Vago, T., Villa, M. L., Shearer, G. M., & Norbiato, G. (1994). An immunoendocrinological hypothesis of HIV infection. *Lancet*, *343*, 1552–1553.

Coe, C. L., Rosenberg, L. T., Fischer, M., & Levine, S. (1987). Psychological factors capable of preventing the inhibition of antibody responses in separated infant monkeys. *Child Development*, *58*, 1420–1430.

Cohen, S., & Wills, T. A. (1985). Stress, social support, and the buffering hypothesis. *Psychological Bulletin*, *98*, 310–357.

Corley, P. A. (1996). Acquired immune deficiency syndrome: The glucocorticoid solution. *Medical Hypotheses*, *47*, 49–54.

Crary, B., Borysenko, M., Sutherland, D., Kutz, I., Borysenko, J., & Benson, H. (1983). Decrease in mitogen responsiveness of mononuclear cells from peripheral blood after epinephrine administration in humans. *Journal of Immunology*, *130*, 694–697.

Das, M., & Berrios, G. E. (1984). Dexamethasone suppression test in acute grief reaction. *Acta Psychiatrica Scandinavica*, *70*, 278–281.

Dekaris, D., Sabioncello, A., Mazuran, R., Rabatic, S., Svoboda-Beusan, I., Racunica, N. L., & Tomasic, J. (1994). Multiple changes of immunological parameters in prisoners of war. Assessments after release from a camp in Manjaca, Bosnia. *Journal of the American Medical Association*, *270*, 595–599.

Evans, D. L., Folds, J. D., Petitto, J. M., Golden, R. N., Pedersen, C. A., Corrigan, M., Gilmore, J. H., Silva, S. G., Quade, D., & Ozer, H. (1992). Circulating natural killer cell phenotypes in men and women with major depression. Relation to cytotoxic activity and level of depression. *Archives of General Psychiatry, 49,* 388–395.

Evans, D. L., Leserman, J., Perkins, D. O., Stern, R. A., Murphy, C., Tamul, K., Liao, D., van der Horst, C. M., Hall, C. D., Folds, J. D., Golden, R. N., & Petitto, J. M. (1995). Stress-associated reductions of cytotoxic T lymphocytes and natural killer cells in asymptomatic HIV infection. *American Journal of Psychiatry, 152,* 543–550.

Evans, D. L., Leserman, J., Perkins, D. O., Stern, R. A., Murphy, C., Zheng, B., Gettes, D., Longmate, J. A., Silva, S. G., van der Horst, C. M., Hall, C. D., Folds, J. D., Golden, R. N., & Petitto, J. M. (1997). Severe life stress as a predictor of early disease progression in HIV infection. *American Journal of Psychiatry, 154,* 630–634.

Fawzy, F. I., Cousins, N., Fawzy, N. W., Kemeny, M. E., Elashoff, R., & Morton, D. (1990). A structured psychiatric intervention for cancer patients. I. Changes over time in methods of coping and affective disturbance. *Archives of General Psychiatry, 47,* 720–725.

Fawzy, F. I., Fawzy, N. W., Hyun, C. S., Elashoff, R., Guthrie, D., Fahey, J. L., & Morton, D. L. (1993). Malignant melanoma. Effects of an early structured psychiatric intervention, coping, and affective state on recurrence and survival 6 years later. *Archives of General Psychiatry, 50,* 681–689.

Fawzy, F. I., Kemeny, M. E., Fawzy, N. W., Elashoff, R., Morton, D., Cousins, N., & Fahey, J. L. (1990). A structured psychiatric intervention for cancer patients. II. Changes over time in immunological measures. *Archives of General Psychiatry, 47,* 729–735.

Feaster, D. J., Goodkin, K., Blaney, N. T., Baldewicz, T., Tuttle, R., Woodward, C., Szapocznik, J., Eisdorfer, C., Baum, M., & Fletcher, M. A. (2000). Longitudinal psychoneuroimmunological relationships in the natural history of HIV-1 infection: The stressor-support-coping model. In K. Goodkin & A. P. H. Visser (Eds.), *Psychoneuroimmunology: Stress, Mental Disorders, and Health* (pp. 153–194). Washington, DC: American Psychiatric Press.

Fleishman, J. A., & Fogel, B. (1994). Coping and depressive symptoms among young people with AIDS. *Health Psychology, 13,* 156–169.

Folkman, S., Chesney, M., Collette, L., Boccelari, A., & Cooke, M. (1996). Postbereavement depressive mood and its prebereavement predictors in HIV+ and HIV− gay men. *Journal of Personality and Social Psychology, 70,* 336–348.

Folkman, S., Chesney, M., Pollack, L., & Coates, T. (1993). Stress, control, coping, and depressive mood in human immunodeficiency virus-positive and -negative gay men in San Francisco. *Journal of Nervous & Mental Disease, 181,* 409–416.

Franke, G. H., Jager, H., Thomann, B., & Beyer, B. (1992). Assessment and evaluation of psychological distress in HIV-infected women. *Psychology and Health, 6,* 297–312.

Garssen, B., & Goodkin, K. (1999). The role of immunologic factors as mediators between psychosocial factors and cancer progression. *Psychiatry Research, 85,* 51–61.

Gass, K. A. (1987). The health of conjugally bereaved older widows: The role of appraisal. *Research in Nursing and Health, 10,* 39–47.

Goodkin, K. (1989). A preliminary report of cross sectional studies of stress, social support, and coping style indices in HIV spectrum disorders. In *Abstracts of Papers, AAAS Annual Meeting* (pp. 51–52). Washington, DC: AAAS.

Goodkin, K. (1990). Psychoneuroimmunology and viral infection with a special note on AIDS. In H. Balner (Ed.), *Publications of the Helen Dowling Institute for Biopsychosocial Medicine. 1. A New Medical Model A challenge for Biomedicine?* (pp. 53–64). Rockville, MD: Swets & Zeitlinger.

Goodkin, K., Antoni, M. H., Helder, L., & Sevin, B. (1993). Psychoneuroimmunological aspects of disease progression among women with human papillomavirus-associated cervical dysplasia and human immunodeficiency virus type 1 co-infection. *International Journal of Psychiatry in Medicine, 23,* 119–148.

Goodkin, K., Antoni, M. H., Sevin, B.-U., & Fox, B. H. (1993a). A partially testable, predictive model of psychosocial factors in the etiology of cervical cancer. I. Biological, psychological, and social aspects. *Psycho-oncology, 2,* 79–98.

Goodkin, K., Antoni, M. H., Sevin, B.-U., & Fox, B. H. (1993b). A partially testable, predictive model of psychosocial factors in the etiology of cervical cancer. II. Bioimmunological, psychoneuroimmunological, and socioimmunological aspects, critique and prospective integration. *Psycho-oncology, 2,* 99–121.

Goodkin, K., & Appels, A. (1997). Behavioral-neuroendocrine-immune interactions in myocardial infarction: An etiological role? *Medical Hypotheses, 48,* 209–214.

Goodkin, K., Baldewicz, T., Blaney, N. T., Austin, P. A., & Molina, R. (1998). Bereavement support group intervention for HIV+ and at risk women. *Book of Abstracts of the XIIth World AIDS Conference* (p. 571). Geneva: International AIDS Society.

Goodkin, K., Baldewicz, T. T., Asthana, D., Khamis, I., Blaney, N. T., Kumar, M., Burkhalter, J. E., Leeds, B., & Shapshak, P. (in press). Intervention affects plasma burden of HIV-1: Report of a randomized controlled trial. *Journal of Human Virology.*

Goodkin, K., Baldewicz, T. T., Kumar, M., Kumar, A., Blaney, N. T., Asthana, D., Cohen, J., & Shapshak, P. (1999). *Prevalence of depressive disorders in bereaved HIV-1+ and HIV-1− homosexual men: Implications for clinical disease progression.* Paper presented at the XXVIIIth ISPNE Congress International Society of Psychoneuroendocrinology, Orlando, FL, July 29–Aug. 2.

Goodkin, K., Blaney, N. T., Feaster, D. J., Baldewicz, T., Burkhalter, J. E., & Leeds, B. (1999). A randomized controlled trial of a bereavement support group intervention in human immunodeficiency virus type 1-seropositive and seronegative homosexual men. *Archives of General Psychiatry, 55,* 52–59.

Goodkin, K., Blaney, N. T., Feaster, D., Fletcher, M. A., Baum, M. K., Mantero-Atienza, E., Klimas, N. G., Millon, C., Szapocznik, J., & Eisdorfer, C. (1992). Active coping style is associated with natural killer cell cytotoxicity in asymptomatic HIV-1 seropositive homosexual men. *Journal of Psychosomatic Research, 36,* 635–650.

Goodkin, K., Blaney, N. T., Nelson, R., Fletcher, M. A., Uselmann, M., & Feaster, D. (1995). Bereavement support group intervention for HIV+ and at risk women—A preliminary report. *First Dutch Conference on Psychology and Health, Abstracts Book,* 158. Kerkrade, The Netherlands: Health Psychology Consortium.

Goodkin, K., Blaney, N. T., Tuttle, R. S., Nelson, R. H., Baldewicz, T., Kumar, M., Fletcher, M. A., Leeds, B., & Feaster, D. J. (1996). Bereavement and HIV infection. *International Review of Psychiatry, 8,* 201–216.

Goodkin, K., Burkhalter, J., Blaney, N. T., Leeds, B., & Feaster, D. J. (1997). Bereavement support group techniques for the HIV infected: Integration of research with clinical practice. *Omega: Journal of Death and Dying, 34,* 279–300.

Goodkin, K., Feaster, D. J., Asthana, D., Blaney, N. T., Kumar, M., Baldewicz, T., Tuttle, R. S., Maher, K. J., Baum, M. K., Shapshak, P., & Fletcher, M. A. (1998). A bereavement support group intervention is longitudinally associated with salutary effects on the CD4 cell count and on number of physician visits. *Clinical and Diagnostic Laboratory Immunology, 5,* 382–391.

Goodkin, K., Feaster, D. J., Tuttle, R., Blaney, N. T., Kumar, M., Baum, M. K., Shapshak, P., & Fletcher, M. A. (1996). Bereavement is associated with time-dependent decrements in cellular immune function in asymptomatic HIV-1 seropositive homosexual men. *Clinical and Diagnostic Laboratory Immunology, 3,* 109–118.

Goodkin, K., Fletcher, M. A., & Cohen, N. (1995). Clinical aspects of psychoneuroimmunology. *Lancet, 345,* 183–184.

Goodkin, K., Fuchs, I., Feaster, D., Leeka, J., & Rishel, D. D. (1992). Life stressors and coping style are associated with immune measures in HIV-1 infection—a preliminary report. *International Journal of Psychiatry in Medicine, 22,* 155–172.

Goodkin, K., Mulder, C. L., Blaney, N. T., Ironson, G., Kumar, M., & Fletcher, M. A. (1994). Psychoneuroimmunology and HIV-1 infection revisited. *Archives of General Psychiatry, 51,* 246–247.

Goodkin, K., Tuttle, R., Blaney, N. T., Feaster, D., Baldewicz, T., Uselmann, M., Nelson, R. H., Baum, M., Shapshak, P., Kumar, M., & Fletcher, M. A. (2000). Bereavement, immunity, and the impact of bereavement support groups in HIV-1 infection. In K. Goodkin & A. P. H. Visser (Eds.), *Psychoneuroimmunology: Stress, Mental Disorders and Health* (pp. 357–394). Washington, DC: American Psychiatric Press.

Gruber, B., Hall, N., Hersh, S., & Dubois, P. (1988). Immune system and psychologic changes in metastatic cancer patients while using ritualized relaxation and guided imagery. *Scandinavian Journal of Behavior Therapy, 17,* 25–46.

Helsing, K. J., & Szklo, M. (1981). Mortality after bereavement. *American Journal of Epidemiology, 114,* 41–52.

Hodgson, D. M, Yirmiya, R., Chiapelli, F., & Taylor, N. (1999). Intracerebral interleukin-1beta impairs response to tumor invasion: involvement of adrenal catecholamines. *Brain Research, 816,* 200–208.

Holsboer, F. (1988). Implications of altered limbic-hypothalamic-pituitary-adrenocortical (LHPA)-function for neurobiology of depression. *Acta Psychiatrica Scandinavica, 77*(Suppl.), 72–110.

Irwin, M., Brown, M., Patterson, T., Hauger, R., Mascovich, A., & Grant, I. (1991). Neuropeptide Y and natural killer cell activity: Findings in depression and Alzheimer caregiver stress. *Federation of American Societies of Experimental Biology (FASEB) Journal, 5,* 3100–3107.

Irwin, M., Daniels, M., Risch, S. C., Bloom, E., & Weiner, H. (1988). Plasma cortisol and natural killer cell activity during bereavement. *Biological Psychiatry, 24,* 173–178.

Irwin, M., Daniels, M., Smith, T. L., Bloom, E., & Weiner, H. (1987). Impaired natural killer cell activity during bereavement. *Brain, Behavior, and Immunity, 1,* 98–104.

Jacobs, S. C. (1993). *Pathologic Grief: Maladaptation to Loss.* Washington, DC: American Psychiatric Press.

Jacobs, S., Bruce, M., & Kim, K. (1997). Adrenal function predicts demoralization after losses. *Psychosomatics, 38,* 529–534.

Jacobs, S., Kasl, S., Schaefer, C., & Ostfeld, A. (1994). Conscious and unconscious coping with loss. *Psychosomatic Medicine, 56,* 557–563.

Jacobs, S. C., Mason, J. W., Kosten, T. R., Wahby, V., Kasl, S. V., & Ostfeld, A. M. (1986). Bereavement and catecholamines. *Journal of Psychosomatic Research, 30,* 489–496.

Kaprio, J., Kosenvuo, M., & Rita, H. (1987). Mortality after bereavement: A prospective study of 95,647 widowed persons. *American Journal of Public Health, 77,* 283–287.

Kavelaars, A., Ballieux, R. E., & Heijnen, C. (1988). Modulation of the immune response by proopiomelanocortin derived peptides. II. Influence of adreno-corticotropic hormone on the rise in intracellular free calcium concentration after T cell activation. *Brain, Behavior, and Immunity, 2,* 57–66.

Kavelaars, A., Ballieux, R. E., & Heijnen, C. J. (1990). Differential effects of beta-endorphin on cAMP levels in human peripheral blood mononuclear cells. *Brain, Behavior, and Immunity, 4,* 171–179.

Kay, M., & Portillo, C. (1989). Nervios and dysphoria in Mexican-American widows. *Health Care Women's International, 10,* 273–293.

Keller, S. E., Schleifer, S. J., Liotta, A. S., Bond, R. N., Farhoody, N., & Stein, M. (1988). Stress-induced alterations of immunity in hypophysectomized rats. *Proceedings of the National Academy of Sciences, 85,* 9297–9301.

Keller, S. E., Weiss, J. M., Schleifer, S. J., Miller, N. E., & Stein, M. (1983). Stress-induced suppression of immunity in adrenalectomized rats. *Science, 221,* 1301–1304.

Kemeny, M. E., & Dean, L. (1995). Effects of AIDS-related bereavement on HIV progression among New York City gay men. *AIDS Education and Prevention, 7(s),* 36–47.

Kemeny, M. E., Weiner, H., Duran, R., Taylor, S. E., Visscher, B., & Fahey, J. L. (1995). Immune system changes after the death of a partner in HIV-positive gay men. *Psychosomatic Medicine, 57,* 547–554.

Kemeny, M. E., Weiner, H., Taylor, S. E., Schneider, S., Visscher, B., & Fahey, J. L. (1994). Repeated bereavement, depressed mood, and immune parameters in HIV seropositive and seronegative gay men. *Health Psychology, 13,* 14–24.

Kertzner, R. M., Goetz, R., Todak, G., Cooper, T., Lin, S. H., Reddy, M. M., Novacenko, H., Williams, J. B., Ehrhardt, A. A., & Gorman, J. M. (1993). Cortisol levels, immune status, and mood in homosexual men with and without HIV infection. *American Journal of Psychiatry, 150,* 1674–1678.

Kessler, R. C., Foster, C., Joseph, J., Ostrow, D., Wortman, C., Phair, J., & Chmiel, J. (1991). Stressful life events and symptom onset in HIV infection. *American Journal of Psychiatry, 148,* 733–738.

Kiecolt-Glaser, J. K., Dura, J. R., Speicher, C. E., Trask, J., & Glaser, R. (1991). Spousal caregivers of dementia victims: Longitudinal changes in immunity and health. *Psychosomatic Medicine, 53,* 345–362.

Kiecolt-Glaser, J. K., Fisher, L. D., Ogrocki, P., Stout, J. C., Speicher, C. E., & Glaser, R. (1987). Marital quality, marital disruption, and immune function. *Psychosomatic Medicine, 49,* 13–34.

Kiecolt-Glaser, J. K., & Glaser, R. (1988). Methodological issues in behavioral immunology research with humans. *Brain, Behavior, and Immunity, 2,* 67–78.

Kiecolt-Glaser, J. K., Glaser, R., Shuttleworth, E. C., Dyer, C. S., Ogrocki, P., & Speicher, C. E. (1987). Chronic stress and immunity in family caregivers of Alzheimer's disease victims. *Psychosomatic Medicine, 49,* 523–535.

Klein, S. J. (1994). AIDS-related multiple loss syndrome. *Illness, Crisis and Loss, 1,* 13–25.

Kosten, T. R., Jacobs, S., & Mason, J. W. (1984). The dexamethasone suppression test during bereavement. *Journal of Nervous and Mental Disease, 172,* 359–360.

Kumar, M., Kumar, A. M., Morgan, R., Szapocznik, J., & Eisdorfer, C. (1993). Abnormal pituitary-adrenocortical response in HIV-1 infection. *Journal of Acquired Immune Deficiency Syndrome, 6,* 61–65.

Kumar, M., Morgan, R., Szapocznik, J., & Eisdorfer, C. (1991). Norepinephrine response in early HIV infection. *Journal of Acquired Immune Deficiency Syndrome, 4,* 782–786.

Laudenslager, M. L., Aasal, R., Adler, L., Berger, C. L., Montgomery, P. T., Sandberg, E., Wahlberg, L. J., Wilkins, R. T., Zweig, L., & Reite, M. L. (1998).

Elevated cytotoxicity in combat veterans with long-term post-traumatic stress disorder: Preliminary observations. *Brain, Behavior, and Immunity, 12,* 74–79.

Laudenslager, M., Captitanio, J. P., & Reite, M. (1985). Possible effects of early separation experiences on subsequent immune function in adult macaque monkeys. *American Journal of Psychiatry, 142,* 862–864.

Lennon, M. C., Martin, J. L., & Dean, L. (1990). The influence of social support on AIDS-related grief reaction among gay men. *Social Science and Medicine, 31,* 477–484.

Leserman, J., Jackson, E. D., Petitto, J. M., Golden, R. N., Silva, S. G., Perkins, D. O., Cai, J., Folds, J. D., & Evans, D. L. (1999). Progression to AIDS: The effects of stress, depressive symptoms, and social support. *Psychosomatic Medicine, 61,* 397–406.

Leserman, J., Petitto, J. M., Perkins, D. O., Folds, J. D., Golden, R. N., & Evans, D. L. (1997). Severe stress, depressive symptoms, and changes in lymphocyte subsets in human immunodeficiency virus-infected men. A 2-year follow-up study. *Archives of General Psychiatry, 54,* 279–285.

Linn, M. W., Linn, B. S., & Jensen, J. (1984). Stressful events, dysphoric mood, and immune responsiveness. *Psychological Reports, 54,* 219–222.

Livnat, S., Felten, S. Y., Carlson, S. L., Bellinger, D. L., & Felten, D. L. (1985). Involvement of peripheral and central catecholamine systems in neural-immune interactions. *Journal of Neuroimmunology, 10,* 5–30.

Lucey, D. R., Clerici, M., & Shearer, G. M. (1996). Type1 and type2 cytokine dysregulation in human infectious, neoplastic, and inflammatory diseases. *Clinical Microbiology Review, 9,* 532–562.

Lundin, T. (1984). Mortality following bereavement. *British Journal of Psychiatry, 144,* 84–88.

Lyketsos, C. G., Hoover, D. R., Guccione, M., Senterfitt, W., Dew, M. A., Wesch, J., VanRaden, M. J., Treisman, G. J., & Morgenstern, H. (1993). Depressive symptoms as predictors of medical outcomes in HIV infection. Multicenter AIDS cohort study. *Journal of the American Medical Association, 270,* 2563–2567.

Marmar, C. R., Horowitz, M. J., Weiss, D. S., Wilner, N. R., & Kaltreider, N. B. (1988). A controlled trial of brief psychotherapy and mutual-help group treatment of conjugal bereavement. *American Journal of Psychiatry, 145,* 203–209.

Martin, J. L. (1988). Psychological consequences of AIDS-related bereavement among gay men. *Journal of Consulting and Clinical Psychology, 56,* 856–862.

Martin, J. L., & Dean, L. (1993). Effects of AIDS-related and HIV-related illness on psychological distress among gay men: A 7-year longitudinal study, 1985–1991. *Journal of Consulting and Clinical Psychology, 61,* 94–103.

McCallum, L. M., Dykes, J. N., Painter, L., & Gold, J. (1989). The Ankali project: A model for the use of volunteers to provide emotional support in terminal illness. *Medical Journal of Australia, 151,* 33–34.

McKinnon, W., Weisse, C. S., Reynolds, C. P., Bowles, C. A., & Baum, A. (1989).

Chronic stress, leukocyte subpopulations, and humoral response to latent viruses. *Health Psychology, 8,* 389–402.

Meyaard, L., Otto, S. A., Keet, I. P. M., Van Lier, R. A. W., & Miedema, F. (1994). Changes in cytokine patterns of CD4+ T-cell clones in human immunodeficiency virus infection. *Blood, 84,* 4262–4268.

Mulder, C. L., Antoni, M. H., Duivenvooden, H. J., Kauffmann, R. H., & Goodkin, K. (1995). Active coping predicts decreased clinical progression over a one-year period in HIV-infected homosexual men. *Journal of Psychosomatic Research, 39,* 957–965.

Nemeroff, C. B., Krishnan, K. R., Reed, D., Leder, R., Beam, C., & Dunnick, N. R. (1992). Adrenal gland enlargement in major depression. A computed tomography study. *Archives of General Psychiatry, 49,* 384–387.

Neugebauer, R., Rabkin, J. G., Williams, J. B. W., Remien, R. H., Goetz, R., & Gorman, J. M. (1992). Reactions among homosexual men experiencing multiple losses in the AIDS epidemic. *American Journal of Psychiatry, 149,* 1374–1379.

Norbiato, G., Bevilacqua, M., Vago, T., Taddei, A., & Clerici, M. (1997). Glucocorticoids and the immune function in the human immunodeficiency virus infection: a study in hypercortisolemic and cortisol-resistant patients. *Journal of Clinical Endocrinology and Metabolism, 82,* 3260–3263.

Norris, F., & Murrell, S. (1987). Transitory impact of life-event stress on psychological symptoms in older adults. *Journal of Health and Social Behavior, 28,* 197–211.

Pakenham, K. I., Dadds, M. R., & Terry, D. J. (1994). Relationships between adjustment to HIV and both social support and coping. *Journal of Consulting and Clinical Psychology, 62,* 1194–1203.

Parkes, C. M., Benjamin, B., & Fitzgerald, R. G. (1969). Broken heart: A statistical study of increased mortality among widowers. *British Medical Journal, 1,* 740–743.

Parkes, C. M., & Brown, R. J. (1972). Health after bereavement: A controlled study of young Boston widows and widowers. *Psychosomatic Medicine, 34,* 449–461.

Perry, S., Fishman, B., Jacobsberg, L., & Frances, A. (1992). Relationships over 1 year between lymphocyte subsets and psychosocial variables among adults with infection by human immunodeficiency virus. *Archives of General Psychiatry, 49,* 396–401.

Pert, C. B., Smith, C. C., Ruff, M. R., & Hill, J. M. (1988). AIDS and its dementia as a neuropeptide disorder: Role of VIP receptor blockade by human immunodeficiency virus envelope. *Annals of Neurology, 23*(s), S71–S73.

Rabkin, J. G., Williams, J. B. W., Remien, R. H., Goetz, R. R., Kertzner, R., & Gorman, J. M. (1991). Depression, lymphocyte subsets, and human immunodeficiency virus symptoms on two occasions in HIV-positive homosexual men. *Archives of General Psychiatry, 48,* 111–119.

Rees, W., & Lutkins, S. (1967). Mortality of bereavement. *British Medical Journal, 4,* 13–16.

Rodin, J. (1986). Aging and health: Effects of the sense of control. *Science, 233,* 1271–1276.

Roy, A., Gallucci, W., Avgerinos, P., Linnoila, M., & Gold, P. (1988). The CRH stimulation test in bereaved subjects with and without accompanying depression. *Psychiatry Research, 25,* 145–146.

Rynearson, E. K. (1990). Pathologic grief: The Queen's croquet ground. *Psychiatric Annals, 20,* 295–303.

Sahs, J. A., Goetz, R., Reddy, M., Rabkin, J. G., Williams, J. B. W., Kertzner, R., & Gorman, J. M. (1994). Psychological distress and natural killer cells in gay men with and without HIV infection. *American Journal of Psychiatry, 151,* 1479–1484.

Sapolsky, R. M., & Pulsinelli, W. A. (1985). Glucocorticoids potentiate ischemic injury to neurons: Therapeutic implications. *Science, 229,* 1397–1400.

Schaefer, C., Quesenberry, C. P., & Wi, S. (1995). Mortality following conjugal bereavement and the effects of a shared environment. *American Journal of Epidemiology, 141,* 1142–1152.

Schedlowski, M., Jacobs, R., Stratmann, G., Richter, S., Hadicke, A., Tewes, U., Wagner, T. O., & Schmidt, R. E. (1993). Changes of natural killer cells during acute psychological stress. *Journal of Clinical Immunology, 13,* 119–126.

Schleifer, S. J., Keller, S. E., Camerino, M., Thornton, J. C., & Stein, M. (1983). Suppression of lymphocyte stimulation following bereavement. *Journal of the American Medical Association, 250,* 374–377.

Shavit, Y., Terman, G. W., Martin, F. C., Lewis, J. W., Liebeskind, J. C., & Gale, R. P. (1985). Stress, opioid peptides, the immune system and cancer. *Journal of Immunology, 135,* 834s–837s.

Sheline, Y. I., Wang, P. W., Gado, M. H., & Csernansky, J. G., & Vannier, M. W. (1996). Hippocampal atrophy in recurrent major depression. *Proceedings of the National Academy of Sciences (USA), 93,* 3908–3913.

Shuchter, S. R., Zisook, S., Kirkorowicz, C., & Risch, C. (1986). The dexamethasone suppression test in acute grief. *American Journal of Psychiatry, 143,* 879–891.

Sikkema, K. J., Kalichman, S. C., Kelly, J. A., & Koob, J. J. (1995). Group intervention to improve coping with AIDS-related bereavement: model development and an illustrative clinical example. *AIDS Care, 7,* 463–475.

Smith, E. M., Harbour-McMenamin, D., & Blalock, J. E. (1985). Lymphocyte production of endorphins and endorphin-mediated immunoregulatory activity. *Journal of Immunology, 135*(2, Suppl), 779s–782s.

Spiegel, D., Bloom, J. R., Kraemer, H. C., & Gottheil, E. (1989). Effect of psychosocial treatment on survival of patients with metastatic breast cancer. *Lancet, 2,* 888–891.

Spiegel, D., Bloom, J. R., & Yalom, I. (1981). Group support for patients with metastatic cancer. *Archives of General Psychiatry, 38,* 527–533.

Spurrell, M. T., & Creed, F. H. (1993). Lymphocyte response in depressed patients and subjects anticipating bereavement. *British Journal of Psychiatry, 162,* 60–64.

Stein, J. A., Newcomb, M. D., & Bentler, P. M. (1994). Psychosocial correlates of AIDS risk behaviors, abortion, and drug use among a community sample of young adult women. *Health Psychology, 13,* 308–318.

Stroebe, W., & Stroebe, M. S. (1993). Determinants of adjustment to bereavement in younger widows and widowers. In M. S. Stroebe, W. Stroebe, & R. O. Hansson (Eds.), *Handbook of Bereavement* (pp. 208–226). New York: Cambridge Univeristy Press.

Sweeting, H. N., & Gilhooly, M. L. (1990). Anticipatory grief: A review. *Social Science and Medicine, 30,* 1073–1080.

Theorell, T., Blomkvist, V., Jonsson, H., Schulman, S., Berntorp, E., & Stigendal, L. (1995). Social support and the development of immune function in human immunodeficiency virus infection. *Psychosomatic Medicine, 57,* 32–36.

Uksila, J. (1985). Human NK activity is not inhibited by pregnancy and cord serum factors and female steroid hormones in vitro. *Journal of Reproductive Immunology, 7,* 111–120.

Vedhara, K., Schifitto, G., McDermott, M., & the Dana Consortium on Therapy for HIV Dementia and Related Cognitive Disorders. (1999). Disease progression in HIV-positive women with moderate to severe immunosuppression: the role of depression. *Behavioral Medicine, 25,* 43–47.

Visser, A. P. H., Vingerhoets, A., Goodkin, K., Peters, L., Boon, M., Garssen, B., & Fletcher, M. A. (2000). Cervical cancer: Psychosocial and psychoneuroimmunological issues. In K. Goodkin & A. P. H. Visser (Eds.), *Psychoneuroimmunology: Stress, Mental Disorders and Health* (pp. 41–76). Washington, DC: American Psychiatric Press.

Williamson, S. A., Knight, R. A., Lightman, S. L., & Hobbs, J. R. (1987). Differential effects of β-endorphin fragments on human natural killing. *Brain Behavior and Immunity, 1,* 329–335.

Windholz, M. J., Marmar, C. R., & Horowitz, M. J. (1985). A review on the research in conjugal bereavement: Impact on health and efficacy of intervention. *Comprehensive Psychiatry, 26,* 433–447.

Wortman, C. B., & Silver, R. C. (1989). The myths of coping with loss. *Journal of Consulting and Clinical Psychology, 57,* 349–357.

Wybran, J., Schandene, L., VanVooren, J., Vandermoten, G., Latinne, D., Sonnet, T., de Bruyere, M., Toelman, H., & Plotnikoff, N. (1987). Immunologic properties of methionine-enkephalin, and therapeutic implications in AIDS, ARC, and cancer. *Annals of the New York Academy of Sciences, 496,* 108–113.

Yehuda, M. (1997). Stress and glucocorticoid. (Letter). *Science, 275,* 1662–1663.

Young, M., Benjamin, B., & Wallis, C. (1963). Mortality of widowers. *Lancet, 2,* 254–256.

Zisook, S., & Shuchter, S. R. (1991). Depression through the first year after the death of a spouse. *American Journal of Psychiatry, 148,* 1346–1352.

30

THE EFFICACY OF BEREAVEMENT INTERVENTIONS: DETERMINING WHO BENEFITS

HENK SCHUT, MARGARET S. STROEBE, JAN VAN DEN BOUT,
AND MAAIKE TERHEGGEN

In the last quarter of the twentieth century numerous intervention programs for bereaved persons were developed, ranging from mutual-help groups open for anyone suffering a loss to full-blown therapeutic programs for complicated or pathological forms of grief. Likewise, strategies have ranged from individual to group interventions. The basic idea behind offering help is to benefit the bereaved individual, to help him or her to deal with the emotional and practical problems following the loss of a loved one. If societal developments are taken as the criterion, it must be concluded that there has been uncritical acceptance of the assumption that help is beneficial. In the United States, Australia, and Europe social workers, psychologists, funeral organizations, hospitals, organizations of bereaved individuals, and various religious and humanistic organizations offer grief counseling and therapy. Undoubtedly they have done so with good intentions, but there is reason to doubt whether what they are trying to achieve is actually being achieved. A substantial number of grief intervention efficacy studies have resulted in disappointing, sometimes even negative, results, as we shall see later in this chapter. A critical review of intervention efficacy studies therefore seems timely.

Two evaluations of the bereavement intervention literature have recently been published (Kato & Mann, 1999; Litterer Allumbaugh & Hoyt, 1999). These were highly valuable reviews. However, it is important to examine the empirical studies from a number of different perspectives. Kato and Mann (1999) focused on an important comparison—namely, the efficacy of group versus individual interventions, but there are a number of further aspects that need to be addressed (e.g., differences in effects of primary, secondary, and tertiary intervention). Their main conclusions were that most studies suffered from methodological flaws and that neither group nor individual intervention was particularly helpful. Litterer Allumbaugh and Hoyt (1999) conducted an insightful in-depth review, including meta-analysis. Their general conclusion was that intervention is helpful, and in particular they argued for providing help as soon as possible after loss. However, a number of concerns remain. First, we query whether the overall quality of the (reports of) efficacy studies of grief counseling and therapy conducted to date permit a meta-analysis. The differences between studies are huge, making detailed comparison hazardous if not impossible. Second, important information gets lost in meeting the criteria for conducting meta-analyses. For instance, follow-up effects of intervention were excluded by Litterer Allumbaugh and Hoyt, because too few of the selected studies included follow-up data. Yet the information from follow-up data is critical to assessing enduring benefits, which, after all, is the general aim of intervention. Including this information may in fact shed a less positive light on efficacy. Third, the type of the interventions was not addressed in these reviews. This too is highly relevant in evaluating grief intervention.

In this chapter we present a narrative review and critical assessment of efficacy studies, categorizing (cf. Caplan, 1964) these into general or primary preventive interventions, preventive interventions for high-risk groups or secondary prevention, and interventions aimed at the treatment of complicated grief (tertiary prevention).

SCOPE

Grief intervention is a broad term, potentially covering help offered by family, friends, and neighbors after the loss of a loved one. However, it is more useful from a scientific perspective to consider informal help separately, as social support. Discussion in this chapter is confined to organized or institutionalized help.

Also excluded are interventions not explicitly aimed at ameliorating grief—for instance, palliative care that is not subsequently followed by bereavement care. There are studies indicating that palliative care of dying patients has positive effects on their survivors too (e.g., Cameron & Parkes, 1983; Kane, Klein, Bernstein, & Rothenberg, 1986; McCorkle, Robinson, Nuamah, Lev, & Benoliel, 1998; Parkes, 1979; Sherwood, Kastenbaum, Morris, & Wright, 1988; Steele, 1990). However, because the primary aim of palliative care concerns the quality of life of the dying patient, it falls outside the range of interventions included in this chapter.

The third inclusion criterion is that the intervention program has to be tested for its effects empirically and in a methodologically sound way. This excludes descriptions of interventions and case studies (e.g., Balk, Tyson-Rawson, & Colletti-Wetzel, 1993; Hodgkinson, 1982; Ramsay, 1977; Rubin, 1999). Such descriptions are valuable and a necessary step toward developing intervention programs. However, an empirical test of the extent to which what is tried is indeed accomplished is often still missing.

Including only empirically tested interventions also excludes potentially important categories or sources of help for bereaved individuals, such as pastoral care and help being offered by general practitioners and funeral directors. The reason is that, to our knowledge, such help has never been put to the test. The conclusions drawn from the overview presented do not necessarily apply to these categories.

In this chapter we address effects of intervention on psychological and social well-being rather than satisfaction with an intervention. Thus if assessment of effects is confined to satisfaction of participants with intervention (e.g., Longman, 1993) or is operationalized in terms of perceived helpfulness of meetings (e.g., Lund & Caserta, 1992; Murphy et al., 1996; Souter & Moore, 1989), these are omitted, because they say little about actual effects in terms of changes.

The demand that testing has to be done in a *methodologically correct way* is an exclusion criterion in itself. Although many of the interventions have been reported to be effective by those who conducted the intervention, shortcomings in the design often preclude valid scientific evaluation of the actual effects. We turn to such problems next, addressing major methodological issues and statistical criteria for sound empirical evaluation.

METHODOLOGICAL ISSUES

As we shall see, the major methodological and statistical issues concern control groups, procedures for assignment to conditions, nonresponse and attrition, and adherence to intervention.

Lack of Control Groups

One of the major shortcomings is the absence of a nonintervention control group (e.g., Horowitz, Marmar, Weiss, Kaltreider, & Wilner, 1986;

Longman, 1993; Quarmby, 1993; Rognlie, 1989; Souter & Moore, 1989). In other disorders this may be less of a problem, but because grief itself is a process that is expected to change over time, pre- and posttreatment comparison without a reference group makes the attribution that change is a result of the intervention difficult, if not impossible. However, lacking a control group does not always prevent authors from making claims about the effects of the intervention.

Participant Assignment Procedures

It is important that assignment procedures to conditions are methodologically correct (i.e., random or matched assignment). Assignment processes should lead to comparable groups, because systematic differences threaten validity. Lieberman and Videka-Sherman (1986) studied the effects of a mutual help program based on a comparison of bereaved persons who had accepted or had declined an invitation to join. Such a procedure is likely to lead to systematic differences between groups. In retrospect, if such similar groups are not established, controlling or neutralizing statistical steps need to be taken.

Nonresponse and Attrition

Nonresponse and attrition can seriously influence results. Bereavement research often suffers from low response, which affects generalizability (Stroebe & Stroebe, 1989), but intervention studies often have even lower acceptance rates (see Table 30-1, 30-3, and 30-5 for an overview). This is particularly threatening in the case of primary preventive interventions for bereaved individuals. To illustrate, Levy and Derby (1992) found that those who joined bereavement support groups were more depressed than nonparticipants.

Adherence

Low adherence is another potential cause of bias. There are major differences between studies. Although Reif, Patton, and Gold (1995) had only 30% regular attendance at group meetings in their intervention study, Murphy, Aroian, and Baugher (1989) reported hardly any absences in their treatment groups. Such differences need to be taken into consideration when data are interpreted. High dropout ratios in control conditions can also seriously threaten validity. In Marmar, Horowitz, Weiss, Wilner, and Kaltreider's (1988) study the comparison group lost 77% of its participants. Fortunately, these investigators succeeded in getting both completers and dropouts back for the follow-up.

The problem of low adherence in efficacy studies is twofold. First, it negatively influences the power of the study. This is a serious problem, because most grief intervention studies already suffer from low sample sizes. Second, dropping out of the intervention often implies dropping out of the research project. However, if the ones who resign from the intervention can be retained for the study (as was the case in Marmar et al., 1988), they offer a valuable opportunity for answering questions on how their symptoms develop, compared with completers. In addition, such comparisons are potentially valuable for examining basic scientific questions: Do they not attend because, as Parkes (1987) suggested, they have achieved the benefit they sought (cf. Tudiver, Hilditch, Permaul, & McKendree, 1992)? Alternatively, could it be, as Levine, Toro, and Perkins (1993) suggested, that those who benefit the least from intervention, or who are the most disturbed, drop out? A third explanation for nonadherence may have little to do with the intervention. Caserta and Lund (1993) found that the majority of nonattenders in their study of whom they had information did so because of relocation, change of work, and so on. Systematic comparison of regular and irregular participants in sessions, as well as background information on their motives for not attending, is crucial for a valid interpretation of intervention results.

A control condition should consist of a nonintervention group or a placebo intervention, because such comparisons most rigorously assesses intervention effects. But nonintervention and placebo controls present a problem: For ethical reasons (cf. Sales & Folkman, 2000) it is difficult to prevent persons who are in distress and in need of support from getting help (e.g., Levy, Derby & Martinowski, 1993). An alternative to an nonintervention control condition could be to compare the efficacy of intervention with that of a well-established program with known effects (i.e., to enable a comparison of effect sizes). Unfortunately, thus far such well-established intervention programs (i.e., well-described and transferable, tested, replicated, and found effective, and accompanied by indications and counter indications) are not available in the area of grief counseling and grief therapy. In the Mawson, Marks, Ramm, and Stern (1981) and Sireling, Cohen, and Marks (1988) studies, the control intervention has such apparent countertherapeutic elements that relatively favorable effects of the experimental intervention are expected. In these studies the control groups were instructed to avoid thoughts of the deceased. The therapists in this condition focused more on problems of daily life and the necessity of carrying on with life. Although the widows and widowers in this study were bereaved between 1 and 20 years when the intervention took place, such an approach is unlikely to be beneficial.

A waiting list condition can also solve the control group problem, although this is a disadvantage with respect to long-term assessment of effects. Because intervention tries to establish lasting effects, this information is critical.

AN OVERVIEW OF EFFICACY STUDIES

The variety of grief interventions can be subdivided into general or primary preventive interventions, selective interventions for high-risk bereaved persons or secondary prevention and psychotherapeutic treatment modalities specifically aimed at treating complicated or pathological grief (tertiary prevention). We follow this structure. It is important to note that such subdivision is structured around the *target group* of the intervention and does not necessarily follow the *therapeutic techniques* used in the intervention. For example, psychotherapeutic techniques can be used in normal samples, in which case this would be categorized under primary preventive interventions.

Primary Preventive Interventions

Primary preventive interventions are in principle open to all bereaved people, the criterion for participation being simply that one has experienced a loss through death. However, for reasons of homogeneity of groups, or for research purposes, several of these programs have actually been aimed at specific categories of bereaved individuals (e.g., widows, partners of those who have died of cancer). Such selection strategies should not be confused with selection of other specific target groups, such as bereaved people who suffered a suicide or homicide loss, which are generally regarded as being risk factors of complicated grief and are therefore reviewed in the section on secondary preventive interventions.

Primary preventive intervention efficacy has been evaluated mainly for widowed spouses and for bereaved children. As we shall see, studies suggest greater benefits among the latter than the former group. We consider first the extent to which serious methodological weaknesses account for a number of generally disappointing results and then discuss the validity of more positive findings. A summary of the design characteristics of these studies is presented in Tables 30-1 and 30–2. In these and all other tables division has been made according to methodological aspects (the general design of the study; sample characteristics, acceptance, and attrition rates) and aspects of intervention (timing, type, and duration of interventions; control conditions).

As can be seen from Table 30-1 and 30-2, most information is available for the widowed and bereaved children.

Widows and Widowers

Indications of noneffectiveness, even counter-effective results of general preventive interventions were already evident in one of the first studies of intervention efficacy (Polak, Egan, Vandenbergh, & Williams, 1973, 1975;

Williams, Lee, & Polak, 1976; Williams & Polak, 1979). Polak et al. evaluated a crisis intervention program in which family members of a deceased person (all sudden deaths) were visited in the first few hours after the loss. This first contact was followed up by telephone contact and visits during subsequent months. The information of these bereaved individuals was compared with that of a group that had not received intervention. Contrary to expectations, the analyses suggested negative effects of the crisis intervention. This study raised much criticism. The main problem was poor matching of the controls with the intervention group (cf. Parkes, 1980). The supported group was at systematically greater risk of having problems during the grieving process because of factors that distinguished them from the control group (i.e., the former were significantly closer to the deceased, had a greater drop in income, and rated economic losses as significantly more important than the latter group). The results cannot be regarded as conclusive evidence of noneffectiveness of a primary preventive intervention. But it is certainly not the only study leading to disappointing results.

Some years later Barrett (1978) reported on a comparison of several forms of group interventions for widows. Self-help groups were compared with groups that were designed to develop friendship between group members and groups that were focused on developing awareness of gender roles and their impact. Changes that took place in these groups were contrasted with a waiting list control group. There appeared to be very few differences between the effects of the four conditions. Improvements over time were found for some dimensions (e.g., self-esteem and attention to others) for all four groups and, rather unexpectedly, there was an increase in the intensity of grief reactions in all four groups too. Barrett's study has also been criticized for its low retention rate and the fact that the time between the loss and intervention varied tremendously in the study.

Nevertheless, the conclusion that outreaching primary intervention does *not* help fits the general picture emerging from subsequent studies. Sabatini (1985, 1988) came to similar conclusions, based on a systematic evaluation of the effectiveness of the American Red Cross First Step Program, an educationally oriented program directed at the tasks of working through grief in a group intervention context. She gathered pre- and post-intervention scores on the Texas Revised Inventory of Grief (Faschingbauer, Zisook, & DeVaul, 1987) and compared the data of 25 widows and widowers attending First Step with those of 25 on a waiting list. The analyses again showed that the intervention group was in fact no better off than the control group.

Walls and Meyers (1985) compared three group interventions for widows: cognitive restructuring, behavioral skills, and a self-help program following Silverman's widow to widow approach. These three conditions were again contrasted with a nonintervention control group. Immediate posttreatment results revealed only a group-specific positive change for the

TABLE 30-1
Methodological Aspects of

Authors	Design	Category of Bereaved	Age	Data Collection Points
Barrett (1978)	Pre–post control	Widows (100%)	$M = 56$	Pre-, post-, 3 and 5 months follow-up
Black & Urbanowicz (1987)	Pre–post control	Children (<17)	$M = \pm 29$	2–3, 12, and 24 months after loss
Constantino (1981)	Pre–post control	Widows (100%)	30–69	Pre- and postintervention
Gerber et al. (1975)	Pre–post control	Widows (72%) and widowers	70% >60	2, 5, 8 and 15 months after loss
Levy et al. (1993)	Posttest control	Widows (72%) and widowers	$M = 61$	1–5, 6, 13, and 18 months after loss
Lieberman & Videka-Sherman (1986)	Posttest control	Widows (93%) and widowers	Unspecified	43 and 55 months after loss
Lieberman & Yalom (1992)	Pre–post control	Widows (72%) and widowers	$M = 57$	Preintervention and 1-year follow-up
Lund & Caserta (1992)	Pre–post control	Widows (76%) and widowers	$M = 67$	2, 4–8, 14–17, and 24 months after loss
Morrison Tonkins & Lambert (1996)	Pre–post control	Preadolescent children (56% female)	7–11, $M = 9$	Pre- and post-intervention
Polak et al. (1975)	Posttest control	Families	Bereaved: $M = 43$ Nonbereaved: $M = 45$	6 and 18 months after loss
Reich & Zautra (1989)	Pre–post control	Widows (77%) and widowers	$M = 71$	Pre- and post-intervention
Sabatini (1985)	Pre–post control	Widows (88%) and widowers	$M = 57$	Pre- and post-intervention
Sandler et al. (1992)	Pre–post control	Children (43% female)	$M = 12$	Preintervention and 6 months follow-up)
Tudiver et al. (1992)	Pre–post control	Widowers (100%)	$M = \pm 63$	Preintervention, 2 and 8 months after entrance
Vachon et al. (1980)	Pre–post control	Widows (100%)	$M = 52$	1, 6, and 24 months after loss
Walls & Meyers (1985)	Pre–post control	Widows (100%)	$M = 53$	Pre-, 2, and 12 months post-intervention

[a] Percentage of T1 (first data collection point).
[b] Not specified per condition.
[c] A = Mutual help; B = confinement group; C = consciousness-raising group.
[d] A = Cognitive restructuring; B = behavioral; C = mutual help.

Primary Preventive Interventions

Recruitment	N Contacted	n Accepted (%)	Assignment	n Experimental Conditions T-last (%)[a]	n Control T-last (%)[a]
Outreaching	239	126 (53%)	Random	A: 18[c] B: 15 C: 20 (62% overall)	17 (61%)
Outreaching	80 families	57 families (71%)	Random	21 families (64%)	18 families (75%)
Outreaching	27	17 (63%)	Order of entrance self-selection	7 (100%)	10/10 (100%)
Outreaching	Unspecified	228 (between 75–94%)	Semi-random	116 (unspecified %)	53/59 (unspecified %)
Outreaching	283	159 (56%)	Self-selection	37 (80%)[b]	90 (80%)[b]
Outreaching	1478	721 (49%)	Self-selection	376 (78%)[b]	100 (78%)[b]
Outreaching	78	67 (86%)	Random	34 (72%)	19 (95%)
Outreaching	1150	339 (30%)	Random and self-selection	A: 39 B: 43 C: 25 D: 27 (56% overall)	98 (unspecified %)
Outreaching	21	16 (76%)	Order of entrance	10 (100%)	6 (100%)
Outreaching	Bereaved families: 204 Nonbereaved families: 158	Bereaved experimental: 39 (72%) Bereaved control: 66 (54%) Nonbereaved families: 56 (35%)	Matching	32 families (82%)	Bereaved families: 54 (81%) Nonbereaved families: 40 (71%)
Outreaching	Bereaved: 62 Nonbereaved: 60–62	Bereaved experimental: 19 Bereaved placebo: 9 Bereaved noninterventions: 29 Nonbereaved experimental: 20 Nonbereaved placebo: 9 Nonbereaved noninterventions: 27	Matching with nonbereaved, random to condition	90%[b]	90%[b]
Help-seekers	—	—	Nonrandom	25 (100%)	25 (100%)
Outreaching	Unspecified	72 (unspecified %)	Random	13 (54%)	31? (unspecified %)
Outreaching	113	113 (100%)	Random	56 (78%)	38 (69%)
Outreaching	185	162 (88%)	Random	24 (61%)[b]	38 (61%)[b]
Outreaching	Unspecified	38 (unspecified %)	Stratified sampling	A = 5[d] (50%) B = 7 (88%) C = 5 (50%)	4 (40%)

TABLE 30-2
Aspects of Primary Preventive Intervention

Authors	Time Since Bereavement	Type of Intervention	Description of Intervention	Number of Sessions	Type of Control
Barrett (1978)	M = ±5 years (1 month–22 years)	Group	A: Mutual help B: Confident group C: Consciousness-raising group	4–7	Waiting list
Black & Urbanowicz (1987)	3–5 months after bereavement	Group	Family therapy	6	Nonintervention
Constantino (1981)	1–24 weeks after bereavement	Group	Crisis intervention	Unspecified	Socialization group and nonintervention
Gerber et al. (1975)	<6 months after bereavement	Individual	Crisis intervention and brief therapy	Unspecified	Nonintervention
Levy et al. (1993)	Unspecified	Group	Mutual help	Median: 5 (2–25)	Nonparticipants
Lieberman & Videka-Sherman (1986)	Unspecified	Group	Mutual help	Unspecified	Nonparticipants
Lieberman & Yalom (1992)	4–8 months after bereavement	Group	Brief psychotherapy	8	Nonintervention
Lund & Caserta (1992)	A + B: 1–4 months after bereavement C + D: 1–12 months after bereavement	Group	Mutual help	A + B: 6.5 C + D: 15	Nonintervention
Morrison Tonkins & Lambert (1996)	6 months after bereavement (1–12 months)	Group	Child group psychotherapy	8	Waiting list
Polak et al. (1975)	Immediately after bereavement	Individual and group	Crisis intervention for families	5.5	Nonintervention and nonbereaved
Reich & Zautra (1989)	4 months after bereavement	Individual	Cognitive control oriented	4	Bereaved: placebo (social visits) and nonintervention Nonbereaved: experimental intervention, placebo, and nonintervention
Sabatini (1985)	3–24 months after bereavement (M = 7)	Group	Mutual help	14	Waiting list
Sandler et al. (1992)	15 months after bereavement	Group	Family adviser program	15	Waiting list
Tudiver et al. (1992)	3–12 months after bereavement	Group	Mutual help	9	Waiting list
Vachon et al. (1980)	Starting ±1 month after bereavement	Individual and group	Individual help and mutual help	Unspecified	Nonintervention
Walls & Meyers (1985)	M = 12 months after bereavement	Group	A: Cognitive restructuring B: Behavioral C: Mutual help	10	Waiting list

cognitive restructuring condition on social anxiety. In this condition the occurrence and appreciation of pleasant events decreased, as was the case with the behavioral skills group. At follow-up one year later, no difference was found between conditions whatsoever, despite the relevance of the outcome measures (e.g., depression, social anxiety, irrational beliefs, and life satisfaction). This may have been caused by lack of power, because groups were very small already at the start and drop out rates were high (see Table 30-1). The results are therefore inconclusive, but suggest that psychological intervention can have harmful effects.

Tudiver et al. (1992) followed a promising new track. Intervention was focused specifically on widowers. This was innovative, because studies thus far included widows only or, in rare cases, only a minority of widowers (see Table 30-1). Stroebe and Stroebe (1983) had, however, demonstrated that widowers suffer relatively more from the loss of the partner than widows do. Help specifically for widowers therefore seems a valuable addition, even though in industrialized western societies widows outnumber widowers by far. Using a randomized control design Tudiver et al. assessed effects of nine weekly peer group sessions on several psychological and psychosocial measures. The sessions focused primarily on information giving, sharing of emotions, and mutual support. Eight months after the beginning of group intervention all participating widowers had improved, but no between-group differences over time were observed. In fact, depression and anxiety were slightly higher in the experimental condition, although that did not reach statistical significance. Based on the scores of the dropouts, the authors suggested that more-recovered participants may not have attended all meetings. But as the authors also suggested, the results may indicate that "focusing widowers' attention on their own and others' grief may have hindered recovery from their grief" (p. 160).

Levy, Derby, and Martinkowski (1993) came to a similar conclusion in a study including widows and widowers. Using a posttest control design, they found no differential effects of mutual support group attendance, compared with nonattendance. This study, however, suffered from substantial methodological flaws, systematic and posthoc assignment to the conditions being the most critical. Attendees were defined as having attended at least two sessions, and all other widows and widowers (not showing up or dropping out after one session) were assigned to the control condition. Such a procedural weakness makes it difficult to evaluate the study, even though the results are in line with the bulk of studies.

Lund and Caserta (1992; Caserta & Lund, 1993) attributed disappointing results of studies to constraints concerning the number of sessions of interventions. They thus compared short-term (maximum eight sessions) and long-term (maximum 18 sessions) mutual help and compared results with a nonintervention control condition. Nevertheless, their conclusion was similar to that of the studies described thus far: Neither intervention had much effect on depression. Attending more sessions was only associated with less intrusion in the case of low perceived support. Furthermore, their data even suggest a negative effect of mutual help: There was an inverse relationship between the number of meetings and reductions in anger and medication use.

Lieberman and Yalom (1992) also came up with negative results. Although the widows and widowers in their study were not suffering from complicated grief or high distress, they offered brief group psychotherapy led by experienced senior clinicians 4 to 10 months after the loss of the partner and compared the group that attended the sessions with a nonintervention control group. They found a modest positive effect of the treatment condition on self-esteem and single role strain, but no difference on any of the variables having to do with grief symptomatology and overall mental health. The authors went a step further, analyzing the patterns of high-risk participants (showing clinical signs of pathology) in the experimental condition compared with low-risk bereaved individuals in the same condition and with the control group. Even these comparisons did not show favorable results for the intervention program. The overall conclusion was that, "for the vast majority of bereaved spouses 'recovery' is the rule and . . . brief preventive intervention early in bereavement may be unnecessary" (p. 128).

A similar conclusion can be drawn from the study conducted by Reich and Zautra (1989). They conducted a sophisticated study, offering a four-session intervention aimed at improving perceived control to elderly widows and widowers. They compared the results with a placebo condition and a nonintervention condition, as well as with nonbereaved controls receiving such an experimental intervention, a placebo treatment, and a nonintervention control group. Although multiple dimensions of psychosocial functioning (e.g., mastery, distress, well-being, positive and negative affect) were used to assess intervention effects, the intervention hardly resulted in any positive result for bereaved individuals. Striking is that the experimental intervention appeared to be efficacious for nonbereaved and for disabled elderly people (which was a subgroup in the same study), indicating that the bereaved individuals may have been more resistant to change.

The review thus far is rather disappointing in two ways. First, many studies lack a sound methodological basis, even though only controlled intervention projects were included. Second, it emerges that early primary preventive interventions for the widowed hardly show any positive effects. Worse still, there are indications that what is achieved is actually the opposite of what is desired. There are, however, studies that claim positive results.

Gerber, Weiner, Battin, and Arkin (1975) were the first ones to offer widows and widowers solely *individual* support and, like Polak et al. (1975), they did that almost immediately after the loss. Results were compared with a nonintervention control group. Results indicated that immediately after the intervention, the supported bereaved individuals compared favorably with the nonintervention controls: They felt unwell less often, had fewer contacts with doctors, and used medication less frequently. In addition, the positive effect appeared to be significantly stronger among the widowers than the widows. So not only were the bereaved people who received crisis intervention better off on subjective measures, but also on more objective and very relevant variables. The effects, however, appeared to be of short duration. At follow-up, hardly any significant difference between the groups was found, and the number of doctor visits and use of medication had risen above baseline in both conditions. At best, the intervention seemed to lead to temporary positive results.

The study by Vachon, Lyall, Rogers, Freedman-Letofsky, and Freeman (1980) is often referred to as the one that unambiguously proved the efficacy of primary preventive interventions. They used an appropriate randomized experimental design (see Table 30-1), and succeeded in contacting a substantial number of widows and in keeping the refusal rate to a minimum: 88% of the 185 participated in the first interview, one month after bereavement. However, at follow-up two years later, 39% had dropped out, which is not unfavorable compared with other studies (see Table 30-1). However, dropouts were different from those who remained in the study (not specified according to condition). The former had lost younger husbands, were of lower socioeconomic class, and seemed to have more psychological problems and less social support available. Positive effects of this widow-to-widow program following the principles of Silverman (1969) were reported regarding a limited number of items of the General Health Questionnaire (GHQ) only, although the authors mentioned using a number of other measures as well. No mention is made of whether the other indices substantiate or differ from the results found with the GHQ. It is noteworthy that the positive results of the intervention appeared to be almost totally confined to the group of widows with high distress at baseline. Therefore, the conclusion to draw from Vachon et al.'s study is not that general preventive intervention works, but that it works for a selection of bereaved individuals—namely those initially suffering from high distress. As such, the authors have shown the effects of secondary preventive interventions, a category of interventions that will be discussed later in the chapter.

Constantino (1981) came to different conclusions. She compared depression and social adjustment among groups who either received crisis intervention or who attended a socialization group. A nonintervention group was added to the design. Assignment to conditions was based on order of acceptance of the intervention. Constantino observed more positive functioning (both on depression and on social adjustment) in the experimental as compared to the socialization group. Scores for the nonintervention group remained the same or even worsened. However, Constantino only made comparisons of the three groups based on pre–post intervention difference scores, despite the fact that there were large differences between the groups at pretest. Furthermore, assignment to conditions was not based on chance or matching. Constantino's conclusions must be considered with caution and cannot be considered evidence of effectiveness of primary preventive interventions.

Lieberman and Videka-Sherman (1986) presented results of a large-scale survey of participating and nonparticipating widows and widowers in mutual help groups. Comparing the participants with a normative sample, the latter showed deterioration over time on anxiety, somatization, self-esteem, coping mastery, medication, and general well-being, whereas the mutual help group participants improved on mental health status in the covered one-year period (except depression, which got worse). A second analysis involved only the 502 participants in the survey. This showed that the more one participated in the program, the better the outcome. Lieberman and Videka-Sherman interpreted these results in support of the efficacy of the program, but one crucial problem was that participants were not randomly assigned to conditions but were self-selected. That resulted in some differences between groups (for instance, participants were likely to be more socially active in organizations and clubs), which was controlled for but which nevertheless suggests that other initial differences confounded the results. People asking for help may be better motivated and have more trust in the counselor (which is often regarded as a predictor of intervention outcome; Garfield, 1994). Furthermore, those bereaved individuals who asked for help are likely to have suffered from more problems or distress in the first place (Caserta & Lund, 1992; Rynearson, 1995; Videka-Sherman & Lieberman, 1985), leaving more room for improvement. Nevertheless, the results do seem to support the value of mutual help for bereaved persons who seek help.

What emerges from the studies supporting the rationale for primary preventive interventions for widows and widowers is that serious methodological weaknesses feature in most of them. Positive findings can therefore not be said to be corroborated by methodologically sound research. The most convincing result from the studies is that intervention offered might be appropriate for the ones who are in high distress. Whether this conclusion holds will be seen later. First, we focus on what emerges from studies addressing the efficacy of intervention for bereaved children.

Bereaved Children

Programs aimed at helping bereaved children cope with the loss of a parent or sibling generally show more favorable results than the adult intervention studies, although, as we shall see, "children" may be too broad a term to use, and the number of studies exploring the effects of intervention on children is still very small.

Black and Urbanowicz (1987) studied 45 families with at least one child under 16 years of age in which one of the parents had died. A random selection was offered six family therapy sessions, aimed at facilitating grief in both the surviving parent and child and improving communication between them. During the first follow-up, the treatment group showed some improvement. The parents were less depressed and the children less restless, less nail biting, and less needy of help from professional agencies. At the second follow-up two years after treatment, the only significant difference in favor of the treatment group was in parents' health problems. Most positive changes thus appeared to be of short duration.

Sandler et al. (1992) reported a carefully conducted study on effects of a 12-session family advisory program aimed at reducing risk for children after the death of a parent. The program was focused on parental demoralization, parental warmth, stable positive events, and negative stress events. A total of 72 children were randomly assigned to a treatment or waiting list condition. The intervention increased *parental report* of warmth of their relationship with their children, increased satisfaction with social support, and prevented a decrease in the discussion of grief-related issues, whereas such a decrease was evident in the control group. With regard to symptomatology (e.g., depression, misconduct) no improvement was found compared with the controls, but taking age into account older children in the treatment group showed more improvement in depression and conduct according to parental report. In contrast, in the control group the conduct of the younger children improved over time. An important suggestion coming from this study is that what is appropriate for adolescents is not necessarily so for preadolescents (see also chapter 9, this volume). Age-specific interventions seem to be required.

Morrison Tonkins and Lambert (1996) also put preventive grief intervention for children to the test. Their intervention was specifically aimed at preadolescents, a limited range of 7- to 11-year-old children. The professionally led intervention group met on eight weekly occasions. The group format was designed to offer children a sense of safety to facilitate exploration of thoughts and feelings and different methods for expressing them. Despite the small number of children, results in this study were strongly in favor of the intervention. The treatment group showed more improvement in the areas of self-reported overall emotions and depression and symptoms reported by parents and teachers.

Primary Preventive Interventions: Conclusions About Efficacy

The overall picture emerging from the studies of the effects of primary preventive interventions hardly calls for optimism. In line with the conclusions to Kato and Mann's (1999) review, we have seen that most studies suffer from methodological weaknesses, sometimes very serious ones, but what we nevertheless found is that primary preventive interventions receive hardly any empirical support for their effectiveness. The positive effects that are found often seem temporary, and sometimes negative results of the intervention have been reported too. At this point the only clear conclusion emerging from the studies seems to be that none of the primary interventions can be called evidence-based. With regard to intervention studies for bereaved children, the picture emerging is somewhat more positive. Research in that area is beginning to show promise that primary preventive interventions for bereaved children can be effective.

Secondary Preventive Interventions

As we have seen in the previous section, some of the primary preventive intervention studies have differentiated low and high risk. In this section we focus on studies that were confined to high-risk groups or secondary preventive interventions. As noted previously, secondary preventive interventions are designed for bereaved individuals who, through screening or assessment, for example, can be regarded as more vulnerable to the risks of bereavement than those bereaved individuals who do not fall into the particular category (e.g., high levels of distress, traumatic loss, concurrent life events, loss of a child). The effects of this category of intervention are indeed more promising, although not equivocal. Details of the studies are presented in Tables 30-3 and 30-4.

An Overview of Secondary Preventive Intervention Efficacy Studies

Raphael (1977, 1978) undertook the first investigation offering intervention to bereaved individuals at higher risk of later complications in the grieving process. She introduced selection criteria into the study of the efficacy of grief interventions, in this case the occurrence of a traumatic, usually sudden death of the partner. Further selection criteria were low social support, an ambivalent relationship with the deceased, or experience of many concurrent stressful life events. Bereaved persons in the intervention condition were offered counseling in the first three months of their bereavement, which was aimed at providing support, encouragement of expression of emotions, and focus on positive and negative aspects of the lost relationship. Approximately a year after therapy ended, persons in the supported group had fewer symptoms than those in the high-risk nonsupported group but more than those in the low-risk nonsupported group. Furthermore, participants in the intervention group had significantly fewer doctor visits than bereaved participants in the control group. However, if therapy visits are included, the difference disappeared. Although Raphael drew her conclusions on cross-sectional comparisons between groups after the intervention and, rather broadly, compared groups on the ratio of bereaved persons with "good" versus "bad" health, the study presents useful evidence of the effectiveness of intervention for high-risk bereaved individuals.

A nonintervention control posttest-only design was used by Parkes (1981) too, who evaluated support after hospice care. He compared scores on autonomic and physical symptoms, depression, worrying, habit change (e.g., smoking, alcohol, and medication consumption) of high-risk bereaved persons who did or did not receive grief support after their loved one had died. An interviewer collected the data 20 months after bereavement. The two groups differed significantly on autonomic symptom scores, habit change, and overall outcome, all in favor of the supported group. It is interesting to note that all positive results seemed attributable to the men in the study, which contrasts with Raphael's results, because her study was confined to women and she did find favorable results. Parkes's study suffered from the same methodological problem as Raphael's (1977): cross-sectional posttest comparison. Parkes, however, did use more fine-grained indicators of distress. On the other hand, psychometric properties of the assessment instrument are not clear. Neither is it evident whether the interviewer was blind to the study condition in which the bereaved individual was placed.

Forrest, Standish, and Baum (1982) found a similar pattern, although this study was focused on mothers who had lost a child and who received practical and emotional support from professionals in a hospital. Six months later there were fewer psychiatric cases (measured using the General Health Questionnaire and the Leeds Anxiety Scale) in the intervention group than among the controls who got "the usual care." But the positive effect disappeared almost half a year later. One of the problems in this study is an obscure dropout pattern. At six months follow-up 70% of original participants still participated (64% in the intervention and 76% in the control condition). During the 14 months follow-up this dropped to 60%, but no information was given about the spread over conditions. This, together with lack of information about how many mothers declined the help offered and how they differed from those who accepted, makes it difficult to evaluate the results of the study.

One of the most impressive studies of the effects of intervention after child loss was done by Murphy et al. (1998). This was apparently designed for multiple risk loss, because it was aimed at parents having recently lost a child by accident, homicide, or suicide. This study nicely combines a pre–post control design and multiple risk factors with relatively large samples, and low drop out rates over the course of the study (see Table 30-3). Parents were randomly assigned to the intervention group ($n = 153$) or the control group ($n = 108$), the only exception being that spouses were as-

TABLE 30-3
Methodological Aspects of Secondary

Authors	Design	Category of Bereaved	Age	Data Collection Points
Forrest et al. (1982)	Posttest control	Mothers (100%)	18–49	6 and 14 months after bereavement
Lake et al. (1987)	Posttest control	Parents (100% female)	M = 24	6 months after bereavement
Murphy et al. (1998)	Pre–post control	Parents (66% female)	M = 45	Pre-, post-, and 6 months after intervention
Parkes (1981)	Posttest control	Miscellaneous (49% female)	M = 66	20 months after bereavement
Raphael (1977)	Posttest control	Widows (100%)	<60	13 months after bereavement
Schut et al. (1997)	Pre–post control	Widows (76%) and widowers	M = 54	11, 18, and 25 months after bereavement
Videka-Sherman & Lieberman (1985)	Posttest control	Parents (74% female)	Unspecified	6–24 and 18–36 months after bereavement

[a]Percentage of T1 (first data collection point).
[b]Not specified per condition.
[c]A = Problem-focused behavior therapy; B = emotion-focused client-centered therapy.

signed to the same treatment condition. At follow-up, six months after the intervention, 86% of the intervention group and 79% of the control group still participated in the study. In both conditions, dropouts reported less dyadic interactions than completers did, and mothers with higher levels of grief tended to drop out more in the control condition. At first sight, the results indicate slow decline of symptoms on all outcome measures in the study and hardly any difference between the conditions immediately after intervention and six months later. Further analyses, however, revealed that mothers with relatively high mental distress and grief symptomatology at baseline improved more than those in the control condition. By contrast, women with relative low levels of grief and mental distress were worse after intervention compared with the control group. For fathers samples sizes were too small for such detailed analyses, but they did not appear to benefit from the intervention at all. In fact, posttraumatic stress symptoms among fathers appeared to decline in the control group while staying stable in the intervention condition, suggesting some negative effects for fathers. This was the first time indications of negative effects of intervention were found in selective preventive interventions. The results run counter to the gender-specific intervention Parkes (1981) reported.

An explanation for this gender inconsistency may lie in the content of the intervention, a notion for which Schut, Stroebe, Van den Bout, and De Keijser (1997; Schut, 1992) present indications. They compared emotion-oriented with problem-oriented individual intervention for widows and widowers with relatively high levels of distress 11 months after bereavement and compared these results with those of a matched control group. The course of distress only marginally differed between condition when pre-, post-, and follow-up data were compared: The problem-focused

Preventive Interventions

Recruitment	N Contacted	n Accepted (%)	Assignment	n Experimental T-last (%)	n Control T-last (%)[a]
Outreaching	Unspecified	50 (unspecified %)	Random	15 (60%)[b]	15 (60%)[b]
Outreaching	Unspecified	78 (unspecified %)	Random	18 (44%)[b]	16 (44%)[b]
Outreaching	329 families	204 families (62%)	Random	131 (86%)	85 (79%)
Screening	Unspecified	Unspecified	Random	32 (unspecified %)	35 (unspecified %)
Screening	200	64 (32%)	Random	27 (87%)	29 (88%)
Screening	358	79 (22%)	Random for treatment/ matching for control	A: 23 (70%)[c] B: 23 (70%)	59 (89%)
Outreaching	2242	667 (28%)	Self-selection	246 (59%)[b]	140 (59%)[b]

group reported less distress than the emotion-focused, which in turn compared favorably with the control group. However, gender-specific analyses revealed that men gained substantially more from emotion-oriented intervention, and widows had more to gain from problem-focused intervention. The main problems in this study, however, were small samples and the fact that the study was not designed to test gender differences, so that baseline differences appeared to be present between men and women in the two conditions. Therefore, we cannot say that this study presents conclusive evidence with regard to gender-specific effects of intervention.

Two studies focusing on high-risk groups have not found positive results of intervention: Videka-Sherman and Lieberman (1985) and Lake, Johnson, Murphy, and Knuppel (1987). Videka-Sherman and Lieberman's (1985) study had a similar design as their previously described study of mutual help after partner loss (Lieberman & Videda-Sherman (1986). But in this instance they studied effects of mutual help after child loss using a posttest only design. The sample was subdivided, posthoc, in six groups with different involvement levels in Compassionate Friends, the mutual help support system being the topic in this project. The rigorous and sophisticated analyses revealed no effect of involvement in the mutual help organization on any of the dependent measures included (e.g., mental health, marital role strain, parental distress, and attitudes toward expression of emotions). However, because the acceptance rate was low and attrition rather high (see Table 30-3), it is difficult to draw firm conclusions. Furthermore, Compassionate Friends members were more depressed and anxious, reported more somatic complaints, less life satisfaction, and lower mastery compared with the nonmembers. Although Videka-Sherman and Lieberman controlled for these differences, systematic differences between groups could have interfered with a pure analysis of effects of the intervention. Furthermore, planning to continue attending meetings was part

TABLE 30-4
Aspects of Secondary Preventive Intervention

Authors	Time Since Bereavement	Risk Factor	Type of Intervention	Description of Intervention	Number of Sessions	Type of Control
Forrest et al. (1982)	Immediately after bereavement	Loss of a child	Individual	Practical and emotional support	2–8	Nonintervention
Lake et al. (1987)	Immediately after bereavement	Loss of a child	Individual	Practical and emotional support	4	Nonintervention
Murphy et al. (1998)	4 months after bereavement (1–7)	Loss of a child through suicide, homicide, or accident	Group	Problem-focused and emotion-focused support	12	Nonintervention
Parkes (1981)	First period after bereavement	Combination of age, occupation, anticipation of loss, pining, anger, self-reproach, support and expectations of coping	Individual	Practical and emotional bereavement counseling	Unspecified	Nonintervention
Raphael (1977)	First 3 months after bereavement	Low social support, ambivalent relationship, or concurrent life events	Group	Aimed at emotional support, expression of emotions and on aspects of the relationship: "selective ego support"	4 (1–9)	Nonintervention
Schut et al. (1997)	14–17 months after bereavement	High distress	Individual	A: Problem-focused behavior therapy B: Emotion-focused client centered therapy	7	Nonintervention
Videka-Sherman & Lieberman (1985)	Unspecified	Loss of a child	Group	Mutual help	Unspecified	Nonparticipants

of the operationalization of involvement in Compassionate Friends. That obviously makes a self-selection bias plausible, because those who continue attending meetings are more likely to still grieve. This does not emerge from the results presented in the article, but grief symptoms were not specifically assessed in this project. Thus we should not attach too much weight to these results.

Lake et al. (1987) studied effects of a perinatal grief support program for mothers who had experienced stillbirth. In this study 78 mothers were either randomly assigned to grief counseling (two sessions with a grief support team before discharge, one session one month and one four to six months after discharge from the hospital) or a nonintervention control group. The data suggested effects on items of subclinical relevance (diarrhea and constipation), but overall no differences were found at follow-up between the groups. A major difficulty in this study was that attrition was high (see Table 30-3), influencing the power of the study.

Secondary Preventive Interventions: Conclusions About Efficacy

The review of high-risk interventions presents mixed results: Effects, if found, are generally rather modest and there are some indications that improvement is only temporary. Furthermore, what becomes apparent in this section is the relevance of gender-specific analyses. Not all studies have addressed this issue, but several (Murphy et al., 1998; Parkes, 1981; Schut et al., 1997) found strong, though inconsistent, indications of men and women reacting differently to the interventions. Although this could partially account for the mixed results presented in this section (effects can be masked by opposing gender effects), it seems unlikely to be the case. Most of the remaining studies were confined to women (Forrest et al., 1982; Lake et al., 1987; Raphael, 1977), and in this case the results are inconsistent too.

In several of these studies participants were screened for risk level before being offered intervention. This coincides almost completely with whether or not positive results were found, suggesting that selecting participants raises the chances of the intervention leading to positive results. On the other hand, screening was not done in studies confined to parents who had lost a child, because that was the factual risk factor. Possibly loss of a child is not such a good indicator of risk (child loss may be too massive a bereavement for intervention to be effective). More likely, as Murphy et al. (1998) suggested, we need to differentiate within that category of parents and make more fine-grained comparisons.

Another point to keep in mind is that defining "risk factors" is complex (see chapter 16, this volume) and is operationalized in a simplified way in several studies. This might also explain some of the inconsistency between studies.

Tertiary Preventive Interventions

Interventions with individuals who suffer from complicated grief usually take place longer after bereavement, primarily because most forms of complicated or traumatic grief take time to develop. Furthermore, studies of the efficacy of tertiary interventions usually take place through processes of help-seeking, with referred or screened and selected participants instead of recruitment, as in most of the studies described previously. As we will demonstrate, most studies addressing tertiary intervention conclude that the intervention is helpful.

An Overview of Tertiary Preventive Intervention Efficacy Studies

Based on the impressive clinical work of Ramsay (1977), Mawson et al. (1981) and Sireling et al. (1988) studied the impact of so-called guided mourning, which uses exposure to painful stimuli and avoided memories and situations. Although Ramsay made use of flooding techniques for treating complicated grief, Mawson et al. and Sireling et al. used systematic desensitization (see Gauthier & Marshall, 1977; Gauthier & Pye, 1979), which is less confrontive and keeps bereaved individuals more in control of the situation. In both Mawson et al.'s and Sireling et al.'s (1988) studies the major inclusion criterion was the presence of so-called "morbid grief," indicating that the most prominent symptoms had to relate in time and content to the loss of a significant other (having started subsequently and persisting longer than a year). In Sireling et al.'s study, participants were referred by psychiatrists and general practitioners. In the Mawson study referral is unclear, but two thirds of the patients were on antidepressant medication, indicating referral too. This suggests that established pathology was probably being dealt with in these studies. Treatment consisted of 6 to 10 sessions, and both Sireling et al. and Mawson et al. found guided mourning patients to improve more than controls on some dimensions. Right after therapy ended, Mawson et al. found less phobic avoidance, bereavement avoidance task performance, and distress. However, several weeks after treatment ended, the experimental condition only did slightly better on the Texas Inventory of Grief. Sireling et al. reported that only the treatment by time interaction on avoidance reached significance. On some other variables supporting trends were observed, but on others (e.g., grief symptomatology and depression) no differences were found between the conditions. Specially, as was mentioned before, if one considers the debatable therapeutic rationale for the antiexposure condition (in Mawson et al. bereavement avoidance task distress worsened in the controls, causing the difference from guided mourning), one can conclude that these results are modest, although this might be explained by the small samples (see Tables 30-5 and 30-6).

Brom and his colleagues (Brom, Kleber, & Defares, 1986) compared four treatment modalities: hypnotherapy, dynamic therapy, behavior therapy (systematic desensitization), and a waiting list condition. Their study was presented as a trauma intervention study, but in 74% of the cases the trauma had been the loss of a loved one, so it can be considered among grief intervention studies. Controlling for initial differences in level of symptoms, the three therapy conditions did appear to lead to notably greater reduction in symptomatology with respect to intrusion and avoidance of the experience. An exception was the decrease of intrusion in the psychodynamic group, which failed to differ from the control condition. On the other hand, dynamic therapy was the only type of intervention to have an impact on certain personality variables: Feelings of inadequacy and trait anxiety were reduced, and dominance increased among the members of the psychodynamic group. On other symptoms, the intervention programs did not evoke more positive results than the control condition. Thus the different interventions did improve functioning on a number of dimensions, with some, but modest, differences between treatment modalities.

With a much smaller scope Azhar and Varma (1995) reported on a study of the efficacy of religious-oriented psychotherapy. This study was conducted in Malaysia, where Islam is a major religion. Thirty bereaved persons diagnosed with major depression were randomly assigned to regular psychotherapy (although it is unclear what this consisted of), combined with antidepressant medication, or to this treatment plus additional religious psychotherapy on a cognitive–behavioral basis. The additional religious psychotherapy consisted of discussions of religious issues specific to the patient (e.g., reading verses of the Koran and encouraging prayers). The results suggested that the additional treatment had a positive effect on depression, especially short-term. However, the authors analyzed all variables separately, although these variables probably shared common factors. They also analyzed the data cross-sectionally, despite the fact that they had gathered longitudinal data. Both of these procedures can lead to an exaggeration of differences between the therapy conditions. Therefore, the results of this study are interesting, but not convincing.

Schut, de Keijser, van den Bout, and Stroebe (1996) studied the effects of so-called cross-modality grief therapy, an integration of group behavior therapy and art therapy. This program was designed for bereaved persons with diagnosed bereavement-related psychopathology (e.g., complicated bereavement, psychosomatic, and anxiety disorders) who were referred to a health care center. Results of the experimental treatment were compared with the regular health care center treatment modality for complicated grief and grief-related disorders at this center before cross-modality treatment was experimentally implemented. Results at follow-up, three to four months after discharge, indicated that both treatment programs were

TABLE 30-5
Methodological Aspects of Tertiary

Authors	Design	Category of Bereaved	Age	Data Collection Points
Azhar & Varma (1995)	Pre–post control	Unspecified (63% female)	$M = 38$	Pre-, 1, 3, and 6 months after intervention
Brom et al. (1989)	Pre–post control	Miscellaneous (79% female)	$M = 42$	Pre- and postintervention and 3 months follow-up
Marmar et al. (1988)	Pre–post control	Widows (100%)	$M = 58$	Pre- and 4 and 12 months after intervention
Mawson et al. (1981)	Pre–post control	Miscellaneous (92% female)	$M = \pm50$	Pre-, 1, 3, and 7 months after intervention
McCallum & Piper (1990)	Pre–post control	Miscellaneous (67% female)	$M = 30$	Pre-, post-, and 6 months after intervention
Schut et al. (1996)	Pre–post control	Miscellaneous (88% female)	$M = 53$	Pre-, post-, and 4 months after intervention
Sireling et al. (1988)	Pre–post control	Miscellaneous (70% female)	$M = 42$	Pre-, post-, 1, 3, and 9 months after intervention

[a]Percentage of T1 (first data collection point).
[b]Not specified per condition.
[c]First figures about targeted 12 sessions, second about 8 sessions, which was post-hoc defined as criterion.
[d]A = hypnotherapy; B = dynamic therapy; C = behavior therapy.

efficacious (although there was substantial relapse between discharge and follow-up) but that the experimental treatment was more effective with regard to the outcome measure used (General Health Questionnaire). At follow-up, the best results were established in the areas of anxiety, insomnia, and problems with daily functioning. A problem of this study, however, is the small sample of the control condition. Again, caution is needed in generalizing from these results.

The psychotherapy studied by McCallum and Piper (1990, McCallum, Piper, & Morin, 1993; Piper & McCallam, 1991) was psychoanalytically oriented. Short-term group intervention focused on the treatment of prolonged or delayed grief (mainly manifested in terms of affective disorders and adjustment disorders) triggered by bereavement or divorce (14%) and included only self-referred participants. After matching, participants were randomly assigned to direct treatment or a waiting list condition. The therapy proved favorable, compared with the waiting list condition, on a very broad range of variables, such as self-esteem, neuroticism, depression, and life satisfaction. A rather low adherence (23% dropped out after at least one session) does however threaten this otherwise excellent study.

Finally, Marmar et al. (1988) compared help-seeking widows who were randomly assigned to individual brief dynamic psychotherapy or mutual help groups. These treatment modalities were available for pathological grief only, which was operationalized in terms of adjustment disorder, posttraumatic stress disorder, and major depressive episode triggered by the death of the spouse. Analyses showed the conditions to be equally effective

Preventive Interventions

Recruitment	N Contacted	n Accepted (%)	Assignment	n Experimental T-last (%)[a]	n Control T-last (%)[a]
Help-seekers	—	—	Random	15 (100%)	15 (100%)
Screening	—	—	Random	A: 26 (90%)[d] B: 26 (90%) C: 28 (90%)	20 (87%)
Outreaching	91	76 (84%)	Random	21 (68%) 27 (87%)[c]	7 (23%) 19 (63%)[c]
Referred	—	—	Random	4 (66%)	2 (33%)
(self) referred	—	—	Matching and random	36 (67%)[b]	
Referred	—	—	Order of entrance	38 (73%)	12 (100%)
Referred	—	—	Random	11 (79%)	9 (75%)

in terms of stress-specific and general symptoms immediately after intervention. Adaptation at work and social functioning improved only later, at 4 and 12 months after treatment, and did not differ between conditions either. A comparison including dropouts indicated superior results for brief dynamic therapy, suggesting that dropouts in the mutual help condition were actually doing worse than the completers.

One of the difficulties in Marmar et al.'s study is that at least three systematic differences exist between the conditions: professional versus nonprofessional led, group versus individual therapy, and dynamic psychotherapy versus mutual help. This leaves the question of which factors caused the differences unanswered. Another major problem is the fact that the mutual help condition suffered from extremely high premature termination of treatment (77%). In the dynamic condition this was lower but still substantial (32%). On the other hand, the authors were able to obtain follow-up information from many of the dropouts too, thereby establishing an important source of information on the differences between completers and dropouts. Nevertheless, because only seven completed treatment in the mutual help condition, it is doubtful whether this type of intervention was really put to the test.

Tertiary Preventive Interventions: Conclusions About Efficacy

Most studies of interventions for complicated grief find positive and lasting results, although the effects are often modest. Methodologically, most of the studies present problems: small samples, inconsistent inclusion criteria (also a result of complicated grief not being included in the DSM), and dubious control interventions make it difficult to draw firm conclu-

TABLE 30-6
Aspects of Tertiary Preventive Intervention

Authors	Time Since Bereavement	Risk Factor	Type of Intervention	Description of Intervention	Number of Sessions	Type of Control
Azhar & Varma (1995)	Unspecified	Major depression	Individual	Additional religious interventions	12–16	Regular treatment
Brom et al. (1989)	<5 years	PTSD	Individual	A: hypotherapy B: dynamic therapy C: behavior therapy	A: 14 B: 19 C: 15	Waiting list
Marmar et al. (1988)	±1 years	Depressive episode, adjustment disorder, or PTSD	Individual	Brief dynamic psychotherapy	12	Mutual help
Mawson et al. (1981)	1–10 years	"Morbid grief"	Individual	Guided mourning	6	Antiexposure
McCallum & Piper (1990)	M = 7 years (3 months–20 years)	Affective disorder or adjustment disorder	Group	Brief dynamic psychotherapy	12	Waiting list
Schut et al. (1996)	±3 years	Major depression, adjustment disorder, or PTSD	Group	Behavior therapy and art therapy combined	20	Regular treatment
Sireling et al. (1988)	1–20 years	"Morbid grief"	Individual	Guided mourning	10	Antiexposure

sions. On the other hand, all studies use a pre–post control design, which is much more robust than the posttest control design used in some of the general preventive and almost all of the high-risk preventive intervention studies.

CONCLUSION

The general pattern emerging from this review is that the more complicated the grief process appears to be or to become, the better the chances of interventions leading to positive results. Based on the evidence to date, outreaching primary preventive intervention for bereaved people cannot be regarded as being beneficial in terms of diminishing grief-related symptoms, with a possible exception for interventions being offered to bereaved children. Secondary interventions stand a better chance of ameliorating distress, although there are some indications that the improvement in well-being is only temporary. Furthermore, the results indicate gender differences in the effects of different types of interventions for high-risk bereaved people. Tertiary preventive interventions generally seem to lead to favorable results, although this conclusion is not unequivocally substantiated by the empirical studies either. Thus our conclusions contrast with those of Litterer Allumbaugh and Hoyt (1999), who claimed that intervention should take place as soon as possible after the loss to be efficacious. A likely explanation for this is that Litterer Allumbaugh and Hoyt systematically excluded follow-up data, which, as we have demonstrated, typically indicates that there is a reduction in the magnitude of the effectiveness.

A plausible explanation for this pattern of differences in intervention effects has to do with recruitment. A feature of almost all primary preventive intervention studies (with the exception of Sabatini, 1985) is that participants were recruited for intervention. In other words, the bereaved persons themselves did not ask for help but were offered support. The same is true for almost half of the high-risk bereaved intervention studies and one of the complicated grief studies. Closer examination reveals that almost without exception the studies with less favorable results are those that use such an "outreach" procedure. Thus the pattern found may have less to do with the target group of the intervention than with the way contact is made with the bereaved person. Intervention programs using an active, outreaching approach are much more likely to have no or negative effects than programs in which one waits for the bereaved person to initiate contact. This may be explained by the likelihood that people asking for help will probably be more motivated and have more trust in the counselor or therapist. Furthermore, bereaved persons asking for help will probably need it more. They will be likely to suffer more in the first place (Caserta & Lund, 1992; Rynearson, 1995; Videka-Sherman & Lieberman, 1985), so that help is probably more appropriate. Furthermore, high distress at baseline leaves more room for improvement during and after the intervention too, which inflates a comparison with primary preventive interventions. Many organizations for helping bereaved individuals do initiate contact with them shortly after the loss and offer their support, though in most cases less obtrusively than the way it is done in most studies reviewed in this chapter. Based on the empirical evidence presented, one can conclude that such a procedure is highly questionable with respect to its beneficial effects, and might even lead to the opposite of what is desired.

Another confound preventing a straightforward conclusion based on the review of the literature is timing of the intervention. The bulk of the primary and secondary preventive interventions take place fairly soon after the loss, whereas tertiary preventive interventions usually take place at longer durations. It seems plausible that early interventions have less effect because the emotional, social, and practical consequences of the loss still need to take their natural course. Furthermore, early after the loss of a loved one, help from friends and family is more likely to be available than later in the grief process. Early interventions could also interfere with support from the natural social environment and trigger friends and family to withdraw (de Keijser, 1997). Bereaved people are probably also more inclined to accept help offered early after loss, because they are distressed and in need of support. But the other side of the coin may be that such outreaching early interventions prevent people from finding their own solutions and ways of dealing with the problems they encounter. This could explain the negative effects that are found in some studies. The evidence for this is, however, inconclusive, and the scope of the assessment of intervention effects is still narrow (despite the fact that very diverse—sometimes hardly comparable—outcome measures are being used). Too few studies have extended investigation beyond grief symptomatology, general health, depression, or social support. Self-esteem, personal independence, personal growth, insecurity, flexibility, and hardiness, just to mention some, should be the focus of attention too to be able to draw broad-range conclusions. This should be assessed at longer durations following intervention. Also needed for better control would be an assessment of naturally occurring social support before, during, and after the intervention takes place. Such information could be used to develop and test explanations of *why* intervention has the differential effects that we have identified and *what* the underlying processes associated with these might be.

The general conclusions emerging from this review concern intervention as well as the study of its effects. Parallel to the ethical guidelines for conducting bereavement research (Parkes, 1995), it may be timely to develop guidelines for implementing grief counseling and therapy, as well as for studying its effects. Based on our current knowledge, the American

Psychological Association's do-not-harm obligation (APA, 1992) may in the case of grief interventions be less easy to prove than we think.

REFERENCES

American Psychological Association. (1992). Ethical principles of psychologists and code of conduct. *American Psychologist, 47*, 1597–1611.

Azhar, M. Z., & Varma, S. L. (1995). Religious psychotherapy as management of bereavement. *Acta Psychiatrica Scandinavica, 91*, 233–235.

Balk, D. E., Tyson-Rawson, K., & Colletti-Wetzel, J. (1993). Social support as an intervention with bereaved college students. *Death Studies, 17*, 427–450.

Barrett, C. J. (1978). Effectiveness of widows' groups in facilitating change. *Journal of Consulting and Clinical Psychology, 46*, 20–31.

Black, D., & Urbanowicz, M. A. (1987). Family interventions with bereaved children. *Journal of Child Psychology, 28*, 467–476.

Brom, D., Kleber, R. J., & Defares, P. B. (1989). Brief psychotherapy for posttraumatic stress disorders. *Journal of Consulting and Clinical Psychology, 57*, 607–612.

Cameron, J., & Parkes, C. M. (1983). Terminal care: Evaluation of effects on surviving family of care before and after bereavement. *Postgraduate Medical Journal, 59*, 73–78.

Caplan, G. (1964). *Principles of preventive psychiatry.* New York: Basic Books.

Caserta, M. S., & Lund, D. A. (1992). Bereaved older adults who seek early professional help. *Death Studies, 16*, 17–30.

Caserta, M. S., & Lund, D. A. (1993). Intrapersonal resources and the effectiveness of self-help groups for bereaved older adults. *The Gerontologist, 33*, 619–629.

Constantino, R. E. (1981). Bereavement crisis intervention for widows in grief and mourning. *Nursing Research, 30*, 351–353.

De Keijser, J. (1997). *Sociale steun en professionele begeleiding bij rouw* [Social support and professional counseling for the bereaved]. Doctoral thesis, Utrecht University, The Netherlands.

Faschingbauer, T. R., Zisook, S., & DeVaul, R. (1987). The Texas Revised Inventory of Grief. In S. Zisook (Ed.), *Biopsychosocial aspects of grief and bereavement.* Washington, DC: American Psychiatry Press.

Forrest, G. C., Standish, E., & Baum, J. D. (1982). Support after perinatal death: A study of support and counseling after perinatal bereavement. *British Medical Journal, 285*, 1475–1479.

Garfield, S. L. (1994). Research on client variables in psychotherapy. In A. E. Bergin & S. L. Garfield (Eds.), *Handbook of psychotherapy and behavior change* (pp. 190–228). New York: Wiley.

Gauthier, J., & Marshall, W. L. (1977). Grief: A cognitive–behavioral analysis. *Cognitive Therapy and Research, 1*, 39–44.

Gauthier, J., & Pye, C. (1979) Graduated self-exposure in the management of grief. *Behavioral Analysis and Modification, 3,* 202–208.

Gerber I., Weiner A., Battin, D., & Arkin, A. M. (1975). Brief therapy to the aged bereaved. In B. Schoenberg, I. Gerber, & A. Wiener (Eds.), *Bereavement, its psychological aspects* (pp. 310–333). New York: Columbia University Press.

Hodgkinson, P. E. (1982). Abnormal grief: The problem of therapy. *British Journal of Medical Psychology, 55,* 29–34.

Horowitz, M. J., Marmar, C. R., Weiss, D. S., Kaltreider, N. B., & Wilner, N. R. (1986). Comprehensive analysis of change after brief dynamic psychotherapy. *American Journal of Psychiatry, 143,* 582–589.

Kane, R. L., Klein, S. J., Bernstein, L., & Rothenberg, R. (1986). The role of hospice in reducing the impact of bereavement. *Journal of Chronic Diseases, 39,* 735–742.

Kato, P. M., & Mann, T. (1999). A synthesis of psychological interventions for the bereaved. *Clinical Psychology Review, 19,* 275–296.

Lake, M. F., Johnson, T. M., Murphy, J., & Knuppel, N. (1987). Evaluation of a perinatal grief support team. *American Journal of Obstetrics and Gynecology, 157,* 1203–1206.

Levine, M., Toro, P. A., & Perkins, D. V. (1993). Social and community interventions. *Annual Review of Psychology, 44,* 525–558.

Levy, L. H., & Derby, J. F. (1992). Bereavement support groups: Who joins; who does not; and why? *American Journal of Community Psychology, 20,* 649–662.

Levy, L. H., Derby, J. F., & Martinkowski, K. S. (1993). Effects of membership in bereavement support groups on adaptation to conjugal bereavement. *American Journal of Community Psychology, 21,* 361–381.

Lieberman, M. A., & Videka-Sherman, L. (1986). The impact of self-help groups on the mental health of widows and widowers. *American Journal of Orthopsychiatry, 56,* 435–449.

Lieberman, M. A., & Yalom, I. (1992). Brief group psychotherapy for the spousally bereaved: A controlled study. *International Journal of Group Psychotherapy, 42,* 117–132.

Litterer Allumbaugh, D., & Hoyt, W. T. (1999). Effectiveness of grief therapy: A meta-analysis. *Journal of Counseling Psychology, 46,* 370–380.

Longman, A. J. (1993). Effectiveness of a hospice community bereavement program. *Omega, 27,* 165–175.

Lund, D. A., & Caserta, M. S. (1992). Older bereaved spouses' participation in self-help groups. *Omega, 25,* 47–61.

Marmar, C. R., Horowitz, M. J., Weiss, D. S., Wilner, N. R., & Kaltreider, N. B. (1988). A controlled trial of brief psychotherapy and mutual-help group treatment of conjugal bereavement. *American Journal of Psychiatry, 145,* 203–209.

Mawson, D., Marks, I. M., Ramm, L., & Stern, R. S. (1981). Guided mourning for morbid grief: A controlled study. *British Journal of Psychiatry, 138,* 185–193.

McCallum, M., & Piper, W. E. (1990). A controlled study of effectiveness and patient suitability for short-term group psychotherapy. *International Journal of Group Psychotherapy, 40,* 431–452.

McCallum, M., Piper, W. E., & Morin, H. (1993). Affect and outcome in short-term group therapy for loss. *International Journal of Group Psychotherapy, 43,* 303–319.

McCorkle, R., Robinson, L., Nuamah, I., Lev, E. & Benoliel, J. Q. (1998). The effects of home nursing care for patients during terminal illness on the bereaved's psychological distress. *Nursing Research, 47,* 2–10.

Morrison Tonkins, S. A., & Lambert, M. J. (1996). A treatment outcome study of bereavement groups for children. *Child & Adolescent Social Work Journal, 13,* 3–21.

Murphy, S. A., Aroian, K., & Baugher, R. (1989). A theory-based preventive intervention program for bereaved parents whose children have died in accidents. *Journal of Traumatic Stress, 2,* 319–335.

Murphy, S. A., Baugher, R., Lohan, J., Scheideman, J., Heerwagen, J., Johnson, L. C., Tillery, L., & Grover, M. C. (1996). Parents' evaluation of a preventive intervention following sudden, violent deaths of their children. *Death Studies, 20,* 453–468.

Murphy, S. A. Johnson, C., Cain, K. C., Das Gupta, A., Dimond, M., Lohan, J., & Baugher, R. (1998). Broad spectrum group treatment for parents bereaved by the violent deaths of their 12 to 28 year-old children. *Death Studies, 22,* 209–236.

Parkes, C. M. (1979). Terminal care: Evaluation of in-patient service at St. Christopher's Hospice. Part II: Self-assessment of effects of the service on surviving spouses. *Postgraduate Medical Journal, 55,* 523–527.

Parkes, C. M. (1980). Bereavement counseling: Does it work? *British Medical Journal, 28,* 3–6.

Parkes, C. M. (1981). Evaluation of a bereavement service. *Journal of Preventive Psychiatry, 1,* 179–188.

Parkes, C. M. (1987). Models of bereavement care. *Death Studies, 11,* 257–261.

Parkes, C. M. (1995). Guidelines for conducting ethical bereavement research. *Death Studies, 19,* 171–181.

Piper, W. E., & McCallum, M. (1991). Group interventions for persons who have experienced loss: Description and evaluative research. *Group Analysis, 24,* 363–373.

Polak, P. R., Egan, D. J., Vanderbergh, R. H., & Williams, W. W. (1973). Crisis intervention in acute bereavement: A controlled study of primary prevention. *Community Mental Health Journal, 12,* 128–136.

Polak, P. R., Egan, D., Vandenbergh, R., & Williams, W. V. (1975). Prevention in mental health: A controlled study. *American Journal of Psychiatry, 132,* 146–149.

Quarmby, D. (1993). Peer group counselling with bereaved adolescents. *British Journal of Guidance and Counselling, 21,* 196–211.

Ramsay, R. W. (1977). Behavioural approaches to bereavement. *Behaviour Research and Therapy, 15,* 131–135.

Raphael, B. (1977). Preventive intervention with the recently bereaved. *Archives of General Psychiatry, 34,* 1450–1454.

Raphael, B. (1978). Mourning and the prevention of melancholia. *British Journal of Medical Psychology, 51,* 303–310.

Reich, G. W., & Zautra, A. G. (1989). A perceived control intervention for at-risk older adults. *Psychology and Aging, 4,* 415–424.

Reif, L. V., Patton, M. J., & Gold, P. B. (1995). Bereavement, stress, and social support in members of a self-help group. *Journal of Community Psychology, 23,* 292–306.

Rognlie, C. (1989). Perceived short- and long-term effects of bereavement support group participation at the hospice of Petaluma. *The Hospice Journal, 5,* 39–53.

Rubin, S. S. (1999). Psychodynamic therapy with the bereaved: Listening for conflict, relationship and transference. *Omega, 39,* 83–98.

Rynearson, E. K. (1995). Bereavement after homicide: A comparison of treatment seekers and refusers. *British Journal of Psychiatry, 166,* 507–510.

Sabatini, L. (1985). The First Step Program: A bereavement service for widowed people. *Crisis Intervention, 14,* 72–83.

Sabatini, L. (1988). Evaluating a treatment program for newly widowed people. *Omega, 19,* 229–236.

Sales, B., & Folkman, S. (2000). *Ethical issues in the conduct of research with human participants.* Washington, DC: American Psychological Association.

Sandler, I. N., West, S. G., Baca, L., Pillow, D. R., Gersten, J. C., Rogosch, F., Virdin, L., Beals, J., Reynolds, K. D., Kallgren, C., Tein, J., Kriege, G., Cole, E., & Ramirez, R. (1992). Linking empirically based theory and evaluation: The family bereavement program. *American Journal of Community Psychology, 20,* 491–521.

Schut, H. A. W. (1992). *Omgaan met de dood van de partner: Effecten op gezondheid en effecten van rouwbegeleiding* [Coping with the death of the partner: Effects on health and effects of grief counseling]. Doctoral dissertation, Utrecht University. Amsterdam, The Netherlands: Thesis Publishers.

Schut, H. A. W., de Keijser, J., van den Bout, J., & Stroebe, M. S. (1996). Cross-modality grief therapy: Description and assessment of a new program. *Journal of Clinical Psychology, 52,* 357–365.

Schut, H. A. W., Stroebe, M. S., van den Bout, J., & de Keijser, J. (1997). Intervention for the bereaved: Gender differences in the efficacy of two counselling programmes. *British Journal of Clinical Psychology, 36,* 63–72.

Sherwood, S., Kastenbaum, R., Morris, J. N., & Wright, S. M. (1988). The first months of bereavement. In V. Mor, D. Greer, & R. Kastenbaum (Eds.), *The hospice experiment* (pp. 147–186). Baltimore: Johns Hopkins University Press.

Silverman, P. R. (1969). The widow-to-widow program: An experiment in preventive intervention. *Mental Hygiene, 53,* 333–337.

Sireling, L., Cohen, D., & Marks, I. (1988). Guided mourning for morbid grief: A controlled replication. *Behavior Therapy, 19,* 121–132.

Souter, S. J., & Moore, T. E. (1989). A bereavement support program for survivors of cancer deaths: A description and evaluation. *Omega, 20,* 31–41.

Steele, L. L. (1990). The death surround: Factors influencing the grief experience of survivors. *Oncology Nursing Forum, 17,* 235–241.

Stroebe, M. S., & Stroebe, W. (1983). Who suffers more? Sex differences in health risks of the widowed. *Psychological Bulletin, 93,* 279–301.

Stroebe, M. S., & Stroebe, W. (1989). Who participates in bereavement research? A review and empirical study. *Omega, 20,* 1–29.

Tudiver, F., Hilditch, J., Permaul, J. A., & McKendree, D. J. (1992). Does mutual help facilitate newly bereaved widowers? Report of a randomized controlled trial. *Evaluation & The Health Professions, 15,* 147–162.

Vachon, M. L. S., Lyall, W. A. L., Rogers, J., Freedman-Letofsky, K., & Freeman, S. J. J. (1980). A controlled study of self-help intervention for widows. *American Journal of Psychiatry, 137,* 1380–1384.

Videka-Sherman, L., & Lieberman, M. (1985). The effects of self-help and psychotherapy intervention on child loss: The limits of recovery. *American Journal of Orthopsychiatry, 55,* 70–82.

Walls, N., & Meyers, A. W. (1985). Outcome in group treatments for bereaved: Experimental results and recommendations for clinical practice. *International Journal of Mental Health, 13,* 126–147.

Williams, W. V., Lee, J., & Polak, P. R. (1976). Crisis intervention: Effects of crisis intervention on family survivors of sudden death situations. *Community Mental Health Journal, 12,* 128–136.

Williams, W. V., & Polak, P. R. (1979). Follow-up research in primary prevention: A model of adjustment in acute grief. *Journal of Clinical Psychology, 35,* 35–45.

VII

RETROSPECTIVE ON THE NEW HANDBOOK: EDITORIAL VIEW

31

FUTURE DIRECTIONS FOR BEREAVEMENT RESEARCH

MARGARET S. STROEBE, ROBERT O. HANSSON,
WOLFGANG STROEBE, AND HENK SCHUT

In this volume we have provided a comprehensive overview of the
state of knowledge on bereavement at the beginning of the twenty-first
century. The volume offers a critical, historical analysis of theoretical and
empirical discoveries across the decades of the past century, placing current
developments in perspective. The adequacy of our methodologies is examined, and ethical dilemmas encountered in conducting research are
brought into focus. Detail is provided regarding the diverse vulnerabilities
and manifestations following very different types of loss, extending the
scope of analysis beyond detriments to mental and physical health. We also
move beyond examination of the grieving individual to consideration of
group and societal influences and impact. The volume provides a fine-
grained analysis of how bereaved people go about their grieving and how
such ways of coping may affect their adaptation to loss. It critically reviews
the intervention needs of bereaved persons, including the physiological
impact of intervention, and presents suggestions for theory-guided counseling and therapy programming. Finally, it examines from many points of
view the emerging conceptual and practical issues, such as the differenti-

ation between normal and pathological grief and the necessity to develop diagnostic criteria for the latter.

Despite the scope and depth of contributions to this volume, coverage has still been selective. In this respect, our previous volume (M. Stroebe, Stroebe, & Hansson, 1993) offers some complementarity, for example, in its extensive treatment of phenomenological aspects of bereavement and its exploration of physiological changes as an outcome of bereavement. Nevertheless, much remains for future exploration—for example, theoretical and empirical investigation of commonalties versus diversities between loss through death and other extremely stressful life events (e.g., war experiences, divorce), or the integration of the still-separate research fields of terminal care and bereavement (cf. Parkes, Relf, & Couldrick, 1996). It is also evident that, even within the areas covered in this volume, new questions are raised for further investigation, and differences of opinion between our contributors continue to be voiced.

The purpose of this concluding chapter, then, is to identify core themes emerging from contemporary research and to suggest directions for future investigation. We also highlight the major controversies in the field today and provide editorial commentary where appropriate and useful. After a discussion of general issues having to do with theory, methodology, and ethical practices, the focus of the chapter shifts to the three themes, consequences, coping, and care.

GENERAL THEORETICAL AND CONCEPTUAL ISSUES

Contemporary empirical research on bereavement is more theory-driven than it ever has been. Perusal of this handbook shows that even if projects were originally "issue-generated," no substantive research these days is conducted in a theoretical vacuum. Thus the question to be addressed is not whether analysis at the theoretical level is relevant, because there is general consensus among leading researchers that it is, but rather *what* theories are useful and in what manner should these guide our research.

Determining What Type of Theoretical Approach Bereavement Research Should Follow

It is interesting to note that our contributors differ considerably regarding the type and scope of the theoretical frameworks that they now consider necessary in the bereavement field. Some call for an integrative approach, arguing that we still have a fragmented view (and database) on bereavement (cf. chapters 2 and 4, this volume). There are also arguments that bereavement phenomena should be understood within the framework of a broader theory, such as emotion theory (e.g., chapters 4 and 22, this volume), and others already adhere closely to different general theories, such as attachment theory, from which to derive their predictions (e.g., chapter 3, this volume), or cognitive stress theory (e.g., chapter 25, this volume). Finally, some investigators adopt highly specific models—which may or may not be integrative and which may or may not draw on the more general theories such as those just mentioned (cf. chapters 10 and 17, this volume).

Do we really need an integrative theory of bereavement? This is a realistic and useful goal (see chapter 4, this volume). At this point in its development, however, the field might also benefit from (a) a multiplicity of approaches, (b) more cross-fertilization between theoretical positions, and (c) theoretical analysis at both general and grief-specific levels. These emphases would seem essential to the ultimate goal of developing an integrative theory.

On the Multiplicity of Approaches

We do not have to look far to illustrate the contrasting potential of different theoretical approaches. As Parkes points out in chapter 2, we have studies of loss and its consequences and completely separate studies of attachments preceding these losses. Both of these are currently influential approaches. The former is gaining momentum through the work of Harvey (e.g., 1998; Harvey & Miller, 1998), who has argued the case for a broadly construed field of loss research, to complement other stressor-specific approaches (e.g., loss of vision; mental capacity; intimate relationships). The study of loss offers a framework with which to search for commonalities versus differences with respect to the nature of these life events and ways of coming to terms with them. It also encourages comparison of theoretical analyses of the different types of stressors. Our understanding of bereavement phenomena can be enhanced by plotting similarities and contrasts with other types of loss in each of these respects. A psychology of loss, then, would incorporate comparative trauma-bereavement theorizing and the analysis of a broad range of stressful life events including burns; divorce/ separation; spinal/brain injury or loss of limb; rape victimization; and so on.

By contrast, attachment theory enables more specific analysis of the personal and interpersonal impact of the termination of a relationship, owing much to the seminal work of Bowlby (1980; cf. Cassidy & Shaver, 1999; chapter 4, this volume). As Parkes commented, "No serious student of bereavement or of child development can afford to ignore this major work whose influence continues" (chapter 2). A central focus of this viewpoint would involve exploring how secure versus insecure patterns of attachment—shown to be reasonably stable from childhood onward and generalizable from the primary attachment figure to other attachment figures—influence bereavement reactions. The chapters by Parkes (chapter 2) and by Shaver and Tancredy (chapter 4) link these to different types of disordered grieving, positing a relationship between style of attachment and the forms of complicated grieving.

Both Parkes (personal communication, 1998), and Shaver and Tancredy (chapter 4, this volume) draw an intriguing link between types of secure versus insecure attachment and ways of coping. As these authors have pointed out, in terms of M. Stroebe and Schut's dual process model (cf. chapter 17, this volume), securely attached persons are likely to grieve normally and to oscillate between confronting and avoiding loss and restoration stressors. In fact, exploration of the hypotheses deriving from this points to a potential integration of attachment and coping research, suggesting a paradigm for future research. In our view, then, attachment research remains central to understanding the phenomena of grief and grieving, and attachment theory will continue to influence thinking in the field. This does not, however, preclude the usefulness of other approaches such as the loss, stress, or trauma perspectives, because these may offer more relevant hypotheses for other, specific interests. For example, the cognitive stress perspective may be more useful for analyzing the impact of secondary stressors associated with bereavement (e.g., social support deficits; financial burdens).

On Cross-Fertilization Among Theoretical Positions

Bereavement researchers from different traditions have much to learn from one other. For example, the body of research on psychopathology and phenomenology of loss might benefit from a consideration of ideas from the attachment and child development areas or from the psychology and physiology of stress (e.g., chapter 2, this volume). Such integrations are evident already in the volume—for example, Oltjenbruns's (chapter 8, this volume) incorporation of developmental theory in the study of the phenomenon of "regrief" among children, or Moss, Moss, and Hansson's (chapter 11, this volume) use of gerontological theory to understand grief among elderly individuals. Also in evidence are efforts to develop integrated models of coping (cf. chapters 17 and 22, this volume). Finally, to take a very different example, Nadeau (chapter 15, this volume) interestingly converges intrapersonal with interpersonal perspectives in her focus on family process (meaning making), her message being that making sense of the death is not just an individual task, as we have come to regard it, but also a collaborative process of social cognition. In all these examples, the quality of understanding is enriched by merging knowledge from different approaches.

744   STROEBE ET AL.

On Generic Versus Specific Theorizing

Our argument for pluralism extends to types of specific versus generic theorizing. There is currently room for knowledge derived at these two levels. For example, a specific model of coping with bereavement may enable identification of patterns and functions of, say, denial or emotional dissociation (e.g., chapter 22, this volume) that would be overlooked in a more general theoretical approach (e.g., dissociation may serve different functions in bereavement than following other traumas such as loss of livelihood). Specific bereavement models may also have the potential for broader application, as a "prototype" for ways of coping with loss in general. Conversely, take the case of attachment theory: As Shaver and Tancredy argue in chapter 4, a person's reaction to a particular loss may not be separate from that person's characteristic way of handling threats to self and to relationships. It makes sense, then, to understand the loss reaction in terms of general attachment principles. Or with respect to emotion theory, because the general body of literature on emotions has shown that emotions are generally functional, it also makes sense to postulate this for the emotion of grief and to attempt to identify the adaptive functions of grief. Archer (chapter 12) provides an excellent example of how researchers go about probing this notion both theoretically and empirically.

Summary

The importance of the scientific endeavor is its search for patterns, to understand such basic issues as why people grieve, the nature of their reactions, and how individual and social factors interact during the process of adaptation. The value of general and specific theories should be measured according to their potential for deriving testable predictions with respect to such patterns. The chapters in this volume show that steps are already being taken toward theoretical integration, but there are also good arguments for theoretical pluralism at this stage, because useful predictions are being derived at both specific and general levels, and cross-fertilization is improving the scope of predictions and our understanding of grief and grieving.

As we continue to test theories in the coming decades, it will be useful to follow the unusual example of Folkman (1997) in her "Rashomon study." Folkman invited four teams of investigators, representing distinct perspectives, to independently analyze a qualitative data set using narratives of 30 bereaved men following the death of their partners from AIDS. This provided an opportunity to compare theoretical and methodological approaches and to explore bereavement processes. Given that the study was longitudinal, the investigators could use analyses of data collected early on to predict scores 12 months later. Thus the predictive power of one approach could be compared with that of another, and the researchers could identify advantages and limitations in the data set for the investigation of their own particular interests. Such a format provides an invaluable opportunity for researchers to learn from one another.

Conceptual Issues: The Nature of Grief

The chapters in this volume reflect a number of advances in our understanding of the nature of grief. For example, we more fully appreciate the role of individual and cultural heterogeneity. Also, the multidimensionality of bereavement reactions is by now well-accepted. "Stages" or phases of grief are no longer viewed to follow a fixed and prescriptive course. People are cautious about pathological interpretation of the absence of distress. There is an awareness that, in the long-term, the bereaved do not simply "return to baseline" following their loss.

Yet as Weiss (chapter 3, this volume) cautions, our descriptions of grief have far outstripped our ability to explain it. We lack a general theory of grief that explains a number of basic questions: Why does it happen in response to only certain losses? What is the role of security and attachment? What are the links between symptoms of grieving and affective or cognitive systems? How and why does it abate? Is it indeed functional, as other emotions are? What is the nature and explanation of individual differences in grief experience? Can others really help, and if so, how? These are all questions for continued investigation.

On a fundamental level, we also need to consider whether there is a need to redefine grief in light of the broad spectrum of reactions that investigators in this volume have found to be associated with it. For example, is "relief" part of the concept of grief? Or, as Weiss (1999) asked, "Is finding comfort through the continued presence of the lost other an aspect of grief?" (p. 2). Chapters in this volume have testified to increased self-understanding and maturity (e.g., among bereaved adolescents; chapter 9), and to gains achieved through the regulation of negative affect with positive affect or reappraisal (cf. chapters 17, 22, 24, and 25, this volume). Do we need to balance our models of bereavement experience by adding features such as potential for personal growth and transformations following a period of successful coping and adaptation? It has become evident that well-being is not simply the other side of depression: A bereaved person may take pride in new achievements but still be very depressed about the loss of his or her loved one.

In our view, it is essential to recognize that such phenomena are components or aspects of grief. However, it is also important to remember that grief is primarily associated with severe distress in our society. We need to be able to identify the most "grief-stricken" for theoretical and applied purposes. This would speak for retaining the narrower, traditional definition of grief that we adopted previously (see chapter 1, this volume).

METHODOLOGICAL ISSUES: THE MEASURABILITY OF "GRIEF"

Remarkable improvements have been made in research design and in measurement in the study of bereavement. Highly diverse methods are now used for examining the experience of bereavement, reflecting a range of new questions and understandings of the nature of grief. Noteworthy still is the broad range of approaches, characteristic of the different disciplinary affiliations, from clinical psychology to sociology and physiology. It is evident too that we are moving beyond the use of nonvalidated measures and inadequate methodologies. Advancements in both measurement and methodology are, however, balanced by certain limitations, which we elaborate next.

Measurement

Progress is evident in the quality of measures used to assess the phenomena and manifestations of bereavement. Previously, a proliferation of single-study instruments hampered progress and limited understanding. However, these have been replaced by psychometrically more respectable techniques, with respect to such properties as reliability, validity, and factor structures. Stringent evaluations of the available measures of bereavement reactions and ways of coping confirm this (see chapters 5 and 20, this volume) for measures at different levels of assessment (symptomatic, cognitive, affective, physiological, and social), although there is room for further refinements.

An interesting concern arising frequently, and reflected in Neimeyer and Hogan's chapter (chapter 5, this volume), is the comparative value of quantitative and qualitative methodologies. Neimeyer and Hogan deplore an unbalanced reliance on quantitative instruments, which foregoes the kinds of insights into "process" that might result from complementary use of qualitative assessments. Discussion often tends to take the form of "either quantitative or qualitative," and researchers typically adhere to one or the other approach. Yet quantitative and qualitative research complement each other. Our own preference is for quantitative evaluation to be preceded by qualitative, in-depth assessment, perhaps in extensive pilot interviews with bereaved persons. In this way, the advantages of both approaches can be realized, yielding a rich data set. We strongly agree with Neimeyer and Hogan on the need for methodological pluralism.

An emerging criticism concerns the use of generic psychiatric measures (e.g., depression) indicative of a psychopathological conceptualization of grief. This limits the focus, it is frequently argued, to a "medical model" and leads to a psychopathology conceptualization of bereavement. For example, criticisms have been made of the reliance on depression measures as indicators of (lack of) adjustment. These criticisms are justified to some extent, because such an approach does reflect extreme restriction when considering the multidimensional, multifaceted nature of the phenomena of grief. Sometimes, however, the benefits of adopting a certain strategy must be weighed against costs. The choice of measure will depend on the hypothesis under investigation. As an example, depression measures permit a comparison with nonbereaved controls that grief inventories do not (cf. chapter 16, this volume). Responses on the two types of scales tend to correlate very highly. Thus if one wishes to compare bereaved with nonbereaved controls, using the former makes sense (see also the section on the duration of grief, vulnerabilities, and "recovery" later in this chapter).

In addition, it is striking how investigators have broadened the focus of assessment over the past decade. The chapters in this volume show that bereavement research now includes assessments of specific coping processes (e.g., chapter 20, this volume), detailed physiological sequelae (e.g., chapters 21 and 29, this volume), qualitative methods of construed and shared meanings of loss (chapters 15 and 19, this volume), and of positive growth (e.g., chapter 7, this volume). It seems likely that research will continue along these lines. Acknowledging this trend, however, it is important not to lose sight of the basic "medical model" concerns: We still need to improve assessment and understanding of the mental and physical health consequences of bereavement. We still do not have answers in sufficient detail to the questions raised in the 1970s and 1980s about differential vulnerabilities (e.g., causes of death of bereaved subgroups across the duration of bereavement).

Despite conceptual advancements, much remains to be improved in the measurement of bereavement. Further examination of the reliability of instruments is necessary. However, this is complex in the case of bereavement, because symptomatology is expected to fluctuate across the course of the bereavement reaction. Likewise, there has been insufficient examination of the relationships between the most used instruments or between more generic and specialized (e.g., perinatal, sibling) bereavement measures. Also, qualitative measurement techniques need to keep abreast of contemporary insights into meaning reconstruction following loss or into posttraumatic growth. A variety of innovative methods for examining construed and shared meanings is now available, as evidenced, for example, by Nadeau (chapter 15, this volume).

Finally, we must continue to explore the adequacy of our measures in capturing the essence of grief and grieving in all its complexity. In this connection, it is useful to compare and contrast two recent monographs, both by contributors to this volume, to place measurement issues in the broader context of the culture and historical period within which we conduct our work, namely Walter's (1999) "On Bereavement: The Culture of Grief," and Archer's (1999) "The Nature of Grief: The Evolution and Psychology of Reactions to Loss."

Research Design

Rigorous methodology and sophisticated designs have become the standard against which we can now measure empirical research on bereavement. Exemplary is the set of studies in the area of coping included in this volume, in which we see the advantages of longitudinal before-, after-, and follow-up bereavement designs (e.g., chapter 25, this volume), creative techniques (e.g., Bonanno's empty chair technique and examination of smiling as a positive emotion), operationalization of new concepts and teasing out of patterns of causality (e.g., chapter 24, this volume), and the buildup across time of programs of research, not single isolated studies, as some questions are answered and others created (e.g., chapter 23, this volume).

However, complaints about design and methodology that we raised a decade ago still pertain (cf. M. Stroebe & Stroebe, 1989; M. Stroebe et al., 1993). To illustrate, W. Stroebe and Schut (chapter 16, this volume) looked closely at the methodology and state of knowledge about risk factors to assess how well-established our conclusions about differential personal or situational vulnerabilities really are. It is indicative that the body of evidence in this area is still insufficient to justify meta-analyses—indeed, this is characteristic of the bereavement research field in general, although notable beginnings have been made (cf. Kato & Mann, 1999; Litterer Allumbaugh & Hoyt, 1999, for the evaluation of intervention efficacy studies). It is also surprising that false conclusions are still reached, for example, about gender patterns in bereavement reactions—the conclusion frequently being that women "have it harder." Main effects of gender on health variables are still ignored when making such statements, as are the differential proportions of bereaved women and men in many bereaved subgroups. Selection biases that lead more grief-stricken women but less grief-stricken men to participate in face-to-face studies are frequently ignored, as are gender differences in the expression (compared to the experience) of grief (the former being measured, the latter being assumed). It is impossible to test theoretical explanations of gender differences (or any other variable), unless such patterns are established on sound empirical basis. Thus our concerns about such issues as sample characteristics, their representativeness, implications of attrition and drop-out during investigation, and generalizability of results remain (cf. M. Stroebe & Stroebe, 1989). It is not sufficient to discount problems of attrition (selection into a study) or drop-out (during the course of a study) simply by citing, as many do, a study by Levy, Derby, and Martinkowski (1992) that "suggested little substantive difference between participants and non-participants in bereavement research" (p. 225). Examining the latter reassuring results (no differences) in comparison with our own disturbing ones (critical differences; M. Stroebe & Stroebe, 1989) leaves much room for further discussion. Again, further examination of such basic methodological issues seems indicated.

THE ETHICS OF BEREAVEMENT RESEARCH

It is a concern that ethical issues often have been neglected in bereavement research, given the potential vulnerability of our bereaved respondents. Formal ethics guidelines for research on bereavement were only recently put forward in a *Death Studies* special issue in 1995 (Parkes, 1995; Rosenblatt, 1995). In this volume, an important further step is the systematic approach to ethical considerations provided by Cook (chapter 6, this volume). This encourages an overdue debate on critical ethical concerns. Some of the most critical of these emerge from reviews in specific chapters of the volume—for example, should we outreach to give help when the efficacy of this has not been established (cf. chapter 30, this volume)? Can we assign bereaved individuals randomly to control conditions in a study of the evaluation of intervention? Do researchers really have an ethical obligation (or are they qualified by training) to apply the lessons of their scholarship to assist persons in need, as Balk and Corr (chapter 9, this volume) claim? Or is it the task of others to pick up research findings and apply them? Many questions apply more broadly—for example, How do we protect the rights, dignity, and well-being of research participants when asking them questions about their most personal emotions? Do we have adequate procedures should they become unduly upset after sharing their experiences with us? Are bereavement researchers themselves skilled and qualified enough to conduct this sensitive work? Indeed, what skills and competencies are *necessary*? Are we rigorous in matters of confidentiality and the storing of data?

There are a number of additional focal concerns for the future. Systems for protecting informed consent and participants' rights need to be systematically developed among the community of bereavement researchers. Inclusion of diverse samples of bereaved people in research investigations, across age, minority, cross-cultural, and gender groups, extending scope beyond the predominant investigation of reactions of White, female, middle-class Westerners is necessary. Likewise, we need systematic assessment of the risks versus benefits of conducting bereavement research: The simple principle that it "does no harm" is an inadequate criterion and is possibly based on a false conclusion (cf. chapter 30, this volume). Cook argues for the inclusion in future studies of participants actually in the discussion of research ethics (chapter 6, this volume). Although this has potential benefits, it also needs careful consideration. We need to assess the impact of such involvement on the respondent him- or herself, and we need to evaluate the specific uses of this strategy for research. In this connection, bereavement researchers would do well to learn how similar concerns have been resolved by our colleagues in the medical and clinical research communities.

A few comments that have been generally helpful are worth mentioning in conclusion. A golden rule is to "do what you think is right" (Folkman, personal communication, 1999; see also Sales & Folkman, in press). Although this may sound simplistic and nebulous, undoubtedly those researchers who have been in the field for some years can think back to occasions when such a guiding principle has helped toward making the most difficult of ethical decisions. A further guideline for ethical conduct of researchers themselves is to recognize the value of consultation within the bereavement research community. Although the responsibility for dealing with ethical dilemmas lies with the investigator, it is invaluable to share concerns with more experienced colleagues, not only to hear new angles on a problem but to realize that personal doubts have resonance among others.

THE CONSEQUENCES OF BEREAVEMENT

Two themes were central in examining the consequences of bereavement in this volume, following our previous assessment of necessary developments (M. Stroebe et al., 1993)—namely, the life span and the social context of bereavement. Before turning to issues arising in these two areas, some general points about the course and consequences of grief need to be made.

The Duration of Grief, Vulnerabilities, and "Recovery"

Through their empirical studies, researchers have done much to change assumptions about the duration of and "recovery" from the impact of bereavement. However, misinterpretations of Lindemann's (1944/1979) statements still occur in some sources, promoting the idea that intense grief is resolved after a few weeks ("With eight to ten interviews in which the psychiatrist shares the grief work, and with a period of from four to six weeks, it was ordinarily possible to *settle an uncomplicated and undistorted grief reaction*" Lindemann, 1944/1979, p. 67; emphasis ours). In general, expectations are no longer that it takes a calendar year, nor that one returns to a baseline state of well-being. Rather, contemporary understanding is that most people adapt over time, usually taking a year or two, but even then that they are different after their loss. Most bereaved persons get used to their loss, but they do not get over it. It is now well-recognized that some aspects of grief may never end, even among those who appear to adapt and get on with their lives (e.g., chapter 10, this volume). It is also recognized that distress after bereavement does not decrease monotonically: "The level of distress can rise as well as fall" (Weiss, 1999, p. 3). Exciting new statistical techniques are being used to identify such fluctuations within longitudinal data sets (cf. Folkman, 1999). Through these, it should be possible to "plot" the course of grief more intricately.

There is continued discussion about use of the various terms *recovery*, *resolution*, and so on, these having become unpopular because they are inaccurate. It is more important now to increase understanding of the course of grief and its fluctuations, for example, in emotional states and current life adaptations, and for this we need further refinement to make better predictions. In this context, it would be useful to follow a distinction suggested in the chapters of Pennebaker, Zech, and Rimé (chapter 23, this volume) and of W. Stroebe and Schut (chapter 16)—namely, to distinguish the consequences of bereavement in terms of (a) *emotional recovery from loss* and (b) *vulnerability to mental and physical health consequences*. Put simply, the former measures "grief" and the latter, general health detriments, including illnesses and ailments. Until now, researchers have tended to select from the range of potential (mostly negative) dependent variables (depression; visits to doctors; mortality; grief symptoms, and so forth) and to treat these as alternatives (a matter of the researcher's choice), and somewhat equivalent (comparable duration effects; equal impact across risk factors). These generic versus grief-specific measures have been distinguished, the latter being regarded as "better" than the former mainly for their ability to capture the complexity of grief and grieving (chapter 5, this volume). Yet, more fundamentally, they reflect different coping mechanisms (including different physiological correlates), and there may be differential predictions with respect to their manifestation over the course of time. To take a hypothetical (but plausible) example: A bereaved woman may openly express her emotions of grief. In general, one would expect the emotional impact to be greater, nearer to the onset of bereavement. Over time, there would be decline in symptoms and gradual emotional recovery. By contrast, a bereaved man may suppress his emotions, the overt "baseline" of emotional impact being, then, lower. But his suppression of grief may be associated with higher physiological arousal (cf. chapter 22, this volume), which in turn, may affect the neuroendocrine and immune systems, causing increased vulnerability to physical (and stress-related) health consequences. Compared to emotional recovery variables, these bereavement-related health vulnerabilities might *increase* in time, at least for those whose etiology (course of illness) takes time to develop. Clearly, such predictions and their pathways need further scrutiny, but ultimately, it seems likely that an integral part of future research will be to make differential predictions according to more precisely specified types of variables.

If the extraordinary recent research is anything to go by, we can expect a major drive of new investigation in this area to focus on further identification of physiological mechanisms in the pathway from the psychological experience of bereavement to the onset of physiological, health, and disease processes (cf. chapters 21 and 29, this volume). Physiological mechanisms need to be examined not only in relationship to these health detriments but also in relationship to emotional upset and recovery, as distinguished previously. In the next 10 years, work at this interface could change much of our thinking about bereavement.

Risk Factors

As pointed out previously, research on risk factors for poor bereavement outcome has been hampered by methodological shortcomings. It is surprising how little is still known about relative vulnerabilities, in particular those reflecting personality differences. It is intuitively convincing that personality factors make a critical difference in the way a person comes to terms with loss. Yet the list of factors that we know little or nothing about is long: perceived control; perceived just-world beliefs; perceived social support (who, whom, when); religiosity; perhaps "counterfactual thinkers"; self-esteem and self-perception; confronters versus avoiders (or monitors–blunters; sensitizers–repressors), and so on. As W. Stroebe and Schut point out in chapter 16, we also still need to disentangle the effects that are bereavement-specific from general personality styles. For example, the preoccupied–attached individuals after bereavement were probably preoccupied–attached individuals in marriage (e.g., chapter 4, this volume). Similarly, although it is true to say, as Parkes does in chapter 2, that "women are much more likely to admit to psychiatric symptoms and to seek psychiatric help during the first year after bereavement than men," women in general are more likely to admit to such symptoms and seek psychiatric help. It is widowers who are relatively more vulnerable during bereavement. Thus care must be taken in interpreting such differences as main effects or as interactions.

Bereavement Across the Life Span

The contributors in Part III clearly demonstrate that developmental–life span considerations need to be taken into account to understand the experience of bereavement among children and adolescents, and younger versus older adults. Identifying these factors is more important than trying to establish a hierarchy of types of grieving, as reflected in the claim that loss of a child is "the worst" type of bereavement that can happen to one. Following the leads suggested by Oltjenbruns (chapter 8), Balk and Corr (chapter 9), Rubin and Malkinson (chapter 10), and Moss, Moss, and Hansson (chapter 11), future research needs to address such questions as,

How is bereavement in childhood (adolescence, etc.) different from other types of bereavement? What makes this type of loss unique? How can we understand the phenomena from a life span perspective and intervene where necessary?

There is, for example, still surprisingly little sound empirical research on bereavement in childhood. In particular, very little empirical research assesses the implications for the bereavement experience of developing capacities according to age, experience, and cognitive capacity (e.g., chapter 8, this volume). To this end, such research as that of van Essen (1999) should prove useful. Van Essen's approach differs from many in that, rather than imposing an adult interpretation on children's grief, her research has concentrated on listening to the voices of young children, to capture the nature of their unique experience of grief. Furthermore, we need to place childhood and adolescent grief in its family context, to increase understanding of how grieving parents and siblings may ameliorate or complicate the course of grieving in a young child. Similar concerns arise for research among elderly individuals, complicated as bereavement is at this stage of life by the experience of multiple and sequential losses and bereavement overload, and frequent social isolation. Research among elderly bereaved people, then, needs to take more account of the social context and of age-related declines that may exacerbate the bereavement experience.

The Social and Cultural Context of Grief and Grieving

The need to account for the social and cultural contexts of bereavement has already become evident. As the chapters in Part IV demonstrate, grief is in many ways both a social and an intrapersonal event. Bereavement research has long included "social" aspects such as the role of social support in bereavement outcome, or the effects of disclosure on health, or the impact of intervention. However, the emphasis has remained largely intrapersonal in focus (e.g., researchers have examined the contribution of these variables to individual recovery). Only recently have researchers extended the interpersonal perspective to examine such topics as the interpersonal regulation of emotion, social construction of the life and death of the deceased, and impact on ongoing relationships (e.g., chapters 13, 14, and 15, this volume). These represent important new themes for future research.

To take three examples: There is considerable evidence that the meaning of a death is, in part, socially constructed (e.g., chapters 13, 15, and 19, this volume). However, questions remain about the impact of interpersonal constructions on the course of both family and individual grieving. Likewise, we need to know how one bereaved person's way of grieving may affect—and be affected by—that of another. Grieving does not take place in isolation but among other grievers and nongrievers. Finally, it is evident that bereavement affects ongoing relationships, which in turn affect the experience of grief. Yet some writers argue for positive, others for negative effects. To illustrate, in different studies following the death of a child, parental relationships have been found to deteriorate, to show no changes, or to improve (Dijkstra & Stroebe, 1998). Plausible explanations for these apparent discrepancies might be advanced in terms of potential *polarization effects* (e.g., some couples experience greater closeness; others greater conflict) or of *enhancement–aggravation phenomena* (e.g., couples may be more mutually supportive but still feel relationship conflict). These proposals need empirical examination (M. Stroebe & Schut, 1999).

A number of authors also argue the need for cross-cultural expansion of bereavement research (e.g., chapters 2, 13, and 14, this volume). We need studies of grief in cultures very different from our own using culturally sensitive techniques and involving researchers who are themselves from these cultures. We also need studies of ethnic minority groups within Western cultures, particularly to enhance understanding of their support needs. Even subgroups within our own culture, such as males versus females or older versus younger generations, are insufficiently represented in research, although we know that there are different meanings ("cultures") of bereavement between such groups. To put it another way, we need to address the concern that our model of grief is based on reactions of a Western, middle-class, White female.

What about the question, Is grief universal?? According to Parkes, "There is something that all who suffer a major loss have in common and the word 'grief' does have a universal meaning which transcends culture" (chapter 2). The search for evolutionary functions of grief would seek to establish adaptive features of these supposed universals (chapter 12, this volume), whereas a social constructionist perspective would deny the "essentiality and universality of thoughts, feelings, and words said in and about bereavement" (Rosenblatt, chapter 13). However, the latter perspective does not deny commonality among grieving humans. It seeks instead to explore malleability in cross-cultural perspective. At this point, it would seem more useful to ask "How malleable is grief?" rather than "Is it universal?" The impact of death rituals, cultural constructions of the ongoing relationship with the deceased, and notions of culturally deviant grieving provide fascinating leads in this connection (e.g., chapter 13, this volume). A Western observer's account of traditional Tibetan customs and reactions, for example, underscores the influence of cultural variation: "Grieving over the deceased as we [Westerners] do . . . is unknown in Tibet. Grief at the loss *is overcome* through the thought of a quick rebirth, Buddhists are not afraid of death. Lamps are left burning in the house of the deceased for forty-nine days, following which the deceased is no longer spoken of. Widows and widower are allowed to remarry after a lapse of time, and then normal life continues" (Harrer, 1997, p. 266; our translation; emphasis ours).

UNDERSTANDING COPING PROCESSES IN COMING TO TERMS WITH LOSS

In the limited space of this chapter, it seems important in considering coping to focus on (a) the controversy around broken versus continuing bonds and (b) the related, and more fundamental, discussions on "grief work" and adaptive coping. It is accurate to say that research on coping processes, involving the identification of mechanisms underlying ways that bereaved people grieve, is one of the most exciting new fields of research at the start of this new century.

Relinquishing and Retaining Bonds

The controversy about broken versus continued bonds has not so much to do with which of these pertains but about the interpretation of established theorists' views on retaining versus breaking bonds. Have we (including some of the editors—see M. Stroebe, Gergen, Gergen, & Stroebe, 1992) represented earlier theorists properly? Did they really mean that ties to the deceased need to be relinquished? At particular issue there is criticism of continuing bonds theorists' distortion of attachment theory. Shaver (see Fraley & Shaver, 1999; chapter 4, this volume) argues that Bowlby (e.g., 1980) himself recognized the adaptive functions of retained bonds: Historically, he had already said what others later presented afresh. Shaver is correct to point out that credit should have been given where it was due. In his later writing, Bowlby (1980) made reference to ways that deceased persons continue to be remembered and referred to. However, much of Bowlby's theoretical reasoning focused on understanding how and why persons come to detach and withdraw from deceased loved ones. This is a major theme in his work, deriving from his observations of young children separated from their mothers and reflected in the title of his book, *The Making and Breaking of Affectional Bonds* (Bowlby, 1979). His early work established phases of reactions to separation, including as a third "detachment." In general, the chapters of this volume show evidence of the continued impact of Bowlby's attachment theory on contemporary bereavement research. It is now important to move the field forward by examining to what extent and under what circumstances bonds continue to be retained versus relinquished, and to look into the functions (both sustaining and distressing) that these might serve for bereaved individuals (e.g., chapter 19, this volume).

Theoretical predictions are needed to structure the research on continuing bonds. Attachment theory provides an appropriate framework (e.g., chapters 2 and 4, this volume). Rubin and Malkinson's (chapter 10, this volume) theoretical analysis of bereaved individuals' evolving and resolving experience of the relationship with the deceased fits into an attachment-continued–broken bonds framework well too. Our suggestion to further such theoretical reasoning is the following: It could be predicted that differences in the ways that bereaved individuals retain or relinquish bonds will depend on their style of attachment. Secure individuals would be expected to differ from insecure ones, and different types of insecure attachments should differ in bonding, just as Parkes (chapter 2, this volume) and Shaver and Tancredy (chapter 4, this volume) predicted for different types of complicated bereavement reactions. Secure individuals might be expected to oscillate between relinquishing and retaining bonds—perhaps best described as a healthy "relocation" of the deceased; insecure–anxious/ambivalent people would be expected to retain their bond in an extreme (clinging) manner, whereas the insecure–avoidant people would be likely to relinquish their ties completely. Insecure–disorganized/disoriented people would display disturbed, somewhat incoherent attempts to retain versus break the bond with the deceased. Such hypotheses can be further explored and empirically tested.

Grief Work and Adaptive Coping Processes

Grief work has been one of the most important concepts within the scientific discipline of bereavement, as well as among lay communities in Western culture. But is it not, in fact, redundant? Critical appraisal of the concept goes back beyond the usual citations, to the early work of Rosenblatt (see Rosenblatt, 1983; Rosenblatt, Walsh, & Jackson, 1976). The chapters in Parts V and VI continue to query its validity (e.g., chapter 18, this volume). In our view, the concept is now no longer useful, because it is too broadly defined in theoretical and empirical terms. It has been superseded by a number of more narrowly defined terms to describe components of coping, such as "rumination," "dissociation," "confrontation–avoidance." Methodological advancements (e.g., diary monitoring, video analyses, physiological measures) have provided more differentiated analyses of the coping process. Theoretical analysis has identified component parts of coping and differentiated them from outcome variables—for example, depression (or rumination, yearning, pining). These are either well-controlled for as confounding variables, or clearly specified as either coping or outcome variables.

In the coping domain, the examination of process is now based on theoretical models (see chapter 17, this volume). Intriguing results are emerging. For example, Folkman in chapter 25 pinpointed the adaptive functions of positive affect during the stress of bereavement, identified meaning-based coping processes that support positive affect, and incorporated these concepts into cognitive stress theory. Bonanno in chapter 22 showed that in contrast to the predictions of the grief work approach, minimization of the experience and nonexpression of emotion was associated with improved functioning over the first two years of bereavement. Hall and Irwin in chapter 21 were able, for the first time, to pit the hypothesis that changes in physiology mediate the relationship between bereavement and increased risk to health with the alternative one, integrating physiological changes into the coping process, that physiological measures act as a signal, or index, of danger to current and future functioning and are not necessarily a mechanism for adverse health outcomes.

Such studies encourage new questions: Should we conclude that the expression of negative affect is maladaptive? Should people hide their emotions of grief? Evidence does, though, seem to suggest that negative emotions need to be confronted and possibly expressed. Traditional notions seem still to be viable to some extent, but current knowledge is beginning to show that there is more to adaptive coping. For example, we need to incorporate analyses of the role of avoidant processing into research, following the lead of Bonanno and others. Fine-grained analysis should help dissipate the "myth" that the failure to experience distress is problematic (e.g., chapter 18). By now it is well-recognized that "no grief" can indeed mean an instance of delayed grief, indicating defensive refusal to experience grief early after bereavement (as Parkes suggested in chapter 2). Alternatively, those who never display grief, either early on or later, may be characterized as not attached in the first place or as distancing–attached (Weiss, 1999; chapter 3, this volume). What we need now is "identification of the dynamics that underlie different grief trajectories" (Weiss, 1999, p. 4). Contemporary research is making inroads. For example, Folkman (1999) has recently adopted an approach that looks at a wide range of predictor variables of the various styles of distress over time (ascending grief over time is not "delayed grief"). This work is more promising than the earlier labeling of a category of bereaved individuals as "deniers" because it addresses process variables. Consequent research also needs to examine the mutual impact of such grief trajectories: What is the impact of one person's grieving on that of another? How do people with different ways of going about their grieving do so in the company of each other? What are the implications of this social context of grieving?

We also need to understand the role of positive affect more precisely: Is it enough to feel positive affect, or is it positive (re)construction of the meaning of loss and related experience that enhances adjustment? Research suggests the latter (e.g., chapter 17, this volume). There are good reasons to argue that it is the *change* in thinking patterns over time, not simply thinking positively about the loss, that predicts adjustment and improved health. Indeed, thinking without cognitive restructuring has been characterized as equivalent to rumination, which is associated with poor adjustment (e.g., chapters 4 and 23, this volume). Cross-cultural studies would also provide invaluable extensions to this research. For example, some societies encourage overt expression of grief by rituals, traditions, and belief systems, and others do not, some permitting only positive expressions, others negative. It should be possible to study the reasons for and advantages versus disadvantages associated with each type of response or cultural prescription.

It should be evident by now that research has become much more focused on specific dimensions of coping that affect the bereavement process (in contrast to the wide variety incorporated into generic coping inventories), rather leaving behind discussion of phases or tasks. Key dimensions are confrontation–avoidance; emotion- versus problem-focus (potentially adapted to loss- versus restoration-oriented); control (regulatory) and (re)appraisal mechanisms. These are becoming integrated into our models of coping with bereavement, but further specification is needed, and we need to develop valid measures that keep abreast of theorizing (see chapter 20, this volume). For example, with respect to confrontation–avoidance, leads can be taken from Horowitz's formulation of intrusion–avoidance and operationalization within the Impact of Event Scale (IES; Horowitz, Wilner, & Alvarez, 1979). However, as Parkes (chapter 2, this volume) points out, the IES does not distinguish between intrusion–preoccupation of happy memories versus memories of painful or life-threatening events. The former are normal reactions, the latter are diagnostic symptoms of posttraumatic stress disorder. Thus for bereavement research purposes, further differentiation is needed between obsessive preoccupation with painful versus happy memories, and the scale needs adaptation from general focus on trauma to specific focus on bereavement.

In conclusion, it is interesting to note that nearly two decades ago Rosenblatt (1983) called for revision of our ideas on processes of discontinuity and emotional control in grieving: "It seems an appropriate amendment to the [grief work] theory to state that people will typically withdraw at times, that this withdrawal is related to social and subsistence demands and perhaps to the demands of the grief work process itself, and that periodic withdrawal may facilitate grief work" (Rosenblatt, 1983, p. 154). As we have seen, these aspects are at the center of contemporary theoretical and empirical investigation.

IMPLICATIONS FOR THE CARE OF BEREAVED INDIVIDUALS

We have stressed throughout that this volume is primarily a research-oriented rather than an applied volume. Yet the theme "care" is as important as "consequences" and "coping" because care of bereaved individuals needs to be guided by a sound body of theoretical and empirical knowledge. This is well-illustrated by selecting major contemporary issues.

Pathological Grief as a Diagnostic Category

There is no doubt that providing adequate clinical, psychiatric, and medical care for bereaved individuals who need it is a concern for researchers, because this needs to be directed from sound understanding of the complications of grief. Should pathological grief be a separate diagnostic category? Can it be reliably distinguished from other forms of grief or disorders, including uncomplicated grief? Prigerson and Jacobs's answer in chapter 27 to these questions is yes. They further argue for the need to have traumatic grief included in diagnostic classification systems such as the *DSM* (American Psychiatric Association, 1994). There are good arguments for this. It would standardize clinical assessment, treatment planning, and qualifying for third-party (insurance) payment for services. Yet consideration of the implications of a diagnostic category (and further research) is also called for (see M. Stroebe et al., 2000). It is a major concern that diagnostic status may bring about a "medicalization" of grief and cause a shift beyond the realms of family context and care. Also there are currently a number of different proposals for diagnostic criteria deriving from attachment theory on the one hand and stress response syndrome theory on the other (cf. Horowitz et al., 1997; Jacobs, 1993, 1999; Hartz, 1986; Raphael, 1989; chapter 27, this volume). Thus scientists need to reach formal consensus on core components, diagnostic criteria, even perhaps theoretical underpinnings for different pathologies of grief. Furthermore, there is the danger of losing sight of the fact that family and friends can meet the needs of most bereaved people (see chapter 2, this volume), which may bias research investigation. A valid comparison is the creation of posttraumatic stress disorder as a diagnostic category. Following its entry into *DSM-III*, "The condition received so much attention that it is sometimes, mistakenly, thought to be the commonest consequence of psychological trauma" (chapter 2).

The relationship (overlap–distinction) of pathological grief with other disorders such as anxiety, depression, and PTSD needs further specification and theoretical understanding (e.g., with respect to differential etiological factors). We need to examine further the extent to which other disorders are manifestations of grief or separate disorders in vulnerable bereaved individuals. For example, it seems clear from the contributions of this volume (e.g., chapters 2, 26, and 28, this volume) that complicated grief is a qualitatively different phenomenon from PTSD, with distinct causes and features, though PTSD may coexist with grief (making Prigerson & Jacobs's term *traumatic grief* a little confusing with reactions to traumatic bereavement, as Parkes points out in chapter 2). Future research needs to establish what types of grief and what types of traumas have convergent versus discrepant symptomatology. What treatment strategies are indicated by this? Should they be different for different disorders?

When (Not) to Intervene

There is consensus among the researchers represented in this volume that methods of counseling and therapy are only needed and effective for a minority of high-risk bereaved people. According to current indications (more studies are needed) the category "high-risk" notably includes bereaved children (see chapter 30, this volume). Parkes (1998) put the argument for such a high-risk focus of intervention succinctly:

> There is no evidence that all bereaved people will benefit from counseling and research has shown no benefit to arise from the routine referral of people to counseling for no other reason than that they have suffered a bereavement. Such routine offers of help may cause family members and others to feel superfluous and to back off when they are most needed. (p. 18)

Raphael, Dobson and Minkov endorse this in chapter 26, arguing strongly that there is no justification for routine intervention in terms of any therapeutic modalities, either psychotherapeutic or pharmacological. This does not mean that people should not ask for help (informal support; professional counseling; medical advice) when they feel they need it. It also does not mean that all those who are needy are provided with help or that an offer or suggestion of help should not be initiated when need is perceived. It simply emphasizes the point that intervention should not be offered on a routine basis. There are a number of considerations that underline this. Extrapolating from contemporary research on coping, it seems likely that retaining internal control, being active rather than passive in grieving, and not being placed in a "victim" role would all be conducive to adaptation. Finally, concern about withdrawal of the family is not just speculation. In a recent study in The Netherlands (de Keijser, 1997), the role of the social network was shown to decrease during and after grief counseling, compared to a nonintervention control group. Further studies of the social implications of care-giving policy developments are called for.

The fact that intervention is not indicated for bereaved persons in the "no–low risk" categories (see chapter 30, this volume) raises intriguing questions for future research: Why do others *not* make a difference? Does normal grief simply run some (culturally appropriate) inevitable course that is impervious to outside influence? Could it be that leaving control over emotional reactions firmly in the hands of grief-stricken individuals actually furthers the adjustment process? Even more fundamentally, we can ask, What is wrong with suffering grief over the loss of a loved one—in other words, why should bereaved people be urged to get over loss quickly, even painlessly, and get on with life?

What Type of Care for Whom

Research has progressed a long way from the simple belief that support of others is needed to help people through grief in cases of uncomplicated bereavement, whereas complicated forms need professional assistance to guide them toward normalization of working through grief (Hansson, Stroebe, & Stroebe, 1988). Understanding of the coping process has suggested specific cognitive components and dual processing (see chapter 17, this volume) that have implications for the provision of care. Research is still needed to determine precisely what works in particular interventions, if it is not just the facilitation of grief work that is instrumental. Hall and Irwin (chapter 21, this volume) argued the need for further research to focus also on teaching coping skills, extending social support networks, stabilizing sleep–wake routines, and preventing bereavement-related depression. Potential clinical benefits would include improved physiological as well as psychological functioning.

A great stride forward in research is the theoretically based intervention program of Fleming and Robinson (chapter 28, this volume). Their approach highlights the need to increase efforts to understand bereavement as a process of meaning reconstruction and of the rebuilding of previously held assumptions–assumptive worlds. This intervention-oriented chapter resonates with others in the volume (cf. chapters 2, 13, and 15, this volume), applying theoretical ideas on meaning reconstruction to assessment of and intervention for complications of bereavement.

Another important question concerns whether we are offering the right kind of care to the right bereaved people. Our own research (Schut, Stroebe, van den Bout, & de Keijser, 1997) suggested that this is not necessarily the case. We may be supporting bereaved individuals in the way that they *want* rather than the way that they *need*. For example, women tend to talk about their feelings and to seek counseling, whereas men tend to avoid counseling and to suppress their feelings. Yet distressed widows benefited from practical advice, and widowers from encouragement to focus on their emotions. A small independent study by Hopmeyer and Werk (1994) indicated, however, that widows and widowers look for and expect precisely the opposite to what they actually need (according to our results) from bereavement groups (women emotional support; men practical solutions). We must be cautious in generalizing from the Schut et al. (1997) results to other types of losses and to uncomplicated bereavements (those in the study had elevated rates of symptomatology). Patterns of male–female expression of emotions may also be changing in Western culture (cf. Walter, 1999). In fact, exploration of the generalizability of these results needs to be high on the research agenda. The broader societal implications of such research also require further investigation. What, for example, are the implications of such results for the workplace? Should we be arguing for the extension of compassionate leave to provide a conducive environment for the confrontation of emotions? Scientific judgments differ on this point. Eyetsemitan (1998) argued,

> By allowing time off only for funerals and expecting their bereaved workers to resume full-blown responsibilities immediately afterwards, organizations promote "Stifled Grief"; that is, grief denied its normal course. (p. 469)

Russell's (1998) conclusion was different:

> Those who have suffered a bereavement may feel that their work gives them a sense of purpose as something which is still part of their life and which has not been lost. (p. 11)

We must continue to question whether our care-giving and intervention programming is based on an outdated myth that grief work simply needs to be done.

CONCLUSION

From an editorial vantage point, this volume has provided a remarkable contrast with the previous one (M. Stroebe et al., 1993). Then it seemed that the chapters provided a representative body of knowledge of basic principles, informing readers across the range of fundamental issues about bereavement. What was necessary, it emerged, was not more of the same for the future, but the investigation of new themes that could be addressed once these basics were reasonably well-established (given, of course, that controversies remained). The identification of important new themes in that earlier Handbook led to the planning for the current volume. In concluding this volume, however, the vision is somewhat different: What is needed now is an extension, not a major change, in the scope of forthcoming bereavement research. Although this concluding chapter has identified a great number of new research questions, basically these reflect important continuations of the research described and issues raised in this volume. Of course, there is room for extension to new topics. As we noted at the outset, coverage has necessarily been selective. Nevertheless, the themes of consequences, coping, and care constitute fruitful areas for further investigation. At the same time, it needs to be recognized that societal changes are likely to alter the bereavement experience in ways that we can only speculate on now, and these, in turn, will affect its scientific investigation. We need only mention the growing tolerance toward euthanasia and assisted suicide in some societies and the role of the Internet in the bereavement area (e.g., public memorials; distribution of information about the grieving process; offers of bereavement services). In other words, the culture within which people grieve will continue to evolve and demand sensitivity on the part of researchers.

REFERENCES

American Psychiatric Association. (1994). *Diagnostic and statistical manual of mental disorders* (4th ed.). Washington, DC: Author.

Archer, J. (1999). *The nature of grief: The evolution and psychology of reactions to loss.* London: Routledge.

Bowlby, J. (1979). *The making and breaking of affectional bonds.* London: Tavistock.

Bowlby, J. (1980). *Attachment and loss. Vol. 3. Loss: Sadness and depression.* London: Hogarth.

Cassidy, J., & Shaver, P. R. (1999). *Handbook of attachment: Theory, research and clinical applications.* New York: Guilford Press.

de Keijser, J. (1997). *Sociale steun en professionele begleiding bij rouw.* [Social support and professional counseling for the bereaved]. Amsterdam: Thesis.

Dijkstra, I., & Stroebe, M. (1998). The impact of a child's death on parents: A myth (not yet) disproved? *Journal of Family Studies, 4,* 159–185.

Eyetsemitan, F. (1998). Stifled grief in the workplace. *Death Studies, 22,* 469–479.

Folkman, S. (1997). Use of bereavement narratives to predict well-being in gay men whose partners died of AIDS—Four theoretical perspectives. *Journal of Personality and Social Psychology, 72,* 851–854.

Folkman, S. (1999, August 20–24). *Characterizing bereavement response: Form matters.* Paper presented at the American Psychological Association Annual Conference, Boston.

Fraley, R. C., & Shaver, P. (1999). Loss and bereavement: Attachment theory and recent controversies concerning "grief work" and the nature of detachment. In J. Cassidy & P. R. Shaver (Eds.), *Handbook of attachment: Theory, research, and clinical applications* (pp. 735–759). New York: Guilford Press.

Hansson, R. O., Stroebe, M., & Stroebe, W. (1988). Bereavement and widowhood. *Journal of Social Issues, 44,* whole issue.

Harrer, H. (1997). *Zeven jaar in Tibet.* Amsterdam, The Netherlands: Pandora.

Hartz, G. (1986). Adult grief and its interface with mood disorder: Proposal for a new diagnosis of complicated bereavement. *Comprehensive Psychiatry, 27,* 60–64.

Harvey, J., (1998). *Perspectives on loss: A sourcebook.* Philadelphia: Brunner/Mazel.

Harvey, J. H., & Miller, E. D. (1998). Toward a psychology of loss. *Psychological Science, 9,* 429–434.

Hopmeyer, E., & Werk, A. (1994). A comparative study of family bereavement groups. *Death Studies, 18,* 243–256.

Horowitz, M., Siegel, B., Holen, A., Bonanno, G., Milbrath, C., & Stinson, C.

(1997). Diagnostic criteria for complicated grief disorder. *American Journal of Psychiatry, 137*, 1157–1160.

Horowitz, M., Wilner, N., & Alvarez, W. (1979). Impact of Event Scale: A measure of subjective stress. *Psychosomatic Medicine, 41*, 209–218.

Jacobs, S. (1993). *Pathologic grief: Maladaptation to loss.* Washington DC: American Psychiatric Press.

Jacobs, S. (1999). *Traumatic grief: Diagnosis, treatment, and prevention.* New York: Taylor & Francis.

Kato, P. M., & Mann, T. (1999). A synthesis of psychological interventions for the bereaved. *Clinical Psychology Review, 19*, 275–296.

Levy, L. H., Derby, J. F., & Martinkowski, K. S. (1992). The question of who participates in bereavement research and the bereavement risk index. *Omega: Journal of Death and Dying, 25*, 225–238.

Lindemann, E. (1979). Symptomatology and management of acute grief. *American Journal of Psychiatry, 101*, 141–148. (Original work published 1944)

Litterer Allumbaugh, D., & Hoyt, W. T. (1999). Effectiveness of grief therapy: A meta-analysis. *Journal of Counseling Psychology, 46*, 370–380.

Parkes, C. M. (1995). Guidelines for conducting ethical bereavement research. *Death Studies, 19*, 171–181.

Parkes, C. M. (1998). Editorial. *Bereavement Care, 17*, 18.

Parkes, C. M., Relf, M., & Couldrick, A. (1996). *Counselling in terminal care and bereavement.* Leicester, UK: British Psychological Society Books.

Raphael, B. (1989, May). *Diagnostic criteria for bereavement reactions.* Paper presented at the International Symposium on Pathologic Bereavement, Seattle, WA.

Rosenblatt, P. (1983). *Bitter, bitter tears: Nineteenth century diarists and twentieth century grief theories.* Minneapolis: University of Minnesota Press.

Rosenblatt, P. (1995). Ethics of qualitative interviewing with grieving families. *Death Studies, 19*, 139–155.

Rosenblatt, P., Walsh, R., & Jackson, D. (1976). *Grief and mourning in cross-cultural perspective.* New Haven, CT: Human Relations Area Files.

Russell, K. (1998). Returning to employment after bereavement. *Bereavement Care, 17*, 11–13.

Sales, B., & Folkman, S. (in press). *Ethical issues in the conduct of research with human participants.* Washington, DC: American Psychological Association.

Schut, H., Stroebe, M., van den Bout, J., & de Keijser, J. (1997). Intervention for the bereaved: Gender differences in the efficacy of grief counselling. *British Journal of Clinical Psychology, 36*, 63–72.

Stroebe, M., Gergen, M., Gergen, K., & Stroebe, W. (1992). Broken hearts: Love and death in historical perspective. *American Psychologist, 47*, 1205–1212.

Stroebe, M., & Schut, H. (1999). The dual process model of coping with bereavement: Rationale and description. *Death Studies, 23*, 197–224.

Stroebe, M., & Stroebe, W. (1989). Who participates in bereavement research? A review and empirical study. *Omega, 20,* 1–29.

Stroebe, M., Stroebe, W., & Hansson, R. (Eds.). (1993). *Handbook of Bereavement: Theory, Research and Intervention.* New York: Cambridge University Press.

Stroebe, M., van Son, M., Stroebe, W., Kleber, R., Schut, H., & van den Bout, J. (2000). On the classification and diagnosis of pathological grief. *Clinical Psychology Review, 20,* 57–75.

Van Essen, I. (1999). *Ik krijk tranen in mijn ogen als ik an je denk* [I get tears in my eyes when I think of you]. Amsterdam: Bezig Bee.

Walter, T. (1999). *On bereavement: The culture of grief.* Buckingham: Open University Press.

Weiss, R. (1999, August 20–24). *What's new in bereavement research: Discussant's comments.* Paper presented at the American Psychological Association Annual Conference, Boston.

AUTHOR INDEX

Numbers in italics refer to listings in the reference sections; *n* following a page number indicates a listing in a note.

Berry, J. O., 242, 256

Berry, L. C., 40, 44, 95, 117, 617, 619, 620, 622, 632, 635

Berry, S., 474, 491

Bersoff, D. N., 139, 140

Berson, R. J., 210, 215

Best, K. M., 213, 215

Beutler, L., 222, 234, 650, 666

Bevilacqua, M., 674, 676, 694, 701

Beyer, B., 684, 695

Bierhals, A. J., 40, 44, 94, 95, 96, 98, 99, 117, 266, 281, 482, 491, 603, 606, 610, 611, 614, 615, 616, 617, 619, 620, 622, 632, 634, 635, 636

Bierhals, E. J., 614, 615, 616, 617, 618, 619, 623, 632, 635

Bierie, M., 177, 197

Bifulco, A., 180, 194, 306, 322

Billings, A. G., 360, 367, 379, 399, 455, 466

Biondi, M., 266, 279

Birenbaum, L. K., 186, 187, 193, 194

Birtchnell, J., 180, 181, 193

Bisson, J., 422, 428

Black, D., 596, 601, 607, 712, 714, 719, 733

Black, H. K., 248, 255

Blalock, J. E., 673, 677, 693, 702

Blaney, N. T., 266, 267, 279, 483, 488, 671, 675, 676, 677, 680, 681, 683, 684, 685, 686, 687, 688, 689, 690, 691, 692, 693, 695, 696, 697

Blaney, P. H., 549, 559

Blank, A., 656, 667

Blankenship, M., 100, 114

Blatt, S. J., 222, 228, 234

Blazer, D. G., 245, 255, 473, 474, 488

Blehar, M. C., 37, 38, 42, 73, 74, 83, 304, 320

Blisett, S. E., 506, 513

Bloch, S., 153, 164, 302, 313, 323, 596, 608

Block, D., 304, 305, 306, 324

Blomkvist, V., 681, 703

Bloom, E., 480, 481, 482, 489, 675, 676, 679, 698

Bloom, H., 83, 83

Bloom, J. R., 531, 543, 686, 702

Bluhm, H. P., 357, 368

Boca, S., 518, 519, 542

Boccellari, A., 554, 558, 560, 567, 568, 578, 581, 685, 695

Bochner, A. P., 109, 115

Bodnar, J. C., 481, 488

Bogaards, J. A., 534, 536, 543

Bohannon, J. R., 357, 368

Bohne, J. B., 153, 164

Bolger, N., 407, 419, 422, 429

Bonanno, G. A., 18, 63, 66, 68, 69, 70, 77, 83, 83, 222, 235, 306, 307, 308, 320, 323, 356, 368, 384, 385, 388, 389, 390, 393, 394, 399, 400, 405, 407, 409, 410, 411, 412, 413, 425, 493, 494, 495, 499, 500, 501, 504, 505, 508, 509, 511, 535, 538, 539, 548, 559, 573, 580, 598, 603, 608, 749, 757, 758, 760, 764

Bond, L. A., 180, 195

Bond, R. N., 676, 698, 699

Boninger, D. S., 659, 665

Bonne, O., 207, 213

Boon, M., 683, 703

Borgquist, A., 267, 279

Borne, G. J. A., 156, 162

Bornstein, M. C., 221, 234

Bornstein, P., 354, 355, 368

Borton, W., 52, 61

Borysenko, J., 676, 694

Borysenko, M., 676, 694

Boscolo, L., 332, 345, 346

Bosley, G., 126, 132, 140

Boss, P., 131, 140

Bouchard, T. J., 75, 86, 273–274, 274n, 275, 277, 282

Bourne, H. R., 676, 693–694

Bouts, P., 520, 540

Bowen, M., 312, 320

Bower, A., 252, 254

Bower, G. H., 520, 539, 548, 559

Bowes, J. M., 478, 479, 491, 603, 612

Bowker, J., 445

Bowlby, J., 9, 12, 17, 22, 29–30, 36–37, 38, 42, 45, 47–48, 51, 55, 59, 61, 64, 69, 71, 72, 73–74, 75, 78, 81–82, 84, 171–174, 193, 220, 221, 222, 223, 224, 231, 233, 234, 264, 268, 270, 279, 304, 305, 320, 356, 362, 364, 368, 376, 383, 384, 385, 399,

Bowlby, J. (*continued*)
    405, 408, 416, 416n, *425*, 432,
    445, 494, 496, 497, 498, 502,
    509, 527, *539*, 545, *559*, 564,
    571, 572, 576, *581*, 589, 607,
    616, *634*, 743, 756, *764*
Bowlby-West, L., 312, *320*
Bowles, C. A., 676, *700*
Bowman, K., 251, *254*
Boyce, T., 350, *367*
Boyer, E. L., 212, *215*
Boyle, F. M., *612*
Brabant, S., 437, *445*
Bradburn, N. M., 568, *581*
Brandon, R., 434, *445*
Braun, K. L., 108, *114*
Braun, M. L., 106, *114*
Breckenridge, J., 354, 355, *368*, 684, *694*
Brehm, J. W., 552, *562*
Brehm, S. S., 549, *560*
Brent, D. A., 615, 619, 620, *635*
Brent, S. B., 172, *196*, 265, *282*
Bretherton, I., 74, *84*, 304, 305, *320*, *321*
Breznitz, S., 221, *234*
Bricker, S. I., 80, 81, *85*
Bridge, J., 615, 619, 620, *635*
Briggs, C. L., 297, *299*
Briggs, D., 598, *611*
Bright, P. D., 202, *215*
Brill, S., 405, *425*
Brison, K. J., 293, 294, 298, *299*, 449, *466*
Broadhead, W. E., 474, *488*
Brock, D. B., 245, 249, 250, *254*, *255*
Broderick, C., 331, *346*
Brody, D. S., 575, *582*
Brody, J. L., 138, *140*
Brom, D., 380, *400*, 600, 601, *609*, 727, 728, 730, *733*
Brönfenbrenner, U., 315, *321*
Brown, B. H., 202, *215*
Brown, E., 180, *193*
Brown, G., 180, *194*, 592, 604, *607*
Brown, L. B., 207, *217*
Brown, M., 675, 677, 679, *698*
Brown, R., 525, *539*, 571, *583*
Brown, R. J., 266, *281*, 483–484, *490*, 494, *513*, 681, 682, *701*
Bruce, M., 477, *489*, 675, *698*
Bruce, M. L., 409, 418, *425*, 473, 474, *488*

Bruner, J., 252, *254*
Brunswick, E., 452, *466*
Bryant, R. A., 602, *607*
Bryer, K. B., 161, *162*
Buck, R., 500, *509*
Buhrfeind, E. D., 530, 533, *543*
Bulman, R., 527, *539*
Burack, J. H., 679, *694*
Burant, C. J., 96, *117*, 251, *259*
Burgin, D., 221, *234*
Burkhalter, J. E., 671, 686, 691, 696, *697*
Burks, V. K., 357, *368*
Burnam, M. A., 474, *491*
Burnett, P., 93, 94, 95, 97, 98, *114*, *116*, 276, *281*, 289, 410, 411, 418, 427, 598, 604, 605, *609*, 614, 616, 633, *634*, *635*
Burns, D. D., 556, *559*
Burns, L. H., 221, *237*
Burton, R., 26, *43*
Buskirk, J. R., 494, 496, 497, 503, *509*
Buss, D. M., 271, 273, *279*
Buswell, B. N., 498, *511*
Butcher, J. N., 455, *466*
Butler, L. D., 549, *559*
Butler, R. N., 244, *255*
Butterfield, P. A., 264, *279*
Buysse, D. J., 480, 481, 482, 484, 485, 486, 488, 489, 490, *491*, 604, *610*
Buysse, M. K., 617, *635*
Byng-Hall, J., 221, *234*, 305, *321*
Byrne, G., 92, 97, *97n*, *115*, 578, *581*, 597, 605, *607*

Cacioppo, J. T., 505, *510*
Cai, J., 681, *700*
Cain, A., 181, *193*, 232, *234*
Cain, B. S., 232, *234*
Cain, C. K., 229, 230, *236*
Cain, K. C., 32, *44*, 92, *116*, 721, 722, 724, 725, *735*
Caldwell, N. D., 549, 550, 552, *561*
Calhoun, L., 92, *118*
Calhoun, L. G., 145, 146, 158, *162*, *166*, *167*
Callahan, J. M., 134, *142*
Calter, N., 302, 306, *321*
Camerino, M., 267, *281*, 480, *491*, 675, 678, *702*

De Graauw, K. P., 594, 608
Deimling, G. T., 276, 278
Dekaris, D., 685, 694
de Keijser, J., 33, 34, 35, 45, 712, 714,
719, 722, 724, 725, 727, 728,
730, 732, 733, 736, 761, 762,
764, 765
Delie, F., 520, 540
de Longis, A., 376, 400, 575, 577, 581,
582
DeMaso, D., 651, 667
Demi, A. S., 175, 184, 231, 236
Denney, D. R., 480, 481, 491
Denour, A., 207, 213
Derby, J. F., 357, 358, 369, 708, 709,
712, 714, 715, 734, 749, 765
de Ridder, D., 17, 379, 388, 401, 449,
452, 456, 459, 460, 462, 463,
466, 468
Derogatis, L. R., 207, 215
DeRosa, A. P., 596, 612
DeSantis, L., 101, 103, 107–108, 115,
147, 163, 200, 210, 212, 216
Desbiens, N., 251, 257
Desmarais, L., 267, 279
Deutsch, H., 410, 425, 496, 509
DeVaul, R. A., 200, 215, 458, 467, 494,
515
Deveau, E. J., 177, 194
De Vries, B., 148, 162, 226, 229, 234,
247, 248, 254, 255
Dew, M. A., 480, 481, 482, 484, 486,
488, 489, 617, 636, 679, 700
Dewey, J., 331, 346
DeWitt, K., 225, 235, 600, 608
Diamond, M., 229, 230, 236
Dichterman, D., 222, 230, 234
Dicks, H., 307, 322
Dieker, T. E., 138, 142
Diekstra, R., 157, 163, 408, 425
Diener, E., 505, 509
Dietrich, D. R., 432, 445
Digiulio, R. C., 147, 167
Dijkstra, I., 398, 399, 755, 764
Dillon, D. R., 334, 347
Dimond, M., 32, 44, 92, 116, 152, 163,
357, 359, 369, 457, 466, 548,
560, 721, 722, 724, 725, 735
Dimond, M. R., 246, 257
Dise-Lewis, J. E., 455, 467
Dobson, K., 651, 665

Dobson, M., 20, 587, 761
Docherty, J., 307, 324
Dodge, K. A., 498, 512
Doka, K., 233, 234, 251, 253, 255, 257,
652, 667
Doman, J., 94, 95, 96, 98, 99, 117, 614,
615, 616, 617, 618, 619, 623,
632, 635
Domittner, G., 354–355, 356, 371
Donnelly, D. A., 531, 539
Dorrity, K., 233, 234
Douglas, A., 435, 445
Douglas, J. D., 252, 255
Douglas, V., 180, 193
Dowe, D., 302, 313, 319, 323
Dozier, S., 523, 542
Drantell, J. J., 146, 149, 166
Dubois, P., 686, 697
Dubois, R., 200, 209, 214
Dubrow, N., 316, 322
Duchenne de Bologne, G. B., 504, 509
Duck, S., 436, 445
Duffy, E., 434, 445
Duivenvooden, H. J., 681, 683, 701
Dunahoo, C. L., 463, 467
Dunham, K., 100, 101, 103, 114
Dunkel-Schetter, C., 577, 581
Dunne, E. J., 597, 608
Dunnick, N. R., 678, 701
Dupuy, D. F., 207, 215
Dura, J. R., 682, 699
Duran, R., 267, 280, 483, 490, 680, 699
Dworkin, D. S., 137, 140, 171, 193
Dyer, C. S., 682, 699
Dykes, J. N., 686, 700
Dyregrov, A., 102n, 132, 140
Dyregrov, K., 132, 140

Easterling, L. W., 95, 97, 115, 157, 163
Edbril, S. D., 155, 166
Eddins, C., 399
Edmonds, S., 148, 163
Edwards, K., 498, 511
Egan, D. J., 710, 711, 712, 714, 716, 735
Egeland, B., 74, 87
Egelhoff, C., 436, 447
Ehrenpreis, L., 247, 260
Ehrhardt, A. A., 676, 699
Eich, E., 500, 510
Eisdorfer, C., 671, 677, 681, 683, 684,
693, 695, 697, 699

Eisenbruch, M., 207, *215*, 620, 633, *634*
Ekman, P., 69, *84*, 494, 498, 500, 502,
    504, 507, *509*, *510*
Ekstrand, M. L., 679, *694*
El-Ahmadi, A., 525, *540*
Elashoff, R., 686, *695*
Elde, C., 245, *259*, 439, *447*
Elizur, E., 161, *163*, 174, 177, 190, *194*,
    195
Ellard, J. H., 131, *140*, 551, *560*, 659,
    661, *665*
Ellis, A., 648, 654, *665*
Ellis, A. P., 452, 462, *469*
Ellis, C., 109, *115*
Ellsworth, P. C., 66, *87*, 498, 507, *510*,
    511
Embleton, G., 594, *612*
Emde, R., 317, *326*
Emery, G., 556, *559*, 649, 651, *665*
Emmons, R. A., 572, *581*
Emons, R. A., 505, *509*
Endler, N. S., 449, 453, 454, 456, 459,
    463, *467*, *468*, 565, 577, *581*,
    584
Engel, G. L., 222, *234*
Epston, D., 312, *327*, 657, *669*
Erenpreis, L., 616, *636*
Erickson, M., 181, *193*
Erikson, E., 171, 172, *194*
Erikson, E. H., 213, *215*
Espin, O., 206, *217*
Esterling, B. A., 480, 481, 482, *488*, 531,
    540
Eth, S., 34, 40, *45*
Evans, D. L., 473, 474, *490*, 679, 681,
    693, 694, 695, *700*
Everett, D. F., 245, *255*
Ewalt, P. L., 201, *215*
Exline, J. J., 233, *234*
Eyetsemitan, F., 763, *764*
Eysenck, H. J., 547, *560*
Eysenck, M. W., 547, *560*

Fadiman, A., 314, *322*
Fahey, J. L., 267, *280*, 483, *490*, 679,
    680, 686, 695, *699*
Fair, P. L., 500, *514*
Fairbanks, L., 155, *165*
Fairburn, C., 650, *665*
Fairchild, S. K., 90, 96, *115*, 242, *256*,
    494, *510*

Falck, V., 248, *255*
Falicov, C., 311, *322*
Fanos, J. H., 232, *234*
Farberow, N., 266, *279*, 355, *368*
Farhoody, N., 676, 698, *699*
Farmer, M. E., 245, *255*
Faschingbauer, T. R., 93, 94, 95, 96, *115*,
    200, *215*, 458, *467*, 711, *733*
Fasiczka, A., 94, 95, 96, 98, 99, *117*, 614,
    615, 616, 617, 618, 619, 623,
    632, *634*, *635*
Fasiczka, A. L., 485, *490*
Fast, I., 181, *193*
Fata, M., 119, *142*
Fawzy, F. I., 686, *695*
Fawzy, N. W., 686, *695*
Feaster, D., 671, 677, 683, 684, 693, *697*
Feaster, D. J., 266, 267, *279*, 483, *488*,
    675, 676, 677, 680, 681, 683,
    685, 686, 687, 688, 689, 690,
    692, 695, 696, *697*
Feifel, H., 455, *467*
Feld, S., 363, *368*
Feldman, W., 595, 597, 606, *611*
Felten, D. L., 676, *700*
Felten, S. Y., 676, *700*
Fenichel, O., 432, *445*
Fennell, M. J., 549, *560*
Fenster, L., 267, *279*
Festinger, L., 658, *665*
Field, J., 596, 603, *610*
Field, N., 306, 318, *322*
Field, N. P., 68, *84*, 356, *368*, 411, 413,
    417, *425*
Field, T., 264, *279*
Finch, A. J., Jr., 155, *164*
Fineberg, T., *422*
Finkbeiner, A., 49, *61*
Finke, L. M., 187, *194*
Finkenauer, C., 381, 382, *399*, *401*, 520,
    521, 523, 524, 525, 526, *540*,
    542
Finucane, R. C., 434, *445*
Fischer, C., 442, *445*
Fischer, K. R., 505, *513*
Fischer, K. W., 66, 67, 69, *84*
Fischer, L. R., 333, 334, *347*
Fischer, M., 678, *694*
Fischhoff, B., 661, *665*
Fish, W. C., 248, *255*
Fisher, L. D., 678, *699*

Fisher, R. A., 270, 271, 272, *279*
Fishman, B., 681, *701*
Fitzgerald, M., 250, *255*
Fitzgerald, R. G., 41, *43*, 678, 681, *701*
Fivas-Depersuing, E., 221, *234*
Flack, V. D., 226, 229, *234*
Fleishman, J. A., 684, *695*
Fleming, S. J., 20, 171, *194*, 200, 201, 203, 204, 212, *215*, 647, 651, 652, 654, 666, 668
Fletcher, M. A., 266, 267, *279*, 483, 488, 531, *540*, 675, 676, 677, 680, 681, 683, 685, 686, 687, 688, 689, 690, 692, 695, 697, *703*, 762
Floerchinger, D. S., 208, *215*
Florian, V., 80, *86*, 461, *468*
Foa, E. B., 414, 415, *425*
Fogel, B., 684, *695*
Folds, J. D., 679, 681, 693, 694, 695, *700*
Foley, D. J., 249, 250, *254*
Folkman, S., 19, *22*, 73, 107, *117*, 154, 156, 157, 160, *163*, *165*, 166, 243, 256, 350, 360, 362, *367*, *368*, 369, 376, 378, 379, 380, 387, 389, 394, 396, 399, 400, 407, 408, 409, 410, 426, 428, 449, 450, 453, 454, 455, 456, 467, 495, 497, *510*, *514*, 554, 558, 560, 564, 566, 567, 568, 570, 571, 572, 573, 575, 577, 578, 579, 581, 582, 583, 584, 683, 685, *695*, 709, 736, 745, 751, 752, 757, 758, 764, 765
Fonagy, P., 651, *669*
Forrest, A. D., 180, *194*
Forrest, G. C., 721, 722, 724, 725, *733*
Fortes, M., 433, *445*
Fortner, B., 392, *400*
Fortner, B. V., 110, *117*
Fortner, M., 219, 230, 236, 484, *489*
Foster, C., 681, *699*
Foster, W. J., 594, *612*
Foster, Y. M., 210, *216*
Fox, B. H., 683, *696*
Fraley, R. C., 72, 74, 76, 78, *81n*, 82, *84*, 385, 400, 407, 416, *416n*, 417, *426*, 432, *445*, 756, *764*
Frances, A., 681, *701*
Francis, D., 437–438, *445*
Francis, M., 382, *401*

Francis, M. E., 79, 86, 389, *401*, 412, 413, 428, 537, *541*
Frank, A. W., 440, *445*
Frank, E., 95, *117*, 222, 237, 247, 258, 415, 424, 426, 484, 485, *488*, 490, 491, 598, 600, 603, 604, 608, 609, 610, *613n*, 614, *614n*, 615, 616, 617, 618, 619, 620, 622, 623, *624n*, 626, *629n*, 632, 635, 636
Frank, M., 504, *510*
Franke, G. H., 684, *695*
Frankiel, R., 302, *322*
Frantz, T., 93, 95, *115*, 313, *325*
Fraser, R. H., 180, *194*
Frederick, C., 34, 40, *45*, 155, *165*
Fredrickson, B. L., 506, *510*, 546, 547, 548, *561*
Fredriksen, K. I., 252, *259*
Freedman, B. A., 33–34, *45*
Freedman, M., 500, *514*
Freedman-Letofsky, K., 712, 714, 717, *737*
Freeman, A., 650, 656, 665, *666*
Freeman, S. J., 33–34, *45*, 355, *371*, 548, 562, 712, 714, 717, *737*
Frets, P., 101, *116*
Freud, E. L., 233, *234*
Freud, S., 4, 17, *22*, 27, 30, *43*, 63, 70, 71–72, 77, 81, 84, 222, *234*, 303–304, *322*, 376, 383, 384, 385, 400, 405, 408, 415, *416n*, 426, 496, *510*, 545, 560, 576, 582, 603, 608, 616, 634
Fried, M., 41, *43*
Friedlander, Y., 247, *257*
Friedman, S., 267, 280, 312, *322*, 476, 477, 489, *491*
Friesen, W. V., 502, 504, *510*
Frijda, N. H., 64, 65, 66, 68, 84, 495, *510*
Fristad, M. A., 478, 479, *491*, 603, *612*
Fromm, K., 155, *163*
Fry, P. S., 246, 249, *255*
Frydman-Helfant, S., 232, *234*
Fuchs, I., 683, *697*
Fulton, R., 247, 251, *258*, 276, *281*
Fung, H. H., 243, *255*
Furman, E., 178, 181, *194*
Futterman, A., 247, 260, 266, *279*

428, 431, 432, 438, 439, 443, 446, 647, 651, 669
Kleban, M. H., 243, 244, 256
Kleber, R., 380, 400, 621, 636
Kleber, R. J., 600, 601, 609, 727, 728, 730, 733
Klein, S. J., 682, 685, 699, 707, 734
Kleinman, A., 440, 446
Klerman, J. L., 500, 514
Kliman, G. W., 181, 195
Klimas, N. G., 683, 697
Klinger, E., 69, 85, 269, 280
Knapp, J. H., 405
Knapp, M., 494, 514
Knapp, R. J., 226, 236
Knight, R. A., 673, 677, 703
Knuppel, N., 722, 723, 724, 725, 734
Knutson, B., 556, 562
Kohut, H., 308, 323
Komar, A. A., 210, 216
Koob, J. J., 598, 611, 686, 702
Koocher, G. P., 138, 141, 172, 195, 265, 280
Koppelman, K. L., 439, 446
Koren-Kane, N., 222, 236
Korenman, S., 359, 368
Kosenvuo, M., 681, 698
Kost, K. A., 658, 659, 666
Kostelny, K., 316, 322
Kosten, T., 92, 116, 477–478, 489, 490, 675, 676, 698, 699
Kowalski, N. C., 250, 252, 256
Kozak, M. J., 500, 511
Kraemer, H. C., 531, 543, 626, 635, 686, 702
Kral, M. J., 100, 101, 103, 114
Kranzler, E. M., 596, 609
Kraus, A. S., 361, 369
Kraus, D. R., 146, 156, 163, 312, 323
Krause, N., 363, 369
Kreling, B., 251, 257
Kreuger, B., 505, 511
Kriege, G., 712, 714, 719, 736
Krishnan, K. R., 678, 701
Kriss, M., 649, 666
Krohne, H. W., 454, 455, 467, 500, 511
Krokoff, L. J., 506, 511
Kruise, D. A., 464, 468
Krupnick, J., 50, 61, 179, 195, 222, 225, 235, 306, 323
Kubany, E. S., 661–662, 663, 666

Kübler-Ross, E., 105, 116, 564, 582
Kuhl, J., 548, 560
Kulenkamp, E. J., 149, 164
Kulik, J., 525, 539
Kumar, A., 671, 677, 683, 687, 693, 696, 699
Kumar, M., 266, 267, 279, 483, 488, 531, 532, 540, 541, 671, 675, 676, 677, 680, 681, 683, 685, 686, 687, 688, 689, 690, 691, 692, 693, 696, 697, 699
Kunonen, M., 114n, 116
Kupfer, D. J., 95, 11, 222, 237, 247, 258, 480, 481, 482, 484, 485, 486, 488, 489, 490, 491, 598, 603, 610, 613n, 614, 614n, 615, 616, 617, 618, 619, 620, 622, 624n, 626, 629n, 632, 635, 636
Kutscher, A. H., 518, 542
Kutz, I., 676, 694
Kvelde, H., 596, 603, 610

Labi, N., 422, 426
Lachman, E., 309, 320
Lachman, M., 154, 158, 162
Lachmann, F., 309, 323
Laferty, M. E., 245, 255
LaGrand, L. E., 201, 208, 216
Lake, M. F., 722, 723, 724, 725, 734
Lambert, M. J., 224, 239, 712, 714, 719, 735
Lamnin, A. D., 531, 541
Lampe, S., 200, 209, 214
Lana, R. D., 226, 229, 234
Lancee, W. J., 355, 371, 548, 562
Land, S., 484, 488
Landman, J., 658, 666
Lang, A., 276–277, 280
Lang, B., 434, 435, 446
Lang, E. L., 149, 164, 221, 235
Lang, F. R., 243, 256
Lang, L. A., 210, 216
Lang, P. J., 500, 511, 520, 540
Langer, E. J., 656, 667
Langosch, D., 596, 608
LaRossa, R., 126, 140
Larson, A., 356, 369
Larson, J., 65–66, 70, 73, 77n, 80, 80n, 86, 153, 165, 314, 322, 388, 401, 407, 412, 413, 427, 463, 464,

Meyaard, L., 674, *701*
Meyèrs, A. W., 711, 712, 714, *737*
Michaels, T. F., 138, *141*
Middleton, W., 93, 94, 95, 97, 98, *114,*
116, 175, *195,* 276, *281,* 384,
401, 410, 411, 418, *427,* 497,
513, 589, 598, 604, 605, 609,
614, 616, 633, *635*
Miedema, F., 674, *701*
Mihalecz, M. C., 494, *509*
Mikulincer, M., 80, 86, 461, *468*
Milbrath, C., 222, *235,* 495, *511,* 598,
603, 608, 614, 616, 618, 619,
626, 631, 632, 634, 760, *764*
Miler, E. D., 418, *427*
Miles, G. B., 333, *347*
Miles, M. S., 148, *164,* 175, *194,* 231,
236
Miller, D. T., 660, 663, *667*
Miller, E. D., 743, *764*
Miller, G. A., 500, *511*
Miller, L. C., 527, *539*
Miller, M., 94, 95, 96, 98, 99, *117,* 614,
615, 616, 617, 618, 619, 623,
632, *635*
Miller, M. A., 178, *195*
Miller, M. D., 604, 606, 609, *611,* 617,
636
Miller, N., 307, *324*
Miller, N. E., 676, *699*
Miller, S. M., 455, *468,* 552, 560, 575,
582
Miller, W. R., 158, *164*
Millon, C., 671, 683, 684, 693, *697*
Milo, E. M., 107, *116,* 458, *468*
Mineka, S., 264, *281*
Minkov, C., 587, 591, 598, 603, *611,*
761
Mireault, G. C., 180, *195*
Misso, V., 175, *195,* 384, *401,* 497, *513*
Mitchell, J., 422
Mitchell, S., 308, *325*
Moen, P., 315, *321*
Moffitt, T., 498, *511*
Moles, E. L., 251, *258*
Molina, R., 687, *696*
Monarch, N. M., 505, 506, *511*
Monnier, J., 463, *467*
Montgomery, P. T., 685, *699*
Moody, C. P., 171, *195*
Moody, R. A., 171, *195*

Moon, S. M., 334, *347*
Moore, I. M., 91, *115*
Moore, T. E., 707, 708, *737*
Moorey, S., 651–652, *667*
Moos, B., 160, *164*
Moos, N., 310, *325*
Moos, R. H., 13, 145, 150, 151, 152,
157, *163, 164,* 166, 208, *217,*
360, *367,* 379, *399,* 455, 460,
466, *468*
Moos, R., 160, *164*
Morgan, D. L., 123–124, *141*
Morgan, H., 77, 86
Morgan, R., 671, 677, 683, 684, 693, *699*
Morgan, R. O., 683, *693*
Morgenstern, H., 679, *700*
Morin, H., 728, *735*
Morris, J. N., 707, *736*
Morrison Tonkins, S. A., 712, 714, 719,
735
Morrow, J., 546, 547, 548, 549, *561*
Morse, J. M., 107, *116,* 135, *141,* 146,
163
Morton, D. L., 686, *695*
Moskowitz, J., 389, 396, 400, 563n, 568,
571, 572, 579, 582, *583*
Moss, M. S., 14, 96, *117,* 148, *165,* 220,
229, 236, 241, 245, 246, 247,
249, 250, 251, 252, 256, 257,
258, 259, 744, *754*
Moss, S. Z., 14, 148, *165,* 220, 229, *236,*
241, 245, 246, 247, 249, 250,
251, 252, 256, *257,* 258, 744,
754
Mougey, E., 65, 86
Moylan, A., 410, 411, 418, *427,* 589,
598, *609*
Mrazek, P. J., 588, 590, 591, *609*
Mulder, C. L., 680, 681, 683, 697, *701*
Mulhern, R. K., 153, *164*
Mullan, J. T., 251, 252, 254, 568, *583*
Mullen, B., 454, *468*
Mulvihill, M., 154, *167*
Mumford, E., 531, *541*
Munholland, K., 74, 84, 305, *321*
Murakami, M., 270, *282*
Murch, R. L., 159, *165*
Murdock, M. E., 597, *609*
Murphy, C., 693, *695*
Murphy, J., 722, 723, 724, 725, *734*
Murphy, K., 597, *609*

Murphy, S. A., 32, *44*, 92, *116*, 229, 230, *236*, 363, *369*, 407, 408, 409, *427*, 594, 609, 707, 708, *735*
Murray, E. J., 531, *539*, *541*
Murray, J., 594, *610*
Murrell, S., 153, *165*, 244, 245, 258, 363, 369, 568, 583, 684, *701*
Murtha, J. M., 136, *142*
Musselman, D. L., 473, 474, *490*
Musson, R. F., 548, *561*

Nabe, C. M., 496, *509*
Nachshon, O., 80, 86
Nadeau, J. W., 107, *117*, 252, 258, 329, 330, 332, 338, 341, 347, 392, *403*, 539, 744, *748*
Nader, K., 34, 40, 45, 155, *165*
Nader, K. O., 654, *667*
Nagy, M., 172, *195*, 265, *281*
Nahemow, L., 243, *258*
Najman, J. M., 594, *612*
Nanni, S. E., 572, *584*
Nassar, H. Z., 232, *238*
Neal, M. B., 123–124, *141*
Neale, J. M., 459, *469*, 548, *562*
Nelson, B., 313, *325*
Nelson, G., 148, *165*
Nelson, J. C., 617, *634*
Nelson, R., 676, 677, 683, 685, 686, 687, 689, *697*
Nemeroff, C. B., 473, 474, *490*, 678, *701*
Nerken, I. R., 147, 158, *165*
Nesse, R. M., 267, *281*
Neufeldt, S., 222, *234*
Neugebauer, R., 684, *701*
Newcomb, M. D., 687, *703*
Newman, B. M., 173, 178, *195*
Newman, M. G., 449, 459, 461, 464, 455, *469*, 577, *584*
Newman, P. R., 173, 178, *195*
Newsom, J., 614, 615, 616, 617, 618, 619, 622, 623, 632, 635, 636
Newsom, J. T., 40, *44*, 266, *281*, 482, *491*, 603, *610*, 614, 615, 616, 617, 619, 620, 622, 632, *634*, 635
Newson, J., 94, 95, 96, 98, 99, *117*
Newson, J. T., 95, *117*
Newton, T. L., 500, *513*
Nezu, A. M., 506, *513*

Nezu, C. M., 506, *513*
Nichols, C., 306, 318, *322*, 417, *425*
Nichols, R., 108, *114*
Nickman, S. L., 41, *43*, 50, *61*, 184–185, 189, 192, *195*, *196*, 204, 209, *217*, 220, 233, *235*, *239*, 302, 314, *323*, 416, 416n, 417, 421, 426, *427*, *428*, 432, 437, 446, 447
Niebor, A. P., 360, *369*
Niedenthal, P. M., 662, *668*
Niemeyer, R. A., 12, 89, 91, 105, 110, 112, *117*, 219, 230, *236*, 392, 400, 414, 423, *427*, 440, 446, 458, 576, 583, 647, 648, 650, 653, 655, 667, *747*
Noaghiul, S., 614n
Noël, M. P., 520, *542*
Noelker, L. S., 276, *278*
Nofzinger, E. A., 485, *490*
Nolen-Hoeksema, S., 19, 65–66, 70, 73, 77n, 80, 80n, 86, 153, *165*, 314, *322*, 357, 358, 362, 363, 364, 369, 388, 389, 396, *401*, 407, 412, 413, *427*, 463, 464, 468, 497, 498, *513*, 570, 576, *583*
Noll, J. L., 494, 501, *509*, 546, 547, 548, 549, 550, 551, 552, 557, *559*, *561*, *562*
Norbiato, G., 674, 676, 694, *701*
Normand, C. L., 50, *61*, 184–185, 189, *195*, 416, 417, *427*
Norris, F., 684, *701*
Norris, F. H., 153, 155, *165*, *166*, 244, 258, 363, *369*, 568, *583*
Notarius, C., 306, 320, 535, *539*
Novacenko, H., 676, *699*
Nuamah, I., 707, *735*
Nuechterlein, K., 315, *325*
Nuñez, F., 34, 40, *45*
Nunley, E. P., 494, 508, 620, 621, *634*
Nurcombe, B., 526, *539*

Oatley, K., 65, 68, 69, 70, 86, 494, *513*
O'Brien, J. M., 206, *217*
O'Bryant, S. L., 156, *165*, 246, 247, *258*
O'Connor, C., 66, 67, 68, 69, 70, *87*
Oetting, E. R., 138, *141*
Offer, D., 213, *217*
Ogrocki, P., 678, *699*

Perlow, J. J., 65, 86
Perls, F., 34, *44*
Permaul, J. A., 709, 712, 714, 715, *737*
Perrez, M., 456, 457, 459, 464, *468*
Perry, S., 597, 681, *701*
Persons, J., 650, *668*
Pert, S., 677, *701*
Peter, D., 136, *140*
Peters, L., 683, *703*
Peterson, J., 247, *260, 266, 279*, 354,
    355, 368, 568, 584, 684, 694
Peterson, P. A., 436, *447*
Petitto, J. M., 679, 681, 693, 694, 695,
    700
Phair, J., 681, *699*
Phifer, J. F., 155, *166*
Philippot, P., 381, 382, *401*, 518, 519,
    520, 521, 524, 525, *540, 542*
Phillips, D. S., 186, *193*
Phillips, R. S., 251, 253, *257, 260*
Piaget, J., 170, 172, *196*
Picardi, A., 266, *279*
Pickett, M., 90, *118*
Pickrel, S., 319, *322*
Pieper, C., 267, *279*
Piercy, F., 310, 311, *325*
Pike, J., 267, *280*
Pilkonis, P. A., 598, *610*, 613n, 614n,
    624n, 629n
Pillow, D. R., 595, 596, *611, 612*, 712,
    714, 719, *736*
Pincus, L., 253, 258, 307, *325*
Piper, W. E., 728, 730, *735*
Pizer, S., 308, *325*
Plotkin, J., 136, *140*
Plotnikoff, N., 673, *703*
Poijula, S., 102n
Polak, P. R., 710, 711, 712, 714, 716,
    735, 737
Polan, H. J., 77, *86*
Pollack, L., 683, *695*
Pollock, G., 225, *237*, 264, *281*
Portillo, C., 686, *698*
Potvin, L., 100, 101, *117*
Poulton, J. L., 548, *560*
Powell, M., 226, 232, *237*
Powell-Griner, E., 250, *256*
Powers, L. E., 651, *668*
Prasad, A., 594, *609*
Pratt, D., 190–191, *195*
Price, R., 657, *666*

Priest, R. G., 180, *194*
Prigerson, H. G., 20, 40, *44*, 92, *117*,
    222, 237, 247, 258, 260, 266,
    281, 305, *327*, 415, 424, 426,
    480, 481, 482, 486, 488, 489,
    491, 598, 600, 603, 604, 606,
    608, *610, 611*, 613, 613n, 614,
    614n, 615, 616–617, 618, 619,
    620, 622, 623, 624n, 626, 629n,
    632, *634, 635, 638*, 636, *760*
Procidano, M. E., 207, *217*
Provine, R. R., 505, *513*
Pruchno, R. A., 96, *117*, 251, *259*
Pulsinelli, W. A., 677, *702*
Purisman, R., 357, *370*
Putnam, F., 494, 499, 501, 508, *509*
Pye, C., 651, 666, 726, *734*
Pynoos, R., 34, 40, *45*, 155, *165*, 306,
    316, *321, 325*
Pyszczynski, T., 549, *562*

Quade, D., 679, *694*
Quarmby, D., 708, *735*
Quesenberry, C. P., 681, *702*
Qureshi, H., 442, *447*

Rabatic, S., 685, *694*
Rabkin, J. G., 681, 684, *701, 702*
Rachman, S., 558, *562*, 648, *668*
Rachmiel, T. B., 548, *562*
Racioppo, M. W., 577, *581*
Racunica, N. L., 685, *694*
Radloff, L., 359, *370*, 568, *583*
Rajagopal, D., 243, 244, *256*
Ramey, S., 315, 316, *321*
Ramirez, R., 712, 714, 719, *736*
Ramm, L., 34, *44*, 414, *427*, 651, 667,
    709, 726, 728, 730, *734*
Ramos, M. C., 126, *141*
Ramsay, R. W., 34, *45*, 707, 726, *736*
Ramsey, R., 651, *668*
Rando, T. A., 34, *45*, 156, *166*, 175, *196*,
    221, 229, 233, *237*, 247, 248,
    249, *259*, 411, 412, 415, 416,
    418, 424, *428*, 458, *468*, 496,
    502, *513*, 653, 655, *668*
Range, L. M., 154, 155, 156, *166*
Raphael, B., 20, 31–33, *45*, 92, 93, 94,
    95, 97, 97n, 98, *114, 115, 116*,

SUBJECT INDEX

Attachment theory (*continued*)
 described, 73–74
 development, 37–39
 future implications, 743–744, 756–757
 grief work, 385–386
 interventions, 20, 589
 kinds of loss, 74–76
 kinship, 364–365
 loss reactions, 77–80, 356, 362–363
 psychic structure and, 304–306
 psychoanalytic theory versus, 385
Autonomic function studies, 475
Autonomy, 120
Avoidant children, 38
Avoidant coping strategies, 415, 600
Avoiders, 40

Beck Depression Inventory, 91
Behavior therapy, 727
Behavioral skills, 711, 715
Behavioral therapy, 600
Beneficence, 120
Bereavement
 age-specific, 36–37, 147–150
 affective and cognitive manifestations, 7
 contextual factors, 152–158
 cross-cultural differences, 15, 34–35,
  285–299
 culturally specific, 8
 defined, 6, 672
 gender differences, 34, 35–36, 358–
  361
 health consequences, 8, 361–362,
  473–488
 modern, 441–442
 postmodern, 442–443
 previous, 154
 reactions, 7–8
 social context, 15–16
 successful adaptation, 146–147
 traumatic, 39–40, 316, 601
Bereavement counseling, 30–34, 606
Bereavement overload, 14, 244
Bereavement pathologies, 589
 early intervention, 598–599
 psychotherapeutic treatments, 599–601
Bereavement Phenomenology Questionnaire (BPQ), 97, 98
Bereavement research

attachment theory, 73–82
care implications, 759–763
concepts and issues, 3–21, 742–746
consequences, 7–8, 751–755
coping assessment, 449–465
coping myths, 407–408
coping processes, 756–759
cross-cultural, 755
design, 749–750
determining theoretical approach,
  742–746
emotion therapy and, 64–73
ethical decision-making, 119–139,
  750–751
future direction, 158–162, 185–192,
  741–764
historical overview, 11, 25–42
measurement, 89–114, 747–750
outcome risk factors, 16, 349–367
participants, 120–124, 131–133, 137–
  138
support group intervention, 685–692
Bereavement risk. *See* Risk factors
Bereavement-specific coping scales, 457–
  458
Bereavement-specific effects, 350
Bereavement-specific risk factors, 350,
  352–353
Bias
 cultural, 34–35, 135
 emotional, 135
 ethical, 122
 hindsight, 661–662
 low adherence, 708–709
 researcher, 134–135
 self-selection, 725
Bonds
 grief and, 47–61
 relationships versus, 53–55
 See also Attachment bonds
Boston Normative Aging Study, 243
Boundaries, 331–332
Brief Symptom Inventory (BSI), 91, 207
Bumpita Arapesh (Papua New Guinea),
  290

Caplan's Laboratory of Community Psychiatry, 31, 33
Care, 10–11

biased views, 34–35
continued bonds, 431, 432–435
diversity, 15, 290–292
family, 248
political power, 433–435
religious beliefs, 432–435
social constructionist view, 285–299
universality, 15, 264–266, 755
writing as disclosure, 533
Cultural norms, 130
Cultural pluralism, 207
Cytokines, 674

Death, mode of, 155–156, 354–355
Death rituals, 294–295, 314–315
Death Studies ethical guidelines, 119–120,
    750
Debriefing, 422, 602
Decathexis, 71, 81
Defense, 565
Dehydroepiandrosterone (DHEA), 673
Delayed grief, 356–357, 411
Denial, 498
Depression
    attachment and, 39
    bereavement-related, 7, 66, 123, 408–
        411, 420, 473–476
    disrupted sleep and, 483–486
    immune system and, 481, 678–679
    intervention efficacy, 716
    kinship and, 364
    normal bereavement versus, 603–605
    in old age, 36
    persistent, 684
    reactive, 48
Depressive symptoms, 473–476, 548
Despair syndrome, 48, 49
Detachment, 81
Developmental psychopathology, 315
Deviant grieving, 296–297
Dexamethasone, 673
Dexamethasone suppression test (DST),
    476, 478–479, 673
Disabling grief, 175–176
Disclosure
    of emotion, 18–19, 376, 517–539
    health effects, 528–529
    interventions, 381–382
    outcome measure effects, 530–531

unanticipated, 128
Disclosure paradigm, 529–533
Disease, bereavement-induced, 473–476
Disengagement, 269, 311
Disordered mourning, 498
Disorganized children, 38–39
Dispositional coping styles, 450–451
Distress
    defined, 672
    prolonged, 548–552
Down-regulation, 673
Dual process model (DPM), 73, 80, 363,
    394–398, 744
Duchenne smile or laughter, 410, 504–
    505
Dyadic Adjustment Scale, 504
Dynamic therapy, 727
Dysphoria, 409, 548–551
Dysphoric rumination, 548–551

Education, 357, 533
Efficacy studies, 705–733
Efficacy studies review
    methodology, 707–709
    overview, 710–719
    preventive interventions, 719–731
    scope, 706–707
Ego processes, 565
Elderly, bereaved. *See* Old age and be-
    reavement
Emergency reactions, 48, 51
Emotion
    cognition and, 70–72
    disclosing and sharing, 517–539
    distinguished from grief, 494–495
    dual process theory, 72
    evolutionary function, 69–70
    grief work and, 70–72, 495–498
    intensity after loss, 49
    positive, 19, 410
    regulation, in old age, 243–244
    religion and, 571
    repressed, 36
    social-functional perspective, 493–494,
        498–506
Emotional disclosure, 381–383
Emotional dissociation, 18, 499–502, 757
Emotional events, 518
Emotional expression, 497, 502–505

General Self-Report Scales, 455–457
General Well-Being Scale, 207
Generalizability, in qualitative study, 333, 334
Gestalt therapy, 34
Grandparent bereavement, 249
Grant Foundation Bereavement Inventory, 458
Graveside behavior, 437–438
Grief
   absence of, 405, 410–411, 498
   bonds and relationships, 47–61, 756–757
   characteristics, 47–51
   chronic, 28, 356, 418, 597, 602
   coerced denial of, 291–292
   complicated, 247, 597, 615, 675, 677
   defined, 6, 672
   delayed, 356–357, 411
   disabling, 175–176
   early views, 26
   evolutionary function, 69–70, 263–278
   malleability, 292–294
   morbid, 27
   normal, 6–7, 29–30, 600
   pathological, 6–7
   social constructionist view, 285–299
   social-functional perspective, 493–508
   societal assumptions and beliefs, 405–407
   subtypes, 7
   traumatic, 20, 39–40, 597, 600
   symptomatology, 7
   Weiss theory, 47–61
   See also Bereavement
Grief counseling, 443
   described, 10–11, 440
   efficacy, 21, 413–415
   emotion-focused, 599
   gender differences, 36
   problem-focused, 599
Grief Experience Inventory (GEI), 94–95, 96–97, 458
Grief measurement. See Measurement
Grief phases or tasks, 9–10, 29–30
Grief Resolution Index, 458
Grief scales, 92–105
Grief states, 49
Grief therapy, 10–11, 218, 413–415

Grief universality, 288–290, 298, 588, 755
Grief work
   attachment theory, 385–386
   as coping process, 9, 757–759
   emotion in, 70–72, 495–498
   Freudian, 27, 63, 77, 384, 385–386
   future issues, 757–759
   rumination versus, 19
   theories, 375, 380
Grieving processes
   continued bonds, 431–444, 756–757
   conceptualization and measurement, 65–68, 89–114
Grounded theory, 106–107, 330, 332
Group behavior therapy, 727
Group counseling, 211
Group interventions, 319
Growth hormone, 673, 677
Guided discovery, 650
Guided mourning, 34, 600
Guilt, 521–522, 662

Hamilton Rating Scale for Depression (HRSD), 478
Harvard Bereavement Study, 30–31
Harvard Childhood Bereavement Study, 184–185, 189
Healthy grief, 80
Highly active antiretroviral therapies (HAART), 682, 685
Hindsight bias, 661–662
Hippocampus, 672
HIV
   caregiver effects, 685
   clinical health outcomes, 681–682
   depression, 684
   disclosure, 528
   elder issues, 597–598
   immunological function, 675–676, 677–678, 679–680, 683
   multiple loss syndrome, 684–685
   physiological effects, 482–483, 484
   support group intervention, 686–687
Hogan Grief Reactions Checklist (HGRC), 114
Hogan Sibling Inventory of Bereavement (HSIB), 100–101, 102–103
Homicide, 592, 594, 597, 601

Hopelessness Scale, 452
Hopi (North America), 440
Hormones, 672
Hospice services, 30–34, 249
Human Relations Area Files, 264
Hypercathexis, 71–72, 432
Hypercortisolemia, 677
Hyphothalamic-pituitary-adrenocortical (HPA) dysregulation, 478
Hypnotherapy, 600, 727
Hypothalamus, 672

Immune system, 21, 66, 133, 267
    bereavement-related, 479–483, 673–674
    depression and, 678–679
    disrupted sleep and, 484, 485, 486
    function, 673–674, 678–680
    writing effects, 530
Impact of Events Scale (IES), 39–40, 452, 759
Inclusive fitness, 270, 365
Incremental grief model, 391
Indicated interventions, 588
Infant attachment, 305
Information-processing theory, 304
Informed consent, 125–127, 750
In-law effect, 339
Insecure attachments, 38, 39
Insomnia, 483
Institutional review boards (IRBs), 135–136
Integrative coping models, 393–398
Interpersonal construction, 15–16, 301–320
    defined, 302–303
    family therapy, 310–311
    social–systems developmental models, 315–316
    sociocultural context, 313–315
    theoretical sources, 303–310
Interpersonal coping models, 390–393
Interpersonal model of grief, 307–310
Interpersonal psychoanalysis, 308
Interpersonal risk factors, 362–365
    kinship, 363–365
    lack of social support, 362–363
Intervention
    adolescent, 210–211

child, 595–597
cognitive–behavioral, 647–664
disclosure, 382
efficacy, 21, 705–733
family, 318–320, 345–346
group, 319
higher-risk individuals, 592–593
indicated, 588
interpersonal, 318–320
parent, 230, 593–595
pharmacological, 20, 589, 604–605
physiological effects, 671–693
preventive, 591–593, 710–731
psychotherapeutic, 20, 587–590, 599–606
research, 129–130
selected, 588
spectrum, 588, 590–591
universal, 588
widows, 593
Intrapersonal coping models, 387–390
Intrusion–avoidance reactions, 380–381
Intrusion scale, 39–40
Inventory of Complicated Grief (ICG), 94–95, 98–99, 112
Inventory of Traumatic Grief, 98, 615
Item pool, 461

Japanese ancestor rituals, 431, 433
Jewish Shiva, 440
Justice, 120

Kinship, 56, 58, 156–157
    grief and, 270–271, 273–274
    as interpersonal factor, 363–365
Kwanga (Papua New Guinea), 293, 294, 298

Laughter, 501, 505–506, 507
Learned helplessness, 39
Leeds Anxiety Scale, 721
Life course perspective, 160–161
Life Events and Coping Inventory for Children, 455
Life scheme, 655, 567
Life Situations Inventory, 455, 456

Life span developmental theory, 13, 753–754

Life stressors, 681, 682, 683, 685–686

Life Stressors and Social Resources Inventory (LISRES), 160

Life tasks, 460

Limbic-hypothalamic-pituitary-adrenal (LHPA) axis, 672, 675, 676, 677, 678, 688

Liminality, 314

Linking objects, 34

Littleton, Colorado, debriefing, 422

Loneliness, 36, 246, 362–363

Longevity, 442

Longitudinal designs, 351–352

Loss and affiliations, 57–58

Loss situations, 41

Lymphocytes, 480, 673

Lymphoid-adrenal axis, 673

Mainz Coping Inventory, 455, 456

Maisin (Papua New Guinea), 287, 295, 296, 297

Marital relationships, 54

Mass trauma, 602

Maternal deprivation, 38

Maternal grief, 594, 725. *See also* Parent bereavement

Meaningful variation, 111–112

Meaning making, 655–657

Meaning making inhibitors, 339

Meaning making qualitative study
    findings, 336
    implications, 343–346
    limitations, 334–335
    locating families, 335–336
    methods, 332–333
    theories, 330–332
    two families contrasted, 336–343
    validity, reliability, generalizability, 333–334

Meaning making stimulator, 339

Meaning reconstruction model, 392–393

Measurement
    coping, 16–17
    efficacy, 707–709
    focus, 111
    future issues, 747–748
    general purpose, 92–99

lack of comparative analysis, 112
    methodological pluralism, 113
    mixed methods, 113
    psychiatric symptom scale, 91–92
    qualitative, 105–110
    quantitative, 92–105
    reliability and validity, 111
    scope, 89–91
    Spanish language, 93
    specialized, 99–105

Melbourne Family Grief Study, 313

Memory, 521–522, 525–526

Mental imagery, 686

Metabolites, 672

Methodological issues, 707–709
    adherence, 708–709
    future considerations, 747–750
    lack of control groups, 707–709
    nonresponse and attrition, 708
    participant assignment, 708

Methodological pluralism, 113

Milan circular questioning, 332, 335, 344, 346

Miller Behavioral Style Scale, 455, 456, 575

Moral guidance, 438–439

Morbid grief, 27, 28, 34

Morbidity, 678

Mortality, 8, 680–682

Mourning
    communal, 442
    defined, 6
    disordered, 498
    forced or guided, 34, 600
    pathological, 418, 760
    public, 291
    traditional, 441
    varieties of emotion, 64, 73
    work of, 496

Multicultural research, 161

Multiple bonds, 59

Multiple loss syndrome, 14, 684–685

Munson Family study, 337–340

Mutual help programs, 11, 34

Myocardial infarction, 682

National Association for Loss and Grief (NALAG), 33, 42

support group interventions, 671–693
Phytohemagglutinin (PHA), 674, 675, 676, 678–680
Polarization effects, 755
Positive affect, 19, 569–573
Positive affect scale, 568, 569
Positive coping, 684
Positive emotion, 19, 410, 497–498, 504–505
Positive psychological states, 389
Positive reappraisal, 570, 571
Positive States of Mind Scale, 568
Postmodernism, 648–649
Posttraumatic stress disorder (PTSD)
  bereavement and, 685
  child and adolescent, 207, 316
  cognitive–behavioral therapy, 653–664
  as diagnostic category, 760
  preventive intervention, 592
  symptomatology, 40, 616
  traumatic grief and, 601
Pre- and postcrisis environment, 160
Preventive interventions, 588–598
  higher risk individual, 592–593
  whole population, 591–592
Primary preventive interventions, 710–718
  bereaved children, 718–719
  efficacy studies, 719–720
  widow and widower, 710–718
Privacy, 127–128
Problem-focused coping, 379, 569–570, 599
Prolactin, 673, 677
Protest syndrome, 48, 49
Psychiatric symptom scale, 91–92
Psychoanalysis, 37, 303
Psychoanalytic theory, 383–384, 576
Psychological distress, 672
Psychopharmacology, 604–605
Psychosocial transitions, 41, 386
Psychotherapeutic intervention, 20, 34, 158, 230, 308, 716, 727
Purgatory, 434

Rapid eye movement (REM) sleep, 484
Rashomon study, 745–746
Reactive depression, 48, 603
Re-grief, 14, 178

Relationships
  affiliative, 55–57
  bonds versus, 53–55
  multiple bonds and, 59
Relaxation training, 686
Reliability, in qualitative study, 333, 334
Religion-oriented psychotherapy, 727
Religiosity
  bereavement influence, 154–155, 357–358
  continued bonds and, 432–435
  emotion and, 571
  intervention and, 687
  scholarly inattention to, 208
  social constructionist perspective, 296–297
Remembrance formation, 438–439
Reproductive values, 271, 272, 274–276, 365
Research design, 749–750
Researcher qualifications, 133–135
Research-induced distress, 128–130
Research methodologies, 129, 182–183
Residential emotional intensity, 523–524
Residential social sharing, 523–524
Residential treatment, 210
Response Styles Questionnaire, 546
Restoration orientation, 40, 395
Revised coping theory, 573–580
  application, 573–575
  focal stressful encounter, 575–576
  outcomes, 578–580
  supplemental measurement, 576–578
Risk assessment
  research-induced distress, 128–130
  threats to confidentiality, 127–128
  unanticipated disclosures, 128
  unethical application of findings, 130–131
  violation of cultural norms, 130
Risk factors, 349–367
  bereavement-specific, 350, 482, 592–593
  conceptual methodology, 350–353
  empirical findings, 353–365
  future research, 753
  general, 350
  interpersonal, 362–365
  personal, 355–362

religious, 358
for ruminators, 550–551
significant others, 462–463
Social systems developmental models,
315–316
Sociocultural bereavement, 313–315
Socratic method, 650
Spirituality, 208, 687
Spousal bereavement. *See* Conjugal be-
reavement
Spousal death, 147–148
Stereotypes, 135
Stillbirth, 594, 725
Storytelling, 314, 340, 345
Strange Situation Test, 37, 38
Strategic Approach to Coping, 463
Stress, 481
Stress and coping model, 65–66, 564–
567
Stress and Coping Process Questionnaire,
456, 457, 459, 464
Stress-coping theory, 12
Stress management, 29
Stressors, 672, 676–678
Stressor-support-coping (SCC) model,
671, 680, 682–685
Stress proliferation, 160
Stress Related Growth Scale (SRGS),
159
Stress response syndrome, 306, 380–381
Stress studies, 28–29
Stress theories, 364, 378–379
Sudden Infant Death Syndrome (SIDS)
counterfactual thinking, 658–659
parental grief, 225–226, 231, 594
social support, 358
positive affects, 571
Suicidal ideation, 247
Suicide, 355, 594, 597
Support group intervention, 685–692
Support programs. *See* Intervention; So-
cial support
Survivor guilt, 206, 249
Symbolic interactionism, 314, 330–331,
391
Sympathetic adrenomedullary system,
672, 688–689
Symptom Checklist (SCL), 91
Systematic desensitization, 727

Tallensi (Ghana), 432–433
Task model, 387–388
Tavistock Center, 304, 307
Tertiary preventive interventions, 726–
731
Test–retest reliability, 92, 111
Texas Revised Inventory of Grief
(TRIG), 93–96, 112, 458, 711,
726
Thanatology, 105, 241
Thematic Apperception Test (TAT), 209
3-methoxy-4-hydroxyphenylglycol
(MHPG), 672, 688–690
T lymphocytes, 674
Toraja (Indonesia), 291
Traumatic distress, 615, 616
Traumatic grief (TG)
assessment tools, 628
clinical description, 39–40, 615–616
consensus criteria, 622–628, 630, 631–
633
delimitation from other disorders, 617–
619
as distinct disorder, 613–633, 760
family studies, 620–622
follow-up studies, 619–620
interventions, 597, 600, 601
laboratory studies, 616–617
normal grief versus, 633
symptomatology, 20
Traumatic stressors, 685
Tübingen Study of Bereavement, 354,
356
Twin studies, 273–274
Two-Track Model of Bereavement, 220,
222–225, 386–387, 576

UCSF Coping Project, 157
Uncooperative interrupting, 342
Universal interventions, 588
Up-regulation, 673, 677

Validity, in qualitative study, 333–334
Values clarification, 438
Veracity, 120
Verbal–autonomic response dissociation,
500–502

ABOUT THE EDITORS

Margaret S. Stroebe is associate professor of psychology at Utrecht University, The Netherlands. She received her PhD at the University of Bristol, United Kingdom. Her long-term interests in bereavement have to do with theoretical approaches to grief and grieving, interactive patterns of coping, and the efficacy of bereavement intervention. She is coauthor (with Wolfgang Stroebe) of *Bereavement and Health* (1987) and *Social Psychology and Health* (1995) and editor (with Wolfgang Stroebe and Robert O. Hansson) of *The Handbook of Bereavement: Theory, Research, and Intervention* (1993).

Robert O. Hansson is professor of psychology at the University of Tulsa, Oklahoma. He earned an MBA and his PhD in social psychology from the University of Washington in 1973. His research interests focus on successful aging, aging families, and coping with loss and stressful life transitions in old age. He is coeditor (with Margaret S. Stroebe and Wolfgang Stroebe) of *The Handbook of Bereavement: Theory, Research, and Intervention* (1993) and coauthor (with Bruce N. Carpenter) of *Relationships in Old Age: Coping With the Challenge of Transition* (1994).

Wolfgang Stroebe is professor of social, organizational, and health psychology at Utrecht University, The Netherlands. He received PhDs from the University of Münster, Germany, and London University (London School of Economics), United Kingdom. He has previously held academic positions in the United States, England, and Germany. His research interests span social and health psychology. He has written and edited in both fields, including volumes on bereavement (with the editors of this volume) and the *European Review of Social Psychology* (with Miles Hewstone).

Henk Schut is associate professor of psychology at Utrecht University, The Netherlands. He received his PhD in clinical psychology at Utrecht University in 1992. His research interests cover processes of coping with loss and the efficacy of grief therapy and counseling of bereaved persons. He also works as a trainer for professionals (e.g., funeral directors and medical specialists) in dealing with dying and bereaved individuals. He is one of the authors of the Dutch publication *Suicide and Grief* (1983) and coauthor (with Jos de Keijser, also in Dutch) of *Individual Grief Counseling* (1991).